WEST'S LEGAL ENVIRONMENT OF BUSINESS

Text
Cases
Ethical and Regulatory Issues

WEST'S LEGAL ENVIRONMENT OF BUSINESS

Text
Cases
Ethical and Regulatory Issues

FRANK B. CROSS
MSIS Department
and
Associate Director, Center for Legal and Regulatory Studies
University of Texas at Austin

ROGER LeROY MILLER
Center for Policy Studies
Clemson University
and
School of Law
University of Miami

WEST PUBLISHING COMPANY
St. Paul   New York   Los Angeles   San Francisco

A study guide has been developed to assist you in mastering the concepts presented in the text. The study guide includes pre-study questions, brief chapter introductions, checklists of what the reader should be able to do after reading the chapters, lists of the cases excerpted in the chapters, review questions, and programmed review. This workbook is available from your local bookstore under the title, *Mastering West's Legal Environment of Business: With Programmed Review to Accompany West's Legal Environment of Business,* prepared by Roger LeRoy Miller and William Eric Hollowell.

The Uniform Commercial Code is reproduced with permission of the American Law Institute and the National Conference of Commissioners on Uniform State Laws. Copyright © 1991.

Composition: Parkwood Composition
Copy Editing: Beverly Peavler and Mary Berry, Naples Editing Services
Artwork: Randy Miyake, Miyake Illustration

Library of Congress Cataloging-in-Publication Data

Cross, Frank B.
   West's legal environment of business: text, cases, ethical, and regulatory issues / Frank B. Cross, Roger LeRoy Miller.
   p. cm.
   ISBN 0-314-89333-4
   1. Industrial laws and legislation—United States.
   2. Trade regulation—United States.
   3. Commercial law—United States.
   I. Miller, Roger LeRoy.
   II. West Publishing Company.
   III. Title.
   IV. Title: Legal environment of business.
KF1600.C76 1991
346.73'07—dc20
[347.3067]

91-23488

CIP

Contents in Brief

Contents

Preface

Many students preparing for a career in business, accounting, government, law, as well as a variety of other careers in today's world need little convincing that the legal and regulatory environment of business is an important area of study. Now, more than ever before, a basic knowledge of our legal and regulatory environment is an important part of a student's general education, for the law touches just about every individual at one time or another. It is not an exaggeration to state that the law provides an all-encompassing framework in our society.

While we cannot in any way dictate how the legal environment of business should be taught, we can attempt, and have attempted, to present a text that allows maximum flexibility for the instructor. To that end, you will find this text extremely comprehensive. Instructors can choose those areas that they wish to emphasize, rather than depend on our—the authors'—personal preferences. We have made every attempt to present the legal environment of business in the most authoritative and accurate manner possible. Specifically, all case and statutory law and all appendices are current up to the date of printing.

Some of you who are familiar with our previous textbooks will notice a similarity in "look and feel" between *West's Legal Environment of Business* and *West's Business Law*. This similarity is by design. We have kept all of the features that the users of *West's Business Law* have told us are strong points, including its thoroughness and flexibility for different types of teaching philosophies. The same care and desire for extreme precision also permeate *West's Legal Environment of Business*.

■ Overview of the Contents

West's Legal Environment of Business is broken into seven units. They start with the foundations and work their way through the public and private environment, the employment and regulatory environment, and conclude with the contemporary and international environment. While we believe the flow of subjects is logical, instructors can easily assign chapters in a different order.

■ Important Chapters and Special Topics

While every chapter in this text has been designed to correspond to the needs of a complete course in the legal and regulatory environment of business, some stand out as especially timely. They are as follows:

- **Alternative Dispute Resolution (Chapter 4)**—Because alternative dispute resolution (ADR) is becoming increasingly popular, we devote one full chapter to it. Information on mediation and arbitration is included, as well as on mini-trials and other private solutions to dispute resolution.
- **Torts and Crimes Related to Business (Chapter 8)**—Traditional torts and crimes affecting business, as well as recent trends in the liability of corporations and corporate personnel for torts and crimes committed while undertaking business activities, are singled out for special attention in this chapter.
- **Financial Transactions (Chapter 24)**—This chapter summarizes the rights and liabilities of consumers and banking institutions under federal legislation covering electronic fund transfers undertaken by consumers. It also includes important information on the liability for the consequences of loans. This chapter explores the relatively new area of legal liability of lenders and describes the common law and statutory law framework for such liability.
- **Takeovers and Mergers (Chapter 25)**—The area of takeovers and mergers has been headline news for the last few years. In this chapter we examine the methodology used by those individuals and institutions that engage in takeovers and mergers. The most common anti-takeover tactics are also discussed.
- **Intellectual Property and Computer Law (Chapter 26)**—This chapter looks in detail at some pressing legal issues in today's business world—particularly, how to protect against infringement of rights in patented, trademarked, or copyrighted property—as well as the evolving legal framework surrounding computerized business transactions and ownership rights in computer software.

■ Other Special Features of This Text

In addition to offering coverage of the topics of special concern discussed above, our text provides many other unique features for the student and the instructor.

Cases

Special attention is given in *West's Legal Environment of Business* to case selection and presentation, as well as to simplifying the task of finding and analyzing case law.

CLASSIC AND CONTEMPORARY CASES You will find a diverse selection of case excerpts in the chapters that follow. We have attempted to provide tried-and-true classic and landmark cases, as well as some of the most modern examples of applications of points of the legal and regulatory environment of business. Many of the cases in this edition are from 1990 and 1991.

CASES FULLY INTEGRATED Our cases are fully integrated into the surrounding text. That is, they directly follow and illustrate the points of law that are being discussed within the text rather than appearing at the ends of the chapters.

A PROVEN CASE FORMAT Each case presented in *West's Legal Environment of Business* follows this proven format:

- *Case Title and Full Case Citation*—The case title and full case citation (including all parallel citations) are presented in the margin at the beginning of each case.
- *Background and Facts*—This section contains a summary, in the authors' own words, of the events leading up to the lawsuit.
- *Case Excerpt*—Following the summary of the background to the case, an excerpt from the actual court opinion is presented—in a contrasting type size to differentiate it from the surrounding textual material. Whenever the court opinion contains a term or phrase that may be difficult for the student to understand, a brief explanation

is provided in brackets. Important phrases and sentences are italicized, and a bracketed note clearly indicates that the emphasis was added by the authors, not the court.

- *Decision and Remedy*—In this section, the authors summarize, in their own words, the outcome of the case.
- *Comments*—Special comments by the authors are added following the *Decision and Remedy* section whenever the student might benefit from additional information regarding the case or its outcome.
- *Ethical Considerations*—This section discusses ethical aspects of the law, or laws, under consideration. Such concerns have become an increasingly important part of the legal and regulatory environment of business. *Ethical Considerations* are appended to numerous cases in this text.

CASE CITATIONS FULLY EXPLAINED   In Chapter 1, we use a comprehensive format to explain case citations. In addition to our explanatory text, we offer an exhibit in four-color graphics to lead the student to a full understanding of how to read and understand case citations in this text and in other legal references. If a citation used within the text has not been explained in this section of Chapter 1, we explain it in brackets or in a footnote where it appears.

CASE BRIEFING ASSIGNMENTS   Many professors prefer to have their students brief cases. To make these assignments more manageable for both students and professors, we provide in Appendix A a short explanation of how to brief a case, followed by twenty-seven cases for briefing. Case briefing assignments, including questions that should be answered for each of the cases for briefing, are found at the ends of the problem sets in each chapter in the text. Sample answers to the questions listed in the case briefing assignments are found in the free manual *Answers to Questions and Case Problems.*

Ethics

Few people today can remain unaware of the importance of ethics. Questions of political ethics in

the Congress confront us on an all-too-regular basis. Ethical issues have arisen with respect to the management of numerous failed savings and loan associations. The ethics of how we do business in other countries has been an issue at various times. Indeed, every individual who has any notion of becoming a part of the American business world must have an understanding of ethics. To this end, we have integrated ethics throughout the text.

ETHICAL ISSUES DESCRIBED IN UNIT OPENERS   At the beginning of each unit of this text, the student is introduced to the ethical issues that may arise concerning the materials presented in the chapters within that unit. These ethical issues tie in with three other ethically oriented features which will be discussed below—the *Ethical Considerations* sections appended to some of the cases, the ethical problems presented at the ends of the *Questions and Case Problems* sections in many of the chapters, and the *Focus on Ethics* section that concludes each unit.

CASE ETHICAL CONSIDERATIONS   As already mentioned, numerous cases contain special concluding sections called *Ethical Considerations.* These sections expose and define the ethical issues brought out in the cases.

A QUESTION OF ETHICS   After Chapter 3, all chapters of *West's Legal Environment of Business* have a special problem at the end of the chapter entitled *A Question of Ethics.* A real-world case is summarized, and then ethical questions are presented for the student to answer. Suggested answers to these questions are included in the *Answers to Questions and Case Problems.*

FOCUS ON ETHICS   At the end of each of the seven units in this text is a special section entitled *Focus on Ethics.* Each of these sections addresses ethical aspects of the law discussed in the preceding unit. While these sections are not intended to substitute for a course in ethics, each section is designed to elicit comments and discussion from the student-readers on ethical issues. For this reason, each *Focus* ends with a set of discussion questions. Brief suggested answers to these questions can be found in the *Instructor's Manual.* Additionally, further comments on, and references for, these sections are given in the *Instructor's Manual.*

Emerging Trends

A number of chapters include a feature entitled *Emerging Trends.* These two-page spreads emphasize policy issues that have arisen, or will arise, with respect to certain aspects of the legal environment of business. Each feature concludes with the following two sections:

- *Implications for the Businessperson*—A list of the steps that businesspersons might take to prevent legal problems in the particular area being discussed.
- *For Critical Analysis*—A set of two or three questions that require the student-readers to analyze critically aspects of the emerging trend being discussed.

The following *Emerging Trends* are included in this edition:

- Codes of Ethics—Do They Work? (Chapter 4).
- The Boundaries of Free Commercial Speech (Chapter 5).
- How to Imprison a Corporation (Chapter 8).
- Tort Reform (Chapter 11).
- The Growing Rights of Independent Contractors (Chapter 15).
- Privacy Rights versus Worker Safety and Efficiency (Chapter 17).
- Toward Stricter Enforcement of Antitrust Laws (Chapter 20).
- Facing a United Europe (Chapter 27).

Unit Opening Notes

Each of the seven units in this text begins with a listing of the chapters in the unit, followed by a discussion of the importance of the topics to be discussed. The student can read about the broad concepts, including traditional business practices and public-policy considerations, on which the legal environment covered in the unit is based.

Immediately following the introductory comments is the section on ethical issues discussed above, under ethics.

Concept Summaries

Whenever key areas of the law need special emphasis, we provide a *Concept Summary.* There are many such summaries, including the following:

- Courts and Procedures (Chapter 2).
- Common Basic Torts (Chapter 7).
- Comparison of Negligence and Strict Liability in the Area of Product Liability (Chapter 11).

Exhibits

When appropriate, we have illustrated important aspects of the law in graphic or summary form in exhibits. In numerous instances, to make sure that the student fully understands the concept being illustrated, we have added explanatory legends. In addition, we have included a number of sample forms for the student's reference. In all, thirty-four exhibits are featured in *West's Legal Environment of Business,* including the following:

- Exhibit 1–6: How to Read Citations.
- Exhibit 2–5: A Typical Complaint.
- Exhibit 4–1: Ethical Decision Making.
- Exhibit 5–1: Federal Legislation Relating to Privacy.
- Exhibit 10–1: A Sample Negotiable Bill of Lading.
- Exhibit 13–1: Articles of Incorporation.
- Exhibit 13–2: Results of Cumulative Voting.
- Exhibit 15–1: Sample Power of Attorney.
- Exhibit 22–1: How Do Stocks and Bonds Differ?
- Exhibit 24–1: A Sample Stop-Payment Order.
- Exhibit 26–1: Federal Legislation Relating to Privacy.

Vocabulary Stressed

One of the major stumbling blocks in the study of the legal environment of business is legal vocabulary. In addition to including bracketed explanations of difficult terms and phrases within the court opinions presented in the text, this text has been completely edited to ensure that every important legal term used by the authors is fully defined when it is first introduced.

At the end of each chapter, all terms that were boldfaced in the chapter are listed in alphabetical order under the heading *Terms and Concepts to Review*. The page on which the term is defined is given after each term. Students can briefly examine the list to make sure they understand all important terms introduced in the chapter and can immediately review terms that they do not completely understand by referring to the page number given. All boldfaced terms are listed and again defined in the glossary at the end of the text.

Questions and Case Problems

Every chapter of this text ends with ten to fourteen questions and case problems. The first four to six of these are hypothetical questions. The remainder are actual case problems, many from 1990 and 1991. A large number of the case problems are based on cases that can be found in their entirety in the LEGAL CLERK Research Software System (discussed below). Complete answers are given in a separate manual for all questions and case problems in the text, including the ethical questions and case briefing assignments. The *Answers to Questions and Case Problems* is free to adopters and can be placed on reserve in the library, if desired.

Appendices

Because the majority of students keep their legal environment of business text as a reference source, we have included a full set of appendices. They are as follows:

A. Briefing Cases—Instructions and Selected Cases.
B. The Constitution of the United States.
C. The Uniform Commercial Code (excerpts).
D. Restatement (Second) of Torts (excerpts).
E. Sherman Anti-trust Act (excerpts).
F. Clayton Act (excerpts).
G. Federal Trade Commission Act (excerpts)
H. Robinson Patman Act (excerpts)
I. Securities Act of 1933 (excerpts)
J. Securities Exchange Act of 1934 (excerpts).
K. Title VII of the Civil Rights Act of 1964 (excerpts).
L. Americans with Disabilities Act of 1990 (excerpts).
M. The Uniform Partnership Act.
N. Guide to Research in Legal Environment.
O. Spanish Equivalents for Important Legal Terms in English.

A SPECIAL NOTE ON THE RESEARCH GUIDE Increasingly, legal and regulatory environment instructors are requiring their students to do research projects covering legal topics studied in the text. Appendix N, our research guide, is designed to let students know the sources available to help them conduct their research. Many publications deal with legal environment issues, and these are categorized in this appendix and tied where appropriate to chapters in the text.

■ Supplements

West's Legal Environment of Business provides the largest and most comprehensive supplements package ever to be offered for a legal environment of business text. We understand that instructors face a difficult task in finding the time necessary to teach the material that they wish to cover during each term. Individually and in conjunction with a number of our colleagues, we have developed supplementary teaching materials that we believe are the best available today. Each component of the supplements package is described below.

West's Legal Environment of Business Instructor's Planning Guide

To simplify and make more efficient the work effort of the instructor using *West's Legal Environment of Business* we have developed a complete planning guide that integrates all of the print, video, and computer software supplements. For each chapter in this guide, you will find helpful suggestions on what parts of the complete learning/teaching package to use.

Other Printed Supplements

The remaining printed supplements for *West's Legal Environment of Business* have a single goal in mind: to make the task of teaching and the task of learning more enjoyable and more efficient.

INSTRUCTOR'S MANUAL The *Instructor's Manual* has been written by text author Roger

LeRoy Miller, together with William Eric Hollowell. Having one of the co-authors of the main text write the *Instructor's Manual* has resulted in complete agreement between what is stressed in the text and what is fully outlined in the *Instructor's Manual*. We believe that the *Instructor's Manual* is the best that has ever been made available for a legal environment professor. Each chapter of the manual contains the following features:

- An introductory section, which highlights the main concepts and importance of the law covered in the chapter.
- A detailed explanatory outline of the chapter contents, which is keyed very closely to the text.
- Synopses of all cases, often accompanied by additional notes and comments, as well as questions to ask in class and brief answers to these questions.
- Additional background on significant persons and statutes that are mentioned or referred to in the text.
- Teaching suggestions, including points to be stressed, hypothetical questions to elicit class discussion, and discussion questions keyed closely to the text and based on information contained in the text.
- Suggested activities and research assignments.
- Explanations of selected footnotes. Cases, statutes, and other references cited in footnotes of the chapter are briefly summarized or explained so that the relationship between the footnote and the text is clear.

A computerized version of the *Instructor's Manual* is now also available (this version is described below, under software).

MASTERING WEST'S LEGAL ENVIRONMENT OF BUSINESS   The study guide, which is entitled *Mastering West's Legal Environment of Business: With Programmed Review,* has been prepared by text author Roger LeRoy Miller together with William Eric Hollowell. This study guide contains an introductory study skills section, and a chapter-by-chapter review of *West's Legal Environment of Business.* The chapter-by-chapter review offers the following for each chapter of the text:

- Pre-study questions.
- Brief chapter introduction.
- Checklist of what each student should be able to do after finishing the chapter.
- Chapter outline (including helpful pneumonics).
- A list of cases excerpted in the chapter.
- True-false questions.
- Fill-in questions.
- Multiple-choice questions.
- Short essay problems (with answers in the *Instructor's Manual*).
- Programmed Review.

A computerized version of this study guide—called *Microguide*—is also available (see below, under software supplements).

CASE PRINTOUTS   Most of the cases in the main body of the text have been reprinted *in their entirety* and published in a separate book, called *Case Printouts to Accompany West's Legal Environment of Business.* This book is available free to adopters. It provides readily accessible and complete information on all the cases selected for detailed discussion in the classroom. Instructors may also copy any of the cases in their entirety to hand out to their students.

ANSWERS MANUAL   A complete answers manual entitled *Answers to Questions and Case Problems* is available to all adopters. Each answer is presented in a standard format.

- *Point of Law and Page Reference*—The point of law to which the problem relates is first stated in boldface, followed by the page number or numbers at which the point of law is discussed in the text.
- *Issue*—The legal issue or question raised by the problem is briefly described.
- Specific answers to questions or problems.

ADVANCED TOPICS AND CONTEMPORARY ISSUES: EXPANDED COVERAGE   A specially prepared paperback text entitled *Advanced Topics and Contemporary Issues: Expanded Coverage to Accompany West's Legal Environment of Business* has been created by text author Frank B. Cross. This book adds a unique element to the total teaching/learning package for *West's Legal Environment of Business.* The book is available to students free of charge at their instructor's option. *Advanced Topics and Contemporary Issues: Expanded Coverage,* keyed to *West's Legal Environment of Business,* provides supplemental detailed coverage of the most pressing legal issues confronting business today. The chapters in this text are as follows:

1. Business Ethics
2. International Business Law
3. Individual Employee Rights
4. Employment Discrimination Law
5. Occupational Safety and Workers' Compensation
6. Accountant Liability
7. Securities Law and Regulation
8. Mergers and Acquisitions
9. Insurance Law
10. Real Estate Law
11. Banking Regulation and Liability
12. Unfair Competition
13. Advertising Law
14. Environmental Liability
15. Health Care Law
16. Sports and Entertainment Law
17. Hospitality Management Law
18. Communications Law
19. Government Contracts
20. Legal Representation of Business

Additionally, each chapter ends with *Ethical Perspectives* and *International Perspectives.*

HANDBOOK ON CRITICAL THINKING AND WRITING   A booklet entitled *Handbook on Critical Thinking and Writing in the American Legal Environment* provides students with an overview of techniques used in critical thinking. It allows students to examine and analyze legal assumptions and arguments. The *Handbook* is closely tied to many of the examples given in the chapters of *West's Legal Environment of Business.* Additionally, the student is given 12 steps to effective writing. Free copies are available to adopters and their students when requested.

A COMPREHENSIVE TEST BANK   Again, to ensure consistency between the teaching materials and the text, one of the authors, Roger LeRoy Miller, has co-written the test bank. There are approximately 1,500 multiple-choice questions with answers and about 1,000 true-false questions with answers. These questions are available in book form or, as discussed below, on software.

TRANSPARENCY ACETATES   The supplements package contains over thirty transparency acetates for overhead projection in the classroom. Included in this package are key actual business forms.

REGIONAL REPORTERS   West's regional reporters cover all state appellate court decisions. The following reporters are available to qualified adopters: Pacific, North Western, South Western, North Eastern, Atlantic, South Eastern, and Southern.

Software Supplements

Software supplements represent an increasingly significant portion of the *West's Legal Environment of Business* teaching/learning package. We offer for adopters and students a wide variety of software supplements.

LEGAL CLERK SOFTWARE   The LEGAL CLERK Research Software System is a user-friendly, interactive software package that simultaneously introduces students to the rudiments of computer-aided legal research and reinforces the underlying concepts of business law. LEGAL CLERK provides a valuable learning tool to help your school meet AACSB recommendations for using microcomputers in business law courses.

To provide instructors with maximum flexibility, LEGAL CLERK covers three major subject areas of business law and the legal environment: UCC/Article 2—Sales, Government Regulation and the Legal Environment of Business, and Contracts. Instructors may select one version or all three versions for their classes. Cases appearing in LEGAL CLERK are clearly identified in the text with a computer logo. The logos are color coded to help users easily identify which version of LEGAL CLERK contains specific cases.

Uniform Commercial Code/Article 2—Sales Version 1.0)

Government Regulation and the Legal Environment of Business (Version 1.0)

Contracts (Version 1.0)

A site license for all three versions of LEGAL CLERK is free to qualified adopters. Each version is accompanied by an *Instructor's Resource Guide* and, for student purchase, a *Student User's Guide*.

LEGAL REVIEW SOFTWARE   This new software allows students to review legal concepts found in all three LEGAL CLERK versions: Contracts, Government Regulation and the Legal Environment of Business, and Uniform Commercial Code/Article 2—Sales. LEGAL REVIEW runs on IBM PCs and compatible microcomputers and is available to qualified adopters. A *Legal Review Student User's Manual* can be purchased by the student. The manual contains specific questions about the legal concepts covered in the software.

COMPUTERIZED INSTRUCTOR'S MANUAL For those instructors who wish to modify the *Instructor's Manual* to add their own notes, we provide a fully computerized version of the *Instructor's Manual*. You may order the manual in the following formats:

- ASCII format for IBM, on 5-¼ inch diskettes.
- ASCII format for IBM, on 3-½ inch diskettes.
- ASCII format for Macintosh, on 3-½ inch diskettes.
- Microsoft Word 4.0 format for Macintosh, on 3-½ inch diskettes.

This software allows the *Instructor's Manual* to be imported into any popular word-processing program, such as WordPerfect. Instructors wishing to obtain these diskettes may request them directly from their West sales representative.

COMPUTERIZED STUDY GUIDE   Your students can test their knowledge of chapter material with the computerized study guide called *Microguide*. The questions from the printed study guide described above are on diskette, allowing your students to practice taking computerized tests. Multiple-choice, true-false, and fill-in test questions are included. *Microguide* runs on IBM PCs and compatible microcomputers or Macintosh microcomputers (with Hypercard). *Microguide* is available free to qualified adopters of the text.

COMPUTERIZED TEST BANK—WESTEST The test bank is available on the latest version of WESTEST 2.0, a highly acclaimed computerized testing system, which is offered for IBM PCs and compatible microcomputers or the Macintosh family of microcomputers. WESTEST allows instructors to do the following:

- Import and export graphs.
- Add or edit questions, instructions, and answers.
- Select questions by previewing the question on the screen.
- Let the system select questions randomly.
- Select questions by question number.
- View summaries of the exam or the examination-bank chapters.
- Set up the page layout for exams.
- Print exams in a variety of formats.

INTERACTIVE SOFTWARE—CONTRACTS The use of computers in learning many subjects has increased dramatically at the college level. For those students who have their own computers or who have access to computers through friends or learning labs, we have developed a unique interactive program for the teaching/learning of contracts. This program uses HyperText, and in this manner, it allows for flexibility in learning the subject matter based on each user's level of understanding.

"YOU BE THE JUDGE" SOFTWARE   This software provides case problems for ten topic areas. The user is given the facts, and is then asked how the issue should be decided. A word processor, which is integrated in the software, allows users to key in their response, and print it. A glossary of legal terms is also included.

PROBLEM CASES ON DISKETTE   Virtually all the case problems found at the ends of all twenty-seven chapters of the text are now available in ASCII format on diskette. These can be imported into any word-processing program, such as Microsoft Word or WordPerfect. The diskettes are available in the following formats:

- 5-¼ inch diskettes for IBM PCs and compatible microcomputers.
- 3-½ inch diskettes for IBM PCs and compatible microcomputers.
- 3-½ inch diskettes for all Macintosh computers.

WESTLAW WESTLAW, the premiere computerized legal-research system, is renowned for its ability to help law professors, law students, attorneys, and paralegals do research in the law. Qualified adopters of *West's Legal Environment of Business* are allowed six free hours of WESTLAW. Contact your West sales representative for more details.

Videocassettes and Videodiscs

No legal environment of business text would be complete without supplemental video and audio materials. We are proud to announce the addition of an extensive videocassette library that is being made available for adopters of *West's Legal Environment of Business*. These instructional videos can help you in the teaching of legal and regulatory environment or business in a variety of areas, including ethics and social responsibility, employment law, and others.

Technology has provided instructors of legal environment of business with yet another way to present teaching materials: the laser videodisc. We are making available for this edition a complete videodisc that provides you with the latest method for presenting important topics to your students.

For more information, contact your West sales representative.

EQUAL JUSTICE FOR ALL VIDEOS The PBS series *Equal Justice Under Law* is available free to adopters of this text. The videos cover the following landmark cases:

- *Marbury v. Madison*
- *McCulloch v. Maryland*
- *Gibbons v. Ogden*

INSTRUCTOR'S VIDEO NOTES TO EQUAL JUSTICE UNDER LAW There is also an instructor's manual for use with the three videocassettes. In that manual, there are teaching notes that may be of help to you if you choose to use these videos. For each video you will find the following:

- An introduction and overview
- Learning objectives
- Critical thinking questions
- Implications and effects on business

■ Acknowledgments

Numerous individuals spent countless hours helping with this edition. We especially wish to thank Lavina Leed Miller for her extensive editorial skills. Much of the research was masterfully undertaken and completed by William Eric Hollowell, who also appropriately worked on the *Instructor's Manual,* the *Test Bank,* and the *Study Guide.* The copyediting services of Beverly Peavler and Mary Berry will not go unnoticed by the casual—as well as the careful—reader. Proofreading lasted many, many months. Our thanks for their meticulous work go to Lavina Leed Miller, William Eric Hollowell, and Jeff Weaver, as well as to Marie-Christine Loiseau. We wish to thank our long-time editor, Clyde Perlee, Jr., for his numerous suggestions for this text. Our developmental editor, Jan Lamar, skillfully added to the planning of this project and oversaw the preparation and production of the supplements. We also thank our production manager and designer at West, John Orr, who worked many months to make sure that this project came out on time. Bette Darwin, production assistant, also deserves our sincere gratitude for her help.

As always, all errors that remain in this text are solely our own responsibility. You can write us with your ideas about how we can improve this book. We welcome all such comments and promise to respond. It is by incorporating your ideas that we continue to write a legal environment of business text that is best for you and for your students.

DEDICATION

Frank B. Cross dedicates this
book to his parents and sisters.

RLM dedicates this book to
Judy and Julian Kreeger
(25 years and counting)

UNIT ONE

The Foundations

◾ The Importance of the Legal Environment of Business

The world of business today is subject to an increasing number of laws and regulations. Business activities are governed by local rules enacted by municipal commissioners; by state and federal laws enacted by state and federal legislatures; by administrative rules promulgated by local, state, and federal agencies; by legal principles developed over the years through our judicial system; and, increasingly, as the global dimension of the business environment expands, by an emerging body of international laws and treaties.

In its broadest sense, the legal environment of business—both domestic and international—includes every rule or regulation that even slightly affects the way in which individuals and organizations conduct business. After all, any law that touches on commerce becomes part of the legal environment of business. Therefore, that environment includes contracts, sales, the formation of partnerships, corporate transactions, business properties, and, of course, all government regulations. No individual engaged in any aspect of commerce can escape the legal environment of business. Knowledge of that environment is essential to success in the modern world of business.

In this unit, we discuss many of the laws and procedures affecting the legal environment of business. In Chapter 1, we look at the sources of American law, including the common law tradition and the rapidly changing international legal environment. We examine court systems and legal procedures in Chapter 2; no businessperson can realistically assume that he or she will not at some time over the course of a business career be exposed to the mechanics of a lawsuit. In Chapter 3, we examine the many recent efforts to find more efficient means of resolving disputes through alternatives to traditional, adversarial courtroom litigation. We conclude Unit One by looking in Chapter 4 at an increasingly important aspect of the American legal environment—business ethics.

Ethical Issues in the Legal Environment of Business

Ethical issues in the legal environment of business commonly arise over just how much regulation of business is necessary or even beneficial for society. A considerable amount of debate centers on whether business is subject to too much "lawyering." Many argue that the erosion of America's competitiveness in world markets is directly attributable to the tremendous increase in legal restrictions placed on business over the last fifty years. Others counter that, left unfettered by governmental oversight, business cannot be relied on to police itself into doing what is right for all of society.

But what duties does business owe society? In free and open competition, business produces the most innovative products for the least cost. Should society demand more? And how can the legal environment protect competition while ensuring that business does the "right thing"? As you will read in Chapter 4, an action may be perfectly legal but still be perceived as "wrong" by some members of society. Later, in the *Focus on Ethics* at the end of this unit, you will learn that business firms that wish to be socially responsible and do the "right" thing usually find it difficult to please everybody at all times because different groups within American society disagree as to what constitutes right or wrong business actions.

Ethical issues arise not only with regard to the nature of laws business should be subject to but also over the process of enforcing those laws. Ethical problems have come about because of changes in our society's attitudes about the legal process itself. The litigation process has become extremely complex and, many would argue, inefficient. A more fundamental criticism is that litigation simply does not produce fair and just results for the parties—at least not at a reasonable cost to the litigants. Others counter that the complexity of the legal system simply mirrors the increased complexity of modern society.

1

Chapter 1

Business and Its Global Legal Environment

Imagine living in a world without laws. The term *chaos* would perhaps best describe the state of such a society. You would not know what your rights were, and you would not know what your duties were. If something went wrong with a product that you had purchased only recently, you would not know what redress was available to you. If there were no laws, you would not know which business agreements had any validity and which did not. Law is necessary to the smooth functioning of any modern society. Society needs certain standards to govern relationships among individuals and between the people and their government. That is why law developed. Law works within the social order, an order containing numerous activities—including business activities.

■ Business and Law

Business activities create some of society's most complex relationships. These relationships involve dealings between firms and their customers; between the firms themselves, which variously compete or cooperate with one another; and between private firms and the many governmental institutions that regulate the firms' activities. This complex web of relations is governed by rules and institutions that collectively comprise the legal environment of business and that are the focus of this text.

When this environment is realistically adapted to the commercial needs of all the parties—government, firms, and consumers alike—it can provide important benefits to society. One important benefit is the degree of certainty that the legal environment produces by enforcing the rights and responsibilities of the various parties in their dealings with one another; advance knowledge of their rights and duties can aid individuals and organizations in formulating and carrying out various complex commercial interactions. When the legal environment is not well adapted to commercial realities, however, it can produce unintended and even detrimental consequences.

Whether or not the current legal environment is the one best suited for our society is a difficult question. The legal environment reflects the interests of various groups, many of which have divergent interests and different degrees of power in influencing the institutions that create the legal environment of business. One point over which there can be no doubt, however, is that no one involved in any phase of commerce can succeed without a sound understanding of the legal and regulatory environment in which business is conducted.

■ The Globalization of the Legal Environment of Business

Another point that is beyond dispute is that the legal environment of business is taking on ever more international dimensions. Approximately 16 percent of the world's total output is currently sold in a country other than the one in which it was produced. This is nearly double what the portion was only twenty years ago. The United States, which because of its population and geography has enormous domestic markets, has seen the international trade portion of its annual national output grow to around 10 percent during the last twenty-five years—more than double what that share was in 1965.

But aggregate statistics belie the full impact of international trade on the U.S. economy. Various sectors and regions have been disproportionately affected by the trend toward internationalization. For example, recent estimates indicate that one-quarter of all jobs in California are related to foreign trade. The automobile and the electronics industries are just two of many that face increased competition from foreign firms, not only in overseas markets, but in domestic markets as well. Moreover, the globalization trend is likely to accelerate in the years ahead as Europe moves toward full economic integration after December 31, 1992, and as the industrial and financial power of Japan and the newly industrialized countries of the Pacific Rim continues to grow. In addition, the United States will continue to face international challenges as it looks abroad to obtain scarce resources such as crude oil.

The "New Look" in International Trade

An important factor in the globalization of the legal environment is the increasingly sophisticated way in which that trade is facilitated as well as the changing nature of the trade involved in international commerce. New technology in communi-

cation, for example, has spawned an international currency market that is not limited by political borders. Countries' currencies are traded twenty-four hours a day merely by revising entries on spools of magnetic tape and hard-disk drives. Technical advances in transportation have allowed business firms to transcend national boundaries. Where, for instance, is the "home" of a firm that produces components in one part of the world, assembles them in another, and eventually sells a finished product in yet a third region of the globe? What is the true nationality of a firm that operates subsidiaries in several countries?

The other wrinkle in the new look to international trade is in the nature of the traded products themselves. America's share of world output of traditional manufactured goods such as steel and textiles has declined, but its export of "cultural" products—everything from films to food franchises—and technological know-how has risen dramatically. Services and information now are traded across national boundaries just as any other set of "commodities." Century 21 agents sell French real estate, and American law firms are clamoring to open branches in Japan. Teriyaki McBurgers are sold in 750 McDonald's franchises throughout Japan. MTV Europe reaches an estimated 20 million European viewers. U.S. television programs are earning an estimated $1 billion a year in the European entertainment market, while 70 percent of the American music industry's current $20 billion in revenues are earned in foreign markets.

The Tasks of the Law in an International Setting

A **trademark** is a legal device to protect the investment made in making an innovative product of specific quality; the trademark identifies a product, distinguishing it from imitators and making the owner's investment in innovation and quality profitable. A trademark protects many forms of **intellectual property**—creations and innovations that result from the mental processes.

But there are many other property interests that are affected and involved in the many business activities carried on throughout the world. Consumers expect that the products they use will work properly and safely. Businesses that extend credit expect to be repaid the amount of the loan plus more after an appropriate interval. Firms that order inputs from other suppliers expect to have those orders fulfilled in a timely manner and according to specifications. Even individuals not directly involved in commerce either as producers or consumers have interests that are affected by business activity. You, for example, may live down the street from a factory that generates smoke or noise that interferes with your enjoyment of your property; though you may not interact with the owners of the factory directly, their business activities do affect you. These are just some of the many interests affected by business, and it is the task of the law to harmonize all of the individual interests so that business activity can function properly. This task is made increasingly complicated by the internationalization of business. Not only are various interests affected, but these interests are filtered through differences in custom and language, and above all, are complicated by the absence of a single source of authority over international business matters. Before beginning our examination of the legal environment, though, we begin by looking at the nature and origin of law itself from both a home vantage point and an international perspective.

■ What Is Law?

There have been and will continue to be different definitions of *law*. Aristotle saw law as a rule of conduct. Plato believed law was a form of social control. Cicero contended that law was the agreement of reason and nature, the distinction between the just and the unjust. The British jurist Sir William Blackstone described law as ''a rule of civil conduct prescribed by the supreme power in a state, commanding what is right, and prohibiting what is wrong.'' In America, jurist Oliver Wendell Holmes, Jr., contended that law was a set of rules that allowed one to predict how a court would resolve a particular dispute—''the prophecies of what the courts will do in fact, and nothing more pretentious, are what I mean by the law.''

Although these definitions vary in their particulars, note that all are based on the following general observation: *Law consists of enforceable rules governing relationships among individuals and between individuals and their society.* In the study of law, often referred to as **jurisprudence,** this very broad statement concerning the nature of

law is the point of departure for all legal scholars and philosophers.

■ Schools of Jurisprudential Thought

The court opinions in this book show that judges often refer to logic, history, custom, or a philosophy of what is right in making their decisions. These opinions also show that different judges—for example, a trial court judge and a reviewing court judge—when examining the same case, sometimes arrive at different conclusions about how the law should apply. That judges differ in their philosophies of law should come as no surprise to Americans. We frequently read or hear about the differences in legal philosophy among United States Supreme Court justices, especially when a significant, controversial case—such as one relating to abortion—is before the court. Part of the study of law, or jurisprudence, is discovering how different approaches to law affect judicial decision making.

All legal philosophers agree that ideals, logic, history, and custom have influenced the development of law in some way. They disagree, however, on the importance that each of these influences should have in shaping law, and their disagreements have produced different schools of jurisprudence. The three most influential schools of legal thought are described below and then illustrated by an hypothetical court case.

The Natural Law School

The oldest and one of the most significant schools of jurisprudence is the **natural law school.** Those who adhere to the natural law school of thought believe that government and the legal system should reflect universal moral and ethical principles that are inherent in human nature.

The natural law school traces its origins to ancient Greece. The Greek philosopher Aristotle (384–322 B.C.) made the distinction between natural law and conventional law (**positive law,** or written law). He pointed out that natural law has the same force everywhere and is not a function of individual situations, cultures, or history. A law prohibiting murder, for example, does not reflect the values accepted by a particular society at a particular time but is based on a universally accepted precept that murder is wrong. To murder someone is thus a violation of natural law.

Because natural law is universal, it takes on a higher order than positive, or conventional, law. It was this higher law to which the international tribunal of judges at Nuremburg appealed when convicting Nazi German war criminals of "crimes against humanity" at the end of World War II. Although these "criminals" may not have disobeyed any positive law of their country and were merely following their government's (Hitler's) orders, they were deemed by the tribunal to have violated a natural law that transcends any particular country's written laws. The natural law school of thought encourages individuals to disobey conventional, or written, laws if those individuals believe that the laws are in conflict with natural law. Protesters who felt that America's involvement in Vietnam (1964-1973) was wrong, for example, used natural law as their reason to violate written laws as they protested America's war effort.

At the basis of natural law is the concept that all persons have natural rights. John Locke, an important English political philosopher, writing in 1689, argued that no one was born with an obligation to obey rulers. He argued that all individuals were born free, equal, and independent, that they had a natural right to life, liberty, and property. The purpose of government was to secure those rights. The authors of the Declaration of Independence relied heavily on Locke's notion of natural law. In the first paragraph of the Declaration of Independence, for example, we read that people have to assume the "separate and equal Station to which the Laws of Nature and of Nature's God entitle them." In the first paragraph are also listed the "unalienable rights" of humans, including the right to life, liberty, and the pursuit of happiness.

In essence, the natural law tradition presupposes that the legitimacy of conventional, or positive, law derives from natural law. Whenever it conflicts with natural law, conventional law loses its legitimacy and should be changed.

The Positivist School

At the other end of the spectrum exists the **positivist school.** Those who adhere to this school believe that there can be no higher law than a nation's positive law—law created by a particular society at a particular point in time.

Thomas Hobbes, an English philosopher who lived from 1588 to 1679, is viewed by many as the founder of the positivist approach to law. Because Hobbes believed that in the original state of nature humans were no better than monkeys killing each other to get at the few bananas on the banana tree, he concluded that sovereign power was necessary for stability and peace—in fact, for survival. No rights existed prior to the creation of a sovereign power (government) that could make and enforce laws, and it was governmental authority—not nature or a deity—that conferred rights on individuals. In other words, individuals do not have any "natural" rights, only those acquired as a result of the existence of enforceable law. This is why, in the positivist view, positive law takes on a greater significance and finality than it does in the natural law tradition. Essentially, from the positivist perspective, the law is the law and must be obeyed on pain of punishment. Whether a particular law is bad or good is irrelevant. The merits or demerits of a given law can be discussed, and laws can be changed—in an orderly manner through legitimate lawmaking process—but as long as a law exists, it must be obeyed.

The Legal Realists

Legal realism was a school of legal thought popular in the 1920s and 1930s, one that left a strong imprint on American jurisprudence. The legal realists were in a sense rebels. They were rebelling against some of the common assumptions of the legal theorists and jurists of their time. One such assumption was that judges, at least ideally, apply the law impartially, logically, and uniformly. Thus, in theory at least, all cases involving similar circumstances and issues should have similar outcomes. But in fact, reality rarely demonstrated such consistency—issues involving identical facts would often be decided differently by different courts, even when the same legal principles were applied. Why was this? For the legal realists, different outcomes resulted from the fact that judges are human beings with unique personalities, value systems, and intellects. It would be impossible, given this obvious fact, for any two judges to engage in an identical reasoning process when evaluating the same case. In other words, it would be impossible for the law to be applied in a completely impartial, logical, and uniform manner. The task of jurists, from the legal realist's point of view, was to acknowledge this fact and become as objective as possible by becoming aware of, and clarifying, the ways in which their reasoning in particular cases was affected by their personal biases and values.

The legal realists further believed that, just as each judge is influenced by the beliefs and attitudes unique to his or her personality, so, too, is each case attended by a unique set of circumstances. That is, no two cases, no matter how similar, are ever exactly the same. Therefore, judges should tailor their decisions to take account of the specific circumstances of each case, rather than rely on some abstract rule that may not relate to those particular circumstances. Extra-legal sources, such as economic and sociological data, could also be considered in making decisions, to the extent that such sources illuminated the circumstances and issues involved in specific cases.

United States Supreme Court Justice Oliver Wendell Holmes, Jr., who lived from 1841 to 1935, was an influential proponent of legal realism. In one of his best known works, *The Common Law,* Holmes emphasized the practical nature of the law: "The life of law has not been logic; it has been experience." Another proponent of this legal school of thought was Karl Llewellyn, who lived from 1893 to 1962. He, too, viewed judges' decisions as being necessarily shaped by the judges' value judgments and their interpretations of the outcomes of previous cases. Llewellyn is best known for his dominant role in drafting the Uniform Commercial Code, a set of rules for commercial transactions that will be discussed shortly. This code, which governs most contracts for the sale of goods, reflects the influence of legal realism in its emphasis on practicality, flexibility, reasonability, and customary trade practices.

The Case of the Speluncean Explorers

To illustrate how philosophies of law affect judicial decisions, Lon Fuller, a professor of Law at Harvard, devised a hypothetical court case entitled *The Case of the Speluncean Explorers.*[1] The "facts" of this hypothetical case, briefly, are as follows.

1. 62 *Harvard Law Review* 616 (1949).

In May of the year 4299, five members of the Speluncean Society, a society of cave explorers, were exploring a deep cavern when a landslide blocked the entrance to the cave. When the men failed to return to their homes, a rescue effort was launched at the site, and for days the workers attemped to clear the entrance. Further landslides made the task extremely difficult and dangerous, and several members of the rescue team were killed during the rescue operation.

Twenty days elapsed before the explorers inside the cave discovered that they had brought a wireless machine into the cave with them. They immediately made contact with the rescuers and asked a physician, who had come to the cave with the rescue party, whether they could survive for ten more days without food, as their provisions were now so scant. The physician said that there was little possibility of this. They then asked the physician if they could survive ten days longer if they consumed the flesh of one of their number. The physician, albeit reluctantly, said yes. The men then asked whether they should cast lots to decide who should be eaten. No one outside the cave would respond to this question. The wireless was silent from that time until the thirty-second day, when the rescuers finally succeeded in clearing the entrance and reaching the men trapped inside. The rescue team then learned that the five men had cast lots by a throw of the dice, and the man who threw the losing number was put to death and eaten by the others.

The four survivors were given medical treatment and then indicted for murder and tried and sentenced to death by the Court of General Instances of the County of Stowfield. The four men petitioned the Supreme Court of Newgarth to hear the case. The relevant statute stated, "Whoever shall willfully take the life of another shall be punished by death." The decisions reached by the judges were essentially as described below. As you read them, try to relate each judge's reasoning to one of the schools of legal thought discussed above.

Judge Truepenny held that the men should be sentenced to death, in accordance with the statute— which "permits of no exception—but suggested that the court should also petition the Chief Executive of the state of Newgarth to extend clemency. "If this is done, then justice will be accomplished without impairing either the letter or spirit of our statutes and without offering any encouragement for the disregard of law.''

Judge Foster held the men to be innocent of any crime for two reasons. First, the positive law of the state of Newgarth was inapplicable to the situation in which the men found themselves. They were not in civil society but in a ''state of nature.'' Therefore, ''the law applicable to them is not the enacted and established law of this Commonwealth, but the law derived from those principles that were appropriate to their condition.'' In effect, the men had to create a ''new charter of government,'' and their agreement to cast lots represented this effort. Second, even if the men's action violated the letter of the law of Newgarth, it did not violate the spirit of the law, because self-defense is permitted by the law, and the men acted in self-defense—that is, they killed so that they could survive.

Judge Tating stated that he was ''wholly unable to resolve the doubts that beset me about the law of this case'' and withdrew from the decision.

Judge Keen agreed with Judge Truepenny, holding that the men violated the statute and therefore should be sentenced to death accordingly. The moral rightness or wrongness of the men's action was irrelevant, he felt, ''to the discharge of my office as a judge sworn to apply, not my conceptions of morality, but the law of the land.'' In Judge Keen's opinion, the court should not even petition the Chief Executive for clemency, as Judge Truepenny had recommended. That was a decision for the Chief Executive alone; it is not the role of the judge to make or advise on policy but simply to apply the law.

Judge Handy concluded that the men were innocent of any crime and that the lower court's ruling should be set aside. He approached the problem as follows: ''The problem before us is what we, as officers of the government, ought to do with these defendants. That is a question of practical wisdom, to be exercised in a context, not of abstract theory, but of human realities.'' Law is a practical, ''human affair,'' and flexibility is ''essential if we are to keep our actions in reasonable accord with the sentiments of those subject to our rule.'' Handy based his decision largely on two ''realities'': First, public opinion was 90 percent in favor of pardoning the defendants or letting them off with only a token punishment. Second, the Chief Executive, as all on the court knew, would very likely not pardon the men or commute their sentences if the issue was left up to him.

Because the court was evenly divided, the lower court's ruling remained unchanged, and the men were put to death.

Obviously, both Judge Truepenny and Judge Keen are legal positivists. Although they differ in some of their views, both stress that the law is the law, and no exceptions are to be made. Because the explorers violated the law by killing their companion, they must pay the consequences and be sentenced to death, as the law requires. Judge Foster believes that applying the law of the Commonwealth of Newgarth would be inappropriate, because the deed occurred outside the bounds of civilized society. Given the extraordinary circumstances, the only law appropriate to the situation was natural law. From this perspective, the men's actions were reasonable and excusable, according to Judge Foster. Judge Handy's approach is that of the legal realist. If the court fails to take ''human realities''—such as public opinion or the Chief Executive's predilections—into account, it will not serve the needs of society.

■ Sources of American Law— The Common Law Tradition

Because of our colonial heritage, much of American law is based on the English legal system. Without a knowledge of this legal heritage, one cannot understand the nature of our legal system today.

The English Origins of Common Law

In 1066, following the Normans' conquest of England, William the Conqueror and his successors began the process of unifying the country under their rule. One of the means they used to this end was the establishment of the *King's Court*. Before the conquest, disputes had been settled according to local custom. The King's Court sought to establish a common, or uniform, set of customs for the whole country. The body of rules that evolved under the King's Court, called the *Curia Regis,* was the beginning of the **common law**—law that was common to the entire realm. As the number of courts and cases increased, the more important decisions of each year were gathered together and recorded in Year Books. Judges, when settling disputes similar to ones that had been decided before, used decisions recorded in the Year Books as the basis for their decisions. If a case was unique, judges had to create new laws, but they based their decisions on the general principles suggested by earlier cases. Each interpretation became part of the authoritative law on the subject and served as a legal **precedent.** Later cases that were similar in legal principles or in facts would be decided with reference to that precedent. The practice of deciding new cases with reference to former decisions is called the doctrine of *stare decisis.*

Stare Decisis

The practice of deciding new cases with reference to former decisions eventually became a cornerstone of the English and American judicial systems. As noted, it forms the doctrine of ***stare decisis***[2] (Latin for "to stand on decided cases").

The doctrine of *stare decisis* performs many useful functions. First, it helps the courts to be more efficient. It would be very time consuming if each judge had to reason out the policies for deciding what the law should be for each case brought before the court. If other courts have confronted the same issue and reasoned through the case carefully, their opinions can serve as guides.

Second, *stare decisis* creates a more just and uniform system. The rule of precedent tends to neutralize the prejudices of individual judges. If judges feel pressure to use precedent as the basis for their decisions, they will be less influenced by any personal biases. Different states and regions, however, often follow different precedents, and so rules of law do vary.

Third, *stare decisis* makes the law more stable and predictable. If the law on a given subject is well settled, someone bringing a case to court can usually rely upon the court to make a decision based on what the law has been. Finally, *stare decisis* reflects the experience of the past and is based on the wisdom of the past.

Sometimes a court departs from the rule of precedent because it has decided that the precedent is incorrect. For example, if changes in technology, business practices, or society's attitudes necessitate a change in the law, courts may depart from precedent. Judges are reluctant to overrule precedent, however, and whether they do so depends on the subject of the case, the number and prestige of prior decisions, the degree of social change that has occurred, and the identity of the deciding court.

Sometimes there is no precedent on which to base a decision, or there are conflicting precedents. In these situations, a court will: (1) refer to past decisions that involved somewhat similar issues and decide the case by reasoning through *analogy* (discussed below); (2) look at social factors—changes in the status of women, for example—that might influence the issues involved; and (3) consider what the fairest result would be.

Cases that overturn precedent often receive a great deal of publicity. In *Brown v. Board of Education,*[3] for example, the United States Supreme Court expressly overturned precedent when it concluded that separate educational facilities for African Americans were inherently unequal. Previously, in *Plessy v. Ferguson,*[4] as well as in numerous other cases, the Court had upheld as constitutional the provision of separate but equal accommodations. The Supreme Court's departure from precedent in *Brown* received a tremendous amount of publicity as people began to realize the ramifications of this change in the law. Although such cases receive the most attention, in reality the majority of cases are decided according to precedent because of the application of the doctrine of *stare decisis.*

Stare Decisis and Legal Reasoning

When applying, overruling, or creating precedent, judges use many forms of reasoning. Generally, a judge writes an opinion in the form of a *syllogism*—that is, deductive reasoning consisting of a major premise, a minor premise, and a conclusion. For example, a plaintiff comes before the court alleging *assault* (a wrongful action, or tort, in which one person makes another fearful of immediate physical harm). The judge might point out in a particular case that "under the common law, an individual must be *aware* of a threat of danger for the threat to constitute civil assault" (major premise); "the plaintiff in this case was unaware of the threat at the time it occurred" (minor premise); and "therefore, the circumstances do not amount to a civil assault" (conclusion).

A second important form of commonly employed legal reasoning might be thought of as a

---

2.   Pronounced *ster*-ay dih-*si*-ses.

3.   347 U.S. 483, 74 S.Ct. 686, 98 L.Ed. 873 (1954).
4.   163 U.S. 537, 16 S.Ct. 1138, 41 L.Ed. 256 (1896).

section of knotted rope, with each knot tying together separate pieces of rope to form a tight length. As a whole, the rope represents a logical progression of connected points, and the last knot represents the conclusion.

For example, imagine that a tenant in an apartment building sues the landlord for damages for an injury resulting from an allegedly dimly lit stairway. The landlord, who was on the premises the evening the injury occurred, testifies that none of the other nine tenants who used the stairway that night complained about the lights. The court concludes that the tenant is not entitled to compensation on the basis of the stairway's lighting. The ''pieces of rope'' might be stated as follows:

1. The landlord testifies that none of the tenants who used the stairs on the evening in question complained about the lights.
2. The fact that none of the tenants complained is the same as if they had said the lighting was sufficient.
3. That there were no complaints does *not* prove that the lighting was sufficient but proves that the landlord had no reason to believe that it was not.
4. The landlord's belief was reasonable, because no one complained.
5. Therefore, the landlord acted reasonably and was not negligent in providing adequate lighting.

In the majority of cases, the two methods of legal reasoning discussed above predominate, and it is unnecessary to look beyond them. There are, however, two other important forms of reasoning that judges use in deciding cases: reasoning by analogy and the process of determining which rules and policies to apply.

To reason by analogy is to compare the facts in the case at hand to the facts in other cases and, to the extent the *patterns* are similar, apply the same rule to the case at hand. To the extent the facts are unique, or ''distinguishable,'' different rules may apply. For example, in case A, it is held that a driver who crosses a highway's center line is negligent. In case B, a driver crosses the line to avoid hitting a child. In determining whether case A's rule applies in case B, a judge would consider what the reasons were for the decision in A and whether B is sufficiently similar for those reasons to apply. If the judge holds that B's driver is not liable, that

judge must pinpoint a policy and explain a rule that is not inconsistent with the decision in case A.

Simply put, legal reasoning means that a judge must harmonize his or her decision with decisions that have been made before. Of course, judges have a seemingly infinite array of precedential decisions from which to choose. When determining which rules and policies to apply in a given case, and in applying them, a judge may examine any or all of the following:

1. Previous case law and the legal principles and policies behind the decisions, as well as their historical setting.
2. Statutes and the policies—legal, historical, and social—underlying the legislature's decision to enact a particular statute.
3. Society's values (for example, fairness).
4. Custom (for example, when a controversial business transaction involves a contract, a judge might ask what the participants expected, based on the usual and customary practices within their trade).
5. Other sources, including data and principles from the fields of economics, psychology, sociology, and philosophy.

Which of these sources is chosen, or receives the greatest emphasis, will depend on the nature of the case being considered and the particular judge hearing the case. Although judges always strive to be free of subjectivity and personal bias in deciding cases, each judge has his or her own unique personality, set of values or philosophical leanings, and intellectual attributes—all of which necessarily frame the decision-making process.

The Common Law Today

The body of law that developed under the English system and that is still used today consists of the rules of law announced in court decisions, including court interpretations of statutes, regulations, and provisions in constitutions. Today this law is known variously as judge-made law, the common law, or **case law.**

Common law, or case law, must be distinguished from **statutory law,** which generally consists of those laws enacted by state legislatures and, at the federal level, by Congress. In all areas not covered by statutory law, common law governs and generally has the same force as statutory law. The history and circumstances of the fifty states differ, and this has given rise to differences among the courts' decisions and thus in the common law among states. Even when legislation has been substituted for common law principles, courts often rely on common law to interpret the legislation, on the theory that the people who drafted the statute intended to codify an existing common law rule.

■ Other Sources of American Law

In addition to case law, or common law, courts have numerous other sources of law to consider when making their decisions.

Constitutions

The U.S. Constitution is the supreme law of the land. A law in violation of the Constitution, no matter what its source, will be declared unconstitutional and will not be enforced. The U.S. Constitution delineates how federal powers are divided among the three governmental branches, establishing a system of checks and balances. Article I vests the legislative power (power to make laws) in the Congress; Article II vests the executive power (power to see that laws are carried out) in the president; and Article III vests the judicial power (power to determine what the law is and whether laws are valid) in the courts.

Each state also has its constitution which sets forth the general organization, powers, and limits of the state government. Generally, state governments are organized in the same way as the federal government. The Tenth Amendment to the U.S. Constitution, which defines the powers and limitations of the federal government, reserves all powers not granted to the federal government to the states or to the people. Thus, each state constitution, unless it conflicts with the U.S. Constitution, is supreme within each state's borders. The U.S. Constitution, for example, gives the federal government the power to regulate *interstate* commerce (commerce between or among states), but the states retain the power to regulate *intrastate* commerce (commerce within a state).

The regulation of interstate commerce is one of the chief ways in which the U.S. Constitution

affects business. This and other aspects of constitutional law as it relates to business will be discussed in detail in Chapter 5. The complete text of the U.S. Constitution is contained in Appendix B.

Statutes and Ordinances

Statutes enacted by the U.S. Congress and the various state legislative bodies constitute another source of law, which is generally referred to as *statutory law,* as noted above. The statutory law of the United States further consists of the ordinances passed by cities, counties, and other political subdivisions. None of these laws can violate the U.S. Constitution or the relevant state constitution.

Administrative Law

An administrative agency is created when the executive or legislative branch of the government delegates some of its authority to an appropriate group of persons, usually called an agency or a commission. Administrative agencies exercise legislative, executive, and judicial power. In their **rulemaking,** they use legislative power; in their regulation and supervision, they use executive power; and in their adjudication procedures, they use judicial power. Unlike legislators, presidents, governors, and many judges, administrative agency personnel are rarely chosen by popular elections, and many do not serve fixed terms. As a result, great power is given to people who may not be responsive to the public.

Administrative law is the branch of public law concerned with the executive power and actions of administrative agencies, their officials, and their employees. When an individual has a dispute with such an agency, administrative law applies. The scope of administrative law has expanded enormously in recent years, and the scope of administrative agencies has increased so much that their activities have come to be called **administrative process,** in contrast to **judicial process.** Administrative process involves the administration of law by nonjudicial bodies, such as the Federal Trade Commission, whereas judicial process is the administration of law by judicial bodies (the courts). Administrative law will be discussed in further detail in Chapter 18.

Commercial Law Codes

The body of law that pertains to commercial dealings is commonly referred to as commercial, or business, law. It includes many of the topics in this text—contracts, partnerships, and corporations, for example. For business students, the most important codification of commercial law is the Uniform Commercial Code (UCC).

CODIFICATION OF COMMERCIAL LAW In the interests of uniformity and reform, in the late nineteenth century the legal profession suggested that comprehensive codes of laws concerning specific subject areas be adopted by the states. (When adopted by a state, these codes of laws become statutory law.)

The National Conference of Commissioners on Uniform State Laws started to meet in the late 1800s to draft uniform statutes. Once these uniform codes had been drawn up, the commissioners urged each state legislature to adopt them. Adoption of uniform codes is a state matter, and a state may reject all or part of a code or rewrite it as the state's legislature sees fit. Hence, even when a proposed code is said to have been adopted in many states, those states' laws may not be entirely "uniform."

The first uniform code, or act, was the Uniform Negotiable Instruments Law, which was finally approved in 1896 and was adopted in every state by the early 1920s (though not all states used exactly the same wording). Afterwards, other acts were drawn up in a similar manner; they included the Uniform Sales Act, the Uniform Warehouse Receipts Act, the Uniform Bills of Lading Act, the Uniform Partnership Act, the Model Business Corporation Act (drafted by the American Bar Association), and the Uniform Stock Transfer Act. More recently, a Uniform Probate Code was prepared. The most ambitious uniform act of all, however, was the Uniform Commercial Code (UCC).

THE UNIFORM COMMERCIAL CODE (UCC) The National Conference of Commissioners on Uniform State Laws and the American Law Institute sponsored and directed the preparation of the Uniform Commercial Code. These two organizations were assisted by literally hundreds of law professors, businesspersons, judges, and lawyers. Excerpts from the official 1991 text of the UCC can be found in Appendix C in this book. The District of Columbia, the Virgin Islands, and forty-nine states have adopted all articles of the UCC (with numerous changes to the specific wording, however). Louisiana, the only state that has not adopted the UCC in its entirety, has adopted all but Article 2.

The UCC is designed to facilitate the legal relationship of parties involved in modern commercial transactions by helping to determine the intentions of the parties to a commercial contract and by giving force and effect to their agreement. Moreover, the UCC is meant to encourage business transactions by assuring businesspersons that their contracts, if validly entered into, will be uniformly enforced.

Restatements of the Law

Notwithstanding the movement toward uniform, statutory laws, the common law remains a significant source of legal authority. To summarize and clarify common law rules, the American Law Institute drafted and published compilations of the common law called Restatements of the Law. There are Restatements of the Law in the areas of contracts, torts, agency, trusts, property, restitution, security, judgments, and conflict of laws. Many of the Restatements are now in their second edition. The *Restatement of the Law of Contracts,* for example, was first published in May 1932. Thirty years later, a second edition was undertaken. It was completed in 1979 and is referred to as the *Restatement (Second) of the Law of Contracts,* or, more simply, as the *Restatement (Second) of Contracts.*

The Restatements, which generally summarize the common law rules followed by most states, do not in themselves have the force of law but are an important secondary source of legal analysis and opinion to which judges often refer in making their decisions. We refer to them frequently in subsequent chapters of this text. Excerpts from the *Restatement (Second) of Torts* can be found in Appendix D.

International Doctrines and Agreements

Because business is becoming increasingly global in scope, numerous cases now brought before the courts involve issues concerning foreign parties or governments. But there is no single supreme authority in the international arena; thus the laws of all nations are potential sources of law. Which law is applicable depends uniquely on the facts of each individual case. International doctrines, treaties, and other agreements pertaining to business are also important sources of law that pertain to the international legal environment. The international component of the legal environment of business is examined more fully throughout the text, but it is perhaps worthwhile at this point to examine the sources of international law as well as compare the legal systems operating throughout the world.

■ Sources of International Law— Treaties, Customs, National Law, and International Institutions

For a rule of action or conduct to take on the quality of law rather than mere admonishment, there must be some force that compels individuals and organizations to adhere to the rule. Sometimes that force is provided by an institution that has a monopoly over the use of coercion—that is, government. At other times, adherence is based on custom or the perception that rules should be followed for the common good of society, even without the threat of sanctions. Self-interest also can create compliance: individuals comply so as to induce others to reciprocate. Usually, law is established in society by a combination of factors.

The international arena, however, is unique because such elements are weak or nonexistent; there is no single-source, one-world government, and language and customs are too diverse to ensure complete voluntary compliance with a uniformly accepted set of norms. Still, international law does exist. But it is really an intermingling of rules and constraints derived from a variety of sources. The laws of individual nations, international treaties, custom, and various international organizations— the United Nations (UN), the International Bank of Reconstruction (the World Bank), and the General Agreement on Trade and Tariffs (GATT)—all comprise the present international legal environment of business. International law affects the acts of both nations and the individual citizens of nations.

The Public-Private International Law Distinction

Most scholars of international law make a distinction between public and private international law. Public international law concerns rules that govern the actions of nations in their dealings with one another and, in some circumstances, the actions of nations in their dealings with individuals of a foreign country. The rules are based on principles that are generally accepted as binding on nations as members of the international community. Private international law, in contrast, concerns the rules that affect the dealings between individual citizens of one country and individual citizens of another country.

While this distinction between public and private international law exists in theory, in practice it is sometimes difficult to make. Individuals make international transactions that are affected by the trade treaties entered into by their respective governments. Similarly, governments frequently intervene to promote the private commercial affairs of their citizens.

Public International Law

Nations rely on public international law in conducting diplomatic relations, negotiations, and policymaking. Public international law includes issues that relate to justifications and conduct in the use of military force. Other issues include how investments by foreigners and sales of foreign products should be treated by the host government. Most of these issues may be analyzed with reference to the various treaties, conventions, and domestic laws of a nation, as well as to the policies and regulations of international organizations.

THE INTERNATIONAL COURT OF JUSTICE The International Court of Justice, also known as the World Court, is a fifteen-member judicial tribunal whose jurisdiction is established in a statute annexed to the Charter of the United Nations. The World Court is the principal judicial arm of the United Nations. The fifteen judges are elected by the UN General Assembly and the UN Security Council for a term of nine years. All member nations of the UN automatically have standing to bring disputes before the World Court, but no country may be compelled to submit to the World Court's jurisdiction. This lack of compulsory jurisdiction is a major institutional weakness of the World Court. (Nations that are not members of the UN may submit to the World Court's jurisdiction under conditions prescribed by the UN.)

Despite the World Court's status as the judicial arm of the UN, the court has not been a decisive factor in resolving international legal issues, particularly in the area of commercial activity. First, only nations can appear before the World Court—though sometimes governments have appeared as representatives of private parties to contest the actions of another government. Second, the World Court's decisions are binding only on the parties to a particular case; there is no precedent value in a decision of the World Court to bind future actions of countries that did not participate directly in a proceeding. Third, as noted above, nations are free to choose whether or not to subject themselves to the World Court's jurisdiction in any particular case; thus they tend to pick and choose which international disputes to submit to the World Court and when to simply ignore the World Court's jurisdiction. Finally, there is no effective power to enforce compliance with the World Court's decision—if a nation chooses not to abide by a decision (assuming it consented to the World Court's jurisdiction to begin with), there is no international police officer to enforce a penalty for the failure to comply.

TREATIES   Treaties provide a source of international law. A treaty is an agreement or contract between two or more nations, which creates rights and duties binding on the parties to the treaty just as a private contract creates rights and duties binding on the parties to the contract. To give effect to a treaty, the supreme power of each sovereign nation that is a party to the treaty must ratify it. For example, Article II, Section 2, of the United States Constitution requires approval by two-thirds of the Senate before a treaty executed by the president will be binding on the United States government.

One treaty of particular significance to the international legal environment of business is the United Nations Convention on Contracts for the International Sale of Goods (CISG). Essentially, the CISG is to international sales contracts what

the Uniform Commercial Code is to domestic sales contracts. It governs the international sale of goods between firms or individuals located in different countries if the respective countries of the parties to the contract have ratified the CISG. Although the list of countries that have ratified the convention is small, the list does include many of the world's leading economic powers, including the United States, and it is expected to grow rapidly.

Note that the treaty does affect individuals engaged in international dealings; this is an example of the overlap of public and private international law described earlier. Other treaties and conventions important to private international commerce and litigation include the following: United Nations Convention on the Recognition and Enforcement of Foreign Arbitral Awards; Hague Convention on Service Abroad of Judicial and Extra-Judicial Documents in Civil and Commercial Matters; Hague Convention on the Taking of Evidence Abroad in Civil and Commercial Matters; and Inter-American Convention on Letters Rogatory.

Private International Law

Apart from the international treaties and conventions discussed in the preceding section, private international law—at least insofar as the legal environment of business is concerned—centers around private parties' right to choose the law that will govern their transactions. Within certain limitations, parties can choose not only the law that will govern their transaction (for instance, the law of California or the law of Nigeria), but also the forum in which future disputes will be decided (for example, a U.S. court or a Nigerian court). Also common in international agreements involving parties that speak different languages are clauses specifying the language that will be used in interpreting the agreement's terms.

CHOICE OF LAW   A contractual provision designating the applicable law, called a **choice-of-law clause,** is typically included in every international contract. At common law (and in European civil law systems, discussed later in this chapter), parties are allowed to choose the law that will govern their contractual relationship as long as they choose the law of a jurisdiction that has a substantial relationship to the parties and to the international business transaction. Under Section 1-105 of the Uniform Commercial Code, parties may choose the law that will govern the contract as long as the choice is "reasonable." Article 6 of the CISG, however, imposes no limitation on the parties in their choice of what law shall govern the contract, and the Hague Convention on the Law Applicable to Contracts for the International Sale of Goods—often referred to as the "Choice-of-Law Convention"—allows unlimited autonomy in the choice of law. Whenever a choice of law is not specified in a contract, the Hague Convention indicates that the governing law is the law of the country in which the *seller's* place of business is located.

CHOICE OF FORUM   A private international contract involves parties of different nationalities and transactions that occur in different countries. Thus if a dispute arises between the parties, litigation may be sought in courts in different nations. There are no universally accepted rules regarding the jurisdiction of a particular court over subject matter or parties to a dispute. Consequently, parties to an international transaction normally include in the contract a **forum-selection clause** designating the forum in which a dispute will be litigated. A forum-selection clause should indicate not only what country but what court has jurisdiction and, if applicable, should indicate which court has exclusive jurisdiction, so as to preclude other courts from entering the case. The forum does not necessarily have to be within the geographical boundaries of either of the parties' own countries.

CHOICE OF LANGUAGE   A deal struck between a U.S. company and a company in, say, Argentina normally involves two languages—English and Spanish. The complex contractual terms involved may often not be understood by one party in the other party's language. Typically, many phrases in one language are not readily translatable into another. To make sure that no disputes arise out of this language problem, an international sales contract normally has a **choice-of-language clause** designating the official language by which the contract is to be interpreted in the event of disagreement. Such a clause might state that the agreement is being written in English, which shall be regarded as the authoritative and official text. The clause

may further allow for the agreement to be translated into, say, Spanish, such translation to be ratified by both parties, and may state that the foreign company can rely on the translation. If arbitration is anticipated, an additional clause must be added to indicate that the arbitration will be in, say, English, Spanish, or French—or whatever the case may be.

■ The Global Perspective: Law around the World

The common law system discussed in this chapter is only one of the judicial systems found in the world today. Another major form is the *civil law system*. Most of the legal systems that exist today are characterized as either common law or civil law systems.[5] These two systems differ in their historical beginnings and in some of their characteristics.

The common law system has its roots in medieval England and owes its early development to the courts of the English kings of the twelfth century A.D. The civil law system grew out of ancient Roman law. The civil law system reached the zenith of its development within the Roman Empire during the first and second centuries A.D. Over the course of time, many developments brought substantial modifications in the civil law system; the modern form of the civil law system is very different from that of the ancient Roman system.

Today, the civil law system is followed in most of the continental European countries, as well as in the Latin American, African, and Asian countries that were once colonies of the continental European nations. Japan and South Africa also have civil law systems. Ingredients of the civil law system are found in the Islamic courts of predominantly Muslim countries. Courts in the former Soviet Union use a system similar to that of the civil law. In the United States, the state of Louisiana,

---

5.   When we are speaking about different legal systems, *civil law* refers to one of the various *systems* of law. When we use the term *civil law* within the context of a single system of law, however, it is used to distinguish all the *areas* of law other than the area of criminal law. Thus, within the common law *system*, civil law is that area of law distinct from the area of criminal law and includes tort law, contract law, and the law of real property.

with its historical ties to France, has a system that can be characterized in part as a civil law system. The legal systems of Puerto Rico, Quebec, and Scotland are similarly characterized as having elements of the civil law system.

The starting point for deciding a controversy in a civil law proceeding is almost always a statute. In the common law system, legal arguments center around earlier judicial decisions. In the civil law system, in contrast, courts avoid giving special consideration to how earlier cases were decided. The decisions of judges in earlier cases are afforded no more regard than the opinions of other legal writers.

The judges in a civil law system take an active role in questioning witnesses and conducting court proceedings. This reduces the role that attorneys play in a civil law proceeding. The civil law system is often referred to as an ''inquisitorial'' system because of the dominant role played by judges. In a common law system, the attorneys play a more active role in shaping the content and course of a case. For this reason the common law system is characterized as ''adversarial.''

Despite the differences in the two systems, distinctions are beginning to blur. For example, in theory, case law precedent is not to play any special role in the civil law system. In fact, however, case precedents are widely followed by the civil law courts. Similarly, judges in the common law system have shown an increased willingness to emulate their civil law system counterparts by playing a more active role in court proceedings; for example, American law judges increasingly act to develop facts and issues during trial proceedings.

Yet another trend in the coalescence of the two systems is the increasing importance of statutes and administrative rules in the common law system. As noted earlier, recent decades have witnessed a proliferation of statutes and administrative rules that have modified or wholly superseded the earlier common law. As will be seen throughout our text, this trend has had particular impact on the legal and regulatory environment of business. This is especially true with regard to commercial transactions subject to the statutory provisions of the Uniform Commercial Code and with regard to business activities subject to the administrative rules of numerous federal and state regulatory agencies.

■ Classification of Law

The body of law is huge. To study it, one must break it down by some means of classification. No single classification system can cover such a large mass of information; consequently, those systems that have been devised tend to overlap. Moreover, they are, of necessity, arbitrary in some respects. A discussion of the best-known systems follows.

Substantive versus Procedural Law

Substantive law includes all laws that define, describe, regulate, and create legal rights and obligations. For example, a rule stating that promises are enforced only when each party has received something of value from the other party is part of substantive law. So, too, is a rule stating that a person who has injured another through negligence must pay damages.

Procedural law establishes the methods of enforcing the rights established by substantive law. Questions about how a lawsuit should begin, what papers need to be filed, which court will hear the suit, which witnesses can be called, and so on are all questions of procedural law. In brief, substantive law tells us our rights; procedural law tells us how to exercise them.

Exhibit 1–1 classifies law in terms of its subject matter, dividing it into law covering substantive issues and law covering procedural issues. Most of this text concerns substantive law.

Public versus Private Law

Public law addresses the relationship between persons and their government, whereas **private law** addresses direct dealings between persons.

Criminal law and constitutional law, for example, are generally classified as public law because they deal with persons and their relationships to government. Criminal acts, though they may involve only one victim, are seen as offenses against society as a whole and are prohibited by governments for the purpose of protecting the public. Constitutional law is frequently classified as public law, because it involves questions of whether the government—federal, state, or local— has the power to act in a particular fashion; often the issue is whether a law, duly passed, exceeds

■ **Exhibit 1–1 Subject Matter of Substantive and Procedural Law**

The importance of the distinction between substantive and procedural law is more than academic. The *result* of a case may well depend upon the determination that a rule is substantive rather than procedural.

Substantive (Policy)	Procedural (Method of Enforcement)
Administrative law	Administrative procedure
Agency	Appellate procedure
Bailments	Civil procedure
Commercial paper	Criminal procedure
Constitutional law	Evidence
Contracts	
Corporation law	
Criminal law	
Insurance	
Partnerships	
Personal property	
Real property	
Sales	
Taxation	
Torts	
Trusts and wills	

the limits set on the government. See Exhibit 1–2 for examples of private and public law.

Civil versus Criminal Law

Civil law concerns the duties that exist between persons or between citizens and their governments, excluding the duty not to commit crimes. Contract law, for example, is part of civil law. The whole body of *tort law,* which has to do with the infringement by one person of the legally recognized rights of another, is an area of civil law. Tort law is discussed in Chapter 6, as well as in Chapter 8, which deals with torts related to business.

Criminal law, in contrast to civil law, is concerned with wrongs committed against the public as a whole. Criminal acts are prohibited by local, state, or federal government statutes. Criminal law is always public law, whereas civil law is sometimes public and sometimes private. In a criminal case, the government seeks to impose a penalty on

■ **Exhibit 1–2 Examples of Public and Private Law**

Public law governs the relationship between persons and their government. Private law governs the relationships among individuals.

Public Law	Private Law
Administrative law	Agency
Civil, criminal, and appellate procedure	Commercial paper
	Contracts
Constitutional law	Corporation law
Criminal law	Partnerships
Evidence	Personal property
Taxation	Real property
	Sales
	Torts
	Trusts and wills

an allegedly guilty person. In a civil case, one party (sometimes the government) tries to make the other party comply with a duty or pay for the damage caused by failure to so comply.

Exhibit 1–3 lists the areas of law falling within each of these classifications.

■ Remedies at Law versus Remedies in Equity

In the early English King's Courts, the kinds of remedies that the courts could grant were severely restricted. If one person wronged another in some way, the King's Courts could award as compensation one or more of the following: (1) land, (2) items of value, or (3) money. The courts that awarded this compensation became known as **courts of law,** and the three remedies were called **remedies at law.** Even though the system introduced uniformity in the settling of disputes, when *plaintiffs* (parties suing) wanted a remedy other than economic compensation, the courts of law could do nothing, so "no remedy, no right." When individuals could not obtain an adequate remedy in a court of law because of strict technicalities, they petitioned the king for relief. Most of these petitions were decided by an adviser to the king, called a *chancellor.* The chancellor was said to be the "keeper of the king's conscience." When the chancellor thought that the claim was a fair one, new and unique remedies were granted. In this way,

■ Exhibit 1–3 Criminal and Civil Law

An important feature distinguishing criminal and civil law is the sanction imposed on the wrongdoer. Criminal sanctions may include imprisonment while civil sanctions emphasize payment of money.

Criminal Law	Civil Law
Administrative law	Agency
Antitrust	Bailments
Constitutional law	Bankruptcy
Criminal law	Business organizations
Environmental law	Commercial paper
Labor law	Contracts
Securities law	Insurance
	Property
	Sales
	Secured transactions
	Torts
	Trusts and wills

a new body of rules and remedies came into being, and eventually formal courts of chancery, or **courts of equity,** were established.

Equity Courts

The distinction between law and equity courts is now primarily of historical interest, but it is still relevant to students of business law because legal and equitable **remedies** differ. (*Remedies* are the legal means to recover a right or redress a wrong.) To seek the proper remedy for a wrong, one must know what remedies are available.

Equity is that branch of law, founded on what might be described as notions of justice and fair dealing, that seeks to supply a remedy when there is no adequate available remedy at law. Thus, two distinct systems were created, each having a different set of judges. Two bodies of rules and remedies existed at the same time, remedies at law and **remedies in equity.** Plaintiffs had to specify whether they were bringing an ''action at law'' or an ''action in equity,'' and they chose their courts accordingly. Only one remedy could be granted for a particular wrong, and even in equity the wrong had to be of a type the court could recognize as remediable.

Courts of equity had the responsibility of using discretion in supplementing the common law. Even today, when the same court can award both legal and equitable remedies, such discretion is often guided by so-called *equitable principles and maxims.* Maxims are propositions or general statements of rules of law that courts often invoke. Listed below are a few of the maxims of equity.

1. Whoever seeks equity must do equity. (Anyone who wishes to be treated fairly must treat others fairly.)
2. When there is equal equity, the law must prevail. (The law will determine the outcome of a controversy in which the merits of both sides are equal.)
3. One seeking the aid of an equity court must come to the court with clean hands. (Plaintiffs must have acted fairly and honestly.)
4. Equity will not suffer a right to exist without a remedy. (Equitable relief will be awarded when there is a right to relief and there is no adequate remedy at law.)
5. Equity regards substance rather than form. (Equity is more concerned with fairness and justice than with legal technicalities.)
6. Equity aids the vigilant, not those who rest on their rights. (Individuals who fail to look out for their rights until after a reasonable period of time has passed will not be helped.)

The last maxim is worthy of discussion. It has become known as the equitable doctrine of **laches,** and it can be used as a **defense** (an argument raised by the defendant to defeat the plaintiff's cause of action or recovery). The doctrine arose to encourage people to bring lawsuits while the evidence was fresh. What constitutes a reasonable time, of course, varies according to the circumstances of the case. Time periods for different types of cases are now usually fixed by **statutes of limitations.** After the time allowed under a statute of limitations has expired, no action can be brought, no matter how strong the case was originally.

Equitable Relief

A number of equitable remedies are available. Three of them—specific performance, injunctions, and rescission—are briefly discussed here. These and other equitable remedies are discussed in more detail at appropriate points in the chapters that follow.

DECREES OF SPECIFIC PERFORMANCE   Previously, courts of law and equity were separate. Hence, a plaintiff might come into a court of equity asking it to order a defendant to perform within the terms of a contract. A court of law could not issue such an order because its remedies were limited to payment of money or property as compensation for damages. A court of equity, however, could issue a decree of **specific performance**—an order to perform what was promised. This remedy was, and still is, only available when the dispute before the court involves a *contractual* transaction.

INJUNCTIONS   If a person wanted to prevent the occurrence of a certain activity, he or she would have to go to the chancellor in equity to ask that the person doing the wrongful act be ordered to stop. The order was called an injunction. An **injunction** is usually an order to a specific person, directing that person to do or to refrain from doing a particular act.

RESCISSION   Often the legal remedy of the payment of money for damages is unavailable or inadequate when disputes occur over agreements. In such cases, the equitable remedy of rescission is frequently given. **Rescission**[6] is an action to undo an agreement—to return the parties to their *status quo* prior to the agreement. If rescission is granted, all duties created by the agreement are abolished. If, for example, a sales agreement is made because a seller misrepresents the quality of goods but the fraud is discovered before any money changes hands, the buyer might want merely to rescind the agreement.

The Merging of Law and Equity

During the nineteenth century, most states adopted rules of procedure that resulted in combined courts of law and equity—although some states, such as Arkansas, still retain the distinction. Today, a plaintiff or a petitioner in equity (the person bringing the action) may request both legal and equitable remedies in the same action, and the trial court judge may grant either or both forms of relief.

Despite the merging of the courts, it is still important to distinguish between actions at law and actions in equity. As mentioned, the primary importance is in the remedy sought. Vestiges of the procedures used when the courts were separate still exist. Today, differences in procedure depend on whether the civil lawsuit involves an action in equity or an action at law. Exhibit 1–4 is illustrative and applies to most states.

The major practical difference between law and equity today is the right to demand a jury trial in actions at law. In the old courts of equity, the chancellor heard both sides of an issue and decided what should be done. Juries were considered inappropriate. In actions at law, however, juries heard evidence and made determinations regarding questions of fact, including the amount of damages to be awarded. Today, in a case involving equitable rights, a judge may impanel a jury to serve in an advisory capacity.

■ How to Find Case Law

Laws pertaining to business consist of case law and statutory law. A substantial number of cases are presented in this text to provide you with concise, real-life illustrations of the interpretation and application of the law by the courts. Many other court decisions have been referenced in footnotes throughout the text. Because of the importance of knowing how to find these and other court opinions, this section offers a brief introduction to the case reporting system and to the legal "shorthand" employed in referencing court cases.

State Court Decisions

Most state trial court decisions are not published. Except in New York and a few other states, which publish selected opinions of their trial courts, decisions from the state trial courts are merely filed in the office of the clerk of the court; they are available there for public inspection.

Written decisions of the appellate (reviewing) courts, however, are published and distributed. At one time, each state published the decisions of its own appellate courts. Many states still publish these decisions, in consecutively numbered volumes called *Reports*.

Additionally, state court opinions appear in regional units of the *National Reporter System*, published by West Publishing Company. Most lawyers

---

6.   Pronounced reh-*sizh*-en.

■ **Exhibit 1–4**
Procedural Differences between an Action at Law and an Action in Equity

Procedure	Action at Law	Action in Equity
Initiation of lawsuit	By filing of a complaint	By filing of a petition
Decision	By jury or judge	By judge (no jury)
Result	Judgment	Decree
Remedy	Monetary damages	Injunction, decree of specific performance, or rescission

and libraries have the West reporters because they report cases more quickly and are distributed more widely than the state-published reports. In fact, many states have eliminated their own reports in favor of West's National Reporter System. The National Reporter System divides the states into the following geographical areas: Atlantic (A. or A.2d), Southeastern (S.E. or S.E.2d), Southwestern (S.W. or S.W.2d), Northwestern (N.W. or N.W.2d), Northeastern (N.E. or N.E.2d), Southern (So. or So.2d), and Pacific (P. or P.2d). The states included in each of these regional divisions are indicated in Exhibit 1-5, which illustrates West's National Reporter System. The "2d" after any of the abbreviations in the National Reporter System refers to the second series for that particular reporter.

After appellate decisions have been published, they are normally referred to (cited) by the name of the case; the volume, name, and page of the state's official report (if different from West's National Reporter System); the volume, unit, and page number of the *National Reporter;* and the volume, name, and page number of any other selected reporter. This information constitutes what is called the **citation.** For example, consider the following case: *Hoffman v. Red Owl Stores, Inc.,* 26 Wis.2d 683, 133 N.W.2d 267 (1965). We see that the opinion in this case may be found in volume 26 of the official *Wisconsin Reports, Second Series,* on page 683 and in volume 133 of the *North Western Reporter, Second Series,* on page 267. When, as in this case, two or more citations are given for the same case, they are called *parallel citations.* In reprinting appellate opinions in this text, in addition to the reporter, we give the name of the court hearing the case and the year of the court decision.

A few of the states—including those with intermediate appellate courts, such as California, Il-

linois, and New York—have more than one report for opinions given by courts within their states. Sample citations from these courts, as well as others, are listed and explained in Exhibit 1–6.

Federal Court Decisions

Federal trial court decisions are published unofficially in West's *Federal Supplement* (F.Supp.), and opinions from the circuit courts of appeal are reported unofficially in West's *Federal Reporter* (F. or F.2d). Cases concerning federal bankruptcy law are published unofficially in West's *Bankruptcy Reporter* (Bankr.). Opinions from the United States Supreme Court are reported in the *United States Reports* (U.S.), West's *Supreme Court Reporter* (S.Ct.), the *Lawyers' Edition of the Supreme Court Reports* (L.Ed.), and other publications.

The *United States Reports* is the official edition of all decisions of the United States Supreme Court for which there are written opinions. Published by the federal government, the series includes reports of Supreme Court cases dating from the August term of 1791, although originally many of the decisions were not reported in the early volumes.

West's *Supreme Court Reporter* (S.Ct.) is an unofficial edition dating from the Court's term in October 1882. Preceding each of its case reports are a summary of the case and *headnotes* (brief editorial statements of the law involved in the case, numbered to correspond to numbers in the report). The headnotes are also given classification numbers that serve to cross-reference each headnote to other headnotes on similar points throughout the National Reporter System and other West publications to facilitate research of all relevant cases on a given point. This is important because, as may be evident from the discussion of *stare decisis,* a lawyer's goal in undertaking legal research is to

■ Exhibit 1–5 National Reporter System—Regional/Federal

Regional Reporters	Coverage Beginning	Coverage
Atlantic Reporter (A. or A.2d)	1885	Connecticut, Delaware, Maine, Maryland, New Hampshire, New Jersey, Pennsylvania, Rhode Island, Vermont, and District of Columbia.
North Eastern Reporter (N.E. or N.E.2d)	1885	Illinois, Indiana, Massachusetts, New York, and Ohio.
North Western Reporter (N.W. or N.W.2d)	1879	Iowa, Michigan, Minnesota, Nebraska, North Dakota, South Dakota, and Wisconsin.
Pacific Reporter (P. or P.2d)	1883	Alaska, Arizona, California, Colorado, Hawaii, Idaho, Kansas, Montana, Nevada, New Mexico, Oklahoma, Oregon, Utah, Washington, and Wyoming.
South Eastern Reporter (S.E. or S.E.2d)	1887	Georgia, North Carolina, South Carolina, Virginia, and West Virginia.
South Western Reporter (S.W. or S.W.2d)	1886	Arkansas, Kentucky, Missouri, Tennessee, and Texas.
Southern Reporter (So. or So.2d)	1887	Alabama, Florida, Louisiana, and Mississippi.

Federal Reporters		
Federal Reporter (F. or F.2d)	1880	U.S. Circuit Court from 1880 to 1912; U.S. Commerce Court from 1911 to 1913; U.S. District Courts from 1880 to 1932; U.S. Court of Claims from 1929 to 1932 and from 1960 to 1982; U.S. Claims Court since 1982; U.S. Courts of Appeals since 1891; U.S. Court of Customs and Patent Appeals since 1929; U.S. Emergency Court of Appeals since 1943.
Federal Supplement (F.Supp.)	1932	U.S. Court of Claims from 1932 to 1960; U.S. District Courts since 1932; U.S. Customs Court since 1956.
Federal Rules Decisions (F.R.D.)	1939	U.S. District Courts involving the Federal Rules of Civil Procedure since 1939 and Federal Rules of Criminal Procedure since 1946.
Supreme Court Reporter (S.Ct.)	1882	U.S. Supreme Court since the October term of 1882.
Bankruptcy Reporter (Bankr.)	1980	Bankruptcy decisions of U.S. Bankruptcy Courts, U.S. District Courts, U.S. Courts of Appeals, and U.S. Supreme Court.
Military Justice Reporter (M.J.)	1978	U.S. Court of Military Appeals and Courts of Military Review for the Army, Navy, Air Force, and Coast Guard.

NATIONAL REPORTER SYSTEM MAP

■ **Exhibit 1–6 How to Read Citations**

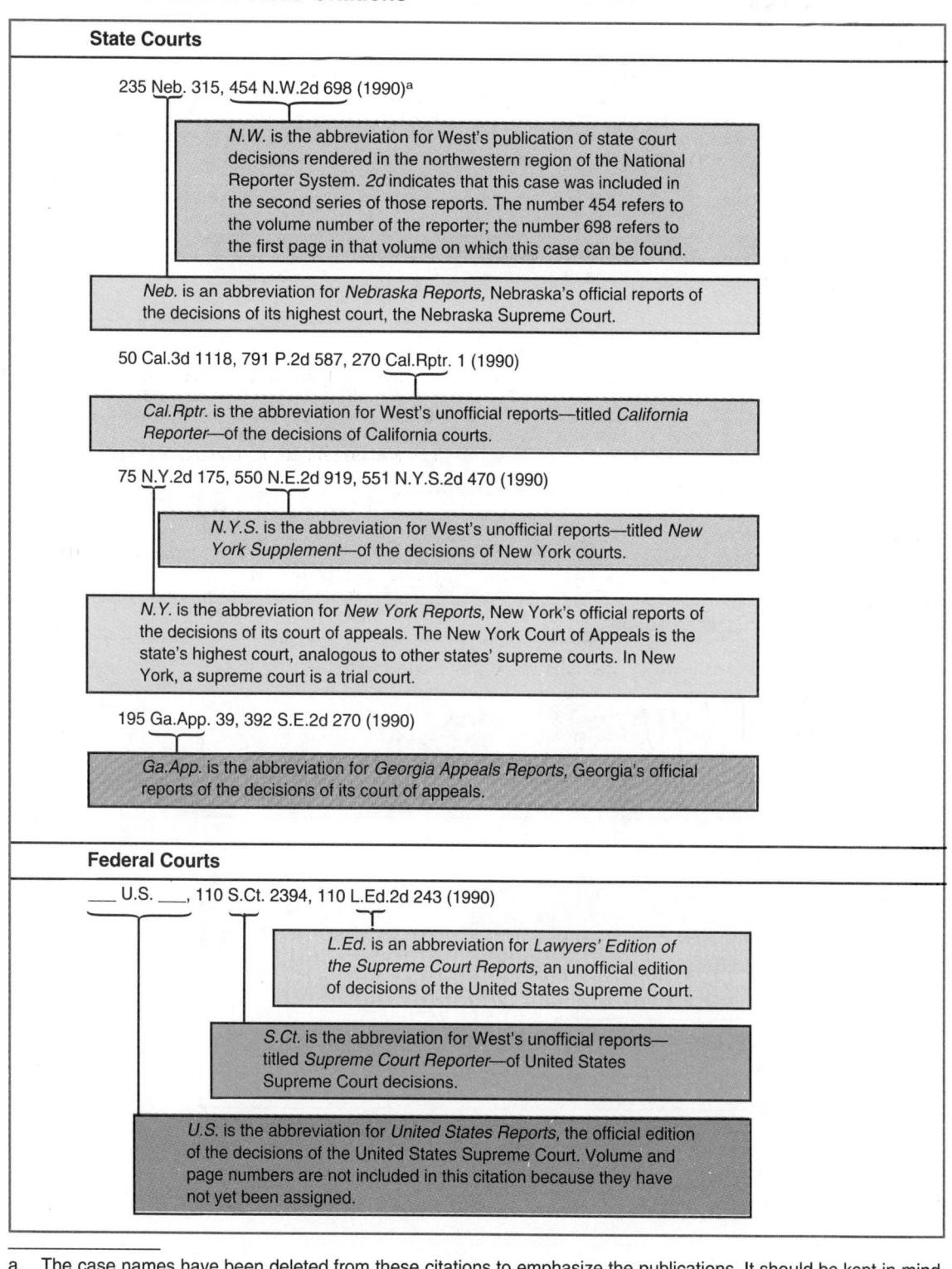

a. The case names have been deleted from these citations to emphasize the publications. It should be kept in mind, however, that the name of a case is as important as the specific page numbers in the volumes in which it is found. If a citation is incorrect, the correct citation may be found in a publication's index of case names. The date of a case is also important because, in addition to providing a check on error in citations, the value of a recent case an authority is likely to be greater than that of earlier cases.

■ **Exhibit 1–6 How to Read Citations (Continued)**

Federal Courts (continued)

901 F.2d 1550 (11th Cir. 1990)

> *11th Cir.* is an abbreviation denoting that this case was decided in the United States Court of Appeals for the Eleventh Circuit.

744 F.Supp. 1118 (M.D.Fla. 1990)

> *M.D.Fla.* is an abbreviation indicating that the United States District Court for the Middle District of Florida decided this case.

English Courts

9 Exch. 341, 156 Eng.Rep. 145 (1854)

> *Eng.Rep.* is an abbreviation for *English Reports, Full Reprint,* a series of reports containing selected decisions made in English courts between 1378 and 1865.

> *Exch.* is an abbreviation for *English Exchequer Reports,* which included the original reports of cases decided in England's Court of Exchequer.

Statutory and Other Citations

18 U.S.C. Section 1961(1)(A)

> *U.S.C.* denotes *United States Code,* the codification of *United States Statutes at Large.* The number 18 refers to the statute's U.S.C. title number and 1961 to its section number within that title. The number 1 refers to a subsection within the section and the letter A to a subdivision within the subsection.

UCC 2-206(1)(b)

> *UCC* is an abbreviation for *Uniform Commercial Code.* The first number 2 is a reference to an article of the UCC and 206 to a section within that article. The number 1 refers to a subsection within the section and the letter b to a subdivision within the subsection.

Restatement (Second) of Torts, Section 568

> *Restatement (Second) of Torts* refers to the second edition of the American Law Institute's *Restatement of the Law of Torts.* The number 568 refers to a specific section.

17 C.F.R. Section 230.505

> *C.F.R.* is an abbreviation for *Code of Federal Regulations,* a compilation of federal administrative regulations. The number 17 is a reference to the regulation's title number and 230.505 to a specific section within that title.

find an authority that cannot be factually distinguished from his or her case.

The Lawyers Cooperative Publishing Company of Rochester, New York, publishes the *Lawyers' Edition of the Supreme Court Reports* (L.Ed.), an unofficial edition of the entire series of the Supreme Court reports that contains many of the decisions not reported in the early official volumes. Also, among other editorial features, the *Lawyers' Edition,* in its second series, precedes the report of each case with a full summary, includes excerpts from briefs of counsel, and discusses in detail selected cases of special interest to the legal profession.

Sample citations for federal court decisions are listed and explained in Exhibit 1–6.

Old Case Law

On a few occasions, the opinions cited in this text are from old, classic cases dating to the nineteenth century or earlier; some of these are from the English courts. The citations to these cases appear not to conform to the descriptions given above because the reports in which they were published have since been replaced. Whenever citations to old case law are made in this text, the citations will be explained in footnotes.

Case Digests and Legal Encyclopedias

The body of American case law consists of nearly 5 million decisions, to which more than 40,000 are added each year. Because judicial decisions are published in chronological order, finding relevant precedents would be a Herculean task if it were not for case digests, legal encyclopedias, and many other publications that classify decisions according to subject.

Case digests consist of alphabetical arrangements of legal topics. Collected under each topic heading are very short statements of relevant points of law in reported cases. Citations to the cases are included. The American Digest System, the most comprehensive in its coverage, condenses and arranges cases reported in West's National Reporter System.

Legal encyclopedias also arrange topics alphabetically and provide case citations, but legal encyclopedias include more detailed consideration of

the law than digests. A legal encyclopedia editorially synthesizes rules from groups of cases and discusses majority and minority views, historical developments, and so on. The text of *Corpus Juris Secundum,* the most comprehensive legal encyclopedia, is based on all reported cases from 1658 to date.

■ How to Find Administrative and Statutory Law

This text also includes numerous citations to federal and state laws and regulations. When Congress passes laws, they are collected in a publication titled *United States Statutes at Large.* When state legislatures pass laws, they are collected in similar state publications. These publications arrange laws by date of enactment. Most frequently, however, laws are referred to in their codified form—that is, the form in which they appear in the federal and state codes. These references are called citations. This section offers a brief introduction to the abbreviations used in citations to statutory and administrative law.

In these codes, laws are compiled by subject. For example, the *United States Code* (U.S.C.) arranges by subject all existing federal laws of a public and permanent nature. Each of the fifty subjects into which the laws have been arranged is given a title and a title number. For example, laws relating to commerce and trade are collected in Title 15, which is titled "Commerce and Trade." Within each subdivision (title), statutes are assigned numbers, which are referred to as section numbers. A U.S.C. citation includes title and section numbers. Thus, a reference to "15 U.S.C. Section 1" means that the statute can be found in Section 1 of Title 15. ("Section" may also be designated by the symbol §.)

State codes follow the U.S.C. pattern of law arranged by subject. They may be called Codes, Revisions, Compilations, Consolidations, General Statutes, or Statutes, depending on the preference of the states. In some codes, subjects are designated by number. In others, they are designated by name. For example, "13 Pennsylvania Consolidated Statutes Section 1101" means that the statute can be found in Section 1101 of Title 13 of the Pennsylvania code. "California Commercial Code Section

1101'' means that the statute can be found in Section 1101 under the commercial heading of the California Code. Abbreviations may be used. For example, "13 Pennsylvania Consolidated Statutes Section 1101" may be abbreviated "13 Pa. C.S. § 1101," and "California Commercial Code Section 1101" may be abbreviated "Cal. Com. Code § 1101."

Rules and regulations adopted by federal administrative agencies are compiled in the *Code of Federal Regulations* (C.F.R.). Like the U.S.C., the C.F.R. is divided into fifty titles. Rules within each title are assigned section numbers. A full citation to the C.F.R. includes title and section numbers. For example, a reference to "17 C.F.R. Section 230.504" means that the rule can be found in Section 230.504 of Title 17.

Commercial publications of these laws and regulations are available and are widely used. For example, West Publishing Company publishes the *United States Code Annotated* (U.S.C.A.). The U.S.C.A. contains the complete text of laws included in the U.S.C., as well as notes of court decisions that interpret and apply specific sections of the statutes, plus the text of presidential proclamations and executive orders. The U.S.C.A. also includes research aids, such as cross-references to related statutes, historical notes, and library references. A citation to the U.S.C.A. is similar to a citation to the U.S.C.: "15 U.S.C.A. Section 1."

■ How to Analyze Case Law

Knowing how to read and analyze a court opinion is an essential step in undertaking accurate legal environment research. A further step involves "briefing" the case. Legal researchers routinely brief cases by summarizing and reducing the texts of the opinions to their essential elements. How to brief a case is discussed in Appendix A, which also includes excerpts of selected cases for briefing.

The cases presented in this text have already been analyzed and edited by the authors. For each case presented, we have provided a "Background and Facts" section so that you may quickly perceive the issue or issues before the court. These sections are strictly our own summaries—in our own words—of information given in the full written opinion of the court. We conclude each case presentation with the court's "Decision and Rem-

edy"—again, in our own words. Occasionally, we also add "Comments" or "Ethical Considerations" or "International Considerations" at the end of a case presentation. This format is illustrated in the sample court case at the end of this section.

Case Titles

In the title of a case, such as *Adams v. Jones,* the *v.* or *vs.* stands for versus, which means "against." In the trial court, Adams was the plaintiff—the person who filed the suit. Jones was the defendant. If the case is appealed, however, the appellate court will sometimes place the name of the party appealing the decision first, so that the case may be called *Jones v. Adams.* Because only some appellate courts retain the trial court order of names, it is often impossible to distinguish the plaintiff from the defendant in the title of a reported appellate court decision. The student must carefully read the facts of each case to ascertain the identity of each party. Otherwise, the discussion by the appellate court will be difficult to understand.

Terminology

The following terms and phrases are frequently encountered in court opinions and legal publications. Because it is important to understand what is meant by these terms and phrases, we define and discuss them here.

DECISIONS AND OPINIONS Most decisions reached by appellate courts are explained in written **opinions**. The opinion contains the court's reasons for its decision, the rules of law that apply, and the judgment. There are four possible types of written opinions for a case decided by an appellate court. When all judges or justices unanimously agree on an opinion, the opinion is written for the entire court and can be deemed a *unanimous opinion.* When there is not a unanimous opinion, a *majority opinion* is written, outlining the views of the majority of the judges or justices deciding the case. Often a judge or justice who feels strongly about making or emphasizing a point that was not made or emphasized in the unanimous or majority opinion will write a *concurring opinion.* That means the judge or justice agrees (concurs) with the judgment given in the unanimous or majority opinion, but for different reasons. In other than unanimous opinions, a *dissenting opinion* is usually written by a judge or justice who does not agree with the majority. The dissenting opinion is important because it may form the basis of the arguments used years later in overruling the precedent of the majority opinion.

JUDGES AND JUSTICES   The terms *judge* and *justice* are usually synonymous and represent two designations given to judges in various courts. All members of the United States Supreme Court, for example, are referred to as justices. Justice is the formal title usually given to judges of appellate courts, although this is not always the case. In New York, a justice is a trial judge of the trial court (which is called the Supreme Court), and a member of the Court of Appeals (the state's highest court) is called a judge. The term *justice* is commonly abbreviated to J., and *justices* to JJ. A United States Supreme Court case might refer to Justice Kennedy as Kennedy, J., or to Chief Justice Rehnquist as Rehnquist, C. J.

APPELLANTS AND APPELLEES   The **appellant** is the party who appeals a case to another court or jurisdiction from the court or jurisdiction in which the case was originally brought. Sometimes, an appellant who appeals from a judgment is referred to as the **petitioner** (which is also the term used to refer to a party who initiates a proceeding in equity, as previously mentioned). The **appellee** is the party against whom the appeal is taken. Sometimes, an appellee is referred to as the **respondent.**

ABBREVIATIONS   In court opinions, as well as in other areas of this text, certain terms appearing in the names of firms or organizations will often be abbreviated. The terms *Company, Incorporated,* and *Limited,* for example, will frequently appear in their abbreviated forms as *Co., Inc.,* and *Ltd.,* respectively, and *Brothers* is commonly abbreviated to *Bros.* Certain organizations or legislative acts are also frequently referred to by their initials or acronyms. In all such cases, to prevent confusion, we will give the complete name of the organization or act upon first mentioning it in a given section of the text.

A Sample Court Case

To illustrate how to read and analyze a court opinion, we have annotated an actual case that was heard by the United States Court of Appeals for the Fifth Circuit in 1991. The lawsuit was initiated by Betty Ann Ferguson, who apparently disagreed with an Internal Revenue Service determination regarding her taxes. At the hearing, she refused to "swear" before testifying, and that became the issue on her appeal.

You will note that triple asterisks (* * *) and quadruple asterisks (* * * *) frequently appear within the opinion. The triple asterisks indicate that we have deleted a few words or sentences from the opinion for the sake of readability or brevity. Quadruple asterisks mean that an entire paragraph (or more) has been omitted. Also, when the opinion cites another case or legal source, the citation to the referenced cases or sources has been omitted to save space and to improve the flow of the text. These editorial practices are continued in the other court opinions presented in this text. In addition, whenever a case opinion presented in this text includes a term or a phrase that may not be readily understandable, we have added a bracketed definition or paraphrase of the term or phrase. In the sample case below, important sections are defined or discussed in the margins.

■ Case Briefing Assignments

At the end of this chapter and all that follow, you will find one case briefing assignment. You are referred to a specific case excerpted in Appendix A. At the beginning of Appendix A there is an explanation of how to brief a case. The cases that follow are in the same format as the one excerpted on the following page, except that we have not included marginal notes.

This section indicates the parties to the lawsuit, the court rendering the opinion on the issue, the date the decision was made, and that the decision can be found in volume 921 of West's *Federal Reporter, Second Series,* on page 588.

Per curiam means "by the court."

The U.S. Tax Court is a federal court that hears disputes between taxpayers and the Internal Revenue Service.

This paragraph opens with a statement of the issue to be decided by the court. An *issue* is a disputed point of fact or law (such as a constitutional right). The rest of this paragraph explains the point of view of the party appealing the lower court's ruling.

A Latin term [pronounced *proh say*] meaning for himself or herself. In lawsuits, one who represents himself or herself without an attorney.

This paragraph describes the events that created the issue before the court.

This paragraph sets forth the general boundaries of the First Amendment rights as applied to religious beliefs. It does not address the specific facts or issue before the court but serves as a foundation for the decision.

FERGUSON v. COMMISSIONER OF INTERNAL REVENUE
United States Court of Appeals, Fifth Circuit, 1991.
921 F.2d 588.

PER CURIAM
* * * *

I.

This First Amendment case ironically arose out of a hearing in Tax Court. Although the government's brief is replete with references to income, exemptions, and taxable years, the only real issue is Betty Ann Ferguson's refusal to "swear" or "affirm" before testifying at the hearing. Her objection to oaths and affirmations is rooted in two Biblical passages, Matthew 5:33-37 and James 5:12. The passages refer only to oaths and swearing, but Ms. Ferguson explains her objection to affirmations in her brief to this court: Appellant is forbidden to swear as evidenced by the Bible directive from her God, and * * * the word "oath" has become synonymous and interchangeable with the word "affirmation," and the word "swear" [has] become synonymous and interchangeable with the word "affirm," as is evidenced in 1 U.S.C. 1 and many other authorities. * * * Also, "affirmation" is the chosen form of those who denounce the very existence of God. Because of these things, "swear" and "affirm" are very repugnant to appellant.

Ms. Ferguson, proceeding pro se, requested that Judge Korner consider the following statement set forth by the Supreme Court of Louisiana in *Staton v. Fought* as an alternative to an oath or affirmation:

> I, [Betty Ann Ferguson], do hereby declare that the facts I am about to give are, to the best of my knowledge and belief, accurate, correct, and complete.

Judge Korner abruptly denied her request, commenting that "[a]sking you to affirm that you will give true testimony does not violate any religious conviction that I have ever heard anybody had" and that he did not think affirming "violates any recognizable religious scruple." Because Ms. Ferguson could only introduce the relevant evidence through her own testimony, Judge Korner then dismissed her petition for lack of prosecution. She now appeals to this court.

II.

The right to [the] free exercise of religion, guaranteed by the First Amendment to the Constitution, is one of our most protected constitutional rights. The Supreme Court has stated that "only those interests of the highest order and those not otherwise served can overbalance legitimate claims to the free exercise of religion." The protection of the free exercise clause extends to all sincere religious beliefs; courts may not evaluate religious truth.

Fed.R.Evid. 603, applicable in Tax Court under the Internal Revenue Code, requires only that a witness "declare that [she] will testify truthfully, by oath or affirmation administered in a form calculated to awaken the witness' conscience and impress the witness' mind with the duty to do so." As evidenced in the advisory committee notes accompanying Rule 603, Congress clearly intended to minimize any intrusion on the free exercise of religion: The rule is designed to afford the flexibility required in dealing with religious adults, atheists, conscientious objectors, mental defectives, and children. Affirmation is simply a solemn undertaking to tell the truth; no special verbal formula is required.

> This is a citation to Rule 603 of the Federal Rules of Evidence. These rules govern the admissibility of facts and testimony to establish or disprove an issue in lawsuits brought in federal courts. (These rules are the model followed by states in their own rules of evidence.)

The courts that have considered oath and affirmation issues have similarly attempted to accommodate free exercise objections. In *Moore v. United States*, for example, the Supreme Court held that a trial judge erred in refusing the testimony of witnesses who would not use the word "solemnly" in their affirmations for religious reasons.

> This paragraph provides a more specific backdrop against which to evaluate the issue by setting out the rule under which all witnesses in federal court must state that they will testify truthfully and the intent underlying the rule.

In *United States v. Looper*, the Fourth Circuit held that the trial judge erred in refusing the testimony of a defendant who would not take an oath that referred to God. Specifically, Looper had told the trial judge, "I can't [take the oath] if it has God's name in it. If you ask me if I'll tell the truth, I can say that." The Fourth Circuit concluded that any form or statement that impressed on the mind and conscious[ness] of the witness the necessity for telling the truth would suffice as an oath, citing proposed Rule 603. The opinion closed by advising trial judges faced with religious objections to an oath or affirmation "to make inquiry as to what form of oath or affirmation would not offend defendant's religious beliefs but would give rise to a duty to speak the truth."

In *Gordon v. State of Idaho*, the Ninth Circuit cited both *Moore* and *Looper* in reaching a similar conclusion.

*   *   * Like Ms. Ferguson, Gordon objected to using either the word "swear" or "affirm" and offered an alternative statement. The Ninth Circuit held that the trial judge abused his discretion by refusing to even consider Gordon's proposed alternative.

> These paragraphs note what a number of courts have done when confronted with similar issues.

The cases cited by the government, *United States v. Fowler* and *Kaltenbach v. Breaux*, are not contrary. In both cases, the witnesses completely refused to cooperate. Fowler would not accept even the simple statement, "I state that I will tell the truth in my testimony." And Kaltenbach's witness refused the very alternative proposed by Ms. Ferguson, the statement set forth in *Staton*.

> The "government" here means the Internal Revenue Service.

These paragraphs present the court's consideration of the point of view on appeal of the party who was successful in the lower court proceeding.

A *brief* is a document that concisely states the (1) issues in a lawsuit, (2) facts that bring the parties to court, (3) laws that can affect the subject of the dispute, and (4) arguments that explain how the law applies to the facts so that the case will be decided in favor of the party submitting the brief.

These paragraphs represent the final conclusions and decision of the court. The court of appeals reversed the lower court's decision, holding that the failure of that court to accommodate the appellant's beliefs, in regard to the oath to be taken before testifying, was inconsistent with the First Amendment and with the Federal Rules of Evidence.

Send back.

The government offers only two justifications for Judge Korner's refusal to consider the *Staton* statement. First, the government contends that the Tax Court was not bound by a Louisiana decision. This argument misses the point entirely; Ms. Ferguson offered *Staton* as an alternative to an oath or affirmation and not as a precedent.

The government also claims that the *Staton* statement is insufficient because it does not acknowledge that the government may prosecute false statements for perjury. The federal perjury statute makes the taking of "an oath" an element of the crime of perjury. However, Ms. Ferguson has expressed her willingness to add a sentence to the *Staton* statement acknowledging that she is subject to penalties for perjury. * * *

The parties' briefs to this court suggest that the disagreement between Ms. Ferguson and Judge Korner might have been nothing more than an unfortunate misunderstanding. * * *

* * * *

If Judge Korner had attempted to accommodate Ms. Ferguson by inquiring into her objections and considering her proposed alternative, the entire matter might have been resolved without an appeal to this court. Instead, however, Judge Korner erred not only in evaluating Ms. Ferguson's religious belief, and concluding that it did not violate any "recognizable religious scruple," but also in conditioning her right to testify and present evidence on what she perceived as a violation of that belief. His error is all the more apparent in light of the fact that Ms. Ferguson was proceeding pro se at the hearing.

We therefore REVERSE the decision of the Tax Court and REMAND this case for further proceedings not inconsistent with this opinion.

■ Terms and Concepts to Review

■ Questions and Case Problems

1-1. In the middle of the last century, the United States declared war on Mexico and levied taxes to support the war effort. Henry David Thoreau, who felt that the war was unjust, refused to pay taxes to support it and was subsequently imprisoned for violating the law. Thoreau maintained that obeying the law in these circumstances would be unethical. Which of the schools of legal philosophy discussed in this chapter would be the most sympathetic toward Thoreau's views on law? Explain.

1-2. How does statutory law come into existence? How does it differ from the common law? If statutory law conflicts with the common law, which law will govern?

1-3. What is substantive law? What is procedural law? Are there reasons for the two to exist side by side?

1-4. Should judges have the same authority to overrule statutory law as they have to overrule common law? Explain.

1-5. Joe Caldor entered a hardware store to purchase an item. While he was there, a mounted display shelf holding gallon cans of paint fell on him. He suffered numerous injuries as a result and could not work for three months. He sued the owner of the hardware store for damages. Explain why this is a civil, and not a criminal, proceeding.

1-6. The concept of *equity* was mentioned in this chapter. Courts of equity tend to follow general rules or maxims rather than common law or *stare decisis* as courts of law do. Some of those maxims are: whoever seeks equity must do equity; one seeking the aid of an equity court must come to the court with clean hands; and equity aids the vigilant, not those who rest on their rights. (The last maxim is the equitable doctrine of laches, and it refers to those who do not pursue a remedy within a reasonable time.) Why would equity courts give more credence to such maxims than to a hard-and-fast body of law?

1-7. Law is constantly changing to reflect the attitudes and beliefs of society. Therefore, a society ultimately determines what rules govern the conduct of persons within that society. Briefly discuss how social attitudes and beliefs—and, consequently, the law—concerning the following topics has changed over time.
   (a) The shooting of a trespasser.
   (b) Laws governing minors.

1-8. A student is interested in reading the entire court opinion in the case of *U.S. v. Sun and Sand Imports, Ltd., Inc.,* 725 F.2d 184 (2d Cir. 1984). The case deals with the transportation, via interstate commerce, of flammable sleepwear for children in violation of the Flammable Fabrics Act. Explain specifically where the student would locate the court's opinion.

1-9. The equitable principle "Equity aids the vigilant, not those who rest on their rights" means that courts will not aid those who do not pursue a cause of action while the evidence is fresh and while the true facts surrounding the issue can be discovered. The statute of limitations, discussed in Section 2-725 of the Uniform Commercial Code (see Appendix C), is based on this principle. Under the statute of limitations, the period of time within which a party can bring an action for breach of a contract covering the sale of goods is four years—although the parties (the seller and the buyer) can reduce this period by agreement to only one year. As a practical matter, discuss which party would benefit more by a one-year period and which would benefit more by a four-year period.

1-10. Most states hold that a manufacturer who sells a defective product that causes harm to a person is strictly liable for damages, even though the manufacturer used reasonable care in the production and sale of the product and was unaware of the defect. Most state constitutions and statutes do not provide for such liability. Where, then, does such a law come from, and on what basis can such liability be imposed?

1-11. Briefly discuss whether an action at law or an action in equity is more appropriate in the following situations:
   (a) Divorce.
   (b) Automobile accident.
   (c) Preventing future trespass on your property by a neighbor.
   (d) Bankruptcy.
   (e) Libel or slander (defaming a person's reputation).

1-12. The text of this chapter stated that the doctrine of *stare decisis* became a cornerstone of the English and American judicial systems. What does *stare decisis* mean, and why has this doctrine been so fundamental to the development of our legal tradition?

1-13. Different courts sometimes reach opposite conclusions when deciding cases involving similar, if not identical, issues. Assuming that the laws and case precedents pertaining to the issues are identical in the jurisdictions in question, how can such differences in legal reasoning and consequent decisions be accounted for?

1-14. What is the difference between a concurring opinion and a majority opinion? Between a concurring opinion and a dissenting opinion? Why do judges and justices write concurring and dissenting opinions, although they will not affect the outcome of the case at hand which has already been decided by majority vote?

1-15. Case Briefing Assignment

Examine Case A.1 [In re Vermont Supreme Court Administrative Directive No. 17 v. Vermont Supreme Court, *579 A.2d 1036 (Vt. 1990)*] *in Appendix A. The case has been excerpted there in great detail. Review and then brief the case, making sure that you include answers to the following questions in your brief.*

1. Why did the Vermont Supreme Court issue Administrative Directive No. 17?
2. Why did the petitioners claim that the directive was unconstitutional?
3. Upon what case precedent did the petitioners base their argument? What was the basic issue and the court's ruling in that case precedent?
4. How did the Vermont Supreme Court rule on the issue?

Chapter 2

The Court System

Today in the United States there are fifty-two separate court systems. Each of the fifty states, in addition to the District of Columbia, has its own fully developed, independent system of courts. Additionally, there is a separate federal court system. It is important to understand that the federal court system taken as a whole is not necessarily superior to the state courts. The federal courts simply are an independent system set up to handle matters of particular federal interest and authorized by Article III, Section 2, of the United States Constitution. The federal court system extends beyond the boundaries of the United States to U.S. territories such as Guam, the Virgin Islands, and Puerto Rico. (In Guam and the Virgin Islands, territorial courts serve as both federal and state courts, whereas in Puerto Rico they serve only as federal courts.) U.S. territorial courts are established by Congress, by its authority under Article I of the U.S. Constitution. As we shall see, the United States Supreme Court is the final controlling voice over all these fifty-two systems, at least when questions of federal law are involved.

This chapter examines both the state and the federal court systems and then follows a typical case through the courts. Remember that an important step in the use of the courts or in the process of adjudication is *determining which rules apply to the facts in the case.* These rules can be *substantive* or *procedural.* They may come from several sources and can cover several areas of the law.

In studying the courts and their procedures, the first question should be which courts have the power to decide a particular case—that is, which courts have jurisdiction.

■ Jurisdiction

Juris means "law"; *diction* means "to speak." Thus, "the power to speak the law" is the literal meaning of the term **jurisdiction.** Before any court can hear a case, it must have jurisdiction—that is, the power to hear and decide the case. Without jurisdiction, a court cannot exercise any authority in the case. For a court to exercise valid authority, it must have jurisdiction both over the person against whom the suit is brought or the property involved in the suit and over the subject matter of the case.

In personam and *In rem* Jurisdiction

Before it can consider a case, a court must have power over the *person* or the *property* involved in the action. Power over the person is often referred to as ***in personam* jurisdiction.** *In personam* jurisdiction is required before a court can enter a personal judgment against a party to the action. This type of jurisdiction may be contrasted with ***in rem* jurisdiction.** An *in rem* proceeding is taken directly against property. In an *in rem* proceeding, for example, a court may use property within a state to help satisfy a general debt.

In all cases in which a court exercises jurisdiction, the parties must be served with notice that they are involved in a suit. The parties may receive actual notice (usually by service of a summons), or, when the parties cannot be located, notice may be published in a newspaper or in some other manner if permitted by statute.

Generally, a court's power is limited to the territorial boundaries of the state in which it is located. Thus, a court has jurisdiction over the person of anyone who can be served with a summons within those boundaries. Additionally, the court has jurisdiction over a person who is a resident of the state or does business within the state. Finally, in some cases in which an individual has committed a wrong, such as causing an automobile injury or selling defective goods within the state, a court can exercise jurisdiction using the authority of a *long arm statute,* even if the individual is outside the state. A **long arm statute** is a state law permitting courts to obtain jurisdiction over nonresident defendants. A court can further exercise jurisdiction over a corporation in the state in which it is incorporated, in the state in which it has its main plant or office, and in any state in which it does business.[1]

Subject Matter Jurisdiction

Subject matter jurisdiction involves a limitation on types of cases a court can hear. **Probate courts** that handle only matters relating to wills and estates offer a common example of limited subject matter jurisdiction. The subject matter jurisdiction of a court is usually defined in the statute or constitution that created the court. A court's subject matter jurisdiction can be limited not only by the subject of the lawsuit but also by the amount of money in controversy, by whether a case is civil or criminal, and by whether the proceeding is a trial or an appeal. Courts that have limited jurisdiction are sometimes said to have ''special'' jurisdiction.

The distinction between courts of general jurisdiction and courts of limited jurisdiction lies in the subject matter of cases heard. A court of general jurisdiction can decide virtually any type of case, including some cases that involve matters of federal law. Every state has courts of general jurisdiction, which may be called county courts, circuit courts, district courts, or some other name. In contrast, at both federal and state levels there are courts that hear only cases of limited subject matter. For example, one court may handle only cases dealing with divorce or child custody. Another may handle disputes over relatively small amounts of money (called a small claims court). Courts of general jurisdiction will not handle cases that are appropriate for these courts of limited jurisdiction.

Original and Appellate Jurisdiction

The distinction between courts of original jurisdiction and courts of appellate jurisdiction normally lies in whether the case is being heard for the first time. Courts having original jurisdiction are those of the first instance. In other words, they are the courts in which the trial of a case begins. In contrast, courts having appellate jurisdiction act as reviewing courts. In general, cases can be brought to them only on appeal from an order or a judgment of a lower court.

■ Venue

Jurisdiction is concerned with whether a court has authority over a specific subject matter or individual. More than one court may have jurisdiction over a case. **Venue**[2] is concerned with the most appro-

---

1. For an example of the minimum contacts required for a court to exercise jurisdiction over a corporation that is not based within its state, see *International Shoe Co. v. Washington,* 326 U.S. 310, 66 S.Ct. 154, 90 L.Ed. 95 (1945).

---

2. Pronounced *ven*-yoo.

priate location for a trial. Venue is a question that arises after a determination of jurisdiction. A particular court may have jurisdiction but not venue.

Basically, the concept of venue reflects the policy that a court trying a suit should be in the geographic neighborhood in which the incident leading to the suit occurred or in which the litigating parties reside. That neighborhood is usually the county in which the incident occurred or in which the parties live. Pretrial publicity or other factors may, however, require a change of venue to another community, especially in criminal cases, if the defendant's right to a fair and impartial jury is impaired.

The proper venue for a suit is defined by statute. Sometimes the parties to a contract designate in the contract the venue in which any future contractual disputes will be heard. Improper venue does not deprive the court of power to hear a case, but a party can request a change of venue if the venue is not proper.

■ Standing to Sue

Standing is a jurisdictional issue that affects the power of courts to hear and decide cases. A party that has *standing to sue* has a sufficient "stake" in a controversy to seek judicial resolution of it. In other words, a party must have a legally protectible and tangible interest at stake in the litigation to have standing. The party must have been injured or threatened with injury by the action about which he or she complained.

The question is whether the **litigant**—an active party in a lawsuit—is the proper party to fight the suit, not whether the matter at issue is *justiciable.* (A **justiciable controversy** is real and substantial, as opposed to hypothetical or academic.) To illustrate: A conservation organization wanted to challenge a government agency's approval of locating a ski complex near a national wilderness area. Before the court would consider whether the challenge involved justiciable issues, the organization needed to show that it was a proper party to bring the suit. To show that it was a proper party—that is, to show that it had standing—the organization alleged that some of its members used, hiked in, and enjoyed the wilderness area that the development threatened. The organization also alleged

that the ski complex compromised these members' enjoyment of the area.[3]

■ The State Court Systems

Many state court systems are based on a three-tiered model. Any person who is a party to a lawsuit typically has the opportunity to plead the case before a trial court and then, if he or she loses, before two levels of appellate courts. Consider the state court system represented in Exhibit 2–1. It has three main tiers: (1) state trial courts of general or limited jurisdiction, (2) the state appellate court or courts, and (3) the state supreme court. If a federal constitutional issue is involved in the decision of the state supreme court, yet another level may be added: the decision may be appealed to the United States Supreme Court.

One can view the typical state system, then, as being made up of trial courts and appellate courts (also called courts of appeals or reviewing courts).

Trial Courts

Trial courts are exactly what their name implies—courts in which trials are held and testimony is taken. Trial courts may be courts of record, in which case a written record is taken, or courts not of record. Today, most are courts of record. Every state has trial courts that have original jurisdiction. Most states have trial courts of both limited and general jurisdiction.

Trial courts that have *limited jurisdiction* as to subject matter are often called special inferior trial courts or minor judiciary courts. Some typical courts of limited jurisdiction are **domestic relations courts,** which handle only divorce actions and child custody cases; local **municipal courts,** which handle mainly traffic cases; probate courts, which handle the administration of wills and estate settlement problems; and **small claims courts** and **justice of the peace courts.** Typically, the minor judiciary courts do not keep complete written records of trial proceedings.

Trial courts that have *general jurisdiction* as to subject matter may be called county, district,

---

3. *Sierra Club v. Morton,* 348 F.Supp. 219 (N.D.Cal. 1972).

■ **Exhibit 2–1 A State Court System**

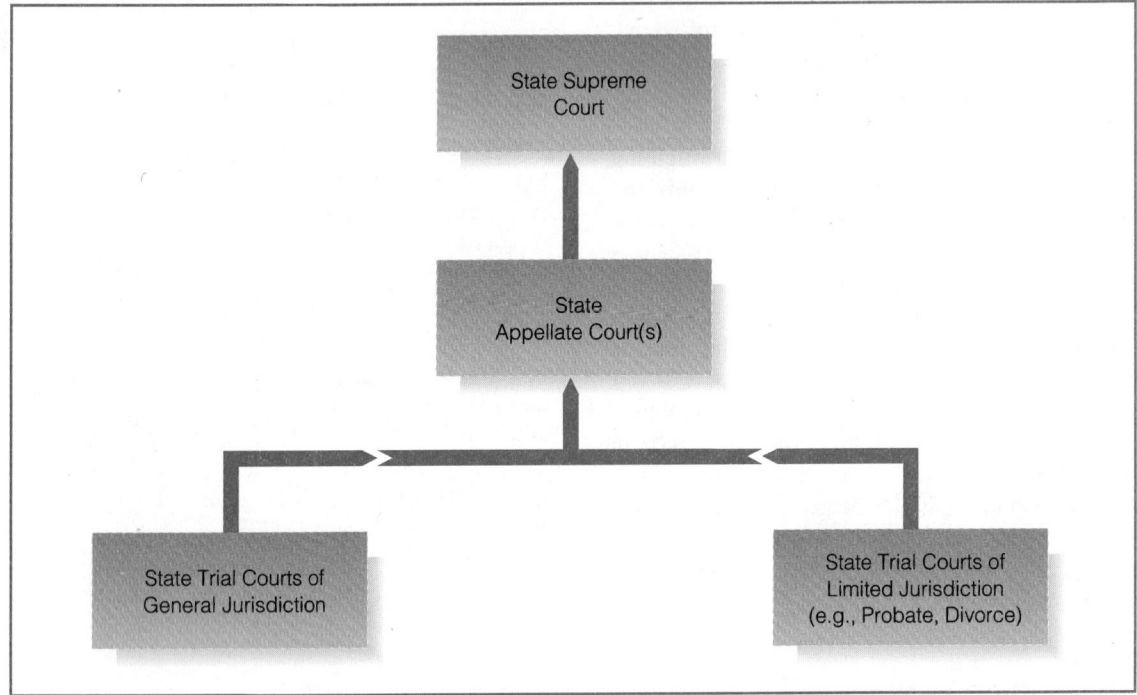

superior, or circuit courts.[4] General-jurisdiction trial courts have authority to hear and decide cases involving nearly every subject matter. These courts of general jurisdiction may be supplemented by the courts of limited jurisdiction, or minor judiciary courts, discussed above.

At the trial level, the parties to a controversy may dispute the particular facts, what law should be applied to those facts, and how that law should be applied. Generally, with some exceptions, as discussed below, it may be said that judges decide **questions of law** and juries decide **questions of fact.** If a party is entitled to and requests a trial by jury, the appropriate issues will be tried before a jury at the trial level, not on appeal. In an appeal, what is at issue is the initial tribunal's legal procedures and application of the law to the facts.

Appellate Courts

Appellate courts, or courts of review, are not usually trial courts—although in some states trial courts of general jurisdiction also have limited ju-

risdiction to hear appeals from the minor judiciary (for example, small claims and traffic cases).

Every state has at least one appellate court. The jurisdiction of these courts is substantially limited to hearing appeals. Many states have intermediate reviewing courts and one court at the highest level. The intermediate appellate court is often called the court of appeals. The highest court of the state is normally called the supreme court.[5] Appellate courts try few cases. Most appellate courts have multijudge panels that examine the record of the case on appeal and determine whether the trial court committed an error. They look at questions of law and procedure, not questions of fact. The only time an appellate court looks at a trial court's finding of fact is when the finding is clearly erroneous (that is, when it is contrary to the evidence presented at trial) or when there is no evidence to support the finding. The decisions of each state's highest court in all questions of state law are final. It is only when questions of federal law are in-

---

4. The name in Ohio is Court of Common Pleas; the name in New York is Supreme Court, Trial Division; the name in Massachusetts is Trial Court.

5. In New York, Maryland, and the District of Columbia, it is called the Court of Appeals. In Maine and Massachusetts, it is called the Supreme Judicial Court. In West Virginia, it is called the Supreme Court of Appeals.

volved that a state's highest court can be overruled by the United States Supreme Court.

■ The Federal Court System

The federal court system is similar in many ways to most state court systems. It is a three-tiered model consisting of: (1) trial courts, (2) intermediate courts of appeals, and (3) the Supreme Court. Exhibit 2–2 shows the organization of the federal court system.

All federal judges and justices, including the nine justices of the United States Supreme Court, are appointed by the president, with the advice and consent of the Senate. Federal district and appellate court judges and United States Supreme Court justices receive lifetime appointments (because under Article III of the U.S. Constitution they "hold their Offices during good Behaviour'').

U.S. District Courts

At the federal level, the equivalent of a state trial court of general jurisdiction is the district court. In fact, United States district courts are often referred to as federal trial courts. There is at least one federal district court in every state. The number of judicial districts is determined by Congress and varies over time, primarily because of population changes and corresponding case loads. Thus, a state can com-prise a single district or be divided into several districts. When there are two or more district courts within a state, the geographical jurisdiction in each court is limited. The state of Florida, for example, has district courts for northern, middle, and southern Florida.

In the Judicial Improvements Act of 1990, Congress took the opportunity to increase the total number of federal judgeships in the United States. The law provides for 629 district court judgeships within the ninety-six judicial districts.[6]

U.S. district courts have original jurisdiction in federal matters. In other words, district courts are the courts in which most federal cases originate. There are other trial courts with original, albeit limited, jurisdiction, in federal matters. These include the U.S. Tax Court, the U.S. Bankruptcy Courts, and the U.S. Claims Court (which hears suits against the United States). Certain administrative agencies and departments having judicial power also have original jurisdiction.

U.S. Courts of Appeals

Congress has established twelve judicial circuits. Each of the fifty states, the District of Columbia,

---

6.   See Sections 44(a) and 133 of Title 28 of the United States Code.

■ Exhibit 2–2 A Simplified Organization Chart of the Federal Court System

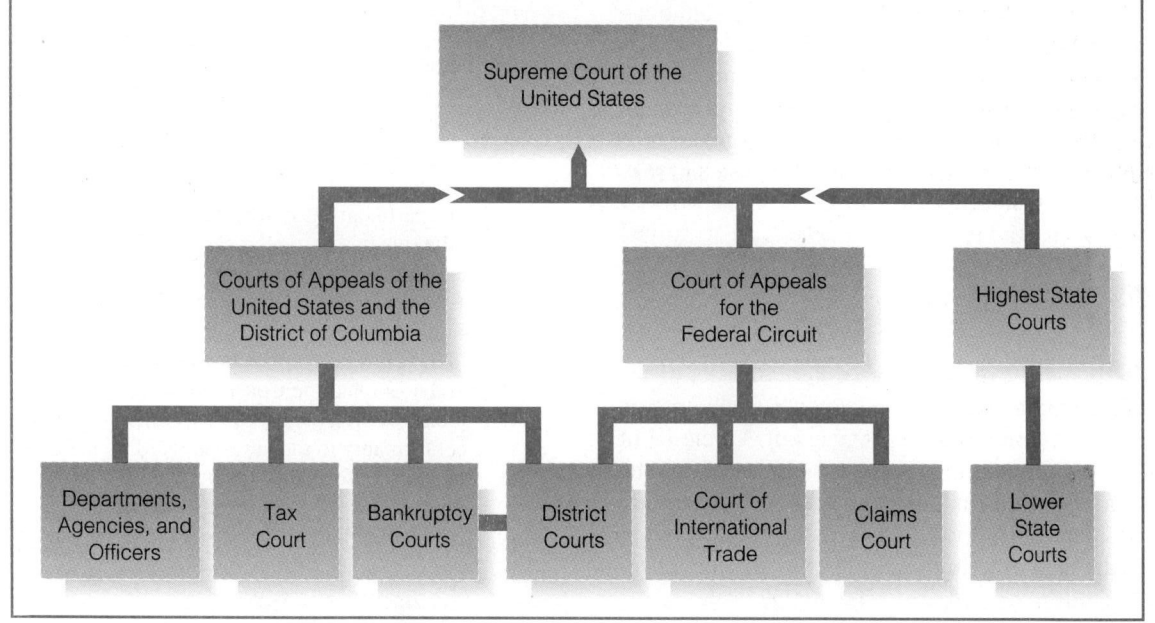

and the territories are assigned to one of these circuits. The circuit courts (U.S. courts of appeals, or U.S. circuit courts of appeals) hear appeals from the district courts located within their respective circuits. The decisions of the courts of appeals are final in most cases, but appeal to the United States Supreme Court is possible. Appeals from federal administrative agencies, such as the Federal Trade Commission, are made directly to the U.S. courts of appeals.

There is also a thirteenth circuit, the federal circuit, which was created by the Federal Courts Improvement Act of 1982. The federal circuit court of appeals, unlike the other U.S. courts of appeals, has *national* jurisdiction over certain types of subject matter. It hears appeals involving special topics such as public contracts, patents, international trade, and other matters in which the uniform application of legal principles on a nationwide basis is highly desirable.

Judicial opinions on cases heard in one of the U.S. courts of appeals are binding on the federal courts within that jurisdiction, but they are not binding on courts in other circuits. Other circuits can use such opinions as precedents if they wish, but they are not legally bound to do so. Exhibit 2–3 shows the geographical boundaries of U.S. district courts and U.S. courts of appeals.

The law provides for 191 appellate court judgeships within the thirteen circuits, and each of the nine justices of the United States Supreme Court is a circuit justice. Courts of appeals normally hear cases in panels consisting of three judges, although the court may sit *en banc* (from the French, "on the bench"). Cases heard *en banc* require that all judges be present, rather than the usual quorum. In the federal circuit court of appeals, judges also sit in panels of three or more in each case and may also hear or rehear a case *en banc*.

The Supreme Court of the United States

The highest level of the three-tiered model of the federal court system is the United States Supreme Court. According to the language of Article III of the U.S. Constitution, there is only one Supreme Court. All other courts in the federal system are considered "inferior." Congress is empowered to create such other inferior courts as it deems nec-

essary. Thus, according to this language, the inferior courts that Congress has created include the second tier in our model (the U.S. courts of appeals), as well as the first tier (the district courts and any other courts of limited jurisdiction).

The Supreme Court was created by the U.S. Constitution. Although it has original, or trial, jurisdiction in rare instances, set forth in Article III, Section 2, most of its work is as an appeals court. The Supreme Court can review any case decided by any of the federal courts of appeals, and it also has appellate authority over some cases decided in the state courts.

■ Judicial Review

A problem often arises as to whether a law is contrary to the mandates of the Constitution. **Judicial review** is the process for resolving such a problem. The term *judicial review* means that the judicial branch of the government has the authority and power to determine if a particular law violates the Constitution. Thus, any state or federal court may refuse to enforce a statute that it concludes is in violation of the U.S. Constitution. Assuming the jurisdictional criteria are satisfied, both state and federal courts may rule on the validity of state and federal statutes and executive acts. Also, federal courts may rule that provisions of state constitutions are unconstitutional under the U.S. Constitution.

The power of judicial review was first established in *Marbury v. Madison*. In determining that the United States Supreme Court had the power to decide that a law passed by Congress violated the Constitution, the Court stated:

> It is emphatically the province and duty of the Judicial Department to say what the law is. Those who apply the rule to a particular case, must of necessity expound and interpret that rule. If two laws conflict with each other, the courts must decide on the operation of each.
>
> So if the law be in opposition to the Constitution, if both the law and the Constitution apply to a particular case, so that the court must either decide that case conformably to the law, disregarding the Constitution; or conformably to the Constitution, disregarding the law; the court must determine which of these conflicting rules governs the case. This is of the very essence of judicial duty.

■ **Exhibit 2–3 United States Courts of Appeals and United States District Courts**

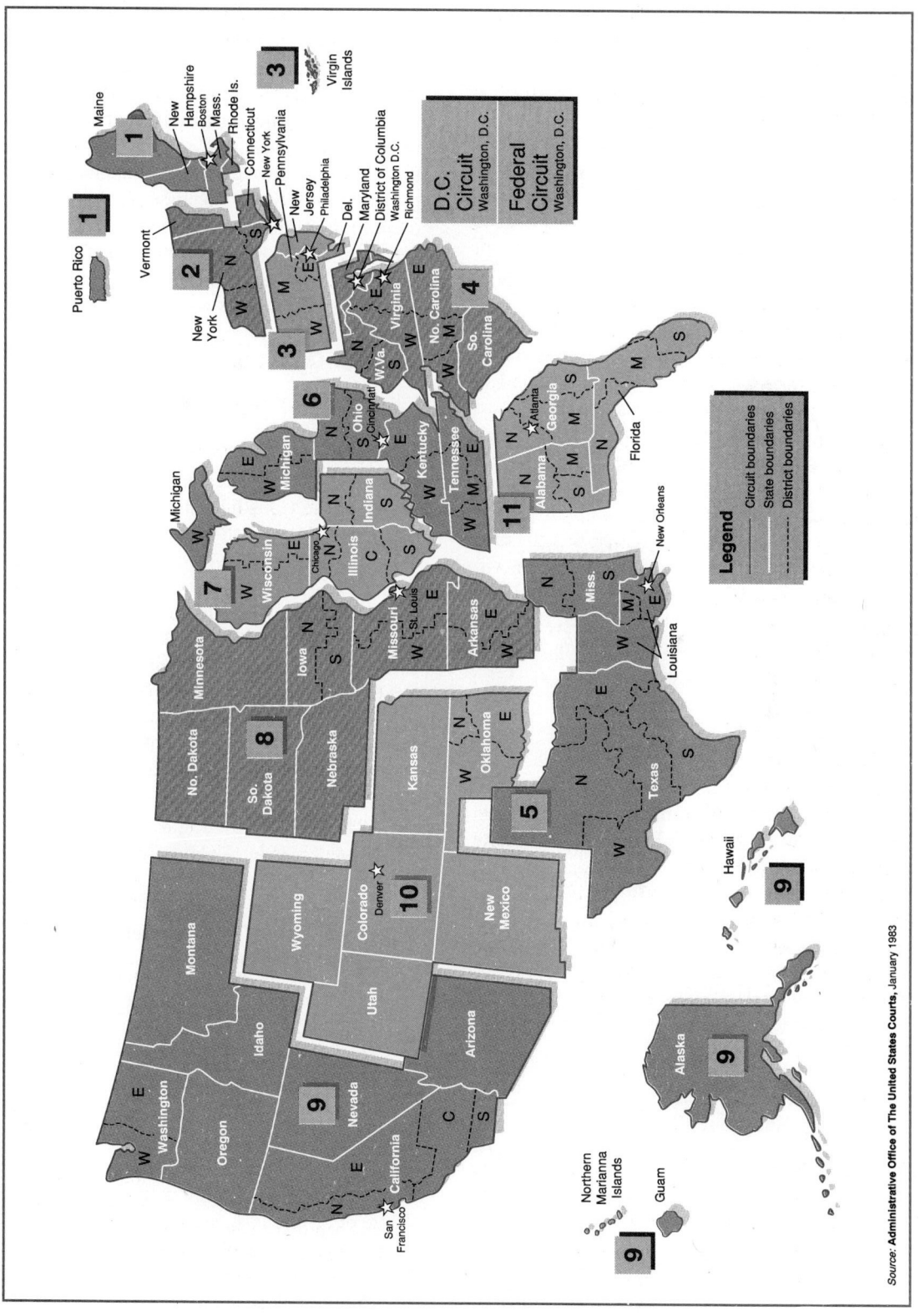

Source: Administrative Office of The United States Courts, January 1983

If, then, the courts were to regard the Constitution and the Constitution is superior to any ordinary Act of the Legislature, the Constitution, and not such ordinary Act, must govern the case to which they both apply.[7]

In another famous case, *United States v. Nixon,*[8] the United States Supreme Court established its power over actions of the president. In 1974, a grand jury indicted seven individuals for obstruction of justice and conspiracy to defraud (among other things). President Nixon was ordered by the special prosecutor to produce tapes, memoranda, papers, and transcripts. The president attempted to avoid the subpoena on the ground of "executive privilege," but this ground was denied him by the district court.

The president's view of the privilege was broad, and he claimed the courts lacked the power to demand the records sought. The Supreme Court subsequently heard the case, denied the claim of executive privilege that was at the heart of the controversy, and affirmed the order of the district court. Among other things, the Court balanced the president's claim against the needs of the defendants and the courts to have the records.

■ Jurisdiction of the Federal Courts

Because the federal government is a government of limited powers, the jurisdiction of the federal courts is limited.

The Constitutional Boundaries of Federal Judicial Power

Section 1 of Article III states that "The judicial Power of the United States shall be vested in one supreme Court and in such inferior Courts as the Congress may from time to time ordain and establish." Section 2 states that "The judicial Power shall extend to all Cases in Law and Equity arising under this Constitution, the Laws of the United

States, and Treaties made, or which shall be made, under their Authority."

In line with the checks and balances system of the federal government, Congress has the power to control the number and kind of inferior courts in the federal system. Congress can also regulate the appellate jurisdiction of the United States Supreme Court. Although the Constitution sets the outer limits of federal judicial power, Congress can set other limits on federal jurisdiction. Furthermore, the courts themselves can promulgate rules that further narrow the types of cases they will hear.

Federal Questions

"The judicial Power shall extend to all cases . . . arising under this Constitution, the Laws of the United States and Treaties made . . . under their Authority." This statement from Article III, Section 2, of the Constitution defines a **federal question** as a cause of action based, at least in part, on the U.S. Constitution, a treaty, or a federal law. Such cases come under the judicial power of federal courts. People whose claims are based on rights granted by an act of Congress can sue in a federal court. People who claim that their constitutional rights have been violated can begin their suits in federal court. For example, a woman who believes that her employer has discriminated against her in violation of a federal law may sue the employer in a federal court.

Any lawsuit involving a federal question can originate in a federal court. As will be discussed below, in lawsuits involving *diversity of citizenship*, the amount in controversy must exceed $50,000 if the case is to proceed in federal court. In federal question cases, however, there is no dollar-amount requirement.

Diversity of Citizenship

Article III, Section 2 of the Constitution establishes another basis for federal district court jurisdiction: **diversity of citizenship.** Diversity of citizenship cases are those arising between (1) citizens of different states, (2) a foreign country and citizens of a state or different states, and (3) citizens of a state and citizens or subjects of a foreign country. Under Title 28 of the United States Code, Section 1332, the amount in controversy must be more than $50,000 before a federal district court can take ju-

---

7. 5 U.S. (1 Cranch) 137, 2 L.Ed. 60 (1803).
8. 418 U.S. 683, 94 S.Ct. 3090, 41 L.Ed.2d 1039 (1974); *certiorari* denied 431 U.S. 933, 97 S.Ct. 2641, 53 L.Ed.2d 250 (1977), rehearing denied 433 U.S. 916, 97 S.Ct. 2992, 53 L.Ed.2d 1103 (1977).

risdiction, as indicated above. This amount is determined by Congress. For purposes of diversity of citizenship jurisdiction, a corporation is a citizen of the state in which it is incorporated and of the state in which it has its principal place of business. Cases involving diversity of citizenship can commence in the appropriate federal court or, if they have started in a state court, can sometimes be transferred to federal court.

Diversity jurisdiction originated in 1789. The authors of the Constitution felt that a state court might be biased toward its own citizens. Hence, the option of using the federal courts provided by the principle of diversity of citizenship is a means of protecting the out-of-state party. A large percentage of the more than 70,000 cases filed in federal courts each year are based on diversity of citizenship.

Consider an example. Ortega is driving from his home state, New York, to Florida. In Georgia he runs into a car owned by Flanders, a citizen of Georgia. Flanders's new Mercedes is demolished, and, as a result of the personal injuries she sustains in the accident, Flanders is unable to work for six months. Thus, the case in question involves more than $50,000 worth of damages. Flanders can therefore bring suit in a federal district court on the basis of diversity of citizenship.

Concurrent versus Exclusive Jurisdiction

When both federal and state courts have the power to hear a case, as when there is diversity of citi-

zenship of the parties, **concurrent jurisdiction** exists. In contrast, when cases can be tried only in federal courts or only in state courts, **exclusive jurisdiction** exists. Federal courts have exclusive jurisdiction in cases involving federal crimes, bankruptcy, patents, and copyrights; in suits against the United States; and in some areas of admiralty (maritime) law. States have exclusive jurisdiction in certain subject matters also—for example, in divorce and in adoption. The concepts of concurrent and exclusive jurisdiction are illustrated in Exhibit 2–4.

When concurrent jurisdiction exists, a party may choose to bring suit in either a state court or a federal court. In making that decision, the party might consider a number of factors, including the location of the courts, the procedural rules of the courts, the expertise of the respective judges, and whether the judge has a lifetime appointment (which means he or she may be subject to fewer outside pressures than a judge who is elected).

In the following case, the court considered whether state and federal courts have concurrent jurisdiction over employment discrimination claims brought under Title VII of the Civil Rights Act of 1964.

BACKGROUND AND FACTS *In March of 1985, the plaintiff, Colleen Donnelly, filed charges with the Equal Employment Opportunity Commission (EEOC). One of her charges was that Yellow Freight System, Inc., had discriminated against her on the basis of sex by failing to offer her employment as a dockworker. On March 15, Donnelly received a "Notice of Right to Sue within Ninety Days" from the EEOC. This notice is required by federal procedures governing claims based on Title VII of the Civil Rights Act of 1964. If a plaintiff fails to initiate an action within this ninety-day period, he or she loses the right to sue. Donnelly filed suit against Yellow Freight within the ninety-day period, but the suit was filed in an Illinois state court, and the complaint alleged that Yellow Freight had violated the Illinois Human Rights Act, which prohibits employment discrimination. Later, after the ninety-day period had elapsed, Donnelly amended her complaint to premise her claims under Title VII. The suit*

Case 2.1

YELLOW FREIGHT SYSTEM, INC. v. DONNELLY

Supreme Court of the United States, 1990.
494 U.S. 820,
110 S.Ct. 1566,
108 L.Ed.2d 834.

was then moved to a federal district court. Yellow Freight contended that the state court lacked jurisdiction over a Title VII claim and thus the original filing in state court was not an effective filing during the required ninety-day period. The district court held, and the appellate court affirmed, that state and federal courts have concurrent jurisdiction over Title VII claims; therefore, Donnelly had met the requirement of filing her claim within ninety days from her receipt of the EEOC notice. Yellow Freight then appealed to the United States Supreme Court.

Justice *STEVENS* delivered the opinion of the Court.
        *   *   *   *

We begin with the text of Title VII itself. The enforcement provisions of Title VII provide that "[e]ach United States district court and each United States court of a place subject to the jurisdiction of the United States shall have jurisdiction of actions brought under this subchapter." Unlike a number of statutes in which Congress unequivocally stated that the jurisdiction of the federal courts is exclusive, Title VII contains no language that expressly confines jurisdiction to federal courts or ousts state courts of their presumptive jurisdiction. The omission of any such provision is strong, and arguably sufficient, evidence that Congress had no such intent.
        *   *   *   *

It may be assumed that federal judges will have more experience in Title VII litigation than state judges. That, however, is merely a factor that the plaintiff may weigh when deciding where to file suit, or that may motivate a defendant to remove a case to federal court. We have no reason to question the presumption that state courts are just as able as federal courts to adjudicate Title VII claims.

In sum, without disagreeing with petitioner's [Yellow Freight's] persuasive showing that most legislators, judges, and administrators who have been involved in the enactment, amendment, enforcement, and interpretation of Title VII expected that such litigation would be processed exclusively in federal courts, we conclude that such anticipation does not overcome the presumption of concurrent jurisdiction that lies at the core of our federal system.

DECISION AND REMEDY   *The United States Supreme Court affirmed the appellate court's decision. Actions alleging violations of Title VII of the Civil Rights Act of 1964 may be brought in either a state or a federal court. Concurrent jurisdiction exists over Title VII claims.*

■ Which Cases Reach the Supreme Court?

The United States Supreme Court is given original, or trial court, jurisdiction in a small number of situations. In all other cases, its jurisdiction is appellate "with such Exceptions, and under such Regulations as the Congress shall make."

Original Jurisdiction

The United States Supreme Court has original and exclusive jurisdiction over all controversies between two or more states. In addition, the Supreme Court has original, but not exclusive, jurisdiction over all actions or proceedings (1) to which ambassadors, other public ministers, consuls, or vice consuls of foreign states are parties; (2) involving controversies between the United States and a state; and (3) commenced by a state against the citizens of another state or against aliens.

Appellate Jurisdiction

Many people are surprised to learn that in a typical case there is no absolute right of appeal to the United States Supreme Court. Thousands of cases

■ Exhibit 2–4 Exclusive and Concurrent Jurisdiction

Exclusive federal jurisdiction (cases involving federal crimes, federal antitrust law, bankruptcy, patents, copyrights, trademarks, suits against the United States, some areas of admiralty law, and certain other matters specified in federal statutes)

Concurrent jurisdiction (federal questions; diversity-of-citizenship cases)

Exclusive state jurisdiction (all matters not subject to federal jurisdiction)

are filed with the Supreme Court each year; yet it hears less than two hundred. To bring a case before the Supreme Court, a party requests the Court to issue a writ of *certiorari*.[9]

A **writ of *certiorari*** is an order issued by the Supreme Court to a lower court requiring the latter to send it the record of the case for review. Parties can petition the Supreme Court to issue a writ of *certiorari,* but whether the Court will issue one is entirely within its discretion. In no instance is the Court required to issue a writ of *certiorari.*

Listed below are some of the situations in which the Supreme Court may issue a writ of *certiorari:*

1.   When a state court decides a substantial federal question that has not been determined by a federal court or the Supreme Court or when a state court decides such a question in a way that is probably in disagreement with the trend of the Supreme Court's decisions.
2.   When two or more federal courts of appeals disagree with each other.
3.   When a federal court of appeals decides an important state question in a way that conflicts with state law, decides an important federal question not yet addressed by the Court but which should be decided by the Court, decides a federal question in a way that conflicts with applicable decisions of the Court, or departs from the accepted and usual course of judicial proceedings.
4.   When a federal court of appeals holds that a state statute is invalid because it violates federal law.
5.   When the highest state court of appeals holds a federal law invalid or upholds a state law that has been challenged as violating federal law.
6.   When a federal court holds an act of Congress unconstitutional.

Most petitions for writs of *certiorari* are denied. A denial is not a decision on the merits of a case, nor does it indicate agreement with the lower court's opinion. Furthermore, denial of the writ has no value as a precedent.[10] The Court will not issue a writ unless at least four justices approve of it. This is called the **rule of four.** Typically, only the petitions that raise the possibility of important constitutional questions are granted.

■ Judicial Procedures: Following a Case through the Courts

American and English courts follow the *adversary system of justice.* The judge's role is viewed as nonbiased and mostly passive. The lawyer functions as the client's advocate, presenting the client's version of the facts in order to convince the judge or the jury (or both) that this version is true. Judges do not have to be entirely passive. They

---

9.   Pronounced sur-shee-uh-*rah*-ree. Between 1790 and 1891, Congress allowed the United States Supreme Court almost no discretion over which cases to decide. After 1925, the Court could choose in almost 95 percent of appealed cases to decide whether to hear arguments and issue an opinion. Beginning with the term in October 1988, mandatory review was eliminated altogether.

---

10.   *Singleton v. Commissioner of Internal Revenue,* 439 U.S. 940, 99 S.Ct. 335, 58 L.Ed.2d 335 (1978).

are responsible for the appropriate application of the law. They do not have to accept the legal reasoning of the attorneys. They can base a ruling and a decision on a personal study of the law. Judges sometimes ask questions of witnesses, sometimes limit the amount of information that can be introduced about an expert witness's qualifications, and sometimes even suggest types of evidence to be presented. For example, if a defendant chooses to act as his or her own counsel, the judge will often play a role more like that of an advocate, intervening during the trial proceedings to help the defendant.[11]

A large body of law—procedural law—establishes the rules and standards for determining disputes in courts. The rules are very complex, and they vary from court to court. There is a set of federal *rules of procedure,* and there are various sets of procedural rules in the state courts. Rules of procedure differ in criminal and civil cases.

We now present a hypothetical *civil* case. The case involves an automobile accident in which a car driven by John Jones, a resident of New Jersey, collided with a car driven by Jane Adams, a resident of New York. The accident occurred at an intersection in New York City. Adams suffered personal injuries, incurring medical and hospital expenses as well as lost wages for four months. Jones and Adams are unable to agree on a settlement, and Adams sues Jones. Adams is the *plaintiff,* and Jones is the *defendant.* Both are represented by lawyers.

The Pleadings

The *complaint* and *answer* (and the *counterclaim* and *reply*)—all of which are discussed below—taken together are called the **pleadings.** The pleadings inform each party of the claims of the other and specify the issues (disputed questions) involved in the case. Pleadings remove the element of surprise from a case. They allow lawyers to gather the most persuasive evidence and to prepare better arguments, thus increasing the probability that a just and true result will be forthcoming from the trial.

COMPLAINT AND SUMMONS   Adams's suit, or action, against Jones will commence when her law-

yer files a **complaint** (sometimes called a petition or declaration) with the clerk of the trial court in the appropriate geographic area (the proper venue). In most states, it will be a court having general jurisdiction; in others, it may be a court having special jurisdiction with regard to subject matter. The complaint will contain (1) a statement alleging the facts necessary for the court to take jurisdiction, (2) a short statement of the facts necessary to show that the plaintiff is entitled to a remedy, and (3) a statement of the remedy the plaintiff is seeking. A typical complaint is shown in Exhibit 2–5.

The complaint will state that Adams was driving her Ford through a green light at the specified intersection, exercising good driving habits and reasonable care, when Jones negligently drove his Cadillac through a red light and into the intersection from a cross street, striking Adams and causing serious personal injury and property damage. The complaint will go on to state that Adams is entitled to $85,000 to cover medical bills, $10,000 to cover lost wages, and $5,000 to cover property damage to the car.

After the complaint has been filed, the sheriff or a deputy of the county (or other person empowered to do so) will serve a **summons** and a copy of the complaint on the defendant, Jones. The summons notifies Jones that he is required to prepare an answer to the complaint and to file a copy of his answer with both the court and the plaintiff's attorney within a specified time period (usually twenty to thirty days after the summons has been served). The summons also informs Jones that failure to answer will result in a **default judgment** for the plaintiff—in which case the plaintiff would be awarded the damages alleged in her complaint. The summons is not part of the pleadings. A typical summons is shown in Exhibit 2–6.

Rules governing the service of a summons vary, but usually *service* is made by handing the summons to the defendant personally or by leaving it at the defendant's residence or place of business. A summons can be served by certified or registered mail. When the defendant cannot be reached, special rules sometimes permit serving the summons by leaving it with a designated person, such as the secretary of state.

CHOICES AVAILABLE AFTER RECEIPT OF THE SUMMONS AND COMPLAINT   Once the defendant has been served with a copy of the summons

---

11.   See *Faretta v. California,* 422 U.S. 806, 95 S.Ct. 2525, 45 L.Ed.2d 562 (1975).

■ **Exhibit 2–5 A Typical Complaint**

IN THE UNITED STATES DISTRICT COURT
FOR THE ——— Southern ——— DISTRICT OF ——— New York

CIVIL NO. 9-1047

——————————————
Jane Adams
Plaintiff

vs.   COMPLAINT

——————————————
John Jones
Defendant.

Comes now the plaintiff and for his cause of action against the defendant alleges and states as follows:

1. This action is between plaintiff, who is a resident of the State of New York, and defendant, who is a resident of the State of New Jersey. There is diversity of citizenship between parties.

2. The amount in controversy, exclusive of interest and costs, exceeds the sum of $50,000.

3. On September 10th, 1992 plaintiff, Jane Adams, was exercising good driving habits and reasonable care in driving her car through the intersection of Broadwalk and Pennsylvania Ave. when defendant, John Jones, negligently drove his vehicle through a red light at the intersection and collided with plaintiff's vehicle.

4. As a result of the collision plaintiff suffered severe physical injury, that prevented her from working, and property damage to her car. The cost she incurred included: $85,000 in medical bills, $10,000 in lost wages, $5,000 automobile repair.

WHEREFORE, plaintiff demands judgment against the defendant for the sum of $100,000 plus interest at the maximum legal rate and the costs of this action.

                                    By ——————————————
                                         Joseph Roe
                                    Attorney for Plaintiff
                                    100 Main Street
                                    New York, New York

1/2/93

Exhibit 2–6 A Typical Summons

SUMMONS IN A CIVIL ACTION

United States District Court

FOR THE Southern DISTRICT OF: New York

CIVIL ACTION FILE NO. 91047

Jane Adams

Plaintiff

v.

John Jones

Defendant

SUMMONS

To the above named Defendant:

You are hereby summoned and required to serve upon Joseph Roe

plaintiff's attorney, whose address is 100 Main Street
New York, New York

an answer to the complaint which is herewith served upon you, within 20* days after service of this summons upon you, exclusive of the day of service. If you fail to do so, judgment by default will be taken against you for the relief demanded in the complaint.

Tom Smith
Clerk of Court

Mary Doakes
Deputy Clerk.

Date: 1/10/93

[Seal of Court]

NOTE:—This summons is issued pursuant to Rule 4 of the Federal Rules of Civil Procedure.

and complaint, the defendant must respond by filing a *motion to dismiss* or an *answer.* If a defendant does not respond, either by choice or for some other reason, the court may enter a default judgment against him or her, as mentioned above.

MOTION TO DISMISS   If the defendant challenges the sufficiency of the plaintiff's complaint, the defendant can present to the court a **motion to dismiss** for failure to state a claim on which relief can be granted, or a *demurrer.* (The rules of civil procedure in many states do not use the term *demurrer;* they use only *motion to dismiss.*) The motion to dismiss for failure to state a claim on which relief can be granted is an allegation that even if the facts presented in the complaint are true, their legal consequences are such that there is no reason to go further with the suit and no need for the defendant to present an answer (discussed below). It is a contention that the defendant is not legally liable even if the facts are as the plaintiff alleges. If, for example, Adams's complaint had alleged facts that excluded the possibility of negligence on Jones's part, Jones can move to dismiss, and he will not be required to answer if his motion is granted.

If the court denies the motion to dismiss, the judge is indicating that the plaintiff has stated a recognized cause of action, and the defendant is given an extension of time to file a further pleading. If the defendant does not do so, a judgment will normally be entered for the plaintiff. If, in contrast, the court grants the motion to dismiss for failure to state a claim on which relief can be granted, the judge is saying that the plaintiff has failed to state a recognized cause of action, and the plaintiff generally is given time to file an amended complaint. If the plaintiff does not file this amended complaint, a judgment will be entered against the plaintiff solely on the basis of the pleadings, and the plaintiff will not be allowed to bring suit on the matter again.

In addition to a plaintiff's failure to state a claim on which relief can be granted, a defendant's pre-answer motion to dismiss may be based on the court's lack of subject matter or personal jurisdiction, improper venue, and other specific reasons. The motion to dismiss is often used for purposes of delay.

If Adams wishes to discontinue the suit because, for example, an out-of-court settlement has been reached, she can likewise move for dismissal. The court can also dismiss on its own motion.

ANSWER AND COUNTERCLAIM   If the defendant has not filed a motion to dismiss or has filed a motion to dismiss that has been denied, then an **answer** must be filed with the court. This document either admits the statements or allegations set out in the complaint or denies them and sets out any defenses that the defendant may have. If Jones admits to all of Adams's allegations in his answer, a judgment will be entered for Adams. If Jones denies Adams's allegations, the matter will proceed to trial.

Jones can deny Adams's allegations and set forth his own claim that Adams was in fact negligent and therefore owes Jones money for damages to the Cadillac. This is appropriately called a **counterclaim.** If Jones files a counterclaim, Adams will have to answer it with a pleading, normally called a **reply,** that has the same characteristics as an answer.

ANSWER AND AFFIRMATIVE DEFENSES   Jones can also admit the truth of Adams's complaint but raise new facts that will result in dismissal of the action. This is called raising an **affirmative defense.** For example, Jones could admit that he was negligent but plead that the time period for raising the claim has passed and that Adams's complaint must therefore be dismissed because it is barred by the statute of limitations (a statutory limit on the time during which one can raise a claim).

Dismissals and Judgments before Trial

Many actions for which pleadings have been filed never come to trial. There are numerous procedural avenues for disposing of a case without a trial. Many of them involve one or the other party's attempts to get the case dismissed through the use of **pretrial motions.** We have already mentioned the motion to dismiss. Another equally important motion is the motion for a judgment on the pleadings.

MOTION FOR JUDGMENT ON THE PLEADINGS   After the pleadings are closed—after the complaint, answer, and any counterclaim and reply have been filed—either of the parties can file a **motion for judgment on the pleadings.** This motion may be used when no facts are disputed and, thus, only questions of law are at issue. For example, this motion would be appropriate if the facts as shown in the pleadings revealed that the time limit allowed for bringing the lawsuit has in fact run out.

Discovery

After the pleadings have been filed and while motions are being argued, the parties can use a number of procedural devices to obtain information and gather evidence about the case. Adams, for example, will want to know how fast Jones was driving, whether or not he had been drinking, whether he saw the red light, and so on. The process of obtaining information from the opposing party or from other witnesses is known as **discovery.**

Discovery serves several purposes. It preserves evidence from witnesses who might not be available at the time of the trial or whose memories will fade as time passes. It can pave the way for summary judgment (discussed below) if it is found that both parties agree on all facts. It can lead to an out-of-court settlement if one party decides that the opponent's case is too strong to challenge. (A civil case can normally be settled at any time, often without the court's permission.) Even if the case does go to trial, discovery prevents surprises by giving parties access to evidence that might otherwise be hidden, and it serves to narrow the issues so that trial time is spent on the main questions in the case. In addition, discovery procedures may serve to establish a witness's testimony so that the witness's credibility can be attacked at trial if that testimony is changed.

The federal rules of civil procedure and similar rules in the states set down the guidelines for discovery activity. Discovery includes gaining access to witnesses, documents, records, and other types of evidence.

DEPOSITIONS AND INTERROGATORIES Discovery can involve the use of depositions or interrogatories, or both. A **deposition** is sworn testimony by either party or any witness, recorded by a court official. The person deposed appears before a court officer and is sworn. That person then answers questions asked by the attorneys from both sides. The questions and answers are taken down, sworn to, and signed. These answers will, of course,

help the attorneys prepare their cases. They can also be used in court to challenge a party or a witness who changes testimony at the trial. Finally, they can be used as testimony if the witness is not available at trial. Depositions can also be taken with written questions from both sides prepared ahead of time.

Interrogatories are a series of written questions for which written answers are prepared and then signed under oath. The main difference between interrogatories and depositions with written questions is that an interrogatory is directed only to a party, not to a witness, and the party can prepare answers with the aid of an attorney. The scope of interrogatories is broader, because parties are obligated to answer questions even if the answer requires disclosing information from their records and files. Interrogatories are also usually less expensive than depositions.

REQUEST FOR ADMISSIONS A party can serve a written request to the other party for an admission of the truth of matters relating to the trial. Any matter admitted under such a request is conclusively established as true for the trial. For example, Adams can ask Jones to admit that he was driving at a speed of forty-five miles an hour. A request for admission saves time at trial because parties will not have to spend time proving facts on which they already agree.

REQUEST FOR DOCUMENTS, OBJECTS, AND ENTRY UPON LAND A party can gain access to documents and other items not in his or her possession in order to inspect and examine them. Likewise, a party can gain "entry upon land" to inspect the premises. Jones, for example, can gain permission to inspect and duplicate Adams's repair bills.

REQUEST FOR PHYSICAL AND MENTAL EXAMINATION When the physical or mental condition of one party is in question, the opposing party can ask the court to order a physical or mental examination. For example, to prepare for trial, Jones would want to have his own medical professionals examine Adams. If the court is willing to make the order, the opposing party can obtain the results of the examination. It is important to note that the court will make such an order only when the need for the information outweighs the right to privacy of the person to be examined.

The rules governing discovery are designed to make sure that a witness or party is not unduly harassed, that privileged material is safeguarded, and that only matters relevant to the case at hand are discoverable.

Motion for Summary Judgment

A lawsuit can be shortened or a trial can be avoided if there are no disagreements about the facts in a case and the only question is which laws apply to those facts. Both sides can agree to the facts and ask the judge to apply the law to them. In this situation, it is appropriate for either party to move for **summary judgment.** Summary judgment will be granted when there are no genuine *questions of fact* (which, as mentioned earlier in this chapter, may be decided by judge or a jury) and the only question is a *question of law* (on which only a judge, not a jury, can rule). Motions for summary judgment can be made before or during a trial, but they will be granted only if it is clear that there are no genuine factual disputes.

When the court considers a motion for summary judgment, it can take into account evidence outside the pleadings. This distinguishes the motion for summary judgment from the motion to dismiss and from the motion for a judgment on the pleadings. To support a motion for summary judgment, one party can bring in an **affidavit** (a sworn statement) that refutes the other party's claim. Unless the second party brings in affidavits of conflicting facts, the first party will normally receive summary judgment. Jones, for example, can bring in the sworn statement of a witness that Jones was in California at the time of the accident. Unless Adams can bring in other statements raising the possibility that Jones was at the scene of the accident, Jones will normally be granted his motion for summary judgment. As mentioned above, a motion for summary judgment will be granted only if there is no dispute concerning the facts of the case.

Pretrial Hearing

Either party or the court can request a pretrial hearing. Usually the hearing consists of an informal discussion between the judge and the opposing at-

torneys after discovery has taken place. The purpose of the hearing is to identify the matters that are in dispute and to plan the course of the trial. The pretrial hearing is not intended to compel the parties to settle their case before trial, although judges may encourage them to settle out of court if circumstances suggest that a trial would be a waste of time.

Jury Trials

A trial can be held with or without a jury. If there is no jury, the judge determines the truth of the facts alleged in the case. The Seventh Amendment to the U.S. Constitution guarantees the right to a jury trial in federal courts in all "suits at common law" when the amount in controversy exceeds $20. Most states have similar guarantees in their own constitutions, although many states put a higher minimum dollar restriction on the guarantee. For example, Iowa requires the dollar amount of damages to be at least $1,000 before there is a right to a jury trial. If this threshold requirement is met, either party may normally request a jury trial.

The right to a trial by jury does not have to be exercised, and many cases are tried without one. In most states and in federal courts, one of the parties must request a jury or the right is presumed to be waived. The decision to exercise the right to a jury trial usually depends on the complexity of the case, the nature of the party's legal theory, and the disposition of the judge assigned to the trial.

Jury Selection

In the case between Adams and Jones, both parties want a jury trial. Each state has a system for the selection of prospective jurors to hear cases. Once the prospective jurors have been selected, then the judge and both attorneys examine the prospective jurors to ensure that their judgment will be impartial. This examination is called *voir dire,*[12] a French phrase meaning "to speak the truth." In most jurisdictions, *voir dire* consists of oral questions that attorneys for the plaintiff and the defendant ask a group of prospective jurors (one at a time) in order to determine whether a potential jury member is biased or has any connection with a

---

12.   Pronounced vwahr-*deer.*

party to the action or with a prospective witness. During *voir dire,* a party may challenge *peremptorily*—that is, without providing any reason—a certain number (the number is determined by statute) of prospective jurors and ask that these individuals not be sworn in as jurors. Alternatively, a party may challenge a prospective juror *for cause*—that is, provide a reason why this individual should not be sworn in as a juror. If the judge grants the challenge, the individual is asked to step down. After the jurors have been selected, they are impaneled and sworn in, and the trial is ready to begin.

Note that there are two types of juries: the ordinary (*petit,* or small) jury and the **grand jury**. The latter is called grand because it consists of a greater number of jurors than the ordinary trial jury. A grand jury is convened in criminal cases. Potential grand jurors are usually drawn from lists of qualified residents. Minors, persons who have been convicted of a crime, and those who are biased toward the subject of the investigation are not qualified. Those who are chosen are sworn in by the court and sit to hear the evidence presented by the prosecutor. A grand jury does not determine the guilt or innocence of an accused party; rather, its function is to determine, after hearing the state's evidence, whether probable (reasonable) cause exists to believe that a crime has been committed and whether a trial ought to be held. If the jury finds probable cause, it will return a ''bill of indictment,'' and the case will be heard by an ordinary jury; if no probable cause is found, it will return ''no bill,'' and the accused is released from the criminal charge.

The Trial

Both attorneys are allowed to make *opening statements* concerning the facts that they expect to prove during the trial. Because Adams is the plaintiff and has the burden of proving that her case is correct, Adams's attorney begins the case by calling the first witness for the plaintiff and examining (questioning) the witness. (For both attorneys, the type of question and the manner of asking are governed by the rules of evidence.) This examination is called *direct examination.* After Adams's attorney is finished, the witness will be questioned by Jones's attorney on *cross-examination.* After that,

Adams's attorney has another opportunity to question the witness in *redirect examination,* and Jones's attorney can then follow with *recross-examination.* When both attorneys have finished with the first witness, Adams's attorney will call the succeeding witnesses in the plaintiff's case, each of whom is subject to cross-examination (and redirect and recross, if necessary).

The plaintiff must prove her case through a *preponderance of the evidence.* That is, she need not provide indisputable proof that she is entitled to a judgment. She need only show that her factual claim is more likely to be true than the defendant's. In a criminal trial, the prosecution has a higher standard of proof to meet—it must prove its case *beyond a reasonable doubt.* Some claims must be proved by *clear and convincing evidence*—evidence that is more than usually convincing. In these situations, the proof must show that the truth of the party's claim is highly probable. These situations include suits involving charges of fraud, suits to establish the terms of a lost will, some suits involving oral contracts, and other suits involving circumstances in which there is thought to be a particular danger of deception.

At the conclusion of the plaintiff's case in a jury trial, the defendant's attorney may ask the judge to direct a verdict for the defendant on the ground that the plaintiff has failed to present a *prima facie*[13] **case** (a case in which the plaintiff has produced sufficient evidence of his or her conclusion that the case can go to a jury) and, thus, there can be only one verdict as a matter of law— a verdict in the defendant's favor. This is called a **motion for a directed verdict.** In considering the motion, the judge will look at the evidence that is favorable to the plaintiff and the unquestionable evidence that is favorable to the defendant and will grant the motion only if he or she believes that a reasonable jury could not find for the plaintiff. (Motions for directed verdicts at this stage of trial are seldom granted.)

The defendant's attorney will then present the evidence and witnesses for the defendant's case. Witnesses are called and examined. The plaintiff's attorney has a right to cross-examine them, and there is a redirect and recross-examination if nec-

---

13. Pronounced *pry*-muh *fay*-shee.

essary. At the end of the defendant's case, either attorney can again move for a directed verdict, and the test will again be whether the jury could, under any reasonable interpretation of the evidence, find for the party against whom the motion is made.

After the defendant's attorney has finished presenting evidence, the plaintiff's attorney can present additional evidence to refute the defendant's case in a **rebuttal.**[14] The defendant's attorney can meet that evidence in a **rejoinder.** After both sides have rested their cases, each attorney presents a **closing argument,** urging a verdict in favor of his or her client. The judge instructs the jury (assuming it is a jury trial) in the law that applies to the case. The instructions to the jury are often called *charges.* Then the jury retires to the jury room to deliberate the case and return a verdict. In the *Adams v. Jones* case, the jury will not only decide for the plaintiff or for the defendant but, if it finds for the plaintiff, will also decide on the amount of money to be paid to her. Let us assume that the jury does decide for Adams, the plaintiff.

MOTION FOR NEW TRIAL   At the end of the trial, a **posttrial motion** can be made to set aside an adverse verdict and to hold a new trial. The motion will be granted if the judge is convinced, after looking at all the evidence, that the jury was in error. A new trial can also be granted on the grounds of newly discovered evidence, prejudicial misconduct by the participants during the trial, or prejudicial error by the judge.

MOTION FOR JUDGMENT *N.O.V.* (NOTWITH-STANDING THE VERDICT)   If Jones's attorney previously moved for a directed verdict, this attorney can now make a posttrial motion for a **judgment** *n.o.v.* (from the Latin *non obstante veredicto,* or notwithstanding the verdict). In other words, Jones can state that even if the evidence is viewed in the light most favorable to Adams, a reasonable jury should not have found a verdict in Adams's favor. If the judge finds this contention to be correct or decides that the law requires the opposite result, the motion will be granted. The standards for granting a judgment *n.o.v.* are the

same as those for granting a motion to dismiss or a motion for a directed verdict. We will assume here that this motion is made and denied and that Jones appeals the case. These events are illustrated in Exhibit 2–7.

The Appeal

When a case as appealed, as it is by Jones in our example, a notice of appeal must be filed with the clerk of the trial court within the prescribed time. Jones now becomes the *appellant,* or *petitioner.* His attorney files in the reviewing court (usually an intermediate court of appeals) the record on appeal, which contains the following: (1) the pleadings, (2) a transcript of the trial testimony and copies of the exhibits, (3) the judge's rulings on motions made by the parties, (4) the arguments of counsel, (5) the instructions to the jury, (6) the verdict, (7) the posttrial motions, and (8) the judgment order from which the appeal is taken. Jones may also be required to post a bond for the appeal.

In some courts, Jones's attorney will be required to prepare a condensation of the record, known as an *abstract.* The abstract and a brief are filed with the reviewing court. Generally, an appellant's **brief** contains (1) a short statement of the facts, (2) a statement of the issues, (3) the rulings by the trial court that the appellant contends are erroneous and prejudicial, (4) the grounds for reversal of the judgment, (5) a statement of the applicable law, and (6) arguments on the appellant's behalf, citing applicable statutes and relevant cases as precedent. The attorney for the *appellee,* or *respondent,* Adams, must now file an answering brief. Jones's attorney can file a reply (although this is not required). The reviewing court then considers the case.

NO EVIDENCE HEARD   Appeals courts do not hear any evidence. An appeals court's decision concerning a case is based on the abstracts, the record, and the briefs. Any error that the appellant brings up on appeal must appear clearly in the trial court record, and the appellant must have objected promptly to the ruling in the trial court. After the appellate court has reviewed the records submitted to it, the attorneys can present oral arguments. The appellate court then takes the case under advisement. After the court reaches a decision, the de-

---

14.   A rebuttal is an attempt by any party (not just the plaintiff) to refute an adverse party's evidence.

■ **Exhibit 2–7 A Typical Lawsuit**

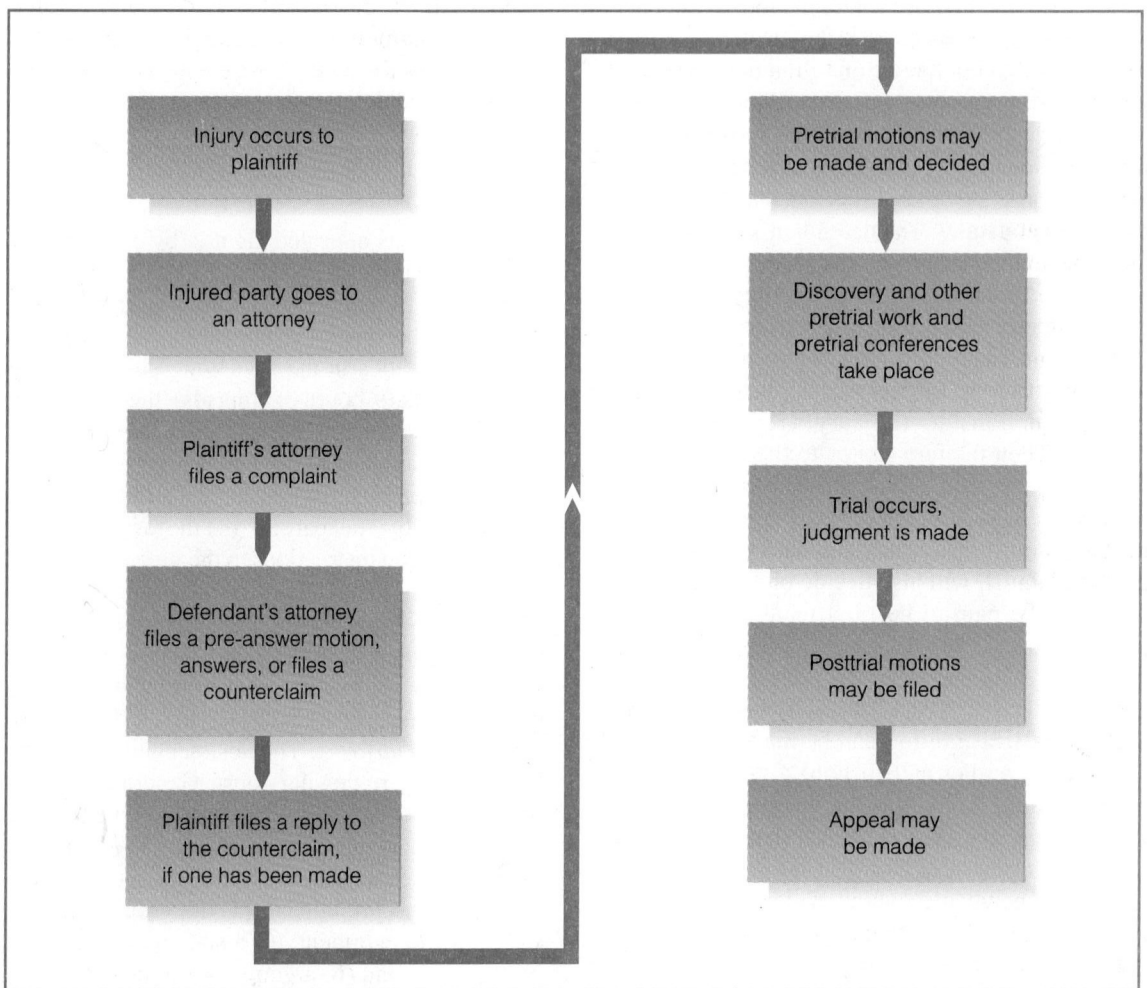

cision is usually published. It contains the court's reasons for its decision, the rules of law that apply, and the court's ultimate decision. In general, appellate courts do not reverse findings of fact unless the findings are unsupported or contradicted by the evidence. Rather, they review the record for errors of law. If the reviewing court believes that a **reversible error** was committed during the trial or that the jury was improperly instructed, the judgment will be reversed. Sometimes the case will be **remanded** (sent back to the court that originally heard the case) for a new trial. In many cases the decision of the lower court is *affirmed,* resulting in the enforcement of that court's judgment or decree.

HIGHER APPEALS COURTS   If the reviewing court is an intermediate appellate court, the party who has lost in that court may seek a reversal of its decision by filing within the prescribed time period a petition for leave to appeal to a higher court.[15] Such a petition corresponds to a petition for a writ of *certiorari* in the United States Supreme Court. The winning party in the intermediate appellate court can file an answer to the petition for leave to appeal. If the petition is granted, the complete record is certified and forwarded to the higher

---

15.   In most states, the appeal from the court of original jurisdiction up to the state supreme court is a matter of right.

court. New briefs must be filed before the state supreme court, and the attorneys may be allowed or requested to present oral arguments. If the state supreme court concludes that the judgment of the intermediate appellate court is correct, it affirms the judgment. If it decides otherwise, it reverses the appellate court's decision and enters an appropriate order of remand. At this point, unless a federal question is at issue or there is some other jurisdictional ground for an appeal to a federal court, the case has reached its end. If a new trial is ordered, it will start again at the court of origin.

It is important to know that the vast majority of disputes are settled out of court, mainly because of the time and expense of trying a case. Furthermore, of those cases that go to trial, about 97 percent are finally resolved at the trial level, as relatively few trial court decisions are changed on appeal.

■ CONCEPT SUMMARY 2.1 Courts and Procedures

Types of Jurisdiction	1. *Jurisdiction over persons/property*—Power of a court over the defendant or the defendant's property; generally limited by territorial boundaries.
	2. *Jurisdiction over subject matter*—Restriction on the types of cases a court can hear.
	  a. Limited jurisdiction—Exists when a court is limited to specific subject matter, such as probate or divorce.
	  b. General jurisdiction—Exists when a court can hear any kind of case.
	3. *Original jurisdiction*—Exists with courts that have authority to hear a case first (trial courts).
	4. *Appellate jurisdiction*—Exists with courts of appeals; generally, appellate courts do not have original jurisdiction.
	5. *Federal jurisdiction*—Arises in the following situations:
	  a. When a federal question is involved (when the plaintiff's cause of action is based at least in part on the U.S. Constitution, a treaty, or a federal law).
	  b. In diversity-of-citizenship cases between (1) citizens of different states; (2) a foreign country and citizens of a state or different states; or (3) citizens of a state and citizens or subjects of a foreign country. The amount in controversy must exceed $50,000.
	6. *Concurrent jurisdiction*—Exists when two different courts have authority to hear the same case.
	7. *Exclusive jurisdiction*—Exists when only one court has authority to hear a case.

Types of Courts	1. *Trial courts*—Courts of original jurisdiction, in which actions are initiated.
	  a. State—Courts of general jurisdiction can hear any case; courts of limited jurisdiction include divorce courts, probate courts, traffic courts, small claims courts, etc.
	  b. Federal—The federal district court is the equivalent of the state trial court. Federal courts of limited jurisdiction include the U.S. Tax Court, the U.S. Bankruptcy Court, and the U.S. Claims Court.
	2. *Intermediate appellate courts*—Courts of appeals (reviewing courts), generally without original jurisdiction. Many states have an intermediate appellate court; in the federal court system, the U.S. circuit courts of appeals are the intermediate appellate courts.
	3. *Supreme court*—The highest court. Each state has a supreme court, although it may be called by some other name, from which appeal to the United States Supreme Court is only possible if a federal question is involved. The United States Supreme Court is the highest court in the federal court system and the final arbiter of the Constitution and federal law.

■ CONCEPT SUMMARY 2.1
Courts and Procedures *(Continued)*

Rules of Procedure	Rules of procedure prescribe how disputes are handled in the courts. Rules differ from court to court, and separate sets of rules exist for federal and state courts, as well as for criminal and civil cases. A sample civil court procedure involves the following steps:
	1. *The pleadings:*
	a. Complaint or petition—A statement of the cause of action and parties involved, filed with the court by the plaintiff's attorney. After the filing, a summons is delivered to the defendant.
	b. Pre-answer motion, such as a motion to dismiss for failure to state a claim on which relief can be granted.
	c. Answer—Can take the form of (1) an admission; (2) an affirmative defense; (3) a counterclaim; or (4) an answer denying some or all of the allegations, which may also contain an admission, an affirmative defense, and a counterclaim.
	2. *Dismissal or judgment before trial:*
	a. Motion for judgment on the pleadings—May be made by either party; will be granted if no cause of action exists or if the defendant fails to answer.
	b. Motion for summary judgment—May be made by either party; will be granted if the parties agree on the facts. Judge applies law in rendering judgment.
	3. *Discovery*—The process of gathering evidence concerning the case; involves *depositions* (sworn testimony by either party or any witness) and *interrogatories* (in which parties to the action write answers to questions with the aid of their attorneys).
	4. *Pretrial hearing*—Either party or the court can request a pretrial hearing to identify the matters in dispute after discovery has taken place and to plan the course of the trial.
	5. *Trial*—Involves jury selection, opening statements from both parties' attorneys, and then:
	a. Plaintiff's introduction and direct examination of witnesses and cross-examination by defendant's attorney; possible redirect by plaintiff's attorney and recross-examination by defendant's attorney.
	b. Defendant's introduction and direct examination of witnesses and cross-examination by plaintiff's attorney; possible redirect by defendant's attorney and recross-examination by plaintiff's attorney.
	c. Possible rebuttal of defendant's argument by plaintiff's attorney, who presents more evidence.
	d. Possible rejoinder by defendant's attorney to meet that evidence.
	e. Closing arguments by both plaintiff's and defendant's attorneys in favor of their respective clients.
	f. Judge's instructions to the jury.
	g. Jury verdict.
	6. *Postrial options:*
	a. Motion for a new trial—Will be granted if the judge is convinced that the jury was in error.
	b. Motion for judgment *n.o.v.* (notwithstanding the verdict)—Movant (party making the motion) must have filed a motion for a directed verdict at the close of all the evidence during the trial; motion will be granted if the judge is convinced that the jury was in error.
	c. Appeal—Either party can appeal the trial court's judgment to an appropriate court of appeals. After posting of bond(s), briefs are filed, a hearing is held, and the appellate court renders a written opinion.

■ Terms and Concepts to Review

affidavit 47
affirmative defense 45
answer 45
brief 49
closing argument 49
complaint 42
concurrent jurisdiction 39
counterclaim 45
default judgment 42
deposition 46
discovery 46
diversity of citizenship 38
domestic relations
    courts 33
exclusive jurisdiction 39
federal question 38
grand jury 48
in personam jurisdiction 32
in rem jurisdiction 32

interrogatories 46
judgment *n.o.v.* 49
judicial review 36
jurisdiction 31
justice of the peace
    courts 33
justiciable controversy 33
litigant 33
long arm statute 32
motion for a directed
    verdict 48
motion for judgment on the
    pleadings 45
motion to dismiss 45
municipal courts 33
pleadings 42
posttrial motion 49
pretrial motions 45

prima facie case 48
probate courts 32
questions of fact 34
questions of law 34
rebuttal 49
rejoinder 49
remanded 50
reply 45
reversible error 50
rule of four 41
small claims courts 33
standing 33
summary judgment 47
summons 42
trial courts 33
venue 32
voir dire 47
writ of *certiorari* 41

■ Questions and Case Problems

2-1. (a) Before two parties go to trial, an involved process called pleadings and discovery takes place. In the past, the rules of discovery were very formal, and trials often turned on elements of surprise. For example, a plaintiff would not necessarily know until the trial what the defendant's defense was going to be. Does this seem like a fair way to conduct a trial? (b) Within the last twenty-five years, new rules of discovery have substantially changed all this. Now each attorney can discover practically all the evidence that the other will be presenting at trial. Certain information, however, is still not available to a party—namely, the opposing attorney's work product. *Work product* is not a clear concept. Basically, it includes all the attorney's thoughts on the case. Can you see any reason why such information should not be made available to the opposing attorney?

2-2. Quite often, trials are concluded before they are begun. If the parties do not disagree on the facts, they simply relate those facts to the judge, and then, through a motion for judgment on the pleadings, they ask the judge to decide what the law is and how it applies to this set of facts. How is it possible that two parties can agree on the facts yet disagree as to which party is liable?

2-3. Once a case is appealed, most appellate courts do not have the power to enter judgment or to award damages to a party who should have received them at trial. Consequently, if the appellate court disagrees with the trial court's decision, it will reverse and remand for retrial and, in effect, order the trial court judge to change the judgment. Why

should an appellate court not take a trial court judge's word as final?

2-4. Sometimes on appeal there are questions of whether the facts presented in a trial support the conclusion reached by the judge or the jury. The appellate court will reverse on the basis of the facts only when it concludes that no reasonable person, from the evidence presented at trial, could have reached the conclusion that the judge or jury reached. Appellate courts normally defer to a trial court's decision with regard to the facts. Can you see any reason for this?

2-5. Marya Callais, a citizen of Florida, was walking near a busy street in Tallahassee, Florida, one day when a large crate flew off a passing truck and hit her, causing her to suffer numerous injuries. She incurred a great deal of pain and suffering plus numerous medical expenses, and she could not work for six months. She wishes to sue the trucking firm for $300,000 in damages. The firm's headquarters are in Georgia, although the company does business in Florida. In what court can Marya bring her suit—in a Florida state court, a Georgia state court, or a federal court? What factors might influence her decision?

2-6. In January of 1983, Colleen Cote, a Wisconsin resident, hired a Michigan lawyer, Peter Wadel, to represent her in a medical malpractice action in a Michigan state court. Wadel scheduled a court appearance for her on February 10, 1983, and sent her a bill for $118.25 for court costs that he had paid on her behalf. She paid him the following month. In July she learned from the defendant's lawyer that the court had dismissed her case in April for lack of prosecution. On checking with Wadel's office, she was told that settlement negotiations were under way with the defendant's insurer—which Cote knew to be untrue, because the defendant was uninsured. She then contacted another lawyer to look into the matter, but the lawyer could obtain no information from Wadel or his law firm concerning the issue. Cote then brought suit in a Wisconsin federal court (there is at least one federal trial court in each state) against Wadel, alleging malpractice in handling her case. Under Wisconsin's long arm statute, jurisdiction is conferred on Wisconsin state and federal courts over nonresident defendants "in any action claiming injury to person or property within or without this state arising out of an act or omission within this state by the defendant." The federal district court in Wisconsin dismissed Cote's suit for lack of personal jurisdiction over the defendant, whose business and residence were in Michigan. Cote appealed, claiming that Wisconsin's long arm statute gave her jurisdiction or that, if it did not, the district should have transferred her case to a court with jurisdiction. Discuss her claims. [*Cote v. Wadel,* 796 F.2d 981 (7th Cir. 1986)]

2-7. A former probationary employee of the Ohio Department of Mental Retardation brought suit in the Ohio Court of Claims against her employer. The employee claimed that her discharge constituted a violation of her right to freedom of speech, guaranteed by the First Amendment, in that she was fired because she vocally disagreed about the treatment received by a particular mentally retarded person. Without ruling on her constitutional claims, the state court dismissed her action as a valid personnel decision. Following the dismissal by the Ohio court, the plaintiff brought suit in federal district court. The federal district court dismissed the constitutional claim against the state officials on the ground that the employee's previous state action constituted "a knowing, intelligent, and voluntary waiver" of her federal action. An Ohio statute provides that "filing a civil action in the Court of Claims results in a complete waiver of any cause of action, based on the same act or omission . . . against any state officer or employee." The employee appealed. The question before the appellate court is whether a state statute can limit jurisdiction granted by federal law. What should the court decide, and why? [*Leaman v. Johnson,* 794 F.2d 1148 (6th Cir. 1986)]

2-8. Martin brought a civil rights action against his employer, the New York Department of Mental Hygiene, when it failed to promote him on several occa-

sions. His complaint stated only that the defendant had discriminated against him on the basis of race by denying him "the authority, salary, and privileges commensurate with his position." The employer made a motion to dismiss the claim for failure to state a cause of action. Discuss whether the employer could be successful. [*Martin v. New York State Department of Mental Hygiene,* 588 F.2d 371 (2d Cir. 1978)]

2-9. On June 16, 1986, the director of the Administrative Office of the U.S. Courts notified the ninety-four federal district courts that no civil jury trials could be initiated until the end of the fiscal year (September 30) due to lack of funds with which to pay jurors. The petitioners in this case (Armster) claimed that the consequent delay of three and a half months in scheduling a jury trial violated the Seventh Amendment right to a civil jury trial. The Justice Department maintained that unlike the Sixth Amendment, which guarantees a speedy *criminal* jury trial, the Seventh Amendment does not guarantee a speedy *civil* jury trial. The Justice Department further noted that district courts have postponed civil jury trials before, although for other reasons—such as court-calendar congestion, lack of a sufficient number of judges, and the priority accorded to trying criminal cases before civil actions. Discuss whether the suspension of civil jury trials for a period of three and a half months due to lack of funds to pay jurors violates the constitutional right to a trial by jury. Are people always entitled to a jury trial in civil law suits? [*Armster v. United States District Court for the Central District of California,* 792 F.2d 1423 (9th Cir. 1986)]

2-10. Case Briefing Assignment

U.S.
? F2d
Examine Case A.2 [Goeller v. Liberty Mutual Insurance Co., *568 A.2d 176 (Pa. 1990)*] *in Appendix A. The case has been excerpted there in great detail. Review and then brief the case, making sure that you include in your brief answers for the following questions.*

1. The Pennsylvania Supreme Court acknowledged that a strong presumption exists in favor of an arbitration panel's award. What must occur before that presumption is applied?

2. What statutory authority guided the court in its deliberations?

3. What two reasons underlie the court's decision that the arbitration panel's award was a nullity?

Chapter 3

Alternative Dispute Resolution

Trials are costly and time-consuming. Many people would say that this is the result of "too many laws, too many lawsuits, and too many lawyers." Some people believe that these have created a logjam in the courts that cannot be overcome.

It is true that the number of lawsuits filed has grown rapidly in recent years, but only 5 to 10 percent of lawsuits filed actually go to trial. Most cases are settled or dismissed long before the parties enter a courtroom. Moreover, the number of cases that are litigated does not appear to be increasing any faster than the population is growing. When compared with the large number of transactions that occur in our highly complex society, the rate of litigation appears low.

Nevertheless, in any individual case, it may be months before a hearing can even be scheduled. Depending on the complexity of the case, the extent of discovery proceedings required, and the delaying tactics of the opposing party, years may be spent in litigation. Even in the best of situations, the civil procedures discussed in Chapter 2 all require time and money.

■ The Problems of Cost and Complexity

Part of the problem is the complexity of litigation. The steps leading to a final decision in a case are numerous and often complicated. Trials are governed by intricate rules of procedure and evidence. Complex rules govern the venue of the trial, the discovery proceedings, the order in which the litigation proceeds, and the type of evidence that may be used, as well as the manner in which it is presented. The facts behind the legal issues that courts face have also become more complicated. As the complexity of the process has grown, so has the cost in time and money.

The Social Goals of Rules for Litigation

The social values served by the rules of procedure and evidence are important, but many of the rules are designed to support goals other than achieving a resolution most efficiently. Do the results of litigation subject to these rules justify the costs? The problem is one of trade-offs. No one favors a set of rules designed to produce a quick judgment regardless of fairness to the parties or correctness of the result. As in most things, an appropriate balance has to be struck. How much of one goal should be sacrificed to achieve another? Is the outcome of the dispute so important that the parties would want to pay any cost to make sure that every *t* was crossed and every *i* dotted along the way to a final decision?

The Role of Experts

Another issue is whether litigation will produce the correct result. Lawyers and judges understand the rules of procedure and evidence, but this does not necessarily prepare them to deal with complex technical problems. For example, how many of them could claim to have an expert's understanding of genetic engineering or organic chemistry? Similarly, among those of us who may someday serve on a jury, who has the time to become familiar with, let alone expert in, industrial organization, labor relations, or sophisticated financial dealings?

Yet as the complexity of social interactions and the level of technical knowledge grow, the courts are increasingly called on to resolve disputes involving issues that confound even the experts. Having an expert testify before a judge or jury is not the same as having an expert direct and decide a case.

As the cost and complexity of litigation have grown, businesspersons and other individuals have asked, "Is there a more appropriate way to resolve disputes?"

■ The Search for Alternatives to Litigation

A number of solutions have been proposed, and some have been implemented, to reduce the congestion in our court system and to reduce the litigation costs facing all members of society. The enforcement of arbitration clauses, court-referred arbitration, and the emergence of an increasing number of private forums for dispute resolution have all helped to reduce the caseload of the courts. Another solution to the problem involves putting caps on damage awards, particularly for pain and suffering. Without the probability of obtaining multimillion-dollar judgments for pain and suffering, some potential litigants will be deterred from undertaking lawsuits to obtain damages. (See the *Emerging Trends* on tort reform in Chapter 11.)

Another avenue of attack is to penalize those who bring frivolous lawsuits. Rule 11 of the Federal Rules of Civil Procedure allows for disciplinary sanctions against lawyers and litigants who bring frivolous lawsuits in federal courts. In the last few years, federal judges have issued hundreds of opinions on motions by attorneys requesting sanctions against opposing counsel. More than 60 percent of those requests were granted. The United States Supreme Court even upheld a $21,000 fine against a Washington, D.C., law firm.

There are now proposals that would supposedly reduce delay and expenses in federal civil cases, and such proposals are being considered by the states as well. All of the proposals can be viewed as case-management plans. One proposal, for example, would require each federal district court to appoint a local advisory committee and to put into place procedures for placing cases on different tracks, with simple cases being handled more quickly than complex ones.

Politics and Law

Because reforms of any system affect individuals and groups differently, they seldom are accomplished easily and quickly. Reform of the court system is a prime example. At the federal level, members of Congress long have been concerned with bringing court costs and delay under control. These concerns gave rise to the enactment of legislation in 1990 that requires the federal courts to develop within one year and implement over three following years a plan to cut costs and reduce delay within the federal judicial system.

Though all ninety-four federal district courts were directed to implement some kind of plans for addressing the problems of cost and delay, the contents of the plans were made mandatory in only ten of the district courts. Regardless of the motives of those involved in efforts to improve the court systems, it is clear that the search for efficient new means to resolve disputes is racing ahead of reform of the traditional methods of litigation.

New Methods and Arrangements

The search for alternative means to resolve disputes has produced several distinct methods and arrangements. These range from neighbors sitting down over a cup of coffee to work out their differences to huge multinational corporations agreeing to resolve a dispute through a formal hearing before a panel of experts. All of these alternatives to traditional litigation comprise what is broadly termed alternative dispute resolution. **Alternative dispute resolution (ADR)** describes any procedure or device for resolving disputes other than the traditional judicial process. ADR is normally a less expensive and less time-consuming process than formal litigation. In some cases, it also has the advantage of being more private. Except in cases involving court-annexed arbitration (a relatively recent innovation discussed later in this chapter), no public record of ADR proceedings is created; only the parties directly involved are privy to the information presented during the process. This is a particularly important consideration in many business disputes because such cases may involve sensitive commercial information.

◾ Negotiation and Mediation

Alternative dispute resolution methods differ in the degree of formality involved and the extent to which third parties participate in the process. Generally, negotiation is the least formal method and involves no third parties. Mediation may be similarly informal but does involve the participation of a third party.

Negotiation

Negotiation is one alternative means of resolving disputes. In the process of negotiation, the parties come together informally, with or without attorneys to represent them. Within this informal setting the parties air their differences and try to reach a settlement or resolution without the involvement of independent third parties. Because no third parties are involved and because of the informal setting, negotiation is the simplest form of ADR.

Mediation

Mediation is another alternative means of resolving disputes. Mediation is similar to negotiation. In the mediation process, as in negotiation, it is up to the parties themselves to reach agreement over their dispute. The major difference between negotiation and mediation is that the latter involves

the presence of a third party called a mediator. The **mediator** assists the parties in reaching a mutually acceptable agreement. The mediator talks face to face with the parties and allows them to discuss their disagreement in a usually informal environment. The mediator's role, however, is limited to assisting the parties. The mediator does not decide a controversy; he or she only aids the process by helping the parties more quickly find common ground on which they can begin to reach an agreement for themselves.

ADVANTAGES OF MEDIATION   There are few procedural rules involved in the mediation process, far fewer than in a courtroom setting. Disputes are often settled far more quickly in mediation than in formal litigation.

There are other benefits. Because the parties reach agreement by mutual consent, there is not the same bitterness that often flows from the winner-take-all outcome of a formal trial decision. Hard feelings are also minimized by the less stressful environment provided by mediation; the absence of the formal rules and adversarial tone of courtroom proceedings lessens the hostility the parties may feel toward one another. This can be very important when the parties have to go on working with one another while the controversy is being resolved or after it has been settled. This is frequently the case when two businesses, say a supplier and a purchaser, have a long-standing, mutually beneficial relationship that they would like to preserve despite their controversy. Similar considerations are found in the context of management and labor disputes; employee disciplinary matters and grievances are subjects that invite mediation as an alternative to formal litigation.

Another important benefit of mediation is that the mediator is selected by the parties. In litigation the parties have no control over the selection of a judge. In mediation the parties may select a mediator on the basis of expertise in a particular field as well as for fairness and impartiality. To the degree that the mediator has these attributes, he or she will more effectively aid the parties in reaching an agreement over their dispute.

DISADVANTAGES OF MEDIATION   Mediation is not without disadvantages. A mediator is likely to charge a fee. (This can be split between the parties, though, and thus may represent less expense than both sides' hiring lawyers.)

Informality and the absence of a third-party referee can also be disadvantages. (Remember that a mediator can only help the parties reach a decision, not to make a decision for them.) Without a deadline hanging over the parties' heads, and without the threat of sanctions if they fail to negotiate in good faith, they may be less willing to make concessions or otherwise strive honestly and diligently to reach a settlement. This can slow the process or even cause it to fail.

■ Arbitration

A third method of dispute resolution combines the advantages of third-party decision making—as provided by judges and juries in formal litigation—with the speed and flexibility of rules of procedure and evidence less rigid than those governing courtroom litigation. This is the process of **arbitration**—the settling of a dispute by an impartial third party (other than a court) who renders a *legally binding* decision. The third party who renders the decision is called an **arbitrator**. When a dispute arises, the parties can agree to settle their differences informally through arbitration rather than formally through the court system. Alternatively, the parties may agree ahead of time that, if a dispute should arise, they will submit to arbitration rather than bring a law suit. Both parties are obligated to follow the arbitrator's decision regardless of whether or not they agree with it; this is what is meant by saying the decision is legally binding.

The Modern Approach

Until well into this century, the common law rule was that agreements to arbitrate a dispute were void as attempts to oust the courts from their jurisdiction. The rationale was that individuals were protected from depriving themselves of the safeguards of the courts. The modern view, however, is that individuals are free to submit their disputes to arbitration by mutual assent just as they are free to contract for other lawful objectives.

Today the federal government and many state governments favor arbitration over litigation. The federal policy favoring arbitration is embodied in the Federal Arbitration Act (FAA) of 1925.[1] The FAA requires that courts give deference to all voluntary arbitration agreements in cases governed by federal law. Virtually any dispute can be the subject of arbitration. A voluntary agreement to arbitrate a dispute normally will be enforced by the courts if the agreement does not compel an illegal act or contravene public policy. In a recent case before the United States Supreme Court, Chief Justice Rehnquist summarized the purpose of the FAA: ''The Act was designed to overrule the judiciary's long standing refusal to enforce agreements to arbitrate, . . . and to place such agreements upon the same footing as other contracts.'' [2]

The Federal Arbitration Act

The Federal Arbitration Act (FAA) does not establish a set arbitration procedure. The parties themselves must agree on the manner of resolving their disputes. The FAA provides the means for enforcing the arbitration procedure that the parties establish for themselves.

Section 2 of the FAA establishes the strong federal policy favoring arbitration by mandating that written agreements to arbitrate are ''valid, irrevocable, and enforceable [in a court of law] save upon such grounds as exist at law or equity for the revocation of any contract.''

Section 4 allows a party to petition a federal district court for an order compelling arbitration under an agreement to arbitrate a dispute. If the judge is ''satisfied that the making of the agreement for arbitration or the failure to comply therewith is not in issue, the court shall make an order directing the parties to proceed with arbitration in accordance with the terms of the agreement.''

Under Section 9 of the FAA, the parties to the arbitration may agree to have the arbitrator's decision confirmed in a federal district court. Through confirmation, one party obtains a court order directing another party to comply with the terms of the arbitrator's decision. Section 10 establishes the grounds by which the arbitrator's decision may be

---

1. 9 U.S.C. Sections 1 through 15.
2. *Volt Information Sciences, Inc. v. Board of Trustees of Leland Stanford Junior University,* 489 U.S. 468, 109 S.Ct. 1248, 103 L.Ed.2d 488 (1989). See Case 3.5.

set aside (canceled). The grounds for setting aside a decision are limited to misconduct, fraud, corruption, or abuse of power in the arbitration process itself; a court will not review the merits of the dispute or the arbitrator's judgment.

The FAA covers any arbitration clause in a contract that involves interstate commerce. Business activities that have even remote connections or minimal effects on commerce among two or more states are within interstate commerce. Thus

arbitration agreements involving transactions only slightly connected to the flow of interstate commerce may fall under the FAA.

The following case illustrates how a party who refuses to arbitrate a dispute may be compelled by a court of law under the FAA to arbitrate if he or she has agreed in an arbitration clause to do so. Note the wide range of issues that parties can be forced to arbitrate under an agreement to arbitrate their disputes.

BACKGROUND AND FACTS *Eugene and Julia McMahon, individually and as trustees for various pension and profit-sharing plans, were customers of Shearson/American Express, Inc., a securities brokerage firm registered with the Securities and Exchange Commission. Two customer agreements signed by the McMahons provided that any dispute that arose between Shearson and the McMahons over Shearson's management of the McMahons' accounts would be subject to arbitration. When a dispute arose, the McMahons brought suit in a federal district court alleging that Shearson, through one of its representatives, had violated Section 10(b) of the Securities Exchange Act of 1934 by "churning" the McMahons' accounts (that is, by excessive trading so as to generate commissions). The McMahons also asserted that Shearson was guilty of violating the Racketeer Influenced and Corrupt Organizations Act (RICO). Relying on the arbitration clause of the parties' agreement, Shearson petitioned the court to compel the McMahons to have the dispute resolved through arbitration. The district court held that under the terms of the arbitration clause the McMahons' Section 10(b) claim was arbitrable (that is, the parties could be compelled to arbitrate rather than litigate them) but that the RICO claim was not. The district court concluded that the RICO claim was not arbitrable "because of the important federal policies inherent in the enforcement of RICO by federal courts." On appeal, the court of appeals held that neither claim was arbitrable. The case proceeded to the United States Supreme Court, which granted* certiorari *to resolve the issue of whether Section 10(b) claims and RICO claims were arbitrable.*

Case 3.1

SHEARSON/AMERICAN EXPRESS, INC. v. McMAHON
United States Supreme Court, 1987.
482 U.S. 220,
107 S.Ct. 2332,
96 L.Ed.2d 185.

Justice *O'CONNOR* delivered the opinion of the Court.

This case presents two questions regarding the enforceability of predispute arbitration agreements between brokerage firms and their customers. The first is whether a claim brought under [Section] 10(b) of the Securities Exchange Act of 1934 (Exchange Act) must be sent to arbitration in accordance with the terms of an arbitration agreement. The second is whether a claim brought under the Racketeer Influenced and Corrupt Organizations Act (RICO) must be arbitrated in accordance with the terms of such an agreement.

*   *   *   *

The Federal Arbitration Act provides the starting point for answering the questions raised in this case. *   *   * The Arbitration Act *   *   * provid[es] that arbitration agreements "shall be valid, irrevocable, and enforceable, save upon such grounds as exist at law or in equity for the revocation of any contract.'' The Act also provides that a court must stay [that is, suspend or delay] its proceedings if it is satisfied that an issue before it is arbitrable under the agreement; and it authorizes a federal district court to issue an order compelling arbitration if there has been a ''failure, neglect, or refusal'' to comply with the arbitration agreement.

The Arbitration Act thus establishes a ''federal policy favoring arbitration.'' * * *

The Arbitration Act * * * mandates enforcement of agreements to arbitrate statutory claims. Like any statutory directive, the Arbitration Act's mandate may be overridden by a contrary congressional command. The burden is on the party opposing arbitration, however, to show that Congress intended to preclude a waiver of judicial remedies for the statutory rights at issue. * * * To defeat application of the Arbitration Act in this case, therefore, the McMahons must demonstrate that Congress intended to make an exception to the Arbitration Act for claims arising under RICO and the Exchange Act, an intention discernible from the text, [legislative] history, or purposes of the statute. * * *

* * * *

* * * Congress did not intend * * * to bar enforcement of all predispute arbitration agreements. In this case, where the SEC has sufficient statutory authority to ensure that arbitration is adequate to vindicate Exchange Act rights, enforcement does not effect a waiver of ''compliance with any provision'' of the Exchange Act * * *. Accordingly, we hold the McMahons' agreements to arbitrate Exchange Act claims ''enforce[able] in accord with the explicit provisions of the Arbitration Act.''

* * * *

Unlike the Exchange Act, there is nothing in the text of the RICO statute that even arguably evinces congressional intent to exclude civil RICO claims from the dictates of the Arbitration Act. This silence in the text is matched by silence in the statute's legislative history. [RICO's] private treble-damages provision * * * was added to the House version of the bill after the bill had been passed by the Senate, and it received only abbreviated discussion in either House. There is no hint in these legislative debates that Congress intended for RICO treble-damages claims to be excluded from the ambit of the Arbitration Act.

* * * *

[W]e find no basis for concluding that Congress intended to prevent enforcement of agreements to arbitrate RICO claims. The McMahons may effectively vindicate their RICO claim in an arbitral forum, and therefore there is no inherent conflict between arbitration and the purposes underlying [the treble-damages provision]. Moreover, nothing in RICO's text or legislative history otherwise demonstrates congressional intent to make an exception to the Arbitration Act for RICO claims. Accordingly, the McMahons, ''having made the bargain to arbitrate,'' will be held to their bargain. Their RICO claim is arbitrable under the terms of the Arbitration Act.

DECISION AND REMEDY *The United States Supreme Court reversed the judgment of the court of appeals. The Supreme Court held that both the Section 10(b) Securities Exchange Act claim and the RICO claim should be sent to arbitration pursuant to the arbitration clause in the parties' contract.*

STATE ARBITRATION STATUTES   Virtually all states follow the federal approach to voluntary arbitration. Thirty states and the District of Columbia have adopted the Uniform Arbitration Act, which was drafted by the National Conference of Commissioners on Uniform State Laws in 1955. Those states that have not adopted the uniform act none-theless follow many of the practices contained in it.

Under the uniform act, the basic approach is to give full effect to voluntary agreements to arbitrate disputes between private parties. The act supplements private arbitration agreements by providing explicit procedures and remedies for enforcing arbitration agreements. Unlike the FAA, however, the uniform act does not dictate the terms of the agreement. Moreover, under both federal and state statutes, the parties are afforded considerable latitude in deciding the subject matter of the arbitration and the methods for conducting the arbitration process.

In the absence of a controlling statute, the rights and duties of the parties are established and limited by their agreement.

The Arbitration Process

The arbitration process begins with a *submission*. **Submission** is the act of referring a dispute to an arbitrator. The next step is the *hearing*, in which evidence and arguments are presented to the arbitrator. The process culminates in an *award*, which is the decision of the arbitrator.

The right to appeal the award to a court of law is limited. If the award was made under a voluntary arbitration agreement, a court normally will not set it aside even if it was the result of an erroneous fact determination or incorrect interpretation of law by the arbitrator.

This seemingly harsh approach is founded on at least two grounds. First, if an award is not treated as final, then, rather than speeding up the dispute resolution process, arbitration may merely add one more layer to the process of litigation. Second, and more fundamentally, the basis of arbitration—the freedom of parties to agree among themselves how to settle a controversy—supports treating an award as final. Having had the opportunity to frame the issues and to set out the manner for resolving their dispute, the parties should not complain if the result was not what they had hoped it would be.

SUBMISSION The parties may agree to submit questions of fact or questions of law or both to the arbitrator. The parties may even agree to leave the interpretation of the arbitration agreement to the arbitrator. In the case of an existing agreement to arbitrate, the clause itself is the submission to arbitration.

The submission typically states the identities of the parties, the nature of the dispute to be resolved, the monetary amounts involved in the controversy, the place at which the arbitration is to take place, and a signed statement that the parties intend to be bound by the arbitrator's award. Exhibit 3–1 contains a sample Submission to Arbitration prepared by the American Arbitration Association.

Most states require that an agreement to submit a dispute to arbitration be in writing. Moreover, because the goal of arbitration is speed and efficiency in resolving controversies, most states require that matters be submitted within a definite period of time, generally six months from the date that the dispute arises.

THE HEARING Because the parties are free to construct the method by which they want their dispute resolved, they must state the issues that will be submitted and the powers that the arbitrator will exercise. The arbitrator may be given power at the outset of the process to establish rules that will govern the proceedings. Typically, these rules are much less restrictive than those governing formal litigation. Regardless of who establishes the rules, the arbitrator will apply them during the course of the hearing.

Restrictions on the kind of evidence and the manner in which it is presented may be less rigid in arbitration partly because the arbitrator is likely to be an expert in the subject matter involved in the controversy. Less stringent restrictions are also possible because there is less fear that the arbitrator will be swayed by improper evidence. In contrast, evidence in a jury trial must sometimes be presented twice: once to the judge, outside the presence of the jury, to determine if the evidence may be heard by the jury; and, depending on the judge's ruling, again, to the jury.

In the typical hearing format, the parties begin as they would at trial by presenting opening arguments to the arbitrator and stating what remedies should or should not be granted. After the opening statements have been made, evidence is presented. Witnesses may be called and examined by both sides. After all the evidence has been presented, the parties give their closing arguments. On com-

■ **Exhibit 3–1 Sample Submission Form**

American Arbitration Association
SUBMISSION TO DISPUTE RESOLUTION

Date: _____

The named parties hereby submit the following dispute for resolution under the _____
_____ Rules* of the American Arbitration Association:

Procedure Selected: ☐ Binding arbitration   ☐ Mediation settlement

☐ Other _____
(Describe)

FOR INSURANCE CASES ONLY:

_____ _____ to _____ _____
Policy Number   Effective Dates   Applicable Policy Limits

_____   _____
Date of Incident   Location

Insured: _____   Claim Number: _____

Name(s) of Claimant(s)	Check if a Minor	Amount Claimed
_____	☐	_____
_____	☐	_____

Nature of Dispute and/or Injuries Alleged (attach additional sheets if necessary):

Place of Hearing: _____

We agree that, if binding arbitration is selected, we will abide by and perform any award rendered hereunder and that a judgment may be entered on the award.

To Be Completed by the Claimant	*To Be Completed by the Respondent*
_____	_____
Name of Party	Name of Party
_____	_____
Address	Address
_____	_____
City, State, and ZIP Code	City, State, and ZIP Code
( ) _____	( ) _____
Telephone Fax	Telephone Fax
_____	_____
Signature†	Signature†
_____	_____
Name of Party's Attorney or Representative	Name of Party's Attorney or Representative
_____	_____
Address	Address
_____	_____
City, State, and ZIP Code	City, State, and ZIP Code
( ) _____	( ) _____
Telephone Fax	Telephone Fax
_____	_____
Signature†	Signature†

Please file three copies with the AAA.

* *If you have a question as to which rules apply, please contact the AAA.*
† Signatures of all parties are required for arbitration.

Form G1–7/90

Reprinted with permission from American Arbitration Association.

pletion of the closing arguments, the arbitrator closes the hearing.

THE AWARD   After each side has had an opportunity to present evidence and to argue its case, the arbitrator will reach a decision. The final decision of the arbitrator is called an **award**, even if no money is conferred on a party as a result of the proceedings. Under most statutes, the arbitrator must render an award within thirty days of the close of the hearing.

In most states, the award does not need to state the arbitrator's findings regarding factual questions in the case. Nor must the award state the conclusions that the arbitrator reached on any questions of law that may have been presented. All that is required for the award to be valid is that it completely resolve the controversy.

Most states do, however, require that the award be in writing, regardless of whether any conclusions of law or findings of fact are included. If the arbitrator does state his or her legal conclusions and factual findings, then a letter or an opinion will be drafted containing the basis of the award. Even though there may not be a statutory requirement that the arbitrator state the factual and legal basis of the award, the parties may impose the requirement in their submission or in their pre-dispute agreement to arbitrate.

Enforcement and Appeal

The role of the courts in the arbitration process is limited. One important role is played at the pre-arbitration stage. A court may be called on to order one party to an arbitration agreement to submit to arbitration under the terms of the parties' agreement. The court in this role is essentially interpreting a contract. The court must determine what the parties have committed themselves to before ordering that they submit to arbitration.

The other important role played by the courts is at the post-arbitration stage. If the arbitration has produced an award, one of the parties may seek a court's order compelling the other party to comply with the award. Again, the court does not look at the merits of the underlying dispute, and the court will not add to or subtract from the remedies pro-

vided by the award. The court's role is limited to determining whether there exists a valid award with which the parties can be made to comply. If a valid award was given, the court will order the parties to comply with the terms.

ENFORCEMENT OF AGREEMENTS TO SUBMIT TO ARBITRATION   When a dispute arises as to whether or not the parties have agreed in an arbitration clause to submit a particular matter to arbitration, one party may file suit to compel arbitration. The court before which the suit is brought will not decide the basic controversy but must decide the issue of arbitrability—that is, whether the issue is one that must be resolved through arbitration. If the court finds that the subject matter in controversy is covered by the agreement to arbitrate, then a party may be compelled to arbitrate the dispute involuntarily.

Although the parties may agree to submit the issue to an arbitrator, the agreement must be explicit; a court will never *infer* an agreement to arbitrate. Unless a court finds an explicit agreement to have the arbitrator decide whether a dispute is arbitrable, the court will decide the issue. This is an important initial determination, because no party will be ordered to submit to arbitration unless the court is convinced that the party has consented to do so.

In the following case, the United States Supreme Court considered a contract containing an arbitration clause that designated the arbitrator as the sole interpreter of the parties' agreement. At issue in the case was whether a court must first determine that the parties intended to arbitrate the dispute, or whether that determination is left to the arbitrator.

As you read this case, ask yourself what are the proper issues for an arbitrator to decide and what are issues that only the courts should decide.

Case 3.2

AT&T TECHNOLOGIES, INC. v. COMMUNICATIONS WORKERS OF AMERICA

United States Supreme Court, 1990.
475 U.S. 643,
106 S.Ct. 1415,
89 L.Ed.2d 648.

BACKGROUND AND FACTS *In 1981, AT&T laid off seventy-nine workers in the Chicago area purportedly because of a slowdown in economic activity. The Communications Workers of America, a union representing some AT&T workers, argued that there was no lack of work and objected to the layoffs as violations of the terms of a collective bargaining agreement between the union and AT&T. The agreement provided that "differences arising with respect to the interpretation of this contract or the performance of any obligation" under the agreement would be resolved through arbitration. The agreement reserved to AT&T the free exercise of managerial functions such as hiring, placement, and termination of employees. The agreement conditioned the exercise of managerial functions on compliance with the terms of the contract but expressly excluded disputes over those decisions from the arbitration clause. AT&T relied on the express exclusion to avoid the union's demand for arbitration over the layoffs. The union sought a federal district court order to compel arbitration. The district court held that the issue of whether a dispute over the layoffs was subject to arbitration should be decided by the arbitrator. The court ordered the parties to proceed to arbitration and to submit the question of whether the layoffs were subject to arbitration to the arbitrator. A federal appellate court affirmed the district court's holding, and AT&T appealed the case to the United States Supreme Court.*

Justice *WHITE* delivered the opinion of the Court.

* * * *

The first [applicable] principle * * * is that "arbitration is a matter of contract and a party cannot be required to submit to arbitration any dispute which he has not agreed so to submit." This axiom recognizes the fact that arbitrators derive their authority to resolve disputes only because the parties have agreed in advance to submit such grievances to arbitration.

The second rule, which follows inexorably from the first, is that the question of arbitrability—whether a collective-bargaining agreement creates a duty for the parties to arbitrate the particular grievance—is undeniably an issue for judicial determination. Unless the parties clearly and unmistakably provide otherwise, the question of whether the parties agreed to arbitrate is to be decided by the court, not the arbitrator.

* * * *

The third principle derived from our prior cases is that, in deciding whether the parties have agreed to submit a particular grievance to arbitration, a court is not to rule on the potential merits of the underlying claims. * * *

Finally, * * * it has been established that where the contract contains an arbitration clause, there is a presumption of arbitrability in the sense that "[a]n order to arbitrate the particular grievance should not be denied unless it may be said with positive assurance that the arbitration clause is not susceptible of an interpretation that covers the asserted dispute. Doubts should be resolved in favor of coverage." Such a presumption is particularly applicable where the clause is as broad as the one employed in this case, which provides for arbitration of "any differences arising with respect to the interpretation of this contract or the performance of any obligation hereunder. . . ." In such cases, "[i]n the absence of any express provision excluding a particular grievance from arbitration, we think only the most forceful evidence of a purpose to exclude the claim from arbitration can prevail."

* * * *

With these principles in mind, it is evident that the [court] erred in ordering the parties to arbitrate the arbitrability question. It is the court's duty to interpret the agreement and to determine whether the parties intended to arbitrate grievances concerning layoffs predicated on a ''lack of work'' determination by [AT&T]. If the court determines that the agreement so provides, then it is for the arbitrator to determine the relative merits of the parties' substantive interpretations of the agreement. It was for the court, not the arbitrator, to decide in the first instance whether the dispute was to be resolved through arbitration.

The United States Supreme Court held that the issue of arbitrability should have been resolved by the district court; the issue should not have been submitted to the arbitrator. The Supreme Court set aside the appellate court's decision, and the case was remanded for proceedings in conformity with the Supreme Court's opinion.

DECISION AND REMEDY

SETTING ASIDE AN ARBITRATION AWARD

After the arbitration has been concluded, the losing party may appeal the arbitrator's award to a court. The scope of review is much more restricted than an appellate court's review of a trial court decision. The general view is that because the parties were free to frame the issues and set the powers of the arbitrator at the outset, they cannot complain about the result.

Fact Findings and Legal Conclusions The arbitrator's fact findings and legal conclusions are normally conclusive. That the arbitrator may have erred in a ruling during the hearing or made an erroneous fact finding is normally no basis for setting aside an award: the parties agreed that the arbitrator would be the judge of the facts. Similarly, no matter how obviously the arbitrator was mistaken in a conclusion of law, the award is normally nonetheless binding: the parties agreed to accept the arbitrator's interpretation of the law. A court will not look at the merits of the dispute, the sufficiency of the evidence presented, or the arbitrator's reasoning in reaching a particular decision.

This approach is consistent with the underlying view of all voluntary arbitration—that its basis is really contract law. If the parties freely contract with one another, courts will not interfere simply because one side feels it received a bad bargain. This view supports the view that any party challenging an award must face the presumption that a final award is valid.

Public Policy and Illegality In keeping with contract law principles, no award will be enforced if compliance with the award would result in the commission of a crime or would conflict with some greater social policy mandated by statute. A court will not overturn an award, however, simply because the arbitrator was called on to resolve a dispute involving a matter of important public concern.[3] For an award to be set aside, it must call for some action on the part of the parties that would conflict with or in some way undermine public policy.

Defects in the Arbitration Process There are some bases for setting aside an award when there is a defect in the arbitration process. These bases are typified by those set forth in the Federal Arbitration Act. Section 10 of the act provides four grounds on which an arbitration award may be set aside:

1. The award was the result of corruption, fraud, or other ''undue means.''
2. The arbitrator exhibited bias or corruption.
3. The arbitrator refused to postpone the hearing despite sufficient cause, refused to hear evidence pertinent and material to the dispute, or otherwise acted to substantially prejudice the rights of one of the parties.
4. The arbitrator exceeded his or her powers or failed to use them to make a mutual, final, and definite award.

The first three bases for setting aside the award include actions or decisions that are more than simply mistakes in judgment. Each requires some ''bad faith'' on the part of the arbitrator. Bad-faith actions or decisions are ones that affect the integrity

---

3. See, for example, *Faherty v. Faherty,* 97 N.J. 99, 477 A.2d 1257 (1984).

of the arbitration process. The honesty and impartiality rather than the judgment of the arbitrator are called into question.

Sometimes it is very difficult to make the distinction between honest mistakes in judgment and actions or decisions made in bad faith. A bribe is clearly the kind of "undue means" included in the first basis for setting aside an award. Letting only one side argue its case is likewise a clear violation of the second basis. Meetings between the arbitrator and one party outside the presence of the other party also taints the arbitration process. While meetings might not involve the kind of corruption that results from taking a bribe, they do affect the integrity of the process, against which the third basis for setting aside an award is meant to protect.

Not every refusal by an arbitrator to admit certain evidence is grounds for setting aside an award under the third basis. Remember that the parties have agreed to have the arbitrator decide all issues in the dispute, which includes ruling on the evidence. It is within the arbitrator's proper discretion to decide which evidence is pertinent and material to the dispute. To provide a basis for overturning an award, the arbitrator's decision must be more than an error in judgment, as obviously incorrect as that judgment might appear to another observer. The decision must be so obviously wrong or unfair as to imply bias or corruption. Otherwise, the decision cannot be a basis for setting aside an award.

The fourth basis for setting aside an award is that the arbitrator exceeded his or her powers in arbitrating the dispute. This issue involves the question of arbitrability. An arbitrator exceeds his or her powers and authority by attempting to resolve an issue that is not covered by the agreement to submit to arbitration.

Waiver Although a defect in the arbitration process is sufficient grounds for setting aside an award, a party can sometimes forfeit the right to challenge an award by failing to object to the defect in a timely manner. The party must object when he or she learns of the problem. After making the objection, the party may still proceed with the arbitration process and still challenge the award in court after the arbitration proceedings have concluded. If, however, a party makes no objection and proceeds with the arbitration process, then a later court challenge to the award may be denied on the ground that the party *waived* the right to challenge the award on the basis of the defect.

Frequently, this occurs when a party fails to object that an arbitrator is exceeding his or her powers in resolving a dispute because the subject matter is not arbitrable or because the party did not agree to arbitrate the dispute. As in the *AT&T Technologies* case above, the question of arbitrability is one for the courts to decide. If a party does not object on this issue at the first demand for arbitration, however, a court may consider the objection waived. The following case demonstrates that a party's failure to object to arbitration, even if the party does not participate in the proceedings, may constitute a waiver to object to an award rendered by the arbitrator.

Case 3.3

COMPREHENSIVE ACCOUNTING CORP. v. RUDELL

United States Court of Appeals, Seventh Circuit, 1985. 760 F.2d 138.

BACKGROUND AND FACTS *In 1980, Glenn and Jean Rudell signed a contract with Comprehensive Accounting Corporation to acquire an accounting franchise. The contract contained an arbitration clause. In 1983, Comprehensive terminated the franchise agreement and invoked the arbitration clause, claiming that the Rudells had defaulted on their obligations under the agreement. The Rudells were notified of the arbitration but chose not to participate or attend the proceedings. Rudell wrote to Comprehensive that "I can't afford to go to Chicago [for the arbitration] and can't see that there is anything left to arbitrate." The arbitration went forward in the Rudells' absence, and an award granting damages and equitable relief was rendered in favor of Comprehensive. Comprehensive then sought to have the award confirmed in a federal district court according to Section 9 of the Federal Arbitration Act—that is, Comprehensive sought a court order directing the Rudells to comply with the terms of the award. The*

Rudells opposed the confirmation on several grounds, all of which were rejected by the district court, which ruled, among other things, that the Rudells were too late to argue that they did not know about the arbitration clause. The Rudells appealed to the decision. They argued that the district court should not have rejected, as too late, their offer to prove that they did not know about the arbitration clause.

POSNER, Circuit Judge.
    *   *   *   *

    *   *   * [I]f the Rudells had claimed that the clause was invalid and nevertheless the arbitrator had gone ahead and made an award against them, he might well *   *   * have exceeded his powers. But that is not this case. There is an arbitration clause, and the Rudells concede that it covers this dispute. They were notified of the arbitration, and while refusing to participate in it did not challenge the arbitrator's authority to proceed in their absence, as the clause *   *   * allowed if the Rudells had notice of the arbitration—as they did—and refused to participate—as they also did.

    They now say that they did not agree to the arbitration clause, which seems hard to believe, given the evidence of their signatures. In the absence of fraud or duress, a person who signs a contract cannot avoid his obligations under it by showing that he did not read what he signed. *   *   * [A]fter an award has been entered, *   *   * section 10 [of the Federal Arbitration Act] does not permit the person resisting enforcement of the award to go back and litigate the question whether there was an agreement to arbitrate. He must show *   *   * that the arbitrator exceeded his powers, and the Rudells have failed to show this.

    *   *   * No one should be forced into arbitration without an opportunity to show that he never agreed to arbitrate the dispute that is the subject of the arbitration. The Rudells had that opportunity when they were notified of the arbitration, and they let it pass by. It was then too late for them to sit back and allow the arbitration to go forward, and only after it was all done, and enforcement was sought, say: oh by the way, we never agreed to the arbitration clause. That is a tactic that the law of arbitration, with its commitment to speed, will not tolerate.

    *   *   * [I]t may be asked, what concretely could the Rudells have done when they were notified of the arbitration, given that the arbitration clause allowed the arbitration to proceed in their absence? They might have brought suit to enjoin the arbitration. At the very least, they could have told the arbitrator that they did not recognize his authority to proceed, because they had not agreed to arbitration. That would have put the arbitrator and Comprehensive on notice that the arbitrator's jurisdiction was questioned. Comprehensive might then have moved *   *   * for an order to arbitrate, and the Rudells would have gotten their day in court to challenge the existence of an agreement to arbitrate, before Comprehensive was put to the expense of the arbitration. If Comprehensive had *   *   * gone ahead with the arbitration in the Rudell[s'] absence, then the Rudells, having put Comprehensive on notice of their reservation, might be allowed in the confirmation proceeding to litigate the question whether there was a valid agreement to arbitrate *   *   * . They did neither. They waited too long.

The Rudells' challenges to the arbitration proceedings were lost by their failure to object to the arbitration proceedings at the time they arose. Having waited until after the proceedings were completed, the Rudells could not challenge the award on the basis of the validity of the arbitration agreement. The district court's decision to enforce the award against the Rudells was affirmed.

DECISION AND REMEDY

CONFLICTS OF LAW   Parties are afforded wide latitude in establishing the manner in which their disputes will be resolved. Nevertheless, an agreement to arbitrate may be governed by the Federal Arbitration Act (FAA) or one of the many state arbitration acts even though the parties do not refer to a statute in their agreement. Recall that the FAA covers any arbitration clause in a contract that involves interstate commerce. Frequently, however, transactions within interstate commerce also have substantial connections to particular states which may have their own arbitration acts. In such transactions involving arbitration agreements, unless the FAA and state arbitration law are nearly identical, the acts may conflict. How are these conflicts to be resolved? As a general principle, the Supremacy Clause and the Commerce Clause of the U.S. Constitution are the basis for giving federal law preeminence; when there is a conflict, state law is preempted by federal law. Thus, in cases of arbitration, the strong federal policy favoring arbitration can override a state's laws that might be more favorable to normal litigation. The following case is representative of the conflicts that can arise between state law and the FAA.

Case 3.4

SOUTHLAND CORP. v. KEATING

United States Supreme Court, 1984.
465 U.S. 1,
104 S.Ct. 852,
79 L.Ed.2d 1.

BACKGROUND AND FACTS   *Southland Corporation is owner and franchisor of 7-Eleven convenience stores. Southland's franchise agreement contained a clause requiring that any dispute between Southland and 7-Eleven franchisees would be settled by arbitration. Several franchisees, including Richard Keating, who operated 7-Eleven stores in California, brought suit in California state court against Southland, alleging, among other things, that Southland had violated California's Franchise Investment Law. Southland asserted that under the franchise agreement the dispute had to be resolved through arbitration. The trial court ordered arbitration of all claims, except those under the Franchise Investment Law. Southland appealed. The appellate court ordered arbitration of all claims, including those under the Franchise Investment Law, but on further appeal the California Supreme Court ruled that the Franchise Investment Law required the parties to litigate claims under that statute rather than submit them to arbitration. The California Supreme Court also ruled that the Franchise Investment Law did not undermine the Federal Arbitration Act (FAA). Southland appealed to the United States Supreme Court, arguing that the Franchise Investment Law, which invalidated certain arbitration agreements covered by the FAA, violated the Supremacy Clause of the U.S. Constitution.*

Chief Justice *BURGER* delivered the opinion of the Court.
　　*   *   *   *
　　[Section 31512 of the] California Franchise Investment Law provides:
　　"Any condition, stipulation or provision purporting to bind any person acquiring any franchise to waive compliance with any provision of this law or any rule or order hereunder is void."
　　The California Supreme Court interpreted this statute to require judicial consideration of claims brought under the State statute and accordingly refused to enforce the parties' contract to arbitrate such claims. So interpreted the California Franchise Investment Law directly conflicts with *   *   * the Federal Arbitration Act and violates the Supremacy Clause.
　　In enacting *   *   * the federal Act, Congress declared a national policy favoring arbitration and withdrew the power of the states to require a judicial forum for the resolution of claims which the contracting parties agreed to resolve by arbitration.

*   *   *   *

*   *   * We see nothing in the Act indicating that the broad principle of enforceability is subject to any *   *   * limitations under State law.

The Federal Arbitration Act rests on the authority of Congress to enact substantive rules under the Commerce Clause. *   *   *

In *Moses H. Cone Memorial Hospital v. Mercury Construction Corp.*, we reaffirmed our view that the Arbitration Act "creates a body of federal substantive law" [that is] applicable in state and federal court. *   *   *

*   *   * [T]here are strong indications that Congress had in mind something more than making arbitration agreements enforceable only in the federal courts. The House Report plainly suggests the more comprehensive objectives: "The purpose of this bill is to make valid and enforceable agreements for arbitration contained in contracts involving interstate commerce or within the jurisdiction or admiralty, or which may be the subject of litigation in the Federal courts."

*   *   *   *

The problems Congress faced [included] *   *   * the failure of state arbitration statutes to mandate enforcement of arbitration agreements. To confine the scope of the Act to arbitrations sought to be enforced in federal courts would frustrate what we believe Congress intended *   *   *.

*   *   *   *

*   *   * We are unwilling to attribute to Congress the intent, in drawing on the comprehensive powers of the Commerce Clause, to create a right to enforce an arbitration contract and yet make the right dependent for its enforcement on the particular forum in which it is asserted. And since the overwhelming proportion of all civil litigation in this country is in the state courts, we cannot believe Congress intended to limit the Arbitration Act to disputes subject only to federal court jurisdiction. Such an interpretation would frustrate Congressional intent to place "[a]n arbitration agreement . . . upon the same footing as other contracts, where it belongs."

In creating a substantive rule applicable in state as well as federal courts, Congress intended to foreclose state legislative attempts to undercut the enforceability of arbitration agreements. We hold that [S]ection 31512 of the California Franchise Investment Law violates the Supremacy Clause.

The decision of the California Supreme Court was reversed. The case was remanded with directions to order arbitration pursuant to the arbitration clauses in the franchise agreements. **DECISION AND REMEDY**

CHOICE OF LAW Notwithstanding federal preemption of conflicting state laws, the Federal Arbitration Act has been interpreted as allowing the parties to choose a particular state law to govern their arbitration agreement. The parties may choose to have the laws of a specific state govern their agreement by including in the agreement a *choice-of-law* clause. The Federal Arbitration Act does not mandate any particular set of rules that parties must follow in arbitration; the parties are free to agree on the manner best suited to their needs.

Consistent with this view that arbitration is at heart a contractual matter between private parties, the United States Supreme Court has upheld arbitration agreements containing choice-of-law provisions.

In the following case, one party to an arbitration agreement sought to compel arbitration under an arbitration clause, but because the agreement contained a choice-of-law provision, the United States Supreme Court upheld an order that state law governed and that the state law provisions did not compel arbitration.

Case 3.5

VOLT INFORMATION SCIENCES, INC. v. BOARD OF TRUSTEES OF LELAND STANFORD JUNIOR UNIVERSITY

United States Supreme Court, 1989.
489 U.S. 468,
109 S.Ct. 1248,
103 L.Ed.2d 488.

BACKGROUND AND FACTS *Volt Information Sciences, Inc., contracted with the Board of Trustees of Stanford University in California to install a system of electrical conduits on the campus. The contract contained an agreement to arbitrate all disputes over the project and a choice-of-law provision providing that the law of California would govern the terms of the contract. A dispute developed over the payment of compensation for extra work. Volt demanded that the matter be submitted to arbitration. Stanford responded by suing in a California court. In the suit Stanford alleged fraud and breach of contract against Volt and sought indemnity from two other parties to the contract. The other parties were not subject to the arbitration agreement. The trial court stayed (stopped) the arbitration and ordered the litigation to proceed. California law allows for a stay of arbitration if third parties not covered by an agreement to arbitrate are involved and if litigation against the third parties might produce a ruling that would conflict with a ruling on the same issue in arbitration. Volt appealed, and the appellate court affirmed the ruling of the trial court. Volt appealed to the California Supreme Court, which declined to review the case. Volt appealed to the United States Supreme Court.*

Chief Justice *REHNQUIST* delivered the opinion of the Court.

*   *   *   *

Appellant first suggests that the Court of Appeal's construction of the choice-of-law clause was in effect a finding that appellant had "waived" its "federally guaranteed right to compel arbitration of the parties' dispute," a waiver whose validity must be judged by reference to federal rather than state law. This argument fundamentally misconceives the nature of the rights created by the FAA. The Act was designed "to overrule the judiciary's long-standing refusal to enforce agreements to arbitrate," and place such agreements " 'upon the same footing as other contracts.' " Section 2 of the Act therefore declares that a written agreement to arbitrate in any contract involving interstate commerce or a maritime transaction "shall be valid, irrevocable, and enforceable, save upon such grounds as exist at law or in equity for the revocation of any contract," and section 4 allows a party to such an arbitration agreement to "petition any United States district court . . . for an order directing that such arbitration proceed in the manner provided for in such agreement."

But section 4 of the FAA does not confer a right to compel arbitration of any dispute at any time; it confers only the right to obtain an order directing that "arbitration proceed *in the manner provided for in* [*the parties'*] *agreement.*" [Emphasis added]. Here the Court of Appeal found that, by incorporating the California rules of arbitration into their agreement, the parties had agreed that arbitration would not proceed in situations which fell within the scope of [the California statute that allowed for a stay of arbitration]. This was not a finding that appellant had "waived" an FAA-guaranteed right to compel arbitration of this dispute, but a finding that it had no such right in the first place, because the parties' agreement did not require arbitration to proceed in this situation. Accordingly, appellant's contention that the contract interpretation issue presented here involves the "waiver" of a federal right is without merit.

Second, appellant argues that we should set aside the Court of Appeal's construction of the choice-of-law clause because it violates the settled federal rule that questions of arbitrability in contracts subject to the FAA must be resolved with a healthy regard for the federal policy favoring arbitration. *   *   *

But we do not think the Court of Appeal offended the *Moses Cone* principle [set forth in *Moses H. Cone Memorial Hospital v. Mercury Construction Corp.* which requires courts to ''rigorously enforce agreements to arbitrate''] by interpreting the choice-of-law provision to mean that the parties intended the California rules of arbitration, including the stay provision, to apply to their arbitration agreement. There is no federal policy favoring arbitration under a certain set of procedural rules; the federal policy is simply to ensure the enforceability, according to their terms, of private agreements to arbitrate. Interpreting a choice-of-law clause to make applicable state rules governing the conduct of arbitration—rules which are manifestly designed to encourage resort to the arbitral process—simply does not offend the rule of liberal construction set forth in *Moses Cone*, nor does it offend any other policy embodied in the FAA.

The United States Supreme Court sustained the decision upholding the choice-of-law provision mandating that California law govern the terms of the parties' agreement. Under California law, the parties had to litigate issues involving third parties not covered by the arbitration clause. Because the parties had chosen to have California law control, there was no conflict with the FAA in ordering the parties to proceed to litigation.

DECISION AND REMEDY

■ The Integration of ADR and Formal Court Procedures

Because of the congestion within the judicial system, many jurisdictions at both the state and federal levels are integrating alternative dispute resolution into the formal legal process. It is hoped by many that utilizing methods such as arbitration within the traditional framework can relieve the worsening logjams afflicting most of the nation's court systems.

Court-Annexed Arbitration

At present, approximately one-third of the states employ some form of court-annexed arbitration. Some states compel the arbitration of certain types of disputes, and many states and some federal court jurisdictions have adopted programs that allow them to refer certain types of cases for mediation or arbitration. Since 1984, for example, ten federal district courts have experimented with court-annexed, nonbinding arbitration for cases involving amounts less than $100,000. Only 10 percent of the cases thus far referred for arbitration have gone to trial.

Court systems in Colorado, Hawaii, Texas, and other states have adopted mandatory mediation or nonbinding arbitration programs for certain types of disputes, usually involving less than a specified threshold dollar amount. Only if the parties fail to reach an agreement, or if one of the parties disa-

grees with the decision of a third party mediating or arbitrating the dispute, will the case be heard by a court. South Carolina was the first state to institute a voluntary arbitration program at the *appellate* court level. In the South Carolina system, litigants must waive a court hearing when requesting arbitration. All decisions by the arbitrators are final and binding.

Court-annexed arbitration differs significantly from the voluntary arbitration process discussed above. Most states, for example, do not allow court-annexed arbitration in disputes involving title to real estate or in cases in which a court's equity powers are involved.

A FUNDAMENTAL DIFFERENCE The fundamental difference between voluntary arbitration and court-annexed arbitration is the finality and reviewability of the award. In respect to court-annexed arbitration, either party may reject the award for any reason. In the event that one of the parties does reject the award, the case will proceed to trial and the court will hear the case *de novo*, reconsidering all the evidence and legal questions as though no arbitration had occurred.

Everyone who has a recognizable cause of action or against whom such an action is brought is entitled to have the issue decided in a court of law. Because court-annexed arbitration is not voluntary, there must be some safeguard against denying an individual his or her day in court. This safeguard is provided by permitting either side to the court-annexed arbitration to reject the award regardless of the reason for so doing.

It is permissible, however, to penalize the party rejecting the award: many statutes directing court arbitration impose court costs and fees on a party who rejects an arbitration award but does not improve his or her position by going to trial. Thus, for example, if the award was more favorable to the rejecting party than is the subsequent jury verdict, the party may be compelled to pay the costs of the arbitration or some fee for the costs of the trial.

In court-annexed arbitration, discovery of evidence occurs before the hearing. After the hearing has commenced, a party seeking to discover new evidence must usually secure approval from the court that mandated the arbitration. This is intended to prevent the parties from using arbitration as a means of previewing each other's case and then rejecting the arbitrator's award.

THE ROLE OF THE ARBITRATOR Notwithstanding the differences between voluntary and court-annexed arbitration, the role of the arbitrator is essentially the same in both types of proceedings. The arbitrator determines issues of both fact and law. The arbitrator also makes all decisions concerning applications of the rules of procedure and evidence during the hearing.

WHICH RULES APPLY Regarding the rules of evidence, however, there are differences among the states. Most states impose the same rules of evidence on an arbitration hearing as on a trial. Other states, such as New Jersey, allow all evidence relevant to the dispute regardless of whether the evidence would be admissible at trial. Still other jurisdictions, such as Washington, leave it to the arbitrator to decide what evidence should be admissible.

WAIVER Once a court directs that the dispute is to be submitted to court-annexed arbitration, the parties must proceed to arbitration. As noted above, either side may reject the award that results from the arbitration for any reason. If a party fails to appear or participate in the arbitration proceeding as directed by the court, however, that failure constitutes a waiver of the right to reject the award.

Summary Jury Trials

Another means by which the courts have integrated alternative dispute resolution methods into the traditional court process is through the use of summary jury trials. A **summary jury trial** is a mock trial that occurs in a courtroom before a judge and jury. Evidence is presented in an abbreviated form along with each side's major contentions. The jury then presents a verdict.

The fundamental difference between a traditional trial and a summary jury trial is that in the latter the jury's verdict is only advisory. The goal of a summary jury trial is to give each side an idea of how it would fare if it pressed the case to a full-blown jury trial with a more elaborate and detailed presentation of evidence and arguments. At the end of the summary jury trial, the presiding judge meets with the parties and encourages them to settle their dispute without going through the extended procedures of a standard jury trial.

■ ADR Forums and Services

Services facilitating dispute resolution outside the courtroom are provided by both government agencies and private organizations. The major source of private arbitration services is the American Arbitration Association (AAA). Most of the largest law firms in the nation are members of this association. Founded in 1926, the AAA now settles more than 50,000 disputes a year in its thirty-one offices throughout the country. Cases brought before the AAA are heard by an expert or a panel of experts—of whom usually about half are lawyers—in the area relating to the dispute. To cover its costs, this nonprofit organization charges a fee, paid by the party filing the claim. In addition, each party to the dispute pays a price for each hearing day, as well as a special additional fee in cases involving personal injuries or property loss.

In addition to the AAA, there exist numerous other state and local nonprofit organizations that provide arbitration services. For example, the Arbitration Association of Florida provides ADR services in that state. The Better Business Bureau offers ADR programs to aid in the resolution of certain types of disagreements. Its latest ADR process involves a mediation program called ComputerCare, through which buyers and sellers of computer equipment and software can settle their disputes. Many industries—including the insurance, automobile, and securities industries—also now have mediation or arbitration programs to facilitate timely and inexpensive settlement of claims. In all, there exist over 600 alternative-dispute-resolution entities in the United States.

Mini-Trials

A recent development in the area of ADR is the use of mini-trials to facilitate dispute settlement. A **mini-trial** is similar to a summary jury trial except that it is a *private* proceeding. In a mini-trial, each party's attorney briefly argues the party's case before the other party. Often, a neutral third party, who acts as an adviser, is also present. If the parties fail to reach an agreement, the adviser renders an opinion as to how a court would likely decide the issue.

For-Profit Alternatives

Those who seek to settle their disputes quickly now have yet another alternative—they can pay private, for-profit organizations to act as mediators or arbitrators. Leading firms in the for-profit justice industry include Endispute of Washington, D.C.; Judicial Arbitration and Mediation Services of California; and Judicate, a Philadelphia-based firm that offers nationwide services and a network of approximately 450 judges—retired judges who are paid an hourly fee for their services—to assist its clients.

Procedures in these private courts are fashioned to meet the desires of the clients seeking their services. With Judicate, for example, the parties decide on the date of the hearing, the presiding judge, whether the judge's decision will be legally binding, and the site of the hearing—which could be a conference room, a law-school office, or a leased courtroom complete with flag and Bible. The judges follow procedures similar to those of the federal courts and use similar rules. Each party to the dispute pays a filing fee and a designated fee for a half-day hearing session or a special, one-hour settlement conference.

■ Caveat: ADR Is Not a Painless Cure

Some have complained that mandatory arbitration deprives individuals of their right to trial by jury; but so far, courts have held that access to the courts is not denied, because appeal of an arbitrator's decision to the courts is always possible. Others have criticized the enforcement of arbitration clauses as unfair to consumers. For example, arbitration clauses in contracts for the purchase of securities (stocks and bonds) usually require investors to agree to submit any disputes arising under the contracts to arbitration. Because the arbitration forums in which these disputes must be settled are largely sponsored by the securities industry, investors may not be given the opportunity to have their problems heard by a truly impartial arbitrator. To protect investors, Massachusetts enacted regulations that prohibited securities brokers from requiring investors to enter into pre-dispute arbitration agreements when purchasing securities. The securities industry brought suit in federal court, claiming that the regulations were unconstitutional because they conflicted with the provisions and policies of the Federal Arbitration Act. The court agreed and struck down the legislation as unconstitutional.[4] The judge compared the court system, with its swollen court calendars, to a body suffering from hypertrophy (pathologic swelling or overgrowth). Arbitration is a way to relieve the swelling, just as a medical shunt (a surgical diversion of the flow of blood from one area of the body to another) is a way to relieve pressure on the body. Although the patient often resists such treatment, it is necessary for regaining health.[5]

---

4. *Securities Industry Association v. Connolly,* 883 F.2d 1114 (1st. Cir. 1989).
5. Investors gained some protection, however, in New York. In a case decided by the New York Court of Appeals, an investor was allowed to bring a dispute with a broker to an independent arbitration panel rather than to the forum subsidized by the securities industry [*In the Matter of Cowen & Co. v. Anderson,* 559 N.Y.S.2d 225, 76 N.Y.2d 318, 558 N.E.2d 27 (1990)].

■ Terms and Concepts to Review

alternative dispute resolution (ADR) 57	**award** 63	**mini-trial** 73
arbitration 58	**mediation** 57	**submission** 61
arbitrator 58	**mediator** 57	**summary jury trial** 72

■ Questions and Case Problems

3-1. In an arbitration proceeding, the arbitrator need not be a judge or even a lawyer. How, then, can the arbitrator's decision have the force of law and be binding on the parties involved?

3-2. Two private U.S. corporations enter into a joint venture agreement to conduct mining operations in the newly formed Middle Eastern nation of Euphratia. As part of the agreement, the companies include an arbitration clause and a choice-of-law provision. The first states that any controversy arising out of the performance of the agreement will be settled by arbitration. The second states that the agreement is to be governed by the laws of the location of the venture, Euphratia. A dispute arises and the parties discontinue operations. One of the parties claims sole ownership to the Euphratia mines and orders the other party to remove its equipment from the mines. The other party disputes the claim of sole ownership and seeks an order from a federal court compelling the parties to submit to arbitration over the ownership and alleged breaches of the joint venture agreement. How should the court rule if the laws of Euphratia state that, while arbitration agreements are to be enforced generally, matters of ownership of natural resources can only be resolved in a Euphratia court of law? Does it matter that two U.S. companies engaged in international commerce would be governed by the Federal Arbitration Act?

3-3. Two brothers, both of whom are certified public accountants, form a professional association to provide tax accounting services to the public. They also agree, in writing, that any disputes that arise between them over matters concerning the association will be submitted to an independent arbitrator, whom they designate to be their father, who is also a CPA. A dispute arises and the matter is submitted to the father for arbitration. During the course of arbitration, which occurs over several weeks, the father asks the older brother, who is visiting one evening, to explain a certain entry in the brothers' association accounts. The younger brother learns of the discussion at the next meeting for arbitration; he says nothing about it, however. The arbitration is concluded in favor of the older brother, who seeks a court order compelling the younger brother to comply with the award. The younger brother seeks to set aside the award, claiming that the arbitration process was tainted by bias because "Dad always liked my older brother best." The younger brother also sought to have the award set aside on the basis of improper conduct in that matters subject to arbitration were discussed between the father and older brother without the younger's being present. Should a court confirm the award or set it aside? Why?

3-4. After resolving their dispute, the two brothers encountered in problem 3 decide to resume their tax accounting practice according to the terms of their original agreement. Again a dispute arises, and again it is decided by the father (now retired except for numerous occasions on which he acts as an arbitrator) in favor of the older brother. The older brother files a petition to confirm the award. The younger brother seeks to set aside the award and offers evidence that the father as arbitrator made a gross error in calculating the accounts that were material to the dispute being arbitrated. If the court is convinced that the father erred in the calculations, should the award be set aside? Why?

3-5. Gates worked for Arizona Brewing Co. and was a member of the International Union of United Brewers, Flour, Cereal, and Soft Drink Workers of America. A contract between Gates's employer and the union stated that the employer and the union were to try to settle their differences, but if the parties could not reach a settlement, the matter was to be decided by arbitration. Claiming that the arbitration clause was void under an Arizona arbitration statute, Gates brought a lawsuit against Arizona Brewing Co. to recover wages. Gates had not made any attempt to submit the dispute between him and the employer to arbitration. The employer argued that Gates could not bring a lawsuit until after arbitration had occurred. A provision in the Arizona arbitration statute, which generally enforced arbitration clauses in contracts, stated that "this act shall not apply to collective contracts between employers and ... associations of employ[ees]." Must Gates undergo arbitration before bringing a lawsuit? Explain. [*Gates v. Arizona Brewing Co.,* 54 Ariz. 266, 95 P.2d 49 (1939)]

3-6. When Roger and Susan Faherty divorced, they entered into a property settlement agreement that was incorporated into the final divorce decree. The property settlement agreement contained a clause that mandated arbitration of any dispute arising out of the agreement. Roger failed to make several alimony and child support payments, and Susan sought court enforcement of the property settlement agreement. Roger's consequent motion to have the court compel arbitration was granted by the court, and the dispute was arbitrated. The arbitrator's decision required Roger to pay Susan $37,648 for back alimony payments and $12,284 for overdue child support. Roger, although he had been the one to petition the court for arbitration, now challenged the validity of the arbitration clause in alimony and child support matters. He claimed that as a matter of public policy such matters should be settled by the courts, not by arbitration. Will the court agree with Roger? Discuss. [*Faherty v. Faherty,* 97 N.J. 99, 477 A.2d 1257 (1984)]

3-7. Hembree purchased a home from Broadway Realty and Trust Co. In the contract of sale, the buyer and seller agreed to arbitrate any claim or controversy "arising out of or relating to this contract." Hembree later claimed that the roof was defective, and the case was arbitrated. The arbitrator decided in favor of Hembree on the basis that the seller had breached an implied warranty. The seller appealed the arbitrator's decision, claiming that the arbitrator had exceeded his authority because only claims arising out of or relating to the contract were to be arbitrated, and an implied warranty claim did not arise out of or relate to "this contract." Discuss whether the arbitrator was within his authority in addressing the implied warranty claim. [*Hembree v. Broadway Realty and Trust Co.,* 151 Ariz. 418, 728 P.2d 288 (1986)]

3-8. Colorado's Mandatory Arbitration Act, which went into effect in January 1988, required that all civil lawsuits involving damages of less than $50,000 be arbitrated rather than tried in court. The statutory scheme, which was a pilot project to continue until July 1, 1990, affected eight judicial districts in the state. It provided for a court trial for any party dissatisfied with an arbitrator's decision. It also provided that if the trial did not result in more than a 10 percent improvement in the position of the party who demanded the trial, that party had to pay the costs of the arbitration proceeding. The constitutionality of the act was challenged by a plaintiff who maintained in part that it violated litigants' rights of access to the courts and to trial by jury. What will the court decide? Explain your answer. [*Firelock, Inc. v. District Court, 20th Judicial District,* 776 P.2d 1090 (Colo. 1989)]

3-9. New York state recently revised its New Car Lemon Law to allow consumers who complain of purchasing a "lemon" to have their disputes arbitrated before a professional arbitrator appointed by the New York attorney general. Before it was revised, the Lemon Law allowed for arbitration of disputes, but the forum in which arbitration took place was sponsored by trade associations within the automobile industry, and consumers often complained of unfair awards. The revised law also provided that con-

sumers had the option of arbitration before a professional arbitrator or suing the manufacturer in court. Manufacturers, however, were *compelled* to arbitrate claims, if a consumer chose to do so, and could not resort to the courts. Trade associations representing automobile manufacturers and importers brought an action seeking a declaration that the alternative arbitration mechanism of the Lemon Law was unconstitutional because it deprived them of their right to trial by jury. How will the court decide? Discuss. [*Motor Vehicle Manufacturers Association of the United States v. State,* 75 N.Y.2d 175, 550 N.E.2d 919, 551 N.Y.S.2d 470 (1990)]

3-10. Case Briefing Assignment

Examine Case A.3 [Rodriguez de Quijas v. Shearson/American Express, Inc. *490 U.S. 477, 109 S.Ct. 1917, 104 L.Ed.2d 379 (1989)]* in Appendix A. The case has been excerpted there in great detail. Review and then brief the case, making sure that your brief answers the following questions.

1. What is the legislative policy "embodied in the Arbitration Act"?
2. How did the court reconcile the protections afforded investors under the Securities Act and the legislative policy advanced by the Arbitration Act? Did the Court believe that, by submitting to arbitration, investors forego "substantive rights" given under the Securities Act?
3. Did the Supreme Court interpret the Securities Act differently than it had in the *McMahon* case (3.1)?

Chapter 4

Business Ethics

Businesspersons receive more extensive media coverage today than perhaps at any other time in our history. We constantly read and hear about business improprieties relating to insider trading activities, hostile takeovers, drug testing and discrimination in the workplace, product liability suits, or investments in South Africa. Indeed, because the media often focus on the improprieties of businesspersons, rather than the *ethical* activities that occur daily in the business arena, one might easily conclude that the men and women in business today are more unethical than businesspersons were in the past. In reality, this is probably not so.

Compare today's business practices, for example, with those of the nineteenth and early twentieth centuries. Gone now is the era of robber barons, cutthroat competition, and a nation run by large business trusts. Society's concern with business ethics today stems in part from a greater awareness of the not-so-ethical practices that occur in the business world and how these business practices and business decisions generally affect our welfare as consumers, our political well-being, and the health of planet Earth. As a result of these concerns, businesspersons face increasing pressure to conduct their affairs more responsibly and ethically.

In preparing for your career in business, you may find a background in business ethics and a commitment to ethical behavior just as important as a knowledge of the specific laws that you will read about in the remainder of this text. Furthermore, if you wish to truly understand the law, you need to be aware of the ethical framework within which it operates. This chapter first examines the nature of business ethics and the relationship between ethics and the law. Then it discusses some of the traditional approaches to ethical reasoning that have guided others in their ethical decision making. No chapter in business ethics would be complete without addressing one of the major ethical issues facing every businessperson—how to justify the self-interested search for profits. Related to this question is another important ethical issue: How can businesspersons act in an ethically responsible manner and at the same time make profits for their firms or their firms' owners?

The ultimate goal of this chapter is to provide you with the basic tools necessary for analyzing ethical issues in business contexts. It cannot tell you how to decide ethical issues. That is something you alone must do—on the basis of your own ethical convictions. As you read this chapter, and this book, examine carefully the ethical dimensions of specific laws and of specific court cases or hypothetical situations. Also examine closely your own ethical standards. What are your ethical criteria? How would you apply these criteria to a particular case or business situation? How can you best adapt your personal ethical standards to the kinds of ethical issues you will face in the business world? Although you can never be fully prepared for the task of ethical decision making—because no two situations are ever exactly alike—the more you analyze ethical issues relating to business that have arisen in the past, the better prepared you will be to make any ethical decisions you may face in the future.

■ The Nature of Business Ethics

Before we can talk about ethics, we need to define it. **Ethics** can be defined as the study of what constitutes right or wrong behavior. It is the branch of philosophy that focuses on morality and the way in which moral principles are applied to daily life. Ethics has to do with fundamental questions such as What is fair? What is just? What is the right thing to do in this situation?—essentially with any question relating to the fairness, justice, rightness, or wrongness of an action. Often, ethical questions or statements contain the words ''should'' or ''ought to.'' For example, when we say that someone ''ought to'' do something, we are not saying that he or she is forced to do it; merely that the person ''should'' do it because it is the fair, just, or right thing to do.

Ethics is not an abstract or a static concept. On the contrary, ethics affects, and gives meaning to, our everyday life and the decisions we make. We constantly apply our values and moral convictions to our actions and decisions, frequently without even being aware of the fact that we are doing so. The clothes we buy, the music we prefer, the way we treat our friends, the books we choose to read— these and a thousand other everyday activities and decisions, if you analyze them carefully, ultimately relate to ethical values and goals.

Defining Business Ethics

Business ethics focuses on what constitutes right or wrong behavior in the world of business and on how moral principles are applied by businesspersons to situations that arise in their daily work and during their careers. It is important to remember that business ethics is not a different *kind* of ethics. That is, businesspersons do not necessarily adopt one set of ethical principles to guide them in their business decisions and another set to guide them in their personal lives. The ethical standards that we set up for our behavior as, say, mothers, fathers, or students apply equally well to our activities as businesspersons. Business activities are just one part of the human enterprise, and business ethics is a subset of ethics that relates specifically to the kinds of situations that arise in the everyday world of business.

The Complexity of Business Ethics

Ethical decision making in the business world is somewhat more complicated than it is in our personal lives, however. In private life, it is not always necessary to analyze your ethical convictions too closely. As mentioned, personal ethical decisions are frequently made almost unconsciously and often from sheer habit. This usually presents no problem, because you are not normally called upon to explain the ethical reasoning underlying your personal decisions to others—except possibly your family or good friends. Even then, if you said you made a certain decision because you felt it was the ''right'' thing to do at the time, this would very likely be an acceptable ''reason'' for your decision.

The business world is a little different. One decision on the part of a businessperson can have repercussions throughout the entire society. Therefore, you need to be prepared to justify—to your superiors, to your colleagues or employees, to corporate shareholders, or even in a court of law— whatever decisions you make. It is not enough to say, ''I felt that it was the best decision in the circumstances'' or ''It seemed like the right thing to do at the time.'' You will need to demonstrate the rational basis for your decision and explain why, given the alternatives facing you, you concluded that your decision was the right one. In the business context, ethical behavior requires that you decide ethical issues on the basis of clearly defined ethical standards. Clearly defined ethical standards are especially important in today's world because businesspersons are increasingly being held to higher standards of accountability for their actions and decisions than they were in the past. To assist employees in making ethical decisions, many business firms today issue ethical policy guidelines or codes of conduct. The use and effectiveness of ethical codes are discussed in the *Emerging Trends* feature in this chapter.

Reasons for Unethical Business Behavior

Unethical behavior in the business context occurs in some cases because employers or owners implicitly condone such behavior. For example, an employee may go along with an unethical decision that economically benefits the company because the employee assumes that the company will reward him or her for increasing company profits. In other situations, unethical conduct may occur because of the belief that one can ''get away with it''—that the unethical activity will not be discovered. According to some, another reason for unethical business behavior is the corporate structure itself. By its very nature, the corporate structure might promote unethical behavior because it tends to protect corporate actors from personal responsibility for what they do.

For example, if a corporation markets a product that results in a consumer's death, the corporate officer who made the decision to market the product may not be deemed a ''murderer'' in the same sense that an individual who intentionally killed another would be. Nor would that corporate officer, in all likelihood, condone the killing of others. In effect, corporate decision makers are shielded from the consequences of their decisions by the corporate entity—that is, they do not witness or deal directly with the harm or injuries generated by their decisions. To a certain extent, they are also shielded from personal responsibility for their actions by the corporate collectivity. In other words, normally no *one* individual makes a corporate decision and therefore no one individual ever has to assume total responsibility for a corporate action (although in recent years, the courts have been increasingly willing to look behind the ''corporate veil'' and hold individual corporate actors liable for actions resulting in harm to others—see Chapter 7).

It is important to realize, though, that much unethical business behavior occurs simply because it is not always clear what ethical standards and behaviors are appropriate or acceptable in the business context. How can you learn what is appropriate or inappropriate behavior in the business world? One important source is business law itself.

■ Ethics and the Law

Virtually every law you read about in this book is related in one way or another to business ethics. Why? Because the law in a broad sense is itself an expression of ethical principles; it expresses what society—through its courts and other governmental bodies—has deemed to be right and proper behavior in the marketplace.

Ethics, as stated above, involves an active process of applying values, which may range from religious principles to customs and traditions. A *social ethic* expresses the dominant ethical values, or shared beliefs, of society in general. Indeed, it is the sharing of beliefs and the desire to spread these beliefs that cause people to organize as groups—pressure groups lobbying Congress to create or amend a law, social groups urging Americans to be for or against abortion, and so on. When enough people are convinced, say, that a certain law is wrong, sufficient pressure will be exerted on government to change that law so that it more effectively represents the social ethic. Because ethics and the law go hand in hand, a careful study of business law will help you to understand what is, and is not, considered by society to be ethical behavior in business.

Business Law as a Guide to Ethical Behavior

Business law rests on the premise that businesspersons should act ethically in their dealings with one another. It requires that people in business honor their contractual commitments, cooperate with one another in the performance of contracts, act reasonably and in good faith, and exercise due care and consideration for others in their undertakings. Although a law may seem arbitrary at first glance, if you look closely, you will very likely find the connection between that particular law and the broad, underlying ethical premise on which it ultimately rests. Insofar as possible, we will help you see this connection by indicating, as we discuss particular laws in this text, how these laws relate to broad social policies and ethical principles.

The Limits of the Law

Because the law reflects and codifies our society's ethical values, many of our ethical decisions are made for us—by our laws. Our laws force us to behave ethically or face undesirable consequences—a fine or even imprisonment. But in the interest of preserving personal freedom, as well as for practical reasons, the law does not, and cannot, codify all ethical requirements. No law says, for example, that it is *illegal* to lie to one's family, but it may be *unethical* to do so. Similarly, in the business world, numerous actions might be unethical but not necessarily illegal. Mere compliance with the law does not always equate with ethical behavior.

Consider the following hypothetical example. The U.S. government has discovered that a child's toy is dangerous and has caused the deaths of some children. Consequently, the government has banned sales of the toy, leaving the manufacturer with a large unsold inventory. Although sales of the product are banned in the United States, it may be perfectly legal to export this toy to nations that have little consumer protection legislation. But would it be ethical to do so?

It is also possible that an individual may consider a particular law to be immoral. In such a situation, should the individual obey the law even if he or she thinks it would be unethical to do so? As discussed in Chapter 1, adherents of the natural law school believe that there is a higher law than that prescribed by a particular society at a particular point in time. If a law accepted by courts and embodied in statutes conflicts with natural law, it loses its legitimacy and "deserves" to be disobeyed. This is the basis for the theory of civil disobedience espoused by Henry David Thoreau, Martin Luther King, Jr., Mahatma Gandhi, and others.

In short, the law has its limits—it cannot make all our ethical decisions for us. When it does not, personal ethical standards must guide the decision-making process. We now examine some of the traditional ways in which ethical standards have been derived.

■ The Derivation of Ethical Standards

Although it would be nice to think that ethical standards simply exist, just as the law of gravity does, such is not the case. Ethical standards are not discoverable, like some universal law of nature. Indeed, the many scientific and technological achievements of the modern world offer us no guidance when it comes to establishing ethical standards of behavior. Ethical standards are by nature subjective; they are derived from basic religious beliefs or philosophical postulates concerning the nature of the good, fair, right, or just. We each have to decide what we believe in and how to translate our beliefs into action.

This is not to say that there are no resources to which we can turn for ethical guidance. On the contrary, religious and philosophical inquiry into the nature of "the good" is an age-old pursuit, and the amount written on this subject could fill a library. Broadly speaking, though, ethical reasoning relating to business has traditionally been characterized by two fundamental approaches. One approach defines ethical behavior in terms of *duty*. The other approach determines what is ethical, or good, in terms of the *consequences* of any given action. We examine each of these approaches below.

Duty-Based Ethics

Is it wrong to cheat on an examination, if nobody will ever know you cheated and if it helps you get into law school so that you can eventually represent *pro bono* (without pay) the needy? Is it wrong to lie to your parents, if the lie harms nobody but helps to keep family relations congenial? These kinds of ethical questions implicitly weigh the "end" of an action against the "means" used to attain that end. If you believe that you have an ethical *duty* not to lie or cheat, then lying and cheating can never be justified by the consequences—no matter how benevolent or desirable those consequences may be. In American culture, the dominant duty-based ethical standard derives from religious sources.

RELIGIOUS ETHICS The Western religious tradition—more specifically, the Judeo-Christian religious tradition—is rooted in the belief that certain absolute truths have been revealed through the prophets, the Bible, and religious institutions. Who among us has not been exposed to the "Thou shalt nots" of the Ten Commandments, the "seven deadly sins," and Christ's instruction to help and care for others ("Love one another as I have loved you"; "Love thy neighbor as thyself"; "He who shall lay down his life for a friend . . . "). These teachings establish for all who believe in them an *absolute ethical duty* to act in accordance with them. It is not the consequences of an act that determine how ethical the act is, but the nature of the act itself. For example, if, like Robin Hood, an individual decides to rob the rich to help the poor, that individual's benevolent motive does not alter the fact that he or she has acted unethically ("sinned"), because stealing violates the Seventh Commandment ("Thou shalt not steal").

Religious ethical standards are *absolute*. When an act is prohibited by religious teachings, it is unethical and should not be undertaken—regardless of its consequences. Telling a lie, for example, for the sake of gaining a promotion is unethical—even though no one would be harmed by the lie and your future would be rosier. Religious ethical standards also involve an element of *compassion*. Therefore, even though it might be profitable for a firm to lay off a less productive employee, if that employee would find it difficult to find employment elsewhere and his or her family would suffer as a result, this potential suffering would be given substantial weight by the decision makers. A compassionate manager or employer might decide to keep the employee and attempt to increase profits in another way. Compassionate treatment of others is also mandated—to a certain extent, at least—by the Golden Rule of the ancients ("Do unto others as you would have them do unto you"), which has been adopted by most religions.

KANT AND DUTY-BASED ETHICS What we have been describing is an other-oriented, duty-based system of ethics. A duty-based approach to ethics is also characteristic of the philosophy of Immanual Kant (1724–1804). This philosopher identified some general guiding principles for moral behavior based on what he believed to be the fundamental nature of human beings. Kant held that it is rational to assume that human beings are qualitatively different from other physical objects occupying space, such as CD players, sofas, and computers. Persons are *moral* agents—that is, they are endowed with moral integrity and the capacity to reason and conduct their affairs rationally; therefore, their thoughts and actions should be re-

spected. When human beings are treated merely as means, they are being treated as the equivalent of objects and are being denied their basic humanity.

A central postulate in Kantian ethics is that individuals should evaluate their actions in light of the consequences that would follow if *everyone* in society acted in the same way. This "categorical imperative" can be applied to any action. For example, say that you are deciding whether to cheat on an examination. If you have adopted Kant's categorical imperative, you will decide not to cheat, because if everyone cheated, the examination would be meaningless. Similarly, you would not cut in line to purchase a ticket for a rock concert, because if everyone else did the same thing, the concept of a line would disappear and chaos would reign.

Kant's ethics impose a duty to respect the moral integrity of others at all times and to act only as we would have all others act. In its effect, Kantian ethical reasoning gives philosophical weight to the Golden Rule mentioned above, but note the distinction: The Golden Rule merely exhorts us to "do unto others as we would have them do unto ourselves." Kant's categorical imperative forces us to look at the larger picture: What would *society* be like if everybody acted as we did? It forces us to look at and evaluate, from a more objective point of view, *social* goals as well as our personal desires and welfare.

PROBLEMS WITH DUTY-BASED ETHICS Sometimes, applying religious or Kantian ethics can pose difficulties. This is especially true in the business context. For example, a business executive negotiating with another firm's representatives may feel it necessary to "stretch the truth" or "hold back" information to obtain the best "deal" for his or her employer. Is this a violation of the religious precept that one should not lie or of Kant's categorical imperative? In some absolute sense, yes, it is unethical in both religious and Kantian terms. But remember that the executive also owes an ethical duty to his or her employer to make decisions that are profitable for the firm. Furthermore, what if the executive knows that, unless the deal is struck, his or her employer will have to lay off a number of long-time employees who depend on the firm to look after their economic welfare? Would "stretching the truth" in negotiating the deal then be consistent with the religious ethical duty to be compassionate toward others? Or the Kantian imperative to act only as we would have all others act?

You can see how, in the business context, ethical decision making may involve fulfilling not just one ethical responsibility but a number of ethical responsibilities simultaneously. When one ethical duty conflicts with another, you have to decide which duty is the most fundamental and act accordingly. In the situation here, the executive may conclude that the ethical duty to be fully honest with others is more fundamental than the duty owed to the firm (even though the cost of this decision may include a personal cost, such as a future promotion or pay raise, which will affect not only the executive but also his or her family). Alternatively, the executive might decide that the ethical duty owed to the firm and its employees (and possibly to his or her family) is more fundamental than, and thus overrides, the duty to be fully honest with the other negotiators. As this example illustrates, frequently the ethical decisions faced by businesspersons are not clear cut; that is, the decisions involve choices not between good and bad alternatives but between good and less good alternatives.

Utilitarianism

''Thou shalt act so as to generate the greatest good for the greatest number.'' This is a paraphrase of the major premise of utilitarian theory. **Utilitarianism** is a philosophical theory first developed by Jeremy Bentham (1748–1832) and then advanced, with some modifications, by John Stuart Mill (1806–1873)—both British philosophers. In contrast to religious ethics and Kant's moral theory, utilitarianism is *outcome oriented*. It focuses on the consequences of an action, not on the nature of the action itself or on any set of preestablished moral values or religious beliefs.

RIGHT AND WRONG IN UTILITARIANISM Under a utilitarian model of ethics, an action is morally correct or right when, among the people it affects, it produces the greatest amount of good for the greatest number. When an action affects the majority adversely, it is morally wrong. Applying the utilitarian theory thus requires (1) a determination of what individuals will be affected by the action in question; (2) an assessment, or **cost-benefit analysis,** of the negative and positive effects of alternative actions on these individuals; and (3) a choice among alternative actions that will produce maximum societal utility—or, in other words, the greatest positive benefits for the greatest number of individuals.

How does a utilitarian determine what constitutes the general welfare or happiness of individuals? Jeremy Bentham's approach to this question was to define happiness strictly in terms of physical pleasure or pain. By thus quantifying happiness, he felt it would be possible to calculate scientifically, by a kind of moral mathematics, the human costs and benefits of any legislative decision. Mill argued that qualitative factors, such as psychological and spiritual well-being, also play a significant role in creating happiness and need to be considered in calculations of the positive and negative effects of a decision. With Mill and later followers of the utilitarian school of thought, what constitutes happiness is individually determined. Therefore, the successful application of the utilitarian welfare-maximization principle depends on the freedom—and physical, mental, social, and financial ability—of all individuals to make and express their choices.

A brief digression: Freedom of choice is at the heart of Mill's philosophy, and it stems from his libertarian outlook. Mill believed that a person should have the liberty to think and do as he or she likes, without government interference, so long as that individual's actions do not infringe on another's rights. Mill's concern with individual liberty has had a profound influence on Western political and legal thought. The right to privacy, for example, is grounded to a certain extent in Mill's philosophical principles concerning individual rights.

PROBLEMS WITH UTILITARIANISM While interesting in principle, utilitarianism suffers from a major problem: Any true calculation of overall welfare, happiness, or utility requires a knowledge of what the *actual* consequences, both negative and positive, of a given decision will be—and rarely, if ever, can all of the possible ramifications of a decision be predicted with total accuracy. This is especially true with decisions that may affect millions of people.

Another problem with utilitarianism is that it always involves both winners and losers—that is, it is impossible to satisfy everybody with a policy action based on the principle of utility. Consider the following example: Johnson, a manufacturer, owns many plants. One of the plants is much older than the others. Equipment at the old plant is outdated and inefficient, and the costs of production at that plant are now twice what they are at any of Johnson's other plants. The price of the product cannot be increased because of competition, both domestic and international. What should Johnson do? In a utilitarian analysis of the problem, the costs of closing the plant (the financial insecurity of those who would be laid off) would be weighed against the benefits of closing the plant (the future financial security of the firm and of those workers who would retain their jobs at the other plants). If Johnson decides the issue from a utilitarian perspective, he will very likely close the plant, because closing the plant will yield the greatest benefit for the greatest number of people. The winners are the majority who will be aided by the decision; the losers are the workers at the old plant, now without jobs.

Utilitarianism is often criticized because its objective, calculated approach to problems tends to reduce the welfare of human beings to plus and minus signs on a cost-benefit worksheet. Utilitarian reasoning has also been used to ''justify'' human costs that many find totally unacceptable.

There are other theories of moral responsibility, but all of them involve making difficult choices in a world in which information is imperfect. Frequently, ethical choices in the business context involve choosing between self-interest (of the businessperson or of the business firm) and perceived ethical obligations. In the business context, self-interest is usually equated with profit-seeking behavior. Not surprisingly, the question of profits and how to justify them ethically has been, and continues to be, a fundamental concern of the business world.

■ Ethics and the Search for Profits

Unethical and, often, illegal business behavior makes good press in America today, but businesspersons in general are respected members of Western society. Profit-making activities are not deemed unethical—so long as no laws or fundamental eth-

ical principles are violated. In fact, successful businesspersons often rank among the most admired individuals in our society. This was not always the case. Historically (and still in our time in those nations that have adopted a communist political ideology), the self-interested pursuit of profits was ethically suspect because it pitted self-gain against community-oriented behavior.

Merchants and Society: A Brief History

Two thousand years ago in ancient Greece, the businessperson ranked about the same as a slave on the social ladder. Greek society allowed businesses to exist, but business profits could only be used to serve the community. Businesspersons who did well were not allowed to display their wealth or success by altering their material standard of living. They had to live in the same manner as others in their class. Whenever a Greek businessperson was suspected of violating this strict standard of morality, the upper classes severely criticized and socially censured that person. Although merchants fared somewhat better in the Roman era, there was little significant change in social status.

In the medieval world, which was dominated by Christian institutions and ethics, merchants presented a perplexing challenge from an ethical point of view. On the one hand, the profit motive and self-interest that it represented were considered anti-Christian *per se* (inherently; in itself)—one's duty was to serve God and others, not one's own material well-being. On the other hand, the trading activities of merchants increased social welfare by making more products available, some of which were vitally necessary. Generally, from about 700 A.D. to 1500 A.D., merchants were therefore regarded as a kind of necessary evil in society. Commerce was deemed acceptable, but only insofar as it served the public interest. And certain types of business activities that are common today were prohibited—charging interest on loans, for example, was forbidden by the Church. One was not allowed to make ''profits'' from loaning money. The concept of a *just price* was also established. Businesspersons accused of setting other than a just price, of using profits irresponsibly, or of acting dishonestly were severely punished.

In the wake of the social and religious activities of the sixteenth century, business activity became more respectable. The religious reformer John Calvin (1509–1564) was particularly influential in this respect. Some of the tenets of Calvinism had profound social implications. Calvin, for example, placed a high value on thrift, industry, and hard work and regarded business success as evidence of God's grace. The spread of Calvinism across Europe was accompanied by an ethical climate favorable to trade and commerce, and businesspersons for the first time began to make their way into the upper social classes. Although the Calvinist doctrine encouraged trade, it did not condone unethical business practices, but held that immoral business behavior should be punished. Also, because businesspersons achieved success only through the grace of God, they were morally obligated to make substantial contributions to the Church and to charitable causes that furthered the welfare of the needy.

From about 1800 to the Great Depression in the 1930s, during the era of the Industrial Revolution, the businessperson moved up to the highest notch on the social ladder. The corporation grew in importance and, with it, the importance of corporate leaders in the political, social, and moral life of this nation, as well as in Western Europe. Profit-seeking activity was fully justified, from an ethical point of view, not only by the Calvinist work ethic but by an economic theory in which the self-interested search for profits was firmly united with social welfare: the theory of capitalism.

Capitalism and the Ethical Justification of Profits

In 1776, Adam Smith, a Scottish economist and the so-called father of capitalism, published his *Wealth of Nations.* In this treatise, Smith firmly linked self-interest to "other-interest" by arguing that the self-interested behavior of individuals in an unfettered marketplace results in maximum social welfare.

Implicitly, the *laissez-faire*[1] ("let them do as they please") world of capitalism described by Smith was a form of utilitarianism. Adam Smith "proved" that individuals acting in their own self-interest generate the greatest social welfare for the greatest number of citizens. According to Smith, this is because an "invisible hand" (the forces of

supply and demand) regulates the free market to ensure that only socially worthwhile profit-seeking enterprises survive. In a nutshell, capitalist theory can be described as follows: The only way that businesses can sell their services or products is if people want them. People show their preferences for goods and services by agreeing to purchase them at whatever the market price is. The market price is determined by the forces of supply and demand—the actions of all suppliers taken together and all consumers taken together, interacting with each other. There is no such thing as a "just" price, only the price generated by the forces of supply and demand. Businesspersons who produce commodities that individuals want at the lowest price survive in this highly competitive marketplace; others do not. Businesses use resources to produce commodities. The difference between the cost of those resources and the revenues businesses receive from the buying public is what we define as profit.

Because consumers are not forced to purchase any particular product, they never pay more than the highest subjective valuation they place on a product. That is, if good *X* costs $20 but a consumer only values it at $18, the consumer will never buy it. Hence, the total revenues received by the businessperson represent the minimum valuation that society places on the commodity that the businessperson sells. The difference between those revenues and the cost of providing the commodity—profits—represents an indication of the social desirability of producing the commodity. High profits are good because they show that resources are being put to highly valued uses. Low profits and losses are bad because they indicate that businesspersons made incorrect decisions about which commodities consumers really wanted.

Presumably, we do not have to worry about high profits lasting forever because such profits encourage new producers to enter the marketplace or old producers to expand output. When output increases, prices fall, and so, too, do profits. In the long run, firms tend to make only a competitive rate of return, or a normal rate of profit. Resources are constantly moving from lower-valued uses to higher-valued uses as businesspersons constantly search for highly profitable opportunities. In the world of Adam Smith, profits are therefore good,

---

1. Pronounced leh-say *fair.*

morally acceptable, and indeed necessary for the material well-being of society.

Today's Marketplace

Adam Smith's theory rested on a vision of a marketplace characterized by perfect competition. But in reality, we live in a world of imperfect competition. Some of the reasons for market imperfections are as follows:

1. When a firm becomes large and powerful enough to control a substantial share of the market, it need not be as sensitive to the dollar votes of consumers. This is because consumers will be unable to purchase the same product from the firm's competitors—there will be no significant competition. Therefore, high profits will not be reduced.
2. It is difficult, if not impossible, for firms to obtain perfect information about what consumers really want or about optimal production techniques. It is also difficult for consumers to obtain perfect information on product availability, price, and quality. As a result of imperfect information, profits in the marketplace do not necessarily go hand in hand with consumer welfare.
3. The existence of **externalities**—the costs or benefits of an action that are not known or properly accounted for by the parties to that action—also results in market imperfections. Environmental pollution is a good example of an externality. If a business firm releases chemicals into a river, pollution results. But the business firm does not pay the "cost" of that pollution; society does. Although the product produced by the firm may be a life-saving drug and thus a benefit to society, the pollution that is produced by the firm mitigates against the social welfare.

Because of market imperfections, the search for profits is not always in society's best interests. To the extent that the ethics of capitalism and the free enterprise system lead to social harm, a socially responsible firm modifies those ethics by applying other ethical standards. The business manager in today's world typically looks at more than just the profit side of the picture when making decisions. The profitability of a given action or decision is still the first consideration, to be sure—after all, the reason a business firm exists is to make profits. It goes without saying that the second primary consideration is the legality of the proposed action. The final consideration is whether the proposed action is ethically justifiable. Exhibit 2–1 illustrates graphically how these three factors—profitability, legality, and ethical considerations—interrelate in the decision-making process.

▧ Tradeoffs and Ethical Decision Making

Ideally, each decision you make as a businessperson would fall readily into the center area of the diagram shown in Exhibit 4–1. Frequently, however, to ensure that a decision or action is at once profitable, legal, and ethical, some profitability or some ethical considerations must be sacrificed—or *traded off*—in the decision-making process. Thus, the concept of a **tradeoff** is intimately involved in ethical decision making.

No matter what your approach to ethics in the business world or in your personal life, you will be faced with the necessity of making tradeoffs

▧ Exhibit 4–1 Ethical Decision Making
This diagram illustrates how legality, profitability, and ethical factors interrelate in the ethical decision-making process in the business context. Ideally, business decisions will fall within the shaded area in which all circles overlap. If they do not, ethically responsible decision making requires that tradeoffs be made so that all three criteria are satisfied.

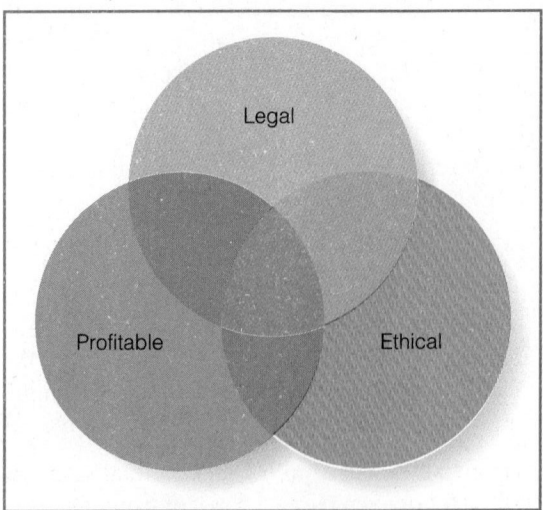

between equally desirable goals. Recognizing the nature of the tradeoff required to resolve an ethical conflict is the first step in the ethical decision-making process. The next step necessarily requires you to bring your own—or your firm's—ethical standards to bear on the decision. You must decide whether one goal is more important or fundamental than the other or others and minimize, to the extent possible, any modification or sacrificing of that goal.

It is important to stress that the ethical tradeoffs normally faced by businesspersons are not clear-cut tradeoffs between "good" and "bad" alternatives. By definition, ethical dilemmas only arise when two or more *ethical* goals come into conflict. For example, assume that a corporate executive has to decide whether to approve the sale of a new product that would be beneficial for most consumers but that might have undesirable side effects for a small percentage of its users. In this situation, the tradeoff becomes relatively obvious: expose an unknown but extremely small number of individuals to possible harm while allowing all other consumers to enjoy the benefits of the new product (and in the process, probably make higher profits) or protect that small number of individuals from possible harm and not allow all other consumers to enjoy the benefits of the new product.

In statistics, this tradeoff is known as a tradeoff between Type I and Type II errors. A *Type I error* occurs because of the sin of *commission*. When the new product is sold and there is an undesirable side effect—a customer becomes sick or is injured—the harm occurs because of the sin of commission. In contrast, if the product is not entered into the marketplace, a *Type II error* will occur. Type II errors result from the sin of *omission*. All of the benefits that people would have derived had the product been introduced do not exist if the product is not marketed.

Let us take a specific example that involves a pharmaceutical company. The firm has developed a new medication that is very effective in the treatment of high blood pressure. The only problem is that the company estimates that one person in a million using the product may have a violent allergic reaction to the medication and might even suffer death. The tradeoff here is between the Type I error (the one-in-a-million chance that someone will suffer or even die as a result of using the med-

ication) and the Type II error (that people may die from cardiovascular disease or other problems resulting from high blood pressure if the new medication is never introduced into the marketplace).

Obviously, because Type I errors can be observed and linked directly to the new medication, they are usually the ones that make the headlines. Type II errors resulting from the nonintroduction of the new medication into the marketplace are not easily calculated, however. There is simply no accurate and widely acceptable way to measure how much suffering and dying occur because the new medication was not introduced into the marketplace.

■ Ethical Issues in Business

It would be impossible to describe all of the different kinds of ethical issues that arise in the business world. As you will discover in reading through this text, ethics relates to all aspects of business activity. Broadly speaking, ethical issues can be categorized as internal issues or external issues. Because many ethical issues internal to the firm concern the relationship between the firm and its employees, we offer here a few examples of ethical issues that have arisen in the employment relationship. Ethical issues external to the firm predominantly relate to the products or services marketed by the firm and how marketing decisions affect the welfare of the ultimate consumers of those products and services. We briefly examine here some of the ethical dimensions of marketing decisions.

It is important to keep the tradeoff concept in mind as you consider the ethical issues discussed below because often what is at issue is the extent to which the employer's profit-making goals should be traded off to fulfill a perceived ethical duty toward employees or consumers.

Employment Relationships

One of the primary concerns of every employer is the ability to control the workplace environment. After all, it is the employer who is responsible for making the business firm a success, and success requires qualified, competent, loyal employees and efficient operations. But employees also have concerns. They want to earn a fair wage; they want to

One way for everyone in a company to be aware of the ethical standards expected of employees is for that company to create, print, and distribute among the employees a code of ethics. Such a code may be called a code of ethics, a code of conduct, a mission statement, a policy statement, or by some other name. In 1968, 32 percent of companies polled had ethical codes. By 1970, 75 percent had such codes, and today well over 90 percent of the Fortune 500 companies have ethical codes of conduct. Indeed, such codes have become a permanent fixture in the business policy-making landscape.

What Are Ethical Codes?

In general, ethical codes provide employees with the knowledge of what the firm expects in terms of their responsibilities and behavior. Relationships that are covered include employee-employee, employee-manager, employee-consumer, and employee-supplier relationships. Some ethical codes offer a lengthy and detailed set of guidelines for employees. Others are not really "codes" at all but summary statements of goals, policies, and priorities.

The Pro Side of Ethical Codes

Do ethical codes work? Do they really result in more ethical behavior on the part of employees? Many believe that they do. A good example of the effectiveness of an ethical policy statement is the guidance offered by such a statement to employees of Johnson & Johnson Company (J&J) when that company was faced with a crisis in 1982.

The crisis arose when some of J&J's popular nonaspirin pain reliever, marketed under the name of Tylenol, was "spiked" with cyanide, causing the deaths of several persons in Chicago. When top management at J&J was informed of the problem, it immediately formed a committee to handle the crisis. Following the company's ethical guidelines, the committee created a set of priorities, the first one being to assure the safety of its customers. To this end, the committee recalled Tylenol from the market until the company could develop tamper-resistant packaging for its product. The second priority was to communicate openly with the buying public about what had happened and why it had happened. This was done through numerous press releases, press conferences, and printed statements, as well as television and radio interviews.

The third priority was to maintain J&J's goodwill and reputation.

Some thought, at the time, that J&J would never recover its former hegemony over the pain-reliever market. The doubters were wrong. Within only a few months, Tylenol had regained its former share of that market, because of the quick and open action on the part of J&J's top management in the face of the crisis.

The Con Side of Ethical Codes

Critics of ethical codes claim that many of them are simply legalistic documents that forbid specific actions. These critics contend that most ethical codes do not provide a set of guidelines based on ethical values for employees and management. Those ethical codes that do contain more than legalistic rules, they maintain, are often filled with platitudes rather than truly important ethical guidelines because the latter may concern sensitive issues.

Other critics contend that no matter how good an ethical code is, the code itself has little effect on the ethical attitudes and behavioral patterns of the company's employees. Rather, it is the example set by top management that promotes ethical (or nonethical) conduct by other members of the corporate family. Employees learn what acceptable norms of conduct are by observing top management's behavior.

For example, if management emphasizes meeting performance objectives at any cost, then employees will know that ethical considerations are being placed, implicitly, in a secondary role. Also, whenever employees are being treated unfairly, they may doubt whether the employer takes ethical considerations seriously. In such settings, it is difficult for a code of ethics to have any effective impact on workers' behavior.

■ Implications for the Businessperson

1. Businesspersons today have to face the fact that unethical behavior will no longer be excused on the premise that "business will be business" or "it's legal, so it's okay." Indeed, today's businessperson benefits most by *preventive measures*—that is, by looking ahead of the law and anticipating problems (including potential court judgments or legislative restraints) that could result from unethical business practices. Paying attention to the "ethical credentials" of potential employees is one such preventive measure; training current employees in the goals and benefits of ethical behavior is another.

2. Top management in any corporation is well advised to develop a meaningful and appropriate code of ethics, to have it printed, to give every employee a copy, and, most importantly, to explain to employees the importance of ethics and how the specific components of the code relate to the company's overall ethical goals and policies.

3. Traditionally, business managers have framed their responsibilities in response to the firm's environment— particularly in response to consumer demand for their firms' products and the actions of competitors in the marketplace. Today's managers must also evaluate their decisions from the opposite perspective—that is, by looking at how the firm affects the environment in which it operates.

■ For Critical Analysis

1. In many countries, the giving of gifts and side payments in return for political or economic favors is a normal way of doing business. American businesspersons, however, are prohibited from bribing foreign officials to obtain contracts or other favorable treatment. Also, some countries encourage—and even legally require—discrimination in employment on the basis of religion, race, or sex, while such employment discrimination is both unethical and illegal in America. Because of the increasingly international scope of business transactions, many efforts have been directed toward the creation of an effective international code of business ethics. Do the differences in ethical standards among nations mean that a workable international code of business conduct is an impossible dream?

2. To what extent do you believe that ethical codes are adopted simply to make firms look good in the eyes of their employees, shareholders, customers, and suppliers? Is it possible that even if an ethical code was adopted for this reason, it would still be a step in the right direction?

3. Analysts of ethical codes maintain that to be effective, an ethical code should relate to the specific business activities of the firm. But what about a huge conglomerate corporation that owns and ultimately directs the activities of numerous, completely diverse subsidiary companies? Is it possible to create a code of ethics that can apply to all employees in the conglomerate and yet be specific enough to offer practical and useful guidance to the employees?

work in an environment free of health-endangering hazards; they want to be treated fairly and equally by their employers; and, increasingly in recent years, they want employers to respect their personal integrity and privacy rights.

By law, employers are required to provide a safe workplace, to pay a minimum wage, and to provide equal employment opportunities for all potential and existing employees. But does an employer have ethical obligations to employees that go beyond those duties written into the law? This question was implicitly raised by the hypothetical situation discussed earlier in this chapter—in which an employer, Johnson, had to decide whether to close down an old, inefficient plant to increase the profitability of the firm. Johnson's dilemma represents a classic conflict between profit-making goals and perceived ethical duties to employees and, according to some, to the community at large. This conflict frequently faces businesspersons today and was dramatized in the film *Roger and Me,* which concerns the decision by General Motors to close its Flint, Michigan, plant.

"PRICE DISCRIMINATION" IN EMPLOYMENT
In recent years, some firms have been criticized for firing highly paid employees who have worked for—and received annual raises from—the firms for years and then replacing those employees with younger, less experienced persons who are happy to accept lower salaries. Such actions are not necessarily illegal. If the fired employee cannot prove that the employer has breached an employment contract or violated the Age Discrimination in Employment Act (ADEA), he or she will not have a cause of action against the employer. The ADEA prohibits discrimination against workers forty years old and older on the basis of their age, but employers can always say that lack of performance or ability, not age, was the deciding factor.

Increasingly, employers who want to shed older, highly paid employees are avoiding liability for age discrimination by offering the employees early retirement plans, financial incentives, and perhaps job-placement services—in return for a written waiver of the right to sue the firm for age discrimination. To ensure that employees are fully cognizant of the rights they are waiving, the Older Workers Benefit Protection Act, which went into effect in 1990, requires that employees be given forty-five days to consider the waiver agreement and seven days to revoke the waiver after signing it. But from an ethical viewpoint, is it fair to long-time, loyal employees to force them to make a choice between early retirement and continuing on the job when the latter choice may involve a lower salary, a demotion to a less desirable position, or even eventual dismissal on the grounds of some "manufactured" reason other than age?

In deciding this issue, remember that if employers fail to keep their eyes on their profit margins, they may place in jeopardy the financial well-being of the firm. Why should a firm retain highly paid employees if it can obtain essentially the same work output for a lower price by hiring cheaper labor? Does an employer or manager owe an ethical duty to employees who have served the firm loyally over a long period of time? Most people would say yes. Should this duty take precedence over, say, a corporate manager's duty to the firm's owners to maintain or increase the profitability of the firm? Would your answer be the same if the firm faced imminent bankruptcy if it could not lower its operating costs? What if the long-time employees were willing to take a slight reduction in pay to help the firm through its financial difficulties? What if they were not?

THE COMPARABLE WORTH CONTROVERSY
The issue of **comparable worth** also pits profit-making goals against the duty to treat employees fairly and equally. In a nutshell, proponents of comparable worth standards think that employers should pay all employees on a comparable basis—by assessing "objectively" the value of each job classification and paying everybody with the same valuation the same amount of money. Typically, a panel of experts uses a point scale to assign a value to each job category. If, for example, a secretary is valued at 200 points and a truck driver is valued at 220 points, the truck driver's salary should be only 10 percent higher than that of the secretary.

Equal pay laws require equal pay for equal work—a male nurse, for example, must be paid the same salary as a female nurse doing the same job. But equal pay laws do not address the issue of comparable worth. The notion of comparable worth involves equality in pay not just for different persons holding the *same* kind of job but for different persons holding *different* kinds of jobs that require the same degree of education or training or effort. The comparable worth doctrine aims to correct the reality that male-dominated jobs still draw higher salaries than female-dominated jobs, even though the former may not require any more expertise or effort than the latter.

Does the employer have a moral obligation to correct for past discrimination against women by correcting the current inequities in female-male pay standards that have resulted from this discrimination? Those who say yes have to face the fact that this decision may be costly to the firm in terms of profits. This is because relative pay is determined largely by overall supply and demand conditions in the labor market. The quantity supplied of typists, for example, may be so great relative to the quantity demanded that their pay scale is 50 percent lower than that of truck drivers. If an employer adopts a comparable worth standard that requires typists to be paid only 10 percent less than truck drivers, that employer will face higher costs than competing firms who do not adopt a comparable worth pay scale. These higher costs will result in lower profits, which could jeopardize the firm's financial future. If the firm is a corporation, an additional ethical issue arises: Is it fair to divert profits from the shareholders to female employees?

EMPLOYMENT DISCRIMINATION   As will be discussed in Chapter 17, by law employers must offer equal employment opportunities to all job applicants and employees. Today's employers are prohibited from discriminating against existing or potential employees on the basis of race, color, national origin, sex, pregnancy, religion, or age. Discrimination against the handicapped is also prohibited. This means that employers must sometimes treat employees unfairly and unequally. For example, many companies have adopted *affirmative action* policies to make up for past discriminatory practices against protected classes, such as minority groups or women. These policies occasionally result in what has been termed "reverse discrimination"—that is, discrimination against qualified members of the "majority" group. Essentially, the ethical question here is whether it is fair to promote a less qualified employee to a position instead of a more qualified employee simply to correct for past discrimination. Some would say yes; others, no. But the question indicates how employers who are trying to fulfill a perceived ethical obligation to treat employees fairly and equally can sometimes find themselves in a no-win situation.

The following case is illustrative. Even though the employer went substantially beyond minimum legal compliance in attempting to provide a safe workplace for employees, the firm was nonetheless charged by some of its employees with having violated another ethical (and legal) duty—that of providing equal employment opportunities for women.

BACKGROUND AND FACTS   *Johnson Controls, Inc., created its Battery Division in 1978. In 1982, as part of an ongoing attempt to reduce the health hazards that might result from lead exposure, Johnson adopted a "fetal protection policy," under which women of childbearing age were prohibited from working in the Battery Division. This decision was reached after scientific studies indicated that a pregnant woman's exposure to high lead levels could harm the fetus. Johnson adopted this mandatory policy largely because its previous voluntary policy had failed to achieve the desired purpose: protecting pregnant women and their unborn children from dangerously high blood lead levels. Employees and their union, United Auto Workers, brought a suit against Johnson, claiming that the fetal protection policy violated Title VII of the Civil Rights Act of 1964, which prohibits discrimination in employment on the basis of sex. The trial court held for Johnson, and the unions and employees appealed. The appellate court affirmed the trial court's ruling. The United States Supreme Court granted* certiorari.

Case 4.1

UNITED AUTO WORKERS v. JOHNSON CONTROLS, INC.

Supreme Court of the United States, 1991.
_____ U.S. _____
111 S.Ct. 1196,
113 L.Ed.2d 158.

Justice *BLACKMUN* delivered the opinion of the Court.

* * * *

Under * * * Title VII [of the Civil Rights Act of 1964], an employer may discriminate on the basis of "religion, sex, or national origin in those certain instances where religion, sex, or national origin is a bona fide occupational qualification [BFOQ] reasonably necessary to the normal operation of that particular business or enterprise." We therefore turn to the question whether Johnson Controls' fetal-protection policy is one of those "certain instances" that come within the BFOQ exception.

* * * *

Johnson Controls argues that its fetal-protection policy falls within the so-called safety exception to the BFOQ. * * *

* * * *

Our case law * * * makes clear that the safety exception is limited to instances in which sex or pregnancy actually interferes with the employee's ability to perform the job. This approach is consistent with the language of the BFOQ provision itself, for it suggests that permissible distinctions based on sex must relate to ability to perform the duties of the job. Johnson Controls suggests, however, that we expand the exception to allow fetal-protection policies that mandate particular standards for pregnant or fertile women. We decline to do so. Such an expansion contradicts not only the language of the BFOQ and the narrowness of its exception but the plain language and history of the Pregnancy Discrimination Act [PDA].

The PDA's amendment to Title VII contains a BFOQ standard of its own: unless pregnant employees differ from others "in their ability or inability to work," they must be "treated the same" as other employees "for all employment related purposes." * * * In other words, women as capable of doing their jobs as their male counterparts may not be forced to choose between having a child and having a job.

* * * *

We have no difficulty concluding that Johnson Controls cannot establish a BFOQ. Fertile women, as far as appears in the record, participate in the manufacture of batteries as efficiently as anyone else. * * * Title VII and the PDA simply do not allow a woman's dismissal because of her failure to submit to sterilization.

* * * *

Our holding today that Title VII, as so amended, forbids sex-specific fetal-protection policies is neither remarkable nor unprecedented. Concern for a woman's existing or potential offspring historically has been the excuse for denying women equal employment opportunities. Congress in the PDA prohibited discrimination on the basis of a woman's ability to become pregnant. We do no more than hold that the Pregnancy Discrimination Act means what it says.

DECISION AND REMEDY *The Supreme Court reversed the judgment of the appellate court and remanded the case for further proceedings. Johnson Controls' fetal-protection policy was discriminatory in violation of Title VII of the Civil Rights Act and the Pregnancy Discrimination Act.*

OTHER EMPLOYMENT ISSUES An increasingly significant ethical issue in the employment context concerns the privacy rights of employees. To what extent, for example, may employers engage in drug testing, integrity testing, performance monitoring, or other procedures before violating an employee's right to privacy? Another ethical problem arises when an employee is asked to "look the other way" when faced with unethical or illegal practices in the workplace. Should the employee "blow the whistle" on the employer by informing the press or a government agency of the activity—when the consequences would, in all probability, mean losing his or her job? What if the employee's family has no other source of income? What if the employee is older and faces few prospects of finding another job with an equivalent salary? If the employee is not asked to participate directly in any illegal act, does he or she have an ethical responsibility to act? These and other employment-related issues will be discussed in Chapter 18.

Consumer Welfare

Manufacturers and sellers have not only an ethical duty to provide safe products but a legal one as well. During the course of the twentieth century, numerous laws have been enacted to protect the consumer against defective or harmful products. A manufacturer that markets a defective product that is unreasonably dangerous to users may be held liable for any resulting injury to a consumer. (Product liability is discussed in more detail in Chapter 12.)

The law, however, has its limits. For example, no law prohibits a corporation from producing and distributing a food product just because it is not nutritious. If a firm markets, say, a type of baby food that babies like and mothers buy but that is not nutritionally satisfactory for babies because of a high MSG (monosodium glutamate) or sugar content, the law will not intervene, nor could a consumer successfully sue the manufacturer for marketing an unsafe product. Thus, the decision to market the food does not violate the law, but it does raise an ethical question.

A case in point is the Nestlé controversy, which arose in the 1970s over the Nestlé Company's distribution of a baby formula in Third World countries. Mothers frequently mixed the infant formula with impure water or excessively diluted it to make it last longer. As a result, babies suffered from malnutrition, diarrhea, and in some cases even death. By 1974, Nestlé was being accused of "killing babies" by marketing its formula in Third World nations. Although other companies pulled

out of the market, Nestlé continued to distribute its product to those countries. In defense of its action, Nestlé argued that the availability of the formula freed mothers from the task of breastfeeding and thus allowed them to earn money to help raise their income and standard of living. Besides, Nestlé claimed, mothers who drank impure water would pass on these impurities to the babies while breastfeeding anyway. In general, Nestlé's defense rested on a cost-benefit analysis from which Nestlé concluded that the social benefits of the formula outweighed the social costs. Nestlé's opponents were ethically outraged, not because the formula had been marketed initially, but because of Nestlé's utilitarian defense for refusing to leave the market once it was learned that the product, from ignorance or for other reasons, was being misused and harming babies.

There are other situations in which, although it may be legal to market a given product, the ethics of doing so might be called into question. In the case presented below, for example, the Honda Motor Company warned those who purchased its mini-bike of the dangers that could result if the product was not used as directed. The case is representative of numerous situations in which consumer misuse of products leads to harms and injuries. If a court concludes—as it did in this case—that the manufacturer has adequately warned consumers of the possible dangers of product misuse, the manufacturer may escape liability for these harms. Nonetheless, there are some who feel that manufacturers should be legally compelled to withdraw from the market products that are capable of seriously injuring consumers, even if the injuries result from consumer misuse. At the least, these people would hold that Honda's continued marketing of its mini-bike violated that firm's ethical responsibility to consumers.

BACKGROUND AND FACTS *On August 14, 1972, Douglas Bratz and Bradley Baughn were injured while riding a Honda Z50AK3 mini-trail bike. Both boys were just two months shy of their ninth birthdays. Bratz, who was driving the bike while Baughn rode as a passenger behind him, ran three stop signs without stopping and then collided with a truck. Bratz did not see the truck because, at the time of the accident, he was looking behind him at a girl chasing them on another mini-trail bike. Bratz wore a helmet, but it flew off on impact because it was unfastened. Baughn was*

Case 4.2

BAUGHN v. HONDA MOTOR CO.

Supreme Court of Washington, 1986.
107 Wash.2d 127,
727 P.2d 655.

not wearing a helmet. Both boys were seriously injured in the accident. The mini-trail bike had a prominent warning label on it, immediately in front of the operator, stating:

> READ OWNER'S MANUAL CAREFULLY. THIS VEHICLE WAS MANUFACTURED FOR OFF-THE-ROAD USE ONLY. DO NOT OPERATE ON PUBLIC STREETS, ROADS OR HIGHWAYS.

The owner's manual contained similar explicit instructions against driving on public streets and roads and urged users to "Always Wear a Helmet." The parents of the injured boys filed suit against Honda, alleging that the mini-trail bike was unreasonably dangerous. Honda claimed that it had sufficiently warned consumers of the dangers that could result if the bike was not used as directed. The trial court granted Honda's motion for summary judgment,[a] and the plaintiffs appealed.

ANDERSEN, Justice.

    *   *   *   *

There is a considerable degree of overlap in the issues presented in the 415 pages of briefs filed in this case, out of which emerges one ultimate issue. * * * Is a manufacturer liable when children are injured while riding one of its mini-trail bikes on a public road in violation of manufacturer and parental warnings? *   *   *

    *   *   *   *

Baughn and Bratz argue that *   *   * [Honda's] warnings were inadequate because they did not describe what might happen if a child did ride a mini-trail bike on a public street. They also criticize Honda for failing to advise parents how to determine if their child was ready to ride a mini-trail bike.

    *   *   *   *

Honda did not warn of every conceivable danger that could be encountered if children rode its mini-trail bikes on public streets and roadways. It did, however, specifically instruct that they were intended for off-the-road use only and that riders should wear helmets. There was no contention that Douglas or Bradley could not read the sticker prominently displayed on the mini-trail bike. There is no evidence that they read the owner's manual; Vernon Bratz said he only checked it to see how to adjust the mini-trail bike.

Honda did not inform parents how to determine if their child was ready to ride a mini-trail bike. In this case, however, both fathers owned motorcycles and had previously bought mini-trail bikes for their children which their children could ride. We cannot perceive that they did not think their children were ready to ride them.

While Honda did not warn Bradley and Douglas of the precise danger they eventually encountered, their parents did and did so repeatedly. The two boys were almost 9 years old. They were apparently normal children and undoubtedly knew that riding their mini-trail bikes on public roads and ignoring stop signs could cause them injury. Despite Honda's warnings and their parents' warnings, they rode into the street through several stop signs, did not watch where they were going and were injured when they collided with a truck they had not seen. The trial court did not err when it ruled that Honda satisfied its duty to warn under the law of negligence and strict liability.

DECISION AND REMEDY   *The Supreme Court of Washington affirmed the lower court's decision to grant summary judgment to Honda.*

---

a. A judgment entered by a trial court prior to trial, based upon the valid assertion by one of the parties that there are no disputed issues of fact that would necessitate a trial.

■ International Perspectives

As American business becomes increasingly global in scope, so also do ethical considerations. Today's business leaders and decision makers must consider such political issues as human rights in other countries. Firms must decide, for example, whether they should profit from business with—and thus lend economic support to—foreign governments that oppress their citizens. Additionally, in undertaking international transactions, business executives need to be aware of the economic and cultural differences between nations. In the Nestlé controversy discussed above, for example, the marketing of the baby formula in the United States and other economically advanced nations posed no problems. It did cause a problem in the Third World, however, because of the different economic and cultural circumstances of consumers in less-developed nations.

Another example of how differences among nations can affect business decisions is the custom of bribing government officials. In many countries, the practice of bribing officials to gain favorable treatment or lucrative business contracts is not considered unethical—indeed, in many nations it is simply considered to be another cost of doing busi-ness. In the United States, however, such bribery is deemed unethical; indeed, it was prohibited by law in 1977 with the Foreign Corrupt Practices Act (see Chapter 27). The effect of this law on Americans doing business abroad is, of course, that it places American businesspersons at a competitive disadvantage relative to foreign businesspersons who are not so constrained in their tactics.

■ An Ever-Changing Ethical Landscape

It is important to remember that our sense of what is ethical—what is fair or just or right in a given situation—varies not only from individual to individual and from group to group but also over time. Business conduct that might have been considered socially responsible a decade or two ago might not be considered ethical today. Indeed, most of the major ethical and social issues discussed in this chapter and elsewhere in this text either did not exist or were of little public concern at the turn of this century. The ethical businessperson not only seeks to clarify his or her own personal ethical standards but also strives to be aware of the ethical concerns of others in society and to consider those concerns when making business decisions.

■ Terms and Concepts to Review

business ethics 77
comparable worth 88
cost-benefit analysis 81

ethics 77
externalities 84
laissez-faire 83

per se 82
tradeoff 84
utilitarianism 81

■ Questions and Case Problems

4-1. Coach Sharon Youngblood works as an athletic coach and recruiter for State University. Athletic competitions and the recruitment of athletes require Sharon to do a great deal of traveling. The university reimburses Sharon for her travel expenses. Sharon joined a frequent-flyer program and has been receiving credit for her business travels as athletic coach. Solely because of the mileage accumulated from her business travels, Sharon will soon be eligible for a free trip anywhere in the continental United States. She very much wants to travel to Miami, Florida, over her Christmas vacation to visit her daughter and family. Sharon is considering using her free ticket for this personal trip but is not sure whether it would be ethical to do so. Analyze Sharon's ethical responsibilities in this situation.

4-2. John Landers works as a computer programmer for IBC—a large New York company. John is from humble beginnings and was lucky to get the job he has through an old roommate's father. John would like to be an artist, but he knows that he could never earn a living by pursuing his artistic ambitions. John has several friends who are "starving artists," and he is convinced that society oppresses talent rather than encourages it. Through his work at IBC, John learns of a proposed merger and decides to tell his artist friends about it—even though disclosing to outsiders this "inside information" is against the law—so they can make enough money to live on while pursuing their artistic careers. John views his decision as perfectly acceptable because it is simply a way for creative people to survive in an unfair society. Is John's behavior ethical? Why or why not?

4-3. Dagmar Hollifield is a scientific genius. He works for Toys 'n' Stuff creating mechanical devices. Hollifield created an entire war simulation game, complete with robot armies. Each robot can shoot its own ammunition. The game was approved by the company's board of directors, and plans were made to produce and market the game in time to profit from the Christmas rush. Just before the date on which the game was to be distributed on the market, Hollifield developed a safety mechanism for the robot. The safety mechanism would make the product much safer for children to use, and the manufacturing cost involved in adding the safety feature would be minimal. Hollifield told his immediate supervisor about the safety device, but the supervisor told him to keep quiet about it so that production and distribution could continue as planned. Should Hollifield tell someone higher on the management ladder about the safety device? What ethical considerations face Hollifield in making this decision?

4-4. Susan Whitehead serves on the City Planning Commission. The city is planning to build a new subway system and is accepting bids on the proposal. Susan's brother-in-law, Jerry, who owns the Custom Transportation Co., has submitted the lowest bid for the system. The Transportation-We-Make-It Co. has submitted a slightly higher bid. Susan knows that Jerry could complete the job for the estimated amount, but she also knows that if Jerry gets and completes this job he will have enough money to sell his company and quit working. Susan is concerned that Custom Transportation's subsequent management might not be as easy to work with if revisions need to be made on the subway system after its completion. She is torn as to whether she should tell the city about the potential changes in Custom Transportation management. If the city knew about the instability of Custom Transportation, it might prefer to give the contract to Transportation-We-Make-It, whose bid was higher than Custom Transportation's bid by only an insignificant amount. Does Susan have an ethical obligation to disclose the information about Jerry to the City Planning Commission? Discuss.

4-5. Beverly Landrine's infant daughter died after the baby swallowed a balloon while playing with a doll known as "Bubble Yum Baby." When a balloon was inserted into the doll's mouth and the doll's arm was pumped, thereby inflating the balloon, the doll simulated the blowing of a bubble gum bubble. The balloon was made by Perfect Product Co. and distributed by Mego Corp. Landrine brought a suit against the manufacturer and distributor, alleging that the balloon was defectively made or inherently unsafe when used by children and that Perfect had failed to warn of the danger associated with the balloon's use. Discuss whether the producer and distributor of the balloon should be held liable for the harm caused by its product. [*Landrine v. Mego Corp.*, 464 N.Y.S.2d 516, 95 A.D.2d 759 (1983)]

4-6. John Novosel was an employee of Nationwide Insurance Co. for almost fifteen years. He was never reprimanded or disciplined and he rose steadily through the company's

ranks. Toward the end of his tenure, the company circulated a memo requesting employees to assist Nationwide's lobbying efforts in the Pennsylvania House of Representatives. Specifically, employees were asked to collect signatures for a petition urging changes in Pennsylvania's no-fault insurance laws. Novosel refused. Privately, he told others that he did not agree with the company's position. Within a few weeks, he was fired. He filed suit. Pennsylvania law prohibits an employment discharge that "abridges a significant and recognized public policy." Novosel argued that "a significant and recognized public policy" could be derived from the important political freedoms expressed in the Pennsylvania Constitution and the First Amendment of the U.S. Constitution. May an employer's power to hire and fire be used to dictate an employee's political activities? Discuss. [*Novosel v. Nationwide Insurance Co.*, 721 F.2d 894 (3d Cir. 1983)]

4-7. Paul Johnson, a male public transit authority employee in Santa Clara, California, challenged the promotion of a female employee, Diane Joyce, who had lower test scores than some of the employees not promoted. Johnson and Joyce were among the final seven candidates for the position of road dispatcher for the County of Santa Clara, and a strong factor in awarding the job to Joyce was the fact that she was a female. Joyce was promoted to the position pursuant to an affirmative action plan designed to increase the number of females in the higher levels of this governmental agency. At the time of Joyce's promotion, not one of the 238 positions in the pertinent job classification was held by a woman. Johnson contended that this promotion violated Title VII of the 1964 Civil Rights Act, which prohibits discrimination in employment on the basis of race, color, religion, sex, or national origin. The case ultimately reached the United States Supreme Court, which concluded that this promotion was a lawful effort to remedy long-standing imbalances in the work force. What ethical issues and conflicts are generated by affirmative action programs? From an ethical point of view, can affirmative action programs be justified when they result in reverse discrimination, as in this case? [*Johnson v. Transportation Agency, Santa Clara County, California*, 480 U.S. 616, 107 S.Ct. 1442, 94 L.Ed.2d 615 (1987)]

4-8. George Geary was employed by the United States Steel Corp. to sell tubular products to the oil and gas industry. Geary believed that one of the company's new products, a tubular casing, had not been adequately tested and constituted a serious danger to anyone who used it. Even though Geary at all times performed his duties to the best of his ability, he continued to express his reservations with respect to the company's new product. Geary alleged that because of his complaints, he was summarily discharged without notice. Given these facts, and in view of the fact that Geary was not a safety expert and had bypassed ordinary company procedures in his complaints, address the following questions. [*Geary v. United States Steel Corp.*, 456 Pa. 171, 319 A.2d 174 (1974)]

(a) Did the employer act wrongfully in discharging Geary?

(b) Did Geary have an ethical duty to complain about the company's product?

(c) Did the employer's need to maintain internal administrative order and harmony in the company outweigh its duty to do all it could to ensure product safety? Suppose that you were a manager and Geary raised the matter with you. How would you act and what ethical factors would influence your decision?

4-9. A Question of Ethics

On July 5, 1884, Dudley, Stephens, and Brooks—"all able-bodied English seamen"— and an English boy between seventeen and eighteen years of age were cast adrift in a lifeboat following a storm at sea that occurred when they were some sixteen hundred miles from the Cape of Good Hope. The lifeboat was not stocked with food and water, and all they had for sustenance were two one-pound tins of turnips. On July 24, Dudley proposed that one of the four in the lifeboat be sacrificed to save the others. Stephens agreed with Dudley, but Brooks refused to consent—and the boy was never asked for his opinion. On July 25, Dudley killed the boy, and the three men then fed upon the boy's body and blood. Four days later, the men were rescued by a passing vessel. They were taken to the port of Falmouth in England and committed for trial at Exeter for the murder of the boy. If the men had not fed upon the boy's body, they would have probably died of famine within the four-day period. The boy, who was in a much weaker condition, would likely have died before the rest. [Regina v. Dudley and Stephens, 14 Q.B.D.[Queen's Bench Division, England] 273 (1884)]

1. This problem is similar to *The Case of the Speluncean Explorers,* the hypothetical case discussed in Chapter 1. The basic question in that case, as here, is whether the survivors should be subject to penalties under the criminal law given the men's unusual circumstances. You be the judge and decide the issue. Give the reasons for your decisions.

2. Solely from an ethical point of view, had the men acted wrongfully? Evaluate their actions from the three ethical perspectives—religious, Kantian, and utilitarian—discussed in this chapter. Do the different ethical approaches yield different conclusions? If so, in what way?

4-10. Case Briefing Assignment

Examine Case A.4 [Burnell v. General Telephone of Illinois, Inc. 536 N.E.2d 1387 (Ill. 1989)] in Appendix A. The case has been excerpted there in great detail. Review and then brief the case, making sure that you include answers to the following questions in your brief.

1. What four elements was Burnell required to show in making a *prima facie* case of age discrimination under the Age Discrimination in Employment Act?

2. In what sense did Burnell argue that he had been discharged by his employer?

3. On what basis did the trial court grant General Telephone's motion for a directed verdict? Did the Illinois appeals court uphold the trial court's decision? What was the rationale of the appellate court's decision?

Focus on Ethics

Ethics and Social Responsibility

Business ethics and social responsibility are intertwined concepts, but they are not exactly the same thing. *Business ethics* involves the application of ethical standards to business activities. *Social responsibility* involves the fulfillment of social expectations concerning the relationship between business and all individuals—within or outside the firm—who are affected by business actions. What is deemed to be socially responsible business activity varies from culture to culture, from time period to time period within a given culture, and from group to group at any moment in time. For example, even though a business firm may act on the basis of what it considers to be very high ethical standards, there will probably be at least one group of individuals who question the ethical responsibility of that firm. In other words, we cannot tell you here what business actions will receive an A+ in terms of social responsibility, because there is no one definition of the term. It means different things to different people at different times.

The Debate over Social Responsibility

Traditionally in capitalist theory, profit-making activities—insofar

as they provided desired goods and services to society and violated no laws—were *per se* socially responsible. Profit making was and continues to be an essential goal of any business. But in today's world, as mentioned in Chapter 4, a businessperson needs to balance profit-seeking goals against duties owed to other groups—which may include the firm and its employees, the consumers who purchase the firm's products or services, and society as a whole. The determination of whether a given firm is acting in a socially responsible manner will ultimately depend on how the observer answers the following question: When two or more of these duties come into conflict, which duty should take precedence over the other or others?

Duty to Shareholders
At one end of the spectrum in the debate over corporate social responsibility is the notion that the corporation's primary duty is to the firm and its owners. Because the owners of any corporate business firm are the shareholders, corporate directors and officers have an ethical duty to act in the shareholders' interest and not abuse the trust placed in them by the shareholder-owners of the firm. The reason people buy

shares of stock is to make a profit, and many people contend that the primary goal of corporations should therefore be profit maximization. The Nobel-Prize-winning economist Milton Friedman effectively phrases this view:

> In a free enterprise, private property system, a corporate executive is an employee of the owners of the business [shareholders]. He has a direct responsibility to his employers. That responsibility is to conduct the business in accordance with their desires, which generally will be to make as much money as possible while conforming to the basic rules of society, both those embodied in law and those embodied in ethical custom.[1]

Those arguing for profit maximization as the primary corporate goal also point out that it would be inappropriate to use the power of the corporate business world to fashion society's goals. For example, many people refuse to invest in, or buy products produced by, firms that are engaged in certain activities—such as the construction or maintenance of nuclear plants or the production of weapons for the military—or that fail to take definitive steps

1. Milton Friedman, "Does Business Have Social Responsibility?" *Bank Administration*, April 1971, pp. 13–14.

toward the advancement of women and minorities in their work forces. Those who perceive profit maximization to be the primary goal of the corporation would argue that the determination as to whether military or nuclear support is in society's best interest is essentially a political question, and therefore the political process—not the corporate boardroom—is the appropriate forum for such a decision.

Duty to Consumers

Somewhere in the middle of the debate spectrum are those who contend that the corporation has an ethical duty to look beyond profit maximization to the welfare of consumers and that consumer welfare should take precedence over profit maximization if these two duties conflict. Many consumers feel that they have absolutely no effect on the pricing, quality, and nature of the products and services offered by modern-day giant corporations. Therefore, corporations have a strict ethical duty *not* to market unsafe and unhealthful products, even when it is legal to do so.

What really is at issue here? Can the corporation meet its goal of profit maximization if it willfully ignores the well-being of consumers? Some would argue that the ultimate control of the corporation actually lies in the hands of the consumer. After all, they argue, the consumer freely chooses to buy or not to buy a corporation's product. Even in the absence of effective competition, the consumer can purchase a smaller quantity of the product being offered. Thus, it is in the corporation's best interest to attempt to satisfy the consumer.

But even assuming that the consumer can exert control over corporate production decisions, the process of competition takes time. Information is costly to obtain and is never perfect. If corporate leaders know or suspect that certain of their products may have deleterious long-run effects on the consumer, do not such corporate leaders have an ethical responsibility to inform the consumer? Eli Lilly had an arthritis drug, Oraflex, approved for sale in the United States without informing the Food and Drug Administration of thirty-two overseas deaths associated with the use of this drug. The dangers of Oraflex only became apparent to the American public when an eighty-one-year-old woman died as a result of taking the drug and Lilly had to pay $6 million in punitive damages.

Although most people would agree that a corporation has an ethical duty to consumers, there is less agreement on how far that duty should extend. In other words, at what point does corporate responsibility for the safety of consumers end and consumer responsibility begin? If a consumer is harmed by a product because that consumer failed to exercise due care or did not use the product as directed by the manufacturer, who should bear the responsibility for that harm, the consumer or the manufacturer?

To illustrate: The Seven-Up Company, as part of a marketing scheme, placed two glass bottles of "Like" cola on the front entrance of the Gruenemeier residence. Russell Gruenemeier, a nine-year-old boy, began playing while holding one of the bottles. He tripped and fell, and the bottle broke and severely cut his right eye, eventually causing him to lose the eye. Russell's mother brought an action against the Seven-Up Company for damages, claiming that the proximate cause of Russell's injury was Seven-Up's negligence. She claimed that the company was negligent because it placed inherently dangerous instrumentalities— glass bottles—within the reach of small children and that the firm should have used unbreakable bottles for its marketing scheme. Had Seven-Up violated any legal or ethical duty by distributing its product in glass bottles? Are glass bottles so inherently dangerous that Seven-Up should be held liable for the boy's injury? If you were the judge, how would you decide the issue? Would you agree with the court's decision in this case that glass bottles are not inherently dangerous, and therefore Seven-Up should not be held liable?[2] Where would you draw the line between the manufacturer's duty of care in product design and distribution and the consumer's responsibility to exercise common sense and reasonable care in the use of products?

Duty to Society

At the other end of the spectrum in the debate on social responsibility are those who feel that business firms should be concerned not only with the welfare of consumers but also with the welfare of society in general. Those who stress the firm's duty to society maintain that because so much of the wealth and power of this country are controlled by business, business in turn has a

---

2. *Gruenemeier v. Seven-Up Co.,* 229 Neb. 267, 426 N.W.2d 510 (1988).

responsibility to society to use that wealth and power in socially beneficial ways. From this perspective, major corporations and business firms are in a sense trustees, or caretakers, of society. As caretakers, they are charged with a host of ethical duties. They should promote human rights, strive for equal treatment of minorities in the workplace, be concerned with environmental health, and generally not profit from activities that society has deemed unethical. They should also share some of their wealth with society in the form of charity.

Indeed, many who have adopted this view of corporate ethical responsibility claim that businesses can best maximize profits by being socially responsible. This is because individuals may be more likely to invest in, and purchase products from, business firms that act ethically in the marketplace and support socially desirable goals. The upswing in so-called ethical investing—that is, investing in firms on the basis of their corporate conduct (relating to a number of criteria, such as investments in South Africa, participation in military contracts, construction or maintenance of nuclear plants, discrimination against minorities, and so on)—in recent years would seem to confirm this assumption.

It should be stressed that business firms generally have been very responsive to social needs, and they routinely donate to hospitals, medical research, the arts, universities, and programs that benefit society. B. Dalton Bookseller, for example, put up $3 million to launch a massive drive against functional illiteracy. The Bank of

America created a $10 million revolving-loan program in which funds are loaned to community development groups at a 3 percent interest rate. The Coca-Cola company established the National Hispanic Business Agenda—a major program to expand ties with the Hispanic community. And more recently, that firm announced that its private foundation will distribute $50 million over a ten-year period to support educational institutions and programs throughout the United States. As one of its many philanthropic projects, Levi Strauss & Company established an "AIDS Initiatives" program to fund public educational programs concerning AIDS and patient care for the victims of that disease. The list goes on. Indeed, today every major business firm has a branch or foundation that has been established specifically to screen charitable requests and to decide on and manage corporate charitable contributions and programs.

The Corporate Balancing Act

Obviously, it is impossible for corporations to be all things to all people at all times. Each corporate board of directors has to make numerous tradeoffs in determining corporate goals. Directors do have an ethical duty to shareholders, because they control the shareholders' wealth. Society has also deemed that corporate directors and officers have an ethical duty not to market defective or unreasonably dangerous products—this social ethic is written into warranty and product liability laws. Similarly, they have a duty to provide safe working conditions for their employees—and this also is

written into law. But there is no law that says how much weight each duty should be given on the balancing scales beyond the minimum prescribed by law.

The tradeoffs become more complicated when one realizes that these duties overlap considerably. For example, for a corporation to run smoothly and productively, it must recruit qualified personnel. To attract qualified personnel in a competitive marketplace, the firm must offer a competitive salary, a good benefits package, and desirable working conditions. If this is done and the corporation is well managed by its qualified personnel, ideally profits will increase and both shareholders and employees will benefit. But this ideal result is not a certainty. What is certain is that such expenses will mean reduced profits for shareholders in the short run. Similarly, corporate philanthropic activities that receive wide publicity may benefit shareholders in the long run—if the public image of the firm entices more consumers to purchase its products—but such long-run possible benefits are difficult to calculate. In sum, ethical decision making in the business context is not easy. Ideally, each corporate decision would provide equal benefits for all individuals affected by that decision, but this is rarely possible. When it is not, difficult tradeoffs must be made.

Evaluating Social Responsibility

Now you can see why it is difficult to evaluate corporate social responsibility. First of all, no one definition of the term is acceptable to all people. Social responsibility means different things to different persons, depending on their economic and moral convictions. Second, because we live in a world of imperfect information, it is not always possible to acquire a sufficient amount of information about a given business firm's activities to make an informed decision as to whether that firm is acting ethically or not. We might read in the paper, for example, that a certain corporation has made generous contributions toward a worthy social cause and therefore assume the corporation has socially responsible goals. What we might not know is that the same corporation is marketing a product that some corporate officers have reason to suspect may be harmful to many of those who purchase it. A case in point is the A. H. Robins Company. In less than two decades, E. Claiborne Robins, the founder and chairman of the company, and his family gave away more than $100 million in support of educational and other charitable causes, and Robins became widely known for his generosity and concern for his fellow Americans. At the same time, the A. H. Robins Company continued to defend the relative safety of its Dalkon Shield intrauterine device (IUD), even though evidence allegedly known by the company indicated that the device could

harm users—and had in fact caused the deaths of several women.[3]

■ Discussion Questions

1. Assume that you are the president of a growing company. You decide to form a code of ethics to guide the firm's employees in their decision making and workplace behavior. What would your major ethical policies be in regard to each of the following areas of concern, and what ethical reasoning would you use to justify your position in each case?
(a) The advancement of women and minority groups.
(b) Military contracts.
(c) Nuclear power.
(d) Animal testing.
(e) Community outreach (involvement in community education, housing, and other projects benefiting the community).
(f) Direct or indirect investment in South Africa.
(g) Charitable contributions.

---

3. Studies released in 1991 purported to show that most IUDs may never have been harmful to users. In view of these findings, A. H. Robins is reevaluating its position in respect to the use of the Dalkon Shield.

2. In creating a code of ethics for your business firm, to what extent would you solicit input from employees? In other words, do you believe that business codes of ethics should be written by owners alone? Or should key management personnel—and perhaps all employees—have a say in the matter?
3. Many managers of so-called ethical funds believe that business firms can best maximize profits by engaging in ethical business behavior. Discuss what reasons they might give for drawing this conclusion.
4. Should business firms *ever* manufacture products that have deleterious effects on the environment? How do you weigh the benefits of a product (e.g., automobiles) against the negative environmental effects (e.g., smog) caused by the product? Should these kinds of decisions be made by the business sector, or should political bodies be left to determine such policies?

UNIT TWO

The Public Environment

■ The Importance of the Public Environment

Business involves relationships. These relationships may arise casually, as when a consumer walks into a department store to make a purchase. Or business relationships may arise formally, as when the shareholders of two multinational corporations agree to merge their respective enterprises. Business relationships may arise by express consent or by implication.

The private environment of business dealings are the focus of Unit Three. Within this private environment, most of the rights that parties enjoy are granted by mutual consent. But the legal environment of business also encompasses rights and duties that exist for individuals and firms even without explicit consent or agreement between parties. For example, individuals do not enter into a contract with the federal government to protect certain rights from governmental intrusion, yet this protection exists. Conversely, businesses do not formally consent to regulation by various government agencies, but nonetheless, they are subject to regulation. The United States Constitution, including the Bill of Rights, imposes limitations on business conduct in the United States. On the one hand it confers power on the states and federal government to regulate commercial activity, while on the other hand it forbids infringement of certain rights of private individuals and businesses.

The legal environment of business involving torts, crimes, administrative law, and constitutional rights and duties may be termed the *public environment*. It is the focus of the next four chapters. In Chapter 5, we examine the basic principles of the federal Constitution, including the constitutional authority to regulate commercial activity. We examine the legal principles governing the administrative process—the establishment and enforcement of government regulations and agency rules—in Chapter 6. In Chapter 7, we discuss the general area of torts—private, nonconsensual wrongs committed by one party against another. We conclude this unit with Chapter 8, in which we examine torts and crimes that relate specifically to business, including so-called white-collar crimes.

Ethical Issues in the Public Environment

Ethical issues in the public environment commonly arise when there is disagreement about whether a given action is right or wrong. Such disagreement often exists when two fundamental ethical principles come into conflict. For example, a basic ethical precept underlying American society and expressed in the U.S. Constitution is that individuals should be free to speak and act as they like without interference from government. The First Amendment freedoms of speech and religion are zealously guarded by the government and by our courts, as are all other constitutional freedoms. Sometimes, however, the exercise of individual freedom results in harm to others, and thus the right to act freely comes into conflict with another ethical assumption operative in our society—that individuals should not harm one another. The latter principle forms the basis of tort law and criminal law. Tort law and criminal law do restrict individual freedom, but for the most part we accept those restrictions.

The thorniest ethical issues in the public environment arise when there is no definite social consensus as to whether a given action by an individual or a business firm is *sufficiently* harmful to society to warrant the *legal* limitation of that person's or firm's freedom of expression or action. In other words, when should one ethical principle be modified to satisfy another ethical obligation?

Murder and theft are actions that are so inherently wrong that criminal sanctions for such activity raise no ethical concern. But what about agreements to fix prices or insider trading—using not-yet-public information to profit in the stock market. In some industrialized countries such actions are not restricted, let alone criminal. There may be legitimate economic reasons for imposing restrictions on these kinds of behavior, but are they so clearly wrong or injurious to the public that we can unhesitatingly condemn them as criminal actions? We will return to this ethical dilemma in our focus on ethics at the conclusion of this unit.

Chapter 5

Constitutional Law

The U.S. Constitution is the supreme law in this country.[1] Neither Congress nor any state may pass a law that conflicts with the Constitution. Laws that govern business have their origin in the lawmaking authority granted by this document.

Before the Constitution was written, a *confederal* form of government existed. The Articles of Confederation, ratified in 1778, established a confederation of independent states and a central government of very limited powers. The central government could handle only those matters of common concern expressly delegated to it by the member states, and the national congress had no ability to make laws directly applicable to individuals unless the member states explicitly supported such laws. In short, the *sovereign power* to govern rested essentially with the states.[2] The Articles of Confederation clearly reflected the central tenet of the American Revolution—that a government should not have unlimited power.

After the Revolutionary War, however, the states began to pass laws that hampered national commerce and foreign trade by preventing the free movement of goods and services. Consequently, in 1787, the Constitutional Convention convened to **amend** the Articles of Confederation to give the national government the power to address the country's commercial problems. Instead of amending the Articles of Confederation, the Convention created the Constitution and a completely new type of federal government, which they believed was much better equipped than its predecessor to resolve the problems of the nation.

■ Basic Constitutional Concepts

The U.S. Constitution delineates the structure and powers of the government, as well as the limitations on those powers.

Federalism

Federalism is the basis for the structure of the government in the United States. A *federal* form of government is one in which the states form a union

---

1. The U.S. Constitution has been included as Appendix B in this text.
2. *Sovereign power* refers to that supreme power to which no other person or authority is superior or equal.

and the sovereign power is divided between a central governing authority and the member states. The Constitution delegates certain powers to the national government, and the states retain all powers not delegated to the national government. The relationship between the national government and the state governments is a partnership—neither partner is superior to the other except within the particular area of authority granted to it under the Constitution. Hence, the concept of federalism recognizes that society may be best served by a distribution of functions among state governments and the national government on the basis of which government is better equipped to perform these functions. The Constitution reflects the belief that a national government can handle certain problems better than individual state governments can.

Conflicts frequently arise regarding the question of which government—national or state—should be exercising power in a particular area. The United States Supreme Court, as the arbiter of the Constitution, resolves such conflicts by deciding which governmental system is empowered to act under the Constitution.

Delegated Powers

The Constitutional Convention created a federal system of government in which the states delegated certain *enumerated powers* to the national government and reserved all other powers to themselves. Thus, the national government has no powers apart from those delegated to it by the states. The national government has no inherent powers (except in dealings with other nations) and can only exercise those powers that have been enumerated in the Constitution or that are necessary and proper for carrying out those powers. These delegated powers, however, are very broad, as reflected in the growth of the federal (national) government.

The Bill of Rights

For various reasons, proposals related to the rights of individuals made during the Constitutional Convention of 1787 were rejected. Yet the importance of a written declaration of the rights of individuals eventually caused the first Congress to submit ten amendments to the Constitution for the approval of the states. These amendments, commonly known as the Bill of Rights, were adopted in 1791 and embody a series of protections for the individual against various types of interference by the federal government. Among the guarantees provided for by the Bill of Rights are the First Amendment protection of the freedom of religion, speech, and assembly; the Fourth Amendment provisions regarding arrest and searches and seizures; and the Sixth Amendment rights to counsel, confrontation, and cross-examination in criminal prosecutions. Furthermore, through the Fourteenth Amendment, passed after the Civil War, most of these guarantees have been held to be so fundamental as to be applicable at the state level as well.

Also held to be so fundamental as to be applicable at both the state and the federal level is a personal right to privacy. There is no specific guarantee of a right to privacy in the Constitution. The right is derived from guarantees found in the First, Third, Fourth, Fifth, and Ninth Amendments. To date, the right to privacy has been held to apply mainly in cases involving matters of marriage, family relationships, and decisions on whether to bear children.

The rights secured by the Bill of Rights are not absolute. The principles enunciated in the Constitution are given form and substance by the government. Ultimately, it is the United States Supreme Court, as the interpreter of the Constitution, that gives meaning to, and determines the boundaries of, the rights guaranteed by the Constitution. For example, the freedom of speech guaranteed by the Constitution will be restrained whenever speech becomes *defamatory* (wrongfully injurious to another's reputation—see Chapter 7).

Separation of Powers

The federal government is divided into three branches—the executive branch, which enforces the laws; the legislative branch, which makes the laws; and the judicial branch, which interprets the laws. Article I of the Constitution provides for the legislative branch. The duties of the executive branch and the method of electing the president are set forth in Article II. The federal judicial system was created by Article III.

Deriving its power from the Constitution, each branch performs a separate function, and no branch may exercise the authority of another branch. Each branch, however, has some power to *limit* the actions of the other branches. In each article of the Constitution that grants specific powers to one of the three branches of the government, there is also a provision for the limitation of that power by another branch. Congress, for example, has power over spending and commerce, but the president can veto that legislation. The executive branch is responsible for foreign affairs, but treaties with foreign governments require the advice and consent of the members of the Senate. Under Article III, Congress determines the jurisdiction of the federal courts, but the United States Supreme Court has the power to hold acts of the other branches of the federal government unconstitutional.[3] Thus, with this system of checks and balances, no one branch of government can accumulate too much power.

The Commerce Clause

Article I, Section 8, of the United States Constitution expressly permits Congress ''[t]o regulate Commerce with foreign Nations, and among the several States, and with the Indian tribes.'' This clause, referred to as the **commerce clause,** has had a greater impact on business than any other provision in the Constitution. Theoretically, the power over commerce authorizes the federal government to regulate every commercial enterprise in the United States. This power was delegated to the federal government to ensure the uniformity of rules governing the movement of goods through the states.

For some time, the commerce power was interpreted as being limited to *interstate* commerce and not applicable to *intrastate* commerce. The United States Supreme Court, however, now recognizes that Congress has the power to regulate any activity, interstate or intrastate, that *affects* interstate commerce. Wheat production of an individual farmer intended wholly for consumption on his or her own farm, for example, was held to be subject to federal regulation, because such home consumption reduces the demand for wheat and thus may have a substantial effect on interstate commerce.[4]

The following case is illustrative. The case specifically demonstrates the United States Supreme Court's use of the commerce clause to affirm the power of Congress to pass the Civil Rights Act of 1964. The breadth of the commerce clause permits the national government to legislate in areas in which there is no explicit grant of power to Congress.

---

3. See *Marbury v. Madison,* 5 U.S. (1 Cranch) 137, 2 L.Ed. 60 (1803).

4. See *Wickard v. Filburn,* 317 U.S. 111, 63 S.Ct. 82, 87 L.Ed. 122 (1942).

Case 5.1

HEART OF ATLANTA MOTEL v. UNITED STATES

Supreme Court of the United States, 1964.
379 U.S. 241,
85 S.Ct. 348,
13 L.Ed. 2d 258.

BACKGROUND AND FACTS   *The owner of a motel, who refused to rent rooms to African Americans despite the Civil Rights Act of 1964, brought an action to have the Civil Rights Act of 1964 declared unconstitutional. The motel owner alleged that Congress, in passing the act, had exceeded its power to regulate commerce because his motel was not engaged in interstate commerce.*

Mr. Justice *CLARK* delivered the opinion of the Court.
* * * *

This is [an action] attacking the constitutionality of Title II of the Civil Rights Act of 1964 *   *   *. Appellant owns and operates the Heart of Atlanta Motel which has 216 rooms available to transient guests.

*   *   * It is readily accessible to interstate highways 75 and 85 and state highways 23 and 41. Appellant solicits patronage from outside the State of Georgia through various national advertising media, including magazines of national circulation; it maintains over 50 billboards and highway signs within the State, soliciting patronage for the motel; it accepts convention trade from outside Georgia and approximately 75 percent of its registered guests are from out of State. Prior to passage of the Act the motel had followed a practice of refusing to rent rooms to Negroes, and it alleged that it intended to continue to do so. In an effort to perpetuate that policy this suit was filed. [The trial court sustained the Act.] *   *   *.

The sole question posed is, therefore, the constitutionality of the Civil Rights Act of 1964 as applied to these facts. *   *   *

*   *   *   *

While the Act as adopted carried no congressional findings, the record of its passage through each house is replete with evidence of the burdens that discrimination by race or color places upon interstate commerce *   *   *. This testimony included the fact that our people have become increasingly mobile with millions of all races traveling from State to State; that Negroes in particular have been the subject of discrimination in transient accommodations, having to travel great distances to secure the same; that often they have been unable to obtain accommodations and have had to call upon friends to put them up overnight. *   *   * These exclusionary practices were found to be nationwide, the Under Secretary of Commerce testifying that there is ''no question that this discrimination in the North still exists to a large degree'' and in the West and Midwest as well *   *   *. This testimony indicated a qualitative as well as quantitative effect on interstate travel by Negroes. The former was the obvious impairment of the Negro traveler's pleasure and convenience that resulted when he continually was uncertain of finding lodging. As for the latter, there was evidence that this uncertainty stemming from racial discrimination had the effect of discouraging travel on the part of a substantial portion of the Negro community *   *   *. We shall not burden this opinion with further details since the voluminous testimony presents overwhelming evidence that discrimination by hotels and motels impedes interstate travel.

*   *   *   *

It is said that the operation of the motel here is of a purely local character. But, assuming this to be true, ''if it is interstate commerce that feels the pinch, it does not matter how local the operation that applies the squeeze.'' *   *   * Thus the power of Congress to promote interstate commerce also includes the power to regulate the local incidents thereof, including local activities in both the States of origin and destination, which might have a substantial and harmful effect upon that commerce. *   *   *

*   *   *   *

We, therefore, conclude that the action of the Congress in the adoption of the Act as applied here to a motel which concededly serves interstate travelers is within the power granted it by the Commerce Clause of the Constitution, as interpreted by this Court for 140 years.

The United States Supreme Court upheld the constitutionality of the Civil Rights Act of 1964. The power of Congress to regulate interstate commerce permitted the enactment of legislation that could halt local discriminatory practices.

DECISION AND REMEDY

SINCE *HEART OF ATLANTA* Actions are still brought to determine whether a local activity ''substantially affects'' interstate commerce and is thus subject to regulation by Congress. In *McLain v. Real Estate Board of New Orleans, Inc.,* the United States Supreme Court held that local real estate brokers, who were licensed to perform their function only in Louisiana, substantially affected financial transactions and title insurance that were clearly interstate in nature. Thus, the brokers' activities sufficiently affected interstate commerce to be regulated by federal laws. The Court acknowledged that the commerce clause had ''long been interpreted to extend beyond activities actually in interstate commerce to reach other activities, while wholly local in nature, which nevertheless substantially affect interstate commerce."[5]

THE POWER OF STATES TO REGULATE Another problem that frequently arises under the commerce clause concerns a state's ability to regulate matters within its own borders. The U.S. Constitution does not expressly exclude state regulation of commerce, and there is no doubt that states have a strong interest in regulating activities within their borders. As part of their inherent sovereignty, states possess **police powers.** The term does not relate solely to criminal law enforcement but to the right of state governments to regulate private activities to protect or promote the public order, health, safety, morals, and general welfare. Fire and building codes, antidiscrimination laws, parking regulations, zoning restrictions, licensing requirements, and thousands of other state statutes covering virtually every aspect of life have been enacted under the state police power.

When state regulations impinge on interstate commerce, courts must balance the state's interest in the merits and purposes of the regulation against the burden placed on interstate commerce.[6] In *Raymond Motor Transportation, Inc. v. Rice,* for example, the United States Supreme Court invalidated Wisconsin administrative regulations limiting the length of trucks traveling on its highways. The Court weighed the burden on interstate commerce against the benefits of the regulations and concluded that the challenged regulations "place a substantial burden on interstate commerce and they cannot be said to make more than the most speculative contribution to highway safety."[7]

Because courts balance the interests involved, it is extremely difficult to predict the outcome in a particular case. State laws enacted pursuant to a state's police powers and affecting the health, safety, and welfare of local citizens do carry a strong presumption of validity.

---

5.   444 U.S. 232, 100 S.Ct. 502, 62 L.Ed.2d 441 (1980).
6.   See *Southern Pacific Co. v. Arizona,* 325 U.S. 761, 65 S.Ct. 1515, 89 L.Ed. 1915 (1945).
7.   434 U.S. 429, 98 S.Ct. 787, 54 L.Ed.2d 664 (1978).

The Supremacy Clause

Article VI of the Constitution provides that the Constitution, laws, and treaties of the United States are "the supreme Law of the Land." This article, commonly referred to as the **supremacy clause,** is important in the ordering of state and federal relationships. When there is a direct conflict between a federal law and a state law, the state law is rendered invalid. But because some powers are shared by the federal government and the states—because they are concurrent powers—it is necessary to determine which law governs in a particular circumstance.

When concurrent federal and state powers are involved, a state law that conflicts with a federal law is prohibited. A federal action based on a power specifically delegated to the federal government by the Constitution always has the capacity to override a state law on the same matter. A federal regulatory scheme will supersede state law when there is an outright conflict between the two or when the state regulation interferes with federal objectives.

When Congress chooses to act exclusively in a concurrent area, it is said to have *preempted* the area. In this circumstance, a valid federal statute or regulation will take precedence over a conflicting state or local law or regulation on the same general subject. Congress, however, rarely makes clear its intent to preempt an entire subject area against state regulation; consequently, the courts must determine whether Congress intended to exercise exclusive dominion over a given area. Consideration of preemption often occurs in the commerce clause context.

No single factor is decisive as to whether a court will find preemption. Generally, congressional intent to preempt will be found if the federal law is so pervasive, comprehensive, or detailed that the states have no room to supplement it. Also, when a federal statute creates an agency—such as the National Labor Relations Board—to enforce the law, matters that may come within the agency's jurisdiction will likely preempt state laws.

In the following case, the court had to determine whether federal laws preempted a county regulation.

BACKGROUND AND FACTS *Bay Soaring leased a small private airport from Robert Harrison for glider operations. The airport was located on Harrison's farm near the town of Woodbine, Maryland. Bay Soaring gave gliding lessons and rides to the public, and sometimes as many as ninety flights a day took place as aircraft towed the gliders aloft. Harrison's neighbors, Bernard Schwartz and others, were not pleased and protested the noise generated by the aircraft. Their protests were heard by the county zoning board, which concluded that the use of the airport had expanded substantially beyond the limits of the conditional use permit that had been granted to Harrison by the zoning board several years previously. On Bay Soaring's application, the zoning board granted a new conditional use permit but attached to the permit several conditions. Condition 2 stipulated that aircraft takeoffs had to be separated by intervals of at least fifteen minutes, and Condition 3 stipulated that no aircraft takeoffs could be made before 9:00 A.M. or after 7:00 P.M. Bay Soaring claimed, and the trial court held, that these two conditions were unconstitutional regulations by the county because federal noise and aviation laws—specifically, the Federal Aviation Act of 1958 and the Noise Control Act of 1972—preempted this area. The neighbors and the county appealed. The Court of Special Appeals held that the two conditions were not preempted. Harrison and Bay Soaring appealed to the state's highest court.*

Case 5.2

HARRISON v. SCHWARTZ

Court of Appeals of Maryland, 1990.
319 Md. 360,
572 A.2d 528.

ADKINS, Judge.

*   *   *   *

In *City of Burbank*,[a] the city enacted an ordinance that made it unlawful for the operator of the privately owned Hollywood-Burbank Airport to allow any pure jet aircraft to take off between 11:00 P.M. of one day and 7:00 A.M. of the next. This curfew was markedly similar to condition 3 as imposed by the Board in the case before us. The Supreme Court concluded that federal preemption—implied from federal occupation of the field of aircraft noise regulation [by the Federal Aviation Act and the Noise Control Act]—rendered the ordinance unconstitutional.

*   *   *   *

Obviously, the small Woodbine airport is very different from Hollywood-Burbank [Airport]. Both, however, are privately owned. The *City of Burbank* holding applies to privately owned airports as well as publicly owned ones. The Supreme Court did not make an exception for small airports that do not involve inter-airport commercial cargo or passenger flights, or for activities not expressly governed by federal statute or regulation. If we were dealing with the sort of preemption that arises from conflict between federal and state enactments, these considerations might be pertinent. But we are dealing with preemption by occupation of the field. Once the field is occupied by the federal government, neither state nor local government may enter it. And occupation of the field does not mean that every blade of grass within it must be subject to express federal control; it means only that Congressional intent demonstrates that the area is subject to exclusive federal control, whether potential or actual.

---

a.   The court is referring to *City of Burbank v. Lockheed Air Terminal*, 411 U.S. 624, 93 S.Ct. 1854, 36 L.Ed.2d 547 (1973), a precedential authority on the question of federal preemption in the area of aviation.

DECISION AND REMEDY *The appellate court affirmed that the two conditions were preempted by the federal acts and were, therefore, unconstitutional. Bay Soaring prevailed.*

The Taxing Power

Article I, Section 8, further provides that Congress has the "Power to lay and collect Taxes, Duties, Imposts, and Excises . . .; but all Duties, Imposts and Excises shall be uniform throughout the United States." The requirement of uniformity refers to uniformity among the states, and thus Congress may not tax some states while exempting others.

Traditionally, in reviewing cases related to the taxing power, the courts have examined whether Congress was actually attempting to regulate indirectly, by taxation, an area in which it had no authority to regulate directly. If the regulatory effect could have been achieved directly by Congress, then the tax would not be stricken as an invalid, disguised regulation. If Congress was attempting to regulate an area over which it had no authority, however, the tax would be invalidated.

In recent cases, the United States Supreme Court has focused less on the motives of Congress and more on whether the tax can be sustained as a valid exercise of federal regulation. The Court has upheld taxes on dealers in firearms,[8] on the transfer of marijuana,[9] and on persons engaged in the business of accepting wagers.[10] If Congress does not have the power to regulate the activity being taxed, the tax will still be upheld if it is a valid revenue-raising measure. If a tax measure bears some reasonable relationship to revenue production, it is generally held to be within the national taxing power. Moreover, the expansive interpretation of the commerce clause almost always provides a basis for sustaining a federal tax.

The Spending Power

Under Article I, Section 8, Congress has the power "to pay the Debts and provide for the common Defence and general welfare of the United States." Through the spending power, Congress disposes of the revenues accumulated from the taxing power, and thus this power necessarily involves policy choices.

The requirement of *standing to sue* (discussed in Chapter 3) makes it difficult for taxpayers to use the judicial system to object to government spending, and consequently, the spending power is seldom challenged. The doctrine of standing to sue requires a litigant to demonstrate *a direct and immediate personal injury* caused by the challenged action.[11] Thus, a litigant must show that the injury suffered can be fairly traced to the challenged action and will be redressed by the judicial relief sought.[12] Communicating directly with members of Congress has proved to be a more efficient route to curbing or increasing federal allocations.

Congress can spend revenues not only to carry out its enumerated powers but also to promote any objective it deems worthwhile, so long as it does not violate the Bill of Rights. For example, Congress could not condition welfare payments on the recipients' agreements not to criticize government policies.

■ The Bill of Rights in a Business Context

A *business* is a commercial, industrial, or professional activity engaged in for profit. Some business entities, such as corporations, exist as separate legal entities and enjoy many of the same rights and privileges as *natural* persons. A corporation is generally identified as an artificial person, or legal entity, under the law. The Bill of Rights guarantees citizens certain protections, and some constitutional protections apply to business entities as well.

---

8. *Sonzinsky v. United States,* 300 U.S. 506, 57 S.Ct. 554, 81 L.Ed. 772 (1937).

9. *United States v. Sanchez,* 340 U.S. 42, 71 S.Ct. 108, 95 L.Ed. 47 (1950).

10. *United States v. Kahriger,* 345 U.S. 22, 73 S.Ct. 510, 97 L.Ed. 754 (1953).

11. *Sierra Club v. Morton,* 405 U.S. 727, 92 S.Ct. 1361, 31 L.Ed.2d 636 (1972).

12. *Simon v. Eastern Kentucky Welfare Rights Organization,* 426 U.S. 26, 96 S.Ct. 1917, 48 L.Ed.2d 450 (1976).

The first ten amendments prohibit specific actions of the federal government, and the Fourteenth Amendment further prohibits most of the same actions by state governments. The due process clause of the Fourteenth Amendment applies certain rights guaranteed by the first ten amendments to the states. Under the doctrine of *selective incorporation,* only those guarantees of individual liberty that are fundamental to the American system of law must be protected by the states.

Freedom of Speech

All of the First Amendment freedoms of religion, speech, press, assembly, and petition have been applied to the states through the *due process clause* of the Fourteenth Amendment (discussed later in this chapter). As mentioned previously, however, none of these freedoms confers an absolute right. It is unclear what types of speech the First Amendment was designed to protect, but constitutional protection has never been afforded to certain classes of speech. In 1942, for example, the United States Supreme Court held as follows:

> There are certain well-defined and narrowly limited classes of speech, the prevention and punishment of which have never been thought to raise any Constitutional problem. These include the lewd and obscene, the profane, the libelous, and the insulting or "fighting" words—those which by their very utterance inflict injury or tend to incite an immediate breach of the peace. It has been well observed that such utterances are no essential part of any exposition of ideas, and are of such slight social value as a step to truth that any benefit that may be derived from them is clearly outweighed by the social interest in order and morality.[13]

Also, governments may regulate the time, place, and manner of speech so long as they do not favor some ideas over others. In other words, two people can be prohibited from giving speeches at the same location at the same time. Otherwise, freedom of speech would belong only to the one who could shout the loudest.

Although the United States Supreme Court initially took the view that language treated as de-

famatory under state law was not entitled to First Amendment protection, it subsequently concluded that the First Amendment requires that a defense for honest error be allowed when statements are made about *public figures.* We will return to the distinction between private and public figures in the section on defamation in Chapter 7.

POLITICAL SPEECH   Speech that otherwise would be within the protection of the First Amendment does not lose that protection simply because its source is a corporation. For example, in *First National Bank of Boston v. Bellotti,* national banking associations and business corporations sought United States Supreme Court review of a Massachusetts statute that prohibited corporations from making political contributions or expenditures that individuals were permitted to make. The Court ruled that the Massachusetts law was unconstitutional because it violated the right of corporations to freedom of speech.[14]

Recently, a more conservative United States Supreme Court ruled that a similar Michigan statute was *not* unconstitutional. The Michigan statute prohibited corporations from using corporate funds for independent expressions of opinion about political candidates. Although the Court acknowledged that corporate spending to support candidates constitutes political speech and thus falls under the protection of the First Amendment, the limitation on political speech created by the Michigan statute was based on a compelling state interest in preserving the fairness of political debate. The Court stressed that corporations, which are creatures of state law, are given advantages that enable some of them to amass wealth. The statute ensured that the wealth of corporations would not give them a potential for unfair advantage over other voters.[15]

COMMERCIAL SPEECH   Freedom-of-speech cases generally distinguish between commercial and noncommercial messages. Although commercial speech, such as advertising, is protected by the First Amendment, its protection is not as extensive

---

13. *Chaplinsky v. New Hampshire,* 315 U.S. 568, 62 S.Ct. 766, 86 L.Ed. 1031 (1942).

14. 435 U.S. 765, 98 S.Ct. 1407, 55 L.Ed.2d 707 (1978).
15. *Austin v. Michigan Chamber of Commerce,* 497 U.S. 652, 110 S.Ct. 1391, 108 L.Ed.2d 652 (1990).

as that afforded to noncommercial speech. A restriction on commercial speech will generally be considered valid as long as it (1) seeks to implement a substantial government interest, (2) directly advances that interest, and (3) goes no further than necessary to accomplish its objective. The greater protection afforded to noncommercial speech by the First Amendment is stressed in the following case.

Case 5.3

METROMEDIA, INC. v. CITY OF SAN DIEGO
Supreme Court of the United States, 1981.
453 U.S. 490,
101 S.Ct. 2882,
69 L.Ed.2d 800.

BACKGROUND AND FACTS *The city of San Diego enacted an ordinance that imposed substantial prohibitions on the erection of outdoor advertising displays within the city. The stated purpose of the ordinance was "to eliminate hazards to pedestrians and motorists brought about by distracting sign displays" and "to preserve and improve the appearance of the City." The ordinance permitted on-site commercial advertising (defined as a sign advertising goods or services available on the property on which the sign was located) but forbade other commercial advertising and noncommercial advertising using fixed-structure signs. The ordinance did provide for exceptions, such as temporary political campaign signs. Companies that were engaged in the outdoor-advertising business in the city when the ordinance was passed brought suit in state court to prohibit enforcement of the ordinance. The trial court held that the ordinance was an unconstitutional exercise of the city's police power and an abridgment of the companies' First Amendment rights. The California Court of Appeal affirmed the decision, but the California Supreme Court reversed, holding that the ordinance was not invalid under the First Amendment. The companies appealed.*

Justice *WHITE* delivered the opinion of the Court.

* * * *

* * * [O]ur recent commercial speech cases have consistently accorded noncommercial speech a greater degree of protection than commercial speech. San Diego effectively inverts this judgment, by affording a greater degree of protection to commercial than to noncommercial speech. There is a broad exception for onsite commercial advertisements, but there is no similar exception for noncommercial speech. The use of onsite billboards to carry commercial messages related to the commercial use of the premises is freely permitted, but the use of otherwise identical billboards to carry noncommercial messages is generally prohibited. The city does not explain how or why noncommercial billboards located in places where commercial billboards are permitted would be more threatening to safe driving or would detract more from the beauty of the city. Insofar as the city tolerates billboards at all, it cannot choose to limit their content to commercial messages; the city may not conclude that the communication of commercial information concerning goods and services connected with a particular site is of greater value than the communication of noncommercial messages.

Furthermore, the ordinance contains exceptions that permit various kinds of noncommercial signs, whether on property where goods and services are offered or not, that would otherwise be within the general ban. * * * No other noncommercial or ideological signs meeting the structural definition are permitted, regardless of their effect on traffic safety or esthetics.

* * * *

With respect to noncommercial speech, the city may not choose the appropriate subjects for public discourse: "To allow a government the choice of permissible subjects for public debate would be to allow that government control over the search for political truth.'' Because some noncommercial messages may be conveyed on billboards throughout the commercial and industrial zones, San Diego must similarly allow billboards conveying other noncommercial messages throughout those zones.

The United States Supreme Court concluded that the ordinance was unconstitutional on its face because it reached too far into the realm of protected (noncommercial) speech. The judgment of the California Supreme Court was reversed, and the case was remanded to that court.

DECISION AND REMEDY

Freedom of Religion

The First Amendment requires that the government neither establish any religion nor prohibit the free exercise of religious practices. This constitutional provision is referred to as either the **establishment clause** or the **free exercise clause.** Government action, both federal and state, must be consistent with this constitutional mandate. Federal or state regulation that does not promote, or place a significant burden on, religion is constitutional even if it has some impact on religion. ''Sunday closing laws,'' for example, make the performance of some commercial activities on Sunday illegal. These statutes, also known as ''blue laws,'' have been upheld on the ground that it is a legitimate function of government to provide a day of rest. The United States Supreme Court has held that the closing laws, although originally of a religious character, have taken on the secular purpose of promoting the health and welfare of workers.[16] Even though closing laws admittedly make it easier for Christians to attend religious services, the Court has viewed this effect as an incidental, not a primary, purpose of Sunday closing laws.

The First Amendment does not require a complete separation of church and state. On the contrary, it affirmatively mandates *accommodation* of all religions and forbids hostility toward any.[17] For example, the United States Supreme Court held in *Lynch v. Donnelly* that a municipality could include religious symbols, such as a Nativity scene, in its annual Christmas display, as long as the religious symbols constituted just one part of a hol-

iday display in which other, nonreligious symbols (such as reindeer and candy-striped poles) were also featured.[18] The Court applied this same reasoning in *County of Allegheny v. American Civil Liberties Union.* In this case, the presence of a Nativity scene within a county courthouse was held to be unconstitutional because it was not displayed in the same area of the courthouse as other, nonreligious holiday symbols. A menorah (a nine-branched candelabrum used in celebrating Chanukah) positioned on the courthouse steps, however, did not violate the First Amendment because it was situated next to a Christmas tree.[19]

Another freedom-of-religion issue involves the accommodation that businesses must make for the religious beliefs of their employees. Title VII of the Civil Rights Act of 1964 prohibits government employers, private employers, and unions from discriminating against persons because of their religion. The Equal Employment Opportunity Commission—the regulatory agency that interprets and applies Title VII—has required that private employers ''reasonably accommodate'' the religious practices of their employees, unless to do so would cause undue hardship to the employer's business. For example, if an employee's religion prohibits him or her from working on a certain day of the week or at a certain type of job, the employer must make a reasonable attempt to accommodate these religious requirements. Employers must reasonably accommodate an employee's religious belief even if the belief is not based on the tenets or dogma of a particular church, sect, or denomination. The

16. *McGowan v. Maryland,* 366 U.S. 420, 81 S.Ct. 1101, 6 L.Ed.2d 393 (1961).
17. *Zorach v. Clauson,* 343 U.S. 306, 72 S.Ct. 679, 96 L.Ed. 954 (1952).

18. 465 U.S. 668, 104 S.Ct. 1355, 79 L.Ed.2d 604 (1984).
19. 492 U.S. 573, 109 S.Ct. 3086, 106 L.Ed.2d 472 (1989).

The Boundaries of Free Commercial Speech

The First Amendment to the U.S. Constitution guarantees freedom of speech. However explicit this guarantee may seem, the courts have nonetheless imposed limitations on individuals' rights to free speech. For example, one does not have the right to yell "fire" in a crowded movie theater. Nor does one have the right to defame the good name or reputation of others by making false statements about them. Furthermore, there are numerous restrictions on the rights of individuals to publish obscene materials. Businesses have even more stringent restrictions on their rights to free speech.

Limitations on Commercial Speech

A distinction is often made between "normal" speech and "commercial" speech. Commercial speech—speech by business firms—consists of advertising, political endorsements, and the like. This type of speech is protected, but to a much lesser extent than speech by individuals. Whenever corporate or business speech is contrary to a "compelling state interest," it can be restrained. For example, a state has a compelling interest in seeing to it that consumers are not misled by false advertising claims. Therefore, the state can limit commercial speech if it deems that the commercial speech at issue misleads consumers. Another state interest is the beautification of roadsides, and this interest allows the state to place restraints on billboard advertising.

The point at which commercial speech passes over the boundary line that separates protected from unprotected commercial speech depends on whether a court holds that a given state interest in limiting the speech is sufficiently compelling to justify the restraint. Court decisions that limit commercial speech are often the subject of controversy.

The Regulation of Housing Advertisements

The Fair Housing Act of 1968[a] and its amendments make it unlawful to publish any advertisement with respect to the sale or rent of a dwelling that indicates any preference based on race. Publishers of newspapers and those controlling other media that accept advertisements rarely, if ever, willfully violate federal law in this regard. What happens, though, when the models used in an advertisement for a housing development do not reflect a "fair" racial make-up? This issue arose recently when the Open Housing Center, Inc., and several African-Americans in New York City brought suit against the New York Times Company (the Times), alleging that certain real estate ads in the *New York Times* communicated a "whites only" message to potential buyers of the real estate—not in the words used in the ads, but in the illustrations, in which African Americans were depicted as being subservient to whites.[b] The Times claimed that the suit should be dismissed because it would be unconstitutional to require newspapers to monitor their ads. Furthermore, the Times argued, to prohibit it from publishing advertisements for a perfectly legal activity—the selling of real estate—would infringe on its right to free speech. The federal trial court hearing the case did not agree with the Times (nor did the appellate court when the case was appealed). The court pointed out that the Times routinely monitors ads to avoid publishing ads that do not meet its "Standards of Advertising Acceptability." These standards provide, among other things, that the Times will not accept ads that fail to comply with antidiscrimination laws.

The appellate court concluded that "it strains the credibility

---

a. 42 U.S.C. Section 3604(c).

b. *Ragin v. New York Times Co.,* 923 F.2d 995 (2d Cir. 1991).

beyond the breaking point to assert that monitoring ads for racial messages imposes an unconstitutional burden [on the Times]."

The Question of Emotional Injury

The Times pointed out that, given the court's holding, the potential for baseless claims for emotional injury exists. For example, a plaintiff may establish a *prima facie* case for punitive damages for emotional injury simply by *oral* testimony that he or she is a newspaper reader of a race different from that of the models used and was substantially insulted and distressed by a certain ad. The court sympathized with the Times but did not regard such a possibility as a reason to "immunize publishers from any liability." The court stated that "[w]here the claim of an illegal preference is based solely upon the use of models and not upon more directly offensive racial messages, we are confident that courts will be able to keep such awards within reason."

It looks as if the newspaper publisher, rather than the real estate company placing the ads, may be held liable for racial overtones and suggestions implicit in advertisements.

■ Implications for the Businessperson

1. It is now clear that advertisements must be monitored not only by advertisers but also by the publishers of advertisements. Advertisers and those who provide vehicles for advertisements must be careful to monitor the racial (and sexual) makeup of the models used in all advertisements. (Such monitoring has been carried out for many years by publishers of elementary and secondary school books to ensure that a fair representation of American society is presented to student readers.)

2. The issue of restrictions on commercial speech is one that will continue to create controversy within and without the courts. All businesses must be concerned with the extent to which they are abiding by the law and public policy when they express themselves in advertising and in other corporate speech, such as political speech (overtly sponsoring a particular political candidate, for example).

■ For Critical Analysis

1. Is it possible not to discriminate against any group when advertising in a nationwide publication such as the *New York Times?* In other words, because the U.S. population is made up of many ethnic groups, how does one determine what percentage of each group must be depicted in advertisements? What if a firm only places one ad, and in that ad a white person is used as a model? Is the ad discriminatory and thus in violation of the federal Fair Housing Act? If you were the publisher of a newspaper, would you be reluctant to use any models in your advertisements for fear of insulting those among your readership who are from an ethnic background different from that of the model depicted?

2. Models are used in advertisements in television also. To what extent do the owners of television networks have to worry about liability for damages if a viewer is distressed by the fact that one of the network's advertisers consistently uses only white males in its ads?

3. Some people contend that there is an inconsistency between the protection afforded to individual speech and that afforded to commercial speech. For example, "hate messages" and racial slurs are counter to the public policy underlying antidiscrimination laws, yet they continue to be heard daily throughout this country. Why should individuals be allowed to engage in overtly discriminatory speech while publishers are prohibited from allowing ads that are suggestive of discrimination?

only requirement is that the belief be sincerely held by the employee.[20]

In the following case, the sacramental use of peyote by two employees violated both an em-

ployment policy and state law. When the employees were discharged for "misconduct," the state refused to grant them unemployment benefits. Ultimately, the United States Supreme Court had to determine whether a state law prohibiting the use of peyote violated the religious rights of Native Americans whose religion required the sacramental use of this drug.

---

20. *Frazee v. Illinois Department of Employment Security,* 489 U.S. 829, 109 S.Ct. 1514, 103 L.Ed.2d 914 (1989).

Case 5.4

EMPLOYMENT DIVISION, DEPARTMENT OF HUMAN RESOURCES OF THE STATE OF OREGON v. SMITH

Supreme Court of the United States, 1990.
494 U.S. 872,
110 S.Ct. 1595,
108 L.Ed.2d 876.

BACKGROUND AND FACTS *Smith and Black, both Native Americans, worked as drug and alcohol abuse rehabilitation counselors. They were discharged by their employer for ingesting peyote, a hallucinogenic drug, for sacramental purposes during a religious ceremony of the Native American Church. When Smith and Black applied for state unemployment compensation, their applications were denied under an Oregon statute disqualifying employees who were discharged for work-connected misconduct. Smith and Black appealed the Employment Division's decision to the courts, claiming that the sacramental use of peyote did not constitute "misconduct" and that the state's denial of unemployment benefits violated their religious rights under the free exercise clause of the First Amendment. The Supreme Court of Oregon ruled in their favor, notwithstanding the fact that the use of peyote was illegal under Oregon law. According to the Supreme Court of Oregon, the law prohibiting the sacramental use of peyote was itself in violation of the First Amendment. The United States Supreme Court then addressed the issue of the statute's constitutionality.*

Justice *SCALIA* delivered the opinion of the Court.

* * * *

* * * We have never held that an individual's religious beliefs excuse him from compliance with an otherwise valid law prohibiting conduct that the State is free to regulate. On the contrary, the record of more than a century of our free exercise jurisprudence contradicts that proposition. As described succinctly by Justice Frankfurter, in [an earlier case]: "Conscientious scruples have not, in the course of the long struggle for religious toleration, relieved the individual from obedience to a general law not aimed at the promotion or restriction of religious beliefs. The mere possession of religious convictions which contradict the relevant concerns of a political society does not relieve the citizen from the discharge of political responsibilities." * * *

* * * *

* * * The government's ability to enforce generally applicable prohibitions of socially harmful conduct, like its ability to carry out other aspects of public policy, "cannot depend on measuring the effects of a governmental action on a religious objector's spiritual development." To make an individual's obligation to obey such a law contingent upon the law's coincidence with his religious beliefs, * * * — permitting him, by virtue of his beliefs, "to become a law unto himself"—contradicts both constitutional tradition and common sense.

* * * *

* * * It may fairly be said that leaving accommodation to the political process will place at a relative disadvantage those religious practices that are not widely engaged in; but that unavoidable consequence of democratic government must be preferred to a system in which each conscience is a law unto itself or in which judges weigh the social importance of all laws against the centrality of all religious beliefs.

The United States Supreme Court reversed the Oregon court's ruling. The Oregon statute prohibiting the ingestion of peyote was constitutional, and denial of unemployment benefits to Smith and Black—whose employment dismissal resulted from the use of this drug—did not violate their rights under the free exercise clause.

DECISION AND REMEDY

Searches and Seizures

The Fourth Amendment protects the "right of the people to be secure in their persons, houses, papers, and effects." Federal, state, and local governments must obtain search warrants before searching or seizing private property. To obtain a warrant, law enforcement officers must convince a judge that they have *probable cause* to believe a search will reveal a specific illegality. **Probable cause** requires law enforcement officials to have trustworthy evidence that would convince a reasonable person that the proposed search or seizure is more likely justified than not. Furthermore, the Fourth Amendment prohibits general warrants and requires a particular description of that which is to be searched or seized. General searches through a person's belongings are impermissible. The search cannot extend beyond what is described in the warrant.

There are exceptions to the requirement of a search warrant, as when it is likely that the items sought will be removed before a warrant can be obtained. For example, if a police officer has probable cause to believe an automobile contains evidence of a crime and it is likely that the vehicle will be unavailable by the time a warrant is obtained, the officer can search the vehicle without a warrant.

Constitutional protection against unreasonable searches and seizures is important to businesses and professionals. With increased federal and state regulation of commercial activities, frequent and unannounced government inspection to ensure compliance with the law would be extremely disruptive. In *Marshall v. Barlow's, Inc.,*[21] the United States Supreme Court held that government in-

spectors do not have the right to enter business premises without a warrant, although the standard of probable cause is not the same as that required in nonbusiness contexts. A general and neutral enforcement plan will justify issuance of the warrant. Lawyers and accountants frequently possess the business records of their clients, and inspecting these documents while they are out of the hands of their true owners also requires a warrant.

In contrast, no warrant is required for seizures of spoiled or contaminated food. Nor are warrants required for searches of businesses in such highly regulated industries as liquor, guns, and strip mining. General manufacturing is not considered to be one of these highly regulated industries.

Self-Incrimination

The Fifth Amendment guarantees that no person "shall be compelled in any criminal case to be a witness against himself." Thus, in any federal proceeding, an accused person cannot be compelled to give testimony that might subject him or her to any criminal prosecution. An accused person cannot be forced to testify against himself or herself in state courts either, because the Fourteenth Amendment due process clause incorporates the Fifth Amendment provision against self-incrimination.

The Fifth Amendment's guarantee against self-incrimination extends only to natural persons. Because a corporation is a legal entity and not a natural person, the privilege against self-incrimination is inapplicable to it. Similarly, the business records of a partnership do not receive Fifth Amendment protection.[22] No artificial organization may utilize

---

21.   436 U.S. 307, 98 S.Ct. 1816, 56 L.Ed.2d 305 (1978).

22.   The privilege has been applied to some small family partnerships. See *United States v. Slutsky*, 352 F.Supp. 1105 (S.D.N.Y. 1972).

the personal privilege against compulsory self-incrimination. When it is required that records of such organizations be produced, the information must be given even if it incriminates the persons who comprise the business entity.

Sole proprietors and sole practitioners who have not incorporated cannot be compelled to produce their business records. These individuals have full protection against self-incrimination because they function in only one capacity: there is no separate business entity.

In the following case, the sole stockholder in a corporation attempted to assert his Fifth Amendment privilege to avoid having to produce his corporation's records.

Case 5.5

WILD v. BREWER

United States Court of Appeals,
Ninth Circuit, 1964.
329 F.2d 924.

BACKGROUND AND FACTS   *Brewer, an agent of the Internal Revenue Service (IRS), served Wild with a summons requiring Wild to appear and testify about the tax liability of "Albert J. Wild, President, Air Conditioning Supply Company." The company was a corporation wholly owned by Wild, and all books and records requested were those of the corporation. Wild appeared but refused to produce the records on the grounds that they might tend to incriminate him and hence were protected by the Fifth Amendment. When Wild was cited for contempt, he appealed. The majority of the appellate court affirmed, ordering Wild to produce the corporate books and records. One judge, however, found support for Wild's position.*

MADDEN, Judge [dissenting].
* * * *

The privilege guaranteed by the Fifth Amendment, against the Government of the United States, "in any criminal case" not to be compelled to be a witness against one's self, is available not only to defendants in criminal trials but to witnesses in any kind of official proceeding under the auspices of the United States. It applies not only to the giving of oral testimony, but to the production from one's possession of incriminating documents or objects.
* * * *

There is without question a general doctrine that an officer of a corporation who, as such officer, has custody of its records may not successfully refuse to produce those records in response to a subpoena [court-ordered summons] issued to the corporation and served upon him as custodian, on the ground that the records contain material which would incriminate him. * * *

A corporation does not have the Constitutional privilege against self-incrimination. It therefore cannot, if its records are subpoenaed, assert the Fifth Amendment privilege. * * *

* * * [But Wild] did not claim the privilege for the corporation, and could not have done so. He claims it for himself, and says that he, and not any artificial legal entity, will be the one to suffer the punishment if he is obliged to furnish to the Government the evidence which will bring about his conviction. * * *

Wild says that since he is the sole owner of his corporation, the corporation does embody the "purely private or personal interests of its [only] constituent(s)," who is Wild himself.

**DECISION
AND REMEDY**   *The trial court's ruling of contempt was affirmed. Although the dissenting judge was sympathetic to Wild's position, only the majority decision was binding: a corporation does not enjoy the Fifth Amendment privilege against self-incrimination, even when it is claimed for the benefit of the*

sole owner. Wild was therefore unable to invoke the Fifth Amendment to protect company records and was required to produce them in response to the IRS subpoena.

A corporation is a legal fiction; that is, it is considered to be a person for most purposes under the law. An unsettled area of corporation law has to do with the criminal acts of a corporation. It is obvious that a corporation cannot be sent to prison even though, under law, it is a person. Most courts hold a corporation that has violated the criminal statutes liable for fines, although in recent years, other penalties have been imposed (see Chapter 8). When criminal conduct can be attributed to corporate officers or agents, those individuals, as natural persons, are held liable and can be imprisoned for their acts.

COMMENTS

■ Other Constitutional Guarantees

Two other constitutional guarantees of great significance to Americans are mandated by the due process clauses of the Fifth and Fourteenth Amendments and the equal protection clause of the Fourteenth Amendment.

Due Process

Both the Fifth and the Fourteenth Amendments provide that no person shall be deprived "of life, liberty, or property, without due process of law." The **due process clause** of these constitutional amendments has two aspects—procedural and substantive. *Procedural* due process requires that any government decision to take life, liberty, or property must be made fairly, and thus fair procedures must be used in determining whether a person will be subjected to punishment or have some burden imposed on him or her. Fair procedure has been interpreted as requiring that the person have at least an opportunity to object to a proposed action before a fair, neutral decision maker (which need not be a judge). Thus, for example, if a driver's license is construed as a "property" interest, some sort of opportunity to object to its suspension or termination by the state must be provided.

Substantive due process focuses on the content, or substance, of legislation. In general, a law that is not compatible with the Constitution violates substantive due process. If a law or other governmental action limits a *fundamental right,* it will be held to violate substantive due process unless it

promotes a *compelling or overriding interest.* Fundamental rights include interstate travel, privacy, voting, and all First Amendment rights. Compelling interests could include, for example, the public's safety. Thus, laws designating speed limits may be upheld, even though they affect interstate travel, if they are shown to reduce highway fatalities because the state has a compelling interest in protecting the lives of its citizens.

In all other cases, a law or action does not violate substantive due process if it rationally relates to any legitimate governmental end. It is almost impossible for a law or action to fail the "rationality" test. Under this test, virtually any business regulation will be upheld as reasonable—the United States Supreme Court has sustained insurance regulations, price and wage controls, banking controls, and controls of unfair competition and trade practices against substantive due process challenges.

To illustrate: If a state legislature enacted a law imposing a fifteen-year term of imprisonment without allowing a trial on all businesspersons who appeared in their own television commercials, the law would be unconstitutional on both substantive and procedural grounds. Substantive review would invalidate the legislation because it abridges freedom of speech. Procedurally, the law is unfair because it imposes the penalty without giving the accused a chance to defend his or her actions. The lack of procedural due process will cause a court to invalidate any statute or prior court decision. Similarly, a denial of substantive due process requires courts to overrule any state or federal law that violates the Constitution.

Equal Protection

Under the Fourteenth Amendment, a state may not ''deny to any person within its jurisdiction the equal protection of the laws.'' The United States Supreme Court has used the due process clause of the Fifth Amendment to make the **equal protection clause** applicable to the federal government. Equal protection means that the government must treat similarly situated individuals in a similar manner.

Both substantive due process and equal protection require review of the substance of the law or other governmental action rather than the procedures used. When a law or action limits the liberty of all persons to do something, it may violate substantive due process; when a law or action limits the liberty of some persons but not others, it may violate the equal protection clause. Thus, for example, if a law prohibits all persons from buying contraceptive devices, it raises a substantive due process question; if it prohibits only unmarried persons from buying the same devices, it raises an equal protection issue.

Basically, in determining whether a law or action violates the equal protection clause, a court will consider questions similar to those previously noted as applicable in a substantive due process review. Under an equal protection inquiry, when a law or action distinguishes between or among individuals, the basis for the distinction—that is, the *classification*—is examined. If the law or action inhibits some persons' exercise of a fundamental right, the classification must be necessary to promote a compelling interest. Also, if the classification is based on a *suspect* trait—such as race, national origin, or citizenship status—the classification must be necessary to promote a compelling interest. Compelling interests include remedying past unconstitutional or illegal discrimination but do not include correcting the general effects of ''society's'' discrimination. Thus, for example, if a city gives preference to minority applicants in awarding construction contracts, the city must identify the past unconstitutional or illegal dis-

crimination against minority construction firms that it is attempting to correct. (Discrimination and affirmative action are discussed more fully in Chapter 17.)

In matters of economic or social welfare, the classification will be considered valid if there is any conceivable *rational basis* on which the classification might relate to any legitimate government interest. It is almost impossible for a law or action to fail the rational-basis test. Thus, for example, a city ordinance that in effect prohibits all pushcart vendors except a specific few from operating in a particular area of the city will be upheld if the city proffers a rational basis—perhaps regulation and reduction of traffic in the particular area—for the ordinance. On the other hand, a law that provides unemployment benefits only to people over six feet tall would violate the guarantee of equal protection. There is no rational basis for determining the distribution of unemployment compensation on the basis of height. Such a distinction could not further any legitimate government objective.

Another approach is applied in cases involving discrimination based on gender or legitimacy. Laws using these classifications must be *substantially related to important government objectives.* For example, an important government objective is preventing illegitimate teenage pregnancies. Because males and females are not similarly situated in this circumstance—only females can become pregnant—a law that punishes men but not women for statutory rape will be upheld. On the other hand, a state law requiring illegitimate children to bring paternity suits within six years of their birth will be struck down if legitimate children are allowed to seek support from their parents at any time. An important objective behind statutes of limitations is to prevent persons from bringing stale or fraudulent claims, but distinguishing between support claims on the basis of legitimacy has no relation to this objective.

In the following case, the defendant asserted that age discrimination against a government employee was rationally related to a legitimate state interest.

BACKGROUND AND FACTS *Adela Izquierdo Prieto, age forty-two, had worked for a government-owned and operated radio and television station in Puerto Rico for over a decade when, without any prior notice, she was suddenly transferred from her television program to a position in radio. Her replacement in the television program was a twenty-eight-year-old woman with less experience. Agustin Mercado Rosa, the administrator of the television channel, explained to a newspaper reporter that Izquierdo was removed because "we need new faces" and because Izquierdo's replacement "is young, attractive and refreshing." Izquierdo sued Mercado, alleging in part that the transfer discriminated against her on the basis of age and therefore violated her rights under the equal protection clause. Mercado claimed that the transfer was rationally related to furthering a legitimate state interest in maximizing viewership for the public television channel, and therefore it was a permissible action. The trial court held for Izquierdo and awarded damages. Mercado appealed.*

Case 5.6

IZQUIERDO PRIETO v. MERCADO ROSA

United States Court of Appeals, First Circuit, 1990.
894 F.2d 467.

LEVIN H. CAMPBELL, Chief Judge.
* * * *
* * *The Supreme Court has held that constitutional age discrimination claims are subject to the rational basis test * * *.
* * * *
* * * Under the rational basis test, the district court must ask whether the state's objective in effectuating an age-related transfer of Ms. Izquierdo was a valid one and whether the transfer rationally furthered this objective. * * *
An ostensible objective of Mr. Mercado's decision to transfer Ms. Izquierdo to radio was to replace her with someone with greater audience drawing power and appeal. Mr. Mercado could have rationally believed that having "new [and young] faces" would maximize audience drawing power, even though his belief might not be accurate. Plaintiff [Izquierdo] argues that, while the maximization of viewership may be a valid goal in the context of commercial television, it is not an appropriate goal for public television because such considerations as rating, audience appeal, ability to sell advertising spots, and profit maximization do not apply to government-owned television stations. The purpose of a state in owning and operating a television station, however, includes serving the public by providing increased access to information and enhanced opportunities for education. Benefit to the public as a whole is maximized the more people take advantage of the services provided. Thus, to maximize viewership by making programs as appealing as possible is a legitimate objective in the operation of government-owned television stations. We think, therefore, that Mr. Mercado's objectives, even those that were age-related, can be reasonably said to promote a legitimate governmental purpose.
* * * *
* * * There is no right under the equal protection clause for a state employee to be free from age discrimination by her state employer so long as such discrimination is rationally related to furthering a legitimate state interest.

The trial court's decision was reversed in respect to Izquierdo's age discrimination claim. Mercado's actions were held to be rationally related to furthering a legitimate state interest and thus did not violate the equal protection clause.

DECISION AND REMEDY

COMMENTS *The court noted that Congress intended to make age discrimination un-*
lawful by passing the Age Discrimination in Employment Act (ADEA). This
act prohibits discrimination against employees on the basis of their age.
Izquierdo, however, did not bring her claim under the ADEA but under
the equal protection clause. Therefore the court did not address the issue
of whether Mercado's actions had violated the ADEA.

■ Terms and Concepts to Review

amend 102
commerce clause 104
due process clause 117
equal protection clause 118

establishment clause 111
federalism 102
free exercise clause 111

police powers 106
probable cause 115
supremacy clause 106

■ Questions and Case Problems

5-1. The U.S. Constitution, in which the people of the United States give the government the "power to govern," was written by a handful of men who represented the aristocracy of the time. Surprisingly, this group of aristocrats wrote a document giving more freedoms to common people than any other constitution in existence. Look at Appendix B. Name some of the basic guarantees found in the Constitution.

5-2. Suppose that in 1973, when the nation was suffering a fuel shortage, the Public Service Commission of the State of Illinois ordered that all "promotional advertising" by electric utilities cease. Assume that this order was based on the commission's finding that the state in all likelihood did not have sufficient fuel for the upcoming winter. If the Public Service Commission sought to enforce its ban in 1977, when the fuel shortage had eased, would such enforcement be a regulation of commercial speech in violation of the First Amendment? If so, why? (Assume that the commission's interest in conservation could not have been adequately protected by a less restrictive alternative.)

5-3. A Georgia statute requires the use of contoured rear-fender mudguards on trucks and trailers operating within Georgia state lines. The statute further makes it illegal for trucks and trailers to use straight mudguards. In approximately thirty-five other states, straight mudguards are legal. Moreover, in Florida, straight mudguards are explicitly required by law. There is some evidence that suggests that contoured mudguards might be a little safer than straight mudguards. Discuss whether this Georgia statute violates any constitutional provisions.

5-4. A mayoral election is about to be held in a large U.S. city. One of the candidates is Gregory Schumann, and his campaign supporters wish to post campaign signs on lamp posts and utility posts throughout the city. A city ordinance, however, prohibits the posting of any signs on public property. Schumann's supporters contend that the city ordinance

is unconstitutional because it violates their rights to free speech. Do you agree? In your answer, discuss what factors a court might consider in determining the constitutionality of the ordinance.

5-5. Thomas worked in the nonmilitary operations of a large firm that produced both military and nonmilitary goods. When the company discontinued the production of nonmilitary goods, Thomas was transferred to a plant producing war materials. Thomas left his job, claiming that it violated his religious principles to participate in the manufacture of materials to be used in destroying life. In effect, he argued, the transfer to the war-materials plant forced him to quit his job. He was denied unemployment compensation by the state because he had not been effectively "discharged" by the employer but had voluntarily terminated his employment. Does the state's denial of unemployment benefits to Thomas violate the free exercise clause of the First Amendment? Explain. [*Thomas v. Review Board of the Indiana Employment Security Division,* 450 U.S. 707, 101 S.Ct. 1425, 67 L.Ed.2d 624 (1981)]

5-6. A 1988 Minnesota statute required all operators of slow-moving vehicles to display on their vehicles a fluorescent orange-red triangular emblem or, as an alternate, a dull black triangle with a white reflective border, plus seventy-two square inches of permanent red reflective tape. A vehicle operator who chose the alternate emblem still had to carry a regular orange-red emblem in the vehicle and display it externally during times of darkness or low visibility. The state brought charges against Hershberger and other members of the Amish religion (the defendants) because they refused to comply with the statute. The defendants claimed that the statute violated their freedom of religion under the First Amendment because displaying the "loud" colors and "worldly symbols" on their slow-moving vehicles (black, box-like buggies) compromised their religious belief that they should remain separate and apart from the modern world. The defendants stated that they would not object to displaying a sign similar to the alternate symbol, if they could use silver, instead of red, reflective tape, and if they did not have to display the "regular" emblem at night. The state argued that, although the silver tape was as effective as the red, in terms of visibility, the red tape was customarily associated with slow-moving vehicles, and therefore the Amish should comply with the statute as written. What will the court hold? Discuss. [*State v. Hershberger*, 444 N.W.2d 282 (Minn. 1989)]

5-7. 📟 The California Fair Employment and Housing Act requires employers to provide leave and reinstatement to employees disabled by pregnancy. At the federal level, Title VII of the Civil Rights Act of 1964, which prohibits employment discrimination on the basis of sex, was amended by the Pregnancy Discrimination Act (PDA) in 1978. The PDA specifies that sex discrimination includes discrimination on the basis of pregnancy. The PDA does not, though, require employers to provide pregnancy leave and reinstatement of employment. A woman employed as a receptionist by California Federal Savings and Loan Association (Cal Fed) took a pregnancy disability leave in 1982. When she notified Cal Fed that she was able to return to work, she was told that her job had been filled and that there were no similar positions available. She then filed a complaint with the California Department of Fair Employment and Housing, which charged Cal Fed with violating the Fair Employment and Housing Act. Before a hearing was held on the complaint, Cal Fed, joined by other employers, brought an action in federal court seeking a declaration that the California Fair Employment and Housing Act was inconsistent with, and preempted by, Title VII of the Civil Rights Act, as amended, and that Cal Fed was thus entitled to an injunction against its enforcement. How should the court rule? Give the reasons for your conclusion. [*California Federal Savings and Loan Association v. Guerra*, 479 U.S. 272, 107 S.Ct. 683, 93 L.Ed.2d 613 (1987)]

5-8. Eligibility and benefit levels in the Federal Food Stamp Program are determined on a household rather than an individual basis. The statutory definition of the term *household* was amended in 1981 and 1982 so that parents, children, and siblings who lived together were to be generally treated as single households but more distant relatives or groups of unrelated persons living together were not to be treated as households unless they also customarily purchased food and prepared meals together. Families that generally bought food and prepared meals as separate economic units, and not as families, would either lose benefits or have their food stamp allotments decreased as a result of the 1981 and 1982 amendments. Several of these families brought suit, claiming the statutory definition of the term *household* was unconstitutional. Did the statutory distinction between parents, children, and siblings, on the one hand, and all other groups of individuals, on the other, violate the guarantee of equal treatment in the due process clause of the Fifth Amendment? Explain. [*Lyng v. Castillo*, 477 U.S. 635, 106 S.Ct. 2727, 91 L.Ed.2d 527 (1986)]

5-9. 📟 In 1982, Philip Zauderer, an attorney practicing in Columbus, Ohio, placed a series of newspaper ads directed at women who had used the Dalkon

Shield intrauterine device (IUD). In his ads, Zauderer included a drawing of the Dalkon Shield and informed women that they could still sue for any injuries or other harm to their health sustained by its use, even though the IUD was no longer being marketed. As a result of these ads, Zauderer filed lawsuits for 106 women. The Ohio Supreme Court deemed such advertisements unethical, and Zauderer was reprimanded by the court for his actions. He was further reprimanded for not having disclosed in his ads that, although his clients would owe no legal fees if they lost, they might still be faced with other costs involved in litigation. Zauderer appealed, claiming the ads were protected under the First Amendment as "commercial speech" and that failure to disclose other costs was not deceptive. Discuss the probable success of Zauderer's appeal. [*Zauderer v. Office of Disciplinary Counsel*, 471 U.S. 626, 105 S.Ct. 2265, 85 L.Ed.2d 652 (1985)]

5-10. In 1983, Gary Peel, an Illinois attorney, began placing on his letterhead the following statement: "Certified Civil Trial Specialist / By the National Board of Trial Advocacy." In so doing, Peel violated Rule 2-105(a) of the Illinois Code of Professional Responsibility, which prohibits lawyers from holding themselves out as "certified" or "specialists" in fields other than admiralty, trademark, and patent law. The Attorney Registration and Disciplinary Commission (ARDC) censured Peel for the violation. The ARDC claimed that Peel's letterhead was misleading because it implied that Peel had special qualifications as an attorney, although in fact no such thing as a civil trial specialty existed in Illinois; because the word *certified* might be interpreted to mean "licensed," and the National Board of Trial Advocacy (NBTA) did not have the authority to license lawyers; and because given the fact that not all attorneys licensed to practice in Illinois are certified by the NBTA, Peel's assertion might erroneously be construed by some readers to mean that those who are certified by that board are superior to those who are not. Peel argued that Rule 2-105(a) violated his constitutional right to free speech and appealed the ARDC's decision to the United States Supreme Court. What will the Court decide? Discuss. [*Peel v. Attorney Registration and Disciplinary Commission*, 496 U.S. 91, 110 S.Ct. 2281, 110 L.Ed.2d 83 (1990)]

5-11. 📟 Taylor owned a bait business in Maine and arranged to have live baitfish imported into the state. The importation of the baitfish violated a Maine statute. Taylor was indicted under a federal statute that makes it a federal crime to transport fish in interstate commerce in violation of state law. Taylor moved to dismiss the indictment on the ground that the Maine statute unconstitutionally burdened interstate commerce. Maine intervened to defend the validity of its statute, arguing that the law legitimately protected the state's fisheries from parasites and nonnative species that might be included in shipments of live baitfish. Were Maine's interests in protecting its fisheries from parasites and nonnative species sufficient to justify the burden placed on interstate commerce by the Maine statute? Discuss. [*Maine v. Taylor*, 477 U.S. 131, 106 S.Ct. 2440, 91 L.Ed.2d 110 (1986)]

5-12. In 1957, Rhodes and several other Georgia landowners entered into a sixty-five-year timber purchase contract with Inland-Rome, Inc. Thereafter, Inland-Rome cut timber from the landowners' land and then removed it for processing in certain Georgia facilities, after which it was shipped as lumber products to points throughout the country. In 1986, the landowners claimed that Inland-Rome had breached the contract and filed suit. Inland-Rome moved to compel arbitration because the parties had agreed, in their contract, to arbitrate any disputes arising thereunder. Georgia law enforces arbitration clauses only if they are contained in construction contracts. Arbitration clauses are enforceable under the Federal Arbitration Act only if the contracts in which they appear affect interstate commerce. Inland-Rome contended that, because lumber products from the cut timber were shipped throughout the nation, the contract related to interstate commerce, and therefore the Federal Arbitration Act should apply. Will the court agree? Discuss. [*Rhodes v. Inland-Rome, Inc.,* 195 Ga.App. 39, 392 S.E.2d 270 (1990)]

5-13. A Question of Ethics

In 1988, as a result of a general election, Arizona added Article XXVIII to its constitution. Article XXVIII provided that English was to be the official language of the state and required all state officials and employees to use only the English language during the performance of government business. Maria-Kelly Yniguez, an employee of the Arizona Department of Administration, frequently spoke in Spanish to Spanish-speaking persons with whom she dealt in the course of her work. Yniguez claimed that the requirement violated constitutionally protected free speech rights and brought an action in federal court against the state governor, Rose Mofford, and other state officials. [Yniguez v. Mofford, *730 F.Supp. 309 (D.Ariz. 1990)*].

1. Did the requirement prevent Yniguez from engaging in political speech? Ostensibly she spoke English; could she not communicate her political views by speaking English? What if the listener, however, spoke only Spanish? Would Yniguez have been able to communicate her political views?

2. Was the requirement too restrictive in fact? After all, most employers require their employees to avoid outside activities while on the job. Does that not restrict the employee's opportunity to communicate his or her political ideas to others?

3. What if Yniguez had been a state representative representing a constituency that spoke only Spanish? Would not the requirement that all state business be conducted in English interfere with Yniguez's ability to carry out the duties of her office? How could she communicate with constituents if she was forbidden to speak in Spanish? Does the restriction interfere with speech simply because it applies too broadly to different situations?

4. A common language promotes greater unity in society. Is this a strong enough justification for enactment of English-only statutes, or are such restrictions simply unethical regardless of other considerations?

5-14. Case Briefing Assignment

Examine Case A.5 [Austin v. Berryman, 878 F.2d 786 (4th Cir. 1989)] in Appendix A. The case has been excerpted there in great detail. Review and then brief the case, making sure that you include answers to the following questions in your brief.

1. Who were the plaintiff and defendant in this action?

2. Why did Austin claim that she had been forced to leave her job?

3. Why was she refused state unemployment benefits?

4. Did the state's refusal to give her unemployment compensation violate her rights under the free exercise clause of the First Amendment?

5. What logic or reasoning did the court employ in arriving at its conclusion?

Chapter 6

Administrative Law

Hardly a day passes that one does not hear someone inveigh against the government's intrusion into our daily lives. A good part of Ronald Reagan's appeal as a candidate for president in 1980 was his promise to get "government off the backs of the people." The "government" in this and similar usage sentiments, more often than not, is the myriad bureaucratic agencies that we encounter in some form or other in almost every facet of our lives. Although the era of deregulation ushered in with the Reagan administration (actually it began, albeit somewhat hesitantly, during the latter part of the Carter administration) has lessened somewhat the *rate of growth* of government regulation, federal agencies continue each year to issue tens of thousands of pages of regulatory fine print. Whether as consumers or as suppliers of some factor of production, each of us is affected in profound and often subtle ways by the regulations promulgated by federal and state agencies.

Firms, both private and public, have been particularly affected by the regulations established by **administrative agencies.** A variety of agencies administer rules covering virtually every aspect of a business's operation. The Securities and Exchange Commission regulates the firm's capital structure and financing, as well as its financial reporting. The National Labor Relations Board governs its hiring and firing of employees and oversees relations between the firm and any unions with which it may deal. The Environmental Protection Agency and the Occupational Safety and Health Administration may affect the way it manufactures its products. The Federal Trade Commission may affect the way it markets these products. Added to this plethora of federal regulation is a second layer of state regulation that, when not preempted by federal legislation, may cover many of the same activities or regulate independently those activities not covered by federal regulation. Because state and local rules vary widely among the various jurisdictions, even a cursory examination of those rules would present an almost insurmountable task. Hence, this chapter will focus exclusively on federal administrative law.

Administrative agencies occupy an unusual niche in the Anglo-American legal scheme. In one light they may be viewed as quasi-administrative in form and function. In another light they are more aptly viewed as being quasi-legislative. And in yet another light they are more correctly viewed as being quasi-judicial in nature. Most agencies are considered part of the executive branch. Some, however, exist as **independent regulatory agencies.**[1] The significant difference between the two types of agencies lies in the accountability of the regulators. Agencies that are considered part of the executive branch are subject to the authority of the president; independent regulatory agencies are not, and their officials cannot be removed without cause. Notwithstanding this distinction, virtually all agencies have a range

---

1. Most economic regulation is administered by independent agencies (the Interstate Commerce Commission, the Federal Communications Commission, the Federal Maritime Commission, and others). More recently established social regulatory agencies (the Occupational Safety and Health Administration, the Environmental Protection Agency, the Food and Drug Administration, and others) are within the executive branch.

of authority so broad as to make that authority seem legislative and judicial, as well as executive, in nature. This range of authority is at the heart of much of the controversy surrounding the regulatory process.

Federal administrative agencies are created by Congress. Statutes define the limits within which an agency operates, but any statutory delegation of power gives some discretion to the agency. Opponents of the administrative process argue that Congress may not totally delegate its legislative responsibility to an agency, however, without abdicating its responsibility under the U.S. Constitution to make the laws. In the following case, the United States Supreme Court considered whether Congress had delegated too much of its legislative power.

Case 6.1

SCHECHTER POULTRY CORP. v. UNITED STATES

Supreme Court of the United
States, 1935.
295 U.S. 495,
55 S.Ct. 837,
79 L.Ed. 1570.

BACKGROUND AND FACTS *The National Industrial Recovery Act (NIRA) of 1933 provided that trade associations could issue their own codes of "fair competition" that, on the approval of the president, would have the force of law. A trade group in the poultry industry proposed a "poultry code," and President Roosevelt approved it. Aaron and Alex Schechter were wholesale kosher poultry dealers in Brooklyn, New York. They refused to comply with the code and consequently were charged with violating it. At their trial in federal district court, they argued, among other things, that the code system of the NIRA violated the U.S. Constitution by providing for the delegation of legislative power by Congress. The district court held that the NIRA was not an unconstitutional delegation of power. The court reasoned that Congress was simply exercising its traditional authority to establish a general standard and to delegate authority to enforce it. The Schechters were convicted on eighteen counts, including selling diseased chickens. (It was their conviction on this charge that gave this case its popular name, the "Sick Chicken Case.") The Schechters appealed. The United States Court of Appeals sustained the convictions on all counts but one. Both parties appealed to the United States Supreme Court.*

Mr. Chief Justice *HUGHES* delivered the opinion of the Court.
    *   *   *   *

[Under NIRA] the approval of a code by the President is conditioned on his finding that it "will tend to effectuate the policy of this title." *   *   * [In section 1 it is] declared to be "the policy of Congress"—"to remove obstructions to the free flow of *   *   * commerce *   *   *; and to [promote] cooperative action among trade groups *   *   *."
    *   *   *   *

The government urges that the codes will "consist of rules of competition deemed fair for each industry by representative members of that industry—by the persons most vitally concerned and most familiar with its problems." * * * But would it be seriously contended that Congress could delegate its legislative authority to trade or industrial associations or groups so as to empower them to enact the laws they deem to be wise and beneficent for the rehabilitation and expansion of their trade or industries? * * * Such a delegation of legislative power is unknown to our law, and is utterly inconsistent with the constitutional prerogatives and duties of Congress.

The question, then, turns upon the authority which section 3 of the [NIRA] vests in the President to approve or prescribe. * * * [NIRA's] restrictions leave virtually untouched the field of policy envisaged by section 1, and, in that wide field of legislative possibilities, the proponents of a code, refraining from monopolistic designs, may roam at will, and the President may approve or disapprove their proposals as he may see fit. * * *
* * * *

Such a sweeping delegation of legislative power finds no support in the decisions upon which the government especially relies. * * *
* * * *

To summarize and conclude * * * : Section 3 of the [NIRA] is without precedent. It supplies no standards for any trade, industry, or activity. It does not undertake to prescribe rules of conduct to be applied to particular states of fact determined by appropriate administrative procedure. Instead of prescribing rules of conduct, it authorizes the making of codes to prescribe them. For that legislative undertaking, section 3 sets up no standards, aside from the statement of the general aims of rehabilitation, correction, and expansion described in section 1. In view of the scope of that broad declaration and of the nature of the few restrictions that are imposed, the discretion of the President in approving or prescribing codes, and thus enacting laws for the government of trade and industry throughout the country, is virtually unfettered. We think that the code-making authority thus conferred is an unconstitutional delegation of legislative power.

The Supreme Court declared that the code system of the NIRA was unconstitutional because adequate standards were not provided and that, therefore, the Schechters could not be found liable for violations of the poultry code.

DECISION AND REMEDY

■ The Creation of Regulatory Agencies

To create an administrative agency, Congress passes **enabling legislation,** which specifies the name, composition, and powers of the agency being created. The Federal Trade Commission (FTC), for example, was created in 1914 by the Federal Trade Commission Act.[2] The act prohibits unfair and deceptive trade practices. It also describes the procedures the agency must follow to charge persons or organizations with violations of the act, and it provides for judicial review of agency orders. Other portions of the act grant the agency powers to "make rules and regulations for the purpose of carrying out the Act," to conduct investigations of business practices, to obtain reports from interstate corporations concerning their business practices, to investigate possible violations of federal antitrust statutes,[3] to publish findings of its investigations, and to recommend new legislation. The act also empowers the FTC to hold trial-like hearings and to adjudicate certain kinds of trade disputes that involve FTC regulations or federal antitrust laws. Notice that, as described earlier with regard to agencies in general, the

---

2. 15 U.S.C. Sections 45 *et seq.*

3. The FTC shares this task with the Antitrust Division of the U.S. Department of Justice.

FTC's grant of power incorporates functions associated with the legislature (*rulemaking*), the courts *(adjudication)*, and the executive branch (*investigation* and *prosecution*).

◼ The Operation of Administrative Agencies

The three operations—enforcement, rulemaking, and adjudication—make up the basic functions of most administrative agencies. Taken together, and supplemented by broad investigative powers, these three functions constitute what may be termed the **administrative process.**

Combining these functions into a single governmental entity creates the institutional flexibility that provides the salient rationale for creating any administrative agency; but it also concentrates considerable power in a single organization, however. For example, the Securities and Exchange Commission imposes rules regarding what disclosures must be made in a stock prospectus; under its enforcement authority, it also prosecutes alleged violations of these regulations; and finally, it sits as judge and jury in deciding whether its rules have been violated, and if so, what punishment to impose on the offender. Given this concentration of authority, one major policy objective of administrative law is to control the risks of bureaucratic arbitrariness and overreaching without hampering the effective use of agency power to deal with a particular problem area.

The two broad categories of control over the administrative process are (1) judicial control exercised through the courts' review of administrative agency actions and (2) political controls exercised by Congress and the executive branch. The other significant limitation to agency power is found in the Administrative Procedure Act (APA),[4] which imposes procedural requirements on an agency formulating policy under its rulemaking authority[5] or adjudicating the application of general statutory commands or established rules in a formal hearing.[6] The APA is such an integral part of the administrative process that its application

will be examined as we go through the various functions carried out by an administrative agency.

Other legal restraints found in the U.S. Constitution and recognizable from earlier chapters are also applicable and will be examined in this section. The broad controls exercised by the legislature, the judiciary, and the executive branch will be reserved for a subsequent section. Note, however, that most of the legal challenges to agency action discussed in this section are those that are usually brought before an independent court for review. It also should be noted that the APA does not apply to all aspects of the administrative process, but rather only to those that are characterized as being formal in nature—a distinction that will be made clear later. The bulk of administrative decisions, however, are made informally, and to these actions, the provisions of the APA do not apply directly.

Enforcement

The enforcement function of an administrative agency has two aspects. An agency has investigative powers and prosecutorial powers.

COLLECTING FACTS—THE INVESTIGATIVE POWER   Virtually every aspect of the administrative process requires that agencies obtain a wide array of information concerning the activities and organizations that they are charged with overseeing. Agencies, for example, frequently hold hearings before drafting new regulations and thus must have knowledge of facts and circumstances pertinent to the proposed rules. Agencies must obtain information and investigate conduct to ascertain whether the enabling statute or the agency's rules are being violated.

Sometimes the information needed may be provided voluntarily by an interested source such as a public interest group, a dissatisfied consumer, or a disgruntled competitor. When necessary information is not readily available, however, agencies have been accorded wide latitude in compelling its disclosure. The two most important investigative tools available to an administrative agency are **subpoenas** and **searches and seizures.**

Subpoenas   There are two basic types of subpoenas: the subpoena *duces tecum* and the subpoena *ad testificandum.* The subpoena *duces*

---

4.   5 U.S.C. Sections 551–706.
5.   5 U.S.C. Section 553.
6.   5 U.S.C. Section 554.

tecum may be used in any investigation. It is a writ, or order, compelling an individual or organization to hand over specified books, papers, records, or documents. The subpoena *ad testificandum* may be issued as part of an agency's adjudicative function. An *ad testificandum* subpoena compels a witness to appear before an *administrative law judge* in a controversy involving an administrative agency.

Searches and Seizures   Many agencies gather information through on-site inspections. Sometimes a search of a home, an office, or a factory is the only means of obtaining evidence needed to prove a regulatory violation. At other times, physical inspections or testing are used in place of a formal hearing to correct or prevent an undesirable condition. Inspection and testing cover a wide range of activities, including safety inspections of underground coal mines, safety tests of commercial equipment and automobiles, and environmental monitoring of factory emissions.

CHALLENGES TO AGENCY INVESTIGATIVE POWERS—LEGAL REQUIREMENTS   The intrusive nature of an agency's investigatory actions brings into play several legal safeguards against agency abuse in exercising its investigatory powers.

Legal Authorization and Legitimate Purpose First, Section 555(c) of the APA incorporates the general principle that an agency can exercise only such powers as have been delegated to it by Congress. Thus an agency's power to conduct a particular investigation must be based in some way on the powers conferred on the agency by the enabling legislation creating the agency. Generally, this limitation is easy to satisfy in practice, because the grant of regulatory power and investigative authority is usually drafted in broad terms by the legislature. The limitation is also easy to satisfy due to the fact that courts usually decide to let an investigation proceed because a possibly injured party will have the opportunity to challenge the investigation when and if the party challenges a final agency action. More likely to be scrutinized is an investigation that appears to have no legitimate purpose, or that appears to have been pursued for an improper purpose, such as harassment.

Information Sought Must Be Relevant   The Fourth Amendment also provides a limitation on an agency's investigatory powers. Even if the investigation is carried out with legal authorization and for a legitimate purpose, any information sought must be relevant to that purpose. An investigating agency, however, does not need to meet the traditional "probable cause" standard in obtaining an administrative subpoena; rather than needing a good faith belief that a violation has occurred, the agency's investigation is justifiable "merely on suspicion that the law is being violated, or even just because it wants assurance that it is not." [7] This is a lesser standard, more akin to the standard applied to the investigative powers of a grand jury.

Investigative Demands Must Be Specific and Not Unreasonably Burdensome   The Fourth Amendment stricture on unreasonable searches and seizures is also a barrier to abuse of agency investigative powers. But it, too, has been modified in the context of the administrative process. The United States Supreme Court has held that, although an administrative subpoena must adequately describe the material sought, "the sufficiency of the specifications is variable in relation to the nature, purposes, and scope of [the agency's] inquiry." [8] Although claims of unreasonable burden are often raised, seldom are they successful, despite the substantial costs of assembling and copying materials, the disruption to an organization or individual's business activities, and the like. Through the use of protective court orders and other procedural devices, however, a business generally will be protected from the dissemination of proprietary information and trade secrets.

Privileged Information May Be Protected   The common law recognized certain communications, such as those between husband and wife and between lawyer and client, as being privileged. There has also been a trend, at least at the state level, to extend the protection to other types of commu-

---

7.   *United States. v. Morton Salt Co.,* 338 U.S. 632, 70 S.Ct. 357, 94 L.Ed. 401 (1950).
8.   *Oklahoma Press Publishing Co. v. Walling,* 327 U.S. 186, 66 S.Ct. 494, 90 L.Ed. 614 (1946).

nications, such as protecting accountant-client communications and news reporters' confidential sources. These protections, however, have seldom been tested in connection with administrative agency investigations, and it is unclear how and to what extent they apply in the administrative law context. One problem is that there is no general federal law governing the application of protections not directly derived from the U.S. Constitution. Another problem is that enabling legislation and agency regulations seldom address these questions.

The Privilege against Self-Incrimination   More substantial than the preceding privileges is the protection against compelled, self-incriminating testimony afforded by the Fifth Amendment. This too is limited in the context of the administrative process. First, with some limitation, an agency has fairly broad power to require that certain records be kept by an individual or organization and that the records be made available to the agency on demand as part of a regulatory program. Second, the privilege against self-incrimination is available only to the person asserting it; it cannot be asserted on behalf of another individual or an organization.[9] The privilege can be lost if the person asserting it is given immunity from prosecution based on evidence obtained solely from that individual's testimony. Finally, and perhaps most important in the context of administrative law, the privilege is only available if the penalty that might be imposed on the individual as a result of the testimony is criminal rather than civil in nature. For many regulatory regimes, the sanctions imposed for violations of administrative regulations are termed "civil penalties" or "forfeitures." Only those sanctions that are designed to effect some retribution or promote deterrence are likely to be deemed criminal penalties.

The Warrant Requirement   The Fourth Amendment protects against unreasonable searches and seizures by requiring that, in most instances, a physical search for evidence must be conducted under the authority of a warrant. Although it was once thought that administrative inspections were exempt from the warrant requirement, the United States Supreme Court, noting the anomaly of affording protection only in cases of suspected criminal activity, has held that the requirement does apply to the administrative process.

With regard to administrative searches, as in other areas of administrative law, however, the standard principles have been significantly modified. First, the standard of probable cause is different: "it may be based not only on specific evidence of an existing violation *but also on a showing that 'reasonable legislative or administrative standards for conducting an . . . inspection are satisfied with respect to a particular [establishment].' "*[10] [Emphasis added.]

Second, although the United States Supreme Court has recognized a legitimate expectation of privacy in commercial, as well as private, dwellings, it has continued to allow warrantless searches of commercial premises that are part of a "pervasively regulated" industry, provided that (1) there is a substantial government interest in the regulatory scheme under which the search is conducted, (2) a warrantless scheme is necessary to further that regulatory scheme, and (3) the terms of the search program are defined so as to limit the risk that inspectors will abuse their discretion in conducting the search.

The "open field" doctrine is also applicable to administrative searches. It provides an exception to the warrant requirement by allowing searches of areas so open to plain view that no reasonable expectation of privacy could be entertained. In a recent case, the Environmental Protection Agency (EPA), when denied access to make a ground inspection, took an aerial photograph of a Dow Chemical plant without Dow's permission. When Dow brought suit against the EPA, alleging a violation of the Fourth Amendment, the Supreme Court upheld the search under the "open field" doctrine.[11]

In the following case, the court considers the extent of an agency's investigative powers.

---

9.   A corporation is not a "person" for purposes of the self-incrimination provision of the Fifth Amendment.

10.   *Marshall v. Barlow's, Inc.*, 436 U.S. 307, 98 S.Ct. 1816, 56 L.Ed.2d 305 (1978).

11.   *Dow Chemical Co. v. United States*, 476 U.S. 227, 106 S.Ct. 1819, 90 L.Ed.2d 226 (1986).

BACKGROUND AND FACTS *The Federal Home Loan Bank Board (FHLBB) is an independent federal agency that operated the Federal Savings and Loan Insurance Corporation (FSLIC). The agency's regulatory duties included examining all FSLIC-insured institutions to determine whether they were being operated properly under applicable laws and regulations. As part of an investigation of Texas-based Vision Banc Savings and Loan, the FHLBB became suspicious of several large loans made by Vision Banc, including one made to Sandsend Financial Consultants, Ltd. Hoping to trace the proceeds of the loans, the FHLBB subpoenaed Sandsend's financial records from a second bank, West Belt. Sandsend requested that the federal district court quash the subpoena. For reasons not fully articulated, the district court judge did quash the subpoena. The FHLBB appealed the decision. Although the government's ability to subpoena bank records is circumscribed by procedures of the Right to Financial Privacy Act, the central issue before the appellate court was the scope of the FHLBB's investigatory authority.*

Case 6.2

SANDSEND FINANCIAL CONSULTANTS, LTD. v. FEDERAL HOME LOAN BANK BOARD
United States Court of Appeals, Fifth Circuit, 1989.
878 F.2d 875.

GEE, Circuit Judge.
        * * * *

The inquiry that the FHLBB is authorized to make is not whether Sandsend has violated the law, but whether Vision Banc has done so. It is undisputed that the FHLBB's examination of Vision Banc is a legitimate law enforcement inquiry. Sandsend's records may facilitate that inquiry. Properly framed, the threshold issue is whether, pursuant to a legitimate law enforcement inquiry, the FHLBB may subpoena a bank customer's records if neither the bank [West Belt] nor the customer is directly associated with the target of the FHLBB's inquiry. *   *   *

The FHLBB's subpoena power extends to Sandsend's financial records; it is not limited to parties directly associated with the target of an investigation. Although this case presents a question of first impression, we are not without guidance. At the outset we note two important principles that inform our inquiry: First, an administrative agency's power to issue subpoenas is a broad-ranging one which courts are reluctant to trammel. *   *   * Second, when reviewing an administrative subpoena, the court plays a "strictly limited" role. The court's inquiry is limited to two questions: (1) whether the investigation is for a proper statutory purpose and (2) whether the documents the agency seeks are relevant to the investigation. *   *   *

[The court examined the language and legislative history of 12 U.S.C. Section 1730(m)(1), (2) and compared it to the statutory authority conferred on the Federal Deposit Insurance Corporation and that of federal bank examiners.]

We find no basis in the record for quashing the subpoena. First, it is undisputed that the FHLBB's examination of Vision Banc is a legitimate law enforcement inquiry. Second, Sandsend's records are relevant to the FHLBB's inquiry. For purposes of an administrative subpoena, the notion of relevancy is a broad one. An agency "can investigate merely on the suspicion that the law is being violated, or even just because it wants assurance that it is not." So long as the material requested "touches a matter under investigation," an administrative subpoena will survive a challenge that the material is not relevant. Certainly, Sandsend has only a tangential relationship to Vision Banc, the target of the investigation. But the FHLBB suspects that Sandsend is part of a scheme to defraud Vision Banc or to misuse Vision Banc's funds. To investigate this suspicion, the FHLBB is tracing Vision Banc's proceeds through several transactions, including the transactions by which the funds ended up in Sandsend's West Belt account. Sandsend may have only a loose connection with

Vision Banc. Its financial records, however, touch on a matter under investigation and, thus, are relevant to the FHLBB's examination.

The appellate court reversed the district court's decision and directed the district court to enforce the FHLBB's subpoena.

CORRECTING VIOLATIONS—THE PROSECUTORIAL POWERS Having undertaken and concluded an investigation, an agency may bring an administrative action against an individual or organization by issuing a **complaint**, the first step in an administrative action. Complaints also are brought by private citizens and organizations, but are prosecuted by the agency having authority over the particular subject matter. Because the agency is acting as prosecutor, judge, and jury, certain procedural devices have been devised to safeguard against an agency's abuse of authority. These will be discussed in the subsequent subsection on adjudication. At this juncture, nonetheless, it is useful to note that the majority of such actions are resolved at their initial stage, without resorting to the formal adjudicatory process. The fact that regulated industries often want to avoid the appearance of being uncooperative with the regulating agency, the fact that regulators are likely to have acquired pertinent information over a prolonged period of regulation, and the cost of litigation make settlement an appealing option to firms. Because settlements also conserve agency resources, agencies devote a great deal of effort to advising and negotiating so as to avoid formal actions.[12]

Rulemaking

The second major function of an administrative agency is the formulation of new regulations—the so-called **rulemaking** function. The power an agency has to make rules is conferred on it by Congress in the agency's enabling legislation. Enabling legislation is almost always written in very broad terms, but Congress is constitutionally limited in how much power to promulgate regulations

it can delegate to an agency. The standards that are applied in testing whether or not a delegation is too broad to meet constitutional demands have changed over the years from being rather slight initially to being very stringent during the early 1930s and then progressively becoming less stringent again. The most demanding standard was the one applied in the famous "Sick Chicken Case," *Schechter Poultry Corp. v. United States.*[13] Another principle is worth mentioning at this point. Only Congress can establish that certain violations of agency regulations will incur criminal sanctions; it cannot delegate the authority to the agency to decide which regulations will be treated as criminal offenses.

One of the most significant developments in administrative law since the 1970s has been the increased importance of agency rulemaking as a means of formulating public policy. The major advantage of rulemaking is that it can resolve in one proceeding issues that might remain unsettled for years if case-by-case adjudication were the only means of effecting agency policy.

TYPES OF AGENCY RULES There are three types of rules that an agency may create: (1) *legislative rules,* (2) *interpretative rules,* and (3) *procedural rules.*

Legislative Rules **Legislative rules** carry the same weight as congressionally enacted statutes. Their validity, though, depends on certain strict requirements being met. First, a legislative rule will be struck down by the courts if it violates any provision of the U.S. Constitution (for example, if it violates due process or denies equal protection). Second, the rule must not involve an impermissible delegation of legislative authority to the agency; that is, there are certain powers that the U.S. Constitution grants exclusively to Congress and that cannot be delegated by Congress to the judiciary

---

12. One way in which an agency advises on questions of how it interprets a statute and how it will respond to certain actions by private parties is through issuing "interpretative rules." See the discussion of interpretative rules in the subsection on rulemaking below. See also the subsection on the adjudication process.

13. 295 U.S. 495, 55 S.Ct. 837, 79 L.Ed. 1570.

or executive branch of government or to an independent agency. Third, the rule must not operate in a way that exceeds the power conferred on the agency by its enabling legislation. Also important is that the enabling statute itself provide reasonable standards to guide the agency in carrying out its administrative tasks. Finally, unless Congress expressly provides an exemption, legislative rules enacted must be promulgated in accordance with provisions of the APA.

The other two types of agency rules, interpretative and procedural rules, need not be enacted in accordance with the provisions of the APA. Nor do they carry the same force as legislative rules, which, as already noted, carry the same weight as a statutory rule of law enacted by the legislature.

Interpretative Rules   **Interpretative rules** are simply statements and opinions issued by an agency explaining how the agency interprets and intends to apply the statutes it enforces. Such an opinion might be rendered by the Securities and Exchange Commission, for example, about whether a particular security is subject to its registration requirements and, if so, what information must be disclosed in a public offering. Because interpretative rules do not have the force of rules of law, they are not automatically binding on private individuals or organizations. They also are not binding on the courts in the way that rules of law are. In practice, however, the courts tend to give considerable weight to interpretative rules when deciding cases involving other agency regulations.

Procedural Rules   **Procedural rules** describe an agency's methods of operation and establish procedures for dealings with the agency in and through hearings, negotiations, settlements, presentation of evidence, and other activities.

THE RULEMAKING PROCESS   As the number and significance of policy objectives carried out through legislative rules have grown, so too have the rulemaking procedures that must be followed. Under the APA, there are three types of agency rulemaking procedures: (1) *"notice-and-comment" rulemaking,* or *informal rulemaking;* (2) *"rulemaking-on-a-record,"* or *formal rulemaking;* and (3) *exempted rulemaking.*[14] The third

is of limited applicability and applies in special circumstances such as military matters or foreign affairs; thus, it will not be discussed here. Dissatisfaction with aspects of both informal and formal types of procedures has been the impetus for the development of another type of procedural form called *hybrid rulemaking* which is not covered by provisions of the APA.

Notice-and-Comment Rulemaking   **Notice-and-comment rulemaking,** also characterized as informal rulemaking, is the most common type. Although termed informal, it is nonetheless governed by the provisions of the APA. There are three requirements imposed by the APA: (1) notice, (2) opportunity for comment, and (3) a general statement of basis and purpose. These requirements parallel the sequence of events that must occur before a rule is adopted. The informal process begins with publication of a **Notice of Proposed Rulemaking** in the *Federal Register.* The notice must state the time and place for which agency proceedings on the proposed rule will be held, as well as a description of the nature of the proceedings. The notice also must state the legal authority for the proceedings, which is usually the agency's enabling legislation. Finally, the notice must either state the terms of the proposed rule or the subject matter of the proposed rule.

Publication of notice of the proposed rule is followed by a **comment period.** The purpose of publication of notice is to allow private parties to comment in writing on the agency proposal in an effort to influence agency policy. After having received and reviewed the comments, the agency takes them into account in drafting the regulation's final version, which is usually modified from the proposed rule. If the final version of the regulation is dramatically different, it must be reproposed. The agency publishes the final version of the regulation in the *Federal Register.* The regulation does not become binding until at least thirty days after final publication unless there is "good cause" for its becoming effective sooner. There is also an exemption to the notice requirement whenever such is unnecessary, impractical, or contrary to the public's interest.

Rulemaking-on-a-Record   **Rulemaking-on-a-record,** or formal rulemaking, also begins with publication of a notice of proposed rulemaking in

_____
14.   5 U.S.C. Section 533.

the *Federal Register*. In this procedure, though, the announced proceedings are much more extensive, amounting to a public hearing and being conducted in the manner of a trial. At the hearing, the agency presents evidence intended to justify the proposed rule. Anyone opposing the proposed rule may present evidence to counter the agency's claims. Both sides are permitted to examine the evidence presented and to cross-examine each other's witnesses. After the hearing is concluded, the agency is required to prepare a formal written statement describing its findings based on the evidence presented by both sides.

Hybrid Rulemaking   Informal and formal rulemaking both offer special advantages, but each also has distinct disadvantages. Informal rulemaking is efficient in its simplicity. Yet its streamlined procedures afford little opportunity to interested parties to learn and contest the basis of a proposed legislative rule. Formal rulemaking, although providing ample opportunity to interested parties to participate in the formulation of agency rules, is torturously slow in producing public policy responses to pressing problems. A famous example is that of the Food and Drug Administration's attempts to establish a rule setting the minimum peanut content for peanut butter. The agency attempted to set the minimum at 90 percent. When industry countered with a proposal of 87 percent, it produced a series of formal proceedings that delayed regulation for nearly ten years.

As rulemaking became an increasingly important part of agency decision making, and as frustration over the shortcomings of APA procedures increased, the courts and later the legislature began a search for alternatives. The result has been a set of ill-defined procedures referred to as **hybrid rulemaking**. These procedures incorporate advantages of both the formal and informal procedures. Like formal rulemaking, there is an opportunity for direct participation through a public hearing. The right of interested parties to cross-examine witnesses is much more restricted, however. Also, as we will see in the subsection on judicial review, the standard applied by an independent court in reviewing an agency's procedures is different.

Adjudication

As noted already, an agency not only sets the rules pursuant to its enabling statute but also enforces

its own rules through its investigatory powers. Moreover, its enforcement entails prosecuting alleged offenders of agency rules in trial-like proceedings before an **administrative law judge (ALJ)** or, in some instances, before the appointed heads of the agency, its board of commissioners. Thus the agency acts as police officer, prosecutor, judge, and jury in agency **adjudication.**

ADMINISTRATIVE LAW JUDGES   Formally, an ALJ is a member of the very agency prosecuting the case. Certain safeguards exist, however, to promote fairness in the proceedings. The ALJ is separated in the agency's organization from the investigative and prosecutorial staff, according to provisions of the APA. The APA also prohibits private communication (*ex parte*) between the ALJ and anyone who is party to an agency proceeding. Finally, provisions of the APA protect the ALJ from agency discipline except on a clear showing of good cause for such action.

THE PROCESS OF ADJUDICATION   After conducting its own investigation of a suspected rule violation, an agency may decide to take action against specific parties. In some cases (for example, FTC action on alleged false advertising), an agency's actions may be prompted by private individuals or interest groups. Procedures vary among the various agencies, but a typical scenario of adjudication might proceed as follows. (This process is illustrated in Exhibit 6–1.)

The initial investigatory phase might involve taking statements under oath by one of the agency's staff attorneys. (To promote fairness, an agency's investigative and prosecutorial staff is formally separate from the members of its commission. In fact, if these members were to take a prosecutorial role at this stage, they would likely be disqualified from ruling on the case at a later stage.) Alternatively, the agency might request documents or records of some kind. In most instances, the agency's requests are enforceable by an order from a federal court ordering that a party comply with the agency's request; failure to comply with the court order can result in fines or even jail sentences for contempt of court.

During this phase of the process, the agency may make an offer to negotiate and reach some settlement, or agreement, concerning the action with which the agency is concerned. If no settle-

■ **Exhibit 6–1 The Process of Administrative Adjudication**

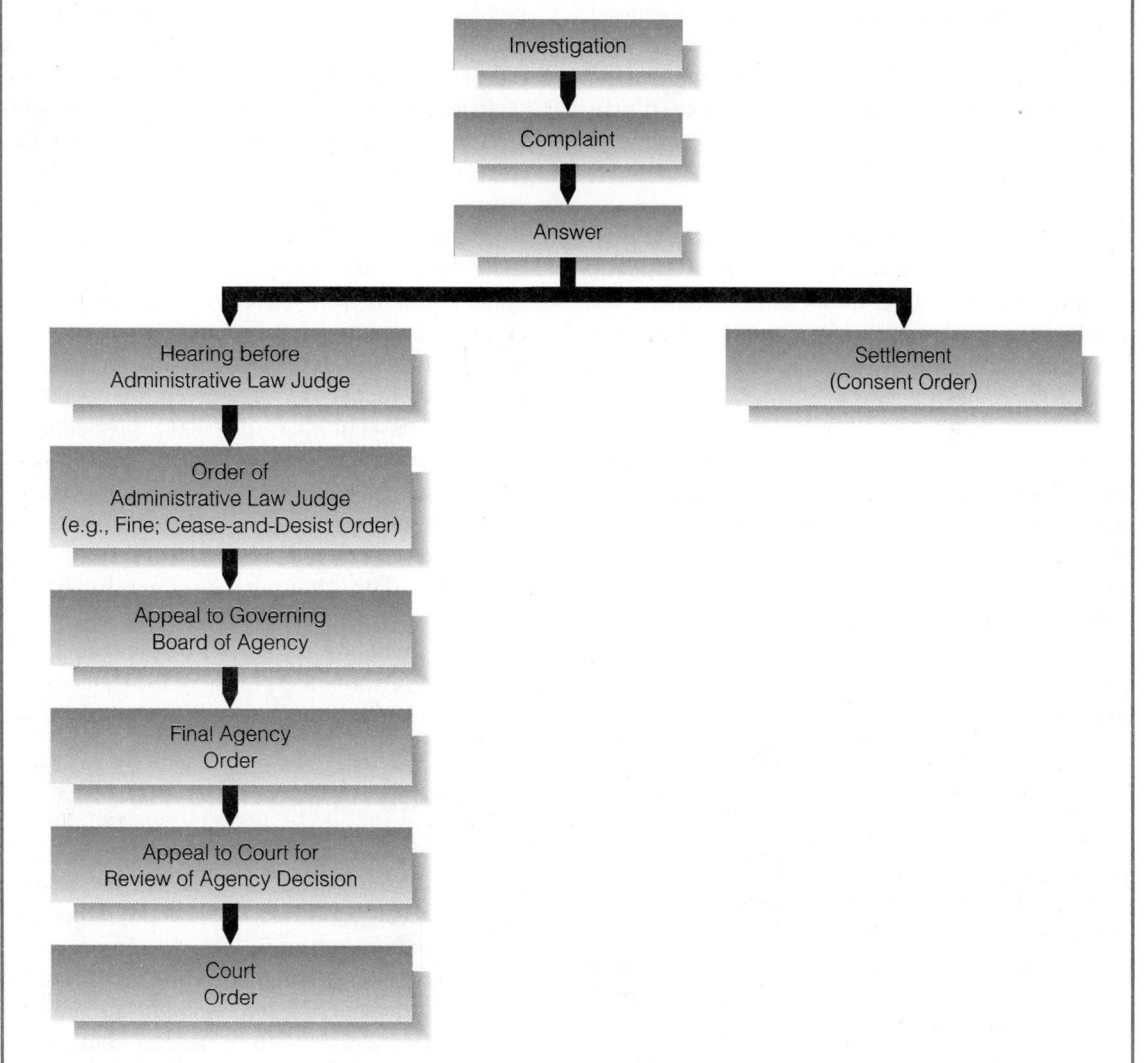

ment between the agency and the parties under investigation is reached, then the agency staff could seek approval of the agency head or commissioners to issue a formal complaint. The complaint is issued as a public document and may be accompanied by a press release. The party charged in the complaint responds by filing an answer. The case then is presented before an ALJ in an administrative hearing.

The Administrative Hearing An administrative adjudication is very much like that of an ordinary trial court proceeding. The charged party may be represented by counsel, cross-examine agency witnesses, and present its own evidence to counter the

agency's. There are important differences, however. Significantly, the ALJ decides both questions of law and fact; there is no jury. Also important is the nature of the evidence: it may be evidence of general circumstances rather than relating solely to the charged party. The ALJ, cognizant of the role that the agency's adjudicative function plays in determining the broader aspects of agency policy, takes into consideration the impact of any decision on the public interest and not just its effect on the individual parties involved in the case.

Initial Order After the case is concluded, the ALJ renders an **initial order.** Either side may appeal the ALJ's initial order. An appeal is usually taken to a federal circuit court, though some intermediate decisions may be appealed to a federal district court. It is also possible in some cases that the commission that governs the agency will decide on its own to review the case. If it does so, it may consider all aspects of the case freshly, as though no prior decisions had been rendered.

Final Order   If no appeal is taken, or if the case is not reviewed or considered anew by the agency commission, the ALJ's initial order becomes the **final order** of the agency. Otherwise, the final order must come from the commission's decision or that of the reviewing court.

Cease-and-Desist Orders   The final order may compel the charged party to pay damages, or it may forbid the party from carrying on some specified activity. The latter is referred to as a **cease-and-desist order** and in effect is identical to an ordinary court's injunction.

■ Control over Administrative Agencies

Agency authority is held in check by several sources of limitation. Some of these we have already encountered. The U.S. Constitution limits agency authority, and the APA significantly affects the formal administrative process. Additionally, the source of agency authority, the enabling legislation of the agency, is by implication a source of limitation as well.

There remains, however, the task of looking at the broader scheme of control over agency power, that is, the political and judicial control over agency power. Political control over agency power is found in both the executive and legislative branches of government. Judicial control is exercised by the independent review of agency action by the United States Supreme Court, the federal courts of appeal, and in more limited instances, the federal district courts.

Executive Control

Executive control over agency power is exercised through several means. First, the president may exercise veto power over any enabling legislation

or subsequent modifications to agency authority that Congress may seek to enact. Another important power over agency affairs is the president's authority to appoint and remove federal officers. In theory, this power is less pronounced in the case of independent agencies whose officers serve for fixed terms and who cannot be removed without just cause. In practice, however, the president's power to exert influence over independent agencies is often considerable.

Typically, agencies that are headed by a set of commissioners have the commissioners' terms of appointment staggered. Because many commissioners do not serve out their full terms, newly elected presidents often are given the opportunity to appoint new commissioners. Moreover, the president generally has the statutory power to designate who among the commissioners will serve as chairperson; a new appointment demotes a sitting commission chairperson to the status of ordinary commissioner. The chairperson generally has the primary responsibility for managing agency operations, including the hiring of personnel. Thus this power affords the president a means of indirectly influencing the policies of an independent agency.

Legislative Control

As Congress gives power to an agency, so too, through subsequent legislation, can it take away power or even abolish an agency altogether. Congress has often moved quickly to counter agency decisions that have inflamed public ire. In the wake of public furor over a controversial National Highway Traffic Safety Administration seat belt requirement, for example, Congress amended the act creating the agency. The amendment prohibited the agency from instituting regulations requiring that cars not start unless the seat belts are fastened or that cars have a warning buzzer that sounds continuously until the seat belts are fastened. Congress's power of the purse (the constitutional taxing and spending powers) also gives it considerable power to influence agency policy. First, there must be legislative authorization for appropriation of government funds to a specific agency. This is usually contained in the enabling legislation and may set certain time and monetary limits for funding particular programs. Congress, of course, can always revise these limits.

In addition to the formal legislating and funding powers that Congress exercises, it has authority to investigate the implementation of its statutory laws and the agencies that it has created. It may also affect agency policy through its "casework" activities. This involves individual legislators' attempts to assist their constituents in dealings with agency staff and officers. Ostensibly, the legislator is performing the role of an "ombudsman" watching over the agency and helping to ensure that the agency treats his or her clients fairly. Performing this role also provides the legislator with an opportunity to identify problem areas that can be corrected through congressional action. There is a fine line, though, between what is considered proper casework and what is construed as an attempt to pressure an agency into making an improper decision in favor of a constituent.

Judicial Review

Through the political process, both the legislative and executive branches exercise considerable influence over the regulatory policies of administrative agencies. The courts, in deciding individual controversies rather than broad policy initiatives, also exercise a considerable amount of control over the regulatory process. The political process requires time and effort in building coalitions entertaining a uniform objective before action is likely to be effective. In contrast, the courts provide a direct avenue for the review of agency action. As will be seen, however, not all agency action is subject to judicial review, nor is every individual entitled to challenge an agency's actions.

THE SCOPE OF JUDICIAL REVIEW   The APA provides for judicial review of most agency action. In its exercise of control over agency actions, a court may compel agency action it deems to have been unlawfully withheld, or it may prevent action it determines to have exceeded agency authority. In reviewing administrative actions, the courts are reluctant to review questions of fact; in most cases, deference is given to the facts found in the initial agency proceeding. This stems partly from the general judicial attitude that those who hear and see the evidence presented firsthand are more suited to judge its value. In the context of administrative process, this attitude is reinforced by the courts'

deference to the expertise of the agency involved. The courts, however, will conduct a hearing to make an independent finding of facts, a *de novo review,* if (1) such a review is required by statute, (2) inadequate fact-finding proceedings were employed by the agency initially adjudicating the case, or (3) new facts are raised in a proceeding to enforce a nonadjudicatory action. Nor are courts generally interested in the merits of policy determinations; thus, review of policy issues is generally limited to ascertaining whether the agency is carrying out the will of Congress as enunciated in the enabling legislation. The court is primarily concerned with the legal issues raised in a controversy over agency actions. But here too there are limits to the scope of its review.

DEFENSES TO AGENCY ENFORCEMENT   Often it is not a defense to an agency action that an individual or organization believes the action to be unlawful. In some cases an intermediate appeal to avoid irreparable harm from delay may be taken to avoid agency action. In other cases, however, the only course available is not to comply and then seek judicial review of the agency's enforcement. The following are the bases to any defense of agency action. The court will review (1) whether the agency has exceeded the authority conferred by the agency's enabling legislation; (2) whether the agency has properly interpreted laws applicable to the agency action under review; (3) whether the agency has violated any constitutional provisions; (4) whether the agency has acted in accordance with procedural requirements of the law; (5) whether the agency's actions were arbitrary, capricious, or an abuse of discretion; and (6) whether any conclusions drawn by the agency are not supported by substantial evidence.

CONDITIONS TO REVIEW OF ENFORCEMENT ACTION   Agency enforcement actions are not automatically subject to review. Parties seeking to have an action reviewed must satisfy several preliminary requirements.

Reviewability   First, the challenger, or plaintiff, must show that the action is of a nature that is reviewable. This is generally quite easy in that the APA creates a presumption in favor of reviewability. To overcome the statutory presumption, the opponent must be able to show either that Congress has enacted a statute that precludes review, thus negating the APA presumption, or that the agency's action is committed to agency discretion as a matter of law. The latter is often difficult to show even apart from the APA because the functioning of the three equal branches of government generally implies the authority of judicial review. Congress does have authority, however, to establish the scope of jurisdiction of the federal courts. Moreover, the judiciary is deferential to the proper functions of the other branches of government. For example, problems of a strictly political nature or involving foreign affairs are generally viewed as being outside the proper scope of judicial review.

Standing   A second requirement for review is that the challenging party have "standing to sue." Challengers must have a direct stake in the outcome of the judicial proceeding by showing their interests have been substantially affected by the agency's action. This requirement, though perhaps not quite as easy to meet as the first requirement, has become more liberalized in recent years. The injury suffered must be to an interest within the range of interests protected by the statute or constitutional provision that provides the basis of the challenge. An injury to an economic interest, or even in some cases to an emotional, environmental, or aesthetic interest, is sufficient to show standing to sue.

Exhaustion of Available Remedies   Courts are reluctant to interfere with the regulatory process, hoping to allow the agencies to correct their own mistakes and to develop fully the regulatory scheme before subjecting the scheme to independent judicial review. Courts, therefore, will not generally review an action until the challenging party has exhausted all possible alternative means of resolving the controversy with the agency.

Ripeness   The final requirement for review is that an actual case or controversy be at issue. This requirement is based on Article III, Section 2, of the U.S. Constitution, which, as interpreted by the United States Supreme Court, prohibits advisory opinions. When considering whether a dispute meets this requirement, courts have been willing to weigh the benefits of allowing time to refine the controversy against the harm of delaying review.

THE STANDARD OF REVIEW   There are two standards of review. Which one is applied depends on whether the procedure under review is a formal agency adjudication or rulemaking, or an informal agency adjudication or rulemaking.

Substantial Evidence Test   In reviewing formal agency adjudications or rulemaking, courts, under the APA, must apply the "substantial evidence" test. Under this test, only those findings that are unsupported by substantial evidence may be overturned. In applying this test, the reviewing courts determine the reasonableness of the challenged agency action as juxtaposed with the facts before the court that could be used to justify the action. Note that this is a different exercise than the *de novo* review described above.

Arbitrary and Capricious Test   A different standard of review is applied with regard to informal agency adjudications and rulemaking. It is the "arbitrary and capricious" test and is the least rigorous standard of judicial review. In applying the test, the court seeks to avoid substituting its judgment for that of the agency's, seeking instead to look for merely an adequate factual basis for the agency's action. Unless the court can point to a "clear error of judgment," it will not strike down the agency's decision. The following case involved an application of the arbitrary and capricious test.

Case 6.3

MARSH v. OREGON NATURAL RESOURCES COUNCIL
Supreme Court of the United States, 1989.
490 U.S. 360,
109 S.Ct. 1851,
104 L.Ed.2d 377.

BACKGROUND AND FACTS   *Four nonprofit organizations brought suit against the Army Corps of Engineers. The organizations claimed that the Corps had violated the National Environmental Policy Act (NEPA) of 1969 by failing to prepare a supplemental environmental impact statement (EIS) based on information contained in two studies—an Oregon Department of Fish and Wildlife (ODFW) memorandum and a U.S. Soil Conservation Service (SCS) survey—regarding a three-dam project that the Corps had begun along Oregon's Rogue River basin. The Corps contended that the EIS was unnecessary; the Corps claimed that on the basis of its own*

*analysis, as well as that of independent research commissioned by the
Corps, the two studies were not indisputable and in any event were of
exaggerated importance in assessing the project. A federal district court
denied the organizations' request that the Corps be enjoined from completing the project. On appeal, the appellate court affirmed part of the
district court's decision, reversed part of the decision, and remanded the
case to the district court. The Corps petitioned for* certiorari, *which was
granted.*

Justice *STEVENS* delivered the opinion of the Court.
    *   *   *   *

The parties disagree *   *   * on the standard that should be applied by a court
that is asked to review the agency's decision. The Government argues that the reviewing court need only decide whether the agency decision was "arbitrary and
capricious," whereas respondents argue that the reviewing court must make its own
determination of reasonableness to ascertain whether the agency action complied
with the law. In determining the proper standard of review we look to *   *   * the
Administrative Procedure Act (APA), 5 U.S.C. [Section] 706, which empowers
federal courts to "hold unlawful and set aside agency action, findings, and conclusions" if they fail to conform with any of six specified standards. We conclude that
review of the narrow question before us of whether the Corps' determination that
the FEISS [Final Environmental Impact Statement Supplement] need not be supplemented should be set aside is controlled by the "arbitrary and capricious standard"
of [Section] 706(2)(A).
    *   *   *   *

The question presented for review in this case is a classic example of a factual
dispute the resolution of which implicates substantial agency expertise. Respondents'
claim that the Corps' decision not to file a second supplemental EIS should be set
aside primarily rests on the contentions that the new information undermines conclusions contained in the FEISS, that the conclusions contained in the ODFW memorandum and the SCS survey are accurate, and that the Corps' expert review of the
new information was incomplete, inconclusive, and inaccurate. *   *   * [R]esolution
of this dispute involves primarily issues of fact. Because analysis of the relevant
documents "requires a high level of technical expertise," we must defer to "the
informed discretion of the responsible federal agencies." ("When examining this
kind of scientific determination . . . a reviewing court must generally be at its most
deferential.") Under these circumstances, we cannot accept respondents' supposition
that review is of a legal question and that the Corps' decision "deserves no deference." Accordingly, as long as the Corps' decision not to supplement the FEISS
was not "arbitrary or capricious," it should not be set aside.
    *   *   * [I]n making the factual inquiry concerning whether an agency decision
was "arbitrary or capricious," the reviewing court "must consider whether the
decision was based on a consideration of the relevant factors and whether there has
been a clear error of judgment." This inquiry must "be searching and careful," but
"the ultimate standard of review is a narrow one." When specialists express conflicting views, an agency must have discretion to rely on the reasonable opinions of
its own qualified experts even if, as an original matter, a court might find contrary
views more persuasive. On the other hand, in the context of reviewing a decision
not to supplement an EIS, courts should not automatically defer to the agency's
express reliance on an interest in finality without carefully reviewing the record
and satisfying themselves that the agency has made a reasoned decision based on
its evaluation of the significance—or lack of significance—of the new
information. *   *   *

[The Court considered the new studies, as well as the opinion of agency experts and of independent experts regarding the new information, and concluded that there was no clear evidence that the agency opinion was erroneous.]

There is little doubt that if all of the information contained in the [OFDW] memorandum and the SCS survey was both new and accurate, the Corps would have been required to prepare a second supplemental EIS. It is also clear that, regardless of its eventual assessment of the significance of this information, the Corps had a duty to take a hard look at the proffered evidence. However, having done so and having determined based on scientific analysis that the new information was of exaggerated importance, the Corps acted within the dictates of NEPA in concluding that supplementation was unnecessary. Even if another decisionmaker might have reached a contrary result, it was surely not ''a clear error of judgment'' for the Corps to have found that the new and accurate information in the documents was not significant and that the significant information was not new and accurate. * * * [T]he Corps conducted a reasoned evaluation of the relevant information and reached a decision that, although perhaps disputable, was not ''arbitrary or capricious.''

DECISION AND REMEDY   *The Supreme Court reversed the appellate court's decision regarding the obligation to prepare a new EIS and remanded the case for further proceedings.*

■ Public Accountability

Over the last two decades, there has been a growing concern over the powers exercised by administrative agencies. As a result, Congress has passed several laws to make agencies more accountable through public scrutiny. The most significant of these laws are the Freedom of Information Act, the Government-in-the-Sunshine Act, and the Regulatory Flexibility Act.

Freedom of Information Act

Enacted in 1966, the Freedom of Information Act (FOIA) requires the federal government to disclose certain ''records'' to ''any person'' on request, even without that person's disclosing the reason for the request.[15] Although the FOIA exempts certain types of records, a request that complies with the FOIA procedures need only contain a reasonable description of the information sought. An agency's failure to comply with a request may be challenged in a federal district court.

The FOIA is utilized by the media, industry trade associations, public interest groups, and even companies seeking information about competitors.

Note that although the FOIA allows agencies to deny requests for exempted information, it does not compel them to do so, and a person cannot compel an agency to refuse disclosure of exempted information about that person.

Government-in-the-Sunshine Act

The Government-in-the-Sunshine Act, or ''open meeting law,'' was passed in 1976. It requires that ''every portion of every meeting of an agency'' that is headed by a ''collegial body'' must be open to ''public observation.''[16] The act also requires procedures to ensure that the public is provided with adequate advance notice of the agency's scheduled meeting and agenda. Like the FOIA, the Sunshine Act contains certain exceptions. There are exceptions that permit closed meetings when (1) the subject of the meeting concerns the accusing of any person of a crime, (2) open meetings would frustrate implementation of future agency actions, or (3) the subject of the meeting involves matters relating to future litigation or rulemaking. Courts interpret these exceptions strictly so as to allow open access whenever possible, as the following case illustrates.

---

15. 5 U.S.C. Section 552.

16. 5 U.S.C. Section 552(b).

BACKGROUND AND FACTS *During the late fall of 1989 the National Economic Commission (NEC) and the administrator of the General Services Administration sought to close upcoming January meetings of the NEC. In those meetings the NEC was to hear expert testimony and discuss economic issues confronting the nation, including "economic assumptions" regarding growth, inflation, interest rates, and unemployment, as well as "budget options," such as revenue sources and budget cuts. The NEC sought closure of all meetings at which these issues would be discussed, alleging fear that participants and witnesses would be inhibited from speaking candidly if the meetings were open to the public. The NEC also asserted a fear that information obtained at open meetings would lead to unwarranted speculation over future economic policy, which in turn might disrupt national markets. Public Citizen, a public-interest group, and others, including the* Washington Post *and the* Wall Street Journal, *sought to prevent the closure of the meetings.*

Case 6.4

PUBLIC CITIZEN v. NATIONAL ECONOMIC COMMISSION

United States District Court, District of Columbia, 1989. 703 F.Supp. 113.

JOYCE HENS GREEN, District Judge.

*   *   *   *

In [a previous case], the Nuclear Regulatory Commission sought to close a series of meetings to discuss preparation of the agency's annual budget request for fiscal year 1982, invoking exemption 9(B) of the Sunshine Act. The Court concluded that there "is no blanket exemption for agency meetings at any stage of the budget preparation process. The availability of exemptions for specific portions of budgetary discussions must be determined upon the facts of each case." The Court recognized that "specific items discussed at Commission budget meetings might be exempt from the open-meeting requirement of the Act, and might justify closing portions of the Commission meetings . . . ." However, [the Court] made it clear beyond any doubt that this could only be done "on an individual and particularized basis." Furthermore, the burden is on the party seeking to close the meeting to establish that the invoked exemption properly applies.

Defendants in the instant case are not seeking to close specific portions of the scheduled meetings on an "individual and particularized" basis. On the contrary, defendants wish to shield the internal debate from the public by closing, in their entirety, all working sessions of the [NEC]. They have not carried their burden of establishing that exemption 9(B) applies to all of the scheduled meetings of the [NEC].

*   *   *   *

*   *   * Rather than singling out discrete portions of some meetings on an individual and particularized basis with justification for such limited closure, defendants assert a sweeping and broad deliberative process privilege, shielding their internal debate and operation from the public. The legislative history of the Sunshine Act as well as the relevant case law prohibits this.

The district court permanently enjoined the NEC from closing its meetings.

DECISION AND REMEDY

Is it possible that the court's reliance on the previous case was misplaced? After all, the NEC was not discussing its, or any particular agency's, budget but rather was seeking to gain information about the nation's economic problems and the overall federal deficit. Moreover, the agency was not establishing policy but only seeking to set the stage for later congres-

COMMENTS

sional action by soliciting a number of independent views. If it were true that the witnesses and participants would be reticent in public meetings, was not closure necessary for the NEC to fulfill its apparent function?

Regulatory Flexibility Act

Concern over the effects of regulation on the efficiency of businesses, particularly smaller ones, led Congress to pass the Regulatory Flexibility Act in 1980. Under this act, whenever a new regulation will have a "significant impact upon a substantial number of small entities," the agency must conduct a regulatory flexibility analysis. The analysis must measure the cost imposed by the rule on small businesses and must consider less burdensome alternatives. The act also contains provisions to alert small businesses about forthcoming regulations. The act has relieved some record-keeping burdens for small businesses, especially with regard to hazardous waste management.

■ Terms and Concepts to Review

adjudication 132
administrative agencies 123
administrative law judge
  (ALJ) 132
administrative process 126
cease-and-desist order 134
comment period 131
complaint 130
enabling legislation 125

final order 134
hybrid rulemaking 132
independent regulatory
  agencies 124
initial order 133
interpretative rules 131
legislative rules 130
Notice of Proposed
  Rulemaking 131

notice-and-comment
  rulemaking 131
procedural rules 131
rulemaking 130
rulemaking-on-a-record 131
searches and seizures 126
subpoena 126

■ Questions and Case Problems

6-1. Assume that the Securities and Exchange Commission (SEC) has a policy not to enforce rules prohibiting insider trading except when the insiders make monetary profits for themselves. Then the SEC modifies this policy by a determination that the agency has the statutory authority to bring an enforcement action against an individual even if he or she does not personally profit from the insider trading. In modifying the policy, the SEC does not conduct a rulemaking but simply announces its new decision. A securities organization objects and says that the policy was unlawfully developed without opportunity for public comment. In a lawsuit challenging the new policy, should the policy be overruled under the Administrative Procedure Act? Discuss.

6-2. Assume that the Food and Drug Administration (FDA), using proper procedures, adopts a rule describing its future investigations. This new rule covers all future cases in which the FDA wants to regulate food additives. Under the new rule, the FDA says that it will not regulate food additives without giving food companies an opportunity to cross-examine witnesses. Some time later, the FDA wants to regulate methylisocyanate, a food additive. In doing so, the FDA conducts a normal notice-and-comment rulemaking, without cross-examination, and regulates methylisocyanate. Producers protest, saying that the FDA promised cross-examination. The FDA responds that the Administrative Procedure Act does not require such cross-examination and that its promise could simply be withdrawn. Discuss fully how the court should rule.

6-3. For decades, the Federal Trade Commission (FTC) resolved fair trade and advertising disputes through individual adjudications. In the 1960s, the FTC began promulgating rules that defined fair and unfair trade practices. In cases involving violations of these rules, the due process rights of participants were more limited and did not include cross-examination. This was because, although anyone found violating a rule would receive a full adjudication, the legitimacy of the rule itself could not be challenged in the adjudication. If a party had violated a rule, it was almost certain to lose the adjudication. Affected parties complained, arguing that their rights before the FTC were unduly limited by the new rules. Were the rules illegal? Explain.

6-4. The Department of Commerce issued a flammability standard that required all mattresses,

141

including crib mattresses, to pass a test that involved contact with a burning cigarette. The manufacturers of crib mattresses petitioned the court to exempt their product from the test procedure, but the department refused to do so. The crib manufacturers sued the department and argued that applying such a rule to crib mattresses was arbitrary and capricious because infants do not smoke. Discuss fully whether this rule should be overturned. [*Bunny Bear, Inc. v. Peterson,* 473 F.2d 1002 (1st Cir. 1973)]

6-5. The Atomic Energy Commission (AEC) was engaged in rulemaking proceedings for nuclear reactor safety. An environmental group sued the commission, arguing that its proceedings were inadequate. The commission had carefully complied with all requirements of the Administrative Procedure Act (APA). The environmentalists argued, however, that the very hazardous and technical nature of the reactor safety issue required more elaborate procedures above and beyond those of the APA. A federal circuit court of appeals agreed and overturned the AEC rules. The commission appealed the case to the United States Supreme Court. How should the Court rule? Discuss. [*Vermont Yankee Nuclear Power Corp. v. Natural Resources Defense Council, Inc.,* 435 U.S. 519, 98 S.Ct. 1197, 55 L.Ed.2d 460 (1978)]

6-6. In 1982, the president of the United States appointed Matthew Chabal, Jr., to the position of U.S. marshal. U.S. marshals are assigned to the federal courts. In the fall of 1985, Chabal received an unsatisfactory annual performance rating, and he was fired shortly thereafter by President Reagan. Given the fact that U.S. marshals are assigned to the federal courts, are these appointees still members of the executive branch? Did President Reagan have the right to fire Chabal without consulting Congress about the decision? [*Chabal v. Reagan,* 841 F.2d 1216 (3d Cir. 1988)]

6-7. A state statute required vehicle dismantlers—that is, persons whose business includes dismantling automobiles and selling the parts—to be licensed and keep records regarding the vehicles and parts in their possession. The statute also authorized warrantless administrative inspections; that is, without first obtaining a warrant, agents of the state department of motor vehicles or police officers could inspect a vehicle dismantler's license, records, and vehicles on the premises. Pursuant to this statute, police officers entered an automobile junkyard and asked to see the owner's license and records. The owner replied that he did not have the documents. The officers inspected the premises and discovered stolen vehicles and parts. Charged with possession of stolen property and unregistered operation as a vehicle dismantler, the junkyard owner argued that the warrantless inspection statute was unconstitutional under the Fourth Amendment. The trial court disagreed, reasoning that the junkyard business was a highly regulated industry. On appeal, the highest state court concluded that the statute had no truly administrative purpose and impermissibly authorized searches only to discover stolen property. The state appealed to the United States Supreme Court. Should the Court uphold the statute? Discuss. [*New York v. Burger,* 482 U.S. 691, 107 S.Ct. 2636, 96 L.Ed.2d 601 (1987)]

6-8. Congress passed legislation in 1966 that required the National Highway Traffic Safety Administration (NHTSA) to adopt automobile safety standards. Among the standards required by Section 203 of the act are rules for grading the quality of automobile tires. In 1975, the NHTSA adopted tread-wear regulations based on certain road-testing procedures. In 1983, as part of the Reagan administration's program of deregulation, the NHTSA indefinitely suspended the tire-quality regulations. The NHTSA contended that the standards were too costly for the economically troubled U.S. automobile industry and that the test procedures were not sufficiently reliable. Public Citizen, a public-interest group, sued the NHTSA, claiming that the suspension of the tire-quality standards was arbitrary and capricious. Will the court agree? Discuss. [*Public Citizen v. Steed,* 733 F.2d 93 (D.C.Cir. 1984)]

6-9. In 1976, the Environmental Protection Agency (EPA) proposed a rule establishing new pollution-control standards for coal-fired steam generators. The agency gave notice and received comments in the manner prescribed by the Administrative Procedure Act. After the public comments had been received, the EPA received informal suggestions from members of Congress and other federal officials. In 1979, the EPA published its final standards. Several environmental groups protested these standards, arguing that they were too lax. As part of this protest, the groups complained that political influence from Congress and other federal officials had encouraged the EPA to relax the proposed standards. The groups went on to argue that these *ex parte* comments were themselves illegal or that such comments at least should have been summarized in the record. What will the court decide? Discuss fully. [*Sierra Club v. Costle,* 657 F.2d 298 (D.C.Cir. 1981)]

6-10. In 1977, the Department of Transportation (DOT) adopted a passive-restraint standard (known as Standard 208) that required new cars to have either air bags or automatic seat belts. By 1981, it became clear that all the major auto manufacturers would install automatic seat belts to comply with this rule. The DOT determined that most purchasers of cars would detach their automatic seat belts, thus making them ineffective. Consequently, the department repealed the regulation. State Farm Mutual Automobile Insurance Co. and other insurance companies sued in the District of Columbia Circuit Court of Appeals for a review of the DOT's repeal of the regulation. That court held that the repeal was arbitrary and capricious because the DOT had reversed its rule without sufficient support. The motor vehicle manufacturers then appealed this decision to the United States Supreme Court. What will result? Discuss. [*Motor Vehicle Manufacturers Association v. State Farm Mutual Automobile Insurance Co.,* 463 U.S. 29, 103 S.Ct. 2856, 77 L.Ed.2d 443 (1983)]

6-11. A Question of Ethics

The Marine Mammal Protection Act was enacted in 1972 to reduce the number of incidental killings of, and injuries to, marine mammals during commercial fishing opera-

tions. Pursuant to the act, commercial fishing vessels are required to allow an employee of the National Oceanic and Atmospheric Administration (NOAA) to accompany the vessels to conduct research and observe operations. In December 1986, after the NOAA had adopted a new policy of recruiting female as well as male observers, the NOAA notified Caribbean Marine Services Co. that female observers would be assigned to accompany two of their fishing vessels on their next voyages. The owners and crew of the ships (the plaintiffs) moved for an injunction against the implementation of the NOAA directive. The plaintiffs contended that the presence of a female on board a fishing vessel would be very awkward because the female would have to share the crew's quarters, and crew members enjoyed little or no privacy with respect to bodily functions. Further, they alleged that the presence of a female would be disruptive to fishing operations because some of the crew members were "crude" men with little formal education and might harass or sexually assault a female observer, and the officers would therefore have to devote time to protecting the female from the crew. Finally, the plaintiffs argued that the presence of a female observer could destroy morale and distract the crew, thus affecting the crew's efficiency and decreasing the vessel's profits. [Caribbean Marine Services Co. v. Baldrige, *844 F.2d 668 (9th Cir. 1988)*]

1. In general, do you think that the public policy of promoting equal employment opportunity should override the concerns of the vessel owners and crew?

If you were the judge, would you grant the injunction? Why or why not?

2. The plaintiffs pointed out that fishing voyages could last three months or longer. Would the length of a particular voyage affect your answer to the above question?

3. The plaintiffs contended that even if the indignity of sharing bunk rooms and toilet facilities with a female observer could be overcome, the observer's very presence in the common areas of the vessel, such as the dining area, would unconstitutionally infringe on the crew members' right to privacy in these areas. Evaluate this claim.

6-12. Case Briefing Assignment

Examine Case A.6 [Penny v. Guiffrida, 897 F.2d 1543 (10th Cir. 1990)] in Appendix A. The case has been excerpted there in great detail. Review and then brief the case, making sure you include answers to the following questions in your brief.

1. What was the basis for Penny's claim against the FEMA?

2. What arguments did FEMA raise on appeal?

3. Did the appellate court address each of FEMA's arguments?

4. What was the appellate court's decision?

Chapter 7

Torts

Part of doing business today and, indeed, part of everyday life is the risk of being involved in a lawsuit. A normal and ever-increasing business operating cost is that of liability insurance to protect against lawsuits. The list of circumstances in which business people can be sued is long and varied. An employee injured on the job may attempt to sue the employer because of an unsafe working environment. The consumer who is injured while using a product may attempt to sue the manufacturer because of a defect in the product. At issue in these examples is alleged wrongful conduct by one person that causes injury to another. Such wrongful conduct is covered by the law of **torts.** (The word *tort* is French for ''wrong.'')

Tort law covers a broad variety of injuries. Society recognizes an interest in personal physical safety, and tort law provides a remedy for acts causing physical injury or interfering with physical security and freedom of movement. Society recognizes an interest in protecting property, and tort law provides a remedy for acts causing destruction or damage to property. Society recognizes other, more intangible interests in such things as personal privacy, family relations, reputation, and dignity. Tort law provides a remedy for invasion of protected interests in these areas.

Tort law is constantly changing and growing with society. Although many torts have their origin in the old common law, new torts are recognized to protect new interests that develop with social change. For example, until recently, because of old notions of family structure, it was not a legally recognizable tort for a husband to negligently injure his wife or child. But today minors, as well as spouses, receive much more protection. Traditionally, one could not recover **damages** for psychological injury unless one had personally risked physical harm. That rule is changing, with more and more courts allowing recovery for emotional damage to those who witness traumatic injury to another.

■ Tort Law versus Criminal Law

Two notions serve as the basis of all torts: wrongs and compensation. Tort law recognizes that some acts are wrong because they cause injuries to persons. Those who commit the acts are to blame, or bear the fault, for these

143

injuries. Of course, torts are not the only type of wrongs that exist in the law; crimes involve wrongs also. In fact, most crimes involve torts. The commission of a tort, however, is not always a crime. A crime is an act so reprehensible that it is considered to be a wrong against the state or against society as a whole. Therefore, the *state* prosecutes the criminal, and the resulting judgment imposes a jail term, a fine, or both. A tort action, in contrast, is a *civil* action in which one person brings a suit of a personal nature against another. The state is not a party to the suit, and the resulting judgment imposes damages but no jail term. In some cases, the same act can be a criminal wrong *and* a civil wrong. Intentionally threatening another, for example, could be the basis for a criminal prosecution as well as the basis of an action in tort for assault (assault will be discussed shortly).

The function of tort law is to provide the injured party with some *remedy*. The law of torts is used to decide when victims must bear the loss themselves and when the responsibility belongs to someone else. A typical tort action involves an intentional or a negligent act of one party that causes personal or property damage to another.

Kinds of Torts

Torts have been traditionally divided into the following three categories:

1. Intentional torts.
2. Negligence.
3. Strict liability.

Intentional torts involve acts that were intended to bring about the consequences that are the basis of the tort. **Negligence** involves matters of risk—sometimes a negligent actor is unaware of the results that will follow from his or her act, and sometimes he or she considers the consequences carefully before acting, but in neither case are the consequences intended. **Strict liability** rules require someone to compensate the injured party without regard to fault.

Intentional Torts: Wrongs against the Person

An intentional tort, as the term implies, requires *intent*. The **tortfeasor** (the one committing the tort)

must intend to commit an act, the consequences of which interfere with the personal or business interests of another in a way not permitted by law. The underlying motive—the reason or impulse behind the intentional act—does not matter. The actor could have been joking or playing around or could even have had some benevolent motive. In tort law, intent only means that the actor intended the consequences of his or her act or knew with substantial certainty that certain consequences would result from the act. The nature of the damage ultimately caused is irrelevant in determining whether there was intent. If Johnson intentionally pushes Adams and Adams falls to the ground and breaks her arm, it does not matter that Johnson never wished to break Adams's arm. It is enough that Johnson intended to bring about harmful or offensive contact to Adams, and Johnson is thus liable for the consequences, including the injury to Adams's arm.

The law generally assumes that one intends the normal consequences of his or her actions. Thus, a push is an intentional tort because the object of the push can ordinarily be expected to go flying; however, a playful pat on the shoulder is not an intentional tort even though, in drawing away suddenly, the person touched may be injured. To recover damages, the injured person must normally prove that real harm has occurred.

Assault

Any intentional, unexcused act that creates in another person a reasonable apprehension or fear of immediate harmful or offensive contact is an **assault.** Apprehension is not the same as fear. If the contact is such that a reasonable person would want to avoid it, and if there is a reasonable basis for believing the contact is coming, then the plaintiff suffers apprehension whether or not he or she is afraid. For example, the *threat* of forceful delivery of an unwanted kiss may constitute an assault.

The interest protected by tort law concerning assault is the freedom from having to expect harmful or offensive contact. The arousal of apprehension is enough to justify compensation. Of course, the *completion* of the act that caused the apprehension, if it results in harm to the plaintiff, also constitutes a tort—a *battery*, discussed below. For example, Jones brings a gun along to an interview with Smith. There is no assault unless she threatens

Smith with it, perhaps by pointing it at him and showing that all she has to do to use it is to cock it. If she fires the gun, and the bullet hits Smith, she has committed a battery.

Battery

A **battery** is an unexcused, harmful or offensive, physical contact intentionally performed. If Jones intentionally punches Smith in the nose, it is a battery. The interest protected by tort law in this case is the right to personal security and safety. The contact can be harmful, or it can be merely offensive (such as an unwelcome kiss). Physical injury does not have to occur. The contact can be to any part of the body or anything attached to it— for example, a hat or other clothing, a purse, or a chair or an automobile in which one is sitting. The contact can be made by the defendant or by some force that the defendant sets in motion—for example, a rock thrown, food poisoned, or a stick swung.

If the plaintiff shows that there was a contact, and the jury agrees that the contact was offensive, that is enough to establish a right to some compensation. Damages from a battery can be for emotional harm or loss of reputation as well as for physical harm.

Defenses to Assault and Battery

A number of legally recognized defenses can be raised by a defendant who is sued for assault or battery, or both. The defenses to be discussed here are (1) consent, (2) self-defense, (3) defense of others, and (4) defense of property.

CONSENT   When a person **consents** to the act that harms him or her, there is no liability for the damage done. A person who voluntarily signs up for a touch football team implicitly consents to the *normal* physical punishment that takes place during such activities. This defense is good only as long as the defendant remains within the boundaries of the consent given—that is, plays football by the normal rules.

SELF-DEFENSE   An individual who is defending his or her life or physical well-being may use the defense of **self-defense.** A person is privileged to use whatever force is *reasonably* necessary to pre-vent harmful contact. This defense extends not only to *real* danger but also to *apparent* danger. Reasonable grounds must exist for believing the danger is real, however. Also, force cannot be used once the danger has passed, and revenge is always prohibited.

DEFENSE OF OTHERS   An individual can act in a reasonable manner to protect others who are in real or apparent danger.

DEFENSE OF PROPERTY   Individuals who use reasonable force in attempting to remove intruders from their homes can use defense of property to counter tort lawsuits for assault or battery, or both. The law does value life, though, more than it values property. In principle, force that is likely to cause death or great bodily injury may never be used just to protect property. Setting a mechanical device that fires a gun if an intruder enters an empty house is not considered reasonable by most courts.

False Imprisonment

False imprisonment is defined as the intentional confinement or restraint of another person without justification. It involves interference with the freedom to move without restraint. The confinement can be accomplished through the use of physical barriers, physical restraint, or threats of physical force. Moral pressure or future threats are not restraints sufficient to constitute false imprisonment. It is essential that the person being restrained not comply with the restraint willingly.

Businesspersons are often confronted with suits for false imprisonment after they have attempted to confine a suspected shoplifter for questioning. Consider, for example, the case in which a store detective locks an alleged shoplifter in one of the store's offices. If the customer can prove that the detention was totally unreasonable, the customer can successfully sue the store for false imprisonment.

The loss to business from shoplifting is estimated to exceed $15 billion a year. Almost all states have adopted so-called merchant-protection legislation, which allows a merchant to detain any suspected shoplifter, provided that there is reasonable cause for suspicion and provided that the confinement is carried out in a reasonable way. Because the risk of real injury to an innocent person is great, however, educational programs should be offered to all employees; these programs explain the exact procedures to be followed when a customer is suspected of shoplifting and help to prevent unlawful detentions and consequent lawsuits. Harm to reputation and emotional distress caused by wrongful imprisonment are believed by the law to be so real that damages are presumed and need not be proved to make a case.

Under the privilege to detain granted to merchants in some states, a merchant can use the defense of *probable cause* to justify delaying a suspected shoplifter. Probable cause exists when there is more evidence for the belief that a person is guilty than against it. The detention, however, must be conducted in a *reasonable* manner and for only a *reasonable* length of time. The following case provides a good example.

Case 7.1

JOHNSON v. K-MART ENTERPRISES, INC.
Court of Appeals of Wisconsin,
1980.
98 Wis.2d 533,
297 N.W.2d 74.

BACKGROUND AND FACTS   *Deborah Johnson, the plaintiff, went to the defendant's store in Madison one evening in September of 1976. She took her small child with her, carrying the child in an infant seat that she had purchased at K-Mart two or three weeks before. After purchasing some diapers and children's clothes, she attempted to leave the store. The store's security officer stopped the plaintiff and asked her to come back into the store because a K-Mart employee reported that she had seen the plaintiff steal the infant seat. To show ownership, the plaintiff pointed to cat hair, food crumbs, and various stains on the seat. After a twenty-minute delay, the security officer apologized and let the plaintiff leave. The trial court dismissed Johnson's action for false imprisonment, and Johnson appealed.*

DYKMAN, Judge.

* * * *

* * * [A merchant may] detain a shopper if certain conditions are met, one of which is that the merchant has probable cause for believing that the shopper stole the merchant's goods. Plaintiff's deposition shows that defendant's security officer believed that plaintiff stole the infant seat because another K-Mart employee told him that she saw plaintiff steal it. There is no conflicting evidence on this point. The question is whether the employee who said she saw plaintiff steal the infant seat was fabricating her story. Our inquiry is whether there is an issue of material fact in dispute as to whether the K-Mart employee who detained the plaintiff had probable cause for believing that plaintiff stole the infant seat.

We find no material facts in dispute, nor reasonable alternative inferences to be drawn from the facts. The merchant received word, through one of its employees, that plaintiff removed an infant seat from the shelf, put her child in it, and left the store without paying for the seat. We hold as a matter of law that the merchant, through its security guard, had probable cause based on this report to believe that plaintiff had shoplifted.

* * * *

Plaintiff argues that her deposition shows that the place of detention made the detention unreasonable, or at least would permit an inference from which a jury could find that the manner of detention was unreasonable.

Few innocent persons who are detained because they are suspected of shoplifting will feel that their detention was accomplished in a reasonable manner. Plaintiff's complaint is that the place she was detained was public. Yet, plaintiff's deposition shows that defendant's only actions were to stop plaintiff, ask her to return to the store, inform her that she was suspected of shoplifting, produce the witness who allegedly saw plaintiff steal the infant seat, apologize to plaintiff for the detention and release her. There is no suggestion in plaintiff's complaint or deposition that she asked to go to a more private place. Defendant's actions do not permit an inference that the detention was accomplished in an unreasonable manner.

*   *   *   *

*   *   * In determining whether a 20-minute detention is reasonable as a matter of law, we must weigh the customer's important liberty interests against a merchant's need for protection against shoplifters. Such a balancing is evident in the language of the statute which gives merchants the power to detain suspected shoplifters while at the same time safeguarding the customer's rights. We hold that a merchant's interest in detaining suspected shoplifters is such that a 20-minute detention is reasonable.

The appellate court upheld the trial court's dismissal of Johnson's claim. The security officer acted reasonably and with probable cause.

DECISION AND REMEDY

Infliction of Emotional Distress

Recently the courts have begun to recognize an interest in freedom from emotional distress as well as an interest in physical security. The tort of *infliction of emotional distress* can be defined as an intentional act that amounts to extreme and outrageous conduct resulting in severe emotional distress to another.[1] For example, a prankster telephones an individual and says that the individual's spouse has just been in a horrible accident. As a result, the individual suffers intense emotional pain or anxiety. This is deemed to be extreme and outrageous conduct that exceeds the bounds of decency accepted by society and is therefore actionable.

As this is a relatively new tort, it poses some problems. One major problem is that it could flood the courts with lawsuits. A society in which individuals are rewarded if they are unable to endure the normal emotional stresses of day-to-day living is obviously undesirable. Therefore, the law usually focuses on the nature of the acts that come under this tort. Indignity or annoyance alone are usually not enough to support a lawsuit based on intentional infliction of emotional distress. Many times, however, repeated annoyances, coupled with threats, are enough. In a business context, for example, the repeated use of extreme methods to collect a delinquent account may be actionable. Also, an unusually severe emotional reaction, such as the extreme distress of a woman incorrectly in-

formed that her husband and two sons have been killed, may be actionable. Because it is difficult to prove the existence of emotional suffering, a court may require that the emotional distress be evidenced by some physical symptom or illness or some emotional disturbance that can be documented by a psychiatric or other consultant.

In recent years, some courts have permitted emotional distress lawsuits for psychic damage if the emotional trauma suffered was sufficiently severe. An issue currently before the courts is whether airline passengers who endure the torture of preparing for a crash landing, or who survive a crash landing without physical injury, should have a cause of action for emotional distress. In some cases, emotional distress actions have been allowed to those who suffer emotionally and psychologically just from having witnessed a horrible accident. For example, a California court recently allowed parties to bring an emotional distress lawsuit after they witnessed the traumatic death of a passenger—a total stranger to the plaintiffs—on a Palm Springs tramway car in which the plaintiffs were riding. The accident occurred when a part of the tramway car broke loose, crashed through the overhead window, and killed the passenger.[2]

Defamation

As discussed in Chapter 5, the freedom of speech guaranteed by the First Amendment is not absolute.

---

1. Restatement (Second) of Torts, Section 46, Comment d.

2. *Ballinger v. Palm Springs Aerial Tramway,* 220 Cal.App.3d 581, 269 Cal.Rptr. 583 (Cal.App. 1990).

In interpreting the First Amendment, the courts must balance the vital guarantee of free speech against another pervasive and strong social interest—preventing and redressing attacks on reputation. When one wrongfully hurts another's good reputation, the tort of **defamation** results. Tort law imposes a general duty on all persons to refrain from making false, defamatory statements about others. Breaching this duty orally involves the tort of **slander**; breaching it in writing or in any form of communication that has "the potentially harmful qualities characteristic of written or printed words" [3] involves the tort of **libel**. Courts have held that the forms of libelous communication include pictures, signs, statues, and films.

The common law has defined four types of false utterances that are considered slanderous *per se,* or on their face. That means that no proof of damages is required before these false utterances become actionable. They are:

1. *A statement that another has a loathsome communicable disease.* Courts have generally limited this tort to imputations that an individual has a venereal disease—although a statement that a person had AIDS has been held to be slanderous *per se.*[4]

2. *A statement that another has committed improprieties while engaging in a profession or trade.* For example, it is actionable to say of an attorney that he or she is unethical, of a merchant that his or her credit is bad, or of a person holding public office that he or she has accepted a bribe. But statements alleging that a clerk has consorted with prostitutes or is a homosexual, that a physician has committed adultery, or that a stenographer's credit is bad have not been held to be actionable— because the clerk, the physician, and the stenographer may still be competent at their work.

3. *A statement that another has committed or has been imprisoned for a serious crime.* Courts generally agree that the crime referred to in the statement must involve "moral turpitude," which has been defined as "inherent baseness or vileness of principle in the human heart." Beating children,

for example, involves moral turpitude, while other forms of battery may not.

4. *A statement that an unmarried woman is unchaste.*

THE PUBLICATION REQUIREMENT   The basis of the tort of defamation is the *publication* of a statement or statements that hold an individual up to contempt, ridicule, or hatred. *Publication* here means that the defamatory statements are made to or within the hearing of persons other than the defamed party. If Thompson writes Andrews a private letter accusing him of embezzling funds, that does not constitute libel. If Peters calls Gordon dishonest, unattractive, and incompetent when no one else is around, that does not constitute slander. In neither case was the message communicated to a third party. Interestingly, the courts have generally held that dictating a letter to a secretary constitutes publication (although a privilege could be involved in this situation—see privileged speech below). Moreover, if a third party overhears defamatory statements by chance, the courts have generally held that this also constitutes publication. Note further that any individual who republishes or repeats defamatory statements is liable even if that person reveals the source of the statements. Most radio stations have instituted seven-second delays for live broadcasts, such as talk shows, to avoid this kind of liability.

DEFENSES TO DEFAMATION   Truth is normally an *absolute* defense against a defamation charge. But the statement at issue must be true in whole, not in part, and if the statement is specific, the truth must also be specific. For instance, if the accusation is that Tony stole a stereo from Sara, it is insufficient to show that Tony is known as a bad character or that Tony stole stereos from Ruth. In contrast, if the statement is substantially true, it is not necessary to prove every detail. For example, saying a politician has wasted $80,000 of the taxpayers' money has been held justified when it was proved that he wasted $17,500.

Other defenses to defamation may exist if the speech concerns a *public figure* or if the speech is *privileged.*

Public Figures   **Public figures** include public officials and employees who exercise substantial

---

3.   Restatement (Second) of Torts, Section 568.
4.   See *McCune v. Neitzel,* 235 Neb. 754, 457 N.W.2d 803 (1990).

governmental power and any persons in the public limelight. Statements made about public figures, especially when they are made via a public medium, are usually related to matters of general public interest; they are made about people who substantially affect all of us. Furthermore, public figures generally have some access to a public medium for answering disparaging falsehoods about themselves; private individuals do not. For these reasons, public figures have a greater burden of proof in defamation cases than do private individuals. In *New York Times Co. v. Sullivan,* the United States Supreme Court held that to recover damages, a public figure must prove that a defamatory statement was made with **actual malice**— that is, *with either knowledge of its falsity or a reckless disregard of the truth.*[5] The following case illustrates a libel case involving a public figure and the extent of liability when actual malice is proved.

---

5. *New York Times Co. v. Sullivan,* 376 U.S. 254, 84 S.Ct. 710, 11 L.Ed.2d 686 (1964).

BACKGROUND AND FACTS *Plaintiff Carol Burnett, the comedienne, believed she had been libeled by an article in* The National Enquirer, *which stated that Burnett was intoxicated and involved in a "row" with Henry Kissinger in a Washington, D.C., restaurant. She sued the* Enquirer, *and the jury awarded her $300,000 in general damages and $1,300,000 in punitive damages. The National Enquirer moved for judgment notwithstanding the verdict and a new trial, claiming, among other things, that there was no actual malice on its part and that the damages were excessive. The trial court judge reduced the general damages to $50,000 and the punitive damages to $750,000. The National Enquirer appealed.*

Case 7.2

BURNETT v. NATIONAL ENQUIRER
California Court of Appeal,
Second District, 1983.
144 Cal.App.3d 991,
193 Cal.Rptr. 206.

ROTH, Presiding Justice.
*   *   *   *

*   *   * [T]he "actual malice" required by *New York Times* to be established by "clear and convincing evidence" refers to that aspect of malice, properly denominated malice in law, necessary to find liability for libel and not to malice in fact, essential to the recovery of punitive damages, which under the cases discussed may be arrived at on the basis of applicable state standards, here on the basis of a preponderance of the evidence. [The court concluded that malice was proved at the trial by a preponderance of the evidence.]
*   *   *   *

It is next contended, however, that regardless of what we have just said, the punitive damages assessed herein are still legally unsupportable. More specifically it is urged (a) the amount of those damages was grossly excessive; (b) such damages were impermissibly disproportionate to the compensatory damages awarded; (c) that the trial court erred in revising the ratio between punitive and compensatory damages on its remittitur [the process by which damages awarded by a jury are reduced]; and (d) that insufficient evidence was present which would show appellant ratified the acts of its employees, so as to justify its liability for punitive damages. *   *   *
*   *   *   *

Viewing the record in the light of these principles, and assuming, as we will hereinafter decide, that the award of compensatory damages was proper, we are of the opinion the award to respondent of $750,000 in order to punish and deter appellant was not justified.

DECISION AND REMEDY	*The appellate court affirmed the trial court's denial of* The National Enquirer's *motions for judgment notwithstanding the verdict and a new trial. The court upheld the general damage reduction to $50,000 but lowered punitive damages from $750,000 to $150,000.*

Privileged Speech   In some circumstances, a person will not be liable for defamatory statements because he or she enjoys a **privilege,** or immunity. Privileged communications are of two types, *absolute* and *qualified.* Only in limited cases, such as in judicial proceedings and legislative proceedings, is absolute privilege granted. For example, statements made by attorneys and judges during a trial are absolutely privileged and therefore cannot be the basis for a defamation charge. Members of Congress making statements on the floor of Congress have an absolute privilege. Legislators have complete immunity from liability for false statements made in debate, even if they make such statements maliciously—that is, knowing them to be untrue. This absolute immunity is granted because judicial and legislative personnel deal with matters that are so much in the public interest that the parties involved should be able to speak out fully and freely and without restriction.

In other situations, a person will not be liable for defamatory statements because he or she has a *qualified* privilege. Qualified, or conditional, privilege is a common law concept based on the philosophy that the right to know or speak is of equal importance with the right not to be defamed. For example, a qualified privilege exists when there is a common interest between the person who makes the statement and the one who receives it. Thus, a statement concerning corporate business made by one corporate director to another is qualifiedly privileged. If a communication is conditionally privileged, to recover damages the plaintiff must show that the privilege was abused.

Another example of a qualified privilege is found in letters of recommendation and in written evaluations of employees. This privilege allows some latitude for making mistakes in the communication without defamation liability. Generally, if the communication statements are made in good faith and the publication is limited to those who have a legitimate interest in the communication, the statements fall within the area of qualified privilege.

Invasion of the Right to Privacy

A person's right to solitude and freedom from prying public eyes is the interest protected by the tort of invasion of privacy. Four different acts qualify as invasions of privacy:

1. *The use of a person's name or picture or other likeness for commercial purposes without permission.* For example, using without permission someone's picture to advertise a product or someone's name to enhance a company name invades the person's privacy.

2. *Intrusion upon an individual's affairs or seclusion.* For example, invading someone's home or illegally searching someone's briefcase is an invasion of privacy. This tort has been held to extend to eavesdropping by wiretap, unauthorized scanning of a bank account, compulsory blood testing, and window peeping.

3. *Publication of information that places a person in a false light.* This could be a story attributing to a person ideas not held or actions not taken by that person. (Publishing such a story could involve the tort of defamation as well.)

4. *Public disclosure of private facts about an individual that an ordinary person would find objectionable.* A newspaper account of a private citizen's sex life could be an actionable invasion of privacy. An example of what would *not* constitute this form of invasion of privacy is an article publicizing what a one-time child star is doing today, so long as nothing is revealed that the community would regard as highly objectionable (unless the objectionable information is truthful and contained in official records that are open to public inspection).

In the following case, the well-known consumer advocate Ralph Nader sued General Motors for the invasion of his right to privacy.

BACKGROUND AND FACTS *When Ralph Nader was about to publish* Unsafe at Any Speed, *a book that severely criticized General Motors Corporation's products from the standpoint of safety and design, General Motors allegedly undertook a campaign of intimidation against him. Nader claimed that General Motors (1) asked Nader's acquaintances about his political and religious views, his integrity, his sexual proclivities and inclinations, and his personal habits; (2) kept him under surveillance in public places for an unreasonable length of time; (3) caused him to be accosted by girls for the purpose of entrapping him into illicit relationships; (4) made threatening, harassing, and obnoxious telephone calls to him; (5) tapped his telephone and eavesdropped, by means of mechanical and electronic equipment, on his private conversations with others; and (6) conducted a continuing and harassing investigation of him. Nader brought an action against General Motors, alleging, among other things, that General Motors had invaded his privacy by these actions. The trial court held for Nader, and General Motors appealed.*

Case 7.3

NADER v. GENERAL MOTORS CORP.

Court of Appeals of New York, 1970.
25 N.Y.2d 560,
255 N.E.2d 765,
307 N.Y.S.2d 647.

FULD, Chief Judge.

* * * *

* * * [T]o sustain a cause of action for invasion of privacy * * * the plaintiff must show that the appellant's conduct was truly "intrusive" and that it was designed to elicit information which would not be available through normal inquiry or observation.

* * * *

Turning, then, to the particular acts charged in the complaint, we cannot find any basis for a claim of invasion of privacy * * * in the allegations that the appellant [General Motors], through its agents or employees, interviewed many persons who knew the plaintiff [Nader], asking questions about him and casting aspersions on his character. Although those inquiries may have uncovered information of a personal nature, it is difficult to see how they may be said to have invaded the plaintiff's privacy. Information about the plaintiff which was already known to others could hardly be regarded as private to the plaintiff. * * *

Nor can we find any actionable invasion of privacy in the allegations that the appellant caused the plaintiff to be accosted by girls with illicit proposals, or that it was responsible for the making of a large number of threatening and harassing telephone calls to the plaintiff's home at odd hours. Neither of these activities, howsoever offensive and disturbing, involved intrusion for the purpose of gathering information of a private and confidential nature. * * *

* * * *

Apart, however, from the foregoing allegations which we find inadequate to spell out a cause of action for invasion of privacy * * *, the complaint contains allegations concerning other activities * * * which do satisfy the requirements for such a cause of action. The one which most clearly meets those requirements is the charge that the appellant and its codefendants engaged in unauthorized wiretapping and eavesdropping by mechanical and electronic means. The Court of Appeals [in a previous case] recognized that such conduct constitutes a tortious intrusion, and other jurisdictions have reached a similar conclusion.

The New York Court of Appeals affirmed the lower court's ruling in favor of Nader, although it held that only the eavesdropping and wiretapping constituted an invasion of Nader's right to privacy.

DECISION AND REMEDY

Fraudulent Misrepresentation

The tort of fraudulent misrepresentation involves the use of fraud and deceit for personal gain. It includes several elements:

1. Misrepresentation of facts or conditions with knowledge that they are false or with reckless disregard for the truth.
2. Intent to induce another to rely on the misrepresentation.
3. Justifiable reliance by the deceived party.
4. Damages suffered as a result of reliance.
5. Causal connection between the misrepresentation and the injury suffered.

In general, the reliance must be on a statement of fact. Reliance on a statement of opinion is not justified unless the person making the statement has a superior knowledge of the subject matter. A lawyer's opinion of the law, for instance, is an example of superior knowledge, and reliance on that opinion will be regarded as reliance on a statement of fact.

For fraud to occur, more than mere *seller's talk,* or **puffing,** must be involved. Fraud exists only when a person represents as a material fact something he or she knows is untrue. For example, it is fraud to claim that a building does not leak when one knows it does. Facts are objectively ascertainable, whereas seller's talk is not. "I'm the best lawyer in town" is seller's talk. The speaker is not trying to represent something as fact, because "best" is a subjective, not an objective, term. (The topic of fraud in contracts is discussed in Chapter 9.)

■ Intentional Torts: Wrongs against Property

Wrongs against property include (1) trespass to land and to personal property, (2) conversion, and (3) nuisance. The wrong is against the individual who has legally recognized rights with regard to real or personal property. The law distinguishes real property from personal property. *Real property,* also called *realty,* is land and things permanently attached thereto. *Personal property,* or *personalty,* includes things that are basically movable. Thus, a house and lot are real property, whereas the furniture inside a house is personal property. Money and securities are also personal property.

Trespass to Land

The civil tort called a **trespass to land** occurs any time a person, without permission, enters onto land that is owned by another, or causes anything or anyone to enter onto the land, or remains on the land, or permits anything to remain on it. Note that actual harm to the land is not an essential element of this tort, because tort law in respect to trespass is designed to protect the right of an owner to exclusive possession. If no harm is done, usually only nominal—in name only, not significant—damages (such as $1) can be recovered by the landowner. Examples of common types of trespass to land include walking or driving on the land, shooting across it with a gun, throwing rocks or spraying water on a building in the possession of another, building a dam across a river that causes water to back up on someone else's land, and placing part of one's building on the adjoining landowner's property.

In the past, the right to land gave exclusive possession of a space that extended from "the center of the earth to the heavens," but this rule has been relaxed. Today, reasonable intrusions are permitted. Thus, aircraft can normally fly over privately owned land. The temporary invasion of the air space over such land is, in effect, considered privileged as to the aircraft owner. Society's interest in air transportation preempts the individual's interest in the air space.

TRESPASS CRITERIA, RIGHTS, AND DUTIES Before a person can be held to be a trespasser, the real property owner (the person who legally controls the realty) must establish that person as a trespasser. For example, ignoring "posted" trespass signs and entering onto the property anyway establish a person as a trespasser. A guest in your home is not a trespasser, but if the guest becomes unruly and you *ask* the guest to leave, however, the guest will become a trespasser. Any person who enters onto another's property to commit an illegal act (such as a thief entering a lumberyard at night to steal lumber) is established as a trespasser without verbal establishment or posted signs.

Once a person is established as a trespasser, certain rights and duties are applied to both the owner of the realty and to the trespasser. Some of these rights and duties are as follows:

1. A trespasser is liable for any damage caused to the property. The owner does not have to prove negligence.
2. A trespasser assumes the risks of the premises and cannot hold the owner liable for injuries sustained. This rule does not permit the owner to lay traps with the intent to injure a trespasser. Under the ''attractive nuisance'' doctrine, infants or young persons do not assume the risks of the premises if they are attracted to the premises by some object or feature thereon. Under some circumstances an owner may even have a duty to warn of dangers on the property, such as guard dogs.
3. As previously discussed, a trespasser can be removed from the premises through the use of reasonable force without the owner being liable for assault and battery. This same basic concept allows an owner to remove, without liability, another's personal property, the presence of which constitutes a trespass, if the removal is accomplished by the exercise of reasonable care.

DEFENSES TO TRESPASS TO LAND   Trespass to land involves wrongful interference with another person's real property rights. But if one can show that the trespass was warranted, as when a trespasser enters to assist someone in danger, a complete defense exists. Consent may also be implied from past behavior. Another defense is to show that the purported owner did not actually have the right to possess the land in question.

In some situations, courts can easily assess damages for trespass to land, especially when the trespasser damages or wrongfully destroys items of value on the land. For example, land purchasers can recover the value of destroyed trees when avoidable errors caused construction crews to knock them down.

Trespass to Personal Property

Whenever any individual unlawfully harms the personal property of another or otherwise interferes with the personal property owner's right to exclusive possession and enjoyment of that property,

trespass to personal property—also called *trespass to personalty*—occurs. Trespass to personal property involves interference with a person's right to possess his or her property and, thus, may entail acts of damage, dispossession, or both. For example, if a student takes another student's business law book as a practical joke and hides it so that the owner is unable to find it for several days prior to the final examination, the student has engaged in a trespass to personal property.

If it can be shown that trespass to personal property was warranted, then a complete defense has been made. Many states, for example, allow automobile repair shops to hold a customer's car (under what is called an artisan's, or possessory, lien) when the customer has refused to pay for repairs rendered.

Conversion

Whenever personal property is taken from its rightful owner or possessor and placed in the service of one who has no legal right to it, or whenever the rightful owner of personal property is otherwise deprived of its use (due to vandalism, for example), the act of **conversion** occurs. Conversion is a trespass to personal property so serious that a converter can be forced to buy the property. A store clerk who steals merchandise from the store commits not only a crime but the tort of conversion as well. Of course, when conversion occurs, the lesser offense of trespass to personal property usually occurs as well. If the initial taking of the property was unlawful, there is trespass. Retention of the property is conversion. Even if the initial taking of the property was permitted by the owner or, for some other reason, is not a trespass, failure to return it may constitute conversion.

Even if a person mistakenly believed that he or she was entitled to the goods, a tort of conversion may take place. In other words, good intentions are not a defense against a charge of conversion, and conversion can be an entirely innocent act. To illustrate: Green loaned her lawnmower to Samuels to mow his lawn. Samuels used the lawn mower and then lent it to his neighbor, Nichols. A thief stole the lawn mower from Nichols. When Green learned what had happened to the mower, she demanded that Samuels pay for it. Samuels is guilty of conversion because he had no right to lend the mower to Nichols. His misuse of the mower renders him liable. He obviously did not intend for the mower to be stolen, but he intentionally took the mower from Green and intentionally and knowingly lent it to his neighbor.

Whoever suffers a conversion is generally entitled to recover the reasonable value of the lost goods. If Henries deliberately smashes a vase that Arts, Inc., exhibits for sale in its store, Henries is liable for the value of the vase. Deliberate destruc-

tion of the personal property of another is conversion. Henries treated the vase as if he owned it when he asserted a right to destroy it. When the goods have not been destroyed, the owner can either try to get them back through a lawsuit or ask for damages for conversion. The court will not give the owner full value for the goods and return the property as well.

The following case illustrates the concept of the tort of conversion.

Case 7.4

RUSSELL-VAUGHN FORD, INC. v. ROUSE

Supreme Court of Alabama,
1968.
281 Ala. 567,
206 So.2d 371.

BACKGROUND AND FACTS   *Plaintiff Rouse was negotiating a new-car purchase with salespersons of Russell-Vaughn, Inc. Rouse gave the salespersons the keys to the car he then owned, which was to be traded for the new automobile. When Rouse decided not to purchase a new car, the sales representatives said they had lost the keys. Rouse summoned the police, and when they arrived, the salespersons produced the missing keys and stated that they "just wanted to see him cry a while." Rouse sued Russell-Vaughn for the conversion of his car. The trial court held for Rouse and awarded him $5,000 in punitive damages. Russell-Vaughn appealed.*

SIMPSON, Justice.
*   *   *   *

*   *   * [A]ppellants argue that there was no conversion since the plaintiff could have called his wife at home, who had another set of keys[,] and thereby gained the ability to move his automobile. We find nothing in our cases which would require the plaintiff to exhaust all possible means of gaining possession of a chattel [an article of personal property] which is withheld from him by the defendant, after demanding its return. On the contrary, it is the refusal, without legal excuse, to deliver a chattel, which constitutes a conversion.

We find unconvincing the appellants' contention that if there were a conversion at all, it was the conversion of the automobile keys, and not of the automobile. In [a previous case] this court sustained a finding that there had been a conversion of cotton where the defendant refused to deliver to the plaintiff "warehouse tickets" which would have enabled him to gain possession of the cotton. The court spoke of the warehouse tickets as a symbol of the cotton and found that the retention of them amounted to a conversion of the cotton. So here, we think that the withholding from the plaintiff after demand of the keys to his automobile, without which he could not move it, amounted to a conversion of the automobile.

It is next argued by appellants that the amount of the verdict is excessive. It is not denied that punitive damages are recoverable here in the discretion of the jury.

DECISION AND REMEDY   *The Alabama Supreme Court upheld the jury verdict for Rouse, and the jury's decision to award $5,000 in punitive damages to Rouse was allowed to stand.*

STOLEN GOODS   As mentioned above, intent to engage in a wrongdoing is not necessary for conversion to exist. Rather, it is the intent to exercise control over property when such control is inconsistent with the plaintiff's rights that constitutes conversion. Therefore, someone who *buys* stolen goods is guilty of conversion even if he or she did not know the goods were stolen—although the buyer is not guilty of a crime in this situation. If the true owner brings a tort action against the buyer, the buyer must pay the owner the full value of the property, despite having already paid some money to the thief.

DEFENSES TO CONVERSION   A successful defense against the charge of conversion is that the purported owner has no title, or right to possess, superior to the holder's rights.

Necessity is another possible defense against conversion. If Abrams takes Stephens's cat, Abrams is guilty of conversion. If Stephens sues Abrams, Abrams must return the cat or pay damages. If, however, the cat has rabies and Abrams took the cat to protect the public, Abrams has a valid defense—necessity (and perhaps even self-defense if he can prove that he was in danger from the cat).

Nuisance

It is possible to commit a tort and be liable because of unreasonable uses you make of your own property. A **nuisance** is an improper activity that interferes with another's enjoyment or use of his or her property. Nuisances can be either *public* or *private*. A public nuisance disturbs or interferes with the public in general, as when the burning of leaves causes smoke to pollute an entire neighborhood. A private nuisance interferes with the property interest of a limited number of individuals, as when a trash pile left next to a neighbor's property creates an attraction for rodents. Reasonable limitations are placed on the use of property in all situations. Such limitations prevent the owner from unreasonably interfering with the health and comfort of neighbors or with their right to enjoy their own private property. The usual remedy is damages for one who suffers as a result of a nuisance. When

damages are unavailable or inadequate, one can have the nuisance stopped by seeking an injunction in the courts. An injunction is an equitable remedy. The court, if it grants the injunction, will prohibit the continuation of the undesirable activity.

Nuisances can also involve indecent, improper, or unlawful personal conduct. Obviously, there is an extremely subjective element in any definition of nuisance, particularly when it involves personal conduct. Moreover, a nuisance may be a crime as well as a tort, and the dividing line is difficult to ascertain. Finally, nuisances may result from intentional types of conduct as well as from negligent (careless) conduct. The defendant may even be held liable on the ground of strict liability (discussed at the end of this chapter). The fact that there is no one, clear-cut definition of nuisance has led to difficulties in applying the doctrine. As William Prosser—a leading scholar in the area of torts—noted, nuisance ''has come to mean all things to all people, and has been applied indiscriminately to everything from an alarming advertisement to a cockroach baked in a pie.'' [6]

■ Unintentional Torts: Negligence

Technological changes during the Industrial Revolution increased the number of injuries to people and their property. Because the injuries were generally unintended, it could not be held that they resulted from intentional torts. Also, to hold the new industries responsible for all of these injuries would have inhibited industrial progress. With these considerations in mind, the courts created negligence law. Today in the United States, negligence is the dominant cause of action for accidental injuries.

In contrast to intentional torts, in negligent torts the tortfeasor neither wishes to bring about the consequences of an act nor believes that they will occur. The actor's conduct merely creates a *risk* of such consequences. Without the creation of a risk, there can be no negligence. Moreover, the risk must be foreseeable; that is, it must be such that a reasonable person would anticipate it and guard

---

6.   W. Page Keeton et al., *Prosser and Keeton on Torts, 5th Ed.* (St. Paul: West Publishing Co., 1984), p. 616.

against it. In determining what is reasonable conduct, courts consider the nature of the possible harm. A very slight risk of a dangerous explosion might be unreasonable, whereas a distinct possibility of burning one's fingers on a stove might be reasonable.

Some of the actions discussed in the preceding section on intentional torts would constitute negligence if the element of intent were missing. For instance, deliberately punching someone in the nose is an intentional tort—battery. But carelessly bumping into someone who then falls and breaks an arm constitutes negligence. Likewise, carelessly, as opposed to intentionally, flooding someone's land constitutes negligence. In a sense, negligence is a *way of committing* a tort rather than a distinct *category* of torts.

Negligence has been committed when someone has suffered an injury caused by the failure of another to live up to a required *duty of care*. Generally, the tort of negligence requires the presence of the following four elements:

1. The defendant owed a duty of care to the plaintiff.
2. The defendant breached that duty.
3. The plaintiff suffered a legally recognizable injury.
4. The defendant's breach of the duty of care caused the plaintiff's injury.

Each of these elements is examined below.

The Duty of Care

Basically, the concept of duty arises from the notion that if we are to live in society with other people, some actions can be tolerated and some cannot, some actions are right and some are wrong, and some actions are reasonable and some are not. For example, drivers of motor vehicles are required to follow certain rules of the road and to exercise care when driving. The basic principle underlying the duty of care is that people are free to act as they please so long as their actions do not infringe upon the interests of others.

If an individual has knowledge, skill, or intelligence superior to that of an ordinary person, the individual's conduct must be consistent with that status. In other words, that individual has a

higher standard of care—his or her duty is that which is reasonable in light of those capabilities. For example, professionals (doctors, dentists, psychiatrists, architects, engineers, accountants, lawyers, and so on) are required to have a standard minimum level of special knowledge and ability. Consequently, the extent of their duty of care is measured by the standards acceptable within their professions.

Breach of the Duty of Care

Tort law relating to negligence measures duty by the **reasonable person standard.** In determining whether a tort has been committed, the courts ask how a reasonable person would have acted in the same circumstances. The reasonable person standard is said to be (although in an absolute sense it cannot be) objective. It is not necessarily how a particular person would act. It is society's judgment on how people should act. If the so-called reasonable person existed, he or she would be careful, conscientious, even-tempered, and honest. This hypothetical "reasonable person" is frequently used by the courts in decisions relating to other areas of law as well.

When someone fails to comply with the duty of exercising reasonable care, a potentially tortious act may have been committed. Failure to live up to the standard of care may involve an act (setting fire to a building) or an omission (neglecting to put out a fire). It may involve an intentional act, a careless act, or a carefully performed but nevertheless dangerous act that results in injury.

Whether or not a person's act or failure to act is unreasonable depends on the interaction of a number of factors. One factor is the nature of the act. Some actions—shooting off a gun in a crowd, for instance—are so outrageous and some acts, like blasting with dynamite, are so dangerous that any damage they cause should be paid for. Another factor in determining whether damages should be awarded is the manner in which an act is performed. Nearly all human acts carry some risk of harm, and individuals are expected to pay attention to their conduct and surroundings when undertaking to do something, rather than to proceed heedlessly. A third factor is the nature of the injury—whether it is serious or slight, extraordinary or simply part of everyday life. Another factor to be considered is whether the activity causing the injury was socially useful. For example, a person may be justified in darting into the path of an oncoming train to save a child, but not to save a hat. Yet another factor to consider is how easily the injury could have been guarded against. Could, for example, a simple, inexpensive warning sign have prevented the injury?

Retail businesses are particularly vulnerable to negligence lawsuits. Unless a retail firm has taken all reasonable precautions against potential injuries to its business invitees (customers), it may be held to have breached its duty of care to those invitees. The following case is illustrative.

BACKGROUND AND FACTS   *Lowell Bray was about to open the door of a restaurant owned by Kate, Inc., when he slipped on some ice and fell, injuring his shoulder. He stated that he could not see the ice but felt it when he slipped. Bray sued Kate, Inc., for damages, alleging that Kate, Inc., by failing to remove the ice from in front of its restaurant door, had breached its duty of care to Bray and was thus negligent. The trial court held for Bray, and Kate, Inc., appealed.*

Case 7.5

BRAY v. KATE, INC.

Supreme Court of Nebraska, 1990.
235 Neb. 315,
454 N.W.2d 698.

WHITE, Justice.
*   *   *   *

Summarized, defendant [Kate, Inc.] contends on appeal that the trial court erred *   *   * because the evidence showed that, as a matter of law, defendant owed no duty to plaintiff. *   *   *

In its brief, defendant urges this court to adopt a possessor's duty of care other than the duty which is now required under Nebraska law. We decline to do so. *   *   *

In view of this court's decisions [in previous cases], the correct statement of Nebraska law is: A possessor of land is subject to liability for injury caused to a business invitee by a condition on the land if (1) the possessor defendant either created the condition, knew of the condition, or by the exercise of reasonable care would have discovered the condition; (2) the defendant should have realized the condition involved an unreasonable risk of harm to a business invitee; (3) the defendant should have expected that a business invitee such as the plaintiff, either (a) would not discover or realize the danger, or (b) would fail to protect himself or herself against the danger; (4) the defendant failed to use reasonable care to protect the plaintiff invitee against the danger; and (5) the condition was a proximate cause of damage to the plaintiff.
*   *   *   *

As to the existence of a duty to the invitee *   *   *, a clear factual issue was presented and resolved by the jury verdict.

The Supreme Court of Nebraska affirmed the lower court's judgment for Bray. Kate, Inc., owed a duty to its patron, Bray, and because it had breached that duty, was liable to Bray for damages.

DECISION AND REMEDY

The Injury Requirement and Damages

For a tort to have been committed, there must be a *legally recognizable injury* to the plaintiff. To recover damages, the plaintiff must have suffered some loss, harm, wrong, or invasion of a protected interest. The reason for the requirement of injury is obvious. Without an injury of some kind, there is nothing to ''recover.''

An injured plaintiff is ordinarily denied recovery for damage that he or she could have avoided by taking reasonable action after the injury occurred. That is, the plaintiff has a duty to take reasonable steps to mitigate (reduce the amount of) damages. Seeking appropriate medical treatment, for example, would be reasonable.

It is important to stress that the purpose of tort law is not to punish people for tortious acts but to compensate the injured parties for damages suffered. Because society wants to discourage some torts, however, occasionally the injured person may be given extra compensation in the form of **punitive damages.** Few negligent acts are so reprehensible that punitive damages are available.[7]

Under some circumstances, one person commits a tortious act and another person is liable to the injured party for the result. For example, an employer is liable for the negligent act of an employee if it was committed within the scope of employment. This liability involves the doctrine of *respondeat superior* (see Chapter 15).

Causation

The fourth element necessary to a tort is causation. If a person fails in a duty of care and someone suffers injury, the wrongful activity must have caused the harm for a tort to have been committed. In deciding whether there is causation, the court must address two questions:

1. Was there *causation in fact?*
2. Was the act the *proximate cause* of the injury?

CAUSATION IN FACT   Did the injury occur because of the defendant's act, or would it have occurred anyway? If an injury would not have occurred without the defendant's act, then there is **causation in fact.** If Johnson carelessly leaves a campfire burning and the fire burns down the forest, there is causation in fact. If Johnson carelessly leaves a campfire burning, but it burns out, and then lightning causes a fire that burns down the forest, there is no causation in fact. In both cases, there is a wrongful act and damage. In the second

case, however, there is no causal connection and thus no liability. Causation in fact can usually be determined by use of the *but for* test: but for the wrongful act, the injury would not have occurred.

In some cases, causation in fact is difficult to determine. What if Johnson's campfire did spread, but at the same time lightning also started a fire? In this type of situation, the courts apply the *substantial factor* test: If Johnson's conduct was a substantial factor in bringing about the damage, Johnson will normally be held liable.

Determining causation in fact entails examining the facts portrayed in evidence at a trial. The plaintiff has the burden of proving causation in fact as well as other elements, such as damages. The plaintiff must prove the case by a *preponderance of the evidence* (see Chapter 2) in a civil suit.

PROXIMATE CAUSE   How far should a defendant's liability extend for a wrongful act that was a substantial factor in causing injury? For example, suppose Johnson's fire not only burns down the forest but also sets off an explosion in a nearby chemical plant that spills chemicals into a river, killing all the fish for a hundred miles downstream and ruining the economy of a tourist resort. Should Johnson be liable to the resort owners? To the tourists whose vacations were ruined? These are questions about the limitation of liability, which is the second element in the general issue of causation. The courts use the term **proximate cause** (or sometimes *legal cause*) to describe this element. Proximate cause is a question not of fact but of law and policy. The question is whether the connection between an act and an injury is strong enough to justify imposing liability.

There is probably nothing in the field of law that has caused more disagreement than the subject of proximate cause. The term is somewhat misleading, because the question is not primarily one of causation and does not arise until causation has been established. Instead, the question concerns a fundamental policy of law: Should a negligent defendant's responsibility extend to consequences that could in no way have been anticipated?

The most discussed and debated of all tort cases, the *Palsgraf* case, which follows, involves what may be called, instead of unforeseeable consequences, the unforeseeable plaintiff. The question before the court is: Does the defendant's duty of care extend only to those who may be injured

---

7. Although punitive damages may be awarded in tort actions, they are usually *not* available in breach of contract actions (to be discussed in the next unit). See the *Emerging Trends* on tort reform in Chapter 11 for a discussion of current issues relating to punitive-damages awards.

as a result of a foreseeable risk, or does it extend also to a person who is outside the zone of danger and whose injury could not reasonably have been foreseen?

Case 7.6

PALSGRAF v. LONG ISLAND RAILROAD CO.

Court of Appeals of New York, 1928.
248 N.Y. 339,
162 N.E. 99.

BACKGROUND AND FACTS   *The plaintiff, Palsgraf, was waiting for a train on a station platform. A man carrying a package was rushing to catch a train that was already moving. As the man attempted to jump aboard the moving train, he seemed unsteady and about to fall. A railroad guard on the car reached forward to grab him, and another guard on the platform pushed him from behind to help him on the train. The man's package, which contained fireworks, fell on the railroad tracks and exploded. There was nothing about the package to indicate its contents. The explosion caused scales located at the other end of the platform to fall on Palsgraf, causing injuries for which she sued the railroad company. At the trial, the jury found that the railroad guards were negligent in their conduct toward the plaintiff, and Palsgraf was awarded damages. The railroad company appealed.*

CARDOZO, C. J. [Chief Justice]
 *   *   *   *

The conduct of the defendant's guard, if a wrong in its relation to the holder of the package, was not a wrong in its relation to the plaintiff, standing far away. Relatively to her it was not negligence at all. Nothing in the situation gave notice that the falling package had in it the potency of peril to persons thus removed. Negligence is not actionable unless it involves the invasion of a legally protected interest, the violation of a right. *   *   * If no hazard was apparent to the eye of ordinary vigilance, an act innocent and harmless, at least to outward seeming, with reference to her, did not take to itself the quality of a tort because it happened to be a wrong, though apparently not one involving the risk of bodily insecurity, with reference to someone else. "In every instance, before negligence can be predicated of a given act, back of the act must be sought and found a duty to the individual complaining, the observance of which would have averted or avoided the injury." *   *   *
 *   *   *   *

 *   *   * What the plaintiff must show is "a wrong" to herself; i.e., a violation of her own right, and not merely a wrong to some one else, nor conduct "wrongful" because unsocial, but not "a wrong" to any one. *   *   * The risk reasonably to be perceived defines the duty to be obeyed[.] *   *   * Here, by concession, there was nothing in the situation to suggest to the most cautious mind that the parcel wrapped in newspaper would spread wreckage through the station. If the guard had thrown it down knowingly and willfully, he would not have threatened the plaintiff's safety, so far as appearances could warn him. His conduct would not have involved, even then, an unreasonable probability of invasion of her bodily security. Liability can be no greater where the act is inadvertent.
 *   *   * One who seeks redress at law does not make out a cause of action by showing without more that there has been damage to his person. If the harm was not willful, he must show that the act as to him had possibilities of danger so many and apparent as to entitle him to be protected against the doing of it though the harm was unintended. *   *   * The victim does not sue derivatively *   *   * to vindicate an interest invaded in the person of another. *   *   * He sues for breach of a duty owing to himself.
 *   *   * [To rule otherwise] would entail liability for any and all consequences, however novel or extraordinary.

**DECISION
AND REMEDY**
Palsgraf's complaint was dismissed. The railroad was not negligent toward her, because injury to her was not foreseeable. Had the owner of the fireworks been harmed, there could well have been a different result if he had filed suit. Chief Justice Cardozo indicated that while the negligent conduct of the defendant's guards may have been a wrong against the holder of the package, it was not a wrong in relation to the plaintiff, who was standing far away.

FORESEEABILITY   Since the decision in the *Palsgraf* case, the courts have used *foreseeability* as the test for proximate cause. The railroad guards were negligent, but the railroad's duty of care did not extend to Palsgraf because she was an unforeseeable plaintiff. According to this view, a defendant's duty of care does not extend to a victim who is not located within a foreseeable zone of danger. Thus, a victim can recover damages only on proving that a reasonable person would have foreseen in the circumstances a risk of injury to him or her.

SUPERSEDING INTERVENING FORCES   A superseding intervening force may break the connection between a wrongful act and injury to another. If so, it cancels out the wrongful act. For example, keeping a can of gasoline in the trunk of one's car creates a foreseeable risk and is thus a negligent act. If lightning strikes the car, exploding the gas tank *and* the gas can, injuring passing pedestrians, the lightning supersedes the original negligence as a cause of the damage, because it was not foreseeable. This example illustrates that the doctrine of superseding intervening forces is also a matter of proximate cause and legal duty.

In other situations, the intervention of a force may not relieve one of liability. If medical mal-

treatment of an injury aggravates the injury, the person whose negligence originally caused the injury is not relieved of liability. If subsequent disease or a subsequent accident is proximately caused by the original injury, the person who caused the original injury will be liable for the injury caused by the subsequent disease or accident. When negligence endangers property and the owner is injured in an attempt to protect the property, the negligent party will be liable for the injury.

In negligence cases, the negligent party will often attempt to show that some act has intervened after his or her action and that this second act was the proximate cause of injury. Typically, in cases in which an individual takes a defensive action, such as attempting to escape by swerving or leaping from a vehicle, the original wrongdoer will not be relieved of liability even if the injury actually resulted from the escape attempt. The same is true under the "danger invites rescue" doctrine. Under this doctrine, if Smith commits an act that endangers Jones, and Brown sustains an injury trying to protect Jones, then Smith will be liable for Brown's injury, as well as for any injuries Jones may sustain. Rescuers can injure themselves, or the person rescued, or even a stranger, but the original wrongdoer will still be liable. The following case illustrates this doctrine.

Case 7.7

**GUARINO v. MINE
SAFETY APPLIANCE
CO.**

Court of Appeals of New York,
1969.
25 N.Y.2d 460,
255 N.E.2d 173,
306 N.Y.S.2d 942.

BACKGROUND AND FACTS   *This case arose out of an accident that killed three men and seriously injured five others. All were sewage treatment workers. After they had corrected a water leakage problem in a New York City sewer, one of the workers, Rooney, was fatally stricken by lethal gas present in the sewer when the protective mask he was wearing failed to operate properly. A coworker attempted to drag Rooney from the sewer tunnel, but finding himself having difficulty breathing, he released Rooney, ripped off his own mask, and yelled for help. Stephen P. Guarino and another coworker were fatally stricken by the lethal gas present in the sewer when they left their posts in the sewer shaft and entered the sewer* *tunnel without masks in response to the call for help. Mary Guarino (the plaintiff), the wife of Stephen P. Guarino, filed suit individually and as administrator of her husband's estate against the manufacturer of the oxygen masks (the defendant). The trial court held for the plaintiff, and the manufacturer appealed.*

JASEN, Judge.
*   *   *   *

Here the defendant committed a culpable [guilty] act against the decedent Rooney, by manufacturing and distributing a defective oxygen-producing mask *   *   *. By virtue of this defendant's culpable act, Rooney was placed in peril, thus inviting his rescue by the plaintiffs who were all members of Rooney's sewage treatment crew. There was no time for reflection when it became known that Rooney was in need of immediate assistance in the dark tunnel some 30 to 40 feet below the street level. These plaintiffs responded to the cries for help in a manner which was reasonable and consistent with their concern for each other as members of a crew. To require that a rescuer answering the cry for help make inquiry as to the nature of the culpable act that imperils someone's life would defy all logic.

As Judge Cardozo so eloquently stated in *Wagner v. International Railway Co.:* ''Danger invites rescue. The cry of distress is the summons to relief. *   *   * The wrong that imperils life is a wrong to the imperilled victim; it is a wrong also to his rescuer.''
*   *   *   *

We conclude that a person who by his culpable act, whether it stems from negligence or breach of warranty, places another person in a position of imminent peril, may be held liable for any damages sustained by a rescuer in his attempt to aid the imperilled victim.

The manufacturer of the malfunctioning oxygen mask was held liable for damages sustained by the coworkers who sought to rescue the worker overcome by sewer gas when the mask failed.

DECISION AND REMEDY

There is no law that says one person must voluntarily come to the aid of, or rescue, another person in danger. You will not be legally liable, for example, if you do not lend assistance to someone being robbed, or even threatened with death or killed, on a subway. Many would hold, however, that individuals have an ethical duty to help, or rescue, others in peril. In a sense, the ''danger invites rescue'' doctrine implicitly recognizes this ethical duty by ensuring that the wrongdoer causing the danger will be liable for the harm caused to rescuers.

ETHICAL CONSIDERATIONS

RES IPSA LOQUITUR   Generally, in lawsuits involving negligence, the plaintiff has the burden of proving that the defendant was negligent. In certain situations, when negligence is very difficult or impossible to prove, the courts may infer that negligence has occurred, in which case the burden of proof rests on the defendant—to prove he or she was *not* negligent. The inference of the defendant's negligence is known as the doctrine of **res ipsa** *loquitur,*[8] which translates as ''the facts speak for themselves.'' This doctrine is applied only when the event creating the damage or injury is one that ordinarily does not occur in the absence of negligence. *Res ipsa loquitur* has been applied to such events as train derailments, wheels falling off mov-

_____

8.   Pronounced rays ihpsuh *loh*-kwuh-duhr.

ing vehicles, falling elevators, and bricks or window panes falling from a defendant's premises. For this doctrine to apply, the event must be caused by an agency or instrumentality within the exclusive control of the defendant, and it must not have been due to any voluntary action or contribution on the part of the plaintiff. Some courts will add still another condition—that the evidence available to explain the event be more accessible to the defendant than to the plaintiff.

Defenses to Negligence

Basic defenses in negligence cases include assumption of risk, contributory negligence, comparative negligence, and the last-clear-chance doctrine.

ASSUMPTION OF RISK   A plaintiff who voluntarily enters into a risky situation, knowing the risk involved, will not be allowed to recover damages. This is the defense of **assumption of risk.** For example, a driver who enters a race knows that there is a risk of being killed or injured in a crash. By entering the race, the driver has thus assumed the risk of injury. The two requirements of this defense are: (1) knowledge of the risk and (2) voluntary assumption of the risk.

The risk can be assumed by express agreement, or the assumption of risk can be implied by the plaintiff's knowledge of the risk and subsequent conduct. Of course, the plaintiff does not assume a risk different from, or greater than, the risk normally carried by the activity. In our example, the race driver assumes the risk of being injured in the race but not the risk that the banking in the curves of the racetrack will give way during the race because of a construction defect.

Risks are not deemed to be assumed in situations involving emergencies. Neither are they assumed when a statute protects a class of people from harm and a member of the class is injured by the harm. For example, employees are protected by statute from harmful working conditions and therefore do not assume the risks associated with the workplace. If an employee is injured, he or she will generally be compensated regardless of fault.

CONTRIBUTORY NEGLIGENCE   All individuals are expected to exercise a reasonable degree of care in looking out for themselves. In some jurisdictions, a person who has failed to exercise such care cannot recover for an injury resulting from negligence. This is the doctrine of **contributory negligence,** according to which both parties have been negligent and their negligence has combined to cause the injury. When one party sues the other in tort for damages for negligence, the defendant can claim contributory negligence, which is a complete defense under common law rules. (Contributory negligence is not, however, a defense to intentional torts or to suits based on strict liability, a topic that will be covered later.) Over the last century, the contributory negligence doctrine has been eroded considerably. Today, most jurisdictions have developed other doctrines—including the doctrines of comparative negligence and last clear chance—to avoid the strict application of the contributory negligence rule.

COMPARATIVE NEGLIGENCE   A majority of the states now allow recovery based on the doctrine of **comparative negligence.** This doctrine permits computation of both the plaintiff's and the defendant's negligence. The plaintiff's damages are reduced by a percentage that represents the degree of his or her contributing fault. To illustrate: Jaime negligently drove through a red light and injured Teresa, who was also driving negligently. Teresa suffered damages of $200,000. The jury found that Jaime was 70 percent negligent and Teresa was 30 percent negligent, so Teresa recovered 70 percent of $200,00, or $140,000. In some states, a plaintiff's negligence must be less serious than the defendant's—that is, the plaintiff can recover only if he or she was 49 percent or less at fault. In other states, a plaintiff's negligence must be no greater than the defendant's—50 percent or less. In still other states, a plaintiff can recover no matter how negligent he or she was—if the defendant was 5 percent at fault, the plaintiff can recover 5 percent of the damages. In some cases, the plaintiff may be subject to a counterclaim by the defendant.

In the following case, an automobile accident victim was held to be comparatively negligent because he failed to wear his seat belt.

BACKGROUND AND FACTS *William Burns was injured in an auto-mobile accident and sought damages from the other party involved in the accident, Ruth Smith, and her insurer. Burns was awarded damages, but the damages were reduced by 75 percent because the trial court jury held that Burns was comparatively negligent to that extent. The jury found Burns to be comparatively negligent because he was not wearing his seat belt at the time of the accident. Burns appealed the decision, contending that the evidence did not adequately support the jury's finding that his failure to use a seat belt made him 75 percent comparatively negligent.*

Case 7.8

BURNS v. SMITH

District Court of Appeal of Florida, Second District, 1985. 476 So.2d 278.

LEHAN, Judge.

*   *   *   *

Mr. Burns contends that the trial court erred in denying his motion for a new trial because the evidence did not adequately support the jury's determination that his failure to use a seat belt made him seventy-five percent comparatively negligent. His contention is to the effect that without any testimony from an accident recon-struction expert there could have been no finding in this case of the requisite causal relationship between the nonuse of a seat belt and the injuries. We do not agree. The evidence showed that Mr. Burns did not use a seat belt and that he was thrown from his seat in the car following the impact. He received head and neck injuries. Under the circumstances of this case we do not believe it was beyond the province of the jury from its common knowledge to conclude that "the failure to use an available and operational seat belt produced or contributed substantially to producing at least a portion of plaintiff's damages."

The verdict of the trial court was affirmed. The jury had reasonable grounds to conclude that Burns's negligence contributed to his injury.

DECISION AND REMEDY

LAST CLEAR CHANCE **Last clear chance** is a doctrine that can excuse the effect of a plaintiff's contributory negligence. If applicable, the last-clear-chance rule allows the plaintiff to recover full damages despite failure to exercise care. This rule operates when, through his or her own negligence, the plaintiff is endangered (or his or her property is endangered) by a defendant who has the last clear chance to avoid the event that causes the damage. For example, if Murphy walks across the street against the light and Lewis, a motorist, sees her in time to avoid hitting her but hits her anyway, Lewis (the defendant) is not permitted to use Murphy's (the plaintiff's) prior negligence as a defense. The defendant negligently missed the opportunity to avoid injuring the plaintiff. The adoption of the comparative negligence rule has effectively abol-ished the last-clear-chance doctrine in most juris-dictions.

[handwritten: Does not apply to case]

■ Strict Liability

The final category of torts is called *strict liability,* or *liability without fault.* Intentional or negligent torts involve acts that depart from a reasonable standard of care and cause an injury. Under the doctrine of strict liability, liability for injury is im-posed for reasons other than fault.

Abnormally Dangerous Activities

Strict liability for damages proximately caused by abnormally dangerous activities is one application of this doctrine. Abnormally dangerous activities have three characteristics:

1. The activity involves potential harm, of a se-rious nature, to persons or property.
2. The activity involves a high degree of risk that

cannot be completely guarded against by the exercise of reasonable care.

3. The activity is not commonly performed in the community or area.

Strict liability is applied because of the extreme risk of the activity. Even when an activity such as blasting with dynamite is performed with all reasonable care, there is still a risk of injury. Balancing that risk against the potential for harm, it is fair to ask the person engaged in the activity to pay for injury caused by the activity. Although there is no fault, there is still responsibility because of the nature of the activity. In other words, it is reasonable to require the person engaged in the activity to carry the necessary insurance or otherwise stand prepared to compensate anyone who suffers.

The following case illustrates a type of abnormally dangerous activity.

Case 7.9

YOMMER v. McKENZIE

Court of Appeals of Maryland,
1969.
255 Md. 220,
257 A.2d 138.

BACKGROUND AND FACTS *The Yommers operated a gasoline station. In December 1967 their neighbors, the McKenzies, noticed a smell in their well water, which proved to be caused by gasoline in the well water. McKenzie complained to the Yommers, who arranged to have one of their underground storage tanks replaced. Nevertheless, the McKenzies were unable to use their water for cooking or bathing until they had a filter and water softener installed. At the time of the trial, in December 1968, they were still bringing in drinking water from an outside source. The McKenzies sued the Yommers for nuisance and recovered damages of $3,500. The Yommers appealed the verdict on the ground that the McKenzies had not proved that there was any negligence and that a gas station is not a nuisance.*

SINGLEY, Judge.
* * * *
We have previously held that the establishment of a gasoline filling station does not constitute a nuisance *per se,* but that it may become a nuisance because of its location or manner in which it is operated.
* * * *
The argument that the McKenzies must prove negligence in order to recover fails to take into account the doctrine of strict liability imposed by the rule of *Rylands v. Fletcher* which has been adopted by our prior decisions. * * *
* * * *
The black letter of [Section 520 of the Restatement (Second) of Torts] sets out the definition:
''520. *Abnormally Dangerous Activities*
In determining whether an activity is abnormally dangerous, the following factors are to be considered.
(a) Whether the activity involves a high degree of risk of some harm to the person, land or chattels of others;
(b) Whether the gravity of the harm which may result from it is likely to be great;
(c) Whether the risk cannot be eliminated by the exercise of reasonable care;
(d) Whether the activity is not a matter of common usage;
(e) Whether the activity is inappropriate to the place where it is carried on; and
(f) The value of the activity to the community.''
We believe that the present case is clearly within the ambit [limits] of this definition. Although the operation of a gasoline station does not of itself involve ''a high degree of risk of some harm to the person, land or chattels of others,'' the

placing of a large underground gasoline tank in close proximity to the appellees' residence and well does involve such a risk * * *. The harm caused to the appellees was a serious one, and it may well have been worse if the contamination had not been detected promptly.

* * * *

The fifth and perhaps most crucial factor * * * as applied to this case is the appropriateness of the activity in the particular place where it is being carried on. No one would deny that gasoline stations as a rule do not present any particular danger to the community. However, when the operation of such activity involves the placing of a large tank adjacent to a well from which a family must draw its water for drinking, bathing and laundry, at least that aspect of the activity is inappropriate to the locale, even when equated to the value of the activity.

* * * *

It is apparent to us that the storage of large quantities of gasoline immediately adjacent to a private residence comes within this rule [of strict liability] and relieved the McKenzies of the necessity of proving negligence.

The Yommers lost on appeal; the judgment for the McKenzies was upheld. There was no need to prove negligence in the case because the nature of the activity and the location of the tank caused the Yommers to be held strictly liable for the gasoline seepage.

DECISION AND REMEDY

Other Applications of Strict Liability

There are other applications of the strict liability principle. Persons who keep dangerous animals, for example, are strictly liable for any harm inflicted by the animals. A significant application of strict liability is in the area of *product liability*. Liability here is a matter of social policy and is based on two factors: (1) the ability of the employer and manufacturer to better bear the cost of injury by spreading it out to society through an increase in the cost of goods and services and (2) the fact that the employer and manufacturer are making a profit from their activities and therefore should bear the cost of injury as an operating expense. Product liability will be considered in depth in Chapter 11.

■ CONCEPT SUMMARY 7.1 Common Basic Torts

Torts	Elements
Intentional Torts against Persons	
Assault	An intentional act that creates in another a reasonable apprehension or fear of immediate harmful or offensive contact.
Battery	An intentional act that brings about harmful or offensive contact to another.
False Imprisonment	An intentional act that confines or restrains another.
Infliction of Emotional Distress	An intentional act amounting to extreme and outrageous conduct that causes severe emotional distress to another.
Defamation	The publication of defamatory factual language concerning, and causing damage to the reputation of, another.

(Continued on next page)

■ CONCEPT SUMMARY 7.1 *(Continued)*

Torts	Elements
Intentional Torts against Persons	
Invasion of Privacy	1. Use of another's name, picture, or other likeness for commercial purposes without permission. 2. Intrusion into another's affairs or seclusion. 3. Publication of information that places another in a false light. 4. Public disclosure of private facts about another.
Fraudulent Misrepresentation	An intentional misrepresentation of facts or conditions, made with knowledge of their falsity or reckless disregard for their truth, to induce another's reliance. The other must have justifiably relied on the misrepresentation, and damage must have been caused by the misrepresentation.
Intentional Torts against Property	
Trespass to Land	An intentional act of physical invasion of another's real property.
Trespass to Personal Property	An intentional act that interferes with another's right to possession of his or her personal property.
Conversion	An intentional act that interferes with another's right to possession of his or her personal property resulting in the destruction of the property or the converting of the property to the tortfeasor's use or benefit.
Nuisance	An intentional act that substantially and unreasonably interferes with another's use or enjoyment of his or her property or with the community's health, safety, or property rights.
Unintentional Torts	
Negligence	A breach, with or without fault, of a duty of care owed to another, causing injury to the other or damage to the other's property.
Strict Liability	A breach of an absolute duty to make something safe, causing injury to another or damage to his or her property.

■ Terms and Concepts to Review

actual malice 149
assault 144
assumption of risk 162
battery 145
causation in fact 158
consent 145
contributory negligence 162
conversion 153
comparative negligence 162
damages 143
defamation 148

intentional tort 144
last clear chance 163
libel 148
negligence 144
nuisance 155
privilege 150
proximate cause 158
public figures 148
puffing 152
punitive damages 158
reasonable person
 standard 156

res ipsa loquitur 161
self-defense 145
slander 148
strict liablity 144
tort 143
tortfeasor 144
trespass to land 152
trespass to personal
 property 153

■ Questions and Case Problems

7-1. Richards is an employee of the Dun Construction Corp. While delivering materials to a construction site, he carelessly runs Dun's truck into a passenger vehicle driven by Green. This is Richard's second accident in six months. When Dun learns of this latest accident, a heated discussion ensues, and Dun fires Richards. Dun is so angry that he immediately writes a letter to the union of which Richards is a member and to all other construction outfits in the community, stating that Richards is the "worst driver in the city" and that "anyone who hires him is asking for legal liability." Richards files suit against Dun, alleging libel on the basis of the statements made in the letters. Discuss the results.

7-2. It is a cold, wintry day. Ken needs to do some shopping on his way home from work. He is running late and is in a hurry. He stops at a drugstore to buy a tube of toothpaste on sale. He sticks the toothpaste in his overcoat pocket, laying the correct amount of change for the purchase on the counter. He is proceeding home when he suddenly remembers his wife's request that he pick up some much-needed groceries. He stops at a grocery store and rushes through the store picking up the groceries. He checks out and in a slow trot starts to leave the store when the checkout clerk sees the toothpaste in his overcoat pocket. Believing Ken is attempting to leave the store without declaring the item, the clerk yells, "Stop, thief!" Two bagboys grab Ken, haul him—struggling and protesting—to a small, dark back room, and lock him in it. One hour later, the store manager gets back from dinner, learns of the events, and, after questioning a distraught Ken, lets him go. Ken starts having nightmares and backaches and becomes extremely nervous when friends and neighbors look at him. Discuss fully whether any torts have been committed against Ken.

7-3. Frank is a former employee of ABC Auto Repair Co. He enters the property of ABC, claiming the company owes him $150 in back wages. An argument ensues, and the ABC general manager, Steward, orders Frank off the property. Frank refuses to leave, and Steward orders two mechanics to throw him off the property. Frank runs to his truck, but on the way he grabs some tools valued at $150. Frank gets into his truck and, in his haste to drive away, destroys a gatepost. Frank refuses to return the tools.
(a) Discuss whether Frank has committed any torts.
(b) If the mechanics had thrown Frank off the property, would ABC be guilty of assault and battery? Explain.

7-4. John is a delivery employee for Crystal Glass, Inc. He is making a delivery when, at an intersection, his van and the passenger car of Jane collide. Jane wants to hold both John and Crystal Glass liable for the damages she has sustained. John claims that Jane was also at fault, at least as much at fault as he, and therefore neither he nor Crystal should be liable. Discuss fully these claims.

7-5. Ruth carelessly parks her car on a steep hill, leaving the car in neutral and failing to engage the parking brake. The car rolls down the hill, knocking down an electric line.

The sparks from the broken line ignite a grass fire. The fire spreads until it reaches a barn one mile away. The barn has dynamite inside, and the burning barn explodes, causing part of the roof to fall on and injure a passing motorist, Jim. Can Jim recover from Ruth? Why or why not?

7-6. Professor Ronald R. Hutchinson received federal funding for animal (monkey) studies on aggression. U.S. Senator William Proxmire bestowed his Golden Fleece of the Month Award on the federal agency that funded Hutchinson's research. The purpose of the award was to publicize wasteful government spending. Senator Proxmire announced the award in a speech prepared for and given to the Senate. The speech was reprinted in a press release mailed to 275 members of the news media and in a newsletter sent to 100,000 people. Among Proxmire's critical comments was a description of the federal grants for Hutchinson's research as "monkey business." Hutchinson sued Proxmire for defamation. The U.S. district court and court of appeals confirmed Senator Proxmire's claims that his communication was privileged and that Professor Hutchinson was a public figure who had not proved that Proxmire acted with malice. Discuss whether either of Senator Proxmire's claims is a valid defense. [*Hutchinson v. Proxmire,* 443 U.S. 111, 99 S.Ct. 2675, 61 L.Ed.2d 411 (1979)]

7-7. H. E. Butt Grocery Co. (H.E.B.) has numerous retail grocery stores scattered throughout the state of Texas. Hawkins went to grocery shop at one of the H.E.B. stores. A heavy rainstorm and north wind had caused water to be tracked into the store by customers and water to be blown through the door each time it was opened. As Hawkins entered through the automatically opened door, she slipped and fell in approximately one-half inch of rain water that had accumulated on the floor. The manager knew of the weather conditions and had had employees mop the floor on numerous occasions. There was no sign posted warning customers of the water hazard. Can Hawkins recover from H.E.B. for injuries sustained from slipping on the water-covered floor? Why or why not? [*H. E. Butt Grocery Co. v. Hawkins,* 594 S.W.2d 187 (Tex.Civ.App. 1980)]

7-8. O'Neill was injured when he was struck in the eye by a softball thrown by Daniels, a teammate, during warm-up activities before an amateur softball game. O'Neill claimed that Daniels was negligent and filed suit. Discuss the probable success of O'Neill's suit in light of the fact that the injury occurred during the warm-up activities. [*O'Neill v. Daniels,* 135 A.D.2d 1076, 523 N.Y.S.2d 264 (1987)]

7-9. One night in August of 1985, Gerrit and Kay Mostert and their daughter went to a movie theater in Cheyenne, Wyoming. While they were in the theater, the National Weather Service warned the community that a severe thunderstorm was imminent and that flash floods and tornadoes could occur. Civil authorities urged citizens to stay indoors in safe areas to avoid injury or death. Although the theater managers were aware of the dangerous weather conditions and the warning that had been issued, they did not inform departing theater-goers of the perilous situation. Shortly after driving away from the theater parking lot, the Mosterts encountered a flooded area. During their attempt to escape, the daughter drowned. The Mosterts brought an action against the theater owners, CBL & Associates, claiming that the theater had been negligent in its failure to warn those leaving the theater of the danger. Discuss whether the theater had a duty to inform the Mosterts and others leaving the theater of the hazardous weather conditions. [*Mostert v. CBL & Associates,* 741 P.2d 1090 (Wyo. 1987)]

7-10. Sharon Lee Glynn, a sixteen-year-old girl, was waiting for a bus in a Peter Pan Bus Lines terminal in Springfield, Massachusetts, when a stranger approached her and stabbed her without warning or provocation. Glynn died as a result of the attack. The bus terminal was in a run-down section of the city, and homeless people and drunks frequented the area. There had been robberies in the terminal's restrooms and assaults in the terminal, and apparently the terminal's managers called the police every week or so because of a security or other problem.' Although the terminal was aware that it needed a uniformed security officer to deter crime on its premises, it had not yet hired any security personnel. The administrator of Glynn's estate, Alfred Sharpe, brought an action against the terminal for damages, claiming that the terminal, by failing to have security personnel present, had breached its duty of care to the patrons of the terminal. In evaluating Sharpe's claim, the court must address the following three questions:

 (a) Did the bus terminal owe a duty of care toward its patrons?

 (b) If so, did it breach this duty by failing to hire a uniformed security officer?

 (c) If it did breach its duty of care, was its breach the proximate cause of Glynn's death?

How will the court decide, and why? [*Sharpe v. Peter Pan Bus Lines, Inc.,* 401 Mass. 788, 519 N.E.2d 1341 (1988)]

7-11. George Giles was staying at a Detroit hotel owned by the Pick Hotels Corp. While a bellboy was removing luggage from the back seat of Giles's car, Giles reached into the front seat to remove his briefcase. As he did so, he supported himself by placing his left hand on the center pillar to which the rear door was hinged, with his fingers in a position to be injured if the rear door was closed. The bellboy closed the rear door, and a part of Giles's left index finger was amputated. Giles sued the hotel for damages. The hotel claimed that it was not liable because Giles, by placing his hand on the car as he did, contributed to the injury. (Under state law, contributory negligence was an absolute defense to liability.) Discuss whether the hotel will succeed in its defense. [*Giles v. Pick Hotels Corp.,* 232 F.2d 887, 6th Cir. 1956)]

7-12. A Question of Ethics

George Ward entered a K-Mart department store in Champaign, Illinois, through a service entrance near the home improvements department. After purchasing a large mirror,

Ward left the store through the same door. On his way out the door, carrying the large mirror in front and somewhat to the side of him, he collided with a concrete pole located just outside the door about a foot and a half from the outside wall. The mirror broke, and the broken glass cut his right cheek and eye, resulting in reduced vision in that eye. He later stated that he had not seen the pole, did not realize what was happening, and only knew that he felt ''a bad pain, and then saw stars.'' Ward sued K-Mart Corp. for damages, alleging that the store was negligent. The Supreme Court of Illinois ultimately decided in Ward's favor and upheld the jury's award of $68,000 in damages. The court held that the store had failed in its duty to its patrons by not maintaining the premises in a reasonably safe condition. The store should have foreseen the risk to its customers posed by the poles and guarded against it. [*Ward v. K-Mart Corp.,* 136 *Ill.2d* 132, 554 *N.E.2d* 223, 143 *Ill.Dec.* 288 (1990)]

 1. What ethical principle underlies the common law doctrine that business owners have a duty of care toward their customers?

 2. K-Mart argued that the pole was such an obvious obstacle that it did not pose any risk, and therefore no warning to customers was needed. Do you agree with this argument? Why or why not?

 3. Can you think of any reasons for the court's conclusion that K-Mart should have foreseen the possibility that a customer could be injured because of the presence of the pole?

 4. Does the duty of care unfairly burden business owners? Discuss.

7-13. Case Briefing Assignment

Examine Case A.7 [Shreve v. Duke Power Co., 97 N.C.App. 648, 389 S.E.2d 444 (1990)] in Appendix A. The case has been excerpted there in great detail. Review and then brief the case, making sure you include answers to the following questions in your brief.

 1. What claim did Shreve raise in his lawsuit?

 2. Who were the defendants?

 3. What was the trial court's decision?

 4. How did the appellate court rule in reviewing the trial court's decision?

 5. Why did the appellate court rule as it did with regard to Duke Power management personnel who discussed the allegation made concerning Shreve?

Chapter 8

Torts and Crimes Related to Business

Our economic system of free enterprise is predicated on the ability of persons, acting either as individuals or as business firms, to compete for customers and for sales. Unfettered competitive behavior has been shown to lead to economic efficiency and economic progress. Businesses may, generally speaking, engage in whatever is *reasonably* necessary to obtain a fair share of a market or to recapture a share that has been lost. But they are not allowed to use the motive of completely eliminating competition to justify certain business activities. Thus, an entire area of what are called business torts has arisen. Remember that a tort is a breach of a duty owed to an individual or to a group. **Business torts** are defined as wrongful interferences with others' business rights. Included in business torts are such vaguely worded concepts as *unfair competition* and *wrongfully interfering with the business relations of others.*

Following a discussion of business torts, we address the subject of crimes, especially so-called *white-collar crime.* A crime is a breach of a duty owed to society as a whole. Although no official definition exists for **white-collar crime,** the term is popularly used to refer to nonviolent crimes committed by individuals or businesses to obtain a personal or business advantage. Bribery, money laundering, insider trading, and corporate crime all fall within the broad category of white-collar crime. We conclude the chapter with a section on the application of the Racketeer Influenced and Corrupt Organizations Act (RICO) to business activities.

■ Torts Related to Business

Because the area of business torts is so broad, we restrict our discussion in this section to the following general categories of business torts: wrongful interference with the business rights of others, appropriation of another's name without permission, and defamation or disparagement of business property or reputation. Other business torts are discussed in Chapter 26, in the context of our discussion of intellectual property and computer law.

Wrongful Interference with the Business Rights of Others

Torts involving wrongful interference with another's business rights generally fall into two categories—interference with a contractual relationship and interference with a business relationship. These two torts and the defenses that can be raised against them are discussed below.

WRONGFUL INTERFERENCE WITH A CONTRACTUAL RELATIONSHIP The body of tort law relating to *intentional interference with a contractual relationship* has increased greatly in recent years. A landmark case in this area involved an opera singer, Joanna Wagner, who was under contract to sing for a man named Lumley for a specified period of years.[1] A man named Gye, who knew of this contract, nonetheless "enticed" Wagner to refuse to carry out the agreement, and Wagner began to sing for Gye. Gye's action constituted a tort because it interfered with the contractual relationship between Wagner and Lumley. (Wagner's refusal to carry out the agreement also entitled Lumley to sue for breach of contract.)

In principle, any lawful contract can be the basis for an action of this type. The plaintiff must prove that the defendant actually *induced* the breach of a contractual relationship, not merely that the defendant reaped the benefits of a broken contract. For example, suppose that Jones has a contract with Smith that calls for Smith to mow Jones's lawn every week for fifty-two weeks at a specified price per week. Miller, who needs gardening services, contacts Smith and offers to pay Smith a wage that is substantially higher than that offered by Jones—although Miller knows nothing about the Smith–Jones contract. Smith breaches his con-

tract with Jones so that he can work for Miller. Jones cannot sue Miller, because Miller knew nothing of the Smith–Jones contract and was totally unaware that the higher wage he offered induced Smith to breach that contract.

Three basic elements are necessary to the existence of wrongful interference with a contractual relationship:

1. A valid, enforceable contract must exist between two parties.
2. A third party must *know* that this contract exists.
3. This third party must *intentionally* cause either of the two parties to the contract to break the contract. Whether this third party acts in bad faith or with malice (the intention to harm another) is immaterial to establishing this tort, even though in most cases bad faith or malice is in evidence. The interference, however, must be for the purpose of advancing the economic interest of the inducer.

The contract may be between a firm and its employees or a firm and its customers, suppliers, competitors, or other parties. Sometimes a competitor of a firm may attempt to draw away a key employee, even to the extent of paying the damages for breach of contract. If the original employer can show that the competitor induced the breach—that is, that the employee would not normally have broken the contract—damages can be recovered.

The following highly publicized case illustrates the requirements for the tort of wrongful interference with a contractual relationship.

---

1. *Lumley v. Gye,* 118 Eng.Rep. 749 (1853).

Case 8.1

TEXACO, INC. v. PENNZOIL CO.

Court of Appeals of Texas— Houston (First District), 1987.
729 S.W.2d 768.

BACKGROUND AND FACTS   *Pennzoil had made an offer to buy control of Getty Oil and had negotiated the offer with the major stockholders, Gordon Getty and the Getty Museum. A Memorandum of Agreement was made subject to the agreement of Getty's board of directors. The board declined to approve the arrangement and made a counteroffer; the board also began looking for other potential bidders. Although some details of the agreement remained unsettled, Pennzoil eventually accepted one of Getty's counteroffers. The news was announced by both companies and reported widely in newspapers, including the* Wall Street Journal, *on January 5, 1984. While the lawyers from each company were negotiating a formal and specific written document, Getty's investment banker continued to look for another bidder. Texaco made a bid that Getty's board promptly* *accepted on January 6. Pennzoil subsequently sued Texaco, alleging tortious (wrongful) interference with its contract with Getty Oil. The trial court jury found that (1) Getty had agreed to Pennzoil's offer to purchase its stock; (2) Texaco knowingly interfered with this agreement; (3) as a result of Texaco's interference, Pennzoil suffered damages of $7.53 billion; (4) Texaco's actions were intentional, willful, and in wanton disregard of Pennzoil's rights; and (5) Pennzoil was entitled to punitive damages of $3 billion. Texaco appealed. Among a number of points of error claimed by Texaco, the appellate court examined (1) whether Pennzoil and Getty actually had a contract, (2) whether Texaco knew that a contract existed between Getty and Pennzoil, and (3) whether Texaco acted to interfere with this contract.*

WARREN, Justice.
* * * *

Texaco contends that under controlling principles of * * * law, there was insufficient evidence to support the jury's finding that at the end of the Getty Oil board meeting * * *, the Getty entities intended to bind themselves to an agreement with Pennzoil.
* * * *

Under [applicable principles of] law, if * * * there is no understanding that a signed writing is necessary before the parties will be bound, and the parties have agreed upon all substantial terms, then an informal agreement can be binding, even though the parties contemplate evidencing their agreement in a formal document later.
* * * *

The record as a whole demonstrates that there was legally and factually sufficient evidence to support the jury's finding * * * that the Trust, the Museum, and the Company intended to bind themselves to an agreement with Pennzoil at the end of the Getty Oil board meeting * * *.
* * * *

* * * Texaco [also] contends that the evidence is legally and factually insufficient to show that Texaco had actual knowledge of any agreement, that it actively induced breach of the alleged contract, and that the alleged contract was valid and capable of being interfered with.
* * * *

Pennzoil responds that * * * the jury could reasonably infer that Texaco knew about the Pennzoil deal from the evidence of (1) how Texaco carefully mapped its strategy to defeat Pennzoil's deal by acting to "stop the train" or "stop the signing"; (2) the notice of a contract given by a January 5 *Wall Street Journal* article reporting on the Pennzoil agreement—an article that Texaco denied anyone at Texaco had seen; (3) the knowledge of an agreement that would arise from comparing the Memorandum of Agreement with the Getty press release; (4) the demands made by the Museum and the Trust for full indemnity from Texaco against any claims by Pennzoil arising out of the Memorandum of Agreement; and (5) the Museum's demand that, even if the Texaco deal fell through, the Museum would be guaranteed the price Pennzoil had agreed to pay for the Museum's shares. * * *
* * * *

The jury was not required to accept Texaco's version of events in this case, and this Court may not substitute its own interpretation of the evidence for the decision of the trier of fact. There was legally and factually sufficient evidence to support an inference by the jury that Texaco had the required knowledge of an agreement.
* * *

*   *   *   *

A necessary element of the plaintiff's cause of action is a showing that the defendant took an active part in persuading a party to a contract to breach it. Merely entering into a contract with a party with the knowledge of that party's contractual obligations to someone else is not the same as inducing a breach. It is necessary that there be some act of interference or of persuading a party to breach, for example by offering better terms or other incentives, for tort liability to arise. The issue of whether a defendant affirmatively took steps to induce the breach of an existing contract is a question of fact for the jury.

*   *   * Texaco argues that it merely responded to a campaign of active solicitation by Getty Oil and the Museum, who were dissatisfied by the terms of Pennzoil's offer.

*   *   *   *

Texaco argues that its testimony shows that Getty Oil and the Museum were the real moving forces that eventually led to the Texaco contract. However, we find that there is legally and factually sufficient evidence in the record to support the jury's finding that Texaco actively induced the breach of the Getty entities' agreement with Pennzoil.

DECISION AND REMEDY   *The appellate court accepted the findings of the jury and affirmed the lower court's decision. The Supreme Court of Texas later found no reversible errors in this decision. Other issues in the case were appealed as high as the United States Supreme Court. In 1988, the case was settled for $3 billion. The day of the payment, Texaco completed its reorganization and emerged from twelve months in bankruptcy proceedings.*

WRONGFUL INTERFERENCE WITH A BUSINESS RELATIONSHIP Individuals devise countless schemes to attract business, but they are forbidden by the courts to interfere unreasonably with another's business in their attempts to gain a share of the market. There is a difference between *competition* and *predatory behavior*. The distinction usually depends on whether a business is attempting to attract customers in general or to solicit only those customers who have already shown an interest in the similar product or service of a specific competitor. If a shopping center contains two shoe stores, an employee of Store A cannot be positioned at the entrance of Store B for the purpose of diverting customers to Store A. This type of activity constitutes the tort of wrongful interference with a business relationship, often referred to as interference with a prospective (economic) advantage, and is commonly considered to be an unfair trade practice. If this type of activity were permitted, Store A would reap the benefits of Store B's advertising.

A salesperson cannot follow another company's salesperson through the city, soliciting the same prospective customers. Even though the people contacted may have purchased nothing from the first salesperson, that salesperson still has a business relationship with them. Courts will issue injunctions against this kind of behavior and will award damages when the business alleging interference can prove it suffered a monetary loss. In the following case a salesperson's activities exceeded the bounds of fair competition.

Case 8.2

AZAR v. LEHIGH CORP.

District Court of Appeal of Florida, Second District, 1978. 364 So.2d 860.

BACKGROUND AND FACTS   *Lehigh Corporation, a developer of real estate, obtained a restraining order (which is similar to an injunction) against one of its former sales representatives, Leroy Azar. Lehigh brought prospective customers to its development, Lehigh Acres, and provided accommodations at its company-owned motel. Azar pursued a practice of following Lehigh purchasers as they entered the motel and persuading them to rescind (cancel) their contracts with Lehigh and purchase less* *expensive property from him. Azar contended that Lehigh's customers had a right under federal law to rescind their contracts within three days and that he was merely providing them with an opportunity to be relieved of their contracts and to obtain comparable property for lower prices. Lehigh asserted that Azar was tortiously interfering with the advantageous business relationship between Lehigh and its customers.*

GRIMES, Chief Justice.
* * * *

There is a narrow line between what constitutes vigorous competition in a free enterprise society and malicious interference with a favorable business relationship. Under the heading of ''Interference with prospective advantage,'' Prosser states:

> Though trade warfare may be waged to the bitter end, there are certain rules of combat which must be observed. . . . W. Prosser, Law of Torts (4th ed. 1971) at [page] 956.

He goes on to say that the courts have generally prohibited such activities as defamation of the competitor, disparagement of his goods and his business methods, and intimidation, harassment and annoyance of his customers. In the final analysis, the issue seems to turn upon whether the subject conduct is considered to be ''unfair'' according to contemporary business standards.

Keeping in mind the trial judge's broad discretion to enter temporary restraining orders, we believe there is sufficient evidence in this record to support the court's decision. Moreover, we believe the terms of the order are precise enough for the appellant to understand what he cannot do. Considering appellant's knowledge of Lehigh's operation, we are confident that he will have no difficulty in ascertaining which of the motel patrons constitute appellees' guests as defined in the temporary restraining order.

The restraining order against Azar was allowed to stand. Azar remained under court order not to solicit business from those customers brought to Lehigh Acres by Lehigh Corporation.

DECISION AND REMEDY

DEFENSES TO WRONGFUL INTERFERENCE A person will not be liable for the tort of wrongful interference with a contractual or business relationship if it can be shown that the interference was *permissible.*

Permissible interferences are interfering actions that the courts have not held to be tortious interferences. For example, bona fide competitive behavior is a privileged (justifiable, or permissible) interference even if it results in the breaking of a contract. If Jones Meats advertises so effectively that it induces Sam's Restaurant Chain to break its contract with Paul's Meat Company, Paul's Meat Company will be unable to recover against Jones Meats on a wrongful interference theory. After all, the public policy that favors free competition in advertising definitely outweighs any possible instability that such competitive activity might cause in contractual relations.

Also, luring customers away from a competitor through aggressive marketing and advertising strategies obviously interferes with the competitor's relationship with his or her customers, but such activity is permitted by the courts. Also, so long as there is no associated illegal activity, a businessperson will not incur tort liability for negotiating secretly behind a rival's back, refusing to do business with a competitor, or refusing to deal with third parties until they stop doing business with a rival.

PERMISSIVE INTERFERENCES VERSUS TORTIOUS INTERFERENCES What the courts consider normal competitive activity is not always easy to ascertain. One might ask when the normal desire to compete and obtain profits ends and when a tortious action begins. The courts often emphasize parties' bad motives, but such cases often involve conduct that would be objectionable anyway—for example, efforts that are directed toward driving a competitor out of business are objectionable for the same reasons that led to the enactment of antitrust laws (see Chapters 20 and 21). The landmark case that follows illustrates how a Minnesota court grappled with the question of malicious injury to business.

Case 8.3

TUTTLE v. BUCK

Supreme Court of Minnesota,
1909.
107 Minn. 145,
119 N.W. 946.

BACKGROUND AND FACTS *The plaintiff, Edward Tuttle, filed suit against the defendant, Cassius Buck, for malicious interference with his barbershop in the small village of Howard Lake, Minnesota. The plaintiff had owned and operated the shop for the previous ten years and had been able to maintain himself and his family comfortably from the income of the business. The defendant was a banker in the same community who "maliciously" established a competitive barbershop. The defendant employed a barber to carry on the business and used his personal influence to attract customers from the plaintiff's barbershop. Apparently, the defendant circulated false and malicious reports and accusations about the plaintiff and personally solicited and persuaded many of the plaintiff's patrons to stop using the plaintiff's services; indeed, the defendant used his personal power as the town's banker to threaten some customers in order to force them to use the defendant's shop instead. The plaintiff charged that the defendant undertook this entire plan with the sole design of injuring the plaintiff and destroying his business, not for serving any legitimate business interest. The trial court's decision for the plaintiff was affirmed by the appellate court, and the defendant appealed.*

ELLIOTT, Justice.
 *   *   *   *
 *   *   * It is not at all correct to say that the motive with which an act is done is always immaterial, providing the act itself is not unlawful. *   *   *
 *   *   * For generations there has been a practical agreement upon the proposition that competition in trade and business is desirable, and this idea has found expression in the decisions of the courts as well as in statutes. But it has led to grievous and manifold wrongs to individuals, and many courts have manifested an earnest desire to protect the individuals from the evils which result from unrestrained business competition. The problem has been to so adjust matters as to preserve the principle of competition and yet guard against its abuse to the unnecessary injury to the individual. So the principle that man may use his own property according to his own needs and desires, while true in the abstract, is subject to many limitations in the concrete. Men cannot always, in civilized society, be allowed to use their own property as their interests or desires may dictate without reference to the fact that they have neighbors whose rights are as sacred as their own. The existence and well-being of society requires that each and every person shall conduct himself consistently with the fact that he is a social and reasonable person. *   *   *
 *   *   * To divert to one's self the customers of a business rival by the offer of goods at lower prices is in general a legitimate mode of serving one's own interest, and justifiable as fair competition. But when a man starts an opposition place of business, not for the sake of profit to himself, but regardless of loss to himself, and for the sole purpose of driving his competitor out of business, and with the intention of himself retiring upon the accomplishment of his malevolent purpose, he is guilty of a wanton wrong and an actionable tort. In such a case he would not be exercising his legal right, or doing an act which can be judged separately from the motive which actuated him. To call such conduct competition is a perversion of terms. It is simply

the application of force without legal justification, which in its moral quality may be no better than highway robbery.

The plaintiff's cause of action was recognized under Minnesota law. The Supreme Court of Minnesota concluded that modern business requires certain protection against abusive business practices.

DECISION AND REMEDY

Appropriation

The use of one person's name or likeness by another, without permission and for the benefit of the user, constitutes the tort of **appropriation.** Under the law, an individual's right to privacy includes the right to the exclusive use of his or her identity. Recently, a number of cases have arisen concerning the use of a famous person's name for the benefit of the user. One case involved the use of "Here's Johnny"—the opening line of the Johnny Carson show. A Michigan corporation that rented and sold portable toilets advertised them as "Here's Johnny" toilets. Carson brought suit, claiming that the Michigan corporation had violated his right to privacy by publicly appropriating his celebrity status for the corporation's commercial benefit. Even though the corporation had not used Carson's name or picture, the court held that the use of "Here's Johnny" was an appropriation of Carson's identity because the phrase was so strongly associated with Carson's public personality.[2] Other cases have involved the unauthorized use of former world heavyweight boxing champion Muhammad Ali's appellation "The Greatest" to describe a nude male model[3] and professional football wide receiver Elroy Hirsch's moniker "Crazylegs" as the name of a shaving gel.[4]

Defamation

As we stated in Chapter 7, the tort of *defamation* occurs when an individual makes a false statement that injures another's reputation. We also divided defamation into its component parts of libel (defamatory statements in written or printed form) and slander (defamatory statements made orally). Defamation becomes a business tort when the defamatory matter injures someone in a profession, business, or trade or when it adversely affects a business entity in its credit rating and other dealings.

When erroneous information from a computer about a person's credit standing or business reputation impairs that person's ability to obtain further credit, *defamation by computer* results. The following case illustrates how this tort can occur.

---

2. *Carson v. Here's Johnny Portable Toilets,* 698 F.2d 831 (6th Cir. 1983).

3. *Ali v. Playgirl, Inc.,* 447 F.Supp. 723 (S.D.N.Y. 1978).
4. *Hirsch v. S. C. Johnson & Son, Inc.,* 90 Wis.2d 379, 280 N.W.2d 129 (1979).

BACKGROUND AND FACTS *Dun & Bradstreet, Inc., the well-known credit-reporting agency, included false information concerning Greenmoss Builders, Inc., in a computerized letter sent to several of its subscribers. The false information was that Greenmoss had filed for bankruptcy, when, in fact, it had not. One of Greenmoss's employees had filed for bankruptcy, and a young, temporary employee of Dun & Bradstreet erroneously concluded that the firm itself had filed for bankruptcy. The inaccurate report resulted in a loss of business and income for Greenmoss, and, because of these damages, Greenmoss sued Dun & Bradstreet for defamation. The trial court held for Greenmoss and awarded $50,000 in compensatory damages and $300,000 in punitive damages to Greenmoss. Dun & Bradstreet appealed, claiming that it was a public figure and its credit report*

Case 8.4

DUN & BRADSTREET, INC. v. GREENMOSS BUILDERS, INC.
Supreme Court of the United States, 1985.
472 U.S. 749,
105 S.Ct. 2939,
86 L.Ed.2d 593.

was a form of speech protected by the First Amendment. Therefore, to recover damages for defamation, Greenmoss would have to prove that Dun & Bradstreet acted with "actual malice." The case was ultimately reviewed by the United States Supreme Court.

POWELL, Justice.
        *   *   *   *

        *   *   * In a related context, we have held that "[w]hether . . . speech addresses a matter of public concern must be determined by [the expression's] content, form, and context . . . as revealed by the whole record." These factors indicate that petitioner's credit report concerns no public issue. It was speech solely in the individual interest of the speaker and its specific business audience. This particular interest warrants no special protection when—as in this case—the speech is wholly false and clearly damaging to the victim's business reputation. Moreover, since the credit report was made available to only five subscribers, who, under the terms of the subscription agreement, could not disseminate it further, it cannot be said that the report involves any "strong interest in the free flow of commercial information." There is simply no credible argument that this type of credit reporting requires special protection to ensure that "debate on public issues [will] be uninhibited, robust, and wide-open."
        *   *   *   *

        We conclude that permitting recovery of presumed and punitive damages in defamation cases absent a showing of "actual malice" does not violate the First Amendment when the defamatory statements do not involve matters of public concern. *   *   *

DECISION AND REMEDY   *The United States Supreme Court held for Greenmoss. The speech did not concern a public matter, and Greenmoss was entitled to the damages awarded by the trial court.*

Disparagement of Property

Disparagement of property occurs when economically injurious falsehoods are made not about another's reputation but about another's *product* or *property*. Disparagement of property is a general term for torts that can be more specifically referred to as *slander of quality* or *slander of title*.

SLANDER OF QUALITY   Publication of false information about another's product, alleging it is not what its seller claims, constitutes a tort of **slander of quality.** This tort has also been given the name **trade libel.** The plaintiff must prove that actual damages proximately resulted from the slander of quality. That is, it must be shown not only that a third person refrained from dealing with the plaintiff because of the improper publication but also that there were associated damages. The economic calculation of such damages—they are, after all, conjectural—is often extremely difficult.

It is possible for an improper publication to be both a slander of quality and a defamation. For example, a statement that disparages the quality of an article may also, by implication, disparage the character of the person who would sell such a product.

The law of trademarks has, to some extent, made it easier for companies to sue other companies on the basis of purported false advertising. In the past, courts often ruled that companies could only be liable for false advertising when they misrepresented their own products. It mattered little what such companies claimed about their competitors' brands, particularly in so-called comparative advertisements. Today, false or misleading statements about another firm's products are actionable.

In the following case, the court evaluates the advertising claims made by the two leading competitors in the U.S. puppy food market.

BACKGROUND AND FACTS *From October 1985 through September 1986, Alpo Petfoods, Inc., and Ralston Purina Company both conducted extensive advertising campaigns for their puppy food products. Ralston claimed in its advertising that its Puppy Chow products helped reduce the incidence of canine hip dysplasia (CHD), a degenerative joint disease. This was a spectacular claim for dog owners and breeders because CHD is one of the most feared dog diseases—it is incurable, difficult to treat, and in its advanced stages, very painful. Because of Ralston's status as the leading puppy food seller in the United States, the claim had a high degree of credibility. Alpo Petfoods, the second largest seller of puppy food in the United States, claimed in its advertising that, based on a survey it had conducted, veterinarians preferred the "formula" in Alpo Puppy Food "2 to 1" over the "leading puppy food" (Ralston's Puppy Chow). In October 1986, Alpo sued Ralston, alleging that Ralston's advertising claims were false, misleading, and deceptive in violation of both the Lanham Act (a federal statute that prohibits false descriptions or representations of goods) and common law. Ralston filed a counterclaim, alleging that Alpo's claims were false, misleading, and deceptive in violation of both the Lanham Act and common law. Ralston further claimed that statements made by Alpo to veterinarians and news media regarding Ralston's CHD claims constituted unfair competition, deceptive trade practices, and defamation. Both parties sought damages and permanent injunctions prohibiting the other party from further publication of the false claims.*

Case 8.5

ALPO PETFOODS, INC. v. RALSTON PURINA CO.

United States District Court, District of Columbia, 1989.
720 F.Supp. 194.

SPORKIN, District Judge.
* * * *
* * * [B]oth parties have made false, deceptive and misleading claims which are actionable. In this respect, both parties are entitled to relief, the extent to which is set out later in this opinion. Because liability has been found and relief has been granted under the Lanham Act, this court does not reach the question of whether the parties' actions constitute common law false advertising or unfair competition. The parties' respective claims, to the extent this court finds the conduct of the parties actionable, can be fully vindicated under the Lanham Act.

The court also finds that Alpo's statements to the media and the public regarding the challenged CHD claims are not defamatory and do not constitute unfair competition or deceptive trade practices.
* * * *
* * * The overwhelming weight of scientific authority indicates CHD is a hereditary disease and there is no reliable evidence that nutritional balance in a puppy's diet affects hip joint laxity, hip joint fit, CHD or degenerative joint disease. Ralston's research does not show that its puppy food reduces hip joint laxity. As a result, Ralston's CHD claims are false.
* * * *
Considering Alpo's veterinarian preference claim against the undisputed fact that veterinarians overwhelmingly preferred Purina Puppy Chow, this court finds that Alpo's veterinarian preference claim was deceptive and misleading.
* * * *
The court is particularly disturbed by its finding that the two leading manufacturers and distributors of dog food in the United States have engaged in serious, deceptive advertising practices. Because of the seriousness of these practices, the court has decided to enjoin both parties from engaging in such practices in the future.

DECISION AND REMEDY *The court entered judgment for Alpo. Ralston was not awarded damages for Alpo's false advertising because of the "magnitude of Ralston's misconduct" compared with that of Alpo. Both parties were enjoined from further publication of their respective false claims, and both were ordered to issue corrective releases to those who had received the false information.*

SLANDER OF TITLE   When a publication denies or casts doubt on another's legal ownership of any property, and when this results in financial loss to that property's owner, the tort of **slander of title** may exist. Usually this is an intentional tort in which someone knowingly publishes an untrue statement about property with the intent of discouraging a third person from dealing with the person slandered. For example, it would be difficult for a car dealer to attract customers after competitors published a notice that the dealer's stock consisted of stolen autos. It would also be difficult for a pizza parlor to attract customers if competitors claimed it used grounded-up cockroaches.

■ Crimes Related to Business

A discussion of criminal law is appropriate to a study of business law because the prevention of crime and the effort of capturing and prosecuting those accused of crimes are time-consuming and costly activities. Consequently, it is important that we understand the nature and extent of such activities and their impact on businesses.

The sanctions used to bring about a peaceful society, in which individuals engaging in business can compete and flourish, include those imposed by the civil law, such as damages for various types of tortious conduct (as discussed in the preceding chapter) and damages for breach of contract (to be discussed in Chapter 9). Chapter 2 also pointed out that courts of equity may restrain certain unlawful conduct or require that things done unlawfully or having certain unlawful effects be undone by issuing injunctions.

These remedies have not been sufficient deterrents in some instances. Consequently, additional sanctions have been developed for particular undesirable activities. As a result, a *criminal law element* exists within the legal environment of business. The prerequisite of *fault* or *guilt* in this area is different from those in the civil law, as are the sanctions and penalties.

The Nature of Crime

Crimes can be distinguished from other wrongful acts in that they are *offenses against society as a whole*. Criminal defendants are prosecuted by a public official, not by their victims. In addition, those who have committed crimes are punished. Tort remedies—remedies for civil wrongs—are generally intended to compensate the injured (except when damages of a punitive nature are assessed), but criminal law is directly concerned with punishing (and, ideally, rehabilitating) the wrongdoer.

A final factor distinguishing criminal sanctions from tort remedies is that the source of criminal law is primarily statutory. Both the acts that constitute crimes and the resulting punishments are formally and very specifically set out in statutes. A crime can thus be defined as a wrong against society proclaimed in a statute and, if intentionally committed, punishable by society.

Classifications of Crimes

Crimes are classified as felonies or misdemeanors according to the punishment provided (the place or the length of confinement).

FELONIES   **Felonies** are punishable by imprisonment in a federal or state penitentiary for more than a year. Extremely serious felonies may even be punishable by death. Felonies can also be classified by type of punishment. The Model Penal Code,[5] for example, provides for four degrees of

---

5.   The American Law Institute issued the Official Draft of the Model Penal Code in 1962. The Model Penal Code is not a uniform code. Rather, it is a rational and integrated body of material drafted for the purpose of assisting state legislatures in reexamining and recodifying state criminal laws. Uniformity among the states is not as important in criminal law as in other areas of the law. Crime varies with local circumstances, and it is appropriate that punishments vary accordingly. The Model Penal Code contains four parts: (1) general provisions, (2) definitions of specific crimes, (3) provisions concerning treatment and correction, and (4) provisions on the organization of correction.

felony: capital offenses, for which the maximum penalty is death; first degree felonies, punishable by a maximum penalty of life imprisonment; second degree felonies punishable by a maximum of ten years' imprisonment, and third degree felonies, punishable by up to five years' imprisonment. (It is important to note that these are maximum penalties. The actual sentence served can be less than the maximum.)

MISDEMEANORS **Misdemeanors** are crimes punishable by a fine or by confinement for up to a year. Misdemeanors are also sometimes defined as offenses punishable by incarceration in a local jail instead of a penitentiary. In practice, the jail confinement usually lasts no more than a year. Disorderly conduct and trespass are common misdemeanors. Some states have different classes of misdemeanors. For example, in Illinois there are Class A misdemeanors (confinement for up to a year), Class B (not more than six months), and Class C (not more than thirty days). A case concerning a crime classified as a misdemeanor may be tried before a justice of the peace, a police court judge, or some other official with limited judicial authority.

PETTY OFFENSES Another kind of wrong is termed a **petty offense** and often is not classified as a crime. Petty offenses include many traffic violations and violations of building codes. Even for petty offenses, a guilty party may be put in jail for a few days, or fined, or both.

FEDERAL AND STATE CRIMES Criminal law is primarily the province of the states, but the federal government also has a criminal code. Federal crimes relate to federal government functions or involve federal personnel or institutions. Counterfeiting, unlawful immigration, spying, robbing a federally insured bank, and assaulting a federal officer are examples of federal crimes. In other instances, the federal government can use its general regulatory powers to aid state law enforcement agencies in combating crimes that have a national impact. Transportation of stolen vehicles across state lines, kidnapping, and civil rights violations are areas that fall under federal criminal law.

The Essentials of Criminal Liability

Two elements are necessary for a person to be convicted of a crime: (1) the performance of a pro-

hibited act and (2) a specified state of mind on the part of the actor.

PERFORMANCE OF PROHIBITED ACTS Every criminal statute prohibits certain behavior. Most crimes require an act of *commission;* that is, a person must *do* something before he or she can be accused of a crime. In criminal law, a prohibited act is referred to as the ***actus reus,***[6] or guilty act. In some cases an act of *omission* can be a crime, but only if what is omitted is a legal duty. Failure to file a tax return is an example of an omission that is a crime.

The *guilty act* requirement is based on one of the premises of criminal law—that a person is punished for *harm done* to society. Thinking about killing someone or about stealing a car may be wrong, but these thoughts in themselves do no harm until they are translated into action. Of course, a person can be punished for attempting murder or robbery, but normally only if substantial steps toward the criminal objective have been taken.

Even a completed act that harms society is not legally a crime unless the court finds that the required state of mind was present.

STATE OF MIND A wrongful mental state *(mens rea)* is as necessary as a wrongful act to establishing criminal liability. What constitutes such a mental state varies according to the wrongful action. Thus, for murder, the *actus reus* (act) is the taking of a life, and the *mens rea*[7] (mental state) is the intent to take life. For theft, the *actus reus* is the taking of another person's property, and the *mens rea* involves both the knowledge that the property belongs to another and the intent to deprive the owner of it. Without the mental state required by law for a particular crime, there can be no crime.

The *mens rea* in which a particular act is committed can vary in the degree of its wrongfulness. The same act—shooting someone—can result from varying mental states. It can be done coldly, after premeditation, as in murder in the first degree. It can be done in the heat of passion, as in voluntary manslaughter. Or it can be done as the result of criminal negligence, as in involuntary manslaughter. In each of these situations, the law recognizes a different degree of wrongfulness, and the harsh-

---

6. Pronounced *ak*-tus *ray*-uhs.
7. Pronounced mehns *ray*-uh.

ness of the punishment depends on the degree to which the act of shooting another was an *intentional* act.

Crimes Affecting Business ·

Numerous forms of crime occur in a business context. In this section, we focus on some of the important crimes affecting business. Other types of crimes relating to business, including white-collar crime, are discussed in the subsequent section.

FORGERY   The fraudulent making or alteration of any writing that changes the legal liability of another is **forgery.** If Samson signs Brewster's name without authorization to the back of a check made out to Brewster, Samson has committed forgery. Forgery also includes changing trademarks, falsifying public records, counterfeiting, and altering any legal document.

Most states have a special statute, often called a *credit-card statute,* to cover the illegal use of credit cards. Thus, the state attorney can prosecute a person who misuses a credit card for violating either the forgery statute or the special credit-card statute.

ROBBERY   At common law, **robbery** was the taking of another's personal property, from his or her person or immediate presence, by force or intimidation. The use of force or fear is this crime's distinguishing characteristic. Thus, picking pockets is larceny (discussed below) and not robbery because the action is unknown to the victim. Typically, states have more severe penalties for *aggravated* robbery—robbery by use of a deadly weapon.

BURGLARY   At common law, **burglary** was defined as breaking and entering the dwelling of another at night with the intent to commit a felony. Originally, the definition was aimed at protecting an individual's home and its occupants. Most state statutes have eliminated some of the requirements found in the common law definition. Thus, the time at which the breaking and entering occurs is usually immaterial, and many state statutes do not require that the building that is entered be a person's dwelling or home. Aggravated burglary, which is defined as burglary with the use of a deadly weapon, and burglary of a dwelling incur greater penalties.

LARCENY   The wrongful or fraudulent taking and carrying away by any person of the personal property of another is **larceny.** It includes the fraudulent intent to permanently deprive an owner of property. Many business-related larcenies entail fraudulent conduct.

The place from which physical property is taken is generally immaterial. Statutes usually prescribe a stiffer sentence, however, when property is taken from buildings such as banks or warehouses. Larceny is differentiated from robbery by the fact that robbery involves force or fear and larceny does not. Therefore, as mentioned above, picking another's pockets is larceny, not robbery.

As society has become more complex, a question has often arisen as to what is property. In most states, the definition of the property that is subject to larceny statutes has been expanded. Stealing computer programs may constitute larceny even though the programs consist of magnetic impulses. Trade secrets can be subject to larceny statutes. Stealing the use of telephone wires by the device known as a ''blue box'' is subject to larceny statutes. So, too, is the theft of natural gas.

In most states, the value of the property taken determines whether the offense is a misdemeanor or a felony. Generally, if the value of the property is less than $50, the crime is a misdemeanor, or *petit larceny.* The states differ as to what amount escalates the crime into a felony, or *grand larceny.* Threshold amounts range from $50 to $2,000.

OBTAINING GOODS BY FALSE PRETENSES   It is a criminal act to obtain goods by means of false pretenses—that is, to represent as true some information or circumstance that is not true, with the intent of deceiving and with the result of defrauding an individual into relinquishing property without adequate compensation. For example, buying groceries with a check knowing that one has insufficient funds to cover it is obtaining goods by false pretenses. Statutes covering such illegal activities vary widely from state to state.

RECEIVING STOLEN GOODS   It is a crime to receive stolen goods. The recipient of such goods need not know the true identity of the owner or of the thief. All that is necessary is that the recipient know or should know that the goods are stolen, which implies an intent to deprive the owner of those goods.

EMBEZZLEMENT   The fraudulent conversion of property or money owned by one person but *entrusted* to another is **embezzlement.** Typically, it involves an employee who fraudulently appropriates money. Banks face this problem, and so do a number of businesses in which corporate officers or accountants ''jimmy'' the books to cover up the fraudulent conversion of money for their own benefit. Embezzlement is not larceny because to commit embezzlement the wrongdoer does not need to carry away the property from the possession of another. In fact, embezzlement involves the conversion of property by a person *in lawful possession* of that property, whereas larceny involves the taking and carrying away of another's property, usually without any right to possession at all. (For example, Stevenson's taking home the company-owned typewriter that he uses in his office is embezzlement. If he gets caught and fired for it and, on the way out, takes a small office pocket calculator, he commits larceny.) Embezzlement is not robbery because there is no taking by use of force or fear.

It does not matter whether the accused takes the money from the victim or from a third person. If, as the comptroller of a large corporation, Saunders pockets a certain number of checks from third parties that were given to her to deposit into the account of another company, she has committed embezzlement.

Often the owner of property will remit money to a contractor specifically for the contractor to use in paying various persons who worked on the owner's building. The contractor who does not use the money for this purpose commits a special form of embezzlement called *misapplication of trust funds.* The funds have been entrusted to the contractor for a specific purpose, and that trust has been violated.

White-Collar Crime

There is a special class of crimes that are especially pertinent to the legal environment of business. These are the so-called white-collar crimes. The classification is not a legal one. Rather, it is a sociological classification, the term probably first having been used by sociologists studying criminal behavior in the 1930s. Thus, a particular crime may or may not be termed a white-collar crime depending on whether it was carried out or accomplished in accordance with certain criteria. One of the hallmarks of a white-collar crime is that it is nonviolent in nature. Also, it is usually committed in the course of a legitimate occupation and often difficult to detect. Larceny, for example, can be a white-collar crime when it is perpetrated in a stealthful, nonviolent manner, such as by a company employee working in the payroll department.

Because it is impossible here to cover the vast range of what are considered to be white-collar crimes, the efforts in this chapter will center on four areas: (1) bribery, (2) money laundering, (3) insider trading and other financial fraud, and (4) corporate crime. As stated above, computer crime, which is also a form of white-collar crime, will be discussed in Chapter 26 in the context of computer law along with the topic of intellectual property.

BRIBERY   Basically, three types of actions called *bribery* are considered crimes. They involve (1) bribery of public officials, (2) commercial bribery, and (3) bribery of foreign officials.

Bribery of Public Officials   The attempt to influence a public official to act in a way that serves a private interest is a crime. As an element of this crime, *intent* must be present and proved. The bribe that is offered can be anything that the recipient of the offer—that is, the public official—considers valuable. The commission of the crime of **bribery** occurs when the bribe is *tendered* (offered or given). The recipient does not have to agree to perform whatever action is desired by the person tendering the bribe; nor does the recipient have to accept the bribe.

Commercial Bribery   In some states, so-called kickbacks and payoffs from an individual working for one company to an individual or individuals working for another company are crimes. No public official need be involved. Such commercial bribes are typically given with the intent of obtaining proprietary information, covering up an inferior product, or securing new business. Industrial espionage sometimes involves this kind of activity—for example, a payoff of some type to an employee in a competing firm in exchange for trade secrets and pricing schedules.

Bribery of Foreign Officials   Bribing foreign officials for the purpose of obtaining favorable business contracts is a crime. This crime and the Foreign Corrupt Practices Act of 1977, which was passed to curb the practice of bribery by American businesspersons securing foreign contracts, are discussed in detail in Chapter 27 in the context of international law.

MONEY LAUNDERING   The profits from illegal activities amount to billions of dollars a year, primarily from illegal drug transactions and also, to a lesser extent, from racketeering, prostitution, and gambling. Under federal law, banks, savings and loan associations, and other financial institutions are required to report currency transactions of over $10,000. Consequently, those who engage in illegal activities face difficulties in placing their cash profits from illegal transactions. Until 1977, Switzerland was a haven for such "flight money." In that year, however, a treaty gave the United States access to Swiss bank-deposit information relating to certain white-collar crimes. Panama City then became a leading haven for such money.

As an alternative to simply placing cash from illegal transactions in bank deposits, wrongdoers and racketeers have invented ways to launder "dirty" money to make it "clean." This **money laundering** is done through legitimate businesses. For example, a successful drug dealer might become partners with a restaurateur. Little by little, the restaurant shows an increasing profit. As a shareholder or partner in the restaurant, the wrongdoer is able to report the "profits" of the restaurant as legitimate income, on which federal and state taxes are paid. The wrongdoer can then spend those monies without worrying about whether his or her lifestyle exceeds the level possible with his or her reported income. The Federal Bureau of Investigation estimates that organized crime alone has invested tens of billions of dollars in as many as a hundred thousand business establishments in the United States.

The most appropriate businesses for laundering dirty money are those that are capable of absorbing large volumes of cash income, which then can be commingled with legitimate income. That is why restaurants, bars, and massage parlors are key businesses—they take in large amounts of cash, as opposed to checks and credit-card charges. Another characteristic of a favorable "laundry" is a business in which fixed expenses do not vary with sales volume. An example of such a business is a pornographic film theatre. The rent, electricity, and wages remain virtually constant regardless of the number of clients. Law-enforcement officials examining a pornographic movie theatre's transactions would have a difficult time proving that the income reported to have been generated by the theatre was more than what was really taken in.

INSIDER TRADING AND OTHER FINANCIAL FRAUD   An individual who obtains "inside information" about the plans of large corporations can often make staggering profits by using such information to engage in "inside trading." An *insider* is an individual with material information about a publicly traded corporation that is not available to the public. **Insider trading**—that is, the buying or selling of corporate securities by a person in possession of material nonpublic information—is covered under Sections 10(b) and 16(b) of the Securities Exchange Act of 1934 and Rule 10b-5 of the Securities and Exchange Commission and is considered more fully in Chapter 22. At this point, it may be said that one who possesses inside information has a duty to disclose it to whoever is on the other side of the transaction.[8]

One of the most famous instances of insider trading involved Ivan Boesky, Dennis Levine, and others in trades that made use of inside information concerning many of the largest corporate takeover attempts in the 1980s. Boesky was sentenced to three years in a federal prison, paid $100 million in penalties, and agreed to work with the government to apprehend other offenders.

The most recent area of white-collar crime has involved scandals in the savings and loan industry. Although actual fraud was not responsible for *all* of the monumental savings and loan failures in the United States, it was evident in many of these failures. A number of heads of failed savings and loan associations have been indicted and will face criminal proceedings. The chairman of the U.S. House Judiciary Subcommittee on Criminal Justice wrote that about "half of the recent bank failures and one-quarter of the thrift failures . . . involved crim-

---

8.   Under the Insider Trading and Securities Fraud Enforcement Act of 1988, insiders may be fined as much as triple the amount of any profit made or loss avoided on each illegal transaction, up to $1 million.

inal activity by insiders, few of whom, according to a congressional survey, were adequately punished.''[9]

CORPORATE CRIME   A corporation is a legal entity created under the laws of a state. It is not a living person and therefore must act through human beings. Hence, any crime committed in the corporate name must be committed by a person or persons in control of the corporation's affairs or in the employment of the corporation.

Because a criminal act requires intent, common law thinking was that a corporation, because it has no mind of its own, could not be guilty of a crime. Corporate officers or employees could and can, however, be charged for committing criminal acts. Moreover, corporations have always been *civilly* liable for the acts of their officers and employees.

Today, the common law view does not prevail. Corporations may be charged with many types of crimes. (They cannot be charged with all types of crimes—for example, a corporation cannot be charged with rape.) The Model Penal Code provides that a corporation may be convicted of a crime in the following situations:

1.   The criminal act by the corporation's agent or employee is within the scope of his or her employment, and the purpose of the statute defining the act as a crime is to impose liability on corporations.
2.   The crime consists of a failure to perform a specific affirmative duty imposed on corporations by law.
3.   The crime was authorized, requested, commanded, committed, or recklessly tolerated by one of the corporation's high managerial agents.

When a law requires intent as an element of a crime, the agent's or employee's intent may be imputed to the corporation. An important factor is how high in the corporate hierarchy the individual stands. Is he or she high enough in the management structure that his or her conduct can be interpreted without proof of authorization as the corporation's acts? This test is known as the ''high managerial agent'' rule.

Crimes for which corporations have been indicted or convicted include manslaughter, homicide, arson, and grand theft.

Liability of Officers and Directors   Although an officer of a corporation cannot be held personally liable for crimes of the corporation or of corporate employees simply because he or she is an officer, if that officer was in a position to prevent the crime, he or she may be held liable. Normally, the court must show that the crimes were committed at the officer's direction or with his or her permission.

This does not mean that it must be proved that the officer had criminal intent. In some instances, when employees under an officer's supervision commit crimes, criminal liability may be imposed on the officer for his or her negligent failure to supervise the employees. In one case, the chief executive officer of a national supermarket chain was held personally liable for sanitation violations in corporate warehouses in which food was exposed to contamination by rodents. The officer admitted that as president he was responsible for the entire operation of the company, including providing sanitary conditions. He testified that he had no choice, however, but to delegate duties, including sanitation, to subordinates. He said that he had no reason to suspect that these subordinates were violating the law, and that when violations came to light, acting through those subordinates, he did everything possible to correct them. Evidence of earlier violations at another warehouse was introduced, however, to show that he was on notice that he could not rely on these subordinates to prevent or correct unsanitary conditions. The court concluded that he was not justified in relying on the subordinates to handle sanitation matters. On appeal, the United States Supreme Court upheld the conviction.[10]

The protection of the safety of workers is another area of potential officer and director liability. The Occupational Safety and Health Act of 1970 established specific regulations concerning safety in the workplace. Criminal penalties for willful violations of the act are, however, limited. Until very recently, even blatant violations of federal workplace guidelines have not met with serious criminal

9.   John Conyers, Jr., ''Don't Water Down the Anti-Fraud Law,'' *New York Times,* December 27, 1987.

10.   *United States v. Park,* 421 U.S. 658, 95 S.Ct. 1903, 44 L.Ed.2d 489 (1975).

How to Imprison a Corporation

 Individuals who commit crimes may be sent to prison. But, as everybody knows, corporations are a different matter. How can you imprison a corporation? Traditionally, judges have not even toyed with the idea, resorting instead to other types of criminal penalties—such as the imposition of fines. But at least one judge has concluded that it is possible to imprison a corporation. On August 30, 1988, in a case heard by the United States District Court for the Eastern District of Virginia, Judge Doumar sentenced a corporation to a three-year term of imprisonment and a $1 million fine.[a] The sentence was imposed on Allegheny Bottling Company (formerly Allegheny Pepsi-Cola Bottling Company) after that firm had been convicted of conspiring with a Coca-Cola distributor to fix prices in violation of the Sherman Antitrust Act of 1890.[b]

In his decision, Judge Doumar took issue with the common assumption that a corporation cannot be imprisoned. That assumption "was made by judges, and not by Congress" and "has lingered in the legal system unexamined and without support." The judge pointed out that Webster's dictionary defines *imprisonment* not in terms of stone walls and iron bars but as a "constraint of a person either by force or by such other coercion as restrains him within limits against his will." Judge Doumar also noted that cases involving false imprisonment entailed not confinement in a jail or prison but rather a forceful restraint of a person against that person's will. Therefore, concluded the judge, corporate imprisonment would require only that a court restrain or immobilize the corporation. Restraints (such as the seizure of corporate assets) are commonly placed on corporations in bankruptcy. Why not effectively "imprison" corporations that commit crimes by applying similar restraints?

After all, the judge reasoned, why should corporations escape imprisonment for criminal offenses when individuals cannot? In no case had any court cited an authority for the proposition that corporations cannot be imprisoned, and no court had ever—to the judge's knowledge—actually held that corporate imprisonment was illegal, unconstitutional, or impossible. The judge maintained that "considerable confusion" attends the concept of corporate imprisonment only because courts mistakenly think that imprisonment "necessarily involves incarceration in jail."

The judge fashioned his sentence so that, insofar as possible, the punishment would fit the crime. After the sentencing, the judge suspended all of the imprisonment and $50,000 of the fine and placed Allegheny on probation for three years. As a special

---

a. *United States v. Allegheny Bottling Co.,* 695 F.Supp. 856 (E.D.Va. 1988).

b. Price fixing and the Sherman Antitrust Act are discussed in Chapter 20.

condition of the probation, Allegheny would not be allowed to ''dispose of any of its franchises, capital assets or plants or facilities in the Norfolk, Richmond or Baltimore areas, without specific permission of this Court through the probation officer.'' In addition, Allegheny was to provide four high-ranking officers or employees to perform community service for forty hours each week for one or two years without compensation. The service was to be performed in the Norfolk, Richmond, and Baltimore areas—the areas affected by the price-fixing agreement. The community service was also to be performed under the direction of the probation office and subject to the approval of the court. The judge emphasized that ''[i]n no event is Allegheny Bottling Company to receive any form of compensation for the community service performed.''

''Stone walls do not a prison make, nor iron bars a cage''—so said Richard Lovelace well over three hundred years ago. Obviously, Judge Doumar

agrees with Lovelace's sentiment—and, very possibly, so might Allegheny Bottling Company.

■ Implications for the Businessperson

The *Allegheny* case discussed here is illustrative—albeit in the extreme—of the general trend to hold corporations and their agents liable for corporate crimes. The implication for the businessperson is that today's corporate directors, officers, and managers can no longer assume that their actions will be sheltered by the corporate veil or that yesterday's standard of reasonable care and oversight will suffice. Today, key corporate personnel must exercise great care to ensure that corporate activities do not violate any law and to avoid the cost of criminal liability. The community service required by Judge Doumar was very costly for Allegheny Bottling Company. In addition, note that the judge did not specify that the ''four top-ranking officers'' had to be themselves guilty of participating in the crime. Even an *innocent* high-ranking officer

or director may have to pay the price of corporate crime.

■ For Critical Analysis

1. What is the logic behind the common assumption that a corporation cannot be imprisoned?
2. Why did the judge include in his order the condition that the guilty corporation could not dispose of any of its assets or franchises in the Norfolk, Richmond, and Baltimore areas?
3. One of the major appeals of the corporation as a form of business organization is the fact that the corporate veil shields the corporation's directors and officers from personal liability. To the extent that courts strip away this veil, the corporation becomes less attractive as a form of business organization. Discuss the tradeoff faced by business and society when corporate shareholders are held personally liable for criminal actions.

penalties. The Justice Department, in 1988, stated that the existence of criminal penalties in the Occupational Safety and Health Act did not preempt state and local criminal laws. Since then, states have successfully prosecuted individual officers for criminal violations of worker safety standards.[11]

Liability of Corporations   Corporate criminal liability is vicarious. That is, one person is punished for the act or acts of another. Thus, the corporation that is found to be criminally responsible for an act committed by an employee can be fined for that offense. Through the fine, stockholders and other employees suffer because of the vicarious liability of the corporation. The justification for such criminal liability involves a showing that the corporation could have exercised control and precluded the act or that persons in supervisory positions within the corporation authorized, consented to, or knew of the act.[12]

■ RICO

In 1970 Congress passed the Organized Crime Control Act. It included the Racketeer Influenced and Corrupt Organizations Act, otherwise known as RICO.[13] The purpose of the act was to curb the apparently increasing entry of organized crime into the legitimate business world. Under RICO, it is a federal crime (1) to use income obtained from racketeering activity to purchase any interest in an enterprise, (2) to acquire or maintain an interest in an enterprise through racketeering activity, (3) to conduct or participate in the affairs of an enterprise through racketeering activity, or (4) to conspire to do any of the preceding.

Racketeering activity is not a new type of crime created by RICO; rather, RICO incorporates by reference twenty-six separate types of federal crimes and nine types of state felonies[14] and states that if a person commits two of these offenses, he or she is guilty of "racketeering activity." Recently, the statute has been rigorously enforced, and the penalties for violations are harsh. The act provides for both civil liability and criminal liability.

Civil Liability

In the event of a violation, the RICO statute permits the government to seek civil penalties, including the divestiture (selling off) of a defendant's interest in a business or the dissolution of the business. Perhaps the most controversial section of RICO is Section 1964(c), under which, in some cases, private individuals are allowed to recover three times their actual loss (treble damages), plus attorneys' fees, for business injuries caused by a violation of the statute.

The broad language of RICO has allowed it to be applied in cases that have little or nothing to do with organized crime, and an aggressive prosecuting attorney may attempt to show that any business fraud constitutes "racketeering activity." Plaintiffs have used the RICO statute in numerous commercial fraud cases because of the inviting prospect of being awarded triple damages if they win. The most frequent targets of civil RICO lawsuits are insurance companies, employment agencies, commercial banks, and stock brokerage firms.

In the case presented below, a plaintiff brought suit against a business firm, claiming that the firm's fraudulent business activities violated RICO. By interpreting RICO provisions very broadly, the United States Supreme Court set a significant precedent for subsequent applications of RICO.

---

11.   See, for example, *People v. Chicago Magnet Wire Corp.*, 126 Ill.2d 356, 534 N.E.2d 962, 128 Ill.Dec. 517 (1989), in which five executives were held criminally liable for allowing workers to become ill from exposure to hazardous chemicals.

12.   Section 2.07 of the Model Penal Code: "Liability of corporations, unincorporated associations, and persons acting, or under a duty to act, in their behalf."

13.   18 U.S.C. Sections 1961-1968.

14.   See 18 U.S.C. Section 1961(A).

BACKGROUND AND FACTS *In 1979 a Belgian corporation, Sedima, S.P.R.L., entered into a contract with another Belgian firm to supply the latter with electronic components. Sedima also formed a joint venture with a U.S. firm, Imrex Company, whereby Imrex would ship the components to Europe and share the proceeds jointly with Sedima. Approximately $8 million in orders had been shipped by Imrex when Sedima concluded that Imrex was fraudulently claiming extra expenses and inflating its bills accordingly—in order to get more than its fair portion of the proceeds. Sedima brought suit against Imrex, alleging, in part, that Imrex had violated RICO. Sedima claimed an injury of at least $175,000 (the amount of alleged overbilling) and asked for treble damages, as allowed by Section 1964(c). Sedima's RICO claims were dismissed by the district court on the ground that Sedima failed to demonstrate it had suffered injury as a result of any "pattern" of "racketeering" activity. The appellate court affirmed, and Sedima appealed to the United States Supreme Court.*

Case 8.6

SEDIMA, S.P.R.L. v. IMREX CO.

Supreme Court of the United States, 1985.
473 U.S. 479,
105 S.Ct. 3275,
87 L.Ed.2d 346.

WHITE, Justice.

* * * *

Underlying the Court of Appeals' holding was its distress at the "extraordinary, if not outrageous," uses to which civil RICO has been put. Instead of being used against mobsters and organized criminals, it has become a tool for everyday fraud cases brought against "respected and legitimate 'enterprises.'" Yet Congress wanted to reach both "legitimate" and "illegitimate" enterprises. The former enjoy neither an inherent incapacity for criminal activity nor immunity from its consequences. The fact that [Section] 1964(c) is used against respected businesses allegedly engaged in a pattern of specifically identified criminal conduct is hardly a sufficient reason for assuming that the provision is being misconstrued. Nor does it reveal the "ambiguity" discovered by the court below. "[T]he fact that RICO has been applied in situations not expressly anticipated by Congress does not demonstrate ambiguity. It demonstrates breadth."

It is true that private civil actions under the statute are being brought almost solely against such defendants, rather than against the archetypal, intimidating mobster. Yet this defect—if defect it is—is inherent in the statute as written, and its correction must lie with Congress. It is not for the judiciary to eliminate the private action in situations where Congress has provided it simply because plaintiffs are not taking advantage of it in its more difficult applications.

We nonetheless recognize that, in its private civil version, RICO is evolving into something quite different from the original conception of its enactors. Though sharing the doubts of the Court of Appeals about this increasing divergence, we cannot agree with either its diagnosis or its remedy. The "extraordinary" uses to which civil RICO has been put appear to be primarily the result of the breadth of the predicate offenses, in particular the inclusion of wire, mail, and securities fraud, and the failure of Congress and the courts to develop a meaningful concept of "pattern." We do not believe that the amorphous standing requirement imposed by the Second Circuit effectively responds to these problems, or that it is a form of statutory amendment appropriately undertaken by the courts.

The appellate court's decision was reversed. The Supreme Court held that a plaintiff does not have to establish that a defendant has been or could be criminally prosecuted under RICO and does not have to show a separate racketeering injury to recover treble damages under Section 1964(c).

DECISION AND REMEDY

COMMENTS   *This case illustrates some of the difficulties faced by the courts in interpreting and applying the RICO statute. Because of the statute's broad
language, it has been applied in ways not anticipated by Congress and,
as Justice White indicated in his opinion above, is "evolving into something quite different from the original conception of its enactors." Congress is currently considering legislation to amend RICO that would restrict the application of RICO to criminal racketeering cases.*

Criminal Liability

Most of the criminal offenses under RICO have
little, if anything, to do with normal business activities, for they involve gambling, arson, and extortion. But securities fraud (involving the sale of
stocks and bonds) and mail fraud are also criminal
violations of RICO, and RICO has become an effective tool in attacking these white-collar crimes
in recent years. Under criminal provisions of
RICO, any individual found guilty of a violation

is subject to a fine of up to $25,000 per violation
or imprisonment for up to twenty years—or both.

In the following case, the owner of a motel was
charged with criminal violations of RICO because
the person to whom he leased the motel operated
it as a place of prostitution. The owner–defendant
was considered by the court to be sufficiently involved in the illegal operation to warrant conviction under the criminal provisions of RICO.

Case 8.7

**UNITED STATES v.
TUNNELL**

United States Court of Appeals,
Fifth Circuit, 1982.
667 F.2d 1182.

BACKGROUND AND FACTS   *In 1967 Tunnell purchased the Pines Motel at Kilgore, Texas. For over three decades, the motel had been known
as a place of prostitution. When Tunnell was imprisoned for tax evasion
in 1974, he leased the motel to Odessa Mae (Mildred) French. The government maintained that Tunnell and French jointly operated the Pines
Motel as a place of prostitution and that they bribed King Russell, a justice
of the peace, and Dwight Watson, a local constable, to permit their operations. Russell testified that he had an arrangement with Tunnell by
which Tunnell reimbursed the sums Russell paid the prostitutes at the motel. The testimony of several witnesses—including prostitutes, motel employees, and law-enforcement officials—linked Tunnell to the prostitution
activities and to the corruption of the constable and the justice of the peace.
Tunnell admitted knowing Russell and Watson and acknowledged the long-
standing reputation of the motel, but he denied knowledge of any bribes
and of the reimbursement scheme. Tunnell was indicted for a RICO offense
(prostitution) and a RICO conspiracy offense, together with French (the
madam) and King Russell. Prior to trial, Russell pleaded guilty to a lesser
charge. The jury found Tunnell and French guilty on both counts. Tunnell
appealed his conviction, claiming that there was no bribery or conspiracy.*

POLITZ, Circuit Judge.
      *   *   *   *
      We *   *   * reject Tunnell's contention that French's action in furnishing the
services of a prostitute free of charge to the peace officers does not constitute the
predicate [asserted or declared] crime of bribery. Tunnell would limit the term "benefit" to pecuniary gain. *   *   *
      The evidence in the record establishes the economic value of the services of a
prostitute. These services were provided at no cost. This constitutes the bestowing

of an economic gain, a benefit, upon the recipient public official. The argument to the contrary is not convincing.

    * * * *

Tunnell challenges the sufficiency of the evidence relating to his aiding and abetting French in her acts of bribery. * * *

Testimony received at trial demonstrated that Tunnell often ran the prostitution business, even though French had leased the motel. He personally passed approval on new prostitutes, bribed the local justice of the peace and constable, told others about the operation, and bragged that if it ''wasn't for his politicking * * * Mildred [French] and Watson wouldn't have a job.'' In short, the record is replete with evidence that Tunnell possessed active knowledge of the racketeering operations conducted on the motel premises and involved himself in these activities.

The appellate court affirmed Tunnell's conviction under RICO's criminal statute provisions.

DECISION AND REMEDY

■ Terms and Concepts to Review

actus reus 179	**embezzlement** 181	**money laundering** 182
appropriation 175	**felonies** 178	**petty offense** 179
bribery 181	**forgery** 180	**robbery** 180
burglary 180	**insider trading** 182	**slander of quality** 176
business torts 169	**larceny** 180	**slander of title** 178
disparagement of	*mens rea* 179	**trade libel** 176
property 176	**misdemeanors** 179	**white-collar crime** 169

■ Questions and Case Problems

8-1. Stevens owns a bakery. He has been trying to obtain a long-term contract with the owner of Martha's Tea Salons for some time. Stevens starts a local advertising campaign on radio and television and in the newspaper. This advertising campaign is so persuasive that Martha decides to break the contract she has had with Hank's Bakery so that she can patronize Stevens's bakery. Is Stevens liable to Hank's Bakery for the tort of wrongful interference with contractual relations? Is Martha liable for this tort? For anything?

8-2. Jenny was stranded in Alaska as the result of a union strike against the airline from which she had purchased a round-trip ticket before leaving her home in Dallas. She was forced to return to Dallas on another airline and incurred additional expense for her return ticket. She sued the union for tortious interference with her contract with the airline and sought to recover the additional expense. Should the union be liable to Jenny for damages? Why or why not?

8-3. After a careful study and analysis, Green Top Airlines decides to expand its operations into Harbor City. Green Top acquires the necessary regulatory authorizations and licenses, negotiates a lease at the airport terminal, and makes substantial capital expenditures renovating airport gates. Immediately thereafter, Red Stripe Airlines, Green Top's major competitor, also undertakes operations in Harbor City even though (1) Harbor City is nowhere near any of Red Stripe's major existing routes, and (2) Red Stripe will lose money by servicing Harbor City. Green Top claims that Red Stripe's entry into Harbor City constitutes a tort. Discuss fully Green Top's claim.

8-4. Assume that Red Stripe Airlines (in Problem 8-3) negotiates a lease at the airport for gates on the same concourse as Green Top Airlines. In fact, for passengers to get to Green Top's gates, they must walk past Red Stripe's gates. Red Stripe puts up a large sign that states, ''Passengers of other airlines—turn in your *tickets* or cancel your *reservations,* and we will give you 25 percent off the price of your trip if you fly on Red Stripe Airlines.'' In addition, Red Stripe's ticket agents solicit business from travelers on their way to Green Top gates. At this time, only Red Stripe and Green Top have operative gates on the concourse. Discuss fully any business tort theories under which Green Top can recover against Red Stripe for the latter's actions. (Remember: A ticket is a contract.)

8-5. Luigi owns and operates a famous Italian restaurant in New York City. Luigi hires chef Toni to prepare the pasta and other dishes on his menu. Toni also contributes a column to *Gourmet Eating* magazine in which he discusses Italian food and restaurants in the area and rates all restaurants with stars. The ratings range from one star (the lowest rating) to five stars (the highest rating). Toni is prohibited from discussing or rating Luigi's restaurant in his column as long as he is employed by Luigi. One day, Luigi and Toni have a dispute over Toni's salary, and Toni, in front of a substantial number of regular customers who are well known in New York society, accuses Luigi of watering his house wine and of not making his own pasta. Luigi has on occasion purchased some pasta from a pasta shop in the neighborhood, but he has never watered his wine. Toni quits on the spot and later, in *Gourmet Eating,* rates Luigi's restaurant with only one star, adding a notation that Luigi's wine and pasta are inferior to the wine and pasta offered by other restaurants. Under what tort theories, if any, can Luigi file suit against Toni? Discuss fully.

8-6. Duggin entered into a contract to purchase certain land from Williams. The contract specified that if the property was not rezoned by June 15, 1981, either party could cancel. Duggin invested a great deal of time and money for engineering studies and surveys that increased the value of the property. Before the June 15 rezoning deadline, Duggin made an agreement to assign the contract to Centennial Development Corp. at a profit. The land was not rezoned as of June 15, but Centennial was prepared to purchase the land without the rezoning. Williams's attorney, Adams, learned of Duggin's deal and convinced Williams to cancel on July 30, 1981, in accordance with the provision in the agreement. Adams also convinced Williams to transfer the property to Adams, after which he sold the land to Centennial. Adams claimed that he was merely working on behalf of his client, Williams. Does Duggin have a claim against Adams for intentional interference with contract rights even though Williams had the right to terminate the contract at will? Explain your answer. [*Duggin v. Adams,* 234 Va. 221, 360 S.E.2d 832 (1987)]

8-7. ▢ Dierdorff was the president of Sun Savings and Loan Association. Sun Savings claimed that over a period of time Dierdorff had received kickbacks from several of Sun's larger loan customers. In relation to the fraudulent kickback scheme, Dierdorff had written letters to four entities—the Internal Revenue Service, the Federal Home Loan Bank Board, the California Savings and Loan commissioner, and the accounting firm of Arthur Young. Sun filed a civil suit alleging that Dierdorff had violated the federal Racketeering Influenced and Corrupt Organizations Act (RICO). The federal district court decided in favor of Dierdorff, holding that the plaintiff, Sun, had failed to allege a "pattern of racketeering activity" and that the acts had not been conducted by an "enterprise." On appeal, how should the appellate court rule on the decision of the district court? Discuss. [*Sun Savings and Loan Association v. Dierdorff,* 825 F.2d 187 (9th Cir. 1987)]

8-8. DBI Services, Inc., provided oil-field trucking services, brine water, and drilling mud to oil producers in the Seminole area of Texas. From 1983 to 1986, the major oil producer in the area, Amerada Hess Corp. (AH), regularly contracted with DBI for its services. AH learned in a 1986 audit of its contractors that DBI had engaged in lavish entertainment of certain AH employees who were responsible for awarding job contracts. Disturbed by this discovery, AH thereafter refused to deal with DBI. AH also refused to accept contract bids from any firms that planned to subcontract work out to DBI, even if the firms had submitted the lowest bids for the contracts. DBI sued AH for tortious interference with its contractual relationships with these other firms. AH claimed that it was not obligated to accept the lowest bids for contracts and that it had a right to determine with whom it would do business. How will the court decide the issue? Discuss. [*DBI Services, Inc. v. Amerada Hess Corp.,* 907 F.2d 506 (5th Cir. 1990)]

8-9. In 1963, Pacific Gas and Electric Co. (PG&E) entered into a contract with the Placer County Water Agency (Agency) under which PG&E would purchase hydroelectric power from the Agency. The contract provided that the agreement would terminate in the year 2013 or at the end of the year in which the Agency completed the retirement of its project bonds, whichever occurred first. As energy prices rose, the Agency wished it could terminate the contract and sell its hydroelectric power in a more favorable market, but it felt it could not do so without breaching its contract with PG&E. Bear Stearns & Co., an investment brokerage firm, approached the Agency and spent several years overcoming the Agency's resistance to making any effort to terminate the contract. Finally it succeeded, and in 1983 the Agency entered into an agreement with Bear Stearns in which Bear Stearns agreed to pay for legal, engineering, and marketing studies on the feasibility of terminating the power contract, in return for 15 percent of any resulting increase in the Agency's revenues above $2.5 million for twenty years. Bear Stearns retained legal counsel to draw up a plan by which the Agency could retire its project bonds and to litigate the question of whether the Agency could terminate the contract. PG&E sued Bear Stearns for tortious interference with PG&E's contract with the Agency. What will the court decide? Explain. [*Pacific Gas and Electric Co. v. Bear Stearns & Co.,* 50 Cal.3d 1118, 791 P.2d 587, 270 Cal.Rptr. 1 (1990)]

8-10. The Electronic Communications Privacy Act (ECPA) of 1986 prohibits the interception of information communicated by electronic means and provides that civil actions for damages may be brought against those who violate the act. Shubert and others (the plaintiffs), who had purchased cellular mobile telephones for use in their cars and other remote locations, brought a class action against their telephone service providers. The plaintiffs alleged that the service providers had intentionally divulged the plaintiffs' cellular telephone communications—and thus violated the ECPA—by transmitting the plaintiffs' cellular telephone communications over public airwaves without the plaintiffs' consent. The plaintiffs further contended that they had never been informed that conversations over these telephones would not be private and had no idea that whatever they said on their car phones could be overheard by anybody tuned to the specific frequencies being used. They had assumed that the service providers would scramble transmission frequencies or encrypt or otherwise render the transmissions incapable of interception. Had the service providers violated the ECPA? Discuss. [*Shubert v. Metrophone, Inc.*, 898 F.2d 401 (3rd Cir. 1990)]

8-11. Leslie R. Barth was president of five corporations. During the course of an investigation for failure to file corporate and personal income tax returns, the Internal Revenue Service (IRS) served an administrative summons (a summons to appear before an administrative agency, here the IRS) requiring Barth to turn over certain corporate records. Barth only partially complied, and the IRS took him to district court. The court ordered the corporations to furnish the requested information and to designate an agent to testify for the corporations. Barth appealed the order, claiming that it violated the ''agent's'' (Barth's) constitutional right against self-incrimination and that this Fifth Amendment protection extended to the corporations. Discuss whether corporations possess Fifth Amendment privileges against self-incrimination and whether Barth's individual privilege against self-incrimination was denied by the district court's order. [*United States v. Barth*, 745 F.2d 184 (2nd Cir. 1984)]

8-12. Fortner LP Gas Co., a Kentucky corporation, was sued by the Commonwealth of Kentucky when a Fortner truck struck two schoolchildren, injuring one and killing the other. The children had just gotten off a school bus and were walking across the street when the truck, unable to stop because the brakes failed to work, hit them. Later inspection of the brakes revealed them to be defective. The Commonwealth of Kentucky prosecuted the corporation, and a grand jury indicted the corporation for manslaughter in the second degree, a felony punishable by a $20,000 fine. Fortner brought a motion for dismissal of the indictment on the ground that it was a corporation and, as such, could not commit manslaughter. Can a corporation commit manslaughter? Discuss. [*Commonwealth v. Fortner LP Gas Co.*, 610 S.W.2d 941 (Ky. 1980)]

8-13. A Question of Ethics

With increasing frequency in recent years, certain acts and omissions committed by corporations—that is, through the officers of the corporation—in violation of regulatory statutes have been made criminal violations. Regulatory violations, in such cases, may result in criminal sanctions against the officers as well as against the corporation. In some instances, criminal liability may arise on the sole basis of the act or omission, without regard to whether or not there was any intent to violate the law or knowledge of the violation. For example, in one case, the president of a family-owned spice importing business was convicted of ten counts of causing adulteration of food products in violation of federal food and drug safety laws even though he had not exercised direct day-to-day management of the plant where the contamination occurred.

The record did show, however, that the defendant was responsible for designing sanitation methods (primarily to control recurring rat infestations) in the plant. [United States v. Gel Spice Co., Inc., *601 F. Supp. 1205 (E.D.N.Y. 1984), aff'd., 773 F.2d 427 (2d Cir. 1985)*]

1. Criminal sanctions under the Food and Drug Act do not require proof of any consciousness of wrongdoing. Is it ethical, though, to convict someone of a crime if that person had no intent to commit the act or the omission? What if the individual was entirely unaware of the criminal violation, as, for example, might be an executive who does not know the conditions at one of his company's plants?

2. Does it seem fair to create criminal liability for the failure to make certain that something is done (for example, that a safe food storage area is maintained)? If there is such a duty, should an alleged offender's knowledge of relevant circumstances be considered? Should one who has such a duty be allowed to delegate that duty to a subordinate and, having done so, avoid all potential liability?

3. Is there a practical aspect to regulatory laws like those imposing criminal liability for causing food adulteration? Such laws impose a duty on executives to seek out and correct conditions that violate regulatory requirements—to safeguard against harming others. Moreover, individuals may avoid criminal liability by producing evidence that they took extraordinary measures to prevent the condition but were not successful. (If such evidence is sufficiently convincing, the government must show *beyond any reasonable doubt* that the condition would not have arisen had the defendant in fact taken such measures.) But is criminal liability and all that it entails—including social stigma—necessary? After all, tort liability imposes similar positive duties to take care not to injure others. Should regulatory violations be limited to civil remedies?

8-14. Case Briefing Assignment

Examine Case A.8 [United States v. O'Connor, *910 F.2d 1466 (7th Cir. 1990)] in Appendix A. The case has been excerpted there in great detail. Review and then brief the case, making sure that you include answers to the following questions in your brief.*

1. O'Connor was charged with having committed two crimes. What were they?

2. What kind of services did O'Connor provide for ''Bill Burns'' and the other agents? What did O'Connor receive from the agents in return for these services?

3. What was O'Connor's defense against the RICO charge?

4. What did the court decide, and why?

Focus on Ethics

The Public Environment

No other area of law engenders as much controversy as that relating to the public environment. This stems from the fact that the law of the public environment, more than any other area, involves searching, ethical questions. All areas of law touch on ethical considerations. But many laws have as their basis practical necessity or commercial need. The law of the public environment, however, concerns issues such as the protection of freedom of speech, the promotion of racial equality, and government regulation of behavior for the public welfare versus individual rights. Little guidance is provided by considerations of practicality in resolving these issues. Moreover, these issues do not merely involve questions of ethics; they are in large measure purely ethical questions. In resolving them, one must rely on basic notions of fairness and justice. Yet conceptions of fairness, justice, and equality differ among individuals. Moreover, each individual's conception is a product of his or her circumstances; as circumstances change over time, so, too, basic conceptions change. Not surprisingly, at any moment in history, there is seldom a broad social consensus over legal issues in the public environment.

Free Speech and the Corporation

Free speech is regarded as one of the basic rights of a democratic society. Yet it has never been considered an absolute right. The right of free speech must be balanced against other important rights and the advancement of other important social goals. In that sense the proper extent of freedom of speech, in its many forms, involves ethical considerations.

Because freedom of speech is not absolute, not all forms of expression are protected. Pornography, for example, is not protected by the First Amendment. Nor are utterances protected that would induce an immediate threat of violence or injury. Even within the context of protected speech, the Supreme Court has historically looked to the nature of the speech involved in determining the extent of the protection afforded. Commercial speech, for example, is afforded less protection from government restriction than is non-commercial speech. The lesser degree of protection means in practical terms that it is easier for government to show that the interest it seeks to promote by regulating the speech is more important than protecting the right of speech. But in balancing such conflicting rights and goals, value judgments must be made.

Judging the Source

The nature of the speech involved may be a legitimate concern in assessing the extent of freedom of speech, but is it legitimate to consider the source of the speech? For example, should it make a difference that the speaker, through either a spokesperson or an advertisement, is a corporation? Most corporate "speech" has as its primary purpose the promotion of a product; that is, it is commercial in nature and, as discussed, is afforded a lesser degree of protection. But what if the speech is political in nature? Should it matter in that case that the speaker is a corporation? This issue was addressed by the United States Supreme Court in *First National Bank of Boston v. Bellotti*, a case referred to in Chapter 5. Although the justices deciding the case were applying their concepts of the free speech clause of the First Amendment, the case raises some difficult ethical questions, which are implicit in the Court's decision and in the opinions of the dissenting justices.

First National Bank of Boston v. Bellotti concerned a Massachusetts law that forbade corporations from using their resources to try to influence public opinion on issues submitted to a referendum vote when those issues did not materially relate to the corporation's business. Controversy arose when five corporations announced their intentions to mount a campaign in opposition to a proposed state individual income tax, which was to be submitted to a referendum vote. The state threatened to fine the corporations and punish their executives if the corporations entered the political debate. The corporations sought protection by asking the courts to declare the Massachusetts law unconstitutional. Ultimately, the case was appealed to the United States Supreme Court.

A divided Court decided in favor of the corporations. The majority held that free speech protections extended to corporations and that the Massachusetts law violated those constitutional protections. In deciding the case, the majority recast the issue involved. For the majority, the issue was *not* whether corporations were protected by the free speech clause but, rather, whether the speech involved was protected. Because the speech was political in nature, the majority concluded that the speech could not be restricted in the manner employed by the state. To the majority, it did not matter that the speaker was a corporation. And indeed, as the majority viewed the case, it was not protecting the corporation.

Instead, it believed that the political nature of the speech meant that it should be heard.

The Ethical Dimensions

The majority's reasoning has some strong points. After all, political debate is the fundamental ingredient of the democratic political process. One of the few areas of virtually uniform agreement over First Amendment rights is that the authors of the Constitution definitely had the public exchange of political views in mind when they constructed the free speech clause. But there are other considerations, largely of an ethical nature, involved when the speaker is a corporation.

There are ethical considerations in a corporation's using its extensive resources to influence the political process. Certainly, bribing officials is wrong both ethically and legally. But other forms of corporate spending that influence the political process also might be abusive. One concern is that a corporation can "leverage" political power through its economic skills. Corporations acquire resources through skills in marketing, management, and technology. Yet these skills, however beneficial to society's material well-being they may be, do not involve political ideas or necessarily indicate a concern for the public welfare. Should the resources garnered in the economic arena be redeployed in the political arena? Is it fair to allow economic skill to be translated into political power? These were concerns raised in dissent to the majority's opinion in *Bellotti,* but they are as much ethical issues as legal ones.

Notwithstanding these concerns, there are ethical as

well as practical considerations that support the majority's view. Recall that the Massachusetts law challenged in *Bellotti* did not ban corporate expenditures on referendum issues that materially related to the corporation's business. The issue was a state individual income tax. The very fact that the corporations would *not* be materially affected by a state *individual* income tax might imply that their political participation was motivated solely by concern for the public welfare rather than their self-interest. Even if they were concerned that the proposed tax might affect the economy of the state and thus the profitability of their businesses, that does not in itself make their views less worthy to be heard. After all, on economic matters, the corporate view of the issues would seem to be extremely relevant. Possibly the corporate view should be heard for that reason alone. And if the corporations choose to subsidize with their own resources the dissemination of important views, maybe they should be praised rather than condemned.

The Unique Nature of the Corporation

Perhaps the basic problem stems from the fact that the corporation is not a natural person. It is a legal fiction created by the state to aid individuals seeking to carry on commercial activities. One danger is that individuals who manage the corporation can use it as a vehicle for their own ends. In theory, managers run the corporation for the benefit of the owners—the shareholders. But it is costly for shareholders to monitor the managers at all times. If managers can use the resources of the owners of the corporation to further their own political views, they will have an unfair advantage over those with different ideas and fewer resources. Even if the law allows that use, is it ethical?

Ethics and the Administrative Process

In Chapter 5 we noted some of the other constitutional protections that apply in the context of business. We looked in Chapter 6 at how some of those protections apply in the administrative process. As noted in Chapter 6, effective governmental regulation necessitates the gathering of relevant information. Often that information can be obtained only by an on-site inspection of business premises or a first-hand examination of business records. When regulatory need conflicts with constitutional principles, not only are legal issues raised, but ethical ones as well.

Recall that the Fourth Amendment protection from unreasonable searches and seizures applies in the context of business. Within the context of administrative law, this protection has been interpreted as requiring that information sought by a regulatory agency be relevant to the matter under scrutiny. Furthermore, any demand for information must be reasonably specific and not unduly burdensome to the business providing the information.

The Need to Know
The ideals embodied in the Fourth Amendment are deeply ingrained in America's political culture. The image of midnight raids in which innocent families watch helplessly as gruff,

heavily armed officers ransack their homes is often invoked when one thinks of a "search and seizure." Protection against such abhorrent practices is fundamental to the American ideal of liberty.

But are the same ideals felt as strongly in other contexts? What about in the business context, especially with regard to agency regulation? Even though the first significant degree of federal economic regulation can be traced as far back as the first half of the nineteenth century, Americans continue to hold extremely ambivalent feelings toward the very idea of government regulation. Americans are prone to look to government to address every new ill society encounters, but then stridently resent, as governmental intrusion, the regulatory schemes designed to cure those ills.

Whatever the sentiments Americans hold regarding government regulation, most accept and many welcome it as an important part of modern society. In accepting such regulation, Americans also accept the fact that regulators must gather information. For example, the Securities and Exchange Commission desires information about proposed stock offerings. The Environmental Protection Agency may request to make an inspection of a chemical plant to ensure compliance with hazardous waste disposal regulations.

Despite acceptance of the need for regulators to gather information, an inherent conflict exists between the regulatory need for information and the individual's right of privacy. Specifically, how much latitude should be afforded to regulators

in gathering information and overseeing private activities?

The United States Supreme Court has attempted to resolve the conflict by balancing the regulators' need to know against individual and corporate expectations of freedom from excessive government prying. An important consideration in resolving the conflict is the less intrusive nature of regulatory searches of businesses: most people simply do not have the same degree of concern about protecting places of business as they do about protecting the family dwelling. As a result, the standards for conducting regulatory investigations and searches are different than those imposed when ordinary police investigations and searches are conducted. For example, even though there may be no suspicion of a regulatory violation, an agency may conduct an investigation or search the premises of a business merely to be assured that no violation is occurring. Within industries subject to a history of extensive regulation, searches may be made even without a warrant. Still, though, as noted in Chapter 6 and above, government is restricted in obtaining private information for regulatory purposes only.

The Ethics of Legal Avoidance
In the face of an agency investigation, a business may prevent or delay agency efforts by asserting legal challenges to the nature or manner of the investigation. There remains, however, the question of whether—in an ethical rather than legal sense—business should challenge any such investigation. We would be expected to challenge an unreasonable search of our

home. We would owe it to our family to challenge such abuse. Arguably, it would be one's civic duty to challenge it to protect future abuse of other families in our community as well. Regulatory investigations may be somehow different, though.

Most regulatory investigations have as their objective ensuring compliance with existing regulatory schemes or gathering information for future ones. Such schemes are designed for the public welfare. Though individuals may disagree about the effectiveness of the scheme or the individual motives of the regulators, society generally accepts the underlying purpose of the regulation—the promotion of public welfare. In such instances, businesses may have an ethical duty not to use legal means to avoid agency action. Indeed, they may have an ethical duty to aid in regulation by compliance, even though they may have a legal right to delay or avoid it.

Yet consider that agency regulation, like all government action, is carried out by individuals—individuals who suffer the same temptations to abuse power that all people suffer. Abuse may even result from a desire to do good; regulators, even though attempting to serve the public good, may become overly zealous in conducting investigations or carrying out a regulatory action. Given these considerations, there may be an ethical duty on the part of individuals and corporations to insist that regulators comply with the letter of the law in carrying out regulatory actions. More directly, they may have an ethical duty to assert a legal right, even if assertion of that right delays or avoids some agency action.

The Ethics of Criminal Sanctions

Criminal law is a means by which private action is controlled for the public's good. Controversy persists in this area of law as well as in other areas of the public environment. In criminal law, debate used to focus almost exclusively on the proper balance between the need to protect the public from antisocial behavior and the desire to protect innocent persons from abuses by the state under the guise of accepted police powers. Increasingly, however, debate has come to include questions about how far society should go in using criminal sanctions to control private behavior in business and the regulatory environment. Most accept the idea that acts such as murder, assault, theft, and robbery are criminal in nature. This is based on the moral outrage produced by such acts.

Today, increasing use is being made of criminal sanctions to control activities that are not generally thought of as being inherently evil. Some crimes that involve violations of economic regulations, for example, are punishable by prison terms or fines. Yet scholars disagree over whether the acts are even necessarily injurious to commerce, let alone morally reprehensible. Lawyers distinguish between acts that are *mala in se* and acts that are *mala prohibita*—that is, between acts that are widely accepted as morally wrong and those that are wrong simply because they violate a statute or regulatory rule. The distinction is important in analyzing ethical issues concerning the use of criminal sanctions to control corporate behavior.

Business Crimes and Conscience

The easiest way to distinguish between acts that are *mala in se* and those that are *mala prohibita* is to ask whether the act is one that would offend the conscience of an average person. If so, the act is *mala in se*—wrong in and of itself, regardless of whether it violates a statute or regulation. Even in the realm of white-collar crimes, which are generally nonviolent acts, there are acts that offend the conscience. Embezzlement, for example, is normally nonviolent. It may be perpetrated by a gray-suited businessperson. It may be unaccompanied by a bloody murder weapon or an outburst of physical violence, but it is reprehensible. We may be repulsed by the hooligans who verbally or physically assault a kindly old woman just for the sake of malicious sport. Yet we are also morally outraged by the bank president who coldly and methodically embezzles the woman's life savings. Violence may generate a greater degree of outrage simply because it is savage and animalistic. Crime need not be violent or brutal to outrage, however; it need only offend our sense of decency.

Many of the business-related crimes we discussed in Chapter 8 fit in this category—embezzlement and bribery are two examples. Money laundering offends the ordinary person's conscience; even if it is not considered extremely evil in and of itself, it is always the adjunct of more reprehensible conduct, such as organized drug dealing. Other crimes discussed in this unit and in later chapters dealing with the regulatory environment are not as easily characterized as morally or intrinsically evil. As noted in the introduction to this unit, some crimes, such as insider trading and price fixing, are not criminal wrongs in other countries. Moreover, as already noted, many experts argue such crimes are not necessarily harmful to the public. Indeed, some of the acts condemned when carried out by private individuals are lauded as essential to the public welfare when carried out by government.

Price fixing is a prime example of an act uniformly condemned as a social evil when pursued by private organizations but praised as essential public policy when pursued by government. During World War II, and again during President Nixon's first term, the federal government fixed prices. It was a crime to sell items or to receive additional money above the ceiling prices set by the government. At different times, various states have made it illegal to sell items such as milk and alcohol below prices prescribed by regulatory boards. If the rationale that condemns price fixing is that it deprives society of the economic benefits of competition, how can it be justified simply because government, as opposed to private parties, does the fixing? It is extremely difficult to characterize price fixing as criminal just because the parties so engaged are private citizens rather than public officials.

The Ethics of Criminal Sanctions
Consider the following piece of testimony given by a corporate executive during a United States Senate hearing on illegal price fixing in the heavy electrical equipment industry during the early 1960s:

Committee attorney: Did you know that these meetings with competitors were illegal?

Executive: Illegal? Yes, but not criminal. I didn't find that out until I read the indictment. . . . I thought that we were more or less working on a survival basis in order to try to make enough to keep our plant and our employees.

Price fixing is illegal under the federal antitrust laws. Strong arguments can be made that such activities do harm society by depriving it of the benefits of free and open competition. Even so, it may be too harsh to brand one who engages in such activity as a criminal.

An Arbitrary Division
Criminal law and the civil law of torts are usually thought of as being separated by a bright, firmly drawn dividing line. Crimes are wrongs against society. Torts are interferences with protected interests of individual members of society. But, in fact, there is a degree of arbitrariness in where the line should be drawn; there is a continuum from torts to crimes, and the two to some degree overlap. Crimes injure individuals in society. Tort law protects individual interests that society deems valuable. Both share as their common end the control of private behavior for the good of the members of society.

A Necessary Distinction
Despite the difficulty in separating civil and criminal wrongs, the distinction is important—ethically if not legally. Criminal sanctions differ substantially from tort liabilities. Criminal sanctions may include

loss of freedoms through imprisonment as well as loss of some other rights, such as the right to participate in certain professions. For example, lawyers convicted of a felony are often barred from practicing law. Moreover, the social stigma of being condemned as a criminal is much worse than the disapprobation of being a tortfeasor.

Consider again the plight of the electrical equipment industry executive. His justification of his actions—that he and the other conspirators were really only concerned with the survival of their companies—may be sincere. If so, his actions seem less criminal in nature. Is it ethical, though, to commit a crime to keep a plant open and employees earning paychecks to support their families? The answer really depends on the nature of the crime. Helping the company or its employees would not justify murder. The answer is less certain regarding price fixing.

The justification for using criminal sanctions against those who violate statutes and regulations is that it is a matter of pure necessity—that civil remedies are simply not sufficiently strong deterrents. But when the action is not so obviously malevolent, we are reluctant to impose a criminal penalty. This can undercut the attempts to control the very behavior that is subject to sanctions. For example, given the possibility that an executive who had engaged in price fixing was merely seeking to protect the jobs of his employees, a judge or jury might be reluctant to convict him of a criminal wrong. Perhaps less reluctance to convict would result if the offense were only a civil wrong.

■ Discussion Questions

1. You serve as chief executive officer of a large corporation. The state in which your company is headquartered has scheduled a state-wide referendum on whether to allow casino gambling to be conducted within the state. Your company is in no way involved in gambling or in the sale of products used in the gaming industry, but you believe that evidence supports the inference that casino gambling, though potentially lucrative for those who operate the casinos, will hurt the state's economy. Some members of the board of directors have expressed similar concerns to you in casual conversation. Should you authorize the use of your company's resources to mount an opposition campaign to the proposal? Why or why not?

2. What if, in the situation described in question 1, you knew of no conclusive evidence to support or refute the proposition that casino gambling had any effect on the overall economy of the state. Suppose, though, you had a strong moral conviction that gambling was wrong. How would that change the ethical dimensions of the question of whether you should authorize the use of corporate resources to oppose the gambling initiative?

3. The company for which you serve as chief executive officer has been informed by a regulatory agency that it is looking into the disposal of hazardous chemicals for the purpose of changing current regulations. The agency requests certain records from your firm. The request is so broad that, according to your vice-president for legal affairs, it could successfully be challenged in court. Your company has spent millions of dollars over the last two years in order to ensure that the company disposes of its chemical wastes in the safest known manner. You know that fulfilling the agency's request for records will be extremely costly to the company and time consuming for several of your top executives. You also know that the information you supply could go a long way toward convincing the agency to impose regulations consistent with the methods your firm is currently using—methods that you believe are very helpful to the environment. What should you do?

UNIT THREE

The Private Environment

■ The Importance of the Private Environment

The noted legal scholar Roscoe Pound once said that "[t]he social order rests upon the stability and predictability of conduct, of which keeping promises is a large item." Contract law deals with, among other things, the formation and keeping of promises (in Latin, *pacta sunt servanda*—agreements shall be kept). The law encourages competent parties to form contracts for lawful objectives. No aspect of modern life is entirely free of contractual relationships. The topics covered in this unit concern the rights and duties that are involved in the myriad voluntary arrangements that arise in the ordinary course of business. Principles of contract law are at the basis of most of these arrangements. Contracts are covered in Chapter 9 of this unit.

The law of sales pertains to a specific area of contracts: the buying and selling of goods, which is essential to most businesses and is the focus of Chapter 10, on sales.

Chapters 11 and 12 concern two other important aspects of commercial activity. We focus in Chapter 11 on the rights that individuals acquire by virtue of having purchased a good and on the corresponding duties that manufacturers and merchants incur as a result of their involvement in the sale of that good. This is the area of product liability. In Chapter 12, we examine the rights and duties of creditors and debtors that arise as a result of one party's lending funds or extending credit to another. The extreme remedy afforded by bankruptcy is the focus of the second half of Chapter 12.

In Chapter 13, we discuss the legal ramifications of the various types of business organizations. In Chapter 14, we examine the rights and duties of the various participants in the most common business form—the shareholders, directors, and managers of the corporation.

198

■ Ethical Issues in the Private Environment

The private environment is rife with ethical questions. The law of contracts in particular is clouded with gray areas that touch on ethical considerations. Because contract principles are at the heart of the consensual relationships discussed in this unit, many of the ethical considerations of contract law carry over into sales, creditor-debtor relations, and business organization.

One of the major ethical considerations in contract law concerns the freedom of contract. At what point should this freedom be limited to achieve justice? For example, in an era dominated by large corporations, consumers frequently have little choice but to contract for their purchases on terms dictated by the seller. At times, injustice results from this unequal bargaining power. But courts will intervene in such contracts only if the contracts are so one-sided or unfair that they "shock the conscience" of the court.

The law of sales has one fundamental guiding principle—the requirement that both parties to a sales contract should act in good faith. The good faith requirement means that individuals shall not manipulate contract terms to their advantage (and to the detriment of other contractual parties), even if they can do so without violating the letter of the law. Good faith exists if a party can meet the subject test of innocence—sometimes called the "pure heart and empty head" test—when entering into the contract.

Ethical considerations lie at the heart of product liability laws and are, to a great extent, responsible for the trend toward product liability litigation in the last several decades. Courts, at least until recently, increasingly sought to compensate consumers harmed by defectively designed or improperly functioning products. Moreover, those same courts awarded ever-increasing amounts in punitive damages to punish companies that were responsible for defective and harmful products.

Chapter 9

Contracts

In the legal environment of business, one of the most significant bodies of private law deals with contracts. Contract law shows what promises or commitments our society believes should be legally binding. It shows what excuses our society will accept for the breaking of such promises. And it shows what kinds of promises will be considered as being against public policy and therefore legally void.

A **contract** may be defined as a promise enforceable at law.[1] A **promise** is an undertaking that something will or will not happen in the future. Thus, a contract may be formed when two or more parties each promise to perform or to refrain from performing some act now or in the future. The promises need not be in writing to constitute a contract, although some contracts must be in writing to be enforceable. On the contract's breach (a **breach of contract** occurs when a contractual promise is not fulfilled), the breaching party may be subject to legal or equitable sanctions. These sanctions may include a payment of money (damages) to the nonbreaching party for the *failure to perform*. Under some circumstances, the breaching party may be required to render the performance promised in the contract.

Contract law is based on the common law and governs all contracts except when the common law of contracts has been modified or replaced by statutory law or administrative agency regulations. Generally, contracts relating to services, real estate, employment, and insurance are governed by the common law of contracts. All contracts for the sale of *goods,* however, are governed by statutory law—particularly the Uniform Commercial Code (UCC).[2]

■ Basic Requirements of a Contract

The many topics that will be discussed in this chapter require an understanding of the basic requirements of a contract and the processes by which

---

1. The American Law Institute defines a *contract* as a ''promise or set of promises for the breach of which the law gives a remedy, or the performance of which the law in some way recognizes as a duty.'' Restatement (Second) of Contracts, Section 1.
2. The UCC is a comprehensive codification of laws that deal with all phases of a commercial transaction. The UCC was devised through the efforts of numerous legal scholars over the course of several decades. Today, most of the sections of the UCC have been adopted by all fifty states and the District of Columbia (with numerous modifications, however).

a contract is created. The following list briefly describes these requirements.

1. **Mutual assent: Offer and acceptance.** An agreement includes a valid offer and a valid acceptance. One party must voluntarily offer to enter into a legal agreement, and another party must voluntarily accept the terms of the offer.
2. **Consideration.** Generally, consideration is the inducement (reason, cause, motive, or price) to enter into a contract. Any promises made by the parties must be supported by legally sufficient and bargained-for consideration.
3. **Contractual capacity.** Both parties entering into the contract must have the contractual capacity to do so; they must be recognized by the law as possessing characteristics that qualify them as competent parties.
4. **Legality.** The contract must be made to accomplish some goal that is legal and not against public policy.

These four requirements constitute what are formally known as the elements of a contract. Also important are possible *defenses* (that is, reasons why a party should not be awarded what he or she seeks in an action or suit) to the formation or enforcement of a contract. These include the following:

1. **Genuineness of assent.** Apparent consent of both parties must be genuine.
2. **Form.** The contract must be in whatever form the law requires, such as in writing, if any special form is required.

■ Objective Theory of Contracts

The intent or apparent intent to contract is of prime importance in the formation of the contract. This intent is determined by what is called the *objective theory of contracts*, not by the personal or subjective intent, or belief, of a party. The theory is that a party's intent to contract is judged by outward, objective facts as they would be interpreted by a reasonable person, rather than by the party's own secret, subjective intentions. Objective facts include: (1) what the party said when entering into the contract, (2) how the party acted or appeared, and (3) the circumstances surrounding the transaction.

■ Types of Contracts

Contracts may be placed in various categories. In studying these categories, it is important to remember that each category signifies a legal distinction regarding a contract's formation, performance, or enforceability.

Bilateral versus Unilateral Contracts

Every contract involves at least two parties. The *offeror* is the party making the offer, and the *offeree* is the party to whom the offer is made. The offeror always promises to do or not to do something and thus is also a promisor. Whether the contract is classified as *unilateral* or *bilateral* depends on what the offeree must do to accept the offer and to bind the offeror to a contract. If the offer requires as acceptance only that the offeree *promise* to perform, the contract formed is called a bilateral contract. Hence, a *bilateral contract* is a promise for a promise. The exchange of mutual promises (called mutuality of obligation) is the basis of the consideration for the contract and the heart of the formation of a bilateral contract.

If the offer is phrased so that the offeree can accept only by complete performance, the contract formed by completion of the act (performance) is called a *unilateral contract.* Hence, a unilateral contract is a promise for an act.

Express versus Implied Contracts

An *express contract* is one in which the terms of the agreement are fully and explicitly stated in words, oral or written. A contract that is implied from the conduct of the parties is called an implied-in-fact contract, or an *implied contract.* Implied-in-fact contracts differ from express contracts in that the *conduct* of the parties, rather than their words, reveals that they *intended* to form a contract and creates and defines the terms of the contract. The following three steps are necessary to establish an implied-in-fact contract: (1) one party furnished some service or property; (2) the party who furnished the service or property expected to be paid and the other party knew or should have known that payment was expected; and (3) the party who received the service or property had a chance to reject it and did not.

Quasi Contracts
(Contracts Implied in Law)

Quasi contracts, or contracts implied in law, do not arise from a mutual agreement between the parties but are imposed by a court to avoid *unjust enrichment.* The doctrine of unjust enrichment holds that people should not be allowed to profit or enrich themselves inequitably at the expense of others.

The quasi contract is, in essence, a legal fiction. It is based neither on an express promise by the defendant to pay for the benefit received nor on conduct of the defendant implying such a promise. Indeed, the recipient of such a benefit not only has not solicited it but often may be unaware that it has been conferred. The doctrine under which the court implies such a contract is called **quantum meruit,** an expression that means "as much as he deserves." *Quantum meruit* essentially describes the extent of compensation owed under a contract implied in law.

Executed versus Executory Contracts

Contracts are also classified according to their stage of performance. A contract that has been fully performed on both sides is called an *executed contract.* A contract that has not been fully performed on both sides is called an *executory contract.* If one party has fully performed but the other has not, the contract is said to be executed on the one side and executory on the other, but the contract is still classified as executory.

Valid, Void, Voidable, and Unenforceable Contracts

A *valid contract* results when all four elements necessary to contract formation—agreement, consideration, contractual capacity, and legality— exist. In other words, the parties agreed, through an offer and an acceptance, to form a contract; the contract was supported by legally sufficient consideration; the contract was for a legal purpose; and the contract was made by parties who had the legal capacity to enter into the contract.

A *void contract* is no contract at all. The terms *void* and *contract* are contradictory. A void contract produces no legal obligations on the part of any of the parties. For example, a contract can be void if one of the parties was adjudged by a court to be mentally incompetent or if the purpose of the contract was illegal.

A *voidable contract* is a *valid* contract in which, by law, one or both of the parties has the option of avoiding his or her legal obligations. The party having this option can elect to avoid any duty to perform or can elect to *ratify* the contract. If the contract is avoided, both parties are released from it. If it is ratified, both parties must fully perform their legal obligations.

Subject to exceptions, contracts made by minors are voidable at the option of the minor. Contracts entered into under fraudulent conditions are voidable at the option of the defrauded party. In addition, some contracts entered into because of mistakes and all contracts entered into under legally defined duress or undue influence are voidable.

An *unenforceable contract* is a valid contract that cannot be enforced because of certain legal defenses against it. For example, a valid contract barred by a statute of limitations is an unenforceable contract. Some oral contracts under the Statute of Frauds are also unenforceable.

■ Mutual Assent

The parties to an agreement are required to manifest to each other their **mutual assent** to the same bargain. Ordinarily, mutual assent is evidenced by an *offer* and an *acceptance.* One party offers a certain bargain to another party, who then accepts that bargain. Because words often fail to convey the precise meaning intended, the law of contracts generally adheres to the objective theory of contracts, as discussed above.

Requirements of the Offer

An **offer** is a promise or commitment to do or refrain from doing some specified thing in the future. Under the common law, three elements are necessary for an offer to be effective: (1) there must be a *serious intention* by the offeror to become bound by the offer; (2) the terms of the contract must be reasonably *certain,* or *definite,* so that they can be ascertained by the parties and a court of law; and (3) the offer must be communicated by the offeror to the offeree.

INTENTION   The first element for an effective offer to exist is a serious intent on the part of the offeror. Offers made in obvious anger, jest, or undue excitement do not meet the intent test. Because these offers are not effective, an offeree's acceptance would not create an agreement.

Expressions of Opinion   An expression of opinion is not an offer. It does not evidence an intention to enter into a binding agreement. Consider Hawkins, who took his son to McGee, a doctor, and asked McGee to operate on the son's hand. McGee said the boy would be in the hospital three or four days and that the hand would *probably* heal within a few days afterward. The son's hand did not heal for a month, but the father did not win a suit for breach of contract. The court held that McGee did not make an offer to heal the son's hand in three or four days. He merely expressed an opinion as to when the hand would heal.[3]

Statements of Intention   No contract is created when Henry says, "I *plan* to sell my stock in Ryder Systems for $150 per share," and Fred "accepts" and tenders (offers or gives) to Henry the $150 per share for the stock. Henry has merely expressed his intention to enter into a future contract for the sale of the stock. No contract is formed, because a reasonable person would conclude that Henry was only *thinking* about selling his stock, not promising to sell.

Invitations to Negotiate   A request or invitation to negotiate is not an offer. It only expresses a willingness to discuss the possibility of entering into a contract. Included are statements such as "Will you sell Blythe Estate?" or "I wouldn't sell my car for less than $1,000." A reasonable person in the offeree's position would not conclude that these statements evidenced an intention to enter into a binding obligation.

In the construction industry, contractors are invited to submit bids. The *invitation* to submit bids is not an offer, and by submitting a bid a contractor does not bind the party who invited the bid. The bids that the contractors submit *are* offers, however, and the offeree can bind the contractor by accepting the bid.

Advertisements, Catalogues, and Circulars   In general, advertisements, mail order catalogues, price lists, and circular letters are treated not as *offers* to contract but as *invitations to negotiate*. Most advertisements are not offers, because the seller never has an unlimited supply of goods. If advertisements were offers, then everyone who "accepted" after the retailer's supply was exhausted could sue for breach of contract. Initial advertisements are treated as *invitations* to make offers, rather than as offers. As further evidence of the lack of intent to offer to sell at the listed prices, the words "prices subject to change" are usually printed somewhere on the price list.

Although most advertisements and the like are treated as invitations to negotiate, this does not mean that an advertisement can never be an offer. *If the advertisement makes a promise so definite in character that it is apparent that the offeror is binding himself or herself to the conditions stated, the advertisement is treated as an offer.* Suppose an advertisement states, "To the first five persons in our store at 8:00 A.M. on May 1, we offer to sell Singer Sewing Machines, Model X, at $100." This statement invites an acceptance of the terms stated rather than an offer to buy. If you were one of the first five in the store at the time specified, your acceptance would create a contract.

Agreements to Agree   Traditionally, agreements to agree—that is, agreements to agree to a material term of a contract at some future date—were not considered to be binding contracts. More recent cases illustrate the view that agreements to agree serve valid commercial purposes and can be enforced if the parties clearly intended to be bound by such agreements. Under the modern view, the emphasis is on the parties' *intent* rather than on form.

For example, when the Pennzoil Company discussed with the Getty Oil Company the possible purchase of Getty's stock, a Memorandum of Agreement was drafted to reflect the terms of the conversations. After more negotiations over the price, both companies issued press releases announcing an agreement in principle on the terms of the memorandum. The next day, Texaco, Inc., offered to buy all Getty's stock at a higher price. The day after that, Getty's board of directors voted to accept Texaco's offer, and Texaco and Getty

---

3.   *Hawkins v. McGee*, 84 N.H. 114, 146 A. 641 (1929).

signed a merger agreement. When Pennzoil sued Texaco for tortious interference with its "contractual" relationship with Getty, a jury concluded that Getty and Pennzoil had intended a binding contract before Texaco made its offer, with only the details left to be worked out. Texaco was held liable for interfering with this contract.[4]

DEFINITENESS   The second element for an enforceable contract is the definiteness of the contract terms. A contract must have reasonably definite terms so that a court can determine if a breach has occurred and can give an appropriate remedy.[5] Courts are sometimes willing to supply a missing term in a contract when the parties have clearly manifested an intent to form a contract. If, in contrast, the parties have attempted to deal with a particular term of the contract but their expression of intent is too vague or uncertain to be given any precise meaning, the court will not supply a "reasonable" term, because to do so might conflict with the intent of the parties. In other words, the court will not rewrite the contract.

COMMUNICATION   A third element for an effective offer is communication of the offer to the offeree, resulting in the offeree's knowledge of the offer. Ordinarily, one cannot agree to a bargain without knowing that it exists.

Termination of the Offer

The communication of an effective offer to an offeree creates a power in the offeree to transform the offer into a binding, legal obligation—a contract. This power of acceptance, however, does not continue forever. It can be terminated by either *action of the parties* or *operation of law*.

TERMINATION BY ACTION OF THE PARTIES The power of the offeree to transform the offer into a binding, legal obligation can usually be terminated by any of the following actions: (1) revocation of the offer by the offeror; (2) rejection of the offer by the offeree; and (3) counteroffer by the offeree.

---

4. *Texaco, Inc. v. Pennzoil Co.*, 729 S.W.2d 768 (Tex.App.—Houston [1st Dist.] 1987).
5. Restatement (Second) of Contracts, Section 33.

Revocation of the Offer by the Offeror **Revocation** is the withdrawal of the offer by the offeror. Generally, an offer may be revoked by the offeror at any time before acceptance. A revocation is not effective until it is received by the offeree. Revocation may be accomplished by express repudiation of the offer (such as "I withdraw my previous offer of October 17.") or by acts inconsistent with the existence of the offer that are made known to the offeree.

Rejection of the Offer by the Offeree   An offer may be rejected by the offeree, in which case the offer is terminated. Any subsequent attempt by the offeree to accept will be construed as a new offer, giving the original offeror (now the offeree) the power of acceptance. A rejection is ordinarily accomplished by words or conduct evidencing an intent not to accept the offer. As in the case of revocation of the offer, rejection is effective only when actually received by the offeror or the offeror's agent.

Merely inquiring about an offer does not constitute rejection. For example, a friend offers to buy your car for $750. If you respond, "Is this your best offer?" or "Will you pay me $1,000 for it?" a reasonable person would conclude not that you had rejected the offer but that you had merely made an inquiry for further consideration of the offer. You can still accept and bind your friend to the $750 purchase price. When the offeree merely inquires as to the firmness of the offer, there is no reason to presume that he or she intends to reject it.

Counteroffer by the Offeree   A **counteroffer** is a rejection of the original offer and the simultaneous making of a new offer. Suppose Stewart offers to sell his home to Twardy for $70,000. Twardy responds, "Your price is too high. I'll offer to purchase your house for $65,000." Twardy's response is termed a counteroffer, because it terminates Stewart's offer to sell at $70,000 and creates a new offer by Twardy to purchase at $65,000. At common law, the **mirror image rule** requires the offeree's acceptance to match the offeror's offer exactly—to mirror the offer. Any material change in, or addition to, the terms of the original offer automatically terminates that offer and substitutes the counteroffer, which, of course, need not be accepted. The original offeror can, however, accept the terms of the counteroffer and create a valid contract.

It is possible for an offeree to make a new offer without intending to reject the original offer. In such a case two offers exist, each capable of being accepted. To illustrate, suppose Frank offers to sell his bicycle for $100. Irene's response is, "I do not have $100 but will try to raise that sum. I do have $75 and offer to purchase your bicycle for that price." Because the offeree did not reject the $100 offer, that offer remains effective. But the offeree did offer to purchase the bicycle for $75. Thus, two offers exist, and the first to be accepted binds the parties to a contract for that amount.

The following case illustrates the rule that, under general contract law, an acceptance must mirror the terms of the offer; if it does not, it will be considered a counteroffer.

BACKGROUND AND FACTS *In October 1983, James Naylor and CEAG Electric Corporation entered into a written agreement under which Naylor would be CEAG's exclusive sales representative in upstate New York. Naylor was to solicit and forward orders for CEAG, and in return CEAG was to pay Naylor commissions up to 7 percent. The contract also provided that it could only be modified by a writing signed by both parties and that it could be terminated by either party without cause on thirty days' written notice. In September 1984, Naylor learned of an opportunity to sell CEAG power supplies to IBM Corporation, and on September 7 CEAG wrote Naylor a letter stating that CEAG would pay Naylor a minimum 2 percent commission on any IBM orders within Naylor's territory. The letter also instructed Naylor to sign both copies of the letter and return one copy to CEAG, which Naylor did not do. Instead, Naylor wrote CEAG a letter in which he demanded higher compensation and a long-term contract. Shortly thereafter, CEAG notified Naylor in writing that it was cancelling its existing October 1983 sales contract. When Naylor later sued CEAG to recover commissions allegedly owed to him under the "contract" of September 7, 1984, one of the issues before the court was whether the written correspondence between CEAG and Naylor in September 1984 constituted a contract. The trial court held that Naylor's letter requesting higher commissions and a long-term contract was a counteroffer, not an acceptance, and therefore no contract or contractual modification was made in September 1984. The appellate court now reviews the issue.*

Case 9.1

NAYLOR v. CEAG ELECTRIC CORP.

Supreme Court of New York, Appellate Division, Third Department, 1990.
158 A.D.2d 760,
551 N.Y.S.2d 349.

HARVEY, Justice.
    *   *   *   *

The crux of plaintiff's [Naylor's] contentions is that two separate and distinct agreements are at issue here; the 1983 sales agreement and the contract allegedly formed by defendant's [CEAG's] September 7, 1984 letter to him. Supreme Court [in New York, the Supreme Court is a trial court] found, however, that the September 7, 1984 letter to plaintiff was merely an offer or proposal to plaintiff to modify the existing October 1983 agreement and plaintiff's September 12, 1984 letter was a rejection and counteroffer. Therefore, no binding contract resulted. With this conclusion we agree. Defendant made its intent quite clear in its September 7, 1984 letter that the exclusive means of acceptance was for plaintiff to sign both copies of the letter and this did not occur. The parties had explicitly stated in their October 1983 agreement that modifications could only be made pursuant to a written instrument signed by both parties. Without mutuality of assent, no contract could be formed as a matter of law.

* * * Because no contract rights were created by the 1984 letter, plaintiff's cause of action seeking commissions pursuant to that letter was properly dismissed.

DECISION AND REMEDY   *The trial court's ruling was affirmed. Naylor could not recover any commissions pursuant to the September 1984 "agreement" because no contract had ever been formed. The only contract in existence was the one created in October 1983, and Naylor provided no evidence that he was owed commissions under that agreement.*

TERMINATION BY OPERATION OF LAW   The power in the offeree to transform the offer into a binding, legal obligation can be terminated by operation of the law through the following: (1) lapse of time; (2) destruction of the subject matter of the contract; (3) death or incompetence (that is, the loss of capacity to contract) of the offeror or the offeree; and (4) supervening illegality of the proposed contract (which occurs when a statute or court decision makes an offer illegal).

An offer terminates automatically when the period of time specified in the offer has passed. The period of time specified in an offer begins to run when the offer is actually received by the offeree, not when it is sent or drawn up. When the offer has been delayed, the period begins to run from the date the offeree would have received the offer, but only if the offeree knows or should know the offer was delayed.[6]

If no time for acceptance is specified in the offer, the offer terminates at the end of a *reasonable* period of time. A reasonable period is determined by the subject matter of the contract, business and market conditions, and other relevant circumstances.

IRREVOCABLE OFFERS   Although most offers are revocable, certain offers can be made irrevocable. Three types of *irrevocable offers* deserve discussion. They are option contracts, offers that induce detrimental reliance in the offeree, and "firm offers" made by merchants. (Firm offers are discussed in the next chapter.)

Option Contracts   As a general rule, offerors may revoke their offers even if they have expressly agreed to hold them open for a specified period of

time. When an offeror promises to hold an offer open for a specified period, however, and the offeree pays for the promise (gives consideration), an *option contract* is created. An option contract is a *separate* contract that takes away the offeror's power to revoke the offer during the period of time specified in the option. If no time is specified, then a reasonable period of time is implied.

Promissory Estoppel   Increasingly, courts are refusing to allow an offeror to revoke an offer when the offeree has changed position in justifiable reliance on the offer. In such cases, revocation is considered unjust to the offeree. Preventing the offeror from revoking the offer is normally called **promissory estoppel.** To *estop* means to bar or impede or to preclude. Thus, promissory estoppel means that the promisor (the offeror) is barred or prevented from revoking the offer, because the offeree has already changed her actions in reliance on the offer. The doctrine of promissory estoppel is discussed again later in this chapter.

Another situation causing detrimental reliance on the part of the offeree involves *partial performance* by the offeree in response to an offer involving a *unilateral* contract. The offer invites acceptance only by full performance; merely promising to perform does not constitute acceptance. Obviously, injustice can result if an offeree expends time and money in partial performance, and then the offeror revokes the offer before performance is complete. Consequently, many courts will not allow the offeror to revoke after the offeree has performed some substantial part of his or her duties.[7] In effect, partial performance renders the offer irrevocable, giving the original offeree reasonable time to complete performance. Of course,

---

6. Restatement (Second) of Contracts, Section 49.

7. Restatement (Second) of Contracts, Section 25.

when performance is complete, a unilateral contract exists.

Acceptance

An **acceptance** is a voluntary act (either words or conduct) by the offeree that shows assent (agreement) to the terms of an offer. The acceptance must be unequivocal and communicated to the offeror. To accept an offer, an offeree must know of the offer, intend to accept it, and accept it *unequivocally.* Unequivocal acceptance is required by the *mirror image rule* previously discussed. If the acceptance is subject to new conditions, or if the terms of the acceptance materially change the original offer, the acceptance may be considered a counteroffer that implicitly rejects the original offer.

Certain conditions, when added to an acceptance, do not qualify the acceptance sufficiently to make it a rejection of the offer. Suppose Childs offers to sell a sixty-five-acre cotton farm to Sharif. Sharif replies, ''I accept your offer to sell the farm, provided that you are the owner.'' This condition does not make the acceptance equivocal. The condition that a seller own the property is normally implied in every offer for the sale of land, so the condition does not add any new or different terms to the offer.

Or suppose that in response to an offer to sell a used bicycle, the offeree replies, ''I accept; please send written contract.'' The offeree has requested a written contract but has not made it a condition for acceptance. Therefore, the acceptance is effective without the written contract. If, however, the offeree replies, ''I accept if you send a written contract,'' the acceptance is expressly conditioned on the request for a writing, and the statement is not an acceptance but a counteroffer. (Notice how important *each* word is!)

SILENCE AS ACCEPTANCE   Ordinarily, silence cannot be acceptance, even if the offeror states, ''By your silence and inaction you will be deemed to have accepted this offer.'' This general rule applies because an offeree should not be obligated to act affirmatively to reject an offer when no consideration has passed to the offeree to impose such a liability. In contrast, silence can operate as an acceptance when an offeree takes the benefit of offered services if he or she had an opportunity to reject them and knew that they were offered with the expectation of compensation.

Silence can also operate as acceptance when the parties have had prior dealings in which the offeree has led the offeror reasonably to understand that the offeree will accept all offers unless the offeree sends notice to the contrary. For example, Brodsky, a sales agent, has previously received shipments of goods from Morales and paid without notifying Morales of his acceptance. Brodsky sells the goods and simply sends Morales a check. Only if the goods are defective does he notify Morales. The last shipment has been neither paid for nor rejected. Four months have passed. Brodsky is bound on a contract and must pay Morales for this last shipment of goods.[8]

COMMUNICATION OF ACCEPTANCE   Whether the offeror must be notified of the acceptance depends on the nature of the contract. In a unilateral contract, no notification or communication is generally necessary. Because a unilateral contract calls for the performance of some act, acceptance is not complete until the act has been substantially performed. Therefore, notice of acceptance is usually unnecessary. When the offeror requests notice of acceptance or has no adequate means of determining whether the requested act has been performed, or when the law requires such notice of acceptance, then notice is necessary.

In a bilateral contract, *communication* of acceptance is necessary because acceptance is in the form of a promise (not performance), and the contract is formed when the promise is made (rather than when the act is performed). The offeree must use reasonable efforts to communicate the acceptance to the offeror. It is possible for a bilateral contract to exist when an offer is accepted by undertaking performance. The beginning of performance by the offeree operates as an *implied* promise. When an offer is accepted by beginning performance, notification to the offeror that performance has begun is needed to trigger the offeror's duty if the offeror would not normally be aware of the beginning of performance.

---

8.   Restatement (Second) of Contracts, Section 72.

■ Consideration

The fact that a promise has been made does not mean the promise can or will be enforced. A promise is not enforceable unless it is supported by consideration. **Consideration** may be defined as the *value* given in return for a promise. In other words, consideration is something that is exchanged for something else. A contract cannot be formed without sufficient consideration.

Often, consideration is broken into two elements: (1) the value of whatever is exchanged for the promise must be *legally* sufficient, and (2) there must be a *bargained-for* exchange. The something of "legally sufficient value" that is bargained for may consist of goods, money, performance, or a return promise. In the following case, one of the classics of contract law, the court found that refraining from certain behavior at the request of another was sufficient consideration to support a promise to pay a sum of money.

Case 9.2

HAMER v. SIDWAY

Court of Appeals of New York,
Second Division, 1891.
124 N.Y. 538,
27 N.E. 256.

BACKGROUND AND FACTS *William E. Story, Sr., was the uncle of William E. Story II. In the presence of family members and guests invited to a family gathering, Story, Sr., promised to pay his nephew $5,000 if he would refrain from drinking, using tobacco, swearing, and playing cards or billiards for money until he became twenty-one. (Note that in 1869, when this contract was formed, it was legal in New York to drink and play cards for money prior to the age of twenty-one.) The nephew agreed and fully performed his part of the bargain. When he reached twenty-one, he wrote and told his uncle that he had kept his part of the agreement and was therefore entitled to $5,000. The uncle replied that he was pleased with his nephew's performance, writing, "I have no doubt but you have, for which you shall have five thousand dollars, as I promised you. I had the money in the bank the day you was twenty-one years old that I intend for you, and you shall have the money certain. . . . P.S. You can consider this money on interest." The nephew received his uncle's letter and thereafter consented that the money should remain with his uncle according to the terms and conditions of the letter. The uncle died about twelve years later without having paid his nephew any part of the $5,000 and interest. The executor of the uncle's estate (Sidway, the defendant in this action) did not want to pay the $5,000 (with interest) to Hamer, a third party to whom the nephew had transferred his rights in the note, claiming that there had been no valid consideration for the promise. The court disagreed with the executor and reviewed the doctrine of detriment and benefit as valid consideration under the law.*

PARKER, Justice.
* * * *

The defendant contends that the contract was without consideration to support it, and therefore invalid. He asserts that the promisee, by refraining from the use of liquor and tobacco, was not harmed, but benefited; that that which he did was best for him to do, independently of his uncle's promise,—and insists that it follows that, unless the promisor was benefited, the contract was without consideration,—a contention which, if well founded, would seem to leave open for controversy in many cases whether that which the promisee did or omitted to do was in fact of such benefit to him as to leave no consideration to support the enforcement of the promisor's agreement. Such a rule could not be tolerated, and is without foundation in the law. The exchequer chamber in 1875 defined "consideration" as follows: "A valuable consideration, in the sense of the law, may consist either in some right, interest, profit, or benefit accruing to the one party, or some forbearance, detriment, loss, or responsibility given, suffered, or undertaken by the other.'' Courts "will not ask whether the thing which forms the consideration does in fact benefit the promisee or a third party, or is of any substantial value to any one. It is enough that something is promised, done, forborne, or suffered by the party to whom the promise is made as consideration for the promise made to him. In general a waiver of any legal right at the request of another party is a sufficient consideration for a promise. Any damage, or suspension, or forbearance of a right will be sufficient to sustain a promise.'' * * * Now, applying this rule to the facts before us, the promisee used tobacco, occasionally drank liquor, and he had a legal right to do so. That right he abandoned for a period of years upon the strength of the promise of the testator [Story, Sr.] that for such forbearance he would give him $5,000. We need not speculate on the effort which may have been required to give up the use of those stimulants. It is sufficient that he restricted his lawful freedom of action within certain prescribed limits upon the faith of his uncle's agreement, and now, having fully performed the conditions imposed, it is of no moment whether such performance actually proved a benefit to the promisor, and the court will not inquire into it; but, were it a proper subject of inquiry, we see nothing in this record that would permit a determination that the uncle was not benefited in a legal sense.

The court ruled that the nephew had provided legally sufficient consideration by giving up smoking, drinking, swearing, and playing cards or billiards for money until he became twenty-one and was therefore entitled to the money.

DECISION AND REMEDY

Adequacy of Consideration

Adequacy of consideration refers to the fairness of the bargain. On the surface, when the values of the items that are exchanged are unequal, fairness would appear to be an issue. Does unfairness negate a bargain?

Under the doctrine of freedom of contract, parties are normally free to bargain as they wish. If people could sue merely because they had entered into an unwise contract, the courts would be overloaded with frivolous suits. In extreme cases, a court of law may consider the adequacy of consideration in terms of its amount or worth, because inadequate consideration may indicate fraud, duress, undue influence, or a lack of bargained-for exchange. It may also reflect a party's incompetency (for example, an individual might have been too intoxicated, insane, or simply too young to make a contract).

As a general principle of contract law, the courts will not ordinarily attempt to evaluate the adequacy of the consideration in an agreed-upon exchange, unless the consideration is so grossly inadequate as to "shock the conscience" of the court.

Under most circumstances, a promise to do what one already has a legal duty to do is not legally sufficient consideration, because no legal detriment or benefit has been incurred or received.[9] For example, if the only thing bargained for is to refrain from committing a crime or a tort against the promisor, there is no consideration. Similarly, promises based on moral duty or obligation are not enforceable, because a moral obligation is not held to be legally sufficient consideration.

Promises made with respect to events that have already taken place are also unenforceable. These promises lack consideration in that the element of bargained-for exchange is missing. In short, you can bargain for something to take place now or in the future, but not for something that has already taken place; past consideration is no consideration.

Detrimental Reliance, or Promissory Estoppel

Notwithstanding the general rule that consideration is an essential element of any contract, there is a

---

9. *Foakes v. Beer,* 9 App.Cas. 605 (1884).

special class of cases in which courts have enforced promises that were not in fact supported by any real consideration. In such cases, the courts have relied on the doctrine of detrimental reliance, or promissory estoppel, to enforce a promise given by one party that induces another party to rely on that promise to his or her detriment. When the promisor can reasonably have expected the promisee to act on the promise, and injustice cannot be avoided any other way, the promise will be enforced.[10] Additionally, the promisee must have acted with justifiable reliance on the promise—that is, must have been justified in relying on it—and in most instances the act must have been of a substantial nature.

Traditionally, promissory estoppel has been applied only to gratuitous promises—that is, when the parties are not bargaining in a commercial setting. The trend, however, is to apply it in any situation if justice so requires. The following classic case illustrates this point.

---

10.   Restatement (Second) of Contracts, Section 90, provides: "A promise which the promisor should reasonably expect to induce action or forbearance on the part of the promisee or a third person and which does induce such action or forbearance is binding if injustice can be avoided only by enforcement of the promise."

 Case 9.3

HOFFMAN v. RED OWL STORES, INC.
Supreme Court of Wisconsin,
1965.
26 Wis.2d 683,
133 N.W.2d 267.

BACKGROUND AND FACTS   *Red Owl Stores, Inc. (defendant), induced the Hoffmans (plaintiffs) to give up their current business and run a Red Owl franchise. The Hoffmans relied on the representations of Red Owl, and when the deal ultimately fell through because of Red Owl's failure to keep its promise concerning the operation of the franchise agency store, the Hoffmans brought this suit to recover their losses, and the trial court found in their favor. Red Owl appealed.*

CURRIE, Chief Justice.
   *   *   *   *
Recognition of a Cause of Action Grounded on Promissory Estoppel.
Sec. 90 of Restatement, 1 Contracts, provides (at p. 110):
"A promise which the promisor should reasonably expect to induce action or forbearance of a definite and substantial character on the part of the promisee and which does induce such action or forbearance is binding if injustice can be avoided only by enforcement of the promise."
   *   *   *   *
Because we deem the doctrine of promissory estoppel, as stated in sec. 90 of Restatement, 1 Contracts, as one which supplies a needed tool which courts may employ in a proper case to prevent injustice, we endorse and adopt it.

Applicability of Doctrine to Facts of this Case.
The record here discloses a number of promises and assurances given to Hoffman by Lukowitz in behalf of Red Owl upon which plaintiffs relied and acted upon to their detriment.
Foremost were the promises that for the sum of $18,000 Red Owl would establish Hoffman in a store. After Hoffman had sold his grocery store and paid the $1,000 on the Chilton lot, the $18,000 figure was changed to $24,100. Then in November, 1961, Hoffman was assured that if the $24,100 figure were increased by $2,000 the deal would go through. Hoffman was induced to sell his grocery store fixtures and inventory in June, 1961, on the promise that he would be in his new store by fall.

In November, plaintiffs sold their bakery building on the urging of defendants and on the assurance that this was the last step necessary to have the deal with Red Owl go through.

We determine that there was ample evidence to sustain the answers of the jury to the questions of the verdict with respect to the promissory representations made by Red Owl, Hoffman's reliance thereon in the exercise of ordinary care, and his fulfillment of the conditions required of him by the terms of the negotiations had with Red Owl.

The trial court's judgment was affirmed. The Hoffmans were entitled to damages, the exact amount to be determined when the case was returned to the trial court

DECISION AND REMEDY

Promissory estoppel does not mean that each and every gratuitous promise will be binding merely because the promisee has changed position. Liability is created only when there is "justifiable reliance on the promise." The promisor must have known or had reason to believe that the promisee would likely be induced to change position as a result of the promise.

COMMENTS

■ Capacity

Although the parties to a contract must assume certain risks, the law indicates that neither party should be allowed to benefit from the other party's lack of *contractual capacity*—the legal ability to enter into a contractual relationship. Courts generally presume the existence of contractual capacity, but there are some situations in which capacity is lacking or may be questionable. In some situations, a party may have the capacity to enter into a valid contract but also have the right to avoid liability under it. For example, minors usually are not legally bound by contracts. Subject to certain exceptions, the contracts entered into by a minor are voidable at the option of that minor. The minor may avoid legal obligations by exercising the option to *disaffirm* the contract. Note, however, that an adult who enters into a contract with a minor cannot avoid his or her contractual duties on the ground that the minor can do so. Unless the minor exercises the option to avoid the contract, the adult party is bound by it.

Intoxication is a condition in which a person's normal capacity to act or think is inhibited by alcohol or some other drug. If the person was intoxicated enough to lack mental capacity, then the transaction is voidable at the option of the intoxicated person even if the intoxication was purely voluntary.

If a person has been adjudged mentally incompetent by a court of law and a guardian has been appointed, any contract made by the mentally incompetent person is void—no contract exists. Only the guardian can enter into binding legal duties on the incompetent person's behalf.

■ Genuineness of Assent

A contract has been entered into for a legal purpose between two parties, each with full legal capacity to form a contract. The contract is also supported by consideration. Nonetheless, the contract may be unenforceable if the parties have not genuinely assented to the terms. **Genuineness of assent** may be lacking because of mistakes, misrepresentation, undue influence, or duress.

Mistakes

It is important to distinguish between mistakes *in judgment as to value or quality* and mistakes *as to facts.* Only the latter have legal significance. Suppose Jane Simpson plans to buy ten acres of land in Montana. If she believes the land is worth $100,000, and it is worth only $40,000, her mistake is one of value or quality. If she believes, however, that the land is the ten acres owned by the Boyds, and it is actually the ten acres owned by the Deweys, her mistake is one of fact. Only a mistake as to fact allows a contract to be avoided.

Mistakes occur in two forms—*unilateral* and *mutual (bilateral). A* unilateral mistake is made by only one of the contracting parties; a mutual, or bilateral, mistake is made by both.

UNILATERAL MISTAKES   A unilateral mistake occurs when one contracting party makes a mistake as to some *material fact*—that is, a fact important to the subject matter of the contract. In general, a unilateral mistake does not afford the mistaken party any right to relief from the contract.[11]

There are two exceptions to the general rule. First, the rule is not applied when the *other* party to the contract knows or should have known that a mistake was made. Second, some states will not enforce the contract against the mistaken party if the error was due to a mathematical mistake in addition, subtraction, division, or multiplication and if it was done inadvertently and without gross

negligence (a mistake of this nature is sometimes referred to as a *scrivener's error*—meaning a writer's, or scribe's, error).

MUTUAL MISTAKES   When both parties are mistaken as to the same material fact, the contract can be rescinded (canceled) by either party at any time.[12] Again, it is important to distinguish between mistakes *in judgment as to value or quality* and mistakes *as to facts.*

To have legal significance, the mistake must be about a material fact—a fact important to the subject matter of the contract. The classic case on mutual mistake of fact involved a ship named *Peerless* that was to sail from Bombay with certain cotton goods on board. More than one ship named *Peerless* sailed from Bombay that winter, however. The consequent mistake as to the identity of the subject matter of the contract was mutual, and it was about a material fact.

---

11.   Restatement (Second) of Contracts, Section 153, liberalizes this rule to take into account the modern trend of allowing avoidance even though only one party has been mistaken.

---

12.   Restatement (Second) of Contracts, Section 152.

Case 9.4

RAFFLES v. WICHELHAUS

Court of Exchequer, England, 1864.
159 Eng.Rep. 375.

BACKGROUND AND FACTS   *The defendant, Wichelhaus, purchased a shipment of Surat cotton from the plaintiff, Raffles, "to arrive ex 'Peerless' from Bombay." The defendant expected the goods to be shipped on the* Peerless *sailing from Bombay in October. The plaintiff expected to ship the goods on another* Peerless, *which sailed from Bombay in December. By the time the goods arrived and the plaintiff tried to deliver them, the defendant was no longer willing to accept them.*

Per Curiam [an opinion by the entire court].
        *   *   *   *
        *   *   * [I]t was agreed between the plaintiff and the defendants   *   *   * at Liverpool, that the plaintiff should sell to the defendants, and the defendants buy of the plaintiff,   *   *   * 125 bales of Surat cotton   *   *   * to arrive ex "Peerless" from Bombay; and that the cotton should be taken from the quay, and that the defendants would pay the plaintiff for the same   *   *   * at the rate of 17-1/4d. per pound, within a certain time then agreed upon after the arrival of the said goods in England.   *   *   * [T]he said goods did arrive by the said ship from Bombay in England,   *   *   * and the plaintiff was then and there ready, and willing and offered to deliver the said goods to the defendants[.]   *   *   * [The plaintiff alleged breach of contract because] the defendants refused to accept the said goods or pay the plaintiff for them.
        [The defendants asserted that the] ship mentioned in the   *   *   * agreement was meant and intended by the defendants to be the ship called the "Peerless," which sailed from Bombay   *   *   * in October; and that the plaintiff was not ready and willing and did not offer to deliver to the defendants any bales of cotton which arrived by the last mentioned ship, but instead thereof was only ready and willing and offered

to deliver to the defendants 125 bales of Surat cotton which arrived by another and different ship, which was also called the ''Peerless,'' and which sailed from Bombay * * * in December.

* * * *

There is nothing on the face of the contract to show that any particular ship called the ''Peerless'' was meant; but the moment it appears that two ships called the ''Peerless'' were about to sail from Bombay there is a latent ambiguity, and parol evidence[a] may be given for the purpose of shewing that the defendant meant one ''Peerless,'' and the plaintiff another. That being so, there was no consensus ad idem [on the point], and therefore no binding contract.

The judgment was for the defendant, Wichelhaus. The court held that no mutual assent existed, because each party attached a materially different meaning to an essential term of the written contract. This being so, oral testimony would have been needed to determine whether the parties had actually meant the same ship. If both had meant the same ship, then the contract would have been enforceable.

DECISION AND REMEDY

a. With respect to contracts, *parol evidence* is evidence that the document itself does not furnish but that other sources (such as, in this case, oral testimony) provide.

Fraudulent Misrepresentation

Although *fraud* is a tort, it also affects the genuineness of the innocent party's consent to the contract. Thus, the transaction is not voluntary in the sense of involving ''mutual assent.'' When an innocent party is fraudulently induced to enter into a contract, the contract normally can be avoided, because that party has not *voluntarily* consented to its terms.[13] Normally, the innocent party can either rescind the contract and be restored to the original position or can enforce the contract and seek damages for any injuries resulting from the fraud.

The word *fraudulent* is used in various senses in the law. Generally, fraudulent misrepresentation refers only to misrepresentation that is consciously false and is intended to mislead another. That is, the perpetrator of the fraudulent misrepresentation must know or believe that the assertion is not true, or must lack confidence in what he or she states or implies to be the truth of the assertion, or must know that he or she does not have the basis stated or implied for the assertion.[14] Typically, fraud consists of the following elements: (1) misrepresentation of a material fact; (2) intent to deceive; and

(3) the innocent party's justifiable reliance on the misrepresentation.

Nonfraudulent Misrepresentation

If a plaintiff seeks to rescind a contract because of *fraudulent* misrepresentation, the plaintiff must prove that the defendant had the intent to deceive. Most courts also allow rescission (cancellation) in cases involving *nonfraudulent* misrepresentation—that is, innocent or negligent misrepresentation—if all of the other elements of misrepresentation exist.

Undue Influence

Undue influence arises from special kinds of relationships in which one party can greatly influence another party, thus overcoming that party's free will. Minors and elderly people are often under the influence of guardians. If the guardian induces a young or elderly ward to enter into a contract that benefits the guardian, undue influence may have been exerted. Undue influence can arise from a number of fiduciary relationships: attorney-client, doctor-patient, guardian-ward, parent-child, husband-wife, or trustee-beneficiary. The essential feature of undue influence is that the party being taken advantage of does not, in reality, exercise free will in entering into a contract. A contract

13. Restatement (Second) of Contracts, Sections 163 and 164.
14. Restatement (Second) of Contracts, Section 162.

entered into under excessive or undue influence lacks genuine assent and is therefore voidable.[15]

Duress

Undue influence involves conduct of a *persuasive* nature; *duress* involves conduct of a *coercive* nature. That is, assent to the terms of a contract is not genuine if one of the parties is *forced* into agreement. Recognizing this, the courts allow that party to rescind the contract. Forcing a party to enter into a contract by threatening the party with a wrongful act is legally defined as *duress.* Duress is both a defense to the enforcement of a contract and a

_____
15. Restatement (Second) of Contracts, Section 177.

ground for rescission. Therefore, the party on whom the duress is exerted can choose to carry out the contract or to avoid the entire transaction. (This is true in most cases in which assent is not real.)

Generally, the threatened act must be wrongful or illegal. Threatening to exercise a legal right is not ordinarily illegal and usually does not constitute duress. The threat of a civil suit, for example, is normally not duress.

Being in need is generally not a circumstance that will lead to a finding of duress, even when one party exacts a very high price for whatever it is the other party needs. If the party exacting the price also creates the need, however, duress may be found. In the following case, the plaintiff claimed that it had signed a release agreement under duress.

Case 9.5

ART STONE THEATRICAL CORP. v. TECHNICAL PROGRAMMING & SYSTEMS SUPPORT OF LONG ISLAND, INC.

Supreme Court of New York,
Appellate Division,
Second Department, 1990.
157 A.D.2d 689,
549 N.Y.S.2d 789.

BACKGROUND AND FACTS *Art Stone Theatrical Corporation purchased a computer software system from Technical Programming & Systems Support of Long Island, Inc. Following a lengthy dispute between the parties over the performance of the software, a representative of Technical Programming removed the source code from the software system without Art Stone's knowledge or consent. The removal of the source code made it impossible for Art Stone to modify or adjust the software system to serve its needs. Without the source code, the system was, for all practical purposes, useless to Art Stone. Shortly thereafter, the parties entered into an agreement, which provided that Technical Programming would make the source code available to Art Stone if the president of Art Stone would, in writing, release Technical Programming from liability for any damages incurred by its removal of the source code from the software. Art Stone signed the release but later sued Technical Programming for damages, claiming that the release was void because it had been procured under duress. The trial court dismissed the action on the ground that the action was barred by the release. Art Stone appealed.*

MEMORANDUM BY THE COURT.
* * * *

The affidavit of the plaintiff's [Art Stone's] president in opposition to the motion to dismiss alleged that the wrongful removal of the source code from the computer software system rendered the system worthless and resulted in the disruption of the plaintiff's business, thereby leaving him no choice but to accede to the defendant's demand and execute the general release in order to obtain the return of the source code. Inasmuch as ''[a] contract may be voided on the ground of economic duress where the complaining party was compelled to agree to its terms by means of a wrongful threat which precluded the exercise of its free will,'' the affidavit was sufficient to raise a factual issue with regard to the plaintiff's claim of duress. Accordingly, a trial on this issue is appropriate.

The appellate court ruled the trial court's judgment was improper. The case was remanded for trial on the issue of duress.

DECISION AND REMEDY

Adhesion Contracts and Unconscionability

Modern courts are beginning to strike down terms dictated by a party with overwhelming bargaining power. *Adhesion contracts* arise in situations in which the signer must agree to certain dictated terms or go without the commodity or service in question. An adhesion contract is written *exclusively* by one party (the dominant party, usually the seller or creditor) and presented to the other party (the adhering party, usually the buyer or borrower) with no opportunity to negotiate. Adhesion contracts usually contain copious amounts of fine print disclaiming the maker's liability for every-

thing imaginable. Standard-form contracts are used by a variety of businesses and include life insurance policies, residential leases, loan agreements, and employment agency contracts. Such standard-form agreements are often challenged as being adhesion contracts. To avoid enforcement of the contract or of a particular clause, the aggrieved party must show substantially unequal bargaining positions and show that enforcement would be manifestly unfair or oppressive. If the required showing is made, the contract or particular term is deemed *unconscionable* and not enforced, as the following classic case illustrates.

BACKGROUND AND FACTS *In June 1947, the Campbell Soup Company entered into a written contract with George and Harry Wentz for delivery by the Wentzes to Campbell of all the Chantenay red-cored carrots to be grown on fifteen acres of the Wentz farm during the 1947 season. The prices specified in the contract ranged from $23 to $30 per ton according to the time of delivery. The contract price for January 1948 was $30 per ton. Early in January of 1948, the Wentzes told a Campbell representative that they would not deliver their carrots at the contract price. The market price had risen to at least $90 per ton, and Chantenay red-cored carrots were virtually unobtainable. The Wentzes harvested 100 tons of Chantenay red-cored carrots and sold 62 tons of the carrots to a neighboring farmer, Lojeski. Lojeski sold approximately half of these carrots to Campbell on the open market. Campbell, suspecting that it was purchasing its "contract carrots" from Lojeski, refused to buy any more and brought suit against the Wentzes and Lojeski to enjoin further sale of the contract carrots to others and to compel specific performance of the contract. The trial court denied Campbell's petition for equitable relief, and Campbell appealed.*

Case 9.6

CAMPBELL SOUP CO. v. WENTZ

United States Court of Appeals, Third Circuit, 1949.
172 F.2d 80.

GOODRICH, Circuit Judge.
* * * *
* * * A party may have specific performance of a contract for the sale of chattels [personal property] if the legal remedy is inadequate. Inadequacy of the legal remedy is necessarily a matter to be determined by an examination of the facts in each particular instance.

We think that on the question of adequacy of the legal remedy the case is one appropriate for specific performance. * * *
* * * *
* * * Here the goods of the special type contracted for were unavailable on the open market, the plaintiff had contracted for them long ahead in anticipation of

its needs, and had built up a general reputation for its products as part of which reputation uniform appearance was important. We think if this were all that was involved in the case specific performance should have been granted.

The reason that we shall affirm instead of reversing with an order for specific performance is found in the contract itself. We think it is too hard a bargain and too one-sided an agreement to entitle the plaintiff to relief in a court of conscience. For each individual grower the agreement is made by filling in names and quantity and price on a printed form furnished by the buyer. This form has quite obviously been drawn by skillful draftsmen with the buyer's interests in mind.

*   *   *   *

*   *   * Paragraph 10 provides liquidated damages to the extent of $50 per acre for any breach by the grower. There is no provision for liquidated or any other damages for breach of contract by Campbell.

The provision of the contract which we think is the hardest is paragraph 9 *   *   *. It will be noted that Campbell is excused from accepting carrots under certain circumstances. But even under such circumstances the grower, while he cannot say Campbell is liable for failure to take the carrots, is not permitted to sell them elsewhere unless Campbell agrees. This is the kind of provision which the late Francis H. Bohlen would call "carrying a good joke too far." *   *   *

We are not suggesting that the contract is illegal. Nor are we suggesting any excuse for the grower in this case who has deliberately broken an agreement entered into with Campbell. We do think, however, that a party who has offered and succeeded in getting an agreement as tough as this one is, should not come to a chancellor and ask court help in the enforcement of its term. That equity does not enforce unconscionable bargains is too well established to require elaborate citation.

DECISION AND REMEDY   *The trial court's ruling was affirmed, not because specific performance was an inappropriate remedy in this case but because the contract was unconscionable. Because the contract was found to be unconscionable, it did not merit enforcement by a court of equity.*

■ Legality

A contract, to be enforced in court, must not call for the performance of an illegal act—that is, any act that is criminal, tortious, or otherwise opposed to public policy. A contract to do something that is prohibited by federal or state statutory law is illegal and, as such, void from the outset. Thus it is unenforceable.

Although contracts are entered into by private parties, some are not enforceable because of the negative impact they would have on society. These contracts are said to be *contrary to public policy*. Numerous examples exist. Any contract to commit an immoral act falls in this category. Contracts that prohibit marriage or promote racial discrimination have been held to be illegal on this basis. Suppose, for example, Dangerfield promises a young man $500 if he will refrain from marrying Dangerfield's daughter. If the young man accepts, the resulting contract is void. Thus, if he married Dangerfield's daughter, Dangerfield could not sue him for breach of contract. It is important to remember that a contract, or a clause in a contract, may be illegal even in the absence of a specific statute prohibiting the action promised by the contract if the contract or clause would be against public policy.

■ Statute of Frauds— the Writing Requirement

In most cases, an oral agreement is valid, but the party seeking to enforce it must establish the existence of the contract as well as its actual terms. Naturally, when the parties have no writing or memorandum about the contract, only oral testimony can be used in court to establish the existence of the terms of the contract. The problem with oral testimony is that parties are sometimes willing to perjure themselves to win lawsuits.

Therefore, at early common law, parties to a contract were not allowed to testify. This led to the practice of hiring third party witnesses. As early as the seventeenth century, the English recognized the many problems presented by this practice and enacted a statute to help deal with it. The statute, passed by the English Parliament in 1677, was known as ''An Act for the Prevention of Frauds and Perjuries.'' The act required that certain types of contracts, to be enforceable, had to be evidenced by a writing and signed by the party against whom enforcement was sought. In the United States, the descendant of the British act is called the **Statute of Frauds.**

Modern Statutes of Frauds

Today almost every state has a statute, modeled after the English act, that stipulates what types of contracts must be in writing. In this text, we refer to these statutes—even if a particular state has more than one statute relating to the topic—as the Statute of Frauds. The name is misleading because the statute does not apply to fraud. Neither does it invalidate any type of contract. Rather, it denies *enforceability* to certain contracts that do not comply with its requirements. The primary purpose of the act is *evidentiary*—to provide reliable evidence of the existence and terms of certain classes of contracts deemed historically to be important or complex. Although the statutes vary slightly from state to state, all states require the types of contracts listed below to be in writing or evidenced by a written memorandum signed by the party against whom enforcement is sought, unless certain exceptions apply. These contracts are said to fall ''under'' or ''within'' the Statute of Frauds.

1. Contracts involving interests in land.
2. Contracts that cannot *by their terms* be performed within one year from the date of formation.
3. Collateral, or secondary, contracts, such as promises to answer for the debt or duty of another and promises by the administrator or executor of an estate personally to pay a debt of the estate—that is, out of his or her own pocket.
4. Promises made in consideration of marriage.
5. Under the Uniform Commercial Code, contracts for the sale of goods priced at $500 or more.

Promissory Estoppel and the Statute of Frauds

Recently, some courts have used the doctrine of promissory estoppel (detrimental reliance) to allow parties to recover under oral contracts that would otherwise be rendered unenforceable under the Statute of Frauds. Section 139 of the Restatement (Second) of Contracts provides that a promise that induces action or forbearance can be enforceable notwithstanding the Statute of Frauds if the reliance was foreseeable to the party making the promise and if injustice can be avoided only by enforcing the promise.

■ Third Party Rights and Duties

Once it has been determined that a valid and legally enforceable contract exists, attention can be turned to the rights and duties of the parties to the contract. Because a contract is a private agreement between the parties who have entered into it, it is fitting that these parties alone should have rights and liabilities under the contract. This idea is referred to as *privity of contract*, and it establishes the basic concept that a third party has no rights in a contract to which he or she is not a party.

There are, however, two exceptions to this rule. The first involves a **third party beneficiary contract.** Here the parties to a contract make it with the intent to benefit a third party, and the third party has rights in the contract and may sue the promisor and under some circumstances the promisee to have it enforced. The second exception involves an **assignment of rights** or a **delegation of duties.** Here one of the original parties *transfers* contractual rights or obligations to a third party, giving the third party the rights or obligations of the transferor.

Third Party Beneficiary Contracts

When the promisee to a contract intends at the time of contracting that the contract performance benefit a third person, the third person becomes a beneficiary of the contract and as a beneficiary has legal rights in the contract. Note that only **intended beneficiaries** have legal rights. Third parties who benefit from a contract only *incidentally* are **incidental beneficiaries** and have no legal rights under the contract; they cannot sue to have the contract enforced. In determining whether a third party beneficiary is an intended or incidental beneficiary, the best question to ask is: To whom is the benefit to be given according to the language of the contract? In other words, according to the language of the contract, was the promisee's purpose to obtain the benefit for himself or herself primarily or to confer a benefit on another directly?

In the following case, a beneficiary to a contract sued the promisor directly for payment of the debt. This case, one of the earliest in a U.S. court in which an exception to the rule of privity was allowed, is a landmark in the law governing third party beneficiary contracts and is often cited by the courts.

Case 9.7

LAWRENCE v. FOX

Court of Appeals of New York,
1859.
20 N.Y. 268.

BACKGROUND AND FACTS *Holly owed Lawrence (the plaintiff) $300. Fox (the defendant) suggested that Holly give him the money and promised to pay it to Lawrence to discharge Holly's debt. (Sufficient consideration was present in this transaction to create a contract between Holly and Fox.) Fox never paid Lawrence, so Lawrence sued the defendant, considering himself a third party beneficiary of the contract between Holly and Fox. The trial court decided that the plaintiff had a legal right to sue the defendant for failing to pay the $300 as promised, even though the plaintiff was never "in privity"; that is, he was not a direct party to the contract. The defendant appealed the decision.*

GRAY, Justice.
* * * *

In this case the promise was made to Holly and not expressly to the plaintiff * * *. As early as 1806 it was announced by the Supreme Court of this State, upon what was then regarded as the settled law of England, "That where one person makes a promise to another for the benefit of a third person, that third person may maintain an action upon it." *Schermerhorn v. Vanderheyden* has often been reasserted by our courts and never departed from.
* * * *

In *Hall v. Marston* the court [said]: "It seems to have been well settled that if A promises B for a valuable consideration to pay C, the latter may maintain assumpsit [an action to enforce the agreement] for the money;" and in *Brewer v. Dyer,* the recovery was upheld, as the court said, "upon the principle of law *long recognized and clearly established,* that when one person, for a valuable consideration, engages with another, by a simple contract, to do some act for the benefit of a third, the latter, who would enjoy the benefit of the act, may maintain an action for the breach of such engagement; that it does not rest upon the ground of any actual or supposed relationship between the parties as some of the earlier cases would seem to indicate, but upon the broader and more satisfactory basis, that the law operating on the act of the parties creates the duty, establishes a privity, and implies the promise and obligation on which the action is founded."
* * * *

In this case the defendant, upon ample consideration received from Holly, promised Holly to pay his debt to the plaintiff; the consideration received and the promise to Holly made it as plainly his duty to pay the plaintiff as if the money had been remitted to him for that purpose, and as well implied a promise to do so as if he had been made a trustee of property to be converted into cash with which to pay.
* * * *

No one can doubt that he [Holly] owes the sum of money demanded of him, or that in accordance with his promise it was his duty to have paid it to the plaintiff; nor can it be doubted that whatever may be the diversity of opinion elsewhere, the adjudications in this State, from a very early period, approved by experience, have established the defendant's liability * * *.

The judgment should be affirmed.

Judgment was for the plaintiff, Lawrence. Fox was required to pay the plaintiff $300 to fulfill his original contract with Holly.   **DECISION AND REMEDY**

Assignment of Rights

In every bilateral contract, the two parties have corresponding rights and duties. One party has a *right* to require the other to perform some task, and the other has a *duty* to perform it. The transfer of *rights* to a third person is known as an *assignment.*

When rights under a contract are assigned unconditionally, the rights of the *assignor* (the party making the assignment) are extinguished.[16] The third party (the *assignee,* or party receiving the assignment) has a right to demand performance from the other original party to the contract (the obligor). The assignee takes only those rights that the assignor originally had.

An assignment need *not* be supported by legally sufficient consideration to be effective. A gratuitous assignment is just as effective as an assignment made for money. The absence of consideration becomes significant, however, when the assignor wants to revoke the assignment. If the assignment was made for consideration, the assignor cannot revoke it. If no consideration is involved, the assignor can revoke, thereby canceling the right of the third party to demand performance or to sue for failure to render that performance.[17]

As a general rule, all rights can be assigned, except in special circumstances. If a statute expressly prohibits assignment, the right in question cannot be assigned. When a contract is uniquely *personal* in nature, the rights under the contract cannot be assigned unless all that remains is a money payment. A right cannot be assigned if assignment will materially increase or alter the risk of the obligor. Also, if a contract stipulates that the rights cannot be assigned, then *ordinarily* they cannot be assigned.

There are several exceptions to the last rule. First, a contract cannot prevent assignment of the right to receive money. This is to encourage the free flow of money and credit in modern business settings. Second, the assignment of rights in real estate normally cannot be prohibited, because this would inhibit the free transfer of real estate, contrary to public policy. Third, the assignment of negotiable instruments (which include checks and notes) cannot be prohibited. Fourth, in a sale-of-goods contract, the right to receive damages for breach of contract or for payment of an account owed may be assigned even though the contract prohibits assignment.

■ Performance and Discharge

Just as rules are necessary to determine when a legally enforceable contract exists, so also are they necessary to determine when one of the parties can justifiably say, ''I have fully performed, so I am now discharged from my obligations under this contract.'' The legal environment of business requires the identification of some point at which one or both parties can reasonably know their duties are at an end.

The **discharge** (termination) of a contract is ordinarily accomplished when both of the parties perform those acts promised in the contract. Although a contract is ordinarily discharged by the parties' performance of their contractual duties, discharge can also occur in other ways. Broadly speaking, contracts can be discharged by the following:

1. The occurrence or failure of a *condition* on which a contract is based.
2. *Performance* (or breach of contract, in which case the nonbreaching party is discharged from the duty of performance).
3. *Agreement of the parties.*
4. *Operation of law* (resulting from material alteration of the contract, the statute of limitations,

---

16. Restatement (Second) of Contracts, Section 317.
17. Restatement (Second) of Contracts, Section 332.

bankruptcy, or impossibility or commercial impracticability of performance).

Conditions

Normally, promises must be performed, or the party promising the act will be in breach of contract. In some cases, however, performance is contingent on the occurrence or nonoccurrence of a certain event. Therefore, a *condition* is inserted into the contract, either expressly by the parties or impliedly by courts. If this condition is not satisfied, the obligations of the parties are discharged. Thus, a **condition** is a possible future event, the occurrence or nonoccurrence of which will trigger the performance of a legal obligation or termination of an existing obligation under a contract.[18]

For example, suppose that I offer to purchase a tract of your land on the condition that your neighbor to the south agrees to sell me her land. You accept my offer. Our obligations (promises) are conditioned on your neighbor's willingness to sell her land. Should this condition not be satisfied (for example, if your neighbor refuses to sell), our obligations to each other are discharged and cannot be enforced.

Performance

The great majority of contracts are discharged by performance. The contract comes to an end when both parties fulfill their respective duties by performing the acts they have promised. Performance can also be accomplished by tender. **Tender** is an unconditional offer to perform by one who is ready, willing, and able to do so.

DEGREE OF PERFORMANCE REQUIRED   It is important to distinguish between *complete performance* and *substantial performance.* Courts typically use a *reasonable expectations test* for determining which of these categories a performance fits. Complete performance occurs when performance is within the bounds of reasonable expectations. Substantial performance occurs

---

18.   Restatement (Second) of Contracts, Section 224, defines a condition as "an event, not certain to occur, which must occur, unless its nonoccurrence is excused, before performance under a contract becomes due."

when performance is slightly below reasonable expectations.

Complete (Strict) Performance   Normally, conditions expressly stated in the contract must fully occur in all aspects for complete, or strict, performance to take place. Any deviation operates as a discharge. For example, a home building contract expressly states that *only* Fuller brand plasterboard is to be used for the walls, and no substitute brand is to be used without the owner's express permission. Suppose that the builder cannot secure the Fuller brand and, without obtaining the owner's permission, installs Honeyrock brand instead. Even though Honeyrock brand may be equivalent in quality to Fuller brand and all other aspects of construction conform to the contract, a court may hold that the failure of the contractor to meet the express contractual condition discharges the owner from his or her contractual obligation to pay for the house on completion.

Substantial Performance   Human nature dictates that performance will not always fully satisfy the parties. Therefore, for the sake of justice and fairness, the courts hold that a party must fulfill his or her obligation to perform as long as the other party has fulfilled the terms of the contract with *substantial performance.* To qualify as substantial, the performance must not vary greatly from the performance promised in the contract. If performance is substantial, the other party's duty to perform remains absolute, less damages, if any, for the minor deviations.

For example, what if, in the example given above, the contract had merely stipulated that Fuller brand plasterboard was to be used for the walls. Fuller brand is unavailable, so the contractor substitutes Honeyrock brand, which the contractor knows is equivalent in quality to Fuller brand. In this case, does the contractor's deviation discharge the buyer from paying for the house on completion? The answer depends on a single question: Does the term in dispute constitute either an express or an implied-in-fact condition? If so, then only complete performance can discharge the promise. If the term of the contract is interpreted as *constructive* (that is, a promise to install plasterboard of Fuller brand quality), then *substantial,* not complete, performance is required. Obviously, if Honeyrock is of similar quality, substantial performance by the builder has taken place, and the buyer may be obligated to pay according to the contract.[19] This kind of deviation from the terms of a contract, however, must not be grossly negligent. The courts differ as to whether an intentional variation from a contract, even if made with good motives, prevents substantial performance.

Although substantial performance does not prevent discharge, a breach of contract—however slight—has occurred. If the plasterboard substituted for Fuller brand had been of a somewhat lower quality than Fuller, reducing the value of the house by $3,000, the contractor would still be allowed to recover the price agreed on in the contract, less that $3,000.

TIME FOR PERFORMANCE   If no time for performance is stated in the contract, a *reasonable time* is implied. If a specific time is stated, the parties must usually perform by that time. Unless time is expressly stated to be vital, however, a delay in performance will not destroy the performing party's right to payment. When time is expressly stated to be vital, or when it is construed to be "of the essence," the time for performance must usually be strictly complied with. The time element becomes a condition.

Discharge by Agreement

Any contract can be discharged by agreement of the parties. *Rescission* is the process by which a contract is canceled and the parties are returned to the positions they occupied prior to forming it. For **mutual rescission** to take place, the parties must make another agreement, which must also satisfy the legal requirements for a contract. There must be an *offer,* an *acceptance,* and *consideration.* Ordinarily, in an executory contract in which neither party has yet performed, if the parties agree to rescind the original contract, their promises not to perform those acts promised in the original contract will be legal consideration for the second contract.

When one party has fully performed, however, an agreement to call off the original contract will not normally be enforceable. Because the performing party has received no consideration for the promise to call off the original bargain, additional consideration will be necessary.

Discharge by Operation of Law

Under certain circumstances, contractual duties may be discharged by operation of law. These circumstances include material alteration of the contract, the running of the statute of limitations, bankruptcy, and the impossibility or impracticability of performance.

To discourage parties from altering written contracts, the law operates to allow an innocent party to be discharged when the other party has materially altered a written contract without consent. Statutes of limitations limit the period during which a party can sue on a particular cause of action. (A cause of action is the basis or reason for suing or bringing an action.) After the applicable limitations period has passed, a suit can no longer be brought in a court of law or equity. Additionally, a discharge in bankruptcy will ordinarily bar enforcement of most of a debtor's contracts by the creditors. Bankruptcy can be entered into voluntarily or involuntarily.[20]

After a contract has been made, performance may become impossible in an objective sense. This is known as *objective impossibility of performance,* or simply as **impossibility of performance,** and may discharge a contract.[21] Certain basic types of situations generally qualify to discharge contractual obligations under this doctrine:

1.   One of the essential parties to a personal contract *dies or becomes incapacitated* prior to performance.[22]

2.   The *specific* subject matter of the contract is destroyed.[23]

3.   A change in *law* renders performance illegal.[24]

---

19.   For an excellent analysis of substantial performance, see Judge Cardozo's opinion in *Jacob & Youngs v. Kent,* 230 N.Y. 239, 129 N.E. 889 (1921).

20.   Some bankruptcies—Chapter 12 and 13 cases—can be initiated *only* by a debtor's filing of a voluntary petition.
21.   Restatement (Second) of Contracts, Section 261.
22.   Restatement (Second) of Contracts, Section 262.
23.   Restatement (Second) of Contracts, Section 263.
24.   Restatement (Second) of Contracts, Section 264.

Occasionally, if circumstances arise after the contract has been formed that make performance *extremely* difficult or costly, courts may allow the contract to be discharged under the **doctrine of commercial impracticability.**[25] For example, the California Supreme Court held that a contract was discharged because it would cost ten times more than the original estimate to excavate a certain amount of gravel.[26] In another case, however, commercial impracticability was not found when a carrier of goods was to deliver wheat from the United States to Iran.[27] The Suez Canal, the usual route, was nationalized by Egypt and closed, forcing the carrier to travel around Africa and the Cape of Good Hope—instead of through the Mediterranean—to get to Iran. The added expense was approximately $42,000 above the contract price of $306,000, and the original journey of 10,000 miles was extended by 3,000 miles. Nevertheless, the court held that the contract was not commercially impracticable to perform, because the closing of the Suez Canal was a foreseeable event in view of the political circumstances of the time—circumstances of which businesspersons were, or should have been, fully aware. Therefore, caution should be used in invoking commercial impracticability. The added burden of performing must be *extreme* and, more importantly, must *not* have been within the cognizance of the parties when the contract was made.

A closely allied theory is the doctrine of **frustration of purpose.** In principle, a contract will be discharged if supervening circumstances make it impossible to attain the purpose both parties had in mind when making the contract. The origins of the doctrine lie in the old English "coronation cases." A coronation procession was planned for Edward VII when he became king of England following the death of his mother, Queen Victoria. Hotel rooms along the procession route were rented at exorbitant prices for that day. When the king became ill and the procession was canceled, the purpose of the room contracts was "frustrated." A flurry of lawsuits resulted. Hotel and building owners sought to enforce the room rent bills against would-be parade observers, and would-be parade observers sought to be reimbursed for rental monies paid in advance on the rooms. Would-be parade observers were excused from their duty of payment. It was from this situation that the court developed its theory of recovery known as *frustration of purpose.*

■ Breach of Contract and Remedies

Whenever a party fails to perform part or all of the duties under a contract, that party is in breach of contract. *Breach of contract* is the failure to perform what a party is under an absolute duty to perform.[28] Once a party has failed to perform or has performed inadequately, the other party—the nonbreaching party—can choose one or more of several remedies. A *remedy* is the relief provided for an innocent party when the other party has breached the contract. It is the means employed to enforce a right or to redress an injury. Strictly speaking, the remedy is not a part of a lawsuit, but the result thereof, the object for which the lawsuit is presented and the end to which all litigation is directed.

The most common remedies available to a nonbreaching party include damages, rescission and restitution, specific performance, and reformation. An award of damages is a remedy at law. The other three remedies are equitable remedies.

Damages

A breach of any contract entitles the nonbreaching party to sue for money (damages). *Damages* are designed to compensate the nonbreaching party for the loss of the bargain. When a party loses the benefit of the bargain or contract, the breaching party must make up this loss to the nonbreaching party. Often, courts say that innocent parties are to be placed in the position they would have occupied had the contract been fully performed.[29] For example, in the famous case of the "hairy hand," a

---

25. Restatement (Second) of Contracts, Sections 265 and 266, and UCC 2-615.
26. *Mineral Park Land Co. v. Howard,* 172 Cal. 289, 156 P. 458 (1916).
27. *Transatlantic Financing Corp. v. United States,* 363 F.2d 312 (D.C. Cir. 1966).

28. Restatement (Second) of Contracts, Section 235(2).
29. Restatement (Second) of Contracts, Section 347, and UCC 1-106(1).

doctor promised to make a boy's scarred hand ''a hundred percent perfect.'' Skin was taken from the boy's chest and grafted onto his thumb and fingers. The hand became infected, and the boy was hospitalized for three months. Use of the hand was greatly restricted, and hair grew out of the grafted skin. In hearing a suit against the doctor, the court explained that the amount of damages was to be determined by the difference between the value to the boy of the ''perfect'' hand that the doctor had promised and the value of the hand in its condition after the operation.[30]

COMPENSATORY DAMAGES Damages compensating the nonbreaching party for the *loss of the bargain* are known as **compensatory damages.** These damages compensate the injured party only for injuries actually sustained and proved to have arisen directly from the loss of the bargain caused by the breach of contract. They simply replace what was lost because of the wrong or injury. To illustrate: Wilcox contracts to perform certain services exclusively for Hernandez during the month of March for $2,000. Hernandez cancels the contract and is in breach. Wilcox is able to find another job during the month of March, but can only earn $1,000. He can sue Hernandez for breach and recover $1,000 as compensatory damages.

CONSEQUENTIAL (SPECIAL) DAMAGES Foreseeable damages that result from a party's

---

30. *Hawkins v. McGee*, 84 N.H. 114, 146 A. 641 (1929).

breach of contract are called **consequential damages**. They differ from compensatory damages in that they are caused by special circumstances beyond the contract itself. They flow from the consequences, or results, of a breach. For example, if a seller fails to deliver goods with knowledge that a buyer is planning to resell these goods immediately, consequential damages will be awarded for the loss of profit from the planned resale. The buyer will also recover compensatory damages for the difference between the contract price and the market price of the goods.

To recover consequential damages, the breaching party must know (or have reason to know) that special circumstances will cause the nonbreaching party to suffer an additional loss. The rationale here is to give the nonbreaching party the whole benefit of the bargain, provided the breaching party knew of the special circumstances when the contract was made. A leading case on the necessity of giving notice of consequential circumstances is *Hadley v. Baxendale,* decided in England in 1854. The case involved a crankshaft used in a mill operation. In the mid-1800s, it was very common for large mills, such as the one the plaintiffs operated, to have more than one crankshaft in case the main one broke and had to be repaired, as it did in this case. Also, in those days it was common knowledge that flour mills had spares. It is against this background that the parties argued whether or not the damages resulting from profits lost while the crankshaft was out for repair were ''too remote'' to be recoverable.

BACKGROUND AND FACTS *The Hadleys (plaintiffs) ran a flour mill in Gloucester. The crankshaft attached to the steam engine in the mill broke, causing the mill to shut down. The shaft had to be sent to a foundry located in Greenwich so that the new shaft could be made to fit the other parts of the engine. Baxendale, the defendant, was a common carrier who transported the shaft from Gloucester to Greenwich. The Hadleys claimed that they had informed Baxendale that the mill was stopped and that the shaft must be sent immediately. The freight charges were collected in advance, and Baxendale promised to deliver the shaft the following day. It was not delivered for several days, however. As a consequence, the mill was closed for several days. The Hadleys sued to recover the profits lost during that time. Baxendale contended that the loss of profits was ''too remote.'' The court held for the plaintiffs, and the jury was allowed to take into consideration the lost profits. The defendant appealed.*

Case 9.8

HADLEY v. BAXENDALE

Court of Exchequer, 1854.
9 Exch. 341,
156 Eng.Rep. 145.

ALDERSON, B.

    *   *   *   *

    *   *   * Where two parties have made a contract which one of them has broken, the damages which the other party ought to receive in respect of such breach of contract should be such as may fairly and reasonably be considered either arising naturally, i.e., according to the usual course of things, from such breach of contract itself, or such as may reasonably be supposed to have been in the contemplation of both parties, at the time they made the contract, as the probable result of the breach of it. Now, if the special circumstances under which the contract was actually made were communicated by the plaintiffs to the defendants, and thus known to both parties, the damages resulting from the breach of such a contract, which they would reasonably contemplate, would be the amount of injury which would ordinarily follow from a breach of contract under these special circumstances so known and communicated. But, on the other hand, if these special circumstances were wholly unknown to the party breaking the contract, he, at the most, could only be supposed to have had in his contemplation the amount of injury which would arise generally, and in the great multitude of cases not affected by any special circumstances, from such a breach of contract. *   *   *

    *   *   *   *

    Now, in the present case, if we are to apply the principles above laid down, we find that the only circumstances here communicated by the plaintiffs to the defendants at the time the contract was made, were, that the article to be carried was the broken shaft of a mill, and that the plaintiffs were the millers of that mill. But how do these circumstances show reasonably that the profits of the mill must be stopped by an unreasonable delay in the delivery of the broken shaft by the carrier to the third person? Suppose the plaintiffs had another shaft in their possession put up or putting up at the time, and that they only wished to send back the broken shaft to the engineer who made it; it is clear that this would be quite consistent with the above circumstances, and yet the unreasonable delay in the delivery would have no effect on the intermediate profits of the mill. Or, again, suppose that, at the time of the delivery to the carrier, the machinery of the mill had been in other respects defective, then, also, the same results would follow. Here it is true that the shaft was actually sent back to serve as a model for a new one, and that the want of a new one was the only cause of the stoppage of the mill, and that the loss of profits really arose from not sending down the new shaft in proper time, and that this arose from the delay in delivering the broken one to serve as a model. But it is obvious that, in the great multitude of cases of millers sending off broken shafts to third persons by a carrier under ordinary circumstances, such consequences would not, in all probability, have occurred; and these special circumstances were here never communicated by the plaintiffs to the defendants. It follows, therefore, that the loss of profits here cannot reasonably be considered such a consequence of the breach of contract as could have been fairly and reasonably contemplated by both the parties when they made this contract.

DECISION AND REMEDY

The Court of Exchequer ordered a new trial. According to the court, the special circumstances that caused the loss of profits had never been sufficiently communicated by the plaintiffs to the defendants. The plaintiffs would have to have given express notice of these circumstances to collect consequential damages.

COMMENTS

When damages are awarded, compensation is given only for those injuries that the defendant could reasonably have foreseen as a probable result of the usual course of events following a breach. If the injury complained of is outside the usual and foreseeable course of events, it must be shown specifically that the defendant had reason to know the facts and foresee the injury.

Rescission and Restitution

Rescission is essentially an action to undo, or cancel, a contract—to return the contracting parties to the positions they occupied prior to the transaction.[31] When fraud, mistake, duress, undue influence, misrepresentation, or lack of capacity to contract is present, unilateral rescission is available.[32] The failure of one party to perform entitles the other party to rescind the contract. The rescinding party must give prompt notice to the breaching party. Generally, to rescind a contract, both parties must make **restitution** to each other by returning goods, property, or money previously conveyed.[33] If the goods or property received can be restored *in specie*—that is, if the actual goods or property can be returned—they must be. If the goods or property has been consumed, restitution must be made in an equivalent amount of money.

---

31.   The rescission discussed here is *unilateral* rescission, in which only one party wants to undo the contract. In mutual rescission, both parties agree to undo the contract. Mutual rescission discharges the contract; unilateral rescission is generally available as a remedy for breach of contract.

32.   The Federal Trade Commission and many states have rules or statutes allowing consumers to unilaterally rescind contracts made at home with door-to-door salespersons. Rescission is allowed within three days for any reason or for no reason at all. See, for example, California Civil Code Section 1689.5.

33.   Restatement (Second) of Contracts, Section 370.

Specific Performance

The equitable remedy of **specific performance** calls for the performance of the act promised in the contract. Although the equitable remedy of specific performance is often preferable to other remedies, specific performance will not be granted unless the party's legal remedy (money damages) is inadequate.[34] For example, contracts for the sale of goods rarely qualify for specific performance. The legal remedy, money damages, is ordinarily adequate in such situations because substantially identical goods can be bought or sold in the market. If the goods are unique, however, a court of equity will decree specific performance. For example, paintings, sculptures, and rare books or coins are so unique that money damages will not enable a buyer to obtain substantially identical substitutes in the market.

Reformation

The equitable remedy of **reformation** is used when the parties have *imperfectly* expressed their agreement in writing. Reformation allows the contract to be rewritten to reflect the parties' true intentions. It applies most often when fraud or mutual mistake (for example, a clerical error) is present.

---

34.   Restatement (Second) of Contracts, Section 359.

■ Terms and Concepts to Review

■ Questions and Case Problems

9-1. Susan contacts Joe and makes the following offer: "When you finish mowing my yard, I'll pay you $25." Joe responds by saying, "I accept your offer." Is there a contract? Is it a bilateral or unilateral contract? What is the legal significance of the distinction?

9-2. Ball writes Sullivan and inquires how much Sullivan is asking for a specific forty-acre tract of land Sullivan owns. In a letter received by Ball, Sullivan states, "I will not take less than $60,000 for the forty-acre tract as specified." Ball immediately sends Sullivan a telegram stating, "I accept your offer for $60,000." Discuss whether Ball can hold Sullivan to a contract for sale of the land.

9-3. After Kira had several drinks one night, she sold Charlotte a valuable fur stole for ten dollars. The next day, Kira offered the ten dollars to Charlotte and requested the return of her stole. Charlotte refused to accept the ten dollars or return the stole, claiming that they had a valid contract of sale. Kira explained that she was intoxicated at the time the bargain was made and thus the contract is voidable at her option. Is Kira correct? Explain.

9-4. Discuss whether any of the following contracts will be unenforceable on the grounds that genuineness of assent is lacking.

   (a) Simmons finds a stone in his pasture that he believes to be quartz. Jenson, who also believes that the stone is quartz, contracts to purchase it for $10. Just before delivery, the stone is discovered to be a diamond worth $1,000.

   (b) Jacoby's barn is burned to the ground. He accuses Goldman's son of arson and threatens to bring criminal action unless Goldman agrees to pay him $5,000. Goldman agrees to pay.

   (c) Kober, a new salesperson, innocently tells Larry that a lawn mower he is selling has a five-year manufacturer's warranty. Larry contracts to purchase the lawn mower in reliance on that information. Larry and Kober are transacting business for the first time. At the time of delivery, it is discovered that the manufacturer only warrants the lawn mower for one year.

9-5. Central Properties entered into a contract with Robbinson and Westside, a real estate development company, whereby Central Properties purchased sixty acres of land. The contract included a "right of first refusal" to purchase the water and sewage system on the remaining property of Westside. Westside wanted to sell the sewage system and over the course of three months exchanged letters with Central asking whether it wished to exercise its "right." Central Properties never affirmatively accepted in any of its responses but requested different terms, price, and so on. Central now wishes to hold Westside to a contract for the system. Westside states no contract was formed. Discuss who is right. [*Central Properties, Inc. v. Robbinson,* 450 So.2d 277 (Fla.App. 1 Dist. 1984)]

9-6. Steven Lanci was involved in an automobile accident with an uninsured motorist. Lanci was insured with Metropolitan Insurance Co., although he did not have a copy of the insurance policy. Lanci and Metropolitan entered settlement negotiations, during which Lanci told Metropolitan that he did not have a copy of his policy. Ultimately, Lanci agreed to settle all claims for $15,000, noting in a letter to Metropolitan that $15,000 was the "sum you have represented to be the . . . policy limits applicable to this claim." After signing a release, Lanci learned that the policy limits were actually $250,000, and he refused to accept the settlement proceeds. When Metropolitan sued to enforce the settlement agreement, Lanci argued that the release had been signed as the result of a mistake and was void. Should the court enforce the contract or void it? Explain. [*Lanci v. Metropolitan Insurance Co.,* 388 Pa.Super. 1, 564 A.2d 972 (1989)]

9-7. In July 1965, Loral Corp. was awarded a $6 million contract to produce radar sets for the Navy. For this contract Loral needed to purchase forty precision gear parts. Loral awarded to Austin Instrument a subcontract to supply twenty-three of the forty gear parts. In May of 1966 Loral was awarded a second contract to produce more radar sets. Loral again solicited bids for forty gear parts. Austin submitted a bid for all forty but was told by Loral that the subcontract would be awarded only for items for which Austin was the lowest bidder. Austin's president told Loral that it would not accept an order for less than forty gear parts and, one day later, told Loral that Austin would cease deliveries on the existing contract unless (1) Loral awarded Austin a contract for all forty gear part units and (2) Loral consented to substantial increases for the prices of all gear parts under the existing contract. Ten days later Austin ceased making deliveries. Loral tried to find other suppliers to furnish the gear parts, but none were available. Because of deadlines and liquidated damage clauses (clauses providing for money damages to be paid in the event of delays) in the Navy contract, plus the possible loss of reputation by Loral with the government, Loral agreed to Austin's terms. After Austin's last delivery, Loral filed suit to recover the increased prices Austin had charged on the grounds that the agreement to pay these prices was based on duress. Discuss Loral's claim. [*Austin Instrument, Inc. v. Loral Corp.,* 29 N.Y.2d 124, 272 N.E.2d 533, 324 N.Y.S.2d 22 (1971)]

9-8. Samuel DaGrossa and others were planning to open a restaurant. At some point prior to August 1985, DaGrossa orally agreed with Philippe LaJaunie that LaJaunie, in exchange for his contribution in designing, renovating, and managing the restaurant, could purchase a one-third interest in the restaurant's stock if the restaurant was profitable in its first year of operations. The restaurant opened in March 1986, and a few weeks later LaJaunie's employment was terminated. LaJaunie brought an action to enforce the stock-purchase agreement. Is the agreement enforceable? Why or why not? [*LaJaunie v. DaGrossa,* 159 A.D.2d 349, 552 N.Y.S.2d 628 (1990)]

9-9. John Agosta and his brother Salvatore had formed a corporation, but disagreements between the two brothers caused John to petition for voluntary dissolution of the corporation. According to the dissolution agreement, the total assets of the corporation, which included a warehouse and inventory, would be split between the brothers by Salvatore's selling his stock to John for $500,000. This agreement was approved, but shortly before the payment was made, a fire totally destroyed the warehouse and inventory, which were the major assets of the corporation. John refused to pay Salvatore the $500,000, and Salvatore brought suit for breach of contract. Discuss whether the destruction of the major assets of the corporation affects John's required performance. [*In the Matter of Fontana v. D'Oro Foods Inc.,* 122 Misc.2d 1091, 472 N.Y.S.2d 528 (1983)]

9-10. Zilg is author of *DuPont: Behind the Nylon Curtain,* an historical account of the DuPont family in America's social, political, and economic affairs. Prentice-Hall, Inc., signed Zilg to a contract to publish the book exclusively. There was no provision to have Prentice-Hall use its best efforts to promote the book; rather, it was left up to the publisher to use its discretion as to the number of copies printed and the level of promotion. Prentice-Hall had originally planned a first printing of 15,000 copies and an advertising budget of $15,000 for the book. Later, having had second thoughts about the sales potential of the book, Prentice-Hall decided to do a first printing of only 10,000 copies and to reduce the amount it had allocated for advertising. In all, Prentice-Hall published a total of 13,000 copies (3,000 beyond the sales volume at which it received the highest royalties), authorized an advertising budget of $5,500, distributed over 600 copies to reviewers, and purchased ads in major newspapers. Zilg later claimed that the reductions in the number of volumes printed and in the advertising budget were evidence that Prentice-Hall had not made a "best effort" to fully promote the book. Prentice-Hall claimed that its reduction came after careful review and was based on sound and valid business decisions. Based on these facts only, discuss whether Prentice-Hall has fulfilled its contractual duty to Zilg. [*Zilg v. Prentice-Hall, Inc.,* 717 F.2d 671 (2d Cir. 1983)]

9-11. Coker International, Inc., entered into a contract with Burlington Industries, Inc., under which Coker agreed to purchase 221 used textile looms from Burlington for a total price of $1,021,000. Under the contract, Coker was required to pay a 10 percent down payment, with the balance to be paid prior to the removal of the looms. Coker planned to resell the looms to a customer in Peru, but the contract was not conditioned on any resale of the looms by Coker. Because of actions of the Peruvian government, Coker's plan to resell the equipment to the Peruvian buyer fell through. Coker sought to rescind the contract with Burlington and recover its down payment, asserting that it should be excused from performance under the doctrine of frustration of purpose. Discuss fully whether Coker can be excused from performance of the contract under this doctrine. [*Coker International, Inc. v. Burlington Industries, Inc.,* 747 F.Supp. 1168 (D.S.C. 1990)]

9-12. A Question of Ethics

 In 1982, in the closing days of Minnesota's gubernatorial campaign, Dan Cohen offered a reporter from the Minneapolis Star and Tribune *some "documents which may or may not relate to a candidate in the upcoming election." Cohen, who was actively promoting one of the gubernatorial candidates, agreed to give the reporter the documents—copies of two public court records of a rival party's candidate for lieutenant governor—if the reporter promised not to reveal the source of the information. The reporter promised to keep the source confidential. The editor of the* Tribune, *however, in spite of the reporter's objections, decided to name Cohen as the source of the information so as not to mislead the public into thinking that the information came from an unbiased source. On the day the newspaper article was published, Cohen was fired by his employer. Cohen sued the newspaper's owner, Cowles Media Co., for breach of contract. Given these facts, discuss the following questions.* [Cohen v. Cowles Media Co., 457 N.W.2d 199 (Minn. 1990)]

1. Do you think that the editor's ethical duty to provide the reading public with unbiased news coverage should have overridden the editor's ethical duty to honor the reporter's promise to Cohen?
2. Did the reporter's promise to keep Cohen's identity confidential create solely an ethical obligation or a contract enforceable in a court of law?
3. If the court decides that an enforceable contract was formed between Cohen and the reporter, how would this affect society's valuation—as expressed in the First Amendment to the Constitution—that freedom of the press should not be constrained?

9-13. Case Briefing Assignment

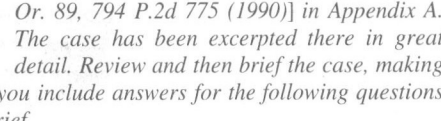 *Examine Case A.9 [Heinzel v. Backstrom, 310 Or. 89, 794 P.2d 775 (1990)] in Appendix A. The case has been excerpted there in great detail. Review and then brief the case, making sure that you include answers for the following questions in your brief.*

1. How did the trial court, the court of appeals, and the Supreme Court of Oregon, respectively, view the document signed by the parties on September 4, 1986?
2. Why did the court of appeals hold that specific performance should be granted, even though that court held that the September 4 document was only an offer to sell the property and not a contract?
3. How did the decision of the Supreme Court of Oregon differ from that of the court of appeals?
4. Why was it significant in this case that Heinzel, and not Backstrom, had drafted the September 4 document? How did this affect the outcome of the case?

Chapter 10

Sales

We noted in Chapter 9 the enormous importance of contract law in coordinating the many cooperative activities undertaken in society. Within the domain of contract law, one area is of particular importance to the legal environment of business—the law governing transactions in tangible commodities, or simply "goods." This chapter builds on the previous one by focusing on one particular type of transaction in goods: the buying and selling of goods. Almost every day of our lives we make purchases—the daily newspaper, groceries, clothes, textbooks, compact discs, a car, and so on. The people from whom we buy our goods are, to us, sellers. But our sellers are in turn buyers from their suppliers, who are in turn buyers from manufacturers. The pervasiveness of activities involving goods would alone make studying the law of sales relevant to our daily lives. But more importantly for our purposes, an understanding of the fundamental rules of sales is imperative for anyone attempting to understand the legal environment of business.

The law of sales is the study of the rights and responsibilities of those in the purchase-and-sale-of-goods chain, from the original maker of the item to the ultimate user. This chapter deals almost exclusively with Article 2 of the Uniform Commercial Code (UCC). Article 2 of the UCC sets out the requirements of sales contracts and how they are formed. It also addresses the sometimes sticky concept of when title passes and who bears the risk of loss for goods in the process of being sold—for example, goods en route from the seller to the buyer—along with the concept of insurable interest. Article 2 regulates performance and obligations required under sales contracts. It also delineates when a breach by either the buyer or the seller occurs and what remedies normally may be sought. A sale of goods usually carries with it at least one type of warranty; sales warranties, express and implied, likewise are governed by the UCC.

■ The Scope of Article 2—the Sale of Goods

No body of law operates in a vacuum removed from other principles of jurisprudence. A sales contract is governed by the same common law principles applicable to all contracts—offer, acceptance, consideration, capacity, and legality—and these principles, described in Chapter 9, should be reexamined when sales are studied. In regard to sales contracts, it is important to remember that when the UCC speaks, its principles will apply; when the UCC is silent on a given issue, then other state statutes and the common law of contracts will apply. The law of sales, found in Article 2 of the UCC, is a part of the law of contracts.

Two other things should be kept in mind. First, Article 2 deals with the sale of *goods,* not real property (real estate), services, or intangible property such as stocks and bonds. Second, in some cases, the rules may vary quite a bit, depending on whether the buyer or seller is a *merchant.* It is always a good idea to note the subject matter of a dispute and the kind of people involved. If the subject is goods, then the UCC will govern. If it is real estate or services, then the common law will apply.

What Is a Sale?

Section 2-102 of the UCC states that Article 2 ''applies to transactions in goods.'' This implies a broad scope for this article, covering gifts, purchases of goods, and bailments. (A bailment involves delivery of personal property without title for a specific purpose, as when, for example, an individual drops off his or her clothes at the cleaner's.) For the purposes of this chapter, we will treat Article 2 as applicable only to an actual sale. A **sale** is officially defined ''as the passing of title from the seller to the buyer for a price'' [UCC 2-106(1)]. The price may be payable in money or in other goods, services, or realty (real estate).

What Are Goods?

To be characterized as a *good,* an item must be *tangible,* and it must be *movable.* A tangible item has physical existence—it can be touched or seen, as can a horse, a car, or a chair. Intangible property, such as corporate stocks and bonds, promissory notes, bank accounts, patents and copyrights, and ordinary contract rights, have only conceptual existence and do not come under Article 2. A *movable* item can be carried from place to place. Hence, real estate is excluded from Article 2.

Who Is a Merchant?

Article 2 governs the sale of goods in general. It applies to sales transactions between all buyers and sellers. In a limited number of instances, however, the UCC presumes that in certain phases of sales transactions involving professional merchants, special business standards ought to be imposed because of the merchants' degree of commercial expertise.[1] Such standards do not apply to the casual or inexperienced seller or buyer.

In general, a person is a merchant when that person, acting in a mercantile capacity, possesses or uses an expertise specifically related to the goods being sold. This basic distinction, however, is not always clear-cut. For example, disagreement has arisen over whether a farmer is a merchant. The answer depends on the particular goods involved, the transaction, and whether, in the particular situation, the farmer has special knowledge concerning the goods involved in the transaction.

■ Formation of a Sales Contract

The policy of the UCC is to recognize that the law of sales is part of the general law of contracts. The UCC often restates general principles or is silent on certain subjects. In these situations, the common law of contracts and applicable state statutes govern. In other situations, the UCC provisions *change* the effect of the general law of contracts.

Offer

In general contract law, the moment a definite offer is met by an unqualified acceptance, a binding contract is formed. In commercial sales transactions, the verbal exchanges, the correspondence, and the actions of the parties may not reveal exactly when a binding contractual obligation arises. The UCC states that an agreement sufficient to constitute a contract can exist even if the moment of its making is undetermined [UCC 2-204(2)].

OPEN TERMS   According to contract law, an offer must be definite enough for the parties (and the courts) to ascertain its essential terms when it is

---

1.   The provisions that apply only to merchants deal principally with the Statute of Frauds, firm offers, confirmatory memoranda, warranties, and contract modification. These special rules reflect expedient business practice commonly known to merchants in the commercial setting. They will be discussed later in this chapter.

accepted. The UCC states that a sales contract will not fail for indefiniteness even if one or more terms are left open, as long as (1) the parties intended to make a contract, and (2) there is a reasonably certain basis for the court to grant an appropriate remedy [UCC 2-204(3)].

The UCC has lessened the requirements for definiteness of essentials in contracts for sale, but it has not removed the common law requirement that the contract be at least definite enough for the court to identify the agreement so as to enforce it or award appropriate damages on its breach. Two factors should be kept in mind. First, the more terms left open, the less likely the courts will find that the parties intended to form a contract. Second, as a general rule, if the *quantity* term is left open, the courts will have no basis for determining a remedy, and the sales contract will fail unless it is either an output or a requirements contract [UCC 2-306].[2] The quantity need not be accurately stated, but a contract will not be enforced beyond the amount stated in the writing.

Open Price Term If the parties have not agreed on a price, the court will determine "a reasonable price *at the time for delivery*" [UCC 2-305(1)]. If either the buyer or the seller is to determine the price, the price is to be fixed in good faith [UCC 2-305(2)].

Sometimes the price fails to be fixed through the fault of one of the parties. In that case, the other party can treat the contract as canceled or fix a reasonable price. For example, Axel and Beatty enter into a contract for the sale of goods and agree that Axel will fix the price, and Axel refuses to fix the price. Beatty can either treat the contract as canceled or can set a reasonable price [UCC 2-305(3)].

Open Payment Term When parties do not specify payment terms, payment is due at the time and place at which the buyer is to receive the goods [UCC 2-310(a)]. Generally, credit is not used when payment terms are unspecified. The buyer can

tender payment in cash or a commercially acceptable substitute, such as a check or a credit card. If the seller demands payment in actual cash, the buyer must be given a reasonable time to obtain it [UCC 2-511(2)]. This is especially important when a definite and final time for performance is stated in the contract.

Open Delivery Term When no delivery terms are specified, the buyer normally takes delivery at the seller's place of business [UCC 2-308(a)]. If the seller has no place of business, then the seller's residence is used. When goods are located in some other place and both parties know it, then delivery is made there. When the time for shipment or delivery has not been clearly specified in the sales contract, the court will infer a "reasonable" time under the circumstances for performance [UCC 2-309(1)].

MERCHANT'S FIRM OFFER The firm offer is in the special category of rules applicable only to merchants. Under common law contract principles, an offer can be revoked any time before acceptance. The major common law exception is an option contract, in which the offeree pays consideration for the offeror's irrevocable promise to keep the offer open for a stated period of time.

The UCC creates a second exception that applies only to **firm offers** for the sale of goods made *by a merchant* (regardless of whether or not the offeree is a merchant). If the merchant gives *assurances* in a *signed writing* that the offer will remain open, the merchant's firm offer is irrevocable, without consideration,[3] for the stated period of time or, if no definite period is specified, a reasonable period (neither period to exceed three months) [UCC 2-205].

Acceptance

Generally, acceptance of an offer to buy or sell goods may be made in any reasonable manner and by any reasonable means. Under Article 2, if the response indicates a definite acceptance of the offer, a contract is formed, even if the response in-

---

2. An *output contract* is a buyer's agreement to purchase a seller's entire output for a stated period; a *requirements contract* is a seller's agreement to supply a buyer with all the buyer's requirements for certain goods used in his or her operations.

---

3. If the offeree pays consideration, then an *option contract* rather than a *merchant's firm offer* is formed. See Chapter 9 for a discussion of option contracts.

cludes additional or different terms—so long as acceptance is not made expressly conditional on the offeror's assent to the new terms. An offeree's additional terms are considered proposals, and the contract is formed on the offeror's terms, unless the parties are both merchants. When both buyer and seller are merchants, the additional proposed terms *automatically* become part of the contract unless:

1. They materially alter the original contract.
2. The offer expressly states that no terms other than those in the offer will be accepted.
3. The offeror objects to the modified terms in a timely fashion [UCC 2-207(2)].

PROMISE TO SHIP OR PROMPT SHIPMENT
The UCC permits acceptance of an offer to buy goods for current or prompt shipment by either a *promise* to ship or *prompt shipment* of the goods to the buyer [UCC 2-206(1)(b)]. This provision of the UCC retains the common law means of acceptance of an offer (performance by delivery of conforming goods—that is, goods that are in accordance with the contract terms—to the carrier) and adds as another means of acceptance the commercial practice of sellers who send promises to ship conforming goods. These promises are effective when sent, if they meet the test of being sent by a medium that is commercially reasonable under the circumstances.

The UCC goes one step further and provides that if the seller does not promise to ship conforming goods but instead ships (in response to the order) *nonconforming goods,* this shipment constitutes both an *acceptance* and a *breach.* This rule does not apply if the seller seasonably (within the time agreed on or within a reasonable time) notifies the buyer that the nonconforming shipment is offered only as an *accommodation.* The notice of accommodation must clearly indicate to the buyer that the shipment does not constitute an acceptance and that, therefore, no contract has been formed.

COMMUNICATION OF ACCEPTANCE   At common law, because a unilateral offer invites acceptance by a performance, the offeree need not notify the offeror of performance unless the offeror would not otherwise know about it. The UCC is more stringent than common law, stating that "Where

the beginning of requested performance is a reasonable mode of acceptance, an offeror who is not notified of acceptance within a reasonable time may treat the offer as having lapsed before acceptance" [UCC 2-206(2)].

■ Consideration

The UCC radically changes the common law rule that contract modification must be supported by new consideration. Section 2-209(1) states that "an agreement modifying a contract needs no consideration to be binding." Of course, contract modification must be sought in good faith [UCC 1-203]. Modifications *extorted* from the other party are in bad faith and therefore unenforceable.

For example, Hal agrees to manufacture and sell certain goods to Betty for a stated price. Subsequently, a sudden shift in the market makes it difficult for Hal to sell the items to Betty at the given price without suffering a loss. Hal tells Betty of the situation, and Betty agrees to pay an additional sum for the goods. Later Betty reconsiders and refuses to pay more than the original price. Under Section 2-209(1) of the UCC, Betty's promise to modify the contract needs no consideration to be binding. Hence, Betty is bound by the modified contract.

In the example above, a shift in the market provides an example of a *good faith* reason for contract modification. Section 1-203 states: "Every contract or duty within this act imposes an obligation of good faith in its performance or enforcement." Good faith in a merchant is defined to mean honesty in fact and the observance of reasonable commercial standards of fair dealing in the trade [UCC 2-103(1)(b)]. But what if there really was no shift in the market, and Hal knew that Betty needed the goods immediately but refused to deliver unless Betty agreed to pay an additional sum of money? This sort of extortion of a modification without a legitimate commercial reason would be ineffective because it would violate the duty of good faith. Hal would not be permitted to enforce the higher price.

■ Statute of Frauds

Section 2-201(1) of the UCC contains a Statute of Frauds provision that applies to contracts for the sale of goods. The provision requires a writing for the contract to be enforceable when the price of the goods is $500 or more. The parties can have an initial oral agreement, however, and satisfy the Statute of Frauds by having a subsequent written memorandum of their oral agreement. In each case the writing must have been signed by the party against whom enforcement is sought.

Written Confirmation between Merchants

Once again the UCC provides a special rule for contracts for the sale of goods between merchants. In transactions between merchants, the requirements of a writing for the Statute of Frauds are satisfied if, after the parties have agreed orally, one of the merchants sends a signed written confirmation to the other merchant. The communication must indicate the terms of the agreement, and the merchant receiving the confirmation must have reason to know of its contents. Unless the merchant who receives the confirmation gives written notice of objection to its contents within ten days after

receipt, the writing will be sufficient against this merchant even though he or she has not signed anything.

Relaxed Requirements

The UCC has greatly relaxed the requirements for the sufficiency of a writing to satisfy the Statute of Frauds. A written contract or a memorandum will be sufficient as long as it indicates that a sales contract was intended and, with the exception for contracts between merchants mentioned above, as long as it is signed by the party against whom enforcement is sought. Except in the case of output and requirements contracts, a contract is not enforceable beyond the quantity of goods shown in the writing. All other terms can be proved in court by oral testimony. Often, terms that are not agreed on can be supplied by the open term provisions of Article 2 itself.

The importance of including some indication of the quantity term in a sales contract is illustrated by the following case.

Case 10.1

THOMAS J. KLINE, INC. v. LORILLARD, INC.

United States Court of Appeals, Fourth Circuit, 1989. 878 F.2d 791.

BACKGROUND AND FACTS   *In December of 1985, Lorillard, Inc., a tobacco products manufacturer, orally agreed with Thomas J. Kline, Inc., to sell tobacco products to Kline and to grant Kline certain credit terms. On January 15, 1986, Lorillard wrote a confirmatory letter to Kline that read as follows: "We are pleased to inform you that your request to purchase Lorillard products on a direct basis has been approved by our New Accounts Committee, and you have been added to our direct list of customers." The letter also stated that credit would be extended to Kline for up to fifteen days following Kline's receipt of any goods ordered. In early February, Kline faced an opportunity to expand its business and placed a large ($30,000) order with Lorillard. Lorillard, however, because it suspected that Kline might be having financial difficulties, suspended its previous credit arrangement with Kline and refused to ship the goods unless Kline wired $30,000 in cash before delivery. Although a few weeks later Kline and Lorillard again agreed on credit arrangements and the transaction went forward, the delay in obtaining the goods resulted in serious losses for Kline. Kline sued Lorillard for damages, alleging, among other claims, that Lorillard had breached a contract. Lorillard contended that the contract was unenforceable under the Statute of Frauds because the only evidence of the deal was the confirmatory letter sent to Kline by Lorillard on January 15, and no quantity term was indicated in the letter. The district court found Lorillard's revocation of credit to be a breach of contract and awarded Kline $2,053,466 in damages. Lorillard appealed.*

CHAPMAN, Circuit Judge.
 *   *   *   *

In Maryland it is well established that a writing satisfies the requirements of the Statute of Frauds if (1) it evidences a contract for the sale of goods, (2) it is signed by the party against whom it is to be enforced, and (3) it specifies the quantity of goods to be sold. Because the writing obviously evidences the sale and was signed by Lorillard's agent, the issue becomes whether the memorandum adequately ''specifies the quantity of goods to be sold.'' *   *   *
 *   *   *   *

A review of decisions on this point reveals that there is not a single Maryland case where terms similar to those used in Lorillard's memorandum have been found to be sufficient written evidence of quantity. *   *   *
 *   *   *   *

The January 15, 1986 letter from Lorillard to Kline is totally silent as to quantity despite Kline's contention that the words ''direct basis'' indicate quantity. *   *   * Precisely how one converts ''direct basis'' into some variety of amount is not adequately explained. There simply is no arguable connection in the law or in the English language between ''direct basis'' and ''amount.'' Under Maryland law, the testimony of Kline, that for a few weeks in December 1985 and January 1986, Lorillard had filled his orders and extended certain credits and discounts, did not supply the missing ingredient—some indication of quantity.
 *   *   * This is not a case where there is a lack of a ''fixed'' written quantity. The Code prevents such restrictions. Here there is a lack of something, anything, in the writing that might evidence the quantity dimension of Kline's claim. The Statute of Frauds was enacted to avoid the potential for injustice in precisely these circumstances. Parol evidence cannot create quantity out of thin air, where the writing relied upon to form the contract is silent as to quantity.

The appellate court reversed the lower court's decision. The Maryland Statute of Frauds barred Kline's claim for breach of contract.

DECISION AND REMEDY

EXCEPTIONS Section 2-201 defines three exceptions to the Statute of Frauds requirement [UCC 2-201(3)]. A contract, if proved to exist, will be enforceable despite the absence of a writing, even if it involves a sale of goods for the price of $500 or more, under the following circumstances:

1. *The oral contract is for (a) specially manufactured goods for a particular buyer; (b) these goods are not suitable for resale to others in the ordinary course of the seller's business; and (c) the seller has substantially started to manufacture the goods or made commitments for the manufacture of the goods.* In this situation, once the seller has taken action, the buyer cannot repudiate the agreement claiming the Statute of Frauds as a defense.

2. *The party against whom enforcement of a contract is sought admits in pleadings (written answers), testimony, or other court proceedings that a contract for sale was made.* In this case the contract will be enforceable even though it was oral, but enforceability is limited to the quantity of goods admitted.

3. *An oral agreement will be enforceable to the extent that payment has been made and accepted or to the extent that goods have been received and accepted.* This is the ''partial performance'' exception. The oral contract will be enforced to the extent of the amount of performance that *actually* took place.

■ Title, Risk, and Insurable Interest

The sale of goods transfers ownership (title) from seller to buyer. Often a sales contract is signed before the actual goods are available. For example, a sales contract for oranges may be signed in May, but the oranges may not be ready for picking and shipment until October. Any number of things can happen between the time the sales contract is signed and the time the goods are actually transferred to the buyer's possession. Fire, flood, or frost may destroy the orange groves. The oranges may be lost or damaged in transit. The parties may want to obtain casualty insurance on the goods. The government may levy a tax on the oranges.

Before the creation of the Uniform Commercial Code (UCC), *title*—right of ownership—was the central concept in sales law, controlling all issues of rights and remedies of the parties to a sales contract. Frequently, however, it was difficult to determine when title actually passed from seller to buyer, and therefore also difficult to predict which party a court would decide had title at the time of a loss. Because of such problems, the UCC divorced the question of title as completely as possible from the question of the rights and obligations of buyers, sellers, and third persons (such as subsequent purchasers, creditors, or the tax collector).

In some situations title is still relevant under the UCC, and the UCC has special rules for locating title. These rules will be discussed in the materials that follow. In most situations, however, the UCC replaces the concept of title with three other concepts: (1) identification, (2) risk of loss, and (3) insurable interest.

Identification

Before any interest in specific goods can pass from the seller to the buyer, two conditions must prevail: (1) the goods must be in existence, and (2) they must be identified to the contract. If either condition is lacking, only a *contract to sell* (not a sale) exists [UCC 2-105(2)]. Goods that are not both existing and identified to the contract are called *future goods*. For example, a contract to purchase next year's crop of hay is a contract for future goods, a crop yet to be grown.

For passage of title, the goods must be identified in a way that will distinguish the particular goods to be delivered under the sales contract from all other similar goods.[4] **Identification** is a des-

---

4. According to UCC 2-401, each provision of Article 2 "with respect to the rights, obligations, and remedies of the seller, the buyer, purchasers or other third parties applies irrespective of title to the goods except where the provisions refer to such title." These provisions referring to title include: UCC 2-312, warranty of title by seller; UCC 2-326(3), consignment sales; UCC 2-327(1)(a), sale on approval and "risk of loss"; UCC 2-403(1), entrustment; UCC 2-501(2), insurable interest in goods; and UCC 2-722, who can sue third parties for injury to goods.

ignation of goods as the subject matter of the sales contract.

There is a general rule that when a purchaser buys a quantity of goods to be taken from a larger mass, identification can be made only by separation of the contracted goods from the mass. Therefore, until the seller separates the 1,000 cases of peas from the 10,000-case lot, title and risk of loss remain with the seller.

When Title Passes

Once goods exist and have been identified, the provisions of UCC 2-401 apply to the passage of title. Parties can expressly agree to when and under what conditions title will pass to the buyer. In virtually all subsections of UCC 2-401, the words "unless otherwise explicitly agreed" appear, meaning that any explicit understanding between the buyer and the seller will determine when title passes.

Unless an agreement is explicitly made, title passes to the buyer at the time and place at which the seller performs the physical delivery of the goods [UCC 2-401(2)]. The delivery terms determine when this occurs.

SHIPMENT CONTRACTS   Under shipment contracts, the seller is required or authorized to ship goods by carrier. Here, the seller is required only to deliver the goods into the hands of a carrier (such as a trucking company), and title passes to the buyer at the time and place of shipment [UCC 2-401(2)(a)].

DESTINATION CONTRACTS   With destination contracts, the seller is required to deliver the goods to a particular destination, usually directly to the buyer but sometimes to another destination designated by the buyer. Title passes to the buyer when the goods are tendered at that destination [UCC 2-401(2)(b)].

DELIVERY WITHOUT MOVEMENT OF THE GOODS   When the contract of sale does not call for the seller's shipment or delivery (when the buyer is to pick up the goods), the passage of title depends on whether the seller must deliver a document of title, such as a bill of lading or a warehouse receipt, to the buyer. A **bill of lading** is a receipt for goods that is signed by a carrier and that serves as a contract for the transportation of the goods. A **warehouse receipt** is a receipt issued by a warehouser for goods stored in his or her warehouse. (See Exhibits 10–1 and 10–2.) When a document of title is required, title passes to the buyer *when and where the document is delivered.* Thus, if the goods are stored in a warehouse, title passes to the buyer when the appropriate documents are delivered. The goods need not move. In fact, the buyer can choose to leave the goods at the same warehouse for a period of time, and the buyer's title to those goods will be unaffected.

When no documents of title are required, and delivery is made without the goods being moved, title passes at the time and place the sales contract was made, if the goods have already been identified. If the goods have not been identified, then title does not pass until identification occurs. Consider an example: Fein sells lumber to Ozo. It is agreed that Ozo will pick up the lumber at the yard. If the lumber has been identified (segregated, marked, or in any other way distinguished from all other lumber), title will pass to Ozo when the contract is signed. If the lumber is still in storage bins with all other lumber at the mill, however, title will not pass to Ozo until the particular pieces of lumber to be sold under this contract are identified [UCC 2-401(3)].

Risk of Loss

Under the UCC, risk of loss does not necessarily pass with title. The question of who suffers a financial risk if goods are damaged, destroyed, or lost is resolved primarily under Sections 2-509 and 2-319.

RISK OF LOSS ABSENT A BREACH OF CONTRACT Risk of loss can be assigned through an agreement by the parties, preferably in writing. Therefore, the parties can generally control the exact moment risk of loss passes from the seller to the buyer. Of course, at the agreed-on time, the goods must be in existence and identified to the contract for this contract provision to be enforceable. In the absence of agreement, risk of loss generally passes to the buyer when the seller delivers, or tenders delivery, of the goods to the buyer.

Delivery of Goods to the Buyer Generally, all contracts are assumed to be shipment contracts if nothing to the contrary is stated in the contract. In

a shipment contract, the seller is required or authorized to ship goods by carrier (that is, not required to deliver them to a particular destination). Risk of loss in shipment contracts passes to the buyer when the seller puts the goods into the carrier's possession [UCC 2-509(1)(a)]. A destination contract requires the seller to deliver the goods to a particular destination. The risk of loss in destination contracts passes to the buyer when the goods are tendered to the buyer at that destination.

Delivery Without Movement of the Goods Frequently, the goods are to be picked up from the seller by the buyer. In the absence of agreement, if the seller is a merchant, risk of loss passes to the buyer only on the buyer's taking physical possession of the goods. If the seller is a nonmerchant, risk passes to the buyer on the seller's tender of delivery [UCC 2-509(3)]. To illustrate: Mellor buys a stereo from Circuit Electronics on Tuesday and tells Circuit that she will pick it up on Thursday. On Wednesday, the electronics store burns down, and the stereo is lost. Because Circuit is a merchant and Mellor had not yet taken possession of the stereo, the loss falls on Circuit. If Mellor had bought the stereo from her neighbor, making the same pick-up arrangements, and the neighbor's house had burned down before Mellor picked up the set, the loss would fall on Mellor—because her neighbor is a nonmerchant.

If a bailee[5] is holding goods for a person who has contracted to sell them and the goods are to be delivered without being moved, the risk of loss passes to the buyer when one of the following occurs: (1) the buyer receives a negotiable (transferable by endorsement or delivery) document of title[6] for the goods; or (2) the bailee acknowledges the buyer's right to possess the goods; or (3) the buyer receives a nonnegotiable document of title *and* has had a *reasonable time* to present the document to the bailee and demand the goods. Obviously, if the bailee refuses to honor the document, the risk

5.   Under the UCC, a bailee is a party who by bill of lading, warehouse receipt, or other document of title acknowledges possession of goods and contracts to deliver them [UCC 7-102(1)(a)]. A warehousing company, for example, or a trucking company that normally issues documents of title for goods it receives is a bailee.

6.   UCC 7-104 states what constitutes negotiable and nonnegotiable documents of title.

■ Exhibit 10–1 A Sample Negotiable Bill of Lading

1st Sheet

UNIFORM MOTOR CARRIER ORDER BILL OF LADING

Shipper's No._____

Original—Domestic

Agent's No._____

CENTRAL FREIGHT LINES INC.

RECEIVED, subject to the classifications and tariffs in effect on the date of the issue of this Bill of Lading,

From _____, Date _____ 19____

At _____ Street, _____ City, _____ County, _____ State

the property described below, in apparent good order, except as noted (contents and condition of contents of packages unknown) marked, consigned and destined as shown below, which said company (the word company being understood throughout this contract as meaning any person or corporation in possession of the property under the contract) agrees to carry to its usual place of delivery at said destination, if within the scope of its lawful operations, otherwise to deliver to another carrier on the route to said destination. It is mutually agreed, as to each carrier of all or any of said property over all or any portion of said route to destination, and as to each party at any time interested in all or any of said property, that every service to be performed hereunder shall be subject to all the conditions not prohibited by law, whether printed or written, herein contained, including the conditions on back hereof, which are hereby agreed to by the shipper and accepted for himself and his assigns.
The surrender of this Original ORDER Bill of Lading properly Indorsed shall be required before the delivery of the property. Inspection of property covered by this bill of lading will not be permitted unless provided by law or unless permission is indorsed on this original Bill of lading or given in writing by the shipper.

Consigned to Order of

Destination _____ Street, _____ City, _____ County, _____ State

Notify

At _____ Street, _____ City, _____ County, _____ State

I. C. C. No. _____   Vehicle No. _____

Routing

No. Pack-ages	Description of Articles, Special Marks, and Exceptions	*Weight (Subject to Correction)	Class or Rate	Check Column	Subject to Section 7 of Conditions, if this shipment is to be delivered to the consignee without recourse on the consignor, the consignor shall sign the following statement:
					The carrier shall not make delivery of this shipment without payment of freight and all other lawful charges.
					(Signature of consignor.)
					If charges are to be prepaid write or stamp here, "To be Prepaid."
					Received $_____ to apply in prepayment of the charges on the property described hereon.
					Agent or Cashier.
					Per_____ (The signature here acknowledges only the amount prepaid.)

*If the shipment moves between two ports by a carrier by water, the law requires that the bill of lading shall state whether it is "carrier's or shipper's weight."
Note—Where the rate is dependent on value, shippers are required to state specifically in writing the agreed or declared value of the property.
The agreed or declared value of the property is hereby specifically stated by the shipper to be not exceeding

Charges advanced:

$_____

_____ per _____

Shipper _____   Agent.

Per _____   Per _____

Permanent address of Shipper _____ Street, _____ City, _____ State

MOORE BUSINESS FORMS, INC., WACO, TEX. M

Source: Reprinted with permission of Central Freight Lines Inc. © 1985 Central Freight Lines, Inc.
Note: This form is printed in yellow to warn holders that it is an order bill of lading. The back of the form permits negotiation by indorsement.

■ Exhibit 10–2 A Sample Nonnegotiable Warehouse Receipt

HART

Warehouse Receipt–Not Negotiable

Agreement No. _____ Vault No. _____ _____ _____ _____

Service Order _____ _____ _____ _____ _____ _____

Receipt and
Lot Number _____   Date of Issue _____ 19 _____

     Received for the account of and deliverable to • _____

whose latest known address is _____ **SAMPLE**

_____ the goods enumerated on the inside or attached schedule to be

stored in Company warehouse, located at _____
which goods are accepted only upon the following conditions set forth below:

READ CAREFULLY That the value of all goods stored, including the contents of any container, and all goods hereafter stored for Depositor's account to be not over $ _____ **per pound † per article** unless a higher value is noted in the schedule, for which an additional monthly storage charge of _____ ¢ on each $ _____ valuation in excess of $ _____ **per pound † per article** or fraction thereof will be made.

     If there are any items enumerated in this receipt valued in excess of the above limitations per pound per article and not so noted in the schedule, return this receipt within 10 days with proper values so indicated in writing in order that the receipt may be re-issued and proper higher storage rates assessed.

OWNERSHIP. The Customer, Shipper, Depositor, or Agent represents and warrants that he is lawfully possessed of goods to be stored and/or has the authority to store or ship said goods. (If the goods are mortgaged, notify the Company the name and address of the mortgagee.)

PAYMENT OF CHARGES. Storage bills are payable monthly in advance for each month's storage or fraction thereof. Labor charges, cartage and other services rendered are payable upon completion of work. All charges shall be paid at the warehouse location shown hereon, and if delinquent, shall incur interest monthly at the rate of _____ per cent ( ) per year.

The Depositor will pay reasonable attorney's fee incurred by The Company in collecting delinquent accounts.

LIABILITY OF COMPANY. The company shall be liable for any loss or injury to the goods caused by its failure to exercise such care as a reasonably careful man would exercise under like circumstances. The company will not be liable for loss or damage to fragile articles not packed, or articles packed or unpacked by other than employees of this company. Depositor specifically agrees that the warehouse will not be liable for contamination of or for insect damage to articles placed in drawers of furniture by the depositor. Periodic spraying of the warehouse premises shall constitute ordinary and proper care, unless the Depositor requests in writing and pays for anti-infestation treatment of articles in drawers and compartments of stored furniture.

CHANGE OF ADDRESS. Notice of change of address must be given the Company in writing, and acknowledged in writing by the Company.

TRANSFER OR WITHDRAWAL OF GOODS. The warehouse receipt is not negotiable and shall be produced and all charges must be paid before delivery to the Depositor, or transfer of goods to another person; however, a written direction to the Company to transfer the goods to another person or deliver the goods may be accepted by the Company at its option without requiring tender of the warehouse receipt.

ACCESS TO STORAGE, PARTIAL WITHDRAWAL. A signed order from the person in whose name the receipt is issued is required to enable others to remove or have access to goods. A charge is made for stacking and unstacking, and for access to stored goods.

BUILDING—FIRE—WATCHMAN. The Company does not represent or warrant that its building cannot be destroyed by fire or that the contents of said buildings including the said property cannot be destroyed by fire. The Company shall not be required to maintain a watchman or sprinkler system and its failure to do so shall not constitute negligence.

CLAIMS OR ERRORS. All claims for non-delivery of any article or articles and for damage, breakage, etc., must be made in writing within ninety (90) days from delivery of goods stored or they are waived. Failure to return the warehouse receipt for correction within ( ) days after receipt thereof by the depositor will be conclusive that it is correct and delivery will be made only in accordance therewith.

FUTURE SERVICE. This Contract shall extend and apply to future services rendered to the Depositor by the Company and to any additional goods deposited with the Company by the Depositor.

WAREHOUSEMAN'S LIEN. The Company reserves the right to sell the goods stored, in accordance with the provisions of the Uniform Commercial Code (Business and Commerce Code if stored in Texas), for all lawful charges in arrears.

TERMINATION OF STORAGE. The Company reserves the right to terminate the storage of the goods at any time by giving to the Depositor thirty (30) days' written notice of its intention so to do, and, unless the Depositor removes such goods within that period, the Company is hereby empowered to have the same removed at the cost and expense of the Depositor, or the Company may sell them at auction in accordance with state law.

DEPOSITOR WILL PAY REASONABLE LEGAL FEES INCURRED BY WAREHOUSE IN COLLECTING DELINQUENT CHARGES.

THIS DOCUMENT CONTAINS THE WHOLE CONTRACT BETWEEN THE PARTIES AND THERE ARE NO OTHER TERMS, WARRANTIES, REPRESENTATIONS, OR AGREEMENTS OF EITHER DEPOSITOR OR COMPANY NOT HEREIN CONTAINED.

Storage per month or fraction thereof	$ _____
Warehouse labor	$ _____
Cartage	$ _____
Packing at residence . . .	$ _____
Wrapping and preparing for storage	$ _____
Charges advanced	$ _____
_____	$ _____
	$ _____

By _____

*Insert "Mr. and/or Mrs." or, if military personnel, appropriate rank or grade.
†Delete the words "per pound" if the declared value is per article.
For goods stored for military personnel under PL 245, the contractor's liability for care of goods is as provided in Basic Agreement with U.S. Government.

THIS PROPERTY HAS NOT BEEN INSURED BY THIS COMPANY FOR FIRE OR ANY OTHER CASUALTY
SCHEDULE OF GOODS ON FOLLOWING PAGE OR ATTACHED

W-1 (1981) Approved by SW H T 4 ©   Re-order from Hart Graphics, Austin, Texas

Source: Reprinted with permission of Hart Graphics, Inc. of Austin, Texas. © 1985 Hart Graphics, Inc.

of loss remains with the seller [UCC 2-509(2), 2-503(4)(b)]. (See Exhibit 10–1 for a sample negotiable bill of lading and Exhibit 10–2 for a sample nonnegotiable warehouse receipt.)

RISK OF LOSS IN A BREACHED SALES CONTRACT   There are many ways to breach a sales contract. The transfer of risk operates differently depending on whether the seller or the buyer breaches. Generally, the party in breach bears the risk of loss.

Seller's Breach   If the goods are so nonconforming that the buyer has the right to reject them, the risk of loss will not pass to the buyer until the defects are cured or until the buyer accepts the goods in spite of their defects (thus waiving the right to reject). For example, a buyer orders blue widgets from a seller under a contract that specifies that the risk of loss will pass to the buyer when the seller gives the goods to a carrier. The seller ships black widgets, giving the buyer the right to reject. The widgets are damaged in transit. The risk of loss falls on the seller (although the risk would have been on the buyer if blue widgets had been shipped) [UCC 2-510].

If a buyer accepts a shipment of goods and later discovers a latent defect, acceptance can be revoked. Revocation allows the buyer to pass the risk of loss back to the seller, at least to the extent that the buyer's insurance does not cover the loss [UCC 2-510(2)].

Buyer's Breach   The general rule is that when a buyer breaches a contract, the risk of loss *immediately* shifts to the buyer. There are three important limitations to this rule:

1. The seller must already have identified the goods under the contract.
2. The buyer will bear the risk for only a *commercially reasonable time* after the seller learns of the breach.
3. The buyer will be liable only to the extent of any *deficiency* in the seller's insurance coverage [UCC 2-510(3)].

SALE ON APPROVAL AND SALE OR RETURN CONTRACTS   A **sale on approval** is not a sale until the buyer accepts (approves) the offer. A **sale or return** is a sale that can be rescinded by the buyer without liability. In each case, passage of title and risk of loss depend on the conditional event's happening or not happening, because these transactions are conditional by their very nature.

Sale on Approval   When a seller offers to sell goods to a buyer and permits the buyer to take the goods on a trial basis, a sale on approval is made. The term *sale* here is a misnomer because only an *offer* to sell has been made, along with a bailment (the holding or storage of another's personal property) created by the buyer's possession.

Therefore, title and risk of loss (from causes beyond the buyer's control) remain with the seller until the buyer accepts the offer. Acceptance can be made expressly, by any act inconsistent with the trial basis purpose or seller's ownership, or by the buyer's election not to return the goods within the trial period. If the buyer does not wish to accept, the buyer may notify the seller of that fact within the trial period, and the return is at the seller's expense and risk [UCC 2-327(1)]. Goods held on approval are not subject to the claims of the buyer's creditors until acceptance.

Sale or Return   The sale or return (sometimes called *sale and return*) is a type of contract by which the seller delivers a quantity of goods to the buyer, on the understanding that if the buyer wishes to retain any portion of those goods (for use or resale), the buyer will consider the portion retained as having been sold to him or her and will pay accordingly. The balance will be returned to the seller or will be held by the buyer as a bailee subject to the seller's order. When the buyer receives possession at the time of sale, the title and risk of loss pass to the buyer. Both remain with the buyer until the buyer returns the goods to the seller within the time period specified. If the buyer fails to return the goods within this time period, the sale is finalized. The return of the goods is at the buyer's risk and expense. The goods held on a sale or return contract are subject to the claims of the buyer's creditors while they are in the buyer's possession.

With certain exceptions, the UCC treats a **consignment** as a sale or return. Under a consignment, the owner of goods (the *consignor*) delivers them to another (the *consignee*) for the consignee to sell. If the consignee sells the goods, he or she must pay the consignor for them. If the goods are not sold, they may simply be returned to the consignor. While the goods are in the possession of the consignee, the consignee holds title to them, and creditors of the consignee will prevail over the consignor in any action to repossess the goods.

Insurable Interest

Buyers and sellers often obtain insurance coverage to protect against damage, loss, or destruction of goods. But any party purchasing insurance must have a ''sufficient interest'' in the insured item to obtain a valid policy. Insurance laws—not the UCC—determine sufficiency. The UCC is helpful, however, because it contains certain rules regarding a buyer's and a seller's **insurable interest** in goods on a sales contract.

Buyers have an insurable interest in *identified* goods. The moment the goods are identified to the contract by the seller, the buyer has this special property interest, which allows the buyer to obtain necessary insurance coverage for the goods even before the risk of loss has passed [UCC 2-501(1)].

Sellers have an insurable interest in goods as long as they retain title to the goods. Even after title has passed to a buyer, however, a seller who has a ''security interest'' in the goods (a right to secure payment) still has an insurable interest and so can insure the goods [UCC 2-501(2)].

Hence, both a buyer and a seller can have an insurable interest in identical goods at the same time. In all cases, one must sustain an actual loss to have the right to recover from an insurance company.

■ Performance and Obligation

To understand the performance that is required of a seller and of a buyer under a sales contract, it is necessary to know the duties and obligations each party has assumed under the terms of the contract. Keep in mind that ''duties and obligations'' under the terms of the contract here include those specified by the agreement, the custom, and the UCC.

The Good Faith Requirement

Sometimes the sales contract leaves open some particulars of performance and permits one of the parties to specify them. The obligations of ''good faith'' and ''commercial reasonableness,'' however, underlie every sales contract within the UCC. These standards are read into every contract, and they provide a framework in which the parties can specify particulars of performance. ''Any such specification must be made in good faith and within limits set by commercial reasonableness'' [UCC 2-311(1)].

Performance of a Sales Contract

A seller has the basic obligation to *transfer and deliver conforming goods.* The buyer has the basic obligation to *accept and pay for conforming goods* in accordance with the contract [UCC 2-301]. Overall performance of a sales contract is controlled by the agreement between the buyer and the seller. When the contract is unclear, or when terms are indefinite in certain respects and disputes arise, the UCC provides built-in standards and rules for interpreting the agreement.

Seller's Obligation—Tender of Delivery

Tender of delivery requires that the seller have and hold *conforming* goods at the buyer's disposal and give the buyer whatever notification is reasonably necessary to enable the buyer to take delivery [UCC 2-503(1)]. Unless the parties have agreed otherwise, the goods must be tendered for delivery at a reasonable time and must be kept available for a reasonable period of time to enable the buyer to take possession of them [UCC 2-503(1)(a)]. What is reasonable depends in part on the subject matter of the contract. All goods called for by a contract must be tendered in a single delivery unless the parties agree otherwise [UCC 2-612] or the circumstances are such that either party can rightfully request delivery in lots [UCC 2-307].

If the contract does not designate the place at which the goods will be delivered, and the buyer is expected to pick them up, the place of delivery is the *seller's place of business* or, if the seller has none, the *seller's residence* [UCC 2-308]. If the contract involves the sale of *identified goods* and the parties know when they enter into the contract that these goods are located somewhere other than at the seller's place of business (such as at a warehouse or in the possession of a bailee), then the *location of the goods* is the place for their delivery [UCC 2-308].

The Perfect Tender Rule

As previously noted, the seller has an obligation to ship or tender *conforming goods,* and this entitles the seller to acceptance by and payment from the buyer according to the terms of the contract. At common law the seller was obligated to deliver goods in conformity with the terms of the contract in every detail. This was called the *perfect tender* doctrine. The UCC, in Section 2-601, preserves the perfect tender doctrine by providing that "if goods or tender of delivery fail *in any respect* to conform to the contract" (emphasis added), the buyer has the right to accept the goods, reject the entire shipment, or accept part and reject part.

Because of the rigidity of the perfect tender doctrine rule, several exceptions to the rule have been created, some of which are discussed here.

AGREEMENT OF THE PARTIES   If the parties have agreed, for example, that defective goods or parts will not be rejected if the seller is able to repair or replace them within a reasonable time, then the perfect tender rule does not apply.

CURE   The term **cure** is not specifically defined in the UCC, but it refers to the seller's right to repair, adjust, or replace defective or nonconforming goods [UCC 2-508].

When any tender or delivery is rejected because of nonconforming goods and the time for performance has not yet expired, the seller can notify the buyer promptly of the intention to cure and can then do so *within the contract time for performance* [UCC 2-508(1)]. Once the time for performance under the contract has expired, the seller can still exercise the right to cure if the seller had *reasonable grounds to believe that the nonconforming tender would be acceptable to the buyer.*

The seller's right to cure substantially restricts the buyer's right to reject. If the buyer refuses a tender of goods as nonconforming but does not

disclose the nature of the defect to the seller, the buyer cannot later assert the defect as a defense if the defect is one that the seller could have cured. The buyer must act in good faith and state specific reasons for refusing to accept the goods [UCC 2-605].

SUBSTITUTION OF CARRIERS   When an agreed manner of delivery (such as particular loading or unloading facilities) becomes impracticable or unavailable through no fault of either party but a commercially reasonable substitute is available, this substitute performance is sufficient tender to the buyer [UCC 2-614(1)].

COMMERCIAL IMPRACTICABILITY   Whenever occurrences unforeseen by either party at the time the contract was made make performance commercially impracticable, the rule of perfect tender no longer holds. According to UCC 2-615(a), delay in delivery or nondelivery in whole or in part is not a breach when performance has been made impracticable "by the occurrence of a contingency the nonoccurrence of which was a basic assumption on which the contract was made." The seller, however, must notify the buyer as soon as it is practicable to do so that there will be a delay or nondelivery.

The notion of commercial impracticability is closely allied with contract law theories of impossibility of performance and frustration of purpose (see Chapter 9). Risks ordinarily assumed by a seller conducting business do not in and of themselves excuse performance. Increased costs resulting from inflation, for example, do not in and of themselves excuse performance. To excuse performance, the unforeseen contingency must alter the essential nature of the performance, such as would occur with a sudden, severe shortage of raw materials.

The following case illustrates the doctrine of commercial impracticability.

Case 10.2

WALDINGER CORP. v. CRS GROUP ENGINEERS, INC.

United States Court of Appeals, Seventh Circuit, 1985. 775 F.2d 781.

BACKGROUND AND FACTS   *In 1977, the Urbana and Champaign Sanitary District was planning two waste-water treatment facilities. The Clark Dietz Division of CRS Group Engineers, Inc., set the specifications for the facilities, and all equipment had to meet with Dietz's approval. Belt filter presses were among the many types of equipment required. Dietz's specifications required certain performance capabilities, as well as exact conformity of the mechanical components. The mechanical specifications* *were set with reference to a machine manufactured by the Ralph B. Carter Company. The Waldinger Corporation, a subcontractor on the project, took bids from four belt filter press manufacturers. Ashbrook, the codefendant, was selected by Waldinger to provide the belt filter presses. Ashbrook's machines could meet the performance specifications, but the mechanical components varied from those required by Dietz. Ashbrook's machine was thus not approved by Dietz, and Waldinger was forced to buy the belt filter presses from the Ralph B. Carter Company at a higher price. Waldinger sued Ashbrook for breach of contract (and CRS Group Engineers for wrongful interference with Waldinger's contract with Ashbrook). Ashbrook claimed that Dietz intentionally or negligently drafted restrictive mechanical specifications and that Dietz's specifications made it commercially impracticable for Ashbrook to fulfill its contract. The Central District Court of Illinois found for Ashbrook, holding that Ashbrook was excused from performance because Dietz had made performance impracticable. Waldinger appealed.*

WOOD, Circuit Judge.
* * * *
The district court found that a basic assumption of the contract between Waldinger and Ashbrook was that Ashbrook equipment was competitive and would comply with the specifications drafted by Dietz. That assumption was based upon the belief that Dietz would interpret its specifications in a competitive and nonrestrictive manner. Because Dietz did not do so, performance by Ashbrook was rendered impracticable.
* * * *
The district court found that it was not foreseeable at the time of contracting that Dietz would require strict compliance with all specifications. * * * True, Ashbrook knew that Dietz's approval was required and that at the time it signed the purchase orders Dietz had not expressly approved its 1-V machine. The refusal of an engineer to waive certain mechanical specifications is foreseeable, and a supplier normally assumes the risk of non-approval. But these general principles cannot be deemed to apply where an engineer's insistence on literal compliance with exclusionary specifications has no scientific or rational basis. Given industry practice on waiver of mechanical specifications and the EPA [Environmental Protection Agency] regulations [the plant was to be built according to EPA standards] prohibiting exclusionary specifications upon which Ashbrook could rightly rely, Ashbrook could not have foreseen the possibility that Dietz would require it to build a Carter machine even if its machine met the performance specifications. The [UCC S]ection 2-615 defense is therefore available to Ashbrook if performance was rendered commercially impracticable by Dietz's insistence upon compliance with the exclusionary specifications.
* * * *
Under the contract documents, then, Ashbrook was required to guarantee performance. This, the evidence shows, it could not do if required to build its [belt] filter press according to Dietz's mechanical specifications. We conclude that Ashbrook's inability to supply a [belt] filter press that would both satisfy Dietz's mechanical specifications and perform as required is sufficient to establish that performance of its contract with Waldinger was commercially impracticable.

The court of appeals affirmed the district court's decision. Ashbrook, the codefendant, did not have to pay any damages to Waldinger because performance of the contract would have been commercially impracticable. Therefore, Ashbrook was excused from fulfilling the terms of the contract.

DECISION AND REMEDY

DESTRUCTION OF IDENTIFIED GOODS   The UCC provides that when a casualty occurs that totally destroys *identified goods* under a sales contract through no fault of either party and *before risk passes to the buyer,* the seller and buyer are excused from performance [UCC 2-613(a)]. If the goods are only partially destroyed, however, the buyer can inspect them and either treat the contract as void or accept the damaged goods with an allowance off the contract price.

ASSURANCE AND COOPERATION   Two other exceptions to the perfect tender doctrine apply equally to the seller and buyer.

The right of assurance—the right to obtain objective indications that performance will occur—stems from the concept that the essential purpose of a contract is performance by both parties, and thus when one party has reason to believe the other party will not perform, forcing the first party to perform creates an undue hardship.

The UCC provides that should a seller (or buyer) have "reasonable grounds" to believe the buyer (or seller) will not perform as contracted, he or she may "in writing demand adequate assurance of due performance" from the other party; and until such assurance is received, he or she may "suspend" further performance without liability. The grounds for such belief and action must be reasonable. Between merchants, the grounds are determined by commercial standards [UCC 2-609]. The assurances requested also must be reasonable. If such assurances are not forthcoming within a reasonable time (not to exceed thirty days), the failure to respond may be treated as a *repudiation* of the contract.

Sometimes the performance of one party depends on the cooperation of the other. The UCC provides that when such cooperation is not forthcoming, the other party can suspend his or her own performance without liability and hold the uncooperative party in breach [UCC 2-311(3)].

Buyer's Obligations

Once the seller has adequately tendered delivery, the buyer is obligated to accept the goods and pay for them according to the terms of the contract. In the absence of any specific agreements to the contrary, the buyer must: (1) furnish facilities reasonably suited for receipt of the goods [UCC 2-503(1)(b)]; and (2) make payment at the time and place the buyer *receives* the goods, even if the place of shipment is the place of delivery [UCC 2-310(a)]. When a sale is made on credit, the buyer is obliged to pay according to credit terms (for example, 60, 90, or 120 days), *not* when the goods are received. The credit period usually begins on the *date of shipment* [UCC 2-310(d)].

Payment can be made by any means agreed on between the parties. Cash can be used, but the buyer can also use any other method generally acceptable in the commercial world. If the seller demands cash when the buyer offers a check, credit card, or the like, then the seller must permit the buyer reasonable time to obtain legal tender [UCC 2-511].

ACCEPTANCE   The buyer can manifest acceptance of the delivered goods in several different ways. The buyer can expressly accept the shipment by words or conduct. For example, there is an acceptance if the buyer, after having had a reasonable opportunity to inspect, signifies agreement to the seller that either the goods are conforming or they are acceptable despite their nonconformity [UCC 2-606(1)(a)].

Acceptance will be presumed if the buyer has had a reasonable opportunity to inspect the goods and has failed to reject them within a reasonable period of time [UCC 2-606(1)(b), 2-602(1)]. The buyer also can accept the goods by performing any act inconsistent with the seller's ownership. For example, any use or resale of the goods will generally constitute an acceptance. Limited use for the sole purpose of testing or inspecting the goods is not an acceptance, however [UCC 2-606(1)(c)].

REVOCATION OF ACCEPTANCE   Acceptance does not in and of itself impair the right of the buyer to pursue remedies, although it does preclude the buyer from exercising the right of rejection. If, however, the buyer accepts nonconforming goods and fails to notify the seller of the breach when it is discovered (or when it should have been discovered), then the buyer is barred from pursuing *any* remedy against the seller. The buyer must inform the seller of the alleged breach within a reasonable time, and the burden is on the buyer to establish the existence of a breach of contract once the goods have been accepted [UCC 2-607(3)].

After a buyer accepts a lot or a *commercial unit,*[7] acceptance can be revoked if nonconformity *substantially* impairs the value of the unit or lot and if one of the following factors also is present: (1) acceptance was predicated on the reasonable assumption that the nonconformity would be cured, and it has not been seasonally cured [UCC 2-608(1)(a)]; or (2) the buyer does not discover the nonconformity, and his or her acceptance was reasonably induced by the difficulty of discovery before acceptance or by the seller's assurances that the goods conform [UCC 2-608(1)(b)].[8]

If some of the goods delivered do not conform to the contract and the seller has failed to cure, the buyer can make a *partial* acceptance [UCC 2-601(c)]. The same is true if the nonconformity was not reasonably discoverable before acceptance. A buyer cannot accept less than a single commercial unit, however.

---

7. A commercial unit is a unit of goods that, by commercial usage, is viewed as a single whole for purposes of sale and that cannot be divided without materially impairing the character of the unit, its market value, or its use [UCC 2-105]. A commercial unit can be a single article (such as a machine), a set of articles (such as a suite of furniture or an assortment of sizes), or a quantity (such as a bale, gross, or carload) or any other unit treated in the trade as a single whole.

8. Prior to the passage of state *lemon laws,* purchasers of automobiles that turned out to be ''lemons'' frequently had no other recourse than to revoke acceptance and request the return of the purchase price. Because of limitations on sellers' liability and the fact that an attempted revocation often led to costly litigation, consumers found it difficult to prevail against the automobile dealer in such disputes. The lemon laws have to a great extent eased this problem. Basically, lemon laws provide that if an automobile under warranty possesses a defect that significantly affects the vehicle's value or use, and the defect has not been remedied by the seller within a specified number of attempts, then the buyer is entitled to a new car, replacement of defective parts, or return of all consideration paid.

Anticipatory Repudiation

The buyer and the seller have concurrent conditions of performance. But what if, before the time for either performance, one party clearly communicates to the other the intention not to perform? Such an action is a breach of the contract by *anticipatory repudiation.* When this occurs, the aggrieved party can, according to UCC 2-610:

1. For a commercially reasonable time await performance by the repudiating parties.
2. Resort to any remedy for breach even if the aggrieved party has notified the repudiating party that he or she awaits the latter's performance and has urged retraction of the repudiation.
3. In either case, *suspend performance* or proceed in accordance with the provisions of Article 2 on the seller's right to identify goods notwithstanding breach or to salvage unfinished goods.

The key to anticipatory breach is that the repudiation takes place before the time that the party is required under contract to tender performance. The nonbreaching party has a choice of two responses. He or she can treat the repudiation as a final breach by pursuing a remedy; or he or she can wait, hoping that the repudiating party will decide to honor the obligations required by the contract despite the avowed intention to renege. Should the latter course be pursued, the UCC permits the breaching party (subject to some limitations) to ''retract'' his or her repudiation. The retraction can be made by any method that clearly indicates an intent to perform. Once retraction has been made, the rights of the repudiating party under the contract are reinstated [UCC 2-611]. The concept of anticipatory repudiation is illustrated in the following case.

BACKGROUND AND FACTS *Neptune Research & Development, Inc., contracted to purchase a high-precision drilling machine for approximately $55,000 from Teknics Industrial Systems, Inc. Although the contract specified a mid-June delivery date, nothing was included in the contract about time being of the essence. In addition, one of the paragraphs within the standard terms and conditions stated that shipping dates were approximate. By late August, the machine had still not been delivered, and Neptune was in desperate need of the machine. Contact with Teknics on August 29 resulted in both parties agreeing to a September 5 delivery date, and Robertson, a Teknics representative, promised to call Neptune on Septem-*

Case 10.3

NEPTUNE RESEARCH & DEVELOPMENT, INC. v. TEKNICS INDUSTRIAL SYSTEMS, INC.

Superior Court of New Jersey, 1989.
235 N.J.Super. 522,
563 A.2d 465.

ber 3 so that delivery arrangements could be made. Robertson did not call Neptune on September 3. On September 4, Neptune's representative called Robertson, who allegedly said that under "no circumstances" would Teknics be able to have the machine ready for pickup until, at the earliest, September 9. As a result of this telephone conversation, Neptune canceled the contract on that same day. Later on September 4, Teknics informed Neptune that the machine could in fact be ready for pickup on September 5, but Neptune refused to go through with the transaction and instead filed suit against Teknics a few weeks later to recover the $3,000 deposit it had paid toward the price of the machine. The trial court held for Neptune, concluding that Teknics had anticipatorily breached the contract on September 4, giving Neptune the right to cancel the contract. Teknics appealed.

KING, P.J.A.D. [Presiding Judge, Appellate Division]
    *   *   *   *

What we *   *   * have is a repudiation by seller that allegedly amounted to an anticipatory breach, followed by a retraction. *   *   *

Until the repudiating party's next performance is due he can retract his repudiation unless the aggrieved party has since the repudiation cancelled or materially changed his position or otherwise indicated that he considers the repudiation final.
    *   *   *   *

*   *   * According to seller, its announcement on September 4 that it could not deliver in time was not an anticipatory breach because it was not material. Seller contends that failure to timely perform is not ordinarily a material breach and a buyer cannot cancel on this basis.
    *   *   *   *

We think under the circumstances here one could reasonably find that the seller's repudiation went to the essence of the contract. Defendant [Teknics] had agreed to a mid-June delivery. Throughout the summer it not only failed to deliver, but it refused to explain its reasons for non-delivery or to give plaintiff adequate assurances that the machine would be delivered soon. By late August buyer *   *   * was in desperate need of the machine. *   *   * We conclude that buyer readily could have cancelled [on August 29] but it did not. Rather, [buyer] agreed to accept the *   *   * machine but only on the express condition that seller have the product available by September 5.

While [buyer] did not expressly state to any of seller's representatives that time had now become of the essence, we conclude this condition can fairly be implied, from the surrounding circumstances. *   *   * Robertson's unequivocal statement on September 4, that under no circumstances would the machine be ready by the promised delivery date, September 5, was a repudiation going to the essence of the contract.
    *   *   *   *

We conclude that Robertson's statement on September 4 constituted an anticipatory repudiation within the meaning of [UCC Section] 2-610.

DECISION AND REMEDY   *The appellate court affirmed the trial court's ruling. The seller's statement on September 4 that it could not deliver the machine by September 5 constituted an anticipatory repudiation of the contract, justifying the buyer's cancellation of the contract. The seller's "retraction" of the repudiation was ineffective because the buyer had already treated the breach as final and canceled the contract prior to the retraction.*

Remedies of Buyer and Seller for Breach

When a sales contract is breached, the aggrieved party may have a number of remedies from which to choose [UCC 2-703, 2-711]. These remedies range from retaining the goods to requiring the breaching party's performance under the contract. The general purpose of these remedies is to put the aggrieved party "in as good a position as if the other party had fully performed." It is important not only that the nonbreaching party know what remedies are available but that he or she know which remedy is most appropriate for a given situation [UCC 1-106(1)].

Remedies of the Seller

A buyer breaches a sales contract by any of the following actions: (1) wrongfully rejecting tender of the seller's goods; (2) wrongfully revoking acceptance of the contract; (3) failing to make payment on or before delivery of the goods; or (4) repudiating the sales contract. On the buyer's breach, the seller is afforded several distinct remedies under the UCC. These include the right to stop or withhold delivery of the goods and the right to recover damages or to recover the purchase price of the goods.

THE RIGHT TO RECOVER DAMAGES The seller is entitled to damages if the buyer wrongfully cancels the sales contract or refuses to accept delivery of goods covered by the contract. The appropriate measure of damages is the difference between the market price at the time and place of delivery and the unpaid contract price, less any expenses the seller may have saved as a result of the buyer's breach. If, however, this measure of damages is not adequate to put the seller in as good a position as he or she would have occupied without

a breach in the contract, then the seller is entitled to recover the profit that would have been earned from complete performance of the contract [UCC 2-708].

THE RIGHT TO RECOVER THE PURCHASE PRICE Before the UCC was adopted, a seller could not sue for the purchase price of the goods unless title had passed to the buyer. Under the UCC, an unpaid seller can bring an action to recover the purchase price and incidental damages, but only under one of the following circumstances:

1. When the buyer has accepted the goods and has not revoked acceptance, in which case title has passed to the buyer.
2. When conforming goods have been lost or damaged after the risk of loss has passed to the buyer.
3. When the buyer has breached after the goods have been identified to the contract and the seller is unable to resell the goods [UCC 2-709(1)].

If a seller sues for the contract price of goods that he or she has been unable to resell to an alternative buyer, the goods must be held for the contract buyer. The seller can resell the goods at any time prior to the collection of the judgment from the buyer, but the net proceeds from the sale must be credited to the buyer.

An action to recover the purchase price and incidental damages is available to the seller only under the circumstances just described and is distinct from an action to recover damages for breach of the sales contract.

In the following case, the court had to determine whether a seller was entitled to recover the purchase price of specially manufactured goods on the buyer's breach of the sales contract.

BACKGROUND AND FACTS *Royal Jones & Associates, Inc., ordered three steel rendering tanks from First Thermal Systems, Inc., for use in its business of constructing rendering plants. The contract provided that First Thermal would manufacture the tanks according to Royal Jones's specifications for a price of $64,350. When the manufacture of the tanks was completed, Royal Jones refused to accept the tanks and refused to pay the contract price. First Thermal brought an action for the contract price of the tanks. The trial court, finding that Royal Jones had breached the con-*

Case 10.4

ROYAL JONES & ASSOCIATES, INC. v. FIRST THERMAL SYSTEMS, INC.

District Court of Appeal of Florida, 1990.
566 So.2d 853.

tract and that the specially manufactured goods were not suitable for sale in the ordinary course of First Thermal's business, awarded First Thermal the full contract price as damages. Royal Jones appealed.

ZEHMER, Judge.

* * * *

* * * Royal Jones contends that the lower court erred in awarding First Thermal the full contract price as damages for the tanks pursuant to section 672.709 [the Florida version of UCC 2-709], because there was no evidence presented at trial that either First Thermal was unable to resell the tanks after making a reasonable effort to do so, or that the circumstances reasonably indicated that such effort would be unavailing. * * *

* * * *

Applying the constructions given to section 2-709 in [previous] cases, we hold that the trial court did not err in awarding First Thermal the full contract price as damages, because the evidence presented at trial by First Thermal was sufficient to meet its burden of proving that the circumstances reasonably indicated that any effort to resell the tanks would have been unavailing. * * * First Thermal proved that any effort at resale would have been unavailing because these were the only rendering tanks First Thermal ever made, the tanks were manufactured according to Royal Jones's specifications, First Thermal had no other customers to which it could resell the tanks, and it was unaware how the tanks could have been marketed for resale. Also, the tanks were built without needed internal components and to a special size in accordance with Royal Jones's specifications and could not be used as rendering tanks without special engineering to which First Thermal had no access. Finally, there was testimony that the tanks had only scrap value to First Thermal of about $700 if they were processed for a scrap dealer. This evidence was sufficient to shift the burden to Royal Jones to show that any effort at resale would not have been unavailing, or that the tanks had some potential market value beyond the salvage value claimed by First Thermal. However, Royal Jones presented no evidence to the contrary at trial, and the lower court did not err in awarding First Thermal the full contract price pursuant to section 672.709.

DECISION AND REMEDY
The appellate court affirmed the trial court's ruling: First Thermal was entitled to the full contract price of the specially manufactured tanks as damages because the evidence showed that efforts to resell the tanks would not have been fruitful.

Remedies of the Buyer

A seller breaches a sales contract by failing to deliver goods conforming to the contract or repudiating the contract prior to delivery. On the breach, the buyer has a choice of several remedies under the UCC. The buyer's remedies include the right to reject noncomforming or improperly delivered goods; to *cover* (that is, to buy the goods elsewhere and recover from the seller the extra cost of obtaining the substitute goods); to recover damages; and, in certain circumstances, to obtain specific performance of the sales contract.

REJECTION If either the goods or the seller's tender of the goods fails to conform to the contract *in any respect,* the buyer can reject the goods. If some of the goods conform to the contract, the buyer can keep the conforming goods and reject the rest [UCC 2-601].

Goods must be rejected within a reasonable time and the seller must be seasonably notified [UCC 2-602]. Notification is seasonable if it occurs before there is any substantial change in the goods not caused by their own defects—for example, before perishable goods perish. Furthermore, the buyer must designate particular defects that are ascertainable by reasonable inspection. Failure to do so precludes the buyer from using such defects to justify rejection or to establish breach when the seller could have cured the defects if they had been stated seasonably [UCC 2-605]. After rejecting the goods, the buyer cannot exercise any right of ownership over them. If the buyer acts inconsistently with the seller's ownership rights, the buyer will be deemed to have accepted the goods [UCC 2-606].

If a *merchant buyer* rightfully rejects goods, and the seller has no agent or business at the place of rejection, the buyer is required to follow any reasonable instructions received from the seller with respect to the goods controlled by the buyer. The buyer is entitled to reimbursement for the care and cost entailed in following the instructions [UCC 2-603]. The same requirement holds if the buyer rightfully revokes acceptance [UCC 2-608(3)].

If no instructions are forthcoming and the goods are perishable or threaten to decline in value quickly, the buyer can resell the goods in good faith, taking the appropriate reimbursement from the proceeds [UCC 2-603(1)]. If the goods are not perishable, the buyer may store them for the seller's account or reship them to the seller [UCC 2-604].

DAMAGES   If a seller wrongfully fails to deliver goods or repudiates the sales contract, or if the buyer is justified in rejecting goods that the seller tenders, then the buyer has several options under the UCC. The buyer may cancel the contract and recover as much of the price as has been paid to the seller. Following cancellation, the buyer may either (1) *cover* by obtaining the goods from another seller and seeking reimbursement for the extra costs incurred or (2) recover damages for breach of the sales contract [UCC 2-711].

If the buyer elects to seek damages rather than cover, then the measure of damages is the difference between the market price at the time the buyer learned of the breach and the contract price, plus, possibly, any consequential damages that result from the seller's breach [UCC 2-713]. Consequential damages flow from (1) any loss resulting from the buyer's unique needs that the seller had reason to know of and that could not be prevented by cover or other action and (2) any injury to person or property that results in a breach of warranty (a

seller's statement or representation concerning the character, quality, or title of the seller's goods and constituting part of the contract of sale) [UCC 2-715].

SPECIFIC PERFORMANCE   A buyer can obtain specific performance if the goods are unique or in other proper circumstances [UCC 2-716(1)]. Although it is not stated in this section of the UCC, an award of specific performance is usually considered inappropriate unless the buyer's remedy at law is inadequate. Ordinarily, a suit for money damages will be sufficient to place a buyer in the position he or she would have occupied if the seller had fully performed. When the contract is for the purchase of a particular work of art, patent, copyright, or similarly unique item, however, money damages may not be sufficient. Under these circumstances, equity will require the seller to perform exactly by delivering the unique goods (a remedy of specific performance).

To illustrate: Casey contracts to sell an antique car to Hammer for $30,000, with delivery and payment due on June 14. Hammer tenders payment on June 14, but Casey refuses to deliver. Can Hammer force delivery of the car? Probably, because the antique car is unique. Therefore, Hammer can obtain specific performance of the contract from Casey.

■ Sales Warranties

In the past, *caveat emptor*—let the buyer beware—was the prevailing philosophy in sales contract law. This may not have been an unrealistic approach when buyers and sellers were more or less equally capable of judging the quality (or lack of it) of the goods that were the subjects of their bargains. In twentieth-century America, however, it is unlikely that any buyer will comprehend the workings of any but a few of the goods he or she purchases, much less grasp all of the risks and be able to assume them intelligently and pay for any resulting injuries or damage. Thus, *caveat emptor* has given way to a consumer-oriented approach. Today, most goods are covered by some type of warranty designed to protect consumers. This change, of course, has not been without cost to consumers, who generally pay higher prices imposed by sellers and their insurers to cover their increased costs.

The concept of *warranty* is based on the seller's assurance to the buyer that the goods will meet certain standards. The UCC designates five types of warranties that can arise in a sales contract:

1. Warranty of title [UCC 2-312].
2. Express warranty [UCC 2-313].
3. Implied warranty of merchantability [UCC 2-314(1), (2)].
4. Implied warranty of fitness for a particular purpose [UCC 2-315].
5. Implied warranty arising from the course of dealing or trade usage [UCC 2-314(3)].

In the law of sales, because a warranty imposes a duty on the seller, a breach of warranty is a breach of the seller's promise. If the parties have not agreed to limit or modify the remedies available to the buyer on the seller's breach of warranty, the buyer can sue to recover damages against the seller. Under some circumstances, a breach can allow the buyer to rescind the agreement.[9]

Warranty of Title

Title warranty arises automatically in most sales contracts. UCC 2-312 imposes three types of warranties of title. In most cases, sellers warrant that they have good and valid title to the goods sold and that transfer of the title is rightful [UCC 2-312(1)(a)]. A second warranty of title provided by the UCC protects buyers who are *unaware* of any encumbrances (claims or liens) against goods at the time the contract is made [UCC 2-312(1)(b)]. This warranty protects buyers who, for example, unknowingly purchase goods that are subject to a creditor's security interest (an interest in property that secures payment to the creditor). If a creditor legally repossesses the goods from a buyer who *had no actual knowledge of the security interest,* then the buyer can recover from the seller for a breach of warranty. (The buyer who has *actual knowledge* of a security interest has no recourse against a seller.) A third category of title warranty is the warranty against infringement. A merchant is deemed to warrant that the goods delivered are

free from any patent, trademark, or copyright claims of a third person [UCC 2-312(3)].

In an ordinary sales transaction, the title warranty can be disclaimed or modified only by the *specific language* in a contract. For example, sellers may assert that they are transferring only such rights, title, and interest as they have in the goods. In certain cases, the circumstances of the sale are sufficient to indicate clearly to a buyer that no assurances as to title are being made. The classic example is a sheriff's sale, when buyers know that the goods have been seized to satisfy debts and it is apparent that the goods are not the property of the person selling them [UCC 2-312(2)].

Express Warranties

A seller can create an **express warranty** by making representations concerning the quality, condition, description, or performance potential of the goods. Under UCC 2-313, express warranties arise when a seller indicates that:

1. The goods will conform to any affirmation or promise of fact that the seller makes to the buyer about the goods. Such affirmations or promises are usually made during the bargaining process. Statements such as ''These drill bits will easily penetrate stainless steel—and without dulling'' constitute express warranties.
2. The goods will conform to any *description* of them—for example, a label that states that a ''crate contains one 150-horsepower diesel engine'' or a contract that calls for delivery of a ''camel's hair coat'' creates an express warranty.
3. The goods will conform to any *sample* or *model.* For example, an express warranty arises when the sales representative of a textile firm says to a prospective customer, ''The bolts of cloth we deliver will match this swatch.''

Express warranties also can be found in a seller's advertisement, brochure, or promotional materials. If an express warranty is not intended, the marketing agent or salesperson should not promise too much.

STATEMENTS OF OPINION AND VALUE According to Section 2-313(2), ''It is not necessary to the creation of an express warranty that the seller

---

9.   Rescission can occur by rejection of goods before acceptance or by revocation by the buyer after acceptance.

use formal words such as 'warrant' or 'guarantee' or that he have a specific intention to make a warranty.'' It is necessary only that a reasonable buyer would regard the representation as part of the basis of the bargain.

On the other hand, if the seller merely makes a statement that relates to the value or worth of the goods or makes a statement of opinion or recommendation about the goods, the seller is not creating an express warranty [UCC 2-313(2)]. What constitutes an express warranty and what constitutes *puffing* is not easy to resolve. (Puffing is the expression of an opinion by a seller that is not made as a representation of fact.) Merely recognizing that some statements are not warranties does not tell us

where one should draw the line between puffs and warranties. The reasonableness of the buyer's reliance is the controlling criterion in many cases.

The context within which a statement is made normally is relevant in determining the reasonableness of the buyer's reliance. For example, any statement made in a written advertisement is more likely to be relied on by a reasonable person than a statement made orally by a salesperson. Another factor is the specificity of the statements made. For example, a car dealer's statement that a vehicle is in ''excellent'' or ''mint'' condition may be too nonspecific for a court to deem it an express warranty—as is illustrated by the following case.

BACKGROUND AND FACTS *The plaintiff, Web Press Services Corporation, purchased a used 1980 Ford Bronco from the defendant, New London Motors, Inc., in July 1984. During the course of the sales negotiation, the defendant told the plaintiff's agent that the truck was ''excellent'' and in ''mint condition.'' The agent took the truck for a test drive and agreed to the purchase. Mechanical troubles developed almost immediately. Many problems were minor and were remedied by the defendant. The Bronco had a major structural defect in the rear axle, however, and the defendant did not remedy this defect. In October 1984, the plaintiff tendered the Bronco back to the defendant and revoked its acceptance of the vehicle. The plaintiff then requested the return of the purchase price, and the defendant refused. The plaintiff brought an action for breach of express warranties, among other actions. The trial court found that the defendant did not breach any express warranties, and Web Press Services Corporation appealed.*

Case 10.5

WEB PRESS SERVICES CORP. v. NEW LONDON MOTORS, INC.

Supreme Court of Connecticut, 1987.
203 Conn. 342,
525 A.2d 57.

DANNEHY, Justice.
*   *   *   *

We next consider the plaintiff's claim that the court should have found a breach of an express warranty. According to the plaintiff, the defendant's repeated statements to the effect that the vehicle was an ''excellent'' and ''unusual'' one, and that it was in ''mint'' and ''very good'' condition, amounted to an express warranty under General Statutes [Section] 42a-2-313(1)(a). *   *   * In concluding that the defendant's statements did not amount to an express warranty, the trial court relied on [a case in which] the court held that words such as ''[t]his car is in A-1 condition'' did not create an express warranty but were merely ''seller's talk.''
*   *   *   *

*   *   * Drawing the line between puffing and the creation of a warranty is often difficult, but several factors have been identified as helpful in making that determination. One such factor is the specificity of the statements made. A statement such as ''this truck will give not less than 15.1 miles to the gallon when it is driven at a steady 60 miles per hour'' is more likely to be found to create an express warranty than a statement such as ''this is a top-notch car.'' Statements to the effect that a truck was in ''good condition'' and that a motor was in ''perfect running order'' have been held not to create express warranties. Another factor to be considered in determining whether a statement creates an express warranty is whether it was written or oral, the latter being more likely to be considered puffing.

The defendant['s] * * * statements certainly cannot be considered specific in nature. Moreover, the plaintiff was allowed to examine and test drive the vehicle prior to purchase. Under the facts of this case the trial court's failure to find an express warranty * * * cannot be considered clearly erroneous.

DECISION AND REMEDY   *The court held that the defendant's statements about the condition of the car did not create an express warranty. The court did remand the case back to the trial court, however, with directions to articulate the legal and factual basis on which it had found that the defendant had not violated the Connecticut Unfair Trade Practices Act, which was one of the other legal theories on which the plaintiff based its action.*

DISCLAIMERS OF EXPRESS WARRANTIES The parol evidence rule protects the seller from a buyer's false claims that an oral warranty was created. Under this rule, if the parties intended the written contract to be the complete expression of their agreement, the buyer cannot offer evidence of an oral warranty. Nevertheless, a court may conclude that the contract was not a complete expression of the parties' intentions and permit proof of oral terms.

The UCC does permit express warranties to be negated or limited by specific and unambiguous language, provided this is done in a manner that protects the buyer from surprise. Therefore, a written disclaimer in language that is clear and conspicuous, and called to a buyer's attention, could negate all oral express warranties not included in the written sales contract [UCC 2-316(1)].

Implied Warranties

An **implied warranty** is one that *the law derives* by implication or inference from the nature of the transaction or the relative situation or circumstances of the parties. For example, Kaplan buys an axe at Enrique's Hardware Store. No express warranties are made. The first time she chops wood with it, the axe handle breaks, and Kaplan is injured. She immediately notifies Enrique. Examination shows that the wood in the handle was rotten but that the rottenness could not have been noticed by either Enrique or Kaplan. Nonetheless, Kaplan notifies Enrique that she will hold him responsible for the medical bills. Enrique is responsible be- cause a merchant seller of goods warrants that the goods he or she sells are fit for the ordinary purposes for which such goods are used. This axe was obviously not fit for those purposes.

IMPLIED WARRANTY OF MERCHANTABILITY An **implied warranty of merchantability** automatically arises in every sale of goods made *by a merchant* who deals in goods of the kind sold [UCC 2-314(1)]. Thus, a retailer of ski equipment makes an implied warranty of merchantability every time the retailer sells a pair of skis, but a neighbor selling skis at a garage sale does not.

Goods that are *merchantable* are "reasonably fit for the ordinary purposes for which such goods are used" [UCC 2-314(2)]. They must at least:

1. Be of average, fair, or medium-grade quality.
2. Pass without objection in the trade or market for goods of the same description.
3. Be adequately packaged and labeled as provided by the agreement.
4. Conform to the promises or affirmations of fact made on the container or label.
5. Be of an even quality and quantity in each unit and among all units.

Some examples of nonmerchantable goods include light bulbs that explode when switched on, pajamas that burst into flames on slight contact with the heating elements of an electric room heater, high heels that break off shoes under normal use, and shotgun shells that explode prematurely.

A sale is also accompanied by an implied warranty of merchantability that imposes on the merchant liability for the safe performance of the product. It makes no difference whether the merchant knew of or could have discovered a defect that makes the product unsafe. (Of course, merchants are not absolute insurers against *all* accidents arising in connection with the goods. For example, a bar of soap is not unmerchantable merely because a user can slip and fall by stepping on it.) In an action based on breach of warranty, it is necessary to show that an implied warranty existed, that the warranty was broken, and that the breach of warranty was the proximate cause of the damage sustained.

IMPLIED WARRANTY OF FITNESS FOR A PARTICULAR PURPOSE   The **implied warranty of fitness** for a particular purpose arises when *any seller* (merchant or nonmerchant) knows the particular purpose for which a buyer will use the goods *and* knows that the buyer is relying on the seller's skill and judgment to select suitable goods [UCC 2-315].

A "particular purpose of the buyer" differs from the "ordinary purpose for which goods are used." Goods can be merchantable—suitable for the use to which such goods are ordinarily put—but still not fit for the buyer's particular purpose. For example, house paints suitable only for painting interior walls are not suitable for painting exterior walls.

A contract can include both a warranty of merchantability and a warranty of fitness for a particular purpose, which relates to a specific use or to a special situation in which a buyer intends to use the goods. For example, a seller recommends a particular pair of shoes, *knowing* that a customer is looking for mountain climbing shoes. The buyer purchases the shoes *relying* on the seller's judgment. If the shoes are found to be not only improperly made but suitable only for walking, not for mountain climbing, the seller has breached both the warranty of fitness for a particular purpose and the warranty of merchantability.

A seller does not need "actual knowledge" of the buyer's particular purpose. It is sufficient if a seller "has reason to know" the purpose. The buyer, however, must have relied on the seller's skill or judgment in selecting or furnishing suitable

goods for an implied warranty of fitness to be created.

For example, Josephs buys a shortwave radio from Hi-Tech Electronics, telling the salesperson that she wants a set strong enough to pick up Radio Luxembourg, which is 8,000 miles away. Hi-Tech Electronics sells Josephs a Model XYZ set. The set works, but it will not pick up Radio Luxembourg. Josephs wants her money back. Here, because Hi-Tech Electronics is guilty of a breach of implied warranty of fitness for the buyer's particular purpose, Josephs will be able to recover. The salesperson knew specifically that she wanted a set that would pick up Radio Luxembourg. Furthermore, Josephs relied on the salesperson to furnish a radio that would fulfill this purpose. Because the salesperson did not do so, the warranty was breached.

IMPLIED WARRANTY ARISING FROM COURSE OF DEALING OR TRADE USAGE   The UCC recognizes in Section 2-314(3) that implied warranties can arise from course of dealing, course of performance, or usage of trade. In the absence of evidence to the contrary, when both parties to a sales contract have knowledge of a well-recognized trade custom, the courts will infer that they both intended that custom to apply to their contract. For example, in the sale of a new car, when the industry-wide custom includes lubricating the car before delivery, a seller who fails to do so can be held liable to a buyer for resulting damages for breach of implied warranty. This, of course, would also be negligence on the part of the dealer.

DISCLAIMERS OF IMPLIED WARRANTIES   Generally speaking, and unless circumstances indicate otherwise, implied warranties (of merchantability and fitness) are disclaimed by the expressions "as is," "with all faults," and other similar expressions that in common understanding for *both* parties call the buyer's attention to the fact that there are no implied warranties [UCC 2-316(3)(a)].

The UCC also permits a seller to specifically disclaim the implied warranty either of fitness or of merchantability [UCC 2-316(2)]. To disclaim the implied warranty of fitness, the disclaimer *must* be in writing and conspicuous. The word *fitness* does not have to be mentioned in the writing; it is sufficient, for example, for the disclaimer to state:

"There are no warranties that extend beyond the description on the face hereof." A merchantability disclaimer must be more specific—it must mention *merchantability*. It need not be written; but if it is, the writing must be conspicuous.

■ Terms and Concepts to Review

bill of lading 234
consignment 238
cure 240
express warranty 248
firm offers 230
identification 234

implied warranty 250
implied warranty of
   fitness 251
implied warranty of
   merchantability 250

insurable interest 239
sale 229
sale on approval 238
sale or return 238
warehouse receipt 235

■ Questions and Case Problems

10-1. A. B. Zook, Inc., is a manufacturer of washing machines. Over the telephone, Zook offers to sell Radar Appliances 100 Model-Z washers at a price of $150 per unit. Zook agrees to keep this offer open for ninety days. Radar tells Zook that the offer appears to be a good one and that it will let Zook know of its acceptance within the next two to three weeks. One week later, Zook sends and Radar receives notice that Zook has withdrawn its offer. Radar immediately thereafter telephones Zook and accepts the $150-per-unit offer. Zook claims, first, that no sales contract was ever formed between it and Radar and, second, that if there is a contract, the contract is unenforceable. Discuss Zook's contentions.

10-2. Flint, a retail seller of television sets, orders 100 Model Color-X sets from manufacturer Martin. The order specifies the price and that the television sets are to be *shipped* by Humming Bird Express on or before October 30. The order is received by Martin on October 5. On October 8 Martin writes Flint a letter indicating that the order was received and that the sets will be shipped as directed, at the specified price. This letter is received by Flint on October 10. On October 28, Martin, in preparing the shipment, discovers it has only 90 Color-X sets in stock. Martin ships the 90 Color-X sets and 10 television sets of a different model, stating clearly on the invoice that the 10 are being shipped only as an accommodation. Flint claims Martin is in breach of contract. Martin claims the shipment was not an acceptance and therefore no contract was formed. Explain who is correct and why.

10-3. On May 1, Peale goes into Carson's retail clothing store to purchase a jacket. Peale finds a jacket he likes for $190 and buys it. The jacket needs alteration. Peale is to pick up the altered jacket at Carson's store on May 10. Consider the following separate sets of circumstances:

   (a) One of Carson's major creditors obtains a judgment on the debt Carson owes and has the court issue a writ of execution (a court order to seize a debtor's property to satisfy debt) to collect on that judgment all clothing in Carson's possession. Discuss *Peale's* rights to the jacket in light of the court's order.

   (b) On May 9, through no fault of Carson, his store burns down, and all contents are a total loss. Between Carson and Peale, who suffers the loss of the jacket destroyed by fire? Explain.

10-4. Mackey orders from Pride 1,000 cases of Greenie brand peas from Lot A at list price to be shipped F.O.B. ["free on board," meaning that shipment is at the seller's expense] via Fast Freight Lines. Pride receives the order and immediately sends Mackey an acceptance of the order with a promise to ship promptly. Pride later separates the 1,000 cases of Greenie peas and prints Mackey's name and address on each case. The peas are placed on Pride's dock, and Fast Freight is notified to pick up the shipment. The night before the pickup by Fast Freight, through no fault of Pride, a fire destroys the 1,000 cases of peas. Pride claims that title passed to Mackey at the time the contract was made and risk of loss passed to Mackey when the goods were marked with Mackey's name and address. Discuss Pride's contentions.

10-5. McDonald has contracted to purchase 500 pairs of shoes from Vetter. Vetter manufactures the shoes and tenders delivery to McDonald. McDonald accepts the shipment. Later, on inspection, McDonald discovers that 10 pairs of the shoes are poorly made and will have to be sold to customers as seconds. If McDonald decides to keep all 500 pairs of shoes, what remedies are available to her? Discuss.

10-6. Loeb & Co. entered into an oral agreement with Schreiner, a farmer, whereby Schreiner was to sell Loeb 150 bales of cotton, each weighing 480 pounds. Shortly thereafter, Loeb sent Schreiner a letter confirming the terms of the oral contract. Schreiner neither acknowledged receipt of the letter nor objected to its terms. When delivery came due, Schreiner ignored the oral agreement and sold his cotton on the open market because the price of cotton had more than doubled (from 37 cents to 80 cents per pound) since the oral agreement was made. In a lawsuit by Loeb & Co. against Schreiner, can Loeb & Co. recover? Explain. [*Loeb & Co. v. Schreiner,* 294 Ala. 722, 321 So.2d 199 (1975)]

10-7. Peggy Holloway, a real estate broker, guaranteed payment for shipment of over $11,000 worth of mozzarella cheese sold by Cudahy Foods Co. to Pizza Pride in Jamestown, North Carolina. The entire arrangement was made orally. Cudahy mailed to Holloway an invoice for the order, and Holloway did not object in writing to the invoice within ten days of receipt. Later, when Cudahy demanded payment from Holloway, Holloway denied having guaranteed payment for the cheese and raised the Statute of Frauds as an affirmative defense. Cudahy claimed that the Statute of Frauds could not be used as a defense, as both Cudahy and Holloway were merchants and Holloway had failed to object within ten days to Cudahy's invoice. Discuss Cudahy's argument. [*Cudahy Foods Co. v. Holloway,* 286 S.E.2d 606 (N.C.App.Ct. 1982)]

10-8. Leemar Steel Co. manufactured counterweight inserts for CMI Corp., according to blueprints from CMI, and shipped them to CMI. CMI prepared an internal memo rejecting the shipment for nonconformance two days after it was received. CMI did not send the rejection notice to Leemar. Instead, a few weeks later, it notified Leemar by phone that there was a "problem with the inserts." CMI paid for the inserts and attempted, with Leemar's aid, to have the inserts ground to the correct tolerances during the next few months. Because this could not be accomplished, CMI filed suit to cancel the contract and to recover the money that it had paid Leemar pursuant to the contract. Discuss whether CMI has accepted the goods. Can it still revoke its acceptance and get its money back? [*CMI Corp. v. Leemar Steel Co.,* 733 F.2d 1410 (10th Cir. 1984)]

10-9. T. W. Oil, Inc., the plaintiff, purchased fuel oil that was still at sea on a tanker. The oil company then contracted to sell to Consolidated Edison Co. (Con Ed), the defendant, this cargo of oil. When the plaintiff purchased the oil shipment, it received a certificate from the foreign refinery that stated the sulfur content of the oil was 0.52 percent. When the oil company then contracted with Con Ed to sell it the oil, the oil company specified that the sulfur content was 0.5 percent, rounding off the 0.52 percent, as was the custom in the trade. During the negotiations with Con Ed, the oil company learned that Con Ed was authorized to buy and burn oil with a sulfur content of up to 1 percent and would mix oils containing more and less than that to maintain that figure. When the oil shipment arrived, its sulfur content was found to be 0.92 percent. Con Ed rejected the shipment. The oil company offered a reduced price, which was also rejected by Con Ed. The next day, T. W. Oil offered to cure with a substitute shipment of conforming oil on a tanker due to arrive approximately one month after the original delivery date. Con Ed rejected the offer to cure. T. W. Oil sued for breach of contract, and the trial court held for the plaintiff, T. W. Oil, holding that the plaintiff's "reasonable and timely offer to cure" was improperly rejected. Discuss whether Con Ed was required to accept the substitute shipment. [*T. W. Oil, Inc. v. Consolidated Edison Co.,* 57 N.Y.2d 574, 443 N.E.2d 932, 457 N.Y.S.2d 458 (1982)]

10-10. Bryant Lewis contracted to sell Ross Cattle Co. 400 head of cattle at $47.50 per hundredweight. Ross made an $8,000 down payment. Before delivery, Lewis heard a rumor that Ross was in poor financial condition, and Lewis demanded that he receive full payment before delivering the animals. Ross told Lewis the balance would be paid on delivery, based on the weight of the cattle delivered. Lewis refused to deliver the cattle and sold them to a third party. Ross filed suit. Lewis claimed that the refusal of Ross to pay was an anticipatory repudiation of the contract. Discuss whether Lewis was correct and what action Lewis could have taken on the basis of the rumor. [*Ross Cattle Co. v. Lewis,* 415 So.2d 1029 (Miss. 1982)]

10-11. Rheinberg-Kellerei GMBH is a German wine producer and export seller who sold 1,245 cases of wine to Vineyard Wine Co. The contract did not specify delivery terms to any specific destination, and Rheinberg, through its agent, selected the port of Wilmington, North Carolina for the port of entry. Rheinberg delivered the wine to the boat carrier in early December 1978. On or about January 24, 1979, Vineyard learned that the wine had been lost in the North Atlantic sometime between December 12 and December 22, when the boat sank with all hands aboard. Vineyard refused to pay Rheinberg. Rheinberg filed an action for the purchase price, claiming that risk of loss had passed to the buyer, Vineyard, on delivery of the wine to the carrier. Vineyard claimed that, because of Rheinberg's failure to give prompt notice of shipment (notice had not been given until after the ship was lost at sea), risk of loss had not passed to the buyer. Discuss fully who is correct. [*Rheinberg-Kellerei GMBH v. Vineyard Wine Co.,* 281 S.E.2d 425 (N.C.App. 1981)]

10-12. Vertis Smith was considering buying a used car from Fitzner Pontiac-Buick-Cadillac, Inc. He particularly liked a 1982 Olds Cutlass on the lot and took it for a test drive. Smith then told Fitzner's sales representative that if Fitzner would fix a rattle he had heard and paint the car, he would purchase it for $7,475. The salesperson agreed to have these things done and assured Smith that when the car was delivered it would be in "first class shape." Fitzner performed as agreed, and the car was delivered shortly thereafter to Smith. During the next few months, Smith had to install a new intake gasket, a new transmission, and a new radiator—repairs that were made by others, not Fitzner. Fitzner repaired a broken taillight and adjusted a window mechanism. In addition, Smith claimed that the car stalled frequently in traffic and got only eleven miles per gallon of gas. Nine months after he had purchased the car, Smith returned it to Fitzner and requested a refund of the purchase price plus the cost of the repairs, alleging, among other things, that Fitzner had breached an express warranty. Discuss fully whether Fitzner's statement that the car would be delivered in "first class shape" constituted an express warranty. [*Fitzner Pontiac-Buick-Cadillac, Inc. v. Smith,* 523 So.2d 324 (Miss. 1988)]

10-13. In 1984, the Lindemann farm's cotton crop fared poorly because of lack of weed control. That year, and every year since the early 1960s, the Lindemanns (plaintiffs) used Treflan, an herbicide manufactured by the defendants, Eli Lilly and Co. The label specifically stated that Treflan would control weeds when used according to label instructions. The Treflan label recommended that the herbicide be incorporated into the soil twice after it had been sprayed. The purpose of the double incorporation was to provide greater uniformity in the herbicide's distribution. The Lindemanns, in an effort to create still greater uniformity in the distribution of the Treflan, made an application by spraying half the amount of a normal application in one direction and half in the opposite direction. Each spraying was incorporated into the soil after it had been applied. If the directions did not contain a specific directive calling for a single application, could the Lindemanns recover for breach of express warranty of the herbicide to control weeds? Discuss. [*Lindemann v. Eli Lilly and Co.*, 816 F.2d 199 (5th Cir. 1987)]

10-14. Robert Levondosky was a patron at Harrah's Marina Hotel Casino, an Atlantic City casino owned by Marina Associates. While playing at one of the casino's tables, he ordered a cocktail, which was served free of charge—it was the casino's custom to give complimentary drinks to patrons at the gambling tables. Levondosky alleged that he swallowed a few thin chips of glass from the rim of the glass in which the drink was served and, as a result, suffered internal injuries. Levondosky sued the casino, contending that the casino had breached an implied warranty of merchantability. In evaluating this claim, the court had to determine (1) whether a "sale" had in fact occurred, which is prerequisite to the creation of an implied warranty of merchantability, and (2) whether the casino gave an implied warranty as to the glass as well as to the drink within it. Review UCC 2-314 and discuss how the court should rule on both issues. [*Levondosky v. Marina Associates*, 731 F.Supp. 1210 (D.N.J. 1990)]

10-15. A Question of Ethics

When Toby and Rita Kahr donated some used clothing to Goodwill Industries, Inc., they were not aware that a small bag containing their sterling silver had been accidentally included within one of the bags of donated clothing. The silverware, which was valued at over $3,500, had been given to them 27 years earlier by Rita's father as a wedding present and had great sentimental value for them. The Kahrs realized what had happened shortly after Toby returned from Goodwill, but when Toby called Goodwill, he was told that the silver had immediately been sold to a customer, Karon Markland, for $15. Although Goodwill called Markland and asked her to return the silver, Markland refused to return it. The Kahrs then brought an action against Markland to regain the silver, claiming that Markland did not have good title to it. In view of these circumstances, discuss the following issues. [Kahr v. Markland, 187 Ill.App.3d 603, 543 N.E.2d 579, 135 Ill.Dec. 196 (1989)]

1. The basic issue in this case is whether the silver was "lost property" (defined as property unintentionally separated from its owner) or property entrusted to a merchant, Goodwill Industries. If the court decides that the silver was lost, this will mean that the party in possession of the property will have good title against all parties except the true owner—in which case, the Kahrs will be able to recover the silver from Markland. If the court decides that the Kahrs entrusted the silver to Goodwill, then the entrustment rule will be applied—in which case, the Kahrs will be unable to recover the silver from Markland, a good faith purchaser. If you were the judge, how would you decide the issue? Why?

2. The entrustment rule can sometimes result in unfair treatment of the entrustor, because the entrustor cannot recover the property from a good faith purchaser (although the entrustor can recover the *value* of the property from the merchant who wrongfully sold the entrusted property). Given this potential for unfair treatment, how can the entrustment rule be justified from an ethical point of view?

3. Did Karon Markland act wrongfully in any way by not returning the silver to Goodwill when requested to do so? What would you have done in her position?

4. Goodwill argued that the entrustment rule should apply. Is this ethical behavior on the part of Goodwill? Why or why not? How might Goodwill justify its argument from an ethical point of view?

10-16. Case Briefing Assignment

Examine Case A.10 [Travel Craft, Inc. v. Wilhelm Mende GmbH & Co., 552 N.E.2d 443 (Ind. 1990)] in Appendix A. The case has been excerpted there in great detail. Review and then brief the case, making sure that you include answers to the following questions in your brief.

1. What were the three issues before the appellate court?

2. Why did the appellate court hold that the implied warranty of merchantability had been effectively disclaimed, even though the word merchantability had not been mentioned, as required under the UCC?

3. The appellate court agreed with the trial court that the written warranty was a "final expression of the parties' agreement on warranties." Why, then, did the appellate court hold that parol evidence was admissible?

4. How might the admissibility of parol evidence affect Travel Craft's chances of recovery?

5. Why did the appellate court reverse the trial court's decision as to the express warranty?

Chapter 11

Product Liability

Often retailers serve simply as go-betweens, selling manufacturers' goods to consumers in prepackaged, sealed containers. Even so, retailers may be liable to purchasers on express or implied warranties despite the fact that they cannot always examine the goods prior to resale. In the past, courts frequently addressed the question of whether the injured party should recover from the manufacturer, the processor, or the retailer for damages caused by the manufacture and marketing of a defective product. Today, liability has been extended to manufacturers and processors through the application of new and old principles of the law.

Manufacturers and sellers of goods can be held liable to consumers, users, and bystanders for physical harm or property damage that is caused by the goods. This is called **product liability,** and it encompasses the contract theory of *warranty* and tort theories of *negligence, misrepresentation,* and *strict liability.*

■ Warranty Law

Today, warranty law is an important part of the entire spectrum of laws relating to product liability. Consumers, purchasers, and even users of goods can recover *from any seller* for losses resulting from breach of implied and express warranties. A manufacturer is a *seller.* Therefore, a person who purchases goods from a retailer can recover from the retailer or the manufacturer if the goods are not merchantable, because in most states *privity of contract* (the connection that exists between contracting parties) is no longer a prerequisite for breach-of-warranty recovery for personal injuries. That is, a product purchaser may sue not only the firm from which he or she purchased a product but also a third party, the manufacturer of the product, in product liability.

Because warranty laws were discussed in Chapter 10, the balance of this chapter will deal with the tort theories of recovery for damages and injuries caused by defective products.

■ Negligence

Negligence is generally defined as the failure to use that degree of care that a reasonable, prudent person would have used under the circumstances. Recall from Chapter 7 that an action in negligence requires the plaintiff to prove that (1) a duty of care existed, (2) this duty was breached, (3) the plaintiff suffered a legally recognizable injury, and (4) the injury was proximately caused by the breach of due care. If the failure to exercise reasonable care in the creation or marketing of a product causes an injury, the basis of product liability is negligence. Thus, the manufacturer of a product must exercise "due care" to make that product safe to be used as intended. Due care must be exercised in designing the product, in selecting the materials, in using the appropriate production process, in assembling and testing the product, and in placing adequate warnings on the label informing the user of dangers of which an ordinary person might not be aware. The duty of care extends to the inspection and testing of products purchased by the manufacturer for use in the final product. The failure to exercise due care is negligence. Failure to exercise due care must be proved in actions based on the theory of negligence—in contrast to actions based on the doctrine of strict liability (discussed below), in which liability does not depend on proof of negligence.

Privity of Contract Not Required

An action based on negligence does not require privity of contract between the injured plaintiff and the negligent defendant-manufacturer. Section 395 of the Restatement (Second) of Torts states:

A manufacturer who fails to exercise reasonable care in the manufacture of a chattel [movable good] which, unless carefully made, he should recognize as involving an unreasonable risk of causing physical harm to those who lawfully use it for a purpose for which the manufacturer should expect it to be used and to those whom he should expect to be endangered by its probable use, is subject to liability for physical harm caused to them by its lawful use in a manner and for a purpose for which it is supplied.

Simply stated, a manufacturer is liable for its failure to exercise due care to any person who sustains an injury proximately caused by a negligently made (defective) product. (The analysis of whether a product is so defective as to be *unreasonably dangerous* applies equally to actions based on strict tort liability and is discussed below.)

In the following landmark case, the New York court dealt with the liability of a manufacturer that failed to exercise reasonable care in manufacturing a finished product. The *MacPherson* case is the classic negligence case in which privity of contract was not required between the plaintiff and the defendant to establish liability. This is a forerunner to product liability, although it does not use product liability theory. Its subject matter, defectively manufactured wooden wheels for automobiles, is dated, but the principles involved are not.

Case 11.1

MacPHERSON v. BUICK MOTOR CO.

Court of Appeals of New York, 1916.
217 N.Y. 382,
111 N.E. 1050.

BACKGROUND AND FACTS *The defendant, Buick Motor Company, was sued by Donald C. MacPherson, the plaintiff, who suffered injuries while riding in a Buick automobile that suddenly collapsed because one of the wheels was made of defective wood. The spokes crumbled into fragments, throwing MacPherson out of the vehicle and injuring him. The wheel itself had not been made by Buick Motor Company; it had been bought from another manufacturer. There was evidence, however, that the defects could have been discovered by reasonable inspection and that no such inspection had taken place. Although there was no charge that Buick knew of the defect and willfully concealed it, MacPherson charged Buick with negligence for putting a human life in imminent danger. Keep in mind that MacPherson sued the manufacturer directly, despite the fact that the automobile was purchased from a retail Buick dealer. The trial court held for MacPherson, and Buick Motor Company appealed.*

CARDOZO, Justice.
* * * *

   The question to be determined is whether the defendant owed a duty of care and vigilance to any one but the immediate purchaser.

The foundations of this branch of the law, at least in this state, were laid in *Thomas v. Winchester*. A poison was falsely labeled. The sale was made to a druggist, who in turn sold to a customer. The customer recovered damages from the seller who affixed the label. ''The defendant's negligence,'' it was said, ''put human life in imminent danger.'' A poison, falsely labeled, is likely to injure any one who gets it. *Because the danger is to be foreseen, there is a duty to avoid the injury.* [Emphasis added.] * * * *Thomas v. Winchester* became quickly a landmark of the law. In the application of its principle there may, at times, have been uncertainty or even error. There has never in this state been doubt or disavowal of the principle itself. * * *

* * * *

We hold, then, that the principle of *Thomas v. Winchester* is not limited to poisons, explosives, and things of like nature, to things which in their normal operation are implements of destruction. If the nature of a thing is such that it is reasonably certain to place life and limb in peril when negligently made, it is then a thing of danger. Its nature gives warning of the consequences to be expected. If to the element of danger there is added knowledge that the thing will be used by persons other than the purchaser, and used without new tests, then, irrespective of contract, the manufacturer of this thing of danger is under a duty to make it carefully. * * * It is possible to use almost anything in a way that will make it dangerous if defective. That is not enough to charge the manufacturer with a duty independent of his contract. * * * There must also be knowledge that in the usual course of events the danger will be shared by others than the buyer. Such knowledge may often be inferred from the nature of the transaction. But it is possible that even knowledge of the danger and of the use will not always be enough. The proximity or remoteness of the relation is a factor to be considered. We are dealing now with the liability of the manufacturer of the finished product, who puts it on the market to be used without inspection by his customers. If he is negligent, where danger is to be foreseen, a liability will follow.

We are not required, at this time, to say that it is legitimate to go back of the manufacturer of the finished product and hold the manufacturers of the component parts. To make their negligence a cause of imminent danger, an independent cause must often intervene; the manufacturer of the finished product must also fail in his duty of inspection. It may be that in those circumstances the negligence of the earlier members of the series is too remote to constitute, as to the ultimate user, an actionable wrong. * * * There is here no break in the chain of cause and effect. In such circumstances, the presence of a known danger, attendant upon a known use, makes vigilance a duty. * * *

* * * *

We think the defendant was not absolved from a duty of inspection because it bought the wheels from a reputable manufacturer. It was not merely a dealer in automobiles. It was a manufacturer of automobiles. It was responsible for the finished product. It was not at liberty to put the finished product on the market without subjecting the component parts to ordinary and simple tests. * * * The obligation to inspect must vary with the nature of the thing to be inspected. The more probable the danger the greater the need of caution.

DECISION AND REMEDY

The New York Court of Appeals, the highest court in the New York state system, affirmed the judgment of the original trial court and the intermediate review court that the defendant, Buick Motor Company, was liable to Donald C. MacPherson for the injuries he sustained when he was thrown from the vehicle.

COMMENTS

This case has been interpreted to cover all articles that imperil life when negligently made. Prior to MacPherson, *manufacturers escaped liability to consumers when their contractual dealings were with distributors or retailers. Since* MacPherson, *that has no longer been true.*

Violation of Statutory Duty

Numerous federal and state laws impose duties on manufacturers of cosmetics, drugs, foods, toxic substances, and flammable materials. These duties involve appropriate description of contents, labeling, branding, advertising, and selling. For example, federal statutes include the Flammable Fabrics Act, the Federal Food, Drug and Cosmetic Act, and the Hazardous Substances Labeling Act. In a tort action for damages, a violation of statutory duty is often held to constitute *negligence per se.*

Consider an example: Jason Manufacturing Company produces pipe fittings *specifically* for use in the construction of homes in Monroe County. The fittings do not comply with county building codes. One of the pipe fittings bursts in a home, allowing hot water to spray on the homeowner. The homeowner can bring a negligence action for personal damages on the ground that failure to comply with the building codes is in and of itself an automatic breach of the manufacturer's duty of reasonable care. Of course, the homeowner has to show proximate cause—that is, he or she must relate the injury to the careless act.

Defenses to Negligence

Any manufacturer, seller, or processor who can prove that due care was used in the manufacture of its product has an appropriate defense against a negligence suit, because failure to exercise due care is one of the major elements of negligence.

But there are other defenses, and their use and application vary from state to state. One area of variation is the tying of the breach (failure to exercise reasonable care) to the injury, referred to as causation (see Chapter 7). Numerous events, involving different people, take place between the time a product is manufactured and the time of its use. If any of these events can be shown to have caused or contributed to the injury, the manufacturer will claim, on the basis of this intervening cause, that it has no liability.

Two other defenses are contributory negligence and, when recognized, assumption of risk (both also discussed in Chapter 7). For example, assume that the manufacturer of an industrial grinder states in its instruction manual that the grinder's operator should wear safety goggles. The owner of a machine tool repair shop purchases a grinder, has her employees read the manufacturer's

instructions, and reminds them to wear safety goggles when they use the machine. Employee Joe Kidd chooses to ignore the warnings. As Kidd begins using the grinder to sharpen a sawblade's cutting edge, a tiny spark of hot metal flies into and causes the loss of his right eye. Kidd files suit, claiming the manufacturer was negligent in failing to warn that the grinder might throw off hot metal sparks. The manufacturer-defendant would claim that Kidd's own knowledge of the risk and voluntary use of the product with such knowledge was a reasonable assumption of risk and that his failure to wear the goggles was the proximate cause of the injury.

Likewise, any time a plaintiff misuses a product or fails to make a reasonable effort at preserving his or her own welfare, the manufacturer or seller will claim that the plaintiff contributed to causing the injuries. The claim is that the plaintiff's negligence offsets the negligence of the manufacturer or seller. In some states, the contributory negligence of the plaintiff is an absolute defense for the defendant-manufacturer or seller. In many others, the negligence of both these parties is compared (under the theory of comparative negligence), and damages are based on the proportion of negligence attributed to the defendant.

■ Misrepresentation

When a fraudulent misrepresentation has been made to a user or consumer and that misrepresentation ultimately results in an injury, the basis of liability may be the tort of fraud. In this case, the misrepresentation must have been made knowingly or with reckless disregard for the facts. Examples are the intentional mislabeling of packaged cosmetics and the intentional concealment of a product's defects.

Nonfraudulent misrepresentation, which occurs when a merchant *innocently* misrepresents the character or quality of goods, can also provide a basis of liability. In this situation, it does not have to be proved that the misrepresentation was made knowingly. A famous example involved a drug manufacturer and a victim of addiction to a prescription medicine called Talwin. The manufacturer, Winthrop Laboratories, a division of Sterling Drug, Inc., innocently indicated to the medical profession that the drug was not physically addictive. Using this information, a physician prescribed the drug for his patient, who developed an addiction that turned out to be fatal. Even though the addiction was a highly unusual reaction resulting from the victim's unusual susceptibility to this product, the drug company was still held liable.[1]

Whether fraudulent or nonfraudulent, the misrepresentation must be of a material fact (a fact concerning the quality, nature, or appropriate use of the product on which a normal buyer may be expected to rely). There must also have been an intent to induce the buyer's reliance. Misrepresen-

tation on a label or advertisement is enough to show an intent to induce the reliance of anyone who may use the product. The buyer must rely on the misrepresentation—if the buyer is not aware of it or if it does not influence the transaction, there is no liability.

In contrast to actions based on negligence and strict liability, in a suit based on fraudulent misrepresentation the plaintiff does not have to show that the product was defective or malfunctioned in any way. This is clearly illustrated in the following case, in which the court stressed that in an action based on fraud, it is only necessary that the plaintiff have suffered a legally recognizable injury as a result of relying on the seller's misrepresentations concerning the product.

1. *Crocker v. Winthrop Laboratories, Division of Sterling Drug, Inc.,* 514 S.W.2d 429 (Tex. 1974).

BACKGROUND AND FACTS *At age 33, Judy Khan had a Bjork-Shiley mechanical heart valve implanted in her heart to replace a diseased valve, after having been told that she would die without the implant. Khan later stated that she had been thoroughly advised of the risks associated with mechanical heart valves, including possible blood clotting, the possible rejection of the valve by her body, and the fact that she would always have to take blood-thinner medication, but that she had never been told that there was a risk that the valve might fracture. A little over two years after the valve was implanted, Khan learned from her surgeon that the implanted valve was within a group of valves being recalled because of numerous reports that the valves were "falling apart and malfunctioning without notice, resulting in death to the patients." The surgeon also told Khan that the risk of open-heart surgery to remove the valve was even greater than the risk of a malfunction. Khan and her husband sued the valve's manufacturer, Shiley, Inc., and its parent company, Pfizer, Inc., alleging numerous causes of action—including negligence, fraud and misrepresentation, breach of warranty, strict liability in tort, and intentional infliction of emotional distress—and seeking both compensatory and punitive damages. The trial court entered summary judgment for Shiley, holding that no liability could exist because Khan's valve had not yet malfunctioned and she could not demonstrate that it was defective. Khan appealed.*

Case 11.2

KHAN v. SHILEY, INC.
California Court of Appeal, Fourth District, Division 3, 1990.
217 Cal.App.3d 848, 266 Cal.Rptr. 106.

SONENSHINE, Associate Justice.
* * * *

[P]laintiffs contend even if product malfunction is a prerequisite in a strict liability context, it has no bearing on causes of action for negligence, breach of warranty, or fraud. They are partly correct. A cause of action does not presently exist under any theory premised on the risk the valve may malfunction in the future. This includes negligence, i.e., failure to warn, and breach of warranty. Allegations of fraud, however, are in a class by themselves.

For purposes of establishing fraud, it matters not that the valve implanted in Khan's heart is still functioning, arguably as intended. Unlike the other theories, in which the safety and efficacy of the product is assailed, the fraud claim impugns defendants' conduct.

* * * *

Plaintiffs assert defendants misrepresented the characteristics and safety of the valve while concealing other material, adverse information. Specifically, they contend defendants misrepresented the valve's propensity to fail, and omitted material facts showing the product had a history of strut failure even before one was implanted into Khan's heart. And they did so with knowledge of the substantial risk of death and without providing adequate warnings which fairly reflected the known risks. Furthermore, defendants allegedly made these misrepresentations with the intention plaintiffs would rely on them in selecting the Shiley valve. Plaintiffs relied on and were induced by these representations in making their selection. They would not otherwise have selected the Shiley valve; indeed, at least six other mechanical heart valves were available at the time of Khan's surgery.

Plaintiffs' complaint contained allegations sufficient to state a cause of action for fraud. In moving for summary judgment, defendants essentially ignored plaintiffs' fraud theory, focusing instead on whether or not the valve had malfunctioned. In so doing, defendants failed to meet their burden to establish there was no triable issue of material fact with respect to the fraud claim. Thus, the motion was erroneously granted as to that cause of action and, accordingly, summary judgment was improper.

DECISION AND REMEDY *The appellate court reversed the trial court's decision. Khan had stated a cause of action for fraud, and therefore the case should proceed to trial; summary judgment was inappropriate.*

ETHICAL CONSIDERATIONS *The defendants asserted that to allow a plaintiff to sue the manufacturer of a mechanical heart valve that had not yet malfunctioned—and had in fact prolonged her life—was contrary to public policy and essentially unfair. Justice Sonenshine responded to this charge as follows: "We recognize the role public policy has played, and continues to play, in the torts arena. However, our decision neither establishes a new cause of action nor drastically extends existing law. It merely confirms that a manufacturer of a product may be liable for fraud when it conceals material product information from potential users. This is true whether the product is a mechanical heart valve or frozen yogurt."*

■ Strict Liability

A fairly recent development of tort law is the revival of the old doctrine of *strict liability.* Under this doctrine, people may be held liable for the results of their acts regardless of their intentions or their exercise of reasonable care. For example, a company that uses dynamite in constructing a road is strictly liable for any damages that it causes, even if it takes reasonable and prudent precautions to prevent such damages. In essence, the blasting company becomes liable for any personal injuries it causes and thus is an absolute insurer—that is, the company is liable for damages regardless of fault.

The English courts accepted the doctrine of strict liability for many years. Often, persons whose conduct resulted in the injury of another were held

liable for damages, even if they had not intended to injure anyone and had exercised reasonable care. This approach was abandoned around 1800 in favor of the *fault* approach, in which an action was considered tortious only if it was wrongful or blameworthy in some respect.

Strict liability was reapplied in several landmark cases involving manufactured goods in the 1960s and has since become a common method of holding manufacturers liable. Section 402A of the Restatement (Second) of Torts, promulgated in 1965 and now adopted by most of the states, clearly espouses the doctrine of strict liability in tort.

The Restatement of Torts

The Restatement (Second) of Torts designates how the doctrine of strict product liability should be applied. It is a precise and widely accepted statement of the liabilities of sellers of goods (including manufacturers, processors, assemblers, packagers, bottlers, wholesalers, distributors, and retailers) and deserves close attention. Section 402A of the Restatement (Second) of Torts states:

> (1) One who sells any product in a defective condition unreasonably dangerous to the user or consumer or to his property is subject to liability for physical harm thereby caused to the ultimate user or consumer or to his property, if
>> (a) the seller is engaged in the business of selling such a product, and
>> (b) it is expected to and does reach the user or consumer without substantial change in the condition in which it is sold.
>
> (2) The rule stated in Subsection (1) applies although
>> (a) the seller has exercised all possible care in the preparation and sale of his product, and
>> (b) the user or consumer has not bought the product from or entered into any contractual relation with the seller.

Under this doctrine, liability does not depend on privity of contract. The injured party does not have to be the buyer or a third party beneficiary, as required under contract warranty theory [UCC 2-318]. Indeed, this type of liability in law is not governed by the provisions of the UCC. Under this doctrine, a plaintiff does not have to prove that there was a failure to exercise due care, as he or she does in an action based on negligence. If certain requirements (discussed in the following section) are met, the seller's liability to an injured party may be virtually unlimited.

Strict liability is imposed by law as a matter of public policy. This public policy rests on the threefold assumption that (1) consumers should be protected against unsafe products; (2) manufacturers and distributors should not escape liability for faulty products simply because they are not in privity of contract with the ultimate users of those products; and (3) manufacturers and sellers of products are in a better position to bear the costs associated with injuries caused by their products—costs that they can ultimately pass on to all consumers in the form of higher prices.

California was the first state to impose strict liability in tort on manufacturers. In the landmark decision that follows, the Supreme Court of California sets out the reasons for applying tort law rather than contract law to cases in which consumers are injured by defective products.

BACKGROUND AND FACTS *The plaintiff, Greenman, wanted a Shopsmith, a combination power tool that could be used as a saw, drill, and wood lathe, after having seen the tool demonstrated by a retailer and having studied a brochure prepared by the manufacturer. The plaintiff's wife bought him one for Christmas. More than a year later, a piece of wood flew out of the lathe attachment of the Shopsmith while the plaintiff was using it, inflicting serious injuries on him. About ten and a half months later, the plaintiff sued both the retailer and the manufacturer for breach of warranties and negligence. The jury found for the plaintiff, and the defendants appealed.*

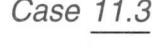 *Case 11.3*

GREENMAN v. YUBA POWER PRODUCTS, INC.
Supreme Court of California, 1962.
59 Cal.2d 57,
377 P.2d 897,
27 Cal.Rptr. 697.

TRAYNOR, Justice.
* * * *

Plaintiff introduced substantial evidence that his injuries were caused by defective design and construction of the Shopsmith. His expert witnesses testified that inadequate set screws were used to hold parts of the machine together so that normal vibration caused the tailstock of the lathe to move away from the piece of wood being turned permitting it to fly out of the lathe. They also testified that there were other more positive ways of fastening the parts of the machine together, the use of which would have prevented the accident. The jury could therefore reasonably have concluded that the manufacturer negligently constructed the Shopsmith. The jury could also reasonably have concluded that statements in the manufacturer's brochure were untrue, that they constituted express warranties, and that plaintiff's injuries were caused by their breach.

* * * *

[But] to impose strict liability on the manufacturer under the circumstances of this case, it was not necessary for plaintiff to establish an express warranty * * *. A manufacturer is strictly liable in tort when an article he places on the market, knowing that it is to be used without inspection for defects, proves to have a defect that causes injury to a human being. Recognized first in the case of unwholesome food products, such liability has now been extended to a variety of other products that create as great or greater hazards if defective.

* * * [The] theory of an express or implied warranty running from the manufacturer to the plaintiff, the abandonment of the requirement of a contract between them, the recognition that the liability is not assumed by agreement but imposed by law, and the refusal to permit the manufacturer to define the scope of its own responsibility for defective products make clear that the liability is not one governed by the law of contract warranties but by the law of strict liability in tort. Accordingly, rules defining and governing warranties that were developed to meet the needs of commercial transactions cannot properly be invoked to govern the manufacturer's liability to those injured by their defective products unless those rules also serve the purposes for which such liability is imposed.

* * * The purpose of such liability is to insure that the costs of injuries resulting from defective products are borne by the manufacturers that put such products on the market rather than by the injured persons who are powerless to protect themselves. Sales warranties serve this purpose fitfully at best. In the present case, for example, plaintiff was able to plead and prove an express warranty only because he read and relied on the representations of the Shopsmith's ruggedness contained in the manufacturer's brochure. Implicit in the machine's presence on the market, however, was a representation that it would safely do the jobs for which it was built. Under these circumstances, it should not be controlling whether plaintiff selected the machine because of the statements in the brochure, or because of the machine's own appearance of excellence that belied the defect lurking beneath the surface, or because he merely assumed that it would safely do the jobs it was built to do. It should not be controlling whether the details of the sales from manufacturer to retailer and from retailer to plaintiff's wife were such that one or more of the implied warranties of the sales act arose. "The remedies of injured consumers ought not to be made to depend upon the intricacies of the law of sales." To establish the manufacturer's liability it was sufficient that plaintiff proved that he was injured while using the Shopsmith in a way it was intended to be used as a result of a defect in design and manufacture of which plaintiff was not aware that made the Shopsmith unsafe for its intended use.

DECISION AND REMEDY *The jury verdict for the plaintiff was upheld. The manufacturer was held strictly liable in tort for the harm caused by its unsafe product.*

Requirements of Strict Product Liability

Just because a person is injured by a product does not mean he or she will have a cause of action against the manufacturer of the product. A cause of action will exist only if the following six basic requirements of strict product liability are met:

1. The product must be in a defective condition when the defendant sells it.

2. The defendant must normally be engaged in the business of selling that product.

3. The product must be unreasonably dangerous to the user or consumer because of its defective condition.[2]

---

2. This element is no longer required in some states—for example, California.

4. The plaintiff must incur physical harm to self or property by use or consumption of the product.
5. The defective condition must be the proximate cause of the injury or damage.
6. The goods must not have been substantially changed from the time the product was sold to the time the injury was sustained.

Thus, in any action against a manufacturer or seller, the plaintiff does not have to show why or in what manner the product became defective. The plaintiff does, however, have to show that at the time the injury was sustained, the condition of the product was essentially the same as when it left the hands of the defendant manufacturer or seller.

The plaintiff normally must also show that the product was so defective as to be an **unreasonably dangerous** product. A court may consider a product so defective as to be unreasonably dangerous if either (1) the product was dangerous beyond the expectation of the ordinary consumer or (2) a less dangerous alternative was economically feasible for the manufacturer, but the manufacturer failed to produce it.

Under the feasible-alternative approach, courts will consider a product's utility and desirability; the availability of other, safer products; the dangers that have been identified prior to an injured user's suit; the dangers' obviousness; the normal expectation of danger, particularly for established products; the probability of injury and its likely seriousness; the avoidability of injury by care in the product's use, including the contribution of instructions and warnings; and the viability of eliminating the danger without appreciably impairing the product's function or making the product too expensive. For example, people often cut themselves on knives, but a court would consider that knives are very useful. Reasoning that there is no way to avoid injuries without making the product useless and that the danger is obvious to users, a court normally would not find a knife to be unreasonably dangerous and would not hold a supplier of knives liable.

In contrast, a court may consider a snowblower without a safety guard over the opening through which the snow is blown to be in a condition that is unreasonably dangerous, even if it carries warnings to stay clear of the opening. The danger may be within the user's expectations, but the court will also consider the likelihood of injury and its probable seriousness, as well as the cost of putting a guard over the opening and the guard's effect on the blower's operation.

Some products are safe when used as their manufacturers and distributors intend but not safe when used in other ways. Suppliers are generally required to expect reasonably foreseeable misuses and to design products that are either safe when misused or marketed with some protective device, for example, a childproof cap.

The following case represents a plaintiff's attempt to recover damages for her son's death which resulted from a dangerous "product"—a handgun. Although unusual, the case clearly illustrates that a fundamental requirement in a strict product liability action is that the product causing the injury must be defective in some way.

BACKGROUND AND FACTS *James Patterson, who worked as a clerk in a convenience store in Dallas, was shot and killed during a robbery of the store in 1980. The revolver used by the robber was a .38 caliber "Saturday Night Special" manufactured by a West German company, Rohm Gesellschaft. Patterson's mother brought a product liability action against Rohm and the Florida distributor of the handgun, claiming that the handgun was "defective and unreasonably dangerous" in design because its potential for injury and death far outweigh any social utility it may have. The defendant moved for summary judgment, contending that it could not be liable for Patterson's death because the handgun was not defective—the gun did not malfunction nor did it lack any essential safety features.*

Case 11.4

PATTERSON v. ROHM GESELLSCHAFT

United States District Court, Northern District of Texas, Dallas Division, 1985. 608 F.Supp. 1206.

BUCHMEYER, District Judge.

* * * *

This claim is totally without merit and totally unsupported by legal precedent. It is a misuse of tort law, a baseless and tortured extension of products liability principles. And, it is an obvious attempt—unwise and unwarranted, even if understandable—to ban or restrict handguns through courts and juries, despite the repeated refusals of state legislatures and Congress to pass strong, comprehensive gun-control measures.

* * * *

* * * [U]nder Texas law, the manufacturer is not required to [e]nsure that its products are completely safe or that they will not cause injury to anyone. Instead, the manufacturer is liable for injuries resulting from a product only if that product is ''defective''—i.e., has a defect in the sense that something is wrong with it. This required defect may be one of three distinct types:

(i) The product may malfunction because of some manufacturing defect.

(ii) The product may be defective because it was sold without sufficient warning or instructions.

(iii) The product may be defective because its basic design is unsafe.

In cases involving the third type of defect, that of defective design, Texas uses the ''risk/utility balancing test'': whether the product is ''unreasonably'' dangerous in the sense that ''the danger-in-fact associated with the use of the product outweighs the utility of the product.'' Typically, this requires the jury to weigh the risks involved in the defective product against the feasibility and cost of an improved design. For example, if placing the gasoline tank in the center of the car ''would reduce the chances of fire in rear end collisions without creating other risks, significantly reducing performance, or significantly increasing costs, then the risk of the rear-end design outweighs its utility, and the car is defective.''

* * * *

But here, the plaintiff's attorneys offer no alternatives and no safer designs for a handgun. Nor can they do so—because a gun, by its very nature, must be dangerous and must have the capacity to discharge a bullet with deadly force. Accordingly, by their unconventional application of the risk/utility test to a nondefective product, the plaintiff's attorneys simply want to eliminate handguns.

Moreover, if this unconventional theory were correct, then it should apply equally to other products besides handguns—to rifles, to shotguns, to switchblade and kitchen and Swiss Army knives, to axes, to whiskey, to automobiles, etc.—even though these products are not defective. The possible consequences of expanding products liability in this manner have been described: ''. . . a plaintiff would need only to prove that the product was a factual cause in producing his injury. Thus, the manufacturer of a match would be liable for anything burned by a fire started by a match produced by him, a gun maker would be liable to anyone shot by the gun, anyone cut by a knife could sue the maker, and a purchaser of food with high calories would have an action for his overweight condition and for an ensuing heart attack.''

**DECISION
AND REMEDY**

The court granted the defendant's motion for summary judgment, holding that the plaintiff had no cause of action under Texas product liability law.

**ETHICAL
CONSIDERATIONS**

If gun manufacturers were held liable for all crimes committed with handguns, in effect handguns would be ''banned''—because no gun manufacturer could profitably produce them. But, as the judge in this case pointed out, such an expansion of product liability law would essentially ban all other products, including automobiles, that can cause harm. Moreover, it is not the function of the courts to write the law. The judge stressed the latter precept in his final comment to his opinion: "As an individual, I believe, very strongly, that handguns should be banned and that there should be stringent, effective control of other firearms. However, as a judge, I know full well that the question of whether handguns can be sold is a political one, not an issue of products liability law—and that this is a matter for the legislatures, not the courts."

Liability Sharing

As with other theories of product liability, a plaintiff using a theory of strict liability in tort has been required to prove that the defective product that caused his or her injury was the product of a specific defendant. In recent years, however, in cases in which plaintiffs could not prove which of many distributors of a harmful product supplied the particular product that caused the plaintiffs' injuries, courts have dropped this requirement. This has occurred in several cases involving DES (diethylstilbestrol), a drug administered in the past to prevent miscarriages. DES's harmful character was not realized until, a generation later, daughters of the women who had taken DES developed health problems, including vaginal carcinoma, that were linked to the drug. Partly because of the passage of time, a plaintiff-daughter often could not prove which pharmaceutical company—of as many as 300—had marketed the DES her mother ingested.

In these cases, some courts applied **industry-wide liability,** holding that all firms that manufactured and distributed DES during the period in question were liable for the plaintiffs' injuries in proportion to the firms' respective shares of the market.[3] In 1989, the New York Court of Appeals went still further and held that even if a firm can prove that it did not manufacture the particular product that caused injuries to the plaintiff, the firm can be held liable based on its share of the national market.[4]

The following case is illustrative of the market-share approach to liability and the application of the rule of apportionment used by the courts in determining each firm's respective liability to the plaintiff.

---

3. This theory of liability was first set out by the California Supreme Court in a 1980 case, *Sindell v. Abbott Laboratories,* 26 Cal.3d 588, 607 P.2d 924, 163 Cal.Rptr. 132 (1980).
4. *Hymowitz v. Eli Lilly and Co.,* 73 N.Y.2d 487, 539 N.E.2d 1069, 541 N.Y.S.2d 941 (1989).

BACKGROUND AND FACTS *Rita Rene Martin (the plaintiff) was born on October 4, 1962. Her mother, Shirley Ann Martin, had obtained a prescription for diethylstilbestrol (DES), which she took from May 1962 until the date Rita Martin was born. On January 4, 1980, Rita was diagnosed as suffering from carcinoma of the vagina. On February 21, 1980, as a result of the cancer, Rita underwent a radical hysterectomy and a partial vaginectomy. Shirley Martin could not remember which drug company had manufactured the DES she ingested. Moreover, because of the passage of time and because DES had been marketed generically, neither Shirley's physician nor her pharmacist could remember which company had manufactured or marketed the drug Shirley ingested. The only thing Shirley Martin could substantiate was that she had taken the drug in 100-milligram doses. Shirley and Rita Martin sued numerous drug companies (the defendants)—on the theories of negligence, strict liability, and breach of warranty—for personal injuries, pain, suffering, and destruction of the parent-child relationship. The Martins alleged that all of the pharmaceut-*

Case 11.5

MARTIN v. ABBOTT LABORATORIES

Supreme Court of Washington, 1984.
102 Wash.2d 581,
689 P.2d 368.

*ical companies were liable for their injuries because of the companies'
concerted, or joint, action to gain FDA approval and to market DES. The
drug companies contended that none of them had been identified as the
actual manufacturer or distributor of the DES ingested by Shirley Martin
and that the plaintiffs had thus failed to state a cause of action for which
relief could be granted. The trial court ruled that the plaintiffs had stated
a valid cause of action, and from this ruling the defendants appealed.*

DORE, Justice.
* * * *

We are presented with a conflict between the familiar principle that a tortfeasor
[one who commits a tort] may be held liable only for damage that it has caused, and
the sense of justice which urges that the victims of this tragedy should not be denied
compensation because of the impossibility of identifying the individual manufacturer
of these generic tablets if their manufacture and distribution were otherwise culpable.
* * * *

Because certain manufacturers and distributors produced or marketed an allegedly
defective drug for accidents of pregnancy, those manufacturers and distributors all
contributed to the risk of injury, even though they may not have contributed to the
actual injury of a given plaintiff. Although the defendants in this case have not acted
in concert, * * * all participated in either gaining approval of DES for use in
pregnancy or in producing or marketing DES in subsequent years. Each defendant
contributed to the *risk* of injury to the public and, consequently, the risk of injury
to individual plaintiffs. Thus, each defendant shares in some measure, a degree of
culpability in producing or marketing DES. Moreover, *as between the injured plaintiff and the possibly responsible drug company, the drug company is in a better
position to absorb the cost of the injury. The drug company can either insure itself
against liability, absorb the damage award, or pass the cost along to the consuming
public as a cost of doing business.* [Emphasis added.] We conclude that it is better
to have drug companies or consumers share the cost of the injury than to place the
burden solely on the innocent plaintiff.

We hold that plaintiff need commence suit against only one defendant and allege
the following elements: that the plaintiff's mother took DES; that DES caused the
plaintiff's subsequent injuries; that the defendant produced or marketed the type of
DES taken by the plaintiff's mother; and that the defendant's conduct in producing
or marketing the DES constituted a breach of a legally recognized duty to the plaintiff.
At the trial, the plaintiff will have to prove each of these elements to the satisfaction
of the trier of fact. We emphasize, however, that the plaintiff need not prove that a
defendant produced or marketed the precise DES taken by the plaintiff's mother.
Rather, the plaintiff need only establish by a preponderance of the evidence that a
defendant produced or marketed the *type* (e.g., dosage, color, shape, markings, size,
or other identifiable characteristics) of DES taken by the plaintiff's mother; the
plaintiff need not allege or prove any facts related to the time or geographic distribution of the subject DES. While the type of DES ingested by the mother should be
within the domain of her knowledge, facts relating to time and distribution should
be particularly within the domain of knowledge of the DES manufacturers and
distributors.
* * * *

The defendants that are unable to exculpate [clear or excuse] themselves from
potential liability are designated members of the plaintiffs' DES market; defined by
the specificity of the evidence as to geographic market area, time of ingestion, and
type of DES. These defendants are initially presumed to have equal shares of the
market and are liable for only the percentage of plaintiff's judgment that represents

their presumptive share of the market. These defendants are entitled to rebut this presumption and thereby reduce their potential liability by establishing their respective market share of DES in the plaintiff's particular geographic market. Upon proof of a market share by a preponderance of the evidence, that particular defendant is only liable for its share of the market as it relates to the total judgment. To the extent that other defendants fail to establish their actual market share, their presumed market share is adjusted so that 100 percent of the market is accounted for.

The Supreme Court of Washington determined that the plaintiffs had stated a valid cause of action, and the case was remanded to the trial court so that it could proceed in accordance with the appellate court's opinion.	**DECISION AND REMEDY**

Limitations on Recovery

Some courts have limited the application of the strict liability doctrine to cases in which personal injuries have occurred. Thus, when a defective product causes only *property damage,* the seller may not be liable under a theory of strict liability, depending on the law of the particular jurisdiction. In addition, until recently, recovery for *economic loss* was not available in an action based on strict liability (and even today it is rarely available). Note, however, that recovery for *breach of warranty* may be available, depending on the type of injury and which alternative section of UCC 2-318 is in effect.

Statutes of limitations restrict the time within which an action may be brought. A typical statute of limitations provides that an action must be brought within a specified period of time after the cause of action accrues. Generally, a cause of action is held to accrue when some damage occurs. Sometimes the running of the prescribed period is tolled (that is, suspended) until the party suffering an injury has discovered it (or should have discovered it).

Many states have passed laws placing outer time limits on some claims so that the defendant will not be left vulnerable to lawsuits indefinitely. These **statutes of repose** may limit the time within which a plaintiff can file a product liability suit. Typically, a statute of repose begins to run at an earlier date and runs for a longer time than a statute of limitations. For example, a statute of repose may proscribe any claims not brought within twelve years from the date of *sale* or *manufacture* of the

defective product. Therefore, it is immaterial that the product is defective or causes an injury if the injury occurs after this statutory period has lapsed. In addition, some of these legislative enactments have limited the application of the doctrine of strict liability to new goods. Some states, such as Massachusetts, have refused to recognize strict product liability. In these states, recovery is gained mainly through breach of warranty or negligence theory.

Strict Liability to Bystanders

All courts extend the strict liability of manufacturers and other sellers to injured **bystanders,** although the drafters of Restatement (Second) of Torts, Section 402A, did not take a position on bystanders. For example, the manufacturer of an automobile was held liable for injuries caused by the explosion of the car's motor while the car was in traffic. A cloud of steam that resulted from the explosion caused multiple collisions because it kept other drivers from seeing well.[5]

In the following case, the court extends the protections of Section 402A to bystanders whose injuries from defective products are reasonably foreseeable. Thus, someone injured by an exploding bottle in a supermarket was able to seek damages from the manufacturer for an injury caused by the defective product.

---

5. *Giberson v. Ford Motor Co.,* 504 S.W.2d 8 (Mo. 1974).

Case 11.6

**EMBS v. PEPSI-COLA
BOTTLING CO. OF
LEXINGTON,
KENTUCKY, INC.**

Court of Appeals of Kentucky,
1975.
528 S.W.2d 703.

BACKGROUND AND FACTS *The plaintiff, Embs, was buying some groceries at Stamper's Cash Market. Unnoticed by her, a carton of 7-Up was sitting on the floor at the edge of the produce counter about one foot from where she was standing. Several of the 7-Up bottles exploded. Embs's leg was injured severely enough that Embs had to be taken to the hospital by a managing agent of the store. Embs brought an action against the manufacturer, but the trial court dismissed her claim. The appellate court now takes up the case.*

JUKOWSKY, Judge.
       *   *   *   *

Our expressed public policy will be furthered if we minimize the risk of personal injury and property damage by charging the costs of injuries against the manufacturer who can procure liability insurance and distribute its expense among the public as a cost of doing business; and since the risk of harm from defective products exists for mere bystanders and passersby as well as for the purchaser or user, there is no substantial reason for protecting one class of persons and not the other. The same policy requires us to maximize protection for the injured third party and promote the public interest in discouraging the marketing of products having defects that are a menace to the public by imposing strict liability upon retailers and wholesalers in the distributive chain responsible for marketing the defective product which injures the bystander. *The imposition of strict liability places no unreasonable burden upon sellers because they can adjust the cost of insurance protection among themselves in the course of their continuing business relationship.* [Emphasis added.]

We must not shrink from extending the rule to the manufacturer for fear that the retailer or middleman will be impaled on the sword of liability without regard to fault. Their liability was already established under Section 402A of the Restatement of Torts 2d. As a matter of public policy the retailer or middleman as well as the manufacturer should be liable since the loss for injuries resulting from defective products should be placed on those members of the marketing chain best able to pay the loss, who can then distribute such risk among themselves by means of insurance and indemnity agreements. *   *   *

The result which we reach does not give the bystander a "free ride." When products and consumers are considered in the aggregate, bystanders, as a class, purchase most of the same products to which they are exposed as bystanders. Thus, as a class, they indirectly subsidize the liability of the manufacturer, middleman and retailer and in this sense do pay for the insurance policy tied to the product.

Public policy is adequately served if parameters are placed upon the extension of the rule so that it is limited to bystanders whose injury from the defect is reasonably foreseeable.

For the sake of clarity we restate the extension of the rule. The protections of Section 402A of the Restatement of Torts 2d extend to bystanders whose injury from the defective product is reasonably foreseeable.

**DECISION
AND REMEDY** *The appellate court reversed the trial court's directed verdict that dismissed Embs's claim. The case was remanded to the lower court for a new trial.*

Crashworthiness Doctrine

Certain courts have adopted the **crashworthiness doctrine**, which imposes liability for defects in the design or construction of motor vehicles that increase the extent of injuries to passengers if an accident occurs. The doctrine holds even when the defects do not actually cause the accident.[6] By accepting the crashworthiness doctrine, the courts reject the argument of automobile manufacturers that involving a car in a collision does not constitute "ordinary use" of the car. There are, however, strong differences of opinion among the courts on this issue.

Other Applications of Strict Liability

Under the rule of strict liability in tort, the basis of liability has been expanded to include suppliers of component parts and lessors of movable goods. Thus, if General Motors buys brake pads from a subcontractor and puts them in Chevrolets without changing their composition, and if those pads are defective, both the supplier of the brake pads and General Motors will be held strictly liable for the damages caused by the defects.

Liability for personal injuries caused by defective goods extends to those who lease such goods. Section 408 of the Restatement (Second) of Torts states that:

> One who leases a chattel as safe for immediate use is subject to liability to those whom he should expect to use the chattel, or to be endangered by its probable use, for physical harm caused by its use in a manner for which, and by a person for whose use, it is leased, if the lessor fails to exercise reasonable care to make it safe for such use or to disclose its actual condition to those who may be expected to use it.

Some courts have held that a leasing agreement gives rise to a contractual *implied warranty* that the leased goods will be fit for the duration of the lease. Under this view, if Hertz Rent-a-Car leases a Chevrolet that has been improperly maintained and a passenger in the Chevrolet is injured in an accident, the passenger can sue Hertz. (Liability here is based on the contract theory of warranty, not tort.)

Defenses

Frequently, negligent misconduct or misuse of the product by the harmed person or a third party, coupled with the product's defect, causes damage or injury. If the misconduct or misuse can be charged

to a claimant, it may be a defense to reduce the claimant's recovery or bar it altogether.

ASSUMPTION OF RISK   In some states, assumption of risk is a defense in an action based on strict liability in tort. For such a defense to be established, the defendant must show the following basic elements:

1. That the plaintiff voluntarily engaged in the risk while realizing the potential danger.
2. That the plaintiff knew and appreciated the risk created by the defect.
3. That the plaintiff's decision to undertake the known risk was unreasonable.

MISUSE OF THE PRODUCT   Similar to the defense of voluntary assumption of risk is that of **product misuse**. Here the injured party did not know that the product was dangerous for a particular use, but the use was not the one for which the product was designed. (Contrast this with assumption of risk.) This defense has been severely limited by the courts, however. If the misuse is reasonably foreseeable, the seller must take measures to guard against it.

COMPARATIVE FAULT   As pointed out in Chapter 7, at common law, in any action based on negligence, contributory negligence of the injured party either completely barred recovery or reduced the amount of recovery under the rule of comparative negligence. In principle, contributory negligence is immaterial in any action based on the theory of strict liability in tort and in fact has been abolished as a defense by most courts.

Recent developments in the area of comparative negligence are affecting the doctrine of strict liability. Whereas previously the plaintiff's conduct was not a defense to strict liability, today a growing number of jurisdictions considers the negligent or intentional actions of the plaintiff in the apportionment of liability and damages. This "comparing" of the plaintiff's conduct to the defendant's strict liability results in an application of the doctrine of comparative negligence. Thus, for example, failure to take precaution against a known defect will reduce a plaintiff's recovery. The majority of states have adopted this doctrine, either legislatively or through court decisions. Its recent growth may have a pervasive effect on strict liability as well.

---

6. *Turner v. General Motors Corp.,* 514 S.W.2d 497 (Tex. Civ.App. 1974).

The percentage of total national income devoted to tort costs is higher in the United States than anywhere else on earth. It is five times what it is in Canada, France, Britain, and Japan. The cost of liability insurance alone is fifteen times higher than in Japan and twenty times higher than in European nations. While tort costs in other nations have remained relatively stable, they have risen dramatically in the United States. For example, medical malpractice costs soared from $1.1 billion in 1978 to $4.2 billion in 1987. Then these costs dropped by $100 million in 1988 and have since continued to fall a little each year. As a consequence, some of the nation's largest underwriters of medical malpractice coverage dropped their rates.

Tort litigation and insurance to protect against tort liability have proved increasingly costly to manufacturers. In 1970 there were seven multimillion-dollar verdicts in tort cases; it is estimated that there will have been six hundred in 1992. As mentioned in the chapter text, tort liability has gone to such an extreme in some areas that even when a company proves that it could not have provided a product to an injured party, it can nonetheless be forced to pay part of the award under a theory of liability sharing.[a] While the costs associated with tort litigation may be assumed to be borne by manufacturers, ultimately these costs fall on consumers. Consider, for example, that approximately 20 percent of the cost of a $40 stepladder goes to insurance. Because federal, state, and local governments are increasingly the objects of lawsuits, taxpayers also find themselves paying for tort litigation.

Caps on Noneconomic Damages

Noneconomic damages traditionally have been awarded in personal-injury actions for the pain and suffering associated with physical injuries. Such damages are also recovered in wrongful-death actions brought by spouses or family members for the pain and suffering and loss of consortium (companionship) associated with the untimely death of loved ones.

Reform measures in state legislatures have sought not to bar recovery of noneconomic damages but rather to limit the extent of damage awards. The state caps range from $100,000 to $1,000,000. The types of lawsuits in which the caps are applied are also restricted. For example, caps in California are applied only to negligence and

---

a. *Hymowitz v. Eli Lilly and Co.,* 73 N.Y.2d 487, 539 N.E.2d 1069, 541 N.Y.S.2d 941 (1989).

malpractice actions involving health-care providers and other professionals, such as lawyers. Because juries are not allowed to know about the caps, if the jury award exceeds the legislative cap, the judge is required to reduce the award by a procedure known as *remittitur.*

Although some state cap laws have been challenged as unconstitutional, more states are imposing such legislative limits in an attempt at tort reform.

Pending Federal Reform Legislation

Approximately 20,000 companies are named as lead defendants in product liability suits each year, and they are subject to a product liability system consisting of different, changing, and often conflicting state product liability laws. To establish consistency, some have argued for federal legislation creating uniform product liability laws. A bill that has been reintroduced on several occasions is the Product Liability Reform Act, sponsored by Senator Robert W. Kasten, Jr., of Wisconsin. If such a bill were enacted, it would supersede state laws on virtually all established issues. Here are some of the provisions of the pending federal tort reform legislation:

■ A two-year statute of limitations after the injury occurs.

- A twenty-five-year statute of repose.
- A requirement that a party rejecting settlement must pay part of the other party's attorneys' fees if the final judgment is not better than the settlement offer.
- A requirement that to obtain punitive damages, a claimant must prove conscious and flagrant indifference to the safety of those harmed by the product.
- A limitation on manufacturers' liability in lawsuits involving products that were approved by the Food and Drug Administration (FDA) or the Federal Aviation Administration (FAA) prior to distribution.
- The elimination of joint and several liability (sometimes called "deep pocket" liability) for noneconomic damages, making each defendant liable only according to its share of responsibility for harm.

Some tort reform advocates recommend that all product liability cases at the state court level be reviewed by federal judges. Occasionally, during the reviewing process, the federal judiciary could proclaim a broad new principle or correct a particularly bad state decision. One tort reform proponent suggests that manufacturers be allowed to disclaim liability in certain states. If a manufacturer does not want to take a chance in a state notorious for its high

product liability awards, it could stamp on its product "not for sale or use in _____" (with the blank filled in with the appropriate state name). If passed at the federal level, such tort reform legislation would allow manufacturers to escape state laws.

Finally, many tort reformers want to put a limit on lawyers' contingency fees—fees that are based on a percentage of the final awards. Personal injury and product liability attorneys, among others, have vociferously argued against such a reform, however.

■ Implications for the Businessperson

1. If one tort reform suggested above—the limitation on lawyers' contingency fees—is instituted, the number of suits brought against business firms and professionals may decline. This would obviously benefit businesspersons and business profit margins.
2. If the continuing trend toward capping punitive damages and noneconomic damages continues, liability insurance rates will fall, and this too will have a beneficial effect on business firms.
3. If the proposed federal Product Liability Reform Act is passed in its current form, businesses may still face punitive damages in product liability suits, but such damages will be harder for plaintiffs to

obtain and will be automatically limited for products approved by the FDA and the FAA.

■ For Critical Analysis

1. Limiting or eliminating attorneys' contingency fees may seem a step in the right direction, at least for beleaguered manufacturers and professionals. On the other hand, the benefit of a contingency-fee system is that it motivates attorneys to take on cases that poorer plaintiffs might not otherwise be able to pay for. On balance, then, will a limitation on contingency fees benefit the nation as a whole?
2. Under the proposed federal tort reform bill, damages awarded for injuries caused by FDA-approved products would be limited. Yet according to one study by consumer groups, over 1,300 deaths and thousands of life-threatening illnesses and permanent injuries have resulted from the use of products approved by the FDA. In view of the fact that FDA approval does not infallibly ensure that a product is safe, is it fair to allow manufacturers to use FDA approval as a defense? A similar question might be raised concerning FAA-certified aircraft.

■ CONCEPT SUMMARY 11.1 Comparison of Negligence and Strict Liability in the Area of Product Liability

	Negligence	Strict Liability
Applicability	All products.	Products dangerously defective in design or manufacture.
Basic test	Considering all of the circumstances, was reasonable care exercised?	Is there a defect making the product unreasonably dangerous?[a]
Elements	1. Duty of care. 2. Breach of the duty. 3. Breach causes injury or damage.	1. Unreasonably dangerous defect. 2. Defect causes[b] injury or damage.[c]

Defenses	1. Exercise of reasonable care.
	2. Intervening or superseding event caused injury or damage.
	3. Claimant unreasonably assumed risk.
	4. Claimant was also negligent:
	  a. Contributory-negligence jurisdiction—absolute defense.
	  b. Comparative-negligence jurisdiction—damages apportioned.
		1. Defect did not exist when product was in defendant's hands.
		2. Claimant misused product in an unforeseeable way.
		3. Claimant unreasonably assumed risk.
		4. Claimant was also negligent:[d]
		  a. Contributory-negligence jurisdiction—absolute defense.
		  b. Comparative-negligence jurisdiction—damages apportioned.

a. As mentioned, some jurisdictions do not require that a defect render a product unreasonably dangerous.
b. In a few jurisdictions, under the crashworthiness doctrine, the defect need not have caused the accident that resulted in an injury. It need only have increased the extent of the injury.
c. Some jurisdictions limit awards to cases involving personal injuries. A few jurisdictions permit recovery of economic losses.
d. This defense is available in only a few states.

■ Terms and Concepts to Review

■ Questions and Case Problems

11-1. Susan buys a television set manufactured by Quality TV Appliance, Inc. She is going on vacation, so she takes the set to her mother's house for her mother to use. Because the set is defective, it explodes, causing considerable damage to her mother's house. Susan's mother sues Quality for the damages to her house. Discuss the theories under which Susan's mother can recover from Quality.

11-2. Perfect Drug Co. manufactures and has placed on the market a drug for airsickness. Jacob purchases the drug from Green's Drug Store. Jacob is going on a trip and takes two of the tablets as directed. Jacob loses consciousness because of the side effects of the drug, and he falls down a flight of stairs at the airport, breaking an arm and a leg. Perfect knew of the possible side effects but did not place any warning on the label. Also, it is learned that Perfect failed to meet minimum federal drug standards in the manufacture of the drug—standards that would have reduced the side effects. Jacob wants to file an action based on Perfect's negligence.

(a) Discuss Jacob's burden of proof.
(b) Discuss how the situation would be different if a warning had been placed on the package and minimum standards had been met.

11-3. Colt manufactures a new pistol. Firing of the pistol is dependent on an enclosed high-pressure device. The pistol has been thoroughly tested in two laboratories in the Midwest, and it has been designed and manufactured according to current technology. Wayne purchases one of the new pistols from Hardy's Gun and Rifle Emporium. When he uses the pistol in the high altitude of the Rockies, the difference in pressure causes the pistol to misfire, resulting in serious injury to Wayne. Colt can prove that all due care was used in the manufacturing process, and it refuses to pay for Wayne's injuries. Discuss Colt's liability in tort.

11-4. Baxter manufactures electric hair dryers. Julie purchases a Baxter dryer from her local Ace Drug Store. Green, a friend and guest in Julie's home, has taken a shower and wants to dry her hair. Julie tells Green to use the new Baxter hair dryer that she has just purchased. As Green plugs in the dryer, sparks fly out from the motor and continue to do so as she operates it. Despite this, Green begins drying her hair. Suddenly, the entire dryer ignites into flames, severely burning Green's scalp. Green sues Baxter on the basis of the torts of negligence and strict liability. Baxter admits the dryer was defective but denies liability, particularly because Green did not purchase the dryer. Discuss the validity of any defense claimed by Baxter.

11-5. Gina is standing on a street corner waiting for a ride to work. Barney has just purchased a new car manufactured by Optimal Motors. Barney is driving down the street when suddenly the steering mechanism breaks, causing him to run over Gina. Gina suffers permanent injuries. Barney's total income per year has never exceeded $15,000. Gina files suit against Optimal under the theory of strict liability in tort. Optimal pleads no liability because (1) due care was used in the manufacture of the car, (2) Optimal is not the manufacturer of the steering mechanism (Smith is), and (3) the Restatement governing strict liability applies only to users or consumers, and Gina is neither. Discuss the validity of the defenses claimed by Optimal.

11-6. Ryder Truck Rental, Inc., leased one of its trucks to Gagliardi Brothers, Inc. While the truck was being operated by one of Gagliardi's employees in the scope of his employment, the brakes failed. The truck struck one car, which then collided with a car driven by Martin. Martin's car was damaged and she received injuries. If Martin wishes to sue Ryder, can she bring her suit under the theory of strict liability? Explain. [*Martin v. Ryder Truck Rental, Inc.,* 353 A.2d 581 (Del. 1976)]

11-7. Ford Motor Co. manufactured and distributed the Ford Cortina, which had only a cardboard shield separating the fuel tank from the passenger compartment. Nanda suffered severe disabling burns when the gas tank in his car exploded on being struck in the rear by another car. In a strict liability action by Nanda against Ford Motor Co., Nanda argued that the absence of a fire wall or metal shield between the fuel tank and passenger compartment constituted an unreasonably dangerous defect in the product and that his injuries were caused by this defect. What was the result? Discuss. [*Nanda v. Ford Motor Co.,* 509 F.2d 213 (7th Cir. 1974)]

11-8. A two-year-old child lost his leg when he became entangled in a grain auger on his grandfather's farm. The auger had a safety guard that prevented any item larger than 4⅝ inches from coming into contact with the machine's moving parts. The child's foot was smaller than the openings in the safety guard. Was such an injury reasonably foreseeable? Discuss. [*Richelman v. Kewanee Machinery & Conveyor Co.,* 59 Ill.App.3d 578, 375 N.E.2d 885, 16 Ill.Dec. 778 (1978)]

11-9. During the 1960s, Aluminum Co. of America (Alcoa) designed, patented, manufactured, and marketed a closure system for applying aluminum caps to carbonated soft-drink bottles. In 1969, Alcoa sold a capping machine to Houston 7-Up Bottling Co. On June 3, 1976, James Alm suffered a severe eye injury when an aluminum bottle cap exploded off a thirty-two-ounce bottle of 7-Up that had come from the Houston 7-Up Bottling Co. Alm sued Alcoa, alleging that, as the manufacturer, Alcoa had a duty to warn consumers of the dangers of a possible bottle-cap explosion. Alcoa argued that it had not had a duty to warn Alm because it had not manufactured or sold any component part or the final product that injured Alm. Alcoa had mentioned possible cap explosions in the machine users' manual, wall charts, and technical information that it had provided to the Houston 7-Up Bottling Co. Which allegation is correct? Explain. [*Alm v. Aluminum Co. of America,* 717 S.W.2d 588 (Tex. 1986)]

11-10. Odell Kennedy was employed by the Georgetown Ice Co. to operate ice-making machinery. Ice was carried up a conveyer from the machine to a freezer for storage, and when the ice became stuck, employees had to climb onto a catwalk over the conveyer to dislodge it. In July 1976, Odell's arm was pulled off when he was accidentally pulled into the conveyer. The accident would not have occurred if protective shields had been incorporated over the top of the machine. The machinery involved in the accident was designed and installed by Custom Ice Equipment Co., and the catwalk was made by Odell's employer, Georgetown. Odell sued Custom for negligently designing the machine in a way that failed to take into account foreseeable dangers and on the basis of strict liability in tort. Discuss whether Odell should succeed against Custom on the theory that Custom should have foreseen that users of the machines would add catwalks or similar devices. [*Kennedy v. Custom Ice Equipment Co.,* 271 S.C. 171, 246 S.E.2d 176 (1978)]

11-11. Frances Ontai entered the Straub Clinic and Hospital to have an x-ray examination of the colon. Ontai was placed in a vertical position on a table manufactured by General Electric. The footrest on the table broke, and Ontai fell to the floor of the examination room, suffering injuries. Ontai filed suit against Straub and General Electric. Ontai's suit against General Electric was based on strict liability in tort, negligence, and implied warranties. Discuss briefly each of these theories of liability. [*Ontai v. Straub Clinic and Hospital, Inc.,* 66 Hawaii 237, 659 P.2d 734 (1983)]

11-12. A Question of Ethics

William Mackowick, who had worked as an electrician for thirty years, was installing high-voltage capacitors in a switchgear room in a hospital when he noticed that a fellow electrician had removed the cover from an existing capacitor manufactured by Westinghouse Electric Corp. Westinghouse had placed a warning label inside the cover of the metal box containing the capacitor on which users were instructed to ground the electricity before handling. Nothing was said on the label about the propensity of electricity to "arc." (Arcing occurs when electricity grounds itself by "jumping" to a nearby object or instrument.) Mackowick walked over to warn the other electrician of the danger associated with the exposed capacitor, and, while talking, pointed his screwdriver toward the capacitor box. The electricity flowing through the fuses arced to the screwdriver and sent a high-voltage electric current through Mackowick's body. As a result, he sustained severe burns and was unable to return to work for three months. Discuss. [Mackowick v. Westinghouse Electric Corp., 575 A.2d 100 (Pa. 1990)]

  1. An appellate court held that even though the manufacturer did not include with its capacitor a warning about arcing, the product was not defective for failure to warn of inherent product dangers. The rationale of the court was that the product would only be used by experienced electricians who would be aware of the dangers of arcing. Was this a reasonable assumption?
  2. Is it ethical for a company not to include such a warning if it is even remotely possible that an inexperi-

enced user of the product would not understand its inherent dangers?

11-13. Case Briefing Assignment

Examine Case A.11 [Bernal v. Richard Wolf Medical Instruments Corp., 221 Cal.App.3d 1326, 272 Cal.Rptr. 41 (1990)] in Appendix A. The case has been excerpted there in great detail. Review and then brief the case, making sure that you include answers to the following questions in your brief.

  1. What product malfunction brought about this product liability suit?
  2. What instructions did the trial court judge give the jury on the design-defect issue, and why did they become the central issue on appeal?
  3. According to the appellate court, which party bore the burden of proving that a safer alternative design was feasible, the plaintiff or the defendant?
  4. Why did the appellate court state that it "would not hesitate to affirm the jury's verdict" if correct instructions had been given to the jury?

Chapter 12

Creditor-Debtor Relations and Bankruptcy

Normally, creditors have no problem collecting the debts owed to them. But when disputes arise over the amount owed, or when the debtor simply cannot or will not pay, what happens then? What remedies are available to creditors when debtors default? And what laws assist and protect debtors? The first part of this chapter provides the answers to these questions. It deals with the various rights and remedies available through statutory laws, common law, and contract law to assist the debtor and creditor in resolving their disputes without the debtor's having to resort to bankruptcy. The second part of this chapter discusses bankruptcy as a last resort in resolving debtor-creditor problems.

▪ Laws Assisting Creditors

Numerous laws create rights and remedies for creditors. We discuss many of them in this section.

Mechanic's Lien on Real Property

When a person contracts for labor, services, or material to be furnished for the purpose of making improvements on real property but does not immediately pay for the improvements, a creditor can place a **mechanic's lien** on the property. This creates a special debtor-creditor relationship wherein the real estate itself becomes security for the debt.

For example, a painter agrees to paint a house for a homeowner for an agreed-on price to cover labor and materials. If the homeowner cannot pay or pays only a portion of the charges, a mechanic's lien against the property can be created. The painter is the lienholder, and the real property is encumbered with a mechanic's lien for the amount owed. If the homeowner does not pay the lien, the property can be sold to satisfy the debt. Notice of the foreclosure and sale must be given to the debtor in advance, however, and the time period within which a mechanic's lien must be filed is normally limited to 60 to 120 days from the last date labor or materials were provided. State law governs mechanics' liens.

Artisan's Lien on Personal Property

An **artisan's lien** is a security device that secures payment of a debt for labor done on, for value added to, or for care provided for personal property. Like the mechanic's lien on real property, the artisan's lien on personal property creates a debtor-creditor relationship. Personal property subject to an artisan's lien serves as collateral for a debt owed to the artisan. Suppose, for example, Cindy leaves her diamond ring at the jeweler's to be repaired and to have her initials engraved on the band. In the absence of an agreement, the jeweler can keep the ring until Cindy pays for the services that the jeweler provides. Should Cindy fail to pay, the jeweler has a lien on Cindy's ring for the amount of the bill and can sell the ring in satisfaction of the lien.

An artisan's lien is a *possessory lien*. The lienholder ordinarily must have retained possession of the property and have expressly or impliedly agreed to provide the services on a cash, not a credit, basis. Usually, the lienholder retains possession of the property. When this occurs, the lien remains in existence as long as the lienholder maintains possession and is terminated once possession is voluntarily surrendered—unless the surrender is only temporary. If it is a temporary surrender, there must be an agreement that the property will be returned to the lienholder. Even with such an agreement, if a third party obtains rights in that property while it is out of the possession of the lienholder, the lien is lost. The only way a lienholder can protect a lien and surrender possession at the same time is to record notice of the lien in accordance with state lien and recording statutes.

Modern statutes permit the holder of an artisan's lien to foreclose and sell the property subject to the lien to satisfy payment of the debt. As with the mechanic's lien, the lienholder is required to give notice to the owner of the property prior to foreclosure and selling. The sale proceeds are used to pay the debt and the costs of the legal proceedings, and the surplus, if any, is paid to the former owner.

Can towing and storage services give rise to an artisan's lien? The court deals with this issue in the following case.

Case 12.1

**CHRYSLER CREDIT
CORP. v. KEELING**

Missouri Court of Appeals,
1990.
793 S.W.2d 222.

BACKGROUND AND FACTS   *Chrysler Credit Corporation had a security interest in a 1988 Dodge pickup that had been purchased by Robert Keeling. When Keeling defaulted on his payments, Chrysler attempted to repossess the vehicle but could not locate it for some time. Finally, the pickup was found in a lot operated by Joe Booth, doing business as Highway Tow Service. Booth had towed the pickup from an apartment complex parking lot to Booth's lot at the request of the apartment manager and had stored the pickup on his auto lot for over two months. Chrysler requested that Booth deliver possession of the car to Chrysler, but Booth refused to do so until he was paid for the towing ($50) and storage ($1,235) services. Chrysler then sued Booth to gain possession of the pickup. Booth contended that he had an artisan's lien on the truck, and that under Missouri law, the common law artisan's lien took priority over Chrysler's perfected security interest. The trial court held for Chrysler, and Booth appealed.*

TURNAGE, Presiding Judge.
    *   *   *   *

Booth is correct that the common law artisan's lien has not been abrogated by statute as held by this court in [a previous case]. The difficulty with Booth's contention is that the artisan's lien is only for one who furnishes labor or materials in the repair of a vehicle. Here, Booth makes no claim that he furnished labor or materials for the repair of the pickup. He makes some claim that towing the vehicle constituted a basis for an artisan's lien, but it is apparent that towing a vehicle does not constitute the furnishing of labor or materials for the repair of a vehicle. Under the facts here Booth did not have a common law artisan's lien.

Booth's claim is for towing and storage. At common law there was no lien for storage. Thus, Booth did not have a common law lien for storage.

What Booth did have was a statutory lien for storage under [Section] 430.020 [a Missouri statute] which provides that every person who stores any vehicle shall have a lien for the amount due. Section 430.040.1 provides that no person shall have the right to take any vehicle out of the possession of any person who has a storage lien without paying the amount lawfully due.

Booth conveniently overlooks [Section] 430.040.2 which provides that a storage lien shall not take precedence over or be superior to any prior lien duly perfected in accordance with the laws of this state without the written consent of the holder of such prior lien.

The appellate court affirmed the trial court's holding that Chrysler was entitled to possession of the pickup. Although under Missouri law, an artisan's lien would be superior to a duly perfected security interest, such as Chryler's, Booth did not have an artisan's lien because he had furnished no labor or materials for the repair of the vehicle.

DECISION AND REMEDY

Writ of Execution

A debt must be past due for a creditor to commence legal action against a debtor. If the creditor is successful in such a legal action, the court awards the creditor a judgment against the debtor (usually for the amount of the debt plus any interest and legal costs incurred in obtaining the judgment). Attorneys' fees are not included in this amount unless provided for by statute or contract.

Frequently, the creditor finds it easy to secure a judgment against the debtor but nevertheless fails to collect the awarded amount. If the debtor will not or cannot pay the judgment, the creditor is entitled to go back to the court and obtain a *writ of execution*, which is an order, usually issued by the clerk of the court, directing the sheriff to seize (levy) and sell any of the debtor's nonexempt[1] real or personal property that is within the court's geographic jurisdiction (usually the county in which the courthouse is located). The proceeds of the sale are used to pay off the judgment and the costs of the sale. Any excess is paid to the debtor. The debtor can pay the judgment and redeem the nonexempt property any time before the sale takes

place. (Because statutes exempt certain property from seizure, however, and because bankruptcy laws supersede and often limit creditors' remedies when a debtor is declared bankrupt, many judgments are virtually uncollectible.)

Attachment

Attachment is a court-ordered seizure and taking into custody of property prior to the securing of a judgment for a past-due debt. Attachment rights are created by state statutes. A *prejudgment* remedy, attachment occurs either at the time of or immediately after the commencement of a lawsuit, but before the entry of a final judgment. By statute, the restrictions and requirements concerning a creditor's right to attach property before judgment are very specific and limited. In addition to the statutory limitations, the due process clause of the Fourteenth Amendment to the Constitution limits the courts' power to authorize seizure of a debtor's property without notice to the debtor or a hearing on the facts. In recent years, a number of state attachment laws have been held to be unconstitutional.

To use attachment as a remedy, the creditor must have an enforceable right to payment of the debt under law and must follow certain procedures. Otherwise, the creditor can be liable for damages

---

1. Under specific statutory provisions certain types of property are exempted from seizure. The subject of exemptions is discussed later in the chapter.

for wrongful attachment. He or she must file with the court an affidavit stating that the debtor is in default and stating the statutory grounds under which attachment is sought. A bond must be posted by the creditor to cover at least court costs, the value of the loss of use of the good suffered by the debtor, and the value of the property attached. When the court is satisfied that all the requirements have been met, it issues a *writ of attachment*, which is similar to a writ of execution in that it directs the sheriff or other officer to seize nonexempt property. If the creditor prevails at trial, the seized property can be sold to satisfy the judgment.

Garnishment

Garnishment is similar to attachment except that it is a collection remedy that is directed not at the debtor but at the debtor's property or rights held by a third person. The third person, the garnishee, owes a debt to the debtor or has property that belongs to the debtor, such as wages or a bank account. Typically, a garnishment judgment will be served on a person's employer so that part of the person's usual paycheck will be paid to the creditor.

Both federal laws and state laws limit the amount of money that can be garnished from a debtor's weekly take-home pay.[2] Federal law provides a minimal framework to protect debtors from losing all their income to pay judgment debts.[3] State laws also provide dollar exemptions, and these amounts are often larger than those provided by federal law. State and federal statutes can be applied together to help create a pool of funds sufficient to enable a debtor to continue to provide for family needs while also reducing the amount of the judgment debt in a reasonable way. Under federal law, garnishment of an employee's wages for any one indebtedness cannot be grounds for dismissal of an employee.

The legal proceeding for a garnishment action is governed by state law. As a result of a garnish-

ment proceeding, the debtor's employer is ordered by the court to turn over a portion of the debtor's wages to pay the debt. Garnishment operates differently from state to state, however. According to the laws in some states, the judgment creditor needs to obtain only one order of garnishment which will then continuously apply to the judgment debtor's weekly wages until the entire debt is paid. In other states, the judgment creditor must go back to court for a separate order of garnishment for each pay period.

Foreclosure

Mortgage holders have the right to foreclose on mortgaged property in the event of a debtor's default. The usual method of **foreclosure** is by judicial sale of the property, although the statutory methods of foreclosure vary from state to state. If the proceeds of the foreclosure sale are sufficient to cover both the costs of the foreclosure and the mortgaged debt, any surplus is received by the debtor. If the sale proceeds are insufficient to cover the foreclosure costs and the mortgaged debt, however, the mortgagee (the creditor-lender) can seek to recover the difference from the mortgagor (the debtor) by obtaining a **deficiency judgment** representing the difference between the mortgaged debt and the amount actually received from the proceeds of the foreclosure sale. A deficiency judgment is obtained in a separate legal action that is pursued subsequent to the foreclosure action. It entitles the creditor to recover from other nonexempt property owned by the debtor.

■ Suretyship and Guaranty

When a third person promises to pay a debt owed by another in the event the debtor does not pay, either a *suretyship* or *guaranty* relationship is created. The third person's credit becomes the security for the debt owed.

Suretyship

A contract of strict suretyship is a promise made by a third person to be responsible for the debtor's obligation. It is an express contract between the **surety** and the creditor. The surety, in the strictest sense, is *primarily* liable for the debt of the principal. The creditor can demand payment from the

2. Some states (for example, Texas) do not usually permit garnishment of wages by private parties except under a child-support order.
3. For example, the federal Consumer Credit Protection Act, 15 U.S.C. Section 1601 *et seq.*, provides that a debtor can retain either 75 percent of the disposable earnings per week or the sum equivalent to thirty hours of work paid at federal minimum wage rates, whichever is greater.

surety from the moment that the debt is due. A suretyship contract is not a form of indemnity; that is, it is not merely a promise to make good any loss that a creditor may incur as a result of the debtor's failure to pay. The creditor need not exhaust all legal remedies against the principal debtor before holding the surety responsible for payment. Moreover, a surety agreement does not have to be in writing to be enforceable, although it usually is.

For example, Robert Delmar wants to borrow money from the bank to buy a used car. Because Robert is still in college, the bank will not lend him the money unless his father, Joseph Delmar, who has dealt with the bank before, will cosign the note. When Mr. Delmar cosigns the note, he becomes primarily liable to the bank. On the note's due date the bank has the option to seek payment from either Robert or Joseph Delmar, or both jointly.

Guaranty

A **guaranty** contract is similar to a suretyship contract in that it includes a promise to answer for the debt or default of another. With a suretyship arrangement, however, the surety is primarily liable for the debtor's obligation. With a guaranty arrangement, the guarantor—the person making the guaranty—is *secondarily* liable. The guarantor can be required to pay the obligation only after the debtor defaults, and then usually only after the creditor has made an attempt to collect from the principal debtor.

For example, a closely held corporation, BX Enterprises, needs to borrow money to meet its payroll. The bank is skeptical about the creditworthiness of BX and requires Dawson, its president, who is a wealthy businessperson and owner of 70 percent of BX Enterprises, to sign an agreement making himself personally liable for payment if BX does not pay off the loan. As a guarantor of the loan, Dawson cannot be held liable until BX Enterprises is in default.

A guaranty contract between the guarantor and creditor must be in writing to be enforceable unless the *main-purpose* exception applies. Briefly, this exception provides that if the main purpose of the guaranty agreement is to benefit the guarantor, then the contract need not be in writing to be enforceable.

The guaranty contract terms determine the extent and time of the guarantor's liability. For example, a guaranty can be *continuing,* designed to cover a series of transactions by the debtor. Also, the guaranty can be *unlimited* or *limited* as to time and amount. In addition, the guaranty can be *absolute,* in which case the guarantor becomes liable immediately on the debtor's default, or *conditional,* in which case the guarantor becomes liable only on the happening of a certain event in addition to the debtor's default.

Defenses of Sureties and Guarantors

The defenses of sureties and guarantors are basically the same. Therefore, the following discussion applies to both. A creditor is obligated to try to prevent certain actions that would release the surety from the obligation. For example, any material change in the terms of the original contract between the principal debtor and the creditor, including the awarding of a *binding* extension of time for making payment, made without the consent of the surety, will discharge the surety either completely or to the extent that the surety suffers a loss.

A release of the principal debtor without the surety's consent releases the surety unless the creditor expressly reserves his or her rights against the surety. A release *with a reservation* is treated as a covenant not to sue rather than a release.

Naturally, if the principal obligation is paid by the debtor or by another person on behalf of the debtor, the surety is discharged from the obligation. Similarly, if valid tender of payment is made, and the creditor for some reason rejects it with knowledge of the surety's existence, then the surety is released from any obligation on the debt.

Most, but not all, defenses available to a principal debtor can be used by the surety to avoid liability on the obligation to the creditor; the defenses that cannot be used are incapacity or bankruptcy of the debtor and the statute of limitations. The ability of the surety to assert the defenses of the debtor against the creditor is the most important concept in suretyship because most of the defenses available to the surety are those of the debtor.

Obviously, a surety may have his or her own defenses—for example, incapacity or bankruptcy of the surety. Another defense is that the creditor fraudulently induced the surety to guarantee the debt of the debtor. In most states, the creditor has a legal duty to inform the surety, prior to the formation of the suretyship contract, of material facts known by the creditor that would materially increase the surety's risk. Failure to so inform is fraud and makes the suretyship obligation voidable.

In addition, if a creditor surrenders or impairs the debtor's collateral while knowing of the surety and without the surety's consent, the surety is released to the extent of any loss that would be suffered from the creditor's actions. The primary reason for this is to protect the surety who agreed to become obligated only because the debtor's collateral was in the possession of the creditor.

Rights of Sureties and Guarantors

The rights of the surety and guarantor are basically the same. Therefore, again, the following discussion applies to both. When the surety pays the debt owed to the creditor, the surety is entitled to certain rights. First, the surety has the legal **right of subrogation.** Simply stated, this means that any right the creditor had against the debtor now becomes the right of the surety. Included are creditor rights in bankruptcy, rights to collateral possessed by the creditor, and rights to judgments secured by the creditor. In short, the surety now stands in the shoes of the creditor and may pursue any remedies that were available to the creditor against the debtor.

Second, the surety has a **right of reimbursement** from the debtor. This right stems either from the suretyship contract or from equity. Basically, the surety is entitled to receive from the debtor all outlays made on behalf of the suretyship arrangement. Such outlays can include expenses incurred as well as the actual amount of the debt paid to the creditor. Third, in the case of *co-sureties* (two or more sureties on the same obligation owed by the debtor), a surety who pays more than his or her proportionate share on a debtor's default is entitled to recover from the co-sureties the amount paid above the surety's obligation. This is the **right of contribution.** Generally, a co-surety's liability either is determined by agreement or, in the absence of agreement, is set at the maximum liability under the suretyship contract.

Assume that two co-sureties are obligated under a suretyship contract to guarantee the debt of a debtor. One surety's maximum liability is $15,000, and the other's is $10,000. The debtor owes $10,000 and is in default. The surety with the $15,000 maximum liability pays the creditor the entire $10,000. In the absence of agreement, this surety can recover $4,000 from the other surety—($10,000/$25,000) x $10,000 = $4,000.

■ Protection for Debtors

In most states, certain types of real and personal property are exempt from levy of execution or attachment. Numerous consumer protection statutes and rules provide special protection for debtors.

Exemptions

Probably the most familiar of the exemptions is the **homestead exemption.** Each state permits the debtor to retain the family home, either in its entirety or up to a specified dollar amount, free from the claims of unsecured creditors or trustees in bankruptcy.[4] The purpose is to ensure that the debtor will retain some form of shelter.

Suppose that Van Cleave owes Goodwin $40,000. The debt is the subject of a lawsuit, and the court awards Goodwin a judgment of $40,000 against Van Cleave. The homestead of Van Cleave is valued at $50,000. There are no outstanding mortgages or other liens on his homestead. To satisfy the judgment debt, Van Cleave's family home is sold at public auction for $45,000. Assume the homestead exemption is $25,000. The proceeds of the sale are distributed as follows:

1. Van Cleave is given $25,000 as his homestead exemption.
2. Goodwin is paid $20,000 toward the judgment debt, leaving a $20,000 deficiency judgment (that is, "leftover debt") that can be satisfied (paid) from any other nonexempt property (personal or real) that Van Cleave may have, if allowed by state law.

In a few states, statutes permit the homestead exemption only if the judgment debtor has a family.

---

4. A *trustee in bankruptcy* is appointed to collect and reduce to money the property of a debtor going through bankruptcy proceedings. Bankruptcy trustees are discussed more fully below.

The policy behind this type of statute is to protect the family. If a judgment debtor does not have a family, a creditor may be entitled to collect the full amount realized from the sale of the debtor's home.

State exemption statutes usually include both real and personal property. Personal property that is most often exempt from satisfaction of judgment debts includes:

1. Household furniture up to a specified dollar amount.
2. Clothing and certain personal possessions, such as family pictures or a Bible.
3. A vehicle (or vehicles) for transportation (at least up to a specified dollar amount).
4. Certain classified animals, usually livestock but including pets.
5. Equipment that the debtor uses in a business or trade, such as tools or professional instruments, up to a specified dollar amount.

Laws Providing Special Protection

There are a number of consumer protection statutes and rules that apply to the debtor-creditor relationship. A brief listing and discussion here of some of the most important of these laws will illustrate their breadth and significance.

CONSUMER CREDIT PROTECTION ACT   Commonly known as the *Truth-in-Lending Act,* Title I of the Consumer Credit Protection Act is basically a *disclosure law.* Administered by the Federal Reserve Board, this law requires sellers and lenders to disclose credit terms on loans so that a consumer-debtor can shop around for the best financing arrangements. Essentially, it requires that the creditor clearly indicate to the consumer-debtor what charges are being made for the privilege of paying the debt over a period of time, including the total annual interest percentage rate and finance charges.

UNIFORM CONSUMER CREDIT CODE   In an attempt to make consumer credit laws at the state level uniform, the National Conference of Commissioners on Uniform State Laws proposed legislation called the Uniform Consumer Credit Code (UCCC). Its essential points are as follows:

1. To place statutory ceilings on interest rates and other charges.

2. To require disclosure similar to that required by the Truth-in-Lending Act.
3. To limit garnishment actions against take-home wages to a certain amount and to prohibit discharge of an employee solely because of garnishment proceedings.
4. To allow cancellation of a contract solicited by a seller in the consumer-debtor's home within three business days of the solicitation.
5. To prohibit referral sales, which are sales in which a seller offers a rebate or discount to a buyer for furnishing the names of other prospective purchasers.
6. To provide criminal as well as civil penalties for violations.

Only a handful of states have adopted the UCCC, even though it has undergone numerous drafts. Some other states have passed laws similar to some of the provisions of the UCCC, such as laws concerning home-solicitation sales.

FEDERAL TRADE COMMISSION RULE   In many modern consumer transactions buyers make purchases on credit, taking the seller's good and promising to pay the full debt at a later time. The buyer in such transactions often becomes a debtor by executing a *note*—a promise to pay a definite amount within a certain time. Such notes are often transferred to a third party, who purchases the notes from the seller-creditor and is then entitled to payment on the notes when due. If the person holding the note is deemed to be a *holder in due course* (HDC), then he or she is free of all claims to and most defenses against payment on the note—including those of the buyer-debtor who executed the note. The Federal Trade Commission (FTC) promulgated a rule that limits the rights of an HDC when the buyer-debtor executes a note as part of a consumer transaction. The FTC rule provides basically that any defenses the buyer can assert against the seller can also be asserted against an HDC. The seller is also required to disclose this information clearly to the buyer in its sales agreement.

The rule basically eliminates the use of a buyer's waiver-of-defense clause in a consumer transaction. These clauses waive any claim or defense the debtor might have against a third party who, for example, purchases the buyer's note from the seller.

■ Bankruptcy and Reorganization

The basic law of bankruptcy in the United States is the federal Bankruptcy Code. The Bankruptcy Code has two goals—to protect a debtor by giving him or her a fresh start, free from creditors' claims, and to ensure equitable treatment to creditors who are competing for a debtor's assets.

The United States Constitution confers on Congress the power to establish uniform laws on bankruptcy.[5] When the Constitution vests power over certain matters in the federal government, as it does with respect to bankruptcy law, the federal law on that subject takes precedence over any state law on the same subject. The Constitution also forbids states from enacting laws that impair contractual obligations, which naturally includes contractual obligations between debtors and creditors.[6] But although the Bankruptcy Code is federal law, the Code incorporates much state law regulating matters important in bankruptcy. State laws on secured transactions, liens, judgments, and exemptions, for example, play a significant role in federal bankruptcy proceedings.

Bankruptcy proceedings are held in specialized federal bankruptcy courts. A bankruptcy court's primary function is to hold *core proceedings*[7] dealing with the procedures required to administer the estate of the debtor in bankruptcy. Bankruptcy courts are under the authority of U.S. district courts, and rulings from bankruptcy courts can be appealed to the district courts. Fundamentally, a bankruptcy court fulfills the role of an administrative court for the district court concerning matters in bankruptcy. Decisions on personal injury, wrongful death, and other civil proceedings affecting the debtor are resolved in other federal or state courts.

The remaining sections in this chapter deal with the most frequently used bankruptcy plans allowed under the various chapters of the Bankruptcy Code: Chapter 7 liquidations, Chapter 11 reorganizations, and Chapter 13 plans. The latter two chapters are sometimes referred to as *rehabilitation chapters.* As you read the following sections on bankruptcy,

be sure to keep in mind that references to Chapter 7, Chapter 11, and Chapter 13 are references to chapters contained in the Bankruptcy Code, not references to chapters within this textbook.

Throughout the various chapters of the Bankruptcy Code, a distinction is made between secured and unsecured creditors. A secured creditor is one in whose favor there is a **security interest**—an interest in personal property or fixtures that secures, or serves as collateral for, payment of a debt. Unsecured creditors do not have a security interest in property that serves as collateral to the underlying debt.

Even though a creditor may have a security interest in certain personal property, additional steps must be taken to ensure that the creditor's security interest in collateral takes *priority* over claims made on the collateral by third parties, such as other secured or general creditors, trustees in bankruptcy, and later purchasers of the collateral. A secured creditor establishes priority over such third party claims by taking steps to *perfect* the security interest. Although there are other means of perfecting a security interest, the most common one is by filing with an appropriate public office a *financing statement*, signed by the debtor, describing the collateral and giving the names and addresses of the debtor and the creditor.[8]

As will be seen, because bankruptcy generally occurs when the debtor's obligations exceed the debtor's assets, the priority of claims to the available assets is frequently crucial to the outcome of a bankruptcy proceeding.

Chapter 7 Liquidations

Chapter 7 liquidation is the most familiar type of bankruptcy proceeding and is often referred to as an *ordinary,* or *straight, bankruptcy.* Put simply, debtors in straight bankruptcies state their debts and turn their assets over to trustees. The trustees sell the assets and distribute the proceeds to creditors. With certain exceptions, the remaining debts are then discharged (extinguished), and the debtors

---

5. U.S. Constitution, Article I, Section 8. See Appendix B.
6. U.S. Constitution, Article I, Section 10. See Appendix B.
7. Core proceedings are procedural functions, such as allowance of claims, decisions on preferences, automatic stay proceedings, confirmation of bankruptcy plans, discharge of debts, and so on.

---

8. There are basically three methods of perfection. First, the debtor may transfer possession of the collateral to the secured creditor. Second, the security interest may be perfected automatically at the time of a credit sale (that is, at the moment the security interest is created under a written security agreement). Third, and most commonly, a security interest may be perfected by the creditor's filing a financing statement.

are relieved of their obligation to pay the debts. Any ''person''—defined as including individuals, partnerships, and corporations[9]—may be a debtor under Chapter 7. Under the Bankruptcy Code, however, railroads, insurance companies, banks, savings and loan associations, and credit unions cannot be Chapter 7 debtors. Other chapters of the Bankruptcy Code or federal or state statutes apply to them.

FILING THE PETITION A straight bankruptcy may be commenced by the filing of either a voluntary or an involuntary petition. The distinction pertains to who may institute bankruptcy proceedings; once the process begins, it is essentially the same proceeding regardless of who initiated it by filing a petition.

Voluntary Bankruptcy A voluntary petition is brought by the debtor, who files official forms designated for that purpose in the bankruptcy court. The Code requires a consumer-debtor who has selected Chapter 7 to state in the petition, at the time of filing, that he or she understands the relief available under other chapters and has chosen to proceed under Chapter 7. If the consumer-debtor is represented by an attorney, the attorney must file an affidavit stating that the attorney has informed the debtor of the relief available under each chapter. Anyone who is liable on a claim held by a creditor can do this. The debtor does not even have to be insolvent to file a petition. (The debtor is insolvent when debts exceed fair market value of assets exclusive of exempt property.)

---

9. The definition of *corporation* includes unincorporated companies and associations. It also covers labor unions.

The voluntary petition contains the following schedules:

1. A list of both secured and unsecured creditors, their addresses, and the amount of debt owed to each.
2. A statement of the financial affairs of the debtor.
3. A list of all property owned by the debtor, including property claimed by the debtor to be exempt.
4. A listing of current income and expenses.

The official forms must be completed accurately, sworn to under oath, and signed by the debtor. To conceal assets or knowingly supply false information on these schedules is a crime under the bankruptcy laws. If the voluntary petition for bankruptcy is found to be proper, the filing of the petition will itself constitute an *order for relief.* (An order for relief is a court's grant of assistance to a complainant. In the context of bankruptcy, relief consists of discharging a complainant's debts.) Once a consumer-debtor's voluntary petition has been filed, the clerk of the court (or person directed) must give the trustee and creditors mailed notice of the order of relief not more than twenty days after entry of the order. A new feature allows a husband and wife to file jointly for bankruptcy under a single petition.

As mentioned previously, debtors do not have to be insolvent to file for voluntary bankruptcy. Debtors do not have unfettered access to Chapter 7 bankruptcy proceedings, however, as the following case illustrates.

BACKGROUND AND FACTS *In 1985 Ronald Walton voluntarily petitioned for Chapter 7 bankruptcy. The bankruptcy court ordered a hearing at which it was determined that Walton's monthly income exceeded his monthly expenses by an amount sufficient to pay off at least a substantial portion of his debts under a sixty-month reorganization plan under Chapter 13. (Chapter 13 of the Bankruptcy Code is an alternative to outright liquidation of debt under Chapter 7; under Chapter 13, individuals in certain circumstances are allowed to pay their debts over an extended period of*

Case 12.2

IN RE WALTON[a]

United States Court of Appeals, Eighth Circuit, 1989.
866 F.2d 981.

---

a. *In re* means concerning or regarding. It is a way to refer to a judicial proceeding in which there are no adversary parties but only some thing on which some action is taken—in this case, a debtor's estate in bankruptcy.

time.) Therefore, the court concluded that granting Walton relief under Chapter 7 would constitute substantial abuse of Chapter 7 and dismissed his petition. (Chapter 7 expressly prohibits "substantial abuse" of its provisions, but it does not indicate what constitutes substantial abuse.) Walton argued on appeal, among other things, that Congress intended "substantial abuse" to mean nothing more than "bad faith" and that because he had brought the petition in good faith, he was not abusing Chapter 7 bankruptcy provisions.

BOWMAN, Circuit Judge.
* * * *

Walton argues essentially that Congress intended "substantial abuse" to mean nothing more than "bad faith." Certainly the court may take the petitioner's good faith and unique hardships into consideration under section 707(b) [of the Bankruptcy Code]. But the cramped interpretation of section 707(b) that Walton advances would drastically reduce the bankruptcy courts' ability to dismiss cases filed by debtors who are not dishonest, but who are also not needy. * * * Several sections [of the Bankruptcy Code] enumerate specific abuses, and the absence of a laundry list of abuses in section 707(b) further suggests that the drafters did not intend a narrow interpretation of "substantial abuse." Although the statute does not mandate a future income test, we are satisfied that it does not preclude the consideration of future income in giving meaning to the "substantial abuse" standard.
* * * *

The record establishes that Walton's monthly income is $1,818 and that his monthly expenses total $1,321. The monthly surplus of $497 would yield a yearly surplus of $5,964. The record also establishes that Walton's unsecured debts total $26,484. Thus, Walton could pay off more than two-thirds of his debts under a three-year plan. And in five years Walton's yearly surplus could repay 100 percent of his outstanding unsecured debt. We conclude, as did the District Court, that these facts adequately rebut the statutory presumption in 11 U.S.C. [Section] 707(b) in favor of granting the relief requested by the debtor.

DECISION AND REMEDY   *The appellate court affirmed the lower court's ruling. Permitting Walton to proceed with Chapter 7 bankruptcy, despite reasonable projections that he could pay all or a substantial portion of his debts without undue hardship, would constitute substantial abuse of Chapter 7 bankruptcy law.*

Involuntary Bankruptcy An involuntary bankruptcy occurs when the debtor's creditors force the debtor into bankruptcy proceedings. Such a case cannot be commenced against a farmer[10] or a charitable institution, however. Nor can it be filed unless the following requirements are met: If the debtor has twelve or more creditors, three or more of those having unsecured claims aggregating at least $5,000 must join in the petition. If a debtor has fewer than twelve creditors, one or more creditors having a claim of $5,000 may file.

If the debtor challenges the involuntary petition, a hearing will be held, and the bankruptcy court will enter an order for relief if it finds either of the following:

10. *Farmers* are defined as persons who receive more than 80 percent of their gross income from farming operations, such as tilling the soil, dairy farming, ranching, or the production or raising of crops, poultry, or livestock. Corporations and partnerships can be *farmers* as well as individuals.

1. The debtor is generally not paying debts as they become due.[11]

2. A custodian either was appointed to take charge or took possession of substantially all of the debtor's property within 120 days before the filing of the petition.

If the court grants an order for relief, the debtor will be required to supply the information in the bankruptcy schedules discussed previously.

An involuntary petition should not be used as an everyday debt-collection device, and the Code provides penalties for the filing of frivolous petitions against debtors. Judgment may be granted against the petitioning creditors for the costs and attorneys' fees incurred by the debtor in defending against an involuntary petition that is dismissed by the court. If the petition is filed in bad faith, damages can be awarded for injury to the debtor's reputation. Punitive damages may also be awarded.

AUTOMATIC STAY The filing of a petition, either voluntary or involuntary, operates as an **automatic stay** (suspension) of virtually all litigation and other action by creditors against the debtor or the debtor's property. In other words, once a petition is filed, creditors cannot commence or continue most legal actions against the debtor to recover claims. Nor can creditors take any action to repossess property in the hands of the debtor. A creditor's failure to abide by an automatic stay imposed by the filing of a petition could be costly. If a creditor *knowingly* violates the automatic-stay provision (a willful violation), any party injured is entitled to recover actual damages, costs, and at-torneys' fees and may also be entitled to recover punitive damages. A secured creditor, however, may petition the bankruptcy court for relief from the automatic stay in certain circumstances.

Underlying the Code's automatic-stay provision is a concept known as *adequate protection,* which holds, among other things, that secured creditors are protected from losing their security as a result of the automatic stay. The bankruptcy court can provide adequate protection by requiring the debtor or trustee to make periodic cash payments or a one-time cash payment (or provide additional collateral or replacement liens) to the extent that the stay causes the value of the property involved to decrease. Or the court may grant other relief that is the ''indubitable equivalent'' of the secured party's interest in the property, such as a guaranty by a solvent third party to cover losses suffered by the secured party as a result of the stay.

For example, G&M Trucking owns two trucks in which Middleton Bank has a security interest. G&M Trucking has failed to make its monthly payments for two months. It files a petition in bankruptcy, and the automatic stay prevents Middleton Bank from repossessing the trucks. Meanwhile, the trucks (whose collective value is already less than the balance due) are depreciating at a rate of several hundred dollars a month. Middleton Bank's inability to repossess and immediately resell the trucks is harming the bank to the extent of several hundred dollars per month. The bankruptcy court may prevent Middleton Bank from being harmed by requiring G&M Trucking to make a one-time cash payment or periodic cash payments (or provide additional collateral or replacement liens) to the extent that the trucks are depreciating in value. If the debtor is unable to provide adequate protection, the court may vacate (remove) the stay and allow Middleton Bank to repossess the trucks.

In the following case, a creditor petitioned the bankruptcy court for, and received relief from, the automatic-stay provision of the Bankruptcy Code.

---

11.   The inability to pay debts as they become due is known as *equitable* insolvency. A balance-sheet insolvency, which exists when a debtor's liabilities exceed assets, is not the test. Thus, it is possible for debtors to be thrown into involuntary bankruptcy even though their assets far exceed their liabilities. This situation may occur when a debtor's cash-flow problems become severe.

BACKGROUND AND FACTS *Max McNeely owed Western States Petroleum, Inc., over $130,000. Western sought and received writs of attachment on all of McNeely's real and personal property. Western also caused a writ of garnishment to be directed to McNeely's bank accounts. Because McNeely's total assets amounted to less than $75,000, McNeely sought protection from Western's collection attempts by filing for Chapter 7 bank-*

Case 12.3

IN RE McNEELY
United States Bankruptcy Court,
District of Utah, 1985.
51 Bankr. 816.

ruptcy. By filing for bankruptcy, McNeely was able to prevent Western's execution of its writs of attachment: because of the bankruptcy filing, Western was unable to execute the writs by having McNeely's property seized and sold in satisfaction of the debt. Western petitioned the bankruptcy court to vacate the automatic stay as it applied to the property subject to the writs on the ground that the writs created a valid lien against the property, giving Western the status of a secured creditor.

CLARK, Bankruptcy Judge.
         *   *   *   *

An attachment is a provisional remedy granted to the plaintiff in an action, which enables him to have property of the defendant seized by an officer and held in the custody of the law as security for the satisfaction of any judgment that he may recover. *   *   * The property attached constitutes security for payment of the debt, if the debt is found to exist. An attachment proceeding is essentially a proceeding for the purpose of establishing a lien to aid in the collection of an unsecured debt *   *   *.
         *   *   *   *

*   *   * The facts of this case demonstrate that the debtor cannot provide adequate protection of the creditor's interest.
         *   *   *   *

Rules 64A, 64C, and 64D of the Utah Rules of Civil Procedure were intended to create a method by which an unsecured creditor, under limited circumstances and by way of the prejudgment writs issued by the state court, could obtain a valid lien in the attached property of a defendant to the lawsuit in which the writs were issued. A lien thus obtained is superior to the interest of the bankruptcy trustee.

Whether or not judgment was actually rendered by the state court prior to entry of the order for relief [under the Bankruptcy Code] does not affect the nature of the creditor's lien acquired pursuant to the writs of attachment. On entry of judgment in favor of the plaintiff, the perfected lien relates back to the levy of attachment. The judgment only determines the value of the creditor's interest. In this case, the state court's summary judgment in the sum of $130,607.27 exceeds the value of the collateral, which is less than $75,000.

For these reasons, Western States Petroleum, Inc. is entitled to relief from the automatic stay with respect to the property subject to the state court writs and shall have a lien against the proceeds of the sale by the trustee of any such property, subject, of course, to the claims of the holders of any superior liens.

DECISION AND REMEDY   *The court granted Western relief from the automatic-stay provision, thus making it a secured creditor in the subsequent bankruptcy action. The court concluded that the writs of attachment were valid and that, if Western were not allowed to execute the attachments, then Western would not attain the status of a secured creditor during the bankruptcy proceedings.*

THE TRUSTEE   Promptly after the order for relief in a Chapter 7 proceeding has been entered, an interim or provisional trustee is appointed by the U.S. Trustee (a government official who performs appointing and other administrative tasks that a bankruptcy judge would otherwise have to perform). The interim or provisional trustee presides over the debtor's property until the first meeting of creditors. At this first meeting, either a permanent trustee is elected or the interim trustee becomes the permanent trustee. The trustee's principal duty is to collect and reduce to money the "property of the estate" and to close up the estate as expeditiously as is compatible with the best interests of the parties.

CREDITORS' MEETING Within a reasonable time after the order of relief is granted (not less than ten days or more than thirty days), the bankruptcy court must call a meeting of creditors listed in the schedules filed by the debtor. The bankruptcy judge does not attend this meeting. The debtor is required to attend this meeting (unless excused by the court) and to submit to examination under oath by the creditors and the trustee. Failing to appear when required or making false statements under oath may result in the debtor's being denied a discharge of bankruptcy.

Proof of claims by creditors must normally be filed within ninety days of this meeting.

PROPERTY OF THE ESTATE On commencement of a Chapter 7 proceeding, an *estate in property* is created. The estate consists of all the debtor's legal and equitable interests in property presently held, wherever located, together with community property, property transferred in a transaction voidable by the trustee, proceeds and profits from the property of the estate, and certain other property acquired after the debtor has filed for bankruptcy. Interests in certain property, such as gifts, inheritances, property settlements (divorce), or life insurance death proceeds to which the debtor becomes entitled *within 180 days after filing* may also become part of the estate. Thus, the filing of a bankruptcy petition generally fixes a dividing line: property acquired prior to the filing of the petition becomes property of the estate, and property acquired after the filing of the petition, except as just noted, remains the debtor's.

EXEMPTIONS Any individual debtor is entitled to exempt certain property from the property of the estate. Prior to the enactment of the Bankruptcy Code, state law exclusively governed the extent of the exemptions. Now, however, the Code establishes a federal exemption scheme. An individual debtor (or a husband and wife who file jointly) may choose between the exemptions provided under the applicable state law and the federal exemptions.[12] The Code exempts the following property:

1. Up to $7,500 in equity in the debtor's residence and burial plot.
2. Interest in a motor vehicle up to $1,200.
3. Interest, up to $200 for any particular item, in household goods and furnishings, wearing apparel, appliances, books, animals, crops, or musical instruments (amendments to the code, however, limit an aggregate total of all items to $4,000).
4. Interest in jewelry up to $500.
5. Interest in any other property worth up to $400, plus any unused part of the $7,500 homestead exemption up to an amount of $3,750.[13]
6. Interest, up to $750, in any tools of the debtor's trade.
7. Any unmatured life insurance contract owned by the debtor.
8. Certain interests in accrued dividends or interest under life insurance contracts owned by the debtor.
9. Professionally prescribed health aids.
10. The right to receive Social Security and certain welfare benefits, alimony and support payments, and certain pension benefits.
11. The right to receive certain personal injury and other awards.

POWERS OF THE TRUSTEE The basic duty of the trustee is to collect the debtor's available estate and reduce it to money for distribution, preserving the interests of both the debtor and unsecured creditors. In other words, the trustee is accountable for administering the debtor's estate. To enable the trustee to accomplish this duty, the Code gives him or her certain powers, stated in both general and specific terms.

General powers are described by the statement that the trustee occupies a position *equivalent* in rights to that of other parties. For example, the trustee has the same rights as a *lien creditor* on a simple contract who could have obtained a judicial lien on the debtor's property or who could have levied execution on the debtor's property. This means that a trustee's claims to the debtor's property have priority over the claims of creditors who have only unperfected security interests in the same

---

12. Individual states are given the power to pass legislation precluding the use of the federal exemptions by debtors in their states. A majority of the states permit a debtor to use only state (not federal) exemptions.

13. The Code places a cap of $3,750 on the unused part of the homestead exemption to prevent some debtors from receiving a complete $7,500 windfall.

property. A trustee also has power equivalent to that of a *bona fide purchaser* of real property from the debtor.

In addition, the trustee has specific powers of avoidance—that is, the trustee can set aside a sale or other transfer of the debtor's property, taking it back as a part of the debtor's estate. These powers include any voidable rights available to the debtor, preferences, certain statutory liens, and fraudulent transfers by the debtor. Each is discussed in more detail in the following subsections.

The debtor shares most of the trustee's avoiding powers. Thus, if the trustee does not take action to enforce one of his or her rights (for example, to recover a preference), the debtor in a Chapter 7 bankruptcy is nevertheless able to enforce that right.[14]

The trustee also has the power to require persons holding the debtor's property at the time the petition is filed to deliver the property to the trustee.

Assumption of Rights   A trustee steps into the shoes of the debtor. Thus, any reason that a debtor can use to obtain the return of his or her property can be used by the trustee as well. These grounds include fraud, duress, incapacity, and mutual mistake.

For example, Rob sells his boat to Inga. Inga gives Rob a check, knowing that there are insufficient funds in the bank account to cover the check. Inga has committed fraud. Rob has the right to avoid that transfer and recover the boat from Inga. Once an order for relief has been entered for Rob, the trustee can exercise the same right to recover the boat from Inga, and it becomes part of the debtor's estate.

Preferences   A debtor is not permitted to transfer property or to make a payment that favors—or gives a *preference* to—one creditor over others. Thus, the trustee is allowed to recover such property or payments, whether made voluntarily or involuntarily.

To constitute a preferential transfer of property that can be recovered, the transfer generally must

have been made by an *insolvent* debtor for a *preexisting* debt within ninety days of filing the petition in bankruptcy. The transfer must give the creditor more than he or she would have received in a Chapter 7 liquidation proceeding. The trustee does not have to prove insolvency, as the Code provides that the debtor is presumed to be insolvent during this ninety-day period.

Sometimes the creditor receiving the preference is an *insider,* meaning an individual, partner, partnership, officer, or director of a corporation (or relative of these) who has a close relationship with the debtor. If such is the case, the avoidance power of the trustee is extended to transfers made within one year of the filing of the petition; however, the presumption of insolvency is confined to the ninety-day period, so the trustee must prove the existence of insolvency before that period.

Only transfers involving something other than current consideration can be preferences. Therefore, it is generally assumed by most courts that payment for services rendered within ten to fifteen days prior to the filing of the petition for current consideration is not a preference. If a creditor receives payment in the ordinary course of business, such as payment of last month's telephone bill, the payment cannot be recovered by the trustee in bankruptcy. To be recoverable, a preference must be a transfer for an antecedent debt, such as a year-old telephone bill. In addition, the Code permits a consumer-debtor to transfer any property to a creditor up to a total value of $600 without the transfer constituting a preference.

If a preferred creditor (one benefitting from a preferential transfer) sells the property to an innocent third party, the property cannot be recovered from the innocent party, but the creditor generally can be held accountable for the value of the property.

Liens on Debtor's Property   The trustee is permitted to avoid the fixing of certain statutory liens, such as a landlord's lien, on property of the debtor. Liens that first become effective at the time of the bankruptcy or insolvency of the debtor are voidable by the trustee. Liens that are not perfected or enforceable on the date of the petition against a bona fide purchaser are also voidable.

Fraudulent Transfers   The trustee may avoid fraudulent transfers or obligations if they were

---

14.   Under Chapter 11 (to be discussed later), for which no trustee generally exists, the debtor has the same avoiding powers as a trustee under Chapter 7. Under Chapter 13 (also to be discussed later) a trustee must be appointed.

made within one year of filing the petition or if they were made with actual intent to hinder, delay, or defraud a creditor. Transfers made for less than a reasonably equivalent consideration are also vulnerable if the debtor thereby became insolvent, was left engaged in business with an unreasonably small amount of capital, or intended to incur debts that would be beyond his or her ability to pay.

The following case illustrates fraudulent transfers made by a debtor to his daughters. The transfers involved no consideration, and after the transfer the debtor retained control and derived benefits from the property. The trustee in bankruptcy sought to set aside the transfers, and the creditors and wife of the debtor filed actions to deny the debtor a discharge in bankruptcy.

BACKGROUND AND FACTS *Ralph I. Lazar (the debtor) was sued for wrongful interference with a contractual relationship. Three weeks later, Lazar made the first of several transfers of his assets to his daughters, Arlene and Betty Lazar. One such transfer was his entire interest in a note and mortgage ($180,000), which was paid to his daughters. His daughters deposited the funds in certificates of deposit for approximately four months. The funds were then withdrawn. With these funds, plus $104,000 transferred from his solely owned pension trust fund, Arlene purchased a yacht. Title to the yacht was held by Arbet Enterprises, Inc., a closely held corporation in which the daughters were the sole shareholders. Arbet Enterprises was formed solely to take title to the yacht. The yacht was then sold, a sixty-foot Chris Craft yacht was purchased (with title held by Arbet Enterprises) with half the proceeds, and the remaining funds were deposited to be used by the debtor and his daughters for their support. The debtor used the Chris Craft as his place of residence and for his personal benefit and enjoyment. Ralph Lazar lost the lawsuit for wrongful interference with a contractual relationship, resulting in a judgment against him for $2 million. When the judgment creditors attempted to execute the judgment, Lazar filed a Chapter 7 bankruptcy petition, having stripped himself of his assets by the transfers to his daughters. The trustee filed a claim against Lazar for fraudulent transfer and sought to have the money held by Arbet Enterprises (as Lazar's* alter ego—*second self) and the Chris Craft yacht turned over to the trustee as part of the debtor's estate. The creditors and wife of Lazar filed independent actions seeking to deny him a discharge in bankruptcy due to his fraudulent actions.*

Case 12.4

IN RE LAZAR
United States Bankruptcy Court,
Southern District of Florida,
1988.
81 Bankr. 148.

WEAVER, Bankruptcy Judge.
*   *   *   *
*   *   * The transfers of the Note and Mortgage and the Pension Trust funds described above are marked by several of the ''badges of fraud'' which the Florida courts have identified as factors tending to indicate the presence of a fraudulent transfer. Specifically, the subject transfers were made to family members for no consideration, and after the transfers the debtor retained full control over, and derived the primary benefit from, the use of the funds and the assets subsequently purchased therewith.

The Court finds that the debtor's intent in making the aforesaid transfers, and the legal effect of said transfers, was to hinder, delay and defraud the creditors. Under these circumstances, the trustee has sufficiently proven his claim.
*   *   *   *
As a separate and independent basis for awarding the turnover of the yacht *   *   * to the trustee, this Court finds that the corporation known as Arbet Enter-

prises, Inc. is the alter ego of the debtor. Arbet Enterprises, Inc. was at all times the mere instrumentality of the debtor [that is, completely under the debtor's control], created to aid the debtor in defrauding the creditors and concealing his ownership of [the yachts].

In addition to the trustee's claim, both the creditors and the debtor's spouse filed independent actions seeking to block the discharge of the debtor. These claims were consolidated for trial with the trustee's claim. The objections to the discharge are mainly premised upon the provisions of 11 U.S.C. [Section] 727(a). In connection with the claimed objections to the debtor's discharge, the Court finds that the debtor, with the intent to hinder, delay and defraud the creditors, did engage in the continuous concealment of his assets during the one year period prior to the filing of the bankruptcy petition, which satisfies the requirements of [Section] 727(a)(2) of the Bankruptcy Code.

DECISION AND REMEDY
The court held that the transfers Ralph Lazar made to his daughters were fraudulent and that the trustee could set aside those transfers, which included the yacht and remaining funds. In addition, Lazar was denied the right to receive a discharge in bankruptcy.

CLAIMS OF CREDITORS Generally, any legal obligation of the debtor is a claim. In the case of disputed or unliquidated claims, the bankruptcy court will set the value of the claim. Any creditor holding a debtor's obligation can file a claim against the debtor's estate.

These claims are automatically allowed unless contested by the trustee, debtor, or another creditor. The Code, however, does not allow claims for breach of employment contracts or real estate leases for terms longer than one year. Such claims are limited to one year's rent or wages, despite the remaining length of either contract in breach. Therefore, an employee who has a three-year employment contract that is breached during the first year by the employer's bankruptcy would be limited to damages accruing during one year from the filing of the petition, or from the date the employment contract was repudiated, whichever is earlier.

PROPERTY DISTRIBUTION Creditors, as mentioned, are either secured or unsecured. A *secured* creditor has a security interest in collateral that secures the debt. The Code provides that a consumer-debtor, within thirty days of the filing of a Chapter 7 petition or before the date of the first meeting of the creditors (whichever is first), must file with the clerk a statement of intention with respect to the secured collateral. That intent must state whether the debtor will retain the collateral or surrender it to the secured party.[15]

The trustee is obligated to enforce the debtor's intent within forty-five days after the intent is filed. If the collateral is surrendered to the secured party, the secured creditor can enforce the security interest either by accepting the property in full satisfaction of the debt or by foreclosing on the collateral and using the proceeds to pay off the debt. In this way, the secured party has priority over unsecured parties to the proceeds from the disposition of the collateral. Indeed, the Code provides that if the value of the collateral exceeds the secured party's claim, the secured party also has priority to the proceeds in an amount that will cover reasonable fees and costs incurred because of the debtor's default. Any excess over this amount is used by the trustee to satisfy the claims of unsecured creditors. Should the secured collateral be insufficient to cover the secured debt owed, the secured creditor becomes an unsecured creditor for the difference.

Bankruptcy law establishes an order of priority for classes of debts owed to *unsecured* creditors,

---

15. Also, if applicable, the debtor must specify whether the collateral will be claimed as exempt property and whether the debtor intends to redeem the property or reaffirm the debt secured by the collateral.

and they are paid in the order of their priority. Each class of debt must be fully paid before the next class is entitled to any of the proceeds—if there are sufficient funds to pay the entire class. If not, the proceeds are distributed *proportionately* to each creditor in a class, and all classes lower in priority on the list receive nothing. The order of priority among classes of unsecured creditors is as follows:

1. Administrative expenses—including court costs, trustee fees, and attorneys' fees.
2. In an involuntary bankruptcy, expenses incurred by the debtor in the ordinary course of business from the date of the filing of the petition up to the appointment of the trustee or the issuance by the court of an order for relief.
3. Unpaid wages, salaries, and commissions earned within ninety days of the filing of the petition, limited to $2,000 per claimant. Any claim in excess of $2,000 is treated as a claim of a general creditor (listed as number 8 below).
4. Unsecured claims for contributions to be made to employee benefit plans, limited to services performed during 180 days prior to the filing of the bankruptcy petition and $2,000 per employee.
5. Claims by farmers and fishermen, up to $2,000, against debtor operators of grain storage or fish storage or processing facilities.
6. Consumer deposits of up to $900 given to the debtor before the petition was filed in connection with the purchase, lease, or rental of property that was not received or provided. Any claim in excess of $900 is treated as a claim of a general creditor (listed as number 8 below).
7. Certain taxes and penalties due to government units, such as income and property taxes.
8. Claims of general creditors.

If any amount remains after the priority classes of creditors have been satisfied, it is turned over to the debtor.

In a bankruptcy case in which the debtor has no assets, creditors are notified of the debtor's petition for bankruptcy but are instructed not to file a claim. In such a case, the unsecured creditors will receive no payment, and most, if not all, of these debts will be discharged.

DISCHARGE From the debtor's point of view, the primary purpose of a Chapter 7 liquidation is to obtain a fresh start through the **discharge of debts.**[16] Certain debts, however, are not dischargeable in bankruptcy. Also, certain debtors may not qualify to have all debts discharged in bankruptcy. These situations are discussed below.

Exceptions to Discharge Discharge of a debt may be denied because of the nature of the claim or the conduct of the debtor. Claims that are not dischargeable under Chapter 7 include the following:

1. Claims for back taxes accruing within three years prior to bankruptcy.
2. Claims against property or money obtained by the debtor under false pretenses or by false representations.
3. Claims by creditors who were not notified of the bankruptcy; these claims did not appear on the schedules the debtor was required to file.
4. Claims based on fraud or misuse of funds by the debtor while he or she was acting in a fiduciary capacity or claims involving the debtor's embezzlement or larceny.
5. Alimony and child support.
6. Claims based on willful or malicious conduct by the debtor toward another or the property of another.
7. Certain fines and penalties payable to governmental units.
8. Certain student loans, unless payment of the loans imposes an undue hardship on the debtor and the debtor's dependents.
9. Consumer debts of more than $500 for luxury goods or services owed to a single creditor incurred within forty days of the order for relief. This denial of discharge may be successfully challenged by the debtor, however, and any debts reasonably incurred to support the debtor or dependents are not classified as luxury goods or services.
10. Cash advances totaling more than $1,000 that are extensions of open-end consumer credit obtained by the debtor within twenty days of the order for relief. A denial of discharge of these debts is also a rebuttable presumption (that is, the denial of discharge may be challenged by the debtor).

---

16. Discharges are granted only to *individuals* who are debtors under Chapter 7, not to corporations or partnerships. The corporations and partnerships may use Chapter 11.

11.   Judgments or consent decrees awarded against a debtor as a result of the debtor's operation of a motor vehicle while legally intoxicated.

In the following case, the question of the discharge of a student loan was at issue.

Case 12.5

IN RE BAKER

United States Bankruptcy Court,
Eastern District of Tennessee,
1981.
10 Bankr. 870.

BACKGROUND AND FACTS   *Mary Lou Baker attended three different institutions of higher learning, the University of Tennessee at Chattanooga, Cleveland State Community College, and the Baroness Erlanger School of Nursing. At these three schools, she received educational loans totaling $6,635. After graduation, she was employed; but her monthly take-home pay was less than $650. Monthly expenses for herself and her three children were approximately $925. Her husband had left town and provided no child or other financial support. She received no public aid and had no other income. In January of 1981, just prior to this action, Mary Lou Baker's church paid her gas bill so that she and her children could have heat in their home. One child had reading difficulty, and another required expensive shoes. Baker had not been well and had been unable to pay her medical bills. She filed for bankruptcy. In her petition, she sought a discharge of her educational loans based on the hardship provision, which is the issue before the court.*

KELLEY, Bankruptcy Judge.

This cause came on to be heard on May 5, 1981, on debtor's complaint to determine dischargeability of certain educational loans. The complaint alleges that debtor is entitled to relief under 11 U.S.C. [Section] 523 (a)(8) which reads as follows:

Exceptions to discharge.

(a) A discharge under section 727, 1141, or 1328(b) of this title does not discharge an individual debtor from any debt—

* * * *

(8) to a governmental unit, or a nonprofit institution of higher education, for an educational loan, unless—

(B) excepting such debt from discharge under this paragraph will impose an undue hardship on the debtor and the debtor's dependents;

* * * *

In 1976 the Congress passed the Educational Amendments which restricted a discharge in bankruptcy. The restriction was designed to remedy an abuse by students who, immediately upon graduation, would file bankruptcy to secure a discharge of educational loans. These students often had no other indebtedness and could easily pay their debts from future wages.

* * * *

The court concludes that under the circumstances of this case, requiring the debtor to repay the debts owed to the *three* defendants in the amount of $6,635.00 plus interest would impose upon her and her dependents an undue hardship. In passing the Educational Amendments of 1976 and including these amendments in the Bankruptcy Reform Act of 1978, Congress intended to correct an abuse. It did not intend to deprive those who have truly fallen on hard times of the ''fresh start'' policy of the new Bankruptcy Code.

DECISION AND REMEDY   *The debtor's student loans were discharged. Given the fact that she had ''truly fallen on hard times,'' Baker should be allowed to have her debts discharged in bankruptcy to avoid undue hardship.*

Objections to Discharge In addition to the exceptions to discharge previously listed, a bankruptcy court may also deny the discharge of the *debtor* (as opposed to the debt). In the latter situation, the assets of the debtor are still distributed to the creditors, but the debtor remains liable for the unpaid portion of all claims. Some grounds for the denial of discharge of the debtor include:

1. The debtor's concealment or destruction of property with the intent to hinder, delay, or defraud a creditor.
2. The debtor's fraudulent concealment or destruction of records, or failure to keep adequate records, of his or her financial condition.
3. The debtor's refusal to obey a lawful order of a bankruptcy court.
4. The debtor's failure to satisfactorily explain the loss of assets.
5. The granting of a discharge to the debtor within six years of the filing of the petition.
6. The debtor's written waiver of discharge, approved by the court.

To encourage legitimate objections, the Code provides that even if the creditor loses on the challenge, the creditor is liable for costs and attorneys' fees only if the challenge was not *substantially justified.*

Effect of Discharge The primary effect of a discharge is to void any judgment on a discharged debt and enjoin any action to collect a discharged debt. A discharge does not affect the liability of a co-debtor.

Revocation of Discharge The Code provides that a debtor may lose his or her bankruptcy discharge by *revocation.* The bankruptcy court may within one year revoke the discharge decree if it is discovered that the debtor was fraudulent or dishonest during the bankruptcy proceedings. The revocation renders the discharge void, allowing creditors not satisfied by the distribution of the debtor's estate to proceed with their claims against the debtor.

Reaffirmation of Debt A debtor may voluntarily wish to pay off a dischargeable debt (such as, for example, a debt owed to a family member or a close friend). This is called a *reaffirmation* of the debt. To be enforceable, such agreements must be made before a debtor is granted a discharge, and they must be filed with the court.

The debtor can rescind the agreement at any time prior to discharge or within sixty days of filing the agreement, whichever is later. This rescission period must be stated *clearly* and *conspicuously* in the reaffirmation agreement.

Chapter 11 Reorganizations

In a **Chapter 11 reorganization,** the creditors and the debtor formulate a plan under which the debtor pays a portion of his or her debts and is discharged of the remainder. Then the debtor is allowed to continue in business. Although this type of bankruptcy is commonly a corporate reorganization, any debtor (except a stockbroker or a commodities broker) who is eligible for Chapter 7 relief is eligible for Chapter 11 relief. In addition, railroads are also eligible for Chapter 11 relief.

The same principles that govern the filing of a Chapter 7 petition apply to Chapter 11 proceedings. The case may be brought either voluntarily or involuntarily. The same principles govern the entry of the order for relief. The automatic-stay and adequate-protection provisions are applicable in reorganizations.

In some instances, creditors may prefer private, negotiated adjustments of creditor-debtor relations, known as **workouts,** to bankruptcy proceedings. Quite frequently these out-of-court workouts are much more flexible and thus more conducive to a speedy settlement. Speed is critical, because delay is one of the most costly elements in any bankruptcy proceeding.

Another advantage of workouts is that they avoid the various administrative costs of bankruptcy proceedings. Thus, under Section 305(a) of the Bankruptcy Code, a court, after notice and a hearing, may dismiss or suspend all proceedings in a case at any time if such a dismissal or suspension would better serve the interests of the creditors of the debtor. Section 1112 also allows a court, at the request of a party in interest and after notice and a hearing, to dismiss a case under Chapter 11 for cause. *Cause* includes an absence of a reasonable likelihood of rehabilitation, the inability to effectuate a plan, and an unreasonable delay by the

debtor that is prejudicial to creditors.[17] In the following case, creditors of Johns-Manville Corpo-

ration sought to dismiss, under Section 1112, a
voluntary Chapter 11 petition filed by Manville.

---

17. See 11 U.S.C. Section 1112(b).

Case 12.6

**IN RE JOHNS-
MANVILLE CORP.**

United States Bankruptcy
Court,
Southern District of New York,
1984.
36 Bankr. 727.

BACKGROUND AND FACTS *On August 26, 1982, Johns-Manville
Corporation, a highly successful industrial enterprise and major producer
of asbestos, filed for protection under Chapter 11 of the Bankruptcy Code.
This filing came as quite a surprise to some of Manville's creditors, as
well as to some of the other corporations that were being sued, along with
Manville, for injuries caused by asbestos exposure. Manville asserted that
the approximately 16,000 lawsuits pending as of the filing date and the
potential lawsuits of people who had been exposed but who would not
manifest asbestos-related diseases until sometime in the future necessitated
its filing. The creditors of Manville, including people harmed by asbestos
exposure who had won lawsuits or settlements, contended that Johns-
Manville had not filed in good faith and that the voluntary Chapter 11
petition should thus be dismissed under Section 1112 of the Bankruptcy
Code.*

LIFLAND, Bankruptcy Judge.
*   *   *   *

In determining whether to dismiss under Code Section 1112(b), a court is not
necessarily required to consider whether the debtor has filed in ''good faith'' because
that is not a specified predicate under the Code for filing. Rather, according to Code
Section 1129(a)(3), good faith emerges as a requirement for the confirmation of a
plan. *   *   * It is thus logical that the good faith of the debtor be deemed a predicate
primarily for emergence out of a Chapter 11 case. It is after confirmation of a concrete
and immutable reorganization plan that creditors are foreclosed from advancing their
distinct and parochial interests in the debtor's estate.

A ''principal goal'' of the Bankruptcy Code is to provide ''open access'' to the
''bankruptcy process.'' *   *   *

Accordingly, the drafters of the Code envisioned that a financially beleaguered
debtor with real debt and real creditors should not be required to wait until the
economic situation is beyond repair in order to file a reorganization petition. The
''Congressional purpose'' in enacting the Code was to encourage resort to the bankruptcy process. This philosophy not only comports with the elimination of an insolvency requirement, but also is a corollary of the key aim of Chapter 11 of the
Code, that of avoidance of liquidation. *   *   *

In the instant case, not only would liquidation be wasteful and inefficient in
destroying the utility of valuable assets of the companies as well as jobs, but, more
importantly, liquidation would preclude just compensation of some present asbestos
victims and all future asbestos claimants. This unassailable reality represents all the
more reason for this Court to adhere to this basic potential liquidation avoidance aim
of Chapter 11 and deny the motions to dismiss. Manville must not be required to
wait until its economic picture has deteriorated beyond salvation to file for
reorganization.
*   *   *   *

In sum, Manville is a financially besieged enterprise in desperate need of reorganization of its crushing real debt, both present and future. The reorganization

provisions of the Code were drafted with the aim of liquidation avoidance by great access to Chapter 11. Accordingly, Manville's filing does not abuse the jurisdictional integrity of this Court.

The motions to dismiss the Manville petition were denied. The court concluded that a bankruptcy proceeding was appropriate in this situation.   **DECISION AND REMEDY**

DEBTOR IN POSSESSION   On entry of the order for relief, the debtor generally continues to operate his or her business as a **debtor in possession.** The court, however, may appoint a trustee to operate the debtor's business if gross mismanagement of the business is shown or if for some other reason appointing a trustee is in the best interests of the estate.

CREDITORS' COMMITTEES   As soon as practicable after entry of the order for relief, a creditors' committee of unsecured creditors is appointed. (Additional creditors' committees may be appointed to represent special-interest creditors.) The committee may consult with the debtor in possession (or the trustee) concerning the administration of the case or the formulation of the plan. Orders affecting the estate generally will not be entered without either the consent of the committee or a hearing in which the judge hears the position of the committee.

THE PLAN   A Chapter 11 plan of rehabilitation is a plan to conserve and administer the debtor's assets in the hope of an eventual return to successful operation and solvency. The plan must be fair and equitable and must:

1. Designate classes of claims and interests.
2. Specify the treatment to be afforded the classes. (The plan must provide the same treatment for each claim in a particular class.)
3. Provide an adequate means for execution.

Filing the Plan   Only the debtor may file a plan within the first 120 days after the date of the order for relief. If the debtor does not meet the 120-day deadline, however, or if the debtor fails to obtain the required creditor consent within 180 days, any party may propose a plan.

Acceptance of the Plan   Once the plan has been developed, it is submitted to each class of creditors

for acceptance. Each class must accept the plan unless the class is not adversely affected by the plan [11 U.S.C. Section 1129(8)]. A class has accepted the plan when a majority of the number of creditors, representing two-thirds of the amount of the total claim, vote to approve it.

Confirmation of the Plan   Each plan submitted is almost a case history in itself, and each plan varies. The plan must be ''in the best interests of the creditors.'' Even when all classes of claims accept the plan, the court may refuse to confirm it if it fails to meet this requirement. Also, even if only one class of claims has accepted the plan, the court may still confirm it under the Code's so-called *cram-down* provision. The plan is binding on confirmation. On confirmation, the debtor is given a Chapter 11 discharge from all claims not protected under the plan. This discharge, however, does not apply to any claims denied discharge under Chapter 7 (as previously discussed).

Chapter 13 Plans

Chapter 13 of the Bankruptcy Code provides for ''Adjustment of Debts of an Individual with Regular Income.'' Individuals (not partnerships or corporations) with regular income who owe noncontingent, liquidated, unsecured debts of less than $100,000 or similar secured debts of $350,000 may take advantage of Chapter 13. Individual proprietors and individuals on welfare, Social Security, fixed pensions, or investment income are included. There are several advantages in filing a **Chapter 13 plan.** One of these advantages is that it is less expensive and less complicated than a Chapter 11 proceeding or a Chapter 7 liquidation.

FILING THE PETITION   A Chapter 13 case can be initiated only by the filing of a voluntary petition by the debtor. Certain Chapter 7 and Chapter 11 cases may be converted to Chapter 13 cases with the consent of the debtor. A trustee must be appointed.

AUTOMATIC STAY   On the filing of a Chapter 13 petition, the automatic stay previously discussed takes effect. It enjoins creditors from taking action not only against the debtor but also against co-obligors of the debtor. Although it applies to all or part of a consumer debt, it does not apply to any business debt incurred by the debtor.

CONTENTS OF THE PLAN   A Chapter 13 plan must:

1.   Provide for the turnover of such future earnings or income of the debtor to the trustee as is necessary for execution of the plan.
2.   Provide for full payment in deferred cash payments of all claims entitled to priority.
3.   Provide for the same treatment of all claims within a particular class. The debtor is permitted to list co-debtors, such as guarantors or sureties, as a separate class.

FILING THE PLAN   Only the debtor may file a plan under Chapter 13. This plan may provide either for the payment of all obligations in full or for payment of an amount less than 100 percent. The time for payment under the plan may not exceed three years unless the court approves an extension. The term, with extension, may not exceed five years.

The Code requires the debtor to make "timely payments," and the trustee is required to ensure that the debtor commences the payments. The law provides that the debtor commence making payments under the proposed plan within thirty days after the plan has been filed. If the plan has not been confirmed, the trustee is instructed to retain the payments until the plan is confirmed and then distribute the payments accordingly. If the plan is denied, the trustee will return the payments to the debtor less any costs. Failure of the debtor to make timely payments or to commence payments within the thirty-day period will allow the court to convert the case to a Chapter 7 bankruptcy or to dismiss the petition.

CONFIRMATION OF THE PLAN   After the plan is filed, the court holds a confirmation hearing at

which interested parties may object to the plan. The court will confirm a plan with respect to each claim of a secured creditor under any of the following circumstances:

1.   If the secured creditors have accepted the plan.
2.   If the plan provides that creditors retain their liens and if the value of the property to be distributed to them under the plan is not less than the secured portion of their claims.
3.   If the debtor surrenders the property securing the claims to the creditors.

OBJECTION TO THE PLAN   Unsecured creditors do not have a vote to confirm a Chapter 13 plan, but they can object to it. The court can approve a plan over the objection of the trustee or any unsecured creditor only in one of the following situations:

1.   The value of the property to be distributed under the plan is at least equal to the amount of the claims.
2.   All the debtor's projected disposable income to be received during the three-year period will be applied to making payments. Disposable income is all income received *less* amounts needed to support the debtor and dependents and/or amounts needed to meet ordinary expenses to continue the operation of a business.

MODIFICATION OF THE PLAN   Prior to completion of payments, the plan may be modified on the request of the debtor, the trustee, or an unsecured creditor. If there is an objection by any interested party to the modification, the court must hold a hearing to determine approval or disapproval of the modified plan.

DISCHARGE   After completion of all payments under a Chapter 13 plan, the court grants a discharge of all debts provided for by the plan. Except for allowed claims not provided for by the plan, certain long-term debts provided for by the plan, and claims for alimony and child support, all other debts are dischargeable. A Chapter 13 discharge is sometimes referred to as a "super-discharge" because debts dischargeable under Chapter 13 include fraudulently incurred debts and claims resulting from malicious or willful injury. Therefore, a Chapter 13 discharge is much more beneficial to some debtors than a Chapter 7 discharge.

Even if the debtor does not complete the plan, a ''hardship'' discharge may be granted if the failure to complete the plan was due to circumstances beyond the debtor's control and if the value of the property distributed with the plan was greater than would have been paid in a Chapter 7 liquidation. A discharge can be revoked within one year if it was obtained by fraud.

■ Terms and Concepts to Review

artisan's lien 276	**deficiency judgment** 278	**right of contribution** 280
attachment 277	**discharge of debts** 291	**right of reimbursement** 280
automatic stay 285	**foreclosure** 278	**right of subrogation** 280
Chapter 7 liquidation 282	**garnishment** 278	**security interest** 282
Chapter 11	**guaranty** 279	**surety** 278
reorganization 293	**homestead exemption** 280	**workouts** 293
Chapter 13 plan 295	**mechanic's lien** 275	
debtor in possession 295		

■ Questions and Case Problems

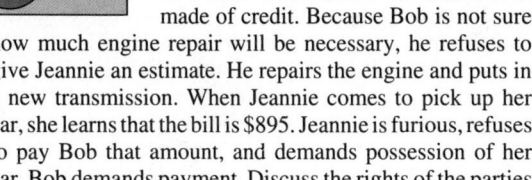

12-1. Jeannie takes her car to Bob's Auto Shop for repairs. A sign in the window states that all repairs must be paid for in cash unless credit is approved in advance. Jeannie and Bob agree that Bob will repair Jeannie's car engine and put in a new transmission. No mention is made of credit. Because Bob is not sure how much engine repair will be necessary, he refuses to give Jeannie an estimate. He repairs the engine and puts in a new transmission. When Jeannie comes to pick up her car, she learns that the bill is $895. Jeannie is furious, refuses to pay Bob that amount, and demands possession of her car. Bob demands payment. Discuss the rights of the parties in this matter.

12-2. Meredith, a farmer, borrowed $5,000 from Farmer's Bank and gave the bank $4,000 in bearer bonds to hold as collateral for the loan. Meredith's neighbor, Peterson, who had known Meredith for years, signed as surety on the note. Due to a drought, Meredith's harvest that year was only a fraction of what it normally was, and he was forced to default on his payments to Farmer's Bank. The bank did not immediately sell the bonds but instead requested $5,000 from Peterson. Peterson paid the $5,000 and then demanded that the bank give him the $4,000 in securities. Can Peterson enforce this demand? Explain.

12-3. Sabrina is a student at Sunnyside University. In need of funds to pay for tuition and books, she attempts to secure a short-term loan from University Bank. The bank agrees to make a loan if Sabrina will have someone financially responsible guarantee the loan payments. Abigail, a well-known businessperson and a friend of Sabrina's family, calls the bank and agrees to pay the loan if Sabrina cannot. Because of Abigail's reputation, the loan is made. Sabrina makes several payments on the loan, but because of illness she is not able to work for one month. She requests that University Bank extend the loan for three months. The bank agrees, raising the interest rate for the extended period. Abigail has not been notified of the extension (and therefore has not consented to it). One month later, Sabrina drops out of school. All attempts to collect from Sabrina have failed. University Bank wants to hold Abigail liable. Will the bank succeed? Explain.

12-4. Delmondo is a retail seller of television sets. He sells Maria a $900 set under a retail installment-loan agreement in which she pays $100 down and agrees to pay the balance in equal installments. Delmondo retains a security interest in the set sold, and he perfects that security interest by filing a financing statement locally. Two months later Maria is in default on her payments to Delmondo and is involuntarily petitioned into bankruptcy by her creditors. Delmondo wants to repossess the television set as provided for in the security agreement, and he wants to have priority over the trustee in bankruptcy to any proceeds from the disposal of the set. Discuss fully Delmondo's right to repossess the set and whether he has priority over the trustee in bankruptcy to any proceeds from disposal of the set.

12-5. Runyan petitions himself into voluntary bankruptcy. He has three major claims against his estate. One is by Calvin, a friend who holds Runyan's negotiable promissory note for $2,500; one is by Ellis, an employee who is owed three months' back wages of $4,500; and one is by the First Bank of Sunny Acres on an unsecured loan of $5,000. In addition, Martinez, an accountant retained by the trustee, is owed $500, and property taxes of $1,000 are owed to Micanopa County. Runyan's nonexempt property has been liquidated, with the proceeds totaling $5,000. Discuss fully what amount each party will receive and why.

12-6. Levinson and Johnson, who had both signed a promissory note, did not pay the note when it was due. Instead, American Thermex, Inc., a corporation in which Johnson had a controlling interest, voluntarily paid the note.

American Thermex later brought suit against Levinson, seeking reimbursement for the payment. American Thermex argued, among other things, that because it had paid the note it had the legal right of subrogation against the note's co-maker, Levinson. Will the court agree that American Thermex has a legal right of subrogation? Why or why not? [*Levinson v. American Thermex, Inc.,* 196 Ga.App. 291, 396 S.E.2d 252 (1990)]

12-7. Harmony Unlimited obtained a judgment against John Chivetta and his company, JMC Enterprises. At the time of the judgment, John lacked sufficient funds to pay. Just before Harmony obtained the judgment, John had transferred $126,000 to his mother, Nettie, who had signed a promissory note. Harmony served a garnishment summons on Nettie, claiming that she was a party to a fraudulent scheme by her son to conceal his assets and was holding funds that belonged to her son. The note for $126,000 was payable on demand, carried no interest, and contained a provision that barred John from obtaining a money judgment against his mother. Nettie paid some of John's bills after the transfer of money from her son to her. Nettie argued that Harmony's rights against her could not be any greater than John's rights against her and that because John could not obtain a judgment against her for the money, Harmony could not do so either. Discuss Harmony's right of garnishment against Nettie. [*Harmony Unlimited, Inc. v. Chivetta,* 743 S.W.2d 884 (Mo.App. 1987)]

12-8. On July 6, 1982, Henry Wilson filed a voluntary petition for Chapter 7 bankruptcy. In October of that year, one of Wilson's creditors, John Milam, filed a complaint with the bankruptcy court objecting to the discharge of a debt owed to him by Wilson. The debt had been incurred in 1978 when Wilson purchased Milam's accounting practice. Wilson made a down payment, and under the terms of their written agreement Wilson was obligated to make monthly payments to Milam until the balance of the debt was paid. When Wilson failed to make the June 1978 payment, Milam brought suit against Wilson and, as a result of the suit, was awarded a judgment against Wilson in the amount of $57,569. This was one of the debts that Wilson sought to discharge in bankruptcy. Milam contended that the debt should not be discharged, because Wilson had failed to keep adequate records on the accounting business from which the financial condition of the business could be ascertained. Wilson admitted that the only business record he maintained for the accounting practice for 1980, 1981, and 1982 was a single checking account from which both business and personal expenses were paid. Was Wilson's debt to Milam discharged by the bankruptcy court? Explain. [*Matter of Wilson,* 33 Bankr. 689 (Bankr.M.D.Ga. 1983)]

12-9. John Patrick Goulding filed for Chapter 7 bankruptcy relief in 1987. In his schedules, he listed assets of $62,000 and debts of over $670,000. The majority of these debts were unsecured and were not consumer debts. The Federal Deposit Insurance Corp. (FDIC), as successor to two banks, was the largest unsecured creditor ($379,000). The FDIC and the trustee learned that Goulding was the beneficiary

of three irrevocable spendthrift trusts (the assets of which cannot be reached by creditors) that provided him with $12,000 per month, and that he would receive from the corpus (principal) of one trust $200,000 on January 30, 1988. The trustee and the FDIC filed a joint motion requesting the court to dismiss Goulding's Chapter 7 petition. Discuss whether the court should have dismissed Goulding's petition and whether any payments made from the trusts were part of the debtor's estate. [*In re Goulding,* 79 Bankr. 874 (W.D.Mo. 1987)]

12-10. In 1983, Beech Acceptance Corp. financed the sale of three airplanes to Gull Air, Inc. Approximately three years later, Gull Air defaulted on its obligations to Beech, and Beech filed suit. Before the trial, Gull Air and Beech negotiated a workout agreement that provided for large monthly payments over a certain period. Despite the workout agreement, Gull Air filed a Chapter 11 petition in bankruptcy. Gull Air claimed that payments made under the workout agreement during the ninety days prior to the filing of the Chapter 11 petition amounted to a preference and must be returned to the debtor in possession (Gull Air). There was no question that Beech had received more than it would have under a Chapter 7 liquidation. Beech claimed that the payments had been made in the ordinary course of business. Discuss who is correct. [*In re Gull Air, Inc.,* 82 Bankr. 1 (D.Mass. 1988)]

12-11. In 1985, the United States, under the Comprehensive Environmental Response, Compensation and Liability Act, filed suit for costs in connection with the cleaning up of asbestos released from a facility owned and operated by Nicolet, Inc. Before the lawsuit was completed, Nicolet filed a petition for Chapter 11 bankruptcy. Nicolet argued that the petition in bankruptcy operated as an automatic stay of the government's right to continue civil proceedings against it to recover the cleanup costs. The Bankruptcy Code provides an exception to the automatic stay order when the debtor has filed the petition. This exception provides that the stay is not available against a governmental unit exercising its police and regulatory powers. Discuss whether the civil action by the United States to recover cleanup costs falls under the automatic stay order or under the exception of a governmental unit exercising its police and regulatory powers. [*United States v. Nicolet, Inc.,* 81 Bankr. 310 (E.D.Pa. 1988)]

12-12. A Question of Ethics

 In September 1986, Edward and Debora Davenport pleaded guilty in a Pennsylvania court to welfare fraud and were sentenced to probation for one year. As a condition of their probation, the Davenports were ordered to make monthly restitution payments to the county probation department, which would forward the payments to the Pennsylvania Department of Public Welfare, the victim of the Davenports' fraud. In May 1987, the Davenports filed a petition for Chapter 13 relief and listed the restitution payments among their debts. The bankruptcy court held that the restitution obligation was a dischargeable debt.

On appeal, the district court reversed, holding that state-imposed criminal restitution obligations cannot be discharged in a Chapter 13 bankruptcy. The Court of Appeals for the Third Circuit reversed the district court's decision, concluding that "the plain language of the chapter" demonstrated that restitution orders are debt within the meaning of the Code and hence dischargeable in proceedings under Chapter 13. Ultimately, the case was reviewed by the United States Supreme Court, which affirmed the Third Circuit's ruling. The Court noted that under the Bankruptcy Code a "debt" is defined as a "liability on a claim" and a "claim" is defined as a "right to payment." Because the restitution obligations clearly constituted a "right to payment," the Court held that the obligations were dischargeable in bankruptcy. [Pennsylvania Department of Public Welfare v. Davenport, *495 U.S. 522, 110 S.Ct. 2126, 109 L.Ed.2d 588 (1990)*]

1. Critics of this decision contend that the Court adhered to the letter, but not the spirit, of bankruptcy law in arriving at its conclusion. In what way, if any, did the Court not abide by the "spirit" of bankruptcy law?

2. Do you think that Chapter 13 plans, which allow nearly all types of debts to be discharged, tip the scales of justice too far in favor of debtors? Explain.

12-13. Case Briefing Assignment

Examine Case A.12 [Allison-Bristow Community School District v. Iowa Civil Rights Commission, *461 N.W.2d 456 (Iowa 1990)*] *in Appendix A. The case has been excerpted there in great detail. Review and then brief the case, making sure that you include answers to the following questions in your brief.*

1. Why did Rowland claim that the back pay, plus interest, that the Civil Rights Commission ordered his employer to pay him were not "earnings" subject to garnishment under Iowa law?

2. How did the relevant Iowa statute define *earnings*?

3. On what grounds did the trial court hold for Rowland?

4. What arguments were advanced by the judgment creditor, Willow Tree, to convince the court that Rowland's award of back pay, plus interest, should be subject to garnishment?

5. What was the reasoning behind the appellate court's conclusion on the issue? In what way did the appellate court's ruling differ from that of the trial court?

Chapter 13

Business Organizations

Every business activity involves—implicitly or explicitly—a form of business organization, whether it be a sole proprietorship, a partnership, a corporation, or some hybrid form. Each form provides different degrees of flexibility and different rights and liabilities, and it is important to be aware of these differences when choosing and structuring one's business organization. In this chapter, we examine the basic features of the three major business forms—sole proprietorships, partnerships, and corporations. We also touch on joint ventures, syndicates, joint stock companies, business trusts, cooperatives, and private franchises.

Note that there is great variety in the sizes and functions of business organizations even within the same category. For example, businesses conducted as sole proprietorships can range from a small mail-order business run out of the owner's home to a multimillion-dollar manufacturing operation occupying acres of an industrial complex. Similarly, partnerships can range from an informal arrangement between two individuals to a formal organization with hundreds of partners. Also, most of the wealthiest U.S. business firms are organized as corporations, but the majority of corporations are small. It has been estimated that over 90 percent of corporations have ten or fewer shareholders.

The sizes of businesses may differ considerably within a category, but tax liabilities and other obligations faced by the businesses within each category typically are constant. A sole proprietorship doing $22,000 worth of business faces the same federal tax laws as a sole proprietorship doing $10 million worth of business.

■ Sole Proprietorships

The simplest form of business is a **sole proprietorship.** In this form, the owner is the business; thus, anyone who does business without creating a formal business entity has a sole proprietorship. Sole proprietorships are very common and constitute over two-thirds of all American businesses. They are also usually small enterprises—less than 1 percent of the sole proprietorships existing in the United States earn over $1 million per year. Sole proprietors can own and manage any type of business from an informal, home-office undertaking to a huge restaurant or construction firm.

Advantages of Sole Proprietorships

A major advantage of the sole proprietorship is that the proprietor receives all the profits (because he or she takes all the risk). In addition, it is often easier and less costly to start a sole proprietorship than to start any other kind of business, as few legal forms are involved. This business form also entails more flexibility than does a partnership or a corporation. The sole proprietor is free to make any decision she or he wishes to concerning the business—whom to hire, when to take a vacation, what kind of business to pursue, and so on. A sole proprietor also pays only personal income taxes on profits. This means that, depending on the amount earned, the applicable tax rate may be lower than the corporate tax rate. Sole proprietors are also allowed to establish tax-exempt retirement accounts in the form of Keogh plans.

Disadvantages of Sole Proprietorships

The major disadvantage of the sole proprietorship is that, as sole owner, the proprietor alone bears the burden of any losses or liabilities incurred by the business enterprise. In other words, the sole proprietor has unlimited liability, or legal responsibility, for all obligations incurred in doing business. The unlimited liability of the sole proprietor, in contrast to the limited liability of the limited partner or corporate shareholder (discussed below), is a major factor to be considered when choosing a business form.

Another disadvantage is that the proprietor's opportunity to raise capital is limited to personal funds and the funds of those who are willing to make loans. The sole proprietorship also has the disadvantage of lacking continuity of business on the death of the proprietor. When the owner dies, so does the business—it is automatically dissolved. If the business is transferred to family members or other heirs, a new proprietorship is created.

■ Partnerships

Partnerships can take the form of general partnerships or limited partnerships. The two forms of partnership differ considerably in regard to legal requirements and the rights and liabilities of partners.

General Partnerships

A **partnership** arises from an agreement, express or implied, between two or more persons to carry on a business for profit. Partners are co-owners of a business and have joint control over its operation and the right to share in its profits. No particular form of partnership agreement is necessary for its creation, although it is desirable that it be in writing. Both partnerships and sole proprietorships are creatures of common law rather than of statute. Basically, the partners may agree to almost any terms when establishing the partnership so long as they are not illegal or contrary to public policy.

A partnership is a legal entity only for limited purposes such as the partnership name and title of ownership and property. The personal net worth of the partners is subject to partnership obligations, and the partnership itself is not subject to levy for federal income taxes, although an *information return* must be filed. A partner's profit from the partnership (whether distributed or not) is taxed as individual income to the individual partner.

Limited Partnerships

A special and quite popular form of partnership is the **limited partnership,** which consists of at least one general partner and one or more limited partners. One of the major benefits of becoming a limited partner is limited liability, both with respect to lawsuits brought against the partnership and money at risk. The maximum money at risk is defined by the limited partnership agreement, which specifically states how much each limited partner must contribute to the partnership.

The limited partnership is created by an agreement; but, unlike a general partnership, the limited partnership does not come into existence until a certificate of partnership is filed appropriately in a state. All states permit limited partnerships. Unlike a general partnership, a limited partnership is completely a creature of statute. If the statute is not followed almost to the letter, the courts will hold that a general partnership exists instead. If a court does hold that a general partnership exists, then those who thought their liability was limited by their investment in a limited partnership will be held generally liable to the full extent of their personal net worth.

The exemptions from personal liability of the limited partners rest on their not participating in management. Active participation in management may render the limited partner just as liable as a general partner to any creditor who knows of the limited partner's management activities. Note that no law expressly bars the participation of limited partners in the management of the partnership. Rather, the threat of personal liability normally deters their participation.

How much actual review and advisement over business matters a limited partner can engage in before being exposed to liability is an unsettled question.[1] In the following case, a limited partner was alleged to have participated in the control of the business by interceding on the partnership's behalf to secure credit.

_____

1. It is an unsettled question partly because there are differences among the laws of different states.

Case 13.1

PITMAN v. FLANAGAN LUMBER CO.

Supreme Court of Alabama, 1990.
567 So.2d 1335.

BACKGROUND AND FACTS *Robert Pitman was one of two limited partners in Ramsey Homebuilders, a limited partnership that engaged in the business of residential construction. Michael Ramsey was the sole general partner in the partnership. Because Ramsey had a poor credit history, he was unable to borrow the money or obtain the credit that was needed to sustain the partnership's business. Pitman, who had a personal account with Flanagan Lumber Company, contacted Flanagan's credit manager and secured an account in the partnership's name. After the partnership failed to pay the account, Flanagan sued Pitman, alleging that although Pitman was a limited partner in Ramsey Homebuilders, he was responsible for the partnership's debt under Section 303 of the Revised Uniform Limited Partnership Act [RULPA 303].[a] Pitman argued that, if anything, he was operating within the waters of the "safe harbor" provided by RULPA 303(b)(3), which states that a limited partner does not participate in the control of the partnership solely by acting as a surety or guarantor for any liabilities incurred by the partnership. The trial court found that Pitman had participated in the control of the business by securing credit for the partnership, that Flanagan had reasonably relied on that participation in extending credit, and that Pitman was therefore liable to Flanagan for the debt subsequently incurred by the partnership. Pitman appealed.*

HOUSTON, Justice.
* * * *

Pitman argues that the evidence does not support the trial court's finding that he participated in the control of the partnership's business. * * * He also contends that he had no written agreement with Flanagan to pay the partnership's account and, therefore, that under [the Alabama Statute of Frauds], he cannot be held responsible for the debt.
* * * *

Flanagan contents, however, that the evidence supports the trial court's finding that Pitman participated in the control of the partnership's business. Furthermore, Flanagan argues, [the Statute of Frauds] is not applicable because the judgment was not predicated upon an agreement between it and Pitman to pay the partnership's account, but, instead, upon Pitman's loss of limited partner status under [RULPA 303(a)]. We agree.

_____

a. The Revised Uniform Limited Partnership Act (RULPA) has been adopted in a majority of states and the District of Columbia to govern limited partnerships.

* * * *

"Control" is defined in Black's Law Dictionary (5th ed. 1979) as the "[p]ower or authority to manage, direct, superintend, restrict, regulate, govern, administer, or oversee." In the present case, the evidence showed that Pitman interceded on behalf of the partnership in order to secure an account with Flanagan. The trial court could have found from this evidence that Pitman participated in the "control" of the partnership's business by securing one of the things that the partnership needed to survive—a source of building materials that would be provided on credit. Furthermore, the evidence supports the trial court's finding that Flanagan reasonably relied on Pitman's participation in the partnership's business by extending credit to the partnership. The trial court's judgment was not plainly and palpably wrong.

With regard to Pitman's second contention (i.e., that [the Statute of Frauds] protects him from liability because he had no written agreement with Flanagan to pay the partnership's debt), the trial court did not adjudge Pitman liable on the ground that he had an agreement with Flanagan to pay the account, but on the ground that he had lost his limited partner status under [RULPA 303(a)], and, therefore became liable as a general partner for the partnership's debt * * *.

The appellate court affirmed the trial court's decision. Pitman's action of securing credit that was vitally necessary to the partnership amounted to sufficient "control" over partnership affairs to hold him liable as a general partner for the debt to Flanagan.   **DECISION AND REMEDY**

■ Corporations

A third and widely used type of business organizational form is the **corporation**. Corporations consist of shareholders, who are the owners. A board of directors, elected by the shareholders, represents the shareholders in directing the affairs of the corporation. The board of directors normally employs officers to oversee the day-to-day operations of the corporation. One of the key features of a corporation is **limited liability**: the liability of its owners (the shareholders) is limited to their investments. Their personal estates are usually not liable for the obligations of the corporation.

The corporation is a creature of statute; it is an artificial being, existing in law only and neither tangible nor visible. The corporation's existence depends generally on state law, although some corporations, especially public organizations, can be created under federal law. Each state has its own body of corporate law, and these laws are not entirely uniform. The Model Business Corporation Act (MBCA), first published in 1946, is a codification of modern corporation law that has been influential in the codification of corporation statutes in many states. Today, the majority of state statutes are guided by the Revised Model Business

Corporation Act (RMBCA). It should be kept in mind, however, that there is considerable variation among the statutes of the states that have used the MBCA or the RMBCA as a basis for their statutes, and there are a number of states that do not follow either act very much, if at all. Because of this, individual state corporation laws should be relied on rather than the MBCA or RMBCA.

Under modern law, except as limited by charters, statutes, or constitutions, *a corporation can engage in all acts and enter into any contract available to a natural person to accomplish the purposes for which it was created.* When a corporation is created, the express and implied powers necessary to achieve its purpose also come into existence. These powers do not give the men and women who run the corporations unlimited management discretion, however.

Nature of the Corporation

A corporation is an artificial person, with its own corporate name, and owned by one or more individual shareholders. It is a legal entity with rights and responsibilities distinct from those of the shareholders. The corporation substitutes itself for its shareholders in conducting corporate business and in incurring liability, yet its authority to act and the liability for its actions are separate and apart from the individuals who own it. (In certain limited situations the "corporate veil" can be pierced; that is, liability for the corporation's obligations can be extended to shareholders. This topic is important for small corporations.)

Responsibility for the overall management of the corporation is entrusted to a board of directors, which is elected by the shareholders. Corporate officers and other employees are hired by the board of directors to run the daily business operations of the corporation. Officers are agents of the corporation. They answer to the board of directors rather than to the shareholders directly.

When an individual purchases a share of stock in a corporation, that person becomes a shareholder and an owner of the corporation. As a general rule, a shareholder is not personally liable for the corporation's business debts; nor is the corporation responsible for a shareholder's personal debts. Each shareholder's liability is limited to the amount of the investment (that is, the money actually paid when the stock was acquired). Unlike the members in a partnership, the body of shareholders can change constantly without affecting the continued existence of the corporation. A shareholder can sue the corporation, and the corporation can sue a shareholder. Also, under certain circumstances, a shareholder can sue on behalf of a corporation. A *shareholder's derivative suit,* for example, is an action brought by a shareholder to enforce a corporate cause of action that is based on a primary right that the corporation has failed, deliberately or not, to act on. This right of shareholders, as well as the rights and duties of all corporate personnel, is discussed in the following chapter.

Because a corporation is a separate legal entity, corporate profits are taxed by state and federal governments. Corporations can do one of two things with corporate profits—retain them or pass them on to shareholders in the form of dividends. The corporation receives no tax deduction for dividends distributed to shareholders. Dividends are again taxable (except when they represent distributions of capital) as ordinary income to the shareholder receiving them. This **double taxation** of corporate income is one of its major disadvantages. Retained earnings, if invested properly, will yield higher cor-

porate profits in the future and thus cause the price of the company's stock to rise. Individual shareholders can then reap the benefits of these retained earnings in the gains they receive when they sell their shares.

Classification of Corporations

The classification of a corporation may depend on its purpose, ownership characteristics, or location. A corporation is referred to as a *domestic corporation* by its home state (the state in which it incorporates). A corporation formed in one state but doing business in another is referred to in that other state as a *foreign corporation.* A corporation formed in another country, say, Mexico, but doing business in the United States is referred to in the United States as an *alien corporation.*

A corporation does not have an automatic right to do business in a state other than its state of incorporation. It must obtain a *certificate of authority* in the states in which it plans to do business. Once the certificate has been issued, the powers conferred on a corporation by its home state generally can be exercised in the other state. Should a foreign corporation do business without obtaining a certificate, the state can fine it, deny it the privilege of using state courts, and even hold its officers, directors, or agents personally liable for corporate obligations incurred in that state.[2]

Before a state court can hear a dispute in which a foreign corporation is the defendant, the state court must have *jurisdiction* over the defendant; and this requires that the foreign corporation have sufficient *contacts* with the state. A foreign corporation that has its home office in the state or has manufacturing plants in the state meets this **minimum-contacts requirement.** A foreign corporation whose only contact with the state is the fact that one of its directors resides there does not have sufficient contact with the state for the state court to exercise jurisdiction over it. This modern view that jurisdiction over foreign corporations is determined by a minimum-contacts standard was established in the following landmark case.

---

2. *Robertson v. Levy,* 197 A.2d 443 (D.C.App. 1964).

BACKGROUND AND FACTS *The state of Washington sought to collect unemployment contributions from the International Shoe Company based on commissions paid by the company to its sales representatives who lived in Washington. International Shoe asserted that its activities within the state of Washington were not sufficient to manifest its "presence" there and thus the state courts could not constitutionally exercise jurisdiction over it. It argued that (1) it had no office in the state of Washington; (2) although it employed eleven to thirteen Washington sales representatives to market its product in Washington, no actual sales or purchase contracts were made in that state; and (3) it maintained no stock of merchandise in Washington. Consequently, it was a denial of due process for the state to subject it to suit. The Supreme Court of Washington held for the state, and International Shoe appealed to the United States Supreme Court.*

Case 13.2

INTERNATIONAL SHOE CO. v. STATE OF WASHINGTON
Supreme Court of the United States, 1945.
326 U.S. 310,
66 S.Ct. 154,
90 L.Ed. 95.

Mr. Chief Justice *STONE* delivered the opinion of the Court.
* * * *
Since the corporate personality is a fiction, although a fiction intended to be acted upon as though it were a fact, it is clear that unlike an individual its "presence" without, as well as within, the state of its origin can be manifested only by activities carried on in its behalf by those who are authorized to act for it. * * * [T]he terms "present" or "presence" are used merely to symbolize those activities of the corporation's agent within the state which courts will deem to be sufficient to satisfy the demands of due process. Those demands may be met by such contacts of the corporation with the state of the forum as make it reasonable, in the context of our federal system of government, to require the corporation to defend the particular suit which is brought there. * * *
* * * *
* * * [T]o the extent that a corporation exercises the privilege of conducting activities within a state, it enjoys the benefits and protection of the laws of that state. The exercise of that privilege may give rise to obligations; and, so far as those obligations arise out of or are connected with the activities within the state, a procedure which requires the corporation to respond to suit brought to enforce them can, in most instances, hardly be said to be undue.
Applying these standards, the activities carried on in behalf of the appellant in the State of Washington were neither irregular nor casual. They were systematic and continuous throughout the years in question. They resulted in a large volume of interstate business, in the course of which appellant received the benefits and protection of the laws of the state, including the right to resort to the courts for the enforcement of its rights. The obligation which is here sued upon arose out of those very activities. It is evident that these operations establish sufficient contacts or ties with the state of the forum to make it reasonable and just according to our traditional conception of fair play and substantial justice to permit the state to enforce the obligations which appellant has incurred there. Hence we cannot say that the maintenance of the present suit in the State of Washington involves an unreasonable or undue procedure.

The United States Supreme Court affirmed the Supreme Court of Washington's decision. International Shoe had sufficient contacts with the state of Washington to allow the state to exercise jurisdiction constitutionally over the foreign corporation.

DECISION AND REMEDY

COMMENTS *In this case, the United States Supreme Court established a new test for jurisdiction over foreign corporations. For a state to exercise jurisdiction constitutionally over a foreign corporation, the corporation must have minimum contacts with the foreign state.*

PUBLIC AND PRIVATE CORPORATIONS A public corporation is one formed by the government to meet some political or governmental purpose. Cities and towns that incorporate are common examples. In addition, many federal government organizations, such as the U.S. Postal Service, the Tennessee Valley Authority, and Amtrak, are public corporations. Private corporations, in contrast, are created either wholly or in part for private benefit. Most corporations are private. Although they may serve a public purpose, such as a public utility does, they are owned by private persons rather than by the government.

NONPROFIT CORPORATIONS Corporations formed without a profit-making purpose are called *nonprofit, not-for-profit,* or *eleemosynary* (charitable) corporations. Although these nonprofit corporations are usually (although not necessarily) private corporations, they can be used with an ordinary for-profit corporation to facilitate making contracts with the government. Private hospitals, educational institutions, charities, religious organizations, and the like are frequently organized as nonprofit corporations. The nonprofit corporation is a convenient form of organization that allows various groups to own property and to form contracts without the individual members being personally exposed to liability.

CLOSE CORPORATIONS A **close corporation** is one whose shares are held by members of a family or by relatively few persons. Close corporations are also referred to as *closely held* or *family-held* corporations. Usually, the members of the small group involved in a close corporation are personally known to each other. Because the number of shareholders is so small, there is no trading market for the shares. In practice, a close corporation is often operated like a partnership. A few states recognize this in special statutory provisions that cover close corporations.

Close Corporation Statutes To be eligible for close corporation status, a corporation has to have a limited number of shareholders, the transfer of corporation stock must be subject to certain restrictions, and the corporation must not make any public offering of its securities.[3] Close corporation statutes provide greater flexibility by expressly permitting corporations that elect to do so to vary significantly from those subject to traditional corporation law.[4]

Management of Close Corporations The close corporation has a single shareholder or a closely knit group of shareholders who usually hold the positions of directors and officers. Management of a close corporation resembles that of a sole proprietorship or a partnership, although, as a corporation, the firm must meet the same legal requirements as other corporations—except when special statutes have been enacted, as mentioned previously.

Statutory close corporations are intended to reduce management formalities. Under the governing statutes, shareholders have unlimited power to restrict decisions of the board of directors. In fact, there need not even be a board of directors; the corporation can be managed by the shareholders. In that circumstance, the shareholders have the same fiduciary duties as directors.

To prevent a majority shareholder from dominating a close corporation, the corporation's charter may require that action can be taken by the board only on approval of more than a majority of the directors. Typically, this would not be required for ordinary business decisions but only for extraordinary actions—such as changing the amount of dividends or dismissing an employee-shareholder.

Transfer of Shares in Close Corporations Because a close corporation, by definition, has a

---

3. See, for example, 8 Del. Code Ann. Section 342, which provides that close corporations can have no more than thirty shareholders.
4. For example, in some states (such as Maryland), the close corporation need not have a board of directors.

small number of shareholders, the transfer of shares of one shareholder to someone else can cause serious management problems. In other words, the other shareholders can find themselves required to share control with someone they may not know or like. To avoid this problem, a few states provide statutes prohibiting the transfer of close corporation shares unless certain persons—including shareholders, family members, and the corporation—have been given the opportunity to purchase the shares for the same price first. These statutes do not apply if shareholders have otherwise specified restrictions. Thus, it may be advisable for the close corporation with several shareholders to specify restrictions on the transferability of stock in its articles of incorporation.

Consider an example: Three brothers, Terry, Damon, and Henry Johnson, are the only shareholders of Johnson's Car Wash, Inc. Terry and Damon do not want Henry to sell his shares to an unknown third person. This problem could be avoided if the articles of incorporation had been

drafted initially to restrict the transferability of shares to outside persons by stipulating that shareholders offer their shares to the corporation itself or to other shareholders of the corporation before selling them to an outside purchaser.

Another way that control of a close corporation can be stabilized is through the use of a shareholder agreement. Agreements among shareholders to vote their stock in a particular way are generally upheld.[5] Shareholder agreements can also provide that when one of the original shareholders dies, his or her shares of stock in the corporation will be divided in such a way that the proportionate holdings of the survivors, and thus their proportionate control, will be maintained. The court evaluated such a shareholder agreement in the following case.

---

5. An important case upholding the validity of shareholders' agreements is *Ringling Bros.–Barnum and Bailey Combined Shows v. Ringling,* 29 Del.Ch. 610, 53 A.2d 441 (1947).

BACKGROUND AND FACTS   *In February 1955, Robert Leihser, Elbert Rench, and Claude Mullen purchased Loyd Trucking Corporation. They divided the fifty corporate shares equally and signed an agreement in 1956 that should any of them die or wish to sell his shares, the remaining stockholder(s) would purchase the shares. A specific procedure was described in the agreement for transferring the shares in such an event. In 1961 Claude Mullen sold his stock, and Leihser and Rench each bought half of Mullen's shares. The specific procedural details outlined in the 1956 agreement were not followed by Mullen, however, when he sold his shares. Also in violation of the 1956 agreement, Leihser and Rench assigned one share of stock each to their respective spouses. Then in 1981 Leihser died. Rench sought to buy Leihser's shares from Leihser's wife, in accordance with the shareholder agreement. Mrs. Leihser was willing to sell, but they could not agree on a price. Finally, Rench initiated this action to compel Mrs. Leihser to sell him the shares. The trial court granted Rench specific performance and ordered Mrs. Leihser to sell the stocks to Rench. Mrs. Leihser appealed.*

Case 13.3

RENCH v. LEIHSER
Appellate Court of Illinois, Fifth District, 1986.
139 Ill.App.3d 889,
487 N.E.2d 1201,
94 Ill.Dec. 324.

HARRISON, Justice.
* * * *

As a general matter, restrictions upon the right to transfer shares of corporate stock are permissible provided that those restrictions are reasonable and not contrary to any law or public policy. Where, as here, the shares are not available on the open market and have no market value, agreements imposing permissible restrictions on their transfer or sale may be enforced by specific performance. *   *   *
* * * *

* * * Considering the language of the 1956 stock purchase agreement itself and the conduct of Robert Leihser and plaintiff Rench subsequent to their purchase of Mullen's stock, we simply cannot accept the circuit court's conclusion that the agreement continued to be valid. The manifest weight of the evidence points to the opposite conclusion: the agreement terminated in 1961, when Mullen sold out. For this reason the circuit court erred in granting specific performance of the agreement * * *.

DECISION AND REMEDY   *The appellate court reversed the finding of the trial court. The 1956 agreement was no longer binding on the shareholders, and Mrs. Rench could therefore not be compelled to sell her shares to Leihser.*

S CORPORATIONS In 1982 Congress enacted the Subchapter S Revision Act, the purpose of which was "to minimize the effect of federal income taxes on choices of the form of business organizations and to permit the incorporation and operation of certain small businesses without the incidence of income taxation at both the corporate and shareholder level."[6] Additionally, Congress decreed that all corporations are divided into two groups: **S corporations** (formerly *Subchapter S corporations*), which have elected Subchapter S treatment, and *C corporations,* which are virtually all other corporations.

Certain corporations can choose to qualify under Subchapter S of the Internal Revenue Code to avoid the imposition of income taxes at the corporate level while retaining all the advantages of a corporation, particularly limited liability. While the S corporation has the advantages of the corporate form without the double taxation of income (corporate income of an S corporation is generally not taxed separately), it does have some disadvantages. One of the most important disadvantages relates to the fact that an S corporation's fringe-benefit payments to employee-shareholders who own more than 2 percent of the stock are nondeductible.

Qualification Requirements for S Corporations Among the numerous requirements for qualification as an S-corporation are the following, more important ones:

1. The corporation must be a domestic corporation.

2. The corporation must not be a member of an affiliated group of corporations.

3. The shareholders of the corporation must be individuals, estates, or certain trusts. Corporations, partnerships, and nonqualifying trusts cannot be shareholders.

4. The corporation must have thirty-five or fewer shareholders.

5. The corporation can have only one class of stock.

6. No shareholder of the corporation can be a nonresident alien.

Benefits of S Corporations At times it is beneficial for a regular corporation to elect S-corporation status, as detailed in the following checklist.

1. When the corporation has losses, the S election allows the shareholders to use such losses to offset other income.

2. Whenever the stockholders are in a lower tax bracket than that applied to a C corporation, the S election causes the corporation's entire income to be taxed in the shareholders' bracket, whether or not it is distributed. This is particularly attractive when the corporation wants to accumulate earnings for some future business purpose.

3. Corporate income is taxed only once. This single tax is imposed at individual income tax rates at the shareholder level and must be paid by shareholders whether or not the income is actually distributed.

Formation of Corporations

The formation of a corporation involves two steps: (1) preliminary organizational and promotional un-

---

6. Senate Committee Report No. 97-640.

dertakings—particularly, obtaining capital for the future corporation—and (2) the legal process of incorporation.

Before a corporation becomes a reality, people invest in the proposed corporation as subscribers, and contracts are frequently made by *promoters* on behalf of the future corporation. Promoters are those who, for themselves or others, take the preliminary steps in organizing a corporation. They issue the *prospectus*[7] for the proposed organization and secure a charter.

It is not unusual for a promoter to purchase or lease property with a view to selling it to the corporation when the corporation is formed. In addition, a promoter may enter into contracts with attorneys, accountants, architects, or other professionals whose services will be needed in planning for the proposed corporation. Finally, a promoter induces people to purchase stock in the corporation.

PROMOTER'S LIABILITY   Some interesting legal questions arise in regard to promoters' activities, the most important centering on whether the promoter is personally liable for contracts made on behalf of a corporation that does not yet have any legal existence. In addition, once the corporation is formed, does it assume liability on these contracts, or is the promoter still personally liable?

As a general rule, a promoter is held personally liable on preincorporation contracts. Courts simply hold that promoters are not agents when a corporation has yet to come into existence. If, however, the promoter secures the contracting party's agreement to hold only the corporation (not the promoter) liable on the contract, the promoter will not be liable in the event of any breach of contract.

Basically, the same rule of personal liability of the promoter continues even after incorporation unless the third party *releases* the promoter. In most states, this rule is applied whether or not the promoter made the agreement in the name of, or with reference to, the proposed corporation.

---

7. A *prospectus* also is a document required by federal or state securities laws and regulations that contains material facts concerning the financial operations of the corporation, thus allowing an investor to make an informed decision. Securities regulation is discussed in Chapter 24.

Once the corporation is formed (the charter issued), the promoter remains personally liable until the corporation assumes the preincorporation contract by *novation*. A novation releases the promoter and makes the corporation liable for performing the contractual obligations. In some cases the corporation *adopts* the promoter's contract by undertaking to perform it. Most courts hold that adoption in and of itself does not discharge the promoter from contractual liability. Obviously, a corporation cannot normally *ratify* a preincorporation contract, as no principal was in existence at the time the contract was made.

SUBSCRIBERS AND SUBSCRIPTIONS   Before the actual formation of the corporation, the promoter can contact potential individual investors, and they can agree to purchase capital stock in the future corporation. This agreement is often called a *subscription agreement,* and the potential investor is called a *subscriber.* Depending on state law, subscribers become shareholders as soon as the corporation is formed or as soon as the corporation accepts the agreement. This way, if Corporation X becomes insolvent, the trustee in bankruptcy can collect the consideration for any unpaid stock from a preincorporation subscriber.

Most courts view preincorporation subscriptions as continuing offers to purchase corporate stock. On or after its formation, the corporation can choose to accept the offer to purchase stock. Many courts also treat a subscription as a contract between the subscribers, making it irrevocable except with the consent of all of the subscribers. A subscription is irrevocable for a period of six months unless otherwise provided in the subscription agreement or unless all the subscribers agree to the revocation of the subscription. In some courts and jurisdictions, the preincorporation subscriber can revoke the offer to purchase before acceptance without liability, however.

Incorporation

Exact procedures for incorporation differ among states, but the basic requirements are similar. Because state incorporation laws differ, individuals have found some advantage in looking for the states that offer the most advantageous tax or incorporation provisions. Delaware has historically had the least restrictive laws. Consequently, many corporations, including a number of the largest, have incorporated there. Delaware's statutes permit firms to incorporate in Delaware and carry out business and locate operating headquarters elsewhere. (Most other states now permit this.) In contrast, closely held corporations, particularly those of a professional nature, generally incorporate in the state in which their principal stockholders live and work.

ARTICLES OF INCORPORATION The primary document needed to begin the incorporation process is called the *articles of incorporation* (see Exhibit 13–1). The articles include basic information about the corporation and serve as a primary

■ **Exhibit 13–1 Articles of Incorporation**

ARTICLE ONE

The name of the corporation is _____ .

ARTICLE TWO

The period of its duration is perpetual (may be a number of years or until a certain date).

ARTICLE THREE

The purpose (or purposes) for which the corporation is organized is (are) _____
_____ .

ARTICLE FOUR

The aggregate number of shares that the corporation shall have authority to issue is _____ of the par value of _____ dollar(s) each (or without par value).

ARTICLE FIVE

The corporation will not commence business until it has received for the issuance of its shares consideration of the value of $1,000 (can be any sum not less than $1,000).

ARTICLE SIX

The address of the corporation's registered office is _____ ,
New Pacum, and the name of its registered agent at such address is _____
_____ .

(Use the street or building or rural route address of the registered office, not a post office box number.)

ARTICLE SEVEN

The number of initial directors is _____ , and the names and addresses of the directors are
_____
_____ .

ARTICLE EIGHT

The name and address of the incorporator is _____
_____ .

(signed) _____
Incorporator

Sworn to on _____ by the above-named incorporator.
      (date)

_____
Notary Public _____ County, New Pacum

(Notary Seal)

---

source of authority for its future organization and business functions.

Corporate Name   Choice of a corporate name is subject to state approval to ensure against duplication or deception. Fictitious-name statutes usually require that the secretary of state run a check on the proposed name in the state of incorporation. Some states require that the incorporators, at their own expense, run a check on the proposed fictional name for the newly formed corporation. Once cleared, a name can be reserved for a short time, for a fee, pending the completion of the articles of incorporation. All corporate statutes require the corporation name to include the word *Corporation, Incorporated,* or *Limited,* or abbreviations of these terms.

A corporate name is prohibited from being the same as, or deceptively similar to, the name of an existing corporation doing business within the state. For example, if an existing corporation is named General Dynamics, Inc., the state will not allow another corporation to be called General Dynamic, Inc., because that name is deceptively similar to the first, and it impliedly transfers a part of the goodwill established by the first corporate user to the second corporation.

Nature and Purpose   The intended business activities of the corporation must be specified in the articles, and, naturally, they must be lawful. A general statement of corporate purpose is usually sufficient to give rise to all of the powers necessary or convenient to the purpose of the organization. The corporate charter can state, for example, that the corporation is organized ''to engage in the production and sale of agricultural products.'' There is a trend toward allowing corporate charters to state that the corporation is organized for ''any legal business,'' with no mention of specifics, to avoid unnecessary future amendments to the corporate charter.

Duration   A corporation can have perpetual existence under most state corporate statutes. A few states, however, prescribe a maximum duration, after which the corporation must formally renew its existence.

Capital Structure   The capital structure of the corporation is generally set forth in the articles. A few state statutes require a relatively small capital investment (for example, $1,000) for ordinary business corporations but a greater capital investment for those engaged in insurance or banking. The number of shares of stock authorized for issuance, their par value, the various types or classes of stock authorized for issuance, and other relevant information concerning equity, capital, and credit must be outlined in the articles.

Internal Organization   Whatever the internal management structure of the corporation, it should be described in the articles, although it can be included in bylaws adopted after the corporation is formed. The articles of incorporation commence the corporation; the bylaws are formed after commencement by the incorporators or the board of directors. Bylaws are subject to and cannot conflict with the incorporation statute and the corporation's charter. Under the RMBCA, shareholders may amend or repeal bylaws. The board of directors may also amend or repeal bylaws unless the articles of incorporation or provisions of the incorporation statute reserve the power to the shareholders exclusively. Typical bylaw provisions describe the voting requirements for shareholders, the election of the board of directors, the methods of replacing directors, and the manner and time of scheduling shareholder and board meetings.

Registered Office and Agent   The corporation must indicate the location and address of its registered office within the state. Usually, the registered office is also the principal office of the corporation. The corporation must give the name and address of a specific person who has been designated as an *agent* and who can receive legal documents on behalf of the corporation. These legal documents include service of process (the delivery of a court order requiring an appearance in court) if the corporation is named in a lawsuit.

Incorporators   Each incorporator must be listed by name and must indicate an address. An incorporator is a person who applies to the state on behalf of the corporation to obtain its corporate charter. The incorporator need not be a subscriber and need not have any interest at all in the corporation. Many states do not impose residency or age requirements for incorporators. States vary on the required number of incorporators; it can be as few as one or as many as three. Incorporators are required to sign the articles of incorporation when they are submitted to the state; often this is their only duty. In some states, they participate at the first organizational meeting of the corporation.

CERTIFICATE OF INCORPORATION   Once the articles of incorporation have been prepared, signed, and authenticated by the incorporators, they are sent to the appropriate state official, usually the secretary of state, along with the appropriate filing fee. In many states, the secretary of state then issues a *certificate of incorporation* representing the state's authorization for the corporation to conduct business. (This may be called the *corporate charter*.) The certificate and a copy of the articles are returned to the incorporators, who then hold the initial organizational meeting that completes the details of incorporation.

CORPORATE FINANCING   Corporations are financed by the issuance and sale of corporate securities—bonds and stock. A detailed description of the types of securities that can be issued and the difference between stocks and bonds is given in Chapter 24.

IMPROPER INCORPORATION   The procedures for incorporation are very specific. If they are not followed precisely, others may be able to challenge the existence of the corporation. Errors in the incorporation procedures can become important when, for example, a third person who is attempting to enforce a contract or bring suit for a tort injury fortuitously learns of them. On the basis of improper incorporation, the plaintiff could seek to make the purported shareholders personally liable.

Also, when the corporation seeks to enforce a contract against a defaulting party, if the defaulting party learns of a defect in the incorporation procedure, he or she may be able to avoid liability on that ground. To prevent the windfall that would occur in giving a contracting party the benefit of the stockholders' personal liability, courts will sometimes attribute corporate existence to an improperly formed corporation by holding it to be a *de jure* corporation or a *de facto* corporation, as discussed below. In some cases, corporation by estoppel may also occur.

In the event of substantial compliance with all conditions precedent to incorporation, the corpo-

ration is said to have *de jure* existence in law. In most states the certificate of incorporation is viewed as evidence that all mandatory statutory provisions have been met. This means that the corporation is properly formed, and neither the state nor a third party can attack its existence. If, for example, an incorporator's address was incorrectly listed, this would mean that the corporation was improperly formed; but the law does not regard such inconsequential procedural defects as detracting from substantial compliance, and courts will uphold the *de jure* status of the corporate entity.

Sometimes there is a defect in complying with statutory mandates—for example, the corporation charter may have expired. Under these circumstances, the corporation may have a *de facto* status, meaning that its existence cannot be challenged by third persons (except for the state). The following elements are required for *de facto* status:

1.   There must be a state statute under which the corporation can be incorporated validly.
2.   The parties must have made a good faith attempt to comply with the statute.
3.   The enterprise must have already undertaken to do business as a corporation.

Corporation by Estoppel

If an association that is neither an actual corporation nor a *de facto* or *de jure* corporation holds itself out as being a corporation, it will be *estopped* (barred, prevented) from denying corporate status in a lawsuit by a third party. This usually occurs when a third party contracts with an association that claims to be a corporation but does not hold a certificate of incorporation. When the third party brings suit naming the so-called corporation as the defendant, the association may not escape from liability on the ground that no corporation exists. When justice requires, the courts treat an alleged corporation as if it were an actual corporation for the purpose of determining the rights and liabilities involved in a particular situation. Corporation by estoppel is thus determined by the situation. It does not extend recognition of corporate status beyond the resolution of the problem at hand.

Disregarding the Corporate Entity

In some unusual situations, a corporate entity is used by its owners to perpetuate a fraud, circumvent the law, or in some other way accomplish an illegitimate objective. In these cases, the court will ignore the corporate structure by ''piercing the corporate veil,'' thereby exposing the shareholders to personal liability.

The following are some of the factors that frequently cause the courts to pierce the corporate veil:

1.   A party is tricked or misled into dealing with the corporation rather than the individual.
2.   The corporation is set up never to make a profit or always to be insolvent, or it is too ''thinly'' capitalized.
3.   The shareholder or director unconditionally guarantees to be personally liable for corporate obligations and/or debts.
4.   Statutory corporate formalities, such as calling required corporation meetings, are not followed.
5.   Personal and corporate interests are commingled to the extent that the corporation has no separate identity.

To elaborate on the fifth factor in the preceding list, consider a close corporation that is formed according to law by a single person or by a few family members. In such a case, the corporate entity and the sole stockholder (or family-member stockholders) must carefully preserve the separate status of the corporation and its owners. Certain practices invite trouble for the one-person or family-owned corporation: the commingling of corporate and personal funds, the failure to hold and record minutes of board of directors' meetings, or the shareholders' continuous, personal use of corporate property (for example, vehicles). When the corporate privilege is abused for personal benefit and the corporate business is treated in such a careless manner that the corporation and the shareholder in control are no longer separate entities, the court will require an owner to assume personal liability to creditors for the corporation's debts. In short, when the facts show that great injustice would result from the use of a corporation to avoid individual responsibility, a court of equity will look behind the corporate structure to the individual stockholder.

General corporation law has no specific prohibition against a stockholder lawfully lending money to his or her corporation. When an officer or director lends the corporation money and takes back security in the form of corporate assets, however, the courts will scrutinize the transaction closely. Any such transaction must be made in good faith and for fair value.

In the following case, two shareholders made a lawful loan of money to a corporation (which later became insolvent) and in return took a security interest in certain pieces of corporate property. When the corporation became insolvent, some creditors charged that the shareholders' loan transaction had not been made in good faith and that their security interest should therefore be set aside.

BACKGROUND AND FACTS   *The plaintiff, InterTherm, Inc., was a creditor of Olympic Homes Systems, Inc. Two of Olympic's shareholders, Langley and Clayton, the defendants, had made a sizable loan to the corporation. In return, they took a security interest in certain corporate property. When the corporation became insolvent, the general creditors attempted to set aside the priority of the defendants' security interest. The defendants argued that the general creditors had failed to show either that there was any fraud involved in the making of the loan or that the loan was not a legitimate transaction. Moreover, according to the defendants, the general creditors had not established that the defendants' relationship to the corporation was fiduciary in nature (having the characteristics of a trust or confidence) or that they showed a lack of good faith in the loan transaction. The trial court entered judgment for the general creditors, and the shareholders appealed.*

Case 13.4

INTERTHERM, INC. v. OLYMPIC HOMES SYSTEMS, INC.

Court of Appeals of Tennessee, 1978.
569 S.W.2d 467.

DROWOTA, Judge.

* * * *

* * * As a fiduciary, the officer or director has a strong influence on how the corporation conducts its affairs, and a correspondingly strong duty not to conduct those affairs to the unfair detriment of others, such as minority shareholders or creditors, who also have legitimate interests in the corporation but lack the power of the fiduciary.

It is also generally held that courts will closely scrutinize the transactions of a majority, dominant, or controlling shareholder with his corporation, and will place the burden of proof upon the shareholder when the good faith and fairness of such a transaction is challenged. * * * It is obvious, however, that the reason for applying the rule to a shareholder is the same as the reason for applying it to an officer or director, that is, that he occupies a fiduciary position with regard to the corporation and those interested in it. Unless it is shown that a shareholder owns a majority of the stock or that he otherwise controls or dominates a corporation, however, a shareholder cannot be said to be a fiduciary and the reason for closely scrutinizing his transactions with the corporation disappears. Further, in reviewing the cases in which the courts have closely scrutinized transactions between a corporation and a shareholder and have put the burden of justifying them on the latter, we find that they almost invariably involve a majority, dominant, or controlling shareholder. Accordingly, it is clear that courts should apply the rule of close scrutiny and place the burden on the shareholder to justify a transaction with his corporation only when the shareholder owns a majority of stock, or is shown to dominate or control the corporation to a significant degree in some other way.

In the instant case, defendants contend that their secured loan to Olympic should be upheld under the general rule that shareholders may lawfully contract with their corporation. Plaintiffs, on the other hand, argue that this Court should scrutinize this transaction closely and put the burden of justifying it on defendants who, plaintiffs further argue, have failed to carry that burden. We hold that the instant transaction should not be subjected to close scrutiny, and that the burden of proof should not be on defendant shareholders, because plaintiffs have offered no evidence from which we could conclude that defendants owned a majority of Olympic's stock or otherwise dominated it in such a way as to justify imposing fiduciary responsibilities on them.

There is no evidence in this record that either defendant Langley or defendant Clayton was ever an officer or director of Olympic. The evidence is that each owned 15% of the capital stock of Olympic. It is clear that both were involved in setting up the corporation, but there is nothing to show that they participated in the business afterward. There is evidence that they did not intend to participate in the corporation's everyday affairs. * * * In short, there is no evidence of any degree of power or control by defendants over the corporation at any time. * * *

Plaintiffs, then, by failing to show that defendants Langley and Clayton had any fiduciary capacity with Olympic, have failed to shift from themselves the burden of proving fraud or absence of good faith in the loan transaction.

DECISION AND REMEDY   *The Supreme Court of Tennessee reversed the lower court's decision and held that the defendants, Langley and Clayton, held a valid security interest in the property of Olympic and were entitled to priority over the general creditors.*

Corporate Management—Shareholders

The acquisition of a share of stock makes a person an owner and shareholder in a corporation. As a shareholder, that person acquires certain powers in the corporation. These powers are discussed here, along with the relationship of the shareholders to the corporation.

SHAREHOLDERS' POWERS Shareholders must approve fundamental changes affecting the corporation before the changes can be effected. Hence, shareholders are empowered to amend the articles of incorporation (charter) and bylaws, approve merger or dissolution of the corporation, and approve the sale of all or substantially all of the corporation's assets. Some of these powers are subject to prior board approval.

Election and removal of the board of directors are accomplished by a vote of the shareholders. The first board of directors is either named in the articles of incorporation or chosen by the incorporators to serve until the first shareholders' meeting. From that time on, selection and retention of directors are exclusively shareholder functions.

Directors usually serve their full term; if they are unsatisfactory, they are simply not reelected. Shareholders have the inherent power, however, to remove a director from office *for cause* (breach of duty or misconduct) by a majority vote.[8] Some state statutes even permit removal of directors *without cause* by the vote of a majority of the holders of outstanding shares entitled to vote.[9]

RELATIONSHIP BETWEEN SHAREHOLDERS AND CORPORATION

As a general rule, shareholders have no responsibility for the daily management of the corporation, although they are ultimately responsible for choosing the board of directors, which does have such control. Ordinarily, corporate officers and other employees owe no direct duty to *individual* stockholders. Their duty is to the corporation as a whole. A director, however, is in a fiduciary relationship to the corporation and therefore serves the interests of the shareholders as a whole.

Generally, there is no legal relationship between shareholders and creditors of the corporation. Shareholders can, in fact, be creditors of the corporation and have the same rights of recovery against the corporation as any other creditor. (See

Case 13.4 above.) The rights and liabilities of shareholders are discussed in detail in the following chapter.

SHAREHOLDERS' FORUM Shareholders' meetings must occur at least annually, and additional, special meetings can be called to take care of urgent matters. Because it is usually not practical for owners of only a few shares of stock of publicly traded corporations to attend a shareholders' meeting, they normally give third persons a written authorization to vote their shares at the meeting. This authorization, called a **proxy,** is often solicited by management, as will be discussed later.

NOTICE OF MEETINGS The notice and time of meetings, including the day and the hour, are announced in writing to each shareholder at a reasonable length of time before the date of the shareholders' meeting.[10] Special-meeting notices must include a statement of the purpose of the meeting; business transacted at a special meeting is limited to that purpose.

SHAREHOLDER VOTING For shareholders to act, a minimum number of them (in terms of number of shares held) must be present at a meeting. This minimum number, called a *quorum,* is generally more than 50 percent. Corporate business matters are presented in the form of *resolutions,* which shareholders vote to approve or disapprove. Some state statutes have set forth voting limits, and corporations' articles or bylaws must remain within these statutory limitations. Some states provide that the unanimous written consent of shareholders is a permissible alternative to holding a shareholders' meeting.

Once a quorum is present, a majority vote of the shares represented at the meeting is usually required to pass resolutions. Assume that Novo Pictures, Inc., has 10,000 outstanding shares of voting stock. Its articles set the quorum at 50 percent of outstanding shares and provide that a majority

---

8. A director can often demand court review of removal for cause.

9. Most states allow *cumulative voting* (which will be discussed shortly) for directors, meaning that no individual director can be removed if the number of votes cast against his or her removal would be sufficient to elect that director if cumulatively voted at an election of the entire board of directors. See, for example, California Corporate Code Section 303A. Also see RMBCA 8.08(c).

---

10. The shareholder can waive the requirement of written notice by signing a waiver form. A shareholder who does not receive written notice, but who learns of the meeting and attends without protesting the lack of notice, is said to have waived notice by such conduct. State statutes and corporate bylaws typically set forth the time within which notice must be sent, what methods can be used, and what the notice must contain.

vote of the shares present is necessary to pass on ordinary matters. At the shareholders' meeting, a quorum of stockholders representing 5,000 outstanding shares must be present to conduct business, and a vote of at least 2,501 of those shares represented at the meeting is needed to pass ordinary resolutions. If more than 5,000 are present, a larger vote will be needed.

At times, a larger-than-majority vote will be required either by statute or by corporate charter. Extraordinary corporate matters, such as merger, consolidation, or dissolution of the corporation, require the approval of a higher percentage of the representatives of all corporate shares entitled to vote, not just a majority of those present at that particular meeting.

VOTING LISTS　Voting lists are prepared by the corporation before each shareholders' meeting. Persons whose names appear on the corporation's stockholder records as owners are the ones ordinarily entitled to vote.[11] The voting list contains the name and address of each shareholder as shown on the corporate records on a given cutoff date, or record date. (RMBCA 7.07 allows a record date to be as much as seventy days before the meeting.) It also includes the number of voting shares held by each owner. The list is usually kept at the corporate headquarters and is available for shareholder inspection.

VOTING TECHNIQUES　Most states permit or require shareholders to elect directors by **cumulative voting,** a method of voting designed to allow minority shareholders representation on the board of directors.[12] Cumulative voting operates as follows: The number of members of the board to be elected is multiplied by the total number of voting shares held. The result equals the number of votes a shareholder has, and this total can be cast for one or more nominees for director. All nominees stand for election at the same time. When cumulative voting

is not required either by statute or under the articles, the entire board can be elected by a simple majority of the voting shares at a shareholders' meeting.

To illustrate: A corporation has 10,000 shares issued and outstanding. The minority shareholders hold only 3,000 shares, and the majority shareholders hold the other 7,000 shares. Three members of the board are to be elected. The majority shareholders' nominees are Mott, Gregory, and Dunsworth. The minority shareholders' nominee is Diamond. Can Diamond be elected by the minority shareholders?

If cumulative voting is allowed, the answer is yes. The minority shareholders have 9,000 votes among them, since the number of directors to be elected times the number of shares equals 3 times 3,000, which equals 9,000 votes. All of these votes can be cast to elect Diamond. The majority shareholders have 21,000 votes (3 times 7,000 equals 21,000 votes), but these votes have to be distributed among their three nominees. The principle of cumulative voting is that no matter how the majority shareholders cast their 21,000 votes, they will not be able to elect all three directors if the minority shareholders cast all of their 9,000 votes for Diamond, as illustrated in Exhibit 13–2.

SHAREHOLDER AGREEMENTS　A group of shareholders can agree in writing before the meeting to vote their shares together in a specified manner. Voting agreements are usually held to be valid and enforceable.

PROXY VOTING　A shareholder can appoint a voting agent. A *proxy* is a written authorization to cast the shareholder's vote, and a person can solicit proxies from a number of shareholders in an attempt to concentrate voting power.

VOTING TRUST　Shareholders can enter into a *voting trust,* which is an agreement (a trust contract) by which legal title (record ownership on the corporate books) is transferred to a trustee who is responsible for voting the shares. The agreement can specify how the trustee is to vote, or it can allow the trustee to use his or her discretion. The trustee takes physical possession of the actual stock certificate and in return gives the shareholder a *voting trust certificate.* The shareholder retains all of the rights of ownership (for example, the right

---

11.　When the legal owner is deceased, bankrupt, incompetent, or in some other way under a legal disability, his or her vote can be cast by a person designated by law to control and manage the owner's property.

12.　See, for example, California Corporate Code Section 708. RMBCA 7.28, however, states that no cumulative voting rights exist unless the articles of incorporation so provide.

■ **Exhibit 13–2 Results of Cumulative Voting**

Ballot	Majority Shareholder Votes			Minority Shareholder Votes	Directors Elected
	Mott	*Gregory*	*Dunsworth*	*Diamond*	
1	10,000	10,000	1,000	9,000	Mott, Gregory, Diamond
2	9,001	9,000	2,999	9,000	Mott, Gregory, Diamond
3	6,000	7,000	8,000	9,000	Gregory, Dunsworth, Diamond

to receive dividend payments) except for the power to vote.

A voting trust is not the same thing as a proxy, for the latter can be revoked more easily. The holder of a proxy has neither legal title to the stock nor possession of the certificates, whereas voting trustees have both.[13]

Corporate Management—Directors

Every corporation is governed by directors. Subject to statutory limitations, the number of directors is set forth in the corporation's articles or bylaws. Historically, the minimum number of directors has been three, but today many states permit fewer. Indeed, RMBCA 8.01 permits corporations with fewer than fifty shareholders to eliminate the board of directors.

DIRECTORS' ELECTION AND TERM OF OF-FICE The first board of directors is normally appointed by the incorporators on the creation of the corporation, or directors are named by the corporation itself in the articles. The first board serves until the first annual shareholders' meeting. Subsequent directors are elected by a majority vote of the shareholders.

The term of office for a director is usually one year—from annual meeting to annual meeting. Longer and staggered terms are permissible under most state statutes. A common practice is to elect one-third of the board members each year for a

three-year term. In this way, there is greater management continuity.

A director can be removed *for cause,* either as specified in the articles or bylaws or by shareholder action. Even the board of directors itself may be given power to remove a director for cause, subject to shareholder review. In most states, unless the shareholders have reserved the right at the time of election, a director cannot be removed without cause.

When vacancies occur on the board of directors due to death or resignation, or when a new position is created through amendment of the articles or bylaws, either the shareholders or the board itself can fill the position, depending on state law or on the provisions of the bylaws.

DIRECTORS' QUALIFICATIONS AND COMPEN-SATION Few legal qualifications exist for directors. Only a handful of states retain minimum age and residency requirements. A director is sometimes a shareholder, but this is not a necessary qualification unless, of course, statutory provisions or corporate articles or bylaws require ownership.

Compensation for directors is ordinarily specified in the corporate articles or bylaws. Because directors have a fiduciary relationship to the shareholders and to the corporation, an express agreement or provision for compensation is necessary for them to receive money from the funds they control or for which they have responsibilities.

DIRECTORS' MANAGEMENT RESPONSIBIL-ITIES Directors have responsibility for all policymaking decisions necessary to the management of all corporate affairs. Just as shareholders cannot act individually to bind the corporation, the directors must act as a body in carrying out routine

---

13. In most states, the term of a voting trust cannot exceed ten years. RMBCA 7.30 provides that it may be extended for an additional term of up to ten years. In contrast, proxies are typically limited to no more than eleven months, unless a proxy specifically provides otherwise [RMBCA 7.22].

corporate business. One director has one vote, and generally the majority rules.

The general areas of responsibility of the board of directors include the following:

1.   Declaration and payment of corporate dividends to shareholders.
2.   Authorization for major corporate policy decisions—for example, the initiation of proceedings for the sale or lease of corporate assets outside the regular course of business, the determination of new product lines, and the overseeing of major contract negotiations and major management-labor negotiations.
3.   Appointment, supervision, and removal of corporate officers and other managerial employees and the determination of their compensation.
4.   Financial decisions such as the declaration and payment of dividends to shareholders or the issuance of authorized shares or bonds.

BOARD OF DIRECTORS' FORUM   The board of directors conducts business by holding formal meetings with recorded minutes. The date on which regular meetings are held is usually established in the articles and bylaws or by board resolution, and no further notice is customarily required. Special meetings can be called with notice sent to all directors.

Quorum requirements can vary among jurisdictions. Many states leave the decision to the corporate articles or bylaws. In the absence of specific quorum requirements thereof, most states provide that a quorum is a majority of the number of directors authorized in the articles or bylaws. Voting is done *in person* (unlike voting at shareholders' meetings, which can be done by proxy).[14] The rule is one vote per director. Ordinary matters generally require a majority vote; certain extraordinary issues may require a greater-than-majority vote.

DELEGATION OF BOARD OF DIRECTORS' POWERS   The board of directors can delegate some of its functions to an executive committee or to corporate officers. In doing so, the board is not relieved of its overall responsibility for directing the affairs of the corporation, but corporate officers and managerial personnel are empowered to make decisions relating to ordinary, daily corporate affairs within well-defined guidelines.

Executive Committee   Most states permit the board of directors to elect an executive committee from among the directors to handle the interim management decisions between board of directors' meetings, as provided in the bylaws. The executive committee is limited to making management decisions about ordinary business matters.

Corporate Officers   The officers and other executive employees are hired by the board of directors or, in rare instances, by the shareholders. In addition to carrying out the duties articulated in the bylaws, corporate and managerial officers act as agents of the corporation, and the ordinary rules of agency (as discussed in Chapter 15) apply or have been applied to their employment (unlike the board of directors, whose powers are conferred by the state).

Qualifications are determined at the discretion of the corporation and are included in the articles or bylaws. In most states, a person can hold more than one office and can be both an officer and a director of the corporation. Corporate officers can be removed by the board of directors at any time with or without cause and regardless of the terms of the employment contract, although it is possible for the corporation to be liable for breach of contract damages.

■ Other Organizational Forms

A business venture does not have to be organized as a sole proprietorship, a partnership, or a corporation. Several other organizational forms exist, although for the most part they are hybrid organizations—that is, they have characteristics similar to those of partnerships or corporations or combine features of both. We look at several of these forms here.

Joint Venture

When two or more persons or entities combine their interests in a particular business enterprise and

---

14.   Except in Louisiana, where a director can vote by proxy under certain circumstances. Some states, such as Michigan and Texas, and RMBCA 8.20 permit telephone conferences for board of director meetings.

agree to share in losses or profits jointly or in proportion to their contributions, they are engaged in a **joint venture.** The joint venture is treated much like a partnership, but it differs in that its creation is in contemplation of a limited activity or a single transaction.

For example, Rusty and Marco pool their resources to buy an old boat, remodel it, and sell it, dividing the profits. This creates not a partnership but a joint venture. The same is true if Rusty, owning a piece of land, and Marco, owning an adjoining piece of land, agree to sell both parcels together as one unit to the highest bidder and then divide the proceeds proportionately to the value of each parcel of land held.

Members of a joint venture usually have limited powers to bind their co-venturers. A joint venture is normally not a legal entity and therefore cannot be sued as such, but its members can be sued individually. Usually joint ventures are taxed like partnerships. They range in size from very small activities to huge, multimillion-dollar joint actions engaged in by some of the world's largest corporations.

Syndicate

A group of individuals getting together to finance a particular project, such as the building of a shopping center or the purchase of a professional basketball franchise, is called a **syndicate** or an *investment group.* The form of such groups varies considerably. They may exist as corporations or as general or limited partnerships. In some cases, the members merely own property jointly and have no legally recognized business arrangement.

Joint Stock Company

A **joint stock company** is a true hybrid of a partnership and a corporation. It has many characteristics of a corporation in that (1) its ownership is represented by transferable shares of stock, (2) it is usually managed by directors and officers of the company or association, and (3) it can have a perpetual existence. Most of its other features, however, are more characteristic of a partnership, and it is usually treated like a partnership. As with a partnership, it is formed by agreement (not statute), property is usually held in the names of the members, shareholders have personal liability, and generally the company is not treated as a legal entity for purposes of a lawsuit. In a joint stock company, however, shareholders are not considered to be agents of each other, as would be the case if the company were a true partnership.

Business Trust

A **business trust** is created by a written trust agreement that sets forth the interests of the beneficiaries and the obligations and powers of the trustees who manage the property placed in trust for the benefit of the beneficiaries. With a business trust, legal ownership and management of the property of the business stay with one or more of the trustees, and the profits are distributed to the beneficiaries.

The business trust was started in Massachusetts in an attempt to obtain the limited-liability advantage of corporate status while avoiding certain restrictions on a corporation's ownership and development of real property. The business trust resembles a corporation in many respects. Death or bankruptcy of a beneficiary, for example, does not terminate the trust, and beneficiaries are not personally responsible for the debts or obligations of the business trust. In fact, in a number of states business trusts must pay corporate taxes.

Cooperative

A **cooperative** is an association, either incorporated or not, that is organized to provide an economic service without profit to its members (or shareholders). An incorporated cooperative is subject to state laws governing nonprofit corporations. It will make distributions of dividends, or profits, to its owners on the basis of their transactions with the cooperative rather than on the basis of the amount of capital they contributed.

Cooperatives that are unincorporated are often treated like partnerships. The members have joint liability for the cooperative's acts. This form of business is generally adopted by groups of individuals who wish to pool their resources to gain some advantage in the marketplace. Consumer purchasing cooperatives are formed to obtain lower prices through quantity discounts. Seller marketing cooperatives are formed to control the market and thereby obtain higher sale prices from consumers. Credit cooperatives and farmers' cooperatives are other examples of this form of business enterprise.

Cooperatives are often exempt from certain federal laws—for example, antitrust statutes—because of their special status.

■ Private Franchises

Times have changed dramatically since Ray Kroc, the late founder of McDonald's, launched the franchising boom more than thirty-five years ago. Today, over a third of all retail sales and an increasing part of the gross national product of the United States are generated by private franchises. A **franchise** is any arrangement in which the owner of a trademark, a trade name, or a copyright has licensed others to use the trademark, trade name, or copyright in selling goods or services. A **franchisee** (a purchaser of a franchise) is generally legally independent but economically dependent on the integrated business system of the **franchisor** (the seller of the franchise). In other words, an individual can operate as an independent businessperson but still obtain the advantages of a regional or national organization. Well-known franchises include McDonald's, Hilton Hotels, Kentucky Fried Chicken, Blockbuster Video, and Burger King.

The Law of Franchising

The growth in franchise operations has outdistanced the law of franchising. There has yet to be developed a solid body of appellate decisions under federal or state laws relating to franchises. In the absence of case law precisely addressed to franchising, the courts tend to apply general common law principles and appropriate federal or state statutory definitions and rules. The franchise relationship has characteristics associated with agency law, employment law, and independent contracting; yet it does not truly fit into any of these traditional classifications.

Some statutory requirements specifically relating to franchising have been enacted at the federal level. Automobile dealership franchisees are protected from automobile manufacturers' bad faith termination of their franchises by the Automobile Dealers' Franchise Act (enacted in 1956), also known as the Automobile Dealers' Day in Court Act.[15] If a manufacturer-franchisor termi-

nates a franchise for a dealer-franchisee's failure to comply with unreasonable demands (for example, failure to attain an unrealistically high sales quota), the manufacturer is liable for damages.

Other federal statutes include the Petroleum Marketing Practices Act (PMPA),[16] which was adopted in 1979 to protect gasoline station franchisees' reasonable expectations in the continuation of their franchises. Before the PMPA's passage, gasoline franchisors were some times known to impose high minimum rents and gallonage requirements, and the situation only worsened during the energy crisis in the early 1970s. The PMPA prescribes the grounds and conditions under which a franchisor may terminate or decline to renew a franchise. Federal antitrust laws (discussed in Chapters 20 and 21) may also apply if there is an illegal price-fixing agreement affecting the relationship between a franchisor and franchisee. In 1979, the Federal Trade Commission (FTC) issued regulations that require franchisors to disclose material facts necessary to a prospective franchisee's making an informed decision concerning the purchase of a franchise.

Many states currently have statutes dealing with franchise law. State legislation tends to be similar to federal statutes and the FTC regulations. That is, state laws are generally designed to protect prospective franchisees from dishonest franchisors and to prohibit franchisors from terminating franchises without good cause. For example, a law might require the disclosure of information that is material to making an informed decision regarding the purchase of a franchise. This could include such information as the actual costs of operation, recurring expenses, and profits earned and facts substantiating these figures.

When a franchise exists primarily for the sale of products manufactured by the franchisor, the law governing sales as expressed in Article 2 of the Uniform Commercial Code (discussed in Chapter 10) applies.

Types of Franchises

Franchises can take the form of distributorships, chain-style business operations, or manufacturing or processing-plant arrangements.

---

15.   15 U.S.C. Sections 1221 *et. seq.*

16.   15 U.S.C. Sections 2801 *et seq.*

1. A *distributorship* is established when a manufacturing concern (franchisor) licenses a dealer (franchisee) to sell its product. Often, a distributorship covers an exclusive territory. An example of this type of franchise is an automobile dealership.

2. A *chain-style business franchise* occurs when a franchise operates under a franchisor's trade name and is identified as a member of a select group of dealers that engages in the franchisor's business. The franchisee is generally required to follow standardized or prescribed methods of operations. Often, the franchisor requires that the franchisee maintain certain standards of operation. In addition, sometimes the franchisee is obligated to deal exclusively with the franchisor to obtain materials and supplies. Examples of this type of franchise include McDonald's and most other fast-food chains.

3. A *manufacturing* or *processing-plant franchise* is created when the franchisor transmits to the franchisee the essential ingredients or formula to make a particular product. The franchisee then markets it either at wholesale or at retail in accordance with the franchisor's standards. Examples of this type of franchise are Coca-Cola and other soft-drink bottling companies.

Franchise Agreement

The franchise relationship is defined by a contract between the franchisor and the franchisee. Each franchise relationship and each industry has its own characteristics, so it is difficult to describe the broad range of details a franchising contract may include. The following sections, however, define the essential characteristics of the franchise relationship.

ENTERING THE FRANCHISE RELATIONSHIP   Prospective franchisees must initially decide on the type of business they wish to undertake. Then they must obtain information about the business from the franchisor. Usually, franchisors have numerous statistics and market studies available for prospective franchisees to examine. Of course, people who acquire franchised businesses vary greatly in their degree of business acumen. Some are experienced businesspersons with a firm grasp of the economic realities of how to operate a franchise. Others have no business experience. Ob-

viously, the inexperienced franchisee must rely heavily on the franchisor in evaluating and setting up the initial business organization.

PAYING FOR THE FRANCHISE   The franchisee ordinarily pays an initial fee or lump-sum price for the franchise license (the privilege of being granted a franchise). This fee is separate from the various products that the franchisee purchases from or through the franchisor. In some industries, the franchisor relies heavily on the initial sale of the franchise for realizing a profit. In other industries, the continued dealing between the parties brings profit to both.

In most situations, the franchisor will receive a stated percentage of the annual sales or annual volume of business done by the franchisee. The franchise agreement may also require the franchisee to pay a percentage of advertising costs and certain administrative expenses incurred under the franchise agreement.

LOCATION AND BUSINESS ORGANIZATION OF THE FRANCHISE   Typically, the franchisor will determine the territory to be served. The franchise agreement may specify whether the premises for the business must be leased or purchased outright. In some cases, construction of a building is necessary to meet the terms of the franchise agreement.

Certainly the agreement will specify whether the franchisor supplies equipment and furnishings for the premises or whether this is the responsibility of the franchisee. When the franchise is a service operation, such as a motel, the contract often provides that the franchisor will establish certain standards for the facility and will make inspections to ensure that the standards are being maintained to protect the franchise name and reputation.

The business organization of the franchisee is of great concern to the franchisor. Depending on the terms of the franchise agreement, the franchisor may specify particular requirements for the form and capital structure of the business. The franchise agreement can provide that certain standards, relating to such aspects of the business as sales quotas or record-keeping, be met by the franchisee. Furthermore, a franchisor may wish to retain stringent control over the training of personnel involved in the operation and over administrative aspects of the business. Although the day-to-day operation of the franchise business is normally left up to the franchisee, the franchise agreement may provide for whatever amount of supervision and control the parties agree on.

PRICE AND QUALITY CONTROLS OF THE FRANCHISE   Franchises provide the franchisor with an outlet for the firm's goods and services. Depending on the nature of the business, the franchisor may require the franchisee to purchase certain supplies from the franchisor at an established price.[17] Of course, a franchisor cannot set the prices at which the franchisee will resell the goods, as this is a violation of state or federal antitrust laws, or both. A franchisor can suggest retail prices but cannot insist on them.

As a general rule, the validity of a provision permitting the franchisor to enforce certain quality standards is unquestioned. Because the franchisor has a legitimate interest in maintaining the quality of the product or service to protect its name and reputation, it can exercise greater control in this area than would otherwise be tolerated.

TERMINATION OF THE FRANCHISE ARRANGEMENT   The duration of the franchise is a matter to be determined between the parties. Generally, a franchise will start out for a short period, such as a year, so that the franchisee and the franchisor can determine whether they want to stay in

---

17.   Although a franchisor can require franchisees to purchase supplies from it, requiring a franchisee to purchase exclusively from the franchisor may violate federal antitrust laws. See Chapter 21.

business with one another. Usually the franchise agreement will specify that termination must be "for cause," such as death or disability of the franchisee, insolvency of the franchisee, breach of the franchise agreement, or failure to meet specified sales quotas. Most franchise contracts provide that notice of termination must be given. If no set time for termination is given, then a reasonable time with notice will be implied. A franchisee must be given reasonable time to wind up the business— that is, to do the accounting and return the copyright or trademark or any other property of the franchisor.

Much franchise litigation has arisen over termination provisions. Because the franchise agreement is normally a form contract drawn and prepared by the franchisor, and because the bargaining power of the franchisee is rarely equal to that of the franchisor, the termination provisions of contracts are generally more favorable to the franchisor. This means that the franchisee, who normally invests a substantial amount of time and money in the franchise operation to make it successful, may receive little or nothing for the business on termination. The franchisor owns the trademark and hence the business.

It is in this area that the lack of statutory law and case law is felt most keenly by the franchisee. Automobile dealerships and gasoline stations subject to franchise contracts now have some statutory protection, however, under the Automobile Dealers' Franchise Act and the Petroleum Marketing Practices Act, respectively. Whether a franchise agreement had been unfairly terminated by the franchisor under the provisions of the PMPA is the subject of the following case.

Case 13.5

RETSIEG CORP. v. ARCO PETROLEUM PRODUCTS CO.
United States Court of Appeals, Ninth Circuit, 1989.
870 F.2d 1495.

BACKGROUND AND FACTS   *In June 1985, Retsieg Corporation entered into a franchise agreement with Arco Petroleum Products Company under which Retsieg would operate an Arco mini market and gas station in Monterey, California. Retsieg was authorized to sell only "Arco branded motor fuels"—which were designated as fuels containing a special Arco additive known as R-585. The required percentage of R-585 in Arco fuels was never made too clear by Arco in its interrogatories but apparently ranged between .05 and .12 percent. In October 1986 Retsieg, after informing Arco of its plans, began to purchase Arco gas (gas containing the R-585 additive) from a cheaper supplier, Caljet. Tests conducted by Arco of the Caljet gas sold by Retsieg showed that the regular gas was "at* *the high end" of the required R-585 content but the unleaded gas and super unleaded gas contained only .02 percent and .03 percent, respectively, of R-585. In November, Arco terminated Retsieg's franchise by written notice on the ground that Retsieg had willfully misbranded the gas in violation of the Petroleum Practices Marketing Act. Retsieg claimed that it had not misbranded the gas, willfully or otherwise, and brought this action against Arco for wrongful termination of the franchise. The district court granted summary judgment for Arco, holding that there was no triable issue of fact. The district court reasoned that under the PMPA "willful" does not require proof of a bad motive; it requires only an intentional act. The court further found it to be "undisputed" that the Caljet gas did not qualify as Arco gas. Thus, because Retsieg "willfully" bought the Caljet gas, it violated the franchise agreement, which Arco could terminate under the PMPA.*

BEEZER, Circuit Judge.

* * * *

The district court's stated reasons for the grant of summary judgment were insufficient. First, it was not "undisputed" that Caljet sold no Arco gasoline. Arco's own tests on the tank of regular gas call that fact into serious question. And if Retsieg received some Arco gasoline, we cannot hold as a matter of summary judgment that Retsieg did not request Arco gasoline from Caljet, despite the absence of any such indication on purchase orders or invoices. It may be coincidence that some of Caljet's gasoline was Arco gasoline, but that is for the trier of fact to determine.

Second, the definition of Arco gasoline is not so clear as to allow us to find that Arco established misbranding (whether willful or not) to the satisfaction of any rational jury. The only test results in the record show that three samples of Retsieg's "Arco" gasoline contained significant amounts of R-585, although two contained less than Arco's specification ranges, as stated in Arco's memorandum. Arco's interrogatory response, however, can reasonably be read as conceding that any amount of R-585 qualifies gasoline as Arco product. Further factfinding appears necessary.

* * * The district court's rationale for granting summary judgment fails because the proper definition of "willful" is more complex than the court's analysis indicates.

We must define "willful misbranding" and apply that definition to the facts before the district court. * * *

* * * *

We adopt [a previous case's] well-reasoned definition for PMPA purposes: A willful adulteration, mislabeling, or misbranding is one involving voluntary action, done either with an intentional disregard of, or plain indifference to the requirements of the franchise agreement. This definition requires, then, either an intent to misbrand—"willful," after all, modifies "misbranding"—or plain indifference to the agreement. It therefore would not have been willful misbranding for Retsieg to sell fuel purchased from a supplier who had promised Arco gasoline, unless Retsieg, by engaging in the transaction, was plainly "indifferent" to the franchisor's requirements. * * *

The evidence is not conclusive.

The appellate court concluded that whether the gas was misbranded and, if so, whether Retsieg had misbranded it willfully were issues that needed to be decided at trial. Holding that summary judgment for Arco was thus inappropriate, that decision was reversed and the case remanded for trial.

DECISION AND REMEDY

■ Terms and Concepts to Review

business trust 319
close corporation 306
cooperative 319
corporation 303
cumulative voting 316
double taxation 304
franchise 320

franchisee 320
franchisor 320
joint stock company 319
joint venture 319
limited liability 303
limited partnership 301

minimum-contacts
   requirement 304
partnership 301
proxy 315
S corporations 308
sole proprietorship 300
syndicate 319

■ Questions and Case Problems

13-1. Suppose Ann, Betty, and Carla are college graduates, and Ann has come up with an idea for a new product that she believes could make the three of them very rich. Her idea is to manufacture purified water dispensers for home use, and her goal is to market them to consumers throughout the Midwest. Ann's personal experience qualifies her to be both first-line supervisor and general manager of the new firm. Betty is a born salesperson. Carla has little interest in sales or management but would like to invest a large sum of money that she has inherited from her aunt. Discuss fully what factors Ann, Betty, and Carla should consider in deciding which form of business organization to adopt.

13-2. In the situation described in Question 13-1, assume that Carla is willing to put her inherited money in the business but does not want any further liability should the purified water dispenser manufacturing business fail. Alternatively, the bank is willing to lend some capital at a 12 percent interest rate, but it will do so only if certain restrictions are placed on management decisions. The bank's plan is not satisfactory to Ann or Betty, and the two decide to bring Carla into the business. Under these circumstances, discuss which types of business organizations are best suited to meet the needs of Carla.

13-3. The limited liability of corporate shareholders is one of the most important reasons that firms choose to organize as corporations rather than as partnerships or sole proprietorships. Limited liability means that if a corporation is not able to meet its obligations with corporate assets, creditors will not be allowed to look to the owners (stockholders) of the corporation to satisfy their claims. Assume that Ann and Betty (in Question 13-1) do not have a wealthy friend like Carla who wishes to go into business with them and they therefore must borrow money to start their business. Ann and Betty decide to incorporate. What do you think a lender will ask them when they seek a loan? What effect does this have on the "advantage" of limited liability under incorporation?

13-4. As a promoter forming a new corporation, Peterson enters into three pre-incorporation subscription agreements with Mary, Anne, and Harry. The three subscribers each agree to purchase a thousand shares of stock of the future corporation for $2,000. Two months later, just before the issuance of the corporate charter, Mary tells Peterson she is withdrawing from the agreement. The charter is issued the next week. Just before the first organizational meeting of the corporation, Harry also withdraws from the agreement. Discuss fully whether Mary or Harry or both can withdraw from their subscription agreements without liability.

13-5. Ann owns 10 shares of Monmouth Corp. Monmouth Corp. has 100,000 outstanding issued common shares. Ann believes that many decisions of the board of directors do not consider the preservation of the environment. Two pending proposals approved by the board deal with the purchase of timberland for conversion into condominiums. Both proposals require an amendment to the corporate charter and need a two-thirds shareholder vote. Ann knows other shareholders who she believes would oppose these proposals. Unfortunately, most shareholders live a considerable distance from the site of the shareholders' meeting and will be unable to attend. Discuss any techniques Ann can use to oppose these proposals.

13-6. Carter Corp. has issued and has outstanding 100,000 shares of common stock. Four stockholders own 60,000 of these shares, and for the past six years their entire slate of nominees for membership on the board has been elected. John and twenty other shareholders, who own 20,000 shares, are dissatisfied with corporate management and want a representative on the board who shares their views. Explain the circumstances under which John and the minority shareholders can elect their representative to the board.

13-7. Pacific Development, Inc., was incorporated in the District of Columbia for the purpose of international brokerage consulting. Pacific's founder, president, and sole shareholder was Tongsun Park, a South Korean who was on close terms with South Korea's president, Park Chung Hee. The U.S. government alleged that Park's main purpose was to influence Congress to give economic and military aid to South Korea. There was initially no board of directors, and later, when appointed by Park, the board rarely met. The Internal Revenue Service (IRS) assessed $4.5 million in back taxes against Park in 1977. It then seized the assets of Pacific Development, Inc., claiming that the company was a mere alter ego of Park. Valley Finance, Inc., was another corporation wholly owned by Park. It had loaned money to Pacific Development, and it held a second deed of trust on the real property that the IRS had seized. Both Pacific Development and Valley Finance attempted to obtain the return of Pacific Development's assets that the IRS had seized. The plaintiffs claimed that the IRS had improperly pierced the corporate veil of Pacific. Do you agree? Why or why not? [*Valley Finance, Inc. v. United States,* 629 F.2d 162 (D.C. Cir. 1980)]

13-8. Harvey's is a group of New York corporations. Five of these entered into an agreement with Flynt Distributing Co. for Flynt to distribute their magazines. Following this agreement, Harvey's failed to pay Flynt or to ship the magazines to Flynt, causing Flynt injury. Two of Harvey's shareholders converted the assets of the five corporations to their own use, which left the corporations undercapitalized. Discuss whether this conduct amounted to an abuse of corporate business, allowing Flynt to pierce the corporate veil to obtain recovery. [*Flynt Distributing Co. v. Harvey,* 734 F.2d 1389 (9th Cir. 1984)]

13-9. Skandinavia, Inc., manufactured and sold polypropylene underwear. In 1981, following two years of poor sales, Skandinavia entered into negotiations to sell the business to Odilon Cormier, an experienced textile manufacturer. On June 15, 1981, Skandinavia and Cormier agreed that Cormier would take Skandinavia's polypropylene underwear inventory and use it in a new corporation, which would be called Polypro, Inc. In return, Skandinavia would receive a commission on future sales from Polypro, Inc. Polypro was established and began selling the underwear. Skandinavia, however, never received any commissions from the sales. It therefore brought suit against Polypro, Inc., and Cormier to recover its promised commissions. The suit against Polypro, Inc., was dismissed by the trial court. In the suit against Cormier, the trial court found Cormier to be personally liable for the commissions owed. Cormier appealed to the Supreme Court of New Hampshire. Is Cormier personally liable for the contract he signed in the course of setting up a new corporation? Explain. [*Skandinavia, Inc. v. Cormier,* 128 N.H. 215, 514 A.2d 1250 (1986)]

13-10. On October 7, 1980, the defendant, Cohen, Stracher & Bloom, P.C., a legal firm organized as a professional corporation under New York law, entered into an agreement with the plaintiff, We're Associates Co., for the lease of office space located in Lake Success, New York. The lease was signed for the landlord by one of the partners of the plaintiff company and for the defendant professional corporation by Paul J. Bloom, as vice-president. Bloom and the two other defendants, Cohen and Stracher, were the sole officers, directors, and stockholders of the professional corporation. The professional corporation became delinquent in paying its rent, and the plaintiff brought an action in May 1983 to recover rents and other charges of approximately $9,000 alleged to be due and owing under the lease. The complaint was filed against the professional corporation and each individual shareholder of the corporation. The individual shareholders moved to dismiss the action against them individually. Will the court grant their motion? Discuss fully. [*We're Associates Co. v. Cohen, Stracher & Bloom, P.C.,* 103 A.D.2d 130, 478 N.Y.S.2d 670 (1984)]

13-11. Pat Daniels, John Daniels, and Bill Mandell (the defendants) planned to purchase a tavern and restaurant business in St. Charles, Illinois, and to organize their business in the form of a corporation under the name of D&M, Inc. The defendants negotiated with Howard Realty Group to lease the premises in which the tavern and restaurant were located. While the sale of the business and negotiation of the lease were proceeding, neither the seller of the business nor Howard contemplated personal guarantees from the defendants. On January 18, 1987, although D&M had not yet been incorporated, the lease was signed in the name of D&M, Inc., by Pat Daniels and Bill Mandell, in their capacity as president and secretary, respectively, of the future corporation. On February 11, 1987, the defendants filed the articles of incorporation for D&M with the secretary of state. The articles were returned by the secretary of state's office because the name "D&M, Inc." was already in use by another Illinois corporation. The defendants then decided to file the articles of incorporation under the name of The Lodge at Tin Cup Pass, Inc., after first checking with the landlord to see if they could use that name because it was similar to the name of the property, Tin Cup Pass. The Lodge was duly incorporated on March 5, 1987. In late 1988, when the Lodge defaulted on its lease payments, Tin Cup Pass Limited Partnership, to whom Howard had assigned the lease, sued the defendants personally to recover the lease payments due, alleging that the defendants should be held liable as corporate promoters for D&M, Inc., a corporation that was never formed. What will result in court? Discuss fully. [*Tin Cup Pass Limited Partnership v. Daniels,* 195 Ill.App.3d 847, 553 N.E.2d 82, 142 Ill.Dec. 732 (1990)]

13-12. Kay Bell, a vice-president of 20th Century Insurance Co., had been employed by that firm for over eleven years when her employment was terminated without notice or justifiable cause in January 1988. During her length of service with the company, she had been continually praised for performance of her duties, had received a promotion, and had been rewarded with continued salary increases, bonuses, and stock grants. 20th Century had agreed to compensate her accordingly and to deal fairly with her in her employment by not terminating her except for justifiable cause. Bell brought an action against 20th Century, alleging that the company had breached an implied employment contract. 20th Century argued that state corporation law barred a corporate officer from claiming breach of an implied contract for wrongful termination. The relevant state statute read, in part, as follows: "Except as otherwise provided by the articles or bylaws, officers shall be chosen by the board and serve at the pleasure of the board, subject to the rights, if any, of an officer under any contract of employment." Did an implied employment contract exist, and, if so, could the company be held liable for breaching that contract? Discuss fully. [*Bell v. Superior Court,* 215 Cal.App.3d 1103, 263 Cal.Rptr. 787 (1989)]

13-13. A Question of Ethics

Francis McQuade was the manager of the New York Giants baseball team. McQuade and John McGraw purchased shares in the National Exhibition Company, the corporation that owned the Giants, from Charles Stoneham, who owned a majority of National Exhibition's stock. As part of the transaction, each of the three agreed to use his best efforts to ensure that the others continued as directors and officers of the organization. Stoneham and McGraw, however, subsequently failed to use their best efforts to ensure that McQuade continued as the treasurer and a director of the corporation, and McQuade sued to compel specific performance of the agreement. A court reviewing the matter noted that McQuade had been "shabbily" treated by the others but refused to grant specific performance on the ground that the agreement was void because it interfered with the duty of the others as directors to do what was best for all the shareholders. Although shareholders may join to elect corporate directors, they may not join to limit the directors' discretion in managing the business affairs of an organization; the directors must retain their independent judgment. Consider the implications of the case and address the following questions. [McQuade v. Stoneham, *263 N.Y. 323, 189 N.E. 234 (1934)*]

1. Given that even the court sympathized with Mc-Quade's plight, was it ethical to put the business judgment of the directors ahead of an otherwise valid promise they had made?

2. Are there practical considerations that support the court's decision? How can directors ever perform the task dictated to them if their judgment is constrained by earlier agreements with some of the corporation's shareholders?

3. Can you think of any circumstances in which it would be fair to the shareholders, as a group, to interfere with the directors' business judgment by holding some of the directors to a similar prior agreement with some or all of the other directors?

13-14. Case Briefing Assignment

Examine Case A.13 [Withers v. Timber Products, Inc., *574 So.2d 1291 (La.App. 1991)*] *in Appendix A. The case has been excerpted there in great detail. Review and then brief the case, making sure that you include answers to the following questions in your brief.*

1. Was Maker personally liable for compensating Withers for the latter's work-related injuries? Why or why not?

2. Under the laws of the state in which the case arose, what must be shown for an individual shareholder to be held liable for debts incurred by the corporation?

3. Is the determination of individual liability a legal or a factual question?

4. What facts and circumstances were important for determining whether "piercing the corporate veil" was appropriate in this case?

Chapter 14

Rights and Duties within the Corporation

No one individual shareholder or director bears sole responsibility for the corporation and its actions. Rather, a corporation joins the efforts and resources of a large number of individuals for the purpose of producing greater returns than those persons could have obtained individually.

Sometimes actions that benefit the corporation as a whole do not coincide with the separate interests of the individuals making up the corporation. In such situations, it is important to know the rights and duties of all participants in the corporate enterprise. This chapter focuses on the rights and duties of directors, managers, and shareholders and the ways in which conflicts between and among them are resolved.

■ The Role of Officers and Directors

Directors, representing the interests of the shareholders, manage the corporation through the officers whom they choose. The directors and officers are deemed to be *fiduciaries* of the corporation; that is, their relationship with the corporation and its shareholders is characterized as one of utmost trust and confidence. The fiduciary duties of the directors and officers include the duty of care and the duty of loyalty.

Duty of Care

Directors are obligated to be honest and to use prudent business judgment in the conduct of corporate affairs. Directors must exercise the same degree of care that reasonably prudent people use in the conduct of their own personal business affairs.

Directors can be held answerable to the corporation and to the shareholders for breach of their duty of care. When directors delegate work to corporate officers and employees, they are expected to use a reasonable amount of supervision. Otherwise, they may be held liable for negligence or mismanagement of corporate personnel. For example, assume that a corporate bank director failed to attend any board of directors' meetings in five and one-half years and never inspected any of the corporate books or records.

Meanwhile, the bank president made various improper loans and permitted large overdrafts. The corporate director could be held liable to the corporation for any losses resulting from the unsupervised actions of the bank president and the loan committee which approved the loans.

The standard of due care has been variously described and codified in many corporation codes and by judicial decisions.[1] The impact of the standard is to require that directors carry out their responsibilities in an informed, businesslike manner.

Directors and officers are expected to act in accordance with their own knowledge and training. Most states, as well as Section 8.30 of the Revised Model Business Corporation Act (RMBCA), however, allow a director to make decisions in reliance on information furnished by competent officers or employees, professionals such as attorneys and accountants, or even an executive committee of the board, without being accused of acting in bad faith or failing to exercise due care if such information turns out to be faulty.

Directors are expected to attend board of directors' meetings, and their votes should be entered into the minutes of corporate meetings. Unless a dissent is entered, the director is presumed to have assented. Directors who dissent are rarely held individually (personally) liable for any losses suffered by the corporation which arise from the board's approval of a particular proposal. For this reason, a director who is absent from a given meeting sometimes registers with the secretary of the board a dissent to actions taken at the meeting.

Directors are expected to be informed on corporate matters and to understand legal and other professional advice rendered to the board. In *Smith v. Van Gorkom*, directors were held liable for accepting an offer for the purchase of a corporation because they had failed to investigate the value of the business and whether a higher price could have been obtained.[2] A director who is unable to carry out such responsibilities must resign. Even when the required duty of care has not been exercised, directors and officers are liable only for the damages caused to the corporation by their negligence.

Duty of Loyalty

One can define loyalty as faithfulness to one's obligations and duties. The essence of the fiduciary duty requires subordination of self-interest to the interest of the entity to which the duty is owed. It presumes constant loyalty to the corporation on the part of the directors and officers. In general, the duty of loyalty prohibits directors from using corporate funds or confidential corporate information for their personal advantage. It requires officers and directors to disclose fully any corporate opportunity or any possible conflict of interest that might occur in a transaction involving the directors of the corporation.

Cases dealing with fiduciary duty typically involve one or more of the following:

1. Competing with the corporation.
2. Usurping a corporate opportunity.
3. Having an interest that conflicts with the interest of the corporation.
4. Engaging in insider trading (using information that is not public to make a profit trading securities).
5. Authorizing a corporate transaction that is detrimental to minority shareholders.
6. Selling control over the corporation.

In the following case, the Alabama Supreme Court reviewed a situation in which officers, directors, and shareholders attempted to secure advantages for themselves at the expense of the corporation.

---

1. See, for example, Section 8.30(a) of the Revised Model Business Corporation Act, which provides that "a director shall perform his duties as a director, including his duties as a member of a committee: (1) in good faith; (2) with the care an ordinarily prudent person in like position would exercise under similar circumstances; and (3) in a manner he reasonably believes to be in the best interests of the corporation." Some courts require the standard of care to be that which an ordinarily prudent person would use in the exercise of his or her personal affairs.

2. 488 A.2d 858 (Del. 1985).

BACKGROUND AND FACTS *The defendants, Morad and Thomson, were officers, directors, and shareholders of Bio-Lab, Inc. Bio-Lab had one additional shareholder, the plaintiff, Coupounas. While serving as officers and directors of Bio-Lab, the defendants incorporated and operated a competing business, Med-Lab, Inc. The plaintiff brought a derivative suit on behalf of Bio-Lab against the defendants and Med-Lab, alleging that, in opening the competing business, they had usurped a corporate opportunity of Bio-Lab. The trial court held for the plaintiff, and the defendants appealed.*

Case 14.1

MORAD v. COUPOUNAS
Supreme Court of Alabama, 1978.
361 So.2d 6.

FAULKNER, Justice.

* * * *

''[I]f there is presented to a corporate officer or director a business opportunity which the corporation is financially able to undertake, [and which] is, from its nature, in the line of the corporation's business and is of practical advantage to it, [and] one in which the corporation has an interest or a reasonable expectancy, and, by embracing the opportunity, the self-interest of the officer or director will be brought into conflict with that of his corporation, the law will not permit him to seize the opportunity for himself.'' * * *

''[N]umerous factors are to be weighed, including the manner in which the offer was communicated to the officer; the good faith of the officer; the use of corporate assets to acquire the opportunity; the financial ability of the corporation to acquire the opportunity; the degree of disclosure made to the corporation; the action taken by the corporation with reference thereto; and the need or interest of the corporation in the opportunity. These, as well as numerous other factors, are weighed in a given case. The presence or absence of any single factor is not determinative of the issue of corporate opportunity.'' * * *

Here the trial court specifically found that one of the corporate purposes of Bio-Lab was to expand into specific new areas, including Tuscaloosa. Ample evidence in the record supports this conclusion. Bio-Lab's certificate of incorporation declared that one of the purposes of the business was ''to have one or more offices.'' * * *

* * * *

* * * [T]estimony revealed that $44,000 had been required to establish Med-Lab. At the end of 1974 Bio-Lab had only $24,300 available for this purpose. But, Raburn [a certified public accountant, familiar with the books of both Med-Lab and Bio-Lab] also testified that in 1974 Bio-Lab had paid a ''rather high'' dividend of $20,000. His testimony indicated that the payment of dividends is often restricted when a corporation wishes to expand. Thus, if the dividend had not been paid, Bio-Lab clearly should have had the financial ability to expand to Tuscaloosa, with or without a loan. In light of this testimony the trial court's finding that defendants improperly formed Med-Lab to the detriment of Bio-Lab is clearly supportable and will not be disturbed by this Court on appeal.

The Alabama Supreme Court determined that the appropriate remedy for the defendants' breach of duty of loyalty was for the court to impose a ''constructive trust,'' which would require all profits of Med-Lab to be paid to Bio-Lab.

DECISION AND REMEDY

Conflicts of Interest

Corporate directors often have many business affiliations, and they can even sit on the board of more than one corporation. Of course, they are precluded from entering into or supporting any business that operates in direct competition with the corporation. The fiduciary duty requires them to make a full disclosure of any potential conflicts of interest that might arise in any corporate transaction.

CONTRACTS BETWEEN DIRECTOR AND CORPORATION Sometimes a corporation enters into a contract or engages in a transaction in which an officer or director has a material interest. The director or officer must make a full disclosure of that interest and must abstain from voting on the proposed transaction.

For example, Pacific Business Corporation needs office space. Louis Allen, one of its five directors, owns the building adjoining the corporation. He negotiates a lease with Pacific for the space, making a full disclosure to Pacific and the other four board directors. The lease arrangement is fair and reasonable, and it is unanimously approved by the corporation's board of directors. In such a case, the contract is valid. The rule is one of reason; otherwise, directors would be prevented from ever giving financial assistance to the corporations they serve.

The various state statutes contain different standards, but a contract will generally not be voidable in the following circumstances:

1. It was fair and reasonable to the corporation at the time the contract was made.
2. There was a full disclosure of the interest of the officers or directors involved in the transaction.
3. The contract is approved by a majority of the disinterested directors or shareholders.

CONTRACTS BETWEEN CORPORATIONS HAVING COMMON DIRECTORS Often contracts are negotiated between corporations having one or more directors who are members of both boards. These transactions require great care, as they are closely scrutinized by courts. Section 8 of the Clayton Act of 1914 specifically states that no person shall be a director in any two or more competing corporations if any one of them has capital surplus and undivided profits aggregating more than $1 million (other than banks, banking associations, trust companies, and common carriers).

The Business Judgment Rule

Directors are expected to use their best judgment in guiding corporate management, but they are not insurers of business success. Honest mistakes of judgment and poor business decisions on their part do not make them liable to the corporation for resulting damages. This is the **business judgment rule.** The rule immunizes directors—and officers—from liability when a decision is within managerial authority, as long as the decision complies with management's fiduciary duties and as long as acting on the decision is within the powers of the corporation. Consequently, if there is a reasonable basis for a business decision, it is unlikely that the court will interfere with that decision, even if the corporation suffers thereby.

To benefit from the rule, directors and officers must act in good faith, in what they consider to be the best interests of the corporation, and with the care that an ordinarily prudent person in a like position would exercise in similar circumstances. This requires an informed decision, with a rational basis, and with no conflict between the decision maker's personal interest and the interest of the corporation.

To be informed, the director or officer must do what is necessary to become informed: attend presentations, ask for information from those who have it, read reports, review other written materials such as contracts—in other words, carefully study a situation and its alternatives. To be free of conflicts of interest, the director must not engage in self-dealing. For instance, a director should not oppose a *tender offer* (an offer made by another company directly to the shareholders to purchase shares in the company) in the corporation's best interest because its acceptance may cost the director her or his position. For a decision to have an apparently rational basis, the decision itself must appear to have been made reasonably. For example, a director should not accept a tender offer with only a moment's consideration based solely on the market price of the corporation's shares.

Whether a defendant's actions could be protected by the business judgment rule was at issue in the following case.

BACKGROUND AND FACTS *Scott McKnight, an ophthalmologist, was employed by Midwest Eye Institute of Kansas City, Inc. The employment contracts for 1987 and 1988 contained a covenant not to compete, which prohibited McKnight from practicing medicine within a defined area for a period of three years after his term of employment expired. When the parties failed to agree on the terms of a proposed 1989 contract, Midwest invoked the restrictive covenant before the termination of the existing employment contract and notified all hospitals and patients served by Mc-Knight that McKnight would be leaving the Kansas City area at the expiration of the contract term. Midwest also terminated all McKnight's on-call duties, prohibited the treatment and consultation of patients, canceled surgeries that McKnight was scheduled to perform, and locked his office. In effect, Midwest consigned McKnight to a compulsory vacation for the rest of the contract term. McKnight sought to enjoin Midwest from enforcing the restrictive covenant. The trial court held that Midwest had breached the employment contract and that, because of the breach, McKnight had no duty under the restrictive covenant. Midwest appealed.*

Case 14.2

McKNIGHT v. MIDWEST EYE INSTITUTE OF KANSAS CITY, INC.
Missouri Court of Appeals, Western District, 1990.
799 S.W.2d 909.

SHANGLER, Presiding Judge.
 *   *   *   *

 *   *   * Midwest argues that the prerogative of the management to idle McKnight or otherwise direct his employment service during the last month of the contract term was a provision explicit in the employment agreement, and thus could not have constituted a breach.

Midwest finds that prerogative in the contract term: ''Employment. Effective from and after July 1, 1988, through June 30, 1989, the Doctor shall faithfully serve the Corporation in the regular ordinary course of the business of the Corporation in such capacity and perform such duties as the executive officers of the Corporation shall determine and direct from time to time.''

It is the argument that this provision embodies the business judgment doctrine: that the business judgment of a corporation vests in the directors and shareholders wide latitude for its exercise in the conduct of the affairs of a corporation, an exercise with which courts will not usually interfere. Accordingly [the argument goes], the judgment of the trial court that Midwest's redirection of McKnight's professional activity during the last month of the employment was a breach of agreement not only misconstrues the contract, but also unduly subjects management decision to judicial oversight, contrary to the business judgment rule.

 *   *   * The business judgment rule protects the directors and officers of a corporation from liability for *   *   * decisions within their authority made in good faith, uninfluenced by any other consideration than the honest belief that the action subserves the best interests of the corporation. It makes immune from court interference such an exercise of independent discretion. The business judgment rule, however, does not operate to relieve a corporation of an obligation of contract merely because the managers hold the honest and disinterested belief that the action benefits the corporation. A corporation, no less than a natural person, is bound by a contract entered with proper authority, and no less than a natural person, may not repudiate the undertaking. * * *

    * * * *

    * * * A suit in equity to enforce a restrictive covenant partakes of a petition for specific performance. Such a redress is not a matter of right, but of discretion. A court of equity will not aid a party who resorts to unjust and unfair conduct.

DECISION AND REMEDY *The appellate court upheld the trial court's ruling. Midwest was barred from enforcing the restrictive covenant against McKnight because it had breached the employment contract.*

■ Rights of Directors

A director of a corporation has a number of rights, including the rights of participation, inspection, indemnification, and compensation.

Participation

Among the rights that a corporate director must have to function properly in that position, the main right is one of participation—meaning that the director must be notified of board of directors' meetings so as to participate in them. As pointed out in the previous chapter, regular board meetings are usually established by the bylaws or by board resolution, and no additional notice of these meetings is required. If special meetings are called, however, notice is required unless waived by the director.

Inspection

A director must have access to all corporate books and records to make decisions and to exercise the necessary supervision. This right is virtually absolute and cannot be restricted.

Indemnification

It is not unusual for corporate directors to become involved in lawsuits by virtue of their position and their actions as directors. Most states (and RMBCA 8.51) permit a corporation to indemnify a director for legal costs, fees, and judgments involved in defending corporation-related suits.

At common law, a director had no right to be indemnified; however, there was little objection to indemnification if the director was absolved of liability. Today, statutes and court decisions allow indemnification even if the director is not absolved of liability, as long as his or her actions were made in good faith and based on a reasonable belief that

such actions were in the best interests of the corporation.

Criminal convictions usually require bad faith, but bad faith is not presumed merely because the director settles the litigation, pleads *nolo contendere* (no contest), or even is found civilly liable. Many states specifically permit a corporation to purchase liability insurance for the directors and officers to cover indemnification. When the statutes are silent on this matter, the power to purchase such insurance is usually considered to be part of the corporation's implied power.

Compensation

Historically, directors have had no inherent right to compensation for their services as directors. Officers receive compensation, and nominal sums are often paid as honoraria to directors. In many cases, directors are also chief corporate officers and receive compensation in their managerial positions. Most directors, however, gain through indirect benefits, such as business contacts, prestige, and other rewards.

There is a trend toward providing more than nominal compensation for directors, especially in large corporations in which directorships can create burdens in terms of time, work, effort, and risk. Many states permit the corporate articles or bylaws to authorize compensation for directors, and in some cases the board can set its own compensation unless the articles or bylaws provide otherwise.

■ Rights of Officers and Managers

As noted earlier, corporate officers' duties are the same as the duties of directors because their respective corporate positions involve both of them in decision making and place them in similar positions of control. Hence, they are viewed as having the same fiduciary duties of care and loyalty in their conduct of corporate affairs. Also, they are subject to the same obligations concerning corporate opportunities and conflicts of interest as directors are.

The rights of corporate officers and other high-level managers are defined by employment contracts, because they are employees of the company.

▇ Rights of Shareholders

As stated in Chapter 13, the acquisition of a share of stock makes a person an owner and shareholder in a corporation. Shareholders thus own the corporation. Although they have no legal title to corporate property vested in the corporation, such as buildings and equipment, they do have an equitable interest in the firm. The rights of shareholders are established in the articles of incorporation and under the state's general incorporation law.

Stock Certificates

A *stock certificate* evidences ownership, and in jurisdictions that require the issuance of stock certificates, shareholders have the right to demand that the corporation issue a certificate and record their names and addresses in the corporate stock record books. In most states (and under RMBCA 6.25), boards of directors may provide that shares of stock be uncertificated (that is, that actual, physical stock certificates not be issued). In that circumstance, it may be required that the corporation send the holders of uncertificated shares letters or some other form of notice containing the same information required to be included on the face of stock certificates.

Stock is intangible personal property—the ownership right exists independently of the certificate itself. A stock certificate may be lost or destroyed, but ownership is not destroyed with it. A new certificate can be issued to replace one that has been lost or destroyed.[3] Notice of shareholder

meetings, dividends, and operational and financial reports are all distributed according to the recorded ownership listed in the corporation's books, not on the basis of possession of the certificate.

Assume that Betty Anderson's certificate showing ownership of corporate stock in Chrysler Corporation is destroyed in a fire on September 1. The corporation declares a dividend on September 5. According to corporate records, Betty Anderson is the ''record owner'' and receives the dividend even though she no longer has the certificate.

Preemptive Rights

A **preemptive right** is a common law concept according to which a preference is given to an existing shareholder over all other prospective purchasers to subscribe to or purchase a proportionate share of a new issue of stock. This allows the shareholder to maintain his or her portion of control, voting power, or financial interest in the corporation. Most statutes either (1) grant preemptive rights but allow them to be negated in the corporation's articles or (2) deny preemptive rights except to the extent that they are granted in the articles. The result is that the articles of incorporation determine the existence and scope of preemptive rights. Generally, preemptive rights apply only to additional, newly issued stock sold for cash and must be exercised within a specified time period (usually thirty days).

For example, National Clothing, Inc., authorizes and issues 1,000 shares of stock, and Paula Gudmundson purchases 100 shares, making her the owner of 10 percent of the company's stock. Subsequently, National Clothing, by vote of its shareholders, authorizes the issuance of another 1,000 shares (amending the articles of incorporation). This increases its capital stock to a total of 2,000 shares. If preemptive rights have been provided, Paula Gudmundson can purchase one additional share of the new stock being issued for each share currently owned—100 additional shares. Thus, she can own 200 of the 2,000 shares outstanding, and her relative position as a shareholder will be maintained. If preemptive rights are not reserved, her proportionate control and voting power will be diluted from that of a 10 percent shareholder to that of a 5 percent shareholder because of the issuance of the additional 1,000 shares.

Preemptive rights are far more significant in a close corporation because of the relatively small

---

3. For a lost or destroyed certificate to be reissued, a shareholder normally must furnish an indemnity bond to protect the corporation against potential loss should the original certificate reappear at some future time in the hands of a bona fide purchaser [UCC 8-302 and 8-405(2)].

number of shares and the substantial interest each shareholder controls.

Stock Warrant Rights

When preemptive rights exist and a corporation is issuing additional shares, each shareholder is usually given **stock warrants,** which are transferable options to acquire a given number of shares from the corporation at a stated price. Warrants are often publicly traded on securities exchanges. When the warrant option is effective only for a short period of time, the stock warrants are usually referred to as *rights.*

Dividend Rights

A *dividend* is a distribution of corporate profits or income *ordered by the directors* and paid to the shareholders in proportion to their respective shares in the corporation. Dividends can be paid in cash, property, stock of the corporation that is paying the dividends, or stock of other corporations.[4]

LEGAL REQUIREMENTS   State laws vary, but every state determines the general circumstances and legal requirements under which dividends are paid. State laws also control the sources of revenue to be used; only certain funds are legally available for paying dividends. Once declared, a cash dividend becomes a corporate debt enforceable at law like any other debt.[5]

---

4.   Technically, dividends paid in stock are not dividends. They maintain each shareholder's proportional interest in the corporation. On one occasion a distillery declared and paid a "dividend" in bonded whiskey.

5.   An insolvent corporation cannot declare a dividend.

Under statutes that limit the sources of funds from which dividends may be paid, prescribed sources include the following:

1.   *Retained earnings.* All states allow dividends to be paid from the undistributed net profits earned by the corporation, including capital gains from the sale of fixed assets. The undistributed net profits are called *earned surplus* or retained earnings.
2.   *Net profits.* A few state statutes allow dividends to be issued from current net profits without regard to deficits in prior years.
3.   *Surplus.* A number of state statutes allow dividends to be paid out of any kind of surplus.

When directors fail to declare a dividend, shareholders can ask a court of equity for an injunction to compel the directors to meet and to declare a dividend. For the injunction to be granted, it must be shown that the directors have acted so unreasonably in withholding the dividend that their conduct is an abuse of their discretion.

Often large money reserves are accumulated for a bona fide purpose, such as expansion, research, or other legitimate corporate goals. The mere fact that sufficient corporate earnings or surplus are available to pay a dividend is not enough to compel directors to distribute funds that, in the board's opinion, should not be paid. The courts are circumspect about interfering with corporate operations and will not compel directors to declare dividends unless abuse of discretion is clearly shown. Thus, directors are not ordinarily forced to declare dividends to shareholders. A striking exception to this rule was made in the following classic case.

Case 14.3

DODGE v. FORD MOTOR CO.

Supreme Court of Michigan, 1919.
204 Mich. 459,
170 N.W. 668.

BACKGROUND AND FACTS *Ford Motor Company was formed in 1903. Henry Ford, the president and owner of most of the firm's stock, attempted to run the corporation as if it were a one-man operation. The firm expanded rapidly and, in addition to regular quarterly dividends, often paid special dividends. Originally, the Ford car sold for more than $900. From time to time, the price was reduced, and in 1916 it sold for $440. For the year beginning August 1, 1916, the price was reduced again, to $360. In the interests of setting aside money for future investment and expansion, the firm announced that it would pay no special dividends after October 1915, even though surplus capital in 1916 exceeded $110,000,000.*

The minority stockholders, who owned one-tenth of the shares of the corporation, petitioned the court to compel the directors to declare a dividend.

OSTRANDER, Chief Justice.

*   *   *   *

*   *   * [I]t is charged that notwithstanding the earnings for the fiscal year ending July 31, 1916, the Ford Motor Company has not since that date declared any special dividends:

"And the said Henry Ford, president of the company, has declared it to be the settled policy of the company not to pay in the future any special dividends, but to put back into the business for the future all of the earnings of the company, other than the regular dividend of five percent (5%) monthly upon the authorized capital stock of the company—two million dollars ($2,000,000)."

This declaration of the future policy, it is charged in the bill, was published in the public press in the city of Detroit and throughout the United States in substantially the following language: "'My ambition,' declared Mr. Ford, 'is to employ still more men; to spread the benefits of this industrial system to the greatest possible number, to help them build up their lives and their homes. To do this, we are putting the greatest share of our profits back into the business.'"

It is charged further that the said Henry Ford stated to plaintiffs [the minority stockholders] personally, in substance, that as all the stockholders had received back in dividends more than they had invested they were not entitled to receive anything additional to the regular dividend of 5 percent a month, and that it was not his policy to have larger dividends declared in the future, and that the profits and earnings of the company would be put back into the business for the purpose of extending its operations and increasing the number of its employees, and that, inasmuch as the profits were to be represented by investment in plants and capital investment, the stockholders would have no right to complain. *   *   *

*   *   *   *

"It is a well-recognized principle of law that the directors of a corporation, and they alone, have the power to declare a dividend of the earnings of the corporation, and to determine its amount. Courts of equity will not interfere in the management of the directors unless it is clearly made to appear that they are guilty of fraud or misappropriation of the corporate funds, or refuse to declare a dividend when the corporation has a surplus of net profits which it can, without detriment to its business, divide among its stockholders, and when a refusal to do so would amount to such an abuse of discretion as would constitute a fraud, or breach of that good faith which they are bound to exercise towards the stockholders."

*   *   *   *

Defendants say, and it is true, that a considerable cash balance must be at all times carried by such a concern. But, as had been stated, there was a large daily, weekly, monthly, receipt of cash. The output was practically continuous and was continuously, and within a few days, turned into cash. Moreover, the contemplated expenditures were not to be immediately made. The large sum appropriated for the smelter plant was payable over a considerable period of time. So that, without going further, it would appear that, accepting and approving the plan of the directors, it was their duty to distribute on or near the 1st of August, 1916, a very large sum of money to stockholders.

DECISION AND REMEDY

Ford Motor Company was ordered by the court to declare a dividend. The court held that, in view of the firm's large capital surplus, to withhold a dividend would violate the directors' duty to the shareholders.

ILLEGAL DIVIDENDS Whenever a dividend is paid while the corporation is insolvent, it is automatically an illegal dividend, and shareholders may be liable for returning the payment to the corporation or its creditors. Dividends are generally required by statute to be distributed only from certain authorized corporate accounts representing profits. Sometimes dividends are improperly paid from an unauthorized account, or their payment causes the corporation to become insolvent. Generally, in this case, shareholders must return illegal dividends only if they knew that the dividends were illegal when they received them.

In all cases of illegal and improper dividends, the board of directors can be held personally liable for the amount of the payment. When directors can show that a shareholder knew a dividend was illegal when it was received, however, the directors are entitled to reimbursement from the shareholder.

Voting Rights

Shareholders exercise ownership control through the power of their votes. In the early development of corporate law, each shareholder was entitled to one vote per share. This rule still holds today, but the voting techniques discussed in the previous chapter (including shareholder agreements, voting trusts, and cumulative-voting methods) all enhance the power of the shareholder's vote.

The articles can exclude or limit voting rights, particularly to certain classes of shares. For example, owners of preferred shares are usually denied the right to vote. Treasury shares, held by the corporation, cannot be voted until they have been reissued by the corporation.

Inspection Rights

Shareholders in a corporation enjoy both common law and statutory **inspection rights.**[6] Shareholders

at common law enjoyed qualified rights to inspect and copy corporate books and records, such as the bylaws and minutes of the board of directors' meetings and the shareholders' meetings, as well as documents such as contracts, correspondence, and tax returns. They even had the right to inspect the corporate headquarters. Nowadays, the shareholder's right of inspection is often limited by statute, however, to the inspection and copying of corporate books and records for a proper purpose, provided the request is made in advance. The shareholder can inspect the books in person, or appoint an attorney, agent, accountant, or other type of assistant to do so on his behalf.

The power of inspection is fraught with potential abuses, and the corporation is allowed to protect itself from them. For example, a shareholder can properly be denied access to corporate records to prevent harassment or to protect trade secrets or other confidential corporate information. Some states require that a shareholder must have held his or her shares for a minimum period of time immediately preceding the demand to inspect or must hold a minimum number of outstanding shares. RMBCA 16.02 provides that every shareholder is entitled to examine specified corporate records.

RMBCA 7.20 requires the corporation to maintain an alphabetical voting list of shareholders with addresses and number of shares owned. This list must be kept open at the annual meeting for inspection by any shareholder of record.

The following case illustrates a court's dilemma in determining whether a stockholder-competitor could inspect the corporate books for limited purposes.

---

6. See, for example, *Schwartzman v. Schwartzman Packing Co.*, 99 N.M. 436, 659 P.2d 888 (1983).

Case 14.4

ULDRICH v. DATASPORT, INC.

Court of Appeals of Minnesota, 1984.

349 N.W.2d 286.

BACKGROUND AND FACTS *Uldrich, the plaintiff, was a shareholder and former director, officer, and employee of Datasport, Inc., a Minnesota corporation. Datasport, the defendant, terminated Uldrich's employment, directorship, and office. Aside from maintaining his status as shareholder, Uldrich was also a competitor of Datasport. While Uldrich was still a director and an officer, he was prohibited from marketing his competing* *product for one year by a court order on Datasport's request. After his dismissal, Uldrich was denied access to Datasport's records and books. Uldrich was concerned about the fact that other shareholders of Datasport were running other businesses using Datasport assets, such as leasing office space to, and sharing it with, Datasport. Uldrich felt that Datasport's revenues were being eaten up by operating expenses. In three and one-half years, Datasport had received income from sales of over $1.5 million; yet Uldrich, over the same period, had received less than $1,000 in return on his investment. Uldrich filed for a writ of* mandamus *(an order issued from a court and directed to a private or municipal corporation or any of its officers commanding the performance of a particular act), which, in this case, would permit Uldrich's inspection. His purpose was to place a monetary value on his shares and to evaluate the conduct and affairs of the other shareholders, directors, and officers. The trial court awarded Uldrich a writ of* mandamus *compelling Datasport to permit inspection. Although the writ enjoined Uldrich from making competitive use of such information, Datasport appealed the order.*

PARKER, Judge.
* * * *
The right to inspect corporate books and records is guaranteed to shareholders by [Minnesota statute, which provides in part:] Every shareholder * * * shall have a right to examine, in person or by agent or attorney, at any reasonable time or times, for any proper purpose, and at the place or places where usually kept or at such other place as the court may order, the share register, books of account and records of the proceedings of the shareholders and directors, and to make extracts therefrom.
* * * *
The trial court found that Uldrich has good faith reasons for seeking access to the corporate books and records of Datasport, i.e., to place a monetary value on his stock interests and to evaluate the conduct and affairs of the other shareholders, officers and directors. In [a previous case] the Supreme Court held such reasons sufficient to compel inspection of corporate books and records by mandamus.
* * * *
Datasport contends that the documents requested are "confidential business information" and that the order directs Datasport to make available "significant portions of its corporate records which cannot be included within any reasonable definition of books of account * * * ."

Neither the statute nor case law defines "books of account." [Datasport] argues that the trial court's order includes information in these various records that are the supporting documentation for the books of account, "but do not themselves form a part of the books of account."

Under the circumstances here, when the shareholders, officers and directors of Datasport have multiple business interests operated on the same premises as, and doing business with, Datasport, and when [Uldrich's] return on his investment appears trivial in view of a substantial sales record, the trial court properly recognized that equity required a broad scope be given to the concept of shareholder access.

The trial court recognized that misuse might be made of some of the information sought and enjoined use of it for any competitive purpose.

The court of appeals affirmed the writ of mandamus *compelling Datasport to allow Uldrich to exercise his shareholder's right of inspection.*

DECISION AND REMEDY

The Right to Transfer Shares

Corporate stock represents an ownership right in intangible personal property. The law generally recognizes the right of an owner to transfer property to another person unless there are valid restrictions on its transferability. Although stock certificates are negotiable and freely transferable by indorsement and delivery, transfer of stock in closely held corporations is generally restricted by contract, the bylaws, or a restriction stamped on the stock certificate. The existence of any restrictions on transferability must always be noted on the face of the stock certificate, and these restrictions must be reasonable.

THE RIGHT OF FIRST REFUSAL Sometimes corporations or their shareholders restrict transferability by reserving the option to purchase any shares offered for resale by a shareholder. This **right of first refusal** remains with the corporation or the shareholders for only a specified time or reasonable time. Variations on the purchase option are possible. For example, a shareholder might be required to offer the shares to other shareholders or to the corporation first.

CORPORATE RECORDS   When shares are transferred, a new entry is made in the corporate stock book to indicate the new owner. Until the corporation is notified and the entry is complete, voting rights, notice of shareholders' meetings, dividend distribution, and so forth, are all held by the current record owner.

Rights on Dissolution

When a corporation is dissolved and its outstanding debts and the claims of its creditors have been satisfied, the remaining assets are distributed on a pro rata basis among the shareholders. Certain classes of preferred stock may be given priority according to the terms of the corporation's bylaws. If no preferences as to distribution of assets on liquidation are given to any class of stock, then the stockholders share the remaining assets.

Suppose a minority shareholder knows that the board of directors is mishandling corporate assets or is permitting a deadlock to threaten or irreparably injure the corporation's finances. The minority shareholder is not powerless to intervene. He or she can petition a court to appoint a receiver and to liquidate the business assets of the corporation.

RMBCA 14.30 permits any shareholder to institute such an action in any of the following circumstances:

1.   The directors are deadlocked in the management of corporate affairs, shareholders are unable to break that deadlock, and irreparable injury to the corporation is being suffered or threatened.
2.   The acts of the directors or those in control of the corporation are illegal, oppressive, or fraudulent.
3.   Corporation assets are being misapplied or wasted.
4.   The shareholders are deadlocked in voting power and have failed, for a specified period (usually two annual meetings), to elect successors to directors whose terms have expired or would have expired with the election of successors.

Shareholder's Derivative Suit

When those in control of a corporation—the corporate directors—fail to sue in the corporate name to redress a wrong suffered by the corporation, shareholders are permitted to do so "derivatively," or "secondarily," in what is known as a **shareholder's derivative suit.** Some wrong must have been done to the corporation, and any damages recovered by the suit usually go into the corporation's treasury. The right of shareholders to bring a derivative action is especially important when the wrong suffered by the corporation results from the actions of corporate directors or officers, because in such cases the directors and officers would probably want to prevent any action against themselves.

The shareholder's derivative suit is singular in that those suing are not pursuing rights or benefits for themselves personally but are acting as guardians of the corporate entity. The derivative nature of this type of lawsuit is stressed in the following case.

BACKGROUND AND FACTS   *Jacob Schachter and Herbert Kulik, the founders of Ketek Electric Corporation, each owned 50 percent of the corporation's shares and served as the corporation's only officers. Arnold Glenn, as trustee, and Kulik brought a shareholder's derivative suit against Schachter, alleging that Schachter had diverted Ketek assets and opportunities to Hoteltron Systems, Inc., a corporation wholly owned by Schachter. The trial court initially held that Kulik failed to prove a breach of duty by Schachter. The appellate court reversed this decision, and the trial court later determined damages and also decided that the damages should be paid to Kulik, not to Ketek Corporation. Schachter appealed, and the appellate court ruled that the damages should be awarded to the injured corporation, Ketek, rather than to the injured shareholder, Kulik. Kulik argued that awarding damages to the corporation was inequitable because Schachter, as a shareholder of Ketek, would ultimately share in the proceeds of the award. Eventually, the case was heard by the New York Court of Appeals.*

Case 14.5

GLENN v. HOTELTRON SYSTEMS, INC.

Court of Appeals of New York, 1989.
74 N.Y.2d 386,
547 N.E.2d 71,
547 N.Y.S.2d 816.

WACHTLER, Chief Judge.

*   *   *   *

It is the general rule that, because a shareholders' derivative suit seeks to vindicate a wrong done to the corporation through enforcement of a corporate cause of action, any recovery obtained is for the benefit of the injured corporation. Where, however, the plaintiff sues in an individual capacity to recover damages resulting in harm, not to the corporation, but to individual shareholders, the suit is personal, not derivative, and it is appropriate for damages to be awarded directly to those shareholders.

In this case, the diversion of Ketek's corporate assets by Schachter for his own profit resulted in a corporate injury because it deprived Ketek of those profits. Kulik, the innocent shareholder, was injured only to the extent that he was entitled to share in those profits. His injury was real, but it was derivative, not direct. Thus, the [lower court] properly ruled that those profits should be returned to Ketek Corp.

The New York Court of Appeals affirmed the lower court's ruling. Damages should be paid to Ketek Corporation and not to Kulik because the injury Kulik suffered was derivative, or secondary to the corporate injury, and not direct.

DECISION AND REMEDY

■ Liabilities of Shareholders

As we have repeated many times now in various contexts, one of the hallmarks of the corporate organization is that shareholders are not personally liable for the debts of the corporation. If the corporation fails, shareholders can lose their investment, but that is generally the limit of their liability. In certain instances of fraud, undercapitalization, or careless observance of corporate formalities, however, a court will pierce the corporate veil (disregard the corporate entity) and hold the share-holders individually liable. But these situations are the exceptions, not the rule.

Although rare, there are certain other instances when a shareholder can be personally liable. One relates to illegal dividends, which were discussed previously. Two others relate to *stock subscriptions* and *watered stock*.

Stock Subscriptions

Sometimes stock-subscription agreements—written contracts by which one agrees to buy capital stock of a corporation—exist before incorporation. Normally, these agreements are treated as continuing offers and are usually irrevocable (for up to six months under RMBCA 6.20). Once the corporation has been formed, it can sell shares to shareholder investors. In either case, once the subscription agreement or stock offer is accepted, a binding contract is formed. Any refusal to pay constitutes a breach resulting in the personal liability of the shareholder.

Watered Stock

Shares of stock can be paid for by property or by services rendered instead of cash. In some states, they cannot be purchased with promissory notes. The general rule is that for **par-value shares** sold (that is, shares that have a specific face value, or formal cash-in value, written on them, such as one penny or one dollar), the corporation must receive a value at least equal to the par-value amount. For any **no par shares** sold (that is, shares that have no face value—no specific amount printed on their face), the corporation must receive the value of the shares as determined by the board or shareholders. When shares are issued by the corporation for less than these stated values, the shares are referred to as **watered stock.** In most cases, the shareholder who receives watered stock must pay the difference to the corporation (the shareholder is personally liable). In some states, the shareholder who receives watered stock may be liable to creditors of the corporation for unpaid corporate debts.

To illustrate the concept of watered stock, suppose that during the formation of a corporation, Gomez, as one of the incorporators, transfers his property, Sunset Beach, to the corporation for 10,000 shares of stock at a par value of $100 per share for a total price of $1 million. After the property is transferred and the shares are issued, Sunset Beach is carried on the corporate books at a value of $1 million. On appraisal, it is discovered that the market value of the property at the time of transfer was only $500,000. The shares issued to Gomez are therefore watered stock, and he is liable to the corporation for the difference.

■ Duties of Major Shareholders

A corporation's majority shareholder is regarded as having a fiduciary duty to the corporation and to the minority shareholders. This fiduciary duty arises when a single shareholder (or a few shareholders acting in concert) owns a sufficient number of shares to exercise *de facto* control over the corporation. Under a fiduciary duty, the controlling shareholder may not exercise his or her influence to oppress or to effect a fraud on the minority shareholders.

In judging whether a majority, or controlling, shareholder has acted fraudulently or has oppressed the minority shareholders, courts normally evaluate the relative fairness of the transaction involved. In determining fairness, courts give great weight to whether the controlling shareholder's actions served a corporate purpose or a personal interest with a corresponding detriment to the corporation or minority shareholders. If the transaction under scrutiny benefits the majority to the exclusion and detriment of the minority, then the majority shareholder bears the burden of showing that the transaction was fair under the circumstances. If, however, the transaction affects the majority and the minority in the same way, then the one challenging the transaction must bear the burden of showing why it was unfair and in breach of the majority's fiduciary duty.

A controlling shareholder can exert influence through his or her voting at shareholders' meetings and by dominating the board of directors (who obtain office by the votes of the shareholders). Many courts have premised the majority's fiduciary duty on the fact that majority control provides opportunities for abuse unless the majority is constrained by a fiduciary duty. Other courts have based the fiduciary duty on the view that because a majority shareholder can control the board of directors, the controlling shareholder should likewise be bound by the same fiduciary duties imposed on the directors.

Sale of Controlling Block of Shares

A controlling block of shares is said to command a **control premium**—an excess in share price over the fair market value of shares sold singly. The premium is considered to be commensurate with the extraordinary control the owner of the block is able to exercise over the affairs of the corporation. Thus, majority shareholders, when they sell a controlling block of shares, are under particular scrutiny for breach of their fiduciary duty because such a sale is, in fact, a transfer of control of the corporation. If control is sold for a premium and the seller knew (or had reason to know) that the purchaser would raid the corporate treasury, commit fraud on the corporation, or otherwise implement policies extremely disadvantageous to the other shareholders, then the seller may be required to forfeit (or disgorge) the premium to the corporation.

Oppression of the Minority and Involuntary Dissolution of the Corporation

When the majority shareholder uses his or her control to prevent other shareholders from having a voice in corporate affairs, the minority is said to have been "frozen out" by the majority. In extreme cases in which the shareholders are unable to resolve their differences, and the disgruntled shareholders cannot sell their shares on the open market, a court may order an extreme remedy—involuntary dissolution of the corporation. In the following case, a minority shareholder—one of the two shareholders in a close corporation—sued to have the corporation dissolved because he had been "frozen out" of the business by the allegedly oppressive tactics of the majority shareholder. Note the court's reluctance to grant the extreme remedy of dissolution, even though it deemed that a "freeze-out" had occurred.

BACKGROUND AND FACTS *In 1984, Elmer Balvik and Thomas Sylvester decided to turn their partnership into a corporation because of the tax benefits that would result. The new Weldon Corporation carried on the partnership's old business of electrical contracting. Sylvester received 70 percent of the stock of the new corporation and Balvik the remaining 30 percent, in proportion to the capital that each contributed. Both took positions as directors and officers of the corporation, and each was entitled to one vote per share of stock owned. Balvik was at all times a minority voice in the company. Although Sylvester and Balvik had had no problems during their years as partners, difficulties emerged soon after incorporation. Sylvester believed that excess profits should be reinvested in the corporation, while Balvik wanted them withdrawn and paid out as bonuses or dividends. Balvik was fired from his job, allegedly because of poor performance, and he began working for another company. Balvik was unable to take any of his capital contribution in the corporation with him and no longer received a salary from the corporation. Balvik sued to have the corporation dissolved under North Dakota law, which allows dissolution for illegal, oppressive, or fraudulent acts by corporate directors or those in control of the corporation toward minority shareholders. The district court ordered dissolution and appointed a receiver, and Sylvester appealed.*

Case 14.6

BALVIK v. SYLVESTER

Supreme Court of North Dakota, 1987.
411 N.W.2d 383.

VANDE WALLE, Justice.
* * * *

"The word 'oppressive,' as used in the statute does not carry an essential inference of imminent disaster; it can contemplate a continuing course of conduct. The word does not necessarily savor of fraud, and the absence of 'mismanagement, or misapplication of assets,' does not prevent a finding that the conduct of the dominant directors or officers has been oppressive. It is not synonymous with 'illegal' and 'fraudulent.' "
* * * *

The limited market for stock in a close corporation and the natural reluctance of potential investors to purchase a noncontrolling interest in a close corporation that has been marked by dissension can result in a minority shareholder's interest being held "hostage" by the controlling interest, and can lead to situations where the majority "freeze out" minority shareholders by the use of oppressive tactics. * * *

Because of the predicament in which minority shareholders in a close corporation are placed by a "freeze out" situation, courts have analyzed alleged "oppressive" conduct by those in control in terms of "fiduciary duties" owed by the majority shareholders to the minority and the "reasonable expectations" held by the minority shareholders in committing their capital and labor to the particular enterprise.
* * * *

* * * [C]onsidering Sylvester's inclination to reinvest profits in the corporation, the possibility of a declaration of dividends in the near future appears remote. We find little relevance in whether Sylvester discharged Balvik from employment for cause, or in the fact that Balvik's removal as a director and officer of the corporation occurred only after Balvik brought the instant suit. The ultimate effect of these actions is that Balvik clearly has been "frozen out" of a business in which he reasonably expected to participate. As a result, Balvik is entitled to relief.
* * * *

We have recognized that forced dissolution of a corporation is a drastic remedy which should be invoked with extreme caution and only when justice requires it. In a sense, a forced dissolution allows minority shareholders to exercise retaliatory "oppression" against the majority.
* * * *

Under the circumstances, we believe the trial court abused its discretion in ordering the extreme remedy of dissolution. Weldon is apparently an on-going business and, under the facts presented, ordering its dissolution and liquidation is unduly harsh. Balvik, in his complaint, sought as an alternative remedy that "the Defendant pay to the Plaintiff the true value of his stock in the Corporation. . . ." * * * [W]e believe [this] is the appropriate remedy here. Consequently, we remand this case for the entry of an order requiring either Weldon or Sylvester to purchase Balvik's stock at a price determined by the court to be the fair value thereof. The court may conduct any further proceedings it deems necessary for resolution of the issue. The parties are, of course, free to agree to other alternative methods of resolving this dispute.

DECISION AND REMEDY   *The Supreme Court of North Dakota affirmed the decision of the lower court that Balvik had been "frozen out" of the corporation. The court refused to dissolve the corporation, however, but remanded the case so that another remedy could be sought.*

■ Terms and Concepts to Review

business judgment rule 330
control premium 340
inspection rights 336
no par shares 340

par-value shares 340
preemptive right 333
right of first refusal 338

shareholder's derivative
   suit 338
stock warrants 334
watered stock 340

■ Questions and Case Problems

14-1. Otts Corp. negotiates with the Wick Construction Co. for the renovation of the Otts corporate headquarters. Wick, owner of the Wick Construction Co., is also one of the five members of the board of directors of Otts. The contract terms are standard for this type of contract. Wick has previously informed two of the other directors of his interest in the construction company. The contract is approved by Otts's board on a three-to-two vote, with Wick voting with the majority. Discuss whether this contract is binding on the corporation.

14-2. Rheingold, Inc., has a board of directors consisting of three members (Evans, Goodrich, and Mortimer) and approximately five hundred shareholders. At a regular meeting of the board, the board selects Green as president of the corporation by a two-to-one vote, with Evans dissenting. The minutes of the meeting do not register Evans's dissenting vote. Later, on an audit, it is discovered that Green is a former convict and has openly embezzled $500,000 from Rheingold, Inc. This loss is not covered by insurance. The corporation wants to hold directors Evans, Goodrich, and Mortimer liable. Evans claims no liability. Discuss the personal liability of the directors to the corporation.

14-3. Ann owns 10,000 shares (10 percent) of Superal Corp. Superal authorized 100,000 shares and issued all of them during its first six months in operation. Later, Superal reacquired 10,000 of these shares. With shareholder approval, Superal amended its articles so as to authorize and issue another 100,000 shares and also, by a resolution of the board of directors, to reissue the 10,000 shares of treasury stock. There is no provision in the corporate articles dealing with shareholders' preemptive rights. Because of her previous ownership of 10 percent of Superal, Ann claims that she has the preemptive right to purchase 10,000 shares of the new issue and 1,000 shares of the stock being reissued. Discuss her claims.

14-4. Lucy has acquired one share of common stock of a multimillion-dollar corporation with over 500,000 shareholders. Lucy's ownership is so small that she is questioning what her rights are as a shareholder. For example, she wants to know whether this one share entitles her to:

(a) Attend and vote at shareholder meetings.
(b) Inspect the corporate books.
(c) Receive yearly dividends.

Discuss Lucy's rights in these three matters.

14-5. Riddle has made a preincorporation subscription agreement to purchase 500 shares of a newly formed corporation. The shares have a par value of $100 per share. The corporation is formed, and Riddle's subscription is accepted by the corporation. Riddle transfers a piece of land he owns to the corporation, and the corporation issues 250 shares for it. One year later, with the corporation in serious financial difficulty, the board declares and pays a $5 per share dividend. It is now learned that the land transferred by Riddle had a market value of $18,000. Discuss any liability shareholder Riddle has to the corporation or to creditors of the corporation.

14-6. Air Engineered Systems and Services, Inc., a company incorporated in Louisiana, had three shareholders, Naquin, Dubois, and Hoffpauir. Each of the shareholders owned one-third of the corporation's outstanding shares. Naquin was fired after he had worked six years as an employee of the firm. He then formed a competing business, hired away one of Air Engineered's employees, tried to hire another, and obtained a contract for his own business that he had originally solicited for Air Engineered. Under Louisiana law, any shareholder who is also a business competitor is entitled to inspect the corporate records if she or he owns 25 percent of the outstanding shares for six months before the demand. When Naquin requested Air Engineered to allow him to inspect the corporate records, however, Air Engineered denied his request because Naquin refused to

sign an indemnity agreement protecting Air Engineered from any damages it might suffer as a result of Naquin's use of the information contained in the corporate records. Shortly thereafter, Dubois and Hoffpauir voted to increase the capital stock of the corporation, and then each of them purchased additional shares. This had the effect of reducing Naquin's percentage to less than 25 percent—which meant that Naquin was not entitled under Louisiana law to inspect Air Engineered's records. Naquin filed suit to require the corporation to permit him to inspect the books, because, at the time his request was made, he had owned more than 25 percent of the outstanding shares of Air Engineered. What was the result? Explain. [*Naquin v. Air Engineered Systems and Services, Inc.,* 463 So.2d 992 (La.App. 1985)]

14-7. Midwest Management Corp. was looking for investment opportunities. Morris Stephens, one of Midwest's directors and chairman of the investment committee, proposed that Midwest provide financing for Stephens's son and his business colleagues, who were in need of funds to open a business. Midwest agreed to propose to the shareholders for their approval an investment of $250,000 in the new business on the condition that Stephens would manage the business and would purchase 100,000 shares of stock in the new firm. At each of two shareholder meetings, the directors informed the shareholders that Stephens had agreed to the condition. Stephens was present at both meetings and did not deny that he had agreed to purchase the 100,000 shares of stock and manage the new corporation. On the shareholders' approval, the $250,000 investment was made, and later another $150,000 was invested when the new business suffered losses. About a year after it had opened, the business closed, and Midwest ended up losing over $325,000. Midwest then learned that Stephens had not kept his agreement to purchase stock in and manage the corporation. Midwest sued Stephens for breaching his fiduciary duties and asked for compensatory and punitive damages. Did Midwest succeed? Explain. [*Midwest Management Corp. v. Stephens,* 353 N.W.2d 76 (Iowa 1984)]

14-8. Frederick Valerino and his family owned 50 percent of the stock in EMA (Electrical-Mechanical of America, Inc.), and the remaining 50 percent was owned by Charles Little. Both Valerino and Little participated actively in operating the corporation until 1979, when a dispute arose, resulting in a stalemate. For two years no shareholders' meeting was held and no board of directors could be elected. Little held a shareholders' meeting in 1981 and sent a telegram to Valerino stating that the purpose of the meeting was "[f]or the sale and purchase of the Capital Stock of EMA." Valerino did not attend and sent a reply letter indicating that he did not wish to sell any of his stock. Actually, Little held the meeting with the intention of issuing more stock to himself and his family, thus reducing Valerino's ownership to 25 percent. Valerino sued to enforce his preemptive rights in the corporation and to set aside the new stock issuance because of fraud. Discuss whether Valerino should succeed in his claim. [*Valerino v. Little,* 62 Md.App. 588, 490 A.2d 756 (1985)]

14-9. Arthur Modell was the president and an 80 percent shareholder of the Cleveland Stadium Corp. (CSC). Modell also served on the board of directors of the Cleveland Browns Football Co. and owned 53 percent of its stock. Aside from Modell, several other members of the board of directors of the Browns also served on the CSC board. At a March 16, 1982, meeting of the Browns' board of directors, the board voted to purchase all of the stock of CSC for $6,000,000. The one person who did not stand to benefit by the purchase of CSC by the Browns was Robert Gries, who, jointly with his business firm, Gries Sports Enterprises, Inc., owned 43 percent of the Browns and was also a director on the board. Gries felt the purchase price was far too high, based on other appraisals that valued CSC at no more than $2,000,000. Not only did the purchase for the price of $6,000,000 increase the debt load of the Browns to a point higher than necessary, the sale of CSC also directly—and, according to Gries, unfairly—benefited Modell. Gries had objected to the purchase at the March meeting but was outvoted by the other Browns' directors. Gries then filed a shareholder's derivative action seeking the rescission of the CSC acquisition. Had Modell breached his fiduciary duty, as a director of the Browns, to the other Browns' shareholders, including Gries? Discuss fully. [*Gries Sports Enterprises, Inc. v. Cleveland Browns Football Co.,* 26 Ohio St.3d 15, 496 N.E.2d 959 (1986)]

14-10. The Federal Deposit Insurance Corp., in an action against the officers and directors of a bank (the defendants), alleged that the defendants had breached their duty of care by failing to exercise reasonable supervision over officers of the bank. Apparently, the bank had suffered losses particularly due to the negligence of one of the defendants, Russell Greenwood, an officer of the bank. The other defendants asserted that they should not be liable for Greenwood's negligence. They argued that no facts had ever been brought to their attention that would have led them to believe that Greenwood was not properly discharging his duties and that in the absence of such information, they were entitled to rely on the judgments of Greenwood and on the appearance that he was properly discharging his duties. The question before the court was whether the directors breached their duty of care because they failed to supervise the actions of one of the bank's officers, Greenwood. How should the court rule? Discuss fully. [*Federal Deposit Insurance Corp. v. Greenwood,* 739 F.Supp. 450 (C.D.Ill. 1989)]

14-11. A Question of Ethics

Abe Schultz, Sol Schultz, and Lawrence Newfeld were the managing directors and officers of Chemical Dynamics, Inc., a close corporation. In 1967, the corporation leased a building in which to house its offices and operations. Included in the lease agreement was a provision giving Chemical Dynamics an option to purchase the property for $300,000. In 1970, because the corporation was experiencing financial problems and could not pay its rent, it assigned the lease and the purchase option to Newfeld in return for Newfeld's loan to the corporation of approximately $21,500. In 1973, Newfeld purchased the property. Eventually, when the corporation's financial sit-

uation had improved and its debts were paid, Abe Schultz sued Newfeld on behalf of the corporation, claiming that Newfeld had breached his fiduciary duty by usurping a corporate opportunity to purchase the property. Given these facts, consider the following questions. [Chemical Dynamics, Inc. v. Newfeld, *728 S.W.2d 590 (Mo.App. 1987)*]

1. In Schultz's suit against Newfeld, the trial court held that Newfeld had not usurped a corporate opportunity because the corporation "knowingly, willingly, and voluntarily sold, bargained, granted and transferred its entire interest in the lease, including the option to purchase the real estate, to Newfeld as consideration for the loan." The court placed emphasis on the language of the corporation's assignment, which was titled a "Bill of Sale," and stated that the corporation was "surrendering ... all benefits of the lease" to Newfeld as consideration for the loan. Schultz countered, however, that the language of the agreement was merely to give Newfeld the greatest degree of protection from creditors—ostensibly, by keeping the lease separate from the corporation's other assets by assigning it wholly to Newfeld. Schultz stated that, notwithstanding the language of the assignment, his understanding was that Newfeld was taking the lease on *behalf of, and in the name of, the corporation.* Is it possible that Newfeld could have led the other directors into this belief and merely demanded the language in the agreement to protect the lease from the corporation's many creditors? If so, was the subsequent purchase a violation of a legal or ethical duty?

2. Neither the trial court nor the appellate court considered it significant that the option to purchase the lease had expired *before* Newfeld's eventual purchase of the property. Because Newfeld had acquired the option in the original loan-for-lease transaction, the court held that it was his right to make the eventual purchase free from any latent interest that the corporation might have. If the option had expired, though, was it not legally required that the corporation be given first opportunity to buy the real estate? Does it matter legally and ethically that the corporation was not in a position to buy the real estate at the time the owners offered it to Newfeld?

14-12. Case Briefing Assignment

Examine Case A.14 [Maschmeier v. Southside Press, Ltd., *435 N.W.2d 377 (Iowa App. 1989)*] *in Appendix A. The case has been excerpted there in great detail. Review and then brief* the case, making sure that you include answers to the following questions in your brief.

1. What was the primary reason for this lawsuit?

2. What restriction did the corporate bylaws place on the transfer of corporate shares? On transfer, how was the price of shares to be determined?

3. How did the majority shareholders (the parents) effectively "freeze out" or "squeeze out" the minority shareholders (the sons)?

Focus on Ethics

The Private Environment

Many aspects of the private environment lend themselves to ethical analysis. Businesspersons certainly face ethical questions when they deal with the application of black-letter law to contracts. (*Black-letter law* is an informal term for the principles of law that courts generally accept or that are embodied in statutes.) Courts, for example, generally will not inquire into the adequacy of the consideration given in a contract. In other words, a court will not reevaluate a contract to determine whether what each party gave is equivalent to what each party received.

Ethical questions are also at the core of many principles of the law of sales. Many of the UCC provisions such as good faith and commercial reasonableness, though designed to meet the practical needs of business dealings, express ethical standards as well. Product liability also involves ethics. Many of the principles of product liability are based on principles designed to aid individuals injured, without extensive inquiry into issues of fault.

Ethical issues are not only prevalent in dealings between the firm and others outside the firm, they also are fundamental to relations within the firm. Ethical considerations, for example, underlie the fiduciary duties owed by corporate directors and managers to shareholders. The fiduciary duties are central to the relationship between the owners of a corporation and those charged with managing its affairs. In this *Focus on Ethics*, we examine selected areas in which ethical problems relate to the private environment of business.

Ethics and Freedom of Contract

In Chapter 4, we pointed out the basic tradeoffs that might exist between ethics and profitability. In general, the responsible business manager will evaluate a business transaction on the basis of three criteria—legality, profitability, and ethics. Any action that is simultaneously legal, profitable, and ethical can certainly put the decision maker's mind at ease. But what does acting ethically really mean in the area of contracts?

If an individual with whom you enter into a contract fails to look after his or her own interests, is that your fault, and should you therefore be doing something about it? That is to say, if the contract happens to be to your advantage and therefore to the other party's detriment, do you have a responsibility to correct the situation? For example, assume that a neighbor whom you have never met places a "for sale" sign on her car, offering to sell it for $2,000. You learn that she is moving to another state and needs the extra cash to help finance the move. You know that she could easily get, with little time or effort on her part, $5,000 for the car, and you congratulate yourself on your good fortune. Even if you do not need a car, you can purchase it and then sell it at a significant profit for yourself.

But you also learn that your neighbor has failed to do the preliminary research—checking blue book prices and so on— that most reasonable individuals would undertake when selling a car, and therefore she is unaware that the car is underpriced. Are you obligated to tell her that she is essentially giving away $3,000 if she sells you the car for only $2,000? Do you have an ethical responsibility toward this woman—whom you will probably never see again— simply because she failed to look after her own interests? This kind of situation, transplanted into the world of

345

commercial transactions, raises an obvious question: At what point should the savvy businessperson cease looking after his or her own economic welfare and become "his brother's keeper," so to speak?

The answer to this question is not simple. On the one hand, a common ethical assumption in our society is that individuals should be held responsible for the consequences of their own actions, including their contractual promises. This principle is expressed in the legal concept called freedom of contract. Applying this ethical precept to the above example, you could justify not saying anything about the true value of the car to your neighbor by stating that you were upholding the principle of freedom of contract. On the other hand, an assumption in our society is that individuals should not harm one another by their actions. If you applied this ethical yardstick to the above example, would you be obligated not to harm your neighbor's interests by taking advantage of her offer? How would you balance these two ethical principles?

In the area of contract law, ethical behavior often involves just such a "balancing act." In the above example, if you purchased the car and the neighbor later learned its true value and sued you for the difference, very likely no court of law would agree that the contract should be rescinded. In other words, the law would not "answer" your ethical question in this case. In all likelihood, the court would not come to the aid of the neighbor, because she could easily have prevented the injustice by learning, as a "reasonable person" would have, the market price of the car. There are times, however,

when courts will hold that the principle of freedom of contract should give way to the principle that people should not be harmed by the actions of others. We look below at some examples of how parties to contracts may be excused from performance under their contracts if that is the only way injustice can be prevented.

Impossibility

The doctrine of impossibility of performance is based to some extent on the ethical question of whether one party should suffer economic loss when it is impossible to perform a contract. The rule that one is "bound by his or her contracts" is not followed when performance is made impossible. The doctrine of impossibility of performance is applied to relieve a contracting party of liability for failure to perform. This doctrine, however, is applied only when the parties themselves did not consciously assume the risk of the events that rendered performance impossible. Furthermore, this doctrine rests on the assumption that the party claiming the defense of impossibility has acted ethically. In other words, a party cannot arrange events intentionally to make performance impossible.

A contract is discharged, for example, if performance of the contract calls for the delivery of a particular car and through no fault of either party this car is stolen and completely demolished in an accident. Yet the doctrine of impossibility of performance is not available if the party agreeing to sell his or her car either crashed the car to avoid performance of the contract or caused the car's destruction by his or her negligence. The well-known

English case of *Taylor v. Caldwell* is also illustrative of the doctrine of impossibility of performance.[1] In *Taylor,* the plaintiff entered into a contract with the defendant to rent the defendant's music hall for a series of concerts. Before the first concert, but after the contract had been entered into, the music hall was destroyed by fire. The court held that the defendant was discharged from performing. Furthermore, because performance was impossible, his failure to perform was not a breach of contract.

Prior to the late nineteenth century, courts were reluctant to discharge a contract even when it appeared that performance was literally impossible. Just as society's ethics change with the passage of time, though, law also makes a transition to reflect society's new perceptions of ethical behavior. Today, courts are much more willing to discharge a contract when its performance has become literally impossible. Holding a party in breach of contract, when performance has become literally impossible through no fault of the party claiming the defense of impossibility, no longer coincides with society's notions of fairness.

Mistake

The notion that mistake in contracts should release the contracting parties from their obligations has gained strength as the ethics of society have changed. If one were to study the court cases of several hundred years ago, one would find much less acceptance of mistake as an excuse to avoid a contractual obligation than exists today.

---

1. 122 Eng.Rep. 309 (K.B. 1863).

Mistakes can arise in numerous contexts surrounding the making of a contract. A mistake may be unilateral in that it is made by only one party. In a case tried early in this century, *Steinmeyer v. Schroeppel*,[2] a bidder on a construction project incorrectly calculated his costs and therefore submitted an offer that was substantially lower than it would have been if he had correctly calculated his costs. The Illinois court held that the bidder was not entitled to rescind the contract. The court further stated that rescission based on a unilateral mistake could not be obtained when the mistake resulted from a failure to exercise reasonable care and diligence. More recent court decisions, however, appear to be less harsh. Some courts have concluded that rescission on account of computation errors is permissible when the only injury to the other party is the loss of the expectancy engendered by a favorably low bid. Thus, ideas of fairness to each of the contracting parties change over time.

Unconscionability

The doctrine of unconscionability represents a good example of how the law attempts to enforce ethical behavior. This doctrine suggests that some contracts may be so unfair to one party as to be unenforceable, even though that party originally agreed to the contract's terms. Section 2-302 of the UCC provides that a court will consider the fairness of contracts and may consider a contract or any clause of a contract to have been

unconscionable at the time it was made. If so, the court may refuse to enforce the contract, or it may enforce the contract without the unconscionable clause, or it may limit the application of the clause so as to avoid an unconscionable result.

The UCC does not define the term *unconscionability*. The drafters of the UCC, however, have added explanatory comments to the relevant sections of the Code, and these comments serve as guidelines to the Code's application. Comment 1 to Section 2-302 suggests that the basic test for unconscionability is whether, under the circumstances existing at the time of the making of the contract, the clause in question was so one-sided as to be unconscionable. This test is to be applied against the general commercial background of the contract. For example, a contract with a marginally literate consumer might be seen as unfair and unenforceable, whereas the same contract with a major business firm would be upheld by the courts. The doctrine of unconscionability could be used broadly to ensure that all contracts appeared perfectly ethical, but the courts have not used it in this way. Only contracts that are so extremely one-sided as to "shock the conscience" of the court have been found unconscionable.

A classic case dealing with unconscionability is *Williams v. Walker-Thomas Furniture Co.*[3] This case involved a consumer who purchased over time, under an installment contract, several items of furniture from a furniture company. Under the

terms of the contract, each time a new item of furniture was purchased, that item, in addition to all of the furniture purchased previously, would be used as collateral (property securing the debt). In 1962, the consumer, Williams, bought a stereo set on which she soon stopped making payments. The furniture company wanted to repossess all of the items that she had purchased from it since 1957. Both the trial court and the intermediate appellate court, even though they felt that the contract was unconscionable, nonetheless held for the furniture company because, the UCC had not yet been adopted by the District of Columbia (the jurisdiction in which this suit was brought), there was no legal basis on which to find the contract unenforceable. On review, however, the District of Columbia Circuit Court of Appeals held that there was no reason why the lower courts could not, under the common law, apply the concept of unconscionability to contracts. The appellate court then remanded the case to the trial court for an examination of whether the terms of the contract were so extreme as to be unconscionable according to business customs and practices.

It may appear that the furniture store acted unethically by including in its standard form for installment sales contracts the provision that all furniture purchased would serve as collateral for future purchases as well. But can you say with certainty that this is necessarily the case? Obviously, Walker-Thomas faced competition in the marketplace from other furniture stores. That it succeeded in using the same contract for so many years indicates that it was engaged in

2. 226 Ill. 9, 80 N.E.564 (1907).

3. 350 F.2d 445 (D.C. Cir. 1965).

business practices that could not be successfully undermined by its competitors. What did this mean? It probably meant that the losses were typically so high in installment sales contracts in terms of defaults and inability to repossess collateral that Walker-Thomas found itself attempting to obtain additional collateral. While to an outsider such an action might seem unconscionable, to the business owner, the action may have appeared to be simply a "good business practice." That means that you cannot develop a general rule as to what constitutes unethical or unconscionable contract terms. You must look at each situation individually and examine carefully the context of each transaction.

Quasi Contract
Quasi contracts, often referred to as contracts implied in law, arise to establish justice and fairness. The term *quasi contract* is misleading because a quasi contract is not really a contract at all. It does not arise from any agreement between two individuals. Rather, a court imposes a quasi contract on the parties when justice requires it. Quasi contracts are used to prevent unjust enrichment. The doctrine of unjust enrichment is based on the theory that individuals should not be allowed to profit or enrich themselves inequitably at the expense of others. This belief is fundamental in our society and is clearly inspired by ethical considerations.

A typical situation in which a court, as a matter of judicial policy, may impose a quasi contract on the parties arises when one person renders emergency services to another person without first entering into

a contract. In these circumstances, courts generally allow the person who renders the emergency services to recover in quasi contract the reasonable fee for those services. This recovery is allowed irrespective of the fact that the parties never entered into a contract.

We have said previously in this text that ethical issues typically involve a tradeoff in one form or another. What tradeoff is involved here? Obviously, by imposing contractual obligations on persons who did not freely enter into those obligations, the government, by way of the courts, is interfering with the personal freedom of individuals to contract as they wish and to be responsible for only those obligations they freely undertake. To a certain extent, when quasi-contractual remedies are granted, this freedom is sacrificed to attain greater justice and fairness by preventing unjust enrichment of one person at the expense of others.

Ethics and Sales: Good Faith and Commercial Reasonableness
"Good faith" and "commercial reasonableness" are two key concepts that permeate the UCC and help to prevent the success of unethical behavior by businesspersons. These two concepts are read into every contract and impose certain duties on all parties. Section 2-311(1) indicates that when parties leave the particulars of performance to be specified by one of the parties, "[a]ny such specification must be made in good faith and within limits set by commercial reasonableness." The requirement of commercial

reasonableness means that the term subsequently supplied by one party should not come as a surprise to the other. The party filling in the missing term may not take advantage of the opportunity to add a contractual term that will be beneficial to himself or herself (and detrimental to the other party) and then demand contractual performance of the other party that was totally unanticipated. In this situation, under the UCC, the party filling in the missing term may not deviate from what is commercially reasonable in the context of the transaction. Courts frequently look to course of dealing, usage of trade, and the surrounding circumstances in determining what is commercially reasonable in a given situation.

Good Faith
The concept of good faith implies that one party will not take advantage of another party by manipulating contract terms. The obligation of good faith is particularly important in so-called requirements and output contracts. UCC 2-306 states "quantity" in these contracts "means such actual output or requirements as may occur in good faith."

For example, if General Motors contracts with Smith's Carburators to purchase all of Smith's output, Smith's cannot then increase its production from one eight-hour shift per day to three eight-hour shifts per day to make greater profits under the contract. As another example, assume that Mary's Machines has fifty employees assembling IBM clones. Mary has a requirements contract with Advanced Tech Circuit Boards under which Advanced Tech is to supply Mary with all of the circuit boards she needs.

If all of a sudden Mary quadruples the size of her business, she cannot insist that Advanced Tech supply her with all her requirements as per the original contract.

In many situations, parties may find it advantageous (profitable) to avoid a legal obligation. Without the counterobligation of good faith, the potential for abuse in the area of sales contracts is tremendous. Suppose, for example, that the market price of the good subject to a requirements contract rises rapidly and dramatically because of a shortage of materials necessary to its production. The buyer could claim that his or her needs are equivalent to the entire output of the seller. Then, after buying all of the seller's output at the contract price, which is substantially below the market price, the buyer could turn around and sell the goods that he or she does not need at the higher market price. Under the UCC, this type of unethical behavior is prohibited—even though the buyer in this instance has not technically breached the contract. Actual requirements must be determined in good faith. No speculation is allowed under requirements contracts.

Commercial Reasonableness

Under the UCC, the concept of good faith is closely linked to commercial reasonableness. All commercial actions—including the performance and enforcement of contract obligations—must exhibit commercial reasonableness. A merchant is expected to act in a reasonable manner according to reasonable commercial customs. Indeed, the words

reasonable, reasonability, and *reasonableness* appear again and again in the UCC. The concept of commercial reasonableness is clearly expressed in the doctrine of commercial impracticability. Under this doctrine, which is related to the common law doctrine of impossibility, a party's nonperformance of a contractual obligation may be excused when, because of unforeseen difficulties, performance of the contract becomes extremely difficult and burdensome. But the UCC makes it clear that the nonperformance must result from difficulties that could not *reasonably* have been foreseen or contemplated at the time of contract formation.

As an example, consider the case of *Maple Farms, Inc. v. City School District of Elmira.*[4] In June of 1973, Maple Farms, Inc., formed an agreement with the school district to supply the school district with milk for the 1973–1974 school year. The agreement was in the form of a requirements contract, under which Maple Farms would sell to the school district all the milk the district required at a fixed price—which was the June market price of milk. By December of 1973, however, the price of raw milk had increased by 23 percent over the price specified in the contract. This meant that if the terms of the contract were fulfilled, Maple Farms would lose $7,350. Because it had similar contracts with other school districts, Maple Farms stood to lose a great deal if it was held to the price stated in the contracts.

---

4. 76 Misc.2d 1080, 352 N.Y.S.2d 784 (1974).

Maple Farms sought to be released from its contractual obligations on the grounds of commercial impracticability, but did not succeed. The court noted that an increase in the price of milk should not have been totally unexpected, given the fact that the price of milk had traditionally varied and in the previous year had risen 10 percent. Also, the general inflation of prices in the United States should have alerted Maple Farms to the possibility of an increased milk price. According to the court, Maple Farms had reason to know these facts and could have placed a clause in its contract with the school district to protect itself from its present situation. Maple Farms could not be excused from performance because it should reasonably have anticipated the possibility that the price of milk might rise at least 10 percent, and possibly more because of the general inflation. In the court's eyes, a price rise of 23 percent was within the range of possibilities that Maple Farms should have anticipated.

The ethical principle expressed in the doctrine of commercial impracticability is that of fairness. In the *Maple Farms* case, essentially the court held that it would not be fair to the school district to excuse Maple Farms from its contractual obligation—because the price rises were not totally unexpected or unreasonable in view of the known facts at the time of contract formation. Maple Farms, in short, had failed to look after its own interests by including in the contract a clause that would have prevented its financial difficulties. But what about the school district? Was it acting reasonably—or ethically—when it refused to release Maple Farms from the contract? The court, at least, found no problem here. It did not escape the court's attention that the primary purpose of the contract, on the part of the school district, was to protect itself (for budgetary reasons) against price fluctuations. Therefore, it would make no sense to expect the school district to release Maple Farms from performance when such fluctuations, in fact, did occur.

Product Liability and Ethics

Ethical questions abound in the area of product liability. As the courts have imposed higher and higher damage awards on manufacturers in product liability lawsuits, so, it would seem, are more consumers bringing lawsuits to obtain damages when they are harmed by a product. In some cases, lawsuits are brought even though it is essentially the consumer who is at fault—if anyone is—and not the manufacturer. Such litigation raises an obvious ethical question: Is it fair that consumers should recover damages for harm caused by their own carelessness or product misuse or for simple accidents for which no one is really at fault?

Consider, for example, the case of *Kemp v. Beneke,* a 1990 Nevada district court case[5] that involved a nine-month-old child, Ryan Kemp, who fell through a toilet seat and suffocated in the water. The Kemp family sued the toilet-seat manufacturer, arguing that a warning sticker should have been placed on the toilet-seat

_____
5. No. A 267563 (Clark Co.).

lid to tell parents to take protective measures, such as buying a so-called "potty lock" to attach to the lid or installing self-closing hinges on the bathroom door. Should the toilet-seat manufacturer be required to warn against the obvious? Although in this case the manufacturer agreed to pay $90,000 to the Kemps, many persons might question the ethics of requiring a manufacturer to warn parents of such an obvious household danger.

In a similar vein, should tobacco companies and liquor companies be held liable for the numerous premature deaths of persons who purchase tobacco or liquor products because they are addicted to these psychoactive drugs? No one forces individuals to become nicotine addicts or alcoholics. Indeed, at least today, virtually no individual can be ignorant of the detrimental effects of consuming tobacco products and alcoholic beverages on a regular basis. Nonetheless, courtrooms in America are still faced with plaintiffs who are suing tobacco companies, and sometimes manufacturers of alcoholic beverages, for the premature deaths of loved ones. To date, no tobacco company has lost a suit, but the fact that such suits can be brought—in spite of the common knowledge of the detrimental effects of cigarette smoking and in spite of the warning labels on cigarette packages—does indicate that the courts are still receptive to a strict liability standard for consumer products.

At the other end of the spectrum is the need to impose strict liability standards on manufacturers to ensure that they will do all they can, within reason, to prevent unsafe

products from entering the marketplace. There is a fine line, however, between an imposition of ethical standards on manufacturers to benefit society and one that has the effect of overprotecting consumers—in the sense that it opens the door to the possibility that consumers may recover damages that are essentially incurred by their own carelessness or product misuse.

The Ethical Considerations of Debt

We are certainly many years away from that period in our history when debtors' prisons existed. Today, debtors are in a much more favorable position. If a creditor fails to exercise care in all aspects of the creditor-debtor relationship, the creditor may end up being accused of fraud, negligence, breach of contract, breach of the duty of good faith, or some other claim that may render the debt uncollectible. If worst comes to worst, the debtor can file for protection under bankruptcy law. Indeed, some now say that we have proceeded too far in the direction of protecting debtors and have made it too easy for debtors to avoid paying what they legally owe. Clearly, it is difficult to ensure the rights of both debtors and creditors at the same time, and laws governing debtor-creditor relationships are frequently perceived by at least one public group as being unfair to either creditors or debtors.

For example, to protect the legitimate interests of creditors, creditors are given numerous remedies under both the common law and statutory law. When these rights and remedies are invoked, however, the creditor is often considered by the general public to be employing unfair tactics. For many, the question of fairness revolves around the purpose for which the debt was incurred. If the debt was incurred for a needed item, such as a refrigerator, then common opinion seems to be that the debtor should be dealt with leniently. In contrast, if the debt was incurred for a trip to the Bahamas, the issue appears to be significantly different.

In contrast, when a debtor is relieved of the obligation to pay a legitimate debt because the creditor technically violated a statutory law, many would claim that this is unfair to the creditor. It also seems unfair to many that creditors who loan money in good faith are frequently precluded from collecting their debts because of the ease with which debtors can now enter into bankruptcy proceedings. In such situations, the law seems unfair to creditors.

There is obviously no way in which the law can protect both debtors and creditors at all times under all circumstances. Tradeoffs must be made in attempting to balance the rights of both groups, and the tradeoffs made often lead to questions of fairness and justice.

Who Pays When the Debtor Defaults?

Although there is clearly a distinction in people's minds between the failure to pay a loan and the theft of personal property, the result is the same—the wealth of the creditor-seller is reduced. Whatever the ethical issue may be when a debtor fails to perform, the economic consequence is clear: the cost

of debtors' nonperformance is imposed on all of those debtors who do perform. This cost takes the form of higher average interest rates. That is, the greater the percentage of loan agreements not consummated according to the agreement, the larger the risk premium added to normal interest rates. Creditors deal in a highly competitive market. They expect to earn a normal rate of return for investment in such an industry. If costs increase because of nonperformance by debtors, those costs will have to be recouped somewhere. In general, the only way to recoup them is to charge all debtors a higher interest rate.

This means that it is not only creditors who are harmed economically when debtors default but ultimately all other debtors or potential debtors, also. Therefore, laws protecting debtors who default may, in fact, not be protecting the interests of all debtors in the long run.

Bankruptcy

The first goal of bankruptcy law is to provide relief and protection to debtors who have "gotten in over their heads." But consider the concept of bankruptcy from the point of view of the creditor. The creditor has extended a transfer of purchasing power from himself or herself to the debtor. That transfer of purchasing power represents a transfer of an asset for an asset. The debtor obtains the asset of money, goods, or services; and the creditor obtains the asset called a *secured* or *unsecured* legal obligation to be repaid. Once the debtor is in bankruptcy, voluntarily or involuntarily, the asset that the creditor owns

most often has a diminished value. Indeed, in many circumstances, that asset has no value. Bankruptcy law attempts to provide a fair means of distributing to creditors the assets remaining in the debtor's possession.

Society has generally concluded that everyone should be given the chance to start over again. Bankruptcy law is a balancing act between providing such a chance and ensuring that creditors are given "a fair shake." But the question of "moral hazard" arises with bankruptcy law just as it does with product liability law. The easier it becomes for debtors to hide behind bankruptcy laws, the greater will be the incentive for debtors to use such laws to avoid payment of legally owed sums of money. That also means that the more easily a debtor can hide behind bankruptcy laws, the more a creditor will charge, because of the increased degree of risk. The fact is that the total number of bankruptcies has increased since the enactment of the Bankruptcy Reform Act of 1978. What this phenomenon means is that creditors incur higher risks in making loans. To compensate for these higher risks, creditors will do one or more of the following: increase the interest rates charged to everyone, require more security (collateral), or be more selective in the granting of credit. Thus, a tradeoff exists: the more lenient bankruptcy laws are, the better off will be those debtors who find themselves in bankruptcy; but those debtors who will never be in bankruptcy will be worse off. Ethical concerns here must be matched with the economic concerns of other groups of individuals affected by the law.

Business and Fiduciary Duties—Revisited

Two important duties that arise within business organizations are the duty of loyalty and the duty of care. As trustees of the shareholders' wealth, corporate directors and officers also have a fiduciary duty to exercise care and maintain loyalty to the shareholders when making decisions affecting the corporate enterprise. Partners owe the same duties to one another within a business partnership. The extreme duties owed, however, are tempered by the *business judgment rule,* which also raises an ethical issue: those engaged in business are not absolute insurers of the success of a venture or even the correctness of their decisions. As long as the decisions are made honestly and in good faith, then partners, managers, and directors have fulfilled their fiduciary duties.

Directors' Duties of Loyalty and Care

Every individual has his or her own personal interests, which may at times conflict with the interests of the partnership or the corporation with which he or she is affiliated. In particular, a partner or a corporate director may face a conflict between personal interests and the interests of the business entity. Corporate officers may find themselves in a position to acquire assets that would also benefit the corporation if acquired in the corporation's name.

In one landmark case, *Guth v. Loft, Inc.,*[6] Charles G. Guth, the president and a director of Loft, Inc., a soft-drink bottling

company, negotiated with the Coca-Cola Company for a discount on its syrups. When negotiations with Coca-Cola failed to result in a discount for Loft, Inc., Guth decided to see what Pepsi Cola could offer. During his investigation of this possibility, Guth set up a new corporation to acquire the secret formula and trademark for the manufacture of Pepsi Cola. He did so without offering the opportunity to Loft. A shareholder brought a suit against Guth, arguing that the shares of the new corporation should belong to Loft, and not to Guth personally. The shareholder prevailed. The court ruled that Guth had *usurped* a corporate opportunity in violation of his duty of loyalty to the corporation.

In addition to the duty of loyalty, every corporate director or officer has a duty of care, which clearly involves a duty to make informed decisions. That means that the partner or director or officer must take sufficient care to make sure that decisions reached are based on an appropriate amount of information.

The Business Judgment Rule

In some situations, directors and officers can escape liability for decisions that are ultimately detrimental to the corporation's interests if they can show that they used their best business judgment in reaching their decisions. A director will normally not be held to have breached his or her fiduciary duty to the corporation or its shareholders for any business judgment that is made in good faith and that seemed reasonable at the time under the circumstances with the information then available.

Unless fraud, bad faith, gross overreaching, or abuse of discretion is present, the judgment of directors is conclusive, and courts are reluctant to interfere, even if a bad decision harms the corporation. The rationale for this rule is that directors are in a better position than either the courts or the shareholders to make business judgments concerning their corporations and that a certain flexibility is necessary if directors are to fulfill their responsibility as the ultimate managers of a corporate enterprise.

Consider, for example, the case of *Shlensky v. Wrigley,*[7] in which the question before the court was whether the director and controlling shareholder of the corporation that owned the Chicago Cubs major league baseball team had exercised sound business judgment when he decided not to install lights for nighttime baseball games. Shlensky, a minority shareholder of the corporation, sued Wrigley and other directors on behalf of the corporation and asked the court to force the board of directors to install lights at Wrigley Field and to hold night games because the Cubs were supposedly losing profits by not doing so, to the detriment of shareholders in the corporation. The reason Wrigley had refused to install the lights and initiate night games was because he felt such a step would result in a deterioration of the surrounding neighborhood and thus a reduction in the property value of Wrigley Field. In this case, the court stated that it was "not their function to resolve for corporations questions of policy and business

6. 5 A.2d 503 (Del. 1939).

7. 95 Ill.App.2d 173, 237 N.E.2d 776 (1968).

management. The directors are chosen to pass upon such questions and their judgment unless shown to be tainted with fraud is accepted as final."

Other courts, however, will not accept the judgment of directors as final, even though it is not "tainted with fraud." Such courts maintain that the business judgment rule, in some circumstances, can be used as a defensive tool by directors to avoid their responsibilities to stockholders. Those who share this attitude feel that there are times when directors' decisions should be closely scrutinized according to the benefit or detriment they cause to the stockholders and the specific conflict of interest involved.

The court took this position in *Koenings v. Joseph Schlitz Brewing Co.*[8] In this case, Schlitz, in the midst of a takeover struggle with another firm, entered into *golden-parachute* employment contracts with its key employees. The contracts stated that if any employee's workload dropped significantly, he or she could consider the contract terminated and collect the rest of the salary due under the contract as liquidated damages. Among the key employees involved in the contracts was Koenings, who was Schlitz's attorney. After the contracts had been formed, Schlitz was acquired by Stroh. When Koenings experienced a drop in his workload, he demanded the remainder of his salary due under the golden-parachute provision in the contract, but Schlitz refused to pay. Koenings then sued for breach of contract.

The Wisconsin Court of Appeals eventually heard the

case and had to determine whether the golden-parachute provision was a reasonable exercise of the board of directors' business judgment and thus enforceable. The appellate court decided that the damages clause was an unreasonable penalty and invalid as a matter of public policy. In this instance, the court regarded "the business judgment rule" as "archaic and unresponsive to fair treatment of stockholders" and ruled that it should not be a basis for upholding contracts that "bear the taint of conflict of interest in favor of the management-beneficiaries to the detriment of the stockholders' interest."

■ Discussion Questions

1. Suppose you contract to purchase steel at a fixed price per ton. There is a lengthy steelworkers' strike, causing the price of steel to triple from the contract price. If you demand that the supplier fulfill the contract, the company will go out of business. Compare the ethical and business aspects of the situation.

2. The courts have often relieved signatories to a valid contract from their obligations on a showing of impossibility of performance. Critics of the doctrine of impossibility argue that the price and other contract terms included in any agreement take into account the possibility that unforeseen difficulties might arise that would render the performance of the contract extremely difficult or costly. Therefore, these critics argue, the promisor should be held to his or her promise even when the performance called for

by the contract would be excused under the doctrine of impossibility. Do you agree with this conclusion?

3. Although the UCC good faith provisions hold merchants to a standard of honesty in fact, such honesty is weighed in the context of commercial customs and habitual practices—course of dealing, usage of trade, commercial reasonableness, and so on. Puffing is a case in point. Merchants may "huff and puff" their wares as they traditionally have and still not—in most instances—violate their duty of dealing honestly and in good faith with the buyers of their products. Do you think that the customary practice of puffing is a fundamentally dishonest practice that should be abandoned? Is there anything the law can, or should, do to ensure that buyers will not be taken in by sellers' statements of opinion?

4. Do you think that the law favors debtors at the expense of creditors, or vice versa? Is there any way a better balance between creditors' and debtors' interests could be achieved?

5. There are laws against "interlocking directorates," in which one individual serves on the board of directors of competing companies. Normally, however, there is no law against a major shareholder in one corporation purchasing the securities of a competing corporation. If a law were passed making such a purchase illegal, who would benefit? Who would lose? Would society be better or worse off, on balance, if such a law were passed?

8.   123 Wis.2d 490, 368 N.W.2d 690 (1985).

UNIT FOUR

The Employment Environment

■ The Importance of the Employment Environment

Very few enterprises are carried on by a single individual. Most businesses rely on employees for conducting the myriad activities that are essential to a commercial organization. Within an organization, there may be several levels of authority for directing activities in the firm. At each stage, there are tasks and duties that are delegated to subordinates. There is a common thread, however: employees are acting on behalf of the corporation—that is, as the agents of the organization. Whenever they are carrying out a function that has been delegated to them by the owners or other agents acting for the owners, the employees are said to be acting in an agency relationship. *Agency* is a relationship between two persons in which one of them, called the *agent,* is authorized to act for and on behalf of the other, called the *principal.* Within the scope of the agency agreement, the agent may negotiate contracts and bind principals to those contracts. Because the agent has the power to bind principals to contracts, the law of agency imposes many obligations on the agent, including the duties of loyalty, obedience, and diligence. Agents, for example, normally must devote their actions exclusively to the principal and promote the interests of the principal.

In Chapter 15, we examine the agency relationship—its formation, the duties of agents and principals, and the liability of both agents and principals to third parties. In Chapter 16, we look at employment law as it relates to industrial relations. Specifically, we examine the legal framework for union organizing and concerted activity in the workplace as well as the process of collective bargaining between management and workers' unions. In Chapter 17, we shift focus from the worker as part of a labor organization and look at the rights of individual employees. In particular, we examine the legislation affecting various forms of discrimination against workers as well as legislation affecting the physical and economic security of individual workers.

◼ Ethical Issues in the Employment Environment

The agent has a duty of loyalty to the principal. This duty requires the agent to promote the interests of the principal. But what if the principal is engaged in unlawful conduct, such as generating pollution along with its production process? An ethical issue arises as to whether there is a greater duty owed to society in general that transcends the duty owed to the principal. In such a situation, if the agent decides to disclose to the authorities the pollution activities of the principal, a conflict may result between the agent and the one to whom he or she owes a duty of loyalty—the principal. Conflicts may also arise even though the principal is not engaged in illegal activities; the agent simply may find the principal's actions violate the agent's own sense of ethics or morality. In such situations, does the agent have a moral obligation or even the right to refuse to be loyal to the principal?

The ethical issues engendered by the agency relationship mostly concern duties owed by the agent to the principal and problems over dealings with third parties outside the employment relationship. There are, however, other ethical considerations within the employment environment. Economically speaking, management must be concerned, as with all productive inputs, over efficiency and productivity in making employment decisions. But there are ethical issues that must be considered because of the human aspect of labor.

A controversial issue concerns the degree to which federal law should invade the workplace in order to undo the harms of past discrimination. Most Americans accept that federal legislation is necessary to ensure equality of opportunity in the workplace. Far fewer, however, are convinced that the workplace can be used as a social laboratory to cure social ills. For example, is it fair, or even practical, to allow affirmative action programs that seek to promote racial equality by giving hiring and promotion preferences to minority candidates? These are but a sample of the ethical issues of the employment environment. We will return to some of them in the *Focus on Ethics* at the end of the unit.

Chapter 15

Agency

One of the most common, important, and pervasive legal relationships is that of agency. In an **agency** relationship between two parties, one of the parties, called the **agent,** agrees to represent or act for the other, called the **principal.** The principal has the right to control the agent's conduct in matters entrusted to the agent. More formally, the Restatement (Second) of Agency[1] defines *agency* as ''the fiduciary relation[2] that results from the manifestation of consent by one person to another that the other shall act in his behalf and subject to his control, and consent by the other so to act.'' In general, the law of agency is based on the maxim that ''one acting by another is acting for himself.''

◼ The Nature of Agency

An agent acts for his or her principal. By using agents, a principal can conduct multiple business operations simultaneously in various locations. Thus, for example, contracts that bind the principal can be made at different places with different persons at the same time. A familiar example of an agent is a corporate officer who serves in a representative capacity for the owners of the corporation. In this capacity, the officer has the authority to bind the principals to a contract. Indeed, agency law is essential to the existence and operation of a corporate entity, because only through its agents can a corporation function and enter into contracts.

◼ Types of Agency Relationships

The first step in analyzing an agency relationship is to determine whether such a relationship exists. Traditional analysis in the law of agency distinguishes three categories of relationships:

---

1. Restatement (Second) of Agency, Section 1(1). The Restatement (Second) of Agency is an authoritative summary of the law of agency. It is often referred to by jurists in decisions and opinions.
2. A fiduciary relationship involves a high degree of trust and a duty to act for someone else's benefit.

1. Principal and agent.
2. Employer and employee.
3. Employer and independent contractor.

It is important to note that at times an employee or an independent contractor may be acting in the capacity of an agent.

Principal–Agent

In a principal–agent relationship, the parties have agreed that the agent will act *on behalf of and instead of* the principal in negotiating and transacting business with third persons. The agent has *derivative authority* in carrying out the principal's business. This relationship will affect the principal's rights and duties. Thus, an agent is empowered to perform legal acts that are binding on the principal.

For example, Earl is hired as a booking agent for the rock group Harry and the Rockets. As the group's agent, Earl can negotiate and sign contracts for the Rockets to appear at concerts. The contracts will be binding and thus legally enforceable against the group.

Employer–Employee

Before the industrial revolution, the terms *employer* and *employee* had no significance in common law rules of agency. The original term used to denote an employer–employee relationship was *master–servant relationship.* The terms *master* and *servant* are now considered archaic, but because they have been traditionally used in the law governing agency relationships, they are still encountered occasionally.

Today, a *servant* is considered to be an employee and a *master* an employer. An **employee** is defined as one whose physical conduct is *controlled,* or subject to control, by the employer. An employee can be an agent if the employee has an appointment or contract for hire with authority to represent the employer.[3]

For example, Dana owns a dress shop. She employs Sandy, Sheila, and Sue as salespeople and Sara as a janitor. Dana is the employer (master);

the other women are the employees (servants). The key feature of the employer–employee relationship is that the employer has the right to control the employee in the performance of the tasks involved in the employment. The employees do not have *independent* business discretion. Dana can thus tell her salespeople not only to sell the dresses but also how to sell them. In selling the dresses, however, they are agents as well as employees. They have been given the authority by Dana to contract for and represent Dana in creating sales with customers. Sara, however, because she is not a salesperson, has no authority with respect to selling dresses and thus is not an agent in that respect. In fact, she may have no authority to represent Dana in any dealings with others, including receiving deliveries of janitorial supplies.

Employer–Independent Contractor

Independent contractors are not employees, because the person for whom they agreed to perform some undertaking has no control over the details of their physical performance. Restatement (Second) of Agency, Section 2, defines an **independent contractor** as follows:

> An independent contractor is a person who contracts with another to do something for him but who is not controlled by the other nor subject to the other's right to control with respect to his physical conduct in the performance of the undertaking. He may or may not be an agent.

The relationship between an employer and an independent contractor may or may not involve an agency relationship. Courts usually determine whether a person is an employee or an independent contractor by asking the following questions:

1. How much control can the employer exercise over the details of the work?
2. Is the employed person engaged in an occupation or business distinct from that of the employer?
3. Is the work usually done under the employer's direction, or is it done by a specialist without supervision?
4. Does the employer supply the tools at the place of work?
5. For how long is the person hired or retained?

---

3. According to the Restatement (Second) of Agency, Sections 2, 14 N, and 25, employees are always agents.

6. What is the method of payment—by time period or at the completion of the job?
7. What is the degree of skill required to do whatever it is the person was hired or retained to do?

Building contractors and subcontractors are independent contractors because a property owner does not control the acts of these professionals. Truck drivers who own their equipment and hire out on an *ad hoc* basis are independent contractors. A collection agency is another example of an independent contractor. In contrast, truck drivers who drive company trucks on a regular basis are

usually deemed employees. An owner of real estate who hires a real estate broker to negotiate a sale of his or her property has not only contracted with an independent contractor (the real estate broker) but has also established an agency relationship for the specific purpose of assisting in the sale of the property.

The following case illustrates a court's application of the above-mentioned criteria in deciding whether an employer–employee or principal–independent contractor relationship existed between the parties.

Case 15.1

AMEAR v. HALL

Court of Appeals of Georgia, 1982.
164 Ga.App. 163,
296 S.E.2d 611.

BACKGROUND AND FACTS *Dr. George Hall, the defendant, normally worked from 8:00 A.M. to 6:00 P.M. on weekdays and frequently on weekends. He had neither the time nor the capacity for household maintenance, so he hired Ivan Davey, who was the partner of the plaintiff, Tom Amear, to do landscaping and other work around the house. Hall would tell Davey what needed to be done, and then Davey, Amear, or other employees would accomplish the work. Davey and Amear controlled their own hours and methods of accomplishing the work. In February of 1977, Hall asked Davey to install fiberglass over four spaces formed by exposed beams connecting the carport and the house. The beams were purely decorative with no structural purpose, and Hall did not instruct Davey how to install the fiberglass. It was Amear's idea to climb out on the beams to install the fiberglass. Once he was on the beams, the nails in each end of the beam supporting him pulled through the beam, and he fell, severely injuring himself. Amear claimed that he was an employee and that Hall had failed to provide and maintain safe working conditions. Hall claimed that Amear was an independent contractor. The trial court entered judgment in favor of Hall, and Amear appealed.*

QUILLIAN, Chief Justice.
  * * * *

The test historically applied by this Court [in determining] whether a person employed is a servant or an independent contractor is whether the employer, under the contract, whether oral or written, has the right to direct the time, the manner, the methods, and the means of the execution of the work, as contradistinguished from the right to insist upon the contractor producing results according to the contract, or whether the contractor in the performance of the work contracted for is free from any control by the employer of the time, manner, and method in the performance of the work. * * * Under either test, the evidence demanded a finding that plaintiff was an independent contractor.
  * * * *

An individual contractor is expected to determine for himself whether his place of employment is safe or unsafe, and ordinarily may not recover against the owner for injuries sustained in the performance of the contract. * * * Unless the owner and an injured employee have a relationship of master–servant, the employer is generally not responsible for injuries occasioned by the method by which work is done by the employee. * * * "It is also the general rule that the employer is under no duty to take affirmative steps to guard or protect the [individual] contractor's employees against the consequences of the contractor's negligence or to provide for their safety.''

The court of appeals found Davey and Amear to be independent contractors. Therefore, Hall was not liable for the injury to Amear, and the judgment of the trial court was affirmed.

DECISION AND REMEDY

■ Formation of Agency Relationships

An agency relationship is a *consensual* relationship; that is, it comes about by voluntary consent and agreement between the parties. It is a consensual relationship because it must be based on some affirmative indication that the agent agrees to act for the principal and the principal agrees to have the agent so act.

Agency by Agreement

Generally, no formalities are required to create an agency. An agency relationship can be created by oral agreement or by written contract. An agency agreement can also be implied from conduct. For example, a hotel expressly allows Jack Andrews to park cars, but Andrews has no employment contract there. The hotel's conduct amounts to a manifestation of its willingness that Jack park its customers' cars, and Jack can infer from the hotel's conduct that he has authority to act as a valet. It can be inferred that, for that purpose, he is an agent for the hotel.

There are two main exceptions to oral agency agreements. In many states, the Statute of Frauds (discussed in Chapter 9) requires that whenever agency authority empowers the agent to enter into a contract that the Statute of Frauds requires to be in writing, the agent's authority from the principal must also be in writing. This is known as the **equal dignity rule.** It applies most frequently to contracts for the sale of an interest in land or contracts that cannot be performed within one year. An exception to the equal dignity rule exists in modern business practice; an executive of a corporation, when acting for the corporation in an ordinary business situation, is not required to obtain written authority from the corporation.

Another agency agreement that must be in writing is a power of attorney. A **power of attorney** grants an agent either full or restricted authority to act in the principal's behalf and often is executed in a notarized writing.[4] The power of attorney can be special—permitting the agent to do specified acts only—or it can be general—permitting the agent to transact all business dealings for the principal. Of course, if the appointment comes within the Statute of Frauds, it must be in writing to be enforceable. See Exhibit 15–1 on page 362.

Agency by Ratification

On occasion, a person who is in fact not an agent, or who is an agent acting outside the scope of his or her authority, may make a contract on behalf of another (a principal). If the principal approves or affirms that contract by word or by action, an agency relationship is created by *ratification*. Ratification is a matter of intent, and intent can be expressed by either words or conduct.

Agency by Estoppel

When a principal causes a third person to believe that another person is his or her agent, and the third person acts in reliance on the belief, the principal is ''estopped from denying'' that an agency relationship exists. In this situation, the courts treat the parties as though an agency relationship existed, because the third party acted on a justifiable belief that this was the case.

Suppose Andrew accompanies Charles to call on a customer, Steve, the proprietor of the General

---

4. An agent who holds the power of attorney is called an *attorney in fact* for the principal. Despite the use of the word ''attorney'' here, *an agent does not have to be an attorney at law to hold a power of attorney.*

The Growing Rights of Independent Contractors

Under copyright law, any work created by an employee during the scope of his or her employment at the request of the employer is called a "work for hire." The employer owns and holds the copyright to such works. But what about the free-lance artist or writer or other worker who is not really an employee in the usual sense? What happens, for example, when a sculptor is commissioned by an organization to create a statue? Who owns the copyright—the sculptor/creator or the organization that commissioned and paid for the work of art? Prior to passage of the Copyright Act of 1976, the courts generally presumed that the commissioning individual or firm held the copyright in such cases. In other words, free-lancers were assumed to be employees, and their works were considered to be "works for hire." If a publishing firm, for example, hired a free-lance photographer to take specifically designated types of photographs for a book the firm was publishing, the presumption would be that the publishing house owned the photographs—unless, of course, the parties had agreed otherwise in writing. The 1976 act changed the rules governing commissioned works and, in effect, reversed the presumption operative prior to 1976. Under the Copyright Act of 1976, the free-lancer who is commissioned to do a work will be the owner of the work created *unless* the parties agree in writing that the work is "for hire" *and* the work falls into one of nine categories stipulated by the act, such as audiovisual works, translations, supplementary works, and others. For publishing houses, advertising agencies, and other firms that routinely farm out work to free-lancers, this change in copyright law obviously has serious consequences.

It takes awhile for the business world to adjust to new laws governing its practices. In the case of the provisions of the Copyright Act of 1976 concerning commissioned works, not until June 1989 did the United States Supreme Court face the task of definitively interpreting the 1976 act in this respect and setting guidelines for determining who owns the copyright to a commissioned work done by a free-lancer. In deciding the case, the crucial issue was whether the party commissioned to do the work was an employee or an independent contractor.

The case before the Supreme Court[a] involved a copyright dispute over a sculpture created by James Earl Reid for the Community for Creative Non-Violence (CCNV), a Washington, D.C., organization dedicated to eliminating homelessness. CCNV conceived of the idea of a modern nativity scene in which, in lieu of the traditional Holy Family, the two adult figures and the infant would appear as contemporary homeless people huddled over a streetside steam grate. The title of the work was to be "Third World America," and the legend on the pedestal would read "and still there is no room at the inn."

CCNV paid Reid $15,000 to cover the actual expenses Reid incurred in creating the statue. Reid donated his services. There was no written contract, and the question of copyright or ownership rights had not been discussed. Initially, the federal district court ruled that the statue was a work for hire, reasoning that Reid had been an employee of CCNV because CCNV was the motivating force in the statue's production. Furthermore, members of CCNV continuously gave Reid direction and suggestions on how to proceed with the statue. In the end, reasoned the court, Reid had produced what CCNV wanted, not what he wanted.[b]

The Court of Appeals for the District of Columbia reversed and remanded the case back to

---

a.   *Community for Creative Non-Violence v. Reid,* 490 U.S. 730, 109 S.Ct. 2166, 104 L.Ed.2d 811 (1989).

---

b.   652 F.Supp. 1453 (D.D.C. 1987).

the district court. The appellate court's decision hinged on "a simple dichotomy in fact between employees and independent contractors."[c] Under agency law, Reid was an independent contractor. The United States Supreme Court agreed. Even though CCNV members directed part of the work to ensure that the statue met their specifications, all other relevant circumstances pointed in the direction of Reid's being an independent contractor. He was already engaged in a skilled occupation; he supplied his own tools; he worked in Baltimore without daily supervision from CCNV members in Washington, D.C.; and he had absolute freedom in deciding when and how long to work to meet his deadline. Additionally, he had total discretion in hiring and paying assistants. Reid was also paid as independent contractors are paid. CCNV did not take out payroll or Social Security taxes, nor did it provide any employee benefits or contribute to unemployment insurance or workers' compensation funds.

CCNV was not left totally empty-handed by the decision—as yet, anyway. The Court indicated that CCNV may still be considered a co-owner of the sculpture, and thus hold copyright jointly with Reid, if on remand the lower court determines that CCNV and Reid

c.   846 F.2d 1485 (D.C. Cir. 1988).

prepared the work "with the intention that their contributions be merged into inseparable or independent parts of a unitary whole."

■ Implications for the Businessperson

1.   Any businessperson who subcontracts with free-lance artists, writers, designers, and others who create "artistic" works must now take special care in crafting appropriate contracts for these subcontractual arrangements. Specifically, contracts with such independent contractors must clearly spell out who has ownership rights in the creative works generated by the free-lancer. Otherwise, the businessperson may find that he or she has paid for a work but does not have property rights in that work.
2.   The independent contractor/free-lancer must examine the issue from the other side. Although the *Reid* decision described above would seem to favor free-lancers, companies hiring free-lancers now routinely include in their contracts provisions that specifically deny the free-lancers any copyright or other property interest in the works created.

■ For Critical Analysis

1.   When an individual has a house built, that person may hire a subcontractor to lay

bricks. The bricklayer is an independent contractor creating a work. Why is the bricklayer not viewed in the same way a sculptor is viewed with respect to rights in the work created? Should there be any distinction made? Indeed, what would be the result if no distinction were made between the work created by a bricklayer and the work created by a sculptor?
2.   In the *Reid* case, a distinction was made between an employee working for hire and a free-lancer/independent contractor. If the type of work generated is substantially the same, is it logical to make a distinction between the work product of the employee and the work product of an independent contractor? In other words, is it logical that the employee should have no property rights in the product produced but the independent contractor—absent contractual terms indicating the contrary—should? Does this distinction create a differential incentive structure with respect to employees and independent contractors? What reasons underlie the law's distinction in this regard?
3.   Analyze the following statement: The *Reid* decision did not help free-lancers; rather, publishing firms and advertising agencies simply rewrote their free-lance contracts to specifically make all free-lance work "work for hire," in which the free-lancer agrees to give up all rights.

■ **Exhibit 15–1 Sample Power of Attorney**

POWER OF ATTORNEY
GENERAL

Know All Men by These Presents: That I, _____

_____

the undersigned (jointly and severally, if more than one) hereby make, constitute and appoint _____

_____

as true and lawful Attorney for me and in my name, place and stead and for my use and benefit:

(a) To ask, demand, sue for, recover, collect and receive each and every sum of money, debt, account, legacy, bequest, interest, dividend, annuity and demand (which now is or hereafter shall become due, owing or payable) belonging to or claimed by me, and to use and take any lawful means for the recovery thereof by legal process or otherwise, and to execute and deliver a satisfaction or release therefor, together with the right and power to compromise or compound any claim or demand;

(b) To exercise any or all of the following powers as to real property, any interest therein and/or any building thereon: To contract for, purchase, receive and take possession thereof and of evidence of title thereto; to lease the same for any term or purpose, including leases for business, residence, and oil and/or mineral development; to sell, exchange, grant or convey the same with or without warranty; and to mortgage, transfer in trust, or otherwise encumber or hypothecate the same to secure payment of a negotiable or non-negotiable note or performance of any obligation or agreement;

(c) To exercise any or all of the following powers as to all kinds of personal property and goods, wares and merchandise, choses in action and other property in possession or in action: To contract for, buy, sell, exchange, transfer and in any legal manner deal in and with the same; and to mortgage, transfer in trust, or otherwise encumber or hypothecate the same to secure payment of a negotiable or non-negotiable note or performance of any obligation or agreement;

(d) To borrow money and to execute and deliver negotiable or non-negotiable notes therefor with or without security; and to loan money and receive negotiable or non-negotiable notes therefor with such security as he shall deem proper;

(e) To create, amend, supplement and terminate any trust and to instruct and advise the trustee of any trust wherein I am or may be trustor or beneficiary; to represent and vote stock, exercise stock rights, accept and deal with any dividend, distribution or bonus, join in any corporate financing, reorganization, merger, liquidation, consolidation or other action and the extension, compromise, conversion, adjustment, enforcement or foreclosure, singly or in conjunction with others of any corporate stock, bond, note, debenture or other security; to compound, compromise, adjust, settle and satisfy any obligation, secured or unsecured, owing by or to me and to give or accept any property and/or money whether or not equal to or less in value than the amount owing in payment, settlement or satisfaction thereof;

(f) To transact business of any kind or class and as my act and deed to sign, execute, acknowledge and deliver any deed, lease, assignment of lease, covenant, indenture, indemnity, agreement, mortgage, deed of trust, assignment of mortgage or of the beneficial interest under deed of trust, extension or renewal of any obligation, subordination or waiver of priority, hypothecation, bottomry, charter-party, bill of lading, bill of sale, bill, bond, note, whether negotiable or non-negotiable, receipt, evidence of debt, full or partial release or satisfaction of mortgage, judgment and other debt, request for partial or full reconveyance of deed of trust and such other instruments in writing of any kind or class as may be necessary or proper in the premises.

Giving and Granting unto my said Attorney full power and authority to do and perform all and every act and thing whatsoever requisite, necessary or appropriate to be done in and about the premises as fully to all intents and purposes as I might or could do if personally present, hereby ratifying all that my said Attorney shall lawfully do or cause to be done by virtue of these presents. The powers and authority hereby conferred upon my said Attorney shall be applicable to all real and personal property or interests therein now owned or hereafter acquired by me and wherever situate.

My said Attorney is empowered hereby to determine in his sole discretion the time when, purpose for and manner in which any power herein conferred upon him shall be exercised, and the conditions, provisions and covenants of any instrument or document which may be executed by him pursuant hereto; and in the acquisition or disposition of real or personal property, my said Attorney shall have exclusive power to fix the terms thereof for cash, credit and/or property, and if on credit with or without security.

The undersigned, if a married woman, hereby further authorizes and empowers my said Attorney, as my duly authorized agent, to join in my behalf, in the execution of any instrument by which any community real property or any interest therein, now owned or hereafter acquired by my spouse and myself, or either of us, is sold, leased, encumbered, or conveyed.

When the contest so requires, the masculine gender includes the feminine and/or neuter, and the singular number includes the plural.

WITNESS my hand this _____ day of _____ , 19____

_____   _____

_____   _____

State of California,
   County of _____ } SS.
On _____ , before me, the undersigned, a Notary Public in and for said
State, personally appeared _____
_____
known to me to be the person _____ whose name _____ subscribed
to the within instrument and acknowledged that _____ executed the same.
                             (Seal) _____
Witness my hand and official seal.   Notary Public in and for said State.

Seed Store. Andrew has done sales work in the past for Charles but is not employed by Charles at the time of the visit with Steve. Charles boasts to Steve that he wishes he had three more assistants "just like Andrew." Steve has reason to believe from Charles's statements that Andrew is an agent for Charles. Steve then places seed orders with Andrew. If Charles does not correct the impression that Andrew is an agent, Charles will be bound to fill the orders just as if Andrew were really Charles's agent. Charles's representation to Steve has created the impression that Andrew is Charles's agent and has authority to solicit orders.

Agency by estoppel does not extend to all acts under all circumstances. For example, the acts or declarations of the purported agent in and of themselves do not create an agency by estoppel. It is the deeds or statements of the principal, not the agent, that create an agency. Suppose Alice walks into Dru's Dress Boutique and claims to be a sales agent for an exclusive Paris dress designer, Pierre Loiseau. Dru has never had business dealings with Loiseau. Based on Alice's claim, however, Dru gives Alice an order and prepays 15 percent of the total sales order. The dresses are never delivered. Dru cannot hold Loiseau liable, because Alice's acts and declarations, in and of themselves, do not create an agency by estoppel.

Note that a third person asserting an agency relationship by estoppel must prove that he or she *reasonably* believed that such a relationship in fact existed. Facts and circumstances must show that an ordinary, prudent person who is familiar with business would have been justified in concluding that the purported agent had authority to bind the supposed principal or to act on the principal's behalf.

Agency by Operation of Law

An agency relationship may arise without any express agreement between the parties involved if, under the relevant circumstances, the law imposes an agency relationship on the basis of necessity or to achieve a specific purpose. When legal principles create an agency in the absence of any private agreement, the agency relationship is said to have come about by operation of law. For example, many state statutes make state officials agents for the *service of process* upon individuals, corpora-

tions, and other legal entities. Service of process is delivery of a summons or other legal papers to the person who is required to respond to them. It is a necessary step in the litigation process. The statutory designation of a state officer for the service of process is an example of an agency relationship created by operation of law to achieve a specific purpose. A corporation with sufficient connections[5] to a state is also subject to receiving service of process in the same state.[6]

Sometimes agency by operation of law is created to give an agent emergency power to act under unusual circumstances that are not covered by the agreement when failure to act would cause a principal substantial loss. If the agent is unable to contact the principal, the courts will often grant this emergency power.

In some cases, an agency relationship by operation of law may occur when family relationships are involved. For example, suppose one spouse purchases certain basic necessities and charges them to the other spouse's charge account. The courts will often rule that the latter is liable for payment for the necessities. These rulings may be based on a social policy of promoting the general welfare of the spouse who made the purchases or on the assumption that the other spouse has a legal duty to supply necessities to family members.

Legal Capacity and Purpose

A principal must have legal capacity to enter into contracts. The logic is simple. A person who cannot legally enter into contracts directly should not be allowed to do it indirectly through an agent. An agent derives the authority to enter into contracts from the principal, and a contract made by an agent is legally viewed as a contract of the principal. It is immaterial whether the agent personally has the legal capacity to make that contract. Thus, a minor can be an agent, but in some states, cannot be a

---

5. See Chapter 13 for a discussion of what connections with a state are sufficient to subject a corporation to a state's court's jurisdiction.
6. In most states, a corporation is required to designate an agent for the service of process. Some states require that this agent be the state's secretary of state. See, for example, New York Business Corporation Law Section 402(a)(7).

principal appointing an agent.[7] In states that permit a minor to be a principal, any resulting contracts will be voidable by the minor principal but not by the adult third party. Thus, any person normally can be an agent, regardless of whether he or she has the capacity to contract. Even a person who is legally incompetent can be appointed an agent.

An agency relationship can be created for any *legal* purpose. One created for an illegal purpose or contrary to public policy is unenforceable. If Jones (as principal) contracts with Smith (as agent) to sell narcotics illegally, the agency relationship is unenforceable, because selling narcotics illegally is a felony and therefore against public policy. It is also illegal for medical doctors and other licensed professionals to employ unlicensed agents to perform professional acts.

■ Duties of Agents and Principals

Once the principal–agent relationship has been created, both parties have duties that govern their conduct. The principal–agent relationship is *fiduciary*—based on trust. In it, each party owes the other the duty to act with the utmost good faith. Neither party may keep from the other information that has any bearing on their agency relationship.

Agent's Duties to Principal

The duties that an agent owes to a principal are set forth in the agency agreement or arise by operation

---

7. Exceptions have been granted by some courts to allow a minor to appoint an agent for the limited purpose of contracting for the minor's necessities of life. See, for example, *Casey v. Kastel,* 237 N.Y. 305, 142 N.E. 671 (1924).

of law. They are implied from the agency relationship *whether or not the identity of the principal is disclosed to a third party.*

Generally, the agent owes the principal the following five duties:

1. Performance.
2. Notification.
3. Loyalty.
4. Obedience.
5. Accounting.

PERFORMANCE   An implied condition in every agency contract is the agent's agreement to use reasonable diligence and skill in performing the work. When an agent fails to perform his or her duties entirely, he or she will generally be liable for breach of contract.

The degree of skill or care required of an agent is usually that expected of a reasonable person under similar circumstances. Although in most cases this is interpreted to mean ordinary care, an agent may have presented himself or herself as possessing special skills (such as those that an accountant or attorney possesses). In these situations, the agent is expected to exercise the skill or skills claimed. Failure to do so constitutes a breach of the agent's duty. For example, an insurance agent who fails to obtain the insurance coverage requested by a principal is guilty of breach of contract. When an agent performs carelessly or negligently, the agent can be liable in tort as well.

The following case raises an interesting question: Did an agent breach his duty to perform by failing to procure a life insurance policy, notwithstanding the fact that no life insurance company would have insured the principal anyway—because he used drugs?

Case 15.2

BIAS v. ADVANTAGE INTERNATIONAL, INC.
United States Court of Appeals, District of Columbia Circuit, 1990. 905 F.2d 1558.

BACKGROUND AND FACTS   *Leonard Bias, a basketball player, entered into an agency agreement with Advantage International, Inc., under which Advantage agreed to advise and represent Bias in his affairs. On June 17, 1986, Bias was picked by the Boston Celtics in the first round of the National Basketball Association draft. On the morning of June 19, 1986, Bias died of cocaine intoxication. Bias's estate sued Advantage, alleging, among other things, that Advantage had failed to procure a $1 million ("jumbo") life insurance policy on Bias, as it had been directed to do. Bias's parents maintained that Advantage had represented to them and to Bias that it had secured the policy, and in reliance on these assur-*

ances, Bias's parents did not independently seek to buy an insurance policy on Bias's life. The trial court granted summary judgment for Advantage, holding that, in effect, the estate did not suffer any damage from Advantage's failure to obtain life insurance for Bias because even if Advantage had tried to obtain the life insurance policy, it would not have been able to do so because of Bias's cocaine use. The estate appealed, arguing that the questions of whether Bias was a drug user and was uninsurable were triable issues of fact and should have gone to the jury.

SENTELLE, Circuit Judge.
* * * *
* * * The testimony of Long and Gregg [former teammates of Bias] clearly tends to show that Bias was a cocaine user. * * * The testimony of Bias's parents to the effect that they knew Bias well and did not know him to be a drug user does not rebut the Long and Gregg testimony about Bias's drug use on particular occasions. * * * Bias's parents and coach did not have personal knowledge of Bias's activities at the sorts of parties and gatherings about which Long and Gregg testified. The drug test results offered by the Estate may show that Bias had no cocaine in his system on the dates when the tests were administered, but, as the District Court correctly noted, these tests speak only to Bias's abstention during the periods preceding the tests. The tests do not rebut the Long and Gregg testimony that on a number of occasions Bias ingested cocaine in their presence.

The Estate could have deposed Long and Gregg, or otherwise attempted to impeach their testimony. The Estate also could have offered the testimony of other friends or teammates of Bias who were present at some of the gatherings described by Long and Gregg, who went out with Bias frequently, or who were otherwise familiar with his social habits. The Estate did none of these things. The Estate is not entitled to reach the jury merely on the supposition that the jury might not believe the defendants' witnesses. We thus agree with the District Court that there was no genuine issue of fact concerning Bias's status as a cocaine user.
* * * *
* * * The defendants offered evidence that every insurance company inquires about the prior drug use of an applicant for a jumbo policy at some point in the application process. * * * The Estate failed to name a single particular company or provide other evidence that a single company existed which would have issued a jumbo policy in 1986 without inquiring about the applicant's drug use. Because the Estate has failed to do more than show that there is ''some metaphysical doubt as to the material facts,'' the District Court properly concluded that there was no genuine issue of material fact as to the insurability of a drug user.

The trial court's judgment was affirmed. Sufficient evidence, which was not rebutted by Bias's estate, existed to indicate that Bias was an illegal drug user and that, because of his illegal drug use, no insurance company would have insured his life for $1 million. Advantage could not be held liable for failing to perform a virtually impossible task.

DECISION AND REMEDY

NOTIFICATION   There is a maxim in agency law that ''all the agent knows, the principal knows.'' This maxim means that a principal will be presumed to know of any statement made by an agent to a third party—because the principal may be bound by it or be liable for any damages resulting from it. Thus, it is only logical that the agent is required to notify the principal of all significant or material matters that come to his or her attention concerning the subject matter of the agency. This is the duty of notification.

For example, Able is Paula's agent for the purchase of a certain property from Tom. In the course of dealing, Able discovers that many years ago Green obtained subsurface mineral rights in this property. Thinking that this is unimportant, Able neglects to tell Paula. The purchase of the land takes place, in any event, subject to Green's right to mine and remove the minerals. Paula does not have recourse against Tom; that is, Paula cannot rescind the sale or use the existence of Green's right to remove minerals as a defense to avoid going through with the sale. Able had the duty to notify Paula. The fact that he failed to do so and breached his fiduciary duty cannot be allowed to prejudice the rights of the innocent third party, Tom. Paula, however, does have recourse against Able for damages.

LOYALTY   Loyalty is one of the most fundamental duties in a fiduciary relationship. Basically stated, the agent has the duty to act solely for the benefit of his or her principal and not in the interest of the agent or a third party.

Numerous principles result from this duty. For example, an agent cannot represent two principals in the same transaction unless both know of the dual capacity and consent to it. Thus, a real estate agent cannot represent both the seller and the buyer, unless the seller and the buyer so agree. A salesperson representing Avon cannot sell products of a competing line at the same time unless both lines consent. In addition, an agent who owns property cannot sell the property to the principal without indicating that ownership before the sale. Furthermore, an agent cannot make ''secret'' profits—that is, an agent employed by a principal to buy cannot buy from himself or herself, and an agent employed to sell cannot become the purchaser without the principal's consent. In short, the agent's loyalty must be undivided. The agent's actions must be strictly for the benefit of the principal and must not result in any secret profit for the agent.

The duty of loyalty means that any information or knowledge acquired through the agency relationship is considered confidential. It would be a breach of loyalty to disclose the information either during the agency relationship or after its termi-

nation. Typical examples of confidential information are trade secrets and customer lists compiled by the principal. Note, however, that an agent has the right to use skills and basic knowledge acquired during the course of agency employment in his or her own behalf (such as sales techniques learned during the agency relationship), so long as the actions do not violate confidentiality.

OBEDIENCE   When an agent is acting on behalf of the principal, a duty is imposed on the agent to follow all lawful and clearly stated instructions of the principal. The agent violates this duty whenever he or she deviates from the instructions. For example an automobile salesperson may be liable to the dealer (the salesperson's principal) if, in an effort to close a sale, he or she makes a more extensive warranty than the dealer has indicated it is willing to make and if the buyer subsequently takes advantage of that warranty to the detriment of the dealer.

During emergency situations, however, when the principal cannot be consulted, the agent may deviate from the instructions without violating this duty if the circumstances so warrant. When instructions are not clearly stated, the agent can fulfill the duty of obedience by acting in good faith and in a manner reasonable under the circumstances.

ACCOUNTING   Unless an agent and a principal agree otherwise, the agent has the duty to keep and make available to the principal an account of all property and money received and paid out on behalf of the principal. This includes gifts from third persons in connection with the agency. For example, a gift from a customer to a salesperson for prompt deliveries made by the salesperson's firm belongs to the firm. The agent has a duty to maintain separate accounts for the principal's funds and for personal funds, and no *commingling* (mixing) of these accounts is allowed. When a licensed professional violates this duty to account, he or she may be subject to disciplinary proceedings by the appropriate regulatory institution. In addition, the agent is liable to the principal for failure to account.

Principal's Duties to Agent

The principal also has certain duties to the agent. Generally these duties include the following:

1. Compensation.
2. Reimbursement and indemnification.
3. Cooperation.
4. Provision of safe working conditions.

The principal's duties to an agent may be expressed, or they may be implied by law.

COMPENSATION   Except in a gratuitous agency relationship, in which one acts as agent solely as a favor to the principal, the principal must pay the agreed-on value (or reasonable value) for an agent's services. When the amount of compensation is agreed on by the parties, the principal owes the duty to pay it on completion of the agent's specified activities. If no amount is expressly agreed on, then the principal owes the agent the customary compensation for the services. If no amount is established either by custom or by law, the principal owes the agent the reasonable value of his or her services.

In general, when a principal requests certain services from an agent, the agent reasonably expects payment. A duty is therefore implied for the principal to pay the agent for services rendered. For example, when an accountant or an attorney is asked to act as an agent, compensation is implied. The principal has the duty to pay that compensation in a timely manner.

REIMBURSEMENT AND INDEMNIFICATION   Whenever an agent disburses sums of money at the request of the principal, and whenever the agent disburses sums of money to pay for necessary expenses in the course of a reasonable performance of his or her agency duties, the principal has the duty to reimburse. Agents cannot, however, recover for expenses they incur through their own misconduct or negligence.

The principal has the duty to reimburse an agent for authorized payments and to **indemnify** (compensate) an agent for liabilities incurred because of authorized and lawful acts and transactions as well as for losses suffered because of the principal's failure to perform any duties. The amount of indemnification is usually specified in the agency contract. If it is not, the courts will look to the nature of the business and the type of loss to determine the amount.

Authorized subagents can recover from either the principal or the agent who hires them, because the subagent is in a fiduciary relationship to both. If the authorized subagent obtains indemnification from the agent who does the hiring, the agent can then seek indemnification from the principal.

COOPERATION   A principal has a duty both to cooperate with and to assist an agent in performing his or her duties. The principal must do nothing to prevent the performance. For example, when a principal grants an agent an exclusive territory, the principal cannot compete with the agent or appoint or allow another agent to so compete in violation of the *exclusive agency*. The competition would expose the principal to liability for the agent's lost sales or profits.

SAFE WORKING CONDITIONS   The common law requires the principal to provide safe premises, equipment, and conditions for all agents and employees. The principal has a duty to inspect working conditions and to warn agents and employees about any unsafe areas. If the relationship is one of employment, the employer's liability is frequently covered by worker's compensation insurance, which is the primary remedy for an employee's injury on the job.

■ Rights and Remedies of Agents and Principals

It is said that every wrong has its remedy. In business situations, disputes between agents and principals may arise out of either contract or tort laws and carry corresponding remedies. These remedies include monetary damages, termination of the agency relationship, injunction, and required accountings.

Agent's Rights and Remedies against Principal

For every duty of the principal, the agent has a corresponding right. Therefore, the agent has the right to be compensated, reimbursed, and indemnified and to work in a safe environment. An agent also has the right to perform agency duties without interference by the principal.

Remedies of the agent for breach of duty by the principal follow normal contract and tort remedies. For example, under appropriate circumstances, an agent can lawfully withhold further performance and demand that the principal give an accounting.

When the principal–agent relationship is not contractual, an agent has no right to specific performance. An agent can recover for past services and future damages but cannot force the principal to allow him or her to continue acting as an agent.

Principal's Rights and Remedies against Agent

In general, a principal has contract remedies for an agent's breach of fiduciary duties. The principal also has tort remedies for fraud, misrepresentation, negligence, deceit, libel, slander, and trespass committed by the agent. In addition, any breach of a fiduciary duty by an agent may justify the principal's termination of the agency. The main actions available to the principal are constructive trust, avoidance, and indemnification.

CONSTRUCTIVE TRUST   Anything an agent obtains by virtue of the employment or agency relationship belongs to the principal. It is a breach of an agent's fiduciary duty secretly to retain benefits or profits that, by right, belong to the principal. Courts in this case will imply a **constructive trust**, under which an agent actually holds the money on behalf of the principal, and the principal can recover it in a lawsuit. For example, Andrews, a purchasing agent, gets cash rebates from a customer. If Andrews keeps the rebates, he violates his fiduciary duty to his principal, Metcalf. On finding out about the cash rebates, Metcalf can sue Andrews and recover them.

An agent is also prohibited from taking advantage of the agency relationship to obtain goods or property that the principal wants to purchase. For example, Peterson (the principal) wants to purchase property in the suburbs. Cox, Peterson's agent, learns that a valuable tract of land has just become available. Cox cannot buy the land for herself. Peterson gets the right of first refusal. If Cox purchases the land for her benefit, the courts will impose a constructive trust on the land; that is, the land will be held for and on behalf of the principal despite the fact that the agent attempted to buy it in her own name.

AVOIDANCE   When an agent breaches the agency agreement or agency duties under a contract, the principal has a right to avoid any contract entered into with the agent. This right of avoidance is at the election of the principal.

In the following case, a real estate agent was supposedly acting on behalf of a landowner for the sale of a piece of property. The trial court ruled that the agent had no cause of action for recovering the lost profits that he could have made had the landowner sold the land to him because the agent's failure to disclose his attempt to resell the land violated the agency agreement.

Case 15.3

RAMSEY v. GORDON

Court of Civil Appeals of
Texas—Waco, 1978.
567 S.W.2d 868.

BACKGROUND AND FACTS   *Ramsey, the plaintiff, was a licensed real estate broker and was also in the business of buying and holding land for resale. Gordon, the defendant, was the owner of approximately 181 acres of land and engaged Ramsey's services as a broker to find a buyer for the property. Ramsey, when he heard that the land was rapidly appreciating in value, told Gordon that he would buy the land himself. Gordon then agreed to sell Ramsey the tract of land for $800 per acre. A contract of sale to convey the property was drawn up; but before the contract was executed, Gordon conveyed the property to a third party for the same price ($800 per acre). Meanwhile, Ramsey, acting for himself, began negotiating for the resale of that property to another customer for a price of $1,250 per acre. Naturally, when Ramsey learned that Gordon had conveyed the property to another buyer, he blamed Gordon for his lost profits. Ramsey claimed that he lost over $90,000 in profits on the resale of the property and brought an action against Gordon to recover this amount. Gordon* *maintained that Ramsey had breached his fiduciary duties as Gordon's agent by not finding a purchaser for the best price available. The trial court held for Gordon, and Ramsey appealed.*

HALL, Justice.

* * * *

Ramsey does not challenge the finding that the property was increasing in value when the contract was being negotiated and made with Gordon, nor the findings that he knew the value was increasing and failed to disclose that fact to Gordon. Indeed, he may not do so because [the findings] are amply supported by the evidence and its inferences. His response to the conclusion that he breached his duties as Gordon's agent is to argue that he was only a purchaser and to cite Gordon's testimony that Gordon believed $800.00 per acre was a fair price when he made the contract. The over-all import of the record is that when it served Ramsey's purposes he would claim that under the contract he was Gordon's agent, but that in fact he used the contract to speculate with the property to his personal advantage without disclosure to Gordon. As we have said, the [trial] court found that Ramsey was Gordon's agent. Ramsey's testimony supports that finding.

Whenever an agent breaches his duty to his principal by becoming personally interested in an agency agreement, the contract is voidable at the election of the principal without full knowledge of all the facts surrounding the agent's interest. [Emphasis added.] * * * [It is a] "settled rule" that "an agent in dealing with a principal on his own account owes it to the principal not only to make no misstatements concerning the subject matter of the transaction, but also to disclose to him fully and completely all material facts known to the agent which might affect the principal; and that unless this duty on the part of the agent has been met, the principal cannot be held to have ratified the transaction."

The judgment of the trial court was affirmed. Ramsey was denied recovery, because an agency relationship existed between Ramsey and Gordon and Ramsey had breached his duties under this relationship.

DECISION AND REMEDY

INDEMNIFICATION   A principal can be sued by a third party for an agent's negligent conduct, and in certain situations the principal can sue the agent for an equal amount of damages. This is called *indemnification.* The same holds true if the agent violates the principal's instructions. For example, Lewis (the principal) tells his agent, Moore, who is a used car salesman, to make no warranties for the used cars. Moore is eager to make a sale to Walters, a third party, and makes a warranty for the car's engine. Lewis is not absolved from liability to Walters for engine failure, but if Walters sues Lewis, Lewis normally can then sue Moore for indemnification for violating his agency instructions.

Sometimes it is difficult to distinguish between instructions of the principal that limit an agent's authority and those that are merely advice. For example, Willis (the principal) owns an office supply company; Jones (the agent) is the manager. Willis tells Jones, "Don't order any more inventory this month." Willis goes on vacation. A large order comes in from a local business, and the present inventory is insufficient to meet it. What is Jones to do? In this situation, Jones probably has the inherent power to order more inventory despite Willis's statement. It is unlikely that Jones would be required to indemnify Willis in the event that the local business subsequently canceled the order.

■ Scope of Agent's Authority

Once the principal–agent relationship has been created, attention focuses on the rights of third persons who deal with the agent. A principal's liability in a contract with a third party arises from the authority given the agent to enter legally binding contracts on the principal's behalf. In certain circumstances, even if an agent contracts outside the scope of his or her authority, the principal may still become liable by ratifying the contract. Many of the concepts employed in ascertaining whether an agency relationship has been formed also relate to determining the scope of authority within the agency relationship.

Actual Authority—Express and Implied

Actual authority can be either *express* or *implied.* **Express authority** is embodied in that which the principal has engaged the agent to do. Express authority can be given orally or in writing. In some cases, as mentioned earlier, express authority must be given in writing. For example, the express authority granted by a *power of attorney* must be in writing. In addition, the *equal dignity rule* in most states requires that if the contract being executed is or must be in writing, then the agent's authority must also be in writing. A principal may, however, ratify in writing an act done originally without written authority. For example, Palmer (the principal) orally asks Larkins (the agent) to sell a ranch that Palmer owns. Larkins finds a buyer and signs a sales contract (a contract for an interest in realty must be in writing) on behalf of Palmer to sell the ranch. The buyer cannot enforce the contract unless Palmer subsequently ratifies Larkins's agency status *in writing.* Once the contract has been ratified, either party can enforce rights under the contract.

Implied authority is conferred by custom, can be inferred from the position the agent occupies, or is implied by virtue of being reasonably necessary to carry out express authority. For example, Adams is employed by Packard Grocery to manage one of its stores. Packard has not specified (expressly stated) Adams's authority to contract with third persons. In this situation, authority to manage a business implies authority to do what is reasonably required (as is customary or can be inferred from a manager's position) to operate the business. This includes making contracts for obtaining employee help, for buying merchandise and equipment, and even for advertising the products sold in the store.

Because implied authority is conferred on the basis of custom, it is important for third persons to be familiar with the custom of the trade. The list of rules that have developed to determine what authority is implied based on custom or on the agent's position is extensive. In general, implied authority is authority customarily associated with the position occupied by the agent or authority that can be inferred from the express authority given to the agent to fully perform his or her duties. The test is *whether it was reasonable for the agent to believe that he or she had the authority to enter the contract in question.*

Apparent Authority and Estoppel

Actual authority (express or implied) arises from what the principal manifests *to the agent.* **Apparent authority** exists when the principal, by either word or action, causes a *third party* reasonably to believe that an agent has authority to act, even though the agent has no express or implied authority. As discussed above, if the third party changes his or her position in reliance on the principal's representations, the principal may be *estopped* from denying that the agent had authority.

For example, suppose a traveling salesperson has been given no express authority to collect for orders solicited from customers. Because the agent neither possesses the goods ordered nor delivers them, the agent also has no implied authority to collect. Assume that a customer, Carla, pays an agent, Adam, for a solicited order. Adam then takes the payment to the principal's accounting department. An accountant accepts payment and sends Carla a receipt. This procedure is thereafter followed for other orders solicited and paid for by Carla. Later Adam solicits an order, and Carla pays Adam as before. This time, however, Adam absconds with the money. Can Carla claim that the payment to Adam was authorized and thus, in effect, a payment to the principal? The answer is yes, because the principal's *repeated* acts of accepting Carla's payment led Carla reasonably to believe that Adam had authority to receive payments for goods solicited. Although Adam did not have express or implied authority, the principal's conduct gave Adam apparent authority to collect. The principal would be estopped from claiming that the agent had no authority to collect in this particular case.

There are other ways that a principal may go beyond mere statements that convince a third party that a certain person is the principal's agent. If, for example, the principal has "clothed the agent" with both possession and apparent ownership of the principal's property, the agent has very broad powers and can deal with the property as if he or she were the true owner.

When land is involved, courts have held that possession alone is not a sufficient indication of ownership. If the agent also possesses the deed to the property, however, and sells the property against the principal's wishes to an unsuspecting buyer, the principal normally cannot cancel the sale or assert a claim to title.

The following case illustrates a situation in which an agency was deemed to exist on the basis of apparent authority.

BACKGROUND AND FACTS *Red River Commodities, Inc., (RRC) en-tered into a contract with Kelby Eidsness under which RRC agreed to purchase 250,000 pounds of sunflowers. Because of a drought, Kelby was only able to deliver 75,084 pounds. The contract contained an excuse clause in which it was stated that if Kelby could not deliver the promised 250,000 pounds because of an event unanticipated at the time the contract was formed, Kelby would be excused from performance only if he season-ably notified RRC of his inability to perform. Kelby orally notified RRC's contracting representative, Richard Frith, whom Kelby assumed was RRC's agent, about his poor crop in September before the harvest. RRC insisted that Frith was not a contracting agent and had no authority to bind RRC in any way. The contract between RRC and Kelby included the following statement: "The contracting representative identified below [Frith] does not have the authority to alter or vary the terms of this agree-ment. He is not an agent of RRC." Nevertheless, after the contract was made, Frith frequently contacted growers for RRC to help with their pro-duction problems. Frith talked to growers, inspected fields, and reported to RRC. RRC's manager testified that Frith was his "go between" with growers such as Kelby. Kelby assumed that Frith was an agent of RRC and therefore that notice to Frith of the drought and Kelby's inability to perform the contract completely would suffice as notice to RRC. In RRC's suit against Kelby for breach of contract, the trial court directed a verdict for RRC, holding, among other things, that Kelby had failed to give notice of his inability to perform because Frith was "an independent sales rep-resentative" and "not an agent . . . insofar as production, acts of God, waivers, and the like are concerned." Kelby appealed.*

Case 15.4

RED RIVER COMMODITIES, INC. v. EIDSNESS

Supreme Court of North Dakota, 1990.
459 N.W.2d 805.

MESCHKE, Justice.

* * * *

RRC's characterization of Frith as "independent" of RRC is not controlling. *How a principal and agent describe their relationship between themselves does not regulate their relationship to others.* [Emphasis added.] * * *

An agency "is ostensible when the principal intentionally or by want of ordinary care causes a third person to believe another to be his agent, who really is not employed by him." An ostensible [apparent] agency exists where the conduct of the supposed agent is consistent with an agency, and where, in a particular transaction, someone is justified in dealing with the supposed agent. An apparent or ostensible agency "must rest upon conduct or communications of the principal which, reasonably interpreted, causes a third person to believe that the agent has authority to act for and on behalf of the principal." * * *

There was evidence that Frith knew about Kelby's poor production, other than through generalized knowledge of drought conditions. Kelby testified that Frith contacted him during the fall before harvest, and that he told Frith that he expected his crop production to be *   *   * between 20% and 50% of the contracted quantity per acre. *   *   *

Notice to an agent is ordinarily notice to the principal. Evidence of Kelby's actual notice to Frith should be reconsidered by the trial court with a correct understanding of the law of agency.

DECISION AND REMEDY   *The Supreme Court of North Dakota reversed the trial court's decision and remanded the case for further proceedings consistent with this opinion. There was sufficient evidence to indicate that an ostensible, or apparent, agency existed between RRC and Frith.*

Emergency Powers

When an unforeseen emergency demands action by the agent to protect or preserve the property and rights of the principal, but the agent is unable to communicate with the principal, the agent has emergency power.

For example, Fisher (the agent) is an engineer for Pacific Railroad (the principal). While Fisher is acting within the scope of his employment, he falls under the train many miles from home and is severely injured. Davis, the conductor (also an agent), directs Thompson, a doctor, to give medical aid to Fisher and to charge Pacific for the medical services. Davis has no express authority to bind Pacific Railroad for the services of Thompson. Yet, because of the emergency situation, the law recognizes him as having authority to act appropriately under the circumstances.

Ratification

Ratification is the affirmation of a previously unauthorized contract or act. Ratification can be either express or implied. Generally, only a principal can ratify. The principal must be aware of all material facts; otherwise, the ratification is not effective. Ratification binds the principal to the agent's acts and treats the acts or contracts as if they had been authorized by the principal *from the outset.* If the principal does not ratify, there is no contract binding the principal, and the third party's agreement with the agent is viewed merely as an unaccepted offer. Because the third party's agreement is treated as an unaccepted offer, the third party can revoke the offer (rescind the agreement) at any time before

the principal ratifies, without liability. The agent, however, may well be liable to the third party for misrepresenting his or her authority.

As noted, the principal's acceptance (that is, the ratification) is binding only if the principal *knows* all the terms of the contract. If not, the principal can thereafter rescind ratification unless, of course, the third party has proceeded to change position in reliance on the contract.

Suppose an agent, without authority, contracts with a third person on behalf of a principal for repair work to the principal's office building. The principal learns of the contract from the agent and agrees to "some repair work," thinking that it will involve only patching and painting the exterior of the building. In fact, the contract includes resurfacing the parking lot, which the principal does not want done. On learning of the additional provision, the principal rescinds the contract. If the third party has made no preparations to do the work (such as purchasing materials, hiring additional workers, or renting equipment), then the principal can still rescind. But if the third party has, to his or her detriment, relied on the principal's ratification by making preparations, the principal must reimburse the third party for the cost of the preparations.

Two important points must be stressed. First, it is immaterial whether the principal's lack of knowledge results from the agent's fraud or is simply a mistake on the principal's part. If the third party has not changed position in reliance on the principal, the principal can repudiate the ratification. The unauthorized contract remains an offer, and the principal's acceptance is not valid, because contract law provides that one cannot accept terms about which one does not know. Second, the entire transaction must be ratified; a principal cannot affirm the desirable parts of a contract and reject the undesirable parts.

Death or incapacity of the third party *before* ratification will void an unauthorized contract. Most courts will also recognize an intervening and extraordinary change of circumstances as a basis for setting aside a principal's ratification to permit a third party to revoke.

Assume that Able, without authority, enters into a contract with a third party who wants to purchase Paula's shopping center. The following night the shopping center is destroyed by fire. Paula's subsequent ratification will not be effective to bind the third party. The courts will reason that it is unjust to hold a third party liable in such a situation and will permit the transaction to be avoided despite ratification.

■ Liability for Contracts

Principals are classified as disclosed, partially disclosed, or undisclosed.[8] A **disclosed principal** is a principal whose identity is known by the third party at the time the contract is made by the agent. A **partially disclosed principal** is a principal whose identity is not known by the third party, but the third party knows that the agent is or may be acting for a principal at the time the contract is made. An **undisclosed principal** is a principal whose identity is totally unknown by the third party, and the third party has no knowledge that the agent is acting in an agency capacity at the time the contract is made.

Disclosed and Partially Disclosed Principals

If an agent acts within the scope of his or her authority, a disclosed or partially disclosed principal is liable to a third party for a contract made by the agent. Ordinarily, if the principal is disclosed, an agent has no contractual liability for the nonperformance of the principal or of the third party.

If the agent has no authority but nevertheless contracts purportedly on behalf of a disclosed principal, the principal cannot be held liable in contract by a third party, but the agent is liable on a warranty theory (see below).

In most states, if the principal is partially disclosed, the principal and agent are both treated as parties to the contract, and the third party can hold either liable for contractual nonperformance.[9]

Undisclosed Principals

When neither the fact of agency nor the identity of the principal is disclosed, a third party is deemed to be dealing with the agent personally, and the agent is liable as a party on the contract.

For example, in a contract for the sale of a horse, a third party knows only that Scammon (the agent) wants to purchase the horse. The third party does not know that Scammon is actually negotiating for Johnson (the principal). Scammon signs a written contract in her own name, not indicating any agency relationship. She obtains and then delivers the horse to Johnson, who is in fact the principal, but Johnson refuses to pay her. Scammon tries to return the horse to the third party, who refuses to take it. The third party is entitled to hold Scammon liable for payment. The agent's subjective intent is not relevant. The third party contracted with the agent on the basis of the *agent's* credit and reputation, not the undisclosed principal's. Therefore, the agent is liable.

In contrast, if the agent has acted within the scope of her authority by disclosing that she was acting in an agency capacity for a third party, then the undisclosed principal would be fully bound to perform just as if the principal had been fully disclosed at the time the contract was made. Exceptions to this rule are made in the following circumstances:

1. The undisclosed principal was expressly excluded as a party in the contract. For example, an agent contracts for a lease of a building with a landlord. The landlord does not know of the agency, and the lease specially lists the agent as tenant, with no right of assignment without the landlord's consent. The undisclosed principal cannot enforce the lease.

2. The contract is a negotiable instrument. Here, the UCC provides that only the agent is liable if

---

8. Restatement (Second) of Agency, Section 4.

9. Restatement (Second) of Agency, Section 321.

the instrument neither names the principal nor shows that the agent signed in a representative capacity.[10]

3. The performance of the agent is personal to the contract, allowing the third party to refuse the principal's performance. Typical examples involve extensions of credit and highly personal service contracts.

4. The third party would not have entered into a contract with the principal had the third party known the principal's identity, the agent or the principal knew this, and the third party rescinds the contract.

If the agent is forced to pay the third party, and if the agent has contracted within the scope of authority granted, the agent is entitled to indemnification by the principal. It was the principal's duty to perform even though his or her identity was undisclosed,[11] and failure to do so will make the principal ultimately liable. Once the undisclosed principal's identity is revealed, the third party has the right to *elect* to hold either the principal or the agent liable on contract. (In some states no election is necessary because the disclosed principal will be automatically held liable on the contract.)

Warranties of Agent

When the agent lacks authority or exceeds the scope of authority, the agent's liability to a third party is based on the theory of breach of implied warranty of authority, not on breach of the contract itself.[12]

The agent's implied warranty of authority can be breached intentionally or by a good faith mistake.[13] The agent's liability remains, as long as the third party has relied on the agency status. Conversely, when the third party knows at the time the contract is made that the agent is mistaken, or when

the agent indicates to the third party *uncertainty* about the extent of authority, the agent is not personally liable for breach of warranty.

■ Liability for Agent's Torts

Obviously, an agent is liable for his or her own torts. A principal may also be liable for an agent's torts if they result from:

1. The principal's own tortious conduct.
2. The principal's authorization of a tortious act.
3. The agent's unauthorized but tortious misrepresentation.

If the agent is an employee, whose conduct the principal–employer controls, the principal–employer may also be liable for torts committed by the employee in the course of employment under the doctrine of *respondeat superior* which is discussed later in this chapter.

Principal's Tortious Conduct

A principal conducting an activity through an agent may be liable for harm resulting from the principal's own negligence or recklessness, which may include giving improper instructions, authorizing the use of improper materials or tools or the like, establishing improper rules, or failing to prevent others' tortious conduct while they are on the principal's property or using the principal's equipment, materials, or tools.

For instance, if Jill knows that Jack cannot drive but nevertheless authorizes him to take the company truck to pick up water pails for her business inventory, she will be liable for her own negligence to anyone injured by his negligent driving.

Principal's Authorization of Tortious Conduct

Similarly, a principal who authorizes an agent to commit a tortious act may be liable to persons or property injured thereby, because the act is considered to be the principal's. For example, if John directs Warren, an agent he retained to oversee the harvest of crops he bought, to cut the corn on specific acreage, which neither of them has the right to, the harvest is a trespass, and John is liable to whoever owns the corn.

---

10. UCC 3-401(1) and 3-403(2)(a). Extrinsic evidence to show an agency relationship is not normally admissible.

11. If Abel is a gratuitous agent, and the principal accepts the benefits of Abel's contract with a third party, then the principal will be liable to Abel on the theory of quasi contract.

12. The agent is not liable on the contract because the agent was never intended personally to be a party to the contract.

13. If the agent intentionally misrepresents his or her authority, then the agent can also be liable in tort for fraud.

In the same light, if Victoria instructs Albert, her real estate agent, to tell prospective purchasers that there is oil beneath her property, when she knows there is not, she will be liable to anyone who buys the property in reliance on the statements.

Misrepresentation

A principal is exposed to tort liability whenever a third person sustains loss due to the agent's misrepresentation. The keys to a principal's liability are whether the agent was actually or apparently authorized to make representations and whether the representations were made within the scope of the agency.

FRAUDULENT MISREPRESENTATION   Assume that Lewis is a demonstrator for Moore's products. Moore sends Lewis to a home show to demonstrate products and to answer questions from consumers. Moore has given Lewis authority to make statements about the products. If Lewis makes only true representations, all is fine; but if he makes false claims, Moore will be liable for any injuries or damages sustained by third parties in reliance on Lewis's false representations.

An interesting series of cases has arisen on the theory that when a principal has placed an agent in a position to defraud a third party, the principal is liable for the agent's fraudulent acts. For example, Pratt is a loan officer at First Security Bank. In the ordinary course of the job, Pratt approves and services loans and has access to the credit records of all customers. Pratt falsely represents to a borrower, McMillan, that the bank feels insecure about McMillan's loan and intends to call it in unless McMillan provides additional collateral, such as stocks and bonds. McMillan gives Pratt numerous stock certificates, which Pratt keeps in her own possession and later uses to make personal investments. The bank is liable to McMillan for losses sustained on the stocks even though the bank had no direct role in or knowledge of the fraudulent scheme.

The legal theory used here is that the agent's position conveys to third persons the impression that the agent has the authority to make statements and perform acts consistent with the ordinary duties that are within the scope of the position. When an agent appears to be acting within the scope of the authority that the position of agency confers but is actually taking advantage of a third party, the principal who placed the agent in that position is liable. In the example above, if a bank teller or a security guard had told McMillan that the bank required additional security for a loan, McMillan would not have been justified in relying on either person's authority to make that representation. McMillan, however, could reasonably expect that the loan officer was telling the truth.

INNOCENT MISREPRESENTATION   Tort liability based on fraud requires proof that a material misstatement was made knowingly and with the intent to deceive. An agent's innocent mistakes occurring in a contract transaction or involving a warranty contained in the contract can provide grounds for the third party's rescission of the contract and the award of damages. Moreover, justice dictates that when a principal knows that an agent is not accurately advised of facts but does not correct either the agent's or the third party's impressions, the principal is directly responsible to the third party for resulting damages. The point is that the principal is always directly responsible for an agent's misrepresentation made within the scope of authority.

Doctrine of *Respondeat Superior*

Under the doctrine of ***respondeat superior***,[14] the principal–employer is liable for any harm caused to a third party by an agent–employee in the scope of employment. This doctrine imposes **vicarious liability** on the employer—that is, liability without regard to the personal fault of the employer for torts committed by an employee in the course or scope of employment.[15]

SCOPE OF EMPLOYMENT   The Restatement (Second) of Agency, Section 229, indicates the fol-

---

14.   The doctrine of *respondeat superior* applies not only to employer–employee relationships but also to principal–agent relationships as long as the principal has the right of control over the agent.

15.   The theory of *respondeat superior* is similar to the theory of strict liability covered in Chapter 7. This doctrine may not apply if the employer has sovereign or charitable-organization immunity. The practice of granting this immunity is diminishing in most states.

lowing general factors that courts will consider in determining whether or not a particular act occurred within the course and scope of employment:

1.   Whether the act was authorized by the employer.
2.   The time, place, and purpose of the act.
3.   Whether the act was one commonly performed by employees on behalf of their employers.
4.   The extent to which the employer's interest was advanced by the act.
5.   The extent to which the private interests of the employee were involved.
6.   Whether the employer furnished the means or instrumentality (for example, a truck or a machine) by which the injury was inflicted.
7.   Whether the employer had reason to know that the employee would do the act in question and whether the employee had done it before.
8.   Whether the act involved the commission of a serious crime.

LIABILITY FOR EMPLOYEE'S NEGLIGENCE
Third persons injured through the negligence of an employee can sue either the employee who was negligent or the employer, if the employee's negligent conduct occurred while the employee was acting within the scope of employment.

At early common law, a servant (employee) was viewed as the master's (employer's) property. The master was deemed to have absolute control over the servant's acts and was held strictly liable for them no matter how carefully the master supervised the servant. The rationale for the doctrine of *respondeat superior* is based on the principle of social duty that requires every person to manage his or her affairs, whether accomplished by the person or through agents or servants, so as not to injure another. Liability is imposed on employers because they are deemed to be in a better financial position to bear the loss. The superior financial position carries with it the duty to be responsible for damages.

Today the doctrine continues, but employers carry liability insurance and spread the cost of risk over the entire business enterprise. Public policy requires that an injured person be afforded effective relief, and recovery from a business enterprise provides far more effective relief than recovery from an individual employee. Liability rights exist under law because of public policy protections of third parties. Thus, a master (employer) cannot contract with a servant (employee) to disclaim responsibilities for injuries resulting from the servant's acts, because such disclaimers are against public policy.

For the employer to be liable, the act causing injury must have occurred within the scope of the employee's employment. For example, Sutton (the employee) is a delivery driver for Schwartz (the employer). Schwartz provides Sutton with a vehicle and instructs him to use it for making company deliveries. Nevertheless, one day Sutton drives his own car instead of the company vehicle and negligently injures Walker. Even though Sutton's act (driving the car) was unauthorized, the negligence occurred as part of Sutton's regular duties of employment (making deliveries). Hence, Schwartz is still liable to Walker for the injuries caused by Sutton, even though Sutton used his own car contrary to Schwartz's instructions. Only if Sutton's acts had exceeded the scope of employment duties in a way that the employer could not reasonably have expected would Schwartz have been relieved of liability.

When an employee goes off on his or her own—that is, departs from the employer's business to take care of personal affairs—is the employer liable? It depends. If the employee's activity is a substantial departure akin to an utter abandonment of the employer's business, then the employer is not liable.

For example, a traveling salesperson is driving the employer's vehicle to call on a customer for a possible sales order. On the way to the customer's place of business, the employee deviates one block to mail a letter at the post office. As the employee approaches the post office, she negligently runs into a parked vehicle owned by Ann. The departure of the employee from the employer's business to take care of a personal affair is not substantial. The employee is still within the scope of employment, and the employer is liable to Ann. If the employee had decided to pick up a few friends for cocktails in another city, and in the process had negligently run her vehicle into Ann, Ann could not have held the employer liable, only the employee.

The following case is a classic in master–servant law. Although it is over 150 years old, the legal principle for which it stands is still viable in employment law today.

BACKGROUND AND FACTS *The plaintiff was walking across Bish-opsgatestreet when he was knocked down by a cart driven negligently by a servant of the defendant. The plaintiff suffered a fractured leg and multiple injuries. The plaintiff took the position that the defendant was liable for his injuries because the defendant's servant was driving the cart that caused the injuries. The defendant argued that his cart was never driven in the neighborhood in which the plaintiff was injured. Moreover, it was suggested that the defendant's servant had gone out of his way for his own purposes and might have taken the cart at a time when it was not wanted for business purposes to pay a visit to some friends.*

Case 15.5

JOEL v. MORISON

Court of Exchequer, England, 1834.
6 Carrington & Payne Reports 501.

PARKE, Judge.

*   *   *   *

His Lordship afterwards, in summing up, said—This is an action to recover damages for an injury sustained by the plaintiff, in consequence of the negligence of the defendant's servant. There is no doubt that the plaintiff has suffered the injury, and there is no doubt that the driver of the cart was guilty of negligence, and there is no doubt also that the master, if that person was driving the cart on his master's business, is responsible. If the servants, being on their master's business, took a detour to call upon a friend, the master will be responsible. If you think the servants lent the cart to a person who was driving without the defendant's knowledge, he will not be responsible. Or, if you think that the young man who was driving took the cart surreptitiously, and was not at the time employed on his master's business, the defendant will not be liable. The master is only liable where the servant is acting in the course of his employment. If he was going out of his way, against his master's implied commands, when driving on his master's business, he will make his master liable; but if he was going on a frolic of his own, without being at all on his master's business, the master will not be liable. As to the damages, the master *   *   * [although not himself] guilty of any offence, *   *   * is only responsible in law, therefore the amount should be reasonable.

The verdict was for the plaintiff, and he was awarded damages of £30 [thirty British pounds sterling]. In this case, the master was held liable for the acts of his servant.

DECISION AND REMEDY

IMPUTED KNOWLEDGE OF DANGEROUS CONDITIONS The employer is charged with knowledge of any dangerous conditions discovered by an employee and pertinent to the employment situation. To illustrate, a maintenance employee in Martin's apartment building notices a lead pipe protruding from the ground in the building's courtyard. The employee neglects either to fix it or to inform the employer of the danger. Sam falls on the pipe and is injured. The employer is charged with knowledge of the dangerous condition regardless of whether or not the employee actually informed the employer. That knowledge *is imputed to the employer* by virtue of the employment relationship.

LIABILITY FOR EMPLOYEE'S INTENTIONAL TORTS Most intentional torts that employees commit have no relation to their employment; and thus, their employers will not be held liable. Under *respondeat superior,* however, the employer is liable for intentional torts of the employee committed within the scope of employment, just as the employer is liable for negligence. For example, an employer is liable when an employee commits assault and battery or false imprisonment while acting within the scope of employment.

An employee acting at the employer's direction can be liable as a *tortfeasor* (one who commits a wrong, or tort), along with the employer, for committing the tortious act even if the employee was unaware of the wrongfulness of the act. For example, an employer directs an employee to burn out a field of crops. The employee does so, assuming that the field belongs to the employer, which it does not. Both can be found liable to the owner of the field for damages.

An employer who knows or should know that an employee has a propensity for committing tortious acts may be liable for the employee's acts even if they would not ordinarily be considered within the scope of employment. For example, the Blue Moon employs Joe Green as a bouncer, knowing that he has a history of arrests for assault and battery. While he is working one night, and within the scope of his employment, he viciously attacks a patron who "looks at him funny." The Blue Moon will bear the responsibility for Green's acts because it knew that he had a propensity for committing tortious acts.

Also, an employer is liable for permitting an employee to engage in reckless acts that can injure others. For example, an employer observes an employee smoking while filling containerized trucks with highly flammable liquids. Failure to stop the employee will cause the employer to be liable for any injuries to others that result.

To reduce the likelihood of liability losses, employers set up stringent work rules. For example, employees who drive company vehicles may be prohibited from giving rides to other passengers. Employees who violate these rules by being careless or committing unlawful or tortious acts may be subject to discipline, including discharge. Almost without exception, employers purchase liability insurance to cover the actions of certain employees.

■ Liability for Independent Contractor's Torts

The general rule concerning liability for the acts of independent contractors is that the employer is not liable for physical harm caused to a third person by the negligent act of an independent contractor in the performance of the contract. An employer who has no legal power to control the details of the physical performance of a contract cannot be held liable. Here again the test is the *right to control.* Because an employer bargains with an independent contractor only for results and retains no control over the manner in which those results are achieved, the employer is generally not expected to bear the responsibility for torts committed by an independent contractor. A collection agency is a typical example of an independent contractor. The creditor is generally not liable for the acts of the collection agency because collection is a distinct business occupation.

Generally, an exception to this doctrine prevails when exceptionally hazardous activities are involved. Typical examples of these activities include blasting operations, the transportation of highly volatile chemicals, and the use of poisonous gases. In these cases, an employer cannot be shielded from liability merely by using an independent contractor. Strict liability is imposed on the employer–principal as a matter of law. Also, in some states, strict liability is imposed by statute.

In the following case, one of the issues before the court is whether the repossession of collateral is an inherently dangerous activity, in which case the secured creditor could be held liable for the damages caused by the independent contractor's tortious actions.

Case 15.6

SANCHEZ v. MBANK OF EL PASO

Court of Appeals of Texas—
El Paso, 1990.
792 S.W.2d 530.

BACKGROUND AND FACTS   *MBank of El Paso contracted with El Paso Recovery Service (El Paso) to have El Paso repossess Yvonne Sanchez's 1978 Pontiac Trans-Am, which had been purchased through MBank financing. Two men hired by El Paso went to Sanchez's home with a tow truck and proceeded to hook the tow truck to the car, which was in the driveway. Sanchez, who was in the yard cutting the grass at the time, asked them their purpose and demanded that they cease their attempt to take the automobile and leave the premises. When they ignored her, she entered and locked herself in the car in an effort to stall them until the police or her husband could arrive. It was only after they got the automobile in the street that they identified their purpose and told her to get* *out of the car, which she refused to do. They then took the vehicle with Sanchez locked in it on a high-speed ride from her home to the repossession lot and parked the car in a fenced and locked yard with a loose guard dog. She was rescued sometime later by her husband and the police. Sanchez filed suit against MBank for damages, alleging that El Paso and its employees were MBank's agents and that they had willfully breached the peace. The trial court granted the bank's motion for summary judgment, holding that the bank could not be liable because El Paso was an independent contractor and not an employee or agent of MBank. Sanchez appealed.*

KOEHLER, Justice.

    *   *   *   *

    *   *   * In the Restatement (Second) of Torts, [Sections] 424, 427 (1965), *   *   * two of the exceptions to the general rule that an employer is not liable for the negligent or tortious acts of an independent contractor are (1) where the employer is by statute or administrative regulation under a duty to provide specific safeguards for the safety of others, he is liable to the others for whose protection the duty is imposed for harm caused by the failure of the contractor employed by him to provide required safeguards, and (2) where the employer employs an independent contractor to do work involving a special or inherent danger to others, he is liable for physical harm to persons resulting from the contractor's failure to take reasonable precautions against the danger.

    *   *   *   *

    MBank contends that neither the specific statutory safeguard exception nor the inherently dangerous work or condition exception applies, since the statute in question does not provide for specific safeguards nor is the repossession of property inherently dangerous. *   *   *

    Our analysis of [the applicable statute] leads us to conclude that the statute does impose a nondelegable duty on a secured party [one who holds an interest in property to secure payment of a debt] who wishes to repossess the collateral property without resorting to judicial process, or as it is sometimes termed "self-help repossession," to do so in a manner as to avoid a breach of the peace. First, the right to take possession of property legally possessed by another person without the need to utilize judicial process is in derogation of the owner's constitutional rights not to be deprived of property except by due process of law. But for the fact that a secured party is given a greater right to possession of the property than the one from whom it is taken, the person taking the property would be guilty of theft. It is therefore a harsh remedy and not being subject to judicial scrutiny, more likely to be abused. Second, the statute in granting this valuable right, imposes a duty on the secured party to repossess only if it can be done without disturbing public tranquility and order. A breach of the peace, for our purposes synonymous under Texas law with disorderly conduct, is a misdemeanor criminal offense.

    We further conclude that there is an element of inherent danger in a nonjudicial repossession. Since there is likelihood that the repossessor will commit a technical trespass by entering upon someone else's property to take possession of the collateral and that the repossession will be done not only without the owner's consent but in many cases against his will, there is a considerable risk that a breach of the peace, assault or worse may occur. If an excavation, properly dug, shored, fenced and lighted, remains inherently dangerous, then a repossession, always bordering on the edge of illegality if not carried out carefully, is also inherently dangerous.

DECISION AND REMEDY   *The trial court's decision was reversed, and the case was remanded for trial. MBank was held liable for the tortious actions of the independent contractor both because MBank had a nondelegable duty to avoid breaching the peace when repossessing collateral and because the repossession of collateral was an inherently dangerous activity.*

■ Liability for Agent's Crimes

Obviously, an agent is liable for his or her own crimes. A principal or employer is not liable for an agent's or employee's crime simply because the agent or employee committed the crime while otherwise acting within the scope of authority or employment, unless the principal or employer participated by conspiracy or other action.

In some jurisdictions, under specific statutes, a principal may be liable for an agent's violating, in the course and scope of employment, such regulations as those governing sanitation, prices, weights, and the sale of liquor.

■ Termination of an Agency

Agency law is similar to contract law in that both an agency and a contract terminate by an act of the parties or by operation of law. Once the relationship between the principal and the agent has ended, the agent no longer has actual authority to bind the principal—that is, he or she lacks the principal's consent to act in the principal's behalf. Under some circumstances, third persons may also need to be notified when the agency has been terminated.

Termination by Act of the Parties

The parties may terminate the authority by including in their agreement some express or implied condition or limitation, the occurrence of which will terminate the agency. This may consist of a certain date or some particular event. Furthermore, at any time, the parties may simply agree to end their relationship.

LAPSE OF TIME   An agency agreement may specify the time period during which the agency relationship will exist. If so, the agency ends when that time expires. For example, Able signs an agreement of agency with Paula "beginning January 1, 1992, and ending December 31, 1995." The agency is automatically terminated on December 31, 1995. Of course, the parties can agree to continue the relationship, in which case the same terms of the agency agreement will apply.

If no definite time is stated, then the agency continues for a reasonable time and can be terminated at will by either party. What constitutes a reasonable time depends on the circumstances and the nature of the agency relationship. For example, Paula asks Able to sell her car. If after two years Able has not sold Paula's car and there has been no communication between Paula and Able, it is safe to assume that the agency relationship has terminated. Able no longer has the authority to sell Paula's car.

PURPOSE ACHIEVED   An agent can be employed to accomplish a particular objective, such as the purchase of stock for a cattle rancher. In that case, the agency automatically ends after the cattle have been purchased.

If more than one agent is employed to accomplish the same purpose, such as the sale of real estate, the first agent to complete the sale automatically terminates the agency relationship for all the others.

OCCURRENCE OF SPECIFIC EVENT   An agency can be created to terminate on the happening of a certain event. For example, Paula appoints Able to handle her business affairs while she is away. When Paula returns, the agency automatically terminates.

Sometimes one aspect of the agent's authority terminates on the occurrence of a particular event, but the agency relationship itself does not terminate. For example, Paula, a banker, permits Able, the credit manager, to grant a credit line of $1,000 to certain depositors who maintain a balance of $1,000 in a savings account. If any customer's savings account balance falls below $1,000, Able can no longer make the credit line available to that customer. But Able's right to extend credit to the other customers maintaining the minimum balance will continue.

MUTUAL AGREEMENT   Recall from basic contract law that parties can cancel (rescind) a contract by mutually agreeing to terminate the contractual relationship. The same holds true in agency law regardless of whether the agency contract is in writing or whether it is for a specific duration. For example, Paula no longer wishes Able to be her agent, and Able does not want to work for Paula any more. Either party can communicate to the other the intent to terminate the relationship. Agreement to terminate effectively relieves each of the rights, duties, and powers inherent in the relationship.

TERMINATION BY ONE PARTY   As a *general* rule, either party can terminate the agency relationship. The agent's act is said to be a renunciation of authority. The principal's act is a revocation of authority. Although both parties may have the *power* to terminate—because agency is a consensual relationship, and thus neither party can be compelled to continue in the relationship—they may not possess the *right* to terminate and may therefore be liable for breach of contract. Wrongful termination can subject the canceling party to a suit for damages.

For example, Able has a one-year employment contract with Paula to act as her agent for $35,000. Paula can discharge Able before the contract period expires (Paula has the *power* to breach the contract); however, Paula will be liable to Able for money damages because Paula has no *right* to breach the contract.

Even in an agency at will (that is, an agency that either party may terminate at any time), the principal who wishes to terminate must give the agent a reasonable notice—that is, at least sufficient notice to allow the agent to recoup his or her expenses and, in some cases, to make a normal profit.

Termination by Operation of Law

Certain events will terminate agency authority automatically, because their occurrence makes it impossible for the agent to perform or improbable that the principal would continue to want performance. These events include death or insanity, loss of the agency's subject matter, changed circumstances, bankruptcy, and war.

Notice Required for Termination

When an agency terminates by operation of law because of death, insanity, or some other unforeseen circumstance, generally there is no duty to notify third persons. If, however, the parties themselves have terminated the agency, it is the principal's duty to inform any third parties who know of the existence of the agency that it has been terminated. The reason for the notice requirement is generally to prevent fraud. If third parties who have relied on the agent's continuing authority are to be dealt with fairly, they must be given notice of the termination of the agent's authority.

An agent's *actual authority* continues until the agent receives some notice of termination. Notice to third-parties, however, follows the general rule that an agent's *apparent authority* continues until the third person is notified (from any source of information) that the authority has been terminated.

The principal is expected to notify *directly* any third person who the principal knows has dealt with the agent. For third persons who have heard about the agency but have not dealt with the agent, *constructive* notice is sufficient.[16]

No particular form of notice is required. The principal can actually notify the agent, or the agent can learn of the termination through some other means. For example, Marshall bids on a shipment of steel, and Smith is hired as an agent to arrange transportation of the shipment. When Smith learns that Marshall has lost the bid, Smith's authority to make the transportation arrangement terminates.

If the agent's authority is written, it must be revoked in writing, and the writing must be shown to all people who saw the original writing that established the agency relationship. Otherwise, the principal may still be bound by the agent's apparent authority. Sometimes a written authorization (like that granting power of attorney) contains an expiration date. The passage of the expiration date is sufficient notice of termination for third parties.

---

16.   *Constructive notice* is information or knowledge of a fact imputed by law to a person if he or she could have discovered the fact by proper diligence. Constructive notice is often accomplished pursuant to statute by newspaper publication.

■ Terms and Concepts to Review

agency 356
agent 356
apparent authority 370
constructive trust 368
disclosed principal 373
employee 357

equal dignity rule 359
express authority 370
implied authority 370
indemnify 367
independent contractor 357
partially disclosed
    principal 373

power of attorney 359
principal 356
ratification 372
respondeat superior 375
undisclosed principal 373
vicarious liability 375

■ Questions and Case Problems

15-1. Adam is hired by Peter as an agent to sell a piece of property owned by Peter. The price to be obtained is not to be less than $30,000. Adam discovers that because a shopping mall is planned for the area of Peter's property, the fair market value of the property will be at least $45,000 and could be higher. Adam forms a real estate partnership with his cousin Carl, and Adam prepares for Peter's signature a contract for $32,000 for sale of the property to Carl. Peter signs the contract. Just before closing and passage of title, Peter learns about the shopping mall and the increased fair market value of his property. Peter refuses to deed the property to Carl. Carl claims that Adam, as agent, solicited a price above that agreed on in the creation of the agency and that the contract is therefore binding and enforceable. Discuss fully whether Peter is bound to this contract.

15-2. John Paul Corp. made the following contracts:

  (a) A contract with Able Construction to build an addition to the corporate office building.

  (b) A contract with a CPA, a recent college graduate, to head the cost accounting section.

  (c) A contract with a salesperson to travel a designated area to solicit orders (contracts) for the corporation.

Able contracts with Apex for materials for the addition; the CPA hires an experienced accountant to advise her on certain accounting procedures; and the salesperson contracts to sell a large order to Green, agreeing to deliver the goods in person within twenty days. Able refuses to pick up the materials, the CPA is in default in paying the hired consultant, and the salesperson does not deliver on time. Apex, the accountant, and Green claim John Paul Corp. is liable under agency law. Discuss fully whether an agency relationship was created by John Paul with Able, the CPA, or the salesperson.

15-3. Alice Adams is a purchasing agent–employee for the A & B Coal Supply partnership. Adams has authority to purchase the coal needed by A & B to satisfy the needs of its customers. While Adams is leaving a coal mine from which she has just purchased a large quantity of coal, her car breaks down. She walks into a small roadside grocery store for help. While there, she runs into Will Wilson. Wilson owns 360 acres back in the mountains with all

mineral rights. Wilson, in need of money, offers to sell Adams the property at $1,500 per acre. On inspection of the property, Adams forms the opinion that the subsurface contains valuable coal deposits. Adams contracts to purchase the property for A & B Coal Supply, signing the contract "A & B Coal Supply, Alice Adams, agent." The closing date is August 1. Adams takes the contract to the partnership. The managing partner is furious, as A & B is not in the property business. Later, just before closing, both Wilson and the partnership learn that the value of the land is at least $15,000 per acre. Discuss the rights of A & B and Wilson concerning the land contract.

15-4. Paula Development Enterprises hires Able to act as its agent to purchase a 1,000-acre tract of land from Thompson for $1,000 per acre. Paula Enterprises does not wish Thompson to know that it is the principal or that Able is its agent. Paula wants the land for a new country housing development, and Thompson might not sell the land for that purpose or might demand a premium price. Able makes the contract for the purchase, signing only Able's name as purchaser and not disclosing to Thompson the agency relationship. The closing and transfer of deed are to take place on September 1.

  (a) If Thompson learns of Paula's identity on August 1, can Thompson legally refuse to deed the property on September 1? Explain.

  (b) Paula gives Able the money for the closing, but Able absconds with the money, causing a breach of Able's contract at the date of closing. Thompson then learns of Paula's identity and wants to enforce the contract. Discuss fully Thompson's rights under these circumstances.

15-5. Able is hired as a traveling salesperson for the ABC Tire Corp. Able has a designated geographic area and time schedule within which to solicit orders and service customers. Able is given a company car to use in covering the territory. One day, Able decides to take his personal car to cover part of his territory. It is 11:00 A.M., and Able has just finished calling on all customers in the city of Tarrytown. Able's next appointment is in the city of Austex, twenty miles down the road, at 2:00 P.M. Able starts out for Austex, but halfway there he decides to visit a former college roommate who runs a farm ten miles off the main highway. Able is enjoying his visit with his former roommate when he realizes that it is 1:45 P.M. and that he will be late for the appointment in Austex. Driving at a high speed down the country road to reach the main highway, Able crashes his car into Thomas's tractor, severely injuring Thomas, a farmer. Thomas claims he can hold the ABC Tire Corp. liable for his injuries. Discuss fully ABC's liability in this situation.

15-6. Evan Smith experienced a heart attack in the emergency room of Baptist Memorial Hospital after being given a dose of penicillin for a sore throat. Smith sued the attending physician as well as the hospital. The hospital called itself a full-service hospital with emergency room facilities. Baptist Memorial considered the doctors as independent contractors, not agents. For example, for tax and accounting purposes the doctors were not treated as employees of the hospital. Based on this information, discuss whether the doctors who treated patients in the emergency room were independent contractors or agents. [*Smith v. Baptist Memorial Hospital System,* 720 S.W.2d 618 (Tex.App.–San Antonio 1986)]

15-7. Broyles signed a sales representative's agreement with NCH Corp. that included covenants not to compete and not to solicit NCH customers after termination of the agreement. NCH maintained detailed and costly records of its routes and customers. It considered this information to be valuable and sensitive, although all the data was readily ascertainable from other sources. Broyles transcribed the names and information with intent to use this material after he left NCH's employ. He later voluntarily terminated his employment with NCH and went to work for a competing firm. Based on the information he had transcribed while an employee of NCH, he solicited business from some of his former customers. NCH sued Broyles, claiming that the use of his list was a breach of his employment contract and a breach of his fiduciary duty to NCH. Discuss whether NCH was successful in its claim that Broyles had breached his fiduciary duty. [*NCH Corp. v. Broyles,* 749 F.2d 247 (5th Cir. 1985)]

15-8. Aztec Petroleum Corp. arranged to have Douglas buy oil and gas leases for Aztec. In return for his services, Douglas was to receive an initial $5,000 plus a royalty interest in the leases he obtained. Douglas obtained a number of leases for Aztec but represented to Aztec that the prices paid for the leases were higher than they actually were. By sending Aztec photocopies of altered checks, both as to payee and amount, and forged receipts, Douglas was able to keep for himself a substantial amount of the money that Aztec had entrusted to him for payment of the leases. This money was used by Douglas for personal purchases, including two new cars, a boat, and other personal items. When Aztec refused to grant Douglas the promised royalty interest in the leases, Douglas brought suit to obtain it. The trial court held for Aztec, and Douglas appealed. In view of Douglas's deceptive activities, is Aztec required to grant the royalty interest? Discuss fully. [*Douglas v. Aztec Petroleum Corp.,* 695 S.W.2d 312 (Tex.App. 1985)]

15-9. Brenda Tarver worked as an independent contractor with Dianne Landers's real estate agency. The agents in the firm worked on a commission basis, and Tarver's contract read that she would receive 30 percent of the agency's commissions for sales for which she was "entitled as either listing and/or selling agent." In the spring of 1984 Charles Smith and his wife contacted the agency concerning some property for sale listed by the agency and advertised in the local newspaper. The Smiths were referred to Tarver, who showed them the property and handled their offer to purchase the property and the seller's counteroffer. In all, Tarver negotiated three offers and three counteroffers between the seller and the buyer. Later, however, the Smiths returned to the agency and, because Tarver was out of the office, negotiated with Dianne Landers concerning the last counteroffer they had rejected. After some modifications were made, they reached an agreement with the seller and purchased the property. Landers would not pay Tarver a commission for the sale because Tarver had not negotiated the final purchase. Tarver sued to recover her commission on the grounds that it was customary in the real estate office that the initial selling agent would be paid the commission and that when the initial selling agent was absent from the office, another agent would handle negotiations—but not receive the commission if a sale resulted. Who will prevail in court? Explain. [*Tarver v. Landers,* 486 So.2d 294 (La.App. 1986)]

15-10. Port Ship Service, Inc., a water taxi service, ferried crew members, customs agents, supplies, and the like between ships and the shore at the Port of New Orleans. Norton, Lilly & Co. acted as an agent for various ships entering the harbor that required water taxi services. Ships needing water taxi services would call Norton, and Norton would communicate the names of the vessels needing the services to Port Ship. Although Norton never informed Port Ship of the names of the vessels' owners, the information was readily available to Port Ship in publications commonly used by port authorities, and in addition, Norton maintained a twenty-four-hour telephone service through which Port Ship could ascertain the identities of any of the ship owners. Port Ship sought to hold Norton liable for unpaid taxi services, and the issue turned on whether the ship owners were fully disclosed principals (in which case Norton could not be held liable) or only partially disclosed principals (in which case Norton could be held liable). The Restatement (Second) of Agency, Section 4, states that "it is the agent's duty to disclose the principal's identity, and not a third party's duty to ascertain that identity." Had Norton disclosed the principals' identities by giving Port Ship the names of the vessels? Discuss fully. [*Port Ship Service, Inc. v. Norton, Lilly & Co.,* 883 F.2d 23 (5th Cir. 1989)]

15-11. Fred Hash worked for Van Stavern Construction Co. as a field supervisor in charge of constructing a new plant facility. Hash entered into a contract with Sutton's Steel & Supply, Inc., to supply steel to the construction site in several installments. Hash gave the name of B. D. Van Stavern, the president and owner of the construction firm, instead of the firm name, as the party for whom he was acting. The contract and the subsequent invoices all had B. D. Van Stavern's name on them. Several loads were delivered by Sutton. All of the invoices were signed by Van Stavern employees, and corporate checks were made out to Sutton. When Sutton Steel later sued Van Stavern personally for unpaid debts totaling $40,437, it claimed that Van Stavern had ratified the acts of his employee, Hash, by allowing payment on previous invoices. Although Van Stavern had had no knowledge of the unauthorized arrangement, had he legally ratified the agreement by his silence? Explain. [*Sutton's Steel & Supply, Inc. v. Van Stavern,* 496 So.2d 1360 (La.App. 1986)]

15-12. Garcia was an employee of Van Groningen & Sons, Inc., which operated an orchard, and one of Garcia's duties was to drive a tractor through the orchard pulling machinery behind. On one particular occasion, Garcia invited his nephew Perez to accompany him on the job as he drove the tractor through the orchard. Perez had to sit on the tool box because there was only one seat on the tractor. Perez was knocked off by a tree branch and was severely injured when the tractor machinery ran over his leg. Perez sued Van Groningen & Sons under the theory of *respondeat superior.* Van Groningen testified that the company forbade anyone but the driver to ride on the tractor because of the danger and that Garcia had personally been advised of this rule. Discuss what chance Perez has of recovering under the doctrine of *respondeat superior.* [*Perez v. Van Groningen & Sons, Inc.,* 41 Cal.3d 962, 719 P.2d 676, 227 Cal.Rptr. 106 (1986)]

15-13. A Question of Ethics

Mallie Brackens consulted Dr. Floyd Jones in April 1983 because of stomach pains. Dr. Jones admitted her to the Detroit Osteopathic Hospital for the purpose of performing a gastrojejunostomy (a surgical joining of the stomach with the middle section of the small intestine). After the surgery, Brackens was readmitted to the hospital twice because of dehydration and other problems and was seen by Drs. Taras and Tobes—whom she had never met before—for upper gastrointestinal examinations. Her problems persisted and finally, in December 1983, she learned from physicians at another hospital that instead of a gastrojejunostomy, Dr. Jones had performed a gastroileostomy, which is a bypass procedure performed on obese persons. Brackens sued the Detroit Osteopathic Hospital, alleging that it was liable for the negligence of its agents, Drs. Taras and Tobes, who had failed to detect the improperly performed gastrojejunostomy when they examined her.

Both the trial court and the appellate court in this case held that, generally speaking, a hospital is not liable for the negligence of a physician who is an independent contractor and merely uses the hospital's facilities to render treatment to his or her patients. Although the trial court granted the hospital's motion for summary judgment, the appellate court held that the case should go to trial and remanded the case. The appellate court reasoned that if an individual looked to the hospital to provide medical treatment and there was a representation by the hospital that medical treatment would be performed by physicians working therein, an agency by estoppel can be found. [Brackens v. Detroit Osteopathic Hospital, *174 Mich.App. 290, 435 N.W.2d 472 (1989)*]

1. Brackens testified that during her confinement in the hospital, she at all times believed that Drs. Taras and Tobes were hospital physicians employed by the hospital. Do you think that, in this case, an agency by estoppel should be found? In your opinion, would this finding be a fair solution? Why or why not?
2. What general ethical principle or principles underlie the theory of agency by estoppel?
3. Why must the *principal* in some way be responsible for creating the appearance of an agency before agency by estoppel will be found? What ethical considerations underlie this requirement?

15-14. Case Briefing Assignment

Examine Case A.15 [Green v. Shell Oil Co., 181 Mich.App. 439, 450 N.W.2d 50 (1989)] in Appendix A. The case has been excerpted there in great detail. Review and then brief the case, making sure that you include answers to the following questions in your brief.

1. Green sued Shell and Lanford on two grounds. What are they?
2. Why did the court hold that summary judgment on the issue of Lanford's agency status was inappropriate?
3. Why did the court hold that the service station attendant was not acting within the scope of his employment while he was participating in the assault and battery?

Chapter 16

Labor Law

Through the first half of the nineteenth century, most Americans were self-employed. For these individuals, problems arising from employment relationships did not exist. For those who were employed, the terms of employment were generally determined by their employers. The nature of employment changed with the Industrial Revolution, beginning about 1760. Fewer Americans were self-employed, and employment relationships lost some of their paternalistic character. Terms of employment came to be determined by bargaining between employees and employers, but because an employer usually bargained from a superior position, the terms tended to favor the employer. Also, most industrial enterprises were in their infancy, and to encourage their development, they were given considerable freedom to respond to changing conditions—freedom to hire and fire and freedom from potentially crippling liability.

With increasing industrialization, the size of corporate employers and the number of workplace hazards increased. The advent of mass production methods produced many rather menial jobs at low wages. Workers came to believe that to counter the power of corporations and to protect themselves they needed to organize into unions to bargain with the employer. Collective activities such as unions were discouraged—sometimes forcibly—by employers. Congress offered some assistance to workers, but early legislation in support of unionization, such as the Railway Labor Act of 1926,[1] was often restricted to a particular industry.

Beginning in 1932, however, a number of statutes were enacted that greatly increased employees' rights to join unions and to engage in collective bargaining to better enable workers to negotiate more favorable working arrangements. At the heart of labor rights is the right to unionize and bargain with management for improved working conditions, salaries, and benefits. The ultimate weapon of labor is, of course, the strike.

This chapter describes the development of labor law and legal recognition of the right to form unions. The laws that govern the management-union relationship are set forth in historical perspective. Then the chapter describes

---

1.   45 U.S.C. Sections 151 *et seq.*

the process of unionizing a company, the collective bargaining required of a unionized employer, the "industrial war" of strikes and lockouts that may result if bargaining fails, and the labor practices that are considered unfair under federal law.

■ Federal Labor Law

Federal labor laws governing union-employer relations have developed considerably since the first law was enacted in 1932. Initially, the laws were concerned with protecting the rights and interests of workers. Subsequent legislation placed some restraints on unions and granted rights to employers. This section summarizes the four major federal labor law statutes.

Norris-LaGuardia Act

Congress protected peaceful strikes, picketing, and boycotts in 1932 in the Norris-LaGuardia Act.[2] The statute restricted federal courts in their power to issue injunctions against unions engaged in peaceful strikes. In effect, this act declared a national policy permitting employees to organize.

National Labor Relations Act

The National Labor Relations Act of 1935 (NLRA),[3] also called the Wagner Act, established the rights of employees to form unions, to engage in collective bargaining, and to strike. The act also created the National Labor Relations Board (NLRB) to oversee union elections and to prevent employers from engaging in unfair labor-union activities and unfair labor practices.

The NLRA states that unequal bargaining power between employees and employers leads to economic instability and refusals of employers to bargain collectively lead to strikes. These disturbances impede the flow of interstate commerce. It is declared to be the policy of the United States, under the authority given to the federal government under the Commerce Clause (Article I, Section 8, Clause 3), to ensure the free flow of commerce by encouraging collective bargaining and unionization.

The purpose of the NLRA was to secure for employees the rights to organize, to bargain collectively through representatives of their own choosing, and to engage in concerted activities for that and other purposes. Section 8(a) of the act specifically defined a number of employer practices as unfair to labor. These unfair labor practices are central to labor law and are discussed throughout the remainder of the chapter.

Another purpose of the act was to promote fair and just settlements of disputes by peaceful processes and to avoid industrial warfare. The NLRB was granted investigatory powers and was authorized to issue and serve complaints against employers in response to employee charges of unfair labor practices. The NLRB was further empowered to issue cease-and-desist orders—which could be enforced by a federal court of appeals if necessary—when violations were found.

Employers viewed the NLRA as a drastic piece of legislation. Those who opposed the act claimed that the Commerce Clause did not grant Congress the power to regulate labor relations. They argued that labor was subject to state, not federal, law. Those who were willing to admit that the NLRA did fall under the Commerce Clause claimed that the NLRA created an undue burden, which rendered the NLRA unconstitutional. The constitutionality of the act was tested in 1937 in *NLRB v. Jones & Laughlin Steel Corporation.*[4] In its decision, the United States Supreme Court held that the act and its application were constitutionally valid.

Labor-Management Relations Act

The Labor-Management Relations Act of 1947 (LMRA, or the Taft-Hartley Act)[5] was passed to proscribe certain union practices. The Taft-Hartley Act contained provisions protecting employers as well as employees. The act was bitterly opposed by organized labor groups. It provided a detailed list of unfair labor activities that unions as well as management were now forbidden to practice. In addition, the law gave the president the authority to intervene in labor disputes and delay strikes that would "imperil the national health or safety."

---

2. 29 U.S.C. Sections 101 *et seq.*
3. 20 U.S.C. Sections 151 *et seq.*

4. 301 U.S. 1, 57 S.Ct. 615, 81 L.Ed. 893 (1937).
5. 29 U.S.C. Section 141 *et seq.*

An important provision of the LMRA regulated the **closed shop**—a firm that requires union membership of its workers as a condition of obtaining employment. Closed shops were made illegal under the Taft-Hartley Act. The act preserved the legality of the **union shop,** which does not require membership as a prerequisite for employment but can, and usually does, require that workers join the union after a specified amount of time on the job. The act also allowed individual states to pass their own **right-to-work laws**—laws making it illegal for union membership to be required for *continued* employment in any establishment. Thus, union shops are technically illegal in states with right-to-work laws.

Labor-Management Reporting and Disclosure Act

The Labor-Management Reporting and Disclosure Act of 1959 (the Landrum-Griffin Act)[6] established an employee bill of rights and reporting requirements for union activities to prevent corruption. The Landrum-Griffin Act strictly regulated internal union business procedures.

Union elections, for example, are regulated by the Landrum-Griffin Act, which requires that regularly scheduled elections of officers occur and that secret ballots be used. Ex-convicts and communists are prohibited from holding union office. Moreover, union officials are made accountable for union property and funds. Members have the right to attend and to participate in union meetings, to nominate officers, and to vote in most union proceedings.

Coverage and Procedures

Coverage of the federal labor laws is broad and extends to all employers whose business activity either involves or affects interstate commerce. Some workers are specifically excluded from these laws. Railroads and airlines are not covered by the NLRA but are covered by a separate act, the Railway Labor Act, which closely parallels the NLRA. Other types of workers, such as agricultural workers and domestic servants, are excluded from the NLRA and have no coverage under separate legislation.

---

6. 29 U.S.C. Section 401 *et seq.*

When a union or employee believes that the employer has violated federal labor law (or vice versa), he or she files a charge with a regional office of the NLRB. The charge is investigated, and if it is found worthy, the regional director files a complaint. The complaint is initially heard by an administrative law judge (ALJ), who rules on the complaint. The Board itself reviews the ALJ's findings and decision. If the NLRB finds a violation, it may issue remedial orders (including requiring rehiring of discharged workers). The NLRB decision may be appealed to a U.S. court of appeals.

■ The Decision to Form or to Select a Union

The key starting point for labor relations law is the decision by a company's employees to form a union, which is usually referred to in the law as a ''bargaining representative.'' Many workplaces have no union, and workers bargain individually with the employer. If the workers decide that they want the added power of collective union representation, they must follow certain steps to have a union certified. Usually, the employer will fight these efforts to unionize.

Preliminary Organizing

Suppose that a national union, such as the AFL-CIO, wants to organize workers who produce semiconductor chips. The union would visit a manufacturing plant of a company, which might be called SemiCo. If some SemiCo workers are interested in joining the union, they must begin organizing. An essential step is to decide exactly which workers will be covered in the planned union. Will all manufacturing workers be covered or just those engaged in a single step in the manufacturing process?

The first step in forming a union is to get the relevant workers to sign **authorization cards**. These cards usually state that the worker desires to have a certain union, such as the AFL-CIO, represent the workforce. If the unionizers can obtain authorization cards from a majority of workers, they may present the cards to the employer and ask the employer, SemiCo, to recognize the union formally. SemiCo is not required to do so, however.

More frequently, authorization cards are obtained to justify an election among workers for unionization. If SemiCo refuses to recognize the union based on authorization cards, an election is necessary to determine whether unionization has majority support among the workers. After the unionizers obtain authorization cards from at least 30 percent of the workers to be represented, the unionizers present these cards to the NLRB regional office with a petition for an election.

This 30 percent support is generally considered a sufficient showing of interest to justify an election on union representation. Union backers are not required to employ authorization cards but generally must have some evidence that at least 30 percent of the relevant workforce supports a union, or at least an election on unionization.

Appropriate Bargaining Unit

The NLRB considers the employees' petition as a basis for calling an election. In addition to a sufficient showing of interest in unionization, the proposed union must represent an **appropriate bargaining unit.**

Not every group of workers can form together into a single union. One key requirement of an appropriate bargaining unit is a *mutuality of interest* among all the workers to be represented. Groups of workers with significantly conflicting interests may not be represented in a single union.

One factor in determining the mutuality of interest is the *similarity of the jobs* of all the workers to be unionized. The NLRB considers factors such as similar levels of skill and qualifications, similar levels of wages and benefits, and similar working conditions. If represented workers have vastly different working conditions, they are unlikely to have the mutuality of interest necessary to bargain as a single unit with SemiCo.

One issue of job similarity has involved companies that employ both general industrial workers and craft workers (those with specialized skill, such as electricians). On many occasions, the NLRB has found that industrial and craft workers should be represented by different unions, although this is not an absolute rule.

A second factor in determining the appropriate bargaining unit is *geographic*. If workers at only a single manufacturing plant are to be unionized, this is not a problem. Even if the workers desire to join a national union, such as the AFL-CIO, they can join together in a single "local" division of that union. Geographic disparity may become a problem if a union is attempting to join workers at many different manufacturing sites together into a single union.

A third factor to be considered is the rule against unionization of *management* employees. The labor laws differentiate between labor and management and preclude members of management from being part of a union. There is no clear-cut definition of management, but many court cases serve as precedents in deciding whether workers are management or labor. One such case held that nurses were not management and could be represented by a union under the NLRA.[7] Professional employees, including legal and medical personnel, may also be considered labor rather than management.

Supervisors are considered management and may not be included in worker unions. A supervisor is an individual who has the discretionary authority as representative of the employer to make decisions such as hiring, suspending, promoting, firing, or disciplining other workers.

Certification

A union, then, becomes certified by first petitioning the NLRB. The proposed union must present authorization cards or other evidence showing employee interest of at least 30 percent. The organization must also show that the proposed union represents an appropriate bargaining unit. If the workers are under the NLRA's jurisdiction and if no other union has been certified within the past twelve months for these workers, the NLRB will schedule an election.

■ Union Election

Labor law provides for an election to determine employee choice regarding whether to be represented by a union and, if so, which union. The NLRB supervises this election, ensuring secret voting and voter eligibility. The election is usually held about a month after the NLRB orders the vote.

---

7. *Noranda Aluminum, Inc. v. NLRB*, 751 F.2d 268 (8th Cir. 1984).

If the election is a fair one, and if the proposed union receives majority support, the Board certifies the union as bargaining representative. Otherwise, the Board will not certify the union.

Sometimes, a plant with an existing union may attempt to *decertify* the union (de-unionize). Although this action may be encouraged by management, it must be conducted by the employees. This action also requires a petition to the NLRB, with a showing of 30 percent employee support and no certification within the past year. The NLRB may grant this petition and call for a decertification election.

Union Election Campaign

Union organizers may campaign among workers to solicit votes for unionization. Considerable litigation has arisen over the rights of workers and outside union supporters to conduct a campaign for recognition of a union.

The employer retains great control over any activities, including unionization campaigns, that take place on company property and company time. Employers may lawfully use this authority to limit the campaign activities of union supporters. For example, an employer's management may prohibit all solicitations and pamphlets on company property as long as it has a legitimate business reason for doing so (such as safety or interference with business). The employer might also reasonably limit the places where solicitation occurs (for example, the lunchroom), limit the times during which solicitation can take place, or prohibit all outsiders from access to the workplace. All these actions are lawful.

Suppose that a union sought to organize clerks at a department store. Courts have found that an employer can prohibit all solicitation in areas of the store open to the public. Union campaign activities in these circumstances could seriously interfere with the store's business.

There are some legal restrictions on management regulation of union solicitation. The key restriction is the *nondiscrimination* rule. An employer may prohibit all solicitation during work time or in certain places but may not selectively prohibit union solicitation during work time. If the employer permits solicitation for a charity, for example, it also must permit union solicitation.

Workers also have a right to some reasonable opportunity to campaign. For example, the Supreme Court held that employees have a right to distribute a pro-union newsletter in nonworking areas on the employer's property during nonworking time. Management had the burden to show some material harm from this action and could not do so.[8]

Management Election Campaign

Management may also campaign among its workers against the union (or for decertification of an existing union). The management's campaign tactics, however, are carefully monitored and regulated by the NLRB. Otherwise, the economic power of management might allow coercion of the workers.

Management still has many advantages in the campaign. For example, management could call all workers together during work time and make a speech against unionization. Management need not give the union supporters an equal opportunity for rebuttal. The NLRB does restrict what management may say in such a speech, however.

In campaigning against the union, the employer may not make threats of reprisals if employees vote to unionize. A supervisor may not state: "If the union wins, you'll all be fired." This would be a threat. Employers must be very careful on this issue. For example, suppose an employer says: "Our competitor's plant in town unionized, and half the workers lost their jobs." The NLRB might consider this to be a veiled threat and therefore unfair.

An interesting controversy arose over a film that employers showed during union campaigns, entitled "And Women Must Weep." This film was prepared to help employers fight unionization efforts. The film was a dramatization of a strike that showed abuses by a union, including attacks on a minister, unionizers vandalizing automobiles, bomb threats, and an infant being accidentally shot and killed. Although this film is arguably inaccurate, courts have found it legal. One court wrote that "the film is a one-sided brief against unionism,

---

8. *Eastex, Inc. v. NLRB*, 437 U.S. 556, 98 S.Ct. 2505, 57 L.Ed.2d 428 (1978).

devoid of significant rational content perhaps, but nevertheless not reasonably to be construed as threatening retaliation or force.''[9]

Obviously, union election campaigns are not like national political campaigns, when a party can make almost any claim. The NLRB tries to maintain ''laboratory conditions'' for a fair election, unaffected by pressure. In establishing such conditions, the Board considers the totality of circumstances in the campaign. The NLRB is especially strict about promises (or threats) made by the employer at the last minute, immediately before the election, because the union lacks an opportunity to respond effectively to these last-minute statements.

There is even a specific rule that prohibits an employer from making any election speech on company time, to massed assemblies of workers, within 24 hours of the time for voting. Such last-

---

9. *Luxuray of New York v. NLRB*, 447 F.2d 112 (2d Cir. 1971).

minute speeches are permitted only if employees attend voluntarily and on their own time.

The employer is also prohibited from taking actions that might intimidate its workers. Employers may not undertake certain types of surveillance of workers or even create the impression of surveilling workers to identify union sympathizers. Management also is limited in its ability to question individual workers about their positions on unionization. These actions are deemed to contain implicit threats.

If the employer issues threats or engages in other unfair labor practices and then wins the election, the NLRB may invalidate the results. The NLRB may certify the union even though it lost the election and direct the employer to recognize the union as the employees' exclusive bargaining representative. The following recent decision illustrates the broad range of employer acts that may be considered unlawful in connection with a unionization campaign.

Case 16.1

ADAIR STANDISH CORP. v. NLRB

United States Court of Appeals, Sixth Circuit, 1990. 912 F.2d 854.

BACKGROUND AND FACTS *Adair Standish Corporation performs printing work in Michigan at its Dexter and Standish plants. In 1984, Adair made plans to increase production capacity at the Standish plant by installing an improved Goss H.V. press, which was scheduled for delivery in September 1985. In July 1985, a local of the AFL-CIO filed with the NLRB a petition for union certification at Adair's Standish facility. Adair opposed the union. An Adair supervisor told several employees that the new Goss press would not be shipped to Standish because of the unionization campaign.*

The union won an election in September 1985. Immediately after the election, two employees asked about revoking their authorization cards in support of the union. The company then posted a notice stating: ''Anyone who is interested in revoking their authorization card which you signed prior to the election may do so now by obtaining a request form from your supervisor.'' A supervisor then informed employees that he had the necessary revocation forms. At the same time, Adair posted a notice stating that it had not enforced ''some of our Company policies as strictly as . . . in the past'' for fear of union complaints but that future tardiness would be enforced strictly. Soon thereafter, employees were disciplined for tardiness. In 1986, Adair decided to ship the new Goss press to its Dexter facility rather than its Standish facility.

The National Labor Relations Board found all these actions to be unfair labor practices and issued cease-and-desist orders directed at a broad range of conduct. The Board also ordered Adair to provide back pay to discharged workers and to transfer the press from the Dexter facility to the Standish plant. Adair appealed these orders.

GUY, Circuit Judge.

* * * *

The first section 8(a)(1) violation challenged by Adair concerns supervisor Ireland's statements prior to the union election that the company might cancel delivery of the press due to unionization activity. Adair contends that the record does not contain substantial evidence indicating that Ireland made such threatening statements. We disagree. * * *

We also accept the Board's conclusion that Ireland's comments were sufficiently coercive to be actionable under section 8(a)(1). We have observed that "[i]n several cases where the defendant employer has asserted that particular statements were opinions and not threats, courts of appeals have upheld the Board order based upon the reasonable inference by employees that such statements were directed toward their decision to join the union. Only when the threats or opinions refer to matters over which the speaker has no control may employees not reasonably conclude that they are being coerced." In this case, [the employees] clearly could have believed that Ireland had some ability to influence the delivery of the press to Standish. * * *

Adair also disputes the Board's finding that the posting of a notice apprising union members of their right to revoke their authorization cards violated section 8(a)(1). We have clearly indicated that "[i]t is a violation of Section 8(a)(1) of the [NLRA] for an employer to sponsor and participate in the circulation of a petition among employees withdrawing support from a union." * * *

Although Adair defines its behavior as innocuously informative, we find that the Board correctly sanctioned the company for violating section 8(a)(1) with respect to revocation of union authorization. * * * In addition, the timing of the company's decision to post the notice—two days after the election and on the same day as the posting of the strict tardiness policy—undermines the beneficent rationale advanced by the company to justify its action.

* * * *

Adair challenges the Board's section 8(a)(3) finding with respect to the tardiness policy and resulting disciplinary actions by contending that the formal policy antedated the union election. The board found that the evidence supports a contrary conclusion, and we agree. Adair had never posted a policy on attendance prior to the union election, and the company's general approach to discipline for tardiness prior to the election was, at best, capricious and vague. More importantly, Adair's decision to post the tardiness policy (along with the union authorization revocation notice) immediately after the union election belies the company's assertion that the posted policy was nothing more than a formal statement of existing protocol. * * *

We likewise find substantial evidence underlying the Board's determination that Adair employees Lachcik and Cummings were disciplined for violating the tardiness policy in contravention of section 8(a)(3). Both employees * * * were well-known union adherents. Under the circumstances, "[a]ntiunion motivation reasonably may be inferred from [Adair's] expressed hostility towards unionization combined with knowledge of the employee[s'] union activities[.]" * * *

DECISION AND REMEDY

The court affirmed the NLRB finding of unfair labor practices and the cease-and-desist orders and back-pay orders. The court vacated the order requiring that the press be moved from Dexter to Standish. The court remanded this issue for a hearing on whether moving the new press was necessary and whether it would impose an "undue or unfair burden" on Adair, in which case the remedy would be inappropriate.

■ Collective Bargaining

If a fair election is held and if the union wins, the NLRB will certify the union as the *exclusive bargaining representative* of the workers polled. Unions may provide a variety of services to their members, but the central legal right of a union is to serve as the sole representative of the group of workers in bargaining with the employer over the workers' rights.

The concept of bargaining is at the heart of the federal labor laws. When a union is officially recognized, it may make a demand to bargain with the employer. The union then sits at the table opposite the representatives of management to negotiate contracts for its workers. The terms of employment that result from the negotiations apply to all workers in the bargaining unit, even those who do not choose to belong to the union. This process is known as **collective bargaining**. Such bargaining is like most other business negotiations, and each side uses its economic power to pressure or persuade the other side to grant concessions.

Bargaining is a somewhat vague term. Bargaining does not mean that either side must give in on demands or even that the sides must always compromise. It does mean that a demand must be taken seriously and considered as part of a package to be negotiated. Importantly, both sides must bargain in ''good faith.''

Subjects of Bargaining

A common issue in collective bargaining concerns the subjects over which the parties can bargain. The law makes certain subjects mandatory for collective bargaining. These topics cannot be ''taken off the table'' but must be discussed and bargained over.

The NLRA requires employers to bargain with workers over wages, hours of work, and other terms and conditions of employment. These are broad terms that cover many employment issues. Suppose that a union wants a contract provision granting all workers four weeks of paid vacation. The company need not give in to this demand but must at least consider it and bargain over it.

Many other employment issues are also considered mandatory subjects of collective bargaining. These include safety rules, insurance coverage, pension and other employee benefits plans, pro-

cedures for employee discipline, and procedures for employee grievances against the company. The Supreme Court has held that an employer must bargain even over the price of food sold in the company cafeteria.[10]

A few subjects are illegal in collective bargaining. Management need not bargain over a provision that would be illegal if included in a contract. Thus, if a union presents a demand for **featherbedding** (the hiring of unnecessary excess workers) or for an unlawful closed shop, management need not respond to these demands.

All other topics are permissive subjects for collective bargaining. Management need not bargain over broad economic issues that are within the business discretion of the managers. For example, management is not required to bargain with a union over the design of products, the location of manufacturing plants or even the decision to close a particular manufacturing facility. Management may choose to bargain over these issues, however, in order to obtain concessions on other mandatory bargaining subjects.

While management need not bargain over a decision to shut down certain facilities, it must bargain over the economic consequences of this decision. Thus, issues such as **severance pay** in the event of plant shut-down or rights of transfer to other plants are considered mandatory subjects of collective bargaining.

Collective bargaining limits the managerial discretion of the employer. While bargaining is going on, management may not make unilateral changes in important working conditions, such as wages or hours of employment. These changes must be bargained over. Once bargaining reaches an impasse, management may make such unilateral changes. The law also includes an exception permitting unilateral changes in cases of business necessity.

Good Faith Bargaining

Parties engaged in collective bargaining often claim that the other side is not bargaining in good faith, as required by labor law. Because neither side is required to compromise on any given issue, it is

---

10. *Ford Motor Co. v. NLRB*, 441 U.S. 488, 99 S.Ct. 1842, 60 L.Ed.2d 420 (1979).

difficult to determine whether a party is bargaining in good faith. This determination involves a judgment about the subjective intent of the bargainer. Good faith is a duty to bargain with an open mind and a sincere aim to reach an agreement if possible.

While good faith is a matter of subjective intent, a party's actions are used to evaluate the finding of good or bad faith in bargaining. Obviously, the employer must be willing to meet with union representatives. Excessive delaying tactics may be proof of bad faith, as is insistence on obviously unreasonable contract terms. Suppose that a company makes a single overall contract offer on a "take-it-or-leave-it" basis and refuses to consider modifications of individual terms. This also is considered bad faith in bargaining.

A series of decisions have found other actions to constitute bad faith in bargaining, including:

- Rejecting a proposal without offering a counterproposal.
- Engaging in a campaign among workers to undermine the union.
- Unilaterally changing wages or terms and conditions of employment during the bargaining process.
- Constantly shifting positions on disputed contract terms.
- Sending bargainers who lack authority to commit the company to a contract.

A party to collective bargaining may be excused from bargaining when the other party commits an unfair labor practice. If, for example, a union refuses to bargain in good faith, the employer is not required to do so. The following case describes this justification.

BACKGROUND AND FACTS *Workers for the Inland Tugs Division of the American Commercial Barge Line Company (I.T.) were represented by the Seafarers International Union of North America (S.I.U.). From September 1979 through April 1980, representatives of I.T. and S.I.U. bargained over a new collective agreement. S.I.U. demanded that the bargaining unit be expanded so that it could represent the workers on a fleetwide basis covering all the employees of the American Commercial Barge Line Company. S.I.U. also insisted that any contract must include a pledge by companies affiliated with the American Commercial Barge Line Company to continue their contributions to S.I.U.-administered trust funds, which provided employee benefits and other union-sponsored activities. The parties could reach no agreement but continued to hold periodic meetings over the following years.*

In 1987, I.T. adopted changes in the system of calculating wages based on employee requests. The company directly polled employees to discover their desires. I.T. also changed its travel policy to encourage employees to use ground transportation on reimbursed trips. S.I.U. claimed that these changes represented an unfair labor practice because the employer had unilaterally changed the terms of employment without bargaining with the union.

The administrative law judge considering the unfair labor practice complaint ruled for S.I.U., finding that I.T. had ignored its duty to bargain. The NLRB reviewed and partially reversed this decision, finding that bargaining had reached an impasse but that I.T. had, nevertheless, committed an unfair labor practice by polling its employees and making unilateral changes without dealing with S.I.U. Both parties appealed this determination.

Case 16.2

INLAND TUGS, A DIVISION OF AMERICAN COMMERCIAL BARGE LINE COMPANY v. NLRB

United States Court of Appeals, Seventh Circuit, 1990.
918 F.2d 1299.

BAUER, Chief Judge.

* * * *

* * * [B]oth the union and the employer can bargain in the best of faith and yet be unable to reach agreement on important issues; just so long as neither side displays an implacable commitment to its demands, totally blocking negotiations. This distinction between lawful "hard bargaining" and unlawful "bad-faith" or "surface" bargaining, although far from crystalline * * * is quite important, as unions and employers not infrequently reach deadlocks in bargaining.

* * * *

S.I.U. has repeatedly made it clear that no contracts will issue unless and until I.T. accepts the fleet-wide bargaining unit and pledges to continue contributing to all the union trust funds. * * * [E]ven before 1984, although the parties traded positions, S.I.U. steadfastly held to its "No trust funds, no contract" demand, and a similar stance regarding its fleet-wide unit demand. * * *

S.I.U.'s demands have clearly caused a deadlock in the bargaining of any successor agreements between S.I.U. and I.T., but how to characterize this deadlock and the issues that have caused it? * * * Yes, S.I.U. could create a good faith impasse as to its demand for continued contributions to those trust funds that involved employee health and pension benefits, as such benefits are mandatory subjects of bargaining. * * * But as to those trust funds that supported industry promotion efforts, S.I.U. could not create an impasse as employer contributions to such efforts are a permissive subject of bargaining. * * *

Moreover, it is clear that S.I.U. could not force an impasse as to the expanded bargaining unit demand, because a demand to change the size or scope of the bargaining unit does not concern a mandatory subject of bargaining. * * *

* * * [W]hile it has shown some willingness to meet and discuss certain issues, S.I.U. has conditioned all meaningful bargaining over a successor agreement on I.T.'s concession to demands that involve permissive subjects of bargaining. By so doing, S.I.U. has violated the Act, and has released I.T. from its duty to bargain "as long as the bargaining is forestalled by the illegal demand[s]." * * *

DECISION AND REMEDY *The court found that S.I.U. had bargained in bad faith and had released I.T. from its duty to bargain with S.I.U. as long as S.I.U. continued to make illegal demands. The court went on to find that S.I.U.'s bad faith bargaining did not excuse I.T. for its direct dealing with and polling of its workers regarding the wage changes, because this was a circumvention of its duty to deal with the certified union.*

If an employer (or a union) refuses to bargain in good faith without justification, it has committed an unfair labor practice, and the other party may petition the NLRB for an order requiring good faith bargaining. Except in extreme cases, the NLRB does not have authority to require a party to accede to any specific contract terms. The NLRB may require a party to reimburse the other side for its litigation expenses.

■ Strikes

The law does not require parties to reach a contract in collective bargaining. Even when parties have

bargained in good faith, they may be unable to reach a final agreement. When extensive collective bargaining has been conducted and the parties still cannot agree, an impasse has been reached.

When bargaining has reached an impasse, the union may call a strike against the employer to pressure it into making concessions. A strike occurs when the unionized workers leave their jobs and refuse to work. They also typically picket the plant, standing outside the facility with signs that complain of management's unfairness.

A strike is an extreme action. Striking workers lose their rights to be paid. Management loses production and may lose customers, whose orders cannot be filled. Labor law regulates the circumstances and conduct of strikes. Most strikes are ''economic strikes,'' which are initiated because the union wants a better contract. A union may also strike when the employer has engaged in unfair labor practices.

The right to strike is guaranteed by the NLRA, within limits, and strike activities, such as picketing, are protected by the free speech guarantee of the First Amendment to the Constitution. Nonworkers have a right to participate in picketing an employer. The NLRA also gives workers the right to refuse to cross a picket line of fellow workers who are engaged in a lawful strike. Not all strikes are lawful, however.

Illegal Strikes

An otherwise lawful strike may become illegal because of the conduct of the strikers. Violent strikes (including the threat of violence) are illegal. The use of violence against management employees or substitute workers is illegal. Certain forms of ''massed picketing'' are also illegal. If the strikers form a massed barrier and deny management or other nonunion workers access to the plant, the strike is illegal. Similarly, ''sitdown'' strikes, in which employees simply stay in the plant without working, are illegal.

Another form of illegal strike is the secondary boycott. A **secondary boycott** is a strike directed against someone other than the strikers' employer such as the companies that sell materials to the employer. Suppose that the unionized workers of SemiCo go out on strike. To increase their economic leverage, the workers picket the leading suppliers or customers of SemiCo in an attempt to hurt the company's business. SemiCo is considered the primary employer, and its suppliers and customers are considered secondary employers. Picketing of the suppliers or customers is a secondary boycott, which was made illegal by the Taft-Hartley Act.

A controversy may arise in a strike when both the primary and secondary employers occupy the same job site. In this case, it may be difficult to distinguish between lawful picketing of the primary employer and an unlawful strike against a secondary employer. The law permits a union to picket a site occupied by both primary and secondary employers, called **common situs picketing**. If evidence indicates that the strike is directed against the secondary employer, however, it may become illegal. For example, if a union sends a threatening letter to the secondary employer about the strike, that fact may show that the picketing includes an illegal secondary boycott.

Most of the litigation over secondary boycotts involves the common situs problem. A key issue in these lawsuits is the creation of separate gates for union and nonunion workers to enter the site. The following case provides an example of this litigation.

BACKGROUND AND FACTS *In 1985, Hoffman Construction Company reached a contract negotiated with Local 29 of the International Association of Bridge, Structural and Ornamental Iron Workers. Later that year, Hoffman decided that it would no longer employ iron workers and other skilled tradesmen directly but would subcontract the work to other companies. After the union was informed of this, it sent Hoffman an application for membership in the Northwest Iron Workers Employers Association, Inc., which had a union contract specifying that members would hire only subcontractors that were unionized.*

At this time, Hoffman was performing work at three job sites: the Performing Arts Center, One Financial Center, and the Good Samaritan Hospital. When Hoffman refused to agree to subcontract only to unionized companies, Local 29 and the Iron Workers District Council of the Pacific Northwest began picketing these sites. Hoffman filed unfair labor charges with the NLRB on the grounds that this picketing extended to secondary employers. The Board agreed and ordered the unions to cease the picketing.

Case 16.3

IRON WORKERS DISTRICT COUNCIL OF THE PACIFIC NORTHWEST v. NLRB
United States Court of Appeals, Ninth Circuit, 1990.
913 F.2d 1470.

The picketing resumed later that year, however, and the unions were held in contempt of court. The unions appealed this ruling.

THOMPSON, Circuit Judge.
* * * *

Sailors' Union of the Pac. (Moore Dry Dock Co.) * * * established a four-part test to determine whether picketing at a common situs is primary or secondary: (a) whether the ''picketing is strictly limited to times when the *situs* of dispute is located on the secondary employer's premises''; (b) whether ''the primary employer is engaged in its normal business at the *situs*''; (c) whether the picketing takes place reasonably close to the *situs*; and (d) ''whether the picketing discloses clearly that the dispute is with the primary employer.'' * * *

* * * The administrative law judge (''ALJ'') and the Board concluded that the August 1986 conduct was unlawful because it violated a *Moore Dry Dock* guideline, namely, a failure to confine the picketing-related activity to the primary gates, when other gates for neutral employers and employees had been established. * * *
* * * *

The evidence before the ALJ included job diary entries, photographs and the uncontradicted testimony of Hoffman employees who were superintendents on each of the three job sites. It was established that on August 18, 1986 at the Performing Arts Center job site there were ten-to-fifteen iron workers standing around near the neutral gate, while picketing was going on at the Hoffman gate. Craft employees generally parked directly east of the neutral gate and to enter the project they had to walk through this congregation of iron workers. Also on August 18, 1986 at the One Financial Center job site, a crowd of men was milling around in the vicinity of an intersection at the corner of the construction site near the neutral gate. Directly in front of the neutral gate were two men wearing Local 29 insignia, hats and union buttons. These men were observed talking to craft employees who approached the gate. Thereafter, the craft employees left the area. * * *

At the Good Samaritan Hospital job site, various subcontractors failed to work during the period of August 19–22, 1986 due to picketing and picketing-related activities. On August 22, 1986 no craft workers worked at the Good Samaritan Hospital job site. The ALJ found this ''total shutdown was due to information being circulated that the strike had been sanctioned by the Columbia Building and Construction Trades Council.'' * * *

There is ''an inference that . . . failure of . . . [neutral] subcontractors to appear and continue their work [is] due to [the union's] picketing at the neutral gate.'' * * * A union agent's statement to neutral employees that another union authorized the picketing is reasonably understood to be a signal or request for the neutral employees to stop work against their own employer.

DECISION AND REMEDY *The court agreed that the unions had engaged in unlawful secondary activity, affirmed the Board's conclusion, and granted an application for enforcement of its order compelling the unions to cease and desist in the picketing.*

One type of illegal secondary boycott is known as a hot-cargo agreement. In a **hot-cargo agreement,** employers voluntarily agree with unions not to handle, use, or deal in non-union-produced goods of other employers. This particular type of secondary boycott was not made illegal by the Taft-Hartley Act, because that act only prevented unions from inducing *employees* to strike or otherwise act to force the employer not to handle these goods. The Landrum-Griffin Act addressed this problem:

It shall be [an] unfair labor practice for any labor organization and any employer to enter into any contract or any agreement . . . whereby such employer . . . agrees to refrain from handling, using, selling, transporting or otherwise dealing in any of the products of any other employer, or to cease doing business with any other person.

Hot-cargo agreements are therefore illegal. Parties injured by an illegal hot-cargo agreement or other secondary boycott may sue the union for damages.

It is legal for a union to urge consumer boycotts of the primary employer, even at the site of a secondary employer. Suppose that a union of food processing workers is on strike against a primary employer called Home Dining, Inc. The products of Home Dining, Inc., are sold at a chain of stores, Peach Groceries. The striking workers can stand outside Peach Groceries and urge consumers not to buy Home Dining's products. The workers cannot urge a total boycott of Peach Groceries, as that would constitute a secondary boycott.

Another form of illegal strike is the **wildcat strike**. A wildcat strike occurs when a minority group of workers, perhaps dissatisfied with a union's representation, call their own strike. But the union is the exclusive bargaining representative of a group of workers, and only the union can call a strike. A wildcat strike, unauthorized by the certified union, is illegal.

In one case, a group of concrete workers left their jobs because it was raining and went on "strike." The court found the strike illegal because it was not preceded by a demand on the employer for action and because the employer had made shelter available for the workers and paid them for waiting time.

The law also places some restrictions on strikes that threaten national health or safety. The law does not prohibit such strikes, nor does it require the settlement of labor disputes that threaten the national welfare. The Taft-Hartley Act simply provides time to encourage their settlement, called the "cooling-off period."

One of the most controversial aspects of the Taft-Hartley Act was the establishment of this **eighty-day cooling-off period**—a provision allowing federal courts to issue injunctions against strikes that would create a national emergency. The president of the United States can obtain a court injunction that will last for eighty days, and presidents have occasionally used this provision. For example, President Eisenhower applied the eighty-day injunction order to striking steelworkers in 1959, President Nixon applied it to striking longshoremen in 1971, and President Carter applied it to striking coal miners in 1978. During these eighty days, the president and other government officials can work with the employer and the union to produce a settlement and avoid a strike that may cause a national emergency.

A strike may also be illegal if it contravenes a **no-strike clause**. The previous collective bargaining agreement between a union and an employer may have contained a clause in which the union agreed not to strike. The law permits the employer to enforce this no-strike clause and obtain an injunction against the strike in some circumstances.

The Supreme Court held that a no-strike clause could be enforced with an injunction if the contract contained a clause providing for arbitration of unresolved disputes.[11] The court held that the arbitration clause was an effective substitute for the right to strike. In the absence of an applicable arbitration provision, however, an employer cannot enjoin a strike, even when the contract contains a no-strike clause.

Replacement Workers

Suppose that Home Dining's workers go out on strike. Home Dining is not required to shut down its operations but may find substitute workers to replace the strikers, if possible. These substitute workers are often called "scabs" by union supporters. An employer may even give the replacement workers permanent positions with the company.

Companies are increasingly employing replacement workers to fight strikes. Even the National Football League, when struck by the players in 1987, found replacement football players to perform for the various NFL teams. While some scoffed at the ability of the replacement players, the tactic was largely successful for management, as the strike was called off after only three weeks.

---

11. *Boys Markets, Inc. v. Retail Clerks Local 770*, 398 U.S. 235, 90 S.Ct. 1583, 26 L.Ed.2d 199 (1970).

Economic Strikes

An important issue is the rights of strikers after the strike ends. In a typical economic strike over working conditions, the strikers have no right to return to their jobs. If satisfactory replacement workers were found, the strikers may find themselves out of work. The law does prohibit the employer from discriminating against former strikers. Even if the employer fires all the strikers and retains all the replacement workers, former strikers must be given preferential rights to any new vacancies that arise and also retain their seniority rights. The following case deals with the issue of worker seniority in the wake of a strike after which not all striking workers were recalled.

Case 16.4

TRANS WORLD AIRLINES, INC. v. INDEPENDENT FEDERATION OF FLIGHT ATTENDANTS

Supreme Court of the United States, 1989.
489 U.S. 426,
109 S.Ct. 1225,
103 L.Ed.2d 456.

BACKGROUND AND FACTS *The Independent Federation of Flight Attendants (respondent) struck Trans World Airlines (TWA) (petitioner) after the two failed to negotiate a new collective bargaining agreement. At the outset, TWA announced its intentions to continue operations by continuing to employ union members who refused to join the strike (crossovers) and by hiring replacement workers to fill vacancies that resulted from the strike. TWA also promised to fill vacancies that occurred during the strike by utilizing its seniority bidding system. The system determined eligibility for job and location assignments among employees of the airline. TWA vowed that the resulting assignments would continue in effect after the strike ended. During the strike some 1,280 flight attendants crossed over while 5,000 honored the picket line. At the conclusion of the strike, TWA had positions available for only 197 strikers, although it eventually recalled some 1,100 other strikers over a two-year period. The union sued TWA, claiming that the more senior striking employees were entitled to preference that would allow them to displace (or "bump") less senior crossovers in the limited number of jobs available once the strike ended. A federal district court held that the senior striking employees were not entitled to such preference over either the crossovers or replacement workers. A circuit court of appeals reversed the decision, and the case was appealed to the United States Supreme Court.*

Justice *O'CONNOR* delivered the opinion of the Court.
* * * *

We first considered the reinstatement rights of strikers under the NLRA in *NLRB v. Mackay Radio & Telegraph Co.* In *Mackay Radio*, radio and telegraph operators working in the San Francisco offices of a national telecommunications firm went on strike. In order to continue operations, the employer brought employees from its other offices to fill the strikers' places. At the conclusion of the strike, the striking operators sought to displace their replacements in order to return to work. We held that it was not an unfair labor practice under [section] 8 of the NLRA for the employer to have replaced the striking employees with others "in an effort to carry on the business," or to have refused to discharge the replacements in order to make room for the strikers at the conclusion of the strike. * * *

The Union relies on [*NLRB v.*] *Erie Resistor* * * * to distinguish junior crossovers from new hires under the NLRA. In *Erie Resistor* we struck down an employer's award of 20 years' super-seniority to new hires and crossovers as an unfair labor practice within the meaning of [Section] 8(a)(1) and [Section] 8(a)(3) of the NLRA. We observed: " . . . Super-seniority affects the tenure of all strikers whereas permanent replacement, proper under *Mackay*, affects only those who are, in actuality, replaced. It is one thing to say that a striker is subject to loss of his job at the strike's end but quite another to hold that in addition to the threat of replacement, all strikers will at best return to their jobs with seniority inferior to that of the replacements and of those who left the strike. . . . Unlike the replacement granted in *Mackay* which ceases to be an issue once the strike is over, the [super-seniority] plan here creates a cleavage in the plant continuing long after the strike is ended. Employees are henceforth divided into two camps: those who stayed with the union and those who returned before the end of the strike and thereby gained extra seniority. This breach is reemphasized with each subsequent layoff and stands as an ever-present reminder of the dangers connected with striking and with union activities in general.''

* * * *

[The union] argues that TWA's refusal to displace junior crossovers will create a ''cleavage'' between junior crossovers and reinstated full-term strikers at TWA ''long after the strike is ended.'' This is the case because desirable job assignments and domiciles that would have been occupied by the most senior flight attendants had there been no strike will continue to be held by those who did not see the strike through to its conclusion. For example, the senior full-term striker who worked in the Los Angeles domicile before the strike may have been replaced by a junior crossover. As poststrike vacancies develop in TWA's workforce, permitting reinstatement of full-term strikers, they are not likely to occur in the most desirable domiciles. Thus, it is unlikely that the senior full-term striker would be reinstated back to her preferred domicile. Resentful rifts among employees will also persist after the strike, the Union argues, because TWA's prestrike assurance of nondisplacement to junior crossovers unlike the same assurance to new hires, ''set up a competition among those individuals who participated in the original decision to strike, and thereby undermined the group's ability to take the collective action that it is the very purpose of the [Railway Labor Act (RLA)] to protect.''

* * * *

None of these scenarios, however, present the prospect of a continuing diminution of seniority upon reinstatement at the end of the strike that was central to our decision in *Erie Resistor*. All that has occurred is that the employer has filled vacancies created by striking employees. Some of these vacancies will be filled by newly hired employees, others by doubtless more experienced and therefore more needed employees who either refused to strike or abandoned the strike. The * * * observation that, ''at the conclusion of the strike'' discrimination in the filling of ''available positions'' based on union activity is impermissible, is beside the point. The positions occupied by newly hired replacements, employees who refused to strike, and employees who abandoned the strike, are simply not ''available positions'' to be filled. As noted above, those positions that were available at the conclusion of the strike were filled ''according to some principle, such as seniority, that is neutral. . . .'' That the prospect of a reduction in available positions may divide employees and create incentives among them to remain at work or abandon a strike before its conclusion is a secondary effect fairly within the arsenal of economic weapons available to employers during a period of self-help.

DECISION AND REMEDY

The Court reversed the decision of the appellate court. The Court held that the senior striking employees were not entitled to preference over those less senior employees who chose not to participate in the strike. The Court did not deny that those strikers who were recalled were entitled to keep their pre-strike seniority—it would be an unfair labor practice for the company to strip them of seniority for having participated in the strike— but they could not bump less senior crossovers or replacements from jobs after the strike ended.

Different rules apply when a union strikes because the employer has engaged in unfair labor practices. If an employer is discriminating against a union's workers, they may go out on an unfair labor practice strike. An economic strike may also become an unfair labor practice strike if the employer refuses to bargain in good faith. In the case of an unfair labor practice strike, the employer may still hire replacements but must give the strikers back their jobs once the strike is over. An employer may, however, refuse to rehire unfair labor practice strikers if the strike was itself unlawful or if there is simply no longer any work for them to do.

■ Lockouts

Lockouts are the employer's counterpart to the worker's right to strike. A **lockout** occurs when the employer shuts down to prevent employees from working. Lockouts are usually used when the employer believes that a strike is imminent.

Lockouts may be a legal employer response. In the leading Supreme Court case, a union and an employer had reached a stalemate in collective bargaining. The employer feared that the union would delay a strike until the busy season and thereby cause the employer to suffer more greatly from the strike. The employer called a lockout before the busy season to deny the union this leverage, and the Supreme Court held that this action was legal.[12]

Some lockouts are illegal, however. An employer may not use its lockout weapon as a tool to break the union and pressure employees into decertification. Consequently, an employer must show some economic justification for instituting a lockout.

■ Unfair Labor Practices

The preceding sections have discussed unfair labor practices in the significant acts of union elections, collective bargaining, and strikes. Many unfair labor practices may occur within the normal working relationship. The most significant of these practices are discussed below.

---

12. *American Ship Building Co. v. NLRB*, 380 U.S. 300, 85 S.Ct. 955, 13 L.Ed.2d 855 (1965).

Recognition, Representation, and Negotiation

As noted above, once a union has been certified as the exclusive representative of a bargaining unit, an employer must recognize and bargain in good faith with the union over issues affecting all employees who are within the bargaining unit. Failure to do so is an unfair labor practice. Because the National Labor Relations Act embraces a policy of majority rule, certification of the union as the bargaining unit's representative binds *all* of the employees in that bargaining unit. Thus, the union must fairly represent all the members of the bargaining unit.

Certification does not, however, mean that a union will continue indefinitely as the exclusive representative of the bargaining unit. If the union loses the majority support of those it represents, an employer is not obligated to continue recognition of or negotiation with the union. As a practical matter, a newly elected representative needs time to establish itself among the workers and to begin to formulate and implement its programs. Therefore, as a matter of labor policy, a union is immune from attack by employers and from repudiation by the employees for a period of one year after certification. During this period, it is *presumed* that the union enjoys majority support among the employees; the employer cannot refuse to deal with the union as the employees' exclusive representative, even if the employees prefer not to be represented by that union.

Beyond the one-year-after-certification period, the presumption of majority support continues, but it is *rebuttable*. An employer may rebut the presumption with objective evidence that a majority of employees do not wish to be represented by the union. If the evidence is sufficient to support a *good faith* belief that the union no longer enjoys majority support among the employees, the employer may refuse to continue to recognize and negotiate with the union.

A delicate question arises during a strike in which an employer hires replacement workers. Specifically, should it be *assumed* that the replacement workers do not support the union? If they do not, and if as a result the union no longer has majority support, the employer need no longer continue negotiating with the union. The following case deals with these complex issues.

BACKGROUND AND FACTS *Teamsters Local 968 (respondent) represented twenty-seven production and maintenance employees of Curtin Matheson Scientific (petitioner), a company engaged in the purchase and sale of laboratory equipment and supplies. Shortly after the collective bargaining agreement between the union and the company expired, the company made a ''final'' offer for a new agreement, which the union rejected. The company then locked out the twenty-seven bargaining unit employees. Later, the company renewed its offer, but the union again rejected it. The union subsequently began an economic strike against the company. Five employees immediately crossed the picket line, however, and reported for work. While the strike was still in effect, the company also hired twenty-nine permanent new employees to replace the twenty-two striking workers. The union later ended its strike and offered unconditionally to accept the company's earlier offer. The company refused, stating the offer was no longer open. The company also refused to bargain further with the union, asserting its doubt that the union was supported by a majority of the employees in the bargaining unit. The union sought help from the National Labor Relations Board, which held that the company lacked a sufficient basis for doubting the union's majority support despite the fact that some workers had crossed the picket line, some had resigned positions within the union, and others had told the company's personnel director that they and other employees did not support the strike. The Board also refused to presume that the replacement workers did not support the union. The company appealed the ruling, and a circuit court overturned the Board's ruling on the theory that there was a presumption that the replacement workers did not support the union. The union appealed the case to the United States Supreme Court.*

Justice *MARSHALL* delivered the opinion of the Court.

* * * *

Upon certification by the NLRB as the exclusive bargaining agent for a unit of employees, a union enjoys an irrebuttable presumption of majority support for one year. During that time, an employer's refusal to bargain with the union is *per se* an unfair labor practice under * * * the National Labor Relations Act. After the first year, the presumption continues but is rebuttable. Under the Board's longstanding approach, an employer may rebut that presumption by showing that, at the time of the refusal to bargain, either (1) the union did not in fact enjoy majority support, or (2) the employer had a ''good faith'' doubt, founded on a sufficient objective basis, of the union's majority support. The question presented in this case is whether the Board must, in determining whether an employer has presented sufficient objective evidence of a good-faith doubt, presume that striker replacements oppose the union.

* * * *

[T]he starting point for the Board's analysis is the basic presumption that the union is supported by a majority of bargaining-unit employees. The employer bears the burden of rebutting that presumption, after the certification year, either by showing that the union in fact lacks majority support or by demonstrating a sufficient objective basis for doubting the union's majority status. Respondent here urges that in evaluating an employer's claim of a good-faith doubt, the Board must adopt a second, subsidiary presumption—that replacement employees oppose the union. Under this approach, if a majority of employees in the bargaining unit were striker replacements, the employer would not need to offer any objective evidence of the employees' union sentiments to rebut the presumption of the union's continuing majority status. The

Case 16.5

NLRB v. CURTIN MATHESON SCIENTIFIC, INC.
Supreme Court of the United States, 1990.
494 U.S. 775,
110 S.Ct. 1542,
108 L.Ed.2d 801.

presumption of the replacements' opposition to the union would, in effect, override the presumption of continuing majority status. In contrast, under its no-presumption approach the Board "take[s] into account the particular circumstances surrounding each strike and the hiring of replacements, while retaining the long-standing requirement that the employer must come forth with some objective evidence to substantiate his doubt of continuing majority status."

We find the Board's no-presumption approach rational as an empirical matter.* * * Although replacements often may not favor the incumbent union, the Board reasonably concluded, in light of its long experience in addressing these issues, that replacements may in some circumstances desire union representation despite their willingness to cross the picket line. * * *

* * * *

The Board's approach to determining the union views of strike replacements * * *limits employers' ability to oust a union without adducing any evidence of the employees' union sentiments and encourages negotiated solutions to strikes. It was reasonable for the Board to conclude that the antiunion presumption, in contrast, could allow an employer to eliminate the union merely by hiring a sufficient number of replacement employees. That rule thus might encourage the employer to avoid good-faith bargaining over a strike settlement, and instead to use the strike as a means of removing the union altogether. * * *

DECISION AND REMEDY   *The Court overturned the circuit court's decision and upheld the National Labor Relations Board's refusal to adopt a presumption that striker replacements oppose the union. The Court concluded that the Board's approach was consistent with the underlying policies of the National Labor Relations Act.*

Employer Interference in Union Activities

The NLRA declares it to be an unfair labor practice for an employer to interfere with, restrain, or coerce employees in the exercise of their rights to form a union and bargain collectively. Unlawful employer interference may take a variety of forms.

Courts have found it an unfair labor practice for an employer to make threats that may interfere with an employee's decision to join a union. Even asking employees about their views on the union may be considered coercive. Employees responding to such questioning must be able to remain anonymous and must receive assurances against employer reprisals.

Employers also may not prohibit certain forms of union activity in the workplace. If an employee has a grievance with the company, the employer cannot prevent the union's participation in support of the employee, for example. If an employer has unlawfully interfered with the operation of a union, the NLRB or a reviewing court may issue a cease-and-desist order halting the practice. The company

typically is required to post the order on a bulletin board and renounce its past unlawful conduct.

Employer Domination of Unions

In the early days of unionization, employers fought back by forming employer-sponsored unions to represent employees. These "company unions" were seldom more than the puppets of management. The NLRA outlawed company unions and any other form of employer domination of workers' unions.

A number of acts are considered unfair labor practices under the law against employer domination. For example, an employer can have no say in which employees belong to the union or which employees serve as union officers. Nor may supervisors or other management personnel participate in union meetings.

Company actions that support a union may be considered improper potential domination. For this reason, a company cannot give union workers pay for time spent on union activities, because this is considered undue support for the union. The company may not provide financial aid to a union and may not solicit workers to join a union.

Discrimination

The NLRA prohibits employers from discriminating against workers because they are union officers or are otherwise associated with a union. When workers must be laid off, the company cannot consider union participation as a criterion for deciding whom to fire.

The prohibition against discrimination in firing workers is a broad one. As illustrated in the following case, this prohibition may extend even to employees who are not otherwise guaranteed unionization rights under federal labor laws.

BACKGROUND AND FACTS *Salvatore Monte was the president of Kenrich Petrochemicals, Inc., a family-owned business. Helen Chizmar had been Kenrich's office manager since 1963. Among the clerical staff that Chizmar supervised were her sister, her daughter, and her daughter-in-law. In May 1987, Chizmar's three relatives and four other clerical staff members designated the Oil, Chemical and Atomic Workers International Union as their bargaining representative. Chizmar was not involved, but when Monte received notice that his office was unionizing, he told Chizmar that someone else could do her job for "$20,000 less" and fired her. Later, he told another employee that one of his reasons for firing Chizmar was that he "was not going to put up with any union bullsh____ ." A few days later, he told the clerical workers that if they voted for the union they would have to "start from scratch. No benefits, no salary, no vacations." Monte shoved one of the women against a filing cabinet. Still later, during negotiations with the union, Monte said that he planned to "get rid of the whole family." Chizmar's family complained to the National Labor Relations Board that Chizmar's firing was an unfair labor practice. The NLRB agreed and ordered that Chizmar be reinstated with back pay. Kenrich appealed.*

Case 16.6

KENRICH PETROCHEMICALS, INC. v. NLRB

United States Court of Appeals, Third Circuit, 1990.
907 F.2d 400.

STAPLETON, Circuit Judge.

* * * *

Kenrich's * * * argument is that the Board may not reinstate a supervisor because the Act does not protect a supervisor who engages in union activity.

* * * While it is uncontestably true that the Act does not protect a supervisor from being discharged for engaging in concerted activity, this does not deprive the Board of the authority to order the reinstatement of a supervisor whose firing resulted not from her own pro-union conduct, but from the employer's efforts to thwart the exercise of * * * rights by protected rank-and-file employees. * * *

* * * *

* * * [W]hen an employer fires a supervisor in order to discourage the exercise of * * * rights by protected employees closely related to the supervisor, the Board, based upon its experience, is entitled to infer in the absence of evidence to the contrary that the intended message was an effective one. Indeed, we do not believe one needs extensive experience with behavior in response to coercive tactics in the workplace to conclude that such a discharge must communicate to rank-and-file employees that the employer is willing to go to any lengths to crush [unionizing] activity. * * *

* * * *

If that discharge is left unremedied, the fears engendered by that discharge and Monte's later threats will not be dispelled. Rather, a powerful message will be sent out to the supervisors and employees of Kenrich that the company may, without fear of redress, use family member supervisors as hostages. * * *

By reinstating Chizmar and compensating her for lost wages, the Board's order protects the * * * rights of Kenrich's employees by assuring them that they need not fear that the exercise of their rights will give the company a license to inflict harm on their family. It also protects the employees by reassuring their relatives who are supervisors that they need not feel that their jobs are dependent on their ability to dissuade their family members from engaging in protected activity.

DECISION AND REMEDY *The court concluded that the NLRB's reinstatement and back-pay order was reasonably calculated to dispel the intimidation caused by Chizmar's firing and ruled that the order be enforced.*

The antidiscrimination provisions also apply to hiring decisions. Suppose that certain employees of Home Dining, Inc., are represented by a union, but the company is attempting to weaken the union's strength. The company cannot require potential new hires to guarantee that they will not join the union.

Discriminatory punishment of union members or officers can be difficult to prove. The company will claim to have good reasons for its action. The NLRB has given a series of factors to be considered in determining whether an action had an unlawful, discriminatory motivation. These include giving inconsistent reasons for the action, applying rules inconsistently and more strictly against union members, failing to give an expected warning prior to discharge or other discipline, and acting contrary to worker seniority.

In one case, an employer, Wright Line, fired an employee, Bernard Lamoureux, for knowingly altering time reports and payroll records. Lamoureux conceded that he had not worked the precise hours he reported on his time card but claimed that he had worked an equivalent number of hours at other times. Lamoureux had been a leading union advocate. The NLRB found that the company had shown particular dislike for Lamoureux because it considered him to be the "union kingpin" in the company. In addition, the company had never before discharged a worker for this type of violation. The NLRB found that this was sufficient evidence of discrimination to shift the burden of proof to the company to demonstrate that it had not had a discriminatory motive. The company could not meet this burden, and the discharge was held unlawful.[13]

The decision to close a facility is generally within the discretion of management, but even this decision cannot be made with a discriminatory motive. If a company has several facilities and only one is unionized, the company cannot shut down the union plant simply because of the union. The company could shut down the union plant if it were demonstrably less efficient than the other facilities, however.

Union Unfair Labor Practices

Certain union activities are declared to be unfair labor practices by the Taft-Hartley Act. Secondary boycotts, discussed above, are one such union unfair labor practice.

One significant union unfair labor practice is coercion or restraint on an employee's decision to participate in or refrain from union activities. Obviously, it is unlawful for a union to threaten an employee or a family with violence for failure to join the union. The law's prohibition includes economic coercion as well. Suppose that a union official declares: "We have a lot of power here; you had better join the union or you may lose your job." This threat is an unfair labor practice.

The NLRA provides unions with the authority to regulate their own internal affairs, which includes disciplining union members. This discipline cannot be used in an improperly coercive fashion. Suppose a disaffected union member feels that the union is no longer providing proper representation for employees and starts a campaign to decertify the union. The union may expel the employee from membership but may not fine or otherwise discipline the worker.

Another significant union unfair labor practice is discrimination. A union may not discriminate

13. *Wright Line*, 251 N.L.R.B. No. 150 (1980).

against workers because they refuse to join a union. This provision also prohibits a union from using its influence to cause an employer to discriminate against workers who refuse to join the union. A union cannot force an employer to deny promotions to workers who fail to join the union.

Other union unfair labor practices include featherbedding, participation in picketing to coerce unionization without majority employee support, and refusal to engage in good faith bargaining with employer representatives.

Unions are allowed to bargain for certain "union security clauses" in contracts, however. While closed shops are illegal, a union can bargain for a provision that requires workers to contribute to the union within thirty days after they were hired. This is typically called an agency shop, or union shop, clause.

The union shop clause can compel workers to begin paying dues to the certified union but cannot require the worker to "join" the union. Dues payment can be required to prevent workers from taking the benefits of union bargaining without contributing to the union's efforts. The clause cannot require workers to contribute their efforts to the union, however, or to go out on strike.

Even a requirement of dues payments to unions has its limits. Excessive initiation fees or dues may be illegal. Unions often use their revenues to contribute to causes or to lobby politicians. A nonunion employee subject to a union shop clause who must pay dues cannot be required to contribute to this sort of union expenditure. The following case addresses these limitations on a union's power to compel dues payments by nonunion employees.

Case 16.7

COMMUNICATIONS WORKERS OF AMERICA v. BECK

Supreme Court of the United States, 1988.
487 U.S. 735,
108 S.Ct. 2641,
101 L.Ed.2d 634.

BACKGROUND AND FACTS *A majority of employees of American Telephone and Telegraph Company (AT&T) and several of its subsidiaries elected to be represented by the Communications Workers of America (CWA) (petitioners). The CWA obtained a union security clause in the collective bargaining agreement negotiated between the CWA and AT&T. Under the clause, employees who did not wish to become union members were required to pay an "agency fee" to the union in amounts equal to the dues paid periodically by union members. Failure to pay the agreement-mandated fee was deemed grounds for discharge from employment with AT&T.*

Twenty employees (respondents) who chose not to join the union brought suit against the CWA, challenging the union's use of the agency fees. Specifically, the employees complained that the funds were used by the union for more than expenses related to the collective bargaining and representation functions of the union. Some of the funds, for example, were used to sponsor social and charitable events. Other portions of the funds were used to promote political ideals and goals of the union membership. The employees complained that such use violated the intent of the National Labor Relations Act. The employees asserted that the act required fees only to the extent necessary to support collective bargaining and representation on the theory that nonmembers, because they reap the benefits of such activity, should be obligated to share the burden of financially supporting it. A federal district court held that the fees violated the employees' constitutional right of free speech. A circuit court of appeals also found fault with the CWA, but not on constitutional grounds; the appellate court held that the union's actions violated provisions of the National Labor Relations Act. The union appealed to the United States Supreme Court.

Justice *BRENNAN* delivered the opinion of the Court.

* * * *

Added as part of the 1947 Labor Management Relations Act, or Taft-Hartley Act, [Section] 8(a)(3) [of the NLRA] makes it an unfair labor practice for an employer "by discrimination in regard to hire or tenure of employment . . . to encourage or discourage membership in any labor organization." * * * Taken as a whole, [Section] 8(a)(3) permits an employer and a union to enter into an agreement requiring all employees to become union members as a condition of continued employment, but the "membership" that may be so required has been "whittled down to its financial core." The statutory question presented in this case, then, is whether this "financial core" includes the obligation to support union activities beyond those germane to collective bargaining, contract administration, and grievance adjustment. We think it does not.

* * * *

* * * [T]he Taft-Hartley Act was "intended to accomplish twin purposes. On the one hand, the most serious abuses of compulsory unionism were eliminated by abolishing the closed shop. On the other hand, Congress recognized that in the absence of a union-security provision 'many employees sharing the benefits of what unions are able to accomplish by collective bargaining will refuse to pay their share of the cost.' " The legislative solution embodied in [Section] 8(a)(3) allows employers to enter into agreements requiring all the employees in a given bargaining unit to become members 30 days after being hired as long as such membership is available to all workers on a nondiscriminatory basis, but it prohibits the mandatory discharge of an employee who is expelled from the union for any reason other than his or her failure to pay initiation fees or dues. * * *

* * * *

[The Court disagreed with the petitioner's interpretation of the legislative history surrounding Section 8(a)(3).] It simply does not follow from this that Congress left unions free to exact dues equivalents from nonmembers in any amount they please, no matter how unrelated those fees may be to collective bargaining activities. On the contrary, the complete lack of congressional concern for the rights of nonmembers in the debate * * * is perfectly consistent with the view that Congress understood [Section] 8(a)(3) to afford nonmembers adequate protection by authorizing the collection of only those fees necessary to finance collective bargaining activities: because the amount of such fees would be fixed by their underlying purpose—defraying the costs of collective bargaining—Congress would have every reason to believe that the lack of any limitations on union dues was entirely irrelevant so far as the rights of nonmembers were concerned. In short, we think it far safer and far more appropriate to construe [Section] 8(a)(3) in light of its legislative justification, i.e., ensuring that nonmembers who obtain the benefits of union representation can be made to pay for them, than by drawing inferences from Congress' rejection of a proposal that did not address the rights of nonmembers at all.

DECISION AND REMEDY

The Court affirmed the decision of the court of appeals. In so doing, the Court held that Section 8(a)(3) of the National Labor Relations Act authorizes the union to exact only those fees and dues necessary to performing the duties of an exclusive representative of the employees in dealing with the employer on labor-management issues.

■ Rights of Nonunion Employees

Most of labor law involves the formation of unions and associated rights. Even nonunion employees have some similar rights, however. Most workers do not belong to unions, so this issue is significant. The NLRA protects concerted employee action, for example, and does not limit its protection to certified unions.

Concerted Activity

Data from the NLRB indicates that a growing number of nonunion employees are challenging employer barriers to their concerted action. Protected concerted action is that taken by employees for their mutual aid and regarding wages, hours, or terms and conditions of employment.

Even an action by a single employee may be protected concerted activity, if that action is taken for the benefit of other employees and if the employee has at least discussed the action with other approving workers. If only a single worker engages in a protest or walkout, the employer will not be liable for an unfair labor practice if it fires the worker unless the employer is aware that this protest or walkout is concerted activity taken with the assent of other workers. Sometimes the mutual interest of other workers should be obvious to the employer, however.

Safety

A common circumstance for nonunion activity is concern over workplace safety. The Labor-Management Relations Act authorizes an employee to walk off the job if he or she has a good faith belief that the working conditions are abnormally dangerous. The employer could not lawfully discharge the employee under these conditions.

Suppose that Knight Co. operates a plant building mobile homes. A large ventilation fan at the plant blows dust and abrasive materials into the faces of workers. The workers have complained, but Knight Co. has done nothing. The workers finally refuse to work until the fan is modified, and Knight fires them. The NLRB will find that the walkout is a protected activity and can command Knight to rehire the workers with back pay.

To be protected under federal labor law, a safety walkout must be *concerted* activity. If a single worker walks out over a safety complaint, other workers must be affected by the safety issue for the walkout to be protected under the LMRA.

Employee Committees

Personnel specialists note that worker problems are often attributable to a lack of communication between labor and management. In a nonunion workforce, a company may wish to create some institution to communicate with workers and act together with them to improve workplace conditions.

This institution, generally called an employee committee, is composed of representatives from both management and labor. The committee meets periodically and has some authority to create rules. The committee gives employees a forum to voice their dissatisfaction with certain conditions and gives management a conduit to inform workers fully of policy decisions.

Creation of an employee committee may be entirely well motivated on the company's part and may serve the interests of workers as well as management. Nevertheless, employee committees are fraught with potential problems under federal labor laws, and management must be aware of these problems.

The central problem with employee committees is that they may become the functional equivalent of a union that is dominated by management, in violation of the NLRA. Thus, these committees cannot perform union functions. The employee representatives on such a committee should not make a package of proposals on wages and terms of employment, because this is the role of a union negotiating committee. Similarly, the committee should not itself perform the function of reviewing employee complaints and grievances but should create a separate grievance system, perhaps with the use of arbitrators to resolve disputes. Nor should the committee members discuss issues related to potential unionization of the covered workforce.

■ Terms and Concepts to Review

appropriate bargaining
  unit 388
authorization cards 387
closed shop 387
collective bargaining 392
common situs picketing 395

eighty-day cooling-off
  period 397
featherbedding 392
hot-cargo agreement 396
lockout 400
no-strike clause 397

right-to-work laws 387
secondary boycott 395
severance pay 392
union shop 387
wildcat strike 397

■ Questions and Case Problems

16-1. A group of employees at the Briarwood Furniture Company's manufacturing plant were interested in joining a union. A representative of the AFL-CIO told the group that her union was prepared to represent the workers and suggested that the group begin organizing by obtaining authorization cards from their fellow employees. After obtaining 252 authorization cards from among Briarwood's 500 nonmanagement employees, the organizers requested the company recognize the AFL-CIO as the official representative of the employees. The company refused. Has the company violated federal labor laws? What should the organizers do?

16-2. The Briarwood Furniture Company, discussed in the preceding problem, employs 400 unskilled workers and 100 skilled workers in its plant. The unskilled workers operate the industrial machinery used in processing Briarwood's line of standardized plastic office furniture. The skilled workers, who work in an entirely separate part of the plant, are experienced artisans who craft Briarwood's line of expensive wood furniture products. Do you see any problems with a single union's representing all the workers at the Briarwood plant? Explain. Would your answers to the preceding problem change if you knew that 51 of the authorization cards had been signed by the skilled workers with the remainder signed by the unskilled workers?

16-3. Suppose that Consolidated Stores is undergoing a unionization campaign. Prior to the election, management says that the union is unnecessary to protect workers. Management also provides bonuses and wage increases to the workers during this period. The employees reject the union. Union organizers protest that the wage increases during the election campaign unfairly prejudiced the vote. Should these wage increases be regarded as an unfair labor practice? Discuss.

16-4. SimpCo was engaged in ongoing negotiations over a new labor contract with the union representing the company's employees. As the deadline for expiration of the old labor contract drew near, several employees who were also active in union activities were disciplined for being late to work. The union claimed that other employees had not been dealt with as harshly and that the company was discriminating on the basis of union activity. When the negotiations failed to prove fruitful and the old contract expired, the union called a strike. The company claimed the action was an economic strike to press the union's demands for higher wages. The union contended the action was an unfair labor practice strike because of the alleged discrimination. What importance does the distinction have for the striking workers and the company?

16-5. [icon] The management of Luxury of New York's production facility in Fort Plain, New York, was trying to discourage employees who were attempting to form a union. To this end, the management sponsored various employee meetings. At one of these meetings, the employees were shown a film that portrayed unions in a very unfavorable light and suggested that union campaigns threatened innocent bystanders with violence. Employees in favor of the union filed a complaint with the National Labor Relations Board. After finding that Luxury had engaged in unfair labor practices, one of which was the showing of the film, the NLRB ordered Luxury to cease such practices. Luxury appealed the NLRB's decision, claiming that its showing of the film was protected under the First Amendment right to freedom of speech. Did prohibiting the film's showing violate the employer's First Amendment rights? Discuss fully. [*Luxury of New York v. National Labor Relations Board,* 447 F.2d 112 (2d Cir. 1971)]

16-6. In June 1979, Castaways Management, Inc., (Castaways) purchased the Castaways Motel in Miami Beach, Florida. The general manager of Castaways actively supported one of the two union locals that sought to represent the motel's employees. Employees were told that voting for the other union could result in demotions, transfers, and pay reductions, and a number of employees who supported the other union were fired before the union election for reasons management claimed were not related to the union campaign. Both unions eventually filed unfair labor practice charges against Castaways, and the National Labor Relations Board found that Castaways had violated federal labor provisions by discharging employees for supporting union activity. Castaways was ordered to reinstate the discharged employees, award them back pay with interest, conduct a new election, and post notice of its violations on motel premises. By the time the initial order was affirmed by an NLRB panel in 1987, the motel had been demolished — although Castaways still existed as a business entity. On appeal, Castaways argued, among other things, that the NLRB's order was rendered moot (of no legal significance) because the motel no longer existed. Under these circumstances, is the NLRB's order enforceable? Discuss. [*National Labor Relations Board v. Castaways Management, Inc.,* 870 F.2d 1539 (11th Cir. 1989)]

16-7. Midland National Life Insurance was engaged in a unionization campaign. To fight the union, Midland distributed campaign literature, including a six-page document distributed the day before the election that described a strike at Meilman Food Company. The document suggested that the Meilman strike had become violent and had caused that plant to shut down. These statements were demonstrably false. In the election, 107 workers cast ballots for the union, and 107 workers voted against the union. The union organizers filed an unfair labor practice complaint against Midland with the National Labor Relations Board, complaining of the inaccuracy of the campaign literature. How should the NLRB decide this issue? Discuss fully. [*Midland National Life Insurance,* 263 N.L.R.B. No. 24 (1982)]

16-8. The employees of J. Weingarten, Inc., were represented by a union. A Weingarten worker was questioned by management about repeated thefts that had occurred at a Weingarten store. The worker asked that she be accompanied by a union representative during her interrogation, but the company refused to permit attendance of the union representative. The union filed an unfair labor practice charge with the National Labor Relations Board. The NLRB found that the employee's right to concerted action had been improperly denied by Weingarten, which had committed an unfair labor practice, and the NLRB issued a cease-and-desist order. Weingarten appealed, and an appellate court reversed the NLRB, holding that the employee had no need for union assistance at the interview. The Board then appealed this decision to the Supreme Court. How should the Supreme Court decide this case? Explain. [*NLRB v. J. Weingarten, Inc.,* 420 U.S. 251 (1975)]

16-9. Jerry Floyd worked for Emerson Electric Company. He had been an active supporter of unionization in 1975. Not long after the union campaign, Floyd was discharged. The employer said that this was because Floyd habitually spent time chatting with other employees about fishing and pornographic movies. Supervisors complained that Floyd was distracting their workers. Floyd claimed that the employer's reason was a pretext and that he had been discharged in retaliation for his unionization actions. The National Labor Relations Board found for Floyd, and Emerson appealed to federal court. Should the court reverse the NLRB decision? Discuss. [*Emerson Electric Co. v. NLRB,* 573 F.2d 543 (8th Cir. 1978)]

16-10. Westvaco operated plants that manufactured printed folding cartons, and its production and maintenance employees were represented by a union. The company hired four new technicians to work at the facility. The union argued that the technicians should be part of the unionized work force. Westvaco disputed this, argument, claiming that the technicians, because of their greater skills, were not properly part of the same bargaining unit as the existing production and maintenance employees, even though the technicians had previously been put through an extensive and specialized training course that lasted about four months. The National Labor Relations Board agreed with the union and added the new technicians to the bargaining unit. Westvaco appealed to court. How should the court rule? Explain fully. [*Westvaco, Virginia, Folding Box Division v. NLRB,* 795 F.2d 1171 (4th Cir. 1986)]

16-11. Employees of Great Dane Trailers, Inc., went out on strike. While the strike was going on, Great Dane offered special vacation benefits but set a cut-off date for accepting the benefits. As a practical matter, employees who came to work during the strike could get the vacation benefits, but those who stayed out on strike missed the cut-off date and lost their opportunity for the benefits. The National Labor Relations Board found that this was an unfair labor practice aimed at breaking the union. The company appealed this decision. Although the company provided no justification for its policy, the company argued that the vacation benefits were a very small benefit and had no significant effect on the decisions of strikers. How should a court rule? Discuss. [*NLRB v. Great Dane Trailers, Inc.,* 388 U.S. 26, 87 S.Ct. 1792, 18 L.Ed.2d 1027 (1967)]

16-12. A Question of Ethics

The employees of First National Maintenance Corporation are represented by a union. First National supplies its customers a contracted-for labor force in return for reimbursement of its labor costs plus a management fee. First National terminated a segment of its business that supplied maintenance work for the Greenpart Care Center, for economic reasons. This required that thirty-five First National workers be laid off. The union contended that this decision was a compulsory subject of bargaining and could not be made unilaterally by the employer. The National Labor Relations Board agreed with the union, but an appeals court reversed the decision, holding that business closings and shutdowns are permissive but not mandatory topics for collective bargaining. [First National Maintenance Corp. v. NLRB, *452 U.S. 666, 101 S.Ct. 2573, 69 L.Ed.2d 328 (1981)*]

1. A company's refusal to bargain over certain working conditions—things such as wages and hours of work—is taken to be a sign of bad faith. Why should not the decision to shut down all or part of a business be treated as a mandatory topic as well?
2. A fundamental change in a corporation, such as the shutting down of operations, normally requires the approval of a majority of the shareholders. In a sense, workers, too, ''invest'' in a firm when they accept employment. They forego other employment opportunities, perhaps. In some cases, they invest their own time in learning special skills suited only for that particular firm. Should, then, workers be afforded rights similar to those of shareholders? Should they at least have a protected right to collectively bargain over the decision to shut down part or all of the business?
3. With reference to the preceding question, what factors distinguish workers from shareholders? What practical considerations weigh against making collective bargaining over business closings a mandatory negotiation topic?

16-13. Case Briefing Assignment

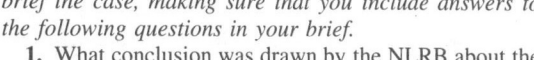

Examine Case A.16 [Teamsters Local Union No. 639 v. NLRB, *924 F.2d 1078 (D.C. Cir. 1991)*] *in Appendix A. The case has been excerpted there in great detail. Review and then brief the case, making sure that you include answers to the following questions in your brief.*

1. What conclusion was drawn by the NLRB about the company's resorting to a lockout in this case? Did the reviewing court agree?
2. What was the basis for concluding that the company's actions were as the NLRB deemed them to be?
3. What factor did the court consider important in determining whether negotiations had reached an impasse?
4. Why did the court reach the conclusion that it reached even though the union was unwilling to accept the company's proposed wage cut in its entirety?

Chapter 17

Employment Law

Historically, employment relationships were primarily governed by contracts. A worker entered into an employment contract with an employer, and the terms of employment were dictated by the terms of the contract. Most employer-employee contracts were considered to be "at will," which meant that the contract had no specified term. Under the **employment-at-will** doctrine, either party may terminate an employment contract at any time and for any reason. In general practice, this meant that employers could fire workers for good, bad, or no cause in response to changing economic conditions. Working employees had no guarantees of safety beyond those negotiated in the contract. If an employee was injured on the job, it was difficult for him or her to recover from the employer, because the employee was considered to have accepted the risks of employment when he or she accepted the job.

With increasing industrialization, corporate employers grew larger and workplace hazards increased. Workers came to believe that to counter the power of corporations and to protect themselves they needed to organize into unions. These collective activities of workers were discouraged, sometimes forcibly, by employers. Eventually, Congress passed laws protecting the rights of workers to organize collectively, as addressed in the preceding chapter.

While the growth of unions gave employees greater bargaining power in contract negotiations, this development also led to greater federal intervention in employer-employee relationships. As labor gained political influence, legislators responded with laws to protect workers, such as minimum wage, maximum hour, child labor, and other statutes. More recently, the legislature has passed additional laws to protect workers, even in the absence of unions. Courts have also modified the traditional at-will doctrine to protect workers from wrongful discharge.

This chapter covers some of the significant laws that regulate the workplace. One of the most significant employment laws is the prohibition on certain forms of discrimination. Other important laws affect occupational safety and the compensation of injured workers. Laws relating to drug testing, lie-detector tests, and the general issue of employees' privacy rights are also important in modern employment relationships.

■ Employment Discrimination

At common law, employment was terminable at will. Any employer could establish all terms and conditions of employment. Labor unions were deemed private associations, so they could determine all membership requirements without oversight of the courts. In the past several decades, however, as a result of judicial decisions, administrative agency actions, and legislation, both employers and unions have been restricted in their ability to discriminate on the basis of race, religion, nationality, age, or sex. Perhaps the most important statute relating to employment discrimination is Title VII of the Civil Rights Act of 1964.[1]

Title VII of the Civil Rights Act of 1964

Basically, Title VII of the Civil Rights Act of 1964 prohibits job discrimination against employees, applicants, and union members on the basis of race, color, national origin, religion, and sex at any stage of employment. A class of persons defined by one or more of these criteria is known as a **protected class.** Title VII prohibits discrimination on the part of employers with fifteen or more employees, labor unions with fifteen or more members, labor unions that operate hiring halls (where members go regularly to be rationed jobs as they become available), employment agencies, and state and local governments, government agencies, political subdivisions, and departments. A special section forbids discrimination in most federal government employment.

PROCEDURES AND REMEDIES   A person who has suffered discrimination may not simply file a lawsuit under Title VII. Compliance with Title VII is monitored by the Equal Employment Opportunity Commission (EEOC). The EEOC has the power to issue guidelines for interpreting the law and to bring lawsuits against organizations that violate the law. Thus, first the victim must file a claim with the EEOC, which investigates the facts and seeks to achieve a voluntary conciliation through which the employer and employee settle the dispute. If conciliation does not occur, the EEOC may sue the employer under Title VII. If the EEOC

chooses not to sue—for example, if it does not believe that the complaining individual was discriminated against—the victim may bring his or her own suit.

Employer liability under Title VII may be extensive. If the plaintiff successfully proves that unlawful discrimination occurred, he or she may be awarded reinstatement, back pay, and retroactive promotions. The court may also grant an injunction prohibiting future violations and correcting for past discrimination. This may even include an affirmative action program, which is discussed more fully below.

DISPARATE-TREATMENT   DISCRIMINATION When one thinks of employment discrimination, one is likely to imagine a job supervisor who is overtly racist or sexist. Blatant discrimination is known as **disparate-treatment discrimination**.

One of its elements is the employer's intent to discriminate. Because intent may sometimes be difficult to prove, courts have established certain special procedures for resolving disparate-treatment cases. Suppose a woman applies for employment with a construction firm and is rejected. If she sues on grounds of disparate-treatment discrimination in hiring, she must meet the following four requirements:

1.   The plaintiff is a member of a protected class.
2.   The plaintiff applied and was qualified for the job in question.
3.   The plaintiff was rejected by the employer.
4.   The employer continued to seek applicants for the position or filled the position with a person not in a protected class.

If the plaintiff can meet these relatively easy tests, she makes out a *prima facie* case of illegal discrimination. Making out a *prima facie* case of discrimination means that the plaintiff has met her initial burden of proof and will win in the absence of an employer response. The burden then shifts to the employer-defendant to articulate a legal reason for not hiring the plaintiff. For example, the employer might say that the plaintiff was not hired because she lacked sufficient experience or training. The employer need only give a reason and need not present proof. The plaintiff must then show that the employer's stated reason is a *pretext*

---

1.   42 U.S.C. Sections 2000e *et seq.*

(not the true reason) and that discriminatory intent actually motivated the employer's decision. Evidence of sexist statements by the employer might be used to show discriminatory intent.

In one case involving charges of discrimination on the basis of national origin, an employer (a Japanese corporation) claimed that its firing of certain employees was a result of its poor financial situation and the necessity that its employees speak the Japanese language. The court found that the employer segregated and classified its managerial work force along national-origin lines, used different evaluation and pay systems, and exempted

Japanese managers from staff cutbacks at the same time that it was laying off American managers. As for the language requirement, the court noted that in the past many employees of American origin who did not speak Japanese had performed the duties that the employer contended could be performed only by employees of Japanese origin.[2]

The following case involves allegations of disparate-treatment discrimination.

---

2. *Fortino v. Quasar Co.*, 751 F.Supp. 1306 (N.D. Ill. 1990).

Case 17.1

PRICE WATERHOUSE v. HOPKINS

Supreme Court of the United States, 1989.
490 U.S. 228,
109 S.Ct. 1775,
104 L.Ed. 2d 268.

BACKGROUND AND FACTS   *Ann Hopkins began working for Price Waterhouse, a professional accounting partnership, in 1978. As a senior manager and officer, Hopkins succeeded in terms of technical skills and client relations, securing a multimillion-dollar contract for the firm. In 1982, Hopkins was proposed for partnership. In evaluations compiled by the partnership committee, however, Hopkins was described as abrasive, overbearing, and "macho," sometimes "bullying" subordinates when she was under pressure. It was suggested that these characteristics were inappropriate in a woman. One partner advised that she "take a course in charm school." Hopkins's promotion was placed on hold, and she was advised to "walk more femininely, talk more femininely, dress more femininely, wear make-up, have her hair styled and wear jewelry." When Hopkins was not reproposed for partnership, she sued Price Waterhouse under Title VII, charging the firm with discrimination on the basis of sex in its partnership decisions. Hopkins claimed that words such as "macho" indicated underlying sexism and that her manner would have been overlooked if she had been a man. The federal district court held Price Waterhouse liable, determining that the partnership decision was infused with stereotypical notions about how women should behave on the job. Price Waterhouse appealed. The appellate court agreed with the district court. Price Waterhouse then appealed to the United States Supreme Court.*

BRENNAN, Justice.
*   *   *   *

The District Court found that sex stereotyping "was permitted to play a part" in the evaluation of Hopkins as a candidate for partnership. Price Waterhouse disputes both that stereotyping occurred and that it played any part in the decision to place Hopkins' candidacy on hold. In the firm's view, in other words, the District Court's factual conclusions are clearly erroneous. We do not agree.
*   *   *   *

*   *   * It takes no special training to discern sex stereotyping in a description of an aggressive female employee as requiring "a course at charm school." Nor *   *   * does it require expertise in psychology to know that, if an employee's flawed "interpersonal skills" can be corrected by a soft-hued suit or a new shade of lipstick, perhaps it is the employee's sex and not her interpersonal skills that has drawn the criticism.

* * * Hopkins showed that the partnership solicited evaluations from all of the firm's partners; that it generally relied very heavily on such evaluations in making its decision; that some of the partners' comments were the product of stereotyping; and that the firm in no way disclaimed reliance on those particular comments, either in Hopkins' case or in the past. Certainly a plausible—and, one might say, inevitable— conclusion to draw from this set of circumstances is that the [partnership committee] in making its decision did in fact take into account all of the partners' comments, including the comments that were motivated by stereotypical notions about women's proper deportment.

* * * *

Price Waterhouse appears to think that we cannot affirm the factual findings of the trial court without deciding that, instead of being overbearing and aggressive and curt, Hopkins is in fact kind and considerate and patient. If this is indeed its impression, petitioner misunderstands the theory on which Hopkins prevailed. * * * [E]ven if we knew that Hopkins had ''personality problems,'' this would not tell us that the partners who cast their evaluations of Hopkins in sex-based terms would have criticized her as sharply (or criticized her at all) if she had been a man. It is not our job to review the evidence and decide that the negative reactions to Hopkins were based on reality; our perception of Hopkins' character is irrelevant. We sit not to determine whether Ms. Hopkins is nice, but to decide whether the partners reacted negatively to her personality because she is a woman.

The Supreme Court concluded that the district court's findings were not clearly erroneous. The Court also concluded, however, that the district court had applied the wrong standard to the employer's burden of proof and remanded the case for a determination under the correct standard as to whether Hopkins would have been denied partnership even in the absence of discrimination. On remand, the district court again held Price Waterhouse liable and ordered the firm to give Hopkins her partnership, retroactive to 1982, and $371,000 in back pay and interest. Price Waterhouse appealed again. The appellate court affirmed the district court's award.

DECISION AND REMEDY

DISPARATE-IMPACT DISCRIMINATION Employers often find it necessary to use interviews and testing procedures to choose among a large number of applicants for job openings. Consequently, personnel tests have been used as devices for screening applicants. Minimum educational requirements are also common. Employer practices such as those involving educational or job requirements may have an unintended discriminatory impact on a protected class. **Disparate-impact discrimination** occurs when, as a result of educational or other job requirements or hiring procedures, an employer's work force does not reflect the same percentage of nonwhites, women, or members of other protected classes that characterizes qualified individuals in the local labor market. If a person who challenges an employment practice that has a discriminatory effect can show a connection between the practice and the disparity, he or she makes out a *prima facie* case, and no evidence of discriminatory intent need be shown. In the following case, the United States Supreme Court evaluated a claim of disparate-impact discrimination in two Alaskan canneries.

Case 17.2

**WARDS COVE
PACKING CO. v.
ATONIO**

Supreme Court of the United
States, 1989.
490 U.S. 642,
109 S.Ct. 2115,
104 L.Ed.2d 733.

BACKGROUND AND FACTS   *At two salmon canneries that operate in
remote areas of Alaska during the summer months, jobs are of two general
types. "Cannery jobs" are unskilled positions filled predominantly by local
nonwhites, Filipinos, and Alaska Natives. "Noncannery jobs" are largely
skilled positions filled predominantly by nonlocal white workers, who are
hired during the winter months from the companies' offices in Washington
and Oregon. Nearly all of the noncannery jobs pay more than the cannery
jobs, and the noncannery workers live in separate dormitories and eat in
separate dining areas. Frank Atonio and other nonwhite cannery workers
brought a Title VII action against the employers, asserting that the employers' hiring and promotion practices—including an English-language
requirement for noncannery jobs and not promoting from within—were
responsible for the racial stratification of the work force and denied to
cannery workers the opportunity to work at noncannery jobs. The district
court held for the employers, but a U.S. court of appeals ruled that the
cannery workers had made out a* prima facie *case of disparate-impact
discrimination. The employers, challenging the use of the numbers of nonwhites in cannery and noncannery positions to measure discrimination,
appealed the case to the United States Supreme Court.*

WHITE, Justice.
*   *   *   *

In holding that respondents had made out a *prima facie* case of disparate impact,
the court of appeals relied solely on respondents' statistics showing a high percentage
of nonwhite workers in the cannery jobs and a low percentage of such workers in
the noncannery positions. Although statistical proof can alone make out a *prima
facie* case, the Court of Appeals' ruling here misapprehends our precedents and the
purposes of Title VII, and we therefore reverse.

[The Court quoted from one of its previous cases involving a similar statistical
comparison:] "There can be no doubt *   *   * that the . . . comparison . . . fundamentally misconceived the role of statistics in employment discrimination cases."
The "proper comparison [is] between the racial composition of [the at-issue jobs]
and the racial composition of the qualified . . . population in the relevant labor
market." *   *   *

*   *   * Measuring alleged discrimination in the selection of accountants, managers, boat captains, electricians, doctors, and engineers—and the long list of other
"skilled" noncannery positions found to exist by the District Court—by comparing
the number of nonwhites occupying these jobs to the number of nonwhites filling
cannery worker positions is nonsensical. If the absence of minorities holding such
skilled positions is due to a dearth of qualified nonwhite applicants (for reasons that
are not petitioners' fault), petitioners' selection methods or employment practices
cannot be said to have had a "disparate impact" on nonwhites.
*   *   *   *

*   *   * [T]he vast majority of these cannery workers did not seek jobs in
unskilled noncannery positions; there is no showing that many of them would have
done so even if none of the arguably "deterring" practices existed. Thus, the pool
of cannery workers cannot be used as a surrogate for the class of qualified job
applicants because it contains many persons who have not (and would not) be noncannery job applicants. Conversely, if respondents propose to use the cannery workers
for comparison purposes because they represent the "qualified labor population"
generally, the group is too narrow because there are obviously many qualified persons
in the labor market for noncannery jobs who are not cannery workers.

The Supreme Court held that comparing the numbers of nonwhites in cannery and noncannery positions was not sufficient to establish a prima facie *case of disparate-impact discrimination. The case was remanded to the lower court for further proceedings.*

DECISION AND REMEDY

DEFENSES   After an employee makes out a *prima facie* case of discrimination, the employer has an opportunity to respond. The employer may attempt to disprove the plaintiff's case, or the employer may use certain defenses to justify employment practices.

Business Necessity Defense   In a disparate-impact case, an employer may assert a **business necessity defense**—that is, the employer may offer a good business reason for a practice that has a discriminatory effect. For example, if requiring a high school diploma is shown to have a discriminatory effect, an employer might argue that a high school education is required for workers to do a good job. Courts have held that educational requirements are a business necessity for some jobs, but they have rejected educational requirements for positions that require primarily manual labor. In one case, a company required certain scores on standardized ability-tests as prerequisites for employment in the company's skilled positions. Use of the tests had a discriminatory effect, because blacks consistently scored lower than whites. When the company asserted a business necessity defense, the court found no relation between the tests and job-performance ability, and thus the requirement did not qualify as a business necessity.[3]

The employer only has to state the business reason that it believes justifies an allegedly discriminatory practice. The person challenging the practice has to show that the practice is not justified by business necessity.[4] This is often a difficult requirement for plaintiffs. Plaintiffs often put forth an alternative, nondiscriminatory test that satisfies the business necessity, but the plaintiffs must show that the alternative test is equally effective and not unduly costly.

BFOQ Defense   Another defense to disparate-treatment discrimination claims applies when discrimination against a protected class is essential to a job—that is, when a particular trait is a **bona fide occupational qualification** (**BFOQ**). For example, a men's fashion magazine might legitimately hire only male models. Under Title VII, race cannot be a BFOQ. The defense applies only to the traits of other protected classes. Much controversy has arisen over this defense, particularly in sex-discrimination cases. Some companies have argued that being male is a BFOQ for jobs requiring heavy lifting,[5] while others have contended that being female is a BFOQ for flight attendants.[6] Courts have rejected both these arguments and have generally restricted the BFOQ defense to instances in which the employee's gender is of the essence of the job.

Seniority System Defense   Another defense protects bona fide seniority systems. An employer with a history of discrimination may have no members of protected classes in upper-level positions. Even if the employer now seeks to be unbiased, it may face a lawsuit seeking an order for minorities to be promoted ahead of schedule to compensate for the past discrimination. If a present intent to discriminate is not shown, and promotions or other job benefits are distributed according to a fair seniority system, the employer has a good defense against the suit.

AFFIRMATIVE ACTION   Title VII and equal opportunity regulations were designed to reduce or eliminate discriminatory practices with respect to hiring, retaining, and promoting employees. Affirmative action programs go a step further and attempt to atone for past discrimination by giving

---

3. *Albemarle Paper Co. v. Moody*, 422 U.S. 405, 95 S.Ct. 2362, 45 L.Ed.2d 280 (1975).

4   *Wards Cove Packing Co. v. Atonio*, 490 U.S. 642, 109 S.Ct. 2115, 104 L.Ed.2d 733 (1989). [Case 17.2 above.]

5. *Rosenfeld v. Southern Pacific Co.*, 444 F.2d 1219 (9th Cir. 1971).

6   *Diaz v. Pan American World Airways, Inc.*, 442 F.2d 385 (5th Cir. 1971).

qualified minorities and women preferential treatment in hiring and promotions. Affirmative action programs are controversial, especially when they are seen as resulting in what is often called "reverse discrimination"—discrimination against members of nonprotected classes, particularly white males. Generally, affirmative action programs that are designed to correct existing imbalances in a work force have been upheld as long as employers con-

sidered factors in addition to race or gender when making employment decisions. In determining whether a challenged plan is legitimate, the United States Supreme Court looks at the circumstances surrounding the case.

In the following case, a male employee who was a candidate for promotion alleged that his employer had engaged in "reverse" gender discrimination by promoting a less qualified female.

Case 17.3

JOHNSON v. TRANSPORTATION AGENCY, SANTA CLARA COUNTY, CALIFORNIA

Supreme Court of the United States, 1987.
480 U.S. 616,
107 S.Ct. 1442,
94 L.Ed.2d 615.

BACKGROUND AND FACTS *Paul Johnson, a male employee of the Transportation Agency of Santa Clara County, California, challenged the promotion of a female employee, Diane Joyce, who had a lower total score on the qualifying test and interviews than he did. Johnson and Joyce were among the final seven candidates for the position of road dispatcher, and a factor in awarding the job to Joyce was that she was a woman. The agency had voluntarily adopted an affirmative action plan designed to increase the number of women in positions in which they "have not been traditionally employed in significant numbers." At the time of Joyce's promotion, not one of the 238 positions in the pertinent job classification was held by a woman. Johnson contended that the promotion violated Title VII. The district court agreed, but the court of appeals reversed, maintaining that the promotion was a lawful effort to remedy long-standing imbalances in the work force. Johnson appealed to the United States Supreme Court.*

BRENNAN, Justice.
    *   *   *   *
    The first issue is *   *   * whether consideration of the sex of the applicants *   *   * was justified by the existence of a "manifest imbalance" that reflected underrepresentation of women in "traditionally segregated job categories." *   *   *
    *   *   *   *
    *   *   * Given the obvious imbalance in the [specific job] category, and given the Agency's commitment to eliminating such imbalances, it was plainly not unreasonable for the Agency to determine that it was appropriate to consider as one factor the sex of Ms. Joyce in making its decision. The promotion of Joyce thus satisfies the first requirement *   *   *, since it was undertaken to further an affirmative action plan designed to eliminate Agency work force imbalances in traditionally segregated job categories.
    *   *   *   *
    We next consider whether the Agency Plan unnecessarily trammeled the rights of male employees or created an absolute bar to their advancement. *   *   * [T]he Plan sets aside no positions for women. *   *   * [The] Plan requires women to compete with all other qualified applicants. No persons are automatically excluded from consideration; all are able to have their qualifications weighed against those of other applicants.
    In addition, petitioner had no absolute entitlement to the road dispatcher position. Seven of the applicants were classified as qualified and eligible, and the Agency Director was authorized to promote any of the seven. Thus, denial of the promotion unsettled no legitimate firmly rooted expectation on the part of the petitioner. Fur-

thermore, while the petitioner in this case was denied a promotion, he retained his employment with the Agency, at the same salary and with the same seniority, and remained eligible for other promotions.

The United States Supreme Court held that the agency appropriately took into account gender in determining that Joyce should be promoted to the road dispatcher position. The Court affirmed the appellate court's judgment.

DECISION AND REMEDY

At the center of the debate over affirmative action programs there are two ethical questions: To what extent, and in what ways, should the government regulate employment conditions to ensure equal opportunity? How much should employees who have not been discriminated against have to pay for those who have been subject to discrimination? In 1989, the United States Supreme Court held that a city ordinance requiring primary contractors on city construction projects to subcontract at least 30 percent of the dollar value of the projects to minority-owned businesses was a violation of the equal protection clause.[7] The Court said that the ordinance was tailored to no goal but "outright racial balancing." The Court added, "While there is no doubt that the sorry history of both private and public discrimination in this country has contributed to a lack of opportunities for black entrepreneurs, this observation . . . cannot justify a rigid racial quota in the awarding of public contracts."

ETHICAL CONSIDERATIONS

---

7. *City of Richmond v. J. A. Croson Co.*, 488 U.S. 469, 109 S.Ct. 706, 102 L.Ed.2d 854 (1989).

As the above case explains, affirmative action programs are not uniformly legal or illegal. To be lawful, such a program must be demonstrably needed because of past discrimination or a statistical disparity in the work force. In addition, any affirmative action plan must be carefully limited to correcting for that past discrimination, or disparity. Furthermore, the affirmative action plan cannot affect other workers too severely (for example, requiring that they be fired or costing them any opportunity for promotion).

SEXUAL HARASSMENT Workers have some protection against sexual harassment in the workplace under Title VII provisions against sex discrimination. Sexual harassment occurs when job opportunities, promotions, and the like are doled out on the basis of sexual favors or when an em-

ployee is subjected to a work environment in which the employee must put up with sexual comments, jokes, or physical contact that is perceived to be sexually offensive.

In a sexual harassment case, the employer may be liable even though an employee did the harassing. If the employee is in a supervising position, the employer will usually be held automatically liable for the behavior. If a lower-level employee is responsible for the harassment, the employer will be held liable only if it knew or should have known about the harassment and failed to take corrective action. The following case is a leading example of the law as applied to sexual harassment and employer liability.

Case 17.4

MERITOR SAVINGS BANK, FSB v. VINSON

Supreme Court of the United States, 1986.
447 U.S. 57,
106 S.Ct. 2399,
91 L.Ed.2d 49.

BACKGROUND AND FACTS   *Mechelle Vinson began work in 1974 as a teller at Meritor Savings Bank. She claimed that Sidney Taylor, a bank vice-president and branch manager, began making sexual advances toward her, to which she ultimately acquiesced out of fear of losing her job. She further testified that Taylor fondled her in front of other employees and even forcibly raped her. Taylor denied these charges. Vinson sued, claiming that she had "constantly been subjected to sexual harassment" by Taylor in violation of Title VII. The district court concluded that any sexual relationship between Vinson and Taylor had no relationship to Vinson's continued employment. Finding no discrimination, the court ruled in favor of the bank. Vinson appealed, and the appellate court ruled in her favor, finding that she had a valid claim of harassing-environment discrimination. The bank appealed to the United States Supreme Court.*

REHNQUIST, Justice.
  * * * *
Respondent argues, and the Court of Appeals held, that unwelcome sexual advances that create an offensive or hostile working environment violate Title VII. Without question, when a supervisor sexually harasses a subordinate because of the subordinate's sex, that supervisor "discriminate[s]" on the basis of sex. Petitioner apparently does not challenge this proposition. It contends instead that in prohibiting discrimination with respect to "compensation, terms, conditions, or privileges" of employment, Congress was concerned with what petitioner describes as "tangible loss" of "an economic character," not "purely psychological aspects of the workplace environment." * * *
  * * * *
Since the guidelines were issued, courts have uniformly held, and we agree, that a plaintiff may establish a violation of Title VII by proving that discrimination based on sex has created a hostile or abusive work environment. As the Court of Appeals for the Eleventh Circuit wrote in [another case]:

> Sexual harassment which creates a hostile or offensive environment for members of one sex is every bit the arbitrary barrier to sexual equality at the workplace that racial harassment is to racial equality. Surely, a requirement that a man or woman run a gauntlet of sexual abuse in return for the privilege of being allowed to work and make a living can be as demeaning and disconcerting as the harshest of racial epithets.

DECISION AND REMEDY   *The Supreme Court affirmed the appellate court's decision in favor of Vinson and remanded the case to district court for further proceedings. The Court held that the bank's liability for the actions of its supervisory employees should be determined by common law principles of agency (see Chapter 15).*

As *Meritor Savings Bank, FSB v. Vinson* illustrates, there may be illegal sexual harassment even if promotions are not conditioned on sexual favors. When a workplace is replete with sexual suggestiveness, a harassing environment—and thus discrimination based on sex—is present. Un-wanted touching, repeated propositions, and the widespread display of "pin-ups" in the office all can constitute sexual harassment. To be actionable, the harassment must be sufficiently pervasive that it affects a term or condition of employment.

PREGNANCY DISCRIMINATION The Pregnancy Discrimination Act of 1978,[8] which amended Title VII, prohibits discriminatory treatment of employees on the basis of pregnancy. Women affected by pregnancy, childbirth, or related medical conditions must be treated—for all employment-related purposes, including the receipt of benefits under employee benefit programs—the same as other persons not so affected but similar in ability to work.

An employer is required to treat an employee temporarily unable to perform her job because of a pregnancy-related condition in the same manner as the employer would treat other temporarily disabled employees. The employer can change work assignments, grant paid disability leaves, or grant leaves without pay, if that is how the employer would treat other temporarily disabled employees. Policies concerning an employee's return to work, accrual of seniority, pay increases, and so on must also result in equal treatment.

Age Discrimination

The Age Discrimination in Employment Act (ADEA) of 1967,[9] as amended, prohibits employment discrimination on the basis of age against individuals forty years of age or older. The act was recently amended to prohibit mandatory retirement for nonmanagerial workers. For the act to apply, an employer must have twenty or more employees, and interstate commerce must be affected by the employer's business activities.

The act is similar to Title VII in that it offers protection against both intentional (disparate-treatment) age discrimination and unintentional (disparate-impact) age discrimination. If a plaintiff can prove that his or her age was a determining reason for an employer's treatment, the employer will be held liable under the ADEA unless the allegedly discriminatory practice is justified by some legitimate and nondiscriminatory business reason.

Numerous cases of alleged age discrimination have been brought against employers who, to cut costs, replace older, higher-salaried employees with younger, lower-salaried workers. In one case, for example, a fifty-four-year-old manager of a plant who earned approximately $15.75 an hour was temporarily laid off when the plant was closed for the winter. When spring came, the manager was replaced by a forty-three-year-old worker who earned approximately $8.05 an hour. The older manager, who had worked for the firm for twenty-seven years, was given no opportunity to accept a lower wage rate or otherwise accommodate the firm's need to reduce costs. The court, which referred to the firm's dismissal of the manager as an exercise in "industrial capital punishment," held that the manager's dismissal in these circumstances violated the ADEA.[10]

In the following case, the plaintiff alleged age discrimination when an employer refused to hire him because he was "overqualified" for the position. The question before the court is whether the employer's refusal to hire the plaintiff for such a reason is merely age discrimination in disguise.

---

8. 42 U.S.C. Section 2000e(k).
9. 29 U.S.C. Sections 621-634.

---

10. *Metz v. Transit Mix, Inc.*, 828 F.2d 1202 (7th Cir. 1987).

BACKGROUND AND FACTS *Thomas Taggart was hired in October 1982 by Preview Subscription Television, Inc., a subsidiary of Time, Inc., as a print manager. Taggart was fifty-eight years old at the time and had worked in the printing industry for over thirty years. A little over six months later, in May 1983, Time notified Preview employees that Preview would be dissolved, and although Preview employees were not guaranteed other jobs at Time, they were told that they would receive special consideration for any available positions. Taggart applied for over thirty positions in various divisions at Time and its subsidiaries but was not offered employment. Taggart noted that younger applicants were chosen for po-*

Case 17.5

TAGGART v. TIME, INC.

United States Court of Appeals, Second Circuit, 1991. 924 F.2d 43.

sitions for which he had applied and was better qualified but for which he was not hired because he was "overqualified." For one position in particular, that of print purchaser for HBO (one of Time's subsidiaries), Taggart was much better qualified than the 41-year-old female who was given the job. Taggart was given no reason for HBO's refusal to hire him for the position, other than that he was "overqualified." Taggart, claiming that the real reason he was not hired was because of his age, brought this action against Time for age discrimination. The trial court granted Time's motion for summary judgment, finding it reasonable that an employer might reject an applicant whose qualifications are excessive because it believed the job would not challenge the employee and therefore the employee would likely continue to seek other employment. Taggart appealed.

CARDAMONE, Circuit Judge.
*   *   *   *

To make out a *prima facie* case of age discrimination, plaintiff must show that (1) he belongs to the protected age group, (2) he applied for and was qualified for the position sought, (3) he was not hired despite his qualifications, and (4) the position was ultimately filled by a younger person. Taggart must therefore show by a preponderance of the evidence that he applied for an available position for which he was qualified, but was rejected because of circumstances which give rise to an inference to unlawful discrimination. *   *   *

Applying Title VII analysis to the present case, it is plain, since Taggart is over 40 years old, that he belongs to the protected age group, he was not offered employment at Time and, at least for some of the openings he was found overqualified, which supports his allegation that he was capable of performing the job, and all of Time's new hirees were younger than he was. Thus, appellant established a *prima facie* case. The issue to be decided therefore is whether the evidence reveals Time did not hire him for reasons which could give rise to an inference of unlawful age discrimination.
*   *   *   *

*   *   * [C]haracterizing an applicant in an age discrimination case as overqualified has a connotation that defies common sense: How can a person overqualified by experience and training be turned down for a position given to a younger person deemed better qualified? Denying employment to an older job applicant because he or she has too much experience, training or education is simply to employ a euphemism to mask the real reason for refusal, namely, in the eyes of the employer the applicant is too old.

An employer might reasonably believe that an overqualified candidate—where that term is applied to a younger person—will continue to seek employment more in keeping with his or her background and training. Yet, that rationale does not comfortably fit those in the age group the statute protects; for them, loss of employment late in life ordinarily is devastating economically as well as emotionally. Instead, an older applicant that is hired is quite unlikely to continue to seek other mostly non-existent employment opportunities.

DECISION AND REMEDY

The appellate court held that refusing to hire Taggart for the sole reason that he was overqualified refuted Time's assertion that it was not discriminating on the basis of age. Therefore, the summary judgment granted by the trial court for the employer was reversed and the case remanded for trial.

ETHICAL
CONSIDERATIONS

In the wake of a corporate merger, takeover, acquisition, consolidation, or other corporate reorganization, and the consequent reshuffling of job positions and personnel, many employees may find themselves "out in the cold." Older employees, such as Taggart, suffer particularly because it is more difficult for them to find other employment, ostensibly because they are "overqualified." Although one cannot help but sympathize with Taggart and others in his position, there is a tradeoff involved in the statutory protection against age discrimination—as there is with other forms of employment discrimination. In selecting potential employees, employers cannot be totally objective. Job interviewers rely, at least to some extent, on their subjective appraisal of a job candidate's personality, energy level, apparent willingness to cooperate with others, and numerous other, often quite subtle factors when making hiring decisions. For the most part, these factors are difficult to document with any specificity and will not hold up in court as sufficient reasons to refuse to hire a member of a protected class. In a sense, antidiscrimination laws force employers to forgo these subjective appraisals or risk being sued for discriminatory hiring practices.

The ADEA contains a special provision that permits employers to offer voluntary retirement plans based on the age of the workers. Thus, a company could offer all employees over fifty-five years of age special benefits if they retired at a certain time. To be legal, however, the plan must be wholly voluntary, and the employer cannot pressure employees to accept the retirement offer.

Americans with Disabilities Act

The Americans with Disabilities Act (ADA) of 1990 prohibits employment discrimination against differently abled persons by businesses with twenty-five or more employees (and after July 1994, businesses with fifteen or more employees). Differently abled persons are persons with a physical or mental impairment that substantially limits "one or more major life activities." Impairments include blindness, paralysis, heart disease, cancer, AIDS, emotional illness, and learning disabilities.

Under the ADA, an employer cannot exclude arbitrarily a person who with *reasonable accommodation* could perform all that is required to do a particular job. This includes employees who become disabled while on the job. A differently abled person who cannot perform a job, however, may be lawfully rejected from employment. For example, a totally blind person who would be re-

quired to drive a truck as part of his or her duties would be unqualified for the job.

What constitutes "reasonable accommodation" is difficult to determine. Under the ADA, ramps must be installed for employees who use wheelchairs, and in some circumstances, readers are required for blind employees and interpreters for the hearing-impaired. Not every employer is required to accommodate all differently abled employees, however. If an employer can show that an accommodation is an undue hardship, it is unlikely that the employer will be ordered to employ a particular differently abled individual.

What constitutes "undue hardship" depends on the employer's size, budget, and profitability and the financial impact of the accommodation on the employer. For example, a small employer may not be required to hire a blind applicant and a reader to fill a single opening, but a large employer may be obligated to do so.

Procedures and remedies under the ADA are the same as under Title VII. If the Equal Employment Opportunity Commission decides not to pursue an individual's complaint, the individual has the right to sue an employer for reinstatement, back pay, and other relief, including reasonable accommodation. If, though, the employer wins the suit or other action, the employer can recover attorney's fees.

■ Rights of Privacy

In the 1980s, the law began to protect the privacy of employees in a number of areas. Lie-detector tests, drug tests, electronic monitoring of work and the workplace, and other practices have been challenged as violations of employees' rights of privacy.

Lie-Detector Tests

At one time, many employers required employees or job applicants to take polygraph, or lie-detector, examinations in connection with their employment. The results of lie-detector tests are not admissible as evidence in criminal trials, and many persons consider the tests to be an invasion of privacy.

In 1988, Congress passed the Employee Polygraph Protection Act.[11] The act prohibits certain employers from: (1) requiring, suggesting, requesting, or causing employees or job applicants to take lie-detector tests; (2) using, accepting, referring to, or asking about the results of lie-detector tests taken by employees or applicants; and (3) taking or threatening negative employment-related action against employees or applicants based on results of lie-detector tests, or because they refused to take the tests.

Employers excepted from these prohibitions include federal, state, and local government employers, certain security service firms, and companies manufacturing and distributing controlled substances. Other employers may use polygraph tests when investigating losses attributable to theft—including embezzlement and stealing of trade secrets.

Drug Testing

Drug and alcohol use has been estimated to cost industry $50 to $100 billion in absenteeism, impaired performance, and accidents each year. Employers are concerned with preventing the deterioration of job performance and other harm that can result from the use of drugs. Some employers have begun testing employees to uncover drug use. In many instances, the tests have proven to be unreliable, but even if their accuracy were unquestion-

able, there is the question as to whether the tests violate employees' rights of privacy.

Constitutional limitations apply to testing of government employees. The tests have been held constitutional when there was a reasonable basis for suspecting that a government employee was using drugs. Also, when drug use in a particular government job could threaten public safety, testing has been upheld. For example, a Department of Transportation (DOT) rule that requires employees engaged in oil and gas pipeline operations to submit to random drug testing was upheld, even though the rule did not require that before being tested the individual must be suspected of drug use.[12] The court held that DOT's interest in promoting public safety in the pipeline industry outweighed the employees' privacy interests.

These federal constitutional limitations do not always restrict private employers, however. In many cases, private employees have no valid protection against drug testing by companies. A drug-testing program is generally a matter of employer discretion, with some exceptions.

Some state constitutions may inhibit private employers' testing for drugs. Some state statutes may restrict private drug testing in any of a number of ways. A collective bargaining agreement may provide protection against testing. In other cases, employees may bring an action for invasion of privacy.

Monitoring Performance

Overseeing employees' performance by electronic means has become more common in the last decade. Today, some employers electronically monitor employees' use of computer terminals or company telephones. In some situations, employers use video cameras to evaluate employees' performance.

Listening to employees' telephone conversations may violate the Omnibus Crime Control Act of 1968 or a state statute. Otherwise, there is little specific government regulation of these activities, and an employer may be able to avoid these laws by simply informing employees that they are subject to monitoring. Nevertheless, in all cases, an employer should consider carefully the need to

---

11.   29 U.S.C. Sections 2001 *et seq.*

12.   *Electrical Workers, IBEW, Local 1245 v. Skinner,* 913 F.2d 1454 (9th Cir. 1990).

monitor employees, especially in areas such as restrooms. An employee may bring an action for invasion of privacy, and a court may decide that the employee's reasonable expectation of privacy outweighs the employer's need for surveillance.

Similarly, an employer should consider alternatives before searching an employee's desk, filing cabinet, or office. If a search is conducted, and the employee sues, a court may balance the purposes of the search against its intrusiveness. The court may also consider the availability of less intrusive alternatives that would have accomplished the same purposes.

■ Employment at Will

Federal statutes have modified the employment-at-will doctrine. Over the last two decades, the doctrine has also been eroded through a series of court rulings that restrict the right of employers to fire workers. Because this is a common law issue, the rules vary from state to state. The trend is to recognize exceptions to the at-will doctrine, however, and some courts have awarded punitive damages against employers in wrongful-discharge litigation. Wise employers will discharge employees only for good cause and will obtain documentation to support their position, in accordance with published company policies.

Statutory Limitations

Whistleblowing occurs when an employee tells the government or the press that his or her employer is engaged in some unsafe or illegal activity. For example, an employee might tell the Environmental Protection Agency (EPA) that his employer has been violating pollution laws.

Employees who blow the whistle often find themselves disciplined or even out of a job. In a state that protects whistleblowers, the employer could not discharge the employee for informing the EPA. Federal law may also protect a whistleblower. For example, if an employee of a defense contractor reveals overcharges on weapons, the employee is protected. In one case, when trucking-company employees were fired for reporting safety violations, the Department of Labor ordered that the employees be reinstated.[13]

Statutory protections for whistleblowers are limited to a few industries. In situations in which neither a whistleblowing statute nor an employment contract protects the worker, the case must be decided on the basis of common law doctrine.

Exceptions Based on Contract Theory

Some courts have used contract theory to protect employees from arbitrary discharge. Many of these courts have held that if an implied employment contract exists between the employer and the employee, then if the employee is fired outside the terms of the implied contract, he or she may succeed in a breach-of-contract action.

For example, an employer's handbook or personnel bulletin may state that, as a matter of policy, workers will be dismissed only for good cause. If the employee is aware of this policy and continues to work for the employer, a court may find that there is an implied contract, based on the terms stated in the handbook or bulletin. If an employer makes promises to employees regarding discharge policy, those promises may also be considered part of an implied contract. If the employer fires the worker in a manner contrary to the manner promised, a court may hold that the employer has violated the implied contract and is liable for damages. Most state courts will consider this claim and judge it by traditional contract standards.

A few states have gone further and held that all employment contracts contain an implied covenant of good faith. This means that both sides promise to abide by the contract in good faith. If an employer fires an employee for an arbitrary or unjustified reason, the employee can claim that the covenant of good faith was breached and the contract violated.

Exceptions Based on Public Policy

A widespread common law exception to the employment-at-will doctrine is the public policy exception. Under this rule, an employer may not fire a worker for reasons that violate a fundamental public policy of the jurisdiction. For example, a court may prevent an employer from firing a worker who serves on a jury and therefore cannot work scheduled hours. Sometimes, an employer will direct an employee to do something that violates the law. If the employee refuses to perform the illegal act, the employer might decide to fire the worker.

---

13. See *Brock v. Roadway Express, Inc.*, 481 U.S. 252, 107 S.Ct. 1740, 95 L.Ed.2d 239 (1987).

Most states have held that firing the worker under these circumstances violates public policy. The public policy theory generally protects employees from being required to violate the law but does not always protect employees when no legal violation is involved.

Whistleblowers may be protected from wrongful discharge for public policy reasons. For example, a bank was held to have wrongfully discharged an employee who pressured the employer to comply with state and federal consumer credit laws.[14] In another case, an at-will employee—a probation officer with the police department of the city of Globe, Arizona—discovered that a man had been arrested for vagrancy under an obsolete statute, had been sentenced to ten days in prison, and had been in jail for twenty-one days. The officer pointed out to a magistrate that this was illegal. The magistrate informed the police chief, the chief fired the officer, and the officer sued the city for wrongful discharge. Holding that the discharge violated public policy, the court said, "So long as employees' actions are not merely private or proprietary, but instead seek to further the public good, the decision to expose illegal or unsafe practices should be encouraged. . . . There is no public policy more important or fundamental than the one favoring the effective protection of the lives, liberty, and property of the people. The officer's successful attempt to free the arrestee from illegal confinement was a refreshing and laudable exercise that should be protected, not punished."[15]

Some states require a clear mandate of public policy to support this cause of action. For example, it has been held that an employee who claimed that he was discharged for reporting environmental violations to his employer was not entitled to recover unless he could show that he was charged with the responsibility of reporting those violations to protect the public interest.[16] The employee alleged that he was fired after he told his superiors that company management may have engaged in a cover-up of a toxic leak. The employee claimed that state and federal "policy recognize the public interest in a cleaner environment" but he acknowledged that he had no responsibility for reporting spills to any public agency.

Exceptions Based on Tort Theory

In a few cases, the discharge of an employee may give rise to a tort cause of action. Abusive discharge procedures may result in intentional infliction of emotional distress or defamation. In one case, a restaurant had suffered some thefts of supplies, and the manager announced that he would start firing waitresses alphabetically until the thief was identified. The first waitress fired said that she suffered great emotional distress as a result. The state's highest court upheld her claim as stating a valid cause of action.[17] Defamation can be a particular concern for employers. If an employer inaccurately believes that an innocent employee is guilty of theft and fires the employee, the employee may be able to sue for defamation.

■ Injury, Compensation, and Safety

Numerous state and federal statutes are designed to protect employees and their families from the risks and effects of accidental injury, death, or disease resulting from their employment. This section discusses state workers' compensation acts and the Occupational Safety and Health Act of 1970, which are specifically designed to protect employees and their families.

State Workers' Compensation Acts

Workers' compensation, which covers employees injured on the job, is increasingly significant to businesses. Total workers' compensation costs in a recent year were $60 billion. Although these losses are covered by insurance, the expenditures have caused insurance rates to rise dramatically and

---

14. *Harless v. First National Bank in Fairmont*, 162 W.Va. 116, 246 S.E.2d 270 (1978).
15. *Wagner v. City of Globe*, 150 Ariz. 82, 722 P.2d 250 (1986).
16. *Smith v. Calgon Carbon Corp.*, 917 F.2d 1338 (3d Cir. 1990).

17. *Agis v. Howard Johnson Co.*, 371 Mass. 140, 355 N.E.2d 315 (1976).

seriously threaten the welfare of many smaller businesses. Because insurance rates are influenced by claim history, companies have a strong incentive to avoid causing workers to file claims for compensation.

Workers' compensation laws establish an administrative procedure for compensating workers injured on the job. Instead of suing in court, an injured worker files a claim with the administrative agency or board that administers the local workers' compensation claims. These agencies have quasi-judicial powers. All of their rulings are subject to review by the courts. In general, the right to recover under workers' compensation laws is determined without regard to the existence of negligence or of fault in the traditional sense. Rather, it is predicated wholly on the employment relationship and the fact that the injury *arose out of or in the course of employment*. A simple, two-pronged test for determining whether an employee can receive workers' compensation consists of the following questions:

1. Was the injury accidental?
2. Did the injury arise out of or in the course of employment?

Intentionally inflicted self-injury, for example, would not be considered accidental and, hence, would not be covered under the workers' compensation laws. If an injury occurs while an employee is commuting to or from work, most workers' compensations schemes would not consider it to have arisen out of or in the course of employment and hence would not cover it. In the past, heart attacks or other medical problems arising out of preexisting disease or physical conditions were not covered, but recently many states have allowed recovery.

Courts have tended to expand the types of injuries covered by workers' compensation, which has compensated more workers but also has contributed to the increased costs of the system. The following decision exemplifies this trend.

BACKGROUND AND FACTS *Rose Wood was a school bus driver employed by Laidlaw Transit, Inc. On the morning of April 29, 1986, while driving a bus of kindergarten children to school, Wood happened upon a gruesome accident scene, in which two high school students, known to her, were killed. She was the first to arrive on the accident scene, where she observed the mangled figure of one of the young victims. She remained on the scene until emergency assistance arrived and then proceeded to take her passengers to school.*

Within weeks, Wood began suffering symptoms of psychological disorder, including insomnia, nightmares, anorexia, and depression. On June 12, 1986, she was driving children to school and nearly collided with an automobile. Her reaction to this episode required her to be hospitalized for post-traumatic stress disorder, and she was unable to return to work as a bus driver.

Wood filed a claim for workers' compensation. The claim was denied by the state workers' compensation law judge but sustained on appeal by the workers' compensation board. The transit company appealed the decision to a court, which reversed the board and held that no accident had occurred for which compensation was due under the workers' compensation law. Ms. Wood appealed the court's decision.

Case 17.6

WOOD v. LAIDLAW TRANSIT

Court of Appeals of New York, 1990.
77 N.Y. 79,
565 N.E.2d 1255,
564 N.Y.S.2d 704.

KAYE, Judge.
* * * *

No one disputes the governing legal standard: employers must provide compensation to their employees for their accidental injuries arising out of and in the course of employment. * * * Nor is there any quarrel as to causal relationship; in this case claimant's injuries unquestionably arose out of and in the course of her employment. But not every job-related injury is compensable. Whether claimant suffered an accident, or "accidental injuries," when she witnessed the events of April 29 is the center of the controversy here. * * *

That same question was the focus of *Wolfe*, where this Court for the first time recognized that psychological injury precipitated by psychic trauma can be an accidental injury compensable to the same extent as a physical injury. Our law had previously allowed workers' compensation claims both in instances where physical impact produced psychic trauma (physical-mental cases) and in instances where psychic trauma produced physical injury (mental-physical cases). * * *

While rejecting any talismanic [magical] effect of physical injury, in *Wolfe* we noted a policy argument that has been raised in the mental-mental cases. As the *Wolfe* respondents argued, absent the requirement of some physical manifestation the floodgates would open to compensation claims by emotionally fragile employees seeing injuries to others, with no rational way for employers to limit their liability. * * *

* * * *

In the present case, Rose Wood was by virtue of her employment an active participant—more than a third party merely witnessing another's injury—in the events of April 29, even though she did not come upon the scene of the accident until after it had occurred. Claimant's job responsibilities involved her in a unique way and distinguished her from others who might have passed on the road. The feeling on claimant's part that she should have been able to help, but couldn't precipitated her psychological injuries in the same way the claimant in *Wolfe* could point to a feeling of inability to prevent her supervisor's suicide as a causative element of her injuries.

DECISION AND REMEDY   *The court reversed the decision of the lower court and reinstated the decision of the workers' compensation board granting benefits to Wood.*

Basically, employers are under a system of strict liability. Few, if any, defenses (including the common law defenses of contributory negligence, assumption of risk, or fellow-servant doctrines) exist for them. Therefore, the costs of treating workers' injuries are considered a cost of production, and the costs of insurance are passed on to consumers.

Employer liability is limited to accidents that arise out of or in the course of employment. Workers' compensation covers most injuries suffered at the work site, but not all. Injuries from intentional torts, such as a fight among employees, are generally considered outside the coverage of workers' compensation.

Most off-site injuries are not covered. Suppose that a white-collar employee is commuting to work and is involved in a traffic accident. Most commuting accidents are not considered to arise out of or in the course of employment. The accident would be covered, though, if the commute was part of the job. If the worker was transacting business on a car phone, the accident probably would be covered under workers' compensation.

In exchange for compensation under these statutes, workers give up the right to sue in court for on-the-job injuries. Even if an injury is caused by an employer's negligence, the injured worker must accept workers' compensation as the sole remedy. The amount of compensation is determined according to a pre-set schedule or set by an administrative review board. On average, recoveries under workers' compensation are less than half what those in comparable successful tort suits would be.

Health and Safety Protection

At the federal level the primary legislation for employee health and safety protection is the Occupational Safety and Health Act of 1970.[18] This act

---

18.   29 U.S.C. Sections 553, 651-678.

was passed to ensure safe and healthful working conditions for practically every employee in the country. The act provides for specific standards that must be met by employers, plus a general duty to keep workplaces safe.

The Occupational Safety and Health Administration (OSHA) was created by the Occupational Safety and Health Act to administer the law. Among the powers of OSHA is the authority to establish specific standards. OSHA has safety standards governing many workplace details, such as the structural stability of ladders, requirements for railings, and the like. OSHA also has some health standards that limit exposures to toxic substances in the workplace.

A separate provision of the Occupational Safety and Health Act is called the **general duty clause**. This clause requires that businesses be maintained free from recognized hazards that may cause serious physical harm to workers and that can be feasibly corrected. All employers that have one or more employees and whose activities significantly affect interstate commerce are covered by the act.

PROCEDURES Employees can file complaints of violations of the Occupational Safety and Health Act to the OSHA, which is part of the Department of Labor. Under the act, an employer cannot discharge an employee who files a complaint or who, in good faith, refuses to work in a high-risk area (where bodily harm or death might result). Employers with eleven or more employees are required to keep occupational injury and illness records for each employee. Each record must be kept and updated for a continuous five-year period and made available for inspection by an OSHA inspector. Whenever a work-related injury or disease occurs, employers are required to report it to OSHA. Whenever an employee is killed in a work-related accident, or if five or more employees are hospitalized in one accident, the Department of Labor must be notified within forty-eight hours. If it is not, the company is fined. Following the accident, a complete inspection of the premises is mandatory.

ENFORCEMENT Three federal agencies were created to develop and enforce the standards set by the act. As mentioned above, OSHA has the authority to promulgate standards, make inspec-

tions, and enforce the act. The National Institute for Occupational Safety and Health is part of the Department of Health and Human Services. Its main duty is to conduct research on safety and health problems and to recommend standards for OSHA administrators to adopt. Finally, the Occupational Safety and Health Review Commission is an independent agency set up to handle appeals from actions taken by OSHA administrators.

OSHA-compliance officers may enter and inspect facilities of any establishment covered by the act. In the past, warrantless inspections were conducted. It is now recognized that such inspections violate the warrant requirement of the Fourth Amendment.[19] Nevertheless, OSHA inspectors can and do conduct surprise inspections. If a violation is discovered, a citation may be issued directing an employer to correct a situation. Civil penalties may also be assessed.

Criminal penalties for willful violation of the federal Occupational Safety and Health Act are very limited. Employers may be prosecuted under state laws, however. For example, PYMM Thermometer Company of Brooklyn, New York, exposed its workers to poisonous mercury. One employee suffered permanent brain damage. A jury convicted two PYMM executives of assault and reckless endangerment. The trial judge set aside the verdict, on the ground that job safety could only be regulated by the federal act. On appeal, the appellate court held that the federal act does not preempt state prosecution of employers whose criminal activity is centered in the workplace or directed against employees.

In 1988, the Justice Department stated its view that criminal penalties in the act did not preempt state and local criminal laws.[20] In other words, the act could no longer be used to shield employers from state criminal prosecution if they showed willful disregard for worker safety. In 1989, the Illinois Supreme Court upheld Cook County's criminal prosecution of five executives at Chicago Magnet Wire Corporation. The executives allegedly allowed workers to become ill from exposure to hazardous chemicals. Suits of a similar nature

19. *Marshall v. Barlow's, Inc.*, 436 U.S. 307, 98 S.Ct. 1816, 56 L.Ed.2d 305 (1978).
20. Letter to Chairman, House Committee on Government Operations, 100th Cong., 2d Sess. (1988).

Privacy Rights versus Worker Safety and Efficiency

A major employment issue today concerns perceived intrusions into employees' rights to privacy. This issue arises when employers feel that they are required to undertake certain actions, such as drug testing, to ensure safety and efficiency in the workplace. The tradeoff here is obvious: employees' privacy rights versus worker safety and efficiency. The trend is obviously toward more intrusion into workers' privacy rights. Today, of businesses with 5,000 or more employees, over 60 percent have some type of drug-testing program. A fourth of those companies test their workers randomly at the job site. The trend is clear, because a mere five years ago, only 3 percent of all private-sector employers had drug-screening programs in progress.

The Issue of Fourth Amendment Rights

To protect the safety of consumers and other employees, does the government have the right to violate the Fourth Amendment's stricture against unreasonable searches and seizures? The question, of course, turns on whether drug testing constitutes an "unreasonable" intrusion upon the rights of employees to be secure in their persons. The United States Supreme Court has ruled, on at least one occasion, that suspicionless testing of train workers following a train accident or other railroad mishap is a reasonable search and seizure.[a] For employers in the private sector, the guidelines are not quite so clear. Private drug-testing programs are governed by state law, which varies widely. Some states have statutes that restrict such testing; others do not.

Blanket, or random, drug testing has posed the greatest challenge to the courts. In 1988, for example, the Justice Department issued a plan that required certain of its employees to submit to random drug testing. Several Justice Department employees challenged the requirement as a violation of the Fourth Amendment. The United States Court of Appeals for the District of Columbia Circuit handed down a decision that said yes for some employees and no for others. Random drug testing was justified only for those employees having access to top-secret classified information; for all others, random drug testing was not justified.[b]

Recently, the Department of Transportation adopted final rules for drug testing applicable to the aviation, rail, mass transit, trucking, and pipeline industries, as well as to the U.S. Coast Guard. Employees in safety-sensitive positions are to be tested for drugs on a random basis. Drug testing is also required for job applicants and upon any reasonable suspicion after an accident.

Wiretapping and Employee Rights

Employers believe that it is necessary to monitor the phone conversations and electronic mail (e-mail) activities of their employees. In a plea-bargaining agreement between the Pennsylvania attorney general's office and R. A. Security Company, the company agreed to pay a $1 million fine for its involvement in the wiretapping of employees' telephone conversations at a western Pennsylvania oil refinery. Pennsylvania state law prohibits the secret tape-recording of

---

a. *Skinner v. Railway Labor Executives Association,* 489 U.S. 602, 109 S.Ct. 1402, 103 L.Ed.2d 639 (1989).

---

b. *Harmon v. Thornburgh,* 878 F.2d 484 (D.C.Cir. 1989).

conversations. R. A. Security monitored over four hundred telephone calls made by employees of United Refining Company and recorded at least one hundred of those conversations. The calls were monitored and recorded as part of a probe by the owner of the company, who suspected executives of engaging in theft. Current federal law recognizes the right of employers to listen in on telephone conversations to monitor employees' performance, but state laws vary.

The issue is even more clouded with respect to e-mail. More than ten million people in the United States use e-mail systems, and most users assume that electronic messages are just as private as letters sent through the U.S. Postal Service. The administrator of the e-mail system for Epson America was fired from her job when she questioned why her supervisors were reading employees' e-mail without their knowledge. The ex-employee's attorney maintained that Epson was reading and printing out e-mail and doing so in violation of California state law, which makes it a crime for a person or a company to eavesdrop on or record confidential communication without the consent of both the sender and

the receiver. Colorado and Florida have similar legislation.

■ Implications for the Businessperson

1. Employers need to be careful in their drug-testing or monitoring practices to avoid lawsuits for violation of employee privacy rights. Therefore, all employers who decide to engage in such activities must first become familiar with the laws of the particular jurisdiction in which they are located. Private drug testing, eavesdropping on employees' telephone conversations and e-mail, and other types of surveillance are governed by widely varying state statutes.

2. Drug testing in the public sector is becoming increasingly accepted and upheld in recent court cases. Such increased acceptability may be a harbinger for the private sector. That means that employers may find themselves freer in the future to take measures that will protect the safety of those affected by employees who use drugs. Again, knowledge of state law is important in this area.

■ For Critical Analysis

1. To what extent should employers have the right to impose drug testing on employees when there is no

evidence of job impairment due to drug use?

2. The costliest psychoactive drug, in terms of lost productivity, absenteeism, and so on, is alcohol. Estimates of the cost of alcohol abuse by employees exceed $50 billion a year. There appear to be more alcohol-related accidents than accidents caused by all other psychoactive drugs combined. Therefore, why is there so much emphasis on testing for the use of illegal drugs as opposed to testing for alcohol abuse and addiction?

3. Are there less intrusive and less personally offensive ways of attaining the same results gained through drug testing? Some argue, for example, that the way to measure performance is by measuring output. The performance of assembly-line workers, for example, can be tested by using time and motion studies, and pilots' performance can be tested at computerized flight simulators. Salespersons can be tested by volume of sales and typists, by words typed per minute. Would such tests truly be alternatives to drug testing?

have been brought in other states. Some courts have held that OSHA does preempt state criminal prosecutions.

■ Retirement and Income Security

Federal and state governments participate in insurance programs designed to protect employees and their families by covering the financial impact of retirement, disability, death, hospitalization, and unemployment. The key federal law on this subject is the Social Security Act of 1935.[21]

Old Age, Survivors, and Disability Insurance (OASDI)

Both employers and employees must contribute under the Federal Insurance Contributions Act (FICA) to help pay for the loss of income benefits on retirement. The basis for the employee's contribution is the employee's annual wage base—the maximum amount of an employee's wages that are subject to the tax. Benefits are fixed by statute but increase automatically with increases in the cost of living if they exceed a certain minimum amount.

Medicare

A health insurance program, Medicare is administered by the Social Security Administration for people sixty-five years of age and older and for some under sixty-five who are disabled. It has two parts, one pertaining to hospital costs and the other to nonhospital medical costs, such as visits to doctors' offices. People who have Medicare hospital insurance can also obtain additional federal medical insurance if they pay small monthly premiums that increase as the cost of medical care increases.

Private Retirement Income Security

There has been significant legislation to regulate retirement plans set up by employers to supplement social security benefits. The major piece of this legislation is the Employee Retirement Income Security Act (ERISA) of 1974.[22] This act empowers the Labor Management Services Administration of

the Department of Labor to enforce its provisions to regulate individuals who operate private pension funds. ERISA does not require an employer to establish a pension plan. When a plan exists, however, ERISA establishes standards for its management.

A key provision of ERISA concerns vesting. **Vesting** gives an employee a legal right to receive pension benefits at some future date when he or she stops working. Before ERISA, some employees who had worked for companies for as long as thirty years received no pension benefits when their employment terminated because those benefits had not vested. ERISA establishes complex vesting rules. Generally, however, all employee contributions to pension plans vest immediately, and employee rights to employer pension-plan contributions vest after five years of employment.

To prevent mismanagement of pension funds, ERISA has established rules on how they must be invested. Pension managers must be cautious in their investments and refrain from investing more than 10 percent of the fund in securities of the employer. ERISA also contains detailed record-keeping and reporting requirements.

Unemployment Compensation

The United States has a system of unemployment insurance in which employers pay into a fund, the proceeds of which are paid out to qualified unemployed workers. The major piece of federal legislation involved is the Federal Unemployment Tax Act of 1939.[23] This act created a state system that provides unemployment compensation to eligible individuals. Employers who fall under the provisions of the act are taxed quarterly. Taxes are typically submitted by the employers to the states, which then deposit them with the federal government. The federal government maintains an Unemployment Insurance Fund, in which each state has an account.

■ Other Employment Laws

Among numerous other employment laws affecting workers and their employers are the Fair Labor Standards Act, the Davis-Bacon Act, and the Walsh-Healey Act.

---

21.   42 U.S.C. Section 301.
22.   29 U.S.C. Sections 1001 *et seq.*

---

23.   26 U.S.C. Section 3301.

Fair Labor Standards Act

The Fair Labor Standards Act of 1938 (FLSA),[24] also known as the Wage-Hour Law, covers employers engaged in interstate commerce. FLSA is concerned with child labor, maximum hours, and minimum wages.

CHILD LABOR   The act prohibits oppressive child labor. Children under sixteen years of age cannot be employed full-time except by a parent under certain circumstances; nor can children between the ages of sixteen and eighteen be employed in hazardous jobs or in jobs detrimental to their health and well-being. Most states require children under sixteen years of age to obtain work permits.

MAXIMUM HOURS   Under FLSA, any employee who agrees to work more than forty hours per week must be paid no less than one and a half times his or her regular pay for all hours over forty. An exception exists for employees (1) whose duties necessitate irregular working hours, (2) who are employed pursuant to a bona fide individual contract or collective bargaining agreement, (3) whose contracts specify a regular rate of pay for up to forty hours a week and one and a half times that rate for hours over forty, and (4) whose contracts provide a weekly pay guarantee for not more than sixty hours. If all four of these elements are present, the employee is exempt. The following case illustrates a court's consideration of these elements.

---

24. 29 U.S.C. Section 201.

BACKGROUND AND FACTS   *Fred Crenshaw was hired by Quarles Drilling Corporation as a drilling-equipment mechanic on September 16, 1980. Crenshaw was provided with a company truck, special tools, and a mobile telephone so that he could do routine maintenance and emergency repairs of Quarles's drilling equipment located in several states. Under the employment contract, Crenshaw was paid a biweekly salary based on a forty-hour regular workweek and twenty hours of overtime per week. Crenshaw often worked more than sixty hours per week but was not given overtime pay for the additional hours. Nor were his hours of travel time between job sites included as "working" hours. In 1983, having left Quarles's employment, Crenshaw filed suit against the company for overtime compensation, claiming it had violated FLSA. The trial court granted judgment for Crenshaw. Crenshaw was awarded $34,082.85 in overtime compensation and an equal amount in liquidated damages. Quarles appealed.*

Case 17.7

CRENSHAW v. QUARLES DRILLING CORP.

United States Court of Appeals, Tenth Circuit, 1986.
798 F.2d. 1345.

TACHA, Circuit Judge.
     *   *   *   *

     [To qualify as an exception to FLSA's overtime pay rule, a] contract must specify a "regular rate of pay." The Supreme Court has interpreted "regular rate" to mean "the hourly rate actually paid for the normal, non-overtime workweek." *   *   *

     At trial, Crenshaw insisted that he did not know the number of hours upon which his salary was based. The chief mechanic, however, who had hired Crenshaw to work for Quarles testified that he had told Crenshaw that his salary would be based on a sixty-hour work week. The district court resolved this factual dispute by adopting Quarles' assertion that the parties had agreed to a sixty-hour work week based on forty hours at a regular hourly rate and twenty hours at one and one-half times the regular rate. We find support for this determination in the record and do not find it to be clearly erroneous.

*   *   *   *

The employment agreement here comes within the *   *   * exception only if there are "irregular hours of work." *   *   *

"*   *   * For hours to be considered to be irregular *   *   *, they must, in a significant number of weeks, fluctuate both below forty hours per week as well as above." *   *   *

*   *   *   *

*   *   * [T]here were only eight weeks in which Crenshaw worked fewer than forty hours out of a total of 119 weeks of work, or 6.7% of the total. *   *   * We hold that the number of weeks that Crenshaw worked fewer than forty hours is not sufficient to satisfy the requirement of "irregular hours" *   *   *. Quarles is therefore liable *   *   * for overtime compensation due to Crenshaw. *   *   *

*   *   *   *

The time that Crenshaw spent traveling to his job sites was included by the district court in calculating the time for which overtime compensation is due.

*   *   * "Employees who transport equipment without which well servicing could not be done, are performing an activity which is so closely related to the work which they and other employees perform, that it must be considered an integral and indispensable part of their principal activities."

The district court here found that travel was an indispensable part of Crenshaw's job. We agree. Quarles provided Crenshaw with a specially equipped truck containing may of the tools that he needed to service drilling rigs scattered across several states.

DECISION AND REMEDY *The appellate court affirmed the trial court's decision that Quarles had violated FLSA but, because of a discrepancy in the factual record concerning the hours worked during a certain period of weeks, the case was remanded to the trial court for further determination of the exact number of hours to be compensated.*

MINIMUM WAGE   The Fair Labor Standards Act provides that a minimum wage of a specified amount ($4.25 per hour as of April 1, 1991) must be paid to employees in covered industries. Congress periodically revises such minimum wages. The term *wages* is meant to include the reasonable cost of the employer in furnishing employees with board, lodging, and other facilities if they are customarily furnished by that employer.

OTHER GOVERNMENT-ENFORCED MINIMUM-WAGE LAWS   In 1931, during the Great Depression, the president signed the Davis-Bacon Act,[25] which requires the payment of "prevailing wages" to employees of contractors or subcontractors working on government construction projects. In 1936 an act that extended the Davis-Bacon Act was put into effect—the Walsh-Healey Act.[26] This act requires a minimum wage as well as overtime pay of time and a half to employees of manufacturers or suppliers entering into contracts with agencies of the federal government.

---

25.   40 U.S.C. Section 276a.
26.   41 U.S.C. Section 35.

▪ Terms and Concepts to Review

bona fide occupational
   qualification (BFOQ) 415
business necessity
   defense 415
disparate-impact
   discrimination 413

disparate-treatment
   discrimination 411
employment at-will 410
general duty clause 427
protected class 411

vesting 430
whistleblowing 423
workers' compensation
   laws 425

■ Questions and Case Problems

17-1. Discuss fully which of the following situations would violate the 1964 Civil Rights Act, Title VII, as amended:

(a) Tennington, Inc., is a consulting firm with ten employees. These employees travel on consulting jobs in seven states. Tennington has an employment record of hiring only white males.

(b) Novo Films, Inc., is making a film about Africa and needs to employ approximately 100 extras for this picture. Novo advertises in all major newspapers in southern California for the hiring of these extras. The ad states that only black persons need apply.

(c) Chinawa, a major processor of cheese sold throughout the United States, employs 100 people at its principal processing plant. The plant is located in Heartland Corners, whose population is 50 percent white and 25 percent black, with the balance Hispanic, Asian, and others. Chinawa requires a high school diploma as a condition of employment for its cleanup crew. Three-fourths of the white population complete high school, compared with only one-fourth of the minority population. Chinawa has an all-white cleaning crew.

17-2. Denton and Carlo were employed at an appliance plant. Their jobs required them to do occasional maintenance work while standing on a wire mesh twenty feet above the plant floor. Other employees had fallen through the mesh, and one had been killed by the fall. When Denton and Carlo were asked by their supervisor to do work that would likely require them to walk on the mesh, they refused because they feared bodily harm or death. Because of their refusal to do the requested work, the two employees were fired. Was their discharge wrongful? If so, under what federal employment law? To what federal agency or department could they turn for assistance?

17-3. Milton Kizer had worked for Lakeway Resort since 1974, maintaining golf carts. During the next decade, he received positive job evaluations and numerous merit pay raises. He was promoted to the position of supervisor of golf cart maintenance at three courses. Then a new employee, McManus, was placed in charge of the golf courses, and he demoted Kizer, who was over the age of forty, to running one of the three cart facilities and froze his salary indefinitely. McManus also demoted five other men over the age of forty. Another cart facility was placed under the supervision of Roger Rodeman. Later, the cart facilities for three courses were again consolidated, but Rodeman—not Kiser—was put in charge. At the time, Kizer was in his forties and Rodeman was in his twenties. Rodeman said that "we are going to have to do away these . . . old and senile" men. Kizer quit and sued Lakeway for employment discrimination. Should he prevail? Explain.

17-4. Gary Segler worked for Caterpillar Tractor Co. in one of its factories. Near his work station there was a conveyor belt that ran through a large industrial oven. Some-times, the workers would use the oven to heat their meals. Thirty-inch-high flasks containing molds were fixed at regular intervals on the conveyor and were transported into the oven. Segler had to walk between the flasks to get to his work station. One morning, the conveyor was not moving, and Segler used the oven to cook a frozen pot pie. As he was removing the pot pie from the oven, the conveyor came on and a flask struck him, seriously injuring him. He sought recovery in workers' compensation. Should he recover? Why or why not?

17-5. Calzoni Boating Co. is an interstate business engaged in manufacturing and selling boats. The company has 500 nonunion employees. Representatives of these employees are requesting a four-day, ten-hours-per-day workweek, and Calzoni is concerned that this would require paying time and a half after eight hours per day. Which federal act might require this? Will it in fact require paying time and a half for all hours worked over eight hours per day if the employees' proposal is accepted? Explain.

17-6. Wise, a female employee of Mead Corp., became involved in a dispute in the lunchroom of her place of employment with another employee, Pruitt. A fight ensued, and Wise kicked and scratched Pruitt and used "abusive and uncivil" language. Because of this behavior, Wise's employment at Mead was terminated by her employer. Wise brought suit, alleging sex discrimination on the part of Mead Corp. in violation of Title VII of the Civil Rights Act of 1964, on the grounds that at least four other fights at Mead had occurred under similar circumstances and none of the participants had been fired. None of the other fights had involved a female. Did Wise's employment termination constitute sex discrimination by Mead Corp.? Discuss. [*Wise v. Mead Corp.*, 614 F.Supp. 1131 (M.D.Ga. 1985)]

17-7. At an REA Express shipping terminal, a conveyor belt was inoperative because an electrical circuit had shorted out. The manager called a licensed electrical contractor. When the contractor arrived, REA's maintenance supervisor was in the circuit breaker room. The floor was wet, and the maintenance supervisor was using sawdust to try to soak up the water. While the licensed electrical contractor was attempting to fix the short circuit, standing on the wet floor, he was electrocuted. Simultaneously, REA's maintenance supervisor, who was standing on a wooden platform, was burned and knocked unconscious. The Occupational Safety and Health Administration (OSHA) sought to fine REA Express $1,000 for failure to furnish a place of employment free from recognized hazards. Will the court uphold OSHA's decision? Explain. [*REA Express, Inc. v. Brennan*, 495 F.2d 822 (2d Cir. 1974)]

17-8. It was the policy of the New York City Transit Authority (TA) not to hire individuals who used narcotics, including methadone—a drug frequently used in the treatment of heroin addiction. Several individuals alleged that they had been either fired or refused employment by TA because of their participation in methadone programs and sued TA under Title VII, claiming that TA's policy was discriminatory in effect. The district court noted that 80 percent of the narcotics users in the New York City area were black or Hispanic, that between 62 and 65 percent of persons receiving methadone treatment in public programs in New York City were black or Hispanic, and that 81 percent of the TA employees referred to TA's medical director for suspected violation of the narcotics rule were black or Hispanic. Based on these statistics, the court held that TA's policy violated Title VII. TA appealed. Did TA's dismissal of and refusal to hire individuals involved in methadone programs constitute discrimination against blacks and Hispanics? [*New York City Transit Authority v. Beazer,* 440 U.S. 568, 99 S.Ct. 1355, 59 L.Ed.2d 587 (1979)]

17-9. Duke Power Co. was sued by a number of its black employees for practicing racial discrimination in the hiring and assigning of employees at its Dan River plant. The plant was organized into five operating departments: (1) labor, (2) coal handling, (3) operation, (4) maintenance, and (5) laboratory testing. Blacks were employed only in the labor department, where the highest-paying jobs paid less than the lowest-paying jobs in the other four departments (which employed only whites). Promotions were normally made within each department on the basis of seniority. Transferees into a department usually began in the lowest position. In 1955 the company began to require a high school education for an initial assignment into any department except the labor department. In addition, it required a high school education for any transfer from the coal handling department to any inside department (operations, maintenance, or laboratory). For ten years, this company-wide policy was enforced. In 1965, when the company abandoned its policy of restricting blacks to the labor department, a high school diploma or equivalency test was nevertheless made a prerequisite to transfer from the labor department to any other department. This requirement rendered a markedly disproportionate number of blacks ineligible for employment advancement in the company. Discuss fully whether these employer practices violated Title VII of the Civil Rights Act. [*Griggs v. Duke Power Co.,* 401 U.S. 424, 91 S.Ct. 849, 28 L.Ed.2d 158 (1971)]

17-10. Patricia Jackson, an African American female and an experienced waitress, applied for a job as a part-time waitress at a restaurant owned by Jackie McCleod in Foley, Alabama. An interview was arranged for the afternoon of June 2, 1989, which was a Friday. During the course of the interview, Jackson and McCleod entered into a verbal contract for Jackson to be hired as a part-time waitress, beginning Monday, June 5. Jackson was to work her first two days in the kitchen, and following that orientation period would start working as a waitress. On Sunday, June 4, McCleod made up the work schedule for the period June 5 through June 11. Jackson was scheduled to work four days during the week and on each of those days would be doing kitchen work. Jackson appeared for work on Monday, June 5, as agreed. When she discovered that she had been scheduled to work in the kitchen for four days, as opposed to the two-day orientation period she expected, she confronted McCleod and asked to be put on the floor as a

waitress. When her request was not granted, Jackson left the restaurant. On that same day, McCleod hired a white female for the position of waitress. Jackson sued McCleod for discrimination on the basis of race in McCleod's hiring procedures, and the issue turned on whether any discrimination occurred during the hiring of Jackson. Will Jackson prevail in court? Discuss fully. [*Jackson v. McCleod,* 748 F.Supp. 831 (S.D. Ala. 1990).]

17-11. Thirty-nine women applicants for firefighting jobs who failed the physical agility test given by the Evanston, Illinois, fire department in 1983 brought an action under Title VII against the city of Evanston. The women claimed that the test they had taken had a discriminatory impact because 85 percent of the women who took the test failed it, while only 7 percent of the men who took the test failed to pass. The test consisted of a group of tasks (carrying and climbing ladders, connecting hoses to fire hydrants, and so on) that had to be performed consecutively by each applicant without a break and while wearing a firefighter's uniform. The complaint focused to a great extent on the way in which the test was scored. The test was timed. In 1983, to obtain a passing score, an applicant had to perform all of the tasks in 628 seconds, as opposed to 890 seconds in 1981 and 915 seconds in 1985. Anyone who failed the physical agility test could not go on to take the two other tests (an intelligence test and a test measuring psychological stability) required of job applicants. The question before the court was whether the test, including the method of scoring, was reasonably related to the fire department's legitimate need for physically strong firefighters. What should the court decide? Discuss fully. [*Evans v. City of Evanston,* 881 F.2d 382 (7th Cir. 1989)]

17-12. Richard Winters was an at-will employee for the Houston Chronicle from April 1977 to June 1986. Beginning in 1980, he became aware of alleged illegal activities carried out by other employees. He claimed that the Chronicle was falsely reporting an inflated number of paid subscribers, that several employees were engaged in inventory theft, and that his supervisor offered him an opportunity to participate in a kickback scheme with the manufacturers of plastic bags. Winters reported all these activities to upper-level management in January 1986 but made no report to law enforcement agencies. He was fired six months later. He sued the Chronicle for wrongful termination. How should the court decide? Discuss fully. [*Winters v. Houston Chronicle Publishing,* 795 S.W.2d 723 (Tex. 1990)]

17-13. A Question of Ethics

Paul Luedtke was employed by Nabors Alaska Drilling, Inc., to work on the company's drilling rigs on Alaska's North Slope. Over the course of his employment, Luedtke was promoted to driller, a position in which he was responsible for overseeing the work of an entire drilling crew. Twice during Luedtke's employment he was accused of violating company drug and alcohol policies, and he was once disciplined for taking alcohol to the North Slope in contravention of company regulations. Sometime later, Luedtke

was ordered to submit to a physical examination, ostensibly to meet the company's physical standards for work on offshore drilling rigs. As part of the examination, Luedtke's urine was tested for drugs. The results indicated marijuana use, and Luedtke was ordered to submit to and pass two subsequent drug tests before continuing employment with the company. Luedtke refused to comply and was fired. Luedtke brought suit against the company on the basis of several legal theories. The Alaska Supreme Court held that the common law of Alaska expressed a public policy of protecting certain "spheres of employee conduct" and " 'private' information" from scrutiny by private employers. The court went on to find, however, that such policy did not protect Luedtke because the drug testing was based on the company's legitimate need to control drug use in a hazardous environment like the one in which Luedtke was employed. [Luedtke v. Nabors Alaska Drilling, Inc., 768 P.2d 1123 (S.Ct. of Alaska, 1989)]

1. The court in this case stated that the public policy of the state protected off-the-job activities and that companies could only test employees at times "contemporaneous with the employee's work time" and only if testing was for the limited purpose of "monitoring drug use that may directly affect employee performance." Legal arguments aside, is this a fair restriction on employers? Society seeks to protect against racial and other forms of discrimination in the workplace but generally leaves employers free to choose workers on the basis of whatever other criteria they deem fit. Should private employers be free to discharge or not hire workers on the basis of characteristics they find objectionable—like drug use, for instance—regardless of the relation between those characteristics and work performance?

2. Even if a worker's off-the-job life-style does not "directly affect employee performance," are there other practical considerations that support an employer's wanting to know about certain employee characteristics? Could not certain "private" activities affect a worker's long-term health and life expectancy? This is certainly a practical concern of an employer, if not a moral one. Should any other social goal—the right to privacy, say—take precedence over such practical considerations?

3. Could investigation into the private affairs of an employee be justified as indicating the employee's propensities for other conduct important to the employer? For example, does illegal drug use demonstrate a propensity to break other laws? What about marital infidelity—are unfaithful spouses likely to be employees prone to stealing or embezzling from an employer? In general, how limited should an employee's expectation of privacy be?

17-14. Case Briefing Assignment

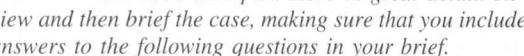

Examine Case A.17 [Johnston v. Del Mar Distributing Co., 776 S.W.2d 768 (Tex.App.—Corpus Christi 1989)] in Appendix A. The case has been excerpted there in great detail. Review and then brief the case, making sure that you include answers to the following questions in your brief.

1. Why did Del Mar Distributing Co. terminate Nancy Johnston's employment?

2. What defense did Del Mar raise against Johnston's claim of wrongful discharge?

3. On what case precedent did the appellate court base its reasoning?

4. Why did the appellate court conclude that, given the circumstances of this case, it was irrelevant whether the act that Johnston was asked to perform was legal or illegal?

The Employment Environment

The employment environment is one in which individuals come together for the purpose of achieving a common purpose. In this sense, the employment environment is like most others we have examined thus far. Yet in spite of the similarities, the employment environment remains unique.

Part of the uniqueness of the employment environment stems from the close nature of the relationship between employers and employees, a relationship that, as seen in this unit, often involves intricate duties of agency. In earlier times, most individuals were self-employed, usually on the family farm. The farm was the center of the family unit. At any given time, several generations might have their entire social and financial security invested in the family farm.

With the onset of the Industrial Revolution, this structure gave way to another—one in which individuals worked with and depended on those individuals that did not share the special bonds of family relationship. Yet because employment relationships typically exist for an extended period, there was inevitably a tendency to incorporate aspects of the family into the employment environment. The result has been that there is sometimes a conflict between the impersonal nature of the market—labor is, after all, a factor of production—and the family-like aspect of the close, long-term relations between an employer and employee. Moreover, the aspects that account for the uniqueness of the employment environment generate numerous ethical issues. In this unit's focus on ethics we examine two such issues. First, we examine the ethical problems surrounding the high degree of loyalty demanded in an agency relationship. Second, we examine the degree to which society should rely on business to utilize affirmative action programs in eliminating the lingering social problem of discrimination against minorities.

The Duties of Agents and Principals

The very nature of the principal-agent relationship is one of trust, which we call a fiduciary relationship. Because of this, it is expected that an agent owes certain duties to the principal. These duties include being loyal and obedient, informing the principal of important facts concerning the agency, accounting to the principal for property or money received, and performing with reasonable diligence and skill. Assuming that agents owe certain fiduciary duties to their principals, do principals have corresponding ethical duties to agents? In the law, principals do have certain defined duties, such as compensation and reimbursement of certain expenses. There are, however, questions concerning the ethical obligations a principal has towards his or her agent.

In this section we look first at the ethical issues associated with the duties owed by an agent to his or her principal. We then turn our focus to issues surrounding those duties the principal owes an agent.

The Duty of the Agent to the Principal

Ethical conduct would prevent an agent from representing two principals in the same transaction, or making a secret profit from the agency relationship, or failing to disclose the interest of the agent in property the principal was purchasing. The expected ethical conduct of the agent has evolved into rules that, if breached, cause the agent to be held liable.

What about looking beyond the duty to the principal and

436

considering one's duty to society? Consider, for example, that some employees of Firestone knew that tires the company was making in the early 1980s were defective. Presumably, they could have divulged that information to the public—at the risk of losing their jobs, of course. Consider also that employees in other industries were aware of deliberate and fraudulent cost overruns on government contracts. They could have made this information public, once again at the risk of losing their jobs. In these and similar circumstances, an employee's duty to follow one's conscience conflicts with the duty of loyalty to the principal. How such conflicts are resolved can have a profound impact on society: some scholars have argued that many of the greatest "evils" in the past twenty-five years have been accomplished in the name of "duty" to the principal. *Duty* in this context means placing the well-being of the principal above that of the public.

It is too simplistic, though, to think that such ethical dilemmas always can be resolved by looking to society's interest ahead of those of a principal's. "Society" seldom has a uniform opinion on where its best interests lie. Everyone may agree that selling defective tires or cheating the government is wrong as well as detrimental to society, but there are other areas that do not present such clear alternatives. In such instances, perhaps the most that can be asked of an agent is that he or she follow his or her own conscience.

The Duty of the Principal to the Agent

Principals owe their agents a duty of cooperation. One might expect most principals to cooperate with their agents out of self-interest, but this is not universally the case. Suppose a principal hires an agent on commission to sell a building, and the agent puts considerable time and expense into the process. If the principal changes his or her mind and decides to retain the building, he or she might want to prevent the agent from completing a sale. Is such action ethical, or does it violate a principal's duty of cooperation? What alternatives would such a principal have?

Another duty of principals is to provide safe working conditions. The principal therefore should not expose agents to unreasonable hazards as they go about their work. The definition of *safe* remains a difficult one, however, as almost every job probably entails some degree of unavoidable risk. Suppose an employer hires a delivery person and supplies a truck. Must the truck contain seat belts to ensure safe working conditions? What about airbags or special safety glass?

Although a principal is legally obligated to fulfill certain duties to the agent, these duties do not include any specific duty of loyalty. Some argue that the lack of employer loyalty to employees leads to a reduction of employee loyalty to employers. After all, they maintain, why should an employee be loyal to an employer's interests over the years when the employee knows that there is no corresponding legal duty on the part of the employer to be loyal to the employee's interests. Employers who do show a sense of loyalty to employees— for example, by not laying off long-time, faithful employees when business is slow or when those employees could be replaced by younger workers at lower cost—base that sense of loyalty primarily on ethical, not legal, considerations.

Significantly, most of the duties described above are negotiable at law. In forming a contract, the principal and the agent can extend or abridge many of the ordinary duties owed in such a relationship. Legal rules generally come into play when the contract is silent or ambiguous on a particular point. Allowing the parties to negotiate their relative duties seems ethically fair, as long as the parties are able to understand their rights and make informed decisions.

Racial Equality in the Workplace

Society has definitely changed its thinking with respect to employment. In the past, employers were not required to hire, retain, and promote employees with equality. Equal opportunity regulations were therefore designed to reduce or eliminate discriminatory practices. Attempts at "making up" for past patterns of discrimination have resulted in affirmative action programs. Many of these affirmative action programs have resulted in what has been termed "reverse discrimination" against majority groups. Such reverse discrimination raises the ethical issue of how far society should go in trying to remedy the effects of past discrimination against minorities.

Striving for Equality

In *United Steelworkers of America v. Weber*,[1] the United States Supreme Court ruled that

---

1. 443 U.S. 193, 99 S.Ct. 2721, 61 L.Ed.2d 480 (1979).

private employers legally can give special preferences to African-American workers to "eliminate racial imbalance" in traditionally white-only jobs. The Court held that voluntary affirmative action plans, even those containing numerical quotas, do not automatically violate the Civil Rights Act of 1964. (Title VII of the act bars employment discrimination on the basis of race.) The Court's decision came a year after the case of *University of California Regents v. Bakke,*[2] in which the Court struck down a rigid quota system for admission to a California state medical school. The *Bakke* decision turned on the proper application of Title VI of the Civil Rights Act, which prohibits discrimination on the basis of race in federally funded programs. In contrast, the *Weber* case, in the Court's view, concerned strictly *private, voluntary* action. But even if that is a valid legal distinction, does it resolve the ethical issues involved?

The Court conceded that the literal language of Title VII of the Civil Rights Act would appear to outlaw racial preferences in hiring. But the Court emphasized the historical context in which Congress enacted the law and the obvious intention of the legislature in writing the law to improve economic conditions of African Americans and other minorities. The view that Title VI "forbade all race-conscious affirmative action," said the Court, "would bring about [a result] at variance with the purpose of the statute and must be rejected."

Ethical Considerations

The *Weber* decision leaves business with considerable discretion in tailoring affirmative action programs. Discretion, however, opens up ethical considerations. Business must strive to balance different, often conflicting goals, in the employment environment if it is to approach the problem ethically.

Consider some of the dominant themes in striving for racial equality within the workforce in light of the *Weber* decision. Do those who have been discriminated against in the past deserve preferential treatment today? Does such preferential status infringe on the rights of others to equal consideration in hiring and promotion? Even though preferential treatment to remedy past discrimination is legal, it nonetheless raises difficult ethical questions.

All antidiscrimination laws carry with them the possibility of leading to reverse discrimination. When they do, they come into conflict with the ethical principle that employees and job candidates should be treated fairly. There is no easy solution.

Laws prohibiting employment discrimination can also come into conflict with other societal goals. Should women, for example, be hired as firefighters by a fire department if they cannot perform firefighting jobs with the same strength and agility as males? Would employing female firefighters jeopardize—to even a small extent—the safety of a town's citizens? What is the trade-off here?

These same questions arose in *Evans v. City of Evanston.*[3]

Thirty-nine women failed to pass an agility test that was required of all candidates for employment as firefighters. The women brought a class-action suit against the city. They claimed that the agility test clearly had a "disparate impact" on women, because 85 percent of the women who took the test failed it, while only 7 percent of the men failed. Consequently, there were no women among Evanston's 106 firefighters (although at one time there had been two women). Because the test had a disparate impact, it was in violation of Title VII— unless the employer could demonstrate that the test served a legitimate interest of the fire department. At trial, the court agreed that the test related to the employer's need for physically strong firefighters. Certain technicalities in the scoring were noted at trial, however, which led to a judgment in favor of the plaintiffs. On appeal, the case was remanded to the trial court for consideration. One of the points made by the appellate court was that the initial agility test prevented most female candidates from taking the other two tests—of intelligence and psychological stability—required of all job candidates.

The ethical issue here is, of course, a touchy one. What if, in fact, the women who could not pass the agility test—but presumably could pass the other two tests—were nonetheless employed as firefighters? Would their employment endanger the safety of the town's citizens? Perhaps it would be more feasible for the fire department to allow all candidates to take all three tests and allocate available jobs on the basis of a combined score. Perhaps some

---

2. 438 U.S. 265, 98 S.Ct. 2733, 57 L.Ed.2d 750 (1978).

3. 881 F.2d 382 (7th Cir. 1989).

other solution is available. The key issue is how society balances its need for safe, efficient fire protection against its duty to provide each individual member the maximum opportunity to participate fully in all phases of society.

Business is a major social institution. It not only provides the goods and services that society desires, but it also is the vehicle by which individuals obtain the means to acquire those goods and services. Jobs and business ownership reflect not only material well-being, but status and a form of self-expression as well. As a major social institution affecting all these aspects of social life, business can play a dominate role in the perpetuation or elimination of discrimination against minorities. But how should business fulfill this role?

As noted, the law has set certain standards for business regarding discrimination in the workplace. As also noted from our reference to the *Weber* case, there remain areas of discretion for business in the matters of employment discrimination. Where the law leaves off, ethical considerations

remain. And because the law is constantly in flux, particularly in the area of civil rights, business's attitutes strongly influence future civil rights laws. These attitudes must be based, at least in part, on ethical considerations.

■ Discussion Questions

1. How much obedience and loyalty does an employee owe an employer? What if the employer engages in an activity—or requests the employee to engage in an activity—that violates the employee's ethical standards but does not necessarily violate any public policy or law? In such a situation, does an employee's duty to abide by his or her own ethical standards override the employee's duty of loyalty to the employer?

2. The termination of an agency agreement can occur by operation of law. In particular, when unforeseen circumstances (such as impossibility of performance or bankruptcy) occur, termination by operation of law may take place. What

ethical considerations are involved here?

3. When an agency is terminated by an act of the parties, the law requires that third parties who have dealt with the agency be notified of the termination. What purpose does notification serve? Are the reasons for this requirement based on any ethical considerations?

4. An employer's affirmative-action policy may conflict with the interests of its current employees and their union. How should such a company balance its duties under labor law with those under discrimination law?

5. The traditional doctrine of at-will employment allows employers to fire whomever they choose for any or no cause. Developments in both statutory and common law have eroded the effectiveness of this doctrine. Do you believe that society has gone too far in the direction of protecting the interests of employees as opposed to the interests of employers? How can these often conflicting interests most appropriately be balanced?

UNIT FIVE

The Regulatory Environment

■ The Importance of Government Regulation

If this text had been written a hundred years ago, it would have had little to say about government regulation. In the 1890s, the beginnings of federal antitrust law were manifested in the form of the Interstate Commerce Commission Act and the Sherman Act, but there was little or no legislation affecting consumer protection or environmental issues. Property law existed in much the same form it had since the 1600s when it was developed as part of the common law of England, to be later carried to the new world by English colonists. Land-use control, however, was virtually nonexistent. Likewise, securities regulation would not begin to develop into its modern form until the 1930s when the Roosevelt administration devised an extensive federal scheme to deal with the perceived abuses of the stock market thought to have brought on the Great Depression.

Today, in contrast, government regulation permeates the entire business community. Administrative agencies generate voluminous rules by which businesses must abide. Indeed, no businessperson can expect to fully understand how business works in America without understanding administrative agencies and regulation. State and federal regulations with respect to packaging and labeling, advertising, and the dumping of toxic waste affect numerous businesses.

Chapter 18, which opens this unit on government regulation, provides an introduction to consumer protection law. The important area of environmental law is covered in Chapter 19. Chapters 20 and 21 deal with antitrust law. Chapter 20 introduces the federal scheme and examines the law governing monopolization, attempts to monopolize, and predatory pricing practices. Chapter 21 extensively covers the various forms of concerted action among firms that threaten free and open competition. Chapter 22 deals with the regulation of transactions in corporate securities. The unit concludes with an examination of the basic framework of real property law and land-use control in Chapter 23.

■ Ethical Issues in Government Regulation

From a very broad perspective, ethical issues in government regulation arise because regulation, by its very nature, means that some traditional rights and freedoms have to be given up to ensure other rights and freedoms. Essentially, government regulation brings two ethical principles into conflict. On the one hand, deeply embedded in American culture is the idea that the government should play a limited role in directing our lives. On the other hand, one of the basic functions of government is to protect the constitutional rights of individuals and, in the business community, the "little guy" from the "big guy." Therefore, Americans have pressured Congress to regulate business activities that result in harm to consumers and thwart competition in the marketplace.

Questions of fairness inevitably arise. Has the government gone too far in regulating a certain industry? Is the way in which regulation is carried out a little too arbitrary? Are the costs of compliance too burdensome for businesses—and for society—to bear? At what point, for example, is increased environmental protection simply too costly? If manufacturers ceased all production and Americans returned to the rural life of earlier times, the environment would certainly benefit. Obviously, Americans do not want to pay that high a "cost." Undoubtedly, we want to enjoy the fruits of our advanced economy. But environmental protection means that some sacrifices will have to be made. How much are we willing to sacrifice today to ensure that future generations have a more healthful world in which to live? In a similar vein, land-use control protects future generations as well as those of the present generation who are affected by the way their neighbors use their land. To what degree should landowners be constrained in putting their land to its most profitable use? These are very broad questions, but they are ethical in nature because they ultimately relate to notions of what is right, just, or good.

Chapter 18

Consumer Law

Many of the agencies and administrative regulatory processes described in Chapter 6 are geared toward what has become a vast area of government regulation: consumer protection. Consumer transactions take a variety of forms but broadly include those that involve an exchange of value for the purpose of acquiring goods, services, land, or credit for personal or family use. Traditionally in disputes involving consumers, it was assumed that the freedom to contract carried with it the obligation to live by the deal made. Therefore, the watchword in most such transactions was *caveat emptor*— "let the buyer beware." Over time, this attitude has changed considerably. Today myriad federal and state laws protect consumers from unfair trade practices, unsafe products, discriminatory or unreasonable credit requirements, and other problems related to consumer transactions.

In this chapter, we focus primarily on federal legislation, partly because of its wider applicability and partly because much state legislation closely parallels the federal laws. As a general rule, state consumer protection is more stringent. An important source of consumer protection on the state level is provided by those portions of the Uniform Commercial Code—adopted by virtually all of the states—that deal with unconscionable sales practices and warranties.

■ Advertising

The earliest federal consumer protection law was the Federal Trade Commission Act, and it is still one of the most important. As discussed in Chapter 6, the act created the Federal Trade Commission (FTC) to carry out the broadly stated goal of preventing unfair and deceptive trade practices.[1]

Unfair and Deceptive Advertising

Advertising will be deemed deceptive if a consumer would be misled by the advertising claim. Vague generalities and obvious exaggerations are permissible. These claims are known as **puffing.** When a claim takes on the

1. 15 U.S.C. Section 45.

appearance of literal authenticity, however, it may create problems. Advertising that would *appear* to be based on factual evidence but that in fact is scientifically untrue will be deemed deceptive. A classic example is provided by a 1944 case in which the claim that a skin cream would restore youthful qualities to aged skin was deemed deceptive.[2] An-

---

2. *Charles of the Ritz Distributing Corp. v. Federal Trade Commission,* 143 F.2d 676 (2d Cir. 1944).

other advertising practice that has been attacked by the FTC as deceptive involves misleading price claims. For example, advertising to sell two cans of paint for the price of one and then setting a very high unit price has been held to be deceptive. The FTC also regulates advertising that contains the endorsements of celebrities. An advertisement may be deemed deceptive if the celebrity actually makes no use of the product. In the following case, advertisements of a sunburn treatment were alleged to be deceptive.

BACKGROUND AND FACTS *The Federal Trade Commission staff's advertising substantiation rule held that advertisements must be substantiated by well-controlled scientific studies, or the claims would be considered deceptive. The staff brought an action against Pfizer, Inc., because the claims made by Pfizer in its advertisements for a sunburn treatment were allegedly unsupported by direct studies on humans. Pfizer argued that it had other forms of evidence sufficient to support its advertising claims. The administrative law judge who heard this adjudication dismissed the complaint against Pfizer, holding that no controlled scientific studies should be required. The staff appealed this dismissal to the commission itself.*

 *Case 18.1*

IN RE PFIZER, INC.
Federal Trade Commission, 1972.
81 F.T.C. 23.

KIRKPATRICK, Commissioner.

The Commission's staff counsel, who have the burden of proving the allegations of the complaint, challenge certain advertising by Pfizer for the product "UN-BURN," a nonprescription product recommended for use on minor burns and sunburn. The complaint cited the following radio and television advertising for Un-Burn as typical and representative:

New Un-Burn actually anesthetizes *nerves* in sensitive sunburned skin.

Un-Burn relieves pain *fast*. Actually *anesthetizes nerves* in sensitive sunburned skin.

* * * Sunburned skin is sensitive skin * * * Sensitive sunburned skin needs * * * UN-BURN. New UN-BURN contains the same local anesthetic doctors often use. * * * Actually anesthetizes nerves in sensitive sunburned skin. I'll tell you what I like about UN-BURN. It's the best friend a blonde ever had! * * * I'm a blonde * * * and I know what it means to have sensitive skin. Why I'm half afraid of moon burn! That's why I'm mad about UN-BURN. It stops sunburn pain in * * * less time than it takes me to slip out of my bikini. * * *

The complaint alleges that the foregoing advertising claims were not substantiated by Pfizer by "adequate and well-controlled scientific studies or tests prior to the making of such statements."

* * * *

Given the imbalance of knowledge and resources between a business enterprise and each of its customers, economically it is more rational, and imposes far less cost on society, to require a manufacturer to confirm his affirmative product claims rather than impose a burden upon each individual consumer to test, investigate, or experiment for himself. The manufacturer has the ability, the knowhow, the equipment, the time and the resources to undertake such information by testing or otherwise— the consumer usually does not.

*   *   *   *

Pfizer's director of Marketing testified that he took three measures to satisfy himself as to the efficacy of the product Un-Burn. First, he received "complete assurance" from Pfizer's medical people that the claims he planned to use for Un-Burn could be supported by the two active ingredients in the quantities in which they were to be used in the product. He was assured that the way a topical anesthetic works is to anesthetize nerves and thereby stop pain. He was also assured by the "medical people" that the product was patterned very closely after the market leader, Solarcaine. Secondly, he was assured that all available literature or information on these two active ingredients had been thoroughly reviewed and favorable conclusions derived from this review as to the efficacy of the ingredients as topical anesthetics. Finally, he personally reviewed all competitive advertising to satisfy himself that Pfizer would not be claiming anything more than other products with the same active ingredients. The director of marketing testified that Pfizer did not conduct tests on humans to determine whether the efficacy claims could be supported, but consciously "accepted another method of satisfying" themselves by going over the history of the ingredients. No specific tests were conducted on human beings to prove that UnBurn anesthetizes nerve ends.

*   *   *   *

While the Commission finds that respondent failed in its attempt to demonstrate affirmatively the existence of a reasonable basis for its Un-Burn advertising, the evidence is not sufficient to prove that respondent in fact *lacked* a reasonable basis for its advertising claims. The record evidence is simply inconclusive with regard to the adequacy of the medical literature and clinical experience relied upon by respondent, and with regard to the reasonableness of such reliance.

DECISION AND REMEDY   *The FTC affirmed the administrative law judge's decision and dismissed the complaint against Pfizer. In so doing, the FTC upheld the concept that advertising must be substantiated, but it went on to hold that the staff had not met its burden of proof in demonstrating that Pfizer's advertising was insufficiently substantiated.*

Bait-and-Switch Advertising

The FTC has promulgated specific rules to govern some advertising techniques. One of the most important rules is contained in the FTC's *Guides on Bait Advertising.*[3] The rule is designed to prevent **bait-and-switch advertising**—that is, advertising a very low price for a particular item that will likely be unavailable to the consumer, who will then be encouraged to purchase a more expensive item. The low price is the "bait" to lure the consumer into the store. The salesperson is instructed to "switch" the consumer to a different item. Under the FTC guidelines, bait-and-switch advertising occurs if the seller refuses to show the advertised

item, fails to have in stock a reasonable quantity of the item, fails to promise to deliver the advertised item within a reasonable time, or discourages employees from selling the item.

FTC Actions against Deceptive Advertising

As described in the last chapter in regard to agency enforcement generally, an FTC action begins with an investigation after the commission receives a complaint. The investigation may lead to a hearing and ultimately a *cease-and-desist order*—an order that the business cease and desist its advertising practice. Under certain circumstances, the FTC may also recover civil penalties. The FTC has also employed three other remedies relating to advertising. First, the FTC may compel **affirmative**

---

3. 16 C.F.R. Part 238.

advertising, which requires a firm to provide specific information in its advertisement so as to prevent consumers from being misled. Second, the FTC may require **counteradvertising**—or corrective advertising—in which the advertiser admits that prior claims about a product were untrue. Finally, the FTC may institute **multiple product orders,** which require a firm to cease and desist from false advertising not only in regard to the product that was the subject of the action but also in regard to all the firm's other products.

Counteradvertising is a harsh remedy and can be a particularly costly one for sellers. But, as the case below indicates, if an advertiser has made false claims about a product for years and years, simply ceasing from making the false claims may not be enough to dispel the illusions created about the product from consumers' minds.

 Case 18.2

WARNER-LAMBERT CO. v. FEDERAL TRADE COMMISSION

United States Court of Appeals, District of Columbia Circuit, 1977.
562 F.2d 749.

BACKGROUND AND FACTS   *Warner-Lambert Company began making Listerine in 1879, using the same formula employed today. As early as 1921, the firm began claiming that Listerine prevented colds and sore throats or lessened their severity. After medical testing conducted by the FTC revealed these claims to be false, the FTC filed a complaint that charged Warner-Lambert with misrepresenting the efficacy of Listerine against colds. On the basis of the evidence obtained through the testing, the administrative law judge sustained the complaint. The FTC affirmed the judge's findings and ordered Warner-Lambert to cease and desist from making the claims. The FTC further ordered Warner-Lambert to ''cease and desist from disseminating any advertisement for Listerine unless it is clearly and conspicuously disclosed in each such advertisement, in the exact language below that: 'Contrary to prior advertising, Listerine will not help prevent colds or sore throats or lessen their severity.' This requirement extends only to the next ten million dollars of Listerine advertising.''   Warner-Lambert appealed the FTC's ruling.*

J. SKELLY WRIGHT, Circuit Judge.

*   *   *   *

The Commission has adopted the following standard for the imposition of corrective advertising:

[I]f a deceptive advertisement has played a substantial role in creating or reinforcing in the public's mind a false and material belief which lives on after the false advertising ceases, there is clear and continuing injury to competition and to the consuming public as consumers continue to make purchasing decisions based on the false belief. Since this injury cannot be averted by merely requiring respondent to cease disseminating the advertisement, we may appropriately order respondent to take affirmative action designed to terminate the otherwise continuing ill effects of the advertisement.

We think this standard is entirely reasonable. It dictates two factual inquiries: (1) did Listerine's advertisements play a substantial role in creating or reinforcing in the public's mind a false belief about the product? and (2) would this belief linger on after the false advertising ceases? It strikes us that if the answer to both questions is not yes, companies everywhere may be wasting their massive advertising budgets. Indeed, it is more than a little peculiar to hear [Warner-Lambert] assert that its commercials really have no effect on consumer belief.

*   *   *   *

*   *   * In this case it has been found that Warner-Lambert has, over a long period of time, worked a substantial deception upon the public; it has advertised

Listerine as a cure for colds, and consumers have purchased its product with that in mind. That the Commission has the authority to prohibit Warner-Lambert from continuing to make such false and deceptive claims in its advertisements is not disputed * * *. Here, however, the FTC has determined on substantial evidence that the deception of the public occasioned by Warner-Lambert's past advertisements will not be halted by merely requiring Warner-Lambert to cease making such claims in the future. To be sure, current and future advertising of Listerine, when viewed in isolation, may not contain any statements which are themselves deceptive. But reality counsels that such advertisements cannot be viewed in isolation; they must be seen against the background of over 50 years in which Listerine has been proclaimed—and purchased—as a remedy for colds. When viewed from this perspective, advertising which fails to rebut the prior claims as to Listerine's efficacy inevitably builds upon those claims; continued advertising continues the deception, albeit implicitly rather than explicitly. It will induce people to continue to buy Listerine thinking it will cure colds. Thus the Commission found on substantial evidence that the corrective order was necessary to "dissipate the effects of respondent's deceptive representations."

DECISION AND REMEDY

The United States Court of Appeals for the District of Columbia affirmed the FTC's ruling, holding that the corrective advertising was necessary and that the duration of the corrective advertising—which had to be continued for the next $10 million worth of advertising for Listerine—was reasonable. The only modification made to the ruling by the court of appeals was that Warner-Lambert did not have to include the words "contrary to prior advertising" in its corrective advertising.

ETHICAL CONSIDERATIONS

The court briefly considered the argument that corrective advertising orders, such as the one issued to Warner-Lambert, could have a "chilling effect" on (act as a disincentive to) free commercial speech—that is, on truthful advertising. A firm might be less likely to engage in advertising, given the possibility that it might be forced, at some future date, to include in its advertising specific disclaimers. The court was not worried. Not only did a substantial government interest—protecting citizens against deception—exist to justify any restraint placed on commercial speech by the requirement of corrective advertising, but also the court believed that no significant chilling effect would likely result from the restraint. Quoting from an opinion of the United States Supreme Court on a similar issue, the court of appeals held that "[s]ince advertising is the sine qua non *of [essential to] commercial profits, there is little likelihood of its being chilled by proper regulation and forgone entirely."*

■ Labeling and Packaging Laws

In addition to the broad restrictions on advertising, a number of federal and state laws deal specifically with the information given on labels and packages. The restrictions are designed to provide accurate information about the product and to warn about possible dangers from its use or misuse. In general, labels must be accurate. That is, they must use words as those words are understood by the ordinary consumer. For example, a box of cereal cannot be labeled "giant" if it would exaggerate the amount of cereal contained in the box. In some instances, labels must specify the raw materials used in the product, such as the percentage of cotton, nylon, or other fibers used in a garment. In other instances, the products must carry a warning. Cigarette packages and advertising, for example, must include one of several warnings about the health hazards associated with smoking.[4]

The numerous federal laws include the Fur Products Labeling Act of 1951, the Wool Products Labeling Act of 1939, the Flammable Fabrics Act of 1953, the Smokeless Tobacco Health Education Act of 1986, and the Fair Packaging and Labeling Act of 1966. The Smokeless Tobacco Health Education Act, for example, requires that producers, packagers, and importers of smokeless tobacco label their product with one of several warnings about the health hazards associated with the use of smokeless tobacco similar to those contained on ordinary tobacco product packages. The Fair Packaging and Labeling Act requires that products possess labels that identify the product; the net quantity of the contents, as well as the quantity of servings, if the number of servings is stated; the manufacturer; and the packager or distributor. The act also provides authority to add requirements concerning words used to describe packages, terms that are associated with savings claims, information disclosures for ingredients in nonfood products, and standards for the partial filling of packages. The most recent standard requires that food products bear labels detailing nutrition, including how much fat a product contains and what kind of fat it is. These restrictions are enforced by the Department of Health and Human Services, as well as the Federal Trade Commission.

■ Sales

Many of the laws that protect consumers concern the disclosure of certain terms in sales transactions and provide rules governing the various forms of sales, such as door-to-door sales, mail-order sales, referral sales, and the unsolicited receipt of merchandise. Much of the federal regulation of sales is conducted by the FTC under its regulatory authority to curb unfair trade practices. Other federal agencies, however, are involved to various degrees. For example, the Federal Reserve Board of Governors has issued Regulation Z, which governs credit provisions associated with sales contracts. Numerous state laws are also relevant. Many states, for example, have enacted laws governing home

sale transactions. Moreover, as noted earlier, states have provided a number of consumer protection provisions through the adoption of the Uniform Commercial Code. Also important is the Uniform Consumer Credit Code,[5] which has been adopted by some states.

Door-to-Door Sales

A door-to-door sale is any transaction that is initiated by a visit to, and concluded at, the buyer's home—as distinct from some other place such as the seller's showroom or office. Certain features of this type of sales activity have prompted concern. For one thing, because repeat purchases are less likely than with store sales, sellers are less constrained by the need to build up goodwill with regular customers. Additionally, individuals may feel more pressure when cornered in their own home by a persistent salesperson; they may simply buy to get rid of an obnoxious salesperson standing at the front door.

For these reasons, door-to-door sales are regulated both at the state level and by the federal government. States have enacted "cooling-off" legislation, which permits a buyer to rescind a door-to-door purchase if the election is made within a certain period of time. The FTC has also mandated a three-day cooling-off period, but when state legislation is more favorable to the buyer, the latter will govern the sale. In addition, the FTC requires the seller to notify the buyer of the right to cancel the sale within the specified time, and if the sale is originally conducted in Spanish, notice must also be given in Spanish.

Telephone and Mail-Order Sales

Sales made by either telephone or mail order are the greatest source of complaints to the nation's Better Business Bureaus. Many mail-order houses are far removed from the buyers to whom the houses sell, thus making the burden greater in bringing a complaint against the seller. Many states, therefore, have enacted consumer protection laws that parallel and supplement the fed-

---

4. 15 U.S.C. Sections 1331 *et seq.*

5. Regulation Z and the Uniform Consumer Credit Code, as well as consumer credit laws generally, are discussed more fully in a subsequent section in this chapter.

eral laws against mail fraud. In addition, the Postal Reorganization Act of 1970 provides that *unsolicited* merchandise sent by U.S. mail may be retained, used, discarded, or disposed of in any manner deemed appropriate, without the recipient incurring any obligation to the sender.

FTC Regulation of Specific Industries

Over the last decade, the FTC has begun to target certain sales practices on an industry-wide basis. Two examples are the used-car business and the funeral-home trade. In 1984 the FTC enacted a rule that requires used-car dealers to affix a "Buyer's Guide" label to all cars sold on their lots. The label must disclose the following: (1) the car's warranty or a statement that the car is being sold "as is," (2) information regarding any service contract or promises being made by the dealer, and (3) a suggestion that the purchaser obtain both an inspection of the car and a written statement of any promises made by the dealer.

In 1984 the FTC also enacted rules requiring that funeral homes provide customers with itemized prices of all charges incurred for a funeral. In addition, the regulations prohibit funeral homes from requiring specific embalming procedures or specific types of caskets for bodies that are to be cremated.

Real Estate Sales

Various federal and state laws apply to consumer transactions involving real estate. These laws are designed to prevent fraud and to provide buyers with certain types of information. In some cases, these protections mirror those provided in non–real estate sales. The disclosure requirements of the Truth-in-Lending Act, which will be discussed in detail shortly, apply to a number of real estate transactions. Differences exist, however, between the disclosure requirements for real estate and for non–real estate transactions. For example, in certain real estate transactions, consumer buyers are given a right to rescind their purchase contract if certain disclosures are not made to them. Moreover, under certain circumstances, the Truth-in-Lending Act provides the consumer with a right to rescind even though a creditor has made all of the required disclosures.[6]

INTERSTATE LAND SALES FULL DISCLOSURE ACT   The Interstate Land Sales Full Disclosure Act[7] was passed by Congress in 1968, and it is administered by the Department of Housing and Urban Development (HUD). The purpose of the act is to ensure disclosure of certain information to consumers so that they can make intelligent decisions about land purchases. The act is similar to the Securities Act of 1933 in both purpose and design. The act requires any seller or lessor of one hundred or more lots of unimproved land, if the sale or lease is part of a common promotional plan, to file an initial "statement of record" with HUD's Office of Interstate Land Sales Registration. The act only applies if the promotional plan can be deemed part of interstate commerce. But, as in cases involving securities, this is generally an easy requirement to meet. For example, even strictly local sales might be considered interstate commerce if transacted in part over the phone; although the calls might be local, the phone lines traverse state boundaries. For the same reason, use of the mail system is likely to ensure that a promotional plan is in the stream of interstate commerce.

Once the initial statement is filed, it must be approved by HUD before the developer can begin to offer the land for sale or lease. The act also provides purchasers with a private right of action for the land promoter's fraud, misrepresentation, or noncompliance with pertinent provisions of the act. Criminal penalties are provided under the act, and HUD is given certain rights with regard to inspections, injunctions, and prosecution of offenses. Three provisions of the act provide purchasers with rights of rescission (cancellation).

REAL ESTATE SETTLEMENT PROCEDURES ACT   For many individuals, purchasing a home involves a bewildering array of settlement procedures and requirements. Settlement may require title insurance, attorneys' fees, appraisal fees, taxes, insurance, and brokers' fees. To aid home buyers, federal legislation requires specific disclosures regarding settlement procedures. The 1976 revisions of the Real Estate Settlement Procedures Act make the following stipulations:

1.   Within three business days after a person applies for a mortgage loan, the lender must send a

---

6. 15 U.S.C. Section 1635. For example, see Case 18.3.

7. 15 U.S.C. Sections 1701 *et seq.*

booklet prepared by HUD that explains the settlement procedures, describes the costs to the potential buyer, and outlines the applicant's legal rights.

2. Within the three-day period, the lender must give an estimate of most of the settlement costs.

3. The lender must clearly identify individuals or firms that the applicant is required to use for legal or other services, including title search and insurance.

4. If the loan is approved, the lender must provide a truth-in-lending statement that shows the annual percentage rate on the mortgage loan.

5. Lenders, title insurers, and others involved in the transaction cannot pay kickbacks for business referred to them.

■ Credit Protection

Because credit has assumed such an important role in consumer transactions, it is not surprising that some of the most important consumer protection laws have to do with credit. We look now at some of the most significant laws regulating consumer credit transactions.

The Truth-In-Lending Act

The Truth-in-Lending Act (TILA), as Title I of the Consumer Credit Protection Act (CCPA) is frequently called, is basically a disclosure law. Administered by the Federal Reserve Board, it requires sellers and lenders to disclose credit or loan terms to debtors so that the latter may shop around for the best available financing terms.

The TILA applies to creditors who, in the ordinary course of business, lend money or either sell on credit or arrange for the extension of credit. Thus sales between two consumers are not subject to the act. Only debtors who are *natural* persons are protected by the TILA; corporations and other entities created by law are not.

DISCLOSURE REQUIREMENTS The disclosure requirements are found in **Regulation Z**, promulgated by the Federal Reserve Board. If the contracting parties are subject to the TILA, the requirements of Regulation Z apply to any transaction involving an installment sales contract in which payment is to be made in more than four installments. These transactions typically include installment loans, retail and installment sales, car loans, home improvement loans, and certain real estate loans if the amount of financing is less than $25,000. Some of the disclosure requirements that may apply to these contracts include the specific dollar amount being financed; the annual percentage rate of interest; any financing charges, premiums, or points; the number, amounts, and due dates of payments; and any penalties imposed on delinquent payments or prepayment.

VIOLATIONS OF THE TILA Various penalties apply to creditors who violate the TILA by either failing to provide the disclosure statement or failing to discover an error in the statement provided. The act confers a *private right of action* on consumers who have been injured by a creditor's violation. If the suit is brought within one year of the date of the violation, the creditor will be liable for twice the amount of the finance charge, plus attorneys' fees. No more than $1,000 in damages may be recovered, but in no event will the penalty be less than $100. Federal agencies, including the Department of Justice and the FTC, may sue violators for criminal, as well as civil, violations. The criminal penalties include as much as a $5,000 fine and up to one year in jail.

The TILA also provides for contract rescission if a creditor fails to follow exactly the procedures required by the act. The following case illustrates how strictly TILA requirements will be enforced.

BACKGROUND AND FACTS *In February 1986, Max and Jacquelyn Elsner met with a representative of Diamond Mortgage to discuss the possibility of obtaining a loan to pay the balance on their land contract and to pay for home improvements. The representative asked the Elsners to sign some preliminary documents, including a loan application, and allegedly advised the Elsners that they would not sign the final binding papers until they received the money. The representative also gave each of the Elsners one copy of a "Notice of Right to Cancel." In fact, the documents*

Case 18.3

ELSNER v. ALBRECHT
Court of Appeals of Michigan, 1990.
185 Mich.App. 72,
460 N.W.2d 232.

signed by the Elsners included a mortgage contract and a promissory note, which Diamond shortly thereafter assigned to Harley and Donna Albrecht in exchange for $26,500. The Elsners never received the money. When the Albrechts sought payment on the note, the Elsners brought an action to rescind the contract, claiming that Diamond had violated the TILA because the representative gave them each only one copy of the "Notice of Right to Cancel"—instead of two copies, as required under the act. The trial court granted rescission, and the Albrechts appealed. The Albrechts argued that, as holders in due course, they were entitled to payment of the note, and therefore the contract could not be rescinded.

PER CURIAM.

    *   *   *   *

First, we find that plaintiffs were entitled to rescind the mortgage contract under the TILA, and Regulation Z. The TILA and Reg. Z provide for rescission until three days after the latest of the following events: (1) consummation of the transactions, (2) delivery of two copies to each borrower of the notice of right to cancel, or (3) delivery of all "material disclosures." We find that plaintiffs were entitled to rescind the transaction because Diamond Mortgage failed to deliver two copies to each borrower of the notice of right to cancel.

This case is virtually identical to a federal district court case involving two other parties victimized by the Diamond-Obie mortgage scheme. In *Stone v. Mehlberg,* the federal district court granted summary disposition to plaintiffs who had rescinded their mortgage transaction. In *Stone,* as in the present case, the trial court found that each plaintiff had not received two copies of their right to cancel as required under [the TILA and Regulation Z]. As the *Stone* court held, this requirement is not a mere technicality and requires that two copies be provided to each spouse since both had an ownership interest in the residence. "The fact that joint obligors may be husband and wife is irrelevant. Spouses are no more interchangeable under the TILA's rescission provisions than any other group of persons. Where the notice of right to cancel is not delivered, plaintiffs' right to rescind continues, subject to the statute of limitations." The *Stone* court went on to note that plaintiffs were not prevented from rescinding their mortgage agreement because of defendants' status as holders in due course, holding the TILA's rescission remedy preempts the holder in due course doctrine.

We choose to follow the holding in *Stone* and find that the trial court did not err in allowing plaintiffs to rescind their mortgage transaction.

DECISION AND REMEDY

The trial court's decision was affirmed. The Elsners were entitled to rescission, notwithstanding the fact that the mortgage contract and note had been transferred to a good faith purchaser for value.

ETHICAL CONSIDERATIONS

It is important to realize that the courts generally assume that the best way to protect the greatest number of consumers is by strict enforcement of consumer protection legislation, such as the TILA, even though occasional injustices are bound to result and even, in this case, at the expense of the holder-in-due-course doctrine—which itself rests on the ethical conviction that innocent third parties should be protected.

EQUAL CREDIT OPPORTUNITY ACT   In 1974, Congress enacted the Equal Credit Opportunity Act (ECOA) as part of the earlier enacted Truth-in-Lending Act. The ECOA prohibits the denial of credit solely on the basis of race, religion, national origin, color, sex, marital status, or age. The act also prohibits credit discrimination on the basis of whether an individual receives certain forms of income, such as public assistance benefits. Under the ECOA, a creditor may not require the signature of an applicant's spouse, other than a joint applicant, on a credit instrument if the applicant qualifies under the creditor's standards of creditworthiness for the amount and terms of the credit request. Creditors are permitted to request any information from a credit applicant except that which would be used for the type of discrimination covered in the act or its amendments.

FAIR CREDIT BILLING ACT   In 1974, Congress also enacted the Fair Credit Billing Act as a part of the Truth-in-Lending Act. Under the terms of the act, a purchaser can withhold payment for a product that was purchased with a credit card and that is alleged to be defective. It is up to the credit card issuer to intervene and attempt to settle the dispute. A purchaser does not have an unlimited right to stop payment, however. The purchaser must first exercise a good faith effort to get satisfaction from the seller. Other provisions of the act relate to disputes over billing. If the debtor believes there is an error in a bill, the debtor may suspend payment until the credit card company investigates the complaint. The credit card holder, within sixty days of receipt of the disputed bill, must write to the company that issued the card and explain the basis of the alleged error. The company must resolve the dispute within ninety days,

during which time it can neither close the account or issue additional financing charges. If, however, the error is unfounded and is resolved against the debtor, the creditor may seek to collect finance charges for the entire period for which payments were not made.

LOST AND UNAUTHORIZED CREDIT CARDS   The TILA contains other provisions regarding credit cards. One of these provisions limits the liability of the cardholder to $50 per card for unauthorized charges made before the credit card issuer is notified that the card has been lost. Another provision prohibits a credit card company from billing a consumer for any unauthorized charges if the credit card was improperly issued by the company.

The Fair Credit Reporting Act

To protect consumers against inaccurate credit reporting, Congress enacted the Fair Credit Reporting Act in 1970. Under the act, consumers can determine and correct any misinformation about their credit standing that is being given out by a credit agency. The act requires that consumers be notified when reporting activities are undertaken, that they be given access to information contained in a consumer report, and that any erroneous information that leads to a denial of credit, employment, or insurance be corrected. Consumers may also request the source of any information being given out by a credit agency, as well as the identity of anyone who has received an agency's report.

The following case illustrates the liability exposure of companies that maintain credit reports and ratings.

BACKGROUND AND FACTS   *The San Antonio Retail Merchants Association (SARMA) maintained credit reports on consumers. In 1974, William* Daniel *Thompson allowed his account at a jewelry store to become delinquent. SARMA placed a derogatory credit rating into Thompson's file but failed to include his Social Security number. In 1978, William* Douglas *Thompson applied for credit with Gulf Oil Corporation and Montgomery Ward in San Antonio. SARMA erroneously reported to both firms the bad-debt record of William Daniel Thompson. As a result, both Gulf and Montgomery Ward denied credit to William* Douglas *Thompson. Initially, Wil-*

 Case 18.4

THOMPSON v. SAN ANTONIO RETAIL MERCHANTS ASSOCIATION
United States Court of Appeals, Fifth Circuit, 1982.
682 F.2d 509.

liam Douglas Thompson believed he had been denied credit because of his 1976 burglary conviction. In 1979, however, he learned the true reason. After discovering the error, William Douglas Thompson attempted to get SARMA to correct the error. SARMA, however, repeatedly sent him letters addressed to William Daniel Thompson and failed to correct the erroneous credit report. William Douglas Thompson sued SARMA, and the district court ruled for him. The court further awarded him $10,000 in damages for mental distress, plus attorneys' fees of $4,485. SARMA appealed this decision.

PER CURIAM.

    *   *   *   *

Under 15 U.S.C. [Section] 1681o of the Fair Credit Reporting Act (Act), a "consumer reporting agency" is liable to "any consumer" for negligent failure to comply with "any requirement imposed" by the Act. In the instant case, the district court determined that SARMA was liable under section 1681o for negligent failure to comply with section 1681e(b) of the Act, which provides:

> When a consumer reporting agency *prepares* a consumer report, it shall follow *reasonable procedures* to assure *maximum possible accuracy* of information concerning the individual about whom the report relates.

Section 1681e(b) does not impose strict liability for any inaccurate credit report, but only a duty of reasonable care in preparation of the report. That duty extends to updating procedures, because "preparation" of a consumer report should be viewed as a continuing process and the obligation to insure accuracy arises with every addition of information. The standard of conduct by which the trier of fact must judge the adequacy of agency procedures is what a reasonably prudent person would do under the circumstances.

Applying the reasonable-person standard, the district court found two acts of negligence in SARMA's updating procedures. First, SARMA failed to exercise reasonable care in programming its computer to automatically capture information into a file without requiring any minimum number of "points of correspondence" between the consumer and the file or having an adequate auditing procedure to foster accuracy. Second, SARMA failed to employ reasonable procedures designed to learn the disparity in social security numbers for the two Thompsons *   *   * .

    *   *   *   *

SARMA asserts that Thompson failed to prove any actual damages, or at best proved only minimal damages for humiliation and mental distress. There was evidence, however, that Thompson suffered humiliation and embarrassment from being denied credit on three occasions. Thompson testified that the denial of credit hurt him deeply because of his mistaken belief that it resulted from his felony conviction:

> I was trying to build myself back up, trying to set myself up, get back on my feet again. I was working sixty hours a week and sometimes seventy. I went back to school. I was going to school at night three nights a week, four nights a week, three hours a night, and [denial of credit] really hurt. It made me disgusted with myself.

DECISION AND REMEDY *The appellate court upheld the district court's finding for Thompson and its estimate of $10,000 in damages for mental distress. Because the Fair Credit Reporting Act specifically authorizes the payment of attorneys' fees, this finding was also affirmed.*

The Fair Debt Collection Practices Act

In 1977, Congress enacted the Fair Debt Collection Practices Act in an attempt to curb what were perceived to be abuses by collection agencies. The act applies only to specialized debt-collection agencies that, usually for a percentage of the amount owed, regularly attempt to collect debts on behalf of someone else. Creditors who attempt to collect a debt are not covered by the act unless, by misrepresenting themselves to the debtor, they cause the debtor to believe they are a collection agency. The act explicitly prohibits a collection agency from using any of the following tactics:

1. Contacting the debtor at the debtor's place of employment if the debtor's employer objects.
2. Contacting the debtor during inconvenient or unusual times (for example, calling the debtor at 3 o'clock in the morning) or at any time if the debtor is being represented by an attorney.
3. Contacting third parties other than the debtor's parents, spouse, or financial advisor about payment of a debt unless a court authorizes such action.
4. Using harassment or intimidation (for example, using abusive language or threatening violence), or employing false and misleading information (for example, posing as a police officer).
5. Communicating with the debtor at any time after receiving notice that the debtor is refusing to pay the debt, except to advise the debtor of further action to be taken by the collection agency.

Enforcement of the act is primarily the responsibility of the FTC. The act allows debtors to recover civil damages, as well as attorneys' fees, in an action against a collection agency that violates provisions of the act.

Garnishment of Wages

Despite the increasing number of protections afforded debtors, creditors are not without their own means of securing payment on a debt. One of these is the right to garnish a debtor's wages after the debt has gone uncollected for a prolonged period. **Garnishment** is the legal procedure by which a creditor may collect on a debt by directly attaching, or seizing, a portion of the debtor's wages. State law provides the basis for a process of garnishment, but the law varies among the states as to how easily

garnishment may be obtained. Indeed, a few states prohibit garnishment of wages altogether. In addition to state law requirements, the Constitution and, more recently, federal legislation under the TILA provide additional protections against abuse. In general, the debtor is entitled to notice and an opportunity to be heard in a process of garnishment. Moreover, wages cannot be garnished beyond 25 percent of the debtor's after-tax earnings and must leave the debtor with at least a specified minimum income.

■ Consumer Health and Safety

Laws discussed earlier regarding the labeling and packaging of products go a long way toward promoting consumer health and safety. These laws enable consumers to make informed choices about the products they choose to consume. But there is a significant distinction between regulating the information dispensed about a product and regulating the content of the actual product. The classic example is tobacco products. Tobacco products have not been altered by regulation nor banned outright despite their obvious hazards (or perhaps because of that obviousness). What has been regulated are the warnings about the hazards of tobacco that producers are required to give consumers.[8] This section focuses on laws that regulate the actual products made available to consumers.

The Federal Food, Drug, and Cosmetic Act

The first federal legislation regulating food and drugs was enacted in 1906 as the Pure Food and Drug Act. That law, as amended in 1938, exists presently as the Federal Food, Drug, and Cosmetic Act. The original act, and the subsequent amendment strengthening its provisions, was intended to protect consumers against adulterated and misbranded foods and drugs. More recent amendments have added additional substantive and procedural requirements to the act. In its present form, the act establishes food standards, specifies safe levels of potentially hazardous food additives, and sets clas-

---

8. We are ignoring recent civil litigation concerning the liability of tobacco product manufacturers for injuries that arise from the use of tobacco.

sifications of food and food advertising. Most of these statutory requirements are monitored and enforced by the Food and Drug Administration (FDA). Under an extensive set of procedures established by the FDA, drugs must be shown to be effective as well as safe before they may be marketed to the public, and the use of some food additives suspected of being carcinogenic is prohibited. In general, the food and drug laws make manufacturers responsible for ensuring that the food and drugs that they offer for sale are free of any substances that could be injurious to the consumer.

The Consumer Product Safety Act

Consumer product safety legislation began in 1953 with enactment of the Flammable Fabrics Act, which prohibits the sale of highly flammable clothing or materials. Over the next two decades, Congress enacted legislation for specific classes of products regarding the design or composition of the products. Then in 1972, Congress, by enacting the Consumer Product Safety Act, created a comprehensive scheme of regulation over matters concerning consumer safety. The act also established far-reaching authority over consumer safety under the Consumer Product Safety Commission (CPSC). The CPSC conducts research on how safe individual products are, and it maintains a clearinghouse on the risks associated with different consumer products. Under the Consumer Product Safety Act, the CPSC is authorized to set standards for consumer products and to ban the manufacture and sale of any product it deems to be potentially hazardous to consumers. The CPSC also has authority to remove from market shelves any products it believes to be imminently hazardous and to require manufacturers to report on any products already sold or intended for sale if the products have proved to be hazardous. The CPSC also has authority to administer other product safety legislation, such as the Child Protection and Toy Safety Act of 1966, the Hazardous Substances Labeling Act of 1960, and the Flammable Fabrics Act.

The CPSC's authority is sufficiently broad to allow it to ban any product that the CPSC believes poses merely an "unreasonable risk" to the consumer. Some of the products that the CPSC has banned include various types of fireworks, cribs,

toys, and many products containing asbestos or vinyl chloride.

State Consumer Protection Laws

Thus far our primary focus has been federal legislation. Our task would be incomplete, however, if at least brief mention were not made of the state laws affecting consumer transactions. Although variation among the state laws prevents making any broad generalizations, it should be noted that state laws often provide more sweeping and significant protections for the consumer than do federal laws. Precisely because of the variation among the states, a businessperson is well-advised to consider all aspects of the laws of the states in which he or she does business. Even remote connections with a state may bring a transaction within the authority of a particular state's laws. Furthermore, basic principles of contract law include the considerable discretion of the contracting parties to choose to have the laws of a particular state govern the terms of their agreement.[9]

The Uniform Commercial Code

Consumers are afforded the protections offered by the sections in the Uniform Commercial Code (UCC) on express and implied warranties. These were covered in detail in Unit Three, and the reader should consider the importance of these protections in the context of our present discussion. The UCC also restricts the ability of sellers to limit their liability for personal injuries caused by defective products. Perhaps the most significant UCC consumer protection, however, is the principle of unconscionability based on UCC 2-302. This section, as interpreted by the courts, prohibits enforcing any contracts that are so one-sidedly unfair that they "shock the conscience" of the court. In discussing consumer protections under the UCC, it is important to note the existence of the Magnuson-Moss Warranty Act. This federal legislation supplements the UCC provisions in cases involving both a consumer transaction of at least $10 and an express written warranty.

---

9. So-called conflicts of law may arise in any transaction that crosses state boundaries.

The Uniform Consumer Credit Code

Far less widely adopted than the UCC is the Uniform Consumer Credit Code (UCCC). Promulgated in 1968 by the National Conference of Commissioners on the Uniform State Laws, the UCCC is an attempt to draft a comprehensive body of rules governing the most important aspects of consumer credit. The UCCC includes sections on truth in lending, maximum credit ceilings, door-to-door sales, and referral sales. The UCCC also contains provisions concerning fine-print clauses and creditor remedies, including provisions regarding deficiency judgments[10] and garnishments. In states that have adopted it, the UCCC applies to most sales, including those involving real estate. Its adoption also displaces the adopting state's consumer credit laws, as well as laws governing installment loans, usury, and retail installment sales. The UCCC is controversial, and it has been adopted in only a handful of states. Even those states that have adopted the UCCC have adopted only portions. Moreover, substantial differences in the various state versions remove much of the uniformity from the act among the various adopting states.

Other State Consumer Protection Laws

Despite the variation among state laws generally, there is a common thread running through most of the consumer protection laws. Most are typically directed at deceptive trade practices, such as a seller's providing false or misleading information to the consumer. As mentioned earlier, some of the legislation is quite broad. A prime example is the Texas Deceptive Trade Practices Act of 1973, which forbids a seller from selling to a buyer anything that the buyer does not need or cannot afford. The California Civil Code permits consumers to keep unsolicited goods without remitting any payment for them.

California is one state that has enacted a broad statute dealing with consumer product warranties generally, but a majority of states—forty-seven at last count—have statutes dealing with warranties on specific types of goods such as new automobiles and new mobile homes. These so-called lemon laws are part of warranty law, but they should be noted for the sake of completeness when considering consumer protection laws. Also discussed in detail in Unit Three are the protections against personal injury and property losses provided by product liability laws based on principles of contract and tort law. Indeed, most consumer disputes are settled by contract law, personal injury being the exception; there are advantages to a plaintiff's bringing a suit on the basis of strict liability under tort law for personal injury from a defective product. Nonetheless, the appearance of government regulators as a kind of third party protector in consumer transactions is an unmistakable trend in recent years.

---

10. A deficiency judgment is a judgment for the portion of a debt not recovered from the forced sale of property securing that debt.

■ Terms and Concepts to Review

affirmative advertising 444
bait-and-switch
   advertising 444
counteradvertising 445

garnishment 453
multiple product orders 445

puffing 442
Regulation Z 449

■ Questions and Case Problems

18-1. Andrew, a California resident, received a flyer in the U.S. mail announcing a new line of regional cookbooks distributed by the Every-Kind Cookbook Co. Andrew was not interested and threw the flyer away. Two days later, Andrew received in the mail an introductory cookbook entitled *Lower Mongolian* *Regional Cookbook,* as announced in the flyer, on a "trial basis" from Every-Kind. Andrew was not interested but did not go to the trouble to return the cookbook. Every-Kind demanded payment of $20.95 for the *Lower Mongolian Regional Cookbook.* Discuss whether Andrew can be required to pay for the cookbook.

18-2. Fireside Rocking Chair Co. advertised in the newspaper a special sale price of $159 on machine-caned rocking chairs. In the advertisement was a drawing of a natural-wood rocking chair with a caned back and seat. The average person would not be able to tell from the drawing whether the rocking chair was machine caned or hand caned. The hand-caned rocking chairs sold for $259. Lowell and Celia Carlisle went to Fireside because they had seen the ad for the machine-caned rocking chair and were very interested in purchasing one. The Carlisles arrived on the morning the sale opened. Fireside's agent said the only machine-caned rocking chairs he had were painted lime green and were priced at $159. He immediately turned the Carlisle's attention to the hand-caned rocking chairs, praising their quality and pointing out that for the extra $100, the hand-caned chairs were surely a good value. The Carlisles, preferring the natural-wood, machine-caned rocking chair for $159 as pictured in the advertisement, said they would like to order the one in the ad. The Fireside agent said he could not order a natural-wood, machine-caned rocking chair. Discuss fully whether Fireside has violated any consumer protection laws.

18-3. On June 28, a sales representative for Renowned Books called on the Petersons at their home. After a very persuasive sales pitch on the part of the sales agent, the Petersons agreed in writing to purchase a twenty-volume set of historical encyclopedias from Renowned Books for a total of $299. An initial down payment of $35 was required, with the remainder of the price to be paid in monthly payments over a one-year period. Two days later the Petersons, having second thoughts, contacted the book company and stated they had decided to rescind the contract. Renowned Books said this would be impossible. Has Renowned Books violated any consumer law by not allowing the Petersons to rescind their contract? Explain.

18-4. Michael and Patricia Jensen purchased a new 1989 Ford Tempo from Ray Kim Ford. The Jensens signed a retail installment contract that provided for an estimated trade-in value of $800 for their old car. When the traded-in car turned out to be worth $1,388.08, Ray Kim prepared a second retail installment contract, without the Jensens' knowledge. The second contract, although it credited the increased trade-in value of the car, compensated for this credit by increasing the interest rate, increasing the sales price of the car, and making other adjustments so that the second contract basically called for future cash payments by the Jensens of about the same amount as the first contract. In effect, the second contract gave the Jensens almost no benefit for the increased value of their traded-in car. The Jensens made payments under the contract until they noticed the five-cent difference in monthly payments, asked for a copy of the contract, and realized that it was not the contract that they had signed. The Jensens sued Ray Kim, alleging that the second contract was a forgery and that Ray Kim had violated the Truth-in-Lending Act by not disclosing to them the credit terms of the second contract. Has Ray Kim violated the Truth-in-Lending Act? If the Jensens choose to adopt the terms of the second contract, despite the forgery, has the act been violated? Discuss fully. [*Jensen v. Ray Kim Ford, Inc.,* 920 F.2d 3 (7th Cir. 1990)]

18-5. Thompson Medical Co. marketed a new cream called Aspercreme that was supposed to help arthritis victims and others suffering from minor aches. Aspercreme contained no aspirin. Thompson's television advertisements stated that the product provided "the strong relief of aspirin right where you hurt" and showed the announcer holding up aspirin tablets as well as a tube of Aspercreme. The FTC held that the advertisements were misleading, because they led consumers to believe that Aspercreme contained aspirin. Thompson Medical Co. appealed this decision and argued that the advertisements never actually stated that its product contained aspirin. How should the court rule? Discuss. [*Thompson Medical Co. v. Federal Trade Commission,* 791 F.2d 189 (D.C. Cir. 1986)]

18-6. Sears, Roebuck & Co. adopted a new advertising program to boost sales of its Lady Kenmore dishwashers. The new ads claimed that these dishwashers "completely eliminated" the need for rinsing dishes before placing them in the dishwasher. The owner's manuals accompanying the machines, however, recommended pre-rinsing. Interviews with consumers indicated that pre-rinsing was still required for truly clean dishes. In an action against Sears, the FTC held that the advertising was misleading. The FTC's remedial order required that Sears keep records to support all future advertising claims for all "major home appliances" and submit them to the FTC. Sears conceded that its dishwasher advertising was misleading but argued that the remedial order, which covered other appliances, was overly broad and unfair. Discuss fully whether the FTC's broad order is legal. [*Sears, Roebuck & Co. v. Federal Trade Commission,* 676 F.2d 385 (9th Cir. 1982)]

18-7. Dennis and Janice Geiger saw an advertisement in a newspaper for a Kimball Whitney spinet piano on sale for $699 by McCormick Piano & Organ Co. Because the style of the piano drawn in the advertisement matched their furniture, the Geigers were particularly interested in the Kimball. When they went to McCormick Piano & Organ, however, they learned that the drawing closely resembled another, more expensive Crest piano, and that the Kimball spinet looked quite different than the piano sketched in the drawing. The salesperson told the Geigers that she was unable to order the spinet piano of the style requested by the Geigers. When the Geigers asked for the names of other customers who had purchased the advertised pianos, the salesperson became hysterical and said she would not, under any circumstances, sell the Geigers a piano. The Geigers then brought suit against the piano store, alleging that the store had engaged in deceptive advertising in violation of Indiana law. Was the McCormick Piano & Organ Co. guilty of deceptive advertising? Explain. [*McCormick Piano & Organ Co. v. Geiger,* 412 N.E.2d 842 (Ind.App. 1980)]

18-8. Branigar Organization, Inc., began a residential development in the 1970s. The development included a large country club with golf courses and tennis courts. The purchase price of a house or lot, however, did not include the initiation fees and dues required for club membership—

although all residents could join the club if they paid these fees. Branigar later transferred the ownership and management of the club, and according to the plan of the new ownership, all members of the club were told that they would lose their usage rights as of December 31, 1990. After that date, only members owning an equity interest in—that is, members who had purchased shares in—the club would be allowed to use the facilities. All non-equity members were offered the right to become equity members. Shirley Rice and others who had purchased lots or houses in the development claimed that Branigar's failure to disclose that the non-equity club members would eventually be required to buy equity membership to use the club violated the Interstate Land Sales Full Disclosure Act. The act requires developers to furnish prospective subdivision-lot purchasers with a property report that includes, among other things, information regarding recreational facilities associated with the subdivision. Will Rice and the others succeed in their claim? Discuss fully. [*Rice v. Branigar Organization, Inc.*, 922 F.2d 788 (11th Cir. 1991)]

18-9. Josephine Rutyna was a sixty-year-old widow who, in late 1976 and early 1977, had incurred a debt for medical treatment for her high blood pressure and epilepsy. She assumed that the cost of the services had been paid by either Medicare or her private insurance company. In July 1978, however, she was contacted by an agent of Collection Accounts Terminal, Inc., who stated that Rutyna still owed a debt of $56 for those services. She denied that she owed the debt and the following month received a letter from the collection agency threatening to contact her neighbors and employer concerning the debt if the $56 was not paid immediately. Discuss fully whether the collection agency's letter violates any consumer protection law. [*Rutyna v. Collection Accounts Terminal, Inc.*, 478 F.Supp. 980 (N.D.Ill. 1979)]

18-10. Sebastian and Maria Shaumyan entered into a home improvement contract with Sidetex Co. Sidetex agreed to install siding, replace windows, and perform other related work at the Shaumyan's home, and the Shaumyans agreed to pay Sidetex a total of $14,800 according to the following schedule: $3,000 as a deposit; $4,000 when Sidetex began the work; $3,900 when the work was half completed; $1,950 on completion of the installation of the siding; and $1,950 on completion of the work on the storm doors and shutters. Although a clause in the agreement referred to the contract as a "consumer credit contract," the Shaumyans' payments were not subject to any finance charges. Sidetex commenced work under the contract, and the Shaumyans made the scheduled progress payments of $3,000, $4,000, and $3,900. Performance was not completed, however, because a dispute arose concerning the quality of the windows that Sidetex was to install. The Shaumyans brought an action against Sidetex to recover damages, claiming that Sidetex violated the antidiscrimination provision of the Equal Credit Opportunity Act (ECOA) by requiring the signature of Mrs. Shaumyan on the home improvement contract. The central issue before the court was whether the home im-

provement contract, which provided for progress payments by the Shaumyans, constituted a "credit transaction" subject to the antidiscrimination provisions of the ECOA. How should the court rule? Discuss fully. [*Shaumyan v. Sidetex Co.*, 900 F.2d 16 (1990)]

18-11. A Question of Ethics

 On July 16, 1982, the Semars signed a loan contract with Platte Valley Federal Savings & Loan Association, offering a second mortgage on their home as collateral. Under the Truth-in-Lending Act (TILA), borrowers are allowed three business days to rescind, without penalty, a consumer loan that uses their principal dwelling as security. The TILA requires lenders in such situations to state specifically the last date on which the borrower can rescind the loan agreement, and if they fail to include this date, the borrower may rescind the loan within three years after it was made. Platte Valley's form omitted the exact expiration date of the three-day period, although it stated that the rescission right expired three business days after July 16. The Semars ceased making monthly payments on the loan in September 1983 and sent a Notice of Rescission to Platte Valley on February 15, 1984. The Semars claimed that Platte Valley had violated the TILA by failing to specify in the loan contract the exact date of the expiration of the three-day rescission period. Because of this violation, the Semars maintained they had three years in which to rescind the contract. Although the court found the Semars to be "unsympathetic plaintiffs," it nevertheless held that rescission was appropriate for the technical violation of the TILA. [Semar v. Platte Valley Federal Savings & Loan Association, 791 F.2d 699 (9th Cir. 1986)]

1. Do you think that the court, by adhering so strictly to the letter of the law, violated the spirit of the law?
2. When deciding issues involving alleged violations of consumer protection legislation, such as the TILA, should courts balance the equities of the cases? That is, should the ethical (or unethical) behavior of the parties to a particular transaction be taken into consideration?
3. How might you justify, on ethical grounds, the court's decision in this case?

18-12. Case Briefing Assignment

Examine Case A.18 [Roberts v. Walmart Stores, Inc., 736 F.Supp. 1527 (E.D.Mo. 1990)] in Appendix A. The case has been excerpted there in great detail. Review and then brief the case, making sure that you include answers to the following questions in your brief.

1. What was the basis of the Roberts' claim?
2. What defense did Walmart raise?
3. What was the court's decision?

Chapter 19

Environmental Law

When the human population was small and dispersed and industry was limited, the earth was relatively unspoiled. Environmental degradation was not a significant problem. People assumed that the environment would absorb whatever they put into it. As the world became more populated, urbanized, and industrialized, however, concerns over the degradation of the environment increased. Industrial society's generation of waste threatened— and continues to threaten—the very existence of human life. The urban industrial society in this century has apparently strained the environment's capacity to handle the pollution discharged into the air and water. In the last two decades, **environmental law**—all law pertaining to environmental protection—has expanded in attempts to control this waste.

■ Common Law Actions

Common law remedies against environmental pollution originated centuries ago in England. Operations that belched dirt, smoke, noxious odors, noise, or toxic substances were sometimes held liable under common law theories of nuisance or negligence. Today, injured individuals continue to rely on the common law to obtain damages and injunctions against business polluters. (Statutory remedies are also available, a topic that we treat later.)

Nuisance

Under the common law doctrine of nuisance, persons may be held liable if they use their property in a manner that unreasonably interferes with others' rights to use or enjoy their property. In these situations, it is common for courts to balance the equities between the harm caused by the pollution and the costs of stopping it.

On the grounds that the hardships to be imposed on the polluter and on the community are relatively greater than the hardships to be suffered by the plaintiff, courts have often denied *injunctive relief.* For example, a factory that causes neighboring landowners to suffer from smoke, dirt, and vibrations may be left in operation if it is the core of a local economy. The injured parties may be awarded only their money damages. These damages may include compensation for the neighbors' total economic loss to their properties, present and future, caused by the factory's operation.

As indicated by the factory example, a property owner may be given relief from pollution in situations in which he or she can identify a distinct harm separate from that affecting the general public. This is referred to as a "private" nuisance. Under the common law, however, citizens were denied *standing* (access to the courts) unless they suffered harm distinct from the harm to the public at large. Some states still require this. Therefore, a group of citizens who wished to stop a new development that would cause significant water pollution were denied access to the courts on the ground that the harm to them did not differ from the harm to the general public.[1] A public authority (such as a state's attorney general) can sue to abate a "public" nuisance.

------

1. *Save the Bay Committee, Inc. v. Mayor of City of Savannah*, 227 Ga. 436, 181 S.E.2d 351 (1971).

Negligence and Strict Liability

An injured party may sue a business polluter in a common law negligence action. The basis for the action is the business's alleged failure to use reasonable care toward the party whose injury was foreseeable and, of course, caused by the failure. For example, employees might sue an employer whose failure to use proper pollution controls contaminated the air, causing the employees to suffer respiratory illnesses.

Injured parties might also recover under a theory of strict liability. Businesses that engage in ultrahazardous activities—such as the transportation of radioactive materials—are liable for whatever injuries the activities cause. In a strict liability action, the injured party does not need to prove that the business failed to exercise reasonable care. In the following case, the court outlines reasons for holding a particular polluter liable under theories of common law negligence and strict liability.

BACKGROUND AND FACTS *In 1964, Velsicol Chemical Corporation began operating a chemical waste burial site on a farm in Tennessee. At the 242-acre site, over the next decade, Velsicol buried more than 300,000 fifty-five-gallon drums and hundreds of boxes filled with chemical waste. In 1973, the state of Tennessee determined the site to be hazardous and closed it. Local residents sued Velsicol on a number of legal theories, including negligence and strict liability, claiming that the aquifer from which they drew their drinking water was contaminated with hazardous chemicals that leaked from the farm. The residents sought damages for a variety of alleged physical and emotional injuries, as well as property damage.*

Case 19.1

STERLING v. VELSICOL CHEMICAL CORP.
United States District Court, Western District of Tennessee, 1986.
647 F.Supp. 303.

HORTON, Judge.

* * * *

Strict Liability * * *

* * * *

* * * [T]he Court concludes that Velsicol's activity on the farm was not only ultrahazardous activity, but also abnormally dangerous activity and therefore the defendant is strictly liable for any damages that have occurred. This conclusion is made for * * * the following reasons:

1. There was a high degree of risk of harm to the person, land or chattels of others * * *;

2. There was a likelihood that the harm that results would be great, such as the increased risk of many diseases including cancer, and the destruction of the plaintiffs' quality of life;

3. The inability to eliminate the risk by the exercise of reasonable care;

4. The extent to which the activity at the dump was not a matter of common usage and as a means of disposal and violated the state of the art;

5. The inappropriateness of the location of the dump where it was carried out; and

6. The extent to which its value to the community (none) was outweighed by its dangerous attributes (great).

Common Law Negligence

The Court concludes that the doctrine of common law negligence applies to this case and Velsicol is clearly guilty of negligence in this case for the following reasons:

1. The Court concludes that there was a duty, a standard of conduct, imposed by law on Velsicol to protect others from unreasonable harm arising from the dumping of chemicals on its farm; and

2. The Court further concludes that defendant breached that duty by its failure to do the following:

a. Defendant failed to investigate the geological makeup or strata under the dumpsite prior to its purchase or operation;

b. Defendant failed to investigate the hydrological, or water bearing zones under the dumpsite prior to its purchase or operation;

c. Defendant failed to hire knowledgeable persons to investigate the geological and hydrogeological area under the dumpsite prior to its purchase or operation;

d. Defendant failed to install proper monitoring procedures in and around the dumpsite prior to commencing dumping operations at the dumpsite;

e. Defendant failed to investigate the geological and hydrogeological situation at the dumpsite after being warned by the [U.S. Geological Survey] in 1967 that their chemicals were escaping from their burial trenches and were in fact contaminating the local water table aquifer;

f. Defendant failed to hire professional geologists or hydrogeologists at the time the 1967 [U.S. Geological Survey] was circulated to properly analyze the data generated therein as any reasonable person would do;

g. Defendant failed to heed the warning in said report by continuing to dump and even expanding the size of the dump;

* * * *

i. Defendant failed in the selection, location, operation and maintenance of the dumpsite under the prevailing state of the art for such operation during the entire length of time the dumpsite was open from 1964 to 1973;

* * * *

k. Defendant failed to take steps in 1967 to halt the leakage that was already occurring from the dumpsite;

l. Defendant failed to properly monitor the dumpsite from its opening in October of 1964 to its closing in June of 1973;

* * * *

n. Defendant failed to operate said dumpsite according to the state of the art methods to protect the plaintiffs by their failure to cover their wastes daily thereby allowing an increase in the infiltration rate;

o. Defendant failed to properly close the dumpsite in 1973 pursuant to the state of the art;

p. Defendant failed to timely register the dumpsite as a hazardous waste disposal site as required by the State of Tennessee;

q. Defendant failed to timely, completely and correctly respond to the requests of governmental agencies as to what was put into the dumpsite;

r. Defendant failed to warn plaintiffs that they should watch their water for the presence of any chemical odors or tastes as early as 1967;

s. Defendant failed to transport the chemicals * * * to the dumpsite * * * in a safe and proper manner to insure the safety of plaintiffs and their property as the defendant allowed said chemicals to spill out of the trucks on to the roadway;

t. Defendant failed to contain their chemicals within the boundaries of their property * * * and did allow them to escape and pollute the drinkable ground water used by plaintiffs; and

u. Defendant failed to contain their chemicals within the boundaries of their property * * * and did allow the fumes from said chemicals to escape into the air which drifted onto the property and into the houses of the plaintiffs.

3. The Court further concludes that defendant's breach of the above duties were in fact the proximate cause of plaintiffs' injuries.

*The district court awarded the residents more than $5.2 million in compensatory damages, $7.5 million in punitive damages, and **prejudgment interest** (interest that accrues on the amount of the judgment from the time of the filing of the suit to the issuing of the judgment) at the rate of 8 percent per year on the compensatory damages. On appeal, the United States Court of Appeals for the Sixth Circuit found that the district court properly held Velsicol liable but that it erred in the damage awards. The case was remanded for recalculation of some of the damages.*[a]

DECISION AND REMEDY

a. *Sterling v. Velsicol Chemical Corp.*, 855 F.2d 1188 (6th Cir. 1988).

■ State and Local Regulation

Many states regulate the degree to which the environment may be polluted. Thus, for example, even when state zoning laws permit a business's proposed development, the proposal may have to be altered to change the development's impact on the environment. State laws may restrict a business's discharge of chemicals into the air or water, or regulate its disposal of toxic wastes. States may also regulate the disposal or recycling of other wastes, including glass, metal, and plastic containers and paper. Additionally, states may restrict the emissions from motor vehicles.

City, county, and other local governments control some aspects of the environment. For instance, local zoning laws control some land use. These laws may be designed to inhibit or direct the growth of cities and suburbs or to protect the natural environment. Other aspects of the environment may be subject to local regulation for other reasons. Methods of waste and garbage removal and disposal, for example, can have a substantial impact on a community. The appearance of buildings and other structures, including advertising signs and billboards, may affect traffic safety, property values, or local aesthetics. Noise generated by a business or its customers may be annoying, disruptive, or damaging to its neighbors. The location and condition of parks, streets, and other public uses of land subject to local control affect the environment and can also affect business.

■ Federal Regulation

Congress has passed a number of statutes to control the impact of human activities on the environment. The major federal environmental statutes discussed in this chapter are listed and summarized in Exhibit 19–1. Some of these statutes have been passed to improve the quality of air and water. Some of them specifically regulate toxic chemicals—including pesticides, herbicides, and hazardous wastes. Some are concerned with radiation.

National Environmental Policy Act

The National Environmental Policy Act (NEPA) of 1969 imposes environmental responsibilities on all agencies of the federal government. NEPA requires that all agencies consider environmental factors when making significant decisions. For every major federal action that significantly affects the quality of the environment, an **environmental impact statement (EIS)** must be prepared. An action qualifies as "major" if it involves a substantial commitment of resources (monetary or otherwise). An action is "federal" if a federal agency has the power to control it. For example, building a new nuclear reactor involves federal action because a federal license is required.

An EIS must analyze (1) the impact on the environment that the action will have, (2) any adverse effects to the environment and alternative actions that might be taken, and (3) irreversible effects the

■ **Exhibit 19–1 Federal Environmental Statutes**

Popular Name	Purpose	Statute Reference
Rivers and Harbors Act (1886)	To regulate the discharge and deposit of refuse in navigable waterways.	33 U.S.C. Sections 407 *et seq.*
Federal Insecticide, Fungicide, and Rodenticide Act (FIFRA) (1947)	To control the use of pesticides and herbicides.	7 U.S.C. Sections 135 *et seq.*
Federal Water Pollution Control Act (FWPCA) (1948)	To eliminate the discharge of pollutants from major sources into navigable waters.	33 U.S.C. Sections 1251 *et seq.*
Atomic Energy Act (1954)	To limit environmental harm from the private nuclear industry.	42 U.S.C. Sections 2011 *et seq.*
Clean Air Act (1963)	To control air pollution from mobile and stationary sources.	42 U.S.C. Sections 7401 *et seq.*
National Environmental Policy Act (NEPA) (1969)	To limit environmental harm from federal government activities.	42 U.S.C. Sections 4321 *et seq.*
Marine Protection, Research, and Sanctuaries Act of 1972 (Ocean Dumping Act)	To regulate the transporting and dumping of material into ocean waters.	16 U.S.C. Sections 1431 *et seq.*
Noise Control Act (1972)	To regulate noise pollution from transportation and nontransportation sources.	42 U.S.C. Sections 4901 *et seq.*
Endangered Species Act (1973)	To protect species that are threatened with extinction.	16 U.S.C. Sections 1531 *et seq.*
Safe Drinking Water Act (1974)	To regulate pollutants in public drinking water systems.	42 U.S.C. Sections 300f *et seq.*
Resource Conservation and Recovery Act (RCRA) (1976)	To establish standards for hazardous waste disposal.	42 U.S.C. Sections 6901 *et seq.*
Toxic Substances Control Act (1976)	To regulate toxic chemicals and chemical compounds.	15 U.S.C. Sections 2601 *et seq.*
Comprehensive Environmental Response, Compensation, and Liability Act (CERCLA) (Superfund) (1980)	To regulate the clean-up of hazardous waste disposal sites.	42 U.S.C. Sections 9601 *et seq.*
Low Level Radioactive Waste Policy Act (1980)	To assign to the states responsibility for nuclear power plants' low-level radioactive waste.	42 U.S.C. Sections 2021b *et seq.*
Nuclear Waste Policy Act (1982)	To provide for the designation of a permanent radioactive waste disposal site.	42 U.S.C. Sections 10101 *et seq.*

action might generate. If an agency decides that an EIS is unnecessary, it must issue a statement supporting this conclusion. EIS's have become instruments for private citizens, consumer interest groups, businesses, and others to challenge federal agency actions on the basis that the actions improperly threaten the environment. Today, almost all environmental litigation under NEPA involves disputes with governmental agencies rather than disputes between private parties.

Complementary Federal Laws

Federal law contains a number of mandates that supplement the obligations expressed in the National Environmental Policy Act to protect environmental values in agency decision making. For example, the Federal Insecticide, Fungicide, and Rodenticide Act (discussed in more detail later in this chapter) requires that an agricultural economy impact analysis be prepared in connection with a suspension or cancellation of the use of any pesticide.

Among the most important of the complementary federal laws are protections for fish and wildlife. Under the Fish and Wildlife Coordination Act,[2] federal agencies proposing to approve the impounding or diversion of the waters of a stream must consult with the Fish and Wildlife Service with a view to preventing the loss of fish and wildlife resources. An important provision is found in the Endangered Species Act of 1973. Under this act, all federal agencies are required to take steps to ensure that their actions "do not jeopardize the continued existence of endangered species" or the habitat of an endangered species. An action may jeopardize the continued existence of a species if it sets in motion a chain of events that reduces the chances that the species will survive.

Environmental Protection Agency

In 1970 the Environmental Protection Agency (EPA) was created to coordinate federal environmental responsibilities. The EPA administers most federal environmental policies and statutes. Other federal agencies with authority for regulating specific environmental matters include the Department of the Interior, the Department of Defense, the Department of Labor, the Food and Drug Administration, and the Nuclear Regulatory Commission.

■ Air Pollution

Federal involvement with air pollution goes back to the 1950s, when Congress authorized funds for air-pollution research. In 1963 the federal government passed the Clean Air Act, which focused on

multistate air pollution and provided assistance to states. Various amendments, particularly in 1970, 1977, and 1990, strengthened the government's authority to regulate the quality of air.

These laws provide the basis for issuing regulations to control pollution coming primarily from mobile sources (motor vehicles) and stationary sources (electric utilities and industrial plants, among others). The EPA sets air quality standards for major pollutants. General guidelines set out requirements for protecting vegetation, climate, visibility, and certain economic conditions. The 1977 amendments to the Clean Air Act establish multilevel standards. For example, they attempt to prevent the deterioration of air quality even in areas where the existing quality exceeds that required by federal law.

Mobile Sources

Regulations governing air pollution from automobiles and other mobile sources specify pollution standards and time schedules. For example, the 1970 Clean Air Act required a reduction of 90 percent in the amount of carbon monoxide and other pollutants emitted by automobiles by 1975. (This did not happen, however, and the 1977 amendments extended the deadline to 1983. Generally, automobile manufacturers have met the 90 percent reduction goal by installing catalytic converters on automobiles.)

An automobile purchased today emits only about 4 percent of the pollutants that a new 1970 model did. Nevertheless, there are so many more automobiles being driven today that urban ground-level ozone, which decreased between the late 1970s and the late 1980s, has risen to former levels. Under the 1990 amendments, automobile manufacturers must cut new automobiles' exhaust emission of nitrogen oxide by 60 percent and emission of other pollutants by 35 percent. Beginning in 1994, increasing percentages of new vehicles must meet these standards. By 1998, all new automobiles must do so. Alternative-fuel vehicles will be introduced in California. Another set of emission controls may be ordered after 2000. To ensure compliance, the EPA certifies the prototype of a new automobile whose emission controls are effective up to 50,000 miles. The EPA may also inspect production models. If a vehicle does not meet the

2. 16 U.S.C. Sections 661 *et seq.*

standards in actual driving, the EPA can order a recall and the repair or replacement of pollution-control equipment at the manufacturers' expense.

Service stations are also subject to environmental regulations. The 1990 amendments required that in 1992 service stations had to sell gasoline with a higher oxygen content in forty-one cities with winter carbon monoxide pollution. This could be accomplished by selling fuel containing

corn ethanol. Beginning in 1995, service stations must sell even cleaner-burning gasoline in Los Angeles and another eight of the most polluted urban areas.

Present regulations are meant to eliminate lead completely in gasoline. In the following case, the court reviewed an EPA order regulating the lead content of gasoline, the validity of which had been challenged by Ethyl Corporation.

Case 19.2

ETHYL CORP. v. ENVIRONMENTAL PROTECTION AGENCY
United States Court of Appeals, District of Columbia Circuit, 1976.
541 F.2d 1.

BACKGROUND AND FACTS *Ethyl Corporation, a leading producer of antiknock compounds for increasing gasoline octane ratings, filed for judicial review of the EPA order that required annual reductions in the lead content of gasoline. The Clean Air Act[a] authorized the agency to regulate gasoline additives that are a danger to public health and welfare.*

WRIGHT, Circuit Judge.
*   *   *   *

[In the EPA's report] on whether lead additives should be regulated for health reasons, [the EPA] candidly discusses the various scientific studies, both pro and con, underlying this information, and ultimately concludes that lead from automobile emissions will endanger the public health. *   *   *

*   *   * Our [scope] requires us to strike "agency action, findings, and conclusions [only if] we find [them] to be "arbitrary, capricious, an abuse of discretion, or otherwise not in accordance with the law *   *   *." This standard of review is a highly deferential one. It presumes agency action to be valid. Moreover, it forbids the court's substituting its judgment for that of the agency *   *   *.

[Ethyl Corporation] vigorously attack[s] both the sufficiency and the validity of the many scientific studies relied upon by the [EPA], while advancing for consideration various studies allegedly supportive of their position. The record in this case is massive—over 10,000 pages. Not surprisingly, evidence may be isolated that supports virtually any inference one might care to draw. *   *   *

*   *   * We find that *   *   * [the EPA's] reasons as stated in its [report] provide a rational basis for its action. Since we reject all of [Ethyl Corporation's] claims [the EPA] may enforce its low-lead regulations.

DECISION AND REMEDY *The court of appeals upheld the EPA regulations. The court accorded substantial deference to the EPA's conclusion, and thus the EPA was permitted to enforce its low-lead regulations.*

a.   Review of agency actions under the Clean Air Act is available only in the U.S. Court of Appeals for the District of Columbia Circuit.

Stationary Sources

The Clean Air Act provides the EPA with authority to establish air quality standards but recognizes that the primary responsibility for preventing and controlling air pollution rests with state and local gov-

ernments. The EPA sets two levels (primary and secondary) of ambient standards—that is, the maximum level of certain pollutants—and the states formulate plans to achieve those standards. The plans are to provide for the attainment of primary standards within three years and secondary standards within a reasonable time. For economic, political, or technological reasons, however, the deadlines are often subject to change.

Different standards apply to existing sources of pollution and major new sources. Different standards also apply to sources in clean areas and sources in polluted areas. Major new sources include existing sources modified by a change in a method of operation that increases emissions. Performance standards for these sources require use of the best available technology to reduce emissions from the combustion of fossil fuels.

Under the 1990 amendments, 110 of the oldest coal-burning power plants in the United States must cut their emissions by 40 percent by the year 2001 to reduce acid rain. Utilities were granted "credits" to emit certain amounts of sulfur dioxide, and those that emit less than required can sell their credits to other polluters. Controls on other factories and businesses are intended to reduce ground-level ozone pollution in ninety-six cities to healthy levels by 2005 (except Los Angeles, which has until 2010). Industrial emissions of 189 hazardous air pollutants must be reduced by 90 percent by 2000. By 2002, production of chlorofluorocarbons, carbon tetrachloride, and methyl chloroform—used in air conditioning, refrigeration, and insulation and linked to depletion of the ozone layer—must stop.

Hazardous air pollutants are those likely to cause an increase in mortality or in serious irreversible or incapacitating illness. As noted, there are 189 of these pollutants, including asbestos, benzene, beryllium, cadmium, mercury, radiation, vinyl chloride, and other cancer-causing materials. These pollutants may also cause neurological and reproductive damage. They are emitted by a variety of business activities, including smelting, dry cleaning, house painting, and commercial baking. Instead of establishing specific emissions standards for each hazardous air pollutant, the new law requires industry to use the best available technology to limit those emissions. The EPA may strengthen this requirement if necessary to protect public health.

The following case was decided before the 1990 amendments, when uniform national standards were provided for air pollutants emitted from any source. The standards included "an ample margin of safety to protect the public health." The case concerns the standard for vinyl chloride (a cancer-causing chemical used in manufacturing plastic) and whether the cost of complying with that standard should be considered in setting it.

BACKGROUND AND FACTS *In 1976, the EPA established emission standards for vinyl chloride. The standards reduced emissions by 95 percent, leaving a risk that 1 of every 100,000 exposed individuals would develop cancer. Environmental groups protested that the standard was not strict enough to protect the public health. In 1977, the EPA responded by starting another rulemaking investigation. No action was taken until 1985, when the EPA determined that a further reduction in emissions would be unreasonably costly for the polluters. The Natural Resources Defense Council, an environmental group, sued the EPA, arguing that the standard did not provide "an ample margin of safety to protect the public health."*

 Case 19.3

NATURAL RESOURCES DEFENSE COUNCIL, INC. v. ENVIRONMENTAL PROTECTION AGENCY
United States Court of Appeals, District of Columbia Circuit, 1987.
824 F.2d 1146.

BORK, Judge.
*   *   *   *

[I]n setting emission standards for carcinogenic pollutants, the [EPA] Administrator has decided to determine first the level of emissions attainable by best available control technology. He will then determine the costs of setting the standard below that level and balance those costs against the risk to health below the level of feasibility. If the costs are greater than the reduction in risk, then he will set the standard at the level of feasibility. This exercise, in the Administrator's view, will always produce an "ample margin of safety."

* * * *

We find that the congressional mandate to provide "an ample margin of safety" "to protect the public health" requires the Administrator to make an initial determination of what is "safe." This determination must be based exclusively upon the Administrator's determination of the risk to health at a particular emission level. * * *

* * * *

We wish to reiterate the limited nature of our holding in this case because it is not the court's intention to bind the Administrator to any specific method of determining what is "safe" or what constitutes an "ample margin." We hold only that the Administrator cannot consider cost and technological feasibility in determining what is "safe." This determination must be based solely on health.

DECISION AND REMEDY *The court held that the EPA had not considered the appropriate factors in setting the vinyl chloride emission limits. The case was remanded to the EPA for reconsideration of the standards.*

Penalties

For violations of emission limits under the Clean Air Act, the EPA can assess civil penalties of up to $25,000 per day. To penalize those for whom this amount makes a violation more cost-effective than compliance, the EPA can obtain a penalty equal to the violator's economic benefits from noncompliance. Private citizens can also sue violators. Those who knowingly violate the act may be subject to criminal fines.

■ Water Pollution

Federal regulations governing the pollution of water can be traced back to the Rivers and Harbors Act of 1886, as amended in 1899. These regulations required a permit for discharging or depositing refuse in navigable waterways.

Navigable Waters

Once limited to waters actually used for navigation, the term *navigable waters* is today interpreted to include coastal and freshwater wetlands and swamps, as well as intrastate lakes and streams used by interstate travelers and industries. In 1948, Congress passed the Federal Water Pollution Control Act (FWPCA), but its regulatory system and

enforcement proved inadequate. In 1972, amendments to the FWPCA—known as the Clean Water Act—established a new system of goals and standards. These amendments established goals to (1) make waters safe for swimming, (2) protect fish and wildlife, and (3) eliminate the discharge of pollutants into the water. They set forth specific time schedules, which were extended by amendment in 1977 and by the Water Quality Act of 1987. Under these schedules, the EPA establishes limitations for discharges of types of pollutants based on the technology available for controlling them. Regulations for the most part specify that the best available technology be installed.

Municipal and industrial polluters must apply for permits before discharging wastes into navigable waters. Under the act, violators are subject to a variety of civil and criminal penalties. Civil penalties for each violation range from as low as a maximum of $10,000 per day, and not more than $25,000 per violation, to as much as $25,000 per day. Criminal penalties range from a fine of $2,500 per day and imprisonment of up to one year to a fine of $1 million and fifteen years' imprisonment. Injunctive relief and damages can also be imposed. The polluting party can be required to clean up the pollution or pay for the cost of doing so. In most cases, explicit penalties are also imposed on parties that pollute the water, as illustrated by the following case.

Case 19.4

UNITED STATES v. ATLANTIC RICHFIELD CO.

United States District Court, Eastern District of Pennsylvania, 1977. 429 F.Supp. 830.

BACKGROUND AND FACTS   *Atlantic Richfield Company (Arco) and other oil companies owned or operated vessels or facilities from which oil was discharged in harmful quantities into navigable waters. The discharges were accidental but nevertheless violated the Clean Water Act. Arco and the others reported the spills to the Coast Guard and cleaned them up. When the Coast Guard assessed monetary civil penalties, Arco refused to pay. In the government's suit to enforce the penalties, Arco argued that the imposition of penalties, over and above clean-up costs, for an accidental oil spill when the reporting and cleaning requirements had been satisfied constituted a criminal action. Arco believed that on that basis it had a right to a jury trial.*

BECKER, District Judge.

   *   *   *   *

   *   *   * [D]efendants claim that, as applied to accidental, reporting, self-cleaners, [the penalty] is really criminal rather than civil because, where defendants are not at fault, the penalty serves none of the ends of civil regulation, but acts only as a punishment. *   *   *

   *   *   *   *

   [Defendants argue that] although the facts reveal "accidental" spills, they do not reveal a basis for inferring that defendants caused the spills through a lack of due care [which could constitute negligence, and] "negligence" is the lowest level of "fault" recognized by our law; i.e., non-negligent conduct is reasonable conduct; therefore, if the spills were not negligent, we can infer that there was no reasonable means for defendants to prevent the spills.

   *   *   *   *

   *   *   * While it is true that the *   *   * facts about the spills themselves would not be sufficient to support an action in negligence, this is not such an action, but rather an action to enforce a penalty.

   The elements of this statutory action are only that defendant violated [the Clean Water Act] and that the Coast Guard following the appropriate procedure assessed the *   *   * penalty. The statute does not make "fault" an element of the cause of action, but rather a factor in the administrative penalty setting procedure. This is proper because there is no principle of law which requires that civil regulability through imposition of penalty be predicated upon a finding of fault. Moreover, a number of factors support civil regulability here in the absence of fault. First, *   *   * the principal goal of [the penalty] is to deter spills. *   *   * Additionally, the Congress obviously believed: (a) that no clean up effort could be complete because, after discharge, it is impossible to guarantee against residual harm from quantities of oil too small or too well dispersed to be detectable; and (b) that even the transitory pollution of waters was deleterious to the environment.

   *   *   *   *

   In view of the foregoing analysis we must reject defendant's contention that, as applied to accidental, reporting, self-cleaners, [the penalty] is really criminal rather than civil because, *   *   * even where defendants are not at fault, the penalty does not act only as a punishment but serves the ends of civil regulation.

The court held that the penalty was civil, not criminal. Therefore, the government could continue to assess and collect fines under the Clean Water Act against oil companies for accidental oil spills.

DECISION AND REMEDY

Drinking Water

Another statute governing water pollution is the Safe Drinking Water Act. Passed in 1974, this act requires the EPA to set maximum levels for pollutants in public water systems. Public water supply system operators must come as close as possible to meeting the EPA's standards by using the best available technology that is economically and technologically feasible. The EPA is particularly concerned with contamination from underground sources. Pesticides and wastes leaked from landfills or disposed of in underground injection wells are among the more than 200 pollutants known to exist in groundwater used for drinking in at least thirty-four states. Many of these substances are associated with cancer and damage to the central nervous system, liver, and kidneys.

Ocean Dumping

The Marine Protection, Research, and Sanctuaries Act of 1972 (known popularly as the Ocean Dumping Act), as amended in 1983, regulates the transportation and dumping of material into ocean waters. (The term *material* is synonymous with the term *pollutant* used in the Federal Water Pollution Control Act.) The Ocean Dumping Act prohibits entirely the ocean dumping of radiological, chemical, and biological warfare agents and high-level radioactive waste. The act establishes a permit program for transporting and dumping other materials. There are specific exemptions—materials subject to the permit provisions of other pollution legislation, wastes from structures regulated by other laws (for example, offshore oil exploration and drilling platforms), sewage, and other wastes. Each violation of any provision or permit may result in a civil penalty of not more than $50,000 or revocation or suspension of the permit. A knowing violation is a criminal offense that may result in a $50,000 fine, imprisonment for not more than a year, or both. Acts amounting to violations can also be enjoined. The Ocean Dumping Act also authorizes the designation of marine sanctuaries for "preserving or restoring such areas for their conservation, recreational, ecological, or esthetic values."

■ Noise Pollution

Regulations concerning noise pollution include the Noise Control Act of 1972. This act requires the EPA to establish noise emission standards (maximum noise levels below which no harmful effects occur due to interference with speech or other activity). The standards must be achievable by the best available technology, and they must be economically within reason. The act prohibits, among other things, distributing products manufactured in violation of the noise emission standards and tampering with noise control devices. Either of these activities can result in an injunction or whatever other remedy "is necessary to protect the public health and welfare." Illegal product distribution can also result in a fine and imprisonment. Violations of provisions of the Noise Control Act can result in penalties of not more than $50,000 per day and imprisonment for not more than two years.

■ Toxic Chemicals

Originally, most environmental clean-up efforts were directed toward reducing smog and making water safe for fishing and swimming. Over time, however, it became clear that chemicals released into the environment in relatively small amounts may pose a considerable threat to human life and health. Control of these toxic chemicals has become an important part of environmental law.

Pesticides and Herbicides

The first toxic chemical problem to receive widespread public attention was that posed by pesticides and herbicides. The federal statute regulating pesticides and herbicides is the Federal Insecticide, Fungicide, and Rodenticide Act (FIFRA) of 1947. Under FIFRA, pesticides and herbicides must be (1) registered before they can be sold, (2) certified and used only for approved applications, and (3) used in limited quantities when applied to food crops. If a substance is identified as harmful, the EPA can cancel its registration after a hearing. If the harm is imminent, the EPA can suspend registration pending the hearing. The EPA may also inspect factories in which these chemicals are manufactured.

Toxic Substances

The first comprehensive law covering toxic substances was the Toxic Substances Control Act, passed in 1976 to regulate chemicals and chemical compounds that are known to be toxic, as well as to institute investigation of any possible harmful effects from new chemical compounds, such as asbestos and polychlorinated biphenyls (popularly known as PCBs). The regulations authorize the EPA to require that manufacturers, processors, and other organizations planning to use chemicals first determine their effect on human health and the environment. The EPA can regulate substances that potentially pose an imminent hazard or an unreasonable risk of injury to health or the environment. The EPA may require special labeling, limit the use of a substance, set production quotas, or prohibit the use of a substance altogether.

Hazardous Wastes

Some industrial, agricultural, and household wastes pose more serious threats. If not properly disposed of, these toxic chemicals may present a substantial danger to human health and the environment. If released into the environment, they may contaminate public drinking water resources. A well-known example of the improper disposal of toxic and hazardous waste involved Hooker Electrochemical Company. Between 1942 and 1953, Hooker dumped more than 20,000 tons of chemical waste in an abandoned canal, known as the Love Canal, near Niagara Falls, New York. Hooker filled in the canal and sold the property to the local school board. An elementary school was built on it, and houses crowded around. In the 1970s, toxic residue bubbled to the surface. The community was abandoned.

RESOURCE CONSERVATION AND RECOVERY ACT   In 1976, Congress passed the Resource Conservation and Recovery Act (RCRA) in reaction to an ever-increasing concern with the effects of hazardous waste materials on the environment. The RCRA required the EPA to establish regulations to monitor and control hazardous waste disposal and to determine which forms of solid waste should be considered hazardous and thus subject to regulation. Under the authority granted by this act, the EPA has promulgated various technical requirements for limited types of facilities for storage and treatment of hazardous waste. It also requires all producers of hazardous waste materials to properly label and package any hazardous waste to be transported.

The RCRA was amended in 1984 and 1986 to add several new regulatory requirements to those already monitored and enforced by the EPA. The

basic aims of the amendments were to decrease the use of land containment in the disposal of hazardous waste and to require compliance with the act by some generators of hazardous waste—such as those generating less than 1,000 kilograms (2,200 pounds) a month—that had previously been excluded from regulation under the RCRA. In 1990, the EPA stiffened its RCRA enforcement policy. Under the new policy, a company may be assessed a civil penalty based on the seriousness of the violation, the probability of harm, and the extent to which the violation deviates from RCRA requirements. The assessment may be up to $25,000 per violation per day. Criminal penalties range from fines of $25,000 per day to $50,000 per day and imprisonment of not more than one year to not more than two years.

SUPERFUND   In 1980, Congress passed the Comprehensive Environmental Response, Compensation, and Liability Act (CERCLA), commonly known as Superfund. The basic purpose of Superfund, which was amended in 1986 by the Superfund Amendments and Reauthorization Act, is to regulate the clean-up of leaking hazardous waste disposal sites. A special federal fund was created for that purpose. Superfund provides that when a release or a threatened release from a site occurs, the EPA can clean up the site and recover the cost of the clean-up from (1) the person who generated the wastes disposed of at the site, (2) the person who transported the wastes to the site, (3) the person who owned or operated the site at the time of the disposal, or (4) the current owner or operator. Liability is usually joint and several—that is, for example, a person who generated only a fraction of the hazardous waste disposed of at the site may nevertheless be liable for all of the clean-up costs.

Recently, courts have focused on the meaning of the words "owner or operator" to determine who is a potentially responsible party. A parent company has been held liable as an "operator" for clean-up costs for a chemical spill at a plant owned by its subsidiary. The court pointed out that the parent company controlled the subsidiary's finances, real estate transactions, and contact with the government, and that the parent company's personnel held most of the subsidiary's officer and director positions.[3] In other cases, courts have held

---

3.   *United States v. Kayser-Roth Corp.*, 910 F.2d 24 (1st Cir. 1990).

officers and shareholders liable based on their authority to exercise control over their corporations.[4] A secured creditor of an operator of a facility has also been held liable on the basis that the creditor participated in the financial management of the facility to a degree indicating a capacity to control the corporation's handling of hazardous waste.[5] In the following case, the court considers whether a successor corporation can be held liable under CERCLA.

---

4. See, for example, *State of New York v. Shore Realty Corp.*, 759 F.2d 1032 (2d Cir. 1985).

5. *United States v. Fleet Factors Corp.*, 901 F.2d 1550 (11th Cir. 1990).

Case 19.5

ANSPEC CO. v. JOHNSON CONTROLS, INC.

United States Court of Appeals, Sixth Circuit, 1991. 922 F.2d 1240.

BACKGROUND AND FACTS   *The Anspec Company purchased a parcel of land from Ultraspherics, Inc., in 1978. After the sale, Ultraspherics merged into the Hoover Group, which was designated as the surviving corporation. Johnson Controls, Inc., is the sole shareholder of the Hoover Group and of Hoover Universal, which was the sole shareholder of Ultraspherics. Prior to the sale of the property to Anspec, Ultraspherics had placed three tanks on the property—one underground and two aboveground—which were used to store hazardous waste materials. Leaks and spills of the hazardous waste contaminated the soil at the site and the groundwater beneath the site. Anspec requested the Hoover Group, as the corporate successor of Ultraspherics, to pay the costs associated with cleaning up the site. When the Hoover Group refused to comply, Anspec brought this action against Ultraspherics and its corporate successors. The trial court held that Ultraspherics could not be liable because it no longer existed. The other defendants—the Hoover Group, Hoover International, and Johnson Controls—moved for dismissal. On the grounds that none of them had ever owned, occupied, or stored chemicals on the property and that CERCLA did not provide that successor corporations were liable for clean-up costs, the trial court granted the motion for dismissal, and Anspec appealed.*

LIVELY, Senior Circuit Judge.
            *   *   *   *
      *   *   * In this dispute between private parties, CERCLA is concerned only that the persons listed in [Section] 9607(a) be responsible for cleanup costs. Since successor corporations are not so listed, the defendants argue, the district court correctly dismissed Hoover Group, Hoover Universal and Johnson Controls.

With respect to Ultraspherics, the plaintiffs contend that this defendant comes within the clear statutory designation of a person potentially liable; that [Section] 9607(a)(2) makes liable for cleanup costs ''any person who at the time of disposal of any hazardous substance owned or operated any facility at which such hazardous substances were disposed of[.]'' *   *   * Moreover, Michigan [corporate law] provides that although the separate existence of every corporation except the surviving corporation in a merger ceases, the surviving corporation has all liabilities of every corporation that was a party to the merger. For purposes of liability, the surviving corporation and the merged corporation are one and the same. If Ultraspherics is not liable for cleanup costs, it is only because Hoover Group stands in its shoes as the surviving party that became liable for its obligations. *   *   *
            *   *   *   *
      *   *   * [C]onstruing the statute [CERCLA] in light of a universally accepted principle of private corporation law, we conclude that Congress included successor

corporations within the description of entities that are potentially liable under CER-
CLA for cleanup costs. That is to say, when Congress wrote ''corporation'' in
CERCLA it intended to include a successor corporation.

  *   *   *   *

  *   *   * [T]he line separating statutory interpretation and judicial lawmaking is
not always clear and sharp. If a statute is found to be abundantly clear and well
defined, a judicial decision that expands or contracts its reach or adds or deletes
remedies fashions federal common law. On the other hand, if the court detects only
gaps in definitions or descriptions, it may fill these interstices of the statute by
exercising its authority to interpret or construe the statute. *   *   * The authority to
construe a statute lies at the very heart of judicial power and is not subject to rigorous
scrutiny. The rule is otherwise with respect to outright judicial lawmaking, however.
Before a federal court may fashion a body of federal common law, it must find either
(1) that Congress painted with a broad brush and left it to the courts to ''flesh out''
the statute by fashioning a body of substantive federal law, or (2) that a federal rule
of decision is necessary to protect uniquely federal interests.

The district court referred to these restrictions on a federal court's power to
fashion common law in granting the defendants' motion to dismiss. We believe the
district court misperceived the judicial function invoked by the plaintiffs' claim in
this case. Rather than deciding whether the case came within its limited authority to
create federal law, the court should have determined whether [Section] 9607(a), when
properly construed[,] includes a claim against a successor corporation in a merger
situation.

*The appellate court reversed the trial court's judgment and remanded the
case for further proceedings consistent with this opinion. The district court
was instructed to follow Michigan law in its application of successor
liability.*

**DECISION
AND REMEDY**

■ Radiation

At the beginning of its development, nuclear energy was regarded as a cleaner and less expensive
alternative to fossil fuels (coal and oil). During the
production of nuclear energy, plutonium, uranium,
and other radioactive materials emit dangerous levels of radiation. Radiation at these levels is believed
to cause cancer and other diseases. The waste produced by a nuclear power plant remains dangerously radioactive for thousands of years. Despite
continuing research, a method for permanent disposal of nuclear waste has not been developed.

Nuclear power plants are built and operated by
private industry. The private nuclear industry is
regulated almost exclusively by the federal government under the Atomic Energy Act of 1954.
The Nuclear Regulatory Commission (NRC) is the
federal agency responsible for regulating the private nuclear industry. The NRC reviews the plans
for each proposed nuclear plant and issues a construction permit only after preparing an environmental impact statement that considers the impact

of an accidental release of radiation. After construction, the NRC licenses the plant's operation.

The Environmental Protection Agency sets
standards for radioactivity in the overall environment and for the disposal of some radioactive
waste. Low-level radioactive waste generated by
private facilities is the responsibility of each state
under the Low Level Radioactive Waste Policy Act
of 1980, as amended in 1986. The NRC regulates
the use and disposal of other nuclear materials and
radioactive waste. Some radioactive waste is buried, burned, or dumped in the ocean. Currently,
however, most of it is stored at the plants in which
it is produced. Under the Nuclear Waste Policy Act
of 1982, the government is looking for a permanent
disposal site scheduled to be opened sometime in
the year 2000.

There is a possibility of injury from exposure
to radioactive substances in other forms. The potential for liability for injuries caused by radiation
exposure begins with the mining of uranium ore.
Hundreds of uranium miners have sued their em-

ployers and the federal government, alleging that they suffered lung cancer or other diseases as a result of exposure in the mines. The processing of uranium ore has also resulted in lawsuits. In one case, for example, it was claimed that exposure to uranium tailings caused the deaths of seven children in Monticello, Utah.[6]

Liability may be predicated on some of the same grounds discussed in other sections of this chapter. A common law theory may serve as the basis for a radiation suit. For example, Safety Light Corporation was held liable under a strict liability theory for the acts of its predecessor company, the United States Radium Company (USRC). USRC had extracted radium from uranium ore and deposited radioactive tailings from the process on vacant portions of its property in New Jersey between 1917 and 1926. T&E Industries, Inc., bought the property in 1974. In 1979, the state advised T&E that radiation levels on the property were excessive. In T&E's suit against Safety Light, the court held that the party creating a radiation hazard

is strictly responsible for its clean-up and any damages.[7]

Liability for injury resulting from radiation may also arise under one of the statutes discussed elsewhere in this chapter. In 1986, the state of Ohio sued the Department of Energy and private contractors who had operated a nuclear weapons facility at Fernald, Ohio, alleging, among other things, that they improperly released radioactive materials into the environment in violation of the Clean Water Act, the Resource Conservation and Recovery Act, and the Comprehensive Environmental Response, Compensation, and Liability Act. In 1988, energy officials admitted that an operator of the facility had been ordered to continue dumping radioactive material at the site over a period of years. Officials agreed to pay Ohio more than $1 million to settle two suits and agreed to allow the state to oversee the clean-up of the site. In 1990, a federal appeals court ordered the Department of Energy to pay $250,000 in civil penalties to Ohio.[8]

---

6. *Maughan v. S. W. Servicing, Inc.,* 758 F.2d 1381 (10th Cir. 1985). Ultimately, it was determined that the children had not received biologically significant doses.

7. *T&E Industries v. Safety Light Corp.,* 123 N.J. 371, 587 A.2d 1249 (1991).
8. *Ohio v. Department of Energy,* 904 F.2d 1058 (6th Cir. 1990).

■ Terms and Concepts to Review

■ Questions and Case Problems

19-1. The EPA has set ambient standards for several pollutants, including sulfur dioxide, specifying the maximum concentration allowable in the outdoor air. One way to meet these standards is to reduce emissions. Companies discovered, however, that they could also meet the standards at less cost by building very high smokestacks. When emitted from such high stacks, pollutants were more widely dispersed and remained below the concentration level specified by the ambient standards. Environmental groups claimed that the Clean Air Act was designed to reduce pollution, not disperse it, and argued that industry should not be allowed to rely on tall stacks. Are the environmental groups correct, or should industry be allowed to use the less expensive dispersal method? Discuss.

19-2. Current scientific knowledge indicates that there is no safe level of exposure to a cancer-causing agent. In theory, even one molecule of such a substance has the potential for causing cancer. Section 112 of the Clean Air Act requires that all cancer-causing substances be regulated to ensure a margin of safety. Some environmental groups have argued that all emissions of such substances must be eliminated in order for such a margin of safety to be reached. Such a total elimination would likely shut down many major U.S. industries. Should the EPA totally eliminate all emissions of cancer-causing chemicals? Discuss.

19-3. Moonbay is a development home building corporation that primarily develops retirement communities. Farmtex owns a number of feedlots in Sunny Valley. Moonbay purchased 20,000 acres of farmland in the same area and began building and selling homes on this acreage. In the meantime, Farmtex continued to expand its feedlot business, and eventually only 500 feet separated the two operations. Because of the odor and flies from the feedlots, Moonbay found it difficult to sell the homes in its development. Moonbay wants to enjoin Farmtex from operating its feedlots in the vicinity of the retirement home development. Discuss under what theory Moonbay would file this action. Discuss fully whether Farmtex has violated any federal environmental laws.

19-4. Fruitade, Inc., is a processor of a soft drink called Freshen Up. Fruitade uses returnable bottles, as well as a special acid to clean its bottles for further beverage processing. The acid is diluted by water and then allowed to pass into a navigable stream. Fruitade crushes its broken bottles and throws the crushed glass into the stream. Discuss fully any environmental laws that Fruitade has violated.

19-5. The EPA canceled the registration of the pesticide diazinon for use on golf courses and sod farms because of concern about the effects of diazinon on birds. The Federal Insecticide, Fungicide, and Rodenticide Act authorizes cancellation of the registration of product's that ''generally cause unreasonable adverse effects on the environment.'' The statute further defines ''unreasonable adverse effects on the environment'' to mean ''any unreasonable risk to man or the environment, taking into account the . . . costs and benefits.'' Thus, in determining whether a pesticide should continue to be used, one must balance the risks and benefits of the use of the pesticide. Does this mean that one must find that the pesticide killed birds more often than not before its use can be prohibited? Or, to prohibit the pesticide's use, is it sufficient to find only that the use of the pesticide results in recurrent bird kills? [*CIBA-Geigy Corp. v. Environmental Protection Agency,* 874 F.2d 277 (5th Cir. 1989)]

19-6. The EPA promulgated water-pollution discharge limits for several mining industries. These standards authorized variances exempting mining operations from coverage by the standards if the operations could show that they used special processes or facilities that made the standards inapplicable. Cost was not a consideration in granting the variances. An industry trade association sued, claiming that the EPA should consider costs in granting variances, and the Fourth Circuit Court of Appeals agreed. Discuss whether the United States Supreme Court should overturn this decision or affirm it and let costs be considered in the granting of variances under the Clean Water Act. [*Environmental Protection Agency v. National Crushed Stone Association,* 449 U.S. 64, 101 S.Ct. 295, 66 L.Ed.2d 268 (1980)]

19-7. 🖳 The Resource Conservation and Recovery Act gives the EPA authority to require a company to clean up a hazardous-waste site that presents an ''imminent and substantial endangerment'' to public health or to the environment. A company disposed of dioxin by discharging it into a pond located on its property. The EPA ordered that the company stop the disposal and clean up the site. The company argued that the EPA had no evidence of any actual harm to the health of nearby residents.

Should the company be compelled to clean up the dioxin even in the absence of evidence of actual harm? Discuss. [*United States v. Vertac Chemical Corp.,* 489 F.Supp. 870 (E.D.Ark. 1980)]

19-8. Taylor Bay Protective Association is a nonprofit corporation established for the purpose of restoring and improving the water quality of Taylor Bay. Local water districts began operating a flood control project in the area. As part of the project, a pumping station was developed. Testimony at trial revealed that the pumps were operated contrary to the instructions provided in the Operation and Maintenance Manual. The pumps acted as vacuums, sucking up increased amounts of silt and depositing the silt in Taylor Bay. Thus, the project resulted in sedimentation and turbidity problems in the downstream watercourse of Taylor Bay. The association sued the local water districts, alleging that the pumping operations created a nuisance. Do the pumping operations qualify as common law nuisance? Who should be responsible for the clean-up costs? Discuss both questions fully. [*Taylor Bay Protective Association v. Environmental Protection Agency,* 884 F.2d 1073 (8th Cir. 1989)]

19-9. Cities Service Co. operated a phosphate rock mine that included large settling ponds for the extraction of phosphate. A dam outside of one of these ponds broke, sending a billion gallons of phosphate slimes into the nearby Peace River. This killed fish and caused other damage. The state of Florida sued Cities Service under strict liability for damages. Given these facts, should Cities Service be liable? [*Cities Service Co. v. State,* 312 So.2d 799 (Fla.App. 1975)]

19-10. Portland General Electric Co. maintained a turbine facility. Nearby residents complained that the facility emitted low-frequency sound waves that caused them to suffer loss of sleep, emotional distress, and mental strain. Consequently, these residents sued the company, claiming that it was creating a nuisance. The defendant contended that the plaintiffs had suffered no special harm. The district court dismissed the plaintiffs' complaint, and the plaintiffs appealed the decision. Should the appellate court affirm the dismissal? Explain. [*Frady v. Portland General Electric Co.,* 55 Or.App. 344, 637 P.2d 1345 (1981)]

19-11. A Question of Ethics

In the 1970s, South Carolina Recycling and Disposal, Inc., (SCRDI) ran a hazardous waste disposal and recycling operation. A number of chemical companies (so-called generators) brought their wastes to the SCRDI facility. Handling of wastes at the site was itself hazardous; 7,200 fifty-five-gallon drums of hazardous substances—including materials that were toxic, carcinogenic, mutagenic, explosive, and highly flammable—accumulated. Stacked without regard to the source or the compatibility of the substances within, many drums deteriorated to the point that their contents spilled onto other drums, mixed with other leaking substances, and oozed into the ground. This caused noxious and toxic fumes and a number of fires and explosions. The EPA began clean-up operations and sued some of the generators (plus others) for the costs. The generators argued that they should not have to pay because there was no evidence linking their specific wastes to the problems. The court granted summary judgment for the EPA, ruling that the EPA needed to show only that the generators sent waste to the site at some time. [United States v. South Carolina Recycling and Disposal, Inc., *653 F.Supp. 984 (D.S.C. 1986)]*

1. The liability imposed on business firms under CERCLA has led to controversy because sometimes it seems unfair that certain businesses should be held liable. In this case, the generators argued that it would be unfair to hold them liable for clean-up costs in the absence of any evidence that their wastes caused any of the problems. In response, the court held that to require specific proof of causation "would . . . effectively 'eviscerate the statute' because of the technological infeasibility of 'fingerprinting' a given generator's substances at a site." What two broad ethical policies or principles are in conflict here?

2. The court also held that the generators were jointly and severally liable for clean-up costs. Joint and several liability under CERCLA means that a company that is responsible for only a fraction of the waste may nonetheless be liable for all of the clean-up costs. From an ethical point of view, evaluate the arguments for and against joint and several liability for the costs associated with environmental clean-up operations.

19-12. Case Briefing Assignment

Examine Case A.19 [Louisiana-Pacific Corp. v. Asarco, Inc., 909 F.2d 1260 (9th Cir. 1990)] in Appendix A. The case has been excerpted there in great detail. Review and then brief the case, making sure that you include answers to the following questions in your brief.

1. Was it proper for Arasco to be held liable for the clean-up costs since it had played no role in selecting IMP's customers?

2. Should IMP or L-Bar Products, Inc., be responsible for cleaning up the contaminated groundwater if they had no prior knowledge of the fact that the slag reacted with acidic wood wastes?

3. Should L-Bar Products, Inc. be responsible for any liabilities that would have otherwise been incurred by IMP due to its subsequent purchase of substantially all of IMP's assets?

Chapter 20

Antitrust and Monopoly

The legal environment of business is generally one of competition among rival firms. In free and open competition, businesses attempt to develop and sell products that are more appealing to customers than are the products of rival firms. Competition among sellers therefore promotes the development of appealing products. When products sold by different firms are similar, firms compete by trying to sell at the lowest price possible while still earning enough after costs to make it worthwhile to remain in that particular endeavor. For example, if Acme, Inc., develops a new laser-printing facsimile transmission machine—a laser fax—that has broad appeal among consumers, it will begin to earn profits greater than those of its rivals that are commensurate with the appeal of the new product. All else equal, the greater the appeal of Acme's laser fax, the greater its profits.

■ Market Power and Antitrust Law

To encourage such innovative behavior, we might feel justified in allowing Acme to have a *monopoly* over the sale of the laser fax—at least for awhile, say seventeen years.[1] The term **monopoly** is generally used to describe a market in which there is a single seller. In that respect, Acme would be a monopolist, albeit for a limited time, in the laser fax market. In legal terms, monopoly may also describe a firm that, although not the sole seller in the market, can nonetheless substantially ignore rival firms in setting a selling price for its product or can in some way limit rivals from competing in the market (possibly by preventing rivals from entering the market altogether). Acme's monopoly would give it such **market power**; Acme would have the power during the term of its monopoly to prevent other firms from selling the laser fax. Acme would be free to charge whatever price it chose to, and it would choose a price that made its profits as large as possible.

Competitive Behavior in Action

Another firm might seek to develop a different type of laser fax, one with equal or greater appeal than Acme's laser fax. If it succeeded, it would draw

---

1. Acme would be given a patent on its newly developed laser fax.

475

customers away from Acme. If its product were sufficiently dissimilar from Acme's, it too might seek a legal monopoly over its product. There would then be two monopolies rather than one, but society would have the benefit of *two* unique and valued products. Moreover, Acme would be concerned that if it charged too high a price for its laser fax, it would lose customers to its rival. Acme's rival would have the same concern over the price of its product.

Eventually, after the legal monopolies expired, numerous firms would be allowed to market identical products. Each firm would seek to attract customers by charging the lowest price. The only thing that would prevent prices from falling ever lower is that at some point the price of a laser fax would be so low that new firms would quit trying to enter the market to compete for fax consumers. They would instead devote their efforts and resources to alternative, more profitable ventures. Ultimately, the laser fax would sell for a competitive price, one that would of course cover the costs of production as well as earn a return equal to that which could be earned by employing the same resources in an alternative industry.

The Goals of Antitrust Law

The simplistic scenario just described highlights the benefits to society of having firms compete in the development, production, and sale of goods and services, even though obtaining those benefits may involve conferring a limited monopoly such as that given to Acme.

Our scenario, simplistic though it may be, should make clear an often overlooked point: market power is not inherently bad. Market power correlates to high profits, and large profits are the reward for innovation, foresight, and good management. It is the prize that motivates firms to benefit society with innovative products and competitive prices. What is at issue is not market power per se but how firms go about acquiring market power and what firms do with that power once they acquire it. **Antitrust law** is that body of statutes and principles that regulate business conduct so as to promote the forms of competition that benefit society while simultaneously seeking to rein in the exercise of market power that often is the fruit of such competition.

■ The Common Law and the Restraint of Trade

Socially beneficial commercial activity involves cooperation as well as competition. A business firm, for example, may compete with certain firms in some markets but cooperate with other firms in other markets. A firm that sells finished goods directly to the public may itself act as a consumer by purchasing intermediate products from a second firm. In this sense, the two firms act cooperatively rather than competitively, at least vis-à-vis one another. Similarly, two firms may cooperate by engaging in a *joint venture,* perhaps to develop or market a new product.

Public Policy and Contracts

Any mutual effort that calls for more than a brief period of sustained cooperation requires commitment from all the parties. The principal means of assuring such a sustained commitment is through a contract between the parties. Most cooperative efforts among business firms, in fact, are embodied in some form of contract. But recall from Chapter 9 that a principle of the common law of contracts is that no contract is enforceable if it is against public policy.

Many contracts between business firms promote competition. Because competition, as noted above, is beneficial to society, such contracts are not against public policy. A contract may provide assurances that one firm will be able to obtain necessary inputs from another on a long-term basis. Likewise, a contract may provide assurances to two firms entering into a joint venture that each will continue fulfilling its obligation on the project beyond the initial investment stage. In both these instances, the rights and remedies afforded by contract law promote economic efficiency. Such agreements are not against public policy.

Some agreements between business firms, however, may reduce competition. An agreement between two bakers to coordinate their production of bread so as to limit output and charge a uniform, higher price in the market might entirely eliminate competition in the affected market. If the two bakers were the only suppliers in the market, their combining together in effect would create a joint monopoly under which they would share exclusive control over the market. Such an agreement would be condemned under the common law as an *unreasonable restraint of trade.*

Consider, though, a baker who decides to sell her bakery to her apprentice. The apprentice might demand that, as a condition to the sale, the baker refrain from opening another bakery across the street. Should such an agreement be condemned as against public policy? At first glance, it is a restraint of trade: it prevents the community from benefiting from the baking skills of the baker. If the agreement were not enforced, however, the apprentice, who was willing to pay a price commensurate with the current earnings of the bakery, would lose out on the deal; customers would probably follow the baker with the established reputation to her new shop across the street from the old one.

If the apprentice knew beforehand that the agreement would not be enforced, it would be the baker who would suffer, because the apprentice would not be willing to pay a price reflecting the expectation that the earnings of the bakery would continue at the current level. Society might consider enforcing such agreements in spite of the restraint of trade so that entrepreneurs who contemplate opening new businesses will be assured of later being able to sell those businesses at full value. If others know that sellers will be held to the promise not to compete, the sellers can sell their businesses for more than they could if such promises were condemned as against public policy.

Interference with Free Trade

Compare the two agreements just discussed. Both interfere with free trade. The first involves outright collusion between two competitors to completely eliminate competition between themselves. Their agreement calls for artificially driving prices higher by restricting output. The second agreement also restrains trade, but the restraint is not the primary purpose of the agreement. The restraint is really the only means of assuring that both parties to the sale of an established bakery can reap the full benefit of their bargain: the sale of the bakery for its highest value. The second agreement thus can be viewed as reasonable given that it is the only means of achieving a legitimate end. It also has offsetting benefits to the restraint of trade in that it encourages

entrepreneurship by allowing the baker to sell her business for its highest value.

■ The Origins of Federal Antitrust Legislation

Despite condemning anticompetitive agreements on the basis of public policy, the common law proved to be an ineffective means of protecting free competition. There are temptations for business firms to agree to limit competition or to harm other rivals. Such agreements, indeed, are unenforceable, because they are held to be against public policy. But the problem under the common law is that such agreements are left unchallenged unless one of the parties to an agreement refuses to abide by its terms. *Unenforceable* means only that a court will not sanction a party that reneges on its promise; it does not mean that a forum will be provided in which anticompetitive agreements can be challenged by others who are not parties to the agreement. These shortcomings became acutely obvious during the latter half of the 1800s as a concentrated group of powerful individuals began to acquire unrivaled market power by combining competing firms under singular control.

The Trend Toward Monopoly

After the Civil War ended, the nation renewed its drive westward. With the movement westward came the expansion of the railroads and the further integration of the economy. The growth of national markets also witnessed the efforts of a number of small companies to combine into large business organizations, many of which gained considerable market power. These large organizations became known as **trusts,** the most famous—or infamous—being John D. Rockefeller's Standard Oil Trust. In general, a trust is an arrangement in which some party, referred to as a trustee, holds legal title to property for the benefit of another. As used by Standard Oil and others around the turn of the century, trusts were a device used to amass market power. The participants transferred their stock to a trustee and in return received trust certificates. The trustee then made decisions fixing prices, controlling output, and allocating geographic markets in which specified members could compete free from competition with other members.

In some cases, an entire industry was dominated by a single organization. The public perception was that the trusts used their market power to drive small competitors out of business, leaving the trusts free to raise prices virtually at will.[2]

The Federal Response

Congress initially dealt with the railroad monopolies by attempting regulation rather than an outright assault on monopoly power. The result was the Interstate Commerce Act of 1887.

Congress next attempted to deal with trusts in a direct, unified way by passing the Sherman Act in 1890. The Sherman Act is a broadly worded pronouncement that prohibits competitors from making agreements that unreasonably restrain trade and condemns conduct leading to or tending to produce monopoly power. Violations of the Sherman Act are criminal offenses as well as civil ones.

The Sherman Act, however, failed to end public concerns over monopolies. The United States Supreme Court initially construed the statute too narrowly to give it much effect and subsequently applied it so rigorously as to make the act unworkable. Lackluster enforcement also contributed to the public's dissatisfaction. Concern over the trust problem continued to the point that it dominated the 1912 presidential election and eventually, in 1914, led to enactment of the Clayton Act and the Federal Trade Commission Act. This legislation sought to deal with the monopoly problem by proscribing specific acts and providing for more aggressive means of enforcement.

The Clayton Act (as amended by the Robinson-Patman Act in 1936 and the Celler-Kefauver Act of 1950) addresses specific acts that are considered to be anticompetitive. The Federal Trade Commission Act created the Federal Trade Commission and invested it with broad enforcement powers to *prevent* as well as correct business behavior broadly defined as *unfair trade practices.*

In the remainder of this chapter, we consider the federal legislation in more detail and examine the means of enforcement. We also examine the

narrower area of antitrust law that deals with individual firms' behavior leading to or tending to create monopolies. We reserve for Chapter 21 the broader area of antitrust law that deals with all forms of joint activities that restrain competition.

■ The Sherman Act

The main provisions of the Sherman Act are contained in Sections 1 and 2 of the act. Both sections describe illegal conduct in very broad terms.

Sections 1 and 2 of the Act

Section 1 prohibits a concerted activity on the part of two or more persons to restrain trade:

> Section 1: Every contract, combination in the form of trust or otherwise, or conspiracy, in restraint of trade or commerce among the several States, or with foreign nations, is hereby declared to be illegal [and is a felony punishable by fine or imprisonment].

Section 2 applies to both unilateral and concerted actions:

> Section 2: Every person who shall monopolize, or attempt to monopolize, or combine or conspire with any other person or persons, to monopolize any part of the trade or commerce among the several States, or with foreign nations, shall be deemed guilty of a felony [and is similarly punishable].

Section 1 of the act prohibits concerted activity that unreasonably restrains trade. Section 2 condemns individual anticompetitive behavior that produces or is intended to produce monopoly power. Both restraint of trade and monopoly power are fundamental concepts in antitrust law.

Antitrust terminology

Because *restraint of trade* and *monopoly power* are phrases encountered throughout the study of antitrust law, they have taken on special meanings as terms of art in the antitrust literature. A **restraint of trade** is any agreement between firms that has the effect of reducing competition in the marketplace. As discussed more completely in the next chapter, some restraints of trade are so blatantly anticompetitive—such as agreements to restrict output or fix prices—that they are condemned as

---

2. There is now a considerable amount of literature that questions whether predatory tactics are economically viable and whether they in fact characterize the activities of Rockefeller and the other "robber barons" of the late nineteenth century.

per se violations, without inquiry into any business justification that may be advanced in defense of the agreements. Other agreements judge the restraints under a rule of reason similar to the common law analysis of the reasonableness of the restraint discussed earlier.

Simply put, **monopoly power** is an extreme amount of market power. The most direct, and perhaps the most useful, way of thinking of *monopoly power* is to recall our initial discussion of Acme's market power in the scenario in which Acme was given, for a time, exclusive control over the laser fax market; specifically, Acme could ignore the effect of raising its product price on the ability of competitors to enter the laser fax market. Such extreme market power is an example of monopoly power. Any firm, even if it is not the sole supplier, that is not completely constrained by the potential response of a rival in deciding what price to charge for its product has some degree of market power. Deciding whether such power is great enough to warrant its being called monopoly power is one of the most difficult tasks encountered in the application of antitrust law.

■ The Clayton Act

In contrast to the Sherman Act's broad proscriptions, set out in Sections 1 and 2 of the act, the Clayton Act's provisions deal with *specific* practices that are not expressly covered by the Sherman Act but that are considered to reduce competition or lead to monopoly power. The substantive provisions of the act deal with four distinct forms of business behavior, which are declared illegal but not criminal. With regard to each of the four, the act's prohibitions are qualified by the general condition that the behavior is illegal only if it substantially tends to lessen competition or create monopoly power. The major offenses under the Clayton Act are set out in sections 2, 3, 7, and 8 of the act.

Section 2: Price Discrimination

Price discrimination occurs when sellers charge different buyers different prices for identical goods. Section 2 of the Clayton Act prohibits certain classes of price discrimination for reasons other than differences in production or transportation

costs. The Clayton Act was amended in 1936 by the Robinson-Patman Act as Congress sought to make it more difficult for businesses to evade the terms of Section 2. To violate Section 2, the seller must be engaged in interstate commerce, and the effect of the price discrimination must be to substantially lessen competition. Under the Robinson-Patman Act, sellers are prohibited from reducing prices to levels substantially below those charged by their competitors unless they can justify the reduction by demonstrating that the lower price was charged "in good faith to meet an equally low price of a competitor."[3]

Section 3: Exclusionary Practices

Section 3 of the Clayton Act prohibits sellers and lessors from selling or leasing "on the condition, agreement or understanding that the . . . purchaser or lessee thereof shall not use or deal in the goods . . . of a competitor or competitors of the seller." Section 3 in effect prohibits two types of vertical arrangements involving exclusionary tactics: exclusive dealing contracts and tie-in sales agreements.

An *exclusive dealing contract* is one in which a seller forbids the buyer from purchasing products from the seller's competitors. Such contracts are prohibited under Section 3 if the effect of the contract will "substantially lessen competition or tend to create a monopoly."

In a *tying arrangement,* or *tie-in sales agreement,* the seller conditions the sale of a product (the tying product) on the buyer's agreeing to purchase another product (the tied product) produced or distributed by the same seller. The legality of such agreements depends on many factors, especially on consideration of the purpose of the arrangement and its likely effect on competition in the relevant markets (consider that there are two markets because the agreement involves both the tying and the tied product). In the next chapter, we deal in depth with both exclusive dealing contracts and tying arrangements as part of our analysis of restraints of trade.

---

3. *United States v. United States Gypsum Co.*, 438 U.S. 422, 98 S.Ct. 2864, 5 L.Ed.2d 854 (1978).

Toward Stricter
Enforcement of Antitrust Laws

During the late 1970s, and for virtually the whole decade of the 1980s under the Reagan administration, the "new" antitrust view in Washington could be summarized, in the words of one official in the Justice Department, as "hands off." The pursuit of alleged antitrust violaters by both the Federal Trade Commission and the Antitrust Division of the Justice Department was, in principle, only to be undertaken if true economic damages were incurred by society. Otherwise, little was done, even if a business was technically violating an antitrust statute. In contrast, the 1990s are seeing increasing attention to antitrust enforcement. Those who make policy in the Justice Department and the FTC have given clear signals, through both their words and their actions, that the current approach to antitrust enforcement is, and will continue to be, more vigorous than in the past.

Court Challenges to Mergers on the Rise

One indication of this more vigorous enforcement of antitrust law has come from the Justice Department's interference with proposed mergers. At the beginning of this decade, for example, court challenges to mergers brought

by the Justice Department's Antitrust Division increased by 100 percent within one year. The current policy of the Justice Department is that a merger will be challenged if it is anticompetitive and if potential entry into the same industry will not be likely, timely, or sufficiently effective to overcome the negative effects of the merger.

The Federal Trade Commission (FTC) similarly has increased its interest in supposed anticompetitive mergers. In 1990, the FTC made thirty-nine requests for information about proposed mergers—up from twenty-five such requests during the previous year. The request for additional information is the first step taken by the FTC toward blocking a merger. The FTC's Bureau of Competition has also added more than 10 percent to the number of attorneys in the Antitrust Enforcement Division.

Professional Associations under Fire

As further evidence of the federal government's renewed interest in antitrust enforcement, a number of professional organizations have recently been under attack. One of the most prominent cases was brought by the Justice Department against three Arizona dentists and two professional corporations for

felonious price fixing.[a] The defendants were accused of conspiring to fix and raise the co-payment fees paid by patient members of four prepaid dental plans.

The Justice Department, speaking through Assistant Attorney General James F. Rill, said that physicians and other medical professionals "enjoy no immunity" from the well-settled rule that price fixing among competitors is a crime. They will be "pursued and prosecuted for the crime." The dentists face eighteen-month prison sentences, as well as monetary penalties, and will be subject to the new, higher maximum penalties for individuals convicted of a felony under the Sherman Act.

On July 5, 1990, the Justice Department took aim at another professional group: the American Institute of Architects (AIA). The government alleged that the trade group illegally restrains competition. The AIA decided not to fight to the bitter end and agreed to establish an antitrust compliance program and to pay $50,000 in costs to the government.

Justice Department antitrust lawyer Robert E. Bloch said that "competition is pretty important in any industry, and professionals are no different." He and others are pursuing antitrust actions against

_____
a. *United States v. Alston,* 1990 W.L. 284741 (D.Ariz. 1990).

obstetricians in Boston. The *Alston* case in Arizona concerning dentists and the case concerning obstetricians in Boston represent the first health-care criminal antitrust cases in fifty years.

Stiffer Penalties

The Comprehensive Crime Control Act of 1990 was passed by Congress on October 27 of that year and approved by the president. New maximum fines for criminal violation of the Sherman Act were included. Any individual convicted of a felony under the Sherman Act now faces a maximum of three years in prison, plus the greatest of three alternatives:

1. A $350,000 fine.
2. Twice the pecuniary gain that the individual derived from the crime.
3. Twice the pecuniary loss suffered by the victims of the crime.

For a corporation, the new maximum penalty is the greatest of three alternatives:

1. A $10 million fine.
2. Twice the pecuniary gain that the corporation derived from the crime.
3. Twice the pecuniary loss suffered by the victims of the crime.

Additionally, the government may collect treble damages for antitrust violations when it is the injured party. Although the Justice Department expressed satisfaction at the increased antitrust penalties, it stated that the Antitrust Division's "first and foremost objective" is to seek jail sentences for those violating antitrust laws.

■ Implications for the Businessperson

1. On the positive side, stricter enforcement of antitrust laws will benefit certain businesspersons because they gain protection against competitors' unfair trade practices that are prohibited by antitrust laws. Those companies that are not involved in anticompetitive practices will definitely gain.
2. In contrast, stricter enforcement of antitrust laws and the imposition of stiffer penalties mean that businesspersons must take greater care in their dealings to ensure that they are not engaging in prohibited practices. More time and resources must be spent with attorneys to determine, ahead of time, whether proposed business actions will be challenged by the Justice Department or the Federal Trade Commission.
3. Those who are members of professional groups or associations must be particularly careful about their policies and practices. Some codes of conduct may be scrutinized by the federal government because of their implicit or explicit anticompetitive requirements. Every professional today is now considered "fair game" by the federal government.

■ For Critical Analysis

1. A distinction can be made between focusing on consumers' interests, as opposed to competitors' interests. Is it appropriate, for example, for the United States to begin to flex its legal muscle on behalf of exporters against foreign companies that collude to exclude U.S. firms from a particular market, when this means that the government's attention is focused on the interests of competitors, as opposed to the interests of consumers?
2. The Robinson-Patman Act, which was originally designed to protect the small businessperson from the buying power of chain stores, has often been used by small stores to extort "tribute" from large firms. In other words, if a large operation was able to undercut the price of a smaller operation in the same line of business, the smaller firm could enter into antitrust litigation, citing violation of the Robinson-Patman Act. Is it possible that some antitrust laws actually end up being anticompetitive?

Section 7: Corporate Mergers

Under Section 7 of the Clayton Act, a person or business organization is forbidden to hold stock or assets in another business if "the effect . . . may be to substantially lessen competition." This section provides the statutory authorization for the government's challenging corporate mergers that could have an anticompetitive effect. Two crucial considerations are the market shares among firms in the relevant market and barriers to a firm's entry into a market.

Section 8: Interlocking Directorates

Section 8 of the Clayton Act deals with *interlocking directorates*—that is, the practice of having individuals serve as directors on the boards of two or more competing companies simultaneously. Specifically, no person may be a director in two or more corporations at the same time if (1) either of the corporations has capital, surplus, or undivided profits aggregating more than $1 million and (2) elimination of competition among the corporations would violate any of the antitrust laws.

■ The Federal Trade Commission Act

The Federal Trade Commission (FTC) Act was enacted in 1914, the same year that the Clayton Act was written into law. Section 5 is the sole substantive provision of the act. It provides, in part, as follows:

> Unfair methods of competition in or affecting commerce, and unfair or deceptive acts or practices in or affecting commerce are hereby declared illegal.

Notice that, whereas the Clayton Act prohibits specific forms of anticompetitive behavior, the FTC Act is a "catchall." Section 5 condemns all forms of anticompetitive behavior that are not covered under other federal antitrust laws.

The FTC Act also created the Federal Trade Commission, an administrative agency with functions that include antitrust enforcement as well as other duties concerning consumer protection.

■ Enforcement of the Antitrust Laws

The federal agencies that enforce the federal antitrust laws are the Department of Justice (DOJ)

and the Federal Trade Commission (FTC). The DOJ can prosecute violations of the Sherman Act as either criminal or civil violations. Violations of the Clayton Act are not crimes, and the DOJ can enforce that statute only through civil proceedings. The various remedies that the DOJ has asked the courts to impose include **divestiture** (making a company give up one or more of its operating functions) and **dissolution.** A group of meat packers, for example, can be forced to divorce itself from controlling or owning butcher shops.

The FTC enforces the Clayton Act and has sole authority to enforce the only substantive provision of the Federal Trade Commission Act, Section 5. FTC actions are effected through administrative cease-and-desist proceedings, but it can seek court sanctions for violations of its administrative orders.

A private party can sue for treble damages and attorney's fees under Section 4 of the Clayton Act if the party is injured as a result of a violation of any of the federal antitrust laws, except Section 5 of the Federal Trade Commission Act. In some instances, private parties may also seek injunctive relief to prevent antitrust violations. The courts have determined that the ability to sue depends on the directness of the injury suffered by the would-be plaintiff. Thus, a person wishing to sue under the Sherman Act must prove (1) that the antitrust violation either directly caused or was at least a substantial factor in causing the injury that was suffered and (2) that the unlawful actions of the accused party affected business activities of the plaintiff that were protected by the antitrust laws.

In recent years, more than 90 percent of all antitrust actions have been brought by private plaintiffs. One reason for this is, of course, that successful plaintiffs recover three times the damages they have suffered as a result of the defendants' antitrust law violations. Such recoveries by private plaintiffs for antitrust violations have been rationalized as encouraging "private attorneys general" who will vigorously pursue antitrust violators on their own initiative. This policy consideration has also prompted the courts to ask, in assessing whether a litigant has standing to sue for an alleged antitrust violation, whether the particular plaintiff is properly suited to fulfill the role of a private attorney general. The following case discusses many of these issues.

BACKGROUND AND FACTS *Dr. Todorov, a neurologist, sought staff privileges at DCH, a state hospital, in order to administer computerized tomograph (CT) scans using the facilities in DCH's radiology department. The hospital followed an elaborate set of procedures in determining which physicians should be granted staff privileges. After several hearings and two appeals, Todorov was denied the privilege of administering head CT scans at DCH. One of the reasons for the denial was DCH's fear that if it permitted one local physician access to its radiology department, others would demand the same opportunity. DCH was afraid that this would interfere with its full-time staff of radiologists at the hospital. The staff of radiologists, an independent group practice under contract with the hospital, served both DCH and West General Hospital. These two hospitals were the only ones serving the community, and Todorov alleged that the independent group of radiologists, with DCH's assistance, had monopolized the market for radiology services in the relevant area by preventing other physicians from using the hospitals' radiology facilities. Todorov brought suit in a federal district court against both DCH and the group of radiologists, alleging a denial of due process and various antitrust violations. The district court granted summary judgment for the defendants on the grounds that DCH, as a state facility, was immune from antitrust liability and that the radiologists enjoyed the same immunity by virtue of their operating under contract for DCH. The court also found that there had been no denial of due process. Todorov appealed the decision. The appellate court agreed that there had been no denial of due process but held that the radiologists did not enjoy the same state organization immunity as did DCH. The appellate court, however, went on to question Todorov's standing to sue.*

Case 20.1

TODOROV, M.D. v. DCH HEALTHCARE AUTHORITY

United States Court of Appeals, Eleventh Circuit, 1991.
921 F.2d. 1438.

TJOFLAT, C.J.
     *   *   *   *

Antitrust standing is best understood in a general sense as a search for the proper plaintiff to enforce the antitrust laws.*   *   *
     *   *   *   *

     *   *   * First, a court should determine whether the plaintiff suffered "antitrust injury"; second, the court should determine whether the plaintiff is an efficient enforcer of the antitrust laws, which requires some analysis of the directness or remoteness of the plaintiff's injury. This two-pronged approach was endorsed by the Supreme Court when it stated that "[a] showing of antitrust injury is necessary, but not always sufficient, to establish standing *   *   *, because a party may have suffered antitrust injury but may not be a proper plaintiff *   *   * for other reasons." *   *   *
     *   *   *   *

We now analyze Dr. Todorov's standing to bring his antitrust claims under sections 4 and 16 of the Clayton Act. *   *   * [W]e must conduct an economic analysis of the market for administering CT scans of the head at DCH. Dr. Todorov alleges that the radiologists control this market and are reaping monopoly, or at least supercompetitive, profits. *   *   *
     *   *   *   *

     *   *   * If Dr. Todorov had been granted the privileges he requested, he would have earned profits as long as the radiologists maintained their inflated price; as competition ensued, he would have been driven from the market. [The court based this assumption on its belief that the in-hospital radiologists could operate more efficiently than Dr. Todorov; their lower cost would allow them to charge a lower price than Dr. Todorov and still make a profit once Dr. Todorov began to compete with them.] Thus, Dr. Todorov's damages are premised on his ability to profit while consumers paid an artificially inflated price; he would have had no profits to lose once price settled at the competitive level. That Dr. Todorov is not the cause of these supercompetitive prices is not relevant to our inquiry; he seeks to benefit from them and urges us to let him use the antitrust laws to forward his cause. We, however, will not afford Dr. Todorov the use of the antitrust laws to recoup these alleged damages.

* * * Dr. Todorov's interests are not aligned with patients' interests; Dr. Todorov is interested in forestalling competition, and thus maintaining an inflated price, because at the competitive price his profit is zero. If we gave Dr. Todorov standing * * *, he would be acting only in his interest. Such an injunction would allow him to enter the market and share the radiologists' supercompetitive profits. * * * As such, Dr. Todorov is a particularly poor representative of the patients; indeed, his interests in this case are so at odds with the patients' interests that it is unlikely that he would have standing under article III of the Constitution to present their claims. Dr. Todorov is thus no champion for the cause of consumers. If the radiologists or DCH are acting anticompetitively and are charging an inflated price, then the patients, their insurers, or the government, all of whom are interested in ensuring that consumers pay a competitive price, may bring an action to enjoin such practice. We thus hold that Dr. Todorov has no standing under either section 4 or 16 of the Clayton Act to assert his * * * claims [under sections 1 and 2 of the Sherman Act].

DECISION AND REMEDY   *The court held that Dr. Todorov had not suffered an antitrust injury for which he would have standing to sue for violations of the Sherman Act. On this basis, the court upheld the trial court's grant of summary judgment for DCH and the group of radiologists.*

■ Exemptions

There are many legislative and constitutional limitations on antitrust enforcement. Most are statutory and judicially created exemptions applying to the following areas:

1. **Labor.** Section 6 of the Clayton Act generally permits labor unions to organize and bargain without violating antitrust laws. Section 20 of the Clayton Act specifies that strikes and other labor activities are not violations of any law of the United States. But a union can lose its exemption if it combines with a nonlabor group rather than acting simply in its own self-interest.

2. **Agricultural Associations and Fisheries.** Section 6 of the Clayton Act (along with the Capper-Volstead Act of 1922) exempts agricultural co-operatives from the antitrust laws. The Fisheries Cooperative Marketing Act of 1976 exempts from antitrust legislation individuals in the fishing industry who collectively catch, produce, and prepare for market their products. Both exemptions allow members of such co-ops to combine and set prices for a particular product, but they do not allow the co-ops to engage in exclusionary practices or restraints of trade directed at competitors.

3. **Insurance.** The McCarran-Ferguson Act of 1945 exempts the insurance business from the antitrust laws in states in which the insurance industry is regulated. This exemption does not cover boycotts, coercion, or intimidation on the part of insurance companies.

4. **Foreign Trade.** Under the provisions of the 1918 Webb-Pomerane Act, American exporters may engage in cooperative activity to compete with

similar foreign associations. Such cooperative activity may not, however, restrain trade within the United States or injure other American exporters. In 1982 the Export Trading Company Act was passed, broadening the Webb-Pomerane Act by permitting the Department of Justice to certify properly qualified export trading companies. Any activity within the scope described by the certificate is exempt from public prosecution under the antitrust laws.

5. **Baseball.** In 1922 the United States Supreme Court held that professional baseball was not within the reach of federal antitrust laws because it was not ''interstate commerce.'' Under modern interpretations of the Constitution's Commerce Clause, this decision is clearly wrong. Nonetheless, professional baseball retains its antitrust exemption; but this exemption applies only to baseball and not to other sports.

6. **Oil Marketing.** The 1935 Interstate Oil Compact allows states to determine quotas on oil that will be marketed in interstate commerce.

7. **Other Exemptions.** Other activities exempt from antitrust laws include the following:

(a) Activities approved by the president in furtherance of the defense of our nation (under the Defense Production Act of 1950 as amended).

(b) Cooperative research among small business firms (under the Small Business Administration Act of 1958 as amended).

(c) Research by consortiums of competitors to cooperate in the development of new computer technology (under special federal legislation, including the National Cooperative Research Act of 1984).

(d) State actions, when the state policy is clearly articulated and the policy is actively supervised by the state.[4]

(e) Activities of regulated industries (such as the transportation, communication, and banking industries) when federal commissions, boards, or agencies (such as the Federal Communications Commission, the Federal Maritime Commission, or the Interstate Commerce Commission) have primary regulatory authority.

(f) Joint efforts by businesspersons to obtain legislative or executive action are protected as promoting legitimate participation in the political process even though such efforts may be selfishly motivated. This is often referred to as the **Noerr-Pennington doctrine.**[5] Though selfish rather than purely public-minded conduct is permitted, there is an exception: conduct that is asserted to be political but that is merely a sham deserves no protection, if it is clear the action is not pursued through legitimate means. The exception, however, is limited to abuse of the political *process.* If legitimate political means are employed, it is irrelevant that the *result* of the process hinders competition or that the efforts were motivated by a self-serving objective such as injuring a competitor. The following United States Supreme Court case deals with this distinction.

---

4. See *Packer v. Brown,* 317 U.S. 341, 63 S.Ct. 307, 87 L.Ed. 315 (1943).
5. *United Mine Workers of America v. Pennington,* 381 U.S. 657, 89 S.Ct. 1585, 14 L.Ed.2d 626 (1965) and *Eastern Railroad Presidents Conference v. Noerr Motor Freight, Inc.,* 365 U.S. 127, 81 S.Ct. 523, 5 L.Ed.2d 464 (1961).

BACKGROUND AND FACTS *After Omni Outdoor Advertising entered the market for billboard advertising in Columbia, South Carolina, Columbia Outdoor Advertising (COA) took a number of actions that seemed designed to make it difficult for Omni to compete with COA. First, COA redoubled its own billboard construction activity and modernized its existing stock. Second, according to Omni, COA offered artificially low rates to customers, while urging Omni's customers to break their contracts with Omni and spreading malicious rumors about Omni. Third, COA met with city officials to urge them to enact zoning ordinances that would restrict billboard construction in the city. On the heels of COA's meeting with city officials, a campaign ensued in which various groups and individuals also joined the call to restrict billboard advertising in Columbia. Omni sued*

Case 20.2

CITY OF COLUMBIA AND COLUMBIA OUTDOOR ADVERTISING, INC. v. OMNI OUTDOOR ADVERTISING, INC.

Supreme Court of the United States, 1991.
____U.S.____,
111 S.Ct. 1344,
113 L.Ed.2d 382.

both the city officials and COA, asserting various antitrust violations. At trial, a jury returned a verdict in favor of Omni, but the trial judge granted defendants' motion for judgment notwithstanding the verdict. An appeals court reversed the trial court's decision and reinstated the jury's verdict. The defendants appealed to the United States Supreme Court, which addressed several issues, including whether COA's lobbying of city officials was legitimate political action protected under the Noerr-Pennington doctrine. Omni contended that COA's activities were not protected because the lobbying efforts were undertaken as a "sham," COA's true intent being to restrict Omni's ability to compete in the billboard advertising market.

SCALIA, J.

*   *   *   *

*   *   *[B]eginning with *Eastern Railroad Presidents Conference v. Noerr Motor Freight, Inc.,* we have [held that] the federal antitrust laws *   *   * do not regulate the conduct of private individuals in seeking anticompetitive action from the government. This doctrine*   *   * rests ultimately upon a recognition that the antitrust laws, "tailored as they are for the business world, are not at all appropriate for application in the political arena." That a private party's political motives are selfish is irrelevant: "*Noerr* shields from the Sherman Act a concerted effort to influence public officials regardless of intent or purpose."

Noerr recognized, however, what has come to be known as the "sham" exception to its rule: "There may be situations in which a publicity campaign, ostensibly directed toward influencing governmental action, is a mere sham to cover what is actually nothing more than an attempt to interfere directly with the business relationships of a competitor and the application of the Sherman Act would be justified." *   *   *

*   *   *   *

Neither of the Court of Appeals' theories for application of the "sham" exception to the facts of the present case is sound. The court reasoned, first, that the jury could have concluded that COA's interaction with city officials "was 'actually nothing more than an attempt to interfere directly with the business relations [sic] of a competitor.' " This analysis relies upon language from *Noerr*, but ignores the import of the critical word "directly." Although COA indisputably set out to disrupt Omni's business relationships, it sought to do so not through the very process of lobbying, or of causing the city council to consider zoning measures, but rather through the ultimate product of that lobbying and consideration, viz., the zoning ordinances. The Court of Appeals' second theory was that the jury could have found "that COA's purposes were to delay Omni's entry into the market and even to deny it a meaningful access to the appropriate city administrative and legislative fora." But the purpose of delaying a competitor's entry into the market does not render lobbying activity a "sham," unless (as no evidence suggested was true here) the delay is sought to be achieved only by the lobbying process itself, and not by the governmental action that the lobbying seeks. *   *   * As for "deny[ing] . . . meaningful access to the appropriate city administrative and legislative fora," that may render the manner of lobbying improper or even unlawful, but does not necessarily render it a "sham." We did hold in *California Motor Transport Co. v. Trucking Unlimited,* that a conspiracy among private parties to monopolize trade by excluding a competitor from participation in the regulatory process did not enjoy *Noerr* protection. But *California Motor Transport* involved a context in which the conspirators' participation in the governmental process was itself claimed to be a "sham," employed as a means of imposing cost and delay. The holding of the case is limited to that situation. To extend it to a context in which the regulatory process is being invoked genuinely, and not in a "sham" fashion, would produce precisely that conversion of antitrust

CHAPTER 20: ANTITRUST AND MONOPOLY   **487**

law into regulation of the political process that we have sought to avoid. Any lobbyist or applicant, in addition to getting himself heard, seeks by procedural and other means to get his opponent ignored. Policing the legitimate boundaries of such defensive strategies, when they are conducted in the context of a genuine attempt to influence governmental action, is not the role of the Sherman Act. In the present case, of course, any denial to Omni of ''meaningful access to the appropriate city administrative and legislative fora'' was achieved by COA in the course of an attempt to influence governmental action that, far from being a ''sham,'' was if anything more in earnest than it should have been. If the denial was wrongful there may be other remedies, but as for the Sherman Act, the Noerr exemption applies.

The Court held that COA's lobbying efforts were, regardless of motive or result, protected political activities not covered by the ''sham'' exception to the Noerr-Pennington doctrine. The Court concluded that COA had not abused the political process *so as to prevent Omni's competing in the billboard market. Instead, COA had used legitimate political lobbying to achieve a legitimate outcome (billboard regulation); motive or effect on competition did not bring the lobbying within the ''sham'' exception to the Noerr-Pennington doctrine. The Court remanded the case to the circuit court for further consideration.*

DECISION AND REMEDY

■ Monopolies

As noted above, the impetus for the initial federal antitrust legislation was concern over monopolies—specifically, concern that in particular markets a single, dominant firm could acquire and use market power to dictate or influence prices and output. Section 2 of the Sherman Act deals broadly with such cases. Section 2 condemns ''every person who shall monopolize or attempt to monopolize.'' (In contrast, Section 1 of the Sherman Act, as described in the next chapter, proscribes certain *concerted* activities in the restraint of trade.) Therefore, Section 2 may be violated by a single entity. The essence of a single entity's violation of Section 2 is the entity's willful acquisition or maintenance of monopoly power, or its specifically intended *attempt* to do so, provided the attempt has a reasonable chance of success.

In the remainder of this chapter we focus on single-firm behavior that is intended either to create or to preserve a monopoly over a particular market. Notice there are actually two distinct types of behavior that are subject to sanction under Section 2. First, conduct that is pursued by a firm that is already a monopolist is condemned as *monopolization* if the conduct interferes with free trade and is intended to preserve the firm's monopoly. Sec-

ond, conduct intended to capture monopoly power is condemned as an *attempt to monopolize.*

Another Section 2 offense is the act of **predatory pricing.** Predatory pricing involves an attempt by one firm to drive its competitors from the market by selling its product substantially *below* normal costs of production; once the competitors are eliminated, the firm will attempt to recapture its losses and go on to earn very high profits by driving prices up far above their competitive level.

Monopolization

In *United States v. Grinnell Corp.,*[6] the United States Supreme Court defined the offense of **monopolization** as involving the following two elements: ''(1) the possession of monopoly power in the relevant market and (2) the willful acquisition or maintenance of the power as distinguished from growth or development as a consequence of a superior product, business acumen, or historic accident.'' A violation of Section 2 requires that both these elements be established.

MONOPOLY POWER   The Sherman Act does not define *monopoly*. In economic parlance, monopoly

---

6.   384 U.S. 563, 86 S.Ct. 1698, 16 L.Ed.2d 778 (1966).

refers to control by a single entity. It is well established in antitrust law, however, that a firm may be a monopoly even though it is not the sole seller in a market. Nor is monopoly a function of size alone (for example, a "mom and pop" grocery located in an isolated desert town is a monopolist if it is the only grocery serving that particular market). Size in relation to the market is what matters because monopoly involves power to affect prices and output. The United States Supreme Court has defined monopoly power as "the power to control prices or exclude competition." This definition is of limited help, though, and most scholars generally consider monopoly power to be simply a *considerable* degree of market power, or, otherwise stated, a *significant* degree of freedom from competitive pressure regarding output and pricing decisions. This generally is the way in which the Court has applied the concept.

As difficult as it is to precisely define market power, it is even more difficult to measure it. As a workable proxy, courts often look to the firm's percentage share of the "relevant market." This is the so-called **market share test.**[7] The relevant market consists of two elements: (1) a relevant product market and (2) a relevant geographic market. A firm generally is considered to have monopoly power if its share of the relevant market is 70 percent or more. This is not an absolute, however. It is only a loose rule of thumb; in some cases, a smaller share may be held to constitute monopoly power.[8]

Product Market   No doubt the relevant product market should include all products that, although produced by different firms, nonetheless have identical attributes. But in determining the relevant market, it must be remembered that products that are not identical may be substituted for one another. Coffee may substitute for tea, cellophane may substitute for wax paper, and so on. In defining the relevant product market, the key issue is the degree of interchangeability between products. If one product is a sufficient substitute for another, the two are considered to be part of the same product market.

In *United States v. E. I. du Pont De Nemours & Co.,*[9] du Pont was sued for monopolizing the cellophane market. Du Pont controlled about 75 percent of cellophane production but contended that it had no monopoly power, because the relevant market included not only cellophane but rather all flexible packaging materials. The Court found that there was indeed a sufficient degree of interchangeability between cellophane and alternatives such as wax paper and aluminum foil. The Court noted, for example, that although 35 percent of the snack food industry used cellophane, an even larger percent used some other packaging material. Consequently, the Court concluded that du Pont did not control a share of the relevant market sufficient to constitute monopoly power. The following case demonstrates another court's efforts to determine the relevant product market in a rather unique setting—the market for advertising bowling balls.

---

7.   Other measures have been devised, but the market share test is the most widely used.
8.   This standard was first articulated by Justice Learned Hand in the famous *Aluminum Co. of America* case discussed below. A 90 percent share was held to be clear evidence of monopoly power. Anything less than 64 percent, said Justice Hand, made monopoly power doubtful, and anything less than 30 percent was clearly not monopoly power. This is merely a rule of thumb, however; it is not a binding principle of law.

---

9.   351 U.S. 377, 76 S.Ct. 994, 100 L.Ed.2d 1264 (1956).

Case 20.3

EUREKA URETHANE, INC. v. PBA, INC.

United States District Court, 1990.
Eastern District of Missouri, 746 F.Supp. 915.

BACKGROUND AND FACTS   *Eureka Urethane (plaintiff) was the manufacturer of the "Bud Ball," a bowling ball bearing the red tie logo of Anheuser-Busch's Budweiser beer. Eureka sought to hire certain professional bowlers to promote the Bud Ball by using it during televised tournaments organized and controlled by PBA, Inc., a subsidiary of the Professional Bowling Association (defendants). PBA had certain rules regarding the tournaments, including specifications on emblems displayed on equip-*

ment used by tournament players. One of the rules stated that bowling ball emblems were restricted to the name or logo of the original manufacturer of the ball. The National Broadcasting Corporation (NBC), which had purchased the rights to televise the tournaments, and several corporate sponsors objected to the use of the Bud Ball during televised play. As a result, PBA refused its permission for players to use the Bud Ball during televised portions of its tournaments. Eureka brought suit against PBA, alleging several antitrust violations under the Sherman Act. PBA moved for summary judgment on several grounds, including its assertion that it lacked monopoly power in the relevant market. The court decided the issue by searching for the proper definition of the relevant market.

LIMBAUGH, District Judge.
    *   *   *   *

The relevant market is determined by reference to both the product market and the geographic market. Plaintiff defines the relevant product market as items used by professional bowlers during televised tournament play. [The court concluded that there was no dispute over the definition of the relevant *geographic* market: because the PBA organized and promoted tournaments throughout the United States, and the tournaments were televised nationwide, the court assumed that the relevant geographic market was the entire United States.] The Court suspects that plaintiff's definition of the relevant market is too narrowly drawn. Defendants, however, have failed to present the Court with sufficient evidence to expand the relevant product market to include other means of advertising a bowling ball.

The essential test for ascertaining the relevant product market involves the identification of those products or services that are either (1) identical to or (2) available substitutes for the defendants' product or service. This comparative analysis has been characterized as the "reasonable interchangeability" standard. The [Supreme Court has] noted that reasonable interchangeability may be gauged by (1) the product's uses, i.e., whether the substitute products or services can perform the same function, and/or (2) consumer response (cross-elasticity of demand). [Cross-elasticity of demand refers to the change in the demand for one product that results from a change in the price of another product.]

Furthermore, a market can be divided into several submarkets. *   *   * A submarket may be determined by examining such practical indicia as (1) industry or public recognition of the submarket as a separate economic entity, (2) the product's peculiar characteristics and uses, (3) unique production facilities, (4) distinct customers, (5) distinct prices, (6) sensitivity to price changes, and (7) specialized vendors.

In the instant matter the product market to be defined is that for the advertisement of a bowling ball. *   *   *

Defendants assert that the plaintiff has many options for the advertisement of a bowling ball: (1) plaintiff may purchase commercial spots advertising the Bud Ball during televised PBA tournaments or other sporting events, (2) plaintiff may purchase the sponsorship of a PBA tournament, (3) plaintiff may purchase print advertisements in bowling journals and other media, and (4) plaintiff may pay professional bowlers to endorse the Bud Ball. Defendants, however, did not carry their burden in broadening the relevant product market by merely listing the options by which plaintiff may advertise the Bud Ball. Only reasonably interchangeable products may be included in the same market. A product is reasonably interchangeable for another if consumers of the products considered them to be reasonable substitutes. The consumer of the product in the instant matter is a purchaser of advertising for a bowling ball. Therefore, the question is whether the purchaser of advertising for a bowling ball considers spot commercials, tournament sponsorships, print advertisements, and paid endorsements as reasonable substitutes for a professional bowler using the ball during a televised tournament. Defendants may prove products are reasonably interchangeable by presenting the Court with a measurement of their cross-elasticities of demand. For example, if the price of a spot commercial increases, do purchasers of advertising for sporting goods purchase endorsements from professional athletes instead. The Court has no evidence of [price] cross-elasticity before it. Instead, defendants merely argue that plaintiff's definition of the relevant product market is untenable given its options in advertising. The Court disagrees.

As narrow as plaintiff's product market appears, plaintiff may still have defined a valid submarket. *   *   * [A professional bowler's] endorsement can have a significant effect on the sale of the product *   *   * [when the product is used in a tournament by the professional bowler].

Furthermore, the PBA is the sole sponsor of televised tournament play for men. Professional bowling does not attract live viewers in significant numbers, and gets no televised coverage except for the tours sponsored by defendants. If a professional bowler cannot use the Bud Ball during televised tournament play, his paid endorsement in a spot commercial or print advertisement would be discounted by the consumer who watches the televised tournament play. The viewer would question the quality of the ball when a professional bowler endorses the ball during a commercial advertisement but uses another ball during televised tournament play.

In sum, although the Court suspects that plaintiffs' submarket may be too narrowly defined, defendant has failed to carry its burden to broaden the relevant product market by proving the substitutability of other means of advertising. For the purposes of the motion for summary judgment, the Court will assume that the relevant product market is the items used by professional bowlers during televised tournament play. *   *   *

DECISION AND REMEDY   *The court refused to define the market as broadly as the defendant contended it should be defined. The defendant possessed considerable control over the more narrowly defined market, and thus the court denied the defendant's motion for summary judgment.*

Geographic Market   The second component of the relevant market is the geographical boundaries of the market. For products that are sold nationwide, the geographical boundaries encompass the entire United States. If transportation costs are significant or if a producer and its competitors sell in only a limited area, one in which customers have no access to other sources of the product, then the geographical market is limited to that area. In this sense a national firm may compete in several distinct areas, having monopoly power in one but not another. Generally, the geographical market is that section of the country within which a firm can increase its price without attracting new sellers or without losing many customers to alternative suppliers outside that area.

CONDUCT AND INTENT—DISTINGUISHING PROCOMPETITIVE FROM ANTICOMPETITIVE BEHAVIOR   Monopoly power is not, in and of itself, illegal. Recall that there are two elements to the monopolization offense. In addition to monopoly power, there is the requirement of "willful acquisition or maintenance of that power." A dominant market share may be the result of business acumen or the development of a superior product or it may be simply the result of historical accident. None of these situations should give rise to antitrust concerns. Indeed, it would be counter to society's interest to condemn a firm that acquired its position on the basis of the first two reasons. If, however, a firm possesses monopoly power as a result of engaging in some purposeful act to acquire or to maintain that power through anticompetitive means, then the firm is in violation of Section 2. The Court has interpreted this second element as requiring some conduct intended to diminish competition.

Some conduct diminishes competition but is not necessarily anticompetitive. Devising new low-cost production methods and developing and producing better products all hurt rival competitors. But they do not injure competition; they are the result of competition. In our initial scenario, even if Acme had not received an exclusive monopoly, its laser fax breakthrough would have given it monopoly power for a period of time until rival firms had had sufficient time to develop and market products that could effectively compete. But ultimately Acme's innovation would have led to increased competition. Thus, only certain acts are condemned under Section 2, even if the acting firm possesses monopoly power. The hallmark of an action that does violate Section 2 is that, without providing better production or products, the firm's action makes competing in the relevant market more difficult for its rivals.

ANTICOMPETITIVE INTENT   The qualifier that the sanctioned action have been "willful" is said to require intent, but the intent requirement is difficult to formulate. In most monopolization cases, intent may be inferred from evidence that the firm had monopoly power and engaged in anticompetitive behavior. For example, in *United States v.*

Aluminum Co. of America,[10] the seemingly innocent act of expanding production demand ran Alcoa afoul of Section 2. The court found that Alcoa had intentionally and artificially stimulated demand and then increased its own capacity to meet that increased demand. The Court of Appeals for the Second Circuit[11] relied on the fact that Alcoa clearly possessed a market share sufficient to give it monopoly power (90 percent of what the court determined to be the relevant market) and that the only apparent reason for its expansion was to prevent competitors from entering the aluminum market. This factual conclusion is often criticized, but the principle set out is now well established. Market domination that results from legitimate competitive behavior—such as foresight, innovation, skill, and good management—will not be condemned unless that domination is abused or acquired through behavior that harms, rather than flows from, competition.

A firm's unilateral refusal to deal with another individual or organization is generally permissible. In the following case, however, the refusal to deal was made by a firm possessing monopoly power, and its apparent intent was to injure competition in the relevant market.

---

10.   148 F.2d 416 (2d Cir. 1945).
11.   The Second Circuit acted as the court of final appeal in place of the Supreme Court because the latter could not muster a quorum of six qualified justices to hear the case. The case was referred to the court of appeals of the circuit from which the case came under a specially drawn statute (28 U.S.C. Section 2109).

BACKGROUND AND FACTS   *Aspen, Colorado, is a leading ski resort, and private investors developed four major facilities there for downhill skiing: Ajax, Aspen Highlands, Buttermilk, and Snowmass. The facilities were owned by independent investors, and they jointly offered an "all-Aspen ticket," which could be used for skiing at any of the facilities. Receipts from the ticket were paid to the various facilities in a manner proportionate to their use, as based on surveys of skiers. By 1977, Aspen Skiing Company (Ski Co.) had acquired ownership of Ajax, Buttermilk, and Snowmass, and Aspen Highlands was owned by the Aspen Highlands Skiing Corporation. At this time, the two companies were engaged in a dispute over the proper distribution of receipts from the all-Aspen ticket. Ski Co. discontinued the all-Aspen ticket and replaced it with a three-area ticket that covered only its own facilities. Aspen Highlands' share of the*

Case 20.4

ASPEN SKIING CO. v. ASPEN HIGHLANDS SKIING CORP.
Supreme Court of the United States, 1985.
472 U.S. 585,
105 S.Ct. 2847,
86 L.Ed.2d 467.

local downhill skiing market declined from over 20 percent in 1976–1977 to 11 percent in 1980–1981. Aspen Highlands filed an antitrust complaint against Ski Co., alleging that Ski Co. had monopolized the market for downhill skiing services at Aspen, in violation of Section 2 of the Sherman Act. Aspen Highlands argued that the discontinuation of the all-Aspen ticket was a purposeful act with intent to monopolize the market. The district court issued a judgment in favor of Aspen Highlands, and the Tenth Circuit Court of Appeals affirmed in all respects. Ski Co. appealed to the United States Supreme Court.

STEVENS, Justice.
* * * *

In this Court, Ski Co. contends that even a firm with monopoly power has no duty to engage in joint marketing with a competitor, that a violation of [Section] 2 cannot be established without evidence of substantial exclusionary conduct, and that none of its activities can be characterized as exclusionary. * * *
* * * *

* * * In the actual case that we must decide, the monopolist did not merely reject a novel offer to participate in a cooperative venture that had been proposed by a competitor. Rather, the monopolist elected to make an important change in a pattern of distribution that had originated in a competitive market and had persisted for several years. The all-Aspen, 6-day ticket with revenues allocated on the basis of usage was first developed when three independent companies operated three different ski mountains in the Aspen area. It continued to provide a desirable option for skiers when the market was enlarged to include four mountains, and when the character of the market was changed by Ski Co.'s acquisition of monopoly power. Moreover, since the record discloses that interchangeable tickets are used in other multimountain areas which apparently are competitive, it seems appropriate to infer that such tickets satisfy consumer demand in free competitive markets.
* * * *

Perhaps most significant, however, is the evidence relating to Ski Co. itself, for Ski Co. did not persuade the jury that its conduct was justified by any normal business purpose. Ski Co. was apparently willing to forgo daily ticket sales both to skiers who sought to exchange the coupons contained in Highlands' Adventure Pack, and to those who would have purchased Ski Co. daily lift tickets from Highlands if Highlands had been permitted to purchase them in bulk. The jury may well have concluded that Ski Co. elected to forgo these short-run benefits because it was more interested in reducing competition in the Aspen market over the long run by harming its smaller competitor.

DECISION AND REMEDY   *The United States Supreme Court affirmed the decision of the lower federal courts. The original jury had found that Aspen Highlands had suffered $2.5 million in actual damages, which were trebled under the Sherman Act to an award of $7.5 million. This award was affirmed by the United States Supreme Court.*

Predatory Pricing

Among monopolization cases, predatory pricing—selling below cost—is one form of conduct that continues to receive considerable attention. One reason for this is that a dominant theme in antitrust is the promotion of consumer welfare. But consumers benefit from low prices. If a firm sells a valuable product for a price below cost, then it is the firm that loses, not the consumer. Despite the fact that consumers benefit from the low price, predatory pricing is still condemned.

Condemnation of predatory pricing is based on the fear that, although it may benefit consumers with low prices in the short term, in the longer run, it will harm competition. The harm feared is that a rich rival, by pricing below its competitors' costs, could drive the competition out of the market by outlasting them during the phase in which prices were below cost. In the subsequent phase, the rich rival would still be in the market but would no longer face any competitors. The firm would then be free to reap large profits by raising the price far above what it had been when the firm faced market competition.

In any event, there are procompetitive reasons not only for low prices but even for prices below cost. Such pricing may be, for example, the only way in which a new firm can gain a "toehold" in a market populated by established firms, especially if the latter have established brand name recognition in the market. To prevent the entry of new competitors into a market by forbidding them from using low prices, perhaps even prices below cost, would hinder rather than promote competition.

Faced with such uncertainty as to the purpose and effect of firms' pricing decisions, courts have struggled to invent a workable standard for judging predatory pricing. Some courts have looked to the costs of firms alleged to have engaged in predatory pricing. Estimates of costs, however, can be highly speculative even with the use of modern cost accounting techniques. Other courts, despairing over the inability to accurately measure costs, have looked to intent. Divining intent is even more subjective than measuring costs, however, and the approach has lost favor in many jurisdictions.

Lastly, some courts have begun to look at market structure in deciding predatory pricing cases. Under this approach, courts look at the potential for harm to consumers created by a firm's below-cost pricing. If it appears that a firm pricing below cost will be unable to capture monopoly profits at a later time, the courts eschew any attempt to discern intent. They also avoid entirely the vexing problems associated with measuring costs. The essence of the market approach is that if the firm is unlikely to capture monopoly profits through high prices in the future, intent does not matter. Consumers benefit from the low prices regardless. Moreover, if the firm is pursuing a legitimate objective of trying to gain access into an established market, the efforts should not be hampered by rivals crying foul simply because they lose business to a competitor selling at a lower price. The following case exemplifies this market approach as well as providing an excellent summary of the other approaches followed among courts looking at predatory pricing.

BACKGROUND AND FACTS   *Rose Acre Farms (defendant) was a relatively recent entry into the midwestern egg suppliers' wholesale market. Through aggressive sales activities, such as offering low prices and "special" discounts to retail purchasers, Rose Acre was able to double its operations over a period of four years—despite the fact that, nationwide, egg sales rose by only 1 percent during the same period. A group of rival wholesale suppliers (plaintiffs) that had lost market shares to Rose Acre brought suit against Rose Acre, contending that its rapid growth in the midwestern markets was the result of predatory pricing practices. The group of wholesalers presented evidence that Rose Acre at times had sold below cost in offering its "specials" to retail supermarket chains. A jury decided the case for the plaintiffs, but the trial judge entered judgment for defendant Rose Acre. The judge ruled that evidence of the economic conditions prevailing in the relevant wholesale market dictated such a ruling. In particular, the judge found that prices in the market were highly competitive and that numerous other firms were entering the market during the same period that Rose Acre was alleged to have perpetrated its predatory*

Case 20.5

A. A. POULTRY FARMS, INC. v. ROSE ACRE FARMS, INC.
United States Circuit Court of Appeals,
Seventh Circuit, 1991.
881 F.2d 1396.

pricing practices. The defendants appealed the decision to the United States Court of Appeals for the Seventh Circuit.

EASTERBROOK, Circuit Judge.

*   *   *   *

Consumers, for whose benefit the antitrust laws are designed, welcome low prices but not monopoly prices. Contentions that firms practice predatory pricing—the sequence low-price-now-high-price-later—accordingly create difficult problems for courts. If a rival files suit during the "low price" period, how can a court tell whether the price is low because the defendant is an efficient producer driving down costs (or just driving price down to cost) as opposed to a predator? *   *   *

One way is to find out whether the defendant's prices exceed its costs. If the price exceeds cost, then it reflects beneficial aggressive competition. If the price is less than cost, then it may reflect a sacrifice in the hope of suppressing competition and collecting a monopoly profit later. *   *   * Often a price below cost reflects only the sacrifice necessary to establish a presence in a competitive market (for example, new magazines lose money for years as they try to increase circulation and attract advertising revenue, without creating the tiniest risk of monopoly) *   *   * Measuring costs creates additional problems. *   *   *

A second approach to separating aggressive competition from predation concentrates on the defendant's intent. If a seller plans to drive out competition by fowl means, then the court infers that its price is unlawfully low now and will be too high later. Frequently courts use intent to resolve ambiguities in interpreting price-cost data; sometimes, though, courts assume that bad intent is unlawful and use price-cost data to infer it. *   *   *

The third approach looks at the back end, the "high price later" part of the predatory sequence. Predatory prices are an investment in a future monopoly, a sacrifice of today's profits for tomorrow's. The investment must be recouped. If a monopoly price later is impossible, then the sequence is unprofitable and we may infer that the low price now is not predatory. More importantly, if there can be no "later" in which recoupment could occur, then the consumer is an unambiguous beneficiary even if the current price is less than the cost of production. Price less than cost today, followed by the competitive price tomorrow, bestows a gift on consumers. Because antitrust laws are designed for the benefit of consumers, not competitors, a gift of this kind is not actionable. *   *   * Only if market structure makes recoupment feasible need a court inquire into the relation between price and cost. *   *   *

Rose Acre could not have recouped a predatory investment in the egg business. Plaintiffs' economic expert witness testified that prices were falling and could not have been expected to rise—at least not because of what Rose Acre did. *   *   * Persistent entry and expansion by other firms at the same time ensures that recoupment cannot occur. *   *   *

Market structure, too, made recoupment impossible. Egg production is unconcentrated. Egg processing is a little more so, but Rose Acre's 1% share on a national basis hardly gave it the power to raise price. *   *   * Every indication in the record *   *   * suggests that [retail buyers had] ample potential sources of supply. *   *   *

Our review of the record leads us to agree with the district court that no rational jury could have found that recoupment took place, could have taken place, or conceivably could take place in the future. To the contrary, the overwhelming impression left by this record is that Rose Acre beat its rivals to the punch in automating production and used its lower costs to take business away from them. New entrants with modern technology have flourished; stodgy firms have stagnated. This is what competition is all about, and to penalize it in the name of antitrust would do a great disservice to consumers.

The appellate court upheld the trial court's decision. Looking at the market structure of the relevant wholesale egg market, the court concluded that there was no danger to competition from Rose Acre's actions—regardless of the firm's intent or the fact that at times it may have sold its product for less than cost.

Attempts to Monopolize

Section 2 also prohibits attempted monopolization of a market. The primary difficulty in developing workable standards for assessing alleged attempts to monopolize is distinguishing anticompetitive conduct from conduct that flows from legitimate competition. This difficulty is encountered in almost every area of antitrust, but identifying attempts to monopolize is one area in which the problem is particularly acute.

Any action challenged as an **attempt to monopolize** must be specifically intended to exclude competitors and garner monopoly power. In addition, a majority of lower courts hold that an attempted violation also requires that the attempt have a "dangerous" probability of success; that is, actual monopolization is not required, but only *serious* threats of monopolization are condemned as violations. Many courts hold that the probability cannot be dangerous unless the alleged offender possesses at least some degree of market power. This latter requirement is apparent in the following case from the United States Seventh Circuit.

BACKGROUND AND FACTS *American Academic Suppliers (plaintiff) and Beckley-Cardy (defendant) were wholesalers engaged in the sale of school supplies. The former's major markets were largely concentrated in the midwestern United States; the latter's markets were more widely dispersed, being on a national rather than regional scale. American Academic had been started by Beckley-Cardy's former president on a small initial investment of less than $500,000. American Academic had also hired a number of salespersons away from Beckley-Cardy. Initially, American Academic had experienced fairly rapid expansion in the markets in which it competed with Beckley-Cardy. Beckley-Cardy eventually responded by considerably reducing the prices of some of its products and, according to Amercian Academic, by making disparaging remarks and starting rumors about the business operations of American Academic. American Academic brought suit against Beckley-Cardy, alleging unfair trade practices under various state laws and alleging that Beckley-Cardy had violated Section 2 of the Sherman Act by attempting to monopolize the school supply market. The trial judge granted summary judgment for Beckley-Cardy, and American Academic appealed the decision. In assessing the trial court's decision in relation to the antitrust allegation, the appeals court looked to whether or not Beckley-Cardy possessed monopoly power—holding that such power was a necessary condition to finding an attempted monopolization offense.*

Case 20.6

AMERICAN ACADEMIC SUPPLIERS, INC. v. BECKLEY-CARDY, INC.
United States Court of Appeals,
Seventh Circuit, 1991.
922 F.2d 1317.

POSNER, Circuit Judge.
* * * *

To say that to be guilty of attempted monopolization a defendant must have monopoly power (because otherwise his attempt does not have a dangerous probability of succeeding) may seem to collapse the two offenses of monopolization and attempted monopolization into one. Not so. To have a monopoly and to monopolize are two separate things. The offense of monopolization is the acquisition of monopoly by improper methods or, more commonly * * * the abuse of monopoly, the latter occurring for example when a monopolist by pricing below cost succeeds in repelling or intimidating new entrants or extending his monopoly into new markets. Firms found guilty of attempting to monopolize are typically, and in predatory pricing cases must always be, monopolists.

The smaller the defendant is in his market and the less time and money it takes for a new firm to enter that market, the less plausible is an inference that the defendant has monopoly power. Beckley-Cardy buys from manufacturers a vast array of educational supplies, ranging from school desks to maps to crayons and excluding only food and textbooks, lists them in its catalog, and resells them to public and private schools throughout the country. It employs a sales force to call on school purchasing agents; the salesmen are empowered to negotiate discounts from the catalog prices. Beckley-Cardy has hundreds of competitors, and its share of the entire educational supplies market (as defined above), nationwide, does not exceed 3 percent although there are categories of supplies in which it has a regional ''market'' share in excess of 25 percent. Not only has Beckley-Cardy a horde of existing competitors, but new entry is exceedingly easy, as the facts of this lawsuit show. In 1984 the then president of Beckley-Cardy left to form his own firm—American Academic Suppliers. The original capital, contributed by him and others, was slightly less than $500,000. His strategy for gaining a foothold in the market was to hire salesmen whom he had known at Beckley-Cardy. * * * Beckley-Cardy responded the following year by reducing its catalog prices nationwide by 5 to 12 percent and by offering a discount of 25 to 40 percent off the catalog prices on approximately 30 percent of its line in those parts of Ohio and other states in which American Academic Suppliers was making heavy inroads. * * *

The price cutting * * * did not drive American Academic Suppliers out of any area. In fact its sales continued to grow during the period in which the discount was in force. It is difficult, to say the least, to see how the discount, steep as it was, contained a hidden menace to the consumers who lapped it up. * * *

The steepness and selectivity of the price discount attest not to the possession of market power by Beckley-Cardy but to the influence of salesmen over purchasing agents in this business. American Academic Suppliers hired salesmen away from Beckley-Cardy in the hope that they would switch the accounts they serviced from their old to their new employer. The hope was largely fulfilled. How was Beckley-Cardy to get the accounts back? It could and did hire new salesmen, but they were placed at a disadvantage by lacking experience with and the personal trust of the school purchasing agents. * * *

* * * [T]he least plausible inference—too implausible to allow a reasonable jury to bring in a verdict for the plaintiff—is that Beckley-Cardy was trying to obtain a monopoly and would unless interrupted have succeeded with enough probability to warrant judicial intervention. * * *

DECISION AND REMEDY   *The court affirmed the trial judge's grant of summary judgment for Beckley-Cardy. The court held that a showing of some degree of monopoly power was a prerequisite to bringing a successful legal action of attempted monopolization against a firm.*

■ Terms and Concepts to Review

antitrust law 476
attempt to monopolize 495
dissolution 482
divestiture 482
market power 475

market share test 488
monopolization 487
monopoly 475
monopoly power 479

Noerr-Pennington
  doctrine 485
predatory pricing 487
restraint of trade 478
trusts 477

■ Questions and Case Problems

20-1. The Southern Motor Carriers Rate Conference is a private organization that lobbies regulatory commissions in various southern states on behalf of national and regional private commercial carriers. A new carrier claims that the organization is really in the business of setting rates and controlling the issuance of licenses through its influence over the members of the various regulatory boards. How might the organization violate antitrust laws? If the organization does no more than lobby the various agencies, does it run afoul of the antitrust laws in light of the Supreme Court's enunciation of the Noerr-Pennington doctrine?

20-2. A car rental firm specializes in renting automobiles to insurance company customers who need temporary replacements while their cars are being repaired. There are several other car rental agencies serving the same geographical area. The specialty agency substantially reduces the daily rental fee on its cars. Other firms in the area contend that the reductions amount to predatory pricing. If an antitrust action is brought against the specialty agency, how should the case be decided? Discuss all factors that must be considered.

20-3. Super-Tech Industries presently controls 55 percent of the market in the manufacture and sale of computers. The balance of the market is controlled by five other manufacturers, with Alcan Corp. having 25 percent of the market. Alcan has an innovative research staff, but every time Alcan introduces a faster, more powerful, and more efficient computer in the market, Super-Tech immediately informs its customers of the upcoming development of a competing computer that it will sell at 30 percent below the Alcan price. Alcan claims that these activities on the part of Super-Tech are an antitrust violation. Discuss fully whether this unilateral action by Super-Tech violates antitrust law.

20-4. Goodfellows, Inc., is a close corporation with only two shareholders. Goodfellows is engaged in the pizza delivery business. There are two other such firms serving the same market, but Goodfellows controls 75 percent share. The two shareholders agree that one will purchase all of the shares that belong to the other. As a condition of the transaction, the shareholder selling the shares agrees not to open a competing pizza delivery business within a seventy-mile radius or become employed by any rival firm within the same designated area. The covenant is to last five years.

Is it an unreasonable restraint of trade? Would a court likely declare the promise not to compete unenforceable?

20-5. Ragu's brand of prepared spaghetti sauce was the best-selling brand in the United States with nearly 70 percent. Hunt-Wesson decided to enter the same market. It conducted extensive research and marketing efforts to develop a product that consumers would differentiate from Ragu's. Before Hunt-Wesson's product was introduced, Ragu introduced its own new spaghetti sauce, which was very similar to Hunt-Wesson's. Hunt-Wesson brought suit, alleging that Ragu had copied many of the features of Hunt-Wesson's product and planned promotional campaign (allegedly using the same slogan and photos similar to the ones Hunt-Wesson had planned to use). Did Ragu violate Section 2 of the Sherman Act, as claimed by Hunt-Wesson? [*Hunt-Wesson Foods, Inc. v. Ragu Foods, Inc.,* 627 F.2d 919 (9th Cir. 1980)]

20-6. The *Lorain Journal,* a daily newspaper, was the only local firm engaged in the business of advertising and disseminating news in its community. The *Journal* faced no viable competitors until a small radio station began operating in a nearby town. The *Journal* set out to eliminate the competition by financially ruining the radio station. To accomplish its purpose, the *Journal* refused to sell ad space to any advertisers who also bought air time from the radio station. The federal government brought an antitrust action against the *Journal,* contending that the *Journal's* actions amounted to an attempt to monopolize the advertising market in violation of Section 2 of the Sherman Act. The *Journal* defended its actions by asserting an absolute right to select its customers and to deal, or not deal, with whomever it chose. How will the case be decided? [*Lorain Journal Co. v. U.S.,* 342 U.S. 143, 72 S.Ct. 181 (1951)]

20-7. American Telephone & Telegraph (AT&T) held an overwhelming share of the telephone service market in both local and long-distance service. AT&T refused to allow fledgling start-ups, like MCI and other smaller phone companies, to connect their long distance lines to the local systems controlled by AT&T's Bell Telephone subsidiaries. Aside from various regulatory standards, the lack of access to AT&T's facilities and the enormous initial capital investments needed to start up a phone service created considerable barriers to entry into the phone services market. The government brought suit, contending that AT&T's refusal to provide an *essential facility* to its competitors violated Section 2 of the Sherman Act. Do you agree? [*United*

States v. American Telephone & Telegraph Co., 552 F.Supp. 131 (D.D.C. 1982)]

20-8. Eastman Kodak controlled a vast share of the photographic film market when it introduced a new pocket-sized camera that used a unique type of film capable of producing photographs that previously could be taken only by much larger cameras. For a year and one-half after Kodak introduced the camera, only Kodak produced the unique type of film. Special equipment was required for developing the special film, and Kodak entered the market for film processing. Berkey Photo, a much smaller firm, also engaged in film processing. Berkey brought suit, alleging that Kodak was attempting to use its monopoly in the camera and film markets to gain a competitive advantage in the film processing market. Berkey claimed that this violated Section 2 of the Sherman Act. Does it? [*Berkey Photo, Inc. v. Eastman Kodak Co.*, 603 F.2d 263 (2d Cir. 1979)]

20-9. Syufy, a movie theater operator, opened a lavish six-screen theater in Las Vegas. All theater owners in Las Vegas obtained films from distributors by submitting bids on first-run movie releases. Successful bidders obtained an exhibition license specifying that the distributor would receive a percentage of the theaters' weekly receipts. Syufy's uniquely opulent theater generated considerable patronage, and soon a price war was under way between Syufy and the other Las Vegas theater owners. Eventually, the competition was reduced to just Syufy and Roberts, a small exhibitor of predominantly second-run films, with the former controlling nearly 100 percent of the Las Vegas theater market. After a major film distributor stopped doing business with Syufy and began to deal exclusively with Roberts, Syufy suffered a reversal of fortunes. Soon thereafter, Roberts became the dominant force in the market. Ultimately, Roberts sold out to a national theater chain. The government sued Syufy, alleging a violation of Section 2 of the Sherman Act. The government argued that Syufy had acquired monopoly power by buying out his competition. Syufy defended by arguing that he could not have violated Section 2 because there were no barriers preventing other firms from entering the Las Vegas theater market. Which side is likely to prevail? [*United States v. Syufy Enterprises*, 903 F.2d 659 (9th Cir 1990)]

20-10. A Question of Ethics

Mr. Furniture, Inc., was a company engaged in the wholesale and retail furniture business. Like many other such companies in its line of business, Mr. Furniture frequently obtained its furniture products from manufacturers by making purchases on credit. Credit usually was not provided by the manufacturers themselves but rather by institutions engaged in "commercial factoring." These institutions typically purchased the manufacturers' accounts receivable at a discount and assumed direct responsibility for collecting the outstanding debts. Moreover, the factored credit institutions often purchased debt on a nonrecourse basis, meaning that they assumed the entire risk of a debtor's failure to repay. The institutions relied on credit ratings and similar criteria in deciding which purchasers

should be extended credit. Barclays American/Commercial was almost certainly the dominant factored credit institution in the market in which Mr. Furniture operated. Barclays refused to extend credit for Mr. Furniture's inventory purchases from furniture manufacturers. Mr. Furniture's president, Howard Cassett, asserted that the refusal was based on two elements: (1) Barclays' attempt to monopolize the factored credit market and (2) the personal animosity that Barclays' manager, Jim Stenhouse, harbored toward Cassett. Mr. Furniture sued Barclays, alleging, among other things, violations of the Sherman Act. The trial court ruled that Mr. Furniture lacked standing to bring the antitrust charge; the court held that any alleged monopolization would directly injure other commercial factoring institutions that competed with Barclays, not Mr. Furniture. [Mr. Furniture Warehouse, Inc. v. Barclays American/Commercial, Inc., *919 F.2d 1517 (11th Cir 1990)]*

1. The court's ruling, affirmed on appeal, that Mr. Furniture lacked standing was based on the contention that any antitrust violations committed by Barclays would injure its competitors—other credit factoring institutions—not Mr. Furniture. Should Mr. Furniture have been allowed to complain simply because, as a "consumer" of credit factoring services, it was harmed by the alleged monopoly over credit extension acquired by Barclays? After all, the antitrust laws are supposed to help consumers, not competitors. Does that mean the court felt that only Barclays' rivals could bring the suit?

2. The court explicitly held that the alleged personal animosity that the Barclays executive had toward Mr. Furniture's president was irrelevant. There is something to be said for preventing the antitrust laws, involving the mechanisms of the judicial process as they do, from being used in such a petty way to settle personal feuds. But if monopoly power, assuming Barclays had such, is used for personal motives, would it be more reasonable to allow standing on that basis? Is such abuse any less troubling just because it is done for personal rather than economic reasons?

20-11. Case Briefing Assignment

Examine Case A.20 [Delaware & Hudson Ry. v. Consolidated Rail Corp., *902 F.2d 174 (2nd Cir. 1990)] in Appendix A. The case has been excerpted there in considerable detail. Review and then brief the case, making sure that you include answers to the following questions in your brief.*

1. What was the make-or-buy policy instituted by Conrail, and how did it allegedly disadvantage the Hudson & Delaware Railway?

2. Did the appellate court agree that a policy designed to maximize short-term profits could not, as a matter of law, violate Section 2 of the Sherman Act? On what United States Supreme Court decision was this argument based?

3. Is a monopolist required to aid a competitor?

4. What is the four-factor test for an "essential facility"?

Chapter 21

Antitrust and Restraints of Trade

Although the common perception of antitrust laws often involves "trustbusting"—that is, breaking up a single, dominant firm—the major thrust of federal antitrust legislation has been directed at various anticompetitive agreements between rival firms. Agreements to fix prices, restrict output, divide markets, exclude other competitors, or otherwise impede the dynamics of a free market have all been condemned as violations of federal antitrust laws. Such joint actions have been prosecuted as impermissible restraints of trade under Section 1 of the Sherman Act and, if the firms possess substantial market power, as conspiracies to monopolize under Section 2 of the same act.

Some agreements may be forced on unwilling firms by another firm possessing substantial market power. Typical of such agreements are exclusive dealing contracts and tying arrangements, described in the preceding chapter. Recall that an exclusive dealing contract conditions one firm's willingness to deal with another on the latter's continued refusal to deal with the former's rivals. Tying arrangements normally require that the purchaser of one product also purchase a second product. Also recall that such agreements violate provisions of the Clayton Act if the contracts or arrangements harm the competitive process or interfere with free trade.

In this chapter we continue our study of antitrust law by examining in detail the various forms of concerted behavior that are condemned as harmful to competition. In particular, we examine how courts attempt to distinguish between those types of trade restrictions that are necessary—perhaps even beneficial—to the competitive process and those that impede competition. We also examine the legal standards for determining whether mergers between firms should be declared illegal on the grounds that the result would be to lessen competition.

■ Restraints of Trade: Overview

The underlying assumption of Section 1 of the Sherman Act is that society's welfare is harmed if rival firms are permitted to join in an agreement that consolidates their market power or otherwise restrains competition. Not all agreements between rivals, however, result in enhanced market power or *unreasonably* restrain trade. It is virtually inconceivable that an agreement

499

to fix prices or restrict output could be designed for any purpose other than to diminish interfirm competition. Yet there are numerous instances when agreements among rivals might actually increase social welfare by making firms more efficient, by making information more readily available, or by creating joint incentives to undertake risky research and development projects.

Characterizing Concerted Action

An agreement that at first glance may appear to be anticompetitive may actually provide legitimate benefits to society. Others are so blatantly and substantially anticompetitive that they are deemed **per se violations** of Section 1. If an agreement is found to be a per se violation, a court is precluded from inquiring whether it should nonetheless be upheld on the ground that it provides benefits that outweigh the anticompetitive effects. Characterization of any form of joint activity as a per se violation implies that the dangers it poses for open competition are so great that no other aspect of the activity can redeem it from condemnation under the antitrust laws. Characterization of an agreement, however, does not always complete the antitrust analysis. If an agreement is not one that is a per se violation of Section 1, then the courts proceed to analyze its legality under what is referred to as a **rule of reason.**

The Rule of Reason

In determining whether a specific agreement that is not a per se violation should nonetheless be condemned as a Section 1 offense, a court will consider several factors. The court must evaluate the purposes the parties have in effecting the agreement, determine whether the parties have power to implement the agreement's purposes, and assess what the effect or potential effect of the agreement is. Some antitrust scholars maintain that case law suggests that courts will also consider a fourth element: whether the parties could have relied on less restrictive means to achieve their goals.

The dividing line between per se violations and agreements judged under a rule of reason is seldom clear. Moreover, in some cases, the United States Supreme Court has stated, or at least implied, that it is applying a per se rule, and yet a careful reading of its analysis suggests that it is weighing benefits

against harms under a rule of reason.[1] Some have termed this a "soft," or "limited," per se rule. Others have termed it a "narrow" rule of reason. Perhaps the most that can be said with certainty is that although the distinction between the two rules seems clear in theory, in the actual application of antitrust laws, the distinction has not always been so clear.

■ Horizontal Restraints

The term **horizontal restraint** is encountered frequently in antitrust law. A horizontal restraint is any agreement that in some way restrains competition between rival firms competing in the same market. Whenever firms at the same level of operation and in direct competition with one another (for example, retailers of a similar product located in the same geographical market) agree to operate in a way that restricts their market activities, they are said to have imposed a horizontal restraint on trade. Some horizontal restraints are per se violations of Section 1, but others may be permissible; those that are not per se violations are tested under the rule of reason.

Price Fixing

Consider again the scenario presented in the preceding chapter involving the introduction of a new laser fax machine. Suppose our hypothetical firm, Acme, had instead sought its reward of large profits by some means other than arduous and financially risky research into innovative laser fax technology. Assume that laser technology has not yet been invented. So we are in the pre–laser fax era. Suppose that Acme's managers decide to make life easy for themselves. Suppose that they go to other fax machine producers who, like Acme, make nonlaser fax machines and say, "Let's not work to one another's disadvantage. There's enough demand for fax machines for all of us to charge higher prices if we don't undercut one another's prices." Acme's plan calls for each producer to charge a price higher than an established minimum. The minimum price

---

1. See, e.g., *Klor's, Inc. v. Broadway-Hale Stores, Inc.,* 359 U.S. 207, 79 S.Ct. 705, 3 L.Ed.2d 741 (1959); *Fashion Originator's Guild of America, Inc. v. FTC,* 312 U.S. 457, 61 S.Ct. 703, 85 L.Ed. 949 (1941); and *Silver v. New York Stock Exchange,* 373 U.S. 341, 83 S.Ct. 1246, 10 L.Ed.2d 389 (1963).

is set as the total cost of the least productive producer plus a 10 percent margin. More efficient firms (that is, firms that can produce at lower cost) will, of course, enjoy higher profits.

Although not all such schemes are as simple or as blatant as our hypothetical example suggests, they all involve some means of eliminating the competition between rivals to sell at the lowest price while still earning a normal profit (that is, one commensurate with the profit that could be earned in some alternative endeavor using the same resources). By eliminating price competition in which firms seek to sell more by charging less than their rivals, firms restrict output. This is the essence of **price fixing.**

Perhaps the definitive case regarding price-fixing agreements remains the 1940 case of *United States v. Socony-Vacuum Oil Co.,* also known as the *Madison Oil* case.[2] In this case, a group of independent oil producers in Texas and Louisiana were caught between falling demand due to the Great Depression and increasing supply from newly discovered oil fields in the region. In response, a group of the major refining companies agreed to buy "distress" gasoline (excess supplies) from the independents so as to dispose of it in an "orderly manner." Although there was no explicit agreement as to price, it was clear that the purpose of the agreement was to limit the supply of gasoline on the market, thereby raising prices.

There may have been good reasons for such an agreement. The refiners may simply have wanted to avoid a temporary situation that would have driven the independent suppliers out of business, thus making it difficult to secure crude oil supplies later after the economic climate had improved. Nonetheless, the threats posed by such agreements to open and free competition are enormous. The United States Supreme Court recognized these dangers in the *Socony-Vacuum* case. The Court held that the asserted reasonableness of a price-fixing agreement is never a defense; any agreement that restricts output or artificially fixes price is a per se violation of Section 1. The rationale of the per se rule was best stated in what is now the most famous portion of the Court's decision: footnote 59 of Justice William O. Douglas's opinion. In it he compared a freely functioning price system to a body's central nervous system, condemning price-fixing agreements as threats to "the central nervous system of the economy."

Price-fixing arrangements are not always easy to identify. An otherwise legitimate arrangement may involve price fixing. It may be an unintentional result of such an arrangement. It also may be difficult to detect because the parties intentionally wish to conceal their scheme. The following case summarizes the United States Supreme Court's views on various practices that have been condemned as attempts to fix prices. It also addresses whether a specific arrangement—an agreement among firms to set uniform terms for, or eliminate entirely, credit extensions to the firms' buyers—is a form of price fixing.

2.   310 U.S. 150, 60 S.Ct. 811, 84 L.Ed.2d 1129 (1940).

BACKGROUND AND FACTS   *After December 1967, retail beer sellers (appellants) in and around Fresno, California, faced a situation in which all local wholesale beer distributors (respondents) refused to sell to the retailers on credit. Instead, the wholesalers demanded payment in advance or on delivery. State law governing all such credit transactions expressly permitted credit extensions without interest for periods of thirty to forty-two days. Prior to the elimination of credit sales, the wholesalers had offered widely differing credit terms to different individual retail buyers. The retailers brought suit, alleging that the elimination of credit sales was the result of an agreement among the wholesalers entered into in secret during 1967. The retailers contended that the purpose of the wholesalers' agreement was to eliminate competition among themselves. According to the retailers, the wholesalers had vigorously competed against one another*

Case 21.1

CATALANO, INC. v. TARGET SALES, INC.

Supreme Court of the United States, 1980.
446 U.S. 643,
100 S.Ct. 1925,
64 L.Ed.2d 580.

by offering favorable credit terms to retail buyers. The issue of whether an agreement among rival firms regarding credit terms was a form of price fixing deemed a per se violation of Section 1 of the Sherman Act was presented to the circuit court of appeals. The appellate court, in a divided decision, held that such an agreement was not a form of price fixing. A majority on the appellate court stated that there could be procompetitive reasons for the elimination of credit sales. First, according to the majority, the elimination might promote competition by "removing a barrier perceived by some sellers to market entry." Second, according to the majority, the elimination would increase information to buyers "by the increased visibility of price made possible by the agreement to eliminate credit." The circuit court's decision was appealed to the United States Supreme Court.

PER CURIAM [by the entire court].
* * * *

* * * It has long been settled that an agreement to fix prices is unlawful per se. It is no excuse that the prices fixed are themselves reasonable. * * *

It is virtually self-evident that extending interest-free credit for a period of time is equivalent to giving a discount equal to the value of the use of the purchase price for that period of time. Thus, credit terms must be characterized as an inseparable part of the price. An agreement to terminate the practice of giving credit is thus tantamount to an agreement to eliminate discounts, and thus falls squarely within the traditional per se rule against price fixing. While it may be that the elimination of a practice of giving variable discounts will ultimately lead in a competitive market to corresponding decreases in the invoice price, that is surely not necessarily to be anticipated. It is more realistic to view an agreement to eliminate credit sales as extinguishing one form of competition among the sellers. In any event, when a particular concerted activity entails an obvious risk of anticompetitive impact with no apparent potentially redeeming value, the fact that a practice may turn out to be harmless in a particular set of circumstances will not prevent its being declared unlawful per se.

The majority of the panel of the Court of Appeals suggested, however, that a horizontal agreement to eliminate credit sales may remove a barrier to other sellers who may wish to enter the market. But in any case in which competitors are able to increase the price level or to curtail production by agreement, it could be argued that the agreement has the effect of making the market more attractive to potential new entrants. If that potential justifies horizontal agreements among competitors imposing one kind of voluntary restraint or another on their competitive freedom, it would seem to follow that the more successful an agreement is in raising the price level, the safer it is from antitrust attack. Nothing could be more inconsistent with our cases.

Nor can the informing function of the agreement, the increased price visibility, justify its restraint on the individual wholesaler's freedom to select his own prices and terms of sale. For, again, it is obvious that any industrywide agreement on prices will result in a more accurate understanding of the terms offered by all parties to the agreement. * * * [T]here is a plain distinction between the lawful right to publish prices and terms of sale, on the one hand, and an agreement among competitors limiting action with respect to the published prices, on the other.

Thus, under the reasoning of our cases, an agreement among competing wholesalers to refuse to sell unless the retailer makes payment in cash either in advance or upon delivery is "plainly anticompetitive." Since it is merely one form of price fixing, and since price-fixing agreements have been adjudged to lack any "redeeming virtue," it is conclusively presumed illegal without further examination under the rule of reason.

The Court reversed the appellate court's decision. The Court concluded that an agreement to eliminate or set terms of credit among rival firms was a form of price fixing. Because price fixing is a per se violation, the credit arrangement violated Section 1 of the Sherman Act regardless of any alleged commercial justification or contention of reasonableness.

DECISION AND REMEDY

Horizontal Market Divisions

Prices can be controlled indirectly through agreements to restrict output, as well as explicitly through agreements to fix prices. Because the former type of agreement operates to decrease the supplies available to consumers, the result has the same effect as a direct agreement to raise prices. Efforts to control prices are often effected by **horizontal market divisions**—that is, by agreements to divide the market up among rival firms. The allocation may be geographical (for example, letting one firm serve the Midwest, another the East Coast, and so on), or it may be functional, by class of customer (for example, having one firm deal exclusively with retailers and a second firm deal solely with wholesalers). In some respects, market divisions may have an even greater impact on competition than do price-fixing agreements. Each firm has a complete monopoly over its allocated share of the market—it is the sole supplier. The sole supplier is free not only from price competition but from competition regarding quality, customer service, and all other dimensions of competition as well.

THE PER SE RULE AND HORIZONTAL MARKET DIVISIONS   Consider once again our hypothetical scenario involving Acme and its rival fax machine producers. Suppose that, flush with the initial success of their price-fixing agreement, the producers agree that each firm that begins selling machines to dealers in remote communities in which fax machines have not been available will thereafter have an exclusive right to sell retail or through dealers in that area. Initially there is intense competition to find such virgin markets. After all the profitable markets have been taken, however, conditions in the exclusive markets change drastically. Suppliers may begin to limit the warranties they offer. Prices may begin to rise despite the lack of warranties. And service among the retailers may noticeably diminish. Because of such effects, agreements like that made by the fax machine producers are generally treated as per se violations of Section 1.

The following case considers whether an allocation of customers is a horizontal restraint that should be treated as a per se violation of Section 1 of the Sherman Act. The case also shows the procedural effects of characterizing conduct as a per se violation.

BACKGROUND AND FACTS   *Suntar Roofing, Inc., was incorporated under the laws of the state of Kansas and engaged in the construction of roofs on new single and multi-family homes in and around Kansas City, Kansas. Suntar agreed to a customer allocation plan that would divide roofing customers in the Kansas City area between Suntar and another Kansas corporation, Ronan's Roofing, Inc. The plan was conceived and implemented by some of the two corporations' officers and owners, who, at a joint meeting, discussed prices for roofing construction, individual roofing projects underway, and the method by which specific customers could be allocated between the two firms. The United States government brought criminal charges against some of the participants in the market allocation conspiracy. In a jury trial, those charged were found guilty of violating federal antitrust laws. The defendants appealed their convictions,*

Case 21.2

UNITED STATES v. SUNTAR ROOFING, INC.

United States Circuit Court of Appeals,
Tenth Circuit, 1990.
897 F.2d 469.

asserting that the trial judge had erred in instructing the jury that all customer allocation schemes are per se violations of Section 1 of the Sherman Act. In a related argument against their convictions, the defendants contended that the judge's conclusion that such agreements were per se violations precluded the defendants' introducing evidence to show the reasonableness of their market allocation agreement. The effect of the trial judge's ruling was that the defendants could be convicted if the evidence showed that they had agreed to allocate customers between the two firms. Because the trial judge ruled such an agreement to be a per se violation, evidence as to the reasonableness of the scheme was deemed irrelevant and thus excluded from the jury's consideration. The appellate court considered the issue of whether such a scheme is a per se violation of Section 1 of the Sherman Act.

BRORBY, J.
*   *   *   *

Appellants contend that the trial court erred when it sustained the government's pre-trial motion to prevent the defendants from offering evidence of the reasonableness and/or economic justification for the alleged activities or evidence of the defendants' lack of intent to violate the law or to restrain trade. Thus, appellants allege that they were deprived of any opportunity to present evidence that the conduct charged was permissible under "rule of reason" analysis and that the jury was deprived of its fact finding function to determine whether the charged conduct unreasonably restrained competition.

Section 1 of the Sherman Act prohibits "[e]very contract, combination, . . ., or conspiracy, in restraint of trade or commerce." Generally, courts apply a "rule of reason" analysis to determine whether particular practices or conduct come within the ambit of the statute. Under "rule of reason" analysis, the factfinder weighs all of the circumstances of a case to decide whether a restrictive practice should be prohibited as imposing an unreasonable restraint on competition.

However, since the passage of the Sherman Act, the courts have formulated and applied a per se rule of illegality for certain restrictive practices that are deemed to be manifestly anticompetitive. As the Supreme Court explained in *Northern Pac. R. Co. v. United States*, "there are certain agreements or practices which because of their pernicious effect on competition and lack of any redeeming virtue are conclusively presumed to be unreasonable and therefore illegal without elaborate inquiry as to the precise harm they have caused or the business excuse for their use." Here, appellants argue that the indictment in this case did not justify the trial court's application of per se analysis in that the restraint charged is not clearly "pernicious" as a matter of law.

In its pre-trial motion, the government argued that the conduct charged in the indictment, a "horizontal" customer allocation agreement, represented conduct which is illegal per se. Prior to trial, the trial court ruled that the indictment did in fact allege a per se violation of the Sherman Act, and that, assuming the government could present evidence establishing the violation charged in the indictment, the defendants would therefore be precluded from introducing evidence of reasonableness or justification at trial. At trial, the court concluded that the government had established the violation charged and therefore precluded defendants' additional evidence. Consistent with the analysis of the Supreme Court and previous holdings of this court and of other circuits, we concur with the determination of the trial court and hold that the activity alleged in the indictment in this case, an agreement to allocate or divide customers between competitors within the same horizontal market, constitutes a per se violation of Section 1 of the Sherman Act.

The appellate court sustained the trial judge's ruling that a customer al-locution scheme is a per se violation of Section 1 of the Sherman Act. Therefore, the trial judge's exclusion of evidence regarding the reason-ableness of, or business justification for, the scheme was not an error; there was no need for the jury to consider such evidence because there is no justification for such a scheme.

DECISION AND REMEDY

CRITICISMS OF APPLYING THE PER SE RULE TO ALL HORIZONTAL MARKET DIVISIONS

The per se rule regarding market divisions has been criticized in certain circumstances, and its future status is uncertain. Some actual cases have involved circumstances very dissimilar to those presented in our hypothetical scenario. In one instance, a group of small- and medium-sized groceries agreed to market a common brand of grocery products by allocating regional territories to members of the group so individual members could focus their marketing efforts on a single territory. The group accounted for only about 6 percent of sales in its market and directly competed with such large chain stores as A&P and Safeway, which carried their own name-brand products.[3] A similar venture using territorial restrictions involved a group of small firms attempting to market mattresses under the trademark *Sealy*.[4] In both these cases the individual firms did not have resources to create their own brands individually and joined together so as to compete with larger, established firms selling their own brand-name products. Nonetheless, both cases were treated as per se violations of Section 1. It is possible that the considerations just discussed will ultimately lead the United States Supreme Court to adopt a rule of reason for judging such horizontal restraints. As shown by some of the cases considered below, the Court has been more willing in recent years to consider economic factors rather than relying solely on mechanical characterizations in judging business conduct.

Trade Associations

The common interests of firms or individuals within an industry or profession are frequently pro-moted by trade associations or professional organizations. These organizations may provide for the exchange of information among the members, the enhancement of the trade or profession's public image, the setting of industry or professional standards, or the pooling of resources to represent the members' interests to various governmental bodies. Some of these activities benefit society as well as the individual members. Even those activities that benefit the members' general economic well-being may not necessarily be anticompetitive.

For example, lumber producers might be concerned about whether or not they are cutting more trees than expected future demand would warrant given the cutting levels of rival firms. The market for lumber might be widely dispersed over the whole nation, making it especially difficult for small firms to gauge the overall demand conditions in the lumber market. Lumber firms might thus decide to form a trade association that could amass data on the output and price levels of its members in various markets.[5] The association would be of economic benefit to lumber firms by reducing the costs of projecting market demand. Such knowledge could also benefit society, however, by making the lumber market function more smoothly, dampening cycles of oversupply and undersupply of lumber output. Even if it did not make the industry function more smoothly, it would be unlikely to harm competition in the industry unless the industry were *concentrated*.

A **concentrated industry** is one in which either a single firm or a small number of firms control a large percentage of market sales. In such concentrated industries, trade associations can be, and have been, used as a means to facilitate anticompetitive actions, such as fixing prices, allocat-

---

3. See *United States v. Topco Associates, Inc.,* 405 U.S. 596, 92 S.Ct. 1126, 31 L.Ed.2d 515 (1972).
4. See *United States v. Sealy, Inc.,* 388 U.S. 350, 87 S.Ct. 1847, 18 L.Ed.2d 1238 (1967).

5. See, for example, *American Column & Lumber Co. v. United States,* 257 U.S. 377, 42 S.Ct. 114, 66 L.Ed.2d 284 (1921).

ing markets, or, as discussed in the next section, conducting boycotts—all with the clear objective of lessening competition. For example, consider again the lumber association. Such an association would be providing information that members could use to determine whether a secret agreement to fix prices was being adhered to by the conspirators. Thus, such associations offer possibilities of both great benefits and substantial harm.

In most instances, the rule of reason is applied in evaluating such practices and agreements. If a court finds that a particular practice or agreement that restrains trade involves no apparent intent to fix prices or limit output and benefits the public as well as the association, then the court will weigh those benefits against the harms to competition under the rule of reason. As in all cases, however, if the harm to competition is substantial, a trade association's activities will be condemned as a Section 1 violation. As shown in the following case, not even action undertaken by a health-care profession allegedly for the sole purpose of protecting the public will escape scrutiny if it is likely to harm market competition.

Case 21.3

WILK v. AMERICAN MEDICAL ASSOCIATION

United States Court of Appeals, Seventh Circuit, 1990. 895 F.2d 352.

BACKGROUND AND FACTS *In 1966, the AMA passed a resolution labeling chiropractic an unscientific cult. (Chiropractors attempt to cure or relieve bodily ailments by making skeletal adjustments.) In effect, this label prevented physicians from associating with chiropractors, because Principle 3 of the Principles of Medical Ethics—the AMA's code of ethical conduct—provided that a "physician should practice a method of healing founded on a scientific basis; and he should not voluntarily associate with anyone who violates this principle." Medical doctors used Principle 3 to justify their refusal to have anything to do with chiropractors or to allow chiropractors to use hospital diagnostic services or become members of hospital medical staffs. Despite the AMA's efforts, chiropractic became licensed in all fifty states, and in a 1980 revision of the ethical code, Principle 3 was eliminated. Chester Wilk and four other chiropractors brought an action against the AMA, claiming that the AMA's actions had violated Section 1 of the Sherman Act; they sought injunctive relief from the "lingering effects" of the AMA's actions on chiropractors. The trial court, holding that the AMA had violated Section 1 of the Sherman Act by conducting what amounted to an illegal boycott in restraint of trade, granted an injunction that required the AMA, among other things, to publish widely the trial court's order. The AMA appealed.*

MANION, Circuit Judge.
* * * *

At trial, the AMA raised the so-called "patient care defense" * * * . That defense required the AMA generally to show that it acted because of a genuine, and reasonable, concern for scientific method in patient care and that it could not adequately satisfy this concern in a way that was less restrictive of competition. The district court rejected the defense. The court found the AMA failed to establish that throughout the relevant period (1966–1980) their [sic] concern for scientific methods in patient care had been objectively reasonable. The court also found the AMA similarly failed to show it could not adequately have satisfied its concern for scientific method in patient care in a manner less restrictive of competition than a nationwide conspiracy to eliminate a licensed profession.
* * * *

As a general rule, [Section] 1 claims under the Sherman Act should be evaluated under the rule of reason unless the challenged action falls into the category of agreements which are deemed so harmful in their effect on competition so as to be conclusively presumed to be unreasonable and thus illegal without a detailed inquiry as to the precise harm they are alleged to have caused. * * *

* * * *

The threshold issue in any rule of reason case is market power. Market power is the ability to raise prices above the competitive level by restricting output. Whether market power exists in an appropriately defined market is a fact-bound question, and appellate courts normally defer to district court findings on that issue. Here, the district court found the relevant market to be the provision of health care services to the American public nationwide, particularly care for the treatment of musculo-skeletal problems. Several facts demonstrated the AMA's market power within the health care services market. * * *

* * * *

The district court also relied on substantial evidence of adverse effects on competition caused by the boycott to establish the AMA's market power. In [a previous case], the United States Supreme Court explained that since "the purpose of the inquiries into market definition and market power is to determine whether an arrangement has the potential for genuine adverse effects on competition, 'proof of actual detrimental effects, such as reduction of output' can obviate the need for an inquiry into market power, which is but a 'surrogate for detrimental effects.' " * * *

* * * Essentially, the AMA argues that the market for medical services is one where there is "information asymmetry." In other words, health care consumers almost invariably lack sufficient information needed to evaluate the quality of medical services. This increases the risk of fraud and deception on consumers by unscrupulous health care providers possibly causing what the AMA terms "market failure": consumers avoiding necessary treatment (for fear of fraud), and accepting treatment with no expectation of assured quality. The AMA's conduct, the theory goes on, ensured that physicians acquired reputations for quality (in part, by not associating with unscientific cultists), and thus allowed consumers to be assured that physicians would use only scientifically valid treatments. This in effect simultaneously provided consumers with essential information and protected competition.

Getting information to the market is a fine goal, but the district court found that the AMA was not motivated solely by such altrustic concerns. Indeed, the court found that the AMA intended to "destroy a competitor," namely, chiropractors. It is not enough to carry the day to argue that competition should be eliminated in the name of public safety.

The appellate court affirmed both the trial court's ruling that the AMA had violated Section 1 of the Sherman Act by conducting an illegal boycott of chiropractors and the trial court's decision to grant an injunction against the AMA. The appellate court also held that the trial court had not abused its discretion in ordering the AMA to widely publish the trial court's findings and decision in the case.

DECISION AND REMEDY

Group Boycotts

Refer again to the fax machine producers and their hypothetical attempts to fix prices and allocate market territories. After their initial success in obtaining greater profits for the industry, they face at least two problems. The first is how to discipline errant firms that attempt to increase their profits by selling for less than the agreed price or by encroaching on another firm's exclusive territory. The second is how to prevent new firms attracted by the large profits in the fax industry from entering the market and reducing each member's share of profits.

Observe the actions of the group members further. They have now formed the High-Quality Facsimile Transmission Machine Association. The function of the association, at least as stated in its charter, is to "promote the interests of the consumer above all other considerations by ensuring that facsimile transmission machines are always manufactured according to the highest possible standards." To facilitate its goals, the association has decided to confer its "seal of approval" on all fax products deemed of worthy quality. In fact, the association has never denied an original producer–member's request for approval except in those instances when the producer happens to have failed to abide by the original price and market-allocation terms the group has set. Things are not so easy, however, for subsequent arrivals into the fax industry. Alleging that the new firms are able to enter the market and compete only by use of "substandard components," the association refuses to bestow any new seals of approval. Moreover, they urge dealers, some of whom have been invited to become members of the association, not to carry or service any products that do not have the association's seal of approval. In concert, the group refuses to have any dealings with any retailers, wholesalers, or other manufacturers who do not exclusively use products carrying the association's seal of approval. This is a group boycott.

A **group boycott,** or concerted refusal to deal, is any agreement by which two or more buyers or sellers refuse to engage in any transactions with a particular person or organization, the object of the boycott. An obvious, and indeed frequent, purpose of a boycott is to eliminate or discipline a competitor of the boycotting group. Boycotts are thus a powerful tool for enforcing anticompetitive arrangements among firms. Sometimes, however, group boycotts are intended to promote economic efficiency, moral or social causes, or the general well-being of the group, without intending to injure competition. For example, a professional organization or a trade association might seek to promote its public image by sponsoring a program to prevent its members from engaging in deceptive advertising or employing high-pressure sales tactics. A member's failure to abide by the program guidelines could be punished by expulsion from the organization or association or by denial of the group's endorsement, such as withholding of the association's "seal of approval." One of the fax producers' means of enforcing its association's restrictive measures, for example, was asking member dealers not to carry, or to boycott, those manufacturers whose products had not received the association's seal of approval.

Despite the possibility of a procompetitive intent or some other socially valuable objective, concerted refusals to deal—group boycotts—are generally said to be per se violations of Section 1. A more accurate statement is that a court will treat a group boycott as a per se violation of Section 1 only in cases in which the group possesses market power and the boycott is intended to restrict or exclude a competitor. If, however, these elements are missing, the court may be inclined to weigh the benefits of the group's efforts against the harm inflicted by the boycott; that is, it will apply a rule of reason analysis, as in the following case.

Case 21.4

FEDERAL TRADE COMMISSION v. INDIANA FEDERATION OF DENTISTS

Supreme Court of the United States, 1986.
476 U.S. 447,
106 S.Ct. 2009,
90 L.Ed.2d 445.

BACKGROUND AND FACTS *In an attempt to control costs, dental health insurers adopted a policy that required dentists to submit diagnostic dental X-rays to the insurance company for review before the company would approve payment for treatment. The Indiana Federation of Dentists objected to this policy and adopted a resolution not to submit X-rays as requested by the insurers. Most dentists complied with this resolution and refused to submit X-rays. In 1978, the Federal Trade Commission (FTC) issued a complaint against the federation and found that the joint refusal to submit X-rays was a violation of antitrust laws. According to the FTC, the policy of not submitting X-rays had the effect of encouraging unnecessary dental procedures and raising costs. The federation appealed this finding, and the Seventh Circuit Court of Appeals overturned the FTC's ruling. The appellate court contended that the FTC had not shown that the federation's policy had an anticompetitive effect. The FTC then appealed to the United States Supreme Court.*

WHITE, Justice.

* * * *

The question remains whether these [facts] are legally sufficient to establish a violation of [Section] 1 of the Sherman Act—that is, whether the Federation's collective refusal to cooperate with insurers' requests for X-rays constitutes an "unreasonable" restraint of trade. * * *

* * * *

Application of the Rule of Reason to these facts is not a matter of any great difficulty. The Federation's policy takes the form of a horizontal agreement among the participating dentists to withhold from their customers a particular service that they desire—the forwarding of X-rays to insurance companies along with claim forms. "While this is not price fixing as such, no elaborate industry analysis is required to demonstrate the anticompetitive character of such an agreement." A refusal to compete with respect to the package of services offered to customers, no less than a refusal to compete with respect to the price term of an agreement, impairs the ability of the market to advance social welfare by ensuring the provision of desired goods and services to consumers at a price approximating the marginal cost [incremental, or additional, cost] of providing them. Absent some countervailing procompetitive virtue—such as, for example, the creation of efficiencies in the operation of a market or the provision of goods and services—such an agreement limiting consumer choice by impeding the "ordinary give and take of the market place" cannot be sustained under the Rule of Reason. No credible argument has been advanced for the proposition that making it more costly for the insurers and patients who are the dentists' customers to obtain information needed for evaluating the dentists' diagnoses has any such procompetitive effect.

The United States Supreme Court reversed the lower court's decision and approved the FTC order. The Court held that the FTC's findings were supported by substantial evidence and that the Indiana Federation of Dentists had violated Section 1 of the Sherman Act. The Court reinstated the FTC's order requiring the federation to cease its practice of jointly refusing to provide dental X-rays to insurers.

DECISION AND REMEDY

Joint Ventures

A **joint venture** is any undertaking by two or more firms or individuals who, while maintaining their distinct identities, come together for the limited purpose of achieving a specific goal. Antitrust analysis of joint ventures involves two issues: first, whether the joining together is itself a violation of antitrust laws; and second, whether the purpose or means of the joint venture is impermissible. The first issue is covered by Section 7 of the Clayton Act as well as Section 1 of the Sherman Act. An important consideration is the joint venture's percentage market share. Here we limit our focus to the legality of the joint venture's purpose and actions.

Unlike price-fixing agreements or market divisions, joint ventures are not necessarily anticompetitive. Indeed, many are likely to provide economic efficiencies. For example, it may be beneficial to society as well as individual firms if resources are pooled by firms engaging in substantial research and development (R&D) efforts. Pooling research and development resources prevents firms' duplicating one another's efforts. Once the R&D phase has been completed, the firms will compete along other dimensions, such as price, quality, and consumer services. Pooling resources also allows the firms to share the risk that the initial efforts may be fruitless. Some ventures that are desirable from society's point of view may involve risks so substantial that no single firm would want to undertake the venture alone. When the risk is spread among many firms, individual risk is reduced, and the venture is more appealing.

This was precisely the rationale advanced in *United States v. Morgan*,[6] which involved the practice among investment bankers of forming underwriting syndicates to bring issues of new securities to the market. During the initial offering, it is common for the underwriters to "make a market" by agreeing to buy back enough of the securities to keep the price above a predetermined minimum if demand is less than anticipated initially. Although such an arrangement has all the earmarks of price fixing, the court held that the arrangement was not an unreasonable restraint of trade. Although sometimes cited as an exception to the rule that price fixing is a per se violation of Section 1, the decision cannot be taken to mean that price fixing is ever reasonable; distinct features of the case make it clear that the court did not view this as ordinary price fixing, which remains a per se violation of Section 1.[7] The court took into consideration several unique aspects of the arrangement: the extremely short-term duration of syndicates; the fact that new syndicates involving different investment houses were continually being formed for new offerings; that there was a competitive process by which investment houses sought to form and join the new syndicates; and that the competitive pressures were sufficient to ensure that those seeking to raise investment capital were provided a relatively low-cost, efficient vehicle for doing so. What is perhaps most significant in the *Morgan* case is that the government, in challenging the practice, was unable to point to any less restrictive means of raising capital as efficiently.

If a joint venture does not involve price fixing or market divisions, the agreement will be analyzed under the rule of reason. Whether the venture will then be upheld under Section 1 depends on an overall assessment of the purposes of the venture, a strict analysis of the potential benefits relative to the likely harms, and in some cases an assessment of whether there are less restrictive alternatives for achieving the same goals.

■ Vertical Restraints

Another distinct set of restraints involves those imposed by the seller on the buyer (or vice versa), as

distinct from those imposed *among* sellers or buyers. These restraints involve what is termed the vertical relationship. Horizontal relationships occur at the same level of operations. Vertical relationships, by comparison, encompass the entire chain of production: the purchase of inputs, basic manufacturing, distribution to wholesalers, and eventual sale of a product at the retail level. For some products, these distinct phases are carried on by different firms. In other instances, a single firm may carry out two or more of the different functional phases. Firms such as the latter are considered to be **vertically integrated firms.**

Even though firms operating at different functional levels do not directly compete with one another, each does compete with other firms operating at its own level of operation. Thus, agreements between firms standing in a vertical relationship do significantly affect competition. For example, a contractual agreement between tire manufacturer Firestone and Billy Ray's Automotive Supplies, an independent retailer, conditioning Billy Ray's future supply of Firestone tires on its willingness to resell only at a price set by Firestone is a form of vertical restraint. Other types of vertical restraints are often encountered, but not all of them necessarily harm competition. Indeed, many are procompetitive. Marketing decisions within a vertically integrated firm are not subject to attack under Section 1. The legality of certain other classes of vertical restraints are judged under a rule of reason. Still others are deemed per se violations of Section 1.

Territorial or Customer Restrictions

In arranging for the distribution of its product, a manufacturing firm may seek to insulate its dealers or retailers from direct competition with one another. As mentioned earlier in the context of separate firms jointly promoting a certain brand of product, there may be legitimate, procompetitive reasons for doing so. One such reason is to prevent a dealer from cutting costs and undercutting rivals by providing the product without promotion or customer service, while relying on a nearby dealer to provide these services. The cost-cutting dealer could thus enjoy the benefits of the promotional and customer service costs expended by his rivals without incurring the associated costs. One way of addressing the problem is to restrict dealers to selling in specific markets or to certain classes of cus-

---

6.   118 F.Supp. 621 (S.D.N.Y. 1953).
7.   The case is more often cited as a classic example of how to judge joint ventures under the rule of reason.

tomers. These restrictions are judged under a rule of reason.

The following case, *Continental T.V., Inc. v. GTE Sylvania, Inc.,* overturned the Court's earlier stance, which had been set out in *United States v. Arnold, Schwinn & Co.*[8] In *Schwinn,* the Court had held such restrictions to be per se violations. The *Continental* case has been heralded as one of the most important antitrust cases since the 1940s. It represents a definite shift away from rigid characterization to a more flexible approach emphasizing economics and efficiency.

_____

8.   388 U.S. 365, 87 S.Ct. 1856, 18 L.Ed.2d 1249 (1967).

Case 21.5

CONTINENTAL T.V., INC. v. GTE SYLVANIA, INC.

Supreme Court of the United States, 1977.
433 U.S. 36,
97 S.Ct. 2549,
53 L.Ed.2d 568.

BACKGROUND AND FACTS   *Before 1962, like most other television manufacturers, GTE Sylvania, Inc., sold its televisions to independent or company-owned distributors, who in turn resold to a large and diverse group of retailers. In 1962, Sylvania phased out its wholesale distributors and began to sell its televisions directly to franchised retailers. Sylvania limited the number of franchises granted for any given area and required each franchisee to sell the Sylvania products from only the locations of the franchise. A franchise did not constitute an exclusive territory, and Sylvania retained sole discretion to increase the number of retailers in an area, depending on the success or failure of existing retailers in developing their market. Continental T.V., Inc., a Sylvania franchisee, withheld all payments due for Sylvania products after a dispute over additional locations sought by Continental. John P. Maguire & Company, the finance company that handled the credit arrangements between Sylvania and its franchisees, sued Continental for payment and for the return of secured merchandise. Continental claimed that Sylvania had violated Section 1 of the Sherman Act by entering into and enforcing franchise agreements that permitted the sale of Sylvania products only in specified locations. The trial court held for Continental, and Sylvania appealed. The court of appeals for the Ninth Circuit reversed, concluding that Sylvania's location restrictions should be judged under a "rule of reason" rather than a per se standard. Continental appealed to the United States Supreme Court.*

POWELL, Justice.
        *   *   *   *

Vertical restrictions reduce intrabrand competition [competition among dealers of the same brand] by limiting the number of sellers of a particular product competing for the business of a given group of buyers. Location restrictions have this effect because of practical constraints on the effective marketing area of retail outlets. Although intrabrand competition may be reduced, the ability of retailers to exploit the resulting market may be limited both by the ability of consumers to travel to other franchised locations and, perhaps more importantly, to purchase the competing products of other manufacturers. None of these key variables, however, is affected by the form of the transaction by which a manufacturer conveys his products to the retailers.

Vertical restrictions promote interbrand competition by allowing the manufacturer to achieve certain efficiencies in the distribution of his products. These "redeeming virtues" are implicit in every decision sustaining vertical restrictions under the rule of reason. Economists have identified a number of ways in which manufacturers can use such restrictions to compete more effectively against other manufacturers. For example, new manufacturers and manufacturers entering new markets can use the restrictions in order to induce competent and aggressive retailers to make the kind of investment of capital and labor that is often required in the distribution of products unknown to the consumer. Established manufacturers can use them to induce retailers to engage in promotional activities or to provide service and repair facilities necessary to the efficient marketing of their products. Service and repair are vital for many products, such as automobiles and major household appliances. The availability and quality of such services affect a manufacturer's goodwill and the competitiveness of his product. Because of market imperfections * * *, these services might not be provided by retailers in a purely competitive situation, despite the fact that each retailer's benefit would be greater if all provided the services than if none did.

DECISION AND REMEDY   *The United States Supreme Court affirmed the appellate court's holding that Sylvania had not violated Section 1 of the Sherman Act. The decision, overturning the Court's earlier ruling in* United States v. Arnold, Schwinn & Co. *that all such restraints would be treated as per se violations, does not mean that all such restraints are necessarily legal but rather that in the future the legality of all such restraints will be tested under a rule of reason.*

Resale Price Maintenance Agreements

Resale price maintenance agreements, also referred to as *fair trade agreements*, occur whenever the manufacturer seeks to establish a minimum price that the retailer or wholesaler may charge for the manufacturer's product. Under these agreements, the manufacturer conditions sales to the retailer or wholesaler on the latter's reselling only at a price allowed by the manufacturer. Although authorized for many years under so-called *fair trade laws*, such agreements are today condemned as per se violations of Section 1. Such a condemnation seems anomalous for at least two reasons. First, the economic justifications are often identical to those that supported the Court's holding in the *Syl-*

vania case which established that vertical territorial and customer restrictions should be judged under a rule of reason. Second, manufacturers can achieve the same result by simply *integrating forward*—that is, by simply selling through their own, rather than independent, dealers. Moreover, manufacturers are legally entitled to *suggest* a retail price to dealers. The manufacturers may refuse to deal with dealers who do not follow that suggestion. The following case involves a manufacturer's right to terminate a relationship with one of its dealers because the dealer is selling the manufacturer's product for a price that other dealers believe is too low.

Case 21.6

BUSINESS ELECTRONICS CORP. v. SHARP ELECTRONICS CORP.

Supreme Court of the United States, 1988.
485 U.S. 717,
108 S.Ct. 1515,
99 L.Ed.2d 808.

BACKGROUND AND FACTS *Business Electronics Corp. was a dealer for Sharp Electronics Corp. and was authorized to sell Sharp calculators in and around Houston, Texas. Business Electronics continuously sold the calculators for prices below those suggested by Sharp. Another dealer authorized to sell Sharp products in the same area complained to Sharp about Business Electronics' pricing policies. In response to the complaint, Sharp terminated Business Electronics' dealership.*

Business Electronics brought suit, contending that the termination was the result of a conspiracy between Sharp and the complaining dealer. Business Electronics argued that the alleged conspiracy was a vertical restraint of trade in violation of Section 1 of the Sherman Act. The trial judge instructed the jury that if it found that the evidence showed an agreement to terminate Business Electronics' dealership, the agreement would amount to a Section 1 violation—that is, that such an agreement is a per se violation of the Sherman Act. On appeal, the circuit court reversed the judge's ruling, holding that such an agreement is not a per se violation of Section 1. The issue was appealed to the United States Supreme Court.

SCALIA, Justice.
    * * * *

Our approach to the question presented in the present case is guided by the premises of *GTE Sylvania* [See Case 21.5 above.] * * * : that there is a presumption in favor of a rule-of-reason standard; that departure from that standard must be justified by demonstrable economic effect, such as the facilitation of cartelizing, rather than formalistic distinctions; that interbrand competition is the primary concern of the antitrust laws; and that rules in this area should be formulated with a view towards protecting the doctrine of *GTE Sylvania*. * * *

There has been no showing here that an agreement between a manufacturer and a dealer to terminate a "price cutter," without a further agreement on the price or price levels to be charged by the remaining dealer, almost always tends to restrict competition and reduce output. Any assistance to cartelizing that such an agreement might provide cannot be distinguished from the sort of minimal assistance that might be provided by vertical nonprice agreements like the exclusive territory agreement in *GTE Sylvania*, and is insufficient to justify a *per se* rule. Cartels are neither easy to form nor easy to maintain. Uncertainty over the terms of the cartel, particularly the prices to be charged in the future, obstructs both formation and adherence by making cheating easier. Without an agreement with the remaining dealer on price, the manufacturer both retains its incentive to cheat on any manufacturer-level cartel (since lower prices can still be passed on to consumers) and cannot as easily be used to organize and hold together a retailer-level cartel.

The Court held that a manufacturer's termination of a dealership because of the dealer's failure to follow the manufacturer's suggested pricing strategy is not a per se violation of Section 1. An agreement between a manufacturer and a dealer to terminate a second dealer's dealership is a per se violation only if the agreement includes some provision for setting prices; no such terms were found in the agreement between Sharp and the dealer that complained about Business Electronics' pricing strategy.

DECISION AND REMEDY

Refusals to Deal

Unlike group boycotts, which, as discussed above, are subject to sharp scrutiny under Section 1, basic freedom of contract has been held to support the rule that manufacturers, acting unilaterally rather than in concert as in a group boycott, are free to deal—or not to deal—with whomever they choose. For example, assume that Acme acts alone to set prices for the resale of its fax machines by refusing to deal with any wholesaler that resells the machines at a different price. Acme has not violated the Sherman Act; it has only exercised its right to

deal with whomever it chooses. There are instances, however, when a refusal to deal will violate antitrust laws. These instances involve offenses proscribed under Section 2 of the Sherman Act and occur only if (1) the firm refusing to deal has, or is likely to acquire, monopoly power and (2) the refusal is likely to have an anticompetitive effect on a particular market.[9]

---

9. A good example is provided by the *Aspen Skiing* case discussed in the preceding chapter (Case 20.4) in relation to the Section 2 offense of monopolization.

Price Discrimination

Whenever a seller charges different buyers different prices for identical goods, the seller is engaging in **price discrimination**. Recall from the preceding chapter that such behavior may violate the Robinson-Patman Act, which was enacted in 1936 and amended Section 2 of the Clayton Act. A violation of Section 2 occurs if a seller discriminates in the prices it charges different customers for commodities of like quality and grade in interstate commerce and the practice results in injury to competition. The act prohibits indirect discrimination, such as variations in the terms of delivery and differences in sales returns, cash discounts, and the like, as well as direct price discrimination.

Although the act appears to embrace the laudable goals of fairness and equality in the marketplace, it has often been criticized as being economically unrealistic. For instance, a difference in packaging, labeling, or product quality normally does not exempt the pricing of the differing products from scrutiny under the act if the difference is deemed to be *negligible*. Thus, orange juice containers that differ by one-eighth inch are considered to be of like grade and quality because they are *functionally* identical in terms of performance. Despite functional equivalence, however, customer perceptions may favor one type of container over another.

In the same vein, identical products sold under different labels are deemed to be of like quality, though experts note that many customers exhibit strong preferences for better-known brand names even though the products are physically identical. In *Federal Trade Commission v. Borden Co.*,[10] the United States Supreme Court addressed the issue of a milk producer's charging different prices for milk sold under different labels. Borden sold evaporated milk under the Borden label, a well-known brand, and at the same time, it packed and marketed evaporated milk under private labels owned by its customers. Although the milk was physically indistinguishable, Borden charged a higher price for its brand-labeled milk. In spite of obvious customer preference for the Borden brand of milk, the Court concluded that the act applied

to the pricing difference because the milk was of like quality and grade in terms of physical attributes. The Court held that preferences due to brand name recognition created through national advertising should not be considered in resolving whether goods are of like grade and quality.

Despite these examples, there are some economic aspects that are taken into account in judging the legality of pricing practices under the Robinson-Patman Act. For example, as noted in the preceding chapter, Section 2 is not violated even though the goods sold are identical if the seller can justify the price differential on the basis of differences in cost, such as in transporting the goods to buyers in disparate locations. Similarly, consideration is given to the fact that prices are not static but fluctuate as market conditions change. Thus, price discrimination occurs only if sales at different price levels are made reasonably close together in time. Close in time is determined by the economic circumstances of the sales. For example, sales of products that are not frequently sold and that incur considerable production costs are considered close in time even though they might be years apart. Conversely, low-cost products sold in high volume may not be close in time for more than a day or even hours. Jet aircraft typify high-cost, low-volume products. Close in time for the sale of aircraft could be two years or more. In contrast, sales of bakery goods occur on an almost continuous basis. Close in time for such products could be several hours or at most a day.

Exclusionary Practices

Recall also from the preceding chapter that Section 3 of the Clayton Act prohibits sellers and lessors from selling or leasing goods, machinery, supplies, etc., "on the condition, agreement or understanding that the . . . purchaser or lessee thereof shall not use or deal in the goods . . . of a competitor or competitors of the seller." Two types of vertical arrangements involving exclusionary tactics—exclusive dealing contracts and tying arrangements—are within the reach of Section 3 of the Clayton Act.

EXCLUSIVE DEALING CONTRACTS Contracts under which a seller forbids the buyer from pur-

---

10.   383 U.S. 637, 86 S.Ct. 1092, 16 L.Ed.2d 153 (1966).

chasing products from the seller's competitors are called **exclusive dealing contracts.** Such contracts are prohibited under Section 3 if the effect of the contract will "substantially lessen competition or tend to create a monopoly."

The leading decision on exclusive dealing contracts remains the 1949 case of *Standard Oil Co. of California v. United States,*[11] in which the then-largest gasoline seller in the United States was challenged by the government under Section 3 for making exclusive dealing contracts with independent stations in seven western states. The United States Supreme Court, in assessing the impact of the exclusive dealing agreement on competition in the retail market, noted that the "independents" covered under the arrangement constituted 16 percent of all retail outlets and 7 percent of all retail gas sales in the area. The Court also noted that the market was substantially concentrated because the seven largest suppliers all used exclusive dealing contracts with their independent retailers and together controlled 65 percent of the market. Looking at market conditions after the arrangements were instituted, the Court noted that market shares were extremely stable and entry into the market was apparently restricted. Thus, the Court found that Section 3 had been violated because competition was "foreclosed in a substantial share" of the relevant market.

TYING ARRANGEMENTS   A seller may condition the sale of a product (the tying product) on the buyer's agreeing to purchase another product (the tied product) produced or distributed by the same seller. As noted in the preceding chapter, the legality of such **tying arrangements** depends on factors such as the purpose of the arrangement and its likely effect on competition in the relevant markets. There are two relevant markets, because the agreement involves two distinct products, the tying and the tied product. In 1936, the United States Supreme Court held that International Business Machines' and Remington Rand's practice of requiring purchase of their own machine cards as a condition to leasing their tabulation machines vi-

olated Section 3 of the Clayton Act. The two firms were the only ones in the market with completely automated tabulation machines, and the Court concluded that each possessed market power sufficient to "substantially lessen competition" through their respective tying arrangements.[12]

The Clayton Act provisions in Section 3 have been held to apply only to commodities, not to services. But tying arrangements also can be considered agreements that restrain trade in violation of Section 1 of the Sherman Act. Cases involving tying arrangements for services have been brought under Section 1 of the Sherman Act. Although the Court continues to state that many tying arrangements are illegal per se, it nonetheless has shown a willingness to look at factors that are important in a rule-of-reason analysis. This is another example of the so-called soft per se rule referred to above in regard to group boycotts.

The United States Supreme Court has recently held that U.S. Steel Corporation's practice of tying its attractive credit services for home builders to the builders' purchase of U.S. Steel's prefabricated houses did not violate antitrust laws, because U.S. Steel did not possess market power in either the credit market or the prefabricated housing market.[13] A similar result was reached in *Jefferson Parish Hospital District No. 2 v. Hyde.*[14] Most courts today generally judge the legality of tying arrangements involving services or commodities by looking at both the firm's market power in the tying product market and the amount of commerce affected in the tied product market. The firm must have sufficient market power in the tying product to coerce the purchase of the tied product, and the tying arrangement must affect a substantial amount of commerce in the market for the tied product.

---

12.   *International Business Machines Corp. v. United States,* 298 U.S. 131, 56 S.Ct. 701, 80 L.Ed.2d 1085 (1936).
13.   *U.S. Steel Corp. v. Fortner Enterprises, Inc.,* 429 U.S. 610, 97 S.Ct. 861, 51 L.Ed.2d 80 (1977).
14.   466 U.S. 2, 104 S.Ct. 1551, 80 L.Ed.2d 2 (1984).

---

11.   337 U.S. 293, 69 S.Ct. 1051, 93 L.Ed. 1371 (1949).

■ Terms and Concepts to Review

concentrated industry 505
exclusive dealing
   contracts 515
group boycott 508
horizontal market
   divisions 503

horizontal restraint 500
joint venture 509
per se violations 500
price discrimination 514
price fixing 501

resale price maintenance
   agreements 512
rule of reason 500
tying arrangements 515
vertically integrated
   firms 510

■ Questions and Case Problems

21-1. Most of the egg wholesalers supplying eggs to grocery stores in a particular area sell eggs to the retailers under various credit terms. The credit terms vary among the different buyers and sellers, but all of the wholesalers follow a common practice of reducing by 10 percent the price charged to a retailer if the retailer pays the wholesaler within three days of delivery. The various wholesalers agree that henceforth the 10 percent discount will be discontinued. If the agreement is indeed carried out by the wholesalers and the discount policy is discontinued, have the wholesalers violated any antitrust laws? Explain. If suit is brought against the wholesalers, what—if any—justification could they offer for the agreement?

21-2. Suppose that the wholesale egg suppliers in the preceding problem agree that the three largest suppliers should sell exclusively to the area's large chain-store groceries, leaving the remaining suppliers to sell solely to local individual "mom and pop" stores. Does the agreement violate any antitrust laws? Is it a defense that the larger suppliers, because of their scale of operations, enjoy a cost advantage that allows them to supply the large chain buyers more efficiently?

21-3. Discuss *fully* whether each of the following situations violates the Sherman Act.

  (a) Trujillo Foods, Inc., is the leading seller of frozen Mexican foods in three southwestern states. The various retail outlets that sell Trujillo products are in close competition, and customers are very price conscious. Trujillo has conditioned its sales to retailers with the agreement that the retailers will not sell below a minimum price nor above a maximum price. The retailers are allowed to set any price within these limits.

  (b) Franklin, Inc., Green, Inc., and Fill-It, Inc., are competitors in the manufacture and sale of microwave ovens sold primarily east of the Mississippi River. As a patriotic gesture and to assist the unemployed, the three competitors agree to lower their prices on all microwave models by 20 percent for a three-month period that includes the Fourth of July and Labor Day.

  (c) Foam Beer, Inc., sells its beer to distributors all over the United States. Foam sends each of its distributors a recommended price list, explaining that past records indicate that selling beer at those prices should ensure the distributor a reasonable rate of return. The price list clearly states that the sale of beer by Foam to the distributor is not conditioned on the distributor's reselling the beer at the recommended price and that the distributor is free to set the price.

21-4. Mickey's Appliance Store was a new retail seller of appliances in Sunwest City. Mickey's innovative sales techniques and financing caused the appliance department of Luckluster Department Store to lose a great many sales. Luckluster was a large department store and part of a large chain with substantial buying power. Luckluster told a number of appliance manufacturers that if they continued to sell to Mickey's, Luckluster would stop purchasing from them. The manufacturers immediately stopped selling appliances to Mickey's. Mickey's filed suit against Luckluster and the manufacturers, claiming their actions constituted an antitrust violation. Luckluster and the manufacturers could prove that Mickey's was a small retailer with a small portion of the market. Because the relevant market was not substantially affected, they claimed they were not guilty of restraint of trade. Discuss *fully* whether there was an antitrust violation.

21-5. Quick Photo, Inc., is a manufacturer of photographic film. At present, Quick Photo has approximately 50 percent of the market. Quick Photo launches a campaign whereby the purchase price of Quick Photo film includes photo processing by Quick Photo, Inc. Quick Photo claims that its film processing is specially designed to improve the quality of the finished photos when Quick Photo film is used. Discuss *fully* whether Quick Photo's combination of film purchase and film processing is an antitrust violation.

21-6. In contracts with television networks for the 1982–1985 football seasons, the National Collegiate Athletic Association (NCAA), a nonprofit organization, gave the ABC, CBS, and Turner broadcasting networks exclusive rights to negotiate with NCAA colleges to televise games. The contracts limited the number of games that could be televised by the networks, the number of appearances that any one team could make on television, and the amount of money a school could have for televising its games. The NCAA plan also required that a certain number of games between small colleges be televised and prohibited any individual institution from contracting separately for television coverage of its games. Not surprisingly, the NCAA plan drew criticism from major college teams, which felt that they deserved more network appearances and more money than teams from smaller schools. Their efforts to gain a greater voice in the NCAA television policy, though supported by the College Football Association, proved unsuccessful. As a result, the Universities of Oklahoma and Georgia brought an action against the NCAA, alleging that its contracts with the television networks violated Sections 1 and 2 of the Sherman Act. Specifically, the NCAA was charged with price fixing, horizontal limitations on production, group boycott, and monopolization. In its defense, the NCAA argued, among other things, that as a nonprofit organization with ''noneconomic'' motives, it should not be subject to antitrust laws. How should the the United States Supreme Court rule? [*NCAA* v. *Board of Regents of the University of Oklahoma,* 468 U.S. 85, 104 S.Ct. 2948, 82 L.Ed.2d 70 (1984)]

21-7. Radial keratotomy is a relatively new surgical procedure to correct myopia (nearsightedness). In 1980, at the recommendation of the National Eye Institute, the American Academy of Ophthalmology, Inc., issued a press release urging ''patients, ophthalmologists and hospitals to approach [radial keratotomy] with caution until additional research is completed.'' Schacher and several other ophthalmologists who specialized in radial keratotomy claimed that the demand for their services declined following issuance of the press release. They brought an action against the Academy, contending that the press release constituted an illegal horizontal trade restraint. The district court held that the Academy had not violated any antitrust law. What will result on appeal? [*Schacher v. American Academy of Ophthalmology, Inc.,* 870 F.2d 397 (7th Cir. 1989)]

21-8. Dr. Beard, an osteopathic physician specializing in radiology, worked for G. S. Bucholz, Inc. Bucholz is the exclusive provider of radiological services to Parkview Hospital. When Dr. Beard resigned from his position at Bucholz, he had every intention of providing radiological services himself to the patients at Parkview, but the Parkview administration informed him that the hospital had an exclusive contract with Bucholz for the provision of radiological services and that Dr. Beard would no longer be permitted to work in Parkview's radiology department. Dr. Beard sued Parkview, alleging that the exclusive contract between the hospital and Bucholz was a tying arrangement in violation of Section 1 of the Sherman Act. Parkview claimed that its arrangement with Bucholz ensured responsibility and accountability for the radiology department and guaranteed the availability of services when needed. Under the terms of the agreement between Bucholz and Parkview, Bucholz bills patients directly for the services it provides; Parkview does not get a portion of any fees charged by Bucholz. Does the exclusive contract between Parkview

and Bucholz violate Section 1 of the Sherman Act? Discuss fully. [*Beard v. Parkview Hospital,* 912 F.2d 138 (6th Cir. 1990)]

21-9. Morton Salt Co. gave quantity discounts to purchasers of its ''Blue Label'' brand of salt. Three different prices for the salt were charged, depending on the quantity purchased. Distributors that purchased more than 50,000 cases were charged $1.35 per case, while distributors that purchased fewer than 50,000 cases were charged between $1.40 and $1.60, depending on how much salt they purchased. The Federal Trade Commission, holding that Morton Salt's discount pricing system was not justified by cost differentials and therefore constituted illegal price discrimination, ordered Morton Salt to discontinue offering the quantity discounts. A circuit court of appeals overturned the FTC ruling, and the case was appealed to the United States Supreme Court. What should the Court decide? [*Federal Trade Commission v. Morton Salt Co.,* 334 U.S. 37, 68 S.Ct. 822, 92 L.Ed. 1196 (1948)]

21-10. To offer a competitive alternative to health maintenance organizations and to promote fee-for-service medicine, members of the Maricopa County Medical Society and another medical society established a schedule that prescribed the maximum fees that the physicians could charge patients who were insured under specified health insurance plans. The state of Arizona filed a complaint against the medical societies, alleging that the fee schedule constituted a horizontal price-fixing conspiracy and a per se violation of Section 1 of the Sherman Act. The medical societies claimed that the per se rule should not apply, because (1) the medical societies were professional organizations, (2) the agreement fixed maximum prices, not minimum or uniform prices, (3) the judiciary had insufficient experience in the medical industry to justify applying the per se rule, and (4) the fee schedule was justified by its procompetitive effects. The district and appellate courts both agreed with the medical societies that the case should not be judged under the per se rule. What will the United States Supreme Court decide? [*Arizona v. Maricopa County Medical Society,* 457 U.S. 332, 102 S.Ct. 2466, 73 L.Ed.2d 48 (1982)]

21-11. Harcourt Brace Jovanovich Legal and Professional Publications (HBJ), the nation's largest provider of bar review materials and lecture services, began offering a Georgia bar review course in 1976 and was in direct, and often intense, competition with BRG of Georgia, Inc., the other main provider of bar review courses in Georgia, from 1977 to 1979. In early 1980, HBJ and BRG entered into an agreement that gave BRG the exclusive right to market HBJ's materials in Georgia and to use its trade name, ''Bar/Bri.'' The parties agreed that HBJ would not compete with BRG in Georgia and that BRG would not compete with HBJ outside of Georgia. Immediately after the 1980 agreement was made, the price of BRG's course was increased from $150 to over $400. Jay Palmer, a former law student, brought an action against the two firms, alleging that the 1980 agreement violated Section 1 of the Sherman Act.

What will the court decide? Discuss fully. [*Palmer v. BRG of Georgia, Inc.,* ___U.S. ___, 111 S.Ct. 401, 112 L.Ed.2d 349 (1990)]

21-12. A Question of Ethics

 A group of lawyers in the District of Columbia regularly acted as court-appointed attorneys for indigent defendants in District of Columbia criminal cases. At a meeting of the Superior Court Trial Lawyers Association (SCTLA), the attorneys agreed to stop providing such representation until the district increased their compensation. Their subsequent boycott had a severe impact on the district's criminal justice system, and the District of Columbia gave in to the lawyers' demands for higher pay. After the lawyers had returned to work, the Federal Trade Commission filed a complaint against the SCTLA and four of its officers and, after an investigation, ruled that the SCTLA's activities constituted an illegal group boycott in violation of antitrust laws. [Federal Trade Commission v. Superior Court Trial Lawyers Association, *493 U.S. 411, 110 S.Ct. 768, 107 L.Ed.2d 851 (1990)*]

1. The SCTLA obviously was aware of the negative impact its decision would have on the district's criminal justice system. Given this fact, do you think the lawyers behaved ethically?

2. On appeal, the SCTLA claimed that its boycott was undertaken to publicize the fact that attorneys were underpaid and that the boycott thus constituted an expression protected by the First Amendment. Do you agree with this argument?

3. Labor unions have the right to strike when negotiations between labor and management fail to result in agreement. Do you think that it is fair for members of the SCTLA to be prohibited from "striking" against their employer, the District of Columbia, simply because the SCTLA is a professional organization and not a labor union?

21-13. Case Briefing Assignment

 Examine Case A.13 [Alan's of Atlanta v. Minolta Corp., *903 F.2d 1414 (11h Cir. 1990)*] *in Appendix A. The case has been excerpted there in considerable detail. Review and then brief the case, making sure that you include answers to the following questions in your brief.*

1. What was the "key dealer" program, and how was it alleged to have harmed the business of Alan's of Atlanta?

2. Why did the trial court grant summary judgment for Minolta and Wolf's?

3. According to the appellate court, what motivated Congress to enact the Robinson-Patman Act?

4. Did the court conclude that price discrimination meant a mere price difference or something more?

Chapter 22

Securities Regulation

After the great stock market crash of 1929, various studies showed a need for regulating securities markets. Basically, legislation for such regulation was enacted to provide investors with more information to help them make buying and selling decisions and to prohibit deceptive, unfair, and manipulative practices. Today, the sale and transfer of securities are heavily regulated by federal and state statutes and by government agencies. This is a complex area of the law. This chapter will first look at corporate financing and the sale of corporate securities, and then at the nature of federal securities regulations and their effect on the business world.

■ Corporate Financing

To obtain financing, corporations issue **securities**—evidence of the obligation to pay money or of the right to participate in earnings and the distribution of corporate trusts and other property. The principal method of long-term and initial corporate financing is the issuance of stocks (equity) and bonds (debt), both of which are sold to investors. **Stocks,** or *equity securities,* represent the purchase of ownership in the business firm. **Bonds** (debentures), or *debt securities,* represent the borrowing of money by firms (and governments). Of course, not all debt is in the form of debt securities. Some is in the form of accounts payable, some is in the form of notes payable, and some is in the form of leaseholds. Bonds are simply a way for the corporation to split up its long-term debt so that it can market it more easily.

Bonds

Bonds are issued by business firms and by governments at all levels as evidence of the funds they are borrowing from investors. Bonds almost always have a designated *maturity date*—the date when the principal or face amount of the bond (or loan) is returned to the investor—and are sometimes referred to as *fixed-income securities,* because their owners receive a fixed-dollar interest payment during the period of time prior to maturity.

The characteristics of corporate bonds vary widely, in part because corporations differ in their ability to generate the earnings and cash flow necessary to make interest payments and to repay the principal amount of the

519

bonds at maturity. Furthermore, corporate bonds are only a part of the total debt and the overall financial structure of corporate business.

Stocks

Issuing *stocks* is another way corporations obtain financing. The ways in which stocks differ from bonds are summarized in Exhibit 22–1. Basically, stocks represent ownership in a business firm, whereas bonds represent borrowing by the firm. Exhibit 22–2 summarizes the types of stocks issued by corporations. The two major types are *common stock* and *preferred stock*.

COMMON STOCK The true ownership of a corporation is represented by **common stock.** It provides a proportionate interest in the corporation with regard to (1) control, (2) earning capacity, and (3) net assets. A shareholder's interest is generally in proportion to the number of shares owned out of the total number of shares issued.

Voting rights in a corporation apply to the election of the firm's board of directors and to any proposed changes in the ownership structure of the firm.[1] For example, a holder of common stock generally has the right to vote in a decision on a proposed merger, because mergers can change the proportion of ownership.

---

1. State corporation law specifies the types of actions for which shareholder approval must be obtained.

Firms are not obligated to return a principal amount per share to each holder of common stock, because no firm can ensure that the market price per share of its common stock will not go down over time. Nor does the issuing firm have to guarantee a dividend; indeed, some business firms never pay dividends.

Holders of common stock are a group of investors who assume a *residual* position in the overall financial structure of a business. In terms of receiving payment for their investment, they are last in line. The earnings to which they are entitled also depend on all the other groups—suppliers, employees, managers, bankers, governments, bondholders, and holders of preferred stock—being paid what is due them first. Once those groups are paid, however, the owners of common stock may be entitled to *all* the remaining earnings. (But the board of directors is not normally under any duty to declare the remaining earnings as dividends.) This return-and-risk pattern is the central feature of ownership in any corporation. The owners of common stock occupy the riskiest position, but they can expect a correspondingly greater return on their investment.

PREFERRED STOCK Stock with *preferences* is called **preferred stock.** Usually, holders of preferred stock have priority over holders of common stock as to dividends and payment upon dissolution of the corporation. Preferred-stock shareholders may or may not have the right to vote.

■ Exhibit 22–1 How Do Stocks and Bonds Differ?

Stocks	Bonds
1. Stocks represent ownership.	1. Bonds represent owed debt.
2. Stocks (common) do not have a fixed dividend rate.	2. Interest on bonds must always be paid, whether or not any profit is earned.
3. Stockholders can elect a board of directors, which controls the corporation.	3. Bondholders usually have no voice in, or control over, management of the corporation.
4. Stocks do not have a maturity date; the corporation does not usually repay the stockholder.	4. Bonds have a maturity date on which the bondholder is to be repaid the face value of the bond.
5. Most corporations issue, or offer to sell, stocks. This is the usual definition of a business corporation.	5. Corporations do not necessarily issue bonds.
6. Stockholders have a claim against the property and income of a corporation after all creditors' (including bond holders) claims have been met.	6. Bondholders have a claim against the property and income of a corporation that must be met before the claims of stockholders.

■ **Exhibit 22–2 Stocks**

Type	Definition
Common Stock	Voting shares that represent ownership interests in a corporation with lowest priorities with respect to payment of dividends and distribution of assets upon the corporation's dissolution.
Preferred Stock	Shares of stock that have priority over common stock shares as to payment of dividends and distribution of assets upon corporate dissolution. Dividend payments are usually a fixed percentage of the face value of the share.
Cumulative Preferred Stock	Shares whose required dividends not paid in a given year must be paid in a subsequent year before any common stock dividends are paid.
Participating Preferred Stock	Shares whose owners are entitled to receive the preferred stock dividend and additional dividends after payment of dividends on common stock.
Convertible Preferred Stock	Preferred shares whose owners have the option to convert their shares into a specified number of common shares either in the issuing corporation or, sometimes, in another corporation.
Redeemable, or Callable, Preferred Stock	Preferred shares issued with the express condition that the issuing corporation has the right to repurchase the shares as specified.
Authorized Shares	Shares allowed to be issed by the articles of incorporation.
Issued Shares	Shares that have been actually transferred to shareholders.
Outstanding Share	Authorized and issued shares still held by shareholders.
Treasury Shares	Shares that are authorized and issued, but are not outstanding (reacquired by the corporation).
No Par Shares	Shares issued with no stated face value. The price is usually fixed by the board of directors or shareholders.
Par-Value Shares	Shares issued and priced at a stated value per share.
Watered Shares	Shares issued (as fully paid) for transfer of property or services rendered, when in fact the value of such property or services is less than the par value or price for no par value shares.

From an investment standpoint, preferred stock is more similar to bonds than to common stock. Preferred shareholders receive periodic dividend payments, usually established as a fixed percentage of the face amount of each preferred share. A 9 percent preferred stock with a face amount of $100 per share would pay its owner a $9 dividend each year. This is not a legal obligation on the part of the firm. Preferred stock is not included among the liabilities of a business, because it is equity. Preferred stock appears in the ownership section of the firm's balance sheet (financial statement). Like other equity securities, preferred shares have no fixed maturity date for when they must be retired by the firm. Although occasionally firms retire preferred stock, they are not legally obligated to do so. A sample cumulative convertible preferred-stock certificate is shown in Exhibit 22–3.

Holders of preferred stock are investors who have assumed a rather cautious position in their relationship to the corporation. They have a stronger position than common shareholders with respect to dividends and claims on assets, but, as a result, they will not share in the full prosperity of the firm if it grows successfully over time.

■ **Investor Protection—The SEC**

The stock market crash of October 29, 1929, and the ensuing economic depression caused the public to focus on the importance of securities markets for the economic well-being of the nation. The fe-

Exhibit 22–3 A Sample Cumulative Convertible Preferred-Stock Certificate

verish trading in securities during the preceding decade became the subject of widespread attention, and numerous reports were circulated concerning the speculative, manipulative, and at times unscrupulous trading that occurred in the stock markets.

The public, irked by such practices, pressured Congress into action. As a result, in 1931 the Senate passed a resolution calling for an extensive investigation of securities trading. The investigation led, ultimately, to the passage by Congress of the Securities Act of 1933, which is also known as the *truth-in-securities* bill. In the following year, the Securities Exchange Act was passed by Congress. This 1934 act created the Securities and Exchange Commission (SEC) as an independent regulatory agency whose function was to administer the 1933 and 1934 acts. Its major responsibilities in this respect are as follows:

1. Requiring disclosure of facts concerning offerings of securities listed on national securities exchanges and offerings of certain securities traded over the counter (OTC).
2. Regulating the trade in securities on the thirteen national and regional securities exchanges and in the OTC markets.
3. Investigating securities frauds.
4. Regulating the activities of securities brokers, dealers, and investment advisers and requiring their registration.
5. Supervising the activities of mutual funds.
6. Recommending administrative sanctions, injunctive remedies, and criminal prosecution against those who violate securities laws. (The Fraud Section of the Criminal Division of the Department of Justice prosecutes violations of federal securities laws.)

From the time of its creation until the present, the SEC's regulatory functions have gradually been increased by legislation granting it authority in different areas. In recent years the SEC has been active in promoting stiffer penalties for *insider trading* and in effecting regulatory changes addressing the problem of the proliferation of hostile takeovers and corporate-control contests, in which outsiders attempt to wrest control of the corporation from its current board of directors. Another current major concern of the SEC is to effect fundamental

changes in the basic regulatory framework applying to the financial services industry. Under the Securities Enforcement Remedies Act of 1990, the SEC was granted substantial new powers, increasing the range of SEC enforcement options to include new cease-and-desist powers and increased penalties.

Securities Act of 1933

The Securities Act of 1933[2] was designed to prohibit various forms of fraud and to stabilize the securities industry by requiring that all essential information concerning the issuance of securities be made available to the investing public. Essentially, the purpose of this act is to require disclosure.

Definition of a Security

Generally, a *security* is any document evidencing a debt or a property interest. Under Section 2(1) of the Securities Act, securities include the following:

> any note, stock, treasury stock, bond, debenture, evidence of indebtedness, certificate of interest or participation in any profit-sharing agreement, collateral-trust certificate, preorganization certificate or subscription, transferable share, investment contract, voting-trust certificate, certificate of deposit for a security, fractional undivided interest in oil, gas, or other mineral rights, or, in general, any interest or instrument commonly known as a ''security,'' or any certificate of interest or participation in, temporary or interim certificate for, receipt for, guarantee of, or warrant or right to subscribe to or purchase, any of the foregoing.[3]

Basically, the courts have interpreted this definition to mean that a security exists in any transaction in which a person (1) invests (2) in a common enterprise (3) reasonably expecting profits (4) derived *primarily* or *substantially* from others' managerial or entrepreneurial efforts.

For our purposes, it is probably most convenient to think of securities in their most common

---

2.   15 U.S.C. Sections 77a–77aa.
3.   15 U.S.C. Section 77b(1). The 1982 amendments added stock options.

form—stocks and bonds issued by corporations. Bear in mind, however, that securities can take many forms and have been held to include whiskey, cosmetics, worms, beavers, boats, vacuum cleaners, muskrats, and cemetery lots, as well as investment contracts in condominiums, franchises, limited partnerships, oil or gas or other mineral rights, and farm animals accompanied by care agreements.

In determining what constitutes a security under the 1933 act, courts have often cited *SEC v. W. J. Howey Co.*[4] In this classic case, in which citrus groves qualified as securities, the United States Supreme Court held that for a security to exist, an investor's profits must be derived *solely* from others' efforts. Later court decisions, however, have required only that the profits be derived *primarily* or *substantially* from the efforts of others.[5]

Registration Requirements

Section 5 of the Securities Act of 1933 broadly provides that if a security does not qualify for an exemption, that security must be *registered* before it is offered to the public either through the mails or through any facility of interstate commerce, including securities exchanges. Issuing corporations must file a *registration statement* with the SEC. Investors must be provided with a *prospectus* that describes the security being sold, the issuing corporation, and the investment or risk attaching to the security. In principle, the registration statement and the prospectus supply sufficient information to enable unsophisticated investors to evaluate the financial risk involved.

The registration statement must include the following:

1. A description of the significant provisions of the security offered for sale, including the rela-

tionship between that security and the other capital securities of the registrant. Also, the corporation must disclose how it intends to use the proceeds of the sale.

2. A description of the registrant's properties and business.

3. A description of the management of the registrant and its security holdings, remuneration, and other benefits, including pensions and stock options. Any interests of directors or officers in any material transactions with the corporation must be disclosed.

4. A financial statement certified by an independent public accounting firm.

5. A description of pending lawsuits.

Before filing the registration statement and the prospectus with the SEC, the corporation is allowed to obtain an underwriter who will monitor the distribution of the new issue. There is a twenty-day waiting period after registration before the sale can take place. During this period, oral offers between interested investors and the issuing corporation concerning the purchase and sale of the proposed securities may take place; very limited written advertising is allowed. At this time, the so-called **red herring** prospectus may be distributed. It gets its name from the red legend printed across it stating that the registration has been filed but has not become effective.

After the waiting period, the registered securities can be legally bought and sold. Written advertising is allowed in the form of a so-called **tombstone ad,** so named because the format resembles a tombstone. Such ads simply tell the investor where and how to obtain a prospectus. Normally, any other type of advertising is prohibited.

Registration violations of the 1933 act are not treated lightly. In the following case, the BarChris Construction Corporation was sued by the purchasers of the corporation's debentures under Section 11 of the Securities Act of 1933. Section 11 imposes liability when a registration statement or a prospectus contains material false statements or material omissions.

---

4. 328 U.S. 293, 66 S.Ct. 1100, 90 L.Ed.1244 (1946).
5. See, for example, *SEC v. Glenn W. Turner Enterprises, Inc.,* 474 F.2d 476 (9th Cir. 1973), *cert.* denied 414 U.S. 821, 94 S.Ct. 117, 38 L.Ed.2d 53 (1973), in which pyramid sales arrangements were held to involve investment contracts and securities, because the profits realized were due primarily or substantially to others' efforts.

BACKGROUND AND FACTS *This lawsuit was brought by purchasers of BarChris Construction Corporation debenture bonds under Section 11 of the Securities Act of 1933. The plaintiffs alleged that the registration statement filed with the SEC, which became effective on May 16, 1961, contained material false statements and material omissions. The defendants fell into three categories: (1) the persons who signed the registration statement, (2) the underwriters (consisting of eight investment banking firms), and (3) BarChris's auditors—Peat, Marwick, Mitchell & Co. Included in the group of defendants who signed the registration statement were (1) BarChris's nine directors, (2) BarChris's controller, (3) one of Bar-Chris's attorneys, (4) two investment bankers who were later named as directors of BarChris, and (5) numerous other persons participating in the preparation of the registration statement. BarChris grew out of a business that was started in 1946 to build bowling alleys. The introduction of automatic pin-setting machines in 1952 sparked rapid growth in the bowling industry. BarChris benefited from this increased interest in bowling, and its construction operations expanded rapidly. It was estimated that in 1960, BarChris installed approximately 3 percent of all bowling lanes built in the United States. BarChris's sales increased dramatically between 1956 and 1960, and the company was recognized as a significant factor in the bowling construction industry. BarChris was in constant need of cash to finance its operations, a need that grew more and more pressing as operations expanded. In 1959, BarChris sold over a half-million shares of its common stock to the public. By early 1961, it needed additional working capital, and this time it decided to sell debentures. BarChris filed a registration statement of the debentures with the SEC and received the proceeds of the financing. Nevertheless, it experienced increasing financial difficulties, which in time became insurmountable. By early 1962, it was painfully apparent that BarChris was beginning to fail. In October of that year, BarChris filed a petition for bankruptcy, and it defaulted on the interest due in November on the debentures. The plaintiffs challenged the accuracy of the registration statement and charged that the text of the prospectus—including many of the figures—was false and that material information had been omitted. The federal district court reviewed all of the figures and statements included in the prospectus.*

Case 22.1

ESCOTT v. BARCHRIS CONSTRUCTION CORP.

United States District Court, Southern District of New York, 1968.

283 F.Supp. 643.

McLEAN, District Judge.

* * * *

It is a prerequisite to liability under Section 11 of the Act that the fact which is falsely stated in a registration statement, or the fact that it is omitted when it should have been stated to avoid misleading, be "material." The regulations of the Securities and Exchange Commission pertaining to the registration of securities define the word as follows:

"The term 'material', when used to qualify a requirement for the furnishing of information as to any subject, limits the information required to those matters as to which an average prudent investor ought reasonably to be informed before purchasing the security registered."

What are "matters as to which an average prudent investor ought reasonably to be informed"? It seems obvious that they are matters which such an investor needs to know before he can make an intelligent, informed decision whether or not to buy the security.

Early in the history of the Act, a definition of materiality was given in *Matter of Charles A. Howard,* which is still valid today. A material fact was there defined as: * * * "a fact which if it had been correctly stated or disclosed would have deterred or tended to deter the average prudent investor from purchasing the securities in question."

The average prudent investor is not concerned with minor inaccuracies or with errors as to matters which are of no interest to him. The facts which tend to deter him from purchasing a security are facts which have an important bearing upon the nature or condition of the issuing corporation or its business.

Judged by this test, there is no doubt that many of the misstatements and omissions in this prospectus were material. This is true of all of them which relate to the state of affairs in 1961, i.e., the overstatement of sales and gross profit for the first quarter, the understatement of contingent liabilities as of April 30, the overstatement of orders on hand and the failure to disclose the true facts with respect to officers' loans, customers' delinquencies, application of proceeds and the prospective operation of several alleys.

DECISION AND REMEDY *BarChris Construction Corporation itself and all the signers of the registration statement for the debentures, the underwriters, and the corporation's auditors were held liable.*

Exemptions under the 1933 Act

A corporation can avoid the high cost and complicated procedures associated with registration by taking advantage of certain exemptions. SEC regulations provide that the following offerings are exempt:

1. Private, noninvestment company offerings up to $500,000 in any twelve-month period are exempt if no general solicitation or advertising is used, the SEC is notified of the sales, and precaution is taken against nonexempt, unregistered resales.[6] The limits on advertising and unregistered resales do not apply if the offering is made solely in states that provide for registration and disclosure and the securities are sold in compliance with those provisions.[7]

2. Noninvestment company offerings up to $5 million in any twelve-month period are exempt, regardless of the number of **accredited investors** (banks, insurance companies, investment companies, the issuer's executive officers and directors, and persons whose income or net worth exceeds certain limits), so long as there are no more than thirty-five unaccredited investors; no general solicitation or advertising is used; the SEC is notified of the sales; and precaution is taken against nonexempt, unregistered resales. If the sale involves *any* unaccredited investors, *all* investors must be given material information about the offering company, its business, and the securities before the sale. The issuer is *not* required to believe that each unaccredited investor "has such knowledge and experience in financial and business matters that he is capable of evaluating the merits and the risks of the prospective investment."[8]

3. Private offerings in unlimited amounts that are not generally solicited or advertised are exempt if the SEC is notified of the sales; precaution is taken against nonexempt, unregistered resales; and the issuer believes that each unaccredited investor has sufficient knowledge or experience in financial matters to be capable of evaluating the invest-

---

6. Precautions to be taken against nonexempt, unregistered resales include asking the investor whether he or she is buying the securities for others; before the sale, disclosing to each purchaser in writing that the securities are unregistered and thus cannot be resold, except in an exempt transaction, without first being registered; and indicating on the certificate that the securities are unregistered and restricted.

7. SEC Regulation D, 17 C.F.R. Section 230.504.

8. SEC Regulation D, 17 C.F.R. Section 230.505.

ment's merits and risks. There may be no more than thirty-five unaccredited investors, although there may be an unlimited number of accredited investors. If there are *any* unaccredited investors, the issuer must provide to *all* purchasers material information about itself, its business, and the securities before the sale.[9]

This last exemption is perhaps most important to those who want to raise funds through the sale of securities without registering them. It is often referred to as the *private placement* exemption, because it exempts "transactions not involving any public offering."[10] This provision applies to private offerings to a limited number of persons who are sufficiently sophisticated and in a sufficiently strong bargaining position so as to be able to assume the risk of the investment (and who thus have no need for federal registration protection); it also applies to private offerings to similarly situated institutional investors.

Also exempt are *intra*state transactions involving purely local offerings.[11] This exemption applies to offerings restricted to residents of the state in which the issuing company is organized and doing business. The exemption requires that 80 percent of the issuer's assets be located in the state of issue, 80 percent of the issuer's gross revenue be from business conducted within the state, and 80 percent of the net income from the sale of the issue be used in the state. Also, for nine months after the last sale, no resale may be made to a nonresident, and precautions must be taken against this possibility. (Precautions include obtaining a statement of residence in writing from each investor, as well as indicating on the securities certificates that they are unregistered and subject to resale only to state residents.) These offerings remain subject to applicable laws in the state of issue.

Among securities exempt from the registration requirement in consideration of the "small amount involved,"[12] other than those mentioned above, is an issuer's offer of up to $1.5 million in securities in any twelve-month period. Under the SEC's Reg-

ulation A,[13] the issuer must file with the SEC notice of the issue and an offering circular, which must also be provided to investors before the sale; but this is a much simpler and less expensive process than the procedures associated with registration.

Also, an offer made *solely* to accredited investors is exempt if its amount is not more than $5 million in any twelve-month period. Any number of accredited investors may participate, but no unaccredited investors may do so. No general solicitation or advertising may be used; the SEC must be notified of all sales; and precaution must be taken against nonexempt, unregistered resales (because these are restricted securities and may be resold only by registration or in an exempt transaction).[14] The exemptions under the Securities Act of 1933 and SEC regulations are summarized in Exhibit 22–4.

Additional Exempt Securities

The following securities are also exempt:[15]

1. All bank securities sold prior to July 27, 1933.
2. Commercial paper if a maturity date does not exceed nine months.
3. Securities of charitable organizations.
4. Securities resulting from a corporate reorganization issued for exchange with the issuer's existing security holders, as well as certificates issued by trustees, receivers, or debtors in possession under the Bankruptcy Act (bankruptcy is discussed in Chapter 12).
5. Securities issued exclusively for exchange with the issuer's existing security holders, provided no commission is paid (for example, stock dividends and stock splits).
6. Securities issued to finance the acquisition of railroad equipment.
7. Any insurance, endowment, or annuity contract issued by a state-regulated insurance company.
8. Government-issued securities.
9. Securities issued by banks, savings and loan associations, farmers' cooperatives, and similar institutions subject to supervision by governmental authorities.

9. SEC Regulation D, 17 C.F.R. Section 230.506.
10. 15 U.S.C. Section 77d(2).
11. 15 U.S.C. Section 77c(a)(11).
12. 15 U.S.C. Section 77c(b).

13. 17 C.F.R. Sections 230.251–230.264.
14. 15 U.S.C. Section 77d(6).
15. 15 U.S.C. Section 77c.

■ **Exhibit 22–4 Exemptions Under the 1933 Act for Securities Offerings by Businesses**

Type of Offering	Required Conditions
Private, noninvestment company offerings up to $500,000 in any twelve-month period	1. No general solicitation or advertising (unless state provides for registration and disclosure). 2. SEC is notified of sales. 3. Precaution is taken against nonexempt, unregistered resales.
Noninvestment company offerings up to $5 million in any twelve-month period	1. Unlimited number of accredited investors. 2. No more than thirty-five unaccredited investors. 3. If *any* unaccredited investors, material information about offering firm must be disclosed to all investors. 4. No general solicitation or advertising. 5. SEC is notified of sales. 6. Precaution is taken against nonexempt, unregistered resales.
Private placement (private offerings in unlimited amounts that are generally not solicited or advertised)	1. Unlimited number of accredited investors. 2. No more than thirty-five unaccredited investors. 3. If *any* unaccredited investors, (a) material information about offering firm must be disclosed, and (b) issuer must reasonably believe that each unaccredited investor is experienced in financial matters and capable of evaluating risks involved in investment. 4. SEC is notified of sales. 5. Precaution is taken against nonexempt, unregistered resales.
Intrastate transactions (offerings restricted to residents of the state in which issuing company is organized and doing business)	1. 80 percent of issuer's assets are located in the state of issue. 2. 80 percent of issuer's gross revenue is from business conducted within the state. 3. 80 percent of net income from the sale of the issue is used in the state. 4. No resale is made to a nonresident for nine months after last sale, and precautions are taken to prevent such resale.
Offerings up to $1.5 million in any twelve-month period (under SEC Regulation A)	Notice of the issue and an offering circular are filed with the SEC and provided to investors.
Offerings up to $5 million in any twelve-month period	1. Unlimited number of accredited investors. 2. No unaccredited investors. 3. No general solicitation or advertising. 4. SEC is notified of sales. 5. Precaution is taken against nonexempt, unregistered resales.

■ Securities Exchange Act of 1934

The Securities Exchange Act of 1934[16] is concerned primarily with the *resale* of securities. The act provides for the regulation and registration of security exchanges, brokers, and dealers, as well as national securities associations, such as the National Association of Securities Dealers (NASD). The 1934 act regulates the markets in which securities are traded by maintaining a continuous disclosure system for all corporations with securities on the securities exchanges and for those companies that have assets in excess of $5 million and five hundred or more shareholders. These corporations are referred to as Section 12 companies, because they are required to register their securities under Section 12 of the 1934 act. The act regulates proxy solicitation for voting, and it allows the SEC to engage in market surveillance to regulate undesirable market practices such as fraud, market manipulation, misrepresentation, and stabilization. (*Stabilization* is a market-manipulating technique in which securities underwriters bid for securities to stabilize their price during their issuance.)

---

16. 15 U.S.C. Sections 77a–78jj.

Insider Trading—
Section 10(b) and SEC Rule 10b-5

One of the most important parts of the 1934 act relates to so-called **insider trading.** Because of their positions, corporate directors and officers often obtain advance inside information that can affect the future market value of the corporate stock. Obviously, their positions can give them a trading advantage over the general public and shareholders. Section 10(b) of the 1934 Securities Exchange Act and SEC **Rule 10b-5** define inside information and extend liability to officers and directors in their personal transactions for taking advantage of such information when they know it is unavailable to the person with whom they are dealing.

APPLICABILITY OF RULE 10b-5 Rule 10b-5 applies in virtually all cases concerning the trading of securities, whether on organized exchanges, in over-the-counter markets, or in private transactions. The rule covers notes, bonds, certificates of interest and participation in any profit-sharing agreement, agreements to form a corporation, and joint-venture agreements; in short, it covers just about any form of security. It is immaterial whether a firm has securities registered under the 1933 act for the 1934 act to apply.

Rule 10b-5 is applicable only when the requisites of federal jurisdiction, such as the use of the mails, of stock exchange facilities, or of any instrumentality of interstate commerce, are present. Virtually no commercial transaction, however, can be completed without such contact. In addition, the states have corporate securities laws, many of which include provisions similar to Rule 10b-5.

Rule 10b-5 covers not only corporate officers, directors, and majority shareholders but also certain "outside" persons having access to, or receiving information of, a nonpublic nature on which trading is based. Those persons to whom the

material information is transmitted are known as *tippees.* (The liability of tippees and other outsiders will be discussed shortly.)

DISCLOSURE UNDER RULE 10b-5 Any material omission or misrepresentation of material facts in connection with the purchase or sale of a security may violate Section 10(b) and Rule 10b-5. The key to liability (which can be civil or criminal) under this rule is whether the insider's information is *material.* Following are some examples of material facts calling for a disclosure under the rule:

1. A new ore discovery.
2. Fraudulent trading in the company stock by a broker-dealer.
3. A dividend change (whether up or down).
4. A contract for the sale of corporate assets.
5. A new discovery of a process or product.
6. A significant change in the firm's financial condition.

Courts have struggled with the problem of when information becomes public knowledge. Clearly, when inside information becomes public knowledge, all insiders should be allowed to trade without disclosure. The courts have suggested that insiders should refrain from trading for a "reasonable waiting period" when the news is not readily translatable into investment action. Presumably, this gives the news time to filter down to, and be evaluated by, the investing public.

The following is one of the landmark cases interpreting Rule 10b-5. The SEC sued Texas Gulf Sulphur Company for issuing a misleading press release. The release underestimated the magnitude and value of a mineral discovery. The SEC also sued several of Texas Gulf Sulphur's directors, officers, and employees under Rule 10b-5 after these persons had purchased large amounts of the corporate stock prior to the announcement of the corporation's rich ore discovery.

BACKGROUND AND FACTS *Texas Gulf Sulphur Company (TGS) drilled an exploratory hole on November 12, 1963, near Timmins, Ontario, that appeared to yield a core with an exceedingly high mineral content. Keeping the results of the test drilling secret, TGS officers, directors, and employees made substantial purchases of company stock or accepted stock options. Test drilling continued. On April 11, 1964, an unauthorized report*

Case 22.2

SEC v. TEXAS GULF SULPHUR CO.

United States Court of Appeals, Second Circuit, 1968.
401 F.2d 833.

*of the discovery appeared in the newspapers. On April 12, TGS issued a
press release that played down the find and stated that it was too early to
tell whether it would be significant. On April 16, after the completion of
test drilling, TGS announced a strike of at least 25 million tons of ore,
substantially driving up the price of TGS stock. The SEC filed suit against
TGS and several of its officers, directors, and employees for violating Rule
10b-5. Included in the complaint were charges that the April 12 press
release was deceptive. The trial court decided that the drilling results were
not "material" until April 9 and that the insider-trading activity before
that date was thus not illegal. The trial court also held that the press
release was not "misleading, or deceptive on the basis of the facts then
known." The SEC appealed.*

WATERMAN, Circuit Judge.
*   *   *   *

I. THE INDIVIDUAL DEFENDANTS
*   *   *   *

In each case, *   *   * whether facts are material within Rule 10b-5 when the
facts relate to a particular event and are undisclosed by those persons who are
knowledgeable thereof will depend at any given time upon a balancing of both the
indicated probability that the event will occur and the anticipated magnitude of the
event in light of the totality of the company activity. Here, *   *   * knowledge of
the possibility, which surely was more than marginal, of the existence of a mine of
the vast magnitude indicated by the remarkably rich drill core located rather close
to the surface (suggesting mineability by the less expensive openpit method) within
the confines of a large anomaly (suggesting an extensive region of mineralization)
might well have affected the price of TGS stock and would certainly have been an
important fact to a reasonable, if speculative, investor in deciding whether he should
buy, sell, or hold. After all, this first drill core was "unusually good and *   *   *
excited the interest and speculation of those who knew about it."
*   *   *   *

Finally, a major factor in determining whether the *   *   * discovery was a
material fact is the importance attached to the drilling results by those who knew
about it. In view of other unrelated recent developments favorably affecting TGS,
participation by an informed person in a regular stock-purchase program, or even
sporadic trading by an informed person, might lend only nominal support to the
inference of the materiality of the *   *   * discovery; nevertheless, the timing by
those who knew of it of their stock purchases and their purchases of *short-term*
calls—purchases in some cases by individuals who had never before purchased calls
or even TGS stock—virtually compels the inference that the insiders were influenced
by the drilling results. *   *   *
*   *   *   *

We hold, therefore, that all transactions in TGS stock or calls by individuals
apprised of the drilling results *   *   * were made in violation of Rule 10b-5.
Inasmuch as the visual evaluation of that drill core (a generally reliable estimate
though less accurate then a chemical assay) constituted material information, those
advised of the results of the visual evaluation as well as those informed of the chemical
assay traded in violation of law. *   *   *
*   *   *   *

II. THE CORPORATE DEFENDANT
*   *   *   *

At 3:00 P.M. on April 12, 1964, evidently believing it desirable to comment upon
the rumors concerning the Timmins project, TGS issued the press release quoted in
pertinent part [as follows:

* * * *

[Recent drilling on one property near Timmins has led to preliminary indications that more drilling would be required for proper evaluation of this prospect. The drilling done to date has not been conclusive, but the statements made by many outside quarters are unreliable and include information and figures that are not available to TGS.

[The work done to date has not been sufficient to reach definite conclusions and any statement as to size and grade of ore would be premature and possibly misleading. When we have progressed to the point where reasonable and logical conclusions can be made, TGS will issue a definite statement to its stockholders and to the public in order to clarify the Timmins project.]

* * * *

* * * It does not appear to be unfair to impose upon corporate management a duty to ascertain the truth of any statements the corporation releases to its shareholders or to the investing public at large. Accordingly, we hold that Rule 10b-5 is violated whenever assertions are made, as here, in a manner reasonably calculated to influence the investing public, e.g., by means of the financial media, if such assertions are false or misleading or are so incomplete as to mislead irrespective of whether the issuance of the release was motivated by corporate officials for ulterior purposes. It seems clear, however, that if corporate management demonstrates that it was diligent in ascertaining that the information it published was the whole truth and that such diligently obtained information was disseminated in good faith, Rule 10b-5 would not have been violated.

* * * *

We conclude, then, that, having established that the release was issued in a manner reasonably calculated to affect the market price of TGS stock and to influence the investing public, we must remand to the district court to decide whether the release was misleading to the reasonable investor and if found to be misleading, whether the court in its discretion should issue the injunction the SEC seeks.

DECISION AND REMEDY

The appellate court ruled in favor of the SEC. All of the trading by insiders who knew of the mineral find violated Rule 10b-5. The questions of whether the press release was misleading and what remedies should be ordered were remanded to the lower court for determination.

COMMENTS

Investors who had sold their TGS stock in reliance on the representations in the April 12 press release also sued TGS. Eventually, they were awarded damages representing the difference between the price at which they sold their stock and the price at which they could have reinvested in TGS after they learned of the April 16 press release.

OUTSIDERS AND RULE 10b-5 The traditional insider-trading case involves true insiders—corporate officers, directors, and majority shareholders who have access to, and trade on, inside information. Increasingly, liability under Section 10(b) of the 1934 act and SEC Rule 10b-5 has been extended to include certain "outsiders"—those who trade on inside information acquired *indirectly*. Two theories have been developed in recent years under which outsiders may be held liable for insider trading: the *tipper/tippee theory* and the *misappropriation theory*.

Tipper/tippee Theory Anyone who acquires inside information as a result of a corporate insider's breach of his or her fiduciary duty can be liable under Rule 10b-5. This liability extends to **tippees** (those who receive "tips" from insiders) and even remote tippees (tippees of tippees).[17] The key to liability under this theory is that inside information was obtained as a result of someone's breach of a

---

17. See the discussion of *SEC v. Musella,* 678 F.Supp. 1060 (S.D.N.Y. 1988), in the *Focus on Ethics* at the end of this unit.

fiduciary duty to the corporation whose shares are traded. Unless there has been a breach of a duty not to disclose inside information, and the tippee knows of this breach (or should know of it), liability under this theory cannot result.

For example, in *Chiarella v. United States*,[18] the United States Supreme Court considered the role Rule 10b-5 plays when there was not breach of duty and no use of interstate commerce, the mails, or any of the facilities of any national securities exchange. Chiarella was a printer who worked at a New York composing room and handled announcements of corporate takeover bids. Even though the documents that were delivered to the printer concealed the identity of the target corporations by blank spaces and false names, Chiarella was able to deduce the names of the target companies. Without disclosing his knowledge, he purchased stock in the target companies and sold the shares immediately after the takeover attempts were made public. He realized a gain of slightly more than $30,000 in the course of fourteen months.

In 1978, Chiarella was indicted on seventeen counts of violating Section 10(b) of the Securities Exchange Act of 1934 and SEC Rule 10b-5. The trial court convicted him on all counts, and the court of appeals affirmed that conviction. The United States Supreme Court, however, reversed the trial court's decision. The Supreme Court held that Chiarella could not be convicted for his failure to dis-

close his knowledge to stockholders or to target companies because he was under no duty to disclose his knowledge. Chiarella was under no duty to disclose because he had no prior dealing with the stockholders and was not their agent, nor was he a person in whom sellers had placed their trust and confidence. Thus, the Court held that Chiarella was not liable as a tippee.[19]

Misappropriation Theory Liability for insider trading may also be established under the misappropriation theory. This theory of liability holds that if an individual wrongfully obtains— misappropriates—inside information and trades on it to his or her personal gain, then the individual should be held liable, because in essence, he or she stole information rightfully belonging to another. This theory has significantly expanded the range of persons who can be held liable for insider trading. (Courts will normally hold that some fiduciary duty must have been violated and some harm to the defrauded party must have occurred for liability to exist.) The following case illustrates an application of the misappropriation theory.

---

18. 445 U.S. 222, 100 S.Ct. 1108, 63 L.Ed.2d 348 (1980).

19. Note, though, that Chiarella might not have escaped liability if the jury had been instructed to find liability under the misappropriation theory discussed in the next section. Under that theory, it could be argued that Chiarella violated his duty of loyalty to his employer, the printing firm, by engaging in actions that could foreseeably be harmful to the printing firm's reputation. Note also that after *Chiarella*, the SEC adopted Rule 14e-3 (17 C.F.R. Section 240.14e-3), which makes it unlawful for a person who acquires advance knowledge of a tender offer to use that information in securities transactions.

Case 22.3

UNITED STATES v. CARPENTER

United States Court of Appeals, Second Circuit, 1986. 791 F.2d 1024.

BACKGROUND AND FACTS *R. Foster Winans, a reporter for the* Wall Street Journal, *co-authored an influential daily financial column called "Heard on the Street." The column discussed selected stocks, and after its publication, there was often a noticeable change in the market price of the company stock that was the subject of the column. Winans entered into a scheme with Kenneth Felis and another stockbroker at Kidder Peabody to give the brokers advance information as to the timing and contents of the "Heard on the Street" column. The brokers would then buy or sell stock based on the probable impact of the column on the market and share the resulting profits. David Carpenter, a news clerk at the* Journal, *also participated in the scheme, acting primarily as a messenger between the conspirators. Over a four-month period, the net profits resulting from this trading activity were about $690,000. Correlations between the "Heard* *on the Street" articles and trading in the Felis account were noted at Kidder Peabody, and inquiries began. Later, the SEC began an investigation. Eventually, Winans and Carpenter revealed the entire scheme to the SEC. Winans and Felis were convicted for participating in an insider-trading scheme based on information misappropriated from the* Journal, *as well as for mail and wire fraud. Carpenter was convicted of aiding and abetting in the commission of securities fraud and mail and wire fraud. On appeal, Winans and the others (the appellants) contended that they could not be held liable under Rule 10b-5 because they were not corporate insiders and did not misappropriate material nonpublic information from corporate insiders.*

PIERCE, Circuit Judge:

    *   *   *   *

Although the facts render the securities fraud issue herein one of first impression, we do not write on a clean slate in assessing whether this case falls within the purview of the "misappropriation" theory of section 10(b) and Rule 10b-5 thereunder. In 1980, the Supreme Court left open the question of the viability of that theory [in] *Chiarella v. United States* with the concurring and dissenting opinions suggesting that had the theory been presented to the jury, Chiarella's conviction might have been affirmed. Since then, the theory has been applied twice by this court. It is clear that defendant Winans, as an employee of the *Wall Street Journal,* breached a duty of confidentiality to his employer by misappropriating from the *Journal* confidential prepublication information, regarding the time and content of certain newspaper columns, about which he learned in the course of his employment. We are presented with the question of whether that unlawful conduct may serve as the predicate [basis] for the securities fraud charges herein.

The core of appellants' argument is that *   *   * the misappropriation theory may be applied only where the information is misappropriated by corporate insiders or so-called quasi-insiders who owe to the corporation and its shareholders a fiduciary duty of abstention of disclosure. Thus, appellants would have us hold that it was not enough that Winans breached a duty of confidentiality to his employer, the *Wall Street Journal,* in misappropriating and trading on material nonpublic information; he would have to have breached a duty to the corporations or shareholders thereof whose stock they purchased or sold on the basis of that information.

Appellants *   *   * interpret the misappropriation theory too narrowly. *   *   * [T]he misappropriation theory more broadly proscribes the conversion by "insiders" or others of material nonpublic information in connection with the purchase or sale of securities. It is precisely such conversion that serves as the predicate for the convictions herein.

    *   *   *   *

We do not say that merely using information not available or accessible to others gives rise to a violation of Rule 10b-5. That theory of 10b-5 liability has been rejected. There are disparities in knowledge and the availability thereof at many levels of market functioning that the law does not presume to address. However, the critical issue is found in the district judge's careful distinction between "information" and "conduct." Whatever may be the legal significance of merely using one's privileged or unique position to obtain material, nonpublic information, here we address specifically whether an employee's use of such information in breach of a duty of confidentiality to an employer serves as an adequate predicate for a securities violation. Obviously, one may gain a competitive advantage in the marketplace through conduct constituting skill, foresight, industry and the like. Certainly this is true in securities law as in antitrust, patent, trademark, copyright and other fields. But one may not gain such advantage by conduct constituting secreting, stealing, purloining, or otherwise misappropriating material nonpublic information in breach of an employer-imposed fiduciary duty of confidentiality. Such conduct constitutes chicanery, not competition; foul play, not fair play. * * *

* * * Winans "misappropriated—stole, to put it bluntly—valuable nonpublic information entrusted to him in the utmost confidence." The information misappropriated here was the *Journal's* own confidential schedule of forthcoming publications. * * * Since section 10(b) has been found to proscribe fraudulent trading by insiders or outsiders, such conduct constituted fraud and deceit, as it would had Winans stolen material nonpublic information from traditional corporate insiders or quasi-insiders. * * *

Nor is there any doubt that this "fraud and deceit" was perpetrated "upon a[ny] person" under section 10(b) and Rule 10b-5. It is sufficient that the fraud was committed upon Winans' employer. Appellants Winans, and Felis and Carpenter by their complicity, perpetrated their fraud "upon" the *Wall Street Journal,* sullying its reputation and thereby defrauding it "as surely as if they took [its] money."

DECISION AND REMEDY   *The trial court's conviction was upheld. The appellants had violated insider-trading laws by trading to their profit on the basis of information obtained by Winans in violation of his fiduciary duty to his employer to keep the information confidential. The mail and wire fraud convictions were also upheld.*

COMMENTS   *This decision was later reviewed by the United States Supreme Court [Carpenter v. United States, 484 U.S. 19, 108 S.Ct. 316, 98 L.Ed.2d 275 (1987)]. Because the Court was evenly divided on the issue of liability under the misappropriation theory (the vote was four to four), the lower court's decision on this issue was upheld "by default." The Supreme Court, however, unanimously affirmed the convictions for mail and wire fraud.*

Insider Reporting and Trading—Section 16(b)

Officers, directors, and certain large stockholders[20] of Section 12 corporations are required to file reports with the SEC concerning their ownership and trading of the corporation's securities.[21] To discourage such insiders from using nonpublic information about their company to their personal benefit in the stock market, Section 16(b) of the 1934 act provides for the recapture by the corporation of all profits realized by the insider on any purchase and sale or sale and purchase of the corporation's stock within any six-month period.[22] It is irrelevant

whether the insider actually uses inside information; all such *short-swing* profits must be returned to the corporation. In other words, Section 16 is a strict liability provision.

Section 16(b) applies not only to stock but to warrants, options, and securities convertible into stock. In addition, the courts have fashioned complex rules for determining profits. Corporate insiders are wise to seek competent counsel prior to trading in the corporation's stock. Exhibit 22–5 compares the effects of Rule 10b-5 and Section 16(b).

If an individual is an "officer" of a corporation, such as a vice-president, but has no access to inside information, should this individual be subject to the provisions of Section 16(b) if he or she realizes short-swing profits by trading in the company's stock? This question arose in the following case, in which the central issue concerned the definition of a corporate officer.

---

20. Those stockholders owning 10 percent of the class of equity securities registered under Section 12 of the 1934 act [15 U.S.C. Section 78*l*].

21. 15 U.S.C. Section 78*l*.

22. 15 U.S.C. Section 78p(b). In a declining stock market, one can realize profits by selling at a high price and repurchasing at a later time at a lower price.

BACKGROUND AND FACTS   *Joseph Crotty was employed by United Artists (UA) in 1969, and by 1980 he had become UA's head film buyer for its western division, which encompassed six western states. Crotty's duties mainly involved negotiating and signing agreements to obtain movies for exhibition, distributing the movies to UA theaters, and supervising the advertising in his division. In 1982, UA made Crotty a vice-president. The appointment was essentially honorary and was accompanied by no change in duties or raise in pay. At no time was Crotty a director of the company, nor did he ever attend any board meetings or receive any information from the directors that was not available to the general public. Between December 19, 1984, and July 24, 1985, Crotty realized a large profit from the purchase and sale of UA shares. C.R.A. Realty Corporation, an organization incorporated to act as a private attorney general and commence actions against corporate officials for violations of federal securities law, sought to recover Crotty's short-swing profits on behalf of UA. The district court dismissed the action, holding that Crotty's transactions were not subject to Section 16(b) because Crotty at no time had access to inside information. C.R.A. Realty appealed.*

Case 22.4

C.R.A. REALTY CORP. v. CROTTY

United States Court of Appeals, Second Circuit, 1989.
878 F.2d 562.

TIMBERS, Circuit Judge.
*   *   *   *

Appellant's [C.R.A. Realty's] starting point in challenging the district court's holding is the Securities and Exchange Commission rule [Rule 3b-2] which defined the term ''officer'' in the 1934 Act as including a vice-president of an issuer. Appellant asserts that, since Crotty is a vice-president of United Artists, this rule places him within the purview of [Section] 16(b). We believe it is significant, however, that the SEC itself does not believe that this rule should be rigidly applied in determining who is an officer within the meaning of [Section] 16. For example, two SEC releases show that the Commission does not consider an employee's title as an officer to bring the employee automatically under [Section] 16. We do not believe that Rule 3b-2 requires us to hold that Crotty is an officer within the purview of [Section] 16(b) merely by virtue of his title as a vice-president of the company.

Moreover the district court's holding is consistent with the law of this Circuit. It relied primarily on *Colby v. Klune.* In *Colby* we held that a corporate employee who did not hold the title of a corporate officer nevertheless could be an officer within the meaning of [Section] 16(b) if he ''perform[ed] important executive duties of such character that he would be likely, in discharging these duties, to obtain confidential information about the company's affairs that would aid him if he engaged in personal market transactions.''

Colby is not factually on all fours with the instant case; indeed it is a correlative of the instant case. Here we must decide whether Crotty's title as a vice-president in and of itself brings him within the purview of [Section] 16(b), whereas the issue in *Colby* was whether an employee's duties could bring him under [Section] 16(b) even if he lacked a title as a corporate officer. We believe that the reasoning of *Colby* applies here. In *Colby* we held that ''[i]t is immaterial how [an employee's] functions are labelled or how defined in the bylaws, or that he does or does not act under the supervision of some other corporate representative.'' In short, *Colby* established as the law of this Circuit that it is an employee's duties and responsibilities—rather than his actual title—that determine whether he is an officer within the purview of [Section] 16(b).
*   *   *   *

To summarize:

We hold that it is the actual functions of an employee—particularly his access to inside information—and not his corporate title that determine whether he is an officer within the purview of [Section] 16(b) of the 1934 Act; Crotty's title of vice-president did not make him an officer. We also hold that the district court's finding that Crotty had no access to inside information is not clearly erroneous.

DECISION AND REMEDY *The appellate court held that Crotty's duties, and not his corporate title, should determine whether he was an officer subject to Section 16(b) provisions. The district court's decision was thus affirmed.*

COMMENTS *In January 1991, the SEC agreed to adopt revisions to the requirements under Section 16 of the 1934 act. The revised rules define ''officer'' in such a way as to make it clear that a person's functions—not simply his or her title—determine the applicability of Section 16.*

Insider-Trading Sanctions

The Insider Trading Sanctions Act of 1984[23] permits the SEC to bring suit in a federal district court against anyone violating, or aiding in a violation of, the 1934 act or SEC rules by purchasing or selling a security while in the possession of material nonpublic information. The violation must occur on or through the facilities of a national securities exchange or from or through a broker or dealer. Transactions pursuant to a public offering by an issuer of securities are excepted.

23.   15 U.S.C. Section 78u(d)(2)(A).

■ Exhibit 22–5 Comparison of Coverage, Application, and Liabilities under Rule 10b-5 and Section 16(b)

	Rule 10b-5	Section 16(b)
1. What is the subject matter of the transaction?	Any security (does not have to be registered).	Any security (does not have to be registered).
2. What transactions are covered?	Purchase or sale.	Short-swing purchase and sale or short-swing sale and purchase.
3. Who is subject to liability?	Virtually anyone with inside information under a duty to disclose—including officers, directors, controlling stockholders, and tippees.	Officers, directors, and certain 10 percent stockholders.
4. Is omission, scheme, or misrepresentation necessary for liability?	Yes.	No.
5. Are any transactions exempt?	No.	Yes, there are a variety of exemptions.
6. Is direct dealing with the party necessary?	No.	No.
7. Who can bring an action?	A person transacting with an insider, or the SEC, or a purchaser or seller damaged by a wrongful act.	Corporation and shareholder by derivative action.

The court may assess as a penalty as much as triple the profits gained or the loss avoided by the guilty party. For purposes of the act, profit or loss is defined as "the difference between the purchase or sale price of the security and the value of that security as measured by the trading price of the security at a reasonable period of time after public dissemination of the nonpublic information." [24]

The Insider Trading and Securities Fraud Enforcement Act of 1988 enlarged the class of persons who may be subject to civil liability for insider trading violations, gave the SEC authority to award bounty payments to persons providing information leading to the prosecution of insider-trading violations, gave the SEC rulemaking authority to require specific policies and procedures to prevent insider trading, and increased the criminal penalties for violations. Maximum jail terms were increased from five to ten years; fines were increased to $1 million for individuals and to $2.5 million for partnerships and corporations. [25] Neither act has any effect on other actions the SEC or private investors may take.

Proxy Statements

Section 14(a) of the Securities Exchange Act of 1934 regulates the solicitation of proxies from shareholders of Section 12 companies. [26] The SEC regulates the content of proxy statements sent to shareholders by corporate managers who are requesting authority to vote on behalf of the shareholders in a particular election on specified issues. Whoever solicits a proxy must fully and accurately disclose all facts that are pertinent to the matter to be voted on. SEC Rule 14a-9 is similar to the antifraud provisions of Rule 10b-5. Remedies for violation are extensive, ranging from injunctions to prevent a vote from being taken to monetary damages.

■ Regulation of Investment Companies

Investment companies, and mutual funds in particular, grew rapidly after World War II.

Investment companies act on behalf of many smaller shareholder-owners by buying a large portfolio of securities and managing that portfolio professionally. A **mutual fund** is a specific type of investment company that continually buys or sells to investors shares of ownership in a portfolio. Such companies are regulated by the Investment Company Act of 1940, [27] which provides for SEC regulation of their activities. It was expanded by the Investment Company Act Amendments of 1970. Further minor changes were made in the Securities Act Amendments of 1975.

The 1940 act requires that every investment company register with the SEC, and it imposes restrictions on the activities of such companies and persons connected with them. For the purposes of the act, an investment company is defined as any entity that (1) "is . . . engaged primarily . . . in the business of investing, reinvesting, or trading in securities" or (2) is engaged in such business and more than 40 percent of the company's assets consist of investment securities. Excluded from coverage of the act are banks, insurance companies, savings and loan associations, finance companies, oil and gas drilling firms, charitable foundations, tax-exempt pension funds, and other special types of institutions, such as closely held corporations.

To register with the SEC, the investment company files a notification of registration. Each year registered companies must file reports with the SEC. In order to safeguard company assets, all securities must be held in the custody of a bank or stock-exchange member, and that bank or stock-exchange member must follow strict procedures established by the SEC.

No dividends may be paid from any source other than accumulated, undistributed net income. Furthermore, there are some restrictions on investment activities. For example, investment companies are not allowed to purchase securities on the margin (pay for only part of the total price, borrowing the rest), sell short (sell shares not yet owned), or participate in joint trading accounts.

■ State Securities Laws

Today, all states have their own corporate securities laws that regulate the offer and sale of securities

---

24. 15 U.S.C. Section 78u(d)(2)(C).
25. 15 U.S.C. Section 78ff(a).
26. 15 U.S.C. Section 78n(a).

27. 15 U.S.C. Sections 80a-1 to 80a-64.

within individual state borders.[28] Often referred to as **blue sky laws,** they are designed to prevent ''speculative schemes which have no more basis than so many feet of blue sky.''

Since the adoption of the 1933 and 1934 federal securities acts, the state and federal governments have regulated securities concurrently. Indeed, both acts specifically preserve state securities laws. Certain features are common to all state blue sky laws. They have antifraud provisions, many of which are patterned after Rule 10b-5. Also, most state corporate securities laws regulate securities brokers and dealers.

---

28.   These laws are cataloged and annotated in the Commerce Clearing House's *Blue Sky Law Reporter,* a loose-leaf service.

Typically, these laws also provide for the registration or qualification of securities offered or issued for sale within the state. Unless an applicable exemption from registration is found, issuers must register or qualify their stock with the appropriate state official, often called a *corporations commissioner.* There is a difference in philosophy among state statutes. Many are like the Securities Act of 1933 and mandate certain disclosures before registration is effective and a permit to sell the securities is issued. Others have fairness standards that a corporation must meet to offer or sell stock in the state. The Uniform Securities Act, which has been adopted in part by several states, was drafted to be acceptable to states with differing regulatory philosophies.

■ Terms and Concepts to Review

accredited investors 526	**investment company** 537	**securities** 519
blue sky laws 538	**mutual fund** 537	**stocks** 519
bonds 519	**preferred stock** 519	**tippee** 531
common stock 519	**red herring** 524	**tombstone ad** 524
insider trading 529	**Rule 10b-5** 529	

■ Questions and Case Problems

22-1. Langley Brothers, Inc., a corporation incorporated and doing business in Kansas, decides to sell $1 million worth of its no par value common stock to the public. The stock will be sold only within the state of Kansas. Joseph Langley, the chairman of the board, says the offering need not be registered with the SEC. His brother, Harry, disagrees. Who is right? Explain.

22-2. Huron Corp. had 300,000 common shares outstanding. The owners of these outstanding shares lived in several different states. Huron decided to split the 300,000 shares two for one. Will Huron Corp. have to file a registration statement and prospectus on the 300,000 new shares to be issued as a result of the split? Explain.

22-3. Leston Nay owned 90 percent of the stock of First Securities Co. Between the years 1942 and 1966, Hochfelder sent large sums of money to Nay to be invested in *escrow accounts*—accounts belonging to one entity but held by another entity—of First Securities. The whole investment scheme was a fraud, and Nay converted the money sent by Hochfelder to his own use. When Hochfelder discovered the fraud, he sued Ernst & Ernst, the auditor of First Securities, for failing to use proper auditing procedures and thus negligently failing to discover the fraudulent scheme. Was the firm of Ernst & Ernst found guilty of

violating Section 10(b) of the 1934 Securities Exchange Act and SEC Rule 10b-5? Explain. [*Ernst & Ernst v. Hochfelder,* 425 U.S. 185, 96 S.Ct. 1375, 47 L.Ed.2d 668 (1976)]

22-4. American Breeding Herds, Inc., (ABH) offered a cattle-breeding plan for which Ronnett contracted to buy thirty-six Charolais cows at $3,000 per head and a one-quarter interest in a Charolais bull at $5,000, totaling $113,000. The ABH agreement described itself as a ''tax shelter program . . . unlike the purchase of securities such as stocks and bonds.'' Ronnett entered into the agreement after receiving investment advice from Shannon, an investment counselor. The cows were tagged and sent to an ABH-approved breeding ranch. Ronnett signed a maintenance agreement and paid a monthly maintenance fee. Was the ABH plan a security, and should it have been registered under Illinois securities law? Explain. [*Ronnett v. American Breeding Herds, Inc.,* 124 Ill.App.3d 842, 464 N.E.2d 1201, 80 Ill.Dec. 218 (1984)]

22-5. Campbell was a financial columnist for a Los Angeles newspaper owned by Hearst Corp. He often bought shares in companies on which he was about to give a favorable report, and then he would sell the shares at a profit after the columns appeared. In June 1969, Campbell interviewed the officers of American Systems, Inc. (ASI). The ASI officers did not disclose to Campbell adverse information concerning its financial condition, and Campbell relied on the officers' presentation of ASI's financial status and made no independent investigation. Planning to write a favorable report, Campbell purchased 5,000 shares of ASI stock for $2 per share. Following the publication of Campbell's favorable, and misleading, article, ASI's stock rose rapidly, and on June 5, Campbell sold 2,000 of his shares at $5 per share. ASI had made plans with another corporation, RGC, in February 1969 whereby RGC would merge with ASI, and ASI would pay RGC stockholders enough ASI stock to equal a market value of $1.8 million on the closing date of June 10, 1969. Zweig and Bruno, who each owned one-third of RGC shares, brought suit against Hearst Corp., alleging that because of the artificial rise in ASI stock due to Campbell's column, they ended up with a smaller percentage of the total outstanding shares of ASI than they would have otherwise received. Discuss whether Hearst is liable under Rule 10b-5. [*Zweig v. Hearst Corp.,* 594 F.2d 1261 (9th Cir. 1979)]

22-6. Ronald Rodeo's investment group purchased limited partnership interests in certain Illinois apartment buildings and separately, by contract, acquired an option to buy out the remaining interests of the general partners. According to the arrangement, the general partners would operate the apartments, and the limited partners would provide essential capital while retaining their limited liability. Rodeo could not actively intervene in the business without losing his limited liability. He therefore had to rely solely upon the general partners for the enterprise's profitability. Two years later, Rodeo became disenchanted with the operation of the apartment enterprise and sued R. Dean Gillman and the other general partners under the Illinois blue sky act. In his claim, Rodeo stated that material misrepresentations and omissions had been made during the negotiation of the limited partnership contracts in violation of the state securities act. The general partners responded that no securities were involved and that, because of the buy-out option, the limited partners actually had ultimate control over the management of the apartments. Discuss the definition of a *security* and whether the limited partnership contracts meet this definition. [*Rodeo v. Gillman,* 787 F.2d 1175 (7th Cir. 1986)]

22-7. U.S. News & World Report, Inc., set up a profit-sharing plan in 1962 that allotted to certain employees specially issued stock known as bonus or anniversary stock. The stock was given to the employees for past services and could not be traded or sold to anyone other than the corporate issuer, U.S. News. This special stock was issued only to employees and for no other purpose than as bonuses. Because there was no market for the stock, U.S. News hired an independent appraiser to estimate the fair value of the stock so that the employees could redeem the shares. Charles Foltz and several other employees held stock through this plan and sought to redeem the shares with U.S. News, but Foltz disputed the value set by the appraisers. Foltz sued U.S. News for violation of securities regulations. What defense would allow U.S. News to resist successfully Foltz's claim? [*Foltz v. U.S. News & World Report, Inc.,* 627 F.Supp. 1143 (D.D.C. 1986)]

22-8. In early 1985, FMC Corp. made plans to buy some of its own stock as part of a restructuring of its balance statement. Unknown to FMC management, the brokerage firm FMC employed—Goldman, Sachs & Co.—disclosed information on the stock purchase that found its way to Ivan Boesky. FMC was one of the seven major corporations in whose stock Boesky allegedly traded using inside information. Boesky made purchases of FMC's stock between February 18 and February 21 and between March 12 and April 4. Boesky's purchases amounted to a substantial portion of the total volume of FMC stock traded during these periods. The price of FMC stock increased from $71.25 on February 20, 1986, to $97.00 on April 25, 1986. As a result, FMC paid substantially more for the repurchase of its own stock than anticipated. Upon the discovery of Boesky's knowledge of FMC's recapitalization plan, FMC sued him for the excess price it had paid—approximately $220 million. Discuss whether FMC should recover under Section 10(b) of the Securities Exchange Act and SEC Rule 10b-5. [*FMC Corp. v. Boesky,* 673 F.Supp. 242 (N.D.Ill. 1987)]

22-9. Emerson Electric Co. purchased 13.2 percent of Dodge Manufacturing Co.'s stock in an unsuccessful takeover attempt in June 1967. Later, when Dodge merged with Reliance Electric Co., Emerson decided to sell its shares. To avoid being subject to the restrictions of Section 16 of the Securities Exchange Act of 1934, which pertain to any purchase and sale by any owner of 10 percent or more of a corporation's stock, Emerson decided on a two-step selling plan. First, it sold off sufficient shares to reduce its holdings to 9.96 percent, and then it sold the remaining stock—all within a six-month period. Because under Section 16(b) of the act, the owner must be a 10 percent owner "both at the time of the purchase and sale . . . of the security involved," Emerson in this way succeeded in avoiding Section 16(b) requirements. Reliance demanded that Emerson return the profits made on both sales. Emerson sought a declaration from that court that it was not liable, arguing that because at the time of the second sale it had not owned 10 percent of Dodge stock, Section 16 did not apply. Does Section 16 of the Securities Exchange Act of 1934 apply to Emerson's transactions, and is Emerson liable to Reliance for its profits? Discuss fully. [*Reliance Electric Co. v. Emerson Electric Co.,* 404 U.S. 418, 92 S.Ct. 596, 30 L.E.2d 575 (1972)]

22-10. The W. J. Howey Co. owned large tracts of citrus acreage in Lake County, Florida. For several years, it planted about five hundred acres annually, keeping half of the groves itself and offering the other half to the public to help finance additional development. Howey-in-the-Hills Service, Inc., was a service company engaged in cultivating and developing these groves, including the harvesting and marketing of the crops. Each prospective customer was offered both a land sales contract and a service contract, after being told that it was not feasible to invest in a grove unless service arrangements were made. Of the acreage sold by Howey, 85 percent was sold with a service contract with Howey-in-the-Hills Service. Howey did not register with the SEC or meet the other administrative requirements that issuers of securities must fulfill. The SEC sued to enjoin Howey from continuing to offer the land sales and service contracts. Howey responded that no SEC violation existed because no securities were issued. Which party will prevail in court, Howey or the SEC? For what reasons? [*SEC v. W. J. Howey Co.*, 328 U.S. 293, 66 S.Ct. 1100, 90 L.Ed. 1244 (1946)]

22-11. Energy Resource Group, Inc., (ERG) entered into a written agreement with Ivan West for West to find an investor willing to purchase ERG stock. West later formed a partnership, called Investment Management Group (IMG), with Don Peters and another person. According to the terms of the partnership agreement, West's consulting work for ERG was excluded from the work of the IMG partnership. West learned through his consulting position with ERG that ERG was to be acquired by another corporation for $6.00 per share. At the time West learned of the acquisition, ERG stock was trading at $3.50 per share. Apparently, Peters learned of the acquisition from papers on West's desk in the IMG office and then shared the information with Ken Mick, his stockbroker. Mick then encouraged several clients to buy ERG stock prior to the public announcement of the acquisition. Mick, in return for leaking this inside information to clients, received a special premium from the enriched investors. Mick then paid a portion of the premium to Peters. The SEC brought an action against Peters for violating Rule 10b-5. Under what theory might Peters be held liable for insider trading in violation of Rule 10b-5? Discuss fully. [*SEC v. Peters*, 735 F.Supp. 1505 (D.Kans. 1990)]

22-12. A Question of Ethics

Between 1970 and 1981, Sanford Weill had served as the chief executive officer (CEO) of Shearson Loeb Rhodes and several of its predecessor entities (collectively "Shearson"). In 1981, Weill sold his controlling interest in Shearson to the American Express Co. and between 1981 and 1985 served as president of that firm. In 1985, Weill developed an interest in becoming CEO for BankAmerica and secured a commitment from Shearson to invest $1 billion in BankAmerica if he was successful in his negotiations with that firm. In early 1986, Weill met with BankAmerica directors several times, but these contacts were not disclosed publicly until February 20, 1986, when BankAmerica announced that Weill had sought to become its CEO but that BankAmerica was not interested in his offer. The day after the announcement, BankAmerica stock traded at prices higher than they had been during the five weeks preceding the announcement. Weill discussed his efforts to become CEO of BankAmerica with his wife, who discussed the information with her psychiatrist, Dr. Willis, prior to BankAmerica's public announcement of February 20. She also told Dr. Willis about Shearson's decision to invest in BankAmerica if Weill succeeded in

becoming its CEO. Willis disclosed to his broker this material, confidential information and purchased BankAmerica common stock. After BankAmerica's public announcement and the subsequent increase in the price of its stock, Willis sold his shares and realized a profit of approximately $27,475.79. The court held that Willis was liable for insider trading under the misappropriation theory. [United States v. Willis, 737 F.Supp. 269 (S.D.N.Y. 1990)]

1. The court stated in its opinion in this case that "[i]t is difficult to imagine a relationship that requires a higher degree of trust and confidence than the traditional relationship of physician and patient" and then quoted the concluding words of the Hippocratic oath: "Whatsoever things I see or hear concerning the life of men, in my attendance on the sick or even apart therefrom, which ought not be noised abroad, I will keep silence thereon, counting such things to be as sacred secrets." The court held that Willis had violated his fiduciary duty to Mrs. Weill, his patient, by investing in BankAmerica stock. Do you agree that Willis's private investments, which were based on information learned through his sessions with Mrs. Weill, constituted a violation of his duty to his patient? After all, Willis had not "noised abroad" Mrs. Weill's secrets—that is, he had not told others (except for his stockbroker) about the information. If you had been in Willis's shoes, would you have felt ethically restrained from trading on the information?

2. Can you think of any ways in which Willis's trading could have been harmful to Mrs. Weill's interests? Does your answer to this question have a bearing on how you would answer Question 1 above?

3. Do you think that Willis's liability for his breach of duty should extend only to Mrs. Weill? In other words, do you think that the misappropriation theory of liability imposes too great a burden on outsiders, such as Willis? Why or why not? How might you justify, from an ethical point of view, the application of the misappropriation theory to "outsider trading"?

22-13. Case Briefing Assignment

Examine Case A.22 [Reves v. Ernst & Young, 949 U.S. 56, 110 S.Ct. 945, 108 L.Ed.2d 47 (1990)] in Appendix A. The case has been excerpted there in great detail. Review and then brief the case, making sure that you include answers to the following questions in your brief.

1. What was the importance of classifying Co-op's notes as securities?

2. What test did the Court apply in determining whether the financial instruments were securities? Briefly describe the elements of the test.

3. What factors lead the Court to conclude what it did about whether the financial instruments were securities?

Chapter 23

Land-Use Control and Real Property

Property ownership confers certain legal rights. We generally think of ownership as conferring on the property's owner the right to possess the property; the right either to use the property or derive profits from another's use of the property; and the right to *alienate* the property—that is, to sell, bequeath (pass on through a will), or give away to others the same rights of ownership. Not all forms of ownership provide such a complete bundle of rights, but one or more of these attributes are normally included when we say that property is "owned."

Yet even for one who possesses the bundle of rights we have delineated, ownership is not truly absolute. The law places restrictions on how property may be used. It also imposes duties on the owners regarding how the land is to be maintained. Also, individual owners may agree with others to restrict or limit the use of their property. Thus, property owners cannot always do with their property whatever they wish. Nuisance and environmental laws, for example, restrict certain types of activities carried out on one's own land. Holding property also may be conditional on the payment of property taxes. Certain uses of property may be contingent on the owner's obtaining a license. If taxes are not paid, ownership of the property will be forfeited to the state. If the license is not obtained, the owner may be sanctioned for the particular use of the property. In addition, if a property owner fails to pay certain debts, the property might be seized to satisfy the owner's creditors. Briefly stated, the rights of every property owner are subject to certain conditions and limitations. In this chapter we focus on restrictions of ownership in a specific type of property—real property.

Real property (sometimes called *realty* or *real estate*) means the land and everything *permanently* attached to the land. When structures are permanently attached to the land, then everything attached permanently to the structures is also realty. Everything else is **personal property** (or *personalty*). Although real property is more than land, it is generally referred to as simply "land." Hence, the control over ownership and use we examine in this chapter is commonly referred to as **land-use control.**

▦ Sources of Land-Use Control

There are basically three sources of land-use control. First, the law of torts places on the owners of land certain obligations that protect both the interests of owners of adjacent or nearby land and individuals who come on another's land. Second, land use is subject to controls imposed by state and local governments as well as by the federal government under the authority each possesses to protect the broader interests of the community. Third, land use is subject to controls that owners impose on themselves as part of agreements entered into with other private individuals. Although such agreements are voluntary, they sometimes ''run with the land'' when its ownership is subsequently transferred to another. Thus, one who acquires ownership of land with actual or *constructive* (imputed by law) notice of a restriction on the land may be bound by an earlier, voluntary agreement to which he or she was not a party.

The principles of tort law relating to *nuisance* and similar legal principles that constrain an owner's use of land were discussed in Chapters 7 and 19. These tort law doctrines provide a significant source of regulation of land use, but they will not be reexamined here. Instead, the reader is urged to review those concepts in the context of our present discussion. Our focus in this chapter is on the remaining two sources of land-use control—privately imposed restrictions and public regulation of land use. We begin with the public control of land use.

■ Public Control of Land Use

Land use is subject to regulation by the state within whose political boundaries the land is located. Most states authorize local control over land use through various planning boards and zoning authorities. Thus, though such bodies act under the authority of the state, most public land-use control is carried out on a local level, by city or county authorities. The federal government does not engage in zoning or other forms of land-use control under normal circumstances, except with respect to federally owned land.

It is worth noting, however, that the federal government does influence state and local regulation, albeit indirectly, through its allocation of federal funds. Stipulations on land use may be a condition to the states' receiving such funds. Federal as well as state laws concerning environmental matters such as air and water quality, the protection

of endangered species, and the preservation of natural wetlands are also a significant source of land-use control.

Authority to Regulate Land Use

The state's power to control the use of land through legislation is derived from two broad sources: the states' *police power* and the doctrine of *eminent domain*. The inherent police power of the states has long been accepted as conferring on state governments the power to enact legislation that promotes the health, safety, and welfare of their citizens. Under their police power, the states have considerable discretion in regulating various activities within their jurisdictions. Provided there is a rational basis for the particular state legislation, and provided that the legislation does not conflict with the Constitution or interfere with the exercise of power delegated to the federal government, state regulation will be upheld by both federal and state courts as a valid exercise of state police power. Land-use control is an area in which the states enjoy particularly wide discretion in enacting regulation.

The second broad source of authority for state control of land use is the power of eminent domain. The power of **eminent domain** is the authority to take private property for public use or purpose without the owner's consenting to the ''taking.'' [1] Like the states' broad police powers, the power of eminent domain is an inherent power of government.

STATE REGULATION A few states have opted to control land use directly, at the state level. In these states, land-use regulation is carried out on a statewide or regional basis. Hawaii, for instance, has employed a statewide land-use classification scheme. Some states have a land-permit process that operates in conjunction with local control.

---

1. The federal government also possesses this authority. With regard to general police powers, however, remember that the federal government is a government of delegated powers. It enjoys broad discretion in carrying out its delegated powers, and its power is supreme in areas delegated to it by the Constitution. But it is somewhat misleading to talk about federal ''police powers,'' precisely because its powers are limited to those conferred on it by the Constitution. The states enjoy all unenumerated implied police powers that do not conflict with the Constitution.

Florida, for example, has used such a scheme in certain land areas of ''critical environmental concern.'' In Florida, the state government has preempted local control in decisions relating to whether an adequate infrastructure (roads, sewers, etc.) exists as a condition to permitting development of the land in question to take place. Vermont also has utilized a land-permit scheme that is applicable on a statewide basis.

REGIONAL REGULATION   A state may create or authorize certain regions to create regional agencies to regulate growth and development in specific areas affected by special environmental problems. In some regions that overlap state boundaries, the United States Congress has approved compacts between the affected states creating just this type of agency. For example, Congress approved a compact between California and Nevada that created the Tahoe Regional Planning Agency.

LOCAL REGULATION   As noted above, most land-use control is implemented and administered at the local level, by either city or county governments. The regulatory powers exercised by such bodies are conferred by the state through some form of *enabling legislation*. Every state, in fact, has enacted some form of enabling legislation that delegates to local governments power to regulate land use in their local communities.

Enabling Acts   Most of the various enabling acts granting local governments land-use control authority contain similar regulatory provisions.

1.   Most provide authority to regulate and limit the height and bulk of buildings.
2.   The majority confer power to establish, regulate, and limit the distances that structures must be located from the street or sidewalk.
3.   Most provide authority to regulate and limit the intensity of the use of lot areas.
4.   The majority confer power to determine the area of open space required around and within structures.
5.   Most grant authority to classify, regulate, and restrict the location of trade and business to certain areas, as well as designate areas for residential use.
6.   The enabling statutes normally authorize decisions to divide the entire municipality or community into districts of various areas and classes to effectuate the purposes of the enabling legislation.
7.   The majority of acts confer power to set standards for the construction of and materials for use in local buildings.

Variances   Enabling statutes normally provide local governments with the authority to grant **variances**. Variances are basically exemptions from land-use regulations and are granted in cases in which application of an ordinance would cause a ''hardship'' because of unique or peculiar circumstances relating to the property at variance with the regulatory scheme. Special circumstances include the property's shape, size, location, surroundings, and topography. The unusual or unique nature of any of these may make a particular land-use regulation inappropriate.

A variance may be denied, however, if the special conditions are not unique to the property but are found throughout the relevant area surrounding the property. A variance also may be denied if the special condition has been caused by the owner of the property. In order to obtain a variance the property owner must show that application of the particular land-use regulation would prevent the owner's earning a reasonable return on his or her investment in the property. We look again at variances and their relation to land-use control in the discussion of specific forms of regulation below.

VOTER REGULATION   Some states permit land-use regulations to be enacted pursuant to a voter initiative and to be reviewed by a voter referendum. The process for such an initiative or referendum might begin with a petition to have the matter placed on the ballot in an upcoming election.

Limitations on Public Control of Land Use

The states' broad powers to control private land use are not without limitation. Significant limitations on both government police powers and the power of eminent domain are found in the United States Constitution. State constitutions and state laws also are sources of limitations on the exercise of these powers. In general, a property owner has the right to challenge the particular restriction as well as the manner in which it is carried out by bringing suit against the appropriate regulatory agency in a state court. When the suit raises federal constitutional issues or involves some aspect of federal law, the suit may be brought in a federal court.

EMINENT DOMAIN AND JUST COMPENSA- TION   Although the government may take land for public use, it must pay for it. The Fifth Amend- ment provides that an owner whose property is taken through the exercise of the power of eminent domain must be given fair and just compensation. Although the Fifth Amendment pertains to actions taken by the federal government, the Fourteenth Amendment has been interpreted as extending this limitation to state actions. Thus, the just compen- sation requirement restricts the states' power of eminent domain as well. As a practical matter, then, eminent domain can be an expensive method of land-use control. The just compensation require- ment was at the heart of the following case, in which the Supreme Court addressed the issue of whether the Fourteenth Amendment requires a state to compensate an owner for a ''temporary'' taking of the owner's property.

Case 23.1

FIRST ENGLISH EVANGELICAL LUTHERAN CHURCH OF GLENDALE v. COUNTY OF LOS ANGELES

Supreme Court of the United States, 1987.
482 U.S. 304,
107 S.Ct. 2378,
96 L.Ed.2d 250.

BACKGROUND AND FACTS   *The First English Evangelical Lutheran Church of Glendale owned twenty-one acres of land in a canyon along the banks of the Middle Fork of Mill Creek in the Angeles National Forest. The church, for a number of years, had used the land as a retreat center and a recreational area for handicapped children. In July 1977, a forest fire destroyed several hundred acres of mountainous forest land upstream from the church's property. The denudation of the forest land created a serious flood hazard, and in February 1978, the runoff from a severe storm overflowed the banks of Mill Creek. The flood destroyed the buildings situated on the church's property. In response to the flooding of the canyon, the County of Los Angeles adopted a temporary ordinance that declared the area a flood zone. Under the terms of the ordinance, the church was forbidden from reconstructing buildings on its property situated in the flood zone. The church sued the county in the California state courts, claiming that the ordinance, though temporary, amounted to a ''taking,'' for which the church was entitled to receive compensation. The trial court dismissed the church's claim for damages on the grounds that under Cal- ifornia law the only available remedy for such action was invalidation of the offending ordinance, not compensation for loss of use of the property. A California appeals court upheld the dismissal. After the California Su- preme Court refused to review the case, the church appealed to the United States Supreme Court.*

REHNQUIST, Chief Justice.
*   *   *   *
We *   *   * have no occasion to decide whether the ordinance at issue actually denied appellant all use of its property or whether the county might avoid the con- clusion that a compensable taking had occurred by establishing that the denial of all use was insulated as a part of the State's authority to enact safety regulations. These questions *   *   * remain open for decision on the remand we direct today. We address the question of whether the Just Compensation Clause [of the Constitution] requires the government to pay for ''temporary'' regulatory takings.

Consideration of the compensation question must begin with direct reference to the language of the Fifth Amendment, which provides in relevant part that ''private property [shall not] be taken for public use, without just compensation.'' As its language indicates, and as the Court has frequently noted, this provision does not prohibit the taking of private property, but instead places a condition on the exercise of that power. * * * This basic understanding of the Amendment makes clear that it is designed not to limit the governmental interference with property rights *per se*, but rather to secure compensation in the event of otherwise proper interference amounting to a taking. Thus, government action that works a taking of property rights necessarily implicates the ''constitutional obligation to pay just compensation.'' * * *

* * * While the typical taking occurs when the government acts to condemn property in the exercise of its power of eminent domain, the entire doctrine of inverse condemnation is predicated on the proposition that a taking may occur without such formal proceedings. * * *

* * * The Court has recognized in more than one case that the government may elect to abandon its intrusion or discontinue regulations. Similarly, a governmental body may acquiesce in a judicial declaration that one of its ordinances has affected an unconstitutional taking of property; the landowner has no right under the Just Compensation Clause to insist that a ''temporary'' taking be deemed a permanent taking. But we have not resolved whether abandonment by the government requires payment of compensation for the period of time during which regulations deny a landowner all use of his land. * * *

* * * The value of [occupying or otherwise using] property for a period of years may be substantial, and the burden on the property owner in extinguishing such an [opportunity] for a period of years may be great indeed. Where this burden results from governmental action that amounted to a taking, the Just Compensation Clause of the Fifth Amendment requires that the government pay the landowner for the value of the use of the land during this period. Invalidation of the ordinance or its successor ordinance after this period of time, though converting the taking into a ''temporary'' one, is not a sufficient remedy to meet the demands of the Just Compensation Clause. * * *

* * * *

* * * Once a court determines that a taking has occurred, the government retains the whole range of options already available—amendment of the regulation, withdrawal of the invalidated regulation, or exercise of eminent domain. * * * We merely hold that where the government's activities have already worked a taking of all use of property, no subsequent action by the government can relieve it of the duty to provide compensation for the period during which the taking was effective.

The Supreme Court reversed the California appellate court's decision. The Court ruled that invalidation of an ordinance without compensation for loss of use of property during the period in which the invalid ordinance remained in effect was an inadequate remedy.

DECISION AND REMEDY

LIMITATIONS ON POLICE POWER A state, as an alternative to an outright taking, may regulate land use through the exercise of its police powers. Under general police powers, states can enact land-use controls that are rationally related to the goal of protecting public health, safety, and general welfare. These laws can affect owners' rights and uses of land without the state's having to compensate the landowner. If, however, a state's restrictions on a landowner's property rights are overly burdensome, the state's regulation may be deemed a *confiscation,* or a taking, and may be subject to the eminent domain requirement that just compensation be paid.

Suppose Perez owns a large tract of land, which she purchased with the intent to subdivide it and develop it into residential properties. At the time of the purchase, there were no zoning regulations restricting use of the land. If, after Perez has undertaken significant steps toward developing the property, the government attempts to zone the entire tract of land as "public parkland only" and thus prohibit Perez's developing any part of it, the action will be deemed confiscatory. This is because the government will be denying her the ability to use her property for any reasonable income-producing or private purpose for which it is suited and because she had reasonable, investment-backed expectations in her development plans. The regulation normally will be held unconstitutional and void unless the government compensates Perez for effectively confiscating her land. Suppose, however, that the government *zones* Perez's parcel of land as "three-fourths residential, one-fourth park area" after her purchase. This zoning regulation is not confiscatory, because she will be able to use most of the property for building residences.

The state's power to regulate the use of land is limited in two other ways, both of which arise from the Fourteenth Amendment. First, the state cannot regulate the use of land arbitrarily or unreasonably, because this would be taking property without due process. There must be a *rational basis* for the classifications that the state imposes on property. Any act that is reasonably related to the health or general welfare of the public is deemed to have a rational basis.

Second, a state's regulation of land-use control cannot be discriminatory. A zoning ordinance is considered discriminatory if it affects one parcel of land in a way in which it does not affect surrounding parcels and if there is no rational basis for the difference. Placing a single parcel or a limited number of parcels in a classification that does not accord with a general zoning scheme or comprehensive plan (referred to as *spot zoning,* discussed below) is often held invalid on grounds of unreasonable discrimination.

Also, a zoning ordinance cannot be racially discriminatory. For example, a small community near a large metropolitan area may not zone itself so as to exclude all low-income housing if the zoning scheme is intentionally designed to exclude minorities. If the community could prove that a legitimate public purpose was served by its zoning classification scheme, however, then the ordinance might be allowed to stand. Similarly, a zoning ordinance cannot prohibit churches or otherwise burden the exercise of religion, but a community can reasonably regulate the churches' location sites.

The following case, which involves an ordinance that was designed to relieve the adverse effects of a local housing shortage in San Jose, California, examines some of the issues related to due process and equal protection in the area of land-use control.

Case 23.2

PENNELL v. CITY OF SAN JOSE

Supreme Court of the United States, 1988.
485 U.S. 1,
108 S.Ct. 489,
99 L.Ed.2d 1.

BACKGROUND AND FACTS *In 1979 the City of San Jose, California, enacted a rent-control ordinance designed to "alleviate some of the more immediate needs created by [the city's] housing situation." These needs included "the prevention of excessive and unreasonable rent increases, the alleviation of undue hardships on individual tenants, and the assurance to landlords of a fair and reasonable return on the value of their property." As part of the regulatory scheme, the ordinance provided that a hearing officer was to determine whether to approve rent increases proposed by area landlords. As part of the determination, the officer was to consider seven factors. Six of the factors were related to objective standards such as the costs to the landlord of maintaining the apartment dwelling. The seventh factor, however, called upon the officer to consider whether the proposed rent increase would create a "hardship" for the tenant as based on the tenant's income and living expenses. A group of landlords (appellants) challenged the ordinance in the California courts. A lower court and an intermediate appellate court decided the case in favor of the landlords, but the decision was reversed by the California Supreme Court. The landlords then appealed their case to the United States Supreme Court, con-*

*tending that the ordinance was in effect a ''taking'' of the landlords' prop-
erty and that the ordinance violated the Due Process Clause and the Equal
Protection Clause of the Fourteenth Amendment. The Court held that the
first argument was not an issue that could properly be brought at the time,
but it did address arguments based on both the Due Process Clause and
the Equal Protection Clause.*

Chief Justice *RENQUIST* delivered the opinion of the Court.
     *   *   *   *

Appellants *   *   * urge that the mere provision in the Ordinance that a Hearing
Officer may consider the hardship of the tenant in finally fixing a reasonable rent
renders the Ordinance ''facially invalid'' under the Due Process and Equal Protection
Clauses *   *   *. The standard for determining whether a state price-control regulation is constitutional under the Due Process Clause is well established: ''Price
control is 'unconstitutional . . . . [i]f arbitrary, discriminatory, or demonstrably irrelevant to the policy the legislature is free to adopt. . . .' '' *   *   *

We reject [the appellants'] contention, however, because we have long recognized
that a legitimate and rational goal of price or rate regulation is the protection of
consumer welfare. Indeed, a primary purpose of rent control is the protection of
tenants. Here, the Ordinance establishes a scheme in which a Hearing Officer considers a number of factors in determining the reasonableness of a proposed rent
increase which exceeds eight percent and which exceeds the amount deemed reasonable under [provisions of the ordinance]. The first six factors [the officer must
consider] focus on the individual landlord—the Hearing Officer examines the history
of the premises, the landlord's costs, and the market for comparable housing. [The
ordinance] also allows the landlord to bring forth any other financial evidence—
including presumably evidence regarding his own financial status—to be taken into
account by the Hearing Officer. It is in only this context that the Ordinance allows
tenant hardship to be considered and *   *   * ''balance[d]'' with the other factors
set out in [the ordinance]. Within this scheme, [the ordinance] represents a rational
attempt to accommodate the conflicting interests of protecting tenants from burdensome rent increases while at the same time ensuring that landlords are guaranteed a
fair return on their investment. We accordingly find that the Ordinance, which so
carefully considers both the individual circumstances of the landlord and the tenant
before determining whether to allow an additional increase in rent over and above
certain amounts that are deemed reasonable, does not on its face violate the Fourteenth
Amendment's Due Process Clause.

We also find that the Ordinance does not violate the Amendment's Equal Protection Clause. Here again, the standard is deferential; appellees need only show that
the classification scheme embodied in the Ordinance is ''rationally related to a legitimate state interest.'' As we stated in *Vance v. Bradley*, ''we will not overturn [a
statute that does not burden a suspect class or a fundamental interest] unless the
varying treatment of different groups or persons is so unrelated to the achievement
of any combination of legitimate purposes that we can only conclude that the legislature's actions were irrational.'' In light of our conclusion above that the Ordinance's tenant hardship provisions are designed to serve the legitimate purpose of
protecting tenants, we can hardly conclude that it is irrational for the Ordinance to
treat certain landlords differently on the basis of whether or not they have hardship
tenants. The Ordinance distinguishes between landlords because doing so furthers
the purpose of ensuring that individual tenants do not suffer ''unreasonable'' hardship; it would be inconsistent to state that hardship is a legitimate factor to be
considered but then hold that appellees could not tailor the Ordinance so that only
legitimate hardship cases are redressed. We recognize, as appellants point out, that

in general it is difficult to say that the landlord "causes" the tenant's hardship. But this is beside the point—if a landlord does have a hardship tenant, regardless of the reason why, it is rational for appellees to take that fact into consideration under * * * the Ordinance when establishing a rent that is "reasonable under the circumstances."

DECISION AND REMEDY *The Court upheld the California Supreme Court's ruling upholding the ordinance. The Court found that the ordinance violated neither the Due Process Clause nor the Equal Protection Clause of the Fourteenth Amendment.*

Forms of Public Control over Land Use

There exist a variety of forms of public land-use control. Most states authorize planning at the local level and have created or authorized the creation of local planning boards to develop and administer land-use regulatory schemes. Similarly, the enabling legislation referred to earlier typically authorizes local bodies to enact zoning ordinances to regulate the use of specific parcels of land, as well as types and specifications of structures erected on the land. Public land-use control also may relate to development of subdivisions, by which private developers subdivide larger tracts of land and construct commercial or residential units on the tracts for resale to private parties. Other forms of land-use regulation include growth management, historical preservation, and similar specific types of controls.

Planning

Most states require that local jurisdictions devise and implement a general development plan as a precursor to specific land-use regulation. In fact, many enabling acts require that local zoning ordinances be in accord with a previously devised comprehensive plan. Although there is no typical plan, all relate to the physical development of an area. The requirement of a master plan does not mean that a special document, labeled as such, exists. Nonetheless, most local jurisdictions have such a document, referred to by various names such as the general plan, city plan, master plan, or comprehensive plan.

A **general plan** is a comprehensive, long-run scheme dealing with the physical development, and in some cases redevelopment, of a city or com-

munity. The plan addresses concerns such as mode of housing, protection of natural resources, provision of public facilities and modes of transportation, and uses to which various pieces of land may be put.

GENERAL PLAN REQUIREMENTS AND PRIVATE DEVELOPERS Any private individuals contemplating development of a parcel of property should consider whether the property is subject to a local general plan. Although some states do not require local communities to adopt such a plan, most do adopt such plans. Regardless of whether required by the state or not, the existence of a general plan can preclude the land use called for by a developer. If the proposed use is not authorized by the general plan, it may be possible to secure an amendment to the plan that would enable the proposed development to proceed. A general plan, however, may be amended to preclude a proposed land use.

Moreover, the plan should be consulted as a valuable source of information before a proposed development is begun: the plan indicates the local jurisdiction's policy regarding further growth in the community; when and where public facilities will be provided and what, if any, contribution toward these facilities must be made by the developer; and whether the developer will be required to provide or contribute to construction of necessary infrastructure (e.g. roads, sewers, etc.).

OTHER REQUIREMENTS Although a proposed land use may comply with a jurisdiction's existing general plan, that fact alone does not guarantee that specific development will be allowed. Most jurisdictions employ other planning requirements in addition to those embodied in the general plan. These additional requirements are contained in specific plans—also called special, area, or community plans. Specific plans typically pertain to only a portion of the jurisdiction's area. Such plans may concern downtown areas subject to redevelopment efforts. They may deal with special environmental concerns in an area or anticipated public transportation needs arising from population growth in the area. Because a proposed development must comply with all applicable specific requirements, a developer should refer to specific plans, when they exist, along with the general plan before beginning any land development.

In addition to complying with the general plan and any applicable specific plans, a proposed development must not entail a particular land use that violates a zoning ordinance.

Zoning

Zoning ordinances are generally part of a zoning law. A typical **zoning law** consists of both an ordinance and a zoning map. The **zoning ordinance** specifies the restrictions on land use to which an area is subject. The **zoning map** indicates the characteristics of each parcel of land within the jurisdiction. The term **zoning** refers more generally to the dividing of a jurisdiction into districts for which specific land-use regulations, or zoning ordinances, are applicable.

Zoning restrictions are generally of two types. First, the restriction may pertain to the kind of land use—such as commercial versus residential—to which property within a particular district may be put. Second, the restriction may dictate the structural features and/or architectural design required of any building erected on property within the particular district. Both types of restrictions are utilized in traditional zoning schemes as well as in more recent schemes employed in land-use control.

FLOATING ZONES Generally, the agency charged with the responsibility of land-use planning can take one of two approaches. The first is to designate, all at one time, use restrictions on each parcel of land located within the entire area to be zoned (usually a city or town). Alternatively, the agency can use **floating zones**, deciding initially how much land should be designated for each

of a variety of particular uses (commercial, residential, park, and farming) and later assigning such designations at the request of landowners. The floating zone concept allows for flexibility in zoning and reduces arbitrariness.

HOLDING ZONES A jurisdiction may not be prepared to comprehensively zone all the land under its control at one time. To preserve some portions of the entire area, a planning agency may temporarily zone the land so as permit only limited development or a low level of intensity of uses. These zones are commonly referred to as **holding zones**. This permits planners to more thoroughly consider the use to which such areas should be put and to await later developments before committing the areas to any one particular use. Note, however, that planning authorities are not permitted to impose holding restrictions on land merely to preserve the land as open space without paying for it; holding zones must be based on a sincere effort by the planning authorities to preserve the land until such time as it may be used most effectively and consistently within the community's general, or master, plan.

SPOT ZONING One method that the agency charged with zoning an area may not use is **spot zoning.** Zoning ordinances are to apply to all property within the zone. Spot zoning occurs when an agency grants a parcel of land a classification different from the one it grants to surrounding property, if the difference between the classifications neither falls within the comprehensive zoning plan nor can be justified on the basis of health, safety, morals, or the community's general welfare. For example, spot zoning might involve granting an owner the right to construct a smelter in a residential neighborhood or limiting an owner to erecting a structure no higher than two stories when the surrounding buildings are fifty-story skyscrapers.

TRADITIONAL TYPES OF ZONING The variety of forms of zoning restrictions reflects the myriad uses to which land may be put and the countless variations possible in designing structures that may be erected on a parcel of land. Perhaps the single common feature among the various types of zoning is that whatever restriction is imposed, absent some special consideration, it must be applied uniformly throughout the district.

Use Zoning Districts are typically zoned for residential, commercial, industrial, or agricultural use. Each such designated district may be further subdivided as to the degree or intensity of such use. For example, districts zoned for residential use are subdivided according to whether multifamily housing units or single family units will be permitted in the district. If a particular district allows multifamily units, the district may be further restricted according to the number of families each distinct unit may house.

Commercial and industrial uses are often zoned according to whether the district permits *heavy* or *light* activity. A zoning for heavy industrial use might permit construction and operation of large steel factories within the district. A zoning for light commercial use might limit land use within the district to such commercial activities as operating professional office buildings or small retail shops. Zoning that specifies the use to which property may be put is referred to as **use zoning.**

Bulk Zoning Bulk regulations, also called land-coverage restrictions, are a common form of zoning. Such zoning is typically referred to as **bulk zoning**. Bulk zoning takes on a variety of forms, including minimum floor-space requirements and minimum lot-size restrictions. Minimum floor-space specifications pertain to area dimensions required for floor space in a building constructed in the district. For example, a district might require that each one-story building contain a minimum of 770 square feet of floor space while each two-story building contain at least 1000 square feet. A minimum lot-size requirement specifies the smallest lot upon which a building in the district may stand. For example, such a zoning ordinance might require that each single family dwelling be built on land at least one acre in size.

Another type of bulk zoning relates to what is called "setback." The setback is the distance between a building and a street, sidewalk, or other boundary. For example, a front setback of 50 feet requires a building to be 50 feet from the street or sidewalk bordering the front of the property. A side-yard setback dictates the distance that must be maintained between the building and the edge of adjacent property; such a restriction ensures that buildings in the district are detached from one another. In addition to setback requirements, zoning ordinances usually require that a building not occupy the entire lot. These are referred to as open-space requirements because they mandate a minimum percentage of land—as much as 80 percent in some suburban areas—that must be preserved.

Another type of ordinance is the cluster zoning ordinance. **Cluster zoning** permits the owner or developer of several parcels of land to comply with all bulk requirements on the basis of an entire development rather than each single lot. Thus, even though an individual lot may not comply with each ordinance, the developer's or owner's land use may yet be permissible under a cluster ordinance. For example, buildings may be constructed too close together for the individual lots to comply with a setback restriction. The plan nevertheless may be allowed under a cluster ordinance if the lots comply with the zoning ordinances on an aggregate basis, say, by including an amount of open space that equals the amount that would result if the setback restrictions had been satisfied.

Height Zoning Districts may also be zoned so as to restrict or regulate the permissible height of buildings constructed on property within a certain area. Typically a jurisdiction will set different height requirements for buildings and even houses located in different regions. The imposition of such restrictions is commonly referred to as **height zoning**. These limits may or may not coincide with the use and bulk restrictions in place for the particular district.

PROTECTION FROM UNDULY BURDENSOME ZONING RESTRICTIONS Zoning, like all government regulation, tends to be inflexible. Inflexibility stems partly from the need to create uniform standards. It also stems from the inability to construct regulations that deal comprehensively with each contingency that may arise in the future. This latter aspect can be particularly burdensome in the area of zoning. Property development usually requires considerable investments in resources and considerable time to be brought to fruition. Thus, there must be continuity in the zoning restrictions that are applied to an area. But, at the same time, conditions are constantly in flux. Communities grow; new commercial demands arise. These and other events may create conflicts when property is subject to existing zoning restrictions. Several mechanisms are employed to balance the need for uniformity and continuity against the need for sufficient flexibility to meet changing conditions concerning land use. The two most common mechanisms are the zoning variance and the process of rezoning.

Zoning Variances As noted above, a landowner whose land has been limited by a zoning ordinance to a particular use cannot make an alternative use of the land unless he or she first obtains a **zoning variance**. A zoning variance permits the owner to engage in some land use that does not comply with existing zoning ordinances. The variance may concern a use restriction, such as a request to construct a bakery shop in a residential zone. Alternatively, the variance may relate to a bulk or height regulation, such as a request for a waiver of the height restriction so that a two-story dwelling may be constructed in a zone prohibiting structures that exceed one floor. Some jurisdictions do not permit variances in use zoning. Other jurisdictions impose stricter requirements before granting variances in use zoning as opposed to variances in bulk or height restrictions.

Most zoning laws provide the means by which a property owner may seek a zoning variance when strict enforcement of an existing ordinance would cause an unreasonable hardship on the owner because of some unique feature associated with the owner's property. A request for a zoning variance is generally made to the board of adjustment, the governmental body that oversees conditional uses and special exceptions. In general, a landowner must meet three criteria to be entitled to a variance:

1. The landowner must find it impossible to realize a reasonable return on the land as zoned.
2. The adverse effect of the zoning ordinance must be particular to the person seeking the variance and not one that has a similar effect on the other landowners within the same zone.
3. Granting of the variance must not substantially alter the essential character of the zoned area.

With regard to the first criterion, it is not sufficient to show that a property would have a greater value absent the zoning restriction; rather, to obtain a variance, it must be shown that the zoning requirement imposes an *undue* hardship on the owner. Hardship generally equates to a deprivation of privileges enjoyed by owners of other property subject to the same restrictions; the hardship must be the result of some unique feature of the property for which the variance is sought, such as its location or topography. Moreover, the hardship may not be the result of the owner's own actions. For example, the owner may not erect a large house and then expect to be granted a variance because the property is too small to meet the open space or setback requirement.

Of the three criteria listed above, perhaps the most important is whether the variance would substantially alter the character of the neighborhood. Courts tend to be more lenient about the first two requirements listed above when reviewing decisions by adjustment boards. As the following case illustrates, courts also tend to defer to the discretion of such boards unless the board clearly has abused its authority.

BACKGROUND AND FACTS *The city of Moline planned to build a new firehouse on land that was appropriately zoned for construction of a firehouse. The proposed firehouse, however, was slightly larger than the zoning ordinances permitted. Thus, in April 1963, Moline filed with the Board of Zoning Adjustment of St. Louis County for variances from the setback and building-line provisions in the ordinance. Alfred and Marie Conner, who owned property adjacent to the site of the new construction, objected to the variance. The variance was granted, and the Conners appealed the board's ruling to the courts.*

Case 23.3
CONNER v. HERD
Court of Appeals of Missouri, 1970.
452 S.W.2d 272.

SMITH, Commissioner.

* * * *

* * * [T]he heart of this appeal [is] appellants' contention that the action of the Board was not based on competent and substantial evidence and was arbitrary and capricious. Neither this court nor the trial court can substitute its judgment on the evidence for that of the Board. We may only determine whether the Board could reach the conclusion it did upon the evidence before it. We hold it could.

* * * *

The most efficient and satisfactory type of fire station for Moline's purposes is one where returning trucks can enter the back of the station from Clairmont Drive, remove the hoses and other equipment for cleaning, put clean equipment on the truck and move the truck into position for exit through the front onto Chambers Road for the next call. * * * There was also testimony that having the station located nearer the road than the old station would allow greater traffic safety in leaving the station in that both the dispatcher and the driver would have greater visibility along Chambers. * * *

The width of the lot is such that a 2 foot variance on the building line of Clairmont Drive would be necessary to get the proposed fire station on the property if the regulation of a 6 foot side yard on the west (next to appellants) is met. The granted variance is less than the previously existing encroachment.

* * * *

The Board could find here that in the absence of a variance Moline would be confronted with substantial additional expense, interruption of fire protection service during the period of construction, and unnecessary inconvenience if not outright danger to the residents of the district. The Board is not required to ignore the source of the funds available to the district (taxpayers) in determining that additional expense constitutes an unnecessary hardship. Under *Rosedale-Skinker,* there exist sufficient ''practical difficulties'' and ''unnecessary hardships'' to the district to permit a variance and these arise from the inadequate size of the lot to contain a fire station. This was the essence of the Board's finding ''that because of the requirements, the proposed new building and facilities cannot be erected as the eighty foot set back line on Chambers Road and the thirty foot building line on Clairmont Drive are intended.''

* * * *

The effect on general welfare finding is supported by the evidence of the need for the new building to render adequate fire protection to the district and by the testimony on the beneficial effect of the proposed construction upon traffic safety on Chambers Road, including the installation of a traffic light on Chambers Road to be controlled by the dispatcher when trucks leave the station.

DECISION AND REMEDY   *The court held that the zoning board had enough evidence to grant the variance in accordance with the requirements of the zoning ordinance. The judgment of the circuit court, which had affirmed the action taken by the zoning board, was affirmed by the appellate court.*

Rezoning   An alternative means of seeking an exemption from existing zoning requirements is through **rezoning**. Rezoning differs from a variance in that the former must be obtained directly from those with ultimate authority over such local matters—usually the city or county board of commissioners—rather than the agencies charged with implementing land-use policy, either the planning board or the adjustment board. A rezoning petition is a request that the zoning ordinances be amended or that a parcel be rezoned to permit a particular use or structural feature.

Rezoning is, in effect, a legislative act, which is subject to judicial review. As in other forms of judicial review of legislative acts, review here is technically limited to inquiry into whether the rezoning exceeds the local agencies' authority, is an abuse of agency discretion, or in some way conflicts with constitutional or other federal or state legal requirements. If none of these deviations are apparent, the agency's decision should be upheld regardless of other considerations; that is, a court should not substitute its discretion for that of the agency on matters of pure policy.

Although, in theory, review of all zoning decisions is to follow the narrow limitations of review of any legislative act, courts tend to scrutinize rezoning decisions more closely. Some courts have required a showing of either a mistake in the original ordinance or a subsequent change in conditions before allowing an amendment to the ordinance or a rezoning plan to be put into effect. Other courts look to whether the modification in zoning will be consistent with the general plan and its effects on the surrounding community. Still other courts have questioned the scope of the rezoning. If the boundaries within which the rezoning applies are too narrowly drawn, the rezoning may be condemned as an impermissible attempt to engage in spot zoning.

Subdivision Regulation

When a developer seeks to subdivide a parcel of land into smaller plots, the developer may be required to comply with certain regulations imposed by the local authority. Subdivision regulation is different from zoning and is usually carried out under the authority of a separate enabling statute, though it may be administered by the same local agencies that oversee the zoning process. This form of land-use control also differs from zoning in that it lacks the same definite standards imposed by zoning restrictions.

Formation of the subdivision typically takes shape according to a process of give and take between the developer and the local authorities. For example, the authorities may demand rearrangement of the proposed layout to allow for public parks or schools. The developer may be required to construct streets that will accommodate a specific level of traffic. Ultimately, the developer must comply with both subdivision ordinances and zoning restrictions applicable to the area in which the development is located.

Developers are frequently required to dedicate parts of the subdivision or pay a fee in lieu of land

dedication for things such as parks and public facilities. In judging whether the local authorities are within their discretion in making such demands, some reviewing courts require that the dedication or fee be specifically and uniquely necessary for the needs of the subdivision. Other courts require only a reasonable relationship between the required dedication and the benefit of the subdivision. Thus, a local demand that a developer set aside space for a public hospital that would serve the entire community as well as the subdivision would be permissible under this latter test but not under the ''specifically and uniquely necessary'' test.

Growth Management

To prevent population growth from racing ahead of the community's ability to provide necessary public services, local authorities may limit the number of residential building permits issued. A property owner may thus be precluded from constructing a residential building on his or her property notwithstanding the fact that the area is zoned for such use and that the proposed structure complies with all other zoning requirements. The growth-management ordinance may prohibit the issuance of residential building permits for a specific period of time or until the occurrence of a specific event, such as a decline in the total number of residents in the community.

Alternatively, the ordinance may require an owner to amass a certain number of *points* before acquiring a residential building permit. Points are normally determined on the basis of the availability of necessary public services, such as the capacity for drainage in the area, the proximity of hospitals and police stations, or any number of other attributes.

Other Types of Public Control of Land Use

Other forms of public control over land use relate to such things as historical preservation, architectural control, and the overall appearance of the community. Local ordinances may prohibit a property owner's tearing down or remodeling an historic landmark or building on his or her property. Local ordinances may require that all proposed building construction be first approved by a design review board composed of local architects. And frequently, for automobile-driver safety, or even for purely aesthetic reasons, a community will restrict the size and placement of outdoor advertising, such as billboards and signs over business establishments.

Most of these types of land-use restrictions have been upheld by the courts. The United States Supreme Court has held that such land-use regulations do not constitute a taking of an owner's property if the restrictions imposed "substantially advance legitimate state interests" and do not "den[y] an owner economically viable use of his land."[2] The Court's decisions have not set a clear standard for what constitutes a "legitimate state interest" or what connection between the regulation and that state interest satisfies the requirement that the regulation "substantially advance" the state interest. Nonetheless, the implication is that the broad range of governmental purposes and regulations that satisfy these requirements include the newer forms of regulations such as scenic zoning[3] and landmark preservation[4] as well as the more traditional forms discussed earlier such as use and bulk zoning.

Even a regulation that completely deprives an owner of the benefit of his or her property is not necessarily invalid. The government may effect such a limitation as long as the owner receives just compensation. Moreover, the government may take the owner's property outright—provided again that the owner receives just compensation. The governmental right to carry out such a "taking" is premised on the doctrine of eminent domain.

_____

2. *Agins v. Tiburon,* 447 U.S. 255, 100 S.Ct. 2138, 65 L.Ed. 2d 106 (1980).
3. Id.
4. *Penn Central Transportation Co. v. New York City,* 438 U.S. 104, 98 S.Ct. 2646, 57 L.Ed.2d 631 (1978).

Condemnation

As noted above, governments have an inherent power to take property for public use or purpose without the consent of the owner. This is the power of eminent domain, and it is very important in the public control of land use.

Every property owner holds his or her interest in land subject to a superior interest. Just as in medieval England the king was the ultimate landowner, so in the United States the government retains an ultimate ownership right in all land. This right, known as eminent domain, is sometimes referred to as the *condemnation power* of the government to take land for public use. It gives a right to the government to acquire possession of real property in the manner directed by the Constitution and the laws of the state whenever the public interest requires it. Property may not be taken for private benefit, but only for public use.

For example, when a new public highway is to be built, the government must decide where to build it and how much land to condemn. After the government determines that a particular parcel of land is necessary for public use, it brings a judicial proceeding to obtain title to the land. Then, in another proceeding, the court determines the *fair value* of the land, which is usually approximately equal to its market value.

The distinction between a rule or ordinance that merely restricts land use and an outright taking is crucial. A restriction is simply an exercise of the state's general police power; even though it limits a property owner's land use, the owner need not be compensated for the limitation. An ordinance that completely deprives an owner of use or benefit of property, or an outright governmental taking of property, however, must be compensated. The following case concerns the distinction between a condition on the use of property and a taking of the property.

Case 23.4

NOLLAN v. CALIFORNIA COASTAL COMMISSION

Supreme Court of the United States, 1987.
438 U.S. 825,
107 S.Ct. 3141,
97 L.Ed.2d 677.

BACKGROUND AND FACTS   *The Nollans sought a permit to demolish an existing single-story dwelling situated on their beachfront property and to erect in its place a two-story, three-room structure approximately three times larger than the existing one. The California Coastal Commission approved the proposed construction but conditioned its approval on the Nollans' dedicating a strip of their land along the beach for public use. Specifically, the strip of land running adjacent to the water's edge along the beach was to be used for a public-access walkway to connect public beaches lying to the north and south of the Nollans' property. The com-*

mission based its ruling on its factual findings that the proposed construction would obstruct the public's view of the ocean, increase private use of the beach, and create a "psychological barrier" to the public's access to the public beaches lying on each side of the Nollans' property. The Nollans went ahead with the proposed construction but challenged the commission's decision as a governmental taking of private property for public use without compensation. The commission contended that the condition was not an outright taking but merely a restriction on use. The case ultimately was brought before the United States Supreme Court.

SCALIA, Justice.

*   *   *   *

Had California simply required the Nollans to make an easement across their beachfront available to the public on a permanent basis in order to increase public access to the beach, rather than conditioning their permit to rebuild their house on their agreeing to do so, we have no doubt there would have been a taking. To say that the appropriation of a public easement across a landowner's premises does not constitute the taking of a property interest but rather, *   *   * "a mere restriction on its use," is to use words in a manner that deprives them of all their ordinary meaning. *   *   * "[O]ur cases uniformly have found a taking to the extent of the occupation, without regard to whether the action achieves an important public benefit or has only minimal economic impact on the owner." We think a "permanent physical occupation" has occurred, for purposes of that rule, where individuals are given a permanent and continuous right to pass to and fro, so that the real property may continuously be traversed, even though no particular individual is permitted to station himself permanently upon the premises.

*   *   * Given, then, that requiring uncompensated conveyance of the easement outright would violate the Fourteenth Amendment, the question becomes whether requiring it to be conveyed as a condition for issuing a land use permit alters the outcome. *   *   *

*   *   * [H]ere, the lack of nexus between the condition and the original purpose of the building restriction converts that purpose to something other than what it was. The purpose then becomes, quite simply, the obtaining of an easement to serve some valid governmental purpose, but without payment of compensation. Whatever may be the outer limits of "legitimate state interests" in the takings and land use context, this is not one of them. In short, unless the permit condition serves the same governmental purpose as the development ban, the building restriction is not a valid regulation of land use but "an out-and-out plan of extortion." *   *   *

*   *   * The Nollans' new house, the Commission found, will interfere with "visual access" to the beach. That in turn (along with other shorefront development) will interfere with the desire of people who drive past the Nollans' house to use the beach, thus creating a "psychological barrier" to "access." The Nollans' new house will also, by a process not altogether clear from the Commission's opinion but presumably potent enough to more than offset the effects of the psychological barrier, increase the use of the public beaches, thus creating the need for more "access." These burdens on "access" would be alleviated by a requirement that the Nollans provide "lateral access" to the beach.

Rewriting the argument to eliminate the play on words makes clear that there is nothing to it. It is quite impossible to understand how a requirement that people already on the public beaches be able to walk across the Nollans' property reduces any obstacles to viewing the beach created by the new house. It is also impossible to understand how it lowers any "psychological barrier" to using the public beaches, or how it helps to remedy any additional congestion on them caused by construction of the Nollans' new house. We therefore find that the Commission's imposition of

the permit condition cannot be treated as an exercise of its land use power for any of these purposes. *   *   *
      *   *   *   *
      *   *   * The Commission may well be right that it (the requirement that land along the beach be dedicated to the public) is a good idea, but that does not establish that the Nollans (and other coastal residents) alone can be compelled to contribute to its realization. Rather, California is free to advance its "comprehensive program," if it wishes, by using its power of eminent domain for this "public purpose," but if it wants an easement across the Nollans' property, it must pay for it.

DECISION AND REMEDY   *The Supreme Court concluded that the Coastal Commission's imposed condition, that the Nollans' property include a public right-of-way, was not rationally related to its asserted interest in reducing obstacles to viewing the public beaches, lowering psychological barriers to use of public beaches, or eliminating congestion on public beaches. Though, as the court said, such right-of-ways might be a good idea, the state's imposing them on property owners would amount to an outright taking of property—which, under the Fourteenth Amendment and, by incorporation, the Fifth Amendment, required that the state justly compensate the owners for the taking.*

■ Private Control of Land Use

The remaining source of land-use control arises out of voluntary agreements reached between private individuals. By agreement, an individual may limit the way in which a landowner uses his property or acquires rights, for example, to cross the landowner's property. These so-called *nonpossessory interests* serve to limit the uses to which private property can be put. We examine the ways in which nonpossessory interests serve as a mechanism for private control of land use.

Nonpossessory Interests

Some interests in land do not include any rights of possession. These **nonpossessory interests,** include *easements, profits,* and *licenses.*

EASEMENTS AND PROFITS Easements and profits are similar, and the same rules apply to both. An **easement** is the right of a person to make limited use of another person's property without taking anything from the property. An easement, for example, can be the right to walk across another's property. In contrast, a **profit** is the right to go onto land in possession of another and take away some part of the land itself or some product of the land. For example, Owen, the owner of Sandy View,

gives Ann the right to go there and remove all the sand and gravel that she needs for her cement business. Ann has a profit. The difference between an easement and a profit is that an easement merely allows a person to use land without taking anything from it, whereas a profit allows a person to take something from the land. Easements and profits can be classified as either *appurtenant* or *in gross.*

Easement or Profit Appurtenant An **easement appurtenant** arises when the owner of one piece of land has a right to go onto an adjacent piece of land owned by another. Suppose Owen, the owner of Whiteacres, has a right to drive his car across Green's land, Greenacres, which is adjacent to Whiteacres. This right-of-way over Greenacres is an easement appurtenant to Whiteacres and can be used only by the owner of Whiteacres. Owen, however, can convey the easement to another when he conveys Whiteacres.

A **profit appurtenant** arises when an owner of one piece of land has the right to take some part or some product of an adjacent piece of land owned by another. For instance, if Owen is entitled to go onto and draw water from a well located on Green's land, Owen enjoys a profit appurtenant because Green's land (Greenacres) is situated adjacent to Owen's land (Whiteacres). In most respects, the rights and limitations of profits appurtenant are identical to those of easements appurtenant. Only Owen enjoys the profit appurtenant, for instance. But as with the easement appurtenant, Owen may convey the profit appurtenant to another as part of a conveyance of Whitcacres.

Easement or Profit in Gross   An **easement in gross** exists when the right to use another's land does not depend on the holder of the easement owning a tract of land adjacent to the burdened land. When a utility company is granted an easement to run its power lines across another's property, it obtains an easement in gross because it will not typically own an adjacent parcel of land.

Similarly, a **profit in gross** does not depend on the holder of the profit's owning a piece of land adjacent to the piece on which the profit exists. For example, suppose Owen owns a parcel of land with a marble quarry. Owen conveys to XYZ Corporation, which owns no land, the right to come onto his land and remove up to five hundred pounds of marble per day. XYZ Corporation owns a profit in gross.

Effect of Sale of Property.   When a parcel of land that is *benefited* by an easement or profit appurtenant is sold, the property carries the easement or profit along with it. (Recall that easements in gross, by contrast, benefit particular parties, not parcels of land.) Thus, if Owen sells Whiteacres to Thomas and includes in the deed to Thomas the appurtenant right-of-way across Greenacres, Thomas will own both the property and the easement that benefits it.

When a parcel of land that has the *burden* of an easement or profit appurtenant is sold, the new owner must recognize its existence only if he or she knew or should have known of it or if it was recorded in the county public records. Thus, if Owen records his easement across Greenacres in the appropriate county office before Green conveys the land, the new owner of Greenacres will have to allow Owen, or any subsequent owner of Whiteacres, to continue to use the path across Greenacres.

Creation of an Easement or Profit   Profits and easements can be created by *deed* or *will* or by *implication, necessity,* or *prescription.* Creation by *deed* or *will* simply involves the delivery of a deed

or a disposition in a will by the owner of an easement stating that the grantee (the person receiving the profit or easement) is granted the rights in the easement or profit that the grantor had. An easement or profit, however, may be created by *implication* when the circumstances surrounding the division of a parcel of property imply its creation. If Barrow divides a parcel of land that has only one well for drinking water and conveys the half without a well to Dan, a profit by implication arises, because Dan needs drinking water. An easement may also be created by *necessity.* An easement by necessity does not require division of property for its existence. A person who rents an apartment, for example, has an easement by necessity in the private road leading up to it.

An easement may be created by one person's continuously and openly using another's land in a certain manner, even though the owner has not given his or her consent to such use. Such an easement is said to have arisen by *prescription.* For example, if Ann continuously drives over or walks across a specific strip of land belonging to Owen, and if Owen is aware or could have learned of Ann's actions, Ann will acquire a right-of-way on the particular strip of land even though Owen has never formally granted such a right to Ann. Ann's continuous and open use will have created an easement by prescription.

Similarly, if Ann continuously and openly goes onto Owen's land and extracts gravel from a rock pit situated there, Ann will after a certain period of time acquire a profit by prescription.

Termination of an Easement or Profit   An easement or profit can be terminated, or extinguished, in several ways. The simplest way is to deed it back to the owner of the land that is burdened by it. Another way is to abandon it and create evidence of intent to relinquish the right to use it. Mere nonuse will not extinguish an easement or profit *unless it is accompanied by an intent to abandon.* Finally, when the owner of an easement or profit becomes the owner of the property burdened by it, then it is merged into the property.

LICENSES   A **license** is the revocable right of a person to come onto another person's land. It is a personal privilege that arises from the consent of the owner of the land and that can be revoked by the owner. A ticket to attend a movie at a theater is an example of a license. If a theater owner issues a ticket entitling the holder to enter the property of the owner and Ann subsequently acquires the ticket and is refused entry into the theater, she has no right to force her way into the theater. The ticket is only a revocable license, not a conveyance of an interest in property.

Covenants Running with the Land

A **covenant running with the land** goes with the land and cannot be separated from it. A covenant runs with the land when the original parties *and* their successors, as opposed to the original parties alone, will be entitled to its benefit or burdened with its obligation. In other words, its benefit or obligation passes with the land's ownership.

Consider an example. Owen is the owner of Grasslands, a twenty-acre estate whose northern half contains a small reservoir. Owen wishes to convey the northern half to Arid City, but before he does, he digs an irrigation ditch connecting the reservoir with the lower ten acres, which he uses as farmland. When Owen conveys the northern ten acres to Arid City, he enters into an agreement with the city. The agreement, which is contained in the deed, states, ''Arid City, its heirs and assigns, promises not to remove more than five thousand gallons of water per day from the Grasslands reservoir.'' Owen has created a *covenant running with the land* under which Arid City and all future owners of the northern ten acres of Grasslands are limited as to the amount of water they can draw from its reservoir.

The four requirements listed below must be met for a covenant running with the land to be enforceable. If they are not met, the covenant will apply to the two original parties to a contract only and will not run with the land to future owners.

1. The covenant running with the land must be created in a written agreement (covenant). It is usually contained in the document that conveys the land.
2. The parties must intend that the covenant *run with the land.* In other words, the instrument that contains the covenant must state not only that the promisor is bound by the terms of the covenant but that all the promisor's ''successors, heirs, or assigns'' will be bound.

3. The covenant must *touch and concern* the land. That is, limitations on the activities of the owner of the burdened land must have some connection with the land. For example, a purchaser of land cannot be bound by a covenant requiring him or her to drive only Ford pickups, because such a restriction has no relation to the land purchased.
4. The original parties to the covenant must be in **privity of estate** at the time the covenant is created. This requirement means that the parties to the covenant must have some close, direct, or successive connection related to the property involved. Relationships such as those of landlord and tenant, or vendor and purchaser result in privity of estate. Landlord and tenant share a direct relationship, the latter being in possession of land owned by the former. A vendor and purchaser have a successive relationship, the former's ownership of the land having immediately preceded the latter's.

Equitable Servitudes

Because there is some confusion over the meaning and application of the privity of estate requirement, covenants running with the land have not always been an effective device for guiding the development of residential and commercial land. Therefore, courts of equity have utilized an alternative means of private land-use control known as **equitable servitudes.** The most significant difference between covenants running with the land and equitable servitudes is that privity of estate is not required for enforcement of an equitable servitude.

An equitable servitude is created by an instrument that complies with the Statute of Frauds (see Chapter 9), an intention that the use of land be restricted, and *notice* of the restriction to the person acquiring the burdened land. The notice may be constructive.

For example, in the course of developing a fifty-lot suburban subdivision, Levitt records a declaration of restrictions that effectively limits construction on each lot to one single-family house. In each lot's deed is a reference to the declaration with a provision that the purchaser and his or her successors are bound to those restrictions. Thus, each purchaser assumes ownership with notice of the restrictions. If an owner attempts to build a duplex (or any structure that does not comply with the restrictions) on a lot, the other owners may obtain a court order enjoining the construction.

In fact, Levitt might simply have included the restrictions on the subdivision's map, filed the map in the appropriate public office, and included a reference to the map in each deed. In this way, each owner would have been held to have constructive notice of the restrictions.

Equitable servitudes and covenants that comply with the requirements just described for each are generally upheld by the courts. As is the case with all contractual arrangements, however, servitudes and covenants that violate public policy are deemed unenforceable. For instance, equitable servitudes and covenants running with the land have sometimes been used to perpetuate neighborhood segregation. Because such discrimination is against the law, these types of servitudes and covenants

have been invalidated by the courts. In the United States Supreme Court case of *Shelley v. Kraemer*,[5] restrictive covenants proscribing resale to minority groups were declared unconstitutional and thus no longer enforceable in courts of law. In addition, the Civil Rights Act of 1968 (also known as the Fair Housing Act) prohibits all discrimination based on race, color, religion, or national origin in the sale and leasing of housing.

Other types of restrictions are not as obviously unenforceable. In such cases, courts ascertain the parties' intent, the notice given, and other aspects of the transaction in determining whether a particular restriction on land use is valid. In the following case, the court had to decide whether a restrictive covenant prohibiting any "outside radio, television, Ham [short-wave] broadcasting, or other electronic antenna or aerial" was intended to prohibit satellite dishes, even though such dishes were not in use at the time the covenant was drafted.

---

5. 334 U.S. 1, 68 S.Ct. 836, 92 L.Ed. 1161 (1948).

BACKGROUND AND FACTS *Claudia Churchill installed a satellite dish in the backyard of her residence, which was located in a residential subdivision called the Piedmont Subdivision. The Piedmont Subdivision was subject to a restrictive covenant that provided in part as follows: "No outside radio, television, Ham broadcasting, or other electronic antenna or aerial shall be erected or placed on any structure or on any lot. If used, any such antenna or aerial shall be placed in the attic of the house or in any other place in the house where it will be concealed from public view from any side of the house." Roy Breeling and a number of other homeowners in the subdivision filed an action, asking that Churchill be required to remove the satellite dish. The trial court held that the covenant applied to the satellite dish, even though such dishes were not in use in the early 1970s when the covenant was drafted. The court therefore granted the homeowners' request and ordered Churchill to remove the dish from her property. Churchill appealed.*

Case 23.5

BREELING v. CHURCHILL

Supreme Court of Nebraska, 1988.
228 Neb. 596,
423 N.W.2d 469.

CHEUVRONT, District Judge.
    *   *   *   *

A restrictive covenant is to be construed in connection with the surrounding circumstances, which the parties are supposed to have had in mind at the time they made it; the location and character of the entire tract of land; the purpose of the restriction; whether it was for the sole benefit of the grantor or for the benefit of the grantee and subsequent purchasers; and whether it was in pursuance of a general building plan for the development of the property.

The restrictive covenants of Piedmont, read as a whole, not only specifically prohibit all outdoor antennas, they evidence a broad concern for aesthetics and prohibit many uses of the property within the subdivision which would detract from the appearance of the area as a whole. It is clear that in light of the surrounding circumstances, the character of the entire area, and the purposes of the restrictions, it was intended that structures such as a satellite dish were not to be permitted. We find that the restriction prohibiting all "outside radio, television, Ham broadcasting, or other electronic antenna or aerial" includes a satellite dish.

DECISION AND REMEDY   *The Supreme Court of Nebraska concluded that the trial court was correct in finding that the restrictive covenant prohibited the erection of a satellite dish. The trial court's judgment was thus affirmed.*

■ Terms and Concepts to Review

bulk zoning 550	general plan 548	real property 541
cluster zoning 550	height zoning 550	rezoning 552
covenant running with the land 558	holding zones 549	spot zoning 549
	land-use control 541	use zoning 550
dedication 553	license 557	variances 543
easement 556	nonpossessory interests 556	zoning 549
easement appurtenant 556	personal property 541	zoning law 549
easement in gross 557	privity of estate 558	zoning map 549
eminent domain 542	profit 556	zoning ordinance 549
equitable servitudes 558	profit appurtenant 556	zoning variance 551
floating zones 549	profit in gross 557	

■ Questions and Case Problems

23-1. The county intends to rezone an area from industrial use to residential use. Land within the affected area is largely undeveloped, but nonetheless it is expected that the proposed action will reduce the market value of the affected land by as much as 50 percent. Will landowners be successful in suing to have the action declared a "taking" of their property, entitling them to just compensation?

23-2. In order to prevent population growth from racing ahead of the local government's ability to provide adequate police and fire protection, as well as road development for the increase in traffic, the local planning board imposes an ordinance limiting the issuance of residential building permits to 1,000 per year for the next three years. A property developer who owns several tracts zoned for residential housing and whose development plans comply with all other existing ordinances challenges the ban in court. Will she succeed? Discuss all the relevant issues. What difference would it make whether the developer had already expended considerable resources and taken the last step toward "discretionary approval" of the development project?

23-3. Suppose that as a condition of a developer's receiving approval for constructing a new residential community, the local authorities insist that the developer dedicate, or set aside, land for a new hospital. The hospital would serve not only the proposed residential community but the entire city. If the developer challenges the condition in court, under what standard might the court invalidate the condition?

23-4. Murray owns 640 acres of rural land. A new highway is being built nearby by Ajax Corporation, Inc. Ajax purchases from Murray the rights to build and use a road across Murray's land for construction vehicles to pass over and to remove sand and gravel required to build the highway. A deed is prepared and filed in the county by Ajax. Later, a dispute arises between Murray and Ajax, and Murray refuses Ajax the right to use the road or to remove sand and gravel. Ajax claims its property rights cannot be revoked by Murray. Discuss fully what property rights Ajax has in this matter.

23-5. St. Bartholomew's church building in New York City was built in 1917 in accordance with the designs of the renowned architect Bertram G. Goodhue. In 1928 a terraced, seven-story building known as Community House was completed by associates of Goodhue. This structure was built adjacent to the church building. In 1967, the city of New York designated the church a landmark structure. Some years later, the church administration sought permission to tear down the seven-story structure so as to construct an office building its place. The city denied permission, claiming that the seven-story structure was an integral part of the landmark and a complement to the church building. The church administrators complained that the denial prevented them from carrying out their religious and social objectives. Comment fully on the legal issues involved. [*Rector, Wardens, and Members of Vestry of St. Bartholomew's Church v. City of New York,* 914 F.2d 348 (2nd Cir. 1990)]

23-6. Ogawa, a licensed dentist practicing in Des Peres, Missouri, was interested in acquiring a certain piece of property from which he intended to conduct his dental practice. Ogawa learned from the city's director of public works that the property was zoned "C-1," meaning that it could be put to commercial use. The applicable zoning ordinance allowed such uses as maintaining "offices for pursuit of any lawful business or profession" on property zoned as C-1. Ogawa, however, was also told that his proposed use of the property would require a site plan approved by the Des Peres Planning and Zoning Commission and that he might need to obtain certain variances from the city's board of adjustments. Shortly thereafter, Ogawa purchased the property, but the site plan he later submitted was not approved. In order to obtain approval for his site plan, Ogawa sought certain variances, all of which related to the distances that had to be maintained between the building on the property and its street, side, and back borders. After two hearings, the board of adjustments granted two of the requested variances but denied two others. The board acknowledged that Ogawa had a vested right in using the property as a rental dwelling, because that was a nonconforming use for which the property had been used prior to its having been zoned for C-1 use. Nevertheless, without obtaining all the requested variances, Ogawa was precluded from using the property for his dental practice, as he had originally intended. A considerable number of other lots in the area failed to meet the ordinance restrictions. Does the fact that other lots were suffering from similar zoning problems help or hurt Ogawa's argument to the court that the board's refusal to approve the variances was an abuse of discretion? Did the board's action amount to a "taking" of Ogawa's property? [*Ogawa v. City of Des Peres,* 745 S.W.2d 238 (Mo. App. 1988)]

23-7. Thimons worked as a public accountant. During three months of the year he divided his professional time equally between his business office and an office located in the basement of his residence. During the remaining nine months of the year he conducted business exclusively out of the office located in his home. Thimons's home office included a reception area for meeting clients. Approximately 60 percent of Thimons's income was derived from business conducted at his residence. Thimons's residential property was subject to a restrictive covenant. Language of the covenant stated that the restrictions were to "run and bind the land." One of the restrictions was that the land was not to be used "for any purpose other than residential uses." Grasso and some of Thimons's other neighbors brought suit seeking to enjoin Thimons's use of his property for an office. Thimons countered that "residential uses," stated in the plural, included his partial use of his residence as an accounting office. What factors must the court consider in the case? Which side is likely to prevail, and why? [*Grasso v. Thimons,* 384 Pa. Super. 593, 559 A.2d 925 (Pa. Superior Ct. 1989).]

23-8. Paul and Barbara Sue Flanagan owned property in Alma, Arkansas, which was purchased by the Smiths under an installment land contract. It had been assumed by all previous owners of the property since 1946 that a fence located at the southern end of the property was in fact the southern boundary of the property. Over the years, all owners had maintained and generally exercised dominion over the property up to the fence. In 1985, when Jerry and Mildred Hicks purchased a lot bordering the southern side of the Flanagan property, a survey showed that the true boundary was approximately eleven feet north of the existing fence. The Hicks asked the Smiths to remove the fence, but they refused to do so. The Hicks then brought an action to compel their neighbors to remove the fence. What will the court decide? Discuss fully. [*Hicks v. Flanagan,* 30 Ark.App. 53, 782 S.W.2d 587 (1990)]

23-9. Michael's Prescriptions was a drugstore located in Detroit. The store had been in operation for over forty years when it was condemned as part of a renovation project covering 465 acres in an area of Detroit known as Poletown. A jury awarded the store's owner $275,000 for the city's taking of the property. The judgment included compensation for the loss of the goodwill the owner had acquired over the years during which the pharmacy operated in Poletown. The city appealed the judgment, arguing that the trial court had erred in ruling that the jury could consider evidence of loss of goodwill in making its determination of the proper award. Who will prevail on appeal? [*City of Detroit v. Michael's Prescriptions,* 373 N.W. 219 (Mich. App. 1985)]

23-10. A Question of Ethics

Lorenz and his wife purchased a home in Florrissant, Missouri. Although the title to the property did not indicate it, the home had been designated as a landmark building. Lorenz later sought a variance that would have allowed him to make certain building changes, such as the installation of vinyl siding on the home. The local council denied the request. Lorenz later learned that the Weslings, an elderly couple whose home was also designated as a landmark building, had been granted a variance similar to the one Lorenz had sought. Lorenz argued that the discrepancy demonstrated that the council's decision had been arbitrary and capricious. The council members contended that they were within their discretion in allowing the Weslings' variance because of the Weslings' advanced ages and because the Weslings had apparently been unaware of the ordinance at the time they made their modifications. A judicial review upheld the council's actions as being a proper exercise of discretion. [Lorenz v. City of Florrissant, 787 S.W.2d 776 (Mo. App. 1990)]

1. Were the Weslings and Lorenz "similarly situated," as Lorenz argued? Lorenz offered evidence that he, too, suffered from physical hardship, but that evidence was contradicted by other evidence. Nonetheless, should the council have limited its inquiry and based its decision solely on property-related issues?

2. Given that the underlying rationale of all zoning and other forms of land-use control is the well-being of the community, did not the council do the ethically "right thing" by allowing special consideration for the Weslings? Alternatively, was Lorenz bearing a disproportionate share of the burden by being denied an identical variance? After all, the city could have uniformly enforced the ordinance and simply used tax dollars collected from the community to pay for the Weslings to change the structure of their home so as to comply with the zoning ordinance. In this way the landmarks would have been conserved *and* the Weslings would have been protected from hardship due to their advanced ages.

23-11. Case Briefing Assignment

Examine Case A.23 [Weihl v. Wagner, 155 Ill. Dec. 297, 569 N.E.2d 297 (Ill. App. 1991)] in Appendix A. The case has been excerpted there in considerable detail. Review and then brief the case, making sure that you include answers to the following questions in your brief.

1. Under Illinois law, how is an easement by prescription obtained?
2. What facts and circumstances were pointed to as support for Weihl's claim that he had acquired an easement over Wagner's land?
3. What arguments were advanced by Wagner to rebut Weihl's claim?
4. What was the court's view of Wagner's arguments?

Focus on Ethics

Government Regulation

Government regulation is pervasive in our economic and legal systems. It includes consumer protection, environmental protection, antitrust law, securities regulation, and other issues. In all areas of government regulation, one can ask the question: Why does government regulation exist? Pure capitalist ideology has as its basis a belief that government intervention in the economic system should be minimal. Yet today virtually every area of economic activity is regulated by government. Is this increased government regulation due to a change in the capitalist ideology or to a change in the ethical concerns of society?

Consumer Ethics: Defaulting on Student Loans

Defaulting on student loans seems to be a national epidemic. In recent years, the government has monitored the repayment of these loans more closely than in the past because of the loss in revenues caused by so many defaulting debtors. Occasionally, colleges and universities fight back, too. They do something to try to force former students to pay their government-guaranteed student loans. One such case involved a student, Mr. Juras, who attended Montana State University and took out a student loan to help foot the educational bill.

As it turned out, Juras defaulted on his loan. When the university eventually assigned Juras's loan to a collection agency, the university agreed that it would not release Juras's transcript until he repaid the loan. In other words, the university would deny Juras the major benefit derived from the loan—proof of his degree. When Juras later requested a copy of his transcript, the university kept its word and refused to give it to him.

Juras sued the university, claiming that such a practice was illegal. He reasoned that the university was treating the transcript as a form of security until the loan was paid. Because the National Defense Student Loan Act required lenders to make student loans on an unsecured basis, the university's retention of the transcript was illegal under that act. He argued that the withholding of his transcript was therefore, in essence, an unfair, coercive, and unconscionable debt-collection practice that violated the Fair Debt Collection Practices Act.

The court did not agree with Juras's claims. The university was not acting counter to the National Defense Student Loan law by withholding Juras's transcript. The transcript belonged to the university, not to Juras, and therefore it could not be considered the secured property of another. A security interest cannot arise in property in which the debtor has no interest, and Juras had no ownership rights or other legal interest in the transcript. Nor did the court find that the university had violated any of the provisions of the Fair Debt Collection Practices Act by withholding the transcript. Juras lost on both counts. He would have to pay the loan if he wanted his transcript.[1]

Protecting the Environment

To what extent is business required to concern itself with the conservation of natural resources? Does a company have to wait until it is besieged by protesters before it acts, as in the case of Weyerhaeuser in the Northwest? This forest

---

1. *Juras v. Aman Collection Service, Inc.,* 829 F.2d 739 (9th Cir. 1987).

products company found itself under attack by protesters who accused it of "raping" the forest. It ultimately set up an extensive program of replanting trees and became more selective in its cutting, thereafter cutting in a manner to conserve natural resources.

Business enterprises generally have emphasized the maximization of profits and thus have observed the minimal environmental protections required by law. But the effect of large corporations' activities on the environment has now become a subject of public concern. The fact is, however, that companies typically cannot protect the environment without incurring higher production costs. This result is generally not happily received by stockholders—even those having environmentalist leanings. For example, pollution control clearly involves costs that must be absorbed somewhere—by shareholders, in the form of smaller dividends; by consumers, in the form of higher prices; or by employees, in the form of lower wages.

In a competitive economic system, companies normally cannot be socially responsible alone. If an individual firm tries to accept this responsibility and other firms do not, the results may be lower profits for the socially responsible firm and its eventual demise. Consequently, we can argue that it is because of our competitive system that we require government regulation and that this need is particularly great in the environmental protection area.

But does this mean that it is only through government regulation of all competitors that we will achieve a reduction in the amount of environmental destruction caused by

production processes? Is it possible to combine profit-making activities *and* environmental protection programs? Dow Chemical thought so. That firm devised and implemented a massive program of pollution control directed toward waste reduction and the conservation of raw materials. Manufacturing processes were closely scrutinized to increase operating efficiency, to recycle raw materials formerly vented into the air or lost to the sewer, and to use waste products. Although in its press releases Dow emphasized its good citizenship, it nonetheless profited by these programs. Pollution control meant savings that could be transformed directly into higher company profits.

Competition and Antitrust Laws

Antitrust policy expresses American attitudes toward big business and government. Current antitrust law stems from public concern in the 1880s over large corporate mergers resulting from new technology and improved transportation links. Indeed, in 1888, the major political parties for the first time put antitrust planks in their presidential campaign platforms. From 1889 to 1891, eighteen states enacted antitrust laws. It was not until 1890 that an antitrust bill, which was introduced by John Sherman for the third time, was passed by Congress. A key feature of the Sherman Act is that it allows private individuals to bring suit against those engaging in unlawful anticompetitive practices and allows those injured individuals to recover treble damages if they prevail. In some sense, the Sherman Act and subsequent antitrust

laws have tried to grapple with the problem of the "little person" versus the "big company," which faces our society at all times today.

Ethics versus Economic Efficiency

The Robinson-Patman Act, which amended and strengthened the prohibition against price discrimination in Section 2 of the Clayton Act, has been criticized by lawyers, businesspersons, and economists alike for many years. In principle, this statute was passed to protect the small businessperson from the buying power of chain stores by limiting price concessions granted to powerful buyers. Thus, the statute prohibited price discrimination unless such discrimination was supported by cost savings or was otherwise necessary to meet a competitor's price. In practice, however, the statute has been used on numerous occasions by small stores to extort tribute from large firms. In other words, every time a large operation was able to undercut the price of a smaller operation in the same line of business, the smaller concern entered into antitrust litigation citing violation of the Robinson-Patman Act. This use of the Robinson-Patman Act has been severely criticized as being anticompetitive and therefore contrary to the guiding principle of the antitrust laws, which is to promote competition.

Antitrust Law versus the Promotion of Technological Progress

In the eyes of many, antitrust law has been a hindrance to international competitiveness. Although antitrust laws have been relaxed, and some areas—for example, certain cooperative research and development projects—are now exempt from antitrust laws, some argue that such relaxation should go even further. These critics of U.S. antitrust law favor a change that would allow industry rivals to jointly produce goods such as high-definition television sets and robotics so as to compete effectively in the world market. The basis of this concept is that today companies face skyrocketing development costs, a high cost of capital, and a very short product life cycle. That means that only the largest companies can afford to go it alone. It is probably for these reasons, more than anything else, that large production consortiums are common both in Europe and in Japan. They are prevented in the United States by antitrust law, however.

Insider Trading

Only in the last few years have Americans seen rich, successful financiers end up in jail because of some violation of securities laws. One law prohibits the use of inside information to profit in the trading of shares of stock in the corporation from which the information was gleaned. Even a *tippee* (an outsider) can be liable for insider trading under securities law if the tippee's acquisition of inside information followed from an officer's or director's breach of his or her fiduciary duties. Tippees of tippees (remote tippees) can also be held liable if they knew, or should have known, that they were trading on improperly obtained inside information.

For example, in *SEC v. Musella*,[2] a manager of a law firm passed inside information

about corporate mergers and acquisitions planned by the firm's clients to a friend and the friend's stockbroker. The stockbroker passed the information on to a third party. That third party then shared the information with his brother, a police officer. The police officer then recommended to two other police officers that they purchase certain securities. All parties involved, including the latter two police officers, profited substantially from their investments, and other tips and investments followed. Could the two police officers, who never were told (and never inquired about) the source of the information, be held liable for insider trading as remote tippees? Yes, according to the court. Their liability was founded not on the fact that they *knew* that they were trading on improperly acquired inside information but on the fact that they *should have known* that such was the case. The court held that the two police officers "did not ask because they did not want to know." The fact that they had consciously avoided knowledge about the source of the information did not mean that they were not guilty under laws prohibiting insider trading.

Outsiders trading on inside information are normally held liable for violating securities laws only if the trading is related to a breach of some duty. Recall from Chapter 22 that in *Chiarella v. United States*,[3] Chiarella was not held liable for trading on information obtained in the course of his work as a printer because the court held that no fiduciary duty had been breached. As mentioned in footnote 19 on page 532,

however, had the jury been instructed to find liability under the misappropriation theory, Chiarella might well have been held liable for violating insider trading laws on the basis that he had violated a duty of loyalty to his employer. In a sense, the development of the misappropriation theory of liability has allowed courts to address more directly the simple ethical question: "Is such behavior right?"

Eminent Domain: Public Good versus Individual Rights

All law-abiding citizens accept government regulation, though sometimes begrudgingly. Usually we accept regulation because it is to our benefit to do so. For example, we willingly comply with the restriction that cars are to be driven on the right side of the road, and we expect the government to ensure that everyone else does as well. The benefit is that we have at least some assurance that a car will not be careening into us head-on just over the bend or around the next corner.

Other forms of regulation are not as uniformly beneficial, however. Most of us are glad that the government imposes some form of control over the quality of the food we eat. Food processors, though, confront higher costs because of it. Depending on supply and demand conditions in the food market, some or all of the additional costs may be passed on to consumers. In general, we accept these burdens because we believe that the greater good of the public is served by such regulation. But when the burdens of regulation are not distributed evenly over the population, how far does the

2. 678 F.Supp. 1060 (S.D.N.Y. 1988).

3. 445 U.S. 222, 100 S.Ct. 1108, 63 L.Ed.2d 348 (1980).

sentiment for the greater public good carry us? The question is particularly difficult with regard to the "taking" of land through the government's power of eminent domain.

All cultures exhibit an attitude approaching reverence toward "the land." Not surprisingly, ownership of land is one of the most important issues governments face. Where, as in the United States, private ownership and reverence for land go hand in hand, the very idea of "taking" land is controversial. The aversion most feel toward such acts is mitigated by the requirement that the government justly compensate those who must forfeit land for the "public use." But the sentimental attachment often felt toward particular pieces of land—land on which stands the home to several generations of a family, for example—is seldom compensable. All such takings are made more acceptable by the condition that they be for the public good. But ethically, is it right to have a single individual incur the lion's share of the burden by having to give up his or her parcel of land for the greater good of all? Moreover, who can say without question precisely what the public's interests are and which are so important as to justify the taking of an individual's land.

Some years ago the United States Supreme Court confronted this issue in *Berman v. Parker*.[4] The District of Columbia condemned certain properties for the purpose of urban renewal in the affected area. Controversy arose because the land was subsequently reconveyed to

private developers. How could private development of the land be a "public use" as required by the Constitution? The Court held that "use" meant purpose, not who would *physically* use or occupy the land. Moreover, the clearing of slums to make an area more attractive is a legitimate exercise of governmental police powers. Thus it is considered appropriate to take property through eminent domain to carry out those powers and achieve the governmental purpose.

Under the Court's broad interpretation of the doctrine of eminent domain, land may be taken for purely commercial and industrial development and use. In the same vein, the Supreme Court of Michigan upheld the taking of property not in fact "blighted" by urban decay so that the land could be resold to General Motors which planned to erect a manufacturing plant on the land.[5] The purpose that sustained the taking was the creation of new jobs and creation of a tax base for the local government. It is in the nature of government that select individuals must define for the many what the public good is, what purposes should be pursued, and how they should be achieved. But given the wide latitude for discretion in exercising the power of eminent domain, the best safeguard against abuse in taking private property is that governments strive to act ethically even if they do not face strict legal constraints.

The Economics of Regulation

Most regulation is motivated by the government's concern for

the social welfare. Corporations may be criticized for using technicalities or loopholes to uphold the letter of the law while violating its spirit. Yet regulation is not always an unmitigated blessing, even for its intended beneficiaries.

Consider the example of rent control. Local governments have placed regulations on landlords to prevent them from raising rents and thereby driving out low-income tenants. Most people are sympathetic to this concern, but the long-run implications of rent control must still be considered. Rent control restricts the profitability of investment in residential housing and discourages the construction of new rental units, which may be needed by the community. Some have even suggested that rent control shares some responsibility for the now-major problem of homelessness. Thus, though rent control may have benefits, its full consequences should be explored.

■ Discussion Questions

1. In view of the many consumer protection laws that exist, should corporations have any ethical obligations to consumers beyond the letter of the law? Don't consumers have the responsibility to bargain for any additional protections?
2. Both environmental and occupational safety laws strive to protect the public health from hazardous substances. Should standards in these two contexts be the same? Or should employees be allowed to voluntarily accept some greater risk in return for a higher wage scale?
3. Some government regulation, such as antitrust law,

4.   348 U.S. 26, 75 S.Ct. 98, 99 L.Ed. 57 (1954).

5.   *Poletown Neighborhood Council v. City of Detroit,* 410 Mich. 617, 304 N.W.2d 455 (1981).

may be enforced by private corporations. Are private suits always ethical and proper, or should we consider the motives of the plaintiff company? For example, when MCI won a large antitrust award from AT&T, some suggested that federal courts were being used as part of market competition. Might not companies be using antitrust laws to enhance their own market share and to restrict competition?

4. The securities industry is heavily regulated not only by the Securities and Exchange Commission but also by numerous state securities commissions. In spite of such regulation, unwary investors may lose millions of dollars each year because of the deceptive tactics of a few corporations, stockbrokers, and others involved in the sale of securities. Does this mean that more regulation and enforcement should be required? Why or why not? Alternatively, is "the nature of the beast" such that no amount of regulation will ever fully protect *all* investors? In either case, what are the tradeoffs involved in additional regulation? In other words, what are the costs and benefits of the securities laws and regulations that are enacted or created for the purpose of protecting investors?

5. There are those who argue that hostile takeovers injure employees, officers, and directors of the target companies. Others contend that such takeovers actually benefit the shareholders of target corporations. After all, the latter group would argue, such corporations would not be "targets" if they were properly managed. Discuss the pros and cons of hostile takeovers. What are the costs and benefits of laws that restrict—or make exceedingly difficult—hostile takeovers?

UNIT SIX

The Contemporary Environment

■ The Importance of the Contemporary Environment

The contemporary environment has been shaped by unprecedented innovations and technological advances over the last several years. These innovations have changed not only the array of products available to consumers but also the fundamental ways in which business is conducted. Advances in telecommunications, for example, have led to innovations ranging from the introduction of the cellular phone to the opening up of global financial markets in which currencies are traded around the clock with virtually instantaneous speed. Computer technology similarly has changed everything from the way in which consumers buy goods and services to the way in which businesses produce these goods and services.

Not all of the recent innovations have involved physical technology. One of the most profound developments has been the devising of new financial instruments, such as the "junk bond," for raising capital in financial markets. In this unit we examine three specific developments which have shaped the contemporary environment. First, in Chapter 24, we look at financial transacting. Specifically we examine the functioning of the modern banking system and the innovations that are propelling us increasingly towards a "cashless society." In the same chapter, we discuss legal aspects of lender liability, a recent trend which has profound implications for both borrowers and lenders in the future.

We then turn, in Chapter 25, to an examination of corporate takeovers and mergers. The use of innovative financial instruments, such as the junk bond, for financing massive takeover contests has brought about important changes in the basic corporate structure of American business. In Chapter 25, we examine in detail the legal and financial issues involved in this controversial means of corporate restructuring. Finally, in Chapter 26, we examine the area of intellectual property, paying particular attention to the emerging legal issues relating to computers.

568

■ Ethical Issues in the Contemporary Environment

The rapid pace at which the contemporary environment is constantly changing poses unique challenges to judges and legislators. Many times the changes occur simply too fast for the law to develop adequate standards for the host of problems encountered. In the area of banking, how far should we go in holding bankers responsible for problems faced by their borrowers? While it was once thought that banks held the upper hand in dealing with borrowers, the law of lender liability has reversed that notion 180 degrees. Ethically, it is difficult to say how far such liability should extend.

If a bank demands strict conditions before loaning money, does that amount to the bank's becoming a virtual partner of the borrower? If the bank is treated as a co-participant with the borrower, the bank may find itself liable for many of the borrower's wrongs unrelated to the latter's relationship to the bank itself. Apart from the economic issues raised by this trend, perplexing ethical questions also arise.

In the contemporary environment, perhaps no other topic has generated more controversy in recent years than that of corporate takeovers and mergers. Many saw the unprecedented size and number of takeovers as a manifestation that, indeed, in corporate America, "greed is good." Others saw takeovers as enormously beneficial to society.

Finally, one of the most important issues in the contemporary environment concerns intellectual property. Ideas are the wellspring from which all the innovations we have been discussing flow. How, then, can society both ethically and legally protect those ideas? Innovations generally are the result of sacrifice and strenuous effort. If there is not a great return on those efforts, society will find the wellspring of ideas quickly running dry. The task for society, then, is to encourage innovation by protecting intellectual property.

Chapter 24

Financial Transactions

For centuries, the exchange of goods and services throughout the world has encompassed more than pure barter between individuals. Individuals do not often trade one good for another. Instead they use various means of payment, such as giving cash for goods or services. But cash is only one of many media of exchange; others of varying complexity are used in the modern business environment. Indeed, the widespread use of checks, credit cards, and the like has prompted many to conclude that we live in a ''cashless'' society.

Not only do individuals use various means of payment to effect transactions—whether simple or sophisticated—they also rely on credit; that is, present wants are matched with future income by other individuals' loaning money or advancing goods on the promise that they will be repaid. Because lenders give up present consumption and accept the risk that they might not be repaid, they are compensated by being paid interest A considerable amount of this commercial financing is undertaken by commercial banks.

In this chapter we examine the legal aspects of this important part of the environment of business—the financial transaction. Specifically, we examine the mechanics of the commercial banking system as well as the legal obligations incurred by banks in extending commercial credit (referred to as lender liability).

■ Checks and the Banking System

Checks are a form of *commercial paper*. **Commercial paper** can be defined as any written promise or order to pay a sum of money. Although the most common, checks are just one of several forms of commercial paper. Other types include drafts, certificates of deposit, and promissory notes. Our discussion will focus exclusively on checks and the banking system.

A check is actually a special kind of draft. A **draft** is an unconditional written order from one party to another, instructing the latter to pay money. The money is usually paid to a third party. In the legal terminology of the Uniform Commercial Code (UCC), discussed in Chapter 10, the party issuing the order to pay is the **drawer**. The party who is ordered to pay is the **drawee**, while the party to whom payment is made is the **payee**. For the draft to have validity, of course, the drawee must be obligated to the drawer—either by prior agreement or preexisting debtor-creditor relationship. A *time draft* is a draft that is payable at a definite future time. A *sight* (or *demand*) *draft* is a draft that is payable either on sight (or demand) when the draft is presented for payment or at a specified time after sight. A **check** is a draft that is drawn on a bank and payable on demand. Note, however, that with certain types of checks, the bank is both the drawer and the drawee. For example, a *cashier's check* is drawn by the bank on itself.

Checks, along with credit cards and charge accounts, are rapidly replacing currency as a means of payment in almost all transactions for goods and services. It is estimated that sixty billion personal and commercial checks are written each year in the United States. Checks are more than a daily convenience; checking account balances are an integral part of the economic system.

Checks are governed by both Article 3 and Article 4 of the UCC. The extent to which any party is either charged with or discharged from liability on a check is established according to the provisions of Article 3; Article 3 governs the use of *all* forms of commercial paper, not merely checks. Article 4 is a statement of the principles and rules of modern bank deposit-and-collection procedures. It governs the relationship of banks with one another as they process checks for payment, and it establishes a framework for deposit and checking agreements between a bank and its customers. A check can therefore fall within the scope of Article 3 and yet be subject to the provisions of Article 4 while it is in the course of collection. In the case of a conflict between Articles 3 and 4, Article 4 controls [UCC 4-102(1)].

The Bank-Customer Relationship

The bank-customer relationship begins when the customer opens a checking account and deposits money that will be used to pay for checks written. The rights and duties of the bank and the customer are contractual and depend on the nature of the transaction.

A creditor-debtor relationship is created between a customer and a bank when, for example, the customer makes cash deposits into a checking account or when final payment is received for checks drawn on other banks. A principal–agent relationship underlies the check collection process. A check does not operate as an immediate legal assignment of funds between the drawer and the payee. The money in the bank represented by that check does not move from the drawer's account to the payee's account, nor is any underlying debt discharged until the drawee bank honors the check and makes final payment. In the transfer of checkbook dollars among different banks, each bank acts as the agent of collection for its customer [UCC 4-201(1)]. (Agency relationships were discussed in Chapter 15.)

A commercial bank serves its customers primarily in the following two ways:

1. By honoring checks for the withdrawal of funds on deposit in its customers' accounts.
2. By accepting deposits in U.S. currency and collecting checks written to or indorsed to its customers that are drawn on other banks.

HONORING CHECKS   When a commercial bank provides checking services, it agrees to honor the checks written by its customers with the usual stipulation that there be sufficient funds available in the account to pay each check. When a drawee bank *wrongfully* fails to honor a check, it is liable to its customer for damages resulting from its refusal to pay. The UCC does not attempt to specify the theory under which the customer may recover for wrongful dishonor; it merely states that the drawee is liable. Thus, the drawer–customer does not have to prove that the drawee bank breached its contractual commitment, or slandered the customer's credit, or was negligent [UCC 4-402]. When the bank properly dishonors a check for insufficient funds, it has no liability to the customer.

In contrast, a bank may charge against a customer's account an *overdraft*—that is, a check that is paid from that account even though the account contains insufficient funds to cover the check [UCC 4-401(1)]. Once a bank makes special arrangements with its customer to accept overdrafts on an account, the payor bank can become liable to its customer for damages proximately caused by its wrongful dishonor of overdrafts.

The customer's agreement with the bank includes a general obligation to keep sufficient money on deposit to cover all checks written. In a civil suit, the customer is liable to the payee or to the holder of a check that is not honored. A holder is a person who is in rightful possession of an instrument that is drawn to that person's order (or drawn to bearer) or that is indorsed to that person (or in blank) [UCC 1-201(20)]. If intent to defraud can be proved, the customer can also be subject to criminal prosecution for writing a bad check.

The following case illustrates that when a bank agrees with a customer to pay overdrafts, the bank's refusal to honor checks on an overdrawn account is a wrongful dishonor.

Case 24.1

KENDALL YACHT CORP. v. UNITED CALIFORNIA BANK

Court of Appeal of California, 1975.
50 Cal.App.3d 949,
123 Cal.Rptr. 848.

BACKGROUND AND FACTS *Lawrence and Linda Kendall were officers and the principal shareholders of Kendall Yacht Corporation, a corporation formed to build yachts on special order from customers. The corporation had never issued stock and was in need of operating funds. The corporation had a payroll checking account and a general business checking account with United California Bank. When the corporation ran into financial problems, Mr. Kendall spoke with Ron Lamperts, a loan officer at the bank, in an effort to obtain financing. The bank agreed to honor overdrafts on the corporate account until such time as the corporation was financially more stable. The Kendalls continued to write checks for supplies, payroll, and other corporate operating expenses from about mid-October through December. The corporate bank account was by then badly overdrawn, and a number of the checks had been dishonored by the bank. The Kendalls' business failed, and they later brought a lawsuit against United California Bank, charging that its wrongful dishonor of checks that it had initially agreed to accept as overdrafts had damaged the Kendalls' personal and credit reputation. The trial court held for the Kendalls, and the bank appealed.*

McDANIEL, Associate Justice.
* * * *

During October, November, and December, the Bank honored overdrafts of the Corporation totaling in excess of $15,000. There were also a number of overdrafts written during these months which were not honored by the Bank. Some of these were to suppliers and others were payroll checks to employees. In addition, the Bank failed to honor a check written to Insurance Company of North America to cover a premium for workmen's compensation insurance. The Kendalls were not aware that this check had been ''bounced'' until after one of their employees had been injured and they had been notified by Insurance Company of North America that their insurance had been terminated for nonpayment of premium.

After the collapse of the business, the Kendalls understandably had a number of enemies in the community. They were accused of having breached the trust of their former suppliers and employees and of having milked the Corporation of its funds and placed them in a Swiss bank account. They were repeatedly threatened with legal action and physical harm; they suffered acts of vandalism such as eggs and oil being thrown at their cars. Mr. Kendall's subsequent employer was contacted and threatened by creditors of the Corporation. Criminal charges were brought against Mrs. Kendall for writing checks against insufficient funds; the charges were dismissed shortly before she was brought to trial on them. The Kendalls were required to appear and answer charges in administrative proceedings involving dishonored payroll checks and the Corporation's failure to carry workmen's compensation insurance. Each testified to experiencing severe emotional distress and humiliation as a result of these matters. They also testified to marital problems which were allegedly caused by the stress brought on by the failure of the business.

*   *   *   *

The Bank contends first that under Commercial Code section 4-402 the wrongful dishonor of a check of a *corporation* does not give a cause of action for damages to individual officers and shareholders of the corporation. Commercial Code section 4402, which represents section 4-402 of the Uniform Commercial Code, reads as follows: ''A payor bank is liable to its customer for damages proximately caused by the wrongful dishonor of an item. When the dishonor occurs through mistake liability is limited to actual damages proved.''

[It] was entirely foreseeable that the dishonoring of the Corporation's checks would reflect directly on the personal credit and reputation of the Kendalls and that they would suffer the adverse personal consequences which resulted when the Bank reneged on its commitments.

*   *   *   *

[It] has been held in this state that a cause of action for wrongful dishonor of a check sounds in tort as well as in contract, and ''if the conduct is tortious, damages for emotional distress may be recovered despite the fact that the conduct also involves a breach of contract.''

The appellate court confirmed the trial court's ruling. The Kendalls were awarded $26,000 each as compensatory damages for the bank's wrongful dishonor of the checks.

DECISION AND REMEDY

Stale Checks The bank's responsibility to honor its customers' checks is not absolute. A bank is not obliged to pay an uncertified check—a check not previously accepted by the bank—presented more than six months from its date [UCC 4-404]. Commercial banking practice regards a check outstanding for longer than six months as a **stale check.** UCC 4-404 gives a bank the option of paying or not paying on a stale check. The usual banking practice is to consult the customer, but if a bank pays in good faith without consulting the customer, it has the right to charge the customer's account for the amount of the check.

Missing Indorsements (Signatures) Banking institutions are allowed to supply any necessary indorsements of a customer. (This rule does not apply if the item expressly requires the payee's indorsement.) The depositary bank places a statement on the item to the effect that it was deposited by a customer or credited to that customer's account [UCC 4-205(1)].

Stop-Payment Orders Only a customer can order his or her bank to pay a check, and only a customer can order payment to be stopped. A customer has no right to stop payment on a check that has been certified or that has been accepted by a bank. A stop-payment order must be received within a reasonable time and in a reasonable manner to permit the bank to act on it [UCC 4-403(1)].

A stop-payment order can be given orally, usually by phone.[1] An oral order is binding on the bank for only fourteen calendar days unless confirmed in writing. (See Exhibit 24–1.) A written stop-payment order or an oral order confirmed in writing is effective for six months only, unless renewed in writing [UCC 4-403(2)]. If the stop-payment order is not renewed, the check can be properly cashed, even though it is a stale check.

Should the drawee bank pay the check over the customer's properly instituted stop-payment order, the bank will be obligated to recredit the account of the drawer–customer. The bank, however, is liable for no more than the actual loss suffered by the drawer because of the wrongful payment.

Cashier's checks are sometimes used in the business community as nearly the equivalent of cash. Except in very limited circumstances, payment cannot be stopped on a cashier's check—once

---

1. Some states do not recognize oral stop-payment orders; they must be in writing.

■ **Exhibit 24–1 A Sample Stop-Payment Order**

© 1991 Bank of America reprinted with permission.

it has been issued by a bank, the bank normally must honor it when it is presented for payment.

Overdrafts   As mentioned above, when the bank receives an item properly payable from its customer's checking account but there are insufficient funds in the account to cover the amount of the check, the bank can either dishonor the item or pay the item and charge the customer's account, creating an overdraft [UCC 4-401(1)]. The bank can subtract the difference from the customer's next deposit because the check carries with it an enforceable implied promise to reimburse the bank.

When a check "bounces," a holder can resubmit the check, hoping that at a later date sufficient funds will be available to pay it. The holder must notify any indorsers on the check of the first dishonor; otherwise they will be discharged from their signature liability.

Payment on a Forged Signature of the Drawer   A forged signature on a check has no legal effect as the signature of a drawer [UCC 3-404(1)]. Banks require signature cards from each customer who opens a checking account. The bank is responsible for determining whether the signature on a customer's check is genuine. The general rule is that the bank must recredit the customer's account when it pays on a forged signature.

The bank has no right to recover from a holder who, without knowledge, cashes a check bearing a forged drawer's signature. The holder merely guarantees that he or she has no knowledge that the signature of the drawer is unauthorized. Unless the bank can prove that the holder has such knowledge, its only recourse is against the forger [UCC 4-207(1)(b)].

ACCEPTING DEPOSITS   A second fundamental service a commercial bank provides for its checking account customers is to accept deposits of cash and checks. Cash deposits made in U.S. currency are received into the customer's account without being subject to further collection procedures. As a matter of routine, banks provisionally credit a customer's account for an item when it is first deposited. More than 99 percent of these items are paid, and the credits become final. In cases in which items are not finally paid, banks are allowed to charge back to customers' accounts the amounts that were provisionally paid [UCC 4-212].

In most situations, deposited checks have come from parties who do business at different banks, but sometimes checks are written between customers of the same bank. Either situation brings into play the bank collection process as it operates within the statutory framework of Article 4 of the UCC.

The Collection Process

The first bank to receive a check for payment is the **depositary bank.**[2] When a person deposits his or her IRS tax refund check into a personal checking account at the local bank, that bank acts as a depositary bank. The bank on which a check is drawn (the drawee bank) is called the **payor bank.** Any bank except the payor bank that handles a check during some phase of the collection process is a **collecting bank.** Any bank except the payor bank or depositary bank to which an item is transferred in the course of this collection process is called an **intermediary bank.**

During the collection process, any bank can take on one or more of the above roles. For example, a buyer in New York writes a check on her New York bank and sends it to a seller in San Francisco. The seller deposits the check in her San Francisco bank account. The seller's bank is both a *depositary bank* and a *collecting bank.* The buyer's bank in New York is the *payor bank.* As the check travels from San Francisco to New York, any collecting bank (other than the depositary bank) holding the item in the collection process is an *intermediary bank.*

CHECK COLLECTION BETWEEN CUSTOMERS OF THE SAME BANK An item payable by the depositary bank that receives it is called an ''on-us item.'' If the bank does not dishonor the check by the opening of the second banking day following its receipt, it is considered paid [UCC 4-213(4)(b)]. For example, Harriman and Goldsmith have checking accounts at First National Bank. On Monday morning, Goldsmith deposits into his own checking account a $300 check from Harriman. That same day, First National issues Goldsmith a ''provisional credit'' for $300. When the bank opens on Wednesday, Harriman's check is considered honored and Goldsmith's provisional credit becomes a final payment.

CHECK COLLECTION BETWEEN CUSTOMERS OF DIFFERENT BANKS Once a depositary bank receives a check, it must arrange to present it either directly or through intermediary banks to the appropriate payor bank. Each bank in the collection chain must pass the check on before midnight of the next banking day following its receipt [UCC 4-202(2)]. Thus, for example, a collecting bank that receives a check on Monday must forward it to the next collection bank before midnight on Tuesday. Unless the payor bank dishonors the check or returns it by midnight on the next banking day following receipt, the payor bank is accountable for the face amount of the check [UCC 4-302].

To facilitate an even flow of the many items handled by banks daily, the UCC permits what is called *deferred posting,* or delayed return. Deferred posting permits posting (recording) of checks received after a certain time (say 2:00 P.M.) to be deferred until the next day. Thus, a check received by a payor bank at 3:00 P.M. on Monday would be deferred for posting until Tuesday. In this case, the payor bank's deadline would be midnight Wednesday [UCC 4-301(1)].

THE FEDERAL RESERVE SYSTEM CLEARS CHECKS The Federal Reserve System serves as the central bank of the nation by transferring funds, handling government deposits, and supervising and regulating banks. The twelve Federal Reserve banks act as clearinghouses and agents in the collection of checks and other instruments. This has greatly simplified the clearing of checks—that is, the method by which checks deposited in one bank are transferred to the banks on which they were written. Suppose Samuel Evans of Chicago writes a check to John Lucky of San Francisco. When Lucky receives the check in the mail, he deposits it in his bank. His bank then deposits the check in the Federal Reserve Bank of San Francisco, which sends the check to the Federal Reserve Bank of Chicago. That Federal Reserve Bank then sends the check to Evans's bank, where the amount of the check is deducted from Evans's account. Exhibit 24–2 illustrates this process.

EXPEDITED FUNDS AVAILABILITY ACT In 1987, Congress passed an act to improve the check-processing system and to shorten the period between the time a customer deposits funds and the time the funds are made available to the customer. The major problem Congress addressed in this legislation was the practice by which depositary banks placed a ''hold'' on deposited checks—that is, did

---

2. All definitions in this section are found in UCC 4-105.

■ Exhibit 24–2 How a Check Is Cleared

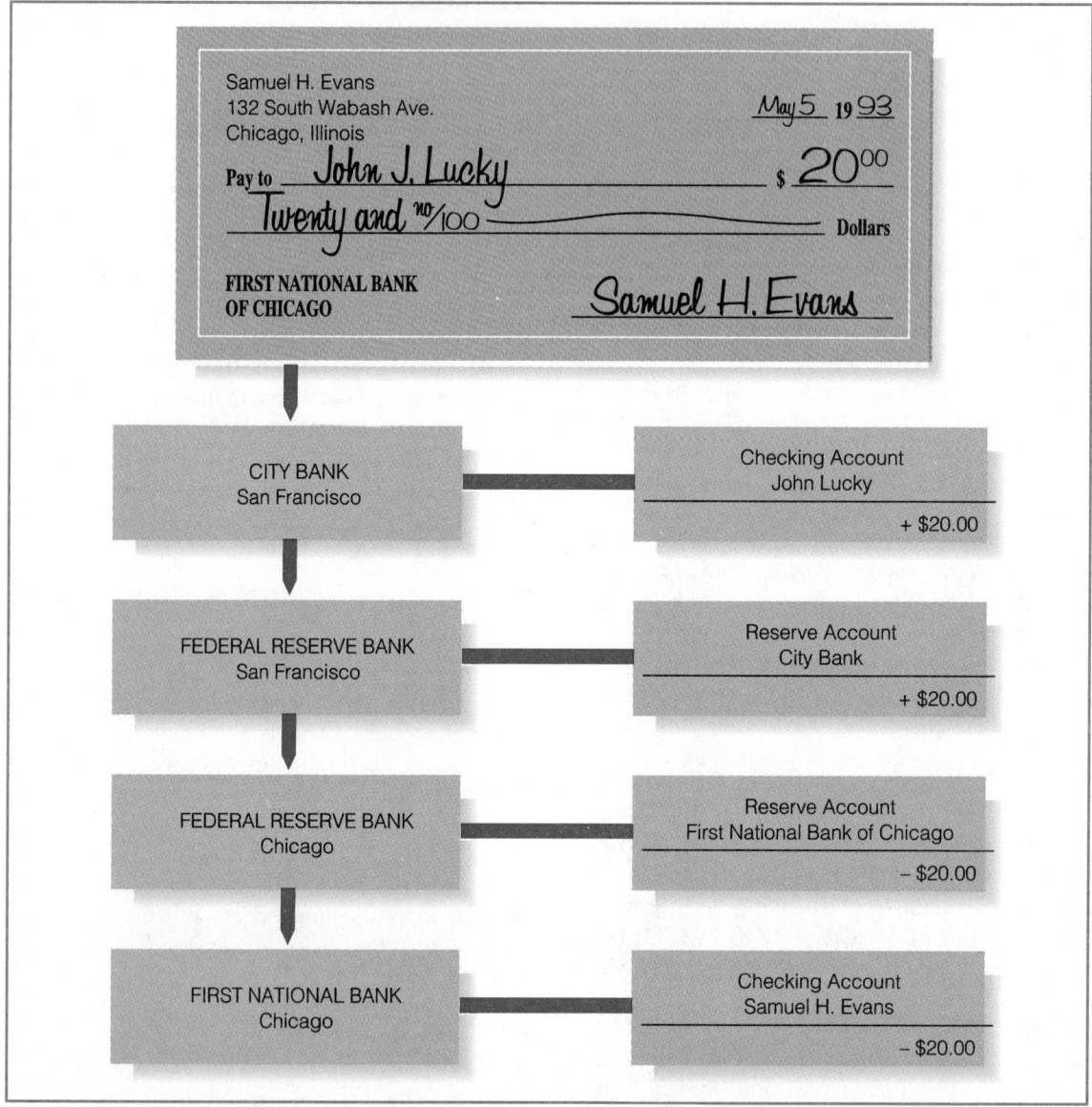

not allow the depositor to draw on these funds (either as cash or by means of a check) until the deposited check had been honored by the payor bank. Many hold periods were lengthy, and many institutions placed holds lasting a week or longer even on deposited government checks.

The act, known as the Expedited Funds Availability Act,[3] requires that any local check deposited must be available for withdrawal by check or as cash within one business day from the date of de-

posit. The Federal Reserve Board of Governors has designated check-processing regions, and if the depositary and payor banks are located in the same region, the check is classified as a local check. For nonlocal checks, the funds are to be available for withdrawal within four business days.

In addition, the act requires the following:

1. That funds be available on the *next business day* for cash deposits and wire transfers, government checks, the first $100 of a day's check deposits, cashier's checks, certified checks, and

---

3. 12 U.S.C. Section 4001 *et seq.*

checks for which the depositary and payor banks are branches of the same institution.

2. That the first $100 of any deposit be available for cash withdrawals on the opening of the next business day after deposit. If the deposit is a local check, the next $400 is to be available for withdrawal by no later than 5:00 P.M. the next business day. If, for example, you deposit a local check for $500 on Monday, you can withdraw $100 in cash at the opening of the business day on Tuesday, and an additional $400 must be available for withdrawal by no later than 5:00 P.M. on Wednesday.

There is a different availability schedule for deposits made at *nonproprietary* automated teller machines (ATMs)—ATMs that are not owned or operated by the banking institution. Basically, a six-day hold is permitted on all deposits, including cash deposits, made at nonproprietary ATMs. Also, a banking institution has eight days to make funds available in new accounts (those open less than thirty days) and an extra four days on deposits over $5,000 (except deposits of government and cashier's checks), on accounts with repeated overdrafts, and on checks of questionable collectibility (but only if the institution tells the depositor it suspects fraud or insolvency).

■ Electronic Fund Transfers

The application of computer technology to banking, in the form of **electronic fund transfer systems (EFTS),** promises to relieve banking institutions of the burden of having to move mountains of paperwork to process fund transfers. An **electronic fund transfer** is a transfer of money made by the use of an electronic terminal, a telephone, a computer, or magnetic tape. Automatic payments, direct deposits, and other fund transfers are now made electronically; no physical transfers of cash, checks, or other negotiable instruments are involved. Through the use of EFTS, transactions that would otherwise take days can now be completed in minutes. For example, Hannah in New York can pay a debt to Barbara in Los Angeles by entering into a computer a bank order to pay it. Chase Manhattan, the drawee bank, can instantly debit Hannah's account and transfer the credit to the Bank of America, Barbara's bank, which can immediately credit her account. EFT transactions

eliminate the **float time** that the drawer of a check currently enjoys. A drawer uses float time by retaining the use of the funds on which the check is written during the period between the check's issuance and final payment.

Commercial electronic fund transfers are governed by contract law and tort law. Consumer transactions utilizing EFTS, however, are subject to the Electronic Fund Transfer Act (EFTA),[4] which went into full effect in 1980. To cover fund transfers that the EFTA and other federal and state laws do not cover, the National Conference of Commissioners on Uniform State Laws and the American Law Institute approved a draft of a new UCC article—Article 4A. Article 4A is primarily intended to cover fund transfers between businesses and financial institutions.

Types of Electronic Transfers

There are four principal types of EFTS in use: (1) automated teller machines, (2) point-of-sale systems, (3) systems handling direct deposits and withdrawals of funds, and (4) pay-by-telephone systems. To initiate a transaction on one of the machines involved, a consumer often uses a card that provides access to the computer system. Each card has an accompanying **personal identification number (PIN)** that is given only to the account holder—a number that is meant to be kept secret so as to inhibit others' use of the card.

AUTOMATED TELLER MACHINES   A major EFTS development has involved the **automated teller machine (ATM),** also called a customer-bank communication terminal or a remote service unit. ATMs are located on banks' premises as well as at convenient locations such as supermarkets, drugstores, and shopping centers. Once the access card activates an ATM, the ATM can receive deposits, dispense funds from checking or savings accounts, transfer funds between accounts, make credit card advances, and receive payments on loan accounts. ATMs are usually connected on-line to the bank's computers.

POINT-OF-SALE SYSTEMS   **Point-of-sale systems** allow consumers to transfer funds to mer-

---

4.   15 U.S.C. Section 1693 *et seq.*

chants to pay for purchases. On-line terminals are located at checkout counters in, for example, grocery stores. Instead of receiving cash or a check from the customer, the checkout person inserts the customer's card into a terminal, which reads the data encoded on the card. The computer at the customer's bank verifies that the card and identification code are valid and that there are enough funds in the customer's account to cover the purchase. After the payment is made, the customer's account is debited for the amount of the purchase.

For the merchant, direct payment from customers by means of point-of-sale systems involves, under current law, less risk of nonpayment or "bounced" checks. For the customer, the electronic transfer makes bills and check writing unnecessary.

DIRECT DEPOSITS AND WITHDRAWALS The main difference between ordinary clearinghouses and automated clearinghouses in which checks are cleared between banks is that entries in automated clearinghouses are made in the form of electronic signals; no checks are used. Thus, these systems do not further automate the handling of checks; they replace checks. This type of EFTS allows a bank to complete a transaction for less than the cost of clearing a check.

A direct deposit may be made to a customer's account through an electronic terminal when the customer has authorized the deposit in advance. The federal government often uses this EFTS to deposit Social Security payments directly into beneficiaries' accounts. Similarly, an employer may agree to make payroll and pension payments directly into an employee's account at specified intervals.

A customer may also authorize a bank (or other financial institution at which the customer's funds are on deposit) to make automatic payments at regular, recurrent intervals to a third party. For example, insurance premiums, utility bills, and home mortgage and automobile installment loan payments may sometimes be made automatically. Additionally, a customer may authorize a bank to make a payment or payments to the Internal Revenue Service for taxes due.

PAY-BY-TELEPHONE SYSTEMS When it is undesirable to arrange in advance for an automatic

payment—as, for example, when the amount of a regular payment varies—some financial institutions permit their customers to pay bills through a pay-by-telephone system. This allows the customer to access the institution's computer system by telephone and direct a transfer of funds. Utility bills sometimes are paid directly by customers using pay-by-telephone systems. Customers may also be permitted to transfer funds between accounts—for example, to withdraw funds from a savings account and make a deposit in a checking account—in this way.

Consumer Transfers: The Electronic Fund Transfer Act

Congress stated in 1978 that the use of electronic systems to transfer funds promised to provide substantial benefits for consumers. But Congress also concluded that, given the unique characteristics of EFTS, existing consumer protection legislation governing the rights and obligations of consumers, financial institutions, and intermediaries was inadequate with respect to the types of fund transfers occurring by means of EFTS. Thus, in 1978, Congress passed the Electronic Fund Transfer Act (EFTA) "to provide a basic framework establishing the rights, liabilities, and responsibilities of participants in electronic fund transfers." The EFTA is essentially a disclosure law designed to benefit consumers; it requires financial institutions to inform consumers of their rights with respect to EFTS. The EFTA is not concerned with *commercial* electronic fund transfers—transfers between businesses or between businesses and financial institutions.

Under the EFTA, the Federal Reserve System's board of governors is authorized to administer the act and to promulgate regulations to carry out the purposes of the act. The board of governors has issued a set of rules, called **Regulation E,** to protect users of EFTS; this regulation should be consulted for a complete understanding of the EFTA. Also, the board has drafted model clauses for financial institutions to use in disclosing information about their electronic systems.

INSTITUTIONS AND TRANSACTIONS COV-ERED The EFTA governs financial institutions that offer electronic fund transfers involving customer accounts. The EFTA defines **financial institutions** to include banks, savings and loan institutions, credit unions, and any other business entities that directly or indirectly hold accounts belonging to consumers. Thus, securities brokerage houses that permit consumers to make electronic transfers to and from money market fund accounts are included. The types of accounts covered include demand accounts, savings accounts, and other asset accounts established for personal, family, or household purposes. All electronic fund transfers involving such accounts are covered by the EFTA. Note that, although telephone transfers are included in the definition of an electronic fund transfer, they are only covered by the EFTA if they are made *pursuant to a prearranged plan under which periodic or recurring transfers are contemplated.*

In the following case, the court examines the purposes of the EFTA and stresses the fact that the act covers only electronic fund transfers made by *consumers.* Transfers between financial institutions are not covered by the act.

BACKGROUND AND FACTS *Shawmut Worcester County Bank, a Massachusetts bank, transferred $10,000 to First American Bank & Trust of Palm Beach, Florida, through an EFTS system known as Fedwire. Shawmut's payment order stated that the beneficiary of the transfer was Fernando Degan and that First American should credit account number 100 205 001 633. It turned out that the First American account under that number was held jointly by Degan and Joseph Merle. When Shawmut discovered its error 106 days after the mistaken transfer, it credited the account of its customer who had requested the transfer with the $10,000 and then asked First American to "reverse" the transfer. First American asked Merle, its customer, if he would authorize the reversal. Merle refused. Accordingly, First American told Shawmut it would not reverse the transfer. Shawmut then sued First American to recover the $10,000, alleging, among other claims, that the transaction fell under the EFTA, which prescribes specific requirements that must be followed in the event of error in a funds transaction.*

Case 24.2

SHAWMUT WORCESTER COUNTY BANK v. FIRST AMERICAN BANK & TRUST

United States District Court, District of Massachusetts, 1990.
731 F.Supp. 57.

YOUNG, District Judge.
* * * *

Shawmut's claim based on rights allegedly secured by the Electronic Fund Transfer Act is * * * without merit. Although the statute does indicate that a subsidiary purpose of the Transfer Act is to "provide a basic framework establishing the rights, liabilities and responsibilities of participants in [electronic fund transfer] systems," the Transfer Act was primarily created for the especial benefit of consumers. The Transfer Act evidently is aimed at providing a framework of law regulating the rights of consumers as against financial institutions in electronic funds transfers. The Transfer Act contains civil remedies only for consumers, with "consumers" being statutorily defined as "natural persons."

This dispute is between two financial institutions and there is no evidence before the Court, even after ample discovery, that First American "directly or indirectly holds an account belonging to a consumer" that conceivably might create the kind of financial institution and consumer relationship between First American and Shawmut that the Act regulates. In the absence of such evidence, it is evident that this sort of funds transfer—a garden-variety wire transfer between financial institutions—is specifically excepted from the Transfer Act coverage by the provisions of section 1693a(6)(B).

DECISION AND REMEDY	*The court granted First American's motion for summary judgment on Shawmut's claim alleging a cause of action under the EFTA. The transfer between the two financial institutions was not covered by the act.*

DISCLOSURE OF TERMS AND CONDITIONS

The EFTA requires that the terms and conditions of electronic fund transfers involving a customer's account must be disclosed in readily understandable language at the time the customer contracts for the services. Included among the required disclosures are:

1. The customer's liability for unauthorized transfers resulting from the loss or theft of the card, code, or other access device.
2. Whom and what phone number to call to report a theft or loss.
3. The charges for using the EFTS.
4. What systems are available and the limits on frequency of use and dollar amounts.
5. The customer's right to see evidence of transactions in writing.
6. How errors can be corrected.
7. The customer's right to stop payments.
8. The financial institution's liability to the customer.
9. Rules concerning disclosure of account information to third parties.

Exhibit 24–3 shows a disclosure form containing the requisite information.

DOCUMENTATION REGARDING TRANSACTIONS

The EFTA considerably reduces the amount of paper used in transferring funds. Financial institutions are required to provide the customer with written documentation—a receipt—of each transfer made from an electronic terminal at the time of the transfer. (Receipts are not required for telephone transfers, even when a telephone transfer is otherwise subject to the EFTA.) The receipt must clearly state the date, the type of transfer, the amount, the identity of the customer's account, the identity of any third party involved (such as a merchant accepting the customer's card as a means of paying for purchased goods), and the location of the terminal involved.

In addition, financial institutions must give customers periodic statements describing types, amounts, dates, transferees, and locations of transfers for each account through which an EFTS provides access. The type of account and the frequency with which the customer uses it determine the timing of the statements. Monthly statements are required for every month in which there is an electronic transfer of funds. Otherwise, statements must be provided quarterly.

The statement must show the amount and date of the transfer, the fees charged, the location or identification of the terminal, and the name of the retailer or third party, if any, involved. Also, the statement must provide an address and phone number for inquiries and error notices.

Financial institutions must also notify customers if an automatic deposit is not made as scheduled. This helps customers to avoid overdrawing their accounts.

PREAUTHORIZED TRANSFERS

A **preauthorized transfer** is a transaction authorized in advance to recur at substantially regular intervals. For example, an employee may be able to arrange with an employer and a bank for the direct deposit of payroll checks into his or her checking account. Similarly, an individual might authorize a monthly transfer from his or her account to pay insurance premiums or installments on a home mortgage or automobile loan.

A situation in which a credit to a customer's account is made from the same payor at least once in each successive sixty-day period requires the financial institution to notify the customer when the credit is made, if the payor does not make the notification. The financial institution must also notify the customer if the deposit is not made as scheduled. The parties can agree on the manner of notice when the service is contracted for. In other words, if an employee has arranged with his or her employer for the direct deposit of weekly payroll checks, the bank handling the receipt of the checks must notify the employee weekly, if the employer does not, whether a check has been deposited as arranged.

This disclosure contains the terms and conditions for all Home Federal electronic banking services, in addition to specific information about pre-authorized electronic payments and deposits.

As someone who uses these services, you should read this information, as it pertains to your rights and responsibilities, as well as the terms and conditions of their use.

Electronic transactions may be payments or deposits, authorized by you, to or from your checking or savings account(s) or loan(s), or to or from a third party. They include:

- AnytimeTeller℠ transactions
- STAR SYSTEM® network transactions
- EXPLORE℠ point-of-sale network (participating gas stations, grocery stores, and other merchants) transactions
- Pre-authorized debits and credits (includes Automatic Payroll Deposit)
- Direct Deposit service
- Telephone Transfer service
- SurePay (automatic loan payments and electronic deposit or payment transactions to or from your checking or savings account)
- Electronic payment or deposit transactions to or from your checking or savings account through an Automated Clearing House (ACH)

Business Days

Our business days are Monday through Friday, except holidays. When allowing processing time, it is important to only count business days. Weekends and holidays are not considered business days.

Privacy

Home Federal may disclose account information to third parties under any of the following conditions:
1. Where it is necessary for completing transfers;
2. To verify the existence and condition of your account for a third party, such as a credit bureau or merchant;
3. To comply with a legitimate request from a government agency, or a court order;
4. With your written permission.

Home Federal Liability/Change of Terms

If Home Federal does not complete a transfer to or from your account at the specified time, or in the specified amount, according to our Agreement with

you, we will be liable for any losses or damages to you, with these exceptions:

Home Federal will not be liable if:
1. There are insufficient funds in your account to make a transfer or payment, for reasons beyond the control of this Association;
2. A transfer would exceed the credit limit on your line of credit;
3. The electronic banking system or terminal was not working properly at the time you initiated a transfer, and you were aware of this malfunction.

Home Federal may cease to offer any electronic banking service at any time. Service users will be given prior notice of any such change in policy.

Home Federal may change any term of the Agreement, including changes which will affect your cost or liability, by giving you at least 21 days written notice.

NOTE: There may be additional exceptions which apply, as stated in our Agreement with you.

Errors and Questions

In case of errors or questions about your electronic transactions, please contact your branch of account.

Home Federal must hear from you within 60 days from the date of the first statement on which the problem or error appears. Failure to do so may result in your being held fully liable for the amount of the error.

Notification by phone or in person requires a written follow-up within 10 working days.

To Resolve an Error

When notifying Home Federal in writing of a suspected error:
1. Include your name, address, and account number.
2. Describe in detail the transaction in question and explain as clearly as you can why you believe it is an error or why you need more information.
3. Indicate the dollar amount of the suspected error.

Home Federal will investigate the error and report to you, usually within 10 business days.

Point-of-sale transactions, however, may take up to 20 business days to investigate.

We may take up to 45 days to investigate a reported error. If so, Home Federal will provisionally recredit your account within 10 business days (or 20 days for point-of-sale transactions) for the amount in question, so that you may have use of the money during the investigation period. This recrediting to your account may not occur if we have not received your notification in writing within the 10 business days.

If it is determined that no error occurred, we will notify you in writing within 3 business days following the completion of the investigation. Any amounts recredited to your account during the course of the investigation will be debited from your account. Copies of documents used in our investigation will be available to you upon request.

Anytimecard℠ Safety

For your protection, please:
1. Be sure to keep your Anytimecard in a safe place, and don't allow anyone to use it.
2. Keep your Personal Identification Number (PIN) a secret. Do not write it on your Anytimecard or otherwise make it available to anyone.
3. Notify Home Federal immediately of any loss, theft, or unauthorized use of your Anytimecard or PIN. Lost or stolen Anytimecards can be reported 24 hours a day, 7 days a week.

Anytimecard Consumer Liability

1. It is your responsibility to notify Home Federal immediately if your Anytimecard and/or Personal Identification Number (PIN) has been lost or stolen. Provided you notify Home Federal within 2 business days of the possible loss or theft, your loss will be limited to a maximum of $50 if your Anytimecard and PIN are used without your permission.
2. If you fail to notify Home Federal within 2 business days of the possible loss or theft of your Anytimecard or PIN, and it can be proven that such notification could have prevented the unauthorized use of your Anytimecard or PIN, your loss could be as much as $500.
3. If you fail to notify Home Federal within 60 days, and it can be proven that such notification could have prevented the unauthorized use of your Anytimecard or PIN, you may not be able to recover

As its name implies, a preauthorized transfer must be authorized by the customer in advance. The authorization must be in writing, and a copy of it must be provided to the customer when it is made. To stop payment of a preauthorized EFT, a customer may notify the financial institution orally or in writing at any time up to three business days before the scheduled date of the transfer. The institution may require the customer to provide written confirmation within fourteen days of an oral notification. For example, suppose Temple has arranged with his bank, Manufacturers Hanover Trust, to have the bank make automatic payments on his automobile installment loan. If Temple wishes to make a given payment on the loan personally, he must order the bank more than three days before the automatic payment is scheduled to be made not to make the payment.

STOPPING PAYMENT AND REVERSIBILITY Under the EFTA, then, a customer may cancel a *preauthorized* transfer before the transfer is made, just as a drawer—the person who signs a check—may stop payment on a check before it is paid. For other EFT transactions, however, the EFTA does not provide for the reversal of an electronic transfer of funds, once it has occurred. This is because the uniquely instantaneous nature of an electronic transfer of funds provides no float time during which an effective reversal of an order to pay can be made.

MISTAKES AND CORRECTIONS Under the EFTA, a customer has a duty to examine the periodic—monthly or quarterly—statements provided by the financial institution handling his or her account or accounts. Within sixty days after the institution has sent a statement, the customer must notify the institution of any errors that appear on it. Whether oral or written, the notice must contain the following information:

1. The customer's name and account number.
2. A sentence stating that an error has been made and its alleged amount.
3. Why the customer believes an error has been made.

The institution is required to investigate and report the results within ten business days. If the institution needs more than ten days, it may take up to forty-five, but it must recredit the customer's account for the amount alleged to be in error until the problem is resolved. If it determines that an error did occur, it has one business day to adjust the customer's account. Even if no mistake has been made, the institution has to give the customer a full written report with conclusions. Failure to investigate in good faith makes the institution liable to the customer for **treble damages**—three times the amount of provable damages.

Banks are held to strict compliance with the terms of the EFTA, and if they fail to adhere to the letter of the law of the EFTA they will be held liable for violation.

CUSTOMER LIABILITY FOR UNAUTHORIZED TRANSFERS Under the EFTA, before a customer can be held liable for any unauthorized transfer, it must be established that the transfer resulted from the use of an accepted means of access and that the customer had been provided with a means of identifying himself or herself to that means of access. For example, a bank's customer will not be held liable for unauthorized withdrawals from the customer's checking account unless the bank has provided the customer with a card and a secret number for access to the bank's EFTS.

In the event that the access card or other device is lost, stolen, or misplaced, the EFTA limits the customer's liability for any unauthorized transfers of funds to $50 if the customer notifies the financial institution within two business days of learning of the loss or theft. If the customer does not inform the institution until after the second day, his or her liability climbs to $500. The customer's liability may be unlimited if notification does not occur within sixty days of the customer's receipt of a periodic statement that reflects an unauthorized transfer.

To avoid liability, the institution must prove first that the customer and the institution had an agreement under which the customer agreed to this liability and second that the customer knew that the access device had been lost, stolen, or misplaced. When an unauthorized transfer has appeared on a statement, the institution must show that any loss of funds due to the unauthorized transfer would not have occurred but for the customer's failure to report the unauthorized transfer's appearance on the statement within sixty days of the statement's transmittal.

To illustrate: On May 1, Wistful goes to an automatic teller machine belonging to Citicorp, his bank, to make a withdrawal from his checking account. He discovers that his access card is missing but fails to tell Citicorp until May 15. Meanwhile, on May 12, Warp, a thief, has made a $100 withdrawal from the account using Wistful's card and number. Wistful, as the account's owner, is liable for the full $100 because he did not notify Citicorp that the card had been stolen or lost prior to Warp's illegal withdrawal. If Wistful had failed to tell Citicorp at all that the card was missing and Warp had continued to use it to withdraw funds, Wistful could have been held liable for the entire amount withdrawn.

Unauthorized use of EFTS access devices constitutes a federal felony. Unauthorized users of EFTS are subject to sanctions, including a $10,000 fine and ten years' imprisonment.

LIABILITY OF THE FINANCIAL INSTITUTION
A financial institution is liable to a customer for all damages *proximately caused* by its failure to make an electronic fund transfer according to the terms and conditions of an account, in the correct amount, or in a timely manner when the customer properly instructs it to do so.

There are exceptions. The institution will not be liable if:

1.   The customer's account has insufficient funds through no fault of the financial institution.
2.   The funds are subject to legal process, such as attachment (see Chapter 12).
3.   The transfer would exceed an established credit limit.
4.   An ATM has insufficient cash.
5.   Circumstances beyond the institution's control prevent the transfer.

The institution is also liable for failure to stop payment of a preauthorized transfer from a customer's account when instructed to do so under the account's terms and conditions.

For an institution's violation of EFTA, a consumer may recover actual damages as well as punitive damages of not more than $1,000 or less

than $100. (Unlike actual damages, punitive damages are assessed to punish a defendant or to set an example for similar wrongdoers.) In a class action suit, the punitive damage limit is the lesser of $500,000 or 1 percent of the institution's net worth.

It is a federal misdemeanor to violate the EFTA. Criminal sanctions for violations of the EFTA by banking institutions may subject an institution or its officials to a $5,000 fine and up to one year's imprisonment.

■ Lender Liability

Twenty-five years ago, in any litigation involving financial institutions, the lender was normally the plaintiff and the borrower the defendant. Generally, the litigation centered on merely determining the rights of the parties on the debtor's default. The court system provided numerous procedural devices that allowed lenders to collect, often without much difficulty, from their debtors.

About fifteen years ago, the lender was still the plaintiff, but the borrower had started to assert affirmative defenses against the lender's attempt at collecting on a debt when the borrower defaulted. Occasionally, a borrower would assert a counterclaim, but rarely would that borrower prevail.

In the last eight to ten years, the tables have been turned, as it were. Financial institutions have become the targets of numerous lawsuits, and the days when financial institutions seemed invulnerable are now in the past. For example, Crocker National Bank was the target of a class-action suit in which the plaintiffs claimed that the fees charged for returned checks—checks returned to account holders when there were insufficient funds in the accounts to cover them—were unconscionable.[5] This case has been cited in numerous other class-action suits against lenders on the grounds that the fees charged for returned checks were unconscionable, as well as in class-action suits challenging other fees that financial institutions charge. The area of **lender liability** has now grown to such an

---

5.   *Perdue v. Crocker National Bank,* 38 Cal.3d 913, 702 P.2d 503, 216 Cal.Rptr. 345 (1985). Although Crocker National Bank had not been held liable after ten years of litigation, in 1985 the bank agreed to a settlement. The bank apparently did not want to risk a jury verdict.

extent that there are even monthly newsletters on the subject. [6]

Typically, lawsuits that are brought against lending institutions involve the following types of claims:

1. The lender failed to lend sufficient funds to the borrower because of negligence in processing the loan.
2. The lender failed to renew short-term loans when the borrower was experiencing financial difficulties.
3. The lender failed to advance funds under a line of credit when the borrower was in a weakened financial situation.
4. The lender failed to solve environmental problems created by the borrower—even though the cost of the clean-up operations exceeded the amount of the loan.

Potential Common Law Liability

Lenders can be potentially liable under the entire body of common law with respect to contracts. To the extent that the borrower can assert and prove breach of contract, the borrower may be able to avoid liability for unpaid debt. Liability of a lender may also be based on the tort theories of misrepresentation, duress, wrongful interference, and negligence. Finally, lender liability may be established if the lender breaches the duty of good faith. We discuss these theories below.

LIABILITY FOR BREACH OF CONTRACT A business relationship between a borrower and a lender comes into existence at the instant when a potential borrower begins to make inquiries about a loan. At any time during the business relationship—from the moment of initial contact to the point at which all of the terms of the loan agreement (if one is formed) have been satisfied—the lender faces potential liability for breach of contract. Credit is the lifeblood of many businesses. A lender's failure to provide credit in a sufficient amount and at the right time may result in the demise of a business. As long as the lender has this ability to determine the financial fate of the borrower, the lender is required to exercise due care and act in good faith at all times.

Loan Applications and Negotiations A loan application is an offer by the borrower, but it is the lender who furnishes the form. Any lender that does not indicate on such an application that it is only seeking information and making no commitment whatsoever to extend credit faces a potential breach of contract suit by an applicant who is turned down.

Lenders have a duty to process all loan applications with due care,[7] and this duty extends to all actions undertaken by the lender in regard to loan negotiations and the processing of loan applications. All procedures relating to loan negotiations and applications should be clearly spelled out by the lender in a loan manual or other written statement of the lending policies. Potential for liability occurs whenever lending practices and procedures undertaken during loan application and negotiation phases are not consistent with what is laid out in written lending policy documents.

The borrower also has an obligation of due care when filling out the loan application and financial statement. If, for example, there is a material change in the borrower's financial statement after the date on which the loan application was submitted, the borrower is normally under an obligation to alert the potential lender to this change in financial circumstances.

Loan Commitments While normally one would think that the commitment for a loan must be reduced to writing to be enforceable, this is not always the case. In many states, a lender who makes an oral agreement must honor that agreement or be subject to a breach of contract suit.[8] Some states do require, however, that a commitment to loan more than a set amount must be in writing to be enforceable. In any event, the prudent loan officer should never make an oral loan commitment. Furthermore, any written letter or document pertaining to loan negotiations should clearly state whether the document is merely a proposal specifying conditions that must be met before a loan can be ob-

---

6. See, for example, Helen Chaitman, ed., *Lender Liability Law Report* (Boston, Mass.: Warren, Gorham & Lamont, Inc.).

7. *Jacques v. First National Bank of Maryland,* 307 Md. 527, 515 A.2d 756 (1986).
8. *Delcon Group, Inc. v. Northern Trust Corp.,* 187 Ill.App.3d 635, 453 N.E.2d 595, 135 Ill.Dec. 212 (1989).

tained or an actual, binding commitment to make the loan. Whenever a letter is simply meant to be a proposal, rather than a commitment, this information should be stated obviously and immediately.

A lender may attempt to back out of a loan commitment by subsequently adding conditions to that commitment that it knows the borrower cannot meet. Normally, once a lender has entered into a loan commitment, it may not add new conditions. In one case, a savings and loan association made a loan commitment for the construction of a hotel and gambling casino. The lender sought participation by other financial institutions but was unable to obtain any. To avoid its commitment, the lender required the borrower to meet additional conditions and delayed the closing of the loan, thus causing the deal to fall through. In the lawsuit that followed, the lender was ordered to pay more than $129 million in damages.[9]

When the loan commitment is for a line of credit, the terms and conditions of the commitment must be defined clearly. Even if a clause appears to grant a lender complete discretion over the termination of funding for the line of credit, the lender does not have absolute right to refuse funding. Discretion must be exercised reasonably and in good faith. Indeed, good faith must permeate the entire loan relationship with respect to the terms of the loan contract. When a lender agrees to a certain credit limit, it may not arbitrarily decide to terminate funding before reaching that limit unless it can be shown that the borrower has not performed according to the terms of the loan agreement.[10]

Liability under a theory of promissory estoppel is also possible in unfulfilled loan commitments, whether they be implied or express. The Restatement (Second) of Contracts, Section 90(1), states as follows:

A promise which the promisor should reasonably expect to induce action or forbearance on the part of the promisee or a third person and which does induce such action or forbearance is binding if in-

justice can be avoided only by enforcement of the promise.

In a well-known Texas case, Ellis Wheeler sought financing from S. E. White to construct a shopping center on a specific site. White assured Wheeler that the money would be available and urged him to demolish the existing building on the site to make way for the construction of the center. White promised that if Wheeler could not obtain the money elsewhere, White would make the loan himself. After Wheeler had razed the old building, White told him that there would be no loan. Wheeler made reasonable efforts to obtain the loan himself but was unsuccessful. The court stated that "where one party has by his words or conduct made to the other a promise or assurance which was intended . . . to be acted on accordingly, then, once the other party has taken him at his word and acted on it, the party who gave the promise cannot afterward be allowed to revert to the previous relationship as if no such promise had been made." [11]

Terminating Loan Agreements Many loan agreements have **acceleration clauses** and other devices that permit the lender to terminate the loan agreement if a debtor fails to meet certain conditions specified in the agreement. An acceleration clause is defined as a clause that allows the holder of a time instrument to demand payment of the entire amount due on the happening of a certain event—for example, on a debtor's failure to make an installment payment when due.

Acceleration clauses and all time notes are subject to the good faith requirement of UCC 1-208. To avoid liability, the lender should accelerate a loan only with valid justification, and there should be clear evidence of default. In other words, the debtor's breach of the loan agreement should be obvious to the reasonable person.

A lender's termination of a loan agreement requires (1) a declaration that the borrower is in default and (2) foreclosure and retaking of the collateral used as security for the loan.

The lender has the ability to declare the borrower in default only if the breach of contract is material. Moreover, the lender must undertake all reasonable means to allow the borrower to avoid

---

9. *Penthouse International, Inc. v. Dominion Federal Savings and Loan Association,* 665 F.Supp. 301 (S.D.N.Y 1987). On appeal, this order was reversed, and the complaint was dismissed. 855 F.2d 963 (2d Cir. 1988).

10. *Carrico v. Delp,* 141 Ill.App.3d 684, 490 N.E.2d 972, 95 Ill.Dec. 880 (1986).

---

11. *Wheeler v. White,* 398 S.W.2d 93 (Tex. 1965).

default before declaring that the loan is in default. The borrower must be presented with a written notice that a default will be declared, and the reasons for the declaration must be included in the notice. These reasons must be tied to specific provisions in the written loan agreement. If a default is declared for an action that does not constitute a default according to the loan agreement, then the lender may be held liable.[12]

Foreclosure or retaking of the collateral used as security for the loan may subject the lender to liability under certain circumstances. For example, if an officer of the lending institution assured the borrower that foreclosure or repossession would not occur, and it does, the lender may be liable. In one case, a bank brought an action to recover on a delinquent promissory note. The borrowers had negotiated the loan to purchase equipment and pay taxes for a restaurant that they were leasing with an option to buy. When they failed to exercise the option, the lease was terminated. Facing unemployment, the borrowers were assured by the bank officer who had arranged the loan that the payment schedule would be adjusted. Because of these assurances, the borrowers were awarded damages when the bank failed to keep its word and sued to collect the debt.[13]

LIABILITY IN TORT Many lender liability cases are based on tort theories. As pointed out in Chapter 7, a tort is a wrongful action by one party that causes injury to another. In general, lenders are more concerned with tort liability than with liability for breach of contract because punitive damages can be, and have been, assessed against lenders when a tort has been committed.

---

12. *In re Werth,* 37 Bankr. 979 (Bankr. D. Colo. 1984); aff'd 54 Bankr. 619 (D.Colo. 1985).
13. *First National Bank of Libby v. Twombly,* 213 Mont. 66, 689 P.2d 1226 (1984).

Misrepresentation and Fraud The tort of misrepresentation occurs when fraud or deceit is employed for personal gain. Actual fraud has four elements: (1) material misrepresentation of fact (not opinion), (2) intentional deceit (involving either knowledge that the misrepresentation is false or reckless disregard for the truth), (3) justifiable reliance on the misrepresentation by the deceived party, and (4) resulting injury or damage.

As noted in Chapter 7, misrepresentation can be accomplished by words or by actions. Intent to deceive can be inferred from circumstances. Reliance on the misrepresentation may be justified if the person to whom the misrepresentation is made does not know the true facts and has no way of finding them out. To recover damages for misrepresentation, proof of injury is universally required—although some courts do not require a showing of injury when the remedy sought is rescission.

Potential acts of fraud on the part of a lender include providing misleading or false information about the borrower to a third party and misrepresenting the effects of legal documents to induce a borrower to execute them. For example, stating that a mortgage is a mere technicality that would not place the mortgaged property at risk of loss through foreclosure could amount to fraud.

Innocent misrepresentation, or constructive fraud, can also be used as a theory on which to base lender liability. Innocent misrepresentation, which occurs without any actual intention to deceive, can be asserted against a lender who has entered into a fiduciary relationship with the borrower. A fiduciary relationship is one of trust and confidence in which one party has a duty to disclose material facts relevant to the relationship to the other. In a fiduciary relationship, therefore, the failure to disclose a material fact can constitute misrepresentation—as the following case illustrates.

Case 24.3

BARNETT BANK OF WEST FLORIDA v. HOOPER

Supreme Court of Florida, 1986.
498 So.2d 923.

BACKGROUND AND FACTS *Dr. Richard Hooper moved to Pensacola, Florida, in 1973 and began doing business with the Barnett Bank of West Florida. In June 1981, Hooper met with Joe Hosner, an attorney and customer of the bank, to discuss investments. Hosner took Hooper to see Edwin Riffel, the loan officer in charge of Hosner's accounts at the bank. Riffel told Hooper that he was familiar with Hosner's investments and that they were sound. Hooper borrowed $50,000 from the bank to invest with*

Hosner. Less than a year later, Harry Stump, an assistant vice-president of the bank, began to suspect that Hosner was involved in a check-kiting scheme.[a] He informed Riffel. By May 14, Stump—believing that the bank was at risk and wishing to protect the bank—returned all Hosner checks presented on May 13 as drawn against uncollected funds. Late in the afternoon of May 14, Hooper returned a call from Hosner, who came on the line with Riffel. During the three-way conversation, Hooper asked to borrow $90,000 to invest with Hosner. A promissory note prepared by Riffel and a check representing the proceeds of the loan in the sum of $89,865 were delivered to Hooper after banking hours by a messenger from Hosner's office. Hooper indorsed the check, and it was deposited in Hosner's account. By May 24, the check-kiting scheme had been confirmed, but because of Hooper's deposit into Hosner's account, the bank lost nothing. Without Hooper's check, Hosner's account would have been overdrawn in the amount of $87,000. Hooper sued to cancel the note on the basis that the bank had a duty to disclose facts material to the loan transaction, or, alternatively, a duty to disclose knowledge of Hosner's fraudulent activity. Based on the rule that a bank owes an implied duty to its depositors not to disclose information to third parties concerning a depositor's account, the trial court directed a verdict against Hooper. The appellate court reversed and remanded for a new trial. The bank appealed to the Supreme Court of Florida.

SHAW, Justice.

* * * *

With these facts in mind, we limit our opinion to the following inquiry:

When a bank enters into a transaction with a customer with whom it has established a confidential or fiduciary relationship, and the transaction is one from which the bank stands to benefit at the expense of the customer, does the bank assume a duty to disclose information material to the transaction which is peculiarly within the bank's knowledge and not otherwise available to the customer?

We see nothing wrong with, but much to commend, a rule of law recognizing that under these special circumstances a bank may by its conduct be found to have assumed a duty of disclosure. Accordingly, we answer the inquiry in the affirmative.

* * * Such "special circumstances" may be found where a bank, having actual knowledge of fraud being perpetrated upon a customer, enters into a transaction with that customer in furtherance of the fraud, or where a bank has established a confidential or fiduciary relationship with a customer.

* * * [W]e are reluctant to formulate a rule of disclosure that will be at tension with the general rule of confidentiality. However, since the usual relationship between a bank and its depositor is one of debtor to creditor, not ordinarily imposing a duty of disclosure upon the bank, we do not feel that our decision herein will overly burden the banking industry. * * * Where the bank defends its breach of duty on the ground that it owes a conflicting duty of confidentiality to a second customer, the jury is entitled to weigh the one duty against the other.

* * * *

In sum, the jury could have found that the bank, having established a confidential or fiduciary relationship with Hooper, entered into a transaction with Hooper from which it was likely to benefit and that at the time of the transaction the bank had

---

a.   A check-kiting scheme involves multiple checking accounts in which, say, a check is written on account number one and deposited in overdrawn account number two, and then a check drawn on account number three is deposited in account number one to cover the "bad" check previously written—and so on.

special knowledge of material facts which were not otherwise available to Hooper. Given these ''special circumstances,'' the jury could have found that Barnett owed Hooper a duty of disclosure against which the jury was entitled to weigh Barnett's duty of confidentiality owed to Hosner.

DECISION AND REMEDY   *The court affirmed the appellate court's decision, and the case was remanded for a new trial consistent with this opinion. A jury could reasonably conclude that the bank's failure to inform Hooper of material facts relating to the loan constituted constructive fraud.*

Duress   Duress includes the following three elements: (1) an unlawful threat, (2) a destruction of free will, and (3) a loss. A threat is unlawful if what is threatened is a crime or a tort. Note, however, that a threat to exercise a legal right, such as a threat to initiate a civil suit, is normally acceptable. Destruction of free will can be established by showing that assent occurred under circumstances that presented no reasonable alternative. For example, a lender that promises to lend funds to a certain borrower at a specified interest rate, but that subsequently threatens to refuse to lend the funds unless the borrower agrees to a higher interest rate, may be found guilty of duress if the borrower is in urgent need of the funds and is unable to obtain them elsewhere.

Hard bargaining between experienced parties possessing relatively equal bargaining power does not establish duress. For example, insisting on a condition that is commonly bargained for would not constitute duress. In cases in which agreements have been invalidated because of duress, the conduct of the party obtaining the advantage has been tainted with some degree of fraud or wrongdoing.

Wrongful Interference and Excessive Control   When a borrower misses payments on a loan or indicates that payments may be missed, a lender may offer to help the borrower out of its financial difficulties. Alternatively, the lender may exercise economic power over the troubled borrower to obtain the required payments. The issue then becomes whether such control and interference is tortious.

For example, a lender may be liable if it requires a financially troubled corporate borrower to take actions that should be decided on only by the officers or directors of the company. Whenever it

can be shown that the lender's influence on the borrower's business will have, or did have, a detrimental effect on the borrower and a beneficial effect on the lender, the lender may be liable.

Sometimes, a lender may become entangled in the business affairs of the borrower to the extent that the lender becomes liable to third parties. At some point, the lender may be considered a joint venturer with the borrower or an agent of the borrower. The extreme case of lender liability under the theory of interference and control occurs when the operation of a borrower's business is so controlled by the lender that the lender becomes liable for the borrower's debts.[14]

Excessive interference and control can also create fiduciary responsibilities between a lender and a borrower. Fiduciary duties can arise if a lender becomes a borrower's financial advisor. A fiduciary relationship imposes on a lender the duties of disclosure and loyalty as well as the duty not to take unfair advantage of the borrower. Once a fiduciary relationship has been established, the lender is no longer able to act in its own best interest but must act in the best interest of the borrower.

In the following landmark case, the principles of wrongful interference and control were applied. This case also marked a turning point in the law of lender liability in general.

---

14. *A. Gay Jenson Farms Co. v. Cargill,* 309 N.W.2d 285 (Minn. 1981).

BACKGROUND AND FACTS *Farah Manufacturing Company (FMC) was a successful apparel manufacturer. In 1964, William Farah became its chief executive officer (CEO). By 1970, FMC had annual sales of $136 million. From 1972 through 1974, however, FMC was the target of a strike and national boycott. By 1976, the company had lost almost $44 million. In that year, FMC's board of directors replaced Farah as CEO, and FMC's banks renegotiated their loan agreements. The new agreements contained clauses that permitted the banks to call in FMC's loans if a management change occurred that the banks opposed. In 1977, Farah tried to regain the CEO position, but the board of directors thwarted the attempt, fearing that the banks would otherwise declare a default under the management-change clause. Over the next year, representatives of the banks became members of FMC's board of directors, and one of the representatives became the CEO of FMC. As CEO, the banks' representative appeared to operate FMC for the benefit of the banks, selling off assets at low prices to make loan prepayments. In 1978, Farah regained control of FMC, threw out the banks' CEO, and sued the banks, alleging fraud, duress, and interference with business relations. The interference allegations were based on charges that the banks had used undue influence (threatening to exercise the management-change clause) to keep out competent management personnel who were loyal to FMC instead of to the banks. The jury awarded FMC more than $18.9 million in damages for lost profits and for losses and damages related to the selling of FMC's assets. One of the banks—State National Bank of El Paso—appealed.*

Case 24.4

STATE NATIONAL BANK OF EL PASO v. FARAH MANUFACTURING CO.
Court of Appeals of Texas—El Paso, 1984.
678 S.W.2d 661.

SCHULTE, J.
* * * *

[Among the reasons] asserted by State National in support of its position that FMC has no legal basis for an actionable claim of interference [is] that the lenders were legally justified and privileged to issue warnings based upon the exercise of contractual rights or upon a financial interest. * * *
* * * *

To maintain the action for interference, it must be established that (1) there was a contract subject to interference, (2) the act of interference was wilful and intentional, (3) such intentional act was a proximate cause of Plaintiff's damage, and (4) actual damage or loss occurred.

The proof of these elements establishes a prima facie case of interference. * * *
* * * *

A justifiable business interest does not grant absolute privilege to interfere with a contractual relationship between others. In determining the propriety of interference, the court in [a previous case stated:] * * * The principal issue [is] whether the social benefits derived in permitting acts of intervention outweigh the harm to be expected therefrom.
* * * *

The central theme of FMC's case is that the lenders interfered with FMC's own business relations and protected rights. Although the lenders may have been acting to exercise legitimate legal rights or to protect justifiable business interests, their conduct failed to comport with the standards of fair play. Upon consideration of the private interests of the parties and of the social utility thereof, the social benefits derived from permitting the lenders' interference are clearly outweighed by the harm to be expected therefrom.

In view of the foregoing principles, the evidence is legally sufficient that the lenders interfered with FMC's business relations, its election of directors and officers and its protected rights. FMC was entitled to have its affairs managed by competent directors and officers who would maintain a high degree of undivided loyalty to the company. * * *

The evidence is factually sufficient that the interference compelled the election of directors and officers whose particular business judgment and inexperience and whose divided loyalty proximately resulted in injury to FMC. The interference by the lenders was done willfully, intentionally and without just cause or excuse. As a matter of law, FMC has established a cause of action for interference. The evidence is legally and factually sufficient to support the jury's finding thereon.

DECISION AND REMEDY   *The appellate court pointed out that the banks could have chosen to exercise or not to exercise the management-change clause, but when they threatened to exercise it to force FMC to act against FMC's interests, they committed wrongful interference. The court affirmed the trial court's judgment in all respects but reduced the amount of the damages awarded by $300,105.*

Negligence   Negligence exists when someone suffers injury because another fails to live up to a required duty of care. To the extent that courts have expanded the areas in which duties are owed by the lender to the borrower, negligence has become an increasingly important theory on which lender liability cases have been based.

Liability for Breach of the Duty of Good Faith   The requirement of good faith in business dealings applies also to lender-borrower relationships. Good faith and fair dealing are required in the creation and performance of all contracts subject to the Uniform Commercial Code [UCC 1-201(19), 1-203, 1-208]. Now, in most states, the duty to act in good faith is implied in all contracts. Good faith requires that both parties to an agreement treat each other honestly, reasonably, and fairly.

The difficulty arises over the extent of the duty, particularly the extent of the duty owed on the part of the lender. The good faith test has not been uniformly applied. In some states, courts apply the good faith doctrine to all aspects of the lender–borrower relationship; in others, to only part of it. In many instances, even loan negotiations—which may include oral commitments and agreements—are included among actions subject to the good faith requirement.

Potential Statutory Liability

Whenever a lender becomes entangled in the business affairs of the borrower, that lender may be subject to statutory liability on a variety of grounds, including violation of federal securities law, racketeering law, tax law, and environmental law. In this section, we examine the potential liability of lenders under environmental laws.

Financial institutions currently face direct and indirect liability under federal and state environmental statutes. Under certain circumstances, because of lender liability, lenders face the same responsibilities as companies that handle, generate, or dispose of hazardous materials. There are over twenty-five major federal environmental laws. Many more state and local laws, which usually impose stricter penalties on polluters, are also important.

At the federal level, the most important environmental legislation affecting lenders has been the Comprehensive Environmental Response, Compensation and Liability Act (CERCLA) of 1980.[15] Lenders taking ownership of real property that served as security for their loans may find themselves liable for the cost of cleaning up toxic waste or chemicals located on the property. Often the

---

15.   42 U.S.C. Sections 9601 *et seq.*

liability exceeds by many times the value of the original loan and certainly the value of the profits that were to be realized from the loan.

Liability Under CERCLA

CERCLA exempts banks and other lenders that have made loans to polluters if the banks or lenders have not partaken in the firms' management. But how far can a lender go in protecting its interests before it will be considered to be participating in management? A landmark case in this area was heard in 1986. Maryland Bank and Trust Company had foreclosed on real estate in which it held a security interest and had then purchased the property at the foreclosure sale.[16] Approximately a year

later, the Environmental Protection Agency (EPA) discovered hazardous waste on the site. The EPA sued the bank for the clean-up costs, which exceeded the value of the loan. The court held that the bank was responsible. Under CERCLA, the EPA has the power to finance toxic waste site clean-up by billing polluters. The court reasoned that whenever a lender qualifies as an owner or operator of a polluted site, the lender can also be deemed responsible.

The scope of lender liability for environmental clean-up costs was greatly expanded in the following case.

---

16. *U.S. v. Maryland Bank and Trust Co.*, 632 F.Supp. 573 (D.Md. 1986).

BACKGROUND AND FACTS *Swainsboro Print Works, Inc., (SPW) operated a cloth-printing facility. In 1976, SPW and Fleet Factors Corporation entered into a financing agreement under which Fleet acquired security interests in SPW's assets, including its printing facility and accounts receivable. In 1979, SPW filed for bankruptcy under Chapter 11. Fleet continued its arrangement with SPW, advancing funds and paying for services, until Fleet determined that the value of the funds advanced exceeded the value of SPW's accounts receivable. In 1981, SPW ceased operations. During the winding up of SPW's affairs, Fleet continued to check the credit of SPW's customers and to collect receivables. Eventually, Chapter 7 (liquidation) proceedings were begun. With the approval of the bankruptcy court, in 1982 Fleet foreclosed on its security interests, selling some of SPW's inventory and equipment at an auction through a liquidator. Fleet permitted unsold equipment to be removed. After 1983, Fleet had no contact with the facility. In 1987, it was sold in a tax foreclosure sale. The federal government filed an action under CERCLA, seeking to impose liability on Fleet for costs associated with the removal of hazardous chemicals and asbestos from the facility. The government alleged that after SPW ceased operations, Fleet became involved in the management of SPW by establishing prices, directing and approving shipments, supervising and laying off employees, processing government forms, and controlling access to the facility. Thus, Fleet was liable either as the "owner or operator" of the facility from 1982 until the tax foreclosure sale or as a participant in management. The federal district court held that only if the government could prove that Fleet's liquidator disturbed the site's hazardous substances, and thereby "operated" the site, could Fleet be held liable. Fleet's motion for summary judgment was denied. Fleet appealed.*

Case 24.5

UNITED STATES v. FLEET FACTORS CORP.

United States Court of Appeals, Eleventh Circuit, 1990. 901 F.2d 1550.

KRAVITCH, Circuit Judge.

* * * *

Although we agree with the district court's resolution of the summary judgment motion, we find its construction of [CERCLA's] exemption [for lenders] too permissive towards secured creditors who are involved with toxic waste facilities. In order to achieve the "overwhelmingly remedial" goal of the CERCLA statutory scheme, ambiguous statutory terms should be construed to favor liability for the costs incurred by the government in responding to the hazards at such facilities. * * *

* * * Under the standard we adopt today, a secured creditor may incur [CERCLA] liability, without being an operator, by participating in the financial management of a facility to a degree indicating a capacity to influence the corporation's treatment of hazardous wastes. It is not necessary for the secured creditor actually to involve itself in the day-to-day operations of the facility in order to be liable—although such conduct will certainly lead to the loss of the protection of the statutory exemption. Nor is it necessary for the secured creditor to participate in management decisions relating to hazardous waste. Rather, a secured creditor will be liable if its involvement with the management of the facility is sufficiently broad to support the inference that it could affect hazardous waste disposal decisions if it so chose.

* * * *

We agree with the court below that the government has alleged sufficient facts to hold Fleet liable under [CERCLA]. * * *

* * * *

Indeed, Fleet's involvement [in 1982 and 1983] would pass the threshold for operator liability under [CERCLA]. Fleet weakly contends that its activity at the facility from the time of the auction was within the secured creditor exemption because it was merely protecting its security interest in the facility and foreclosing its security interest in its equipment, inventory, and fixtures. This assertion, even if true, is immaterial to our analysis. The scope of the secured creditor exemption is not determined by whether the creditor's activity was taken to protect its security interest. What is relevant is the nature and extent of the creditor's involvement with the facility, not its motive.

DECISION AND REMEDY *The appellate court concluded that the district court had properly denied Fleet's motion for summary judgment. The appellate court also concluded that the district court had erred in construing the secured creditor exemption to insulate Fleet from CERCLA liability for its conduct prior to 1982, but it upheld the lower court's ruling that Fleet was liable for its subsequent activities if the government could establish its allegations. The case was remanded.*

SINCE THE *FLEET FACTORS* DECISION More recently, a different circuit court put some limitations on lender liability with respect to environmental clean-up costs in *The East Asiatic Co. v. Port of St. Helens (In re Bergsoe Metal Corp.).*[17] The court held that a lender cannot be held liable under CERCLA unless it exercises "actual management authority" that results in the discharge of hazardous waste. The court further held that the lender cannot be held liable simply because it has the power to get involved in management. The court stated that a secured creditor must participate in the actual management of the facility before liability will be imposed. Some observers have argued that this decision will limit the effectiveness of the *Fleet Factors* decision in future lender liability cases involving CERCLA.

17.   910 F.2d 668 (9th Cir. 1990).

■ Terms and Concepts to Review

acceleration clauses 585
automated teller machine
 (ATM) 577
check 571
collecting bank 575
commercial paper 570
depositary bank 575
draft 570
drawee 570

drawer 570
electronic fund transfer 577
electronic fund transfer
 systems (EFTS) 577
financial institutions 579
float time 577
intermediary bank 575
lender liability 583
payee 570

payor bank 575
personal identification
 number (PIN) 577
point-of-sale systems 577
preauthorized transfer 580
Regulation E 577
stale check 573
treble damages 582

■ Questions and Case Problems

24-1. Daniel drafts a check for $1,000 payable to Paula and drawn on the West Bank. After issue of the check, Paula negotiates the check to Fred. Fred finds an ideal real estate lot for sale, but to close the deal he needs to make a $1,000 down payment by certified check. Fred takes the check to West Bank and requests West Bank to certify Daniel's check.

(a) If West Bank refuses to certify Daniel's check, can either Daniel or Fred hold the bank liable? Explain.

(b) If West Bank certifies the check, explain fully the liability of Daniel as drawer to Fred and to Paula as indorser.

24-2. On January 5, Daniel drafts a check for $3,000 drawn on the East Bank and payable to his secretary, Sylvia. Daniel puts last year's date on the check by mistake. Sylvia has not yet cashed the check at the East Bank when, on January 7, Daniel is killed in an automobile accident. The East Bank is aware of Daniel's death. On January 10, Sylvia presents the check to the East Bank, and the bank honors the check by payment to Sylvia. Daniel's widow, Martha, claims that the East Bank has wrongfully paid Sylvia, because it knew of Daniel's death and because the check was by date over one year old. Martha, as executrix of Daniel's estate and sole heir by his will, demands that East Bank recredit Daniel's estate for the check paid Sylvia. Discuss fully East Bank's liability in light of Martha's demand.

24-3. Just before going home for Christmas vacation, Jim noticed that his November bank statement reflected a $200 shortfall in his account. Upon closer inspection, he noted that on November 28 there had been a $200 cash withdrawal from an automatic teller machine. Jim had not used his ATM card in over two months. He immediately notified the bank by telephone of the error and advised the bank that he was going to be out of town until January 18, but he gave the bank the address and telephone number at which he could be reached. Jim wrote a letter to the bank confirming his telephone conversation and once again gave the bank this address and telephone number. On January 18, when Jim arrived back in town, he still had not heard from the bank. When he called the bank, the bank officer said

that he was sorry that nothing had been done to try to resolve the problem. The reason for the delay, the bank officer stated, was that many bank employees had been on Christmas vacation, causing the bank to be understaffed for about a month. The bank officer told Jim that the bank would try to get back in touch with him within two weeks concerning the matter. Jim, unhappy with this answer, decided to file suit against the bank for violation of the Electronic Fund Transfer Act. Will Jim succeed in his suit? If so, how much money will he be able to recover?

24-4. Kim has a checking account at First National Bank. She has had this bank account for over five years and has never had a check returned for insufficient funds. Kim works at Monmouth Medical Center and has arranged with her employer for direct deposit of her monthly paycheck into her checking account at First National. For an unexplained reason, Kim's July 1 paycheck is not deposited in her checking account. On July 15, Kim receives four notices from the bank stating that four of her checks have not been honored because her account is overdrawn. She incurs late charges from her creditors and charges from the bank for the overdrawn checks. Kim files suit against her bank. Can she recover any money from the bank? If so, under what theory and how much?

24-5. Arkon Corp. and First Bank of Springfield are negotiating a loan for $300,000 to finance Arkon's purchase of a new piece of equipment from Make-It Co. The equipment is usually priced at $350,000, but Make-It is willing to sell the equipment for $300,000 if cash is paid on delivery. Make-It has also agreed that if Arkon cannot pay the full cash price on delivery, Arkon can purchase the equipment for $330,000, payable with a 10 percent down payment and the rest in twelve equal installments, and Make-It will hold a security interest in the equipment until the debt is fully paid. Arkon and First Bank meet to discuss the loan. Substantial progress is made, but no loan contract is signed by the parties. Arkon is led to believe, however, that when the loan negotiation process is concluded, it will receive the loan. Based on this assumption, Arkon agrees with Make-It to purchase the equipment. Three days later, First Bank, after further evaluation, denies approval of Arkon's loan application. Make-It delivers the equipment, but

Arkon cannot pay the full cash price and cannot even raise enough money for the 10 percent down payment that would allow it to retain possession under the terms of the alternative contract. The equipment is repossessed and sold by Make-It for $310,000, leaving a deficiency of $20,000 that Arkon must pay. Arkon claims that First Bank should be liable for the loss because it led Arkon to believe that the loan would be forthcoming. Will Arkon be able to hold First Bank liable under any of the theories of lender liability presented in this chapter? Discuss fully.

24-6. MMM Co. markets its products in a growing and highly competitive market. Because of cash-flow problems, MMM seeks a loan from West Bank. The bank makes the loan. The loan contract provides that because of MMM's history of cash-flow problems, all purchases by MMM of inventory or equipment will require West Bank's approval. MMM has an opportunity to purchase a new piece of equipment that would increase its productivity. West Bank, however, refuses to approve the purchase. Within six months, MMM cannot fulfill its orders, and its customers consequently shift their business to other producers. One year later, MMM has lost so many customers that it is insolvent. MMM seeks to hold West Bank liable for its failure. Discuss fully whether MMM has any cause of action under any of the theories of lender liability discussed in this chapter.

24-7. Robert Parrett was the principal shareholder, president, and chief operating officer of P & P Machinery, Inc., a farm machinery business located in Nebraska. On March 1, 1984, Parrett signed and delivered a check from P & P Machinery to a South Dakota firm. The check was dishonored by the bank even though P & P Machinery had sufficient funds in its account to cover the check. In addition, Parrett had a long-standing relationship with the bank as personal guarantor of corporate obligations to the bank and had never had any previous problems with the bank. As a result of the dishonored check, Parrett was charged with felony theft in South Dakota and extradited for trial in South Dakota. On learning that the bank had dishonored the check erroneously, the trial court dismissed the charge against Parrett. Parrett sued the bank for damages. The trial court held that Parrett had no standing to sue the bank because he was not the bank's ''customer''—the corporation was. Will the appellate court agree that Parrett lacked standing to sue the bank? Discuss fully. [*Parrett v. Platte Valley State Bank & Trust Co.,* 236 Neb. 139, 459 N.W.2d 371 (1990)]

24-8. Susan Wolf forged her employer's name on more than ninety checks drawn on the employer's bank account. The bank cashed the checks, debiting the employer's account, and Wolf wrongfully received a total of more than $22,500. When the forgeries were discovered, the employer brought a criminal action against Wolf but later dropped the charges and settled out of court. The employer also demanded that the bank credit its account for the amount of the forged checks. The bank refused. Assuming there was no evidence that the employer's negligence had substantially contributed to the forgery, discuss whether the employer was entitled to have the bank

credit its account. [*SCCI, Inc. v. U.S. National Bank of Oregon,* 78 Or.App. 176, 714 P.2d 1113 (1986)]

24-9. John Wingo, the owner and president of Specialty Flooring Co., deposited a check for $67,371.32 into the company's bank account at Palmetto Federal Savings Bank of South Carolina. The check had been drawn by U.S.A. Construction Co. on its account with the same bank and represented payment under a subcontracting agreement between the parties. Two days later, U.S.A. advised Specialty that it was going to stop payment on the check because of Specialty's allegedly inferior work under their contract. Wingo immediately went to the bank and requested a cashier's check for $70,000, payable to Specialty. Palmetto issued a bank check in that amount drawn on its account with Citibank, in exchange for which Wingo tendered a $70,000 check written on Specialty's account with Palmetto. When Palmetto learned that payment had been stopped on U.S.A.'s check to Specialty, it revoked the provisional credit of $67,371.32 given to Specialty's account and stopped payment on the $70,000 bank check it had issued to Specialty—as Specialty's account now lacked sufficient funds to cover the $70,000 check that it had issued to Palmetto in exchange for the bank check. Specialty sued Palmetto for wrongful dishonor. Palmetto claimed that it had a legal right to stop payment on the bank check because the check had been drawn on its Citibank account, and therefore, as Citibank's customer, Palmetto could rightfully stop payment. Discuss fully whether in this situation Palmetto could rightfully stop payment on the cashier's check. [*Specialty Flooring Co. v. Palmetto Federal Savings Bank of South Carolina,* 394 S.E.2d 13 (S.C. 1990)]

24-10. Melanie Curde went to the ATM at her bank, Tri-City Bank & Trust Co., checked her account balance, withdrew some funds, and attempted to deposit a $200 check that she had received. She inserted the check and a deposit slip into the ATM slot labeled ''Deposit.'' She later testified that the check and deposit slip disappeared into the slot and were not seen again. Several months later, when the front covering of the ATM was removed for servicing, Curde's check and deposit slip were found between the covering and the machine itself, in an area near the bottom of the machine away from the deposit slot. Although Curde was unable to present any receipts for the ATM transactions of that day, the bank's ATM tape reflected that Curde had indeed checked her account balance, withdrawn funds, and attempted a third transaction that had resulted in an error and was canceled by the customer. Curde filed suit against the bank for damages, alleging, in part, that the bank had violated the Electronic Fund Transfer Act (EFTA). The bank claimed, in part, that it could not be liable under the EFTA because the EFTA governs only when electronic fund transfers are made, and in this case no actual transfer of funds had ever taken place. How should the court decide this issue? Discuss fully. [*Curde v. Tri-City Bank & Trust Co.,* 1990 WL 151211 (Tenn.App. 1990)]

24-11. East Bay Limited Partnership purchased a shopping center for the purpose of renovating the center and reselling it to a third party. The purchase was financed through a loan from American General Life & Accident Insurance Co. The parties agreed in writing that during the first six months of the loan, the property could be sold to a buyer approved by the lender and the loan assumed without payment of any fee, but after six months a 1 percent fee would be required. Prepayment of the loan was precluded during the first six years. The written agreement specifically provided that American had the right to approve a proposed buyer based on the buyer's "net worth, credit worthiness and management expertise." About one and a half years into the loan, East Bay requested American's approval to sell the shopping center to the James W. Hall Corp. In a letter to East Bay, American stated that it would not allow Hall to assume the loan because of the "lack of experience of the company buying the property." East Bay wished to pay off the loan in full so that it could then sell the shopping center without American's approval. American told East Bay that the latter could pay the loan in full only if a prepayment fee of 24.25 percent was paid. In the end there was no sale and no prepayment. East Bay went into default, and American obtained ownership rights in the shopping center, which had been given as security for the loan. East Bay sued American for, among other things, intentional interference with a business relationship and breach of its duty to act in good faith and deal fairly with East Bay. Will the court hold for East Bay on either of these counts? Discuss. [*East Bay Limited Partnership v. American General Life & Accident Insurance Co.*, 744 F.Supp. 1118 (M.D.Fla. 1990)]

24-12. Neal Boge, a dairy farmer, entered into a loan agreement with the United States National Bank of Oregon, giving the bank a security interest in his cows. When Boge fell into arrears on his payments and was unable to meet the bank's subsequent demand for full payment of the loan, the bank sent Boge's file to Portland for foreclosure. Boge and the Rileys, from whom he had purchased the cows, tentatively agreed that the Rileys would repurchase the cows and that Boge would use the proceeds to pay the loan in full and redeem the collateral (the cows). The Rileys would then resell the cows to Boge and finance the purchase themselves. The Rileys and Boge met with a bank representative to obtain information about the specifics of Boge's indebtedness and to make sure that the Rileys could obtain clear title to the cows. The bank representative stated that he could not furnish the information immediately because the file was in Portland. There was evidence, however, that the information was readily available in computers that were at the bank representative's disposal. There was also evidence that the bank representative was hostile and uncooperative. A few days later, the bank demanded that Boge surrender the cows, plus other equipment subject to the bank's security interest, which Boge did shortly thereafter. The cows were then sold by the bank at auction. In the lawsuit that followed, Boge claimed that the bank had breached the implied covenant of good faith and fair dealing by failing to provide promptly the information requested by Boge. Because this information was not provided in time, the Boge-Riley refinancing plan fell through and Boge was unable to pay the loan (and redeem the collateral) before the cows were sold at auction. Had the bank breached the implied covenant of good faith and fair dealing? Discuss fully. [*United States National Bank of Oregon v. Boge*, 102 Or.App. 262, 794 P.2d 801 (1990)]

24-13. Question of Ethics

 *On December 8, 1981, Judico Enterprises, Inc., executed a $460,000 promissory note payable in one year to the First National Bank of Midland, Texas. Willie Coleman and Dwayne Powell, Judico's president and secretary, personally guaranteed the note, giving certain real estate as security for the loan. The guaranty contract contained express waivers of bank obligations regarding the collateral—the bank could obtain a judgment against Coleman and Powell for the full amount of the debt, even if the collateral had been sold to satisfy part of the debt. On October 26, 1982, Judico filed for Chapter 11 bankruptcy. The bank sued Coleman and Powell on their guaranties and moved in the bankruptcy court for relief from the automatic stay to foreclose on the property securing the note. Shortly thereafter, the bank became insolvent, and it was taken over by the Federal Deposit Insurance Corp. (FDIC) in October 1983. In November 1983, the guarantors' attorney sent a letter to the FDIC stating that the property was worth approximately the amount of the debt at that time. The FDIC officer assigned to the Judico account was aware that property prices in the surrounding geographic area were declining. The FDIC obtained from the bankruptcy court an order lifting the automatic stay in August 1984 but did not sell the property until June 1985. By that time, the value of the property had declined substantially, so that after the sale, a deficiency of $500,000 still existed on the debt. The FDIC sued Coleman and Powell to collect the deficiency, and in the litigation that followed, the focal issue was whether the FDIC had breached its duty of good faith by delaying foreclosure and sale of the collateral in a period of declining property prices. Ultimately, the Supreme Court of Texas held that the FDIC had not breached its duty of good faith. The court noted that good faith is defined in the Uniform Commercial Code as "honesty in fact"—and the guarantors did not allege that the FDIC was dishonest. Furthermore, the court said, the UCC "does not require diligence for good faith."* [FDIC v. Coleman, 795 S.W.2d 706 (Tex. 1990)]

1. The Texas Supreme Court pointed out that charging creditors with a good faith obligation to consider market factors—such as declining property prices—in timing the sale of collateral would impose an unfair burden. Creditors would have to be closely attuned to changes in the market prices of any repossessed collateral to be sold. For example, in an era of *rising* property prices, creditors could be held to have violated their duty of good faith if they failed to *delay* selling the collateral so as to obtain the best price—

and so on. Do you believe that this argument justifies the court's decision in this case?

2. In view of the guarantors' waiver of the bank's obligation to sell the collateral at all, would it be fair to hold the FDIC liable for the deficiency? Should the waiver extend to the *timeliness* of the sale, as well as to the sale itself?

3. Solely from an ethical point of view, do you think that the FDIC acted wrongfully in any way in delaying the foreclosure sale? The court maintained that it did not have a legal obligation to sell the collateral as soon as possible, but did it have an ethical duty to do so?

4. If you believe that the FDIC should have been legally obligated to sell the collateral promptly because property values were declining, how would you define "promptly"? In other words, should the FDIC have held the sale at the very earliest possible moment? What if it delayed a week, or a month? At what point would the FDIC be liable for breaching its duty? Do such definitional difficulties constitute a sufficient basis for holding that good faith should not be imposed on the creditor in timing the sale of collateral?

24-14. Case Briefing Assignment

Examine Case A.24 [Mellon Bank, N.A. v. Securities Settlement Corp., 710 F.Supp. 991 (D.N.J. 1989)] in Appendix A. The case has been excerpted there in great detail. Review and then brief the case, making sure that you include answers to the following questions in your brief.

1. Who brought this lawsuit, and why?
2. What was the threshold issue in this case, according to the court?
3. On what grounds did each of the parties move for summary judgment?
4. What did the court mean by its statement that it "must sail between the Scylla of common law and the Charybdis of statute in an attempt to predict what Pennsylvania's highest court would do if confronted with this situation"?
5. What law governed the resolution of this case? Did the provisions of the UCC play a significant role in the court's reasoning?
6. What law or legal duty had Mellon violated?

Chapter 25

Takeovers and Mergers

Corporations often expand the size or scope of their business operations by raising capital in the financial markets for the construction of new plants, the acquisition of new equipment, or the research and development of new products. Alternatively, corporations may accomplish the same expansion by acquiring the assets or shares of other firms. There are also other reasons for a corporation's acquiring the assets or shares of another corporation. A corporation may wish to increase its property or investment holdings or acquire the know-how or goodwill of another corporation. Sometimes acquisition is motivated by a desire to eliminate a competitor or to ensure adequate resources and markets for the acquiring corporation's product.

Whatever its purpose, a corporation may acquire the assets of, or a controlling interest in, another corporation through several different means. A corporation may *merge* with another corporation, in which case the operations of the acquired firm are absorbed into the corporate structure of the acquiring firm. Alternatively, two firms may blend their corporate structures so as to form a new, distinct firm through *consolidation.* And of course, a firm may simply make a direct purchase of the assets of another corporation without going through the process of a merger or consolidation. This chapter examines these various types of corporate acquisitions and transformations, which have become common in the modern corporate environment.

■ Takeovers

The most direct way in which control of another corporation may be acquired is through a **takeover**. The takeover of another corporation is accomplished through the purchase of a substantial number of the voting shares of the firm that is being acquired. The majority shareholder can then control the acquired corporation's assets and dictate its business policies. In effecting the takeover, the acquiring individual, group, or firm deals directly with the shareholders of the corporation whose control is being sought.

Takeovers are of two types: friendly and hostile. A friendly takeover occurs when the management of the firm being acquired does not oppose the acquisition. A hostile takeover, by contrast, occurs when the management of the firm being acquired opposes the acquisition. In both cases, the corporation that is the object of a takeover attempt is usually referred to as the **target firm.** The individual, group, or firm seeking to take over the target is often referred to as the **aggressor.**

Takeover Tactics

A takeover, especially one opposed by the management of the target firm—that is, a hostile takeover—can be an involved process. Some mergers begin with a public offer to buy shares from the shareholders of the target corporation. In other cases, the takeover of a publicly traded corporation may begin with an anonymous purchase of shares on an open stock exchange.

During the "merger mania" that swept Wall Street in the 1980s, corporate takeovers often resembled open warfare. Takeover battles were sometimes launched in a manner comparable to an army's surprise invasion of another country. Corporate "raiders" went to great lengths to keep from tipping opposing management to the fact that their company was "in play." Decoys were sent to board airline jets, for example, while the true parties darted off in the opposite direction to meet in seclusion with their investment advisors and lawyers to map out corporate battle plans. Sometimes *dummy* corporations would be dispersed throughout the United States to make purchases of shares without revealing the names of those parties actually involved.[1] Often smaller blocks of shares would be sold simultaneously with the ongoing purchases so as to avoid running up the price of the stock of the target and alerting others that a takeover attempt was in the making.

Many of these tactics tested the limits of what was legally permissible in waging a takeover battle, and in some instances the limits were exceeded: by the close of the decade, a number of prominent investment bankers and financiers were either behind bars or awaiting sentencing for violations of federal securities laws.

---

1. Secrecy may be carried only so far under federal securities laws. Under the Williams Act, anyone acquiring over 5 percent of any class of a corporation's securities must file a statement with the SEC detailing certain information, such as the source of the funds used for the acquisition, the plans for the corporation that the acquiring party may have in purchasing the securities, and any contracts or agreements the acquiring party may have with the corporation.

"BEACHHEAD" ACQUISITION AND PROXY FIGHT An attempted takeover may begin with a gradual accumulation of a block of the target corporation's shares. Having established a *beachhead* with the block of shares (hence the name, **beachhead acquisition**), the aggressor may then launch a *proxy fight* for control of the corporation. A **proxy fight** resembles a political campaign in that the aggressor must secure the *proxies* of other shareholders. A **proxy** entitles its holder to cast votes on behalf of the individual conferring the proxy; a proxy may be obtained for each share that may be voted. If the shares owned, coupled with the proxies obtained, represent enough votes to outvote all other shareholders, effective control of the corporation will have been obtained. The controlling group usually exercises control by using its majority vote to elect a board of directors that supports its views.

To wage a successful proxy contest, an aggressor must obtain a list of shareholders so that the shareholders may be contacted and their proxies solicited. Federal securities laws require that the corporation's management provide only minimal assistance to the aggressor. Management may even resist providing a list of shareholders; in that event, costly litigation may result. Moreover, even when the aggressor secures a list of shareholders, it must pay the costs associated with contacting the shareholders and mailing the proxy requests. In contrast, management's solicitations to the shareholders may be charged to the corporation—at least insofar as the contest between the group seeking control and the incumbent management is based on issues of corporate policy, rather than being a personality contest between two opposing factions. Most courts have allowed management to charge to the corporation reasonable expenses of "educating" the shareholders about the policy issues raised in a particular proxy fight.

The rules of solicitation and other aspects of a proxy contest are slanted in favor of the incumbent management. Also, the solicitation process can be lengthy and expensive—especially if the incumbent management balks at turning over a list of shareholders from whom proxies may be solicited. Thus, other takeover strategies have been favored over the proxy contest in recent times. Nonetheless, there are some factors that may lessen the one-sidedness of the proxy fight. One factor is the increased importance of the institutional investor in financial markets. Obtaining the support of a handful of institutional investors that hold large blocks of shares obviates the need to contact a multitude of individual investors, each of whom may hold only a small fraction of the corporation's voting shares. In addition, an aggressor that is successful in its proxy fight may recoup the expense of its efforts by having the corporation approve a reimbursement out of corporate funds; again, however, the legality of such action turns on whether the contest involved policy issues rather than personalities.

TENDER OFFER ACQUISITION   A takeover battle frequently begins when the aggressor makes a tender offer to the shareholders of the target company. A **tender offer** is a public offer to all shareholders of the target corporation to purchase from them their shares in the target corporation. The price offered is generally higher than the market price of the target stock prior to the announcement of the tender offer. The higher price induces shareholders to tender (offer to sell) their shares to the acquiring firm.

The tender offer can be conditional on the receipt of a specified number of outstanding shares by a specified date. An offering corporation can make an **exchange tender offer,** in which it offers target stockholders its own securities in exchange for their target stock. In a **cash tender offer,** the offeror offers the target stockholders cash in exchange for their target stock.

Federal securities laws strictly control the terms, duration, and circumstances under which most tender offers may be made. In addition, a majority of states have passed antitakeover statutes that impose additional regulations on tender offers when in-state companies are involved.

The use of the tender offer as a method of gaining corporate control began in the mid-1960s. Highly contested legal battles and enormous expenses involved in complying with federal and state regulations have worked in some cases to discourage the use of tender offers as a vehicle for obtaining control of a corporation through stock purchase.

LEVERAGED BUY-OUTS (LBOS)   In the last decade, a number of corporations have arranged to "go private" through so-called **leveraged buy-outs (LBOs).** In an LBO, the management of a corporation—or any other group, but management is usually included—purchases all outstanding corporate stock held by the public and in this way gains control over the corporate enterprise. The LBO is financed by borrowing against the assets of the corporation, which may include real estate or plant and equipment. The borrowing may take the form of the issuance of bonds, a straight bank loan, or a loan from an investment bank. Because an LBO often results in a high debt load for the corporation, the interest payments on the debt may become so burdensome that the corporation cannot survive. Some corporations have failed to survive following LBOs for this reason.

GREENMAIL   Takeover attempts may prove profitable even when they are unsuccessful. After a takeover attempt is launched—usually beginning with attainment of a beachhead acquisition of a block of shares—negotiations may begin between the aggressor and the target's incumbent management. Out of these negotiations may come an agreement in which the target agrees to pay the aggressor a premium (a price above the current market price) for its block of shares. In return, the aggressor agrees to make no further acquisitions of the target's shares for a definite period. The net result of the agreement is that the aggressor abandons any fight for control of the target in return for what is in effect a peace payment. Such payments are referred to as **greenmail.**

As unseemly as greenmail may appear, it is not illegal. And it may be quite profitable—for the aggressor, anyway. For example, T. Boone Pickens and his small firm, Mesa Petroleum Corporation, launched six different takeover attempts between 1982 and 1985. Even though not a single attempt was successful, the firm earned $978 million merely by collecting its greenmail. Whether greenmailing will continue to generate such enormous profits is open to doubt. In the future, it may be prohibited by legislation. In the meantime, in an effort to curb the use of greenmail, Congress has imposed a nondeductible excise tax on the receipt of such payments.

Takeover Defenses

As discussed in Chapter 14, the directors of a corporation owe a fiduciary duty to the shareholders. In the context of a tender offer, this requires that, after full consideration, the directors of the target firm make a good faith decision as to whether the shareholders' acceptance or rejection of the offer would be most beneficial. In making any recommendation, the directors must fully disclose all *material facts.* A fact is material if there is a substantial likelihood that a reasonable shareholder would consider it important in deciding how to vote. For example, information identifying a good price for the stock would be considered material.

Sometimes, a target firm's board of directors sees a tender offer as favorable and recommend to the shareholders that they accept it. Alternatively, to resist a takeover, a target company may make a *self tender,* which is an offer to acquire stock from its own shareholders and thereby retain corporate control. Alternatively, a target corporation might resort to one of several other tactics.

CROWN JEWEL DEFENSE   Virtually every corporation, and certainly every conglomerate (a firm owning two or more unrelated businesses), possesses a variety of assets. Some of course are more valuable than others. An extreme example would be a firm that owned an aging mining operation in Reno and an extremely valuable parcel of real estate in downtown Manhattan. When a corporation is threatened with an imminent takeover, management may seek to prevent the takeover by making the firm less attractive to the aggressor. One way to do so is to sell off its valuable assets. In our example, the firm would sell its Manhattan real estate. By selling the valuable asset and retaining the undesirable one, the firm becomes less of a prize in a potential takeover. This defense is referred to as the **crown jewel defense** because the firm attempts to avoid a takeover by selling off its most valuable asset—that is, its *crown jewel.*

SCORCHED EARTH TACTICS   A related defense involves *scorched earth tactics.* These tactics work in ways virtually identical to the crown jewel defense by eliminating the valuable assets of the target firm and pursuing other actions designed to make the target less appealing to an aggressor. Under **scorched earth tactics**, the target firm sells off assets or divisions or takes out loans that it agrees to pay in the event of a takeover. These actions make the target less financially attractive to the aggressor.

POISON PILL DEFENSE   Another way in which a firm may make itself less attractive to takeover is by *swallowing a poison pill.* The **poison pill** defense involves the target corporation's issuing to its stockholders shares that may be exchanged for cash upon the occurrence of a successful takeover. This not only makes the target less attractive to take over but also has the potential for making the takeover prohibitively expensive for a successful aggressor; upon consummation of the takeover, the new management will be forced to redeem for cash those shares issued as part of the *poison pill.*

SHARK REPELLANT DEFENSE   A target firm may make a takeover more difficult for an aggressor by changing its articles of incorporation or its bylaws. The target corporation, upon approval of the shareholders, can make fundamental changes in its corporate structure (see Chapters 13 and 14). To make a takeover difficult, the articles or bylaws governing such changes may be amended to require that a large number of shareholders approve any fundamental change such as an acquisition, merger, or consolidation. Because this defense casts the acquiring corporation in the role of a predator, or *shark,* the tactic is called a **shark repellant** defense.

LOBSTER TRAP DEFENSE   Another way in which the target firm may effect a corporate change that makes a takeover more difficult is by preventing the aggressor from acquiring more than 10 percent of the voting shares. This may be accomplished by prohibiting the conversion of convertible securities (corporate bonds or nonvoting, preferred stock that may be converted into common shares) into common shares if the holders already own, or would own after conversion, 10 percent or more of the outstanding voting shares. Because this tactic applies only to holders of large blocks, it is referred to as the **lobster trap** defense; a lobster trap is designed to catch the larger lobsters while allowing the smaller ones to escape.

PAC-MAN DEFENSE   Consistent with the belief that the best defense is a good offense, a takeover perhaps can be avoided by the target firm's turning on the acquiring firm and taking it over. Because this defense involves the prey turning on and consuming the predator, it is commonly referred to as the **Pac-man defense** after the popular video game. In employing this strategy, the target firm may utilize any of the takeover tactics described above and used by any other aggressor.

WHITE KNIGHT DEFENSE   If it is unlikely that the target will be unable to successfully defend against an imminent takeover, it may still avoid the takeover by undertaking a merger with a third corporation, one that it favors over the aggressor. The target corporation usually searches for and solicits a merger with the third corporation. The third corporation then makes a better (often simply a higher) tender offer to the target firm's shareholders. The third corporation is seen as having *rescued* the target from an imminent takeover and is referred to as a *"white knight."* Thus, this defense is called the **white knight** defense.

GREENMAIL TACTICS   If all else is likely to fail, the target may attempt to avoid a takeover simply by paying *greenmail* to the aggressor. Greenmail has already been discussed in the context of takeover tactics. But we mention it here as well because greenmail tactics, though profitable to an aggressor, are not truly takeovers; they in fact prevent takeovers.

Greenmail payments may be justified as a means of avoiding a lengthy contest for corporate control, during which management's attention would be diverted from running the business affairs of the corporation. Whether this justifies the payment of large sums to prevent a transfer of control of the corporation is really a matter that only the majority of shareholders can resolve. Suffice it to say, however, that such payments—if sufficiently large—are an effective defense to a takeover.

GOLDEN PARACHUTE   Although not a takeover defense, the so-called **golden parachute** often comes into play when a company has failed to beat back a takeover attempt. The incumbent management more often than not is opposed to a takeover. This is generally thought to be due to the fact that top management is usually changed after a successful takeover. One way to appease the top management of a corporation, then, is to provide special termination or retirement benefits that must be paid to the management if it is replaced or "retired" following a takeover. In other words, a departing high-level manager's *parachute* will be *golden* if the manager is forced to "bail out" of the firm after a takeover.

These golden parachute arrangements are often criticized as having been extracted from the corporation with the acquiescence of a too-compliant board of directors. In fact, though, it may be in the corporation's best interest to provide such arrangements. Managerial skills are a valuable commodity. If one firm is not willing to pay for a high level of skill, others will be. In the market for managerial talent, offering golden parachutes may be the only way a corporation can secure highly competent managers.

LIMITATIONS ON TAKEOVER DEFENSES   The ultimate responsibility for deciding whether to accept or resist a takeover attempt rests with the target corporation's board of directors. In making its decision, the board must meet the standards imposed under its fiduciary duty to the corporation's shareholders. Whether the board decides to accept or resist the takeover attempt, it must meet high standards of loyalty and care. Indeed, because the directors—especially inside directors, who also serve as officers of the target corporation—may fear being replaced after a successful takeover, the degree of scrutiny used in assessing whether the directors met their standard of duty and care in trying to fend off a takeover may be greater than the degree of scrutiny applied to directors who accept a takeover.

Shareholders frequently benefit from the efforts of the aggressor either through an improvement in management or simply as a result of having the opportunity to sell their shares for a premium to a corporate suitor. Directors may fear being replaced, however. Thus, there is the potential for conflict between the interests of the shareholders and the interests of the directors. This potential conflict may limit the board's efforts in resisting a takeover attempt. The following case discusses the limits to which directors may go in using many of the takeover defenses discussed in this section.

Case 25.1

**REVLON, INC. v.
MacANDREWS &
FORBES HOLDINGS,
INC.**

Delaware Supreme Court,
1986.
506 A.2d 173.

BACKGROUND AND FACTS *In June 1985, Pantry Pride first approached Revlon about the possibility of a friendly acquisition of Revlon. The initiative was rebuffed (possibly because of personal animosity Revlon's chairman harbored against his counterpart at Pantry Pride). In anticipation of a hostile takeover, Revlon's board authorized two defensive tactics: the repurchase of up to 5 million outstanding shares and a poison pill defense. As a poison pill, the board authorized the distribution of $65 promissory notes (one for each share of outstanding stock) at 12 percent interest if an aggressor acquired 20 percent of Revlon's shares. This defensive action was later followed by Pantry Pride's making a hostile tender offer to Revlon's shareholders. Revlon, having been advised by its investment bankers that the Pantry Pride offer did not reflect the intrinsic worth of the company, recommended that its shareholders reject the offer. Revlon also countered with its own offer to purchase 10 million common shares in exchange for a combination of subordinated notes and preferred, convertible stock. The notes contained covenants limiting Revlon's ability to incur additional debt, sell assets, or pay dividends unless approved by nonmanagement members of Revlon's board of directors. In addition, Revlon's board authorized a search for another firm—a white knight—that would be interested in acquiring Revlon. Eventually, Revlon's board authorized a leveraged buyout by Forstmann, Little & Co., an investment banking boutique specializing in LBOs. As part of the LBO plan, Revlon agreed to grant Forstmann a "lock-up" option on valuable Revlon divisions. This option entitled Forstmann to purchase the divisions for a value approximately $100 to $175 million below their estimated market value if another acquiror got 40 percent of Revlon's shares. In addition to other provisions, Revlon was to waive certain restrictions contained in its notes. The announcement of the waiver caused the market value of Revlon's notes to fall dramatically, and many of the note holders threatened to sue Revlon and its directors. All the while, Pantry Pride had continued to raise its bid. The Forstmann proposal finally accepted by Revlon's board was for a higher per share price than the most recent Pantry Pride offer; its approval was aided by the fact that Forstmann's financing was securely in place; and Forstmann agreed to support the notes at their par value (thus avoiding the threatened litigation by the notes' holders). Pantry Pride sought an injunction to prevent the board from carrying out its concessions to Forstmann. The court of chancery held in favor of Pantry Pride and enjoined certain actions by the board. The court concluded that Revlon's directors had breached their duty of loyalty by making concessions to Forstmann out of concern for their potential liability to the noteholders, rather than seeking to maximize the sale price of the company for the benefit of the shareholders. The injunction was appealed to the Delaware Supreme Court.*

MOORE, Justice.
* * * *

The first relevant defensive measure adopted by the Revlon board was the Rights Plan, which would be considered a "poison pill" in the current language of corporate takeovers—a plan by which shareholders receive the right to be bought out by the corporation at a substantial premium on the occurrence of a stated triggering event. Thus, the focus becomes one of reasonableness and purpose.

* * * In adopting the Plan, the board protected the shareholders from a hostile takeover at a price below the company's intrinsic value, while retaining sufficient flexibility to address any proposal deemed to be in the stockholders' best interests.

* * * *

The second defensive measure adopted by Revlon to thwart a Pantry Pride takeover was the company's own exchange offer for 10 million of its shares. The directors' general broad powers to manage the business and affairs of the corporation are augmented by the specific authority conferred under [Delaware statutes], permitting the company to deal in its own stock. However, when exercising that power in an effort to forestall a hostile takeover, the board's actions are strictly held to the fiduciary standards outlined in *Unocal [Corp. v. Mesa Petroleum Co.]*. These standards require the directors to determine the best interests of the corporation and its stockholders, and impose an enhanced duty to abjure any action that is motivated by considerations other than a good faith concern for such interests.

The Revlon directors concluded that Pantry Pride's $47.50 offer was grossly inadequate. In that regard the board acted in good faith, and on an informed basis, with reasonable grounds to believe that there existed a harmful threat to the corporate enterprise. The adoption of a defensive measure, reasonable in relation to the threat posed, was proper and fully accorded with the powers, duties, and responsibilities conferred upon directors under our law.

However, when Pantry Pride increased its offer to $50 per share, and then to $53, it became apparent to all that the break-up of the company was inevitable. The Revlon board's authorization permitting management to negotiate a merger or buyout with a third party was a recognition that the company was for sale. The duty of the board had thus changed from the preservation of Revlon as a corporate entity to the maximization of the company's value at a sale for the stockholders' benefit. This significantly altered the board's responsibilities under the *Unocal* standards. It no longer faced threats to corporate policy and effectiveness, or to the stockholders' interests, from a grossly inadequate bid. The whole question of defensive measures became moot. The directors' role changed from defenders of the corporate bastion to auctioneers charged with getting the best price for the stockholders at a sale of the company.

This brings us to the lock-up with Forstmann and its emphasis on shoring up the sagging market value of the Notes in the face of threatened litigation by their holders. Such a focus was inconsistent with the changed concept of the directors' responsibilities at this stage of the developments. The impending waiver of the Notes covenants had caused the value of the Notes to fall, and the board was aware of the noteholders' ire as well as their subsequent threats of suit. The directors thus made support of the Notes an integral part of the company's dealings with Forstmann, even though their primary responsibility at this stage was to the equity owners.

The original threat posed by Pantry Pride—the break-up of the company—had become a reality which even the directors embraced. Selective dealing to fend off a hostile but determined bidder was no longer a proper objective. Instead, obtaining the highest price for the benefit of the stockholders should have been the central theme guiding director action. Thus, the Revlon board could not make the requisite showing of good faith by preferring the noteholders and ignoring its duty of loyalty to the shareholders. The rights of the former already were fixed by contract. The noteholders required no further protection, and when the Revlon board entered into an auction-ending lock-up agreement with Forstmann on the basis of impermissible considerations at the expense of the shareholders, the directors breached their primary duty of loyalty.

DECISION AND REMEDY *The court held that the "lock-up" and other measures taken by the board are legal under Delaware law. Such actions nonetheless represent a breach of fiduciary duty if they are not pursued in the best interests of the stockholders—specifically, if they are pursued without concern for the maximization of shareholders' profit. The court found that Revlon's board had pursued its actions out of a desire to avoid being sued by the disgruntled noteholders.*

ANTITRUST LAW AS A TAKEOVER DEFENSE

A target may also seek an injunction against an acquiring corporation on grounds that the attempted takeover violates antitrust laws, which are intended to prevent the illegal restraint of competition. This defense may succeed if the takeover would, in the eyes of a court, result in a substantial increase in the acquiring corporation's market power. Because antitrust laws are designed to protect competition rather than competitors, incumbent managers who are able to avoid takeovers by resorting to the use of private antitrust actions are unintended beneficiaries of the laws.

Antitrust challenges to mergers may be brought by the government rather than private parties. Hence, the antitrust considerations involved in a proposed takeover—or, for that matter, a proposed merger or consolidation—exist apart from the consideration of defense tactics. Therefore, we devote a separate section to the antitrust issues involved in takeovers and mergers. First, we continue our discussion of the basic forms of corporate transformations and acquisitions.

■ The Mechanics of Merger and Consolidation

The terms *merger* and *consolidation* are often used interchangeably, but they refer to two legally distinct proceedings. Whether a combination is in fact a merger or a consolidation, however, the rights and liabilities of shareholders, the corporation, and its creditors are the same.

Merger

A **merger** involves the legal combination of two or more corporations. After a merger, only one of the corporations continues to exist. For example, Corporation A and Corporation B decide to merge. It is agreed that A will absorb B; so upon merger,

B ceases to exist as a separate entity, and A continues as the **surviving corporation.** This process is illustrated graphically in Exhibit 25–1.

After the merger, A is recognized as a single corporation possessing all the rights, privileges, and powers of itself and B. A automatically acquires all of B's property and assets without the necessity of formal transfer. A becomes liable for all B's debts and obligations. Finally, A's articles of incorporation are deemed *amended* to include any changes that are stated in the *articles of merger.*

■ Exhibit 25–1 Merger

In this illustration, Corporations A and B decide to merge. They agree that A will absorb B, so that on merging, B ceases to exist as a separate entity, and A continues as the surviving corporation.

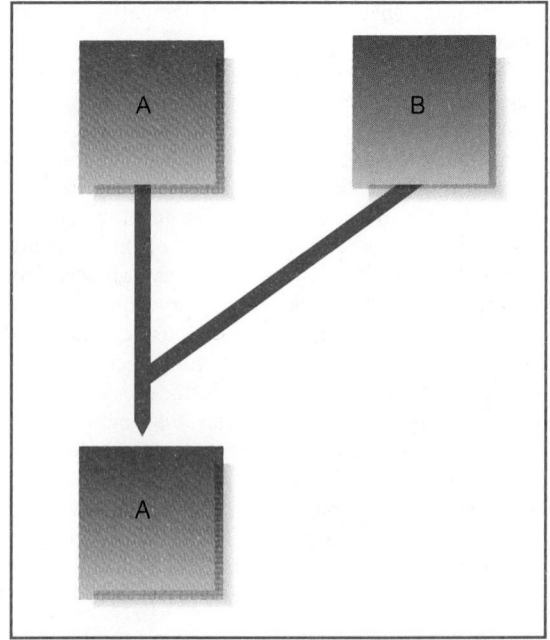

In a merger, the surviving corporation is vested with the disappearing corporation's preexisting legal rights and obligations. For example, if the disappearing corporation had a right of action against a third party, the surviving corporation could bring suit after the merger to recover the disappearing corporation's damages.

Consolidation

In the case of a **consolidation,** two or more corporations combine so that each corporation ceases to exist and a new one emerges. Corporation A and Corporation B consolidate to form an entirely new organization, Corporation C. In the process, A and B both terminate. C comes into existence as an entirely new entity. This process is illustrated graphically in Exhibit 25–2.

The results of consolidation are essentially the same as the results of merger. C is recognized as a new corporation and a single entity; A and B cease to exist. C accedes to all the rights, privileges,

■ Exhibit 25–2 Consolidation
In this illustration, Corporations A and B consolidate to form an entirely new organization, Corporation C. In the process, A and B terminate, and C comes into existence as an entirely new entity.

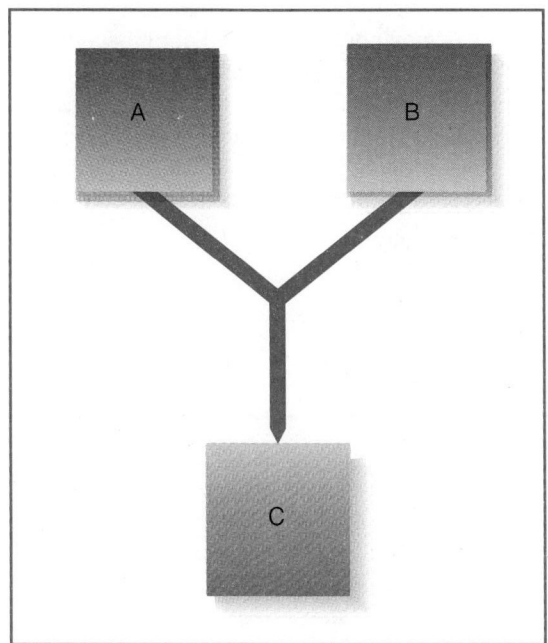

and powers previously held by A and B. Title to any property and assets owned by A and B passes to C without formal transfer. C assumes liability for all debts and obligations owed by A and B. The articles of consolidation *take the place of* A's and B's original corporate articles and are thereafter regarded as C's corporate articles.

When a merger or consolidation takes place, the surviving corporation or newly formed corporation will issue shares or pay some fair consideration to the shareholders of the corporation that ceases to exist.

The Merger and Consolidation Procedure

All states have statutes authorizing mergers and consolidations for *domestic* corporations, and most states allow the combination of domestic (in-state) and foreign (out-of-state) corporations. Although the procedures vary somewhat among jurisdictions, in each case the basic requirements are as outlined below:

1. The board of directors of *each* corporation involved must approve a merger or consolidation plan.
2. The shareholders of *each* corporation must vote approval of the plan at a shareholders' meeting. Most state statutes require the approval of two-thirds of the outstanding shares of voting stock, although some states require only a simple majority, and others require a four-fifths vote. Frequently, statutes require that each class of stock approve the merger; thus, the holders of nonvoting stock must also approve. A corporation's bylaws can dictate a stricter requirement.
3. Once approved by *all* of the directors and the shareholders, the plan (articles of merger or consolidation) is filed, usually with the secretary of state.
4. When state formalities are satisfied, the state issues a certificate of merger to the surviving corporation or a certificate of consolidation to the newly consolidated corporation.

Short-Form Mergers

A number of states provide for what is known as a **short-form merger**—a simplified procedure for the merger of a substantially owned subsidiary corporation into its parent corporation. A short-form merger (also referred to as a *parent-subsidiary merger*) can be accomplished *without approval of the shareholders* of either corporation.

The short-form merger can be used only when the parent corporation owns at least 90 percent of the outstanding shares of each class of stock of the subsidiary corporation. The simplified procedure requires that a plan for the merger be approved by the board of directors of the parent corporation before it is filed with the state. A copy of the merger plan must be sent to each shareholder of record of the subsidiary corporation.

Appraisal Rights

What if a shareholder disapproves of the merger or consolidation but is outvoted by the other shareholders? The law recognizes that a dissenting shareholder should not be forced to become an unwilling shareholder in a corporation that is new or different from the one in which the shareholder originally invested. The shareholder has the right to dissent and may be entitled to be paid *fair value* for the number of shares held on the date of the merger or consolidation. This right is referred to as the shareholder's **appraisal right.** An appraisal right is given by state statute and is available only when the statute specifically provides for it. It is normally extended to regular mergers, consolidations, short-form mergers, sales of substantially all the corporate assets not in the ordinary course of business, and in certain states, adverse amendments to the articles of incorporation.

The appraisal right may be lost if the elaborate statutory procedures are not precisely followed. Whenever the right is lost, the dissenting shareholder must go along with the objectionable transaction.

One of the basic procedures usually followed requires that a written notice of dissent be filed by the dissenting shareholder or shareholders prior to the vote of the shareholders on the proposed transaction. This notice of dissent is also basically a notice to all shareholders of costs that may be imposed by dissenting shareholders should the merger or consolidation be approved. In addition, after the merger or consolidation has been approved, the dissenting shareholders must make a written demand for payment and for fair value.

Valuation of shares is often a point of contention between the dissenting shareholder and the corporation. The Revised Model Business Corporations Act (RMBCA) 13.01 provides that the "fair value of shares" is the value on the day prior to the date on which the vote was taken.[2] The corporation must make a *written* offer to purchase a dissenting shareholder's stock, accompanying the offer with a current balance sheet and income statement for the corporation. If the shareholder and the corporation do not agree on the fair value, a court will determine it.

Once a dissenting shareholder elects appraisal rights under statute, in some jurisdictions, the shareholder loses his or her shareholder status. Without that status, a shareholder cannot vote, receive dividends, or sue to enjoin whatever action prompted his or her dissent. In some of those jurisdictions, statutes provide, or courts have held, that shareholder status may be reinstated during the appraisal process (for example, if the shareholder decides to withdraw from the process and the corporation approves). In other jurisdictions, the status may not be reinstated until the appraisal has concluded. Even if the status is lost, courts may allow an individual to sue on grounds of fraud or other illegal conduct associated with the merger.

The following case illustrates the frequently encountered problem of determining the fair value of shares under appraisal rights.

---

2. Any appreciation or depreciation of the stock in anticipation of the approval is excluded.

Case 25.2

ROSENBLATT v. GETTY OIL CO.

Supreme Court of Delaware, 1985.
493 A.2d 929.

BACKGROUND AND FACTS *In 1976, the defendant, Getty Oil, began negotiating for the merger of that corporation with Skelly Oil. Both acknowledged the desirability of a merger and agreed that an exchange of common stock would be the method of achieving that result. An engineering firm, D & M, and several investment banking and accounting firms were hired to assist in estimating asset values. Getty Oil and Skelly Oil* *immediately took an adversarial approach as each tried to value its own assets as high as possible. Eventually, Skelly agreed to an exchange ratio of 0.5875 shares of Getty stock for 1 share of Skelly stock. The boards of directors of both companies agreed to the merger and submitted the question to their respective shareholders; and with shareholder approval, the companies were merged in 1977. Rosenblatt, a minority shareholder in Skelly Oil, brought a class-action suit on behalf of himself and other Skelly Oil shareholders who disapproved of the merger. The plaintiffs challenged the fairness of the price and asset valuations and sought a review by the courts. Part of their claim was based on the fact that the valuation of Skelly assets was substantially below the liquidation price that the plaintiffs' appraisers had determined. Thus, Rosenblatt claimed that liquidation would be the only fair course for Skelly given the lower price offered by Getty Oil. The court of chancery (court of equity), however, held that the exchange ratio was fair to all shareholders, and the plaintiffs appealed.*

MOORE, Justice.
* * * *

As to the fairness of the merger price, plaintiffs claim that exclusive use of the Delaware Block method [a method of assigning weights to asset value, market value, and earnings potential] yielded a value of $110 per share, considerably less than Skelly's appraised asset value of $195 per share. * * *
* * * *

While the plaintiffs challenge the defendant's use of the Delaware Block method, that was the only valuation technique permitted at that time. * * * We find no legal error or abuse of discretion by the Chancellor's action in accepting its use here.
* * * *

* * * In Delaware a company is valued as a going concern, not on what can be obtained by its liquidation. * * * [T]he trial court properly found that Skelly was in fact depleting its reserves more rapidly than Getty, that Getty was proportionately outspending Skelly in the areas of exploration, development, and production, that Getty was more successful at finding oil, and that Getty's future prospects were superior. As to Skelly's exploration expenditure reductions, the evidence demonstrates that in large part, these reductions were due to Skelly's withdrawal from unprofitable oil and gas lease obligations. With respect to the claimed dilution of earnings and dividends, these issues were raised in the negotiations, and the Getty team agreed to raise Getty's 1977 dividend to prevent dilution. * * *

After an exhaustive review of the facts and evidence relating to the issue of fairness, we conclude that Getty dealt fairly with Skelly's minority shareholders from the genesis of the merger through approval by the respective boards of the two companies. We also conclude that the price received by the Skelly shareholders was fair.

The Supreme Court of Delaware affirmed the decision of the lower court. The exchange ratio was fair to all shareholders.

DECISION AND REMEDY

Shareholder Approval

Shareholders invest in a corporate enterprise with the expectation that the board of directors will man-

age the enterprise and will approve ordinary business matters. Actions taken on extraordinary matters must be authorized by the board of directors and the shareholders. Often, modern statutes require that certain types of extraordinary matters be approved by a vote of the shareholders. Typically, matters requiring shareholder approval include the sale, lease, or exchange of all, or substantially all, corporate assets outside of the corporation's regular course of business. Other examples include amendments to the articles of incorporation, transactions concerning merger or consolidation, and dissolution.

Hence, when any extraordinary matter arises, the corporation must proceed as authorized by law to obtain shareholder and board of director ap-

proval. Sometimes a transaction can be characterized so as not to seem to require shareholder approval, but a court will use its equity powers to require such approval. To determine the nature of the transaction, the courts will look not only to the details of the transaction but also to its consequences.

The following case involves a sale of corporate assets that was negotiated without the shareholders' approval. The shareholders opposing the sale sought injunctive relief from the court.

Case 25.3

SCHWADEL v. UCHITEL

District Court of Appeal of Florida, Third District, 1984.
455 So.2d 401.

BACKGROUND AND FACTS   *Mike and Peter Schwadel, the plaintiffs, were major shareholders in HJU Sales & Investments, Inc. Over several years the assets of the corporation had been sold off until only one asset remained—a restaurant called "The Place for Steak." The plaintiffs sued the president and third major shareholder of the corporation, Hy Uchitel, when he entered into a contract to sell this remaining asset. Florida state law prohibits the sale of all or substantially all of a corporation's assets without shareholder approval. The Schwadels sought an injunction to prevent the sale of the restaurant, but the lower court denied the request. The plaintiffs appealed.*

BASKIN, Judge.
*   *   *   *

The prerequisites of section 607.241 [of Florida statutes] must be satisfied when a contemplated sale of major assets of a corporation will substantially limit the corporate business. The Place for Steak was the sole asset of Southern Caterers of North Bay Village, Inc., the wholly owned subsidiary of HJU, and the last of several restaurants owned by parent corporation HJU. It is undisputed that the fundamental purpose in forming the parent corporation and in operating the corporate enterprise through various subsidiaries was, and continues to be, to engage in the restaurant business. Thus, the sale of The Place for Steak constitutes a sale of "substantially all" the corporate assets and is subject to the statutory rights and protections extended to stockholders under Florida's shareholder "consent" provisions governing such transactions.

The purpose of a shareholder "consent" provision is "to protect the shareholders from fundamental change, or more specifically to protect the shareholders from the destruction of the means to accomplish the purposes or objects for which the corporation was incorporated and actually performs." When Hy Uchitel entered into a contract for the sale of the last major corporate asset, he violated shareholders' statutory rights to receive prior notice to consider the transaction and effectively barred their participation in a decision which fundamentally changes the nature of the corporation. This court must therefore decide whether injunctive relief is appropriate under these circumstances.

The general rule is that a court of equity is empowered to issue injunctive relief to prevent officers or directors of a corporation from wrongfully dealing with corporate assets and to prevent such wrongful actions from infringing upon shareholders' voting rights. The proposed sale of the remaining corporate asset constituted a breach of Uchitel's fiduciary duties to the corporation and to its stockholders, and deprived shareholders of their statutory rights to notice and to vote prior to the transfer of the last corporate asset. Injunctive relief is appropriate because appellants have a clear legal right to prior notice and a vote, and legal remedies are inadequate to prevent the irreparable harm that would result from Uchitel's unilateral decision to change the fundamental nature of the corporate enterprise. An award of damages would not compensate the shareholders for the destruction of the corporation caused by the transfer of the last major corporate asset. The pending sale is therefore enjoined.

The court of appeals reversed the lower court's decision and granted an injunction to the plaintiffs.

DECISION AND REMEDY

■ Purchase of Assets

When a corporation acquires all or substantially all of the assets of another corporation by direct purchase, the purchasing corporation, or *acquiring corporation,* simply extends its ownership and control over more physical assets. Because no change in the legal entity occurs, the acquiring corporation is not required to obtain shareholder approval for the purchase.[3]

Although the acquiring corporation may not be required to obtain shareholder approval for such an acquisition, the U.S. Department of Justice has issued guidelines that significantly constrain and often prohibit mergers that could result from a purchase of assets, including takeover bids. These guidelines are part of the federal antitrust laws to enforce Section 7 of the Clayton Act.

Note that the corporation that is *selling* all its assets is substantially changing its business position and perhaps its ability to carry out its corporate purposes. For that reason, the corporation whose assets are *acquired* must obtain both board of director and shareholder approval. In most states and under the RMBCA, a dissenting shareholder of the selling corporation can demand appraisal rights.

Generally, a corporation that purchases the assets of another corporation is not responsible for the liabilities of the selling corporation. Exceptions to this rule are made in the following circumstances:

1. When the purchasing corporation impliedly or expressly assumes the seller's liabilities.
2. When the sale amounts to what in fact is a merger or a consolidation.
3. When the purchaser continues the seller's business and retains the same personnel (same shareholders, directors, and officers).
4. When the sale is fraudulently executed to escape liability.

In any of these situations, the acquiring corporation will be held to have assumed both the assets and the liabilities of the selling corporation. The following case addresses the issue of whether a corporation that purchased the assets of another firm could be subject to liability for an injury caused by a product manufactured by the selling firm.

3. If the acquiring corporation plans to pay for the assets with its own corporate stock and not enough authorized unissued shares are available, the shareholders must vote to approve issuance of additional shares by amendment of the corporate articles. Also, acquiring corporations whose stock is traded in a national stock exchange can be required to obtain their own shareholders' approval if they plan to issue a significant number of shares, such as a number equal to 20 percent or more of the outstanding shares.

BACKGROUND AND FACTS *In January 1981, Frederick Brandt, a surgeon, purchased a Tredex treadmill from Atlantic Fitness Products. The treadmill was manufactured by American Tredex Corporation. In July 1981, Nissen Corporation purchased all the assets of American Tredex, as well as its goodwill and the name, American Tredex. Subsequently, Brandt obtained replacement parts for the treadmill from Nissen. In the fall of 1986, Brandt was injured when he caught one of his fingers in the tread-*

Case 25.4

MILLER v. NISSEN CORP.

Court of Special Appeals of Maryland, 1990.
83 Md.App. 448,
575 A.2d 758.

mill's operating mechanism while performing an adjustment to the tread-mill. Brandt and his wife sued Nissen and Atlantic Fitness to recover damages, alleging, among other things, negligence and breach of warranty. Nissen moved for summary judgment, contending that it was not responsible for any injuries involving equipment sold or manufactured by American Tredex prior to the date of the asset purchase agreement (July 1981). Atlantic Fitness filed a cross-claim against Nissen for indemnity and contribution, as well as a memorandum in opposition to Nissen's motion for summary judgment. Atlantic Fitness claimed that Nissen was liable as a successor in interest to American Tredex because Nissen essentially continued American Tredex's business. The trial court granted Nissen's motion for summary judgment, and Atlantic Fitness, through Warren Miller, and Brandt appealed.

CATHELL, Judge.
* * * *

At oral argument, counsel for Nissen asked this Court to hold that * * * the grant of summary judgment * * * was appropriate, since the appellees failed to demonstrate a genuine dispute as to the question of Nissen's substantial continuation of the enterprise of American Tredex. * * * We decline to do so.
* * * *

Nissen included a copy of the asset purchase agreement as an exhibit with its motion for summary judgment. It also included an affidavit by its vice president * * * affirming, in pertinent part, that Nissen acquired an interest in American Tredex Corporation on July 31, 1981, and that Nissen neither designed, manufactured or sold any American Tredex treadmill prior to that date. Atlantic Fitness filed a memorandum in opposition to that motion, which relies on the facts contained in the asset purchase agreement as a basis for establishing Nissen's liability. That memorandum asserts that certain provisions in the asset purchase agreement (such as the purchase of its business goodwill, the title and interest in the name "American Tredex Corporation," the total inventory, patents and trademarks, customer lists, contract rights, prepaid receivables, warranties, and the continued employment of two previous high level employees of the predecessor corporation, to name but a few) evidence an intent on the part of Nissen to continue substantially the business of American Tredex. Additionally, the agreement creates an inference that the selling corporation must remain in business for a minimum of five years to "indemnify, reimburse and hold [Nissen] harmless" from liability. An inference could be made that this provision indicates that Nissen would be subject to suit after the expiration of the five-year indemnification period. Appellant, Atlantic Fitness, asserts therefore that "the totality of the transaction . . . demonstrates a basic continuity of the business of American Tredex by Nissen." * * *

Based on this information, we are unable to agree with Nissen's argument that the trial judge correctly granted its motion for summary judgment * * *. There may or may not be a genuine dispute as to the facts relating to this issue. There is, however, a clear dispute as to the inferences which arise from those facts.

DECISION AND REMEDY

The appellate court reversed the trial court's ruling and remanded the case for further proceedings. Summary judgment for Nissen was inappropriate because, based on the evidence presented, a jury could conclude that Nissen continued the business of its predecessor.

■ Financial Considerations in Takeovers and Mergers

One of the factors—indeed, perhaps the most important factor—that has propelled the unprecedented number and magnitude of mergers since the early 1980s is the innovation in corporate financing that has taken place during this same period. Financial instruments and methods of raising capital that once would have been considered unorthodox—if not altogether unsound—are now commonplace among investment bankers and corporate financial officers. Many of these innovations are affected by numerous and subtle economic forces aside from those that drive activities on Wall Street. During economic downturns, for example, financing techniques that would be used unhesitatingly under normal circumstances are employed only infrequently. In general, though, many of the recent financial innovations are now a common feature of modern corporate finance.

JUNK BONDS   The most important and most controversial innovation in corporate finance has been the so-called junk bond. A junk bond, like any bond, is a promise to pay a certain amount to investors after or during a specific period. **Junk bonds** are unique in that they are subject to a high degree of risk—the risk that the borrower will not be able to pay the lender under the terms of the bond. Because the bonds are subject to high risk they are called *junk*. The high degree of risk, however, means that investors must be compensated for taking on the risk; thus the bonds yield inordinately high returns. In theory, because only a fraction of the bonds will go into default (be unpaid in the full amount on schedule), one can still invest in junk bonds safely simply by diversifying one's portfolio (holding a diverse package of different securities).

Junk bonds have frequently been employed to finance takeovers, with the investors' being promised that they would be repaid by the aggressors' selling off some of the target corporations' assets after the acquisition had been completed. Because a takeover attempt's success is uncertain at best, and because even if it succeeds, the value of the target's assets may not be sufficient to repay the debt holders, the bonds issued to finance the attempt were often sold as junk bonds—high-risk, high-yield bonds. For awhile, the junk-bond market

seemed to offer an almost unlimited supply of funds for financing takeover bids. Eventually, though, some of the deals proved too risky. Others proved to be ill-advised for reasons other than mode of financing; some takeovers and mergers simply matched companies with managers not suited for making the resulting businesses profitable. Allegations of impropriety eventually brought down the undisputed master of the junk-bond market, Michael Milken. Milken's fall also brought down his employer, the investment banking firm of Drexel, Burnham, and Lambert, which had dominated the merger and acquisition business for nearly a decade.

These events, together with the startling decline of the stock market in October 1987, cooled the takeover fever that had raged throughout the earlier part of the 1980s. Nonetheless, reports of the demise of the junk-bond market proved to be exaggerated, and it seems likely that, regardless of whether the market is ever dominated as completely as it was under Milken, junk bonds will remain a feature of corporate finance. Thus, there remains the potential that even the largest, most well-established firm can become the target of a small, unknown aggressor.

TWO-TIER FINANCING   In a two-tier process, the aggressor acquires a controlling interest in the target by making a very attractive purchase offer to the shareholders of the target corporation. After obtaining a sufficient number of shares through its initial offer to achieve a controlling interest, the aggressor then merges the acquired firm into one of the aggressor's subsidiaries. The minority shareholders in the target firm are usually helpless to oppose the merger. They are paid less for their shares and are thus eliminated at a lower price. For example, U.S. Steel acquired a controlling interest in Marathon Oil after making a tender offer of $125 per share to the Marathon shareholders. After acquiring its controlling interest, U.S. Steel instigated a merger. According to the terms of the merger Marathon's minority shareholders (those who had elected not to accept the tender offer) were given U.S. Steel stock worth $16 per share. In subsequent litigation, the actions under this two-tier plan were held to have been lawful.[4]

---

4.   *Randal v. Thomas,* 772 F.2d 244 (6th Cir. 1985).

◼ Federal Securities Law and Takeovers and Mergers

The important role played by federal securities laws in the area of corporate finance extends to takeovers and mergers. One of the most important pieces of federal legislation concerning takeovers is the Williams Act. The act, passed by Congress in 1970, amended Sections 13 and 14 of the Securities Exchange Act of 1934. The Williams Act regulates offers to buy stock, specifically tender offers. The provisions of the act apply to all offers to buy more than 5 percent of another corporation's securities.

THE RATIONALE OF THE WILLIAMS ACT The underlying purpose of the Williams Act is to create a level playing field for both the target and the aggressor. The act also is intended to protect shareholders against unfair and deceptive practices in the securities market. Many economists contend that the act is misguided and perhaps counterproductive. Others contend that federal action is necessary to protect less powerful interests and unsophisticated investors. Because so many different groups with divergent interests are affected, the regulation of takeovers is often influenced more by political considerations than by economic ones. As discussed in the subsequent section, this tendency is even more pronounced at the state level.

THE SUBSTANTIVE PROVISIONS OF THE WILLIAMS ACT The important provisions of the Williams Act impose disclosure requirements on aggressors and targets. In addition, the act's provisions establish the basic framework for making a tender offer.

Section 13(d) of the Williams Act focuses on open-market and privately negotiated acquisitions. Under 13(d), any person who acquires more than 5 percent ownership of securities registered under Section 12 of the Securities Exchange Act (the section pertaining to reporting requirements) must file a statement of ownership with the Securities and Exchange Commission. The filing must be made within ten days after the 5 percent ownership level has been reached. The filing must disclose information about the individual or organization making the purchase and the details of any financial arrangements that were made in order to make the purchase. The information disclosure must state the purchaser's intentions regarding the corporation whose stock has been acquired, such as whether or not a tender offer is anticipated and whether or not a merger or consolidation is intended. A purchaser may simply state that the purchase is purely for investment purposes, if in fact that is the purchaser's intent. Section 13(d) is intended to alert a target's shareholders and management to an imminent takeover attempt.

Section 14(d) of the Williams Act pertains to tender offers. Like Section 13(d) of the act, Section 14(d) applies to all securities subject to the reporting requirements of the Securities Exchange Act of 1934. With regard to such securities, Section 14(d) requires that any person planning to make a tender offer file with the Securities and Exchange Commission all solicitations, advertisements, and any other material to be used in making the tender offer. The tender offeror must also disclose information such as financial arrangements and future intentions concerning the target, much as in a Section 13(d) disclosure. The filings and disclosure must precede the distribution of the tender offer materials. Anyone planning to oppose or support the tender offer must likewise file materials relating to the offer prior to distributing the materials.

Section 14(f) of the Williams Act requires that a public disclosure be made of the identities of persons to be elected to the board and any agreements affecting the directors of the target during the transfer of management control should the tender offer succeed.

If a takeover proceeds uncontested, the target company's directors must make one of the following declarations to the shareholders within ten days of the announcement of the tender offer: (1) that it recommends that the shareholders accept the offer or that they reject it, (2) that it has no opinion on the offer, or (3) that it is unable to take any position concerning the offer.

◼ State Law Restrictions on Takeovers and Mergers

Managers and directors are not the only corporate personnel who have reason to fear a takeover or merger. A company's rank and file also face potential hardship from corporate changes. Indeed, the rank and file may have even more to fear than others. Stockholders often walk away from a takeover or merger having sold their shares to the aggressor at a substantial premium. As discussed earlier, the target corporation's directors and top managers may also find a takeover profitable: many either stay on under the new organization or leave after collecting the compensation benefits contained in their golden parachutes. But just as often, the rank and file do not fare so well.

THE BROADER IMPACT When the acquired corporation has served as the major employer in a community, the effects of a takeover or merger can extend far beyond the employees of the company. Businesses that relied on the patronage of the acquired corporation's employees also suffer. Indeed, the closing of a major plant or division of the acquired company can be the death warrant for an entire community.

Most thoughtful observers recognize that the gains from active competition for corporate assets are essential to a modern, dynamic economy. Corporate takeovers and mergers are a necessary component of competition. Without the threat of being replaced by more aggressive, entrepreneurial-minded managers, a company's leaders may become complacent. Without competition for corporate assets, there is no guarantee that labor and capital will be allocated to their most valuable uses. Still, though, when it is your job, your family and community, it is easy to lose sight of the "big picture." What is indisputably beneficial for the overall economy may seem to be an inequitable burden for the individual worker. Moreover, the adverse effects of takeovers and mergers have fallen disproportionately on local communities where plant closings and layoffs have occurred.

Because state governments are inevitably more concerned with regional and local concerns than with the broader issues, it is not surprising that state governments have been the most hostile to unrestrained competition for corporate assets. Over several decades, various states have launched direct legislative assaults on takeovers and mergers. The rationale apparently has been that the best strategy for mitigating the hardships wrought by corporate acquisitions is the outright elimination of takeovers and mergers.

THE STATES' RESPONSE Over a twenty-year span, states have enacted three generations of antitakeover statutes. Illinois enacted a first-generation statute. Under the Illinois law, acquisition of any firm that had substantial assets in Illinois was forbidden unless approved by a public official. The law was declared unconstitutional under the Commerce Clause of the United States Constitution.[5]

Indiana has since enacted a second-generation statute that provides that the aggressor's shares in the target firm lose their voting power unless either the target's directors approve the acquisition or the shareholders not affiliated with the aggressor or management authorize restoration of the shares' voting power. The Supreme Court upheld the law, finding no inconsistency between the state's law and federal law because the Indiana statute allowed any aggressor to acquire shares unhindered.[6] The Indiana statute makes the shares of Indiana corporations less attractive, but it does not interfere with the process of bidding for shares in an attempted acquisition. The Court held that the law does not violate the Commerce Clause of the United States Constitution. The Court instead found that the law deals only with the internal affairs of a corporation. The Court also found the statute potentially beneficial to shareholders because it allows investors to avoid coercion from two-tier bids and similar takeover tactics.

The following case deals with the third generation of state antitakeover statutes. The case involves a Wisconsin law that requires an aggressor to wait three years after buying shares in the target corporation before merging with the company or acquiring more than 5 percent of its assets, unless the board of the target agrees in advance to an earlier takeover.

---

5. *Edgar v. MITE Corp.*, 457 U.S. 624, 102 S.Ct. 2629, 73 L.Ed.2d 269 (1982).

6. *CTS Corp. v. Dynamics Corp. of America*, 481 U.S. 69, 107 S.Ct. 1637, 95 L.Ed.2d 67 (1987).

Case 25.5

**AMANDA ACQUISITION
CORP. v. UNIVERSAL
FOODS CORP.**
United States Court of Appeals,
Seventh Circuit, 1989.
877 F.2d 496.

BACKGROUND AND FACTS   *Amanda Acquisition was a shell corporation formed for the sole purpose of acquiring control of Universal Foods,
a diversified company incorporated under the laws of Wisconsin. Amanda
commenced an all-cash tender offer for Universal shares, conditioned on
at least 75 percent of Universal's shares being tendered. Under Wisconsin
law, no firm incorporated in the state and having its headquarters, substantial operations, or 10 percent of its shareholders there may "engage
in a business combination with an interested stockholder" until three years
after the "interested stockholder's stock-acquisition date" unless approved
in advance by the Wisconsin corporation's directors. Because Amanda's
financing was contingent on a prompt merger with the target, Universal,
the tender offer was also made contingent on a judicial declaration that
the Wisconsin law was unconstitutional or otherwise invalid under federal
law. Amanda filed suit in a federal district court, contending that the Wisconsin statute was preempted by the Williams Act and inconsistent with
the Commerce Clause. The trial court disagreed, and Amanda appealed
to the United States Court of Appeals for the Seventh Circuit.*

EASTERBROOK, Circuit Judge.
*   *   *   *

*   *   * Unless a federal statute or the Constitution bars the way, Wisconsin's
choice must be respected.
*   *   *   *

The Williams Act regulates the process of tender offers: timing, disclosure,
proration if tenders exceed what the bidder is willing to buy, best-price rules. It slows
things down, allowing investors to evaluate the offer and management's response.
Best-price, proration, and short-tender rules ensure that investors who decide at the
end of the offer get the same treatment as those who decide immediately, reducing
pressure to leap before looking. After complying with the disclosure and delay
requirements, the bidder is free to take the shares. *   *   * [The act says] nothing
about the voting power of shares acquired in tender offers. *   *   *
*   *   *   *

Any bidder complying with federal law is free to acquire shares of Wisconsin
firms on schedule. Delay in completing a second-stage merger may make the target
less attractive, and thus depress the price offered or even lead to an absence of bids;
it does not, however, alter any of the procedures governed by federal regulation.
Indeed Wisconsin's law does not depend in any way on how the acquiring firm came
by its stock: open-market purchases, private acquisitions of blocs, and acquisitions
via tender offers are treated identically. Wisconsin's law is no different in effect
from one saying that for the three years after a person acquires 10% of a firm's stock,
a unanimous vote is required to merge. Corporate law once had a generally applicable
unanimity rule in major transactions, a rule discarded because giving every investor
the power to block every reorganization stopped many desirable changes. (Many
investors could use their "hold-up" power to try to engross a larger portion of the
gains, creating a complex bargaining problem that often could not be solved.) Wisconsin's more restrained version of unanimity also may block beneficial transactions,
but not by tinkering with any of the procedures established in federal law.
*   *   * It is not attractive to put bids on the table for Wisconsin corporations,
but because Wisconsin leaves the process alone once a bidder appears, its law may
co-exist with the Williams Act.
*   *   *   *

Buyers of stock in Wisconsin firms may exercise full rights as investors, taking immediate control. No interstate transaction is regulated or forbidden. True, Wisconsin's law makes a potential buyer less willing to buy (or depresses the bid), but this is equally true of [other valid state rules]. Many other rules of corporate law—supermajority voting requirements, staggered and classified boards, and so on—have similar or greater effects on some persons' willingness to purchase stock. States could ban mergers outright, with even more powerful consequences. *   *   *

*   *   *   *

*   *   * A state with the power to forbid mergers has the power to defer them for three years. Investors can turn to firms incorporated in states committed to the dominance of market forces, or they can turn on legislators who enact unwise laws. The Constitution has room for many economic policies. "[A] law can be both economic folly and constitutional." Wisconsin's law may well be folly; we are confident that it is constitutional.

The court affirmed the trial court's decision by holding that the Wisconsin law neither violated the United States Constitution nor was preempted by federal securities law. The case was subsequently appealed to the United States Supreme Court, but the Court denied certiorari *for review, thus giving its tacit approval of the Wisconsin statute.*

DECISION AND REMEDY

■ Terms and Concepts to Review

aggressor 598	**junk bonds** 611	**scorched earth tactics** 600
appraisal right 606	**leveraged buy-outs**	**shark repellant** 600
beachhead acquisition 598	**(LBOs)** 599	**short-form merger** 605
cash tender offer 599	**lobster trap** 600	**surviving corporation** 604
consolidation 605	**merger** 604	**takeover** 597
crown jewel defense 600	**Pac-man defense** 601	**target firm** 598
exchange tender offer 599	**poison pill** 600	**tender offer** 599
golden parachute 601	**proxy** 598	**white knight** 601
greenmail 599	**proxy fight** 598	

■ Questions and Case Problems

25-1. Gretz is chairman of the board of directors of Faraday, Inc., and Williams is chairman of the board of directors of Firebrand, Inc. Faraday is a manufacturing corporation, and Firebrand is a transportation corporation. Gretz and Williams meet to consider the possibility of combining their corporations and activities into a single corporate entity. They consider two alternative courses of action: acquisition by Faraday of all the stock and assets of Firebrand or combination of the two corporations to form a new corporation, Farabrand, Inc. Both chairmen are concerned about the necessity of formal transfer of property, liability for existing debts, and the problem of amending articles of incorporation. Discuss what the two proposed combinations are called and what

legal effect each has on the transfer of property, the liabilities of the combined corporations, and the need to amend the articles of incorporation.

25-2. Ann owns 10,000 shares of Ajax Corp. Her shares represent a 10 percent ownership in Ajax. Zeta Corp. is interested in acquiring Ajax in a merger, and the board of directors of each corporation has approved the merger. The shareholders of Zeta have already approved the acquisition, and Ajax has called for a shareholders' meeting to approve the merger. Ann disapproves of the merger and does not want to accept Zeta shares for the Ajax shares she holds. The market price of Ajax shares is $20 per share the day before the shareholder vote and drops to $16 on the day the shareholders of Ajax approve the merger. Discuss Ann's rights in this matter, beginning with notice of the proposed merger.

25-3. Green Corp. wants to acquire all the assets of Red Dot Corp. Green plans to pay for the assets by issuing its own corporate stock. Green's board of directors has already approved the merger. Discuss whether shareholder approval is required for this merger.

25-4. Alitech Corp. is a small midwestern business that owns a valuable patent. Alitech has approximately 1,000 shareholders with 100,000 authorized and outstanding shares. Block Corp. would like to have use of the patent, but Alitech refuses to give Block a license. Block has tried to acquire Alitech by purchasing Alitech's assets, but Alitech's board of directors has refused to approve the acquisition. Alitech's shares are presently selling for $5 per share. Discuss how Block Corp. might proceed to gain the control and use of Alitech's patent.

25-5. On March 6, 1981, Carolyn Hamaker lost three fingers from her left hand while operating a notcher machine (a lathe) at her place of employment in South Dakota, Pallets and Wood Products. The notching machine had been manufactured by Kenwel Machine Co. On December 31, 1975, Kenwel sold its assets to John and Rosemary Jackson, who created a new company called Kenwel-Jackson Machine Co. Kenwel Machine Co. terminated its existence in August 1977. Kenwel-Jackson Machine Co. continued to manufacture notchers, but it made several design changes and was in fact producing a different machine from the one that injured Carolyn Hamaker. As a result of her injuries, Hamaker brought a suit for damages against Kenwel-Jackson, because Kenwel Machine Co. no longer existed. Discuss whether Kenwel-Jackson is liable for injuries caused by a machine manufactured by a company it purchased. [*Hamaker v. Kenwel-Jackson Machine Co.,* 387 N.W.2d 515 (S.D. 1986)]

25-6. Davis Aircraft Products Co. was engaged in the business of designing, manufacturing, and selling restraints used in aircraft. Prior to November 1984, Davis Aircraft conducted its manufacturing operations out of a building located in Northport, New York. Because the Northport facility required extensive repairs, Davis Aircraft began to search for a new building and subsequently exchanged the Northport building for a building owned by Thomas Mara in Bohemia, New York. Bruce Davis, the president of Davis Aircraft, claimed that the Bohemia facility was "significantly more efficient for manufacturing" than was the Northport facility. The manufacturing operations continued as before. A shareholder of Davis Aircraft, Pamela Dukas, alleged that the transaction was voidable because shareholder approval had not been obtained. The trial court denied Davis Aircraft's request for summary judgment, and Davis Aircraft appealed. Will the appellate court hold that shareholder approval was required for this transaction? Discuss fully. [*Dukas v. Davis Aircraft Products Co.,* 131 A.D.2d 720, 516, N.Y.S.2d 781 (1987)]

25-7. Edward Antar and William Markowitz were the sole stockholders and directors of E.B.M., Inc., a corporation formed for the purpose of buying and managing real estate. Antar and Markowitz were also the controlling shareholders and directors of Acousti-Phase, Inc., a corporation that man-

ufactured and sold stereo speakers. In 1982, Acousti-Phase was effectively shut down when a fire destroyed the manufacturing and storage facility that it was renting from E.B.M. Shortly after the fire, E.B.M. contracted with a New York firm to assemble the speakers, affix the Acousti-Phase name, and sell the final product, primarily to former customers of Acousti-Phase. At the time of the fire, Acousti-Phase owed Cab-Tek, Inc.—a corporation that supplied it with cabinet housings for its stereo speakers—$26,470. In 1985, Cab-Tek sued E.B.M. to recover the debt owed by Acousti-Phase. Discuss fully whether E.B.M. can be held liable for Acousti-Phase's debt. [*Cab-Tek, Inc. v. E.B.M., Inc.,* 153 Vt. 432, 571 A.2d 671 (1990)]

25-8. A Question of Ethics

 The Natomas Corporation merged with the Diamond Shamrock Corporation. Under the terms of the merger, Diamond Shamrock retained its corporate identity and the Natomas Corporation was absorbed into the former's corporate hierarchy. As part of the merger agreement, five inside directors (individuals who serve as officers of the corporation and sit as directors of the corporation's board) of Natomas were offered golden parachutes. The terms of the parachute agreements provided that the five would be paid three years of compensation in the event they resigned or were terminated from their positions at Natomas for any reason other than for just cause. Three of the five voluntarily left their positions after three years. Under the terms of their parachute agreements, they collected over $10 million. A suit challenging the golden parachutes was brought by Gaillard, a shareholder of Natomas. A trial court sustained the golden parachutes on the grounds that the directors were protected by the business judgment rule in effecting the agreement. [Gaillard v. Natomas, 256 Cal. Rptr. 702 (Cal. 1989).]

1. Regardless of the legal issues, are golden parachutes ethical in a general sense?

2. What practical considerations would lead a corporation to *want* to grant its top management such seemingly one-sided agreements?

3. In *Gaillard,* how would your views be affected by evidence showing that the golden parachutes were developed and presented to the board by the very individuals who were the beneficiaries of the agreements; that is, by the five inside directors?

25-9. Case Briefing Assignment

Examine Case A.25 [Greenlee v. Sherman, 142 A.D.2d 472, 536 N.Y.S.2d 877 (1989)] in Appendix A. The case has been excerpted there in great detail. Review and then brief the case, making sure that you include answers to the following questions in your brief.

1. What is the issue raised on appeal in this case?

2. The appellate court held that the successor liability theory did not apply in this case for two basic reasons. What were they?

Chapter 26

Intellectual Property and Computer Law

Most individuals think of wealth in terms of houses, land, cars, stocks, and bonds. But wealth also includes **intellectual property,** which consists of the products of individuals' minds—products that result from intellectual, creative processes. Although it is an abstract term for an abstract concept, intellectual property is nonetheless wholly familiar to virtually everyone. *Trademarks, service marks, copyrights,* and *patents* are all forms of intellectual property. The book you are reading is copyrighted. Undoubtedly, the personal computer you use at home is trademarked and patented. Some of the resident software within that computer might be copyrighted. You see advertisements for trademarked items every day—Xerox, IBM, and the like. The study of intellectual property law is important because intellectual property has taken on an increasing importance, not only within the United States but globally as well. Much of what is sold abroad—including popular American television series, computer programs, and blockbuster films—consists of intellectual property.

The need to protect creative works was voiced by the framers of the U.S. Constitution over two hundred years ago: Article I, Section 8, of the Constitution authorized Congress ''To promote the Progress of Science and useful Arts, by securing for limited Times to Authors and Inventors the exclusive Right to their respective Writings and Discoveries.'' Laws protecting patents, trademarks, and copyrights are explicitly designed to protect and reward inventive and artistic creativity. For example, trademark law provides incentives to companies to invest in the development of goodwill by ensuring that others will not steal and profit from their trade symbols. Although intellectual property law limits the economic freedom of some individuals, it does so to protect the freedom of others to enjoy the fruits of their labors—in the form of profits.

In the last decade, computers have become dominant in the business world, and they are becoming increasingly familiar in every household in America, as well as in the rest of the economically developed world. But the many and diverse advantages brought about by the computer revolution have not been risk free. Not surprisingly, unfair trade practice issues arise constantly in this growth industry. The protection of intellectual property relating to computers—such as computer software—has posed difficulties for legislatures and the courts because computers were not envisioned by the legislators who drafted the previous patent, trademark, and copyright laws. Therefore, previous laws have had to be amended, or new laws created, to serve the needs of a computer generation. In the sections below on patent, copyright, and trademark laws, we discuss how these laws have been applied to computer software. In the final section in this chapter, we address another legal challenge presented by computers—the problem of computer crime.

■ Patents

A **patent** is a grant from the federal government that conveys and secures to an inventor the exclusive right to make, use, and sell an invention for a period of seventeen years. Patents for a lesser period are given for designs, as opposed to inventions. For either a regular patent or a design patent, the applicant must demonstrate to the satisfaction of the patent office that the invention, discovery, or design is genuine, novel, useful, and not obvious in the light of the technology of the time. A patent holder gives notice to all that an article or design is patented by placing on it the word "Patent" or "Pat.," plus the patent number.

Patent Infringement

If a firm makes, uses, or sells another's patented design, product, or process without the patent owner's permission, the tort of patent infringement exists. Patent infringement may exist even though not all features or parts of an invention are copied. (With respect to a patented process, however, all steps or their equivalent must be copied in order for infringement to exist.) Often, litigation for patent infringement is so costly that the patent holder will instead offer to sell to the infringer a license to use the patented design, product, or process. Indeed, in many cases the costs of detection, prosecution, and monitoring are so high that patents are valueless to their owners, because they cannot afford to protect them.

Patents for Computer Software

It is difficult for developers and manufacturers of software to obtain patent protection because many software products simply automate procedures that can be performed manually. In other words, the

computer programs do not meet the "novel" and "not obvious" requirements mentioned above. Also, the basis for software is often a mathematical equation or formula, which is not patentable. It is possible, however, to obtain a patent for a *process* that incorporates a computer program, providing, of course, that the process itself is patentable.[1]

Another obstacle to obtaining patent protection for software is the procedure of obtaining patents. The process can be expensive and slow. The time element is a particularly important consideration for someone wishing to obtain a patent on software: in light of the rapid changes and improvements in computer technology, the delay could undercut the product's success in the marketplace.

International Patent Issues

The scope of manufacturing and distribution is now very much international. Consequently, inventors often file for patent protection in many countries simultaneously. The international patent protection afforded a U.S. national is normally governed by the patent laws in each country in which the American inventor seeks protection. Additionally, the United States may have a treaty with another country, which may govern patents.

Patent practices in other countries normally differ substantially from those in the United States. For example, it took Texas Instruments thirty years to obtain a patent in Japan. Political and economic issues obviously were at play here, for the delay allowed the Japanese computer chip industry to flourish. In the United States, Texas Instruments was granted patent protection for the same invention within four years of the patent application.

The nature of the product for which a patent will be granted differs dramatically from country to country. A number of countries, for example, do not permit invention patents for pharmaceuticals (although some protection may be obtained by a process patent).

■ Copyrights

A **copyright** is an intangible right granted by statute to the author or originator of certain literary or

---

1. See *Diamond v. Diehr*, 450 U.S. 175, 101 S.Ct. 1048, 67 L.Ed.2d 155 (1981).

artistic productions. Works created after January 1, 1978, are automatically given statutory copyright protection for the life of the author plus fifty years. Copyrights owned by publishing houses expire seventy-five years from the date of publication or a hundred years from the date of creation, whichever is first. For works by one or more authors, the copyright expires fifty years after the death of the last surviving author.

The Copyright Act provides that a copyright owner no longer needs to place a © or ℗ on the work to have the work protected against infringement. Chances are, if somebody created it, somebody owns it.

Under the ''fair use'' doctrine, the reproduction of copyrighted material is permitted without the payment of royalties under certain circumstances. Section 107 of the Copyright Act provides as follows:

[T]he fair use of a copyrighted work, including such use by reproduction in copies or phonorecords or by any other means specified by [Section 106 of the Copyright Act], for purposes such as criticism, comment, news reporting, teaching (including multiple copies for classroom use), scholarship, or research, is not an infringement of copyright. In determining whether the use made of a work in any particular case is a fair use the factors to be considered shall include—

(1) the purpose and character of the use, including whether such use is of a commercial nature or is for nonprofit educational purposes;

(2) the nature of the copyrighted work;

(3) the amount and substantiality of the portion used in relation to the copyrighted work as a whole; and

(4) the effect of the use upon the potential market for or value of the copyrighted work.

Because these guidelines as to what constitutes fair use are very broad, the courts determine whether a particular use is fair on a case-by-case basis. Thus, any reproduction can still make its producer subject to a violation.

Copyright Infringement

Whenever the form or expression of an idea is copied, an infringement of copyright has occurred. The reproduction does not have to be exactly the same as the original; nor does it have to reproduce the original in its entirety. If a substantial part of the original is reproduced, a copyright infringement exists. Penalties or remedies can be imposed on those who infringe copyrights. These range from actual damages plus the infringer's profits or statutory damages not exceeding $100,000 imposed at the discretion of the court, to criminal proceedings for willful violations, which may result in fines, imprisonment, or both.

The following case discusses whether recording television broadcasts on home videotape recorders constitutes a copyright infringement.

BACKGROUND AND FACTS *Universal City Studios, the respondent, owns the copyrights on some of the television programs broadcast on the public airwaves. Sony Corporation, the petitioner, manufactures and sells home videotape recorders. Universal alleged that members of the general public used Betamax videotape recorders (VTRs—today, VCRs) to record some broadcasts of Universal's copyrighted works, thereby infringing Universal's copyrights. Universal then maintained that Sony was liable for these copyright infringements because Sony marketed the Betamax VTRs. Universal sought money damages, an accounting for profits, and an injunction against the manufacture and marketing of Betamax VTRs. The district court denied Universal any relief, but the court of appeals held Sony liable for contributory infringement. The United States Supreme Court took up the case.*

Case 26.1

SONY CORP. v. UNIVERSAL CITY STUDIOS

Supreme Court of the United States, 1984.
467 U.S. 417,
104 S.Ct. 774,
78 L.Ed.2d 574.

Justice *STEVENS* delivered the opinion of the Court.

* * * *

The two respondents in this case do not seek relief against the Betamax users who have allegedly infringed their copyrights. Moreover, this is not [an] action on behalf of all copyright owners who license their works for television broadcast, and respondents have no right to invoke whatever rights other copyright holders may have to bring infringement actions based on Betamax copying of their works. As was made clear by their own evidence, the copying of the respondent's programs represents a small portion of the total use of VTRs. It is, however, the taping of respondents' own copyrighted programs that provides them with standing to charge Sony with contributory infringement. To prevail, they have the burden of proving that users of the Betamax have infringed their copyrights and that Sony should be held responsible for that infringement.

* * * *

* * * [T]he sale of copying equipment, like the sale of other articles of commerce, does not constitute contributory infringement if the product is widely used for legitimate, unobjectionable purposes. Indeed, it need merely be capable of substantial noninfringing uses.

* * * *

Even unauthorized uses of a copyrighted work are not necessarily infringing. An unlicensed use of the copyright is not an infringement unless it conflicts with one of the specific exclusive rights conferred by the copyright statute. * * * The most pertinent [section of the copyright statute] in this case is [Section] 107, the legislative endorsement of the doctrine of "fair use."

* * * *

* * * A challenge to a noncommercial use of a copyrighted work [requires] proof either that the particular use is harmful, or that if it should become widespread, it would adversely affect the potential market for the copyrighted work.

DECISION AND REMEDY   *The Supreme Court concluded (1) that a substantial number of television broadcast copyright holders would not object to having their broadcasts recorded and (2) that Universal had failed to demonstrate that the recordings would cause more than minimal harm to the market for, or value of, their copyrighted works. Therefore, the Betamax VTR is capable of noninfringing uses, and Sony was not liable for contributory infringement.*

What Is Protected Expression?

Section 102 of the Copyright Act specifically excludes copyright protection for any "idea, procedure, process, system, method of operation, concept, principle or discovery, regardless of the form in which it is described, explained, illustrated, or embodied." Note that it is not possible to copyright an *idea*. The underlying ideas embodied in a work may be freely used by others. What is copyrightable is the particular way in which an idea is *expressed.* Whenever an idea and an expression are inseparable, the expression cannot be copyrighted.

Consider an example: A video game manufacturer develops a Thai kick-boxing game. The developer cannot prevent a competitor from producing another kick-boxing game that is based on the standard moves and rules of Thai kick-boxing. The idea for the game is not copyrightable. The developer can, however, prevent competitors from copying original graphics whenever they can be separated from the standard treatment of Thai kick-boxing.

Generally, anything that is not an original expression will not qualify for copyright protection. Facts widely known to the public are not copyrightable. Page numbers are not copyrightable because they follow a sequence known to everyone. Mathematical calculations are not copyrightable.

Compilations of facts, however, are copyrightable. Section 103 of the Copyright Act defines a compilation as "a work formed by the collection and assembling of preexisting materials of data that are selected, coordinated, or arranged in such a way that the resulting work as a whole constitutes an original work of authorship."

Does the compilation of "facts" (names, addresses, and telephone numbers) listed in the white pages of a telephone directory qualify for copyright protection? This issue arose in the following case.

BACKGROUND AND FACTS   *The Rural Telephone Service Company provides telephone service to several communities in Kansas. Rural publishes a typical telephone directory, consisting of white pages and yellow pages. Data for the directory is obtained from Rural's subscribers, who must provide their names and addresses to obtain telephone service. Feist Publications, Inc., is a publishing company that specializes in area-wide telephone directories covering a much larger geographic range than directories such as that published by Rural. To obtain white-pages listings for its area-wide directory, Feist approached each of the eleven telephone companies operating in northwest Kansas and offered to pay for the right to use their white-pages listings. Rural was the only company that refused to license its listings to Feist. Rural's refusal created a problem for Feist because omitting Rural's listings would leave an unacceptable "gap" in its area-wide directory, rendering it less attractive to potential yellow-pages advertisers. To overcome this problem, Feist used the listings without Rural's consent. Rural sued Feist for copyright infringement. The trial court granted summary judgment to Rural, holding that telephone directories are copyrightable, and the appellate court affirmed the decision. The United States Supreme Court granted certiorari.*

Case 26.2

FEIST PUBLICATIONS, INC. v. RURAL TELEPHONE SERVICE CO.
Supreme Court of the United States, 1991.
____ U.S. ____,
111 S.Ct. 1282,
113 L.Ed.2d 358.

Justice *O'CONNOR* delivered the opinion of the Court.
*   *   *   *

*   *   * A factual compilation is eligible for copyright if it features an original selection or arrangement of facts, but the copyright is limited to the particular selection or arrangement. In no event may copyright extend to the facts themselves.
*   *   *   *

There is no doubt that Feist took from the white pages of Rural's directory a substantial amount of factual information. At a minimum, Feist copied the names, towns, and telephone numbers of 1,309 of Rural's subscribers. Not all copying, however, is copyright infringement. To establish infringement, two elements must be proven: (1) ownership of a valid copyright, and (2) copying of constituent elements of the work that are original. The first element is not at issue here; Feist appears to concede that Rural's directory, considered as a whole, is subject to a valid copyright because it contains some foreword text, as well as original material in its yellow pages advertisements.

The question is whether Rural has proved the second element. In other words, did Feist *   *   * copy anything that was "original" to Rural? Certainly, the raw data does not satisfy the originality requirement. Rural may have been the first to discover and report the names, towns, and telephone numbers of its subscribers, but this data does not "ow[e] its origin" to Rural. Rather, these bits of information are uncopyrightable facts; they existed before Rural reported them and would have continued to exist if Rural had never published a telephone directory. The originality requirement "rule[s] out protecting . . . names addresses, and telephone numbers of which the plaintiff by no stretch of the imagination could be called the author."

The question that remains is whether Rural selected, coordinated, or arranged these uncopyrightable facts in an original way. * * *

* * * *

Rural's selection of listings could not be more obvious: it publishes the most basic information–name, town, and telephone number—about each person who applies to it for telephone service. This is "selection" of a sort, but it lacks the modicum of creativity necessary to transform mere selection into copyrightable expression. Rural expended sufficient effort to make the white pages directory useful, but insufficient creativity to make it original.

* * * *

Nor can Rural claim originality in its coordination and arrangement of facts. The white pages do nothing more than list Rural's subscribers in alphabetical order. * * * [T]here is nothing remotely creative about arranging names alphabetically in a white pages directory.

DECISION AND REMEDY

The United States Supreme Court reversed the decision of the appellate court. Feist's use of Rural's white-pages listings did not constitute copyright infringement.

ETHICAL CONSIDERATIONS

This case raises an obvious ethical question: Is it fair that Feist should be able to reap the fruits of Rural's labors without any penalty? In addressing just this question, the Court at one point in its opinion pointed out that the "primary objective of copyright is not to reward the labor of authors, but '[t]o promote the Progress of Science and useful Arts.' To this end, copyright assures authors the right to their original expression, but encourages others to build freely upon the ideas and information conveyed by a work. This principle, known as the idea/expression or fact/expression dichotomy, applies to all works of authorship. As applied to a factual compilation, assuming the absence of original written expression, only the compiler's selection and arrangement may be protected; the raw facts may be copied at will. This result is neither unfair nor unfortunate. It is the means by which copyright advances the progress of science and art."

Copyright Protection for Computer Software

The Computer Software Copyright Act of 1980 amended the 1976 Copyright Reform Act to include computer programs in the list of creative works protected by federal copyright law. The 1980 statute defines a computer program as a "set of statements or instructions to be used directly or indirectly in a computer in order to bring about a certain result." Because of the unique nature of computer programs, the courts have had many problems in applying and interpreting the 1980 act. One of the basic problems concerns computer language.

THE LANGUAGE PROBLEM Traditionally, copyright protection was extended only to literary works that were perceptible to humans—that is, to things written or printed in intelligible notation. But computer programs, which are classified as "literary works" under the 1980 act, are expressed in a language "readable" by machines. Should copyright protection be limited to those parts of a computer program that can be read by humans, such as the "high-level" language of a source code? Or should it also extend to the binary-language object code of a computer program, which is readable only by the computer?

In an important 1983 decision, *Apple Computer, Inc. v. Franklin Computer Corp.*, copyright protection was extended to include both the binary object code and the source code of a computer program. In this decision, the Court of Appeals for the Third Circuit held that "a computer program, whether in object code or source code . . . is protected from unauthorized copying whether from its \object or source code version."[2]

PROGRAM STRUCTURE PROTECTION By 1983 it was fairly well established—particularly by the *Apple Computer* decision just mentioned—that a program's computer codes were copyrightable. The next issue that arose in the evolution of computer copyright law was whether copyright protection should cover other elements of computer software, such as the overall structure, sequence, and organization of a program. In a 1986 case, *Whelan Associates v. Jaslow Dental Laboratory,* the Third Circuit Court of Appeals noted that copyrights of other literary works can be infringed upon even when there is no substantial similarity between the works' *literal* elements. The copyright of a play or a book, for example, can be infringed upon if its plot or plot devices are copied. The court applied the same principle to computer programs and held that the structure, sequence, and organization of computer programs were copyrightable.[3]

PROGRAM "LOOK AND FEEL" PROTECTION An issue addressed in *Whelan* has evolved into what is now generally called program "look and feel" protection. Should the "look and feel"—the general appearance, command structure, video images, menus, windows, and other screen displays—of computer programs also be protected by copyright? This is a significant question because the software industry is so highly competitive. If the look and feel of a program makes it easy to learn and use, the manufacturer of that program will have a competitive edge in the marketplace—an edge that will be quickly lost to competitors if such program features cannot be copyrighted. In contrast, some argue that allowing such features as menus or other command structures or visual displays to be copyrighted would be like copyrighting the alphabet.

Program "look and feel" was at issue in a case filed in 1988 by Apple Computer, Inc., against Microsoft Corporation and Hewlett-Packard Company. Apple contended that Microsoft's Windows 2.03 program and Hewlett-Packard's New Wave program infringed Apple's copyright because the programs copied the "look and feel" of the popular Macintosh computer displays. Although the outcome of this lawsuit is not yet known, a federal district court in Boston recently addressed a very similar issue in a case brought by Lotus Development Corporation against Paperback Software International. Lotus claimed that Paperback Software had infringed its copyright in its Lotus 1-2-3 spreadsheet format design and the keystroke sequences used in manipulating information. In what many regard as a significant decision for software manufacturers, the court held that Lotus's menu command structure—including the choice of command terms, the structure and order of those terms, their presentation on the screen, and the long prompts—was copyrightable and that Paperback Software International had infringed Lotus's copyright.[4]

PROTECTION FOR MASK WORKS The Semiconductor Chip Protection Act of 1984 provides protection for the **mask work,** which is defined as a series of images related to the pattern formed by the many layers of a semiconductor-chip product. A mask work must be fixed in the product to qualify for the protection, and within two years of initially taking commercial advantage of the mask work, the owner must register it with the U.S. Copyright Office. On registration, the owner of the protected mask work obtains the exclusive right, for ten years, to reproduce, import, or distribute the work or a semiconductor-chip product that contains it.

International Copyright Issues

To some extent, international copyright issues have become less of a problem for American copyright owners. The United States is now a party to a number of international copyright treaties, including the Berne Convention and the Universal Copyright Convention. Under the Berne Convention, if an

2. 714 F.2d 1240 (3d Cir. 1983).
3. 797 F.2d 1222 (3d Cir. 1986).

4. *Lotus Development Corp. v. Paperback Software International,* 740 F.Supp. 37 (D.Mass. 1990).

American writes a book, his or her copyright in the book must be recognized by every country that has signed the convention. Also, if a citizen of a country that has not signed the convention first publishes a book in a country that has, all other countries that have signed the convention must recognize that author's copyright. Copyright notice is not needed to gain protection under the Berne Convention for works published after March 1, 1989.

■ Trademarks and Related Property

A **trademark** is a distinctive mark, motto, device, or emblem that a manufacturer stamps, prints, or otherwise affixes to the goods it produces, so that they can be distinguished from the goods of other manufacturers and merchants. Bestowing an exclusive trademark right on the originator of a mark yields several benefits, some of which were mentioned at the beginning of this chapter. First, exclusive trademark protection creates incentives for merchants to invest in product development and improvement. Second, trademark law permits consumers to be certain that they are obtaining the same product from the same manufacturer every time that they return to the marketplace. Trademark law therefore reduces "search costs" for consumers and prevents the confusion that would result in the marketplace if trademarks were not protected. Finally, trademark law prevents unjust enrichment by prohibiting unscrupulous merchants from selling inferior imitations under the same trademark as the original.

Normally, personal names, words, or places that describe an article or its use cannot be trade-marked; they are available to anyone. Words that are used as part of a design or device, however, or words that are used in an uncommon or fanciful way may be trademarked. Consider an example. *English Leather* may not be trademarked to describe leather processed in England. In contrast, *English Leather* may be, and is, trademarked as a name for after-shave lotion, because this constitutes a *fanciful* use of the words. Consider also that under some circumstances, even the common name of an individual may be trademarked if purchasers associate the name with the product and not primarily with its status as a name—for example, Campbell Soups.

Trademark Infringement

Once a trademark has been registered, a firm is entitled to its exclusive use for marketing purposes. Whenever that trademark is copied to a substantial degree or used in its entirety by another, intentionally or unintentionally, the trademark has been infringed. The owner of the trademark need not register it with the state or with the federal government to obtain protection from the tort of trademark infringement, but registration does furnish proof of the date of inception of its use. Moreover, registration may prolong the life of the trademark. Registration is renewable between the fifth and sixth years after the initial registration and every twenty years thereafter, as long as the mark remains distinctive and is used.

The defendant firm in the following case was liable for trademark infringement even though it did not manufacture the article.

Case 26.3

VUITTON ET FILS, S.A. v. CROWN HANDBAGS
United States District Court, Southern District of New York, 1979.
492 F.Supp. 1071.

BACKGROUND AND FACTS *The plaintiff, Vuitton et Fils, S.A., is a French corporation that manufactures expensive handbags and distributes them through an exclusive retail network in the United States. (S.A. stands for société anonyme, which is the French equivalent of a corporation.) The handbags are of high quality and bear the Vuitton registered trademark, the firm's initials and a fleur de lis. Robert Cullen was employed by Vuitton as a private investigator and by chance passed the defendant's window display, which featured two handbags bearing the Vuitton trademark. The defendant, Crown Handbags, was not a retail outlet for Vuitton handbags. The defendant offered to sell Cullen six handbags in a bulk transaction. At the trial, the handbags were shown to be cheap imitations of Vuitton's* *product. Vuitton sued Crown Handbags for infringement of its registered trademark.*

BRIEANT, District Judge.
*   *   *   *

[When] an alleged infringing mark is used in connection with the sale of similar goods, the long standing rule in this Circuit has been that the second comer to the marketplace ''has a duty to so name and dress his product as to avoid all likelihood of consumers confusing it with the product of the first comer.'' The second comer has no right to trade upon the good will of the first comer developed over a period of time and at considerable expense. *   *   *

The great weight of the evidence in the case leads to the conclusion that the Vuitton trademark is a strong mark, and as such is entitled to broad protection. The strength of the mark stems from its conspicuously distinctive nature. It is unique in its design and color, and during the more than 46 years of its continuous use in this country it has come to represent a source of product of perceived quality and prestige. *   *   *
*   *   *   *

Both Vuitton and consumers in general would suffer by the purchase of counterfeit bags of inferior quality. Vuitton would soon lose its reputation for quality and exclusivity, and consumers would be deceived into believing they were getting something they were not.

Defendant clearly infringed upon plaintiff's registered trademark *   *   * by offering for sale a combination of product and trademark which exactly mimics that of plaintiff *   *   * . In doing so, defendant acted willfully and with knowledge of the fact that these handbags which it offered for sale infringed upon the trademark rights of plaintiff. *   *   * The counterfeit bags were manufactured with the intention to trade upon the plaintiff's established reputation for quality merchandise. Although defendant apparently did not itself manufacture the infringing articles, it took an active part in their distribution and sale, making use of plaintiff's trademark in the process.

Vuitton was granted permanent injunctive relief from Crown Handbag's commercial practices that violated Vuitton's trademark rights. Crown had to pay damages amounting to the sales price of the six handbags offered to Vuitton's investigator. Crown also had to pay Vuitton's attorneys' fees. **DECISION AND REMEDY**

The Trademark Revision Act

In 1988, the Trademark Revision Act was passed by Congress. This act, which took effect on November 16, 1989, significantly altered the prior registration scheme. That scheme required that the mark be used before an application could be filed. The 1988 act, in contrast, allows an applicant to file on the basis either of use or of the bona fide intention to use the mark in commerce. This is the so-called ''intent to use'' provision, which requires that the mark be put into commerce within six months after filing with the U.S. Patent and Trademark Office. At the end of the six months, the applicant must provide proof that the mark was put into commerce and that the application was not opposed. Under extenuating circumstances, the six-month period can be extended by thirty months, giving the applicant a total of three years from the date of notice of trademark approval to make use of the mark and file the required use statement. Registration under the 1988 act is postponed until actual use of the mark. Nonetheless, during this waiting period, any applicant can legally protect his or her trademark against a third party who previously has neither used the mark nor filed an application for it. The 1988 act's new provision has considerably cut the costs in developing and marketing a new product. It has particularly benefitted small companies.

Trademarks for Computer Hardware and Software

Trademarks for computer hardware and software are protected under federal trademark law, just as trademarks for other products are. Trademark registration provides protection for twenty years and is renewable. Once a trademark has been registered with the U.S. Patent and Trademark Office, its owner has the right to its exclusive and continued use, providing the mark does not become generic (as described below). Trademark infringement occurs when an unauthorized party copies the trademark to a substantial degree or uses it in its entirety, intentionally or unintentionally.

Service, Certification, and Collective Marks

A **service mark** is similar to a trademark but is used to distinguish among services rather than goods. For example, each airline has a particular mark or symbol associated with its name. Titles and character names used in radio and television are frequently registered as service marks. Service marks are registered in the same manner as trademarks.

A **certification mark** is used by one or more persons, other than the owner, to certify the region, materials, mode of manufacture, quality, or accuracy of the owner's goods or services. When used by members of a cooperative, association, or other organization, such a mark is referred to as a **collective mark.** Examples of certification marks are the "Good Housekeeping Seal of Approval" and "UL Tested." Collective marks appear at the ends of the credits of movies to indicate the various associations and organizations that participated in the making of the movies. The union marks found on the tags of certain products are also collective marks. The same policies and restrictions that apply to trademarks and service marks normally apply to certification and collective marks.

■ Trade Names

The term **trade name** is used to indicate part or all of a business's name, whether that business be a sole proprietorship, a partnership, or a corporation. Generally, a trade name is directly related to a business and to its goodwill. As with trademarks, words must be unusual or fancifully used to be protected as trade names. The word *Safeway* was held by the courts to be sufficiently fanciful to obtain protection as a trade name.[5] The decisions of the courts do not give entirely clear guidelines as to when the name of a corporation can be regarded as a trade name. A particularly thorny problem arises when a trade name acquires generic use. For example, *aspirin, thermos, escalator, trampoline, raisin bran, dry ice, cube steak, linoleum, nylon, kerosene,* and *cornflakes* originally were used only as trade names, but they are now used to refer to those products generally. Similarly, other trade names—such as Frigidaire, Scotch Tape, Xerox, and Kleenex—have acquired secondary meanings and are close to becoming generic terms. Even so, the courts will not allow other firms to use those names in such a way as to deceive a potential consumer. Consider, for example, the following case concerning Coca-Cola, decided by the United States Supreme Court.

---

5. *Safeway Stores v. Suburban Foods,* 130 F.Supp. 249 (E.D.Va. 1955).

Case 26.4

THE COCA-COLA CO. v. THE KOKE CO. OF AMERICA
Supreme Court of the United States, 1920.
254 U.S. 143,
41 S.Ct. 113,
65 L.Ed. 189.

BACKGROUND AND FACTS *The plaintiff, Coca-Cola Company, sought to enjoin (prevent) the defendants (The Koke Company of America and other beverage companies) from, among other things, using the word* Koke *for their products. The defendants contended that the Coca-Cola trademark was a fraudulent misrepresentation and that Coca-Cola was therefore not entitled to any help from the courts. The defendants alleged that the Coca-Cola Company, by its use of the Coca-Cola name, represented that the beverage contained cocaine (from coca leaves). The trial court granted the injunction against The Koke Company, but the appellate* *court reversed the lower court's ruling. Coca-Cola then appealed to the United States Supreme Court.*

Mr. Justice *HOLMES* delivered the opinion of the Court.

* * * *

* * * The defense relied on here should be scrutinized with a critical eye. The main point is this: Before 1900 the beginning of the good will was more or less helped by the presence of cocaine, a drug that, like alcohol or caffein or opium, may be described as a deadly poison or as a valuable item of the pharmacopœa according to the rhetorical purposes in view. The amount seems to have been very small,[a] but it may have been enough to begin a bad habit and after the Food and Drug Act of June 30, 1906, if not earlier, long before this suit was brought, it was eliminated from the plaintiff's compound. Coca leaves still are used, to be sure, but after they have been subjected to a drastic process that removes from them every characteristic substance except a little tannin and still less chlorophyl. The cola nut, at best, on its side furnishes but a very small portion of the caffein, which now is the only element that has appreciable effect. That comes mainly from other sources. It is argued that the continued use of the name imports a representation that has ceased to be true and that the representation is reinforced by a picture of coca leaves and cola nuts upon the label and by advertisements, which however were many years before this suit was brought, that the drink is an "ideal nerve tonic and stimulant," * * * and that thus the very thing sought to be protected is used as a fraud.

The argument does not satisfy us. We are dealing here with a popular drink not with a medicine, and although what has been said might suggest that its attraction lay in producing the expectation of a toxic effect the facts point to a different conclusion. Since 1900 the sales have increased at a very great rate corresponding to a like increase in advertising. The name now characterizes a beverage to be had at almost any soda fountain. It means a single thing coming from a single source, and well known to the community. It hardly would be too much to say that the drink characterizes the name as much as the name the drink. In other words Coca-Cola probably means to most persons the plaintiff's familiar product to be had everywhere rather than a compound of particular substances. The coca leaves and whatever of cola nut is employed may be used to justify the continuance of the name or they may affect the flavor as the plaintiff contends, but before this suit was brought the plaintiff had advertised to the public that it must not expect and would not find cocaine, and had eliminated everything tending to suggest cocaine effects except the name and the picture of the leaves and nuts, which probably conveyed little or nothing to most who saw it. It appears to us that it would be going too far to deny the plaintiff relief against a palpable fraud because possibly here and there an ignorant person might call for the drink with the hope for incipient cocaine intoxication. The plaintiff's position must be judged by the facts as they were when the suit was begun, not by the facts of a different condition and an earlier time.

The district court's injunction was allowed to stand. The competing beverage companies were enjoined from calling their products ''Koke.''

**DECISION
AND REMEDY**

a.   In reality, until 1903 the amount of active cocaine in each bottle of Coke was equivalent to one ''line'' of cocaine.

■ Trade Secrets

Some business processes and information that are not, or cannot be, patented, copyrighted, or trademarked are nevertheless protected against appropriation by a competitor as **trade secrets.** Customer lists, plans, research and development, pricing information, marketing techniques, production techniques, and generally anything that makes an individual company unique and that would have value to a competitor constitute trade secrets. The most widely used definition of a trade secret is found in the Restatement of Torts, Section 757(b):

> A trade secret may consist of any formula, pattern, device, or compilation of information which is used in one's business, and which gives him an opportunity to obtain an advantage over competitors who do not know or use it. It may be a formula for a chemical compound, a process of manufacturing, treating or preserving materials, . . . or a list of customers.

Virtually all law with respect to trade secrets is common law. Identical types of information reviewed by different courts in similar factual settings have been classified differently. In an effort to reduce the unpredictability of common law with respect to trade secrets, a model act, the Uniform Trade Secrets Act, was presented to the states in 1979 for adoption. Parts of it have been adopted in over twenty states. Typically, a state that has adopted parts of the act has only adopted those parts that encompass its own existing common law.

Unlike copyright and trademark protection, protection of trade secrets extends both to ideas and to their expression. (For this reason, and because a trade secret involves no registration or filing requirements, trade secret protection may be well suited for software.) Of course, the secret formula, method, or other information must be disclosed to some persons, particularly to key employees. Businesses generally attempt to protect their trade secrets by having all employees who use the process or information agree in their contracts never to divulge it. Thus, if a salesperson tries to solicit the company's customers for noncompany business, or if an employee copies the employer's unique method of manufacture, he or she has appropriated a trade secret and has also broken a contract—two separate wrongs. Theft of confidential business data by industrial espionage, as when a business taps into a competitor's computer, is a theft of trade secrets without any contractual violation and is actionable in itself.

Under Section 757 of the Restatement of Torts, "One who discloses or uses another's trade secret, without a privilege to do so, is liable to the other if (a) he discovered the secret by improper means, or (b) his disclosure or use constitutes a breach of confidence reposed in him by the other in disclosing the secret to him." In the following case, the court had to decide whether aerial photography was an "improper means" of discovering another's trade secret.

Case 26.5

E. I. duPONT de NEMOURS & CO. v. CHRISTOPHER

United States Court of Appeals, Fifth Circuit, 1970. 431 F.2d 1012.

BACKGROUND AND FACTS   *In the words of the court, "This is a case of industrial espionage in which an airplane is the cloak and a camera the dagger." In 1969, Rolfe and Gary Christopher, at the request of an unknown third party, took sixteen aerial photographs of a new plant being constructed by E. I. duPont de Nemours & Company in Beaumont, Texas. Because the plant construction had not yet been completed, a process for making methanol, which DuPont was trying to keep secret, was not yet covered by a roof and so was visible from the air. DuPont, concerned about the flight circling over the plant, conducted an investigation and learned that photographs had been taken and that the Christophers were the photographers. The Christophers refused to tell DuPont the name of the person or corporation requesting the photographs, stating that their client wished to remain anonymous. Having reached a dead end in the investigation, DuPont subsequently filed suit against the Christophers, alleging that they had wrongfully obtained photographs revealing DuPont's trade secrets. The Christophers argued that they had committed no "actionable wrong" in photographing the DuPont facility because "they conducted all of their activities in public airspace, violated no government aviation standards, did not breach any confidential relation, and did not engage in any fraudulent or illegal conduct." The trial court held that DuPont's claim was actionable, and the Christophers appealed.*

GOLDBERG, Circuit Judge:

* * * *

This is a case of first impression, for the Texas courts have not faced this precise factual issue, and * * * we must sensitize our * * * antennae to divine what the Texas courts would do if such a situation were presented to them. The only question involved in this * * * appeal is whether DuPont has asserted a claim upon which relief can be granted. * * * [T]he Christophers argue that for an appropriation of trade secrets to be wrongful there must be a trespass, other illegal conduct, or breach of a confidential relationship. We disagree.

It is true, as the Christophers assert, that the previous trade secret cases have contained one or more of these elements. However, we do not think that the Texas courts would limit the trade secret protection exclusively to these elements. * * * Not limiting itself to specific wrongs, Texas adopted subsection (a) of the Restatement [of Torts] which recognizes a cause of action for the discovery of a trade secret by any ''improper'' means.

* * * *

The question remaining, therefore, is whether aerial photography of plant construction is an improper means of obtaining another's trade secret. We conclude that it is * * *.

* * * [T]he Texas rule is clear. One may use his competitor's secret process if he discovers the process by reverse engineering[a] applied to the finished product; one may use a competitor's process if he discovers it by his own independent research; but one may not avoid these labors by taking the process from the discoverer without his permission at a time when he is taking reasonable precautions to maintain its secrecy.

* * * *

In the instant case DuPont was in the midst of constructing a plant. Although after construction the finished plant would have protected much of the process from view, during the period of construction the trade secret was exposed to view from the air. To require DuPont to put a roof over the unfinished plant to guard its secret would impose an enormous expense * * *. We should not require a person or corporation to take unreasonable precautions to prevent another from doing that which he ought not do in the first place.

DECISION AND REMEDY

The appellate court affirmed the trial court's holding that DuPont had stated a cause of action and remanded the case to the trial court for further proceedings.

ETHICAL CONSIDERATIONS

The decision in this case illustrates a tradeoff between the policy of promoting free competition and the policy of protecting the spirit of inventiveness. A free market requires competitiveness, and being competitive requires an awareness of what the competition is doing. Being competitive also requires inventiveness in the development of new products or processes—and protecting against the attempts of competitors to learn of those new products or processes. The tradeoff occurs at the point when, in the words of the court, ''the protections required to prevent another's spying cost so much that the spirit of inventiveness is dampened.''

a. Reverse engineering is a technique in which a process or secret formula is learned by analysis of the product that results from the process or secret formula.

■ Computer Crime

The American Bar Association defines **computer crime** as any act that is directed against computers and computer parts, that uses computers as instruments of crime, or that involves computers and constitutes abuse. Generally, computer crimes are classified as white-collar crimes, because ordinarily they do not involve physical violence. Recall from the discussion earlier in this chapter the difficulties faced by the courts in applying conventional copyright law to computer software. Similar difficulties exist in attempting to apply traditional criminal law to computer crimes. In some cases, existing laws have been extended—either by amendment or through judicial interpretation—to include computer crimes. In other cases, new legislation has been enacted to specifically address crimes unique to the computer age.

Detecting and Prosecuting Computer Crime

Computer crime is often difficult to detect; and if the crime is cleverly executed, it may go undetected for some time. In some cases, victimized companies, and even the government, have discovered multimillion-dollar thefts only after a considerable lapse of time. Even when it is apparent that a computer crime has occurred, tracing the crime to the individual who committed it can be very difficult,

because the individual's identity is "hidden," as it were, by the anonymous nature of the computer system. It is also frequently true that, in the case of an employee, no one with enough expertise to discover a crime is overseeing the perpetrator's activities.

Even when computer crimes are detected and reported, the complexities of the computer systems involved have often frustrated the attempts of attorneys, police officers, jurors, and others to comprehend the offenses and prosecute the offenders successfully. Computer crimes may also be difficult to prosecute because a particular form of computer-assisted abuse falls outside the traditional definition of a crime. For example, the commonly used definition of larceny (theft) does not encompass intangible property such as the data stored in a computer.

Under existing federal statutes, successful prosecutions include convictions under laws concerning theft and property offenses, transportation of stolen property, wire fraud, and mail fraud. The following case is representative of the types of problems encountered by courts in trying to apply traditional laws to situations involving computers. In this case, the court had to decide whether alterations of accounts payable documents that resulted in the issuance of checks by the computer to an improper payee constituted forgery.

Case 26.6

UNITED STATES OF AMERICA v. JONES

United States Court of Appeals, Fourth Circuit, 1977. 553 F.2d 351.

BACKGROUND AND FACTS *Criminal indictments were returned against Amy Everston Jones, charging her with transporting in interstate and foreign commerce certain checks (securities) that she knew had been "stolen, converted or taken by fraud" in violation of federal law. The purported crime was against a Canadian company, Inglis, Ltd., a subsidiary of Whirlpool Corporation, a U.S. corporation. Michael Everston, an alleged accomplice of Jones, was the supervisor of Inglis's accounting department. Everston directed an accounting clerk to set up an account payable to A. L. E. Jones and, by changing vendor numbers and other computerized data, was able to convert documents properly payable to Whirlpool into the account of A. L. E. Jones. The computer ultimately issued checks to Jones, which she deposited in her account in Maryland. Jones admitted that the checks were forgeries, but since forgeries are excluded as violations under the federal statutes, she moved to dismiss the indictments. The district court agreed and dismissed the indictments against Jones. The United States appealed.*

FIELD, Senior Circuit Judge.

* * * *

* * * [W]e disagree with the district court's conclusion that the acts committed by Everston constituted common law forgery. The Supreme Court has noted that "[f]orgery * * * may * * * be defined [at common law] to be, 'the fraudulent making or alteration of a writing to the prejudice of another man's right' * * * ." Significantly, then, "[a]n essential element of the crime of forgery is making the false writing [a false writing was defined by the court earlier in this opinion to be a writing "which falsely purports to be the writing of another person than the actual maker"] * * *."

In the present case, the district court was of the opinion that Everston, in fact, made a false writing because "the individual who drafted the instrument in a practical sense was Everston, although he employed the computer as the instrumentality [means] by which the checks were physically drawn." We think, however, that the acts of Everston did not constitute the making of a false writing, but rather amounted to the creation of a writing which was genuine in execution but false as to the statements of fact contained in such writing. The distinction is critical to the sufficiency of the indictment.

The district court was of the opinion that the facts did not warrant the conclusion that false statements appeared on the face of the checks issued by Inglis to "A. L. E. Jones." We cannot agree. The checks state that the designated amount is payable "to the order of A. L. E. Jones," and implicit in such an unconditional order was the existence of an obligation running from Inglis, Limited, to the payee. There was, of course, no such obligation, but as the result of Everston's misconduct the accounting department of Inglis was defrauded into believing that the company owed a bona fide obligation to "A. L. E. Jones" and, accordingly, issued a genuine instrument containing a false statement of fact as to the true creditor.

* * * *

Since we conclude that the checks did not fall within the exclusion of the statutes as forgeries, the order of the district court dismissing the indictment must be reversed.

DECISION AND REMEDY

The decision of the district court dismissing the indictments was reversed. The defendant sought review by the United States Supreme Court, but the writ of certiorari *was denied.*

COMMENTS

The common law definition of forgery requires that a writing falsely purport to be the writing of one other than the actual maker. In other words, the crime requires a lie about the genuineness of a document. Thus, the employee who pads a timecard does not commit forgery, because the lie does not relate to the timecard's genuineness but to the truth of the information on it. Similarly, in this case, the court reasoned that since the company actually issued the checks, the checks were genuine; it was the statements on them that were false.

Types of Computer Crime

Crimes committed with or against computers generally fall into five broad categories: financial crimes, theft of computer equipment, theft or unauthorized use of data or services, *software piracy* (the unauthorized copying of another's com-

puter program), and vandalism and destructive programming.

FINANCIAL CRIMES In addition to using computers for information storage and retrieval, businesses increasingly use computers to conduct financial transactions. This is equally true of the government, which handles many of its transactions by computer. These circumstances provide opportunities for employees and others to commit crimes that can involve serious economic losses. For example, employees of accounting and computer departments can, with little effort and without the risk involved in transactions evidenced by paperwork, transfer monies among accounts. The potential for crime in the area of financial transactions is great, and it is in this category of computer crime that most monetary losses are suffered.

With the right computer equipment—desktop-publishing or drawing programs, scanners, laser printers, and so on—checks, stock certificates, gift certificates, identification cards, college transcripts, and even currency can be (and have been) forged. To date, this "desktop forgery" has not resulted in significant financial losses—relative to losses incurred by other types of counterfeiting—but its potential is worrisome for many.

COMPUTER-RELATED THEFT   The theft of computer equipment (hardware) has become easier and more commonplace as computer components have become smaller and thus more readily transportable. Computer-related theft may involve goods that are controlled and accounted for by means of a computer applications program. For example, an employee in a company's accounting department could manipulate inventory records to funnel orders for goods through a phony account and ship the merchandise elsewhere. Payments could also be made on the basis of dummy orders for goods that the company never received. Thefts of computer equipment and thefts of goods with computers are subject to the same criminal and tort laws as thefts of other property (see Chapters 7 and 8).

THEFT OR UNAUTHORIZED USE OF DATA OR SERVICES   Most people would agree that when an individual uses another's computer or computer information system without authorization, the individual is stealing. For example, an employee who used a computer system or data stored in a computer system for private gain and without the employer's authorization would likely be considered a thief, as would a politician who used a government computer to send out campaign brochures.

Once a computer system has been accessed, information contained in the computer's records can be altered. An individual could, for example, remove a bad credit history and obtain loans that otherwise might not be obtainable. Alternatively, an individual could create a bad credit history to prevent or delay another party's receipt of borrowed funds.

The theft or unauthorized use of computer data and services does not fit within the common law definition of larceny or its traditional statutory counterparts. At common law and under most criminal codes, larceny requires a physical taking and carrying away of property from another's possession. Under the common law, criminal statutes are to be strictly construed (that is, a criminal statute cannot be held to include offenses other than those that the statute clearly describes and provides for). Thus, because stealing computer data or services need not involve physically taking and carrying away property from another's possession, it could not be held to constitute larceny.

In a number of states, however, legislation has been passed to abolish or at least limit the application of the common law rule of strict construction of criminal statutes. For example, Model Penal Code Section 1.02(3) provides for construction "according to the fair import of [a statute's] terms." Thus, under an increasing number of revised criminal codes or broad judicial interpretations of existing statutes, the unauthorized use of computer data or services is considered larceny.

Particularly vulnerable to the theft of data or services are systems to which more than one party has access. Even systems accessible only through *passwords* (codes designed to prohibit access to all but authorized users) are often used illegally, especially when the codes are not changed for long periods of time. Breaking a computer's security code or device and perusing the information in the system's records is commonly known as *hacking*. Some instances of hacking have been widely publicized and have generated considerable alarm. Such was the case, for example, in 1983 when a group of Wisconsin high school students discovered the passwords for the computer system at the defense research center in Los Alamos, New Mexico, and thereby gained access to it. More recently, Robert Morris, Jr., a Cornell University student, paralyzed a nationwide computer research network involving six thousand computers. Morris's program unleashed a ''virus'' that copied itself repeatedly and used up much of the memory of the computers. The activities of these and other so-called computer ''hackers'' have brought to the public's attention the alarming vulnerability of computer systems—and the businesses and government agencies that rely on them.

In the following case, two employees used their employer's computer facilities, without the employer's authorization, to develop an outside business interest. As you read the case, note how an existing criminal statute (governing mail fraud) is interpreted very broadly by the court to cover computer-assisted crime.

BACKGROUND AND FACTS   *David Kelly and Mathew Palmer, Jr., while employed at Sperry Univac's applications development center, developed a system—which they called the allegro system—for computerizing the generation of sheet music. In developing the program, they used—without Univac's knowledge or permission—substantial amounts of computer time and storage capacity within the central processing unit of the applications development center. Eventually, Kelly and Palmer mailed promotional materials to music publishers, inviting them to send representatives to an allegro demonstration. Kelly and Palmer's activities were finally discovered by the company, and they were indicted on five counts of mail fraud and one count of conspiracy to commit mail fraud. The indictment alleged that in using Sperry Univac's computer time and storage facilities without authorization, Kelly and Palmer had defrauded Univac of their services as employees and used the U.S. mails to further a fraudulent scheme. After a trial by jury, Kelly and Palmer were found guilty on all counts. They filed posttrial motions contending that their acts did not constitute a scheme or an attempt to defraud within the meaning of the mail fraud statute and that the mails had not been used to execute the scheme.*

Case 26.7

UNITED STATES v. KELLY

United States District Court,
Eastern District of
Pennsylvania, 1981.
507 F.Supp. 495.

DITTER, District Judge.
 *   *   *   *
 *   *   * The essential elements of mail fraud are (1) a scheme or artifice to defraud and (2) the use of the United States mails in execution of the scheme. *   *   *
 *   *   *   *
[I]t is abundantly clear [from the] record that Kelly and Palmer were aware of Univac's policy against the use of its facilities for personal business ventures. They nevertheless made extensive use of the company's computer facilities in furtherance of their own pecuniary interests, took steps to conceal their activities and willfully failed to seek authorization for them. The evidence was more than sufficient to sustain the jury's determination that the defendants acted with intent to defraud.
 *   *   *   *
 *   *   * The defendants contend that the mailing of the promotional materials was related only to their goal of ultimately making money from the completed allegro system. It did not, they assert, further the unauthorized use of Univac's computer facilities and therefore was unrelated to the execution of the fraudulent scheme. In so arguing, defendants posit an unduly restrictive interpretation of the perimeters of their scheme to defraud. Under the terms of the indictment, Kelly and Palmer were charged with defrauding Univac by *using its resources for their own personal gain.* The evidence at trial clearly established that while the defendants were utilizing Univac's facilities to develop the technological viability of the system, they were

actively engaged in attempting to develop a market for the completed allegro program. * * *

* * * *

The obvious purpose of the promotional material was to solicit potential sales for the completed allegro system. Viewed in this context, the mailings were directly related to the achievement of the fruits of defendants' scheme. I therefore conclude that the mailing in question was ''for the purpose of executing'' the scheme to defraud.

DECISION AND REMEDY   *The defendants' posttrial motions were denied and the convictions upheld.*

ETHICAL CONSIDERATIONS   *The defendants might have escaped legal liability for their unauthorized use of Univac's computer if they had not used the mails to further their scheme. But the lack of legal liability would not have changed the fact that Kelly and Palmer had acted unethically. They knowingly used their employer's property for personal gain—certainly in violation of their duty of loyalty to their employer. Ethically, there is no difference between using Univac's computer and using, say, Univac's trucks to run a delivery service on the side.*

SOFTWARE PIRACY   For the average consumer, software is expensive. It can also be expensive to produce. Often, considerable sums are invested in the research and development necessary to create new, innovative software programs. And, once marketed, new software requires that user support be provided during its life on the market. It is not surprising that, given the expense of software and the zealous competition in today's software market, many individuals and business firms have been tempted to steal software by decoding and making unauthorized copies of software programs. This is known as *software piracy*. It has been estimated that the annual loss to developers from this practice is more than $250 million.

Manufacturers have incorporated protective codes into their software to inhibit its duplication. Breaking through these security codes became little more than a game to some individuals, who then made illegal copies of the software. Consequently, some manufacturers ceased attempting to protect their software by this method because little benefit was gained in comparison with the increased cost and software complexity required by the security measures. Many companies now take protective steps against software piracy by stressing the benefits—such as written instructions and user support—associated with using authorized copies. Others are suing the users of unauthorized copies in tort for copyright or patent infringement.

Software piracy is illegal, but the applicability of traditional criminal or tort law is made difficult by the unique nature of computer programs. For example, as with the theft of data or services, statutes designed to prohibit larceny—the taking of property without the owner's consent—may be difficult to apply. These statutes were originally enacted to prohibit the theft of *tangible* property. Computer programs, however, are *intangible,* or intellectual, property. As mentioned in Chapter 8, some states have dealt with the issue of program piracy by expanding their definitions of property to bring the theft of computer programs under their larceny statutes. At the federal level, existing laws protecting intellectual property (such as patent and copyright laws) have been amended in recent years to extend coverage to computer programs—as was discussed earlier in this chapter. In 1990, in an attempt to further control the unauthorized copying of computer programs, the federal government passed a law that prohibits, with some exceptions, the renting, leasing, or lending of computer software without the express permission of the copyright holder.

VANDALISM AND DESTRUCTIVE PROGRAMMING   On occasion, political activists, terrorists, and disgruntled employees have physically damaged computer hardware or ruined computer software. These acts have included such conduct as smashing computer equipment with a crowbar, shooting it with a pistol, and—in an attempt to make a political point—pouring blood over a computer. In one instance, to erase a company's records, an individual merely walked past computer storage banks with a large electromagnet.

Other destructive acts have required greater technical awareness and facility. For example, a computer program can be designed to rearrange, replace, or even destroy data. Further, the program can be time-delayed and set—much like a time-bomb—to "explode" in the future. Similarly, lines can be inserted into an existing program to damage a system or, for example, to have funds transferred into a phony account. Thus, a knowledgeable individual can do a considerable amount of damage.

Some software companies include in their programs mechanisms that will disable programs if, for example, annual license fees are not paid by a certain date. In one case, when a dispute arose between Revlon, Inc., and its software supplier, Logisticon, Inc., over software performance, Logisticon gained telephone access to the computer system and activated software-disabling commands. As a result, operations at two of Revlon's main distribution centers were brought to a standstill for three days. In its still-pending lawsuit against Logisticon, Revlon characterized Logisticon's actions as a form of extortion. Logisticon viewed the matter somewhat differently: it claimed that it "repossessed" the software because Revlon refused to pay the agreed price for the software.[6]

Private Protective Measures

An increasingly common practice among business firms and government institutions is restricting access to, and use of, information in a computer system through the use of various security measures. In some cases, the data's availability can be limited to those with special security clearances. Establishing a system of security clearances may involve organizing data in specific categories. The category to which an individual is given access is related to the information the individual needs to perform his or her job. For example, the names of account holders can be kept separate from the accounts' balances. In this way, a party who needs to work with

the balances can be prevented from learning the holders' identities.

Passwords may be attached to a system or to a portion of the data within a system to preclude unauthorized access. Considering the relative ease with which unauthorized individuals have discovered passwords in the past, however, it is advisable to change the passwords frequently.

Another means of limiting access to computer information is to encode the data contained within the system—that is, to translate the data into a secret code. Data can be encoded before it is stored or communicated to another party. The data is decoded when it is taken from storage or when the other party receives it.

As a further protective measure, a copy of the data can be stored outside the facilities in which a company's computer system is located. Then, if some of the information kept in the system is destroyed or lost, it can be reproduced.

Crime Control Legislation

At the federal level, Congress has enacted legislation directed at specific computer abuses. The most significant federal legislation relating to computer crimes is the Counterfeit Access Device and Computer Fraud and Abuse Act of 1984. This act prohibits the unauthorized access to, or use of, computer systems. Under the act, it is a crime to access a computer knowingly for any of the following reasons:

1. To obtain restricted government information—which includes information protected for reasons of national defense or foreign relations and information restricted under the Atomic Energy Act—with the intent that the information be used to the injury of the United States or the advantage of a foreign nation.
2. To obtain information contained in a financial institution's financial records or in a consumer reporting agency's files on consumers.
3. To use, modify, destroy, or prevent the authorized use of a computer operated for or on behalf of the federal government or to disclose the information that it contains.

Another federal act, the Electronic Fund Transfer Act (EFTA)—discussed in more detail in Chapter 24—concerns electronic fund transfers, such as

---

6. *New York Times,* October 24, 1990, pp. C1, C4.

■ **Exhibit 26–1 Federal Legislation Relating to Privacy**

Title	Provisions Concerning Privacy
Freedom of Information Act (1966)	Provides that individuals have a right to obtain access to information about them collected in government files.
Fair Credit Reporting Act (1970)	Provides that consumers have the right to be informed of the nature and scope of a credit investigation, the kind of information that is being compiled, and the names of the firms or individuals who will be receiving the report.
Crime Control Act (1973)	Safeguards the confidentiality of information amassed for certain state criminal systems.
Family Educational Rights and Privacy Act (1974)	Limits access to computer-stored records of education-related evaluations and grades in private and public colleges and universities.
Privacy Act (1974)	Protects the privacy of individuals about whom the federal government has information. Specifically, the act provides the following: 1. Agencies originating, using, disclosing, or otherwise manipulating personal information must ensure the reliability of the information and provide safeguards against its misuse. 2. Information compiled for one purpose cannot be used for another without the concerned individual's permission. 3. Individuals must be able to find out what data concerning them are being compiled and how the data will be used. 4. Individuals must be given a means through which to correct inaccurate data.
Tax Reform Act (1976)	Preserves the privacy of personal financial information.
Right to Financial Privacy Act (1978)	Prohibits financial institutions from providing the federal government with access to a customer's records unless the customer authorizes the disclosure.
Electronic Fund Transfer Act (1980)	Requires financial institutions to notify an individual if a third party gains access to the individual's account.
Counterfeit Access Device and Computer Fraud and Abuse Act (1984)	Prohibits use of a computer without authorization to retrieve data in a financial institution's or consumer reporting agency's files.
Cable Communications Policy Act (1984)	Regulates access to information collected by cable service operators on subscribers to cable services.
Electronic Communications Privacy Act (1986)	Prohibits the interception of information communicated by electronic means.

direct payroll and social security deposits and transactions conducted at automatic teller machines (ATMs). These transfers provide opportunities for theft through such means as the interception and alteration of data involved in the transfers, the counterfeiting of ATM cards, and the use of stolen code numbers to gain access to financial information and accounts.

Under the EFTA, it is a crime to use, sell, furnish, or transport in interstate commerce any counterfeit, fictitious, altered, forged, lost, stolen, or

fraudulently obtained device (such as an ATM card or code number) used to conduct an electronic fund transfer to obtain money, goods, services, or anything else of value. Penalties for violations include up to ten years' imprisonment and a fine of up to $10,000.

At the state level, computer crime is being controlled both by the expansion of traditional criminal laws to cover computer abuses, as mentioned above, and by the passage of laws prohibiting specific computer uses or abuses. In Idaho, for example, accessing computer information without authorization is a misdemeanor, and illegally changing information is a felony. South Dakota has made it illegal to disclose passwords. All unauthorized computer use is a felony in Hawaii. California, Arizona, and numerous other states have also passed new legislation or revised their laws to cover the specific types of computer offenses discussed in this section.

■ Privacy Rights in a Computer Age

Although computers have greatly facilitated commercial transactions, they have also led to a tradeoff that many have found disturbing: speedier, more efficient transactions at the expense of individual privacy. Today, virtually all institutions with which an individual has dealings—including schools, doctors and dentists, insurance companies, mail-order houses, banking institutions, credit card companies, and mortgage firms—obtain information about that individual and store it in their computer files. In addition, numerous government agencies, such as the Census Bureau, the Social Security Administration, and the Internal Revenue Service, collect and store data concerning individuals' incomes, expenses, marital status, and other personal history and habits. Any time an individual applies for a driver's license, a credit card, or even telephone service, information concerning that individual is gathered and stored. Frequently, this personal information finds its way to credit bureaus, marketing departments and firms, or others without the permission or even the knowledge of the individuals concerned.

As mentioned in previous chapters, an individual's right to privacy is protected under tort law and, to a certain extent, under the U.S. Constitution. In situations involving computers, tort damages may be awarded for unauthorized intrusion into another's private records or unauthorized examination of another's bank account. But how does one demonstrate that private records have been invaded when there has been no physical intrusion into one's home or place of business? In such a case, there is no "evidence" of the invasion of privacy.

In response to society's concern over the potential abuse of personal information collected by the government and other institutions, Congress has enacted several laws (see Exhibit 26–1). In addition, many of the laws that states have enacted to address computer crime are also necessarily concerned to some extent with the issue of privacy. The Privacy Act of 1974 has served as a model for many of the state laws regulating government records and recording practices. Although this legislation has helped to control the collection and dispersal of information contained in computer files, information in computer files is still to a great extent unprotected by rules, laws, or codes of ethics. In general, how to control computer use and abuse remains a significant legal challenge of our time.

■ Terms and Concepts to Review

certification mark 626
collective mark 626
computer crime 630
copyright 618

intellectual property 617
mask work 623
patent 618
service mark 626

trade name 626
trade secrets 627
trademark 624

■ Questions and Case Problems

26-1. Professor Wise is teaching a summer seminar in business torts at State University. Several times during the course, he makes copies of relevant sections from business law texts and distributes them to his students. Unbeknownst to Wise, the daughter of one of the textbook authors is a member of his seminar. She tells her father about Wise's copying activities, which have been done without her father's or his publisher's permission. Her father sues Wise for copyright infringement. Wise claims protection under the "fair use" doctrine. Who will prevail? Explain.

26-2. Adams, who owns and operates a restaurant, has had an account with Uptown Bank for over twenty years. All of Uptown's banking records are computerized. Greed, a competitor of Adams, pays a sum of money to a disgruntled Uptown employee to access Uptown's computer system and provide Greed with information on the financial position and activities of Adams. In addition to giving Greed this information, the employee gives one of Adams's creditors the access code of Uptown's computer system. The creditor, using its own computer, then gathers financial information on Adams. Uptown Bank learns of these activities and discharges the employee. Discuss whether any of the federal laws mentioned in this chapter are specifically applicable to these facts.

26-3. As a college student, you are required to write a term paper. You are currently employed part-time by ABC, Inc. Without ABC's permission, you secure access to ABC's computer and use the computer to generate certain data formulations for your paper. Discuss whether you could and should be liable to ABC for theft.

26-4. One day during algebra class, Diedra, an enterprising fourteen-year-old student, began drawing designs on her shoelaces. By the end of the class, Diedra had decorated her shoelaces with the name of the school, "Broadson Junior High," written in blue and red (the school colors) and with pictures of bears, the school's mascot. After class, Mrs. Laxton, Diedra's teacher, reprimanded Diedra for not paying attention in class and asked Diedra what she had been doing during the lecture. Diedra showed Mrs. Laxton her shoelaces. When Diedra got home that night, she wrote about the day's events in her diary. She also drew her shoelace design in the diary. Mrs. Laxton had been trying to think of how she could build up the school spirit. She thought about Diedra's shoelaces and decided to go into business for herself. She called her business "Spirited Shoelaces" and designed shoelaces for each of the local schools, decorating the shoelaces in each case with the school's names, mascots, and colors. The business became tremendously profitable. Even though Diedra never registered her idea with the patent or copyright office, does she nonetheless have intellectual property rights in the shoelace design? Will her diary account be sufficient proof that she created the idea? Discuss fully.

26-5. Original Appalachian Artworks, Inc., (OAA) makes and distributes the very successful product called Cabbage Patch Kids—soft, sculptured dolls that were in great demand in the early 1980s. The dolls are unique in appearance, and the name is registered as a trademark to OAA. The design, too, is protected under a copyright registration. In 1986, Topps Chewing Gum, Inc., had an artist copy many of the features of the dolls for Topps's new product—stickers that depicted obnoxious cartoon characters called Garbage Pail Kids. The stickers proved very lucrative; in fact, Topps expanded the product line to include T-shirts, balloons, and school notebooks.

(a) Did Topps infringe upon OAA's trademark and copyrighted product? Why or why not?

(b) Topps claimed that its product was actually a satire of OAA's product and therefore a fair use of a protected work. Would this amount to a fair use? Discuss.

[*Original Appalachian Artworks, Inc. v. Topps Chewing Gum, Inc.,* 642 F.Supp. 1031 (N.D.Ga. 1986)]

26-6. McGraw was employed by the city of Indianapolis as a computer operator. The city leased computer services on a fixed-charge, or flat-rate, basis; hence, its expense for computer services was constant, regardless of how much computer time was used. McGraw was provided with a terminal at his desk and assigned a portion of the computer's information storage capacity, or private library. McGraw became involved in a private sales venture and began using a small portion of his assigned library to maintain records associated with the venture. At the time he was hired, he received a handbook disclosing the general prohibition against the unauthorized use of city property, and he was reprimanded several times for selling his products in the office and on "office time." The relevant criminal theft statute reads: "A person who knowingly or intentionally exerts unauthorized control over property of another person with intent to deprive the other of any part of its value or use commits theft." Discuss whether McGraw should be convicted of theft because of his unauthorized use of city facilities. [*State v. McGraw,* 480 N.E.2d 552 (Ind. 1985)]

26-7. On September 21, 1987, Quality Inns International, Inc., announced a new chain of economy hotels to be marketed under the name "McSleep Inns." The response of the owners of McDonald's Corp., the fast-food chain, was immediate. McDonald's wrote Quality Inns a letter stating that the use of "McSleep Inns" infringed upon the McDonald's family of marks characterized by the prefix "Mc" attached to a generic term. Five days later, Quality Inns filed an action seeking a declaratory judgment from the court that the mark "McSleep Inns" did not infringe on McDonald's federally registered trademarks or common law rights to its marks and would not constitute an unfair trade practice. McDonald's counterclaimed, alleging trademark infringement and unfair competition. McDonald's argued that the use of the name "McSleep Inns" by Quality Inns would confuse and mislead the public and allow Quality Inns to trade on the goodwill and reputation of McDonald's. Quality Inns claimed that "Mc" had come into generic use as a prefix and therefore McDonald's had no trademark rights to the prefix itself. Quality Inns further claimed that its use of the prefix for lodging accommodations would not be confusing to the public because McDonald's products were fast foods. Does the use of the prefix "Mc" by Quality Inns for its new "McSleep" chain of economy motels infringe on McDonald's trademarks? Explain. [*Quality Inns International, Inc. v. McDonald's Corp.,* 695 F.Supp. 198 (D.Md. 1988)]

26-8. Vault Corp. produces computer diskettes, under the registered trademark PROLOK, that are designed to prevent the unauthorized copying of programs placed on the diskettes by software computer companies, Vault's customers. A program placed on a PROLOK diskette can be copied onto another diskette, but the computer will not read the program from the copy unless the original PROLOK diskette is also in one of the computer's disk drives. Quaid

Software, Ltd., markets the CopyWrite diskette. Quaid's diskette contains a feature called RAMKEY, which unlocks the PROLOK protective device. Individuals who purchase the CopyWrite diskette can therefore make fully functional copies of any programs placed on PROLOK diskettes. Vault alleged that Quaid's RAMKEY feature contributed to the infringement of Vault's copyright and Vault's customers' copyrights in violation of the Copyright Act. Quaid claimed that because the RAMKEY feature was capable of substantial noninfringing uses—including the making of archival copies of PROLOK diskettes to be used if the original PROLOK diskettes were damaged—Quaid should not be held responsible for any infringing uses of RAMKEY made by those who purchased the CopyWrite diskette. Review *Sony Corp. v. Universal City Studios* (Case 8.1) and discuss the merits of Quaid's claim in light of that decision. [*Vault Corp. v. Quaid Software, Ltd.*, 847 F.2d 255 (5th Cir. 1988)]

26-9. Mead Data Central, Inc., provides a computerized legal research service under the trademark LEXIS. LEXIS is widely known and used by the legal community, but a survey indicated that only about 1 percent of the general population recognized the name. In August of 1987, Toyota Motor Corp. announced a new line of luxury automobiles to be called Lexus. Mead Data Central sought to enjoin Toyota from using the name Lexus, claiming that Toyota's use of that name would dilute the distinctive quality of LEXIS as a mark and thus violate Section 368-d of New York's General Business Law. That statute reads, in part, as follows: "Likelihood of injury to business reputation or of dilution of the distinctive quality of a mark or trade name shall be a ground for injunctive relief in cases of infringement of a mark registered or not registered." What will result in court? Discuss. [*Mead Data Central, Inc. v. Toyota Motor Sales, U.S.A., Inc.*, 875 F.2d 1026 (2d Cir. 1989)]

26-10. A Question of Ethics

Gayle Schreier, a travel agent, has access to the computer reservation system of American Airlines (American). American's frequent-flyer program, called AAdvantage, allows American's passengers who join the program to accumulate mileage credits. When enough credits are accumulated, American issues coupons that can be used to acquire, without any cash payment, tickets for American flights. Passengers who are not members of AAdvantage can also receive mileage credits if they sign up for the program within a twenty-four-hour claim period following their flights. Gayle devised a scheme by which she could take advantage of mileage credits that were not claimed by American's passengers. She enrolled a fictitious person, G. Johnson, in the AAdvantage program. Then she accessed the computer system to replace the name of actual passengers who had made particular flights with that of G. Johnson. AAdvantage issued coupons to G. Johnson and sent them to G. Johnson's address, which Gayle had provided. Eventually, these coupons were exchanged for tickets and used. In no case did Gayle use mileage credits that any passenger of American Airlines had claimed. [U.S. v. Schreier, 908 F.2d 645 (10th Cir. 1990)]

1. In light of the fact that she was not depriving any passenger of mileage credits, and assuming that she has not violated any law, was Gayle acting wrongfully from an ethical point of view? If you were in her position, would you do as she did? Why or why not?
2. Did Gayle's activities in any way harm the interests of American Airlines? Discuss.
3. Has Gayle violated any of the laws discussed in this or the two previous chapters? Explain.

26-11. Case Briefing Assignment

Examine Case A.26 [New Era Publications International, ApS v. Carol Publishing Group, 904 F.2d 152 (2d Cir. 1990)] in Appendix A. The case has been excerpted there in great detail. Review and then brief the case, making sure that you include answers to the following questions in your brief.

1. What was the nature of New Era's claim against Carol Publishing?
2. How had the author of the book published by Carol used the material from Hubbard's works?
3. What are the four factors used in evaluating whether use of copyrighted material is a "fair use" under Section 107?
4. Briefly summarize the appellate court's interpretation of the work published by Carol in light of the four factors delineated in Section 107.

Focus on Ethics

The Contemporary Environment

The contemporary environment of business is marked by innovations and technological advances both in the products available to consumers and the ways in which commerce is conducted. The social and business changes wrought by these innovations present unique ethical problems. In this *Focus on Ethics* we consider a few of the special legal and ethical issues which have come about as a result of these recent changes in the contemporary environment.

Efficiency versus Due Care

A major problem faced by today's banking institutions is how to verify customer signatures on the billions of checks that are processed through the banking system each month. If a bank fails to verify a signature on a check it receives for payment and the check turns out to be forged, the bank will normally be held liable to its customer for the amount paid. But how can banks possibly examine, item by item, each signature on every check that they pay?

The banks' solution to this problem is simply not to examine all signatures. Instead, computers are programmed to verify all signatures only on checks exceeding a certain

threshold amount, such as $1,000 or $2,500 or perhaps some higher amount. Checks for less than the threshold amount are selected for signature verification only on a random basis. In other words, serious attention is restricted to serious matters. The result is that many checks, if not most, are paid without signature verification. This practice, which has become an acceptable standard within the banking industry of today, is economically efficient for banks: even though liability costs are sometimes incurred—when forged checks are paid—the costs involved in verifying the authenticity of each and every signature would be far higher.

From an ethical standpoint, some have claimed that this banking practice is not fair to small depositors, who normally do not write checks exceeding the threshold amount. Although the UCC permits a bank customer to recover from the bank any amounts paid over the customer's forged signature, recovery will be precluded if the customer was negligent in his or her duty to examine canceled checks promptly and then report any forgeries to the bank within the time prescribed by the UCC. But it is the small depositor—and not those whose checks usually exceed the threshold

amount—who is more likely to delay in examining canceled checks and who therefore is more likely to suffer losses as a result of random signature verification.

In view of the effect of random signature verification on small depositors, some people have alleged that banks using such procedures are not exercising due care in the handling of the customers' accounts. Under the UCC, banks are held to a standard of "ordinary care." At one time in the banking industry, ordinary care normally was interpreted to mean that a bank had a duty to inspect *all* signatures on checks. The question is, what constitutes ordinary care in the context of today's world? Does a bank exercise ordinary care if it follows the prevailing industry practice of examining signatures on only a few, randomly selected checks under a certain amount? Or does ordinary care still mean that a bank should examine each signature?

This became a critical issue in a case involving the Rhode Island Trust National Bank and one of its customers, Zapata Corporation.[1] Zapata found itself

<hr>

1. *Rhode Island Trust National Bank v. Zapata Corp.,* 848 F.2d 291 (1st Cir. 1988).

the victim of a series of check forgeries ranging in amount from $150 to $800. In all, over a three-month period, more than $100,000 in forged checks was paid by the bank. None of the checks was examined by the bank, which only verified all signatures on checks for $1,000 or more. Unfortunately, Zapata failed to promptly inspect its canceled checks and report the forgeries to the bank, as required by UCC 4-406(1). Under UCC 4-406(2), Zapata's negligence precluded recovery of the funds from the bank—unless Zapata could show that the bank had failed to exercise ordinary care. Under UCC 4-406(3), if the customer establishes lack of ordinary care on the part of the bank in paying the checks, the customer can recover from the bank regardless of the customer's own negligence.

Zapata alleged that the bank itself was negligent because it did not examine the signatures on all the checks it paid, but the court was not convinced that the bank had violated its duty of care. The First Circuit Court of Appeals ruled that, indeed, the $1,000 signature-verification threshold was within the limits of ordinary care, and therefore the bank was not liable. Not all courts would agree with the First Circuit's conclusion, but that provided no consolation to Zapata, which was left out in the cold. While we may sympathize with Zapata, the other side of the story also deserves to be considered: if banks were required to examine the signature on every $2 or $10 or $150 check that came through the banking system, the system would probably screech to a grinding halt and make everybody worse off. What we see here is a cost imposed on the few—those who are victims

of forgeries similar to the one just described above and who do not inspect their canceled checks—for the benefit of the whole. The tradeoff here can be phrased as follows: the stricter the rule of liability to which banks are held for paying checks over forged signatures, the more expensive banking activities become, and therefore the slower the rate of growth of banking and commerce in the nation.

Ethics and Technology

Everybody knows that we live in the age of the computer, and the use of computers in the banking industry is probably just short of overwhelming. As more and more of the work of the banking system is handled by computers, fewer and fewer transactions are evidenced by a "paper trail." Needless to say, electronic fund transfer systems (EFTS) have posed legal—and ethical—problems, just as computers and computerized transactions have created problems in other areas of the law such as torts and crimes.

Electronic Fund Transfer Act

The Electronic Fund Transfer Act (EFTA) addressed many of the issues that involve the customer's liability with respect to EFTS and the bank's duty of care to the customer. Not all issues have been resolved, however—particularly those that involve disagreement between the customer and the bank's computer. Consider, for example, the following situation.

Mrs. Judd and her husband had a joint checking account at a Citibank branch in New York. They also had Citicards that gave them access to the

computer via the bank's automated teller machines (ATMs) located throughout the city. Each card, before it could access the computer, had to be first "validated" by the bank. Although Mrs. Judd had gone into the bank to receive her personal identification number (PIN) and have her card validated, her husband had not yet done so. Thus, only Mrs. Judd's card could be used to obtain cash or make any other transaction via the ATM, and then only if the user knew her PIN—which she said she had given to no one and which she had not even written down, but memorized.

The Judds were thus stunned to learn that $800 had been charged to their checking account as a result of two transactions, one made on February 26, 1980, between 2:13 and 2:14 P.M., and the other on March 28, 1980, between 2:30 and 2:32 P.M. The bank maintained that there was no way the funds could have been withdrawn without the use of Mrs. Judd's card and PIN. But Mrs. Judd was convinced the bank had made an error—or, rather, that the computer had. She could not have withdrawn the funds at those times, she contended, because she had been at work on both days at those times; a letter from her employer confirmed her statement.

Eventually, the case came before the Civil Court of New York City, and Judge John Marmarellis was faced with the problem of deciding the issue. Whom was he to believe? Mrs. Judd, whom he described as a "credible witness?" Or the bank's computer printout, which, as "translated" by the bank's manager, verified that the amounts could have been withdrawn from her account only by the use of her card and PIN? He opted to believe Mrs. Judd and awarded her $800 plus interest and disbursements, having stated in his opinion the following: "It is too commonplace in our society that when faced with the choice of man or machine, we readily accept the 'word' of the machine every time. This, despite the tales of computer malfunctions that we hear daily."[2]

Stories similar to that of the Judds do not always have happy endings, but courts recognize that machines can err and have shown a willingness, as in the Judds' case, to take the word of a credible witness over that of a computer. Nonetheless, in the absence of paper evidence of fund transactions, there is no foolproof guarantee that truth and fair play will win out in these kinds of situations. Although it is natural to sympathize with a person who loses money at the hands of an erring and uncaring machine, banks can also be victimized by unethical individuals who falsely, but convincingly, allege computer mistakes and seek recovery from the bank.

Fraudulent Wire Transfers

The EFTA covers only consumer transfers. Commercial wire transfers between banking and other institutions are not covered by the act. In the event of an erroneous or fraudulent commercial wire transfer, the courts must therefore wade through a jungle of legal principles and precedents to determine the issue. Article 4A

of the UCC was drafted to fill the need for a uniform law with respect to wire transfers, but, until it is adopted by all of the states, courts will still have to rely on tort and contract law in settling disputes between parties to commercial wire transfers.

Unfortunately, it is relatively easy for a technologically sophisticated and well-placed individual to commit fraud using an EFTS. Unless, however, specific requirements are met, the transfer will not fall under the EFTA, and the bank will not be liable. For example, telephone transfers are covered by the EFTA only if they are made pursuant to a prearranged plan under which periodic or recurring transfers are contemplated. Therefore, if an imposter, posing as an account holder, calls a bank official and requests him or her to transfer funds, the true owner of the account cannot hold the bank liable under the EFTA. The owner may be able to recover the fraudulently transferred funds in a tort or contract lawsuit, but the action will not lie under the EFTA.[3]

A fraudulent wire transfer was central to a scheme cleverly executed by two con artists, aliases Hank and David Friedman. The Friedmans arranged to buy $800,000 worth of rare gold coins and bullion from Colonial Coins, Inc., in Houston. They told Colonial that they would arrange to have the funds transferred from their Boston bank to Colonial's account at the Texas American Bank, and Colonial agreed. The Friedmans then wrote a letter to Bradford Trust Company in

Boston and, over the forged signature of Frank Rochefort, one of Bradford's account holders, authorized Bradford to liquidate $800,000 worth of mutual funds in Rochefort's account and wire the proceeds to his account at the Texas American Bank of Houston. Although the letter stated that the funds should be transferred to the account of Frank S. Rochefort, the account number given in the request was that of Colonial Coins. To expedite the transfer, the Friedmans also included in the letter the account number of the Houston bank. The agent at Bradford that handled the transaction saw nothing unusual or unduly suspicious about the letter and arranged for the $800,000 to be transferred by wire to the Texas bank. When the money arrived at Texas American, the bank failed to investigate the discrepancy between the account number and the account holder's name. Instead, because it had been advised by Colonial to expect the transfer, it immediately deposited the funds into the account number given on the wire and telephoned Colonial to let the merchant know that the funds had been received. At that point, the Friedmans received the gold and coins and left, not to be heard from again.

The matter went unnoted by Bradford Trust until an astonished Frank Rochefort noted the withdrawal on his statement and informed Bradford Trust that he had not authorized the transfer. Bradford credited Rochefort's account with $800,000 and then turned to the Texas bank to recover. Unfortunately for Bradford, it never did retrieve its money. The court would not agree that the Texas bank had been more

2. *Judd v. Citibank,* 107 Misc.2d 526, 435 N.Y.S.2d 210 (1980).

3. *Kashanchi v. Texas Commerce Medical Bank, N.A.,* 703 F.2d 936 (5th Cir. 1983).

at fault than Bradford Trust, and Bradford was thus left holding the proverbial bag—in this case, a very empty one.[4]

Until Article 4A is uniformly in effect, courts will have to continue to apply laws that were drafted before the computer age to disputes involving wire transfers. But sometimes this is difficult. Often, courts will look to Articles 3 and 4 for guidance and apply, by analogy, rules governing transfers via paper to a transfer of funds via an EFTS. In the case just described, the court's conclusion reflected the reasoning implicit in the UCC provisions governing commercial paper: that between two innocent parties, the party in the best position to prevent the fraud should bear the loss. Although the court found the Texas American bank to have been negligent, it held that Bradford Trust should bear the loss because it had dealt more directly with the imposter.

Lender Liability

Lender liability is an issue that has become important only in the last ten or fifteen years. Today, lenders find that they are often liable for more than the size of the loan. In particular, lenders may find themselves held liable by the U.S. government for all costs of cleaning up toxic wastes from real estate on which they have foreclosed. Many have questioned the fairness of holding lenders liable in these circumstances.

Lender liability also poses a long-run tradeoff for society: To the extent that more lenders are held liable for improper

4. *Bradford Trust Co. v. Texas American Bank-Houston,* 790 F.2d 407 (5th Cir. 1986).

repossession of collateral, improper foreclosure, or toxic waste clean-up costs, the amount of total lending will decrease. That is, the higher the total cost of lending, the smaller the amount of credit that will be offered to business firms. This will reduce the amount of commerce in America. The tradeoff is thus relatively obvious.

Ethics and Hostile Takeovers

Merger mania, targets, poison pills, golden parachutes, greenmail, white knights. The shenanigans of corporate raiders, arbitrageurs, boards of directors, and investment banking firms have caught the attention of the press, politicians, and laypersons alike. It is true that in the United States (and now in Europe) the amount of corporate takeover activity seems to have increased. A number of corporate raiders have become famous—some because they have gone to jail for resorting to illegal activities. The unethical nature of actions that violate the law is clear. But what about corporate raiders and arbitrageurs who do not violate the law? Are they acting ethically?

To answer this thorny question, let's take one example. A corporate raider learns, through diligent research and personal contacts, that a certain publicly traded company seems to be undervalued in the marketplace. That is to say, the public, or market, value of the company appears to be less than its true value. The corporate raider starts to acquire shares in the stock of the company. Eventually, word gets out that she is doing this, and typically the market value of

the stock rises. At some point, the corporate raider may make a tender offer to purchase a certain percentage of the outstanding shares of stock at a price that exceeds the current market price. If the corporate raider succeeds, she will acquire voting control of the corporation, oust the board of directors, put in her own people, and take over the corporation. Often, after this is done, the new board of directors will sell off certain parts of the company and restructure other parts. In the process, the lives of the previous managers and employees are altered—many of them are fired. The corporate raider is viewed as a greedy scoundrel. There was even a movie about this called *Wall Street,* in which the character played by Michael Douglas was portrayed as evil incarnate as he went about taking over corporations and then restructuring them.

As always, the ethical question here involves a tradeoff. The corporate raider typically will only go after control of a corporation that is poorly managed. If a corporation is well managed, its profits and its profit potential will be high and therefore will be reflected in a high market value, thus making it an unlikely candidate for a takeover. When a corporate raider chooses a poorly managed company as a target, a certain group of individuals will gain—current shareholders. Another group will lose—current management and some employees.

What about arbitrageurs, those persons who have no true interest in actually taking over corporations but rather engage in buying and selling the stock of companies that are, or will be, the targets of takeover attempts? Is it ethical for these individuals to bid up the price of stock in a company that is a takeover target only to sell that stock at an inflated price? Again, the answer to this question depends on whom you want to benefit. If the arbitrageurs correctly predict what is going to happen, they will make a profit. If they predict incorrectly, a loss will be incurred. At the same time, because of increased buying pressure on the company's stock, current shareholders in the target corporation will gain more than they would have if an arbitrageur had never entered the marketplace.

Sometimes, corporate raiders may go past any well-reasoned ethical boundary. This occurs in the case of greenmail. In a greenmail situation, a so-called corporate raider has no intention of actually making a raid on the corporation, but he or she gives the impression that a takeover attempt is going to occur. A large block of stock is purchased, and a threat is brandished in front of current management. Often, the board of directors, in an attempt to make sure that no corporate raid occurs, will agree to buy back this large block of stock at an inflated price. The purported corporate raider obtains a handsome profit. The shareholders in the company actually lose. The only beneficiaries, besides the raider, seem to be current management, who have made sure that their jobs are protected.

Computer Piracy
Tremendous growth in the microcomputer industry in recent years has raised numerous ethical considerations. Many

people claim that copyright law has failed to keep up with the unethical behavior that is now possible in our legal system. Some types of computer programs are protected under the copyright laws; yet computer software can exist in several forms. In the past, manufacturers of computer software marketed their programs in an unreadable form stored in a silicon chip. But now technology has advanced to the point at which programs stored in these silicon chips can be "pirated."

Manufacturers have sought to "copy protect" their software. This means programming, or "locking," the disk, so that it cannot be copied. Copy protection has largely failed, however, and has created a new market in programs that "crack" the copy-protection codes. Do you think it is ethical for a company to make money by selling computer programs that defeat copy-protection systems?

■ Discussion Questions

1. One often hears about individuals who complain that "the system" is unfair to "the little person." This complaint is nowhere more evident than within the world of banking. The small depositor who is lax about reviewing his or her canceled checks may find out too late that he or she has been the victim of forgery. The customer's negligence in failing to discover the forgery typically gets the bank off the hook, particularly if the forgery involves an amount so small that it clearly falls under any threshold level the bank might have set for examination of checks for unauthorized

signatures. Furthermore, it is the less well-educated and experienced individual who often is taken in by a scam artist or otherwise becomes an innocent victim of fraud. Yet because the UCC offers special protection to those accepting checks without reason to be suspicious of fraud, an innocent party to a fraudulent transaction often has no legal recourse. From an ethical standpoint, how could you justify to the "losers" in the above situations the provisions of the UCC that fail to protect them? How would you explain the trade-offs involved? Can you think of a way in which such problems could be handled more fairly or ethically than they are under the UCC?
2. It would be possible to eliminate an imposter's ability to effectuate telephone fund transfers by simply making it illegal for banks to act on transfer requests made by telephone. If this were done, no one would have to worry about innocent parties being hurt because of fraudulent fund transfers that do not fall under the EFTA. It is clear, then, who the beneficiaries of such a change in the law would be. What would be the costs to society, though, of such a change in the law? Who would pay those costs? What might the ultimate outcome of such a law be?
3. Assume that all lending institutions are held liable for environmental clean-up costs on properties on which they foreclose. What businesses would be affected by such a development, and how would they be affected? [Hint: Dry cleaners; print shops.]
4. There are those who argue that hostile takeovers injure employees, officers, and directors of the target

companies. Others contend that such injuries inure to the benefit of the shareholders of target corporations. After all, the latter group would argue, such corporations would not be "targets" if they were properly managed. Discuss the pros and cons of hostile takeovers. What are the costs and benefits of laws that restrict—or make exceedingly difficult—hostile takeovers?

5. When a corporate insider knows that something positive is going to be announced, if that person uses that information to make a profit by first purchasing the stock in the company and then selling it when the price goes up, that person is guilty of illegal insider trading. In contrast, an astute investor who doggedly pursues the company's activities and correctly guesses that the good event is going to occur cannot be prosecuted for illegal insider trading if he makes a profit. From society's point of view what is the difference in the ultimate result between these two actions?

6. Some have argued that insider trading should be made legal because the more quickly information is disseminated in the marketplace and reflected in the price of stocks, the more efficient the system. What are the pros and cons about making all insider trading legal?

UNIT SEVEN

The International Environment

■ The Importance of the International Environment

Business in general faces an increasingly international economic environment. Many businesspersons find themselves engaged in exporting goods and services. Others find that they are importing goods and services. Additionally, numerous other types of financial dealings with other countries are possible. Often money capital is raised abroad to finance a project at home. And some businesses are discovering that they can make higher profits by investing money capital in other countries or by actually producing goods in other countries for sale in those countries, as well as for sale elsewhere, including the United States. These topics to a certain extent have been treated throughout the text. In this, our final chapter, though, we look exclusively at the international environment of business. In so doing, we pay particular attention to international transactions and the legal environment within which international transactions take place.

■ Ethical Issues in the International Environment

Ethical issues in the international business arena frequently have to do with cultural and political differences between nations. For example, many other countries do not have such extensive consumer protection laws as does the United States. That means that U.S. business firms may export products that might require warnings if distributed in the United States or that may be banned outright in the United States. The decision to distribute such products abroad turns on ethical considerations. Similarly, whereas an employer operating within the United States is prohibited from discriminating against employees, U.S. employers operating abroad are not so constrained in their employment practices. Again, ethical decisions are called for in this area. Different customs in the international landscape pose other ethical problems. Bribery of government officials, for example, is an age-old practice in many countries. But since 1977, when the U.S. Congress passed the Foreign Corrupt Practices Act, U.S. firms and their employees have been prohibited from giving bribes in return for favorable contracts from foreign governments. This obviously puts U.S. firms at a disadvantage and thus raises issues of fairness.

Sales transactions, whether domestic or international, are fraught with ethical considerations that cannot be ignored by the serious student of business law. These considerations take on an extra dimension in the international environment. Differences in culture, language, and laws combine to make the ethical issues of international sales transactions particularly difficult. For example, is it ethical to market pharmaceutical products in other countries when those products have not yet been approved by the U.S. Food and Drug Administration as safe? Is it ethical to sell children's toys in foreign markets when such toys might not pass muster under the watchful eye of the U.S. Consumer Product Safety Commission? We will return to these difficult issues in our final *Focus on Ethics.* First, though, we take an in-depth look at the legal aspects of the international environment of modern business.

647

Chapter 27

The International Legal Framework

Nearly every major business considers the potential of international markets for its products or services. The simplest way to conduct international business is to seek customers abroad. It may be more profitable, however, to manufacture a product in the same country as its market, if access to raw materials is better and labor is less expensive, because customers are closer and barriers to trade may be avoided. One way to arrange production abroad is for a firm to invest in its own facilities; another method is to license the technology associated with a product to an existing foreign company.

Over the last decade, countries competing for international trade have become more evenly matched competitors than in earlier years. In part, this is due to the increased use and success of regional international organizations such as the European Community (EC). Another factor has been the ebbing economic strength of the United States relative to that of the EC, Japan, and the countries of the Middle East.

Transacting business on an international level is considerably different from transacting business within the boundaries of a single nation. Buyers and sellers in the international marketplace face laws that are more complex and uncertain. In competing for international trade, countries regulate more closely foreign investment within their borders; they also provide incentives to stimulate exports to (and foreign investment in) other countries and to inhibit imports. For example, a country may limit ownership of real property by foreigners. Similarly, a country may prohibit the importation of goods that contain an ingredient commonly found in certain exports, thereby keeping those foreign goods from entering the country. For example, in 1988 the European Economic Community banned beef imports from the United States because of concerns over the effect of growth hormones (added to beef by U.S. cattle farmers) on consumers. In contrast, a country may provide tax incentives for domestic firms engaged in export activities.

Because the exchange of goods, services, and ideas on a global level is now a more common phenomenon, it is important for the student of business law to be familiar with the laws pertaining to international business transactions. In this chapter we examine the legal context of international business transactions and then look at U.S. and international regulation of specific international business activities. The chapter concludes with a discussion of the application of U.S. antitrust, patent, and discrimination laws in a transnational setting.

The Legal Context of International Business Transactions

National law is law that pertains to a particular nation. Because the legal system of each country reflects its own unique cultural, historical, economic, and political background, the laws of each nation differ. When disputes arise that cannot be settled by national law, *international law* may come into play.

What Is International Law?

International law can be defined as a body of written and unwritten laws observed by otherwise independent nations and governing the acts of individuals as well as states. The key difference between national law and international law is the fact that national law can be enforced by government authorities. But what government can enforce international law? By definition, a *nation* is a sovereign entity—which means that there is no higher authority to which that nation must submit. If a nation violates an international law, the most that other countries or international organizations can do (if persuasive tactics fail) is resort to coercive actions—from severance of diplomatic relations and boycotts to, at the last resort, war—against the violating nation.

In essence, international law is the result of centuries-old attempts to reconcile the traditional need of each nation to be the final authority over its own affairs with the desire of nations to benefit economically from trade and harmonious relations with one another. Ordinarily, no sovereign nation can be compelled to obey a law external to itself, but nations can, and do, voluntarily agree to be governed in certain respects by international law for the purpose of facilitating international trade and commerce, as well as civilized discourse.

Sources of International Law

One important source of international law consists of international customs that have evolved among nations in their relations with one another. Under

Article 38(1) of the Statute of the International Court of Justice, international custom is referred to as "evidence of a general practice accepted as law." Even though customary law serves as an independent form of law, it is subject to challenges on various applications. When, for example, does a particular custom evolve into a general practice constituting a law? Conversely, when does a custom traditionally accepted as law become so outdated or impractical in a modern context that it should no longer be considered law? Just as customs within a nation change, often necessitating changes in that nation's laws, so do customs among nations change, thus affecting international law.

Treaties and other explicit agreements between or among foreign nations provide another important source of international law. A *treaty* is an agreement or contract between two or more nations that must be authorized and ratified by the supreme power of each nation. Under Article II, Section 2, of the U.S. Constitution, the president has the power "by and with the Advice and Consent of the Senate, to make Treaties, provided two-thirds of the Senators present concur." A *bilateral* agreement, as the term implies, occurs when only two nations form an agreement that will govern their commercial exchanges or other relations with one another. *Multilateral* agreements are those formed by several nations. For example, the European Community (EC), or Common Market, which regulates commercial activities among its European member nations, is the result of a multilateral trade agreement. Other multilateral agreements have led to the formation of regional trade associations, such as the Association of Southeast Asian Nations (ASEAN) and the Andean Common Market (ANCOM).

International organizations and conferences further contribute to what is known as international law. In international law, the term **international organization** generally refers to organizations composed mainly of nations and usually established by treaty. The United States is a member of more than one hundred multilateral and bilateral organizations, including at least twenty through the United Nations (see Exhibit 27–1). These organizations adopt resolutions, declarations, and other types of standards that often require a particular behavior of nations. The General Assembly of the United Nations, for example, has adopted numer-

■ **Exhibit 27–1**
Multilateral International Organizations in which the United States Participates

Name	Purpose
Customs Cooperation Council	Established in 1950. Supervises the application and interpretation of an international code classifying goods and customs tariffs.
General Agreement on Tariffs and Trade (GATT)	Created in 1947, this was the first global commercial agreement in history and currently the principal instrument for regulating international trade. Limits tariffs and other barriers to world trade on particular commodities and other items.
International Bank for Reconstruction and Development	Popularly known as the World Bank, a specialized agency of the United Nations since 1947. Promotes growth, trade, and balance of trade by facilitating investment and providing technical assistance, particularly in agriculture, energy, transportation, and telecommunications.
International Center for the Settlement of Investment Disputes	Established in 1966. Conciliates and arbitrates disputes between private investors and governments of other countries.
International Civil Aviation Organization	Established in 1947 and became a specialized agency of the United Nations seven months later. Develops international civil aviation by issuing rules and policies for safe and efficient airports and air navigation.
International Court of Justice (World Court)	Established in 1922 and became one of the principal organs of the United Nations in 1945. Jurisdiction comprises all cases that are referred to it. Decides disputes in accord with the rules of international law.
International Maritime Organization	Established in 1948. Promotes cooperation in the areas of government regulation, practices and technical matters of all kinds affecting shipping in international trade, the adoption of standards of maritime safety and efficiency, and the abolition of discrimination and unnecessary restrictions.
International Monetary Fund (IMF)	Created in 1944 at the United Nations Monetary and Financial Conference. Promotes economic stability by aiding the growth of international trade and the stability of currency exchange rates, as well as by providing for a system of international monetary assistance.
International Telecommunications Satellite Organization	Established in 1964. Operates an international public communications satellite system on a commercial, nondiscriminatory basis.
Permanent Court of Arbitration	Established in 1899 to facilitate the settlement of international disputes. The court has jurisdiction over all cases that it is requested to arbitrate.
United Nations (UN)	Established in 1945 to maintain international peace and security. Promotes international cooperation.
World Intellectual Property Organization	Established in 1967 and became a specialized agency of the United Nations in 1974. Promotes protection of intellectual property throughout the world.

ous nonbinding resolutions and declarations that embody principles of international law. Disputes with respect to these resolutions and declarations may be brought before the International Court of Justice. In general, however, that court has juris-

diction to settle legal disputes only when nations voluntarily submit to its jurisdiction.

In the past decade, the United Nations Commission on International Trade Law (UNCITRAL) has made considerable progress in establishing more uniformity in international law as it relates to trade and commerce. One of its most significant creations to date is the 1980 Convention on Contracts for the International Sale of Goods (CISG). The CISG is similar to Article 2 of the Uniform Commercial Code in that it is designed to settle disputes between parties to sales contracts. It spells out the duties of international buyers and sellers that will apply if the parties have not agreed otherwise in their contract. The CISG only governs sales contracts between trading partners in nations that have ratified the CISG. These nations include the United States.

Legal Principles and Doctrines

Over time a number of legal principles and doctrines have evolved and have been employed—to a greater or lesser extent—by the courts of various nations to resolve or reduce conflicts that involve a foreign element. The three important legal principles discussed below are based primarily on courtesy and respect and are applied in the interests of maintaining harmonious relations among nations.

THE PRINCIPLE OF COMITY Under what is known as the principle of **comity**, one nation will defer and give effect to the laws and judicial decrees of another country, so long as those laws and judicial decrees are consistent with the law and public policy of the accommodating nation. This recognition is based primarily on courtesy and respect. For example, assume that a Swedish seller and an American buyer have formed a contract, which the buyer breaches. The seller sues the buyer in a Swedish court, which awards damages. But the buyer's assets are in the United States and cannot be reached unless the judgment is enforced by a U.S. court of law. In such a case, if it is determined that the procedures and laws applied in the Swedish court were consistent with U.S. national law and policy, a court in the United States would likely defer to, and enforce, the foreign court's judgment.

THE ACT OF STATE DOCTRINE The **act of state doctrine** is a judicially created doctrine that provides that the judicial branch of one country

will not examine the validity of public acts committed by a recognized foreign government within its own territory. This doctrine is premised on the theory that the judicial branch should not "pass upon the validity of foreign acts when to do so would vex the harmony of our international relations with that foreign nation."[1]

The act of state doctrine can have important consequences for individuals and firms doing business with, and investing in, other countries. For example, this doctrine is frequently employed in cases involving **expropriation**, which occurs when a government seizes a privately owned business or privately owned goods for a proper public purpose and awards just compensation. When a government seizes private property for an illegal purpose and without just compensation, the taking is referred to as a **confiscation.** The line between these two forms of taking is sometimes blurred because of differing interpretations of what is illegal and what constitutes just compensation. To illustrate: Tim Flaherty, an American businessperson, owns a mine in Brazil. The government of Brazil seizes the mine for public use and claims that the profits Tim has realized from the mine in preceding years constitute just compensation. Tim disagrees, but the act of state doctrine may prevent Tim's recovery in a U.S. court of law.

When applicable, both the act of state doctrine and the doctrine of *sovereign immunity,* which we discuss in the next section, tend to immunize foreign nations from the jurisdiction of U.S. courts. What this means is that, generally, firms or individuals who own property overseas have little legal protection against government actions in the countries in which they operate.

The applicability of the act of state doctrine is at issue in the following case.

---

1. *Libra Bank Ltd. v. Banco Nacional de Costa Rica, S.A.,* 570 F.Supp. 870 (S.D.N.Y. 1983).

Case 27.1

W. S. KIRKPATRICK & CO. v. ENVIRONMENTAL TECTONICS CORP., INTERNATIONAL

Supreme Court of the United States, 1990.
493 U.S. 400,
110 S.Ct. 701,
107 L.Ed.2d 816.

BACKGROUND AND FACTS *W. S. Kirkpatrick & Company learned that the Republic of Nigeria was interested in contracting for the construction and equipment of an aeromedical center in Nigeria. Kirkpatrick, with the aid of a Nigerian citizen, secured the contract as a result of bribing Nigerian officials. Nigerian law prohibits both the payment and receipt of bribes in connection with the awarding of government contracts, and the U.S. Foreign Corrupt Practices Act (FCPA) of 1977 expressly prohibits U.S. firms and their agents from bribing foreign officials to secure favorable contracts. Environmental Tectonics Corporation, International (ETC), an unsuccessful bidder for the contract, learned of the bribery and sued Kirkpatrick in a U.S. federal district court for damages. The district court granted summary judgment for Kirkpatrick because resolution of the case in favor of ETC would require imputing to foreign officials an unlawful motivation (the obtaining of bribes) and accordingly might embarrass the sovereign or interfere with the conduct of U.S. foreign policy. ETC appealed. The court of appeals reversed the judgment of the district court and remanded the case for trial. Kirkpatrick appealed to the United States Supreme Court.*

Justice *SCALIA* delivered the opinion of the Court.

* * * *

In every case in which we have held the act of state doctrine applicable, the relief sought or the defense interposed would have required a court in the United States to declare invalid the official act of a foreign sovereign performed within its own territory. * * * In the present case, by contrast, neither the claim nor any asserted defense requires a determination that Nigeria's contract with Kirkpatrick International was, or was not, effective.

* * * *

The short of the matter is this: Courts in the United States have the power, and ordinarily the obligation, to decide cases and controversies properly presented to them. The act of state doctrine does not establish an exception for cases and controversies that may embarrass foreign governments, but merely requires that, in the process of deciding, the acts of foreign sovereigns taken within their own jurisdictions shall be deemed valid. That doctrine has no application to the present case because the validity of no foreign sovereign act is at issue.

DECISION AND REMEDY

The Supreme Court affirmed the judgment of the court of appeals. Because the validity of no foreign sovereign act was at issue, the act of state doctrine did not apply in this case.

THE DOCTRINE OF SOVEREIGN IMMUNITY

When certain conditions are satisfied, the doctrine of **sovereign immunity** immunizes foreign nations from the jurisdiction of the U.S. courts. In 1976, Congress codified this rule in the Foreign Sovereign Immunities Act (FSIA). The FSIA also modified previous applications of the doctrine in certain respects by expanding the rights that plaintiff creditors have against foreign nations.

The FSIA exclusively governs the circumstances in which an action may be brought in the United States against a foreign nation, including attempts to attach a foreign nation's property. One of the primary purposes of the FSIA was to have federal courts, rather than the Department of State, determine claims of foreign sovereign immunity. It was thought that a determination of such an immunity by the courts would increase the degree of certainty in the law of sovereign immunity.

Section 1605 of the FSIA sets forth the major exceptions to the jurisdictional immunity of a foreign state. A foreign state is not immune from the jurisdiction of the courts of the United States when the state has ''waived its immunity either explicitly or by implication'' or when the action is ''based upon a commercial activity carried on in the United States by the foreign state.'' [2]

Issues frequently arise as to what entities fall within the category of *foreign state*. The question of what is a *commercial activity* has also been the subject of dispute. Under Section 1603 of the FSIA, a *foreign state* is defined to include both a political subdivision of a foreign state and an instrumentality of a foreign state. A *commercial activity* is broadly defined under Section 1603 to mean a commercial activity that is carried on by the foreign state having substantial contact with the United States. But the particulars of what constitutes a commercial activity are not defined in the act. Rather, it is left up to the courts to decide whether a particular activity is governmental or commercial in nature.

In the following case, the court had to determine whether the defense of sovereign immunity was available under the FSIA.

---

2.   28 U.S.C. Section 1605(a)(1), (2).

BACKGROUND AND FACTS   *The Bank of Jamaica, which is wholly owned by the government of Jamaica, contracted with Chisholm & Company in January 1981 for Chisholm to arrange for lines of credit from various U.S. banks and to obtain $50 million in credit insurance from the Export-Import Bank of the United States. This Chisholm successfully did, but subsequently the deals arranged for by Chisholm were refused by the Bank of Jamaica. The bank had decided to do its own negotiating while still having Chisholm work as well. When the bank refused to pay Chisholm for its services, Chisholm brought this action to obtain relief for the bank's breach of the implied contract. The Bank of Jamaica filed a motion to dismiss, asserting, among other things, that it was immune from the jurisdiction of the U.S. courts under the doctrine of sovereign immunity.*

Case 27.2

CHISHOLM & CO. v. BANK OF JAMAICA
United States District Court, Southern District of Florida, 1986.
643 F.Supp. 1393.

EDWARD B. DAVIS, District Judge.
    *   *   *   *

    *   *   * [T]he Foreign Sovereign Immunities Act (''FSIA'') *   *   * grants foreign states immunity from suit in federal and state court, subject to certain exceptions. *   *   *
    *   *   *   *

Plaintiffs contend *   *   * that Defendants' activity falls within the exception to sovereign immunity outlined in [FSIA] Section 1605, the ''commercial activity'' exception. Section 1605(a)(2) strips foreign countries of their sovereign immunity in any case—

    in which the action is based upon *   *   * an act outside the territory of the United States in connection with the commercial activity of the foreign state elsewhere and that act causes a direct effect in the United States.
        *   *   *   *

Section 1603(d) *   *   * defines commercial activity as:
    either a regular course of commercial conduct or a particular commercial transaction or act. *   *   *

The legislative history of the FSIA suggests that the drafters intended to cover contracts for lines of credit. *   *   * [I]t is apparent that Congress intended to include all contracts involved in importing and exporting goods to and from the United States. *   *   *

The legislative history also suggests that courts should "inquire whether the activity in question is one which private persons ordinarily perform or whether it is peculiarly within the realm of governments." *   *   * In this case, the general activity, engaging in contracts in order to obtain lines of credit, is one in which private entities generally engage. *   *   *

Defendants argue that, because the bank was acting in furtherance of the Jamaican Economic Recovery Program in seeking foreign credit for importers, its actions were governmental. It is the nature of Defendants' actions, however, which must be scrutinized in determining their character; not their purpose. A contract, implied or otherwise, is inherently commercial, even when the ultimate purpose behind it is government regulation.

*   *   * Once the bank decides to contract with someone to obtain financing, it must follow the rules of the marketplace, and one of those rules is that contracts cannot be breached. Therefore, the Court holds that the bank's implied contract with Chisholm & Co. and its alleged misrepresentations constitute commercial activity.

*   *   * The Court *   *   * [also] finds that the Defendants' acts had a direct effect in the United States *   *   *.

Unlike persons, a corporation can only suffer financial loss. Therefore, *   *   * the relevant inquiry is whether Chisholm & Co. has suffered a direct financial loss in the United States. Such an effect can arise from the cancellation of a contract. Here, the beneficiary of the contract that was breached was an American corporation. Chisholm & Co. had its place of business in the United States and was to be paid in the United States. The failure to pay an American corporation in the United States creates a direct effect "in" the United States.

DECISION AND REMEDY   *The court denied the bank's motion to dismiss as it concerned Chisholm's claim for payment for its services under its contract with the bank.*

■ Doing Business Internationally

There are a number of ways in which a U.S. domestic firm can engage in international business transactions. The simplest way is to seek out foreign markets for domestically produced products (or services). In other words, U.S. firms can look abroad for **export** markets for their goods and services. Alternatively, a U.S. firm can establish foreign production facilities so as to be closer to the foreign market or markets in which its products are sold. The advantages may include lower labor costs, fewer government regulations, and lower taxes and trade barriers. It is also possible to obtain business from abroad by licensing technology developed and owned by the domestic firm to an existing foreign company. Finally, it is possible to expand abroad by selling franchises to overseas entities. The presence of McDonald's, Burger King, and KFC franchises throughout the world attests to the popularity of franchising.

Exporting

The initial foray into international business by most U.S. companies is through exporting—that is, selling their products to buyers located in other countries. Exporting can take two forms: direct exporting or indirect exporting. In *direct exporting,* a U.S. company signs a sales contract with a foreign purchaser that provides for the conditions of shipment and payment for the goods. (How payments are made in international transactions is discussed later in this chapter.) If business develops sufficiently in foreign countries, a U.S. corporation may develop a specialized marketing organization in the foreign market itself. Such *indirect exporting* can be undertaken by the appointment of a foreign agent or a foreign distributor.

FOREIGN AGENT   When a U.S. firm desires a limited involvement in an international market, it will typically establish an *agency relationship* with a foreign firm. In an agency relationship, one person (the agent) agrees to act on behalf of, or instead of, another (the principal)—see Chapter 15. The foreign agent is thereby empowered to enter into contracts in the agent's country on behalf of the U.S. principal.

FOREIGN DISTRIBUTOR   When a substantial market exists in a foreign country, a U.S. firm may wish to appoint a distributor located in that country. The U.S. firm and the distributor enter into a **distribution agreement**, which is a contract between the seller and the distributor setting out the terms and conditions of the distributorship—for example, price, currency of payment, guarantee of supply availability, and method of payment. The terms and conditions primarily involve contract law. Disputes concerning distribution agreements may involve jurisdictional or other issues that are treated in detail later in this chapter. In addition, some **exclusive distributorships** have raised antitrust problems.

A distributor is not normally the same as a foreign agent because the distributor takes title to the merchandise when it is received. Thus the distributor bears the risk connected with commercial sales.

Manufacturing Abroad

An alternative to direct or indirect exporting is the establishment of foreign manufacturing facilities. Typically, U.S. firms desire to establish manufacturing plants abroad if they believe that by doing so they will reduce costs—particularly for labor, shipping, and raw materials—and thereby be able to compete more effectively in foreign markets. As pointed out above, foreign manufacturing facilities may lead to fewer trade restrictions and a lowering of taxes, particularly import taxes, in the country involved. Apple Computer, IBM, General Motors, and Ford are some of the many U.S. companies that have established manufacturing facilities abroad. Foreign firms have done the same in the

United States. Sony, Nissan, and other Japanese manufacturers have established U.S. plants to avoid possible import duties that the U.S. Congress may impose on Japanese products entering this country.

There are several ways in which an American firm can manufacture in other countries. They include licensing and franchising, as well as investing in a wholly owned subsidiary or a joint venture.

LICENSING   It is possible for U.S. firms to license their technologies to foreign manufacturers. **Technology licensing** may involve a process innovation that lowers the cost of production, or it may involve a product innovation that generates a superior product. Technology licensing may be an attractive alternative to establishing foreign production facilities, particularly if the process or product innovation has been patented, because the patent protects—at least to some extent—against the possibility that the innovation might be pirated. Firms may be able to acquire parallel patents in a foreign country, depending on the patent laws of that country, and international agreements protecting intellectual property rights may allow for patent or copyright protection in the countries abiding by such agreements. (International protection for intellectual property rights was discussed in Chapter 26.) As with any licensing agreement, a licensing agreement with a foreign-based firm calls for a payment of royalties on some basis—such as so many cents per unit produced or a certain percentage of profits from units sold in a particular geographical territory.

In certain circumstances, even in the absence of a patent, a firm may be able to license the "know-how" associated with a particular manufacturing process—for example, a plant design or a secret formula. The foreign firm that agrees to sign the licensing agreement further agrees to keep the know-how confidential and to pay royalties. For example, the Coca-Cola Bottling Company licenses firms worldwide to use (and keep confidential) its secret formula for the syrup used in that soft drink, in return for a percentage of the income gained from the sale of Coca-Cola by those firms.

The licensing of technology benefits all parties to the transaction, in that those who receive the license can take advantage of an established reputation for quality, and firms that grant the license receive income from the foreign sales of the firm's products, as well as the establishment of a worldwide reputation. Also, once a firm's trademark is known worldwide, the demand for other products manufactured or sold by that firm may increase—an obviously important consideration.

FRANCHISING   Franchising is a well-known form of licensing. A **franchise** can be defined as an arrangement in which the owner of a trademark, a trade name, or a copyright (the **franchisor**) licenses another (the **franchisee**) to use the trademark, trade name, or copyright under certain conditions or limitations in the selling of goods or services in exchange for a fee, usually based on a percentage of gross or net sales. Examples of international franchises include McDonald's, the Coca-Cola Bottling Company, Holiday Inn, Avis, and Hertz. Because of their franchising arrangements, these firms are known throughout the world.

INVESTING IN A WHOLLY OWNED SUBSIDIARY OR A JOINT VENTURE   One way to expand into a foreign market is to establish a wholly owned subsidiary firm in a foreign country. The European subsidiary would likely take the form of the *société anonyme* (S.A.), which is similar to a U.S. corporation. In German-speaking nations, it would be called an *Aktiengesellschaft* (A.G.). When a wholly owned subsidiary is established, the parent company, which remains in the United States, retains complete ownership of all of the facilities in the foreign country, as well as complete authority and control over all phases of the operation.

The expansion of a U.S. firm into international markets can also take the form of a joint venture. In a **joint venture,** the U.S. company owns only a part of the operation—the rest is owned either by local owners in the foreign country or by another foreign entity. In a joint venture, responsibilities, as well as profits and liabilities, are shared by all of the firms involved in the venture. A joint venture is the only way in which U.S. companies are allowed to have manufacturing facilities in many developing countries. Often, U.S. ownership of joint ventures in these countries cannot exceed 49 percent. Additionally, some less-developed countries require that Americans constitute a minority of the management of the joint venture.

Commercial Contracts in an International Setting

Language and legal differences among nations can create special problems for parties to international contracts when disputes arise. It is possible to avoid these problems by including in a contract special provisions designating the official language of the contract, the legal forum in which disputes under the contract will be settled, and the substantive law that will be applied in settling any disputes. These contractual provisions will be examined in the following sections. It is also important to indicate in the contract whether disputes under the contract will be arbitrated or litigated, and what acts or events will excuse the parties from performance under the contract. In provisions for arbitration, it is important that the forum, choice of law, and expertise of the arbitrator be specified in the contract.

CHOICE OF LANGUAGE   A deal struck between a U.S. company and a company in another country normally involves two languages. The complex contractual terms involved may not be understood by one party in the other party's language. Typically, many phrases in one language are not readily translatable into another. To make sure that no disputes arise out of this language problem, an international sales contract should have a **choice-of-language clause** designating the official language by which the contract will be interpreted in the event of disagreement. Such a clause might state that the agreement is being written in English, which is to be regarded as the authoritative and official language of the contract's text. The clause may further allow that the agreement is to be translated into, say, Spanish; that the translation is to be ratified by both parties; and that the foreign company can rely on the translation. If arbitration is anticipated, an additional clause must be added to indicate that the arbitration will be in, say, English, Spanish, or French—or whatever the case may be.

CHOICE OF FORUM   In international contracts, it is especially important to include a **forum-selection clause**. When several countries are involved, litigation may be sought in courts in different nations. There are no universally accepted rules regarding the jurisdiction of a particular court over subject matter or parties to a dispute. Consequently, parties to an international transaction should always include in the contract a forum-selection clause designating the forum in which a dispute will be litigated. A forum-selection clause should specifically indicate the court that will have jurisdiction. The forum does not necessarily have to be within the geographical boundaries of either of the parties' nations.

Under certain circumstances, a forum-selection clause will not be valid. Specifically, if the clause denies one party an effective remedy, is the product of fraud or unconscionable conduct, causes substantial inconvenience to one of the parties to the contract, or violates public policy, the clause will not be enforced.

In the following case, the United States Supreme Court made it clear that wide latitude should be granted the parties in selecting the forum in which a contractual dispute would be settled.

BACKGROUND AND FACTS *In November 1967, Zapata Off-Shore Company, a Houston-based American corporation, contracted with Unterweser, a German corporation, to tow Zapata's drilling rig from Louisiana to Italy. A clause in the contract contained the following forum-selection clause: "Any dispute arising must be treated before the London Court of Justice." Unterweser's ship, the M/S Bremen, began the towing operation, but on January 9, 1968, a severe storm arose in the Gulf of Mexico. During this storm, the drilling rig was severely damaged, and the rig was towed to the nearest port, which was Tampa, Florida. On January 12, Zapata, ignoring the contract provision, sued in federal district court in Tampa, seeking damages for allegedly negligent towage. Unterweser argued that the U.S. courts lacked jurisdiction because of the contract provision. The district court rejected Unterweser's motion to dismiss the case, and Unterweser appealed. On appeal, a sharply divided Fifth Circuit Court of Appeals affirmed the district court by an eight-to-six vote. Unterweser then appealed to the United States Supreme Court.*

Case 27.3

M/S BREMEN v. ZAPATA OFF-SHORE CO.

Supreme Court of the United States, 1972.
407 U.S. 1,
92 S.Ct. 1907,
32 L.Ed.2d 513.

BURGER, Justice.
 * * * *

 * * * For at least two decades we have witnessed an expansion of overseas commercial activities by business enterprises based in the United States. The barrier of distance that once tended to confine a business concern to a modest territory no longer does so. Here we see an American company with special expertise contracting with a foreign company to tow a complex machine thousands of miles across seas and oceans. The expansion of American business and industry will hardly be encouraged if, notwithstanding solemn contracts, we insist on a parochial concept that all disputes must be resolved under our laws and in our courts. * * *

Forum-selection clauses have historically not been favored by American courts. Many courts, federal and state, have declined to enforce such clauses on the ground that they were "contrary to public policy," or that their effect was to "oust the jurisdiction" of the court. Although this view apparently still has considerable acceptance, other courts are tending to adopt a more hospitable attitude toward forum-selection clauses. This view, advanced in the well-reasoned dissenting opinion in the instant case, is that such clauses are *prima facie* valid and should be enforced unless enforcement is shown by the resisting party to be "unreasonable" under the circumstances. * * *
 * * * *

This approach is substantially that followed in other common-law countries including England. It is the view advanced by noted scholars and that adopted by the Restatement of the Conflict of Laws. It accords with ancient concepts of freedom of contract and reflects an appreciation of the expanding horizons of American contractors who seek business in all parts of the world. Not surprisingly, foreign businessmen prefer, as do we, to have disputes resolved in their own courts, but if that choice is not available, then in a neutral forum with expertise in the subject matter. Plainly, the courts of England meet the standards of neutrality and long experience in admiralty litigation. The choice of that forum was made in an arm's-length negotiation by experienced and sophisticated businessmen, and absent some compelling and countervailing reason it should be honored by the parties and enforced by the courts.

DECISION AND REMEDY   *The Supreme Court held that the contract provision was controlling and that U.S. courts lacked jurisdiction. Consequently, the Court vacated the appellate court's decision and remanded the case for further proceedings consistent with its opinion.*

CHOICE OF LAW   A contractual provision designating the applicable law, called a **choice-of-law clause,** is typically included in every international contract. At common law (and in European civil law systems), parties are allowed to choose the law that will govern their contractual relationship provided that the law chosen is the law of a jurisdiction that has a substantial relationship to the parties and to the international business transaction. Under Section 1-105 of the UCC, parties may choose the law that will govern the contract as long as the choice is "reasonable." Article 6 of the CISG, however, imposes no limitation on the parties in their choice of what law will govern the contract, and the 1986 Hague Convention on the Law Applicable to Contracts for the International Sale of Goods—often referred to as the "Choice-of-Law Convention"—allows unlimited autonomy in the choice of law. Whenever a choice of law is not specified in a contract, the Hague Convention indicates that the governing law is that of the country in which the *seller's* place of business is located.

FORCE MAJEURE   Every contract, particularly those involving international transactions, should have a *force majeure* **clause.** The definition of the French term *force majeure* is "impossible or irresistible force"—which sometimes is loosely identified as "an act of God." In international business contracts, *force majeure* clauses commonly stipulate that a number of other eventualities, in addition to acts of God, may excuse a party from liability for nonperformance. Consider, for example, the following typical *force majeure* clause:

> The parties hereto shall not be liable for failure of performance hereunder if occasioned by undeclared or declared war, flood, fire, embargo, governmental orders, regulations, restrictions, governmental expropriation, fire, flood, accident, interruptions of transportation facilities, labor strikes and disputes, shortages of materials, or production facilities, or any other causes beyond the control of the parties.

■ Making Payment on International Transactions

Currency differences between nations and the geographic distance between parties to international sales contracts add a degree of complexity to international sales that does not exist within the domestic market. Because international contracts involve greater financial risks, special care should be taken when drafting the contract to specify both the currency in which payment is to be made and the method of payment. Additionally, there may be difficulties in repatriating profits made in businesses in wholly owned subsidiaries or joint ventures abroad.

Monetary Systems

While it is true that our national currency, the U.S. dollar, is one of the primary forms of international money, any U.S. firm undertaking business transactions abroad must be prepared to deal with one or more other currencies. After all, just as a U.S. firm wants to be paid in U.S. dollars for goods and services sold abroad, so too does, say, a Japanese firm want to be paid in Japanese yen for goods and services sold outside of Japan. Both firms therefore must rely on the convertibility of currencies.

FOREIGN EXCHANGE MARKETS   Currencies are convertible when they can be freely exchanged one for the other at some specified market rate in a **foreign exchange market**. The foreign exchange market is a worldwide system for the buying and selling of foreign currencies. At any particular point in time, the foreign exchange rate is set by the forces of supply and demand in unrestricted foreign exchange markets. The foreign exchange rate is simply the price of a unit of one country's currency in terms of another country's currency. For example, if today's exchange rate is 100 yen for $1, that means that anybody with 100 yen can obtain $1, and vice versa.

CORRESPONDENT BANKING   Many times, a U.S. company can deal directly with its domestic bank, which will take care of the international money flow problem. Commercial banks sometimes have correspondent branches or banks in other countries, which are called **correspondent banks**. For example, Citicorp might open an account in French francs in *Credit Lyonnais* in Paris. At the same time, *Credit Lyonnais* will open an account in Citibank by depositing U.S. dollars with Citibank. Citibank and *Credit Lyonnais* are correspondent banks.

Correspondent banking is a major means of transferring funds internationally. Suppose, for example, that a customer of Citibank wishes to pay a bill in French francs to a company in Paris. Citibank can draw a bank check payable in francs on its account in *Credit Lyonnais* and then send it to the French company to whom its customer owes the money. Alternatively, Citibank's customer can request a **wire transfer** of the funds to the French company. Citibank instructs *Credit Lyonnais* by wire to pay the necessary amount in French francs. Wire transfers are a major part of electronic fund transfer systems (discussed in Chapter 24). Fedwire, which is operated by the U.S. Federal Reserve

System, is available for wire transfers between banks within the United States. The Clearinghouse Interbank Payment Systems (CHIPS) handles about 90 percent of both national and international interbank transfers of U.S. funds. Finally, the Society for Worldwide International Financial Telecommunications (SWIFT) is a communication system that provides banks with messages concerning transactions. The funds do not, however, accompany the message and therefore must be transferred by some other means.

Letters of Credit

Because buyers and sellers engaged in international business transactions are often separated by thousands of miles, special precautions are often taken to ensure performance under the contract. Sellers want to avoid delivering goods for which they might not be paid. Buyers desire the assurance that sellers will not be paid until there is evidence that the goods have been shipped. Thus, **letters of credit** are frequently used to facilitate international business transactions. In a simple letter-of-credit transaction, the *issuer* (a bank) agrees to issue a letter of credit and to ascertain the occurrence of certain acts by the *beneficiary* (seller). In return, the *account party* (buyer) promises to reimburse the issuer for the amount paid to the beneficiary. There may also be an *advising bank* that transmits information, and a *paying bank* may be involved to expedite payment under the letter of credit. See Exhibit 27-2 for the "life cycle" of a letter of credit.

Under a letter of credit, the issuer is bound to pay the beneficiary (seller) when the beneficiary has complied with the terms and conditions of the letter of credit. The beneficiary looks to the issuer, not to the account party (buyer), when it presents the documents required by the letter of credit. Typically, the letter of credit will require that the beneficiary deliver a *bill of lading* (a document that evidences the transportation of goods) to prove that shipment has been made. Letters of credit assure beneficiaries (sellers) of payment while at the same time assuring account parties (buyers) that payment will not be made until the beneficiaries have complied with the terms and conditions of the credit.

THE VALUE OF A LETTER OF CREDIT   The basic principle behind letters of credit is that pay-

■ Exhibit 27–2 The "Life Cycle" of a Letter of Credit

Although the letter of credit appears quite complex at first, it is not difficult to understand. This exhibit depicts the steps involved in a letter-of-credit procurement cycle. This cycle merely involves the exchange of documents (and money) through intermediaries.

Step 1: The buyer and seller agree on the terms of sale. The sales contract dictates that a letter of credit is to be used to finance the transaction.

Step 2: The buyer completes an application for a letter of credit and forwards it to the buyer's bank, which will issue the letter of credit.

Step 3: The issuing (buyer's) bank then forwards the letter of credit to a correspondent bank in the seller's country.

Step 4: The correspondent bank relays the letter of credit to the seller.

Step 5: Having received assurance of payment, the seller makes the necessary shipping arrangements.

Step 6: The seller prepares the documents required under the letter of credit and delivers them to the correspondent bank.

Step 7: The correspondent bank examines the documents. If it finds them in order, it sends them to the issuing bank and pays the seller in accordance with the terms of the letter of credit.

Step 8: The issuing bank, having received the documents, examines them. If they are in order, the issuing bank will charge the buyer's account and send the documents on to the buyer or the buyer's customs broker. The issuing bank also will reimburse the correspondent bank.

Step 9: The buyer or broker receives the documents and picks up the merchandise from the shipper (carrier).

ment is made against the documents presented by the beneficiary and not against the facts that the documents purport to reflect. Thus, in a letter-of-credit transaction, the issuer does not police the underlying contract: *a letter of credit is independent of the underlying contract between the buyer and the seller.* Eliminating the need for banks (issuers) to inquire into whether actual conditions have been satisfied greatly reduces the cost of letters of credit and encourages the free flow of commerce. Moreover, as mentioned above, the use of a letter of credit protects both buyers and sellers.

COMPLIANCE WITH A LETTER OF CREDIT
In a letter-of-credit transaction, generally at least three separate and distinct contracts are involved: the underlying contract between the account party (buyer) and the beneficiary (seller), the contract between the issuer (bank) and the account party (buyer), and finally the letter of credit itself, which involves the issuer and the beneficiary. Given the fact that these contracts are separate and distinct, the issuer's obligations under the letter of credit do not concern the underlying contract between the buyer and the seller. Rather, it is the issuer's duty to ascertain whether the documents presented by the beneficiary (seller) comply with the terms of the letter of credit.

If the documents presented by the beneficiary comply with the terms of the letter of credit, the issuing bank must honor the letter of credit. Sometimes, however, it is difficult to determine exactly what a letter of credit requires. Moreover, the courts are divided as to whether *strict* or *substantial* compliance with the terms of the letter of credit is required. Traditionally, courts required strict compliance with the terms of a letter of credit, but in recent years some courts have moved to a standard of *reasonable* compliance.

If the issuing bank refuses to pay the seller (beneficiary) even though the seller has complied with all the requirements of the letter, the seller can bring an action to enforce payment. In the international context, the fact that the issuing bank may be thousands of miles distant from the seller's business location can pose difficulties for the seller—as the following case illustrates.

BACKGROUND AND FACTS *Pacific Reliant Industries, Inc., an Oregon company, sold building materials to Paradise Development Company, a company located in American Samoa. Pacific was reluctant to make several large deliveries, totaling more than $1 million in value, without some protection against nonpayment. Accordingly, representatives from Pacific, Paradise, and Amerika Samoa Bank (ASB) met in American Samoa on two occasions to discuss the supply contract and the letter of credit. Following these negotiations, ASB issued a letter of credit in favor of Pacific on Paradise's account. Later, alleging that ASB had wrongfully dishonored the letter of credit, Pacific brought suit against ASB to recover payment. The United States District Court for the District of Oregon dismissed the suit for lack of personal jurisdiction, holding that ASB lacked sufficient "minimum contacts" with the state of Oregon to subject it to a lawsuit in that state. Pacific appealed, contending that this case was not typical of other letter-of-credit cases because ASB had participated in forming the underlying contract, had had personal contact with the beneficiary (Pacific), and had known that Pacific would not extend credit or ship goods from Oregon without the letter of credit.*

Case 27.4

PACIFIC RELIANT INDUSTRIES, INC. v. AMERIKA SAMOA BANK

United States Court of Appeals, Ninth Circuit, 1990.
901 F.2d 735.

CANBY, Circuit Judge:

*   *   *   *

ASB issued its letter of credit on the account of a customer, Paradise. Unlike a guarantor's obligation, ASB's "obligation under the letter of credit is independent of the underlying sales contract" between Paradise and Pacific. In [a previous case], we held that California could not exercise personal jurisdiction over a Philippine bank that had issued a letter of credit to California businesses. Negotiations for the underlying sales contract occurred in California, but negotiations for the letter of credit occurred in the Philippines. The letter of credit specified that a New York bank would be the paying bank. We found that the Philippine bank could not "reasonably have expected the issuance or negotiation of this letter to have effects in California that would make it fair to require it to defend this suit there."

Here, both the negotiations for the underlying contract and the letter of credit occurred in American Samoa. Pacific sent a representative to American Samoa to sell building materials. That representative prompted the buyer to obtain a letter of credit from its local bank, ASB. Although Pacific's representative participated in the negotiations to obtain that letter of credit, the letter of credit is independent of the underlying sales contract. ASB did not initiate the transactions between itself, Paradise, or Pacific. Nor did ASB take any significant actions in Oregon. ASB did not invoke the benefits and protections of Oregon law and could not reasonably have expected to be haled into court there. We conclude that ASB's conduct as an issuing bank of a letter of credit does not subject it to suit in Oregon, the residence of the beneficiary and the shipping point for the ordered goods.

The appellate court affirmed the lower court's ruling. Pacific could not bring suit against ASB in Oregon because ASB lacked sufficient minimum contacts with the state of Oregon to satisfy jurisdictional requirements.

DECISION AND REMEDY

■ Resolving International Contract Disputes

It goes without saying that disputes will arise with international contracts just as they do with domestic ones. Indeed, it might be argued that more disputes will arise internationally, because of cultural differences among nations. Differences in language and custom certainly contribute. Countries may differ distinctly in their attitudes toward contracts. In Japan, for example, it is customarily assumed that the relationship between contracting parties will be long term in nature. This leads to lengthy negotiations and short contracts. The opposite expectation characterizes businesspersons in the United States, and this leads to short negotiation periods and lengthy contracts. In any event, when contract disputes do arise, contractual parties need to decide whether to undertake litigation or arbitration as a method of dispute settlement.

Litigation

If no arbitration clause is contained in the sales contract, litigation may be the method by which a dispute is settled. If forum-selection and choice-of-law clauses were included in the contract, the lawsuit will be heard by a court in the specified forum country, and the specified substantive law will be applied. If no forum and choice of law were specified in the contract, however, legal proceedings will be more complex and attended by much more uncertainty. For example, litigation may take place in two or more countries, with each country applying its own choice-of-law rules to determine which substantive law will be applied to the particular transactions. Furthermore, even if a plaintiff wins a judgment in a lawsuit litigated in the plaintiff's country, there is no guarantee that the court's judgment will be enforced by judicial bodies in the defendant's country. Under the *principle of comity*, an international principle of law founded in the need for courteous interaction among nations, the judgment may be enforced in the defendant's country. This is particularly true if the defendant's country is the United States and the foreign court's decision is consistent with U.S. national law and policy. Other nations, however, may not be as accommodating as the United States, and the plaintiff may be left empty-handed.

Arbitration

As discussed in Chapter 3, the arbitration of civil disputes is becoming an increasingly attractive alternative to costly litigation through the court system. This is true on the international level as well. Arbitration clauses are frequently found in contracts governing the international sale of goods. By means of such clauses, the parties agree in advance to be bound by the decision of a specified third party in the event a dispute should arise. The third party may be a neutral entity such as the International Chamber of Commerce, a panel of individuals representing both parties' interests, or some other group or organization. The 1958 United Nations Convention on the Recognition and Enforcement of Foreign Arbitral Awards—which has been implemented in more than fifty countries, including the United States—assists in the enforcement of arbitration clauses, as do provisions in specific treaties between nations.

In the following case, the plaintiff alleged that the defendant had violated U.S. securities laws and that therefore, in accordance with a ruling case precedent on a similar issue, the arbitration clause should not be enforced. The United States Supreme Court had to decide whether the precedent should apply to an international contractual dispute.

Case 27.5

SCHERK v. ALBERTO-CULVER CO.

Supreme Court of the United States, 1974.
417 U.S. 506,
94 S.Ct. 2449,
41 L.Ed.2d 270.

BACKGROUND AND FACTS *Alberto-Culver Company, an American corporation with its principal office in Illinois, manufactured and sold toiletries and hair products in the United States and abroad. In 1969, to expand its overseas operations, Alberto-Culver purchased from Fritz Scherk three interrelated business entities, organized under the laws of Germany and Liechtenstein, that were engaged in the manufacture of toiletries and the licensing of trademarks for such toiletries. Included in the sale were all the rights held by these enterprises to trademarks in cosmetic*

goods. In the contract, Scherk guaranteed the sole and unencumbered own-
ership of these trademarks. The contract also contained an arbitration
clause, which provided that any controversy or claim arising out of the
agreement would be referred to arbitration before the International Cham-
ber of Commerce in Paris. The clause also stipulated that the laws of the
state of Illinois would "apply to and govern this agreement, its interpre-
tation and performance." When Alberto-Culver later learned that the
trademark rights were subject to substantial encumbrances, it brought an
action for damages and other relief in a federal district court in Illinois,
contending that Scherk's fraudulent representations concerning the status
of the trademark rights violated the Securities Exchange Act of 1934.
Scherk moved to dismiss the action, contending, among other things, that
the dispute should be arbitrated in accordance with the contract. The dis-
trict court denied Scherk's motion and granted a preliminary order en-
joining Scherk from proceeding with arbitration. The district court held
that it was bound by the United States Supreme Court's decision in Wilko
v. Swan, *which held that an agreement to arbitrate could not preclude a*
buyer of a security from seeking a judicial remedy under U.S. securities
laws.[a] *Scherk appealed.*

Mr. Justice *STEWART* delivered the opinion of the Court.

     *   *   *   *

     *   *   * [T]he respondent's [Alberto-Culver's] reliance on *Wilko* in this case
ignores the significant and, we find, crucial differences between the agreement involved in *Wilko* and the one signed by the parties here. Alberto-Culver's contract to
purchase the business entities belonging to Scherk was a truly international
agreement. *   *   *

     Such a contract involves considerations and policies significantly different from
those found controlling in *Wilko*. In *Wilko*, quite apart from the arbitration provision,
there was no question but that the laws of the United States generally, and the federal
securities laws in particular, would govern disputes arising out of the stock-purchase
agreement. The parties, the negotiations, and the subject matter of the contract were
all situated in this country, and no credible claim could have been entertained that
any international conflict-of-laws problems would arise. In this case, by contrast, in
the absence of the arbitration provision considerable uncertainty existed at the time
of the agreement, and still exists, concerning the law applicable to the resolution of
disputes arising out of the contract.

     Such uncertainty will almost inevitably exist with respect to any contract touching
two or more countries, each with its own substantive laws and conflict-of-laws rules.
A contractual provision specifying in advance the forum in which disputes will be
litigated and the law to be applied is, therefore, an almost indispensable precondition
to achievement of the orderliness and predictability essential to any international
business transaction. Furthermore, such a provision obviates the danger that a dispute
under the agreement might be submitted to a forum hostile to the interests of one of
the parties or unfamiliar with the problem area involved.

     A parochial refusal by the courts of one country to enforce an international
arbitration agreement would not only frustrate these purposes, but would invite

---

a. 346 U.S. 427, 74 S.Ct. 182, 98 L.Ed. 168 (1953). The United States Supreme Court has since ruled
that claims alleging violations of securities laws can be arbitrated pursuant to a contractual arbitration
clause. See, for example, *Shearson/American Express, Inc. v. McMahon*, 482 U.S. 220, 107 S.Ct. 2332,
96 L.Ed.2d 185 (1987).

unseemly and mutually destructive jockeying by the parties to secure tactical litigation advantages. * * * [T]he dicey atmosphere of such a legal no-man's-land would surely damage the fabric of international commerce and trade, and imperil the willingness and ability of businessmen to enter into international commercial agreements.

DECISION AND REMEDY   *The United States Supreme Court reversed the judgment of the district court, holding that the arbitration clause was enforceable. The case was remanded for further proceedings consistent with this opinion.*

■ Regulation of Specific Business Activities

Doing business abroad can affect the economies, foreign policy, domestic politics, and other national interests of the countries involved. For this reason, nations impose laws to restrict or facilitate international business. Controls may also be imposed by international agreement.

Exporting

The U.S. Constitution provides in Article I, Section 9, that "No Tax or Duty shall be laid on Articles exported from any State." Thus Congress cannot impose any export taxes. Congress can, however, use a variety of other devices to control exports. Congress may set export quotas on, for example, grain being sold abroad. Under the Export Administration Act of 1979, restrictions can be imposed on the flow of technologically advanced products and technical data. Other export control provisions to inhibit development of the military potential of other countries are found in the Atomic Energy Act of 1954 and the Nuclear Non-proliferation Act of 1978.

Devices to stimulate exports and thereby aid domestic businesses include export incentives and subsidies. The Revenue Act of 1971, for example, gave tax benefits to firms marketing their products overseas through certain foreign sales corporations, exempting income produced by the exports. Under the Export Trading Company Act of 1982, U.S. banks are encouraged to invest in export trading companies. An export trading company consists of exporting firms joined to export a line of goods. The export trading company concept is modeled after a Japanese practice. The Export-Import Bank provides financial assistance, consisting primarily of credit guarantees given to commercial banks. Based on those guarantees, the banks loan funds to U.S. exporting companies.

Importing

All nations have restrictions on imports, and the United States is no exception. Restrictions include strict prohibitions, quotas, and tariffs. Under the Trading with the Enemy Act of 1917, for example, no goods may be imported from nations that have been designated enemies of the United States. Other laws prohibit the importation of illegal drugs, books that urge insurrection against the United States, and agricultural products that pose dangers to domestic crops or animals. Quotas are limits on the amounts of goods that can be imported. For example, at one time, the United States had quotas on the numbers of automobiles that could be imported from Japan. Currently, Japan voluntarily restricts the numbers of automobiles exported to the United States. Tariffs are taxes on imports. Generally, a tariff is a percentage of the value of the imports or is a flat-rate per unit (such as a barrel of oil). Tariffs raise the prices of goods, causing some consumers to purchase less expensive, domestically manufactured goods.

These restrictions are also known as trade barriers. The elimination of trade barriers is sometimes seen as essential to the world's economic well-being. To minimize trade barriers among nations, most of the world's leading trade nations abide by the General Agreement on Tariffs and Trade (GATT). The GATT has become the principal instrument for regulating international trade. Originally negotiated in 1947, the GATT has gone through seven major tariff and trade renegotiations. Between 1964 and 1967, for example, forty-eight countries negotiated tariff reductions of 50 percent on a broad range of products. Between 1973 and 1979, one hundred countries negotiated nearly a dozen agreements relating to other trade barriers. An eighth round of negotiations began in 1986 to consider intellectual property rights, investment policies, dispute resolution, and other topics.

Under Article I of the GATT, each member country agrees to grant most-favored-nation treatment to other member countries. This obligates each GATT member to treat other GATT members at least as well as it treats that country that receives its most favorable treatment with regard to imports or exports.

The United States has specific laws directed at what it sees as unfair international trade practices. **Dumping**, for example, is the sale of imported goods at "less than fair value" (LTFV). "Fair value" is usually determined by the price of those goods in the exporting country. Dumping is designed to undersell U.S. businesses to obtain a larger share of the U.S. market. To prevent this, an extra tariff—known as an antidumping duty—may be assessed on the imports.

The procedure for imposing antidumping duties involves two U.S. government agencies: the International Trade Commission (ITC) and the International Trade Administration (ITA). The ITC is an independent agency that makes recommendations to the president concerning temporary import restrictions. The ITC assesses the effects of dumping on domestic businesses. The ITA is part of the Department of Commerce and decides whether import sales were at LTFV. The ITA determination establishes the amount of antidumping duties, which are set to equal the difference between the price charged in the United States and the price charged in the exporting country. A duty may be retroactive to cover past dumping.

Investing

Investing in foreign nations involves a risk that the foreign government may take the investment property. As explained above, expropriation occurs when property is taken and the owner is paid just compensation for what is taken. This does not violate generally observed principles of international law. Confiscation occurs when property is taken and no (or inadequate) compensation is paid. International law principles are violated when property is confiscated.

Generally, few remedies for confiscation of property by a foreign government are available. In many cases, claims are resolved by lump-sum settlements after negotiations between the United States and the taking nation. For example, investors whose claims arose out of confiscations following the Russian Revolution in 1917 were offered a lump-sum settlement by the Union of Soviet Socialist Republics in 1974. Still outstanding are $2 billion of claims against Cuba for confiscations that occurred in 1959 and 1960.

To counter the deterrent effect that the possibility of confiscation may have on potential investors, many countries guarantee compensation to foreign investors if property is taken. A guarantee can be in the form of national constitutional or statutory laws or provisions in international treaties. As further protection for foreign investments, some countries provide insurance for their citizens' investments abroad. In the United States, for example, the Overseas Private Investment Corporation (OPIC), a government agency, insures U.S. citizens and businesses against losses incurred as a result of confiscation of their assets by foreign governments, war, or other causes. The premium charged by OPIC for coverage depends on the nature and extent of the business risk covered. In addition to OPIC, several private firms offer international investment insurance.

Bribing Foreign Officials

Giving payments in cash or in-kind benefits to foreign government officials to obtain business contracts and other favors is often considered normal practice. To reduce the amount of these bribes given to foreign government officials by representatives of U.S. corporations, Congress enacted the Foreign Corrupt Practices Act[3] (FCPA) in 1977.

The FCPA is divided into two major parts. The first part applies to all U.S. companies and their directors, officers, shareholders, employees, and agents. As noted in Case 27.1, this part of the FCPA prohibits bribery of most officials of foreign governments if the purpose of the payment is to get the official to act in his or her official capacity to provide business opportunities.

The second part of the FCPA is directed toward accountants, because in the past, bribes were often concealed in corporate financial records. All companies must keep detailed records that "accurately and fairly" reflect the company's financial activities. In addition, they must have an accounting system that provides "reasonable insurance" that

---

3. 15 U.S.C. Sections 78 *et seq.*

all transactions entered into by the company are accounted for and legal. These requirements assist in detecting illegal bribes.

The FCPA further prohibits any person from making false statements to accountants or false entries in any record or account. Businesses in violation of the FCPA may be fined up to $1 million. Individual officers or directors who violate the FCPA may be fined up to $10,000 (the fine cannot be paid by the company) and be imprisoned for up to five years.

The FCPA does not prohibit payment of substantial sums to minor officials, whose duties are ministerial. These payments are often referred to as "grease," or facilitating payments. They are meant to ensure that administrative services that might otherwise be performed at a slow pace are sped up. Thus, for example, if a firm makes a payment to a minor official to speed up an import licensing process, the FCPA has not been violated.

U.S. Laws in a Transnational Setting

The internationalization of business raises questions of the extraterritorial effect of a nation's laws. Extraterritorial effect refers to the effect of a country's laws outside the country. To what extent do U.S. domestic laws affect other nations' businesses? To what extent are U.S. businesses affected by domestic laws when doing business abroad? The following sections discuss these questions in the context of U.S. antitrust, patent, and discrimination laws.

Antitrust Laws

U.S. antitrust laws (see Chapter 20) have a wide application. They may *subject* persons in foreign nations to their provisions, as well as *protect* foreign consumers and competitors from antitrust-violation acts committed by U.S. citizens. Consequently, *foreign persons,* a term that by definition includes foreign governments, may sue under U.S. antitrust laws in U.S. courts.

Section 1 of the Sherman Act provides for the extraterritorial effect of the U.S. antitrust laws. The United States is a major proponent of free competition in the global economy, and thus any conspiracy that has a substantial effect on U.S. commerce is within the reach of the Sherman Act. The act of violation may even occur outside the United States, and foreign governments as well as persons can be sued in violation of U.S. antitrust laws. Yet before U.S. courts will exercise jurisdiction and apply antitrust laws, it must be shown that the alleged violation had a *substantial effect* on U.S. commerce. U.S. jurisdiction is automatically invoked, however, when a *per se* violation occurs.[4]

A *per se* violation may consist of resale price fixing and tying, or tie-in, contracts. If a domestic firm, for example, joins a foreign *cartel* (a group of firms organized to control the market for their products) to control the production, price, or distribution of goods, and this cartel has a *substantial restraining effect* on U.S. commerce, a *per se* violation may exist. Hence, both the domestic firm and the foreign cartel have the potential to be sued in violation of the U.S. antitrust laws. Likewise, if foreign firms doing business in the United States enter into a price-fixing or other anticompetitive agreement to control a portion of U.S. markets, a *per se* violation may exist.

In 1982, the United States amended the Sherman Act and the Federal Trade Commission Act to limit their application when unfair methods of competition are involved in U.S. export trade or commerce with foreign nations. The acts are not limited, however, when there is a "direct, substantial, and reasonably foreseeable effect" on U.S. domestic commerce that results in a claim for damages.

An alleged conspiracy on the part of Japanese television manufacturers to gain control of the electronic products market in the United States—in violation of the Sherman Act and other antitrust and tariff legislation—is considered by the United States Supreme Court in the following case.

---

4. Certain types of restrictive contracts are deemed inherently anticompetitive and thus in restraint of trade as a matter of law. These contracts are said to be *per se* violations of the antitrust laws. See Chapter 20.

BACKGROUND AND FACTS *Zenith Radio Corporation and several other U.S. manufacturers of television sets alleged that Matsushita Electric Industrial Company and other Japanese firms "illegally conspired to drive American firms from the consumer electronic products market" by means of a "scheme to raise, fix and maintain artificially high prices for television receivers sold by [Matsushita and others] in Japan and, at the same time, to fix and maintain low prices for television receivers exported to and sold in the United States." The alleged conspiracy began, according to Zenith, in 1953. The American firms claimed that the Japanese were engaged in a "predatory pricing" arrangement whereby the losses sustained by selling at such low prices in the United States were offset by monopoly profits obtained in Japan. Once the Japanese gained control over an overwhelming portion of the American market for electronic products, their monopoly power would enable them to recover their losses by charging artificially high prices in the United States as well. The district court granted summary judgment in favor of the Japanese firms, and the case was appealed. The court of appeals reversed the judgment of the district court, and the case was appealed to the United States Supreme Court.*

Case 27.6

MATSUSHITA ELECTRIC INDUSTRIAL CO. v. ZENITH RADIO CORP.

Supreme Court of the United States, 1986.
475 U.S. 574,
106 S.Ct. 1348,
89 L.Ed.2d 538.

Justice *POWELL* delivered the opinion of the Court.

*   *   *   *

*   *   * Respondents cannot recover antitrust damages based solely on an alleged cartelization of the Japanese market, because American antitrust laws do not regulate the competitive conditions of other nations' economies. *   *   *

Respondents nevertheless argue that [this] supposed [conspiracy is] circumstantial evidence of *   *   * a conspiracy to monopolize the American market by means of pricing below the market level. *   *   *

*   *   *   *

*   *   * [R]espondents allege that a large number of firms have conspired over a period of many years to charge below-market prices in order to stifle competition. Such a conspiracy is incalculably more difficult to execute than an analogous plan undertaken by a single predator. The conspirators must allocate the losses to be sustained during the conspiracy's operation, and must also allocate any gains to be realized from its success. Precisely because success is speculative and depends on a willingness to endure losses for an indefinite period, each conspirator has a strong incentive to cheat, letting its partners suffer the losses necessary to destroy the competition while sharing in any gains if the conspiracy succeeds. *   *   * Yet if conspirators cheat to any substantial extent, the conspiracy must fail, because its success depends on depressing the market price for all buyers *   *   *.

[I]f predatory pricing conspiracies are generally unlikely to occur, they are especially so where, as here, the prospects of attaining monopoly power seem slight. *   *   * Two decades after their conspiracy is alleged to have commenced, petitioners appear to be far from achieving this goal: the two largest shares of the retail market in television sets are held by RCA and respondent Zenith, not by any of the petitioners. Moreover, those shares, which together approximate 40% of sales, did not decline appreciably during the 1970's. Petitioners' collective share rose rapidly during this period, from one-fifth or less of the relevant markets to close to 50%. Neither the District Court nor the Court of Appeals found, however, that petitioners' share presently allows them to charge monopoly prices; to the contrary, respondents contend that the conspiracy is ongoing—that petitioners are still artificially depressing the market price in order to drive Zenith out of the market. *   *   *

The alleged conspiracy's failure to achieve its ends in the two decades of its asserted operation is strong evidence that the conspiracy does not in fact exist.

DECISION AND REMEDY *The United States Supreme Court reversed the decision of the court of appeals and remanded the case.*

Patent Laws

In the United States, inventions are protected by patent law, which is intended to prevent others from copying the invention (see Chapter 26). U.S. patent laws provide no direct protection overseas, however. To be protected in another country, an invention must be patented under the laws of that country. Internationally, an agreement known as the Paris Convention[5] guarantees nondiscrimina-tory treatment under the laws of other nations, but it does not provide independent international patent protection.

The United States may prohibit the importation of products that infringe on patents registered in the United States. The following case addresses the issue of whether a U.S. firm, barred from marketing its product within the United States because of a competitor's superior patent claim, could nonetheless legally market the product abroad.

5. See International Convention for Protection of Industrial Property, March 20, 1883, 21 U.S.T. 1583, T.I.A.S. No. 6923.

Case 27.7

DEEPSOUTH PACKING CO. v. LAITRAM CORP.

Supreme Court of the United States, 1972.
406 U.S. 518,
92 S.Ct. 1700,
32 L.Ed.2d 273.

BACKGROUND AND FACTS *Laitram Corporation held U.S. patents for machinery used in the process of deveining shrimp. (Deveined shrimp are easier and more pleasing to eat.) Under U.S. patent law, only the owner of a patent may "make" or "sell" an item patented in the United States. Deepsouth Packing Company began shipping components of deveining machinery similar to Laitram's to foreign customers. The components were shipped in three separate boxes, but the entire machine could be assembled in less than an hour. Laitram sought an injunction against Deepsouth, arguing that this practice violated its exclusive rights under U.S. patent law. The federal district court ruled for Deepsouth, but the court of appeals reversed and ruled that Deepsouth's foreign sales violated Laitram's patent. Deepsouth appealed to the United States Supreme Court.*

Mr. Justice *WHITE* delivered the opinion of the Court.
     *   *   *   *

     *   *   * Petitioner and respondent both hold patents on machines that devein shrimp more cheaply and efficiently than competing machinery or hand labor can do the job. Extensive litigation below has established that respondent, the Laitram Corp., has the superior claim and that the distribution and use of petitioner Deepsouth's machinery in this country should be enjoined to prevent infringement of Laitram's patents. We granted certiorari to consider a related question: Is Deepsouth, barred from the American market by Laitram's patents, also foreclosed by the patent laws from exporting its deveiners, in less than fully assembled form, for use abroad?
     *   *   *   *

     *   *   * [The] judgment of Laitram's patent superiority forecloses Deepsouth and its customers from any future use (other than a use approved by Laitram or occurring after the Laitram patent has expired) of its deveiners "throughout the United States." The patent provisions taken in conjunction with the judgment below also entitle Laitram to the injunction it has received prohibiting Deepsouth from continuing to "make" or, once made, to "sell" deveiners "throughout the United States." Further, Laitram may recover damages for any past unauthorized use, sale, or making "throughout the United States." This much is not disputed.

But Deepsouth argues that it is not liable for every type of past sale and that a portion of its future business is salvageable. [U.S. patent laws] obviously are intended to grant a patentee a monopoly only over the United States market; they are not intended to grant a patentee the bonus of a favored position as a flagship company free of American competition in international commerce. Deepsouth, itself barred from using its deveining machines, or from inducing others to use them "throughout the United States," barred also from making and selling the machines in the United States, seeks to make the parts of deveining machines, to sell them to foreign buyers, and to have the buyers assemble the parts and use the machines abroad. *   *   *

*   *   *   *

In conclusion, we note that what is at stake here is the right of American companies to compete with an American patent holder in foreign markets. Our patent system makes no claim to extraterritorial effect; "these acts of Congress do not, and were not intended to, operate beyond the limits of the United States," and we correspondingly reject the claims of others to such control over our markets. To the degree that the inventor needs protection in markets other than those of this country, the wording of [the U.S. patent laws] reveals a congressional intent to have him seek it abroad through patents secured in countries where his goods are being used.

The United States Supreme Court reversed the decision of the court of appeals. The Supreme Court held that Deepsouth's practice did not violate U.S. patent laws.

DECISION AND REMEDY

Discrimination Laws

There are laws in the United States against discrimination on the basis of race, color, national origin, religion, and sex. Specifically, Title VII of the 1964 Civil Rights Act regulates employment practices of businesses and covers employees who are employed in any industry affecting commerce. The term *commerce* is defined as "trade, traffic, commerce, transportation, transmission, or communication among the several states; or between a state and anyplace outside thereof." A central question for some employees is whether the Civil Rights Act covers U.S. citizens working abroad for U.S. employers.

This question faced the court when a naturalized U.S. citizen, Ali Boureslan, who was employed in Saudi Arabia by a U.S. corporation, Aramco, claimed that his supervisor at Aramco had undertaken a "campaign of harassment" against him when he first began working in Saudi Arabia in 1980. From then until he was fired in 1984,

Bourselan alleged, he had been continually victimized by his supervisor's racial, religious, and ethnic slurs. Following his employment termination, Boureslan filed a Title VII action, in which he alleged discrimination based on race, religion, and national origin. Boureslan claimed that Congress intended the Civil Rights Act to apply to U.S. citizens working abroad for U.S. employers. The district court held to the contrary, and on appeal, the U.S. Court of Appeals for the Fifth Circuit agreed with the district court that Title VII could not be applied extraterritorially. The court stated that contrasting religious and social customs abroad "could well leave American corporations a difficult choice of either refusing to employ U.S. citizens in such countries or discontinuing business."[6] The United States Supreme Court affirmed the lower courts' decisions in March 1991, holding that the plaintiff failed to demonstrate any clearly expressed con-

---

6. *Boureslan v. Aramco,* 892 F.2d 1271 (5th Cir. 1990).

By the time you read this book, businesspersons in the United States may already be facing a single integrated European market with almost 330 million consumers, a total gross national product of over $4 trillion, and a growth rate that is expected to exceed that in the United States. On December 31, 1992, many of the trade barriers among the twelve European Community (EC) countries[a] will have been eliminated.

A united Europe began in 1951 with the establishment of the European Coal and Steel Community (ECSC), consisting of Belgium, West Germany, France, Italy, Luxembourg, and The Netherlands. In 1957, the European Atomic Energy Community (Euratom) was established, and at the same time the Treaty of Rome[b] formally established the European Economic Community (EEC). The Treaty of Rome outlined three goals: (1) to preserve European peace;

---

a. Belgium, Denmark, France, Germany, Greece, Ireland, Italy, Luxembourg, The Netherlands, Portugal, Spain, and the United Kingdom.
b. Treaty Establishing The European Economic Community, U.K.T.S. 15 (1979), 298 U.N.T.S. 11 (concluded at Rome March 25, 1957; entered into force Jan. 1, 1958).

(2) to establish a European common market—that is, a market in which goods, capital, and labor could move freely from one country to another; and (3) to form a politically unified Europe.

Common Institutions

Originally, the ECSC, Euratom, and the EEC functioned separately. Under the Merger Treaty signed in 1965, however, the three now have common institutions: the European Council of Ministers, the European Commission, the European Parliament, and the European Court of Justice. Reference is now typically made to the European Community, or the EC.

The European Council, to which each EC country appoints one member, has both legislative and executive powers. The votes of the members are weighted to prevent the large countries from outvoting the small countries.

The European Commission is the principal executive body and may exercise legislative power delegated to it by the European Council. Its seventeen members, who are appointed by the European Council, do not take orders from member countries—they act only in the best interests of the EC. The European Commission proposes and drafts EC legislation, which is then submitted to the European Council for adoption.

The European Council may amend the proposals only by unanimous vote. Before enacting EC legislation, the European Council must consult with the European Parliament.

The European Parliament, whose 518 members are elected directly by citizens of the EC countries, has no legislative authority, but it must be heard in an advisory capacity.[c] It may vote European Commission members out of office.

The European Court of Justice has thirteen justices appointed by the European Council. The court enforces EC and other international law (for example, the General Agreement on Tariffs and Trade) and analyzes "general principles of law common to Member States." The court has jurisdiction over EC matters throughout the EC. Its opinions have authority but no means of enforcement—national courts and law enforcement agencies must implement its judgments. Nevertheless, noncompliance has rarely been a problem.

The Single European Act

By 1968, most tariffs within the EC were eliminated. Other trade

---

c. In 1980, the European Court of Justice held that the European Council acts illegally if it legislates without waiting for the European Parliament's opinion. See *S.A. Roquette Freres v. Council,* 1980 Eur.Comm.Rep. 3333.

barriers continued to restrict trade among EC countries, however, preventing achievement of the goal of a real common market. By the mid-1980s, it was clear that a Europe of relatively small, protected national economies was incapable of competing with the United States and Japan.

In June 1985, the European Commission set out a program of nearly three hundred EC-wide legislative measures needed to remove the financial, technical, and physical barriers that obstructed the operation of a true common market in Europe. To implement the program, EC countries ratified the Single European Act in February 1986 as an amendment to the Treaty of Rome. The act took effect in July 1987.

The objective of a unified European market is to make European businesses more competitive in Europe and the rest of the world. A unified market will give European-based companies a larger home market, which will make it possible for larger European-based companies to form. In turn, these companies will be able to undertake research and development on a larger scale. The effect of a unified European market on U.S. businesses may be profound.

■ Implications for the Businessperson

1. The EC is the largest market for exports from the United States, but no other international organization rivals the EC in its detailed rulemaking. Anyone doing business with EC countries will have contact with EC law, which is vast and intricate. There are law school courses devoted entirely to the study of EC law. Businesspersons contemplating doing business with the EC must invest in mastering the new "rules of the game."

2. U.S. businesspersons may have to invest directly in business operations in EC countries to take maximum advantage of expanding economic opportunities because of new licensing rules and other regulations under the Single European Act. For example, previously, each EC member separately licensed the sale of regulated products and services within its territory. Now a company licensed in any member country is permitted to sell its products or provide its services in all the other member countries without meeting further licensing requirements. But this privilege is extended only to individuals and legal entities that are citizens of, and licensed by, another member country. "Third-country" businesses (such as U.S. firms) will need to obtain separate licensing in each EC country in which they wish to do business.

■ For Critical Analysis

1. The Treaty of Rome states that a company organized under the laws of any EC country and "having its registered office, central administration or principal place of business within the Community" is entitled to EC status, regardless of the home country of the EC company's parent company. As noted above, "EC status" means that a company permitted to sell its products or provide its services in one EC country can do so in all member countries without meeting further licensing requirements. Should the mere formality of organizing a company in an EC country entitle the company to EC status when the company is owned and controlled by non-EC persons?

2. Even within a unified European market, there will still remain many differences compared with the U.S. market. What are they, and how will they affect the amount of trade within the EC?

gressional intent that Title VII should apply extra-territorially. The Court pointed out that Congress on numerous occasions has legislated extraterritorially and that Congress may similarly amend Title VII to apply abroad. In other words, any ex-traterritorial application of Title VII will have to be undertaken by the legislature, not the courts.[7]

7. *Equal Employment Opportunity Commission v. Arabian American Oil Co.*, ____ U.S., ____,111 S.Ct. 1227, 113 L.Ed.2d 274 (1991).

■ Terms and Concepts to Review

act of state doctrine 651
choice-of-language
   clause 656
choice-of-law clause 658
comity 651
confiscation 651
correspondent banks 659
distribution agreement 655
dumping 605
exclusive distributorship 655

export 654
expropriation 651
force majeure clause 658
foreign exchange
   market 659
forum-selection clause 656
franchise 656
franchisee 656
franchisor 656

international law 649
international
   organization 649
joint venture 656
letter of credit 659
national law 649
sovereign immunity 652
technology liscensing 655
wire transfer 659

■ Questions and Case Problems

27-1. Air Flight is a U.S. manufacturer of helicopters. Heise, vice-president in charge of sales, wants to sell one hundred helicopters to North Zin, a foreign country. Secretary of Defense Zoro in North Zin has complete authority to purchase helicopters for his country. Zoro usually relies on evaluations made by his subordinates. Air Flight's main competition in the sale of these helicopters is from Top Flight, a European firm. The president of Top Flight has given Zoro his own personal helicopter and deposited $100,000 into Zoro's account. Heise immediately offers Zoro $200,000 in cash, and in addition, gives $10,000 to each of Zoro's subordinates to induce them to process Air Flight's evaluation before they process Top Flight's. ABC accountants, when auditing Air Flight's accounts, discover these payments that have been made to Zoro and his subordinates. Heise and Air Flight claim that without these payments, Air Flight cannot compete in foreign markets. Discuss whether these payments made by Air Flight are illegal.

27-2. Section 1610(d)(1) of the Foreign Sovereign Immunities Act (FSIA) provides that the property of a foreign state that is used for commercial activity in the United States is not immune from attachment prior to the entry of a judgment if the foreign state has "explicitly waived its immunity from attachment prior to judgment." Banco Nacional, an instrumentality of the government of Costa Rica, entered into a written agreement with Libra Bank, Ltd., the plaintiffs. In the agreement, Banco Nacional stated that it did not have "any right of immunity from suit with respect to the Borrower's obligations" under this particular agreement. Did Banco Nacional, the defendant, "explicitly" waive its immunity from prejudgment attachment as re-

quired by the FSIA? [*Libra Bank, Ltd. v. Banco Nacional de Costa Rica, S.A.*, 676 F.2d 47 (2d Cir. 1982)]

27-3. Both Mannington Mills and Congoleum Corp. are American producers of carpets and other floor coverings. Mannington alleged that Congoleum had fraudulently obtained foreign patents through false statements and misrepresentation of data. Mannington sued Congoleum, arguing that these actions violated U.S. antitrust laws. Congoleum argued that the U.S. courts had no jurisdiction. Congoleum contended that issuance of foreign patents came under the act of state doctrine or, at least, required deference to foreign nations. Should the United States exercise jurisdiction over this dispute? [*Mannington Mills, Inc. v. Congoleum Corp.*, 595 F.2d 1287 (3d Cir. 1979)]

27-4. ICC Industries was an importer of potassium permanganate from the People's Republic of China. The International Trade Administration (ITA) of the Department of Commerce conducted an antidumping investigation and concluded that this potassium permanganate was being imported at less than fair value (LTFV), in violation of U.S. law. Fair value is an estimate of the value of the product in the home market—in this case, the People's Republic of China. As a consequence of its investigation of ICC, the ITA imposed retroactive antidumping duties on its imports of potassium permanganate for the period 1981 to 1983. Imposition of these duties required a finding that ICC had known or should have known that the product was being imported at less than fair value. ICC argued that it was unaware of this fact. ICC emphasized that because the People's Republic of China had a nonmarket economy, the company was unable to ascertain a home market value for potassium permanganate. ICC therefore appealed the ITA's order to the Court of Appeals for the Federal Circuit. What will result? Discuss fully. [*ICC Industries, Inc. v. United States,* 812 F.2d 694 (Fed.Cir. 1987)]

27-5. Harris Corp., the plaintiff, entered into a contract with the defendant, National Iranian Radio and Television (NIRT), to manufacture and deliver 144 FM broadcast transmitters to Teheran, Iran. Due to the revolution in Iran, the plaintiff was unable to complete delivery of the transmitters. NIRT attempted to collect on a letter of credit that had been set up to guarantee performance. The plaintiff subsequently brought an action against the defendant, seeking to enjoin receipt of payment on the letter of credit. Bank Melli Iran, the issuer, was also made a defendant. Both defendants alleged that the district court lacked jurisdiction over them. From 1969 to 1982, Melli maintained an office in New York City, where it carried out significant business transactions. Moreover, NIRT had entered into this contract that required performance by Harris in the United States and also the training of NIRT personnel in the United States. Was this action consistent with due process? Was the ''minimum contacts'' standard established for foreign jurisdiction (discussed in Chapter 40) satisfied? [*Harris Corp. v. National Iranian Radio and Television,* 691 F.2d 1344 (11th Cir. 1982)]

27-6. Texas Trading & Milling Corp. and other companies brought an action for breach of contract against the Federal Republic of Nigeria and its central bank. Nigeria, a rapidly developing and oil-rich nation, had overbought huge quantities of cement from Texas Trading and others. Unable to accept delivery of the cement, Nigeria repudiated the contract, alleging immunity under the Foreign Sovereign Immunities Act of 1976. Because the buyer of the cement was the Nigerian government, does the doctrine of sovereign immunity remove the dispute from the jurisdiction of U.S. courts? [*Texas Trading & Milling Corp. v. Federal Republic of Nigeria,* 647 F.2d 300 (2d Cir. 1981)]

27-7. Billy Lamb and Carmon Willis (the plaintiffs) are tobacco growers in Kentucky. Phillip Morris and B.A.T. Industries, PLC, routinely purchase tobacco not only from Kentucky but also from producers in several foreign countries. In 1982, subsidiaries of Phillip Morris and B.A.T. (the defendants) entered into an agreement with *La Fundacion Del Nino* (the Children's Foundation) of Caracas, Venezuela. The president of the Children's Foundation was the wife of the then president of Venezuela. The agreement provided that the two subsidiaries would donate a total of approximately $12.5 million to the Children's Foundation, and in exchange, the subsidiaries were to obtain price controls on Venezuelan tobacco, elimination of controls on retail cigarette prices in Venezuela, tax deductions for the donations, and assurances that existing tax rates applicable to tobacco companies would not be increased. The plaintiffs brought this action, alleging that the Venezuelan arrangement was an inducement designed to restrain trade in violation of U.S. antitrust laws. Such an arrangement, the plaintiffs contended, would result in the artificial depression of tobacco prices to the detriment of domestic tobacco growers, while ensuring lucrative retail prices for tobacco products sold abroad. The trial court held that the plaintiffs'

claim was barred by the act of state doctrine. What will result on appeal? Discuss. [*Lamb v. Phillip Morris, Inc.,* 915 F.2d 1024 (6th Cir. 1990)]

27-8. While in the United States, Scott Nelson was hired as a monitoring systems engineer for the King Faisal Specialist Hospital in Riyadh, Saudi Arabia. Nelson alleged that in the course of performing his duties under his employment contract with the hospital, he was detained and tortured by agents of the Saudi government in Saudi Arabia for reporting safety violations at the hospital. Nelson brought suit for his injuries against Saudi Arabia, the hospital, and Royspec, a corporation owned and controlled by the government of Saudi Arabia (collectively, Saudi Arabia). Saudi Arabia claimed immunity under the doctrine of sovereign immunity. Nelson contended that because his detention and torture resulted from his recruitment within the United States by an agent of the Saudi government as part of a commercial activity, the district court had subject matter jurisdiction under the Foreign Sovereign Immunities Act. What should the court decide? Discuss fully. [*Nelson v. Saudi Arabia,* 923 F.2d 1528 (11th Cir. 1991)]

27-9. Gordonsville Industries, Inc., located in Virginia, entered into a contract with American Artos Corp., a North Carolina corporation, for the design, construction, and installation of a textile drying system. Artos, in turn, contracted with GEA Luftkuhlergesellschaft, a German firm, for the design of a hot oil boiler, one of the system's integral parts. GEA subcontracted the actual construction of the boiler to Industrial Boiler Co., a Georgia corporation. A forum-selection clause in the Artos-GEA contract specified that in the event of a lawsuit, ''it is agreed that the place for litigation shall be the Amtsgericht [civil court] in Bochum, Germany.'' Later, Gordonsville Industries, unhappy with the performance of the textile drying system, filed suit in a U.S. federal court against Artos to recover damages. Artos then filed a complaint, essentially seeking indemnification (reimbursement), against GEA. GEA moved to dismiss the complaint on the grounds that under the forum-selection clause in the Artos-GEA contract, the dispute should be heard in the specified German court. Artos contended that the clause should not be enforced because the construction of the boiler had taken place in the United States, and all of the relevant records and witnesses were located in the United States, not Germany. What will the court decide? Discuss. [*Gordonsville Industries, Inc. v. American Artos Corp.,* 549 F.Supp. 200 (W.D.Va. 1982)]

27-10. Royal Bed and Spring Co., a Puerto Rican distributor of furniture products, entered into an exclusive distributorship agreement with Famossul Industria e Comercio de Moveis Ltda., a Brazilian manufacturer of furniture products. Under the terms of the contract, Royal Bed was to distribute in Puerto Rico the furniture products manufactured by Famossul in Brazil. The contract contained choice-of-forum and choice-of-law clauses, which designated that the judicial district of Curitiba, State of Parana, Brazil, as the judicial forum and the Brazilian Civil Code as the law to be applied in the event of any dispute. Famossul terminated the exclusive distributorship and suspended the shipment of goods without just cause. Puerto Rican law refuses to enforce forum-selection clauses providing for foreign venues as a matter of public policy. In what jurisdiction should Royal Bed bring suit? Discuss fully. [*Royal Bed and Spring Co. v. Famossul Industria e Comercio de Moveis Ltda.*, 906 F.2d 45 (5th Cir. 1990)]

27-11. Panhandle Eastern Pipe Line Co. (PEPL) and another party entered into a contract for the purchase of liquified natural gas (LNG) from the Algerian National Oil & Gas Co. A *force majeure* clause in the contract stated that "chance events affecting the facilities used for the performance of the contract" could reduce the quantities of LNG that PEPL was obligated to purchase. If the purchaser were to claim that full performance under the contract was impossible because of the nationwide recession, the enactment of energy conservation legislation, the warm winter season, the unprecedented reduction in the price of crude oil, and the emergence of increased competition in the sales market, would the purchaser's contractual performance be excused under the *force majeure* clause? Discuss fully. [*United States v. Panhandle Eastern Corp.*, 693 F.Supp. 88 (D.Del. 1988)]

27-12. A Question of Ethics

In a contract between Arthur Young & Co., a New York corporation with a branch office in Hawaii, and Robert Leong, whose only office was in Hawaii, the parties included a forum-selection clause stating that any dispute arising under the contract would be heard before a New York court and New York law would apply. When a dispute did eventually arise, Leong claimed that the forum-selection clause should not be enforced, on the grounds of inconvenience. Not only had the dispute arisen in Hawaii, but all of the relevant records and witnesses were located there, and to transport the records and witnesses to New York would entail a major inconvenience. Discuss the following questions concerning whether the court should enforce the forum-selection clause in these circumstances. [Arthur Young & Co. v. Leong, *53 A.D.2d 515, 383 N.Y.S.2d 618 (1976)*]

1. Is it ethical to compel Leong to have "his day in court" so far from his home? Given that he agreed to the provision, is it ethical to not compel him?

2. What practical considerations could have been motivating factors for the parties to bind themselves to the forum-selection clause? Ethically, which of those factors supports enforcing the clause? Which support not enforcing it?

3. What would be wrong with partially enforcing the clause by having a local court hear the case but apply New York law in reaching its conclusion? Is the fact that a partial enforcement of the clause does not give one of the parties the full benefit of the original bargain an ethical reason for enforcing the clause fully?

27-13. Case Briefing Assignment

Examine Case A.27 [Trans-Orient Marine Corp. v. Star Trading & Marine, Inc., *731 F.Supp. 619 (S.D.N.Y. 1990)*] *in Appendix A. The case has been excerpted there in great detail. Review and then brief the case, making sure that you include answers to the following questions in your brief.*

1. What specific circumstances led to this lawsuit?

2. What was the central international legal issue addressed by the court?

3. How did the court distinguish a "succession of state" from a "succession of government," and what was the effect of the distinction on executory contracts of the state?

4. What "seminal decision" on this issue was referred to by the court? What other cases did the court rely on in its reasoning?

Focus on Ethics

The International Environment

Ethics in International Trade

The American government has become increasingly active in protecting consumers and the environment from hazardous products and industrial processes. Many foreign governments, however, lack the capability or the will to provide similar protections. As a consequence, U.S. firms may sell seemingly hazardous products overseas with little or no regulation.

Suppose that the U.S. government discovers that a pesticide causes cancer and prohibits the use of the chemical in this nation. The pesticide producer may have large stocks of the chemical in inventory. Moreover, sales of the chemical may be quite profitable for the company. Suppose that the producer elects to sell its inventory overseas or even to continue producing the pesticide for foreign sales. Is this action ethical? Should not the company at least warn the foreign buyers of the cancer risk? Or should the company simply leave the matter in the hands of the foreign government?

Some persons have suggested that the United States should prohibit exports of any products banned for domestic use. Bear in mind, however, that foreign circumstances may differ from those in the United States. For example, the United States banned the pesticide DDT, primarily because of its adverse effects on wildlife. In Asia, however, DDT was a critical component of the mosquito control necessary to combat malaria. Perhaps foreign citizens would conclude that the benefits of a hazardous product outweigh the risks that it presents.

The Foreign Corrupt Practices Act

Congress has attempted to legislate international ethics in the Foreign Corrupt Practices Act (FCPA). Broadly speaking, this act prohibits U.S. companies from bribing foreign governments for contracts or other favors. Prior to passage of the act, such payments were relatively commonplace and an accepted cost of doing business.

American firms have voiced frustration with the act. Foreign officials in some countries have traditionally expected payments for consideration in doing business. Such payments are not always considered unethical behavior in some countries but rather a supplemental tax for the use of official services. Higher-level officials may be fully aware of such payments and implicitly authorize them.

The FCPA only prohibits U.S. firms from making such payments—it cannot prevent foreign officials from expecting or demanding them. Thus, the act may not prevent overseas bribery but may merely shift such actions from U.S. to foreign corporations, thus placing American corporations at a competitive disadvantage in international trade. This disadvantage is especially undesirable in view of the ongoing U.S. balance-of-payments deficit.

Business officials have experienced an additional ethical dilemma. An employee of a U.S. corporation has a fiduciary duty to the corporation's shareholders. Yet the FCPA may prevent the employee from making sure the company competes effectively. The problem is further complicated when the U.S. firm can provide the best products or services to the foreign country. In this instance, the FCPA may injure the U.S. company, its workers, and the foreign purchaser as well. Congress recently has amended the FCPA to reduce record-keeping requirements, but the fundamental proscription on bribery remains. Is bribery always unethical, or can it be justified by the benefits that may result?

International Considerations

The problem of diversity of interests and values faced by large corporations is writ large in the international arena. Multinational corporations need to consider not only ethical values of Americans but also those values of the host countries within which they do business. In the event of a conflict, which values should prevail? For example, in some countries discrimination on the basis of race, sex, or religion is required by law. Also, in many countries labor is cheaper and the legal standards for employee health and safety are much lower. U.S. employment laws do not apply abroad, but should U.S firms nonetheless,

for ethical reasons, abide by U.S. standards?

The United Nations recently drafted a code of conduct for multinational corporations that, if accepted, would impose specific ethical requirements on firms involved in foreign business operations. Among other things, these firms would be required to consider the health and safety of consumers and the environment of the host country, to respect human rights and fundamental freedoms, and to disclose whether their products have been banned in other countries. The proposed code has come under much criticism, however. According to officials within the U.S. Department of State, the code will probably not be accepted in its present form by this country because it is "unbalanced." While multinational corporations face numerous restrictions under the code, the host countries are not required to abide by equally restrictive guidelines.

■ Discussion Questions

1. Suppose a foreign government official demands that a U.S. company make a

payment to him before the company can be granted a contract to provide water-supply facilities for the foreign nation. This payment would violate the Foreign Corrupt Practices Act. Company officials know that their company's bid is the lowest and believe that their company can do the best job of constructing the facilities. These officials further believe that the payment can be made secretly. Failure to make the payment will mean that the job will be given to a higher bidder from a European nation. Should the officials make the payment if they are unlikely to be caught?
2. Cigarette consumption in the United States has declined in the face of fears about the effects of smoking on health. Cigarette companies may, however, increase sales in foreign countries, where the health risks of smoking are less well known. Should cigarette companies include health warnings on all packs of cigarettes sold overseas, even though that country's law does not require this action? Is the warning alone enough to fulfill the companies' ethical obligations?

Appendix A

How to Brief a Case and Selected Cases

How to Brief a Case

To fully understand the law with respect to business, you need to be able to read and understand court decisions. To make this task easier, you can use a method of case analysis that is called *briefing*. There is a fairly standard procedure that you can follow when you "brief" any court case. You must first read the case opinion carefully. When you feel you understand the case, you can prepare a brief of it.

Although the format of the brief may vary, typically it will present the essentials of the case under headings such as those listed below.

1. **Citation.** Give the full citation for the case, including the name of the case, the date it was decided, and the court that decided it.
2. **Facts.** Briefly indicate (a) the reasons for the lawsuit; (b) the identity and arguments of the plaintiff(s) and defendant(s), respectively; and (c) the lower court's decision—if appropriate.
3. **Issue.** Concisely phrase, in the form of a question, the essential issue before the court. (If more than one

issue is involved, you may have two—or even more—questions here.)
4. **Decision.** Indicate here—with a "yes" or "no," if possible—the court's answer to the question (or questions) in the *Issue* section above.
5. **Reason.** Summarize as briefly as possible the reasons given by the court for its decision and the case or statutory law relied on by the court in arriving at its decision.

When you prepare your brief, be sure you include all of the important facts. But remember that, by definition, the result should be brief.

Selected Cases for Briefing

Court opinions can run from a few pages to hundreds of pages in length. For reasons of space, only the essential parts of the opinions are presented in the cases that follow. As with the cases presented in the chapters of this text, a series of three asterisks indicates that a portion of the text—other than citations and footnotes—has been omitted. Four asterisks indicate the omission of at least one paragraph.

Case A.1

IN RE VERMONT SUPREME COURT ADMINISTRATIVE DIRECTIVE NO. 17 v. VERMONT SUPREME COURT
Supreme Court of Vermont, 1990.
579 A.2d 1036.

BARNEY, Chief Justice (Ret.), Specially Assigned.

Petitioners brought a petition for extraordinary relief under V.R.A.P. 21 [Vermont Rules of Appellate Procedure] seeking a declaration that an administrative directive of this Court ordering the delay of most civil jury trials until after July 1, 1990 for budgetary reasons is unconstitutional. * * * *

On January 11, 1990 this Court issued Administrative Directive No. 17, entitled "Temporary Postponement of Civil Jury Trials'' which stated as follows:

> The resources available to the Judiciary have been drastically reduced for the remainder of fiscal year 1990. Accordingly, each superior and district court judge and clerk is hereby ordered to postpone until after July 1, 1990 any civil jury case for which the jury has not yet been drawn.
>
> The administrative judge is hereby authorized to permit the trial of any given case where justice requires, but it is envisioned that nearly all civil jury cases will be delayed.
>
> This directive shall become effective on January 22, 1990.

There is no dispute over the motivation for the issuance of Administrative Directive 17. Financial problems within the State of Vermont caused the Governor and Legislature to order rescisions—that is, reductions in the preexisting appropriations for government agencies. *   *   *

*   *   *   *

The central substantive question before this Court is whether Administrative Directive 17 denies the right to trial by jury or fails to keep it ''sacred'' as required by Chapter I, Article 12 or Chapter II, [Section] 38.

*   *   *   *

*   *   * [P]etitioners' position is that a jury trial delayed is equal to a jury trial denied for purposes of the Vermont Constitution. In this case, at least, in the context of a temporary moratorium [suspension] for the time involved, with an exception from the moratorium available where justice requires, we reject this position.

Our precedents do not support the absolutist view of the jury trial right that the petitioners espouse. Vermont courts have long exercised the power to adopt administrative rules having an incidental effect on the availability of jury trials in some cases. *   *   *

*   *   *   *

Delay *per se* is not unconstitutional; it may become such only when an injured plaintiff, ready and eager for trial, or a defendant, seeking vindication and himself ready for trial, are denied for too long his day in court. If a five year delay in a civil action reflects simply the parties' utilization of pre-trial discovery or settlement negotiations there is no constitutional violation. To codify the myriad relevant elements into timetables of general application having constitutional force may well be impossible.

There have been periods in our history when clogged dockets in our superior court meant that a litigant would wait for a trial date far longer than the same litigant would wait today. Although we have no specific record on this point, we believe that it is likely that the petitioners in this case will have the opportunity to go to jury trial sooner than they would have during periods in the past despite the delay occasioned by Administrative Directive 17. The remedy they seek, however, is the instant access to a jury. Such a remedy cannot be found in the constitutional jury trial rights on which they rely. Petitioners have failed to show specific prejudice or that their trials are being delayed unreasonably. Caseloads cannot be managed on the simplistic position that everyone is entitled to an immediate trial whenever they are ready for one.

*   *   *   *

[We now] consider the main precedent relied upon by petitioners, *Armster v. United States District Court for the Central District of California,* holding that that district court and the district court for the district of Alaska could not constitutionally suspend civil jury trials because of fiscal constraints. *Armster* appears at first blush to proclaim a Seventh Amendment civil jury trial right which is infringed by the slightest diminution:

> We must vigilantly protect the right to civil jury trials, and we must scrutinize in the most rigorous manner possible any action that appears to limit in any way the availability of that right.
>
> ... We conclude that the availability of constitutional rights does not vary with the rise and fall of account balances in the Treasury. Our basic liberties cannot be offered and withdrawn as ''budget crunches'' come and go, nor may they be made contingent on transitory political judgments regarding the advisability of raising or lowering taxes, or on pragmatic or tactical decisions about how to deal with the perennial problem of the national debt. ... Rather, our constitutional rights are fixed and immutable, subject to change only in the manner our forefathers established for the making of constitutional amendments.

The court goes on to hold, however, that it is not the moratorium *per se* that offends the Seventh Amendment, but the length of the moratorium:

> Specifically, we conclude that the Seventh Amendment right to a civil jury trial is violated when, because of such a suspension, an individual is not afforded, for any significant period of time, a jury trial

he would otherwise receive. We do not suggest that a suspension of any duration whatsoever would be constitutional. We need only decide here that a suspension for a significant period is barred by the Seventh Amendment . . . . [W]e believe three and a half months constitutes far more than a significant period, given the mandate of the Seventh Amendment.

The *Armster* court appeared at first to treat the deferral of jury trials in the case before it as a power that had been exercised without the need for justification, not as an option chosen in the face of competing claims to judicial resources or limited funding. The court's apparent response was to declare invalid any action that appeared to limit the civil jury trial right "in any way." However, in its holding it conceded that the civil jury right might be limited according to a reasonableness standard *   *   *.

*   *   *   *

Armster and the decisions relying on it are distinguishable because they deal with blanket moratoria and [in one case] a far longer time period. We also cannot accept the analysis that the jury trial right is infringed when access to juries is delayed a relatively short period of time. Finally, we are relying on our own settled interpretations of the nature of the right to trial by jury under the Vermont Constitution. These interpretations do not necessarily apply to the Seventh Amendment to the United States Constitution, which is not applicable to the states.

[The petition] for extraordinary relief is DISMISSED.

_____

Case A.2

GOELLER v. LIBERTY MUTUAL INSURANCE CO.

Supreme Court of Pennsylvania, 1990.
568 A.2d 176.

McDERMOTT, Justice.

This is an appeal from an order of the Superior Court which reversed an order of the Court of Common Pleas of Philadelphia County. The latter order denied appellee's petition to confirm a decision of a panel of arbitrators. It also mandated the convention [a convening; bringing together] of a new panel and re-hearing of appellant's claim under the uninsured motorist provision of an insurance policy. The facts and procedural history of the case are set forth below.

Appellant was injured in an automobile mishap in Connecticut while removing the driver from an overturned automobile. Involved in the accident were two other drivers, one of whom was allegedly uninsured. He entered a claim against appellee, the carrier of his employer's insurance policy, for coverage under an uninsured motorist provision which appellee disputed. The contract provided that disputes would be resolved by arbitration conducted in accordance with the Pennsylvania Arbitration Act *   *   *.

A panel of three arbitrators was assembled, as provided in the agreement, and presided over hearings on September 12 and 25, 1986. On July 28, 1987, the neutral arbitrator mailed a letter to the attorneys of the parties and each of the other panel members. It stated simply to the effect that appellee's arbitrator and the neutral arbitrator found for appellee and that appellant's arbitrator dissented and found for appellant. The neutral arbitrator's was the solitary signature to the letter. The following day, the letter was filed with the Prothonotary [principal court clerk].

Also on the following day, appellant's arbitrator by certified mail, responded with a letter to the neutral arbitrator. In it he made a number of complaints. He stated that he had not agreed to the letter nor had he been consulted. He maintained in effect that the letter misrepresented his opinion. Regarding the deliberations of the panel members, he went on to express shock on learning that the other arbitrators had discussed the case out of his presence. In summary he stated that the letter was absolutely incorrect. He suggested further that the panel withdraw their purported findings and withdraw as the arbitrators in order to allow another panel to take over the matter. He sent courtesy copies to the other addressees of the neutral arbitrator's letter. On August 3, 1987, the neutral arbitrator responded by letter. Its entire text stated, "Because of (sic) you have impugned my integrity, I am withdrawing my award and I am withdrawing from the panel of arbitrators in this case."

On August 7, 1987, appellee filed a petition to confirm the award. On August 24, 1987, appellant answered, and filed new matter, petitioning, *inter alia* [among other things], for an order to convene a new arbitration panel. The court found adequate grounds to conclude that all of the panel members had not participated in the deliberations and that the award was not final in nature. The court therefore denied appellee's petition to confirm the award and ordered the parties to convene a new arbitration panel to try the case.

On appeal, the Superior Court reversed, determining that the lower court erred in its resolution of both the question of whether the panel had issued a final award and that of whether the award was the product of misconduct or other gross irregularity. Appellant petitioned this Court and we granted leave to appeal in order to review the Superior Court's determinations.

With respect to appellant's first contention, he asserts * * * that there was no final award by the arbitrators. The [Pennsylvania Arbitration] Act states in appropriate part:

> Award of Arbitrators
> General Rule—The award of the arbitrators shall be in writing and signed by the arbitrators joining in the award. The arbitrators shall deliver a copy of the award to each party personally or by registered or certified mail or as prescribed in the agreement to arbitrate.

In reply, appellee argues that the neutral arbitrator was without the power to withdraw the award of the arbitrators after it had been issued. We are impressed that the latter argument is non-responsive to the issue raised: whether there was an award in the first instance. We conclude that there was not.

First we note that this arbitration, as agreed by the parties, was to be regulated by the provisions of the Act. The reviewing court is bound to construe the words of the Act according to rules of grammar and according to their common and approved usage. The object of the Court's interpretation is to ascertain and effectuate the intention of the General Assembly [the Pennsylvania legislature]. The word "shall," in the section relied on by appellant, is clearly mandatory [authoritative; compelling] in effect. But it is manifest that a purported award signed by no more than one of the three members of the panel, as herein, does not comply with the plain wording of the Act. The purported award in this case, in failing the formal stat-

utory requirement, failed the requirement of their agreement as well. The "award" was a nullity.

Furthermore we are persuaded that there was no award in this case for another, more substantive, reason. This Court long ago voiced the principle that, "The opportunity to deliberate, and, if possible, to convince their fellows is the right of the minority, of which they cannot be deprived by the arbitrary will of the majority." * * *

The record indicates, and it is not disputed, that one of the members of the panel in this case was denied his opportunity to deliberate. When an arbitrator, properly appointed and entitled to act, is denied access to the deliberations of the other arbitrators, their decision is not a decision. It matters not whose arbitrator he or she may be. What is important is that all viewpoints must at least be heard. Each must be entitled to the opportunity to persuade the others, be permitted to dissent and to maintain his voice in the decision. It is manifest that that principle was violated in this case.

We recognize, as the Superior Court admonishes, that a strong presumption exists in favor of an arbitration panel's final award. However, before the award is paid such deference [courteous submission to another's opinion or judgment] by the courts it must come into existence as a corporate act of the panel. For the reasons set forth above, we conclude that in this case it did not.

Furthermore, the mandate of the trial court, that a new panel be convened and the matter retried, is necessary to afford the parties no less than that to which they agreed, an award by an arbitration panel.

Since we resolve appellant's first contention as we do, it is not necessary to pierce the veil of the panel's deliberations and pass on whether the award was a product of misconduct or other grave irregularity in terms of the Act.

The order of the Superior Court is reversed. The order of the Court of Common Pleas of Philadelphia County is reinstated.

Case A.3

RODRIGUEZ de QUIJAS v. SHEARSON/ AMERICAN EXPRESS, INC.

United States Supreme Court, 1989.
490 U.S. 477,
109 S.Ct. 1917,
104 L.Ed.2d 526.

KENNEDY, Justice.

The question here is whether a predispute agreement to arbitrate claims under the Securities Act of 1933 is unenforceable, requiring resolution of the claims only in a judicial forum.

I

Petitioners are individuals who invested about $400,000 in securities. They signed a standard customer agreement with the broker, which included a clause stating that the parties agreed to settle any controversies "relating to [the] accounts" through binding arbitration that complies with specified procedures. The agreement to arbitrate these controversies is unqualified, unless it is found to be unenforceable under federal or state law. * * * The investments turned sour, and petitioners eventually sued respondent and its broker-agent in charge of the accounts, alleging that their money was lost in unauthorized and fraudulent transactions. In their complaint they pleaded various violations of federal and state law, including claims under § 12(2) of the Securities Act of 1933, * * * and claims under three sections of the Securities Exchange Act of 1934.

The District Court ordered all the claims to be submitted to arbitration except for those raised under § 12(2) of the Securities Act. It held that the latter claims must proceed in the court action under our clear holding on the point in Wilko v. Swan, 346 U.S. 427, 74 S.Ct. 182, 98 L.Ed. 168 (1953). The District Court reaffirmed its ruling upon reconsideration, and also entered a default judgment against the broker, who is no longer in the case. The Court of Appeals reversed, concluding that the arbitration agreement is enforceable because this Court's subsequent decisions have reduced Wilko to "obsolescence." * * *

II

The Wilko case, decided in 1953, required the Court to determine whether an agreement to arbitrate future controversies constitutes a binding stipulation "to waive compliance with any provision" of the Securities Act, which is nullified by § 14 of the Act. * * * The Court considered the language, purposes, and legislative history of the Securities Act, and concluded that the agreement to arbitrate was void under § 14. But the decision was a difficult one in view of the competing legislative policy embodied in the Arbitration Act, which the Court described as "not easily reconcilable," and which strongly favors the enforcement of agreements to arbitrate as a means of securing "prompt, economical and adequate solution of controversies." * * * *

It has been recognized that Wilko was not obviously correct, for "the language prohibiting waiver of 'compliance with any provision of this title' could easily have been read to relate to substantive provisions of the Act without including the remedy provisions." * * * The Court did not read the language this way in Wilko, however, and gave two reasons. First, the Court rejected the argument that

"arbitration is merely a form of trial to be used in lieu of a trial at law." * * * The Court found instead that § 14 does not permit waiver of "the right to select the judicial forum" in favor of arbitration, * * * because "arbitration lacks the certainty of a suit at law under the Act to enforce [the buyer's] rights," * * *. Second, the Court concluded that the Securities Act was intended to protect buyers of securities, who often do not deal at arm's length and on equal terms with sellers, by offering them "a wider choice of courts and venue" than is enjoyed by participants in other business transactions, making "the right to select the judicial forum" a particularly valuable feature of the Securities Act. * * *

* * * The shift in the Court's views on arbitration away from those adopted in Wilko is shown by the flat statement in [a prior case]: "By agreeing to arbitrate a statutory claim, a party does not forgo the substantive rights afforded by the statute; it only submits to their resolution in an arbitral, rather than a judicial, forum." * * * To the extent that Wilko rested on suspicion of arbitration as a method of weakening the protections afforded in the substantive law to would-be complainants, it has fallen far out of step with our current strong endorsement of the federal statutes favoring this method of resolving disputes.

Once the outmoded presumption of disfavoring arbitration proceedings is set to one side, it becomes clear that the right to select the judicial forum and the wider choice of courts are not such essential features of the Securities Act that § 14 is properly construed to bar any waiver of these provisions. Nor are they so critical that they cannot be waived under the rationale that the Securities Act was intended to place buyers of securities on an equal footing with sellers. Wilko identified two different kinds of provisions in the Securities Act that would advance this objective. Some are substantive, such as placing on the seller the burden of proving lack of scienter when a buyer alleges fraud. * * * Others are procedural. The specific procedural improvements highlighted in Wilko are the statute's broad venue provisions in the federal courts; the existence of nationwide service of process in the federal courts; the extinction of the amount-in-controversy requirement that had applied to fraud suits when they were brought in federal courts under diversity jurisdiction rather than as a federal cause of action; and the grant of concurrent jurisdiction in the state and federal courts without possibility of removal.

There is no sound basis for construing the prohibition in § 14 on waiving "compliance with any provision'' of the Securities Act to apply to these procedural provisions. Although the first three meaşures do facilitate suits by buyers of securities, the grant of concurrent jurisdiction constitutes explicit authorization for complainants to waive those protections by filing suit in state court without possibility of removal to federal court. These measures, moreover, are present in other federal statutes which have not been interpreted to prohibit enforcement of predispute agreements to arbitrate. *   *   * [T]he party opposing arbitration carries the burden of showing that Congress intended in a separate statute to preclude a waiver of judicial remedies, or that such a waiver of judicial remedies inherently conflicts with the underlying purposes of that other statute. *   *   * But as Justice Frankfurter said in dissent in Wilko, so it is true in this case: "There is nothing in the record before us, nor in the facts of which we can take judicial notice, to indicate that the arbitral system . . . would not afford the plaintiff the rights to which he is entitled." *   *   *

The language quoted above from § 2 of the Arbitration Act also allows the courts to give relief where the party opposing arbitration presents "well-supported claims that the agreement to arbitrate resulted from the sort of fraud or overwhelming economic power that would provide grounds 'for the revocation of any contract.' " *   *   * This avenue of relief is in harmony with the Securities Act's concern to protect buyers of securities by removing "the disadvantages under which buyers labor" in their dealings with sellers. *   *   *

III

We now conclude that Wilko was incorrectly decided and is inconsistent with the prevailing uniform construction of other federal statutes governing arbitration agreements in the setting of business transactions. Although we are normally and properly reluctant to overturn our decisions construing statutes, we have done so to achieve a uniform interpretation of similar statutory language *   *   * and to correct a seriously erroneous interpretation of statutory language that would undermine congressional policy as expressed in other legislation, *   *   * Both purposes would be served here by overruling the Wilko decision. In this case, for example, petitioners' claims under the 1934 Act were subjected to arbitration, while their claim under the 1933 Act was not permitted to go to arbitration, but was required to proceed in court. That result makes little sense for similar claims, based on similar facts, which are supposed to arise within a single federal regulatory scheme. In addition, the inconsistency *   *   * undermines the essential rationale for a harmonious construction of the two statutes, which is to discourage litigants from manipulating their allegations merely to cast their claims under one of the securities laws rather than another. For all of these reasons, therefore, we overrule the decision in Wilko.

The judgment of the Court of Appeals is AFFIRMED.

_____

Case A.4

BURNELL v. GENERAL TELEPHONE OF ILLINOIS, INC.

Appellate Court of Illinois, Fourth District, 1989.
536 N.E. 2d 1387.

GREEN, Justice.

On August 28, 1986, plaintiff John E. Burnell filed suit in the circuit court of Morgan County seeking reemployment and monetary damages resulting from his discharge from the employment of defendant General Telephone Company (GTE). In his complaint, plaintiff alleged, *inter alia* [among other things], defendant had discriminated against him in violation of section 2 of the Age Discrimination in Employment Act of 1967 (Act) *   *   * and his subsequent termination from employment constituted a constructive discharge. The case was tried before a jury on an amended complaint, and on June 30, 1988, at the close of plaintiff's case, the court allowed defendant's motion for a directed verdict.

On appeal, plaintiff maintains the trial court erred in concluding the evidence received at trial did not raise a sufficient issue that plaintiff was the victim of a constructive discharge to warrant the submission of the case to the jury. We affirm.

A directed verdict is properly entered only in "cases in which all of the evidence, when viewed in its aspect most favorable to the opponent, so overwhelmingly favors movant that no contrary verdict based on that evidence could ever stand." *   *   *

Section 4(a)(1) of the Act provides that it shall be unlawful for an employer to "discharge any individual or otherwise discriminate against any individual with respect to his compensation, terms, conditions, or privileges of employment, because of such individual's age." * * * To establish a prima facie case of discriminatory discharge under the Act, the plaintiff must show (1) he is within the protected age group; (2) he was doing satisfactory work; (3) he was discharged despite the adequacy of his work; and (4) his position was filled by a person younger than he. The burden then shifts to the employer to show a legitimate, nondiscriminatory reason for the challenged action. Finally, the plaintiff must rebut the employer's showing by demonstrating that the proffered justification was a pretext, and that plaintiff's age was the determining factor for the challenged action. * * *

* * * *

Plaintiff testified at trial that (1) he was born in 1932 and worked for GTE continuously from 1950 through 1984, first as a union "craft" employee, and, beginning in 1961, he held a series of management positions; (2) in 1984, he held the position of "Service Manager of Facilities" in the Jacksonville Division of the company; (3) three individuals held the same position in the Bloomington Division; (4) at that time, plaintiff was both the oldest and had the most seniority of the four incumbent service facility managers; (5) in March 1984, Ronald Harpole informed plaintiff he would be replacing plaintiff; (6) at that time, Harpole told plaintiff that plaintiff would be offered the position entitled "DAC supervisor," at the same salary, or he could elect to retire and receive a continuation of his salary for a certain period of time; (7) plaintiff was aware of the consolidation efforts by the company, and he believed that many of the functions of the DAC supervisor would not exist after consolidation; (8) accordingly, he made several attempts to determine the security of the position from Harpole, Harpole's supervisor, and Wineburg; (9) no one was able to give plaintiff any assurance as to the duration of the position, nor could they assure him he could later elect the separation pay benefit he was initially offered if the DAC position were eliminated; and (10) as a result, plaintiff elected early retirement.

Here, in regard to the establishment of a prima facie case, plaintiff's evidence showed: (1) he was within the protected age group; (2) he was doing satisfactory work; and (3) his position was filled by a person younger than he. In regard to the issue upon which the defendant had the burden of going forward, plaintiff's evidence established, as a legitimate, non-

discriminatory reason for defendant's actions, the nationwide consolidation efforts which involved the elimination of unnecessary job positions. (Although the service facility supervisor position was not unnecessary, the division manager position held by Harpole, plaintiff's supervisor, was eliminated when the two divisions were combined.)

However, as defendant was never actually discharged from his employment, he had the burden to make a prima facie showing he was constructively discharged from his employment with defendant and failed to do so. Defendant argued the phrase "constructive discharge" has been interpreted by Federal courts under the Act to require a finding that the defendant deliberately or intentionally made the plaintiff's working conditions so intolerable that a reasonable person, in a similar situation, would be forced to resign his or her employment to escape those intolerable conditions. * * * Defendant concluded plaintiff did not introduce any evidence that plaintiff had been constructively discharged by defendant.

The trial court, in granting defendant's motion for a directed verdict, found the evidence conclusively showed (1) there was no actual discharge since plaintiff was offered a position at a salary approximately equal to that which he had been making; and (2) there was no constructive discharge, because plaintiff's status was not made intolerable by any action on the part of the employer. The court noted plaintiff weighed his options and chose voluntarily to leave the employment and avail himself of the wage continuance plan. The court found that, although plaintiff was concerned about the security of the position, that concern was based on speculation, and such speculation could not be considered in determining whether plaintiff was constructively discharged.

* * * *

The evidence, when viewed most favorably to the plaintiff showed there was no evidence of: (1) a decrease in salary * * *; (2) a loss in prestige * * *; (3) a conflict between plaintiff and a new supervisor * * *; or (4) a demotion * * *. In addition, plaintiff was not "rushed" into making a decision * * *. Here, plaintiff was informed of his options in March 1984, and, as late as August 1984, at least, those options were still available to him. In fact, plaintiff did not actually leave his employment with defendant until January 12, 1985. Under the circumstances, there was insufficient evidence for the jury to determine that a reasonable person, in a similar situation, would find the working conditions so intolerable that he would be forced to resign his employment.

Accordingly, for the reasons stated, the decision of the trial court is affirmed.

_____

Case A.5

AUSTIN v. BERRYMAN

United States Court of Appeals, Fourth Circuit, 1989.
878 F.2d 786.

MURNAGHAN, Circuit Judge.

We have before us for *en banc* reconsideration an appeal taken from an action successfully brought by Barbara Austin in the United States District Court for the Western District of Virginia against the Virginia Employment Commission, challenging a denial of unemployment compensation benefits. * * *

In brief, Austin charged, *inter alia* [among other things], that the denial of her claim for unemployment benefits, based on a Virginia statute specifically precluding such benefits for any individual who voluntarily quits work to join his or her spouse in a new location, was an unconstitutional infringement upon the incidents of marriage protected by the Fourteenth Amendment and an unconstitutional burden on her First Amendment right to the free exercise of her religion. Her religion happened to command that she follow her spouse wherever he might go and the sincerity of her religious belief was not questioned. The district court found in Austin's favor and awarded injunctive relief and retroactive benefits.

On appeal, Judge Sprouse, writing for a panel majority, found that the denial of benefits did not implicate Austin's Fourteenth Amendment rights, but that it did unconstitutionally burden Austin's right to the free exercise of her religion. The panel also found, however, that any award of retroactive benefits was barred by the Eleventh Amendment. One panel member concurred with the panel majority as to the Fourteenth and Eleventh Amendment issues, but dissented as to the existence of a free exercise violation. The panel opinion now, of course, has been vacated by a grant of rehearing en banc.

After careful consideration of the additional arguments proffered by both sides, the Court, *en banc,* is convinced that the panel majority correctly concluded that denying Austin unemployment benefits did not infringe upon fundamental marital rights protected by the Fourteenth Amendment. To this extent, we adopt the majority panel opinion. We also find,

however, that the denial of benefits did not unconstitutionally burden Austin's First Amendment right to the free exercise of her religion. We are persuaded that the views expressed on the First Amendment, free exercise of religion claim in the opinion dissenting in part from the panel majority are correct, and we hereby adopt that opinion as that of the *en banc* court. As we find that Austin is not entitled to any relief, we need not address whether the Eleventh Amendment bars an award of retroactive benefits.

The decisive consideration, as we see it, is that the proximate cause of Austin's unemployment is geographic distance, not her religious beliefs. There is no conflict between the circumstances of work and Austin's religious precepts. Austin's religious beliefs do not ''require'' her ''to refrain from the work in question.'' Austin is unable to work simply because she is now too far removed from her employer to make it practical. In striking contrast, if one, for genuine religious beliefs, moves to a new residence in order to continue to live with a spouse, and that residence is not geographically so removed as to preclude regular attendance at the worksite, no unemployment, and hence no unemployment benefits, will arise. That amounts to proof that extent of geographical non-propinquity, not religious belief, led to Austin's disqualification for unemployment benefits.

Austin voluntarily decided to quit her job and join her spouse in a new geographic location 150 miles away. Virginia has stated that every individual who follows such a course, no matter what the reason, religious or non-religious, is disqualified for unemployment benefits. To craft judicially a statutory exception only for those individuals who profess Austin's religious convictions, particularly in the absence of a direct conflict between a given employment practice and a religious belief, would, in our view, result in a subsidy to members of a particular religious belief, impermissible under the Establishment Clause.

Accordingly, the judgment of the district court is REVERSED.

_____

Case A.6

PENNY v. GUIFFRIDA

United States Court of Appeals, Tenth Circuit, 1990.
897 F.2d 1543.

EBEL, Circuit Judge.

* * * *

In December 1977, Lawrence Penny applied for a Home Loan Guaranty with the Veterans Administration ("VA") on a home in the Norman, Oklahoma area. Using a VA form, Penny's mortgage company submitted to the VA a Request for Determination of Reasonable Value, which included a metes-and-bounds [boundaries and limits] description of the tract and listed the property address as a rural route number. The VA subsequently issued a Certificate of Reasonable Value, which included the following condition: "Flood insurance required in accordance with VA Reg. 4326."

Soon thereafter, Kenneth Bridges, an insurance agent employed by Farmers Insurance Company and authorized to write insurance under the National Flood Insurance Program ("NFIP"), informed Penny that he would need flood insurance in order to qualify for the VA-guaranteed loan. At Penny's request, Bridges subsequently prepared a flood insurance policy application for Penny for $35,000 of coverage. On the application, Bridges described the house as being in Cleveland County, Oklahoma, and added a parenthetical that stated: "(inside city limits of Norman)." In fact, Penny's home was located in Cleveland County, but outside the city limits of Norman. It is undisputed that while Norman, Oklahoma, qualified for the NFIP, the area of Cleveland County located outside Norman's city limits did not.

Bridges submitted the application to the St. Paul Fire and Marine Insurance Company, which, as servicing agent for the NFIP, approved the application on December 30, 1977. Penny paid his first annual premium of $88.00, and FEMA issued him a flood insurance policy. Penny continued to pay his annual premiums for the years 1978 through 1982.

On May 18, 1982, Penny's home was flooded. When Penny reported the loss, an agent from the General Adjustment Bureau surveyed the property and estimated Penny's losses at $35,124.05. In July 1982, the NFIP administrator denied Penny's claim on the ground that Penny's home was not located in a community participating in the NFIP, and, consequently, Penny was not eligible for NFIP coverage. In August 1982, FEMA cancelled Penny's insurance effective March 20, 1982, and returned his last premium.

In 1984, Penny brought suit against Bridges, Farmers Insurance Company, and FEMA. In his complaint, Penny alleged that Bridges and Farmers Insurance Company were liable in tort for their negligence in issuing the flood insurance policy. He further alleged that FEMA was liable in contract and was equitably estopped from denying liability under the policy. * * *

On Penny's negligence claim against Bridges and Farmers, the jury found for Penny in the amount of $40,000. The estoppel claim against FEMA was tried simultaneously to the court, and it held that FEMA was equitably estopped from denying liability to Penny under the policy and that FEMA was jointly and severally liable with Bridges and Farmers to the extent of the $35,000 policy limit. The district court awarded Penny prejudgment interest and costs against FEMA but denied him attorney's fees because it found that FEMA's position had been "substantially justified." FEMA appeals from the judgment against it, and Penny appeals from the denial of attorney's fees.

FEMA raises three arguments on appeal: (1) the district court incorrectly held that FEMA was estopped from denying liability under the policy; (2) the district court erred by awarding Penny recovery on inconsistent theories; and (3) the district court's award of interest was improper because Congress has not authorized interest awards against the United States under the NFIP. Penny appeals on the ground that the district court erred in denying attorney's fees. Because we reverse the district court's conclusion that the government was estopped from denying liability under the policy, we need not address the other issues raised by FEMA.

* * * *

The district court held that the traditional elements of estoppel were present in this case and that FEMA engaged in "affirmative misconduct" so as to warrant a finding that FEMA was estopped from denying coverage under the policy. We disagree.

Historically, equitable estoppel has been used to prevent a party from taking a legal position inconsistent with an earlier statement or action that places his adversary at a disadvantage. * * * In private suits, the traditional elements of equitable estoppel are: (1) the party to be estopped must know the facts; (2) the party to be estopped must intend that his conduct will be acted upon or must so act that the party asserting the estoppel has the right to believe that it was so intended; (3) the party asserting the estoppel must be ignorant of the true facts; and (4) the party asserting the estoppel must rely on the other party's conduct to his injury. * * *

The law of estoppel against the government is considerably less clear. * * * However, recent Supreme Court decisions have at least suggested the possibility that unauthorized official conduct may give rise to an estoppel against the government where the litigant makes out the requisites of private estoppel and additionally shows the existence of ''affirmative misconduct.'' Nevertheless, no Supreme Court case has ever actually applied estoppel against the government for the unauthorized acts of its agents, and a 1984 Supreme Court case has made it clear that the Court still has not resolved whether estoppel may ever be applied against the government. * * *

* * * *

Although the Supreme Court consistently has reversed lower court decisions granting estoppel, it has continued to leave open the possibility that equitable estoppel against the government might apply in some cases. In light of the aforementioned precedent, however, we do not find that the facts in the case before us would satisfy the criteria for equitable estoppel against the government even if the Supreme Court ultimately decides that such a doctrine is viable. Specifically, we do not believe that FEMA's actions rose to the level of affirmative misconduct.

Penny argues that the government's actions constituting affirmative misconduct were: (1) the VA's requirement that Penny obtain flood insurance in order to qualify for a home loan; (2) FEMA's acceptance of Penny's premiums from 1977–1982; (3) FEMA's denial of liability when Penny's home was flooded; and (4) FEMA's retroactive cancellation of Penny's policy as of March 20, 1982, and FEMA's tender of only his last premium.

We do not accept Penny's argument that the government, through the VA, required him to obtain flood insurance through FEMA. The Flood Disaster Protection Act of 1973 requires the purchase of flood insurance as a condition to receiving federal or federally-related financial assistance for the construction

or acquisition of insurable buildings ''within an identified special flood, mudslide (i.e., mudflow), or flood-related erosion hazard area that is located within any community participating in the Program.'' * * * Because the Penny property was outside of the city limits, the VA did not have the authority to require Penny to obtain insurance. Therefore, Penny cannot be heard to say that he relied on the VA's written requirement of insurance, because he is ''expected to know the law and may not rely on the conduct of Government agents contrary to law.'' * * *

Nor do we accept Penny's assertion that FEMA knew that Penny's property was ineligible for flood insurance when it took Penny's premiums. Until the time of Penny's claim, FEMA was unaware that Penny's house was not in the city limits of Norman, and therefore that FEMA was prohibited by statute from insuring it, because FEMA, like Penny, ₁elied on Bridge's written description in Penny's insurance application placing Penny's house ''inside [the] city limits of Norman.'' * * * Similarly, in our case, the law was not in dispute, but FEMA mistakenly believed that the factual circumstances made Penny eligible for insurance. The Supreme Court has indicated that mere negligence on the part of a government agent does not reach the level of affirmative misconduct. * * *

FEMA was acting pursuant to its statutory authority in denying liability to Penny, and it would have acted beyond its authority to extend insurance to Penny. Penny offers no authority to suggest that an agency's conformance with a congressional enactment establishes affirmative misconduct.

Finally, although we do not approve of FEMA's tender of only the last premium paid, that action occurred after any possible reliance by Penny and is not relevant to an estoppel analysis.

The government's actions in this case were less egregious [flagrantly bad] than governmental misconduct that the Supreme Court has found not to constitute affirmative misconduct. We hold, therefore, that the district court was incorrect in concluding that the affirmative misconduct requirement has been met. Because we conclude that there was no showing of affirmative misconduct, we need not consider the other issues raised by FEMA in its appeal. With regard to Penny's appeal of the district court's order denying attorney's fees we find no error in the district court's ruling that FEMA's position was ''substantially justified,'' and therefore we conclude that there was no abuse of discretion in the district court's refusal to award Penny attorney's fees.

Case A.7

SHREVE v. DUKE POWER CO.

Court of Appeals of North Carolina, 1990.
389 S.E.2d 444.

WELLS, Judge.

A motion by a defendant for a directed verdict * * * tests the legal sufficiency of the evidence to take the case to the jury and support a verdict for the plaintiff. * * * On such a motion, the plaintiff's evidence must be taken as true and the evidence must be considered in the light most favorable to the plaintiff, giving the plaintiff the benefit of every reasonable inference to be drawn therefrom. A directed verdict for the defendant is not properly allowed unless it appears as a matter of law that a recovery cannot be had by the plaintiff upon any view of the facts that the evidence reasonably tends to establish.

At trial, plaintiff's evidence tended to show that on 3 February 1984 he was employed by defendant Duke at its Dan River power plant. Plaintiff had been employed by Duke for about 16 years and had a good work record. Defendant Stultz was one of plaintiff's supervisors at the Dan River plant. On 3 February 1984, approximately one week after plaintiff had lodged a complaint about plant safety violations with Duke's safety director from Charlotte, Stultz reported to other Duke management personnel at the plant that plaintiff had threatened him with physical violence. As a result of Stultz' report, plaintiff was fired from his job. Plaintiff testified that he had never threatened Stultz and that he was fired solely because he had voiced concerns about safety at the plant. In their answer to plaintiff's complaint, defendants admit that on the occasion in question defendant Stultz had reported to other Duke management personnel that plaintiff had threatened Stultz.

The speaking of false and defamatory words which tend to prejudice another in his trade, business, or means of livelihood, or which accuse another of committing a crime, constitute slander and are actionable per se. * * * In North Carolina, it is a statutory crime to communicate a threat to physically injure another. * * *

Accordingly, we REVERSE the judgment against FEMA, and we AFFIRM the order of the district court refusing to award Penny attorney's fees.

Plaintiff's evidence was clearly sufficient to take his case to the jury as to defendant Stultz. If believed, it would establish that Stultz slandered plaintiff in two respects: (1) in his trade and means of livelihood, and (2) in accusing him of criminal conduct. We therefore order a new trial as to defendant Stultz.

Defendant Duke asserts that when its other management personnel repeated what Stultz had reported to them, their utterances were privileged under North Carolina law. We agree.

A defamatory statement is qualifiedly privileged when made (1) in good faith, (2) on subject matter (a) in which the declarant has an interest, or (b) in reference to which the declarant has a right or duty, (3) to a person having a corresponding interest, right, or duty, (4) on a privileged occasion, and (5) in a manner and under circumstances fairly warranted by the occasion and duty, right, or interest. * * * The existence of a privilege creates a presumption that the statement was made in good faith and without malice. * * * In order to prevail in the face of such a presumption, plaintiff would have to show actual malice.

At most, plaintiff's evidence shows that Duke's other management personnel discussed Stultz' accusation against plaintiff among themselves, believed Stultz, and fired plaintiff for threatening his supervisor. There is no evidence from which a jury could reasonably infer that defendant Duke acted out of malice or ill-will toward plaintiff. Duke's statements were privileged, and we therefore hold that the trial court properly allowed its motion for a directed verdict.

The result is:
As to defendant Stultz,
NEW TRIAL;
As to defendant Duke,
NO ERROR.

Case A.8

UNITED STATES v. O'CONNOR

United States Court of Appeals, Seventh Circuit, 1990.
910 F.2d 1466.

EASTERBROOK, Circuit Judge.

Daniel J. O'Connor, a crooked policeman, got caught in a sting operation. Federal agents posing as shady auto parts dealers—not above buying stolen cars to satisfy their customers' wants or cannibalize for parts—approached O'Connor and asked for notice of any potential investigations that might affect their business. At the initial meeting O'Connor described the tips he had provided to David Gorzellaney, operator of a bowling emporium cum [combined with] gambling house, who introduced O'Connor to the agents. Gorzellaney was by then cooperating with the FBI. O'Connor boasted to "Bill Burns" (the lead agent's *nom de guerre*) that he had not only tipped Gorzellaney off to raids but also once took part in a raid and hid from fellow police officers evidence that Gorzellaney had overlooked.

Burns told O'Connor that he needed similar aid and also wanted security for legitimate used-parts sales. O'Connor generously offered to use his patrol car to help Burns transport stolen merchandise and to wear a beeper so that Burns could reach him as needed. O'Connor did not come cheap. He asked Burns: "What wouldn't hurt you?," to which the agent replied "Well, three bills [$300 per month] won't hurt me." O'Connor replied: "Maybe we should start at five." Burns agreed, provided the monthly payments were in installments. O'Connor got $300 on the spot. During the next two months he received another $650 in four installments. In exchange O'Connor agreed to give Burns news pronto, to "put a little feeler out" to potential buyers of stolen merchandise, and to obtain information about the addresses of the owners of cars whose license plate numbers Burns would furnish. Burns's "customers" would "shop" for cars by cruising the streets to find models they liked, then furnishing license plate numbers; Burns needed to track down the cars and arrange for their "appropriation." During the two months in which payments continued, O'Connor learned and told Burns that Gorzellaney had become a "pigeon" for the FBI and should be avoided. O'Connor also furnished computer printouts showing registration information for cars to be stolen.

Burns stopped paying O'Connor after two months, pleading ill health and poor business. O'Con-

nor tried to get in touch with Burns, paging him and even once following him in a patrol car. Burns promised to resume payments. He never did; instead a grand jury indicted O'Connor, charging him with engaging in a pattern of racketeering, in violation of the Racketeer Influenced and Corrupt Organizations Act (RICO). Convicted after a bench trial, O'Connor has been sentenced to 2 ½ years' imprisonment, to be followed by 3 years' probation.

O'Connor contends that the evidence is insufficient to establish a "pattern" of racketeering, a necessary ingredient of the RICO offense. He emphasizes that "Burns" and the other agents determined the number and timing of payments that would be made, and he maintains that there must be a "pattern" from his side as well as from the agents'. True enough, but the trier of fact was entitled to conclude that O'Connor was prepared to (and did) undertake an extended series of criminal acts (taking bribes, providing information and protection) that would continue indefinitely, so long as Burns needed his services. Fences do not pay all the money up front; reciprocity—a "pattern" of money for information in increments—is important to maintain trust and loyalty.

Although the inference of a pattern was by no means open and shut (given the leading role played by the FBI), the evidence permitted a reasonable trier of fact to conclude beyond a reasonable doubt that O'Connor had committed himself to an enduring series of criminal acts, sufficient to establish a "pattern" * * *. O'Connor points to other cases in which this court has concluded that the evidence did not make out a pattern. There are many such cases—perhaps there is even a pattern of using the "pattern" requirement to trim off the excesses in civil RICO suits. [A previous case] emphasizes the impossibility of fitting all RICO cases to a single pattern, and nothing of moment could be achieved by surveying and attempting (probably vainly) to reconcile the many cases. Once a case has been tried, the evidence and reasonable inferences must be taken in the light favorable to the verdict. That perspective, when added to our holding in [another previous case], requires affirmance.

As for extortion: * * * [T]his court, in common with several other circuits, * * * has held that a public employee in a position to dole out or withhold official favors who solicits or accepts bribes under color of official right commits the crime of extortion. * * *

AFFIRMED.

Case A.9

HEINZEL v. BACKSTROM

Supreme Court of Oregon, 1990.
310 Or. 89,
794 P.2d 775.

VAN HOOMISSEN, Justice.

Plaintiffs Rodger and Judith Heinzel brought this action for specific performance of an agreement for the sale of real property owned by defendant Backstrom. The first and dispositive issue is whether the agreement is a contract. The trial court found the agreement to be a contract; but it also found that because the Heinzels had not tendered performance by the agreed closing date, Backstrom had been free to sell the property to the defendants Johnson. The Court of Appeals reversed. It found the agreement to be a contract, that the Heinzels had tendered performance within a "reasonable time" after the agreed closing date and, therefore, that they are entitled to specific performance. On de novo review [reviewing a case as if it had not been heard and no decision had been rendered before], we find the agreement to be a mere offer to sell which by its own terms expired before the Heinzels tendered performance. Accordingly, we reverse the decision of the Court of Appeals.

The relevant facts are uncontested. The real property which is the subject of this action consists of one commercial building and lot and two contiguous vacant lots that Backstrom had inherited from her father. After her husband died in 1984, Mrs. Backstrom decided to sell this property.

In August, 1986, the Heinzels contacted Backstrom expressing their interest in buying her property. * * *
* * * *

On September 4, 1986, after verifying the amount of taxes owing on Backstrom's property, Mr. Heinzel drafted the following document:

September 4, 1986
Sales agreement between Rodger and Judith Heinzel and Grace Backstrom.
I Grace Backstrom hereby agree to sell to Rodger and Judith Heinzel my properties described as, Lt. 8 Bl 2 Everests and lt 1 & 2 Bl 2 Everests in the City of Newberg. The property to be free of encumbrances except Yamhill County property taxes both past-due and present. The purchase price to be $45,000 for Lt 8 Bl 2 Everests and $5,000 each for Lt 1 & 2 Bl 2 Everests, the total value for all properties being $55,000. Escrow to be closed on October 1, 1986.

The document was signed by all the parties. The Heinzels paid Backstrom no money at that time.

That same day, Mr. Heinzel opened an escrow for the consummation of the sale. * * *

After signing the agreement, Backstrom had become concerned about the transaction. On September 9, 1986, she consulted her attorney, who told her that he would examine the document. He advised her not to communicate with the Heinzels thereafter and to refer any inquiries about the matter to him.

On September 11, a realtor notified Backstrom that the defendants Johnson wanted to buy her property. Backstrom again consulted her attorney, who told her that her agreement with the Heinzels probably was binding until October 1. He again advised her to refer any inquiries about the matter to him. He also arranged for the Johnsons' offer to remain open until after October 1. Neither Backstrom nor her attorney communicated with the Heinzels. When the October 1 deadline passed with no word from the Heinzels, Backstrom's attorney told her that any agreement she had with them had expired. On October 16, Backstrom sold the property to the Johnsons.

On October 28, 1986, the escrow holder asked the Heinzels to inform Backstrom that the escrow documents on her sale to the Heinzels were ready for her signature. Mr. Heinzel conveyed this information to Backstrom that same day, at which time Backstrom told him that she already had sold the property to the Johnsons. That was the Heinzels' first notice of Backstrom's sale to the Johnsons.

On October 29, 1986, the Heinzels deposited the purchase price in escrow. Backstrom refused to accept it. On November 3, the escrow holder mailed Backstrom the escrow documents on her sale to the Heinzels. When Backstrom did not sign the documents, the Heinzels commenced this action for specific performance * * *.
* * * *

Two facts support the Heinzels' argument that the document they signed obligated them to buy Backstrom's property. First, its caption reads: "Sales agreement between Rodger and Judith Heinzel and Grace Backstrom." That language could support an inference that the document was intended to be an agreement between the parties to sell and to buy the property. However, use of the words "sales agreement" in the caption is not determinative. The meaning of those words must be determined by reading them in the context of the entire document.

Second, the fact that the Heinzels signed the document could support an inference that the Heinzels intended to bind themselves to buy Backstrom's property. On the other hand, the Heinzels' signatures also could be interpreted as being nothing more than their acknowledgment of the terms and conditions of Backstrom's offer. More importantly, the document, which reads: "I Grace Backstrom hereby agree to sell * * *," contains no concomitant unequivocal promise by the Heinzels to buy Backstrom's property. As the Court of Appeals correctly noted, the document "does not contain express mutual promises. Although Backstrom promised to sell, [the Heinzels] did not expressly promise to buy."

Thus, the document provides support for both the Heinzels' and Backstrom's interpretations. Hence, the document is ambiguous. Given this ambiguity, the fact that Mr. Heinzel, who had previous experience in commercial real estate matters, drafted the agreement becomes legally significant. Any ambiguity in an agreement is resolved against the party who drafted it.

As the drafter of the document, Mr. Heinzel had the opportunity to include language which would have clearly shown the parties' intentions. He easily could have included the Heinzels' express promise to buy Backstrom's property, but he did not do so. Application of the rule that any ambiguity in an agreement is to be resolved against the party who drafted it weighs in favor of Backstrom's argument that the document here does not show that the Heinzels intended to bind themselves to buy her property.

On *de novo* review, we find that Backstrom offered to sell her property to the Heinzels on specific terms and conditions. We find further that the Heinzels did not obligate themselves to buy Backstrom's property.

The document here specifically provided: "Escrow to be closed on October 1, 1986." We find that to be a condition of Backstrom's offer, and that the offer terminated after that date. Any attempt by the Heinzels to accept Backstrom's offer after October 1, 1986, was a counter-offer because such "acceptance" necessarily would have involved a closing date different from that specifically stated in Backstrom's offer. We conclude that the trial court correctly determined that the equities were with defendants.

The decision of the Court of Appeals is reversed. The judgment of the circuit court is AFFIRMED.

Case A.10

TRAVEL CRAFT, INC. v. WILHELM MENDE GmbH & CO.

Supreme Court of Indiana, 1990.
552 N.E.2d 443.

SHEPARD, Chief Justice.
* * * *

In 1982, Wilhelm Mende GmbH & Co., a West German Corporation, directed a sales campaign toward Travel Craft, Inc., a manufacturer of motor homes and recreational vehicles. Mende representatives traveled to Travel Craft's plant in Elkhart to persuade Travel Craft to purchase Alu-span, an aluminum-type material. The record indicates that the sales campaign was the first contact between the companies. Travel Craft did not have any prior knowledge of Alu-span.

Travel Craft decided to buy Alu-span for use in constructing its motor homes. After the initial purchase, Travel Craft and Mende negotiated a warranty. Travel Craft drafted the warranty, which stated in pertinent part:

> Seller [Mende] agrees for a period of three (3) years from the date of delivery that product manufactured by it will be free under normal use from substantial defects in materials or workmanship. There are no other warranties, express or implied.

On finished motor homes, Alu-span cracked and separated from its base. As a result, Travel Craft recalled more than 100 motor homes. The cracks and separations apparently resulted from Alu-span's inherent inability to withstand the structural stress associated with its use in motor homes, rather than from any flaw in the material or manufacture.

Travel Craft sued Mende for breach of express and implied warranties. The trial court granted Mende's motions for summary judgment. The Court of Appeals affirmed. Because it appears that this Court has not interpreted the sales provisions of the Uniform

Commercial Code since Indiana adopted them in 1963, we grant transfer.

* * * *

I. Exclusion of Implied Warranties

* * * Travel Craft argues that the disclaimer of the implied warranty of merchantability it drafted in this case * * * was ineffective because it did not contain the word merchantability.

* * * *

The disclaimer in this transaction would normally be inadequate because it does not mention the word merchantability. After reading [Indiana Code Section] 26-1-2-316 [the Indiana equivalent of U.C.C. 2-316] and the Uniform Commercial Code's commentary, however, we conclude that this case is an exception to the rule. The commentary states that U.C.C. [Section] 2-316(2) seeks to:

> [P]rotect a buyer from unexpected and unbargained language of disclaimer by denying effect to such language when inconsistent with language of express warranty and permitting the exclusion of implied warranties only by conspicuous language or other circumstances which protect the buyer from surprise.

Applying [Indiana Code Section] 26-1-2-316(2) in favor of Travel Craft, the buyer and the drafter of the warranty, would subject the seller to the same type of surprise the provision is intended to prevent. Accepting Travel Craft's argument would turn a buyer's shield against surprise into a buyer's sword of surprise. We conclude, consequently, if the buyer drafts the disclaimer it cannot in good faith claim surprise or unexpected and unbargained for language. Our construction follows the drafter's intent that the Code be construed to promote its underlying purposes and policies, and leads us to hold in this case that the implied warranty of merchantability was effectively disclaimed, even though the word "merchantability" was not mentioned.

As for the implied warranty of fitness for a particular purpose, [Indiana Code Section] 26-1-2-316(2) provides the opportunity to disclaim simply by a conspicuous writing. We conclude that the words of this disclaimer were adequate. The trial court properly granted Mende's motion for summary judgment aimed at implied warranties.

II. Use of Parol Evidence

In ruling on the adequacy of the disclaimer and on Mende's motion for summary judgment on the ex-

press warranty, the trial court barred all parol evidence. It treated the written warranty, drafted by Travel Craft and executed by Mende, as a complete and exclusive statement of all of the terms of the agreement. Travel Craft says that this treatment was error; it argues that the trial court should have admitted parol evidence. Mende claims that the "the series of communications and final writing between the parties was only a final expression of their agreement as to warranties." It says parol evidence could not be admitted with respect to that agreement on warranties.

* * * *

We conclude that the written warranty was a final expression of the parties' agreement on warranties, but we believe that the trial court erred in treating the agreement as a final expression on all terms and thus barring all parol evidence. We read U.C.C. § 2-202 to provide that when parties create a complete and exclusive agreement on limited terms, parol evidence is still admissible if it is explanatory or supplemental. We hold that parol evidence was admissible to explain and supplement the warranty words "normal use" and "defects."

III. Summary Judgment on Express Warranty

Travel Craft argues that the trial court erred in finding that there were no genuine issues of material fact and granting summary judgment to Mende. The trial court focused on whether Alu-span was defective, and Mende urges us that there is no evidence of defect.

* * * *

The trial court's summary judgment order states:

> A substantial difference exists between a product that is not merchantable or fit for a particular purpose and one that is defective. If it is defective it is highly unlikely it could be merchantable or fit for the particular purpose. However, it could be unmerchantable or unfit for the particular purpose without being defective. With implied warranties it is only necessary that some malfunction exist[s] that makes it unmerchantable or unfit for the particular purpose rather than showing the existence of some specific dereliction by the manufacturer that constitutes a breach. Whereas the express warranty is that the product is free under normal use from substantial defects in material or workmanship, a specific defect must be shown to constitute a breach of warranty.

We disagree with the trial court's interpretation of the express warranty terms "normal use" and "defect."

The facts before the trial court on summary judgment are subject to conflicting inferences. Who would "normally use" this product and for what purpose would they use it? Was Alu-span "defective" within the meaning of the express warranty? The black-letter definition of "defective" suggests that a good may be defective as the result of some sort of imperfection or dereliction, and it may also be "defective" when the product is not fit for the ordinary purposes for which it was sold or used.

When the facts are viewed most favorably for non-movant Travel Craft, the express warranty may be interpreted as tantamount to an express warranty of fitness for a particular purpose.

We affirm the trial court's decision on implied warranties. We reverse its grant of summary judgment on the express warranty and remand the case for further proceedings, to be conducted in accord with our holding on the admission of parol evidence.

Case A.11

BERNAL v. RICHARD WOLF MEDICAL INSTRUMENTS CORP.

California Court of Appeal, Fourth District, 1990.
221 Cal.App.3d 1326,
272 Cal.Rptr. 41.

TAYLOR, Associate Justice.

Plaintiffs Morris and Rosie Bernal appeal from a judgment for Richard Wolf Medical Instruments Corporation ("Wolf") in their action for personal injuries. During Morris' knee surgery, arthroscopic scissors distributed and warranted by Wolf broke, causing the injury. Plaintiffs' case was predicated, in part, on a strict products liability theory for an allegedly defectively designed instrument * * *. On appeal, they raise instructional error. We reverse.

I.

In March 1980, Wolf sold a pair of arthroscopic scissors to Mercy Hospital. In November 1984, Morris Bernal underwent arthroscopic knee surgery at Mercy.

During the surgical procedure, a scissor blade broke off inside the knee joint, "floated away," and it became imperative to open up the entire knee joint to find it. As a result of the failure of the scissors during surgery, and the subsequent arthrotomy, Bernal developed sympathetic dystrophy. His condition will continue to deteriorate and he will probably require a future total knee replacement. Medical testimony indicated Bernal's problems were proximately caused by complications arising from the failure of the scissors during surgery.

Bernal and his wife sued Wolf on several theories, including strict products liability based on design defect * * *.

Bernal's experts testified at trial the scissors broke due to a condition known as "stress corrosion crack-ing," resulting from a combination of design considerations. The experts did not testify to a "defect" as such, nor did they testify that a reasonable alternative design was possible. * * *

In instructing the jury on Bernal's burden of proof with respect to the alleged design defect, the court gave the version submitted by Wolf, which read *in toto* [entirely] as follows: "With respect to the existence of a defect in the design of the scissors, plaintiff must show by a preponderance of the evidence that a reasonable alternative design was possible, which would have avoided the breakage complained of."

Bernal contends this instruction is erroneous, in that it impermissibly places the burden on him to prove a safer alternative design. He further contends, although Wolf's manager testified the company warranted the scissors to be completely free of defects in material and workmanship, [that] the trial judge refused to give any of Bernal's proffered jury instructions on warranty.

II.

In a case of strict products liability based on a design defect, does the plaintiff have the burden of proving a reasonable alternative design was feasible? We conclude one does not.

We begin with *Baker v. Chrysler Corp.* There the court stated: "Requiring an injured plaintiff who seeks damages against a manufacturer on the basis of strict liability in tort for a defective design to show that alternative designs for the product could reasonably have been developed does not enlarge plaintiff's burden of proof. An injured plaintiff has always had the burden to prove the existence of the defect. The reasonableness of alternative designs, where a design defect is claimed, is part of that burden." Thus, held the court, the burden was upon the injured plaintiff to establish that reasonable alternative designs are possible.

Two years later, however, our [California] Supreme Court decided *Barker v. Lull Engineering Co.* There, the Court articulated a two-pronged definition of a design defect. The tests subsequently have become known as the "consumer expectation" test, and the "risk-benefit" test. The court stated: "[A] product may be found defective in design . . . under either of two alternative tests. First a product may be found defective in design if the plaintiff establishes that the product failed to perform as safely as an ordinary consumer would expect when used in an intended or reasonably foreseeable manner. Second, a product may alternatively be found defective in design if the plaintiff demonstrates that the product's design proximately caused his injury and the defendant fails to establish, in light of the relevant factors, that, on balance, the benefits of the challenged design outweigh the risk of danger inherent in such design."

Noting that past authorities had generally not devoted much attention to the appropriate allocation of the burden of proof, the [California] Supreme Court remarked that the "burden is particularly significant [in that] one of the principal purposes behind the strict product liability doctrine is to relieve an injured plaintiff of many of the onerous evidentiary burdens [problems of presenting needed evidence] inherent in a negligence cause of action. Because most of the evidentiary matters which may be relevant to the determination of the adequacy of a product's design under the 'risk-benefit' standard—e.g., the feasibility and cost of alternative designs—are similar to issues typically presented in a negligent design case and involve technical matters peculiarly within the knowledge of the manufacturer, we conclude that once the plaintiff makes a *prima facie* showing that the injury was proximately caused by the product's design, the burden should appropriately shift to the defendant to prove, in light of the relevant factors, that the product is not defective." * * *

* * * *

* * * [T]here is no question Bernal presented a *prima facie* case that the design of the scissors was a proximate cause of their failure during the surgical procedure, causing disability and the need for future surgery. That is all he had to prove. At that point, Wolf had the burden of proof to show that, on balance, the benefits of the design of the product as a whole outweigh the danger inherent in such design considering, among other enumerated "relevant factors," the feasibility of a safer alternate design. We hold it was error to instruct the jury in the context of design defect that "plaintiff must show by preponderance of the evidence that a reasonable alternative design was possible, which would have avoided the breakage complained of."

Wolf complains to so hold renders it an insurer of its surgical instruments. Not so. Strict liability does not equate with absolute liability. Under the risk-benefit test, the defendant has the burden, and thus the opportunity, to highlight all of the benefits of its product's design before the jury. This would, of course, involve technical information peculiarly within its knowledge, and certainly more readily available to it. Among other things, the defense may show any alternate design would entail unreasonable costs, be uneconomic or impractical, interfere with the product's performance, or create other or increased risks. The case before us is a prime example. Here, the defense produced strong evidence the surgical instrument was made with the best steel available and was reasonably safe for its intended use, but had inherent dangers no human skill or knowledge has yet been able to eliminate. But for the erroneous burden of proof instruction, we would not hesitate to affirm the jury's verdict on this record.

* * * *

Judgment reversed and remanded for retrial on the [issue] of strict liability * * *. Costs awarded to appellant.

———————

Case A.12

ALLISON-BRISTOW COMMUNITY SCHOOL DISTRICT v. IOWA CIVIL RIGHTS COMMISSION

Supreme Court of Iowa, 1990.
461 N.W.2d 456.

SCHULTZ, Justice.

In this appeal the issue is whether back pay and interest awarded to an employee in a civil rights action qualifies as personal earnings which are exempt from garnishment by a judgment creditor under Iowa Code section 642.21 (1989). The district court held that back pay and interest on the award were not exempt under section 642.21 and could be garnished by a judgment creditor. We hold that the exemption applies to the back pay, but not to the interest.

In 1981, Bernard W. Rowland filed a civil rights complaint against his employer for unlawful discrimination in terminating his employment. The Civil Rights Commission held in favor of Rowland and ordered the employer to pay him $65,377, less appropriate deductions for federal and state income taxes and social security. It further ordered that attorney fees and interest be paid by the employer. On April 26, 1989, following appeals, the employer filed a satisfaction of judgment and deposited money for payment of the judgment with the clerk of the district court. It is agreed by the parties that the tax withholdings amounted to $19,838 and that the net back-pay award plus interest amounted to $80,248.

In independent actions, Willow Tree Investment Co. (Willow Tree) obtained judgments against Rowland in state and federal courts. It caused a writ of execution to be issued and garnished the clerk of court for the funds held on behalf of Rowland for back pay and interest. On June 9, 1989, Rowland received notice of the garnishment and promptly resisted, claiming that the funds deposited for back pay and interest were personal earnings which fell within the exemption contained in section 642.21. The district court allowed the garnishment.

* * * *

I. Earnings. Throughout this appeal the underlying issue is whether the civil rights award of back pay qualifies as earnings that fall within the exemption in section 642.21. This section defines "earnings" as "compensation paid or payable for personal services, whether denominated as wages, salary, commission, bonus or otherwise. . . ." The district court relied upon federal cases interpreting the federal Consumer Credit Protection Act and upon language in *MidAmerica Savings Bank v. Miehe* in concluding that the purpose of this legislation is to facilitate an employee's payment of living expenses and support. We agree with this broad assertion of purpose, but cannot agree with the district court's next conclusion.

The district court concluded that the legislature did not intend an amount subsequently received for back pay to be exempt earnings. It reasoned that the back pay was received too late to allow an employee to apply it toward day-to-day living expenses incurred during the time period when the back wages were earned. This conclusion ignores the fact that Rowland had living expenses during the period he was wrongfully unemployed. Exemption laws are to be liberally construed to allow debtors and their families assurance that necessary living expenses can be covered. Rowland should be in a position to use the judgment in his favor to replenish the source from which his living expenses were paid during the period he was deprived of earnings. In other words, a judgment creditor should not gain an advantage caused by the wrongful acts of an employer.

Willow Tree urges that the underlying intent of the exemption section is to provide a continuing means of support for a debtor. Willow Tree emphasizes that the Supreme Court found that the legislative intent behind passage of the federal Consumer Credit Protection Act was to prevent personal bankruptcy filings, to preserve a debtor's employment, and to provide an ongoing means of support for a debtor and his family. We concede that one of the purposes of the federal Act is to ensure a continued means of support for the debtor. In this case, however, the exemption is derived from the additional protection given the debtor under state law. Our state law determines the amount of the exemption on the basis of an individual's expected annual income. This method of annual calculation is less attuned to provide a continued means of support for a debtor than the federal Act, which calculates the amount of disposable income that can be garnished on a weekly basis.

* * * Consideration of the relevant Iowa legislation as a whole demands a broader view than the trial court's narrow focus upon an exemption that is conditioned only on the payment of current living expenses. We believe the more appropriate focus should be upon the true nature of the award in question to determine if it falls within the term "earnings" as defined in section 642.21. A civil rights award is unlike a damage award in a typical contract or tort action. The underlying purpose of allowing damages in a civil rights award is compensation for the injury sustained. In civil rights actions, the legislature gave the courts power to provide a wide variety of relief, most of which is equitable in nature. In unfair employment practices remedial action includes "[h]iring, reinstatement or upgrading of employees with or without pay. . . ." Although part of a civil rights award may be compensation, the real purpose behind a civil rights award is to make the person whole for an injury suffered as a result of unlawful employment discrimination.

In this case, the award not only allowed back pay, but also required the employer to pay the tax withholdings to place the employee in the same position he would have occupied if the wages were received during the period of wrongful discharge. Under these circumstances, we conclude that the judgment entered in Rowland's favor for back pay is an award of earnings paid for personal services as defined in subsection 642.21(3)(a).

Willow Tree * * * claims that Rowland's award of back wages was extinguished and replaced by a judgment debt. Thus, it urges that the back-pay award lost its character as wages and may be garnished as any other judgment. It cites *Stephen O. Cook v. Valentine W. Holbrook* for the proposition that a claim for wages merges into a judgment and becomes a separate and distinct debt losing its character as wages. It also argues that our language in *Chader v. Wilkins* supports the proposition that a judgment is a debt regardless of the nature of the original cause of action.

We cannot agree that the entry of a judgment for back pay resulted in Rowland's losing the exemption provided in section 642.21. *Cook* is distinguishable from this case because the creditor sought to garnish a fund arising from a judgment that was held by an attorney. Likewise, our decision in *Chader* is not controlling. The language in *Chader* does not persuade us to determine that a judgment extinguishes the entire character of the original claim. More important, we believe that stronger authority can be found in those cases holding that an employee's wages remain exempt when he sues an employer and recovers a judgment. We believe that these cases are more consistent with the purposes of Iowa's exemption and civil rights statutes.

* * * *

Willow Tree also urges that time has destroyed the exempt character of the wages. It cites our decision in *Miehe* for authority that the exemption only lasts for a ninety-day period after the wages are paid if the wages can be traced to a checking or savings account in a financial institution. In this case, the funds have not been transferred to Rowland nor has he exercised any control over the funds. He has not been permitted ''a reasonable opportunity to negotiate the paycheck [earnings represented by the judgment] and spend the fund.'' Under these circumstances it would be premature to establish a ninety-day limit as we did in *Miehe*.

II. Interest.   We address Rowland's claim that he is entitled to an exemption in the interest due on the judgment for back pay wages. He urges that the interest should be construed as ''earnings'' for the purposes of section 642.21. We do not agree. Interest is allowed for the use of money or as damages for its detention. We hold that the interest is not exempt under section 642.21.

III. Conclusion.   In summary, we hold that the amount of Rowland's judgment against his employer for back pay is exempt earnings under section 642.21, but that the amount awarded for interest on the judgment is not exempt. We remand for the district court to determine the amount of the exemption and render judgment accordingly.

AFFIRMED IN PART AND REVERSED IN PART.

———————

Case A.13

WITHERS v. TIMBER PRODUCTS, INC.

Court of Appeal of Louisiana, Third Circuit, 1991.
574 So.2d 1291.

GUIDRY, Judge.
    * * * *

Plaintiff, James D. Withers, a truck driver, was injured May 21, 1986, as he attempted to dismount from a front end loader at the Timber Products, Inc. sawmill near Provencal, Louisiana. According to Withers, as he was dismounting from the front end loader, his pants leg snagged on a brake lever, causing him to fall, injuring his back. The accident allegedly took place at approximately 1:30 a.m. with no wit-

nesses present. The record reflects that Withers finished his deliveries early that same morning, but has not worked since. Plaintiff testified that he notified Larry Davis, the mill superintendent, of his accident just before the mill opened on the morning of May 21, 1986. * * *

Following Timber Products' rejection of a worker's compensation recommendation from the State Department of Labor, suit was timely filed against that corporation. By supplemental and amending petition, John Makar, appellant, was added as a defendant. In his supplemental and amending petition, plaintiff alleged that Timber Products was the alter ego [second self] of Makar and prayed for judgment against Makar. * * *

* * * *

Appellant argues that plaintiff, a trucker engaged by Timber Products to haul chips, was an independent contractor and thus Timber Products and John Makar are not liable to him for the payment of worker's compensation benefits.

Withers hauled wood chips from the Timber Products mill to a purchaser designated by Timber Products. The record reflects that Timber Products had the right to control and supervise the hauling and exercised the right to direct when and to whom the wood chips were to be hauled. While plaintiff supplied and paid the expenses of the truck used, the price per ton paid to him took into account the mileage involved in making delivery. Plaintiff was required to load his own truck but always used a front end loader supplied by Timber Products.

* * * The record in this case reveals no clear error in the trial court's conclusion that Withers was an employee of Timber Products and not an independent contractor.

* * *

Plaintiff was injured on May 21, 1986. He first consulted Dr. John P. Sandifer, an orthopaedic surgeon, the next day. Dr. Sandifer found muscle spasms in plaintiff's back and, because of complaints of accompanying leg pain, suspected a herniated disc. X-rays supported the doctor's suspicions. Plaintiff's symptoms worsened and Dr. Sandifer hospitalized Withers for five to six days beginning May 27, 1986. During that period of time, plaintiff showed some improvement and Dr. Sandifer discharged him to continue conservative treatment.* * *

* * * *

It is well settled that the testimony of an injured employee alone can establish the occurrence of a compensable accident by a preponderance of the evidence if his testimony is supported by corroborating circumstances. * * * A plaintiff may prove his claim by presenting his own uncontradicted testimony that establishes a presumption that he suffered a disability as a result of a work accident. If defendant fails to produce any direct evidence to rebut it, then plaintiff is entitled to compensation. * * * In the instant case, Withers' testimony was uncontradicted and unrebutted. His testimony was corroborated by that of his treating physician, who initially saw him on the day following the accident. Accordingly, we find that plaintiff proved his injury, his continuing inability to work and his entitlement to compensation. * * *

* * * *

Makar contends that the trial court erred in finding Timber Products to be his alter ego and in piercing the corporate veil.

Makar admitted that he formed Timber Products a few weeks after foreclosing on Mak-Wee and that he was the sole stockholder and officer at the time of incorporation. In his reasons for judgment, the trial judge observed: ''Mr. Makar testified that, shortly after incorporating the business as Timber Products, Inc., he 'swapped' one hundred percent (100%) of the stock of Timber Products, Inc. to John J. Johnson, III, of Winnfield, Louisiana, for some property in Winnfield. Mr. Johnson is alleged to be judgment proof and to have no assets and no source of business income. Mr. Makar testified that he swapped all of the stock in Timber Products, Inc. for Mr. Johnson's non-revenue producing property as an 'investment.' At the trial of this case, Mr. Makar admitted that there was no Worker's Compensation Insurance in effect covering anyone working for Timber Products, Inc. and testified that the business was not insured because 'it was a calculated risk that no one would get hurt. If someone got hurt and the business was doing good, they got paid. If someone got hurt and the business was not doing good, then they got nothing.' Mr. Johnson, as stated above, lived in Winnfield, some forty-five (45) miles east of the chip mill operated by Timber Products, Inc. Mr. Johnson testified that, although he ostensibly owned one hundred percent of the stock of Timber Products, Inc.; that he had never been to the mill site; had never met or talked to the mill superintendent; did not keep up with the financial operation of the mill; could not say whether or not federal or state income tax returns had been filed or paid; did not know how many employees worked for Timber Products, Inc.; and had no idea of who was being paid what. Mr. Johnson candidly admitted that he had served two felony sentences with the Louisiana Department of Corrections and was a two-time felony offender. He further testified that he was 'judgment proof.' The Court finds that Timber Products, Inc. was located in the precise site of Mr. Makar's previous corporation known as Mak-Wee; the same equipment was being used; the same superintendent, Larry Davis, was in charge of operations.''

It was established that Makar had authority to sign Timber Products checks, but Johnson did not. Further, no evidence of the alleged transfer from Makar to Johnson was made part of the record.

* * * In a few limited situations a party can reach an individual shareholder by "piercing the corporate veil," making the individual liable for debts incurred by the corporation. This can be done when a shareholder practices fraud upon a third person through the corporation or disregards the corporate entity to such an extent that the individualities of the corporation and shareholder cease to exist; the corporation no longer exists as an individual distinguishable from the shareholder. When a party seeks to pierce the corporate veil, the situation must be viewed with regard to the totality of the circumstances. Whether individual liability will be assigned to shareholders is primarily a factual finding to be made by the trial court. In Louisiana the concept of the corporation as a separate entity is felt to be beneficial and is disregarded only in exceptional circumstances. * * *

After closely examining the record, we cannot say that the trial judge clearly erred in finding Timber Products to be the alter ego of defendant, Makar. Inasmuch as we have reached this conclusion, it follows that timely institution of suit and service of process on Timber Products clearly notified Makar of the instant litigation and interrupted prescription against him, individually. Accordingly, the exception of prescription filed by Makar was properly overruled.

* * * *

In this case, it is undisputed that Timber Products had no worker's compensation coverage. The trial judge found that the alleged "transfer" of Timber Products stock to John Johnson was nothing more than a sham transfer in an attempt by Makar to avoid exposure for worker's compensation liability. This being the case, the trial judge's obvious conclusion, that Timber Products' failure to pay plaintiff worker's compensation was arbitrary and capricious, is not clearly wrong. Penalties and attorney's fees were properly assessed.

Accordingly, for the reasons stated, we amend the judgment of the trial court to find plaintiff, John D. Withers, to be temporarily, totally disabled. In all other respects, we affirm the judgment of the trial court. All costs of this appeal are taxed against defendant-appellant, John Makar.

AFFIRMED AS AMENDED.

Case A.14

MASCHMEIER v. SOUTHSIDE PRESS, LTD.
Court of Appeals of Iowa, 1989.
435 N.W.2d 377.

HABHAB, Judge.

Defendant Kenneth E. Maschmeier and Charlotte A. Maschmeier created a corporation, Southside Press, Ltd., that did business at 1220 Second Avenue North in Council Bluffs. This building is owned by Kenneth and Charlotte and was leased by them to the corporation.

Kenneth and Charlotte are the majority shareholders, with each having 1300 shares. They are the only officers and directors of the corporation.

They gifted to their two sons [Marty and Larry] each 1200 shares of stock. All the parties were employed by Southside Press until the summer of 1985 when, because of family disagreements, Marty and Larry were terminated as employees. * * *

The parents on August 2, 1985, created a new corporation, Southside Press of the Midlands, Ltd. They are its only officers and directors. As individuals they terminated the lease of their building * * * with Southside and leased the same premises to Midlands. In addition, Kenneth, as president of Southside, entered into a lease with himself as president of Midlands whereby the printing equipment and two of the vehicles were leased to Midlands for $22,372 per year for five years, with an option to buy such assets at the end of the lease term at their fair market value but not to exceed $20,000. In addition, the inventory and two other vehicles owned by Southside were sold by it to Midlands. Notwithstanding the fact that a substantial part of the assets of Southside had been disposed of, the parents still received an annual salary from it of more than $20,000.

After Marty and Larry's employment with Southside had terminated, each obtained employment with other printing companies in the same metropolitan area. The family disagreement continued. All stockholders were employed by companies that were competitive to Southside. Ultimately, the parents, as majority shareholders, offered to buy the sons' shares of stock for $20 per share. Their sons felt that this amount was inadequate. Thus, this lawsuit.

In 1985, Southside Press had gross sales of more than $600,000. The trial court found that in 1985 the corporate assets had a fair market value of $160,745. Shareholders' equity was found to be $236,502.92, and divided by the number of shares equals $47.30 per share. The court found that the majority shareholders had been abusive and oppressive to the minority shareholders by wasting the corporate assets and leaving Southside Press only a shell of a corporation. The court ordered the majority shareholders to pay $47.30 per share to the sons, or $56,760 to each son, plus interest at the maximum legal rate from the date of the filing of the petition.

 *   *   *   *

 *   *   * [D]efendants state that the shares were valued at $20 pursuant to the corporate bylaws and should be enforced as an agreement of the shareholders. *   *   *

 *   *   *   *

Whenever a situation exists which is contrary to the principles of equity and which can be redressed within the scope of judicial action, a court of equity will devise a remedy to meet the situation though no similar relief has been granted before. The district court has the power to liquidate a corporation under [Iowa Code] section 496A.94(1). This statute also allows the district court to fashion other equitable relief.

It is contended that, in order for the trial court to have properly invoked the powers under section 496A.94(1), it had to find either the majority shareholders were oppressive in their conduct towards the minority shareholders, or that the majority shareholders misapplied or wasted corporate assets.

 *   *   * The alleged oppressive conduct by those in control of a close corporation must be analyzed in terms of "fiduciary duties" owed by majority shareholders to the minority shareholders and "reasonable expectations" held by minority shareholders in committing capital and labor to the particular enterprise, in light of the predicament in which minority shareholders in a close corporation can be placed by a "freeze-out" situation.

 *   *   * The trial court found *   *   * here [that] the majority shareholders attempted to "freeze out" or "squeeze out" the minority shareholders by terminating their employment and not permitting them to participate in the business.

 *   *   *   *

We concur with the trial court's findings that the majority shareholders acted oppressively toward the minority shareholders and wasted corporate assets. In

this respect, we further determine that the trial court properly invoked Iowa Code section 496A.94 when it fashioned the remedy requiring the majority shareholders to purchase the shares of the minority.

But that does not resolve the problem, for as stated above *   *   * [t]he appellant challenges the method fashioned by the trial court in fixing the value of the stock and payment thereof by asserting it should be governed by the bylaws.

The articles of incorporation of Southside vested in the directors of the corporation the "authority to make provisions in the Bylaws of the corporation restricting the transfer of shares of this corporation." This the board of directors did when they adopted the following bylaw that relates to restrictions on the transferability of stock. *   *   *

 *   *   *   *

Section 3 [of the corporate bylaws] is a restriction on stock transfer. If a shareholder intends to sell his stock, he must first offer it to the corporation at a price "agreed upon by the shareholders at each annual meeting." The shareholders must agree on the value of the stock and if they are unable to do so, each has a right to select an appraiser and the appraisers shall appoint another and in this instance the five appraisers are to act as a Board of Appraisers to value the stock.

 *   *   * Since none of the shareholders requested appraisers, we deem this, as the trial court did, to be a waiver. We concur with this statement from the trial court's ruling: "All parties have left the Court with the burden of evaluating the corporate stock."

 *   *   *   *

We agree with the defendants that a contractual formula price is enforceable even if the formula price is less than its fair market value. But here the parties were unable to agree to a price, i.e., at the last meeting of the stockholders. Thus the trial court was called upon to do so.

Courts have generally held that no one factor governs the valuation of shares; but that all factors, such as market value, asset value, future earning prospects, should be considered. In this case, the parties relied rather heavily on what is referred to in the record as book value (shareholders' equity) in arriving at stock value. The trial court likewise used shareholder equity but adjusted that amount by the present day fair market value of corporate assets.

 *   *   *   *

We determine that under the circumstances here the valuation per share as fixed by the trial court and the method it employed in arriving at value is fair and reasonable. However, we further conclude that the amount Larry and Marty are to receive must be re-duced by the total amount of loans made to them as they appear on the corporate books.

*   *   *   *

WE AFFIRM AND MODIFY.

Case A.15

GREEN v. SHELL OIL CO.

Court of Appeals of Michigan, 1989.
181 Mich.App. 439,
450 N.W.2d 50.

FITZGERALD, Justice.

*   *   *   *

At approximately 6:00 P.M. on December 21, 1981, plaintiff drove into a Shell service station owned and operated by defendant Lanford and leased from defendant Shell Oil Company. Plaintiff filled his gas tank and, as he walked from the self-service island to the station's office to pay for the gasoline, was struck by a slow-moving vehicle plaintiff alleges was driven by Monica Gottwald. Plaintiff slapped the hood of the vehicle with his hand and yelled for Gottwald to stop and to be more careful. Immediately thereafter, Leslie Salgado, an occupant of the Gottwald vehicle and employee of the station, exited from the vehicle and began striking plaintiff. An un-identified station attendant joined Salgado in his attack on plaintiff.

On January 2, 1982, plaintiff filed a complaint in Oakland Circuit Court against defendants and Sal-gado, as well as others no longer parties to the instant action, alleging [among other things] vicarious lia-bility [indirect liability] of defendants for *   *   * assault and battery and negligence by defendants in failing to provide a safe place for doing business. The case was remanded to district court after mediation.

Defendants moved for and were granted summary disposition. The district court held that defendants could not be held liable for an intentional tort com-mitted by the service station attendant. The court also held that the attendant owed no duty to stop an assault by a third party. *   *   *

Plaintiff appealed *   *   * to circuit court. The circuit court reversed the district court's grant of sum-mary disposition *   *   *.

*   *   *   *

We believe that *   *   * defendant Lanford's employees were in a position to control the unruly situation, to eject the instigator from the premises and to refrain from increasing plaintiff's injuries. On these facts, a jury could find that defendant Lanford failed to exercise reasonable care for his invitees' protection.

The question *   *   * becomes whether Shell Oil had apparent authority over the service station so as to make it liable for the assault on plaintiff. In *Johnston v. American Oil Co.*, the plaintiff's decedent was shot during an altercation with the proprietor of a Standard service station, who refused to serve him and his companions. The trial court granted defendant American Oil Company's summary judgment motion based on the proprietor's status as an independent contractor. The plaintiff had pointed to the service station's use of American Oil's trademark and its sale of supplies and products obtained from American Oil. On appeal, the panel concluded:

> American Oil's national advertising campaign promoting the Standard Oil name and products, in-cluding the slogans "As you travel ask us" and "You expect more from Standard and you get it," would seem to raise a sufficient question of fact as to the existence of agency by estoppel or by apparent au-thority to defeat the granting of summary judgment.
>
> *   *   *   *
>
> We believe the trial court herein likewise erred in grant-ing the motion for summary judgment. The question, of course, is not whether Murphy is, in fact, an agent of American Oil, the question is whether plaintiff has raised a material issue of fact that requires further proofs before the finding of fact. Here plaintiff has carried that burden.

In his affidavit [a written or printed statement con-firmed by oath or affirmation], plaintiff stated:

> I always assumed that a Shell gas station was op-erated by Shell Oil. I cannot state whether I ever ac-tually considered whether the operators of gas stations have an ownership interest in the business or not, but it was my belief at the time of the assault upon me, and prior, that Shell Oil either owned the facilities and operated them directly, or exercised active control over

the operations of the gas station so as to ensure uniform standards of quality, reliability and conduct of the employees at the stations.

According to defendants, Shell Oil exercised no control over the hiring, firing and supervision of the service station employees and had no authority over the supervision, management and control of the station. In addition, defendant Lanford was not required to purchase any parts from Shell Oil. As defendants state on appeal, ''the most that can be said is that '[Wayne Lanford] displayed [Shell's] brand signs, that he honored [Shell's] credit cards, [and that Shell's] agents from time to time made suggestions as to operation of the station.' ''

In light of the foregoing, we cannot say with any degree of certainty that further factual development of plaintiff's theory of apparent authority would be futile. Accordingly, we believe that plaintiff should be given the opportunity to show that Shell Oil had apparent authority over defendant Lanford's employees.

Defendants also argue that they cannot be held vicariously liable for the attendant's participation in the assault. We agree.

An employer is liable for the intentional tort of his employee if the tort is committed in the course and within the scope of the employment. An employer is not liable if the employee's tortious act is committed while the employee is working for the employer but the act is outside his authority, ''as where he steps aside from his employment to gratify some personal animosity or to accomplish some purpose of his own.''

An employer's liability may also be based upon a finding that the employee acted within the scope or apparent scope of his employment. Generally, the trier of fact determines whether an employee was acting within the scope or apparent scope of his employment. Summary disposition is appropriate, however, where it is apparent that the employee is acting to accomplish a purpose of his own.

Plaintiff testified at a deposition that Salgado struck him on the left side of the head. Plaintiff fell to the ground, dazed by the blow. The next thing he remembered was being kicked, while laying on the ground, by a man in a brown uniform, allegedly the unidentified station attendant. On this testimony, we conclude that the attendant's violent conduct was engaged in for the purpose of assisting Salgado and not for any purpose in furtherance of the employer's business interests. This is not a situation where the employee was attempting to collect plaintiff's payment on behalf of his employer. Nor is it a situation where the attendant's conduct can be reasonably construed as an attempt to end the altercation or eject plaintiff from the employer's establishment in order to restore order. Accordingly, summary disposition on plaintiff's vicarious liability claim was appropriate. The attendant's action could only be construed as an attempt to accomplish his own purpose, not to further his employer's business interests.

* * * *

WE AFFIRM IN PART, REVERSE IN PART AND REMAND. ————————

———————————————————

Case A.16

TEAMSTERS LOCAL UNION NO. 639 v. NLRB

United States Court of Appeals, District of Columbia Circuit, 1991.
924 F.2d 1078.

HENDERSON, Circuit Judge.
* * * *

The Association of D.C. Liquor Wholesalers (the Association) is an organization composed of three businesses that sell wine and liquor in the District of Columbia. One of the Association's functions is to represent its members in negotiating and administer-

ing collective bargaining agreements with the various labor unions that represent the members' employees. In early 1987, the Association entered negotiations with Local 639 of the Teamsters Union (the Union), which represented the Association members' drivers, warehousemen and helpers. * * *

The parties began bargaining for the new contract on January 21, 1987, with Ronald Ross serving as the Union's primary representative and Ronald Tisch bargaining for the Association. * * * The Association sought to reduce its labor-related costs, including its legal aid contributions and contributions to the employees' health and pension plans. Throughout the negotiations, marked disagreement existed between the parties on the questions of the two-tier wage system and the caseload-helper limit. * * *

* * * *

Finally, the Union negotiator informed the Association representative that, at that time, the Union would make no better offer. On learning that the Union planned to offer no further concessions, Tisch, the Association negotiator, declared that the parties had reached impasse. Ross, the Union negotiator, immediately disagreed with the declaration of impasse and accused the Association of "trying to bust the Union." He also stated his intention to seek strike authorization at the Union meeting the next day.

* * * *

Over the weekend following this final bargaining session, the Union membership authorized a strike, but Union officials instructed the members to report for work at the regular time on Monday morning. After the strike vote, Ross and the Union president contacted Tisch in an attempt to resume negotiations. * * * Tisch refused to meet with the Union representatives for further negotiations.

When the employees attempted to report for work on Monday, their employers read them the following statement: "Your contract has expired. There is no agreement between the Union and management on a new contract. No contract, no work. You are locked out." The Association members continued operations with the replacement employees for whom they had arranged earlier. At the federal mediator's urging, the parties met again on March 26. When the meeting began, the Union served Association negotiator Tisch with unfair labor practice charges. The parties argued and the Association negotiators walked out. By letters dated March 27 and June 23, the Union again sought to resume negotiations. The Association refused to respond to either of these overtures.

The Administrative Law Judge (ALJ) concluded that the parties' negotiations had not reached impasse when the Association terminated negotiations on February 27. The finding of no valid impasse proceeded from the ALJ's conclusion that the Association had acted in bad faith during the negotiations: it "entered bargaining in an appraisal of what the Union probably would not ultimately accept and appears to have formulated its position accordingly." * * * Having concluded that the parties had not reached impasse, the ALJ determined that the Association's refusal to bargain after February 27 violated * * * the Na-

tional Labor Relations Act (the Act). * * * Finally, the ALJ concluded that the lockout was an attempt to coerce the Union to accept the Association's unlawfully implemented final offer. * * *

On review, the Board affirmed the ALJ's decision although it rejected the ALJ's "suggesti[on]" that the Association had acted in bad faith throughout the negotiations. Nevertheless, it concluded that, on February 27, the Association had formulated its wage proposals "specifically to avoid its obligation to bargain in good faith." * * *

Having found no impasse, the Board ruled that the Association's refusal to negotiate after February 27 and its unilateral implementation of its final offer violated * * * the Act. It further agreed with the ALJ that the lockout and replacement of employees violated [the Act]. The Board ordered the Association to recognize and bargain with the Union and ordered the employers to offer reinstatement and back pay to all employees terminated as a result of the lockout. These petitions for review followed.

A bargaining impasse is "the deadlock reached by bargaining parties 'after good-faith negotiations have exhausted the prospects of concluding an agreement.' " * * * In the absence of impasse, a party refusing to negotiate on a mandatory bargaining topic violates section * * * of the Act. * * *

* * * *

In determining whether parties have exhausted the possibilities of agreement, the Board has "no fixed definition of an impasse . . . which can be applied mechanically to all factual situations." * * * It considers a number of factors, including the "bargaining history, the good faith of the parties in negotiations, the length of the negotiations, the importance of the issue or issues as to which there is disagreement, [and] the contemporaneous understanding of the parties as to the state of negotiations. * * * Our review of the record reveals substantial evidence of at least two of these factors to support the Board's finding of no impasse.

First, we find support for the Board's conclusion regarding the length of the parties' negotiations on wages. By the time the Association declared impasse, the parties had met twelve times over the course of a month; however, they had agreed to postpone any discussion of wages until the final session. * * * The fact that the wage negotiations lasted only one day supports the Board's conclusion that the parties had had an inadequate opportunity to "fully explore and negotiate [the Association's] finally revealed full hard core economic position.''

The Association would have us hold that, although the parties bargained only for one day on the issue of wages, the negotiations were nonetheless deadlocked because the parties had bargained at length—and unsuccessfully—over other economic issues like the two-tier wage system and the caseload-helper limit. Because all labor-related expenses ''come out of the same pot,'' the Association insists that the parties had reached a bona fide impasse in that several economic issues remained unresolved at the time the Association declared impasse. To accept this argument, however, would negate the deference we are required to extend to the Board's findings of fact. * * *

The last of the Taft factors—the ''contemporaneous [at the same time] understanding of the parties as to the state of negotiations,'' * * * also supports a finding of no impasse. If either negotiating party remains willing to move further toward an agreement, an impasse cannot exist: the parties' perception regarding the progress of the negotiations is of central importance to the Board's impasse inquiry. * * * Both the ALJ and the Board found that, immediately after the Association negotiator declared impasse, Ross, the Union negotiator, ''strongly disagreed'' with that characterization of the negotiations. * * * They further found that Ross stated he had more movement to make. * * * These Union protestations manifest that one party did not view the negotiations as having reached impasse; they provide substantial evidence to support the Board's finding of no impasse and we therefore decline to disturb it. * * * *

Once we have determined that the Board's finding of no impasse rests on substantial record evidence, few questions remain regarding the Association's petition for review. * * * Because the parties did not reach impasse on February 27, we uphold the Board's ruling that the Association's refusal to participate in further negotiations and its unilateral implementation of its final offer violated * * * of the Act.

We also uphold the Board's conclusion that the Association violated the Act when it locked out and replaced its employees. When an employer locks out its employees for the purpose of evading its duty to negotiate with the employees' bargaining representative, the employer violates * * * of the Act. * * * In the case of a ''bargaining'' lockout, however, the lockout, to be permissible, must be for the ''sole purpose of bringing economic pressure to bear in support of [the employer's] legitimate bargaining position.'' * * * Here, the Association employers' lockout and replacement of their employees does not meet this standard. The employers locked out their employees in an attempt to coerce the Union to accept the Association's unilaterally implemented final offer. * * *

The collective bargaining agreement that expired on February 28, 1987, provided for a Union hiring hall. The Union contends that the Association employers violated the Act by hiring replacement employees from outside the hiring hall. By way of remedy, the Union asks us to modify the Board's order to award back pay to those individuals who would have been hired from the hiring hall had the Association employers not obtained their replacement employees elsewhere.

* * * *

In sum, we uphold the Board's ruling that the Association employers' declaration of impasse, their refusal to bargain with the Union and their subsequent lockout and replacement of their employees violated the National Labor Relations Act. We further approve the remedial provisions of the Board's order and decline to modify it as the Union asks us to do. Because we deny both petitions for review, we direct that the Board's order be

ENFORCED.

Case A.17

JOHNSTON v. DEL MAR DISTRIBUTING CO.

Court of Appeals of Texas—Corpus Christi, 1989.
776 S.W.2d 768.

BENAVIDES, Justice.

Nancy Johnston, appellant, brought suit against her employer, Del Mar Distributing Co., Inc., alleging that her employment had been wrongfully terminated. Del Mar filed a motion for summary judgment in the trial court alleging that appellant's pleadings failed to state a cause of action. After a hearing on the motion, the trial court agreed with Del Mar and granted its motion for summary judgment.

* * * *

In her petition, appellant alleged that she was employed by Del Mar during the summer of 1987. As a part of her duties, she was required to prepare shipping documents for goods being sent from Del Mar's warehouse located in Corpus Christi, Texas to other cities in Texas. One day, Del Mar instructed appellant to package a semi-automatic weapon (for delivery to a grocery store in Brownsville, Texas) and to label the contents of the package as "fishing gear." Ultimately, the package was to be given to United Parcel Service for shipping. Appellant was required to sign her name to the shipping documents; therefore, she was concerned that her actions might be in violation of some firearm regulation or a regulation of the United Postal Service. Accordingly, she sought the advice of the United States Treasury Department Bureau of Alcohol, Tobacco & Firearms * * *. A few days after she contacted the Bureau, appellant was fired. Appellant brought suit for wrongful termination alleging that her employment was terminated solely in retaliation for contacting the Bureau.

* * * *

Del Mar asserted in its motion that, notwithstanding the above described facts, appellant's cause of action was barred by the employment-at-will doctrine. Specifically, Del Mar asserted that since appellant's employment was for an indefinite amount of time, she was an employee-at-will and it had the absolute right to terminate her employment for any reason or no reason at all.

It is well-settled that Texas adheres to the traditional employment-at-will doctrine. The Texas Supreme Court [has] held that absent a specific contractual provision to the contrary, either the employer or the employee may terminate their relationship at any time, for any reason.

Today, the absolute employment-at-will doctrine is increasingly seen as a "relic of early industrial times" and a "harsh anachronism." Accordingly, our Legislature has enacted some exceptions to this doctrine * * *.

Recently, the Texas Supreme Court, recognizing the need to amend the employment-at-will doctrine, invoked its judicial authority to create a very narrow common law exception to the doctrine. In [*Sabine Pilot Service, Inc. v. Hauck*] the Texas Supreme Court was faced with a narrow issue for consideration,

i.e., whether an allegation by an employee that he or she was discharged for refusing to perform an illegal act stated a cause of action. The Court held that

> public policy, as expressed in the laws of this state and the United States which carry criminal penalties, requires a very narrow exception to the employment-at-will doctrine * * * [t]hat narrow exception covers only the discharge of an employee for the sole reason that the employee refused to perform an illegal act.

Justice Kilgarlin noted in his concurring opinion to *Sabine Pilot* that it is against public policy to allow an employer "to require an employee to break a law or face termination. . . ." He elaborated that to hold otherwise "would promote a thorough disrespect for the laws and legal institutions of our society."

* * * *

On appeal, appellant alleges that her petition did state a cause of action pursuant to the public policy exception announced in *Sabine Pilot*. In her brief, appellant contends that since Texas law currently provides that an employee has a cause of action when she is fired for refusing to perform an illegal act, it necessarily follows that an employee states a cause of action where she alleges that she is fired for simply inquiring into whether or not she is committing illegal acts. To hold otherwise, she argues, would have a chilling [inhibiting, discouraging] effect on the public policy exception announced in *Sabine Pilot*. We agree.

It is implicit that in order to refuse to do an illegal act, an employee must either know or suspect that the requested act is illegal. In some cases it will be patently obvious that the act is illegal (murder, robbery, theft, etc.); however, in other cases it may not be so apparent. Since ignorance of the law is no defense to a criminal prosecution, it is reasonable to expect that if an employee has a good faith belief that a required act might be illegal, she will try to find out whether the act is in fact illegal prior to deciding what course of action to take. If an employer is allowed to terminate the employee at this point, the public policy exception announced in *Sabine Pilot* would have little or no effect. To hold otherwise would force an employee, who suspects that a requested act might be illegal, to (1) subject herself to possible discharge if she attempts to find out if the act is in fact illegal; or (2) remain ignorant, perform the act and, if it turns out to be illegal, face possible criminal sanctions.

We hold that since the law recognizes that it is against public policy to allow an employer to coerce its employee to commit a criminal act in furtherance of its own interest, then it is necessarily inferred that the same public policy prohibits the discharge of an employee who in good faith attempts to find out if the act is illegal. It is important to note that we are not creating a new exception to the employment-at-will doctrine. Rather, we are merely enforcing the narrow public policy exception which was created in *Sabine Pilot.*

* * * *

Furthermore, it is the opinion of this Court that the question of whether or not the requested act was in fact illegal is irrelevant to the determination of this case. We hold that where a plaintiff's employment is terminated for attempting to find out from a regulatory agency if a requested act is illegal, it is not necessary to prove that the requested act was in fact illegal. A plaintiff must, however, establish that she had a good faith belief that the requested act might be illegal, and that such belief was reasonable. * * *

* * * *

The judgment of the trial court is REVERSED and REMANDED for trial.

Case A.18

ROBERTS v. WALMART STORES, INC.
United States District Court, E.D. Missouri, 1990.
736 F.Supp. 1527.

LIMBAUGH, District Judge.

Plaintiffs are black citizens of the United States. Defendant is a retail department store. On December 5, 1989 plaintiffs were customers at a store operated by defendant in St. Charles, Missouri. During this visit plaintiffs purchased several items and presented defendant with a check in payment for the merchandise. Defendant recorded the race of plaintiffs on the check. Plaintiffs, upon becoming aware that their race was being recorded on the check, returned the merchandise and retrieved the check. Plaintiffs then filed a two-count amended complaint against defendant alleging that defendant's practice of recording the race of black citizens who pay for merchandise by check violates the Thirteenth Amendment. * * *

The Thirteenth Amendment is implicated when it is alleged that a private individual or entity deliberately acted in a way to segregate, humiliate or belittle a person of the black race in a way that prevented such a person from freely exercising a right guaranteed to all citizens. * * * Plaintiffs may not maintain a cause of action against defendant, a private corporation, directly under the Thirteenth Amendment. Instead, plaintiffs must base their claims on one of the implementing statutes of the Thirteenth Amendment. * * *

* * * *

Defendant asserts that its recording the race of the plaintiffs on the check is post-formation conduct which is no longer actionable. * * * After *Patterson* the resolution of this civil rights claim turns on an interpretation of the Missouri Commercial Code to determine whether the contract was formed at the time the alleged violation occurred. The Court does not possess enough information about the retail transaction to ascertain whether a contract was already formed at the time defendant recorded the race of plaintiffs on the check. Therefore, defendant's motion to dismiss plaintiffs' claim * * * is denied.

* * * *

First, defendant asserts that plaintiffs have failed to plead that blacks were treated any differently than whites. Although plaintiffs did not plead that whites purchasing merchandise by check do not have their race recorded on their check, plaintiffs' complaint should not be dismissed unless it appears that plaintiffs could "prove no set of facts in support of the claim which would entitle them to relief." * * *

Second, defendant asserts that plaintiffs failed to plead a cause of action *₁ * * because plaintiffs were able to purchase the merchandise with the check. Therefore, although defendant recorded plaintiffs' race on the check, no civil rights violation occurred because defendant did not refuse to sell plaintiffs the merchandise due to their race. * * * Although defendant was willing to consummate the retail transaction with plaintiffs, defendant is not absolved from liability * * * if defendant's motives in recording the race of plaintiffs was infected with racial discrimination. * * *

* * * *

There is no authority for plaintiffs' argument that payment by check, absent an agreement by the seller to hold the check for a period of time before presentment to the drawee, constitutes an extension of credit rather than a cash transaction. * * *

* * * *

Defendant seeks for the Court to require plaintiffs to file a second amended complaint because "plaintiffs' amended complaint is so vague and ambiguous that defendant cannot reasonably be required to frame a responsive pleading." * * * The Court has reviewed plaintiffs' amended complaint and concludes that plaintiffs' allegations are clear and plain and are undoubtedly sufficient to satisfy the requirements of notice pleading * * *.

[The district court granted defendant's motion to dismiss in part and denied defendant's motion to dismiss in part.]

Case A.19

LOUISIANA-PACIFIC CORPORATION v. ASARCO, INC.

United States Court of Appeals, Ninth Circuit, 1990.
909 F.2d 1260.

WRIGHT, Circuit Judge.

* * * *

For almost 80 years, Asarco had a copper smelter at Ruston, Washington. As part of its operations, it produced a by-product called "slag," a hard rock-like substance. IMP sold the slag to several businesses, including Louisiana-Pacific, from the early 1970s until March 1985 when the copper smelter ceased operations. About nine months after IMP stopped selling the slag, it sold substantially all its assets to L-Bar.

One major use of the slag was as ballast to stabilize the ground at log sort yards in the Tacoma area. Government agencies now assert that the slag reacted with the acidic wood-waste in the log sort yards, causing heavy metals from the slag to leach into the groundwater and soil. It appears that the log yards may require substantial environmental clean up.

Louisiana-Pacific and the Port of Tacoma sued Asarco under CERCLA, claiming that it was liable for the costs of cleaning up and abating the release of the hazardous substances. Asarco brought third-party claims against L-Bar and others for contribution or indemnity in the event that Louisiana-Pacific and the Port of Tacoma succeed in their action against it. It sued L-Bar as successor in interest to IMP.

L-Bar moved for summary judgment, claiming that it was not the successor to IMP and could not be liable under CERCLA for IMP's actions. Judge Bryan * * * granted L-Bar's motion for summary judgment and denied Asarco's motion for reconsideration.

* * * *

Preliminarily, we must decide whether there is successor liability under CERCLA. Although Congress failed to address specifically the issue of corporate successor liability in CERCLA, we find Third Circuit authority persuasive on this issue and hold that Congress did intend successor liability. * * *

We also agree with the Third Circuit that the issue of successor liability under CERCLA is governed by federal law. * * *

Because Congress has not addressed the issue of successor liability under CERCLA, we must look to other circuits and the states for guidance in fashioning the federal law. When examining successor liability under CERCLA in the context of a merger or consolidation, the Third Circuit said: We believe it in line with the thrust of the legislation to permit—if not require—successor liability under traditional concepts. * * * We believe its analysis is equally applicable to successor liability in the context of an asset sale, and hold that the traditional rules of successor liability in operation in most states should govern. * * *

* * * *

Under traditional rules of successor liability, asset purchasers are not liable as successors unless one of the following four exceptions applies: (1) The purchasing corporation expressly or impliedly agrees to assume the liability; (2) The transaction amounts to a "de-facto" consolidation or merger; (3) The purchasing corporation is merely a continuation of the selling corporation; or (4) The transaction was fraudulently entered into in order to escape liability. * * *

Asarco argues that it has established genuine issues of material fact under both the implied assumption of liability and de-facto merger exceptions. It also argues that it has established material facts under an expanded version of the mere continuation exception, known as the continuing business enterprise exception. We disagree.

* * * *

Asarco argues for the first time on appeal that L-Bar may have impliedly assumed IMP's liability. As a general rule, we will not consider issues on appeal that were not raised in the district court. * * * Although the rule permits discretion, we see no reason to depart from it in this case. The question of implied assumption of liability is a fact specific question, rather than a purely legal issue, and additional facts would have to be developed [at the trial level] * * *.

* * * *

Asarco also argues that there are genuine issues of fact as to whether the asset purchase was a de facto merger. Courts have recognized de facto mergers when: (1) there is a continuation of the enterprise of the seller in terms of continuity of management, personnel, physical location, assets, and operations; (2) there is a continuity of shareholders; (3) the seller ceases operations, liquidates, and dissolves as soon as legally and practically possible; and (4) the purchasing corporation assumes the obligations of the seller necessary for uninterrupted continuation of business operations. * * *

Asarco argues that continuity of shareholders is not necessary for finding a de facto merger. Its argument has no merit because courts have consistently required continuity of shareholders, accomplished by paying for the acquired corporation with shares of stock. * * *

Here, there was no continuity of shareholders. The consideration paid by L-Bar for IMP was a combination of cash, a promissory note and payment of some debts. No stock in L-Bar or Reserve Industries Corporation, L-Bar's parent corporation, was exchanged as part of the sale. Although a few IMP shareholders now own stock in Reserve, that was bought on the open market, and no former IMP shareholder holds more than 2½% of Reserve stock. Because there is no genuine issue of material fact as to continuity of shareholders, the district court did not err in finding that the asset purchase was not a de facto merger.

* * * *

* * * Asarco argues that in keeping with the purposes of CERCLA, we should adopt a more expansive version of the mere continuation exception, known as the continuing business enterprise exception. * * * Even were we to adopt the exception, it is inapplicable here.

Two key facts distinguish the circumstances surrounding the transfer of assets in this case * * *. First, L-Bar did not have actual notice of IMP's potential CERCLA liability. At the time of the asset sale, IMP had not been identified as a potentially responsible party by any state or federal agency and no one had asserted or threatened a claim against IMP for clean-up costs. Second, and perhaps more importantly, L-Bar did not continue IMP's slag business. In fact, IMP had ceased its slag business nine months before L-Bar purchased its assets. [As a result,] we need not decide whether to adopt the continuing business enterprise exception under CERCLA.

Asarco has failed to establish that under traditional concepts of successor liability there is a genuine issue of material fact as to L-Bar's liability as successor to IMP.

* * * *

The district court did not err in granting summary judgment to L-Bar because Asarco has failed to establish a genuine issue of material fact as to L-Bar's successor liability under CERCLA.

AFFIRMED.

———————

Case A.20

DELAWARE & HUDSON RY. v. CONSOLIDATED RAIL CORP.

United States Court of Appeals, Second Circuit, 1990.
902 F.2d 174.

TIMBERS, Circuit Judge.

* * * *

The dispute leading to this appeal arose when Canadian shippers and railroads sought to lower rates so that rail carriage of newsprint could compete more readily with carriage by truck. Conrail agreed to lower its rates on trips where it was the sole American carrier. It did not decline outright to cooperate in cases where it was the secondary ("short haul") carrier to

D & H, but instituted a policy, called "make or buy," that achieved the same effect. Under that policy, Conrail would agree to the reduced rate only if its profit, called "contribution," matched its profit on the route where it was the sole carrier.

Conrail's action placed D & H in a bind between giving up almost all of its profits on a given route and losing entirely the ability to carry freight on the route. It decided not to concur in joint rates where the make or buy policy was in effect. It commenced the instant action in July 1986. In June 1988, D & H sought protection under Chapter 11 of the United States Bankruptcy Code.

After surviving a motion to dismiss and after extensive discovery, D & H's antitrust claims were rejected by the district court on Conrail's motion for summary judgment.

From the summary judgment rejecting these claims, this appeal was taken by D & H which asserts that, since there are genuine issues of material fact with respect to the three claims, summary judgment was improper. We agree.

* * * *

We turn first to the question whether the make or buy policy constituted the offense of monopolization under § 2 of the Sherman Act * * * To establish the defendant's liability, the plaintiff must demonstrate "(1) the possession of monopoly power in the relevant market and (2) the willful acquisition or maintenance of that power as distinguished from growth or development as a consequence of a superior product, business acumen, or historic accident."

Addressing the second element first, we must affirm the district court's ruling unless D & H has demonstrated that there is a genuine issue of material fact as to whether Conrail's make or buy policy constituted willful anticompetitive conduct in the relevant newsprint transportation market. Conrail's most significant contention in this regard is that, since the policy was intended to increase short-term, as well as long-term, profits, Conrail is insulated from liability.

* * * *

A monopolist cannot escape liability for conduct that is otherwise actionable simply because that conduct also provides short-term profits. * * * Our review of the record in the instant case satisfies us that there is evidence which would support a jury finding that Conrail is liable for monopolization. * * * In view of the evidence referred to above,

however, we hold that D & H has proffered evidence sufficient to support a verdict in its favor by a reasonable jury on the question whether Conrail's conduct violated § 2. Obviously, therefore, this issue could not properly be decided against D & H on a motion for summary judgment.

* * * *

IV.

We turn next to the question whether the make or buy policy constituted denial of an essential facility and, by implication, a violation of § 2. The alleged essential facility is Conrail's tracks used for short haul routes * * * The district court rejected D & H's claim, relying on the four-factor test set forth [in a previous case]: ((1) control of the essential facility by a monopolist; (2) a competitor's inability practically or reasonably to duplicate the essential facility; (3) the denial of the use of the facility to a competitor; and (4) the feasibility of providing the facility.) * * *

There is no question that Conrail controls the short haul tracks, thus satisfying the first element. With respect to the second element, we agree with the district court's statement that "physical duplication of [Conrail's] lines would be an impractical and unreasonable project to undertake." The fourth element, feasibility, is demonstrated by the fact that D & H was permitted continuous use of the tracks until the make or buy policy foreclosed that use.

The third element—whether Conrail impermissibly denied to D & H the use of the tracks—is the one on which the district court based its decision. The court held correctly that there need not be an outright refusal to deal in order to find that denial of an essential facility occurred. It is sufficient if the terms of the offer to deal are unreasonable. In this context the following passage is particularly appropriate:

"Such plan of reorganization must also provide definitely for the use of the terminal facilities by any other railroad not electing to become a joint owner, upon such just and reasonable terms and regulations as will, in respect of use, character and cost of service, place every such company upon as nearly an equal plane as may be with respect to expenses and charges as that occupied by the proprietary companies."

* * * *

We disagree, however, with the district court's conclusion that the terms of the make or buy policy were reasonable as a matter of law.

* * * *

We need not determine on this appeal the circumstances under which a legitimate business practice will shield a defendant from liability for conduct that otherwise would constitute denial of an essential facility. * * * In our discussion above on the monopolization claim, we held that there is a genuine issue of material fact with respect to the question whether the make or buy policy was a legitimate practice. That holding is equally applicable here.

V.

D & H also contends that the make or buy policy constituted the § 2 offense of attempted monopolization. To make out a successful claim of attempted monopolization, a plaintiff must demonstrate: (1) anti-competitive conduct; (2) intent to monopolize; and (3) a dangerous probability of obtaining monopoly power. * * * These elements essentially track those required for a successful monopolization claim. We held with respect to the monopolization claim that the development and implementation of the make or buy policy raised triable issues on the questions of conduct and intent. Likewise, evidence of Conrail's monopoly power that is sufficient to withstand a motion for summary judgment also suffices to raise a triable issue as to whether there was a dangerous probability that Conrail would obtain monopoly power.

VI.

To summarize:

We hold that there are genuine issues of material fact with respect to whether the development and implementation by Conrail of its make or buy policy constituted the antitrust offenses of monopolization, denial of essential facilities and attempted monopolization.

Nothing in this opinion is to be construed as an expression of our views on the merits of the issues to be tried. All we hold today is that there are genuine issues of material fact which should not be decided by summary judgment.

REVERSED AND REMANDED.

Case A.21

ALAN'S OF ATLANTA v. MINOLTA CORP.

United States Circuit Court, Eleventh Circuit, 1990.
903 F.2d 1414.

ESCHBACH, Senior Circuit Judge.

* * * *

Alan's of Atlanta, Inc. (''AA'') was an Atlanta-based ''specialty'' retailer of cameras and related equipment. It had stores in Atlanta and throughout Georgia and Florida. At the start of 1979 AA had a substantial share of the Atlanta market for Minolta-brand camera sales, about 33%, and an overwhelming share of specialty store sales, about 78%. By the end of 1985 AA's fortunes had taken a turn for the worse. Its Atlanta market share of Minolta camera sales had plummeted to about 4%. Its share of specialty store sales suffered a similar fate. During this same period AA witnessed the dramatic rise of a competing specialty camera retailer, Wolf Camera, Inc. Wolf Camera had captured the 29% of the Minolta camera market lost by AA and then some. Its share of that market rose from about 6% to about 41%. Even more dramatic was the rise in its share of specialty camera store sales, which rocketed from about 14% to over 65%. AA's president, Alan Goodelman, could only guess at the cause of Wolf Camera's rise and AA's fall. He surmised that AA's problems were caused by a faulty computer system, or perhaps by a bad management decision to expand in Florida. In June of 1985 Goodelman was approached by Eugene Grabowski, a former Southeast Region sales manager for Minolta Corporation (''Minolta''). Grabowski brought news that a price discrimination scheme may have led to AA's woes. He told Goodelman that Minolta had market development fund (''MDF'') accounts through which benefits were disbursed by either the national director of sales or the regional sales managers. These benefits had been used prior to 1979 for the equal good of all Minolta retailers. In 1979 Robert Lathrop took over as national director of sales, however, and instituted a ''key dealer'' program in which the MDF benefits were to be channeled disproportionately to ''key dealers'' in various cities. The MDF accounts were to support a program in which these selected dealers would be given free cameras and camera equipment, free advertising, free promotions, and various other benefits not available to non-key dealers.

Grabowski alleged that the key dealer program was motivated by two rationales. First, Minolta promotions could be cheaper if limited to one retailer with a large-volume capacity. For example, instead of making 100 shipments of 100 cameras to 100 retailers during a promotion, Minolta could make 1 shipment of 10,000 cameras to one retailer, saving distribution costs. Although the program was not designed to put non-key dealers out of business, it was designed to concentrate the market and to create a market leader through whom the promotions could be handled efficiently. Second, the program was designed to create a de facto vertical integration of Minolta with selected retailers, at least in some respects. According to Grabowski, Lathrop believed that after helping a retailer achieve success, he could dictate to the retailer what cameras to sell and at what price. Key dealers were usually the highest volume dealers within a defined market area. AA was the highest volume dealer in the Atlanta market at the time the key dealer program was instituted, but it was not chosen by Minolta as the Atlanta area key-dealer. Grabowski alleged that Lathrop personally disliked Goodelman, and, in any case, felt that Wolf Camera had more sales potential. Thus Wolf Camera was chosen in AA's stead.

As beneficiary of the key dealer program, Wolf Camera was slated to receive over non-key dealers a price advantage on purchases. Grabowski alleged that Lathrop and Charles Wolf, the owner and CEO of Wolf Camera, hashed out the range of advantage. The range settled upon was four to seven percent per purchase dollar, generally, with specific instances of up to ten percent. Grabowski told Goodelman of various incidents in which he furtively conferred some of this advantage to Wolf Camera by giving it free goods, advertising, and other benefits.

* * * *

After hearing this tale, Goodelman's thinking changed about why AA had taken a bath in the marketplace. He no longer blamed the faulty computer or a bad management decision, but rather Minolta's alleged "key dealer" scheme. * * * Sometime later AA cut off its relationship with Minolta and on February 18, 1986, it filed a five-count complaint in federal court against Minolta, Lathrop, Wolf Camera, and Wolf ("the Appellees").

The complaint * * * alleged in Count I that Minolta and Lathrop had violated section 2(a) of the Clayton Act, as amended by the Robinson-Patman Act [hereinafter referred to simply as the RPA] by engaging in a scheme of price discrimination. Section 2(a) makes it (potentially) illegal for a seller to discriminate in price between its customers where the discrimination leads to a reasonable possibility that competition in general or competition with the favored customer specifically may be adversely affected, unless the discrimination is justifiable on the basis of the seller's costs. The section does not ban price discrimination per se, but only non cost-justified price discrimination that causes the requisite injury to competition or competitors.

Count V alleged that Minolta and Lathrop, through the same scheme, had violated RPA sections 2(d) and 2(e). Sections 2(d) and (e) are not as generous to discriminating sellers as is section 2(a). Section 2(d) prohibits a seller from paying a customer for "services or facilities" furnished by the customer in connection with the resale of the seller's product, unless the opportunity to receive such a payment is available to all of the seller's customers on "proportionally equal terms." The section has no "competitive injury" or "cost justification" escape clause like section 2(a). To force all price discrimination to take a readily recognizable form—from whence it can be tested under the "competitive injury" and "cost justification" guidelines of section 2(a)—section 2(d) creates liability for certain indirect price discriminations related to resale programs upon the mere showing that the indirection is price discrimination, thus "nipping potentially destructive practices before they reach full bloom." Section 2(e) is similar in scope and language to section 2(d) except it bans a seller from furnishing to a customer a service or facility connected with the resale of the seller's product (rather than paying a customer for so furnishing), unless the opportunity to receive the seller's service or facility is available to all of the seller's customers on "proportionally equal terms."

Count II alleged the corollary of Counts I & V, that Wolf and Wolf Camera knowingly received discriminatory price advantages in violation of section 2(f) of the RPA. * * *

* * * [T]he district court dismissed all motions as moot save Appellees' motions for summary judgment, which it granted. The court explained that summary judgment against AA was warranted because AA had failed to show that it had been harmed by anything done by the Appellees. * * *

* * * *

The Robinson-Patman Act was enacted into law in 1936. It amended the Clayton Act's regulation of price discrimination by making its scope more inclusive and its standards much tougher. The RPA's enactment was motivated by concerns for small, independent distributors, which in the 1930's were threatened by the arrival of chain stores. * * * Although the Clayton Act had prohibited certain price discriminations, it was seen as ineffective in stopping the discriminatory prices granted chain stores by virtue of their size. * * * So far as purchasing was concerned, this discrimination put the more normal "mom and pop" merchants of the day at a competitive disadvantage. Congress sought to alleviate the disadvantage by putting the new-age retailing behemoths on a level "playing-field" with small independent merchants and businessmen. The RPA was Congress's tool for doing so, for leveling competition between these types of competitors. As is obvious from this brief summary of the RPA's history, "it is fairness, as Congress perceives it, that Robinson-Patman is all about." The Act's goal is to abolish unwarranted favoritism among all functional competitors, big or small. Its objective is to assure "that businessmen at the same functional level * * * start on equal competitive footing so far as price is concerned * * * to assure that all sellers regardless of size, competing directly for the same customers . . . receive evenhanded treatment from their suppliers."

In this case, the evenhanded treatment sought by the RPA is missing. In fact, favoritism abounds. The facts show that in selling to AA and Wolf Camera Minolta clearly favored Wolf Camera. The facts establish price discrimination on Minolta's part, for "a price discrimination within the meaning of [the RPA] is merely a price difference," and the facts demonstrate a difference in price between what Minolta charged Wolf Camera and what Minolta charged AA. Making this clear is a comparison of ratios based on the documented benefits received from Minolta by Wolf Camera and AA in relation to their purchases. The evidence indicates * * * Wolf Camera's documented benefit/purchases ratio is .029, or about $.03 on the dollar. * * * AA's ratio * * * is about .0087, or less than $.01 on the dollar. Thus, the competitors' benefit/purchases ratios are not equal.

Despite this and other substantial evidence hinting of Minolta's discrimination in favor of Wolf Camera (and, consequently, against AA), the court below [the federal district court] granted summary judgment against AA's claims. The court seemed to believe that in spite of the evidence indicating favoritism, its reasons, based as they were on the "proportionally equal" test of RPA sections 2(d) and (e), the "meeting competition" defense of RPA section 2(b), and the "antitrust injury" test of Clayton Act section 4, were enough to support summary judgment. While in theory this certainly is true, in the reality of this case, it is not.

[The appellate court reversed the trial court's grant of summary judgment and remanded the case for trial.]

* * * *

Case A.22

REVES v. ERNST & YOUNG.

United States Supreme Court, 1990.
494 U.S. 56,
110 S.Ct. 945,
108 L.Ed.2d 47.

MARSHALL, Justice.

This case presents the question whether certain demand notes issued by the Farmer's Cooperative of Arkansas and Oklahoma are "securities" within the meaning of § 3(a)(10) of the Securities Exchange Act of 1934. We conclude that they are.

The Co-Op is an agricultural cooperative that, at the time relevant here, had approximately 23,000 members. In order to raise money to support its general business operations, the Co-Op sold promissory notes payable on demand by the holder. Although the notes were uncollateralized and uninsured, they paid a variable rate of interest that was adjusted monthly to keep it higher than the rate paid by local financial institutions. * * * Despite these assurances, the Co-Op filed for bankruptcy in 1984. At the time of the filing, over 1,600 people held notes worth a total of $10 million.

After the Co-Op filed for bankruptcy, petitioners, a class of holders of the notes, filed suit against Arthur Young & Co., the firm that had audited the Co-Op's financial statements (and the predecessor to respondent Ernst & Young). Petitioners alleged, inter alia, that Arthur Young had intentionally failed to follow generally accepted accounting principles in its audit, specifically with respect to the valuation of one of the

Co-Op's major assets, a gasohol plant. Petitioners claimed that Arthur Young violated these principles in an effort to inflate the assets and net worth of the Co-Op. Petitioners maintained that, had Arthur Young properly treated the plant in its audits, they would not have purchased demand notes because the Co-Op's insolvency would have been apparent. On the basis of these allegations, petitioners claimed that Arthur Young had violated the antifraud provisions of the 1934 Act as well as Arkansas' securities laws.

Petitioners prevailed at trial on both their federal and state claims, receiving a $6.1 million judgment. Arthur Young appealed, claiming that the demand notes were not "securities" under either the 1934 Act or Arkansas law, and that the statutes' antifraud provisions therefore did not apply. A panel of the Eighth Circuit, agreeing with Arthur Young on both the state and federal issues, reversed. *   *   * We granted *certiorari* to address the federal issue *   *   * and now reverse the judgment of the Court of Appeals.

This case requires us to decide whether the note issued by the Co-Op is a "security" within the meaning of the 1934 Act. Section 3(a)(10) of that Act is our starting point: "The term 'security' means any note, stock, treasury stock, bond, debenture, *   *   * but shall not include currency or any note, draft, bill of exchange, or banker's acceptance which has a maturity at the time of issuance of not exceeding nine months, exclusive of days of grace, or any renewal thereof the maturity of which is likewise limited." *   *   *

The fundamental purpose undergirding the Securities Acts is "to eliminate serious abuses in a largely unregulated securities market." *   *   * In defining the scope of the market that it wished to regulate, Congress painted with a broad brush. It recognized the virtually limitless scope of human ingenuity, especially in the creation of "countless and variable schemes devised by those who seek the use of the money of others on the promise of profits," *   *   * and determined that the best way to achieve its goal of protecting investors was "to define 'the term "security" in sufficiently broad and general terms so as to include within that definition the many types of instruments that in our commercial world fall within the ordinary concept of a security.' " *   *   * [Congress] enacted a definition of "security" sufficiently broad to encompass virtually any instrument that might be sold as an investment.

*   *   *   *

Congress did not, however, "intend to provide a broad federal remedy for all fraud." *   *   * Accordingly, "[t]he task has fallen to the Securities and Exchange Commission (SEC), the body charged with administering the Securities Acts, and ultimately to the federal courts to decide which of the myriad financial transactions in our society come within the coverage of these statutes." *   *   * Congress' purpose in enacting the securities laws was to regulate investments, in whatever form they are made and by whatever name they are called.

*   *   *   *

*   *   * [A] note is a security only if it evidences "(1) an investment; (2) in a common enterprise; (3) with a reasonable expectation of profits; (4) to be derived from the entrepreneurial or managerial efforts of others." *   *   *

*   *   * The demand notes here may well not be "investment contracts," but that does not mean they are not "notes." To hold that a "note" is not a "security" unless it meets a test designed for an entirely different variety of instrument "would make the Acts' enumeration of many types of instruments superfluous," *   *   * and would be inconsistent with Congress' intent to regulate the entire body of instruments sold as investments. *   *   * The other two contenders—the "family resemblance" and "investment versus commercial" tests—are really two ways of formulating the same general approach. Because we think the "family resemblance" test provides a more promising framework for analysis, however, we adopt it. The test begins with the language of the statute; because the Securities Acts define "security" to include "any note," we begin with a presumption that every note is a security. We nonetheless recognize that this presumption cannot be irrebuttable.

*   *   *   *

*   *   * If the seller's purpose is to raise money for the general use of a business enterprise or to finance substantial investments and the buyer is interested primarily in the profit the note is expected to generate, the instrument is likely to be a "security." If the note is exchanged to facilitate the purchase and sale of a minor asset or consumer good, to correct for the seller's cash-flow difficulties, or to advance some other commercial or consumer purpose, on the other hand, the note is less sensibly described as a "security." *   *   * Third, we examine the reasonable expectations of the investing public: The Court will consider instruments to be "securities" on the basis

of such public expectations, even where an economic analysis of the circumstances of the particular transaction might suggest that the instruments are not "securities" as used in that transaction. * * * Finally, we examine whether some factor such as the existence of another regulatory scheme significantly reduces the risk of the instrument, thereby rendering application of the Securities Acts unnecessary. * * *

We conclude, then, that in determining whether an instrument denominated a "note" is a "security," courts are to apply the version of the "family resemblance" test that we have articulated here: a note is presumed to be a "security," and that presumption may be rebutted only by a showing that the note bears a strong resemblance (in terms of the four factors we have identified) to one of the enumerated categories of instrument. If an instrument is not sufficiently similar to an item on the list, the decision whether another category should be added is to be made by examining the same factors.

Applying the family resemblance approach to this case, we have little difficulty in concluding that the notes at issue here are "securities." * * * The Co-Op sold the notes in an effort to raise capital for its general business operations, and purchasers bought them in order to earn a profit in the form of interest. Indeed, one of the primary inducements offered purchasers was an interest rate constantly revised to keep it slightly above the rate paid by local banks and savings and loans. From both sides, then, the transaction is most naturally conceived as an investment in a business enterprise rather than as a purely commercial or consumer transaction.

As to the plan of distribution, the Co-Op offered the notes over an extended period to its 23,000 members, as well as to nonmembers, and more than 1,600 people held notes when the Co-Op filed for bankruptcy. To be sure, the notes were not traded on an exchange. They were, however, offered and sold to a broad segment of the public, and that is all we have held to be necessary to establish the requisite "common trading" in an instrument. * * *

The third factor—the public's reasonable perceptions—also supports a finding that the notes in this case are "securities." We have consistently identified the fundamental essence of a "security" to be its character as an "investment." The advertisements for the notes here characterized them as "investments," see supra, at 948, and there were no countervailing factors that would have led a reasonable person to question this characterization. In these circumstances, it would be reasonable for a prospective purchaser to take the Co-Op at its word.

Finally, we find no risk-reducing factor to suggest that these instruments are not in fact securities. The notes are uncollateralized and uninsured. Moreover, * * * the notes here would escape federal regulation entirely if the Acts were held not to apply.

The court below found that "[t]he demand nature of the notes is very uncharacteristic of a security," on the theory that the virtually instant liquidity associated with demand notes is inconsistent with the risk ordinarily associated with "securities." This argument is unpersuasive. * * * The demand feature of a note does permit a holder to eliminate risk quickly by making a demand, but just as with publicly traded stock, the liquidity of the instrument does not eliminate risk all together. Indeed, publicly traded stock is even more readily liquid than are demand notes, in that a demand only eliminates risk when and if payment is made, whereas the sale of a share of stock through a national exchange and the receipt of the proceeds usually occur simultaneously.

* * * *

For the foregoing reasons, we conclude that the demand notes at issue here fall under the "note" category of instruments that are "securities" under the 1933 and 1934 Acts. * * * Accordingly, we reverse the judgment of the Court of Appeals and remand the case for further proceedings consistent with this opinion.

So ordered.

Case A.23

WEIHL v. WAGNER

Appellate Court of Illinois, Fifth District,1991.
569 N.E.2d 297.

RARICK, Justice.

* * * *

In the spring of 1956, plaintiff, Roy H. Weihl, started farming as a tenant a 40-acre tract of land in Monroe County. In order to get to the land, Weihl used a field road which passed over a parcel of land also consisting of 40 acres directly north of the tract he was farming. This northern parcel of land was owned by the Hedenkamps. Weihl subsequently purchased the 40-acre tract he was farming in 1957 and continued using the field road to get to his acreage. In 1961, Weihl began tenant-farming the Hedenkamp land. Over the years, the Hedenkamp land went through several changes of ownership and one division. Weihl, however, continued farming the majority of the land as a tenant farmer, and at all times, used the same field to access all parcels, including his own. In 1977 the owner of one of the parcels over which the road ran asked Weihl to use a more southerly route in connection with one stretch of the field road. Weihl agreed and accordingly changed his route. In 1985 defendant Wagner purchased the east 17.5 acres of the Hedenkamp land, the parcel through which the field road ran. Wagner found no reference in his deed to any easement over the southerly part of his land corresponding to the field road Weihl used and therefore decided to prohibit Weihl's further use of the road. Weihl, in turn, brought suit to have an easement by prescription found over Wagner's land. The trial court ruled in favor of Weihl.

Wagner argues on appeal the character of Weihl's use of the field road did not establish any prescriptive rights. Furthermore, and even if such rights once existed, they were abandoned in 1977 when the location of the road was changed. We disagree.

In Illinois, in order to acquire an easement by prescription, the party claiming such a right must show that the use of the land was adverse, exclusive, continuous and uninterrupted, and under claim of right for a period of at least 20 years. * * * Having met the other criteria, the primary contention here is whether Weihl sufficiently established that his use of the field road was adverse in nature. To meet the requirement of adversity, a claimant must show the use of the property was with the knowledge and acquiescence of the owner but without his permission. * * * Mere permission to use the land can never ripen into a prescriptive right, regardless of the length of time such permissive use is enjoyed. * * * Permission may be established by written or oral license or may be inferred from the surrounding circumstances. * * * For instance, the use of vacant and unenclosed land is presumed to be permissive * * * as is true when there is evidence of a neighborly relationship between the parties. * * * There is, however, a rebuttable presumption of a grant or

adverse right where the use of the land or way occurred normally, or in other words, has been used openly, uninterruptedly, continuously and exclusively for more than 20 years, and the origin of such way is not shown. * * * Whether the use was adverse or permissive ultimately is a question of fact for the trial court which will not be disturbed on appeal unless manifestly against the weight of the evidence. * * * We see no reason to disturb the finding of adversity in this instance. Weihl began using the field road in 1956. He testified he did not ask anyone's permission to use the road. He knew the road was there and believed he had the right to use it to get to the 40 acres he was farming. His use of the road was open and continuous for over a period of 20 years. Clearly the land was not vacant and unenclosed having both a barn and house on the premises in close proximity to the road. * * * It is true Weihl was a tenant for the majority of the prescriptive period over the land through which the field road ran. While as a tenant Weihl had permission to use the field road to access the rented acreage, we cannot say he necessarily had permission to use the road to access other lands. His use of the field road to reach his own land went beyond the rights of his tenancy and therefore continued to be adverse in nature. We too conclude Weihl met his burden of establishing a prescriptive easement over the field road on Wagner's land.

Wagner argues, however, Weihl abandoned any prescriptive rights when he agreed to a change in the location of the road in 1977. Again, we disagree. By 1977, Weihl had already met the statutory prescriptive period of 20 years. Once the easement existed, it did not matter it was shifted to another location by mutual agreement. Such a request to change the location in fact serves to highlight the landowner's recognition of Weihl's rights. While our research has not brought to light any case in Illinois with a similar fact pattern directly supporting this conclusion, we note several other jurisdictions have encountered such circumstances and consistently have ruled in favor of nonabandonment. * * * We therefore find the trial court's judgment is supported by the evidence.

We do choose, however, to remand this cause for further definition of the prescriptive easement granted in this instance. We agree the order entered by the trial court describing the easement is somewhat vague and uncertain as to specific location. Contrary to Wagner's contentions, however, we see no error in the court's "increasing" the width of the easement over the southern portion of the road to 18 feet as compared to that of the 16½ feet of the northern portion of the road created by express easement. It is true the extent of prescriptive use defines the easement. * * * What Wagner fails to realize is that Weihl's use of the road requires the "additional" width. While Weihl's farm equipment only extends 15½ feet in width, Weihl testified that because of overhangs, fence posts and vegetative growth along a portion of the southerly road his usage exceeds the northern width of 16½ feet in this area. If Weihl is and has been using a wider section on the southerly portion then such use accordingly justifies the wider easement over that portion as the extent of the prescriptive ease-ment. The difficulty lies in the trial court's not adequately defining where this wider section is located. For this reason, we agree with Wagner the judgment must be remanded for further clarification as to the location of the prescriptive easement granted in this instance.

For the aforementioned reasons, we affirm the judgment of the circuit court of Monroe County as to the granting of the prescriptive easement but remand for further clarification of the location of such easement.

AFFIRMED IN PART; REMANDED IN PART.

Case A.24

MELLON BANK, N.A. v. SECURITIES SETTLEMENT CORP.

United States District Court, District of New Jersey, 1989. 710 F.Supp. 991.

CLARKSON S. FISHER, District Judge.

Before the court are the motions of plaintiff, Mellon Bank ("Mellon"), and defendant, Securities Settlement Corporation ("SSC"), for summary judgment. At oral argument, the parties agreed that the facts are not in dispute. The transaction underlying this case is relatively simple. SSC performed clearing services in connection with securities transactions in the accounts of one of its customers, Kobrin Securities ("Kobrin"). One of Kobrin's clients was another entity, Barrett Consultants ("Barrett"), to whom SSC sent monthly statements regarding Barrett's account with Kobrin. On the morning of June 4, 1985, SSC, at Kobrin's request, instructed Mellon to wire transfer $113,080.50 to Barrett's account with the Franklin State Bank ("FSB"). Within several hours after Mellon had sent the wire, SSC learned that Kobrin was incapable of paying the securities' purchase price. Although SSC instructed Mellon to cancel the wire transfer, the money went through to Barrett's account. Mellon filed the instant complaint in October of 1987 in the Superior Court of New Jersey, Law Division, Somerset County, seeking reimbursement for the funds it had sent to FSB. SSC removed the case to this court in November of the same year.

* * * *

The threshold issue is whether Pennsylvania's version of the U.C.C. applies to this action. [Mellon and SSC agreed that Pennsylvania law governed their rights and liabilities.] SSC has cited several cases for the proposition that the U.C.C. does not govern wire transfers and contends that this case must be decided without reference to the statute. Mellon counters that the U.C.C. has been applied by analogy in other jurisdictions and urges the court to do the same. Unfortunately neither party has cited, nor has the court found, decisions from the Pennsylvania state courts which address this question.

There are merits to both positions. On one hand it might be noted that the U.C.C. covers only "items," which 13 Pa.C.S.A. [Pennsylvania Consolidated Statutes Annotated] section 4104 [Pennsylvania's version of U.C.C. 4-104] defines as "any instrument for the payment of money even though it is not negotiable." With this definition as a starting point, it might be added that an instrument is a signed writing which expresses an agreement regarding rights, while the instant case involves an unsigned and electronically-transmitted instruction. It could be asserted that this difference is not merely semantic; it illustrates that the U.C.C. was designed to address paper transactions rather than high-speed financial distributions. According to this argument Pennsylvania's trial courts would not adjudicate this case under 13 Pa.C.S.A. section 4101 et seq.

On the other hand, a "check is no more than an order on the bank to pay a stated amount . . . from the maker's account.'' Although checks are negotiable instruments, it could be argued that Thomas's definition exactly fits a wire transfer, which is nothing more than an order directing the bank to pay money from one account to another. Moreover, it could be argued that the total exclusion of the U.C.C. from this case would leave the court with little current law upon which to base its decision.

Thus the court must sail between the Scylla of common law and the Charybdis of statute [between two equally perilous alternatives] in an attempt to predict what Pennsylvania's highest court would do if confronted with this situation. * * * The court concludes that it should follow those decisions which have applied the common law while at the same time borrowing appropriate rules from the governing version of the U.C.C.

* * * *

SSC had a right to stop the * * * wire transfer, and Mellon was under a corresponding duty to use ordinary care in handling SSC's request. * * * Before the court can determine * * * whether Mellon actually used ordinary care, it must examine the wire transfer at issue here.

The transfer was made under BankWire, a system maintained by Mellon and roughly 100 other banks. BankWire procedure requires a customer's authorized representative to instruct Mellon to transfer money from the customer's account to the recipient's account in another bank. After receiving and verifying an instruction, Mellon personnel would when necessary select a "correspondent" bank. The correspondent bank would then serve as a conduit for the transfer to the recipient's bank.

This process does not transmit the funds themselves; rather, upon making the transfer Mellon would debit the customer for the the amount of the transfer, and credit the correspondent bank's account with Mellon. * * * BankWire funds become available on the day following the transfer.

Because BankWire funds are not immediately obtainable, a cancellation does not require the bank to recapture the wired funds. Essentially, a BankWire cancellation requires two steps. First, Mellon sends a cancellation notice to the "correspondent" bank, which in turn instructs the recipient bank to disregard the transfer. Second, Mellon reverses the credit/debit notation which it made upon receiving the transfer order; the customer's account is recredited and the correspondent bank's account is debited, thereby re-

turning the balances to their pre-transfer sums. * * *

* * * *

SSC instructed Mellon to cancel the wire on the same day it learned that the funds were not covered. * * * Within several hours * * *, Mellon sent a notice to MHT [the correspondent bank] instructing them to cancel the transaction. * * * Shortly after this message was sent Mellon reversed its account entries; it restored the transferred amount to SSC's account, and debited MHT's account with Mellon to the same amount.

Mellon's notice contained two errors. First, it referred to "YR BK WIRE," i.e., a wire transfer sent by MHT rather than one received by it. Second, the notice gave a transaction number of "184B." Transaction numbers are assigned by BankWire to each transfer request. The wire's true number was "06040184B."

* * * SSC heard nothing from Mellon regarding the transfer. Mellon, however, heard from MHT on several occasions. On June 6, 1985, MHT telephoned Mellon to inform the bank that MHT had not received the June 4, 1985 wire. * * * The next day MHT again contacted Mellon and informed the bank that MHT had no record of receiving a wire transfer denominated by [the transaction number] 184B.

Mellon replied to neither of these correspondences. * * *

On July 12, 1985, MHT wired Mellon that it intended to credit FSB with $113,080.50. In the same communication MHT asked Mellon to wire them in return should Mellon not want the transaction to be completed. MHT also asked that Mellon credit MHT's account with $113,080.50. Four days later Mellon wired MHT that cancellation instructions had already been issued by Mellon on June 4, 1985. Mellon's wire contained, for the first time, the correct transaction number. Two days after this, on July 18, 1985, MHT requested that FSB authorize a reversal of the June 4 transfer. The next day FSB informed MHT that Barrett had already withdrawn the money.

No reasonable fact finder could conclude that Mellon acted with ordinary care regarding the cancellation. Mellon incorrectly identified the transaction to be cancelled, both by omitting five digits from the transaction number and by indicating that it sought to cancel a wire sent by MHT. The latter error might be considered inconsequential; after all, MHT did respond to Mellon within forty-eight hours to ask about Mellon's wire. But the inaccurate transaction number persisted throughout MHT's attempts to comply with Mellon's instructions; this error tainted such attempts for over one month.

Mellon's error easily ranks with those considered sufficient to constitute a breach of a bank's duty of ordinary care. The record demonstrates that Mellon inaccurately carried out SSC's instructions and that, even though it was twice given notice of MHT's corresponding inability to cancel the wire, Mellon failed to take prompt remedial action. Indeed, the court notes that Mellon's failures transgressed its own internal guidelines.

* * * *

Upon examining the record and the parties' arguments, the court concludes that no reasonable finder of fact could grant Mellon the relief it seeks. Rather, it is SSC who is entitled to judgment as a matter of law. Summary judgment is granted for SSC against all Mellon's claims.

Case A.25

GREENLEE v. SHERMAN

New York Supreme Court, Appellate Division, Third Department, 1989.
142 A.D.2d 472,
536 N.Y.S.2d 877.

CASEY, Justice Presiding.

[This action arises] out of a 1980 transaction between Horace and Annie Greenlee, plaintiffs * * * and Philip Sherman, the sole proprietor of Sherman Fuel and Oil Burner Service, whereby Sherman installed a combination wood/oil furnace in the basement of the Greenlees' house. The Greenlees used the furnace until March 30, 1984, when a fire substantially destroyed their house. It is alleged that the fire was caused by the improper installation of the flue pipe from the furnace, which resulted in the exposure of a wooden joist to intense radiant heat while the furnace was operating. This exposure to intense heat allegedly caused a chemical process, known as pyrolyisis, in the wooden joist which ultimately lowered the ignition temperature of the wood to the point where it was ignited by the flue pipe.

* * * [T]he Greenlees seek [among other things] to recover damages based upon Sherman's negligent installation of the furnace. Named as defendants * * * are the executor of Sherman's estate and Main Care Heating Service, Inc. (hereinafter Main Care), as the successor in interest to Sherman Fuel and Oil Burner Service. * * * Main Care moved * * * for summary judgment dismissing the Greenlees' complaint and Supreme Court granted the motion. * * * The Greenlees have appealed * * *.

The issue raised by the appeal in [this action] is whether there exists a triable issue of fact on the question of Main Care's liability as a successor in interest to Sherman's business, pursuant to an agreement between Sherman and Main Care, dated November 19, 1980.

It is the general rule that a corporation which acquires the assets of another is not liable for the torts of its predecessor. * * * There are exceptions. * * * A corporation may be held liable for the torts of its predecessor if (1) it expressly or impliedly assumed the predecessor's tort liability, (2) there was a consolidation or merger of seller and purchaser, (3) the purchasing corporation was a mere continuation of the selling corporation, or (4) the transaction is entered into fraudulently to escape such obligations.

Main Care relies upon this general rule, while the Greenlees contend that the second and third exceptions are applicable. In *Grant-Howard Assoc. v. General Housewares Corp.*, the Court of Appeals noted that these two exceptions "are based on the concept that a successor that effectively takes over a company in its entirety should carry the predecessor's liabilities as a concomitant [something that exists concurrently with something else] to the benefits it derives from the good will purchased." But the court prefaced this remark with the following explanation of the genesis of the successor liability theory:

> Allowing recovery in tort against a successor corporation is merely an extension of the concept of products liability, which calls for the burden of consumer injuries to be borne by the manufacturer, who can transfer the costs to the general public as a component of the selling price. Strict liability assures that a responsible source is available to compensate the injured party.

The case at bar does not involve the concept of products liability. The Greenlees' action is based upon the negligence of Sherman in the installation of the furnace; there is no claim that Sherman manufactured or sold a defective product. The Greenlees contracted directly with Sherman for certain services to be performed by him, and their claim for damages is based upon Sherman's negligence in performing those services. In these circumstances, the public policy considerations underlying the concept of products liability are not present. Therefore, based upon the previously quoted language of the Court of Appeals in *Grant-Howard Assoc. v. General Housewares Corp., supra* [above—meaning in this instance the case cited above; the full citation for this case was omitted by the authors when editing this case], it appears that the successor liability theory is not applicable in this case.

In any event, we find no proof in the record to support the Greenlees' contention that there was a consolidation or merger of Main Care and Sherman's business or that Main Care is a mere continuation of Sherman's business. As to the consolidation or merger claim, Sherman, the sole proprietor of the selling business, did not become involved with Main Care, either as a shareholder or as an employee; Main Care did not acquire either the cash on hand or the accounts receivable of Sherman's business; Main Care did not hire any employee of Sherman's business; and Main Care did not install furnaces, which was at least a part of Sherman's business. As to the "mere continuation" claim, that exception refers to corporate reorganization, which did not occur here. Main Care had been in existence for at least 12 years prior to its purchase of Sherman's business and it continued in substantially the same form thereafter, with the addition of Sherman's assets. In short, Main Care cannot be viewed as a "mere continuation" of Sherman's business. Thus, assuming that the successor liability theory is applicable outside the context of products liability, the Greenlees' proof was inadequate to defeat Main Care's motion for summary judgment.

*   *   *   *

ORDERS AND JUDGMENT AFFIRMED.

Case A.26

NEW ERA PUBLICATIONS INTERNATIONAL, ApS, v. CAROL PUBLISHING GROUP

United States Court of Appeals, Second Circuit, 1990.
904 F.2d 152.

FEINBERG, Circuit Judge.

*   *   *   *

The biography at issue in this appeal is entitled A Piece of Blue Sky: Scientology, Dianetics and L. Ron Hubbard Exposed, and was written by Jonathan Caven-Atack. (We will refer to A Piece of Blue Sky as "the book" and to Caven-Atack as "the author.") The subject of the book is L. Ron Hubbard, the controversial founder of the Church of Scientology (the Church), who died in 1986.

*   *   *   *

*   *   * The book paints a highly unflattering portrait of Hubbard as a thoroughgoing charlatan who lied relentlessly about his accomplishments. The author's attitude toward his subject can be gauged by his descriptions of Hubbard as "an arrogant, amoral egomaniac," "a paranoid, power hungry, petty sadist," and—perhaps ironically in light of the claims in this case—"an outright plagiarist." *   *   *

Plaintiff/appellee New Era Publications International is the exclusive licensee of Hubbard's works. After learning that appellant Carol Publishing Group intended to publish the book, appellee sued appellant in the district court. *   *   * [New Era] claimed that the book copied "substantial portions" of certain of Hubbard's works in violation of its exclusive copyright rights *   *   * and accused [Carol] of willful copyright infringement. *   *   * In particular, [New Era] argued that 121 passages of the book were drawn from 48 of Hubbard's works. The complaint sought, among other things, an injunction to stop publication of the book. [New Era] subsequently moved for a temporary restraining order and a preliminary injunction; by stipulation, the proceedings for a permanent and for a preliminary injunction were later merged.

The district court granted a permanent injunction. It held, first, that the copyright had expired on one of the works quoted in the book, the HCO Manual of Justice. The court then went on to determine whether the book's use of passages from Hubbard's other works was protected "fair use" * * *. The district court analyzed the four factors spelled out in [the copyright laws that provide that in "determining whether the use made of a work in any particular case is a fair use the factors to be considered shall include—(1) the purpose and character of the use, including whether such use is of a commercial nature or is for nonprofit educational purposes; (2) the nature of the copyrighted work; (3) the amount and substantiality of the portion used in relation to the copyrighted work as a whole; and (4) the effect of the use upon the potential market for or value of the copyrighted work." The court] found that factor one (purpose and character of the use) "strongly" favored [New Era] because "many of the passages lack any allowable fair use purpose;" factor two (nature of the copyrighted work) favored [New Era] since "so many" of the quoted passages "are expressive rather than factual;" factor three (amount used in relation to copyrighted work as a whole) also favored [New Era], because the quoted passages amount to a "small, but significant element of" the book; and that factor four (effect of use on the market for the copyrighted work) did not favor either party. The district court thus concluded that appellee was entitled to a permanent injunction against publication of the book in its present form, noting that "[t]he book is still in manuscript form, so deletion of the infringing passages will be relatively simple and inexpensive." The district court thereafter entered judgment, listing 103 infringing passages taken from 43 works, all published.

[Carol] now appeals from the judgment granting an injunction, and [New Era] cross-appeals from the district court's determination that the copyright on the HCO Manual had expired.

* * * *

[Carol] asserts that, contrary to the district court's view, all four fair use factors * * * weigh in its favor, while [New Era] argues to the contrary. At the outset, we note that [the relevant statute "requires a case-by-case determination whether a particular use is fair." * * * Furthermore, fair use is a mixed question of law and fact, * * * and thus the district court's conclusion on this point is open to full review on appeal. * * * And, "[w]here the district court has found facts sufficient to evaluate each of the statutory factors, an appellate court 'need not remand for further factfinding,' " but may resolve the issue of fair use as a matter of law. * * *

* * * *

* * * Under the appropriate wide-ranging standard of review, we conclude that all four factors * * * favor appellant, and that appellant's use was fair.

* * * *

As noted above, the book is an unfavorable biography. * * * Our cases establish that biographies in general, and critical biographies in particular, fit "comfortably within" these statutory categories "of uses illustrative of uses that can be fair." * * * [New Era] argues that there is no rule that if an allegedly infringing work is a biography, factor one necessarily operates in the biographer's favor in evaluating whether there has been a "fair use." Nevertheless, "[i]f a book falls into one of these categories [i.e., criticism, scholarship or research], assessment of the first fair use factor should be at an end." * * * [T]he author uses Hubbard's works for the entirely legitimate purpose of making his point that Hubbard was a charlatan and the Church a dangerous cult. To be sure, the author and [Carol] want to make a profit in publishing the book. But the author's use of material "to enrich" his biography is protected fair use, "notwithstanding that he and his publisher anticipate profits."

[New Age] also contends that the book's use of Hubbard's works does not serve any fair use purpose, but was rather unnecessary appropriation of Hubbard's literary expression. We do not agree with this characterization. The author uses the quotations in part to convey the facts contained therein, and not for their expression. More importantly, even passages used for their expression are intended to convey the author's perception of Hubbard's hypocrisy and pomposity, qualities that may best (or only) be revealed through direct quotation. * * *

* * * *

We hold that factor one favors appellant.

* * * Whether or not a work is published is critical to its nature under factor two, because "the scope of fair use is narrower with respect to unpublished works." * * *

Furthermore, the scope of fair use is greater with respect to factual than non-factual works. * * * We have some hesitation in trying to characterize Hubbard's diverse body of writings as solely "factual" or "non-factual," but on balance, we believe that the quoted works—which deal with Hubbard's life, his views on religion, human relations, the

Church, etc.—are more properly viewed as factual or informational.

* * * *

We conclude that factor two favors appellant.

* * * *

Factor three addresses the amount and substantiality of the portion used in relation to the copyrighted work, not to the allegedly infringing work. * * * This factor has both a quantitative and a qualitative component, so that courts have found that use was not fair where the quoted material formed a substantial percentage of the copyrighted work * * *

Here, the book uses overall a small percentage of Hubbard's works. [Carol] calculates that the book quotes only a minuscule amount of 25 of the 48 works that [New Era] claimed were infringed, 5–6% of 12 other works and 8% or more of 11 works, each of the 11 being only a few pages in length. * * *

Appellee also argues that factor three weighs in its favor because the quotations are an important ingredient of the book, pointing out that 2.7% of the book is made up of quotations from Hubbard's works. Appellee asserts that, because of the length of Hubbard's works and because so many of his writings were quoted from, it would be of little value to focus on the amount of infringing material in relation to the copyrighted works * * *.

* * * [T]he use of the quotes here is primarily a means for illustrating the alleged gap between the official version of Hubbard's life and accomplishments, and what the author contends are the true facts. For that purpose, some conjuring up of the copyrighted work is necessary. * * *

We find that factor three favors appellant.

* * * *

Factor four of * * * concerns the "effect of the use upon the potential market for or value of the copyrighted work." According to the Supreme Court, this "is undoubtedly the single most important element of fair use." * * * In evaluating this factor, courts do not focus solely on the market for the work itself, but also on the "harm to the market for derivative works." [New Era] argues strenuously that factor four favors it, asserting that it intends to publish an authorized biography of Hubbard that will include excerpts from all of his works, including material as yet unpublished, and that the book will discourage potential readers of the authorized biography by conveying the flavor of Hubbard's writings. [New Era]

also contends that * * * publication of a similar unfavorable biography would impair the market for, and compete with, its planned biography of Hubbard.

We do not find either argument persuasive. * * * Indeed, it is not "beyond the realm of possibility that" the book "might stimulate further interest" in the authorized biography.

* * * Furthermore, even assuming that the book discourages potential purchasers of the authorized biography, this is not necessarily actionable under the copyright laws. Such potential buyers might be put off because the book persuaded them (as it clearly hopes to) that Hubbard was a charlatan, but the copyright laws do not protect against that sort of injury. Harm to the market for a copyrighted work or its derivatives caused by a "devastating critique" that "diminished sales by convincing the public that the original work was of poor quality" is not "within the scope of copyright protection." * * * Here, the purpose of the book is diametrically opposed to that of the authorized biography; the former seeks to unmask Hubbard and the Church, while the latter presumably will be designed to promote public interest in Hubbard and the Church. Thus, even if the book ultimately harms sales of the authorized biography, this would not result from unfair infringement forbidden by the copyright laws, but rather from a convincing work that effectively criticizes Hubbard, the very type of work that the Copyright Act was designed to protect and encourage.

* * * *

We conclude that factor four favors appellant.

* * * *

In sum, balancing all of the relevant factors, we believe that the present case presents a strong set of facts for invoking the fair use defense: The book is a critical biography, designed to educate the public about Hubbard, a public figure who sought public attention, albeit on his own terms; the book quotes from merely a small portion of Hubbard's works and from only those that have been published; and, it will cause no adverse impact protected by the copyright law on the market for Hubbard's writings. In these circumstances, we conclude that the book's use of passages from Hubbard's work is protected fair use.

* * * *

Conclusion

We hold that each of the four factors * * * favors appellant, and that the book's use of quotations from Hubbard's published works was protected fair use. * * * We thus reverse the judgment of the district court, except to the extent it concludes that the copyright on the HCO Manual expired in 1987, as to which we affirm.

Case A.27

TRANS-ORIENT MARINE CORP. v. STAR TRADING & MARINE, INC.

United States District Court, Southern District of New York, 1990.
731 F.Supp. 619.

CONNER, District Judge.

Defendant Republic of the Sudan moves this Court to dismiss the complaint for failure to state a claim or for summary judgment. It claims that the new Republic of the Sudan, as successor state, is not liable for the alleged breach of a five-year exclusive agency contract entered into by the prior sovereign state of Sudan. Defendant further asserts that a fundamental change in circumstances relieves it of any prior contractual obligations.

FACTS

Plaintiff's cause of action for breach of contract arises from an alleged five-year exclusive agency agreement to represent the Sudan in the United States P.L. 480 program [an agricultural trade development and assistance program]. The alleged October 14, 1983 agreement was effective from October 1, 1984 through September 30, 1989. In April 1985, a military coup deposed the then head of state, declaring a state of emergency and suspending the constitution. A twelve-month transitional military regime followed, which was then replaced by a civilian coalition government. The name of the state was changed from the Sudan to the Republic of Sudan. In June 1989, there was another military coup in which the present military regime overthrew the former civilian administration and suspended the constitution. Both parties agree that the Republic of the Sudan is a foreign sovereign state.

On January 3 and 4, 1985, the then Sudanese government sent letters advising plaintiff that a new agent, CIDCO, had been appointed to handle the contracts under P.L. 480 and that CIDCO would select the shipping agent. This alleged termination of the then-executory contract did not provide the one-year termination notice required under the original contract. Since January 1985, the Sudan has awarded CIDCO a continuing series of contracts to handle the wheat and wheat flour transportation under P.L. 480, in alleged violation of plaintiff's exclusive agency contract. No additional facts are relevant to the present motion.

DISCUSSION

The present Sudanese government asserts that it is not liable for the contractual obligations of the prior sovereign, pointing to the two military coups of 1985 and 1989 to sustain its position that both the 1985 military regime and the present administration are successor states and that there has been a fundamental change in circumstances. Plaintiff contends that neither the 1985 regime nor the present regime is a successor state but that they represent mere changes in government which do not relieve the present regime from the prior government's contractual obligations. Plaintiff further argues that even if either regime is a successor state, they have ratified the prior government's contract. For the following reasons, summary judgment is denied.

Whether a new administration may terminate the executory portions of its predecessor's contracts is based on the succession of state theory. International law sharply distinguishes the succession of state, which may create a discontinuity of statehood, from a succession of government, which leaves statehood unaffected. It is generally accepted that a change in government, regime or ideology has no effect on that state's international rights and obligations because the state continues to exist despite the change. * * *

However, where one sovereign succeeds another, and a new state is created, the rights and obligations of the successor state are affected. The rule with regard to contracts with private foreign individuals involves a balancing of competing interests. While the successor state is permitted to terminate existing contracts originally executed by the former sovereign and the private party, the successor state is liable to that party only for any amount due him as of the date of the change of sovereignty. But if the contract is totally executory, the successor state is released from the contract.

The Restatement of Foreign Relations Law describes a successor state to include: a state that wholly absorbs another state, that takes over part of the territory of another state, that becomes independent of another state of which it had formed a part, or that arises because of the dismemberment of the state of which it had been a part.

Careful study of defendant's submission reveals that the state of Sudan has not (1) wholly absorbed or been wholly absorbed by another state; (2) partly taken over or been partly taken over by another state; (3) become independent from another state of which it had formed a part; or (4) arisen out of dismemberment of a state of which it had been a part since the date of plaintiff's contract. Under the Restatement's definition, the state of Sudan has remained the same entity since its independence in 1956. Defendant's own exhibit in support of its motion substantiates that only a change in government was effected by the two military coups * * *

Accordingly, the only changes in the Sudan since its independence in 1956 have been in the government, with seven distinct successive administrations. But there has been only one state.

Defendant unpersuasively emphasizes various aspects of the relevant transitions to reflect the creation of a new state: that the transitions resulted by way of military coups as opposed to routine, constitutional processes, the re-naming of the nation, the suspension of the constitution, the closing of the borders and the declaration of a state of emergency. Treatises, as well as applicable case law, demonstrate that such features do not effect a succession of state. * * *

Furthermore, the Restatement's comparative chart in a Recognition of States section illustrates that a change in government by armed force or fraud, as well as institution of another regime following a civil war, leaves "no question of the existence of the state." It offers as contemporary examples of mere changes in government: Pinochet's 1973 ouster of Allende in Chile, Franco's 1936-39 takeover of Spain, and the Communist revolution in China.

The seminal decision on the distinction between a succession of state versus a change in government is the U. S. Supreme Court decision in *The Sapphire*. In *The Sapphire*, the Supreme Court considered whether a lawsuit begun by the French Emperor, Napoleon III, was abated by the overthrow of the Emperor during the course of litigation. In holding that the action was not extinguished, the Supreme Court

stated that, "on the [Emperor's] deposition the sovereignty does not change, but merely the person or persons in whom it resides. . . . A change in such representative works no change in the national sovereignty or its rights."

* * * *

* * * In *United States v. National City Bank of New York,* the district court held the post-revolutionary State of Russia liable on the treasury notes of the pre-revolutionary state. Similarly, in *Jackson v. People's Republic of China,* the district court determined that the People's Republic, as successor government to the Imperial Chinese Government, was successor to its obligations, specifically, payment of principal due on the prior government-issued bonds. The law is clear that the obligations of a state are unaffected by a mere change in government. It is of no consequence that the Sudan allegedly breached an executory contract. The distinction between executed and executory contracts only applies where there has been a succession of state. The military coups of 1985 and 1989 did not effect a succession of state of the Sudan but merely changed the state's governing body, leaving the state's obligations undisturbed.

Defendant's alternative claim that a fundamental change of circumstances has occurred since October, 1983 relieving it of any prior contractual obligations is unsubstantiated. Defendant presents no explanation as to what "circumstances constituted an essential basis of the consent of the parties to be bound by the agreement" or what changes have "radically transform[ed] the extent of obligations still to be performed under the agreement." Having failed to demonstrate a fundamental change in circumstances, the present government is therefore contractually obligated to plaintiff under the October 14, 1983 five-year extension of agency contract if its predecessor indeed breached that agreement.

CONCLUSION

For the reasons discussed above, summary judgment is denied. Plaintiff is directed to brief the additional grounds for dismissal or summary judgment raised in defendant's motion papers by March 19, 1990. Defendant shall reply by March 26, 1990.

SO ORDERED.

Appendix B

The Constitution of the United States

PREAMBLE

We the People of the United States, in Order to form a more perfect Union, establish Justice, insure domestic Tranquility, provide for the common defence, promote the general Welfare, and secure the Blessings of Liberty to ourselves and our Posterity, do ordain and establish this Constitution for the United States of America.

ARTICLE I

Section 1. All legislative Powers herein granted shall be vested in a Congress of the United States, which shall consist of a Senate and House of Representatives.

Section 2. The House of Representatives shall be composed of Members chosen every second Year by the People of the several States, and the Electors in each State shall have the Qualifications requisite for Electors of the most numerous Branch of the State Legislature.

No Person shall be a Representative who shall not have attained to the Age of twenty five Years, and been seven Years a Citizen of the United States, and who shall not, when elected, be an Inhabitant of that State in which he shall be chosen.

Representatives and direct Taxes shall be apportioned among the several States which may be included within this Union, according to their respective Numbers, which shall be determined by adding to the whole Number of free Persons, including those bound to Service for a Term of Years, and excluding Indians not taxed, three fifths of all other Persons. The actual Enumeration shall be made within three Years after the first Meeting of the Congress of the United States, and within every subsequent Term of ten Years, in such Manner as they shall by Law direct. The Number of Representatives shall not exceed one for every thirty Thousand, but each State shall have at Least one Representative; and until such enumeration shall be made, the State of New Hampshire shall be entitled to chuse three, Massachusetts eight, Rhode Island and Providence Plantations one, Connecticut five, New York six, New Jersey four, Pennsylvania eight, Delaware one, Maryland six, Virginia ten, North Carolina five, South Carolina five, and Georgia three.

When vacancies happen in the Representation from any State, the Executive Authority thereof shall issue Writs of Election to fill such Vacancies.

The House of Representatives shall chuse their Speaker and other Officers; and shall have the sole Power of Impeachment.

Section 3. The Senate of the United States shall be composed of two Senators from each State, chosen by the Legislature thereof, for six Years; and each Senator shall have one Vote.

Immediately after they shall be assembled in Consequence of the first Election, they shall be divided as equally as may be into three Classes. The Seats of the Senators of the first Class shall be vacated at the Expiration of the second Year, of the second Class at the Expiration of the fourth Year, and of the third Class at the Expiration of the sixth Year, so that one third may be chosen every second Year; and if Vacancies happen by Resignation, or otherwise, during the Recess of the Legislature of any State, the Executive thereof may make temporary Appointments until the next Meeting of the Legislature, which shall then fill such Vacancies.

No Person shall be a Senator who shall not have attained to the Age of thirty Years, and been nine Years a Citizen of the United States, and who shall not, when elected, be an Inhabitant of that State for which he shall be chosen.

The Vice President of the United States shall be President of the Senate, but shall have no Vote, unless they be equally divided.

The Senate shall chuse their other Officers, and also a President pro tempore, in the Absence of the Vice President, or when he shall exercise the Office of President of the United States.

The Senate shall have the sole Power to try all Impeachments. When sitting for that Purpose, they shall be on Oath or Affirmation. When the President of the United States is tried, the Chief Justice shall preside: And no Person shall be convicted without the Concurrence of two thirds of the Members present.

Judgment in Cases of Impeachment shall not extend further than to removal from Office, and disqualification to hold and enjoy any Office of honor, Trust, or Profit under the United States: but the Party convicted shall nevertheless be liable and subject to Indictment, Trial, Judgment, and Punishment, according to Law.

Section 4. The Times, Places and Manner of holding Elections for Senators and Representatives, shall be prescribed in each State by the Legislature thereof; but the Congress may at any time by Law make or alter such Regulations, except as to the Places of chusing Senators.

The Congress shall assemble at least once in every Year, and such Meeting shall be on the first Monday in December, unless they shall by Law appoint a different Day.

Section 5. Each House shall be the Judge of the Elections, Returns, and Qualifications of its own Members, and a Majority of each shall constitute a Quorum to do Business; but a smaller Number may adjourn from day to day, and may be authorized to compel the Attendance of absent Members, in such Manner, and under such Penalties as each House may provide.

Each House may determine the Rules of its Proceedings, punish its Members for disorderly Behavior, and, with the Concurrence of two thirds, expel a Member.

Each House shall keep a Journal of its Proceedings, and from time to time publish the same, excepting such Parts as may in their Judgment require Secrecy; and the Yeas and Nays of the Members of either House on any question shall, at the Desire of one fifth of those Present, be entered on the Journal.

Neither House, during the Session of Congress, shall, without the Consent of the other, adjourn for more than three days, nor to any other Place than that in which the two Houses shall be sitting.

Section 6. The Senators and Representatives shall receive a Compensation for their Services, to be ascertained by Law, and paid out of the Treasury of the United States. They shall in all Cases, except Treason, Felony and Breach of the Peace, be privileged from Arrest during their Attendance at the Session of their respective Houses, and in going to and returning from the same; and for any Speech or Debate in either House, they shall not be questioned in any other Place.

No Senator or Representative shall, during the Time for which he was elected, be appointed to any civil Office under the Authority of the United States, which shall have been created, or the Emoluments whereof shall have been increased during such time; and no Person holding any Office under the United States, shall be a Member of either House during his Continuance in Office.

Section 7. All Bills for raising Revenue shall originate in the House of Representatives; but the Senate may propose or concur with Amendments as on other Bills.

Every Bill which shall have passed the House of Representatives and the Senate, shall, before it become a Law, be presented to the President of the United States; If he approve he shall sign it, but if not he shall return it, with his Objections to the House in which it shall have originated, who shall enter the Objections at large on their Journal, and proceed to reconsider it. If after such Reconsideration two thirds of that House shall agree to pass the Bill, it shall be sent together with the Objections, to the other House, by which it shall likewise be reconsidered, and if approved by two thirds of that House, it shall become a Law. But in all such Cases the Votes of both Houses shall be determined by Yeas and Nays, and the Names of the Persons voting for and against the Bill shall be entered on the Journal of each House respectively. If any Bill shall not be returned by the President within ten Days (Sundays excepted) after it shall have been presented to him, the Same shall be a Law, in like Manner as if he had signed it, unless the Congress by their Adjournment prevent its Return in which Case it shall not be a Law.

Every Order, Resolution, or Vote, to which the Concurrence of the Senate and House of Representatives may be necessary (except on a question of Adjournment) shall be presented to the President of the United States; and before the Same shall take Effect, shall be approved by him, or being disapproved by him, shall be repassed by two thirds of the Senate and House of Representatives, according to the Rules and Limitations prescribed in the Case of a Bill.

Section 8. The Congress shall have Power To lay and collect Taxes, Duties, Imposts and Excises, to pay the Debts and provide for the common Defence and general Welfare of the United States; but all Duties, Imposts and Excises shall be uniform throughout the United States;

To borrow Money on the credit of the United States;

To regulate Commerce with foreign Nations, and among the several States, and with the Indian Tribes;

To establish an uniform Rule of Naturalization, and uniform Laws on the subject of Bankruptcies throughout the United States;

To coin Money, regulate the Value thereof, and of foreign Coin, and fix the Standard of Weights and Measures;

To provide for the Punishment of counterfeiting the Securities and current Coin of the United States;

To establish Post Offices and post Roads;

To promote the Progress of Science and useful Arts, by securing for limited Times to Authors and Inventors the exclusive Right to their respective Writings and Discoveries;

To constitute Tribunals inferior to the supreme Court;

To define and punish Piracies and Felonies committed on the high Seas, and Offenses against the Law of Nations;

To declare War, grant Letters of Marque and Reprisal, and make Rules concerning Captures on Land and Water;

To raise and support Armies, but no Appropriation of Money to that Use shall be for a longer Term than two Years;

To provide and maintain a Navy;

To make Rules for the Government and Regulation of the land and naval Forces;

To provide for calling forth the Militia to execute the Laws of the Union, suppress Insurrections and repel Invasions;

To provide for organizing, arming, and disciplining, the Militia, and for governing such Part of them as may be employed in the Service of the United States, reserving to the States respectively, the Appointment of the Officers, and the Authority of training the Militia according to the discipline prescribed by Congress;

To exercise exclusive Legislation in all Cases whatsoever, over such District (not exceeding ten Miles square) as may, by Cession of particular States, and the Acceptance of Congress, become the Seat of the Government of the United States, and to exercise like Authority over all Places purchased by the Consent of the Legislature of the State in which the Same shall be, for the Erection of Forts, Magazines, Arsenals, dock-Yards, and other needful Buildings;—And

To make all Laws which shall be necessary and proper for carrying into Execution the foregoing Powers, and all other Powers vested by this Constitution in the Government of the United States, or in any Department or Officer thereof.

Section 9.   The Migration or Importation of such Persons as any of the States now existing shall think proper to admit, shall not be prohibited by the Congress prior to the Year one thousand eight hundred and eight, but a Tax or duty may be imposed on such Importation, not exceeding ten dollars for each Person.

The privilege of the Writ of Habeas Corpus shall not be suspended, unless when in Cases of Rebellion or Invasion the public Safety may require it.

No Bill of Attainder or ex post facto Law shall be passed.

No Capitation, or other direct, Tax shall be laid, unless in Proportion to the Census or Enumeration herein before directed to be taken.

No Tax or Duty shall be laid on Articles exported from any State.

No Preference shall be given by any Regulation of Commerce or Revenue to the Ports of one State over those of another: nor shall Vessels bound to, or from, one State be obliged to enter, clear, or pay Duties in another.

No Money shall be drawn from the Treasury, but in Consequence of Appropriations made by Law; and a regular Statement and Account of the Receipts and Expenditures of all public Money shall be published from time to time.

No Title of Nobility shall be granted by the United States: And no Person holding any Office of Profit or Trust under them, shall, without the Consent of the Congress, accept of any present, Emolument, Office, or Title, of any kind whatever, from any King, Prince, or foreign State.

Section 10.   No State shall enter into any Treaty, Alliance, or Confederation; grant Letters of Marque and Reprisal; coin Money; emit Bills of Credit; make any Thing but gold and silver Coin a Tender in Payment of Debts; pass any Bill of Attainder, ex post facto Law, or Law impairing the Obligation of Contracts, or grant any Title of Nobility.

No State shall, without the Consent of the Congress, lay any Imposts or Duties on Imports or Exports, except what may be absolutely necessary for executing its inspection Laws: and the net Produce of all Duties and Imposts, laid by any State on Imports or Exports, shall be for the Use of the Treasury of the United States; and all such Laws shall be subject to the Revision and Controul of the Congress.

No State shall, without the Consent of Congress, lay any Duty of Tonnage, keep Troops, or Ships of War in time of Peace, enter into any Agreement or Compact with another State, or with a foreign Power, or engage in War, unless actually invaded, or in such imminent Danger as will not admit of delay.

ARTICLE II

Section 1.   The executive Power shall be vested in a President of the United States of America. He shall hold his Office during the Term of four Years, and, together with the Vice President, chosen for the same Term, be elected, as follows:

Each State shall appoint, in such Manner as the Legislature thereof may direct, a Number of Electors, equal to the whole Number of Senators and Representatives to which the State may be entitled in the Congress; but no Senator or Representative, or Person holding an Office of Trust or Profit under the United States, shall be appointed an Elector.

The Electors shall meet in their respective States, and vote by Ballot for two Persons, of whom one at least shall not be an Inhabitant of the same State with themselves. And they shall make a List of all the Persons voted for, and of the Number of Votes for each; which List they shall sign and certify, and transmit sealed to the Seat of the Government of the United States, directed to the President of the Senate. The President of the Senate shall, in the Presence of the Senate and House of Representatives, open all the Certificates, and the Votes shall then be counted. The Person having the greatest Number of Votes shall be the President, if such Number be a Majority of the whole Number of Electors appointed; and if there be more than one who have such Majority, and have an equal Number of Votes, then the House of Representatives shall immediately chuse by Ballot one of them for President; and if no Person have a Majority, then from the five highest on the List the said House shall in like Manner chuse the President. But in chusing the President, the Votes shall be taken by States, the Representation from each State having one Vote; A quorum for this Purpose shall consist of a Member or Members from two thirds of the States, and a Majority of all the States shall be necessary to a Choice. In every Case, after the Choice of the President, the Person having the greater Number of Votes of the Electors shall be the Vice President. But if there should remain two or more who have equal Votes, the Senate shall chuse from them by Ballot the Vice President.

The Congress may determine the Time of chusing the Electors, and the Day on which they shall give their Votes; which Day shall be the same throughout the United States.

No person except a natural born Citizen, or a Citizen of the United States, at the time of the Adoption of this Constitution, shall be eligible to the Office of President; neither shall any Person be eligible to that Office who shall not have attained to the Age of thirty five Years, and been fourteen Years a Resident within the United States.

In Case of the Removal of the President from Office, or of his Death, Resignation or Inability to discharge the Powers and Duties of the said Office, the same shall devolve on the Vice President, and the Congress may by Law provide for the Case of Removal, Death, Resignation or Inability, both of the President and Vice President, declaring what Officer shall then act as President, and such Officer

shall act accordingly, until the Disability be removed, or a President shall be elected.

The President shall, at stated Times, receive for his Services, a Compensation, which shall neither be increased nor diminished during the Period for which he shall have been elected, and he shall not receive within that Period any other Emolument from the United States, or any of them.

Before he enter on the Execution of his Office, he shall take the following Oath or Affirmation: "I do solemnly swear (or affirm) that I will faithfully execute the Office of President of the United States, and will to the best of my Ability, preserve, protect and defend the Constitution of the United States."

Section 2. The President shall be Commander in Chief of the Army and Navy of the United States, and of the Militia of the several States, when called into the actual Service of the United States; he may require the Opinion, in writing, of the principal Officer in each of the executive Departments, upon any Subject relating to the Duties of their respective Offices, and he shall have Power to grant Reprieves and Pardons for Offenses against the United States, except in Cases of Impeachment.

He shall have Power, by and with the Advice and Consent of the Senate to make Treaties, provided two thirds of the Senators present concur; and he shall nominate, and by and with the Advice and Consent of the Senate, shall appoint Ambassadors, other public Ministers and Consuls, Judges of the supreme Court, and all other Officers of the United States, whose Appointments are not herein otherwise provided for, and which shall be established by Law; but the Congress may by Law vest the Appointment of such inferior Officers, as they think proper, in the President alone, in the Courts of Law, or in the Heads of Departments.

The President shall have Power to fill up all Vacancies that may happen during the Recess of the Senate, by granting Commissions which shall expire at the End of their next Session.

Section 3. He shall from time to time give to the Congress Information of the State of the Union, and recommend to their Consideration such Measures as he shall judge necessary and expedient; he may, on extraordinary Occasions, convene both Houses, or either of them, and in Case of Disagreement between them, with Respect to the Time of Adjournment, he may adjourn them to such Time as he shall think proper; he shall receive Ambassadors and other public Ministers; he shall take Care that the Laws be faithfully executed, and shall Commission all the Officers of the United States.

Section 4. The President, Vice President and all civil Officers of the United States, shall be removed from Office on Impeachment for, and Conviction of, Treason, Bribery, or other high Crimes and Misdemeanors.

ARTICLE III

Section 1. The judicial Power of the United States, shall be vested in one supreme Court, and in such inferior Courts as the Congress may from time to time ordain and establish. The Judges, both of the supreme and inferior Courts, shall hold their Offices during good Behaviour, and shall, at stated Times, receive for their Services a Compensation, which shall not be diminished during their Continuance in Office.

Section 2. The judicial Power shall extend to all Cases, in Law and Equity, arising under this Constitution, the Laws of the United States, and Treaties made, or which shall be made, under their Authority;—to all Cases affecting Ambassadors, other public Ministers and Consuls;—to all Cases of admiralty and maritime Jurisdiction;—to Controversies to which the United States shall be a Party;—to Controversies between two or more States;—between a State and Citizens of another State;—between Citizens of different States;—between Citizens of the same State claiming Lands under Grants of different States, and between a State, or the Citizens thereof, and foreign States, Citizens or Subjects.

In all Cases affecting Ambassadors, other public Ministers and Consuls, and those in which a State shall be a Party, the supreme Court shall have original Jurisdiction. In all the other Cases before mentioned, the supreme Court shall have appellate Jurisdiction, both as to Law and Fact, with such Exceptions, and under such Regulations as the Congress shall make.

The Trial of all Crimes, except in Cases of Impeachment, shall be by Jury; and such Trial shall be held in the State where the said Crimes shall have been committed; but when not committed within any State, the Trial shall be at such Place or Places as the Congress may by Law have directed.

Section 3. Treason against the United States, shall consist only in levying War against them, or, in adhering to their Enemies, giving them Aid and Comfort. No Person shall be convicted of Treason unless on the Testimony of two Witnesses to the same overt Act, or on Confession in open Court.

The Congress shall have Power to declare the Punishment of Treason, but no Attainder of Treason shall work Corruption of Blood, or Forfeiture except during the Life of the Person attainted.

ARTICLE IV

Section 1. Full Faith and Credit shall be given in each State to the public Acts, Records, and judicial Proceedings of every other State. And the Congress may by general Laws prescribe the Manner in which such Acts, Records and Proceedings shall be proved, and the Effect thereof.

Section 2. The Citizens of each State shall be entitled to all Privileges and Immunities of Citizens in the several States.

A Person charged in any State with Treason, Felony, or other Crime, who shall flee from Justice, and be found in another State, shall on Demand of the executive Authority of the State from which he fled, be delivered up, to be removed to the State having Jurisdiction of the Crime.

No Person held to Service or Labour in one State, under the Laws thereof, escaping into another, shall, in Consequence of any Law or Regulation therein, be discharged from such Service or Labour, but shall be delivered up on Claim of the Party to whom such Service or Labour may be due.

Section 3. New States may be admitted by the Congress into this Union; but no new State shall be formed or erected within the Jurisdiction of any other State; nor any State be formed by the Junction of two or more States, or Parts of States, without the Consent of the Legislatures of the States concerned as well as of the Congress.

The Congress shall have Power to dispose of and make all needful Rules and Regulations respecting the Territory or other Property belonging to the United States; and nothing in this Constitution shall be so construed as to Prejudice any Claims of the United States, or of any particular State.

Section 4. The United States shall guarantee to every State in this Union a Republican Form of Government, and shall protect each of them against Invasion; and on Application of the Legislature, or of the Executive (when the Legislature cannot be convened) against domestic Violence.

ARTICLE V

The Congress, whenever two thirds of both Houses shall deem it necessary, shall propose Amendments to this Constitution, or, on the Application of the Legislatures of two thirds of the several States, shall call a Convention for proposing Amendments, which, in either Case, shall be valid to all Intents and Purposes, as part of this Constitution, when ratified by the Legislatures of three fourths of the several States, or by Conventions in three fourths thereof, as the one or the other Mode of Ratification may be proposed by the Congress; Provided that no Amendment which may be made prior to the Year One thousand eight hundred and eight shall in any Manner affect the first and fourth Clauses in the Ninth Section of the first Article; and that no State, without its Consent, shall be deprived of its equal Suffrage in the Senate.

ARTICLE VI

All Debts contracted and Engagements entered into, before the Adoption of this Constitution shall be as valid against the United States under this Constitution, as under the Confederation.

This Constitution, and the Laws of the United States which shall be made in Pursuance thereof; and all Treaties made, or which shall be made, under the Authority of the United States, shall be the supreme Law of the Land; and the Judges in every State shall be bound thereby, any Thing in the Constitution or Laws of any State to the Contrary notwithstanding.

The Senators and Representatives before mentioned, and the Members of the several State Legislatures, and all executive and judicial Officers, both of the United States and of the several States, shall be bound by Oath or Affirmation, to support this Constitution; but no religious Test shall ever be required as a Qualification to any Office or public Trust under the United States.

ARTICLE VII

The Ratification of the Conventions of nine States shall be sufficient for the Establishment of this Constitution between the States so ratifying the Same.

AMENDMENT I [1791]

Congress shall make no law respecting an establishment of religion, or prohibiting the free exercise thereof; or abridging the freedom of speech, or of the press; or the right of the people peaceably to assembly, and to petition the Government for a redress of grievances.

AMENDMENT II [1791]

A well regulated Militia, being necessary to the security of a free State, the right of the people to keep and bear Arms, shall not be infringed.

AMENDMENT III [1791]

No Soldier shall, in time of peace be quartered in any house, without the consent of the Owner, nor in time of war, but in a manner to be prescribed by law.

AMENDMENT IV [1791]

The right of the people to be secure in their persons, houses, papers, and effects, against unreasonable searches and seizures, shall not be violated, and no Warrants shall issue, but upon probable cause, supported by Oath or affirmation, and particularly describing the place to be searched, and the persons or things to be seized.

AMENDMENT V [1791]

No person shall be held to answer for a capital, or otherwise infamous crime, unless on a presentment or indictment of a Grand Jury, except in cases arising in the land or naval forces, or in the Militia, when in actual service in time of War or public danger; nor shall any person be subject for the same offence to be twice put in jeopardy of life or limb; nor shall be compelled in any criminal case to be a witness against himself, nor be deprived of life, liberty, or property,

without due process of law; nor shall private property be taken for public use, without just compensation.

AMENDMENT VI [1791]

In all criminal prosecutions, the accused shall enjoy the right to a speedy and public trial, by an impartial jury of the State and district wherein the crime shall have been committed, which district shall have been previously ascertained by law, and to be informed of the nature and cause of the accusation; to be confronted with the witnesses against him; to have compulsory process for obtaining witnesses in his favor, and to have the Assistance of Counsel for his defence.

AMENDMENT VII [1791]

In Suits at common law, where the value in controversy shall exceed twenty dollars, the right of trial by jury shall be preserved, and no fact tried by jury, shall be otherwise re-examined in any Court of the United States, than according to the rules of the common law.

AMENDMENT VIII [1791]

Excessive bail shall not be required, nor excessive fines imposed, nor cruel and unusual punishments inflicted.

AMENDMENT IX [1791]

The enumeration in the Constitution, of certain rights, shall not be construed to deny or disparage others retained by the people.

AMENDMENT X [1791]

The powers not delegated to the United States by the Constitution, nor prohibited by it to the States, are reserved to the States respectively, or to the people.

AMENDMENT XI [1798]

The Judicial power of the United States shall not be construed to extend to any suit in law or equity, commenced or prosecuted against one of the United States by Citizens of another State, or by Citizens or Subjects of any Foreign State.

AMENDMENT XII [1804]

The Electors shall meet in their respective states, and vote by ballot for President and Vice-President, one of whom, at least, shall not be an inhabitant of the same state with themselves; they shall name in their ballots the person voted for as President, and in distinct ballots the person voted for as Vice-President, and they shall make distinct lists of all persons voted for as President, and of all persons voted for as Vice-President, and of the number of votes for each, which lists they shall sign and certify, and transmit sealed to the seat of the government of the United States, directed to the President of the Senate;—The President of the Senate shall, in the presence of the Senate and House of Representatives, open all the certificates and the votes shall then be counted;—The person having the greatest number of votes for President, shall be the President, if such number be a majority of the whole number of Electors appointed; and if no person have such majority, then from the persons having the highest numbers not exceeding three on the list of those voted for as President, the House of Representatives shall choose immediately, by ballot, the President. But in choosing the President, the votes shall be taken by states, the representation from each state having one vote; a quorum for this purpose shall consist of a member or members from two-thirds of the states, and a majority of all states shall be necessary to a choice. And if the House of Representatives shall not choose a President whenever the right of choice shall devolve upon them, before the fourth day of March next following, then the Vice-President shall act as President, as in the case of the death or other constitutional disability of the President.—The person having the greatest number of votes as Vice-President, shall be the Vice-President, if such number be a majority of the whole number of Electors appointed, and if no person have a majority, then from the two highest numbers on the list, the Senate shall choose the Vice-President; a quorum for the purpose shall consist of two-thirds of the whole number of Senators, and a majority of the whole number shall be necessary to a choice. But no person constitutionally ineligible to the office of President shall be eligible to that of Vice-President of the United States.

AMENDMENT XIII [1865]

Section 1.   Neither slavery nor involuntary servitude, except as a punishment for crime whereof the party shall have been duly convicted, shall exist within the United States, or any place subject to their jurisdiction.

Section 2.   Congress shall have power to enforce this article by appropriate legislation.

AMENDMENT XIV [1868]

Section 1.   All persons born or naturalized in the United States, and subject to the jurisdiction thereof, are citizens of the United States and of the State wherein they reside. No State shall make or enforce any law which shall abridge the privileges or immunities of citizens of the United States; nor shall any State deprive any person of life, liberty, or property, without due process of law; nor deny to any person within its jurisdiction the equal protection of the laws.

Section 2.   Representatives shall be apportioned among the several States according to their respective numbers, counting the whole number of persons in each State, excluding Indians not taxed. But when the right to vote at any election for the choice of electors for President and Vice President of the United States, Representatives in Congress, the Executive and Judicial officers of a State, or the mem-

bers of the Legislature thereof, is denied to any of the male inhabitants of such State, being twenty-one years of age, and citizens of the United States, or in any way abridged, except for participation in rebellion, or other crime, the basis of representation therein shall be reduced in the proportion which the number of such male citizens shall bear to the whole number of male citizens twenty-one years of age in such State.

Section 3.   No person shall be a Senator or Representative in Congress, or elector of President and Vice President, or hold any office, civil or military, under the United States, or under any State, who having previously taken an oath, as a member of Congress, or as an officer of the United States, or as a member of any State legislature, or as an executive or judicial officer of any State, to support the Constitution of the United States, shall have engaged in insurrection or rebellion against the same, or given aid or comfort to the enemies thereof. But Congress may by a vote of two-thirds of each House, remove such disability.

Section 4.   The validity of the public debt of the United States, authorized by law, including debts incurred for payment of pensions and bounties for services in suppressing insurrection or rebellion, shall not be questioned. But neither the United States nor any State shall assume or pay any debt or obligation incurred in aid of insurrection or rebellion against the United States, or any claim for the loss or emancipation of any slave; but all such debts, obligations and claims shall be held illegal and void.

Section 5.   The Congress shall have power to enforce, by appropriate legislation, the provisions of this article.

AMENDMENT XV [1870]

Section 1.   The right of citizens of the United States to vote shall not be denied or abridged by the United States or by any State on account of race, color, or previous condition of servitude.

Section 2.   The Congress shall have power to enforce this article by appropriate legislation.

AMENDMENT XVI [1913]

The Congress shall have power to lay and collect taxes on incomes, from whatever source derived, without apportionment among the several States, and without regard to any census or enumeration.

AMENDMENT XVII [1913]

Section 1.   The Senate of the United States shall be composed of two Senators from each State, elected by the people thereof, for six years; and each Senator shall have one vote. The electors in each State shall have the qualifications requisite for electors of the most numerous branch of the State legislatures.

Section 2.   When vacancies happen in the representation of any State in the Senate, the executive authority of such State shall issue writs of election to fill such vacancies: *Provided*, That the legislature of any State may empower the executive thereof to make temporary appointments until the people fill the vacancies by election as the legislature may direct.

Section 3. This amendment shall not be so construed as to affect the election or term of any Senator chosen before it becomes valid as part of the Constitution.

AMENDMENT XVIII [1919]

Section 1. After one year from the ratification of this article the manufacture, sale, or transportation of intoxicating liquors within, the importation thereof into, or the exportation thereof from the United States and all territory subject to the jurisdiction thereof for beverage purposes is hereby prohibited.

Section 2. The Congress and the several States shall have concurrent power to enforce this article by appropriate legislation.

Section 3. This article shall be inoperative unless it shall have been ratified as an amendment to the Constitution by the legislatures of the several States, as provided in the Constitution, within seven years from the date of the submission hereof to the States by the Congress.

AMENDMENT XIX [1920]

Section 1. The right of citizens of the United States to vote shall not be denied or abridged by the United States or by any State on account of sex.

Section 2. Congress shall have power to enforce this article by appropriate legislation.

AMENDMENT XX [1933]

Section 1. The terms of the President and Vice President shall end at noon on the 20th day of January, and the terms of Senators and Representatives at noon on the 3d day of January, of the years in which such terms would have ended if this article had not been ratified; and the terms of their successors shall then begin.

Section 2. The Congress shall assemble at least once in every year, and such meeting shall begin at noon on the 3d day of January, unless they shall by law appoint a different day.

Section 3. If, at the time fixed for the beginning of the term of the President, the President elect shall have died, the Vice President elect shall become President. If the President shall not have been chosen before the time fixed for the beginning of his term, or if the President elect shall have failed to qualify, then the Vice President elect shall act as President until a President shall have qualified; and the Congress may by law provide for the case wherein neither a President elect nor a Vice President elect shall

have qualified, declaring who shall then act as President, or the manner in which one who is to act shall be selected, and such person shall act accordingly until a President or Vice President shall have qualified.

Section 4. The Congress may by law provide for the case of the death of any of the persons from whom the House of Representatives may choose a President whenever the right of choice shall have devolved upon them, and for the case of the death of any of the persons from whom the Senate may choose a Vice President whenever the right of choice shall have devolved upon them.

Section 5. Sections 1 and 2 shall take effect on the 15th day of October following the ratification of this article.

Section 6. This article shall be inoperative unless it shall have been ratified as an amendment to the Constitution by the legislatures of three-fourths of the several States within seven years from the date of its submission.

AMENDMENT XXI [1933]

Section 1. The eighteenth article of amendment to the Constitution of the United States is hereby repealed.

Section 2. The transportation or importation into any State, Territory, or possession of the United States for delivery or use therein of intoxicating liquors, in violation of the laws thereof, is hereby prohibited.

Section 3. This article shall be inoperative unless it shall have been ratified as an amendment to the Constitution by conventions in the several States, as provided in the Constitution, within seven years from the date of the submission hereof to the States by the Congress.

AMENDMENT XXII [1951]

Section 1. No person shall be elected to the office of the President more than twice, and no person who has held the office of President, or acted as President, for more than two years of a term to which some other person was elected President shall be elected to the office of President more than once. But this Article shall not apply to any person holding the office of President when this Article was proposed by the Congress, and shall not prevent any person who may be holding the office of President, or acting as President, during the term within which this Article becomes operative from holding the office of President or acting as President during the remainder of such term.

Section 2. This article shall be inoperative unless it shall have been ratified as an amendment to the Constitution by the legislatures of three-fourths of the several States within seven years from the date of its submission to the States by the Congress.

AMENDMENT XXIII [1961]

Section 1. The District constituting the seat of Government of the United States shall appoint in such manner as the Congress may direct:

A number of electors of President and Vice President equal to the whole number of Senators and Representatives in Congress to which the District would be entitled if it were a State, but in no event more than the least populous state; they shall be in addition to those appointed by the states, but they shall be considered, for the purposes of the election of President and Vice President, to be electors appointed by a state; and they shall meet in the District and perform such duties as provided by the twelfth article of amendment.

Section 2.   The Congress shall have power to enforce this article by appropriate legislation.

AMENDMENT XXIV [1964]

Section 1.   The right of citizens of the United States to vote in any primary or other election for President or Vice President, for electors for President or Vice President, or for Senator or Representative in Congress, shall not be denied or abridged by the United States, or any State by reason of failure to pay any poll tax or other tax.

Section 2.   The Congress shall have power to enforce this article by appropriate legislation.

AMENDMENT XXV [1967]

Section 1.   In case of the removal of the President from office or of his death or resignation, the Vice President shall become President.

Section 2.   Whenever there is a vacancy in the office of the Vice President, the President shall nominate a Vice President who shall take office upon confirmation by a majority vote of both Houses of Congress.

Section 3.   Whenever the President transmits to the President pro tempore of the Senate and the Speaker of the House of Representatives his written declaration that he is unable to discharge the powers and duties of his office, and until he transmits to them a written declaration to the contrary, such powers and duties shall be discharged by the Vice President as Acting President.

Section 4.   Whenever the Vice President and a majority of either the principal officers of the executive departments or of such other body as Congress may by law provide, transmit to the President pro tempore of the Senate and the Speaker of the House of Representatives their written declaration that the President is unable to discharge the powers and duties of his office, the Vice President shall immediately assume the powers and duties of the office as Acting President.

Thereafter, when the President transmits to the President pro tempore of the Senate and the Speaker of the House of Representatives his written declaration that no inability exists, he shall resume the powers and duties of his office unless the Vice President and a majority of either the principal officers of the executive department or of such other body as Congress may by law provide, transmit within four days to the President pro tempore of the Senate and the Speaker of the House of Representatives their written declaration and the President is unable to discharge the powers and duties of his office. Thereupon Congress shall decide the issue, assembling within forty-eight hours for that purpose if not in session. If the Congress, within twenty-one days after receipt of the latter written declaration, or, if Congress is not in session, within twenty-one days after Congress is required to assemble, determines by two-thirds vote of both Houses that the President is unable to discharge the powers and duties of his office, the Vice President shall continue to discharge the same as Acting President; otherwise, the President shall resume the powers and duties of his office.

AMENDMENT XXVI [1971]

Section 1.   The right of citizens of the United States, who are eighteen years of age or older, to vote shall not be denied or abridged by the United States or by any State on account of age.

Section 2.   The Congress shall have power to enforce this article by appropriate legislation.

The Uniform Commercial Code (Excerpts)

Article 2
SALES

Part 1 Short Title, General Construction and Subject Matter

§ 2—101. Short Title.

This Article shall be known and may be cited as Uniform Commercial Code—Sales.

§ 2—102. Scope; Certain Security and Other Transactions Excluded From This Article.

Unless the context otherwise requires, this Article applies to transactions in goods; it does not apply to any transaction which although in the form of an unconditional contract to sell or present sale is intended to operate only as a security transaction nor does this Article impair or repeal any statute regulating sales to consumers, farmers or other specified classes of buyers.

§ 2—103. Definitions and Index of Definitions.

(1) In this Article unless the context otherwise requires

    (a) "Buyer" means a person who buys or contracts to buy goods.

    (b) "Good faith" in the case of a merchant means honesty in fact and the observance of reasonable commercial standards of fair dealing in the trade.

    (c) "Receipt" of goods means taking physical possession of them.

    (d) "Seller" means a person who sells or contracts to sell goods.

(2) Other definitions applying to this Article or to specified Parts thereof, and the sections in which they appear are:

"Acceptance". Section 2—606.
"Banker's credit". Section 2—325.
"Between merchants". Section 2—104.
"Cancellation". Section 2—106(4).
"Commercial unit". Section 2—105.
"Confirmed credit". Section 2—325.
"Conforming to contract". Section 2—106.
"Contract for sale". Section 2—106.
"Cover". Section 2—712.
"Entrusting". Section 2—403.
"Financing agency". Section 2—104.
"Future goods". Section 2—105.
"Goods". Section 2—105.
"Identification". Section 2—501.
"Installment contract". Section 2—612.
"Letter of Credit". Section 2—325.
"Lot". Section 2—105.
"Merchant". Section 2—104.
"Overseas". Section 2—323.
"Person in position of seller". Section 2—707.
"Present sale". Section 2—106.
"Sale". Section 2—106.
"Sale on approval". Section 2—326.
"Sale or return". Section 2—326.
"Termination". Section 2—106.

(3) The following definitions in other Articles apply to this Article:
"Check". Section 3—104.
"Consignee". Section 7—102.
"Consignor". Section 7—102.
"Consumer goods". Section 9—109.

"Dishonor". Section 3—507.
"Draft". Section 3—104.

(4) In addition Article 1 contains general definitions and principles of construction and interpretation applicable throughout this Article.

§ 2—104. Definitions: "Merchant"; "Between Merchants"; "Financing Agency".

(1) "Merchant" means a person who deals in goods of the kind or otherwise by his occupation holds himself out as having knowledge or skill peculiar to the practices or goods involved in the transaction or to whom such knowledge or skill may be attributed by his employment of an agent or broker or other intermediary who by his occupation holds himself out as having such knowledge or skill.

(2) "Financing agency" means a bank, finance company or other person who in the ordinary course of business makes advances against goods or documents of title or who by arrangement with either the seller or the buyer intervenes in ordinary course to make or collect payment due or claimed under the contract for sale, as by purchasing or paying the seller's draft or making advances against it or by merely taking it for collection whether or not documents of title accompany the draft. "Financing agency" includes also a bank or other person who similarly intervenes between persons who are in the position of seller and buyer in respect to the goods (Section 2—707).

(3) "Between merchants" means in any transaction with respect to which both parties are chargeable with the knowledge or skill of merchants.

§ 2—105. Definitions: Transferability; "Goods"; "Future" Goods; "Lot"; "Commercial Unit".

(1) "Goods" means all things (including specially manufactured goods) which are movable at the time of identification to the contract for sale other than the money in which the price is to be paid, investment securities (Article 8) and things in action. "Goods" also includes the unborn young of animals and growing crops and other identified things attached to realty as described in the section on goods to be severed from realty (Section 2—107).

(2) Goods must be both existing and identified before any interest in them can pass. Goods which are not both existing and identified are "future" goods. A purported present sale of future goods or of any interest therein operates as a contract to sell.

(3) There may be a sale of a part interest in existing identified goods.

(4) An undivided share in an identified bulk of fungible goods is sufficiently identified to be sold although the quantity of the bulk is not determined. Any agreed proportion of such a bulk or any quantity thereof agreed upon by number, weight or other measure may to the extent of the seller's interest in the bulk be sold to the buyer who then becomes an owner in common.

(5) "Lot" means a parcel or a single article which is the subject matter of a separate sale or delivery, whether or not it is sufficient to perform the contract.

(6) "Commercial unit" means such a unit of goods as by commercial usage is a single whole for purposes of sale and division of which materially impairs its character or value on the market or in use. A commercial unit may be a single article (as a machine) or a set of articles (as a suite of furniture or an assortment of sizes) or a quantity (as a bale, gross, or carload) or any other unit treated in use or in the relevant market as a single whole.

§ 2—106. Definitions: "Contract"; "Agreement"; "Contract for Sale"; "Sale"; "Present Sale"; "Conforming" to Contract; "Termination"; "Cancellation".

(1) In this Article unless the context otherwise requires "contract" and "agreement" are limited to those relating to the present or future sale of goods. "Contract for sale" includes both a present sale of goods and a contract to sell goods at a future time. A "sale" consists in the passing of title from the seller to the buyer for a price (Section 2—401). A "present sale" means a sale which is accomplished by the making of the contract.

(2) Goods or conduct including any part of a performance are "conforming" or conform to the contract when they are in accordance with the obligations under the contract.

(3) "Termination" occurs when either party pursuant to a power created by agreement or law puts an end to the contract otherwise than for its breach. On "termination" all obligations which are still executory on both sides are discharged but any right based on prior breach or performance survives.

(4) "Cancellation" occurs when either party puts an end to the contract for breach by the other and its effect is the same as that of "termination" except that the cancelling party also retains any remedy for breach of the whole contract or any unperformed balance.

§ 2—107. Goods to Be Severed From Realty: Recording.

(1) A contract for the sale of minerals or the like (including oil and gas) or a structure or its materials to be removed from realty is a contract for the sale of goods within this Article if they are to be severed by the seller but until severance a purported present sale thereof which is not effective as a transfer of an interest in land is effective only as a contract to sell.

(2) A contract for the sale apart from the land of growing crops or other things attached to realty and capable of severance without material harm thereto but not described in subsection (1) or of timber to be cut is a contract for the sale of goods within this Article whether the subject matter is to be severed by the buyer or by the seller even though it forms part of the realty at the time of contracting, and the parties can by identification effect a present sale before severance.

(3) The provisions of this section are subject to any third party rights provided by the law relating to realty records, and the contract for sale may be executed and recorded as a document transferring an interest in land and shall then constitute notice to third parties of the buyer's rights under the contract for sale.

Part 2 Form, Formation and Readjustment of Contract

§ 2—201. **Formal Requirements; Statute of Frauds.**

(1) Except as otherwise provided in this section a contract for the sale of goods for the price of $500 or more is not enforceable by way of action or defense unless there is some writing sufficient to indicate that a contract for sale has been made between the parties and signed by the party against whom enforcement is sought or by his authorized agent or broker. A writing is not insufficient because it omits or incorrectly states a term agreed upon but the contract is not enforceable under this paragraph beyond the quantity of goods shown in such writing.

(2) Between merchants if within a reasonable time a writing in confirmation of the contract and sufficient against the sender is received and the party receiving it has reason to know its contents, its satisfies the requirements of subsection (1) against such party unless written notice of objection to its contents is given within ten days after it is received.

(3) A contract which does not satisfy the requirements of subsection (1) but which is valid in other respects is enforceable

(a) if the goods are to be specially manufactured for the buyer and are not suitable for sale to others in the ordinary course of the seller's business and the seller, before notice of repudiation is received and under circumstances which reasonably indicate that the goods are for the buyer, has made either a substantial beginning of their manufacture or commitments for their procurement; or

(b) if the party against whom enforcement is sought admits in his pleading, testimony or otherwise in court that a contract for sale was made, but the contract is not enforceable under this provision beyond the quantity of goods admitted; or

(c) with respect to goods for which payment has been made and accepted or which have been received and accepted (Sec. 2—606).

§ 2—202. **Final Written Expression: Parol or Extrinsic Evidence.**

Terms with respect to which the confirmatory memoranda of the parties agree or which are otherwise set forth in a writing intended by the parties as a final expression of their agreement with respect to such terms as are included therein may not be contradicted by evidence of any prior agreement or of a contemporaneous oral agreement but may be explained or supplemented

(a) by course of dealing or usage of trade (Section 1—205) or by course of performance (Section 2—208); and

(b) by evidence of consistent additional terms unless the court finds the writing to have been intended also as a complete and exclusive statement of the terms of the agreement.

§ 2—203. **Seals Inoperative.**

The affixing of a seal to a writing evidencing a contract for sale or an offer to buy or sell goods does not constitute the writing a sealed instrument and the law with respect to sealed instruments does not apply to such a contract or offer.

§ 2—204. **Formation in General.**

(1) A contract for sale of goods may be made in any manner suffecent to show agreement, including conduct by both parties which recognizes the existence of such a contract.

(2) An agreement sufficient to constitute a contract for sale may be found even though the moment of its making is undetermined.

(3) Even though one or more terms are left open a contract for sale does not fail for indefiniteness if the parties have intended to make a contract and there is a reasonably certain basis for giving an appropriate remedy.

§ 2—205. **Firm Offers.**

An offer by a merchant to buy or sell goods in a signed writing which by its terms gives assurance that it will be held open is not revocable, for lack of consideration, during the time stated or if no time is stated for a reasonable time, but in no event may such period of irrevocability exceed three months; but any such term of assurance on a form supplied by the offeree must be separately signed by the offeror.

§ 2—206. **Offer and Acceptance in Formation of Contract.**

(1) Unless other unambiguously indicated by the language or circumstances

(a) an offer to make a contract shall be construed as inviting acceptance in any manner and by any medium reasonable in the circumstances;

(b) an order or other offer to buy goods for prompt or current shipment shall be construed as inviting acceptance either by a prompt promise to ship or by the prompt or current shipment of conforming or nonconforming goods, but such a shipment of non-conforming goods does not constitute an acceptance if the seller seasonably notifies the buyer that the shipment is offered only as an accommodation to the buyer.

(2) Where the beginning of a requested performance is a reasonable mode of acceptance an offeror who is not notified of acceptance within a reasonable time may treat the offer as having lapsed before acceptance.

§ 2—207. Additional Terms in Acceptance or Confirmation.

(1) A definite and seasonable expression of acceptance or a written confirmation which is sent within a reasonable time operates as an acceptance even though it states terms additional to or different from those offered or agreed upon, unless acceptance is expressly made conditional on assent to the additional or different terms.

(2) The additional terms are to be construed as proposals for addition to the contract. Between merchants such terms become part of the contract unless:

(a) the offer expressly limits acceptance to the terms of the offer;

(b) they materially alter it; or

(c) notification of objection to them has already been given or is given within a reasonable time after notice of them is received.

(3) Conduct by both parties which recognizes the existence of a contract is sufficient to establish a contract for sale although the writings of the parties do not otherwise establish a contract. In such case the terms of the particular contract consist of those terms on which the writings of the parties agree, together with any supplementary terms incorporated under any other provisions of this Act.

§ 2—208. Course of Performance or Practical Construction.

(1) Where the contract for sale involves repeated occasions for performance by either party with knowledge of the nature of the performance and opportunity for objection to it by the other, any course of performance accepted or acquiesced in without objection shall be relevant to determine the meaning of the agreement.

(2) The express terms of the agreement and any such course of performance, as well as any course of dealing and usage of trade, shall be construed whenever reasonable as consistent with each other; but when such construction is unreasonable, express terms shall control course of performance and course of performance shall control both course of dealing and usage of trade (Section 1—205).

(3) Subject to the provisions of the next section on modification and waiver, such course of performance shall be relevant to show a waiver or modification of any term inconsistent with such course of performance.

§ 2—209. Modification, Rescission and Waiver.

(1) An agreement modifying a contract within this Article needs no consideration to be binding.

(2) A signed agreement which excludes modification or rescission except by a signed writing cannot be otherwise modified or rescinded, but except as between merchants such a requirement on a form supplied by the merchant must be separately signed by the other party.

(3) The requirements of the statute of frauds section of this Article (Section 2—201) must be satisfied if the contract as modified is within its provisions.

(4) Although an attempt at modification or rescission does not satisfy the requirements of subsection (2) or (3) it can operate as a waiver.

(5) A party who has made a waiver affecting an executory portion of the contract may retract the waiver by reasonable notification received by the other party that strict performance will be required of any term waived, unless the retraction would be unjust in view of a material change of position in reliance on the waiver.

§ 2—210. Delegation of Performance; Assignment of Rights.

(1) A party may perform his duty through a delegate unless otherwise agreed or unless the other party has a substantial interest in having his original promisor perform or control the acts required by the contract. No delegation of performance relieves the party delegating of any duty to perform or any liability for breach.

(2) Unless otherwise agreed all rights of either seller or buyer can be assigned except where the assignment would materially change the duty of the other party, or increase materially the burden or risk imposed on him by his contract, or impair materially his chance of obtaining return performance. A right to damages for breach of the whole contract or a right arising out of the assignor's due performance of his entire obligation can be assigned despite agreement otherwise.

(3) Unless the circumstances indicate the contrary a prohibition of assignment of "the contract" is to be construed as barring only the delegation to the assignee of the assignor's performance.

(4) An assignment of "the contract" or of "all my rights under the contract" or an assignment in similar general terms is an assignment of rights and unless the language or the circumstances (as in an assignment for security) indicate the contrary, it is a delegation of performance of the duties of the assignor and its acceptance by the assignee

constitutes a promise by him to perform those duties. This promise is enforceable by either the assignor or the other party to the original contract.

(5) The other party may treat any assignment which delegates performance as creating reasonable grounds for insecurity and may without prejudice to his rights against the assignor demand assurances from the assignee (Section 2—609).

Part 3 General Obligation and Construction of Contract

§ 2—301. General Obligations of Parties.

The obligation of the seller is to transfer and deliver and that of the buyer is to accept and pay in accordance with the contract.

§ 2—302. Unconscionable Contract or Clause.

(1) If the court as a matter of law finds the contract or any clause of the contract to have been unconscionable at the time it was made the court may refuse to enforce the contract, or it may enforce the remainder of the contract without the unconscionable clause, or it may so limit the application of any unconscionable clause as to avoid any unconscionable result.

(2) When it is claimed or appears to the court that the contract or any clause thereof may be unconscionable the parties shall be afforded a reasonable opportunity to present evidence as to its commercial setting, purpose and effect to aid the court in making the determination.

§ 2—303. Allocations or Division of Risks.

Where this Article allocates a risk or a burden as between the parties ''unless otherwise agreed'', the agreement may not only shift the allocation but may also divide the risk or burden.

§ 2—304. Price Payable in Money, Goods, Realty, or Otherwise.

(1) The price can be made payable in money or otherwise. If it is payable in whole or in part in goods each party is a seller of the goods which he is to transfer.

(2) Even though all or part of the price is payable in an interest in realty the transfer of the goods and the seller's obligations with reference to them are subject to this Article, but not the transfer of the interest in realty or the transferor's obligations in connection therewith.

§ 2—305. Open Price Term.

(1) The parties if they so intend can conclude a contract for sale even though the price is not settled. In such a case the price is a reasonable price at the time for delivery if

    (a) nothing is said as to price; or

    (b) the price is left to be agreed by the parties and they fail to agree; or

    (c) the price is to be fixed in terms of some agreed market or other standard as set or recorded by a third person or agency and it is not so set or recorded.

(2) A price to be fixed by the seller or by the buyer means a price for him to fix in good faith.

(3) When a price left to be fixed otherwise than by agreement of the parties fails to be fixed through fault of one party the other may at his option treat the contract as cancelled or himself fix a reasonable price.

(4) Where, however, the parties intend not to be bound unless the price be fixed or agreed and it is not fixed or agreed there is no contract. In such a case the buyer must return any goods already received or if unable so to do must pay their reasonable value at the time of delivery and the seller must return any portion of the price paid on account.

§ 2—306. Output, Requirements and Exclusive Dealings.

(1) A term which measures the quantity by the output of the seller or the requirements of the buyer means such actual output or requirements as may occur in good faith, except that no quantity unreasonably disproportionate to any stated estimate or in the absence of a stated estimate to any normal or otherwise comparable prior output or requirements may be tendered or demanded.

(2) A lawful agreement by either the seller or the buyer for exclusive dealing in the kind of goods concerned imposes unless otherwise agreed an obligation by the seller to use best efforts to supply the goods and by the buyer to use best efforts to promote their sale.

§ 2—307. Delivery in Single Lot or Several Lots.

Unless otherwise agreed all goods called for by a contract for sale must be tendered in a single delivery and payment is due only on such tender but where the circumstances give either party the right to make or demand delivery in lots the price if it can be apportioned may be demanded for each lot.

§ 2—308. Absence of Specified Place for Delivery.

Unless otherwise agreed

(a) the place for delivery of goods is the seller's place of business or if he has none his residence; but

(b) in a contract for sale of identified goods which to the knowledge of the parties at the time of contracting are in some other place, that place is the place for their delivery; and

(c) documents of title may be delivered through customary banking channels.

§ 2—309. Absence of Specific Time Provisions; Notice of Termination.

(1) The time for shipment or delivery or any other action

under a contract if not provided in this Article or agreed upon shall be a reasonable time.

(2) Where the contract provides for successive performances but is indefinite in duration it is valid for a reasonable time but unless otherwise agreed may be terminated at any time by either party.

(3) Termination of a contract by one party except on the happening of an agreed event requires that reasonable notification be received by the other party and an agreement dispensing with notification is invalid if its operation would be unconscionable.

§ 2—310. **Open Time for Payment or Running of Credit; Authority to Ship Under Reservation.**

Unless otherwise agreed

(a) payment is due at the time and place at which the buyer is to receive the goods even though the place of shipment is the place of delivery; and

(b) if the seller is authorized to send the goods he may ship them under reservation, and may tender the documents of title, but the buyer may inspect the goods after their arrival before payment is due unless such inspection is inconsistent with the terms of the contract (Section 2—513); and

(c) if delivery is authorized and made by way of documents of title otherwise than by subsection (b) then payment is due at the time and place at which the buyer is to receive the documents regardless of where the goods are to be received; and

(d) where the seller is required or authorized to ship the goods on credit the credit period runs from the time of shipment but post-dating the invoice or delaying its dispatch will correspondingly delay the starting of the credit period.

§ 2—311. **Options and Cooperation Respecting Performance.**

(1) An agreement for sale which is otherwise sufficiently definite (subsection (3) of Section 2—204) to be a contract is not made invalid by the fact that it leaves particulars of performance to be specified by one of the parties. Any such specification must be made in good faith and within limits set by commercial reasonableness.

(2) Unless otherwise agreed specifications relating to assortment of the goods are at the buyer's option and except as otherwise provided in subsections (1)(c) and (3) of Section 2—319 specifications or arrangements relating to shipment are at the seller's option.

(3) Where such specification would materially affect the other party's performance but is not seasonably made or where one party's cooperation is necessary to the agreed performance of the other but is not seasonably forthcoming, the other party in addition to all other remedies

  (a) is excused for any resulting delay in his own performance; and

  (b) may also either proceed to perform in any reasonable manner or after the time for a material part of his own performance treat the failure to specify or to cooperate as a breach by failure to deliver or accept the goods.

§ 2—312. **Warranty of Title and Against Infringement; Buyer's Obligation Against Infringement.**

(1) Subject to subsection (2) there is in a contract for sale a warranty by the seller that

  (a) the title conveyed shall be good, and its transfer rightful; and

  (b) the goods shall be delivered free from any security interest or other lien or encumbrance of which the buyer at the time of contracting has no knowledge.

(2) A warranty under subsection (1) will be excluded or modified only by specific language or by circumstances which give the buyer reason to know that the person selling does not claim title in himself or that he is purporting to sell only such right or title as he or a third person may have.

(3) Unless otherwise agreed a seller who is a merchant regularly dealing in goods of the kind warrants that the goods shall be delivered free of the rightful claim of any third person by way of infringement or the like but a buyer who furnishes specifications to the seller must hold the seller harmless against any such claim which arises out of compliance with the specifications.

§ 2—313. **Express Warranties by Affirmation, Promise, Description, Sample.**

(1) Express warranties by the seller are created as follows:

  (a) Any affirmation of fact or promise made by the seller to the buyer which relates to the goods and becomes part of the basis of the bargain creates an express warranty that the goods shall conform to the affirmation or promise.

  (b) Any description of the goods which is made part of the basis of the bargain creates an express warranty that the goods shall conform to the description.

  (c) Any sample or model which is made part of the basis of the bargain creates an express warranty that the whole of the goods shall conform to the sample or model.

(2) It is not necessary to the creation of an express warranty that the seller use formal words such as ''warrant'' or ''guarantee'' or that he have a specific intention to make a warranty, but an affirmation merely of the value of the goods or a statement purporting to be merely the seller's opinion or commendation of the goods does not create a warranty.

§ 2—314. **Implied Warranty: Merchantability; Usage of Trade.**

(1) Unless excluded or modified (Section 2—316), a warranty that the goods shall be merchantable is implied in a contract for their sale if the seller is a merchant with respect to goods of that kind. Under this section the serving for value of food or drink to be consumed either on the premises or elsewhere is a sale.

(2) Goods to be merchantable must be at least such as

(a) pass without objection in the trade under the contract description; and

(b) in the case of fungible goods, are of fair average quality within the description; and

(c) are fit for the ordinary purposes for which such goods are used; and

(d) run, within the variations permitted by the agreement, of even kind, quality and quantity within each unit and among all units involved; and

(e) are adequately contained, packaged, and labeled as the agreement may require; and

(f) conform to the promises or affirmations of fact made on the container or label if any.

(3) Unless excluded or modified (Section 2—316) other implied warranties may arise from course of dealing or usage of trade.

§ 2—315. **Implied Warranty: Fitness for Particular Purpose.**

Where the seller at the time of contracting has reason to know any particular purpose for which the goods are required and that the buyer is relying on the seller's skill or judgment to select or furnish suitable goods, there is unless excluded or modified under the next section an implied warranty that the goods shall be fit for such purpose.

§ 2—316. **Exclusion or Modification of Warranties.**

(1) Words or conduct relevant to the creation of an express warranty and words or conduct tending to negate or limit warranty shall be construed wherever reasonable as consistent with each other; but subject to the provisions of this Article on parol or extrinsic evidence (Section 2—202) negation or limitation is inoperative to the extent that such construction is unreasonable.

(2) Subject to subsection (3), to exclude or modify the implied warranty of merchantability or any part of it the language must mention merchantability and in case of a writing must be conspicuous, and to exclude or modify any implied warranty of fitness the exclusion must be by a writing and conspicuous. Language to exclude all implied warranties of fitness is sufficient if it states, for example, that "There are no warranties which extend beyond the description on the face hereof."

(3) Notwithstanding subsection (2)

(a) unless the circumstances indicate otherwise, all implied warranties are excluded by expressions like "as is", "with all faults" or other language which in common understanding calls the buyer's attention to the exclusion of warranties and makes plain that there is no implied warranty; and

(b) when the buyer before entering into the contract has examined the goods or the sample or model as fully as he desired or has refused to examine the goods there is no implied warranty with regard to defects which an examination ought in the circumstances to have revealed to him; and

(c) an implied warranty can also be excluded or modified by course of dealing or course of performance or usage of trade.

(4) Remedies for breach of warranty can be limited in accordance with the provisions of this Article on liquidation or limitation of damages and on contractual modification of remedy (Sections 2—718 and 2—719).

§ 2—317. **Cumulation and Conflict of Warranties Express or Implied.**

Warranties whether express or implied shall be construed as consistent with each other and as cumulative, but if such construction is unreasonable the intention of the parties shall determine which warranty is dominant. In ascertaining that intention the following rules apply:

(a) Exact or technical specifications displace an inconsistent sample or model or general language of description.

(b) A sample from an existing bulk displaces inconsistent general language of description.

(c) Express warranties displace inconsistent implied warranties other than an implied warranty of fitness for a particular purpose.

§ 2—318. **Third Party Beneficiaries of Warranties Express or Implied.**

Note: If this Act is introduced in the Congress of the United States this section should be omitted. (States to select one alternative.)

Alternative A

A seller's warranty whether express or implied extends to any natural person who is in the family or household of his buyer or who is a guest in his home if it is reasonable to expect that such person may use, consume or be affected by the goods and who is injured in person by breach of the warranty. A seller may not exclude or limit the operation of this section.

Alternative B

A seller's warranty whether express or implied extends to any natural person who may reasonably be expected to use, consume or be affected by the goods and who is injured in person by breach of the warranty. A seller may not exclude or limit the operation of this section.

Alternative C

A seller's warranty whether express or implied extends to any person who may reasonably be expected to use, consume or be affected by the goods and who is injured by breach of the warranty. A seller may not exclude or limit the operation of this section with respect to injury to the person of an individual to whom the warranty extends. As amended 1966.

§ 2—319. **F.O.B. and F.A.S. Terms.**

(1) Unless otherwise agreed the term F.O.B. (which means "free on board") at a named place, even though used only in connection with the stated price, is a delivery term under which

(a) when the term is F.O.B. the place of shipment, the seller must at that place ship the goods in the manner provided in this Article (Section 2—504) and bear the expense and risk of putting them into the possession of the carrier; or

(b) when the term is F.O.B. the place of destination, the seller must at his own expense and risk transport the goods to that place and there tender delivery of them in the manner provided in this Article (Section 2—503);

(c) when under either (a) or (b) the term is also F.O.B. vessel, car or other vehicle, the seller must in addition at his own expense and risk load the goods on board. If the term is F.O.B. vessel the buyer must name the vessel and in an appropriate case the seller must comply with the provisions of this Article on the form of bill of lading (Section 2—323).

(2) Unless otherwise agreed the term F.A.S. vessel (which means "free alongside") at a named port, even though used only in connection with the stated price, is a delivery term under which the seller must

(a) at his own expense and risk deliver the goods alongside the vessel in the manner usual in that port or on a dock designated and provided by the buyer; and

(b) obtain and tender a receipt for the goods in exchange for which the carrier is under a duty to issue a bill of lading.

(3) Unless otherwise agreed in any case falling within subsection (1)(a) or (c) or subsection (2) the buyer must seasonably give any needed instructions for making delivery, including when the term is F.A.S. or F.O.B. the loading berth of the vessel and in an appropriate case its name and sailing date. The seller may treat the failure of needed instructions as a failure of cooperation under this Article (Section 2—311). He may also at his option move the goods in any reasonable manner preparatory to delivery or shipment.

(4) Under the term F.O.B. vessel or F.A.S. unless otherwise agreed the buyer must make payment against tender of the required documents and the seller may not tender nor the buyer demand delivery of the goods in substitution for the documents.

§ 2—320. **C.I.F. and C. & F. Terms.**

(1) The term C.I.F. means that the price includes in a lump sum the cost of the goods and the insurance and freight to the named destination. The term C. & F. or C.F. means that the price so includes cost and freight to the named destination.

(2) Unless otherwise agreed and even though used only in connection with the stated price and destination, the term C.I.F. destination or its equivalent requires the seller at his own expense and risk to

(a) put the goods into the possession of a carrier at the port for shipment and obtain a negotiable bill or bills of lading covering the entire transportation to the named destination; and

(b) load the goods and obtain a receipt from the carrier (which may be contained in the bill of lading) showing that the freight has been paid or provided for; and

(c) obtain a policy or certificate of insurance, including any war risk insurance, of a kind and on terms then current at the port of shipment in the usual amount, in the currency of the contract, shown to cover the same goods covered by the bill of lading and providing for payment of loss to the order of the buyer or for the account of whom it may concern; but the seller may add to the price the amount of the premium for any such war risk insurance; and

(d) prepare an invoice of the goods and procure any other documents required to effect shipment or to comply with the contract; and

(e) forward and tender with commercial promptness all the documents in due form and with any indorsement necessary to perfect the buyer's rights.

(3) Unless otherwise agreed the term C. & F. or its equivalent has the same effect and imposes upon the seller the same obligations and risks as a C.I.F. term except the obligation as to insurance.

(4) Under the term C.I.F. or C. & F. unless otherwise agreed the buyer must make payment against tender of the required documents and the seller may not tender nor the buyer demand delivery of the goods in substitution for the documents.

§ 2—321. **C.I.F. or C. & F.: "Net Landed Weights"; "Payment on Arrival"; Warranty of Condition on Arrival.**

Under a contract containing a term C.I.F. or C. & F.

(1) Where the price is based on or is to be adjusted according to "net landed weights", "delivered weights",

"out turn" quantity or quality or the like, unless otherwise agreed the seller must reasonably estimate the price. The payment due on tender of the documents called for by the contract is the amount so estimated, but after final adjustment of the price a settlement must be made with commercial promptness.

(2) An agreement described in subsection (1) or any warranty of quality or condition of the goods on arrival places upon the seller the risk of ordinary deterioration, shrinkage and the like in transportation but has no effect on the place or time of identification to the contract for sale or delivery or on the passing of the risk of loss.

(3) Unless otherwise agreed where the contract provides for payment on or after arrival of the goods the seller must before payment allow such preliminary inspection as is feasible; but if the goods are lost delivery of the documents and payment are due when the goods should have arrived.

§ 2—322. **Delivery "Ex-Ship".**

(1) Unless otherwise agreed a term for delivery of goods "ex-ship" (which means from the carrying vessel) or in equivalent language is not restricted to a particular ship and requires delivery from a ship which has reached a place at the named port of destination where goods of the kind are usually discharged.

(2) Under such a term unless otherwise agreed

(a) the seller must discharge all liens arising out of the carriage and furnish the buyer with a direction which puts the carrier under a duty to deliver the goods; and

(b) the risk of loss does not pass to the buyer until the goods leave the ship's tackle or are otherwise properly unloaded.

§ 2—323. **Form of Bill of Lading Required in Overseas Shipment; "Overseas".**

(1) Where the contract contemplates overseas shipment and contains a term C.I.F. or C. & F. or F.O.B. vessel, the seller unless otherwise agreed must obtain a negotiable bill of lading stating that the goods have been loaded on board or, in the case of a term C.I.F. or C. & F., received for shipment.

(2) Where in a case within subsection (1) a bill of lading has been issued in a set of parts, unless otherwise agreed if the documents are not to be sent from abroad the buyer may demand tender of the full set; otherwise only one part of the bill of lading need be tendered. Even if the agreement expressly requires a full set

(a) due tender of a single part is acceptable within the provisions of this Article on cure of improper delivery (subsection (1) of Section 2—508); and

(b) even though the full set is demanded, if the documents are sent from abroad the person tendering an incomplete set may nevertheless require payment upon

furnishing an indemnity which the buyer in good faith deems adequate.

(3) A shipment by water or by air or a contract contemplating such shipment is "overseas" insofar as by usage of trade or agreement it is subject to the commercial, financing or shipping practices characteristic of international deep water commerce.

§ 2—324. **"No Arrival, No Sale" Term.**

Under a term "no arrival, no sale" or terms of like meaning, unless otherwise agreed,

(a) the seller must properly ship conforming goods and if they arrive by any means he must tender them on arrival but he assumes no obligation that the goods will arrive unless he has caused the non-arrival; and

(b) where without fault of the seller the goods are in part lost or have so deteriorated as no longer to conform to the contract or arrive after the contract time, the buyer may proceed as if there had been casualty to identified goods (Section 2—613).

§ 2—325. **"Letter of Credit" Term; "Confirmed Credit".**

(1) Failure of the buyer seasonably to furnish an agreed letter of credit is a breach of the contract for sale.

(2) The delivery to seller of a proper letter of credit suspends the buyer's obligation to pay. If the letter of credit is dishonored, the seller may on seasonable notification to the buyer require payment directly from him.

(3) Unless otherwise agreed the term "letter of credit" or "banker's credit" in a contract for sale means an irrevocable credit issued by a financing agency of good repute and, where the shipment is overseas, of good international repute. The term "confirmed credit" means that the credit must also carry the direct obligation of such an agency which does business in the seller's financial market.

§ 2—326. **Sale on Approval and Sale or Return; Consignment Sales and Rights of Creditors.**

(1) Unless otherwise agreed, if delivered goods may be returned by the buyer even though they conform to the contract, the transaction is

(a) a "sale on approval" if the goods are delivered primarily for use, and

(b) a "sale or return" if the goods are delivered primarily for resale.

(2) Except as provided in subsection (3), goods held on approval are not subject to the claims of the buyer's creditors until acceptance; goods held on sale or return are subject to such claims while in the buyer's possession.

(3) Where goods are delivered to a person for sale and such person maintains a place of business at which he deals in

goods of the kind involved, under a name other than the name of the person making delivery, then with respect to claims of creditors of the person conducting the business the goods are deemed to be on sale or return. The provisions of this subsection are applicable even though an agreement purports to reserve title to the person making delivery until payment or resale or uses such words as "on consignment" or "on memorandum". However, this subsection is not applicable if the person making delivery

(a) complies with an applicable law providing for a consignor's interest or the like to be evidenced by a sign, or

(b) establishes that the person conducting the business is generally known by his creditors to be substantially engaged in selling the goods of others, or

(c) complies with the filing provisions of the Article on Secured Transactions (Article 9).

(4) Any "or return" term of a contract for sale is to be treated as a separate contract for sale within the statute of frauds section of this Article (Section 2—201) and as contradicting the sale aspect of the contract within the provisions of this Article on parol or extrinsic evidence (Section 2—202).

§ 2—327. **Special Incidents of Sale on Approval and Sale or Return.**

(1) Under a sale on approval unless otherwise agreed

(a) although the goods are identified to the contract the risk of loss and the title do not pass to the buyer until acceptance; and

(b) use of the goods consistent with the purpose of trial is not acceptance but failure seasonably to notify the seller of election to return the goods is acceptance, and if the goods conform to the contract acceptance of any part is acceptance of the whole; and

(c) after due notification of election to return, the return is at the seller's risk and expense but a merchant buyer must follow any reasonable instructions.

(2) Under a sale or return unless otherwise agreed

(a) the option to return extends to the whole or any commercial unit of the goods while in substantially their original condition, but must be exercised seasonably; and

(b) the return is at the buyer's risk and expense.

§ 2—328. **Sale by Auction.**

(1) In a sale by auction if goods are put up in lots each lot is the subject of a separate sale.

(2) A sale by auction is complete when the auctioneer so announces by the fall of the hammer or in other customary manner. Where a bid is made while the hammer is falling in acceptance of a prior bid the auctioneer may in his discretion reopen the bidding or declare the goods sold under the bid on which the hammer was falling.

(3) Such a sale is with reserve unless the goods are in explicit terms put up without reserve. In an auction with reserve the auctioneer may withdraw the goods at any time until he announces completion of the sale. In an auction without reserve, after the auctioneer calls for bids on an article or lot, that article or lot cannot be withdrawn unless no bid is made within a reasonable time. In either case a bidder may retract his bid until the auctioneer's announcement of completion of the sale, but a bidder's retraction does not revive any previous bid.

(4) If the auctioneer knowingly receives a bid on the seller's behalf or the seller makes or procures such as bid, and notice has not been given that liberty for such bidding is reserved, the buyer may at his option avoid the sale or take the goods at the price of the last good faith bid prior to the completion of the sale. This subsection shall not apply to any bid at a forced sale.

Part 4 Title, Creditors and Good Faith Purchasers

§ 2—401. **Passing of Title; Reservation for Security; Limited Application of This Section.**

Each provision of this Article with regard to the rights, obligations and remedies of the seller, the buyer, purchasers or other third parties applies irrespective of title to the goods except where the provision refers to such title. Insofar as situations are not covered by the other provisions of this Article and matters concerning title became material the following rules apply:

(1) Title to goods cannot pass under a contract for sale prior to their identification to the contract (Section 2—501), and unless otherwise explicitly agreed the buyer acquires by their identification a special property as limited by this Act. Any retention or reservation by the seller of the title (property) in goods shipped or delivered to the buyer is limited in effect to a reservation of a security interest. Subject to these provisions and to the provisions of the Article on Secured Transactions (Article 9), title to goods passes from the seller to the buyer in any manner and on any conditions explicitly agreed on by the parties.

(2) Unless otherwise explicitly agreed title passes to the buyer at the time and place at which the seller completes his performance with reference to the physical delivery of the goods, despite any reservation of a security interest and even though a document of title is to be delivered at a different time or place; and in particular and despite any reservation of a security interest by the bill of lading

(a) if the contract requires or authorizes the seller to send the goods to the buyer but does not require him to deliver them at destination, title passes to the buyer at the time and place of shipment; but

(b) if the contract requires delivery at destination, title passes on tender there.

(3) Unless otherwise explicitly agreed where delivery is to be made without moving the goods,

(a) if the seller is to deliver a document of title, title passes at the time when and the place where he delivers such documents; or

(b) if the goods are at the time of contracting already identified and no documents are to be delivered, title passes at the time and place of contracting.

(4) A rejection or other refusal by the buyer to receive or retain the goods, whether or not justified, or a justified revocation of acceptance revests title to the goods in the seller. Such revesting occurs by operation of law and is not a "sale".

§ 2—402. **Rights of Seller's Creditors Against Sold Goods.**

(1) Except as provided in subsections (2) and (3), rights of unsecured creditors of the seller with respect to goods which have been identified to a contract for sale are subject to the buyer's rights to recover the goods under this Article (Sections 2—502 and 2—716).

(2) A creditor of the seller may treat a sale or an identification of goods to a contract for sale as void if as against him a retention of possession by the seller is fraudulent under any rule of law of the state where the goods are situated, except that retention of possession in good faith and current course of trade by a merchant-seller for a commercially reasonable time after a sale or identification is not fraudulent.

(3) Nothing in this Article shall be deemed to impair the rights of creditors of the seller

(a) under the provisions of the Article on Secured Transactions (Article 9); or

(b) where identification to the contract or delivery is made not in current course of trade but in satisfaction of or as security for a pre-existing claim for money, security or the like and is made under circumstances which under any rule of law of the state where the goods are situated would apart from this Article constitute the transaction a fraudulent transfer or voidable preference.

§ 2—403. **Power to Transfer; Good Faith Purchase of Goods; "Entrusting".**

(1) A purchaser of goods acquires all title which his transferor had or had power to transfer except that a purchaser of a limited interest acquires rights only to the extent of the interest purchased. A person with voidable title has power to transfer a good title to a good faith purchaser for value.

When goods have been delivered under a transaction of purchase the purchaser has such power even though

(a) the transferor was deceived as to the identity of the purchaser, or

(b) the delivery was in exchange for a check which is later dishonored, or

(c) it was agreed that the transaction was to be a "cash sale", or

(d) the delivery was procured through fraud punishable as larcenous under the criminal law.

(2) Any entrusting of possession of goods to a merchant who deals in goods of that kind gives him power to transfer all rights of the entruster to a buyer in ordinary course of business.

(3) "Entrusting" includes any delivery and any acquiescence in retention of possession regardless of any condition expressed between the parties to the delivery or acquiescence and regardless of whether the procurement of the entrusting or the possessor's disposition of the goods have been such as to be larcenous under the criminal law.

(4) The rights of other purchasers of goods and of lien creditors are governed by the Articles on Secured Transactions (Article 9), Bulk Transfers (Article 6) and Documents of Title (Article 7).

Part 5 Performance

§ 2—501. **Insurable Interest in Goods; Manner of Identification of Goods.**

(1) The buyer obtains a special property and an insurable interest in goods by identification of existing goods as goods to which the contract refers even though the goods so identified are non-conforming and he has an option to return or reject them. Such identification can be made at any time and in any manner explicitly agreed to by the parties. In the absence of explicit agreement identification occurs

(a) when the contract is made if it is for the sale of goods already existing and identified;

(b) if the contract is for the sale of future goods other than those described in paragraph (c), when goods are shipped, marked or otherwise designated by the seller as goods to which the contract refers;

(c) when the crops are planted or otherwise become growing crops or the young are conceived if the contract is for the sale of unborn young to be born within twelve months after contracting or for the sale of crops to be harvested within twelve months or the next normal harvest season after contracting whichever is longer.

(2) The seller retains an insurable interest in goods so long as title to or any security interest in the goods remains in him and where the identification is by the seller alone he

may until default or insolvency or notification to the buyer that the identification is final substitute other goods for those identified.

(3) Nothing in this section impairs any insurable interest recognized under any other statute or rule of law.

§ 2—502. **Buyer's Right to Goods on Seller's Insolvency.**

(1) Subject to subsection (2) and even though the goods have not been shipped a buyer who has paid a part or all of the price of goods in which he has a special property under the provisions of the immediately preceding section may on making and keeping good a tender of any unpaid portion of their price recover them from the seller if the seller becomes insolvent within ten days after receipt of the first installment on their price.

(2) If the identification creating his special property has been made by the buyer he acquires the right to recover the goods only if they conform to the contract for sale.

§ 2—503. **Manner of Seller's Tender of Delivery.**

(1) Tender of delivery requires that the seller put and hold conforming goods at the buyer's disposition and give the buyer any notification reasonably necessary to enable him to take delivery. The manner, time and place for tender are determined by the agreement and this Article, and in particular

    (a) tender must be at a reasonable hour, and if it is of goods they must be kept available for the period reasonably necessary to enable the buyer to take possession; but

    (b) unless otherwise agreed the buyer must furnish facilities reasonably suited to the receipt of the goods.

(2) Where the case is within the next section respecting shipment tender requires that the seller comply with its provisions.

(3) Where the seller is required to deliver at a particular destination tender requires that he comply with subsection (1) and also in any appropriate case tender documents as described in subsections (4) and (5) of this section.

(4) Where goods are in the possession of a bailee and are to be delivered without being moved

    (a) tender requires that the seller either tender a negotiable document of title covering such goods or procure acknowledgment by the bailee of the buyer's right to possession of the goods; but

    (b) tender to the buyer of a non-negotiable document of title or of a written direction to the bailee to deliver is sufficient tender unless the buyer seasonably objects, and receipt by the bailee of notification of the buyer's rights fixes those rights as against the bailee and all third persons; but risk of loss of the goods and of any

failure by the bailee to honor the non-negotiable document of title or to obey the direction remains on the seller until the buyer has had a reasonable time to present the document or direction, and a refusal by the bailee to honor the document or to obey the direction defeats the tender.

(5) Where the contract requires the seller to deliver documents

    (a) he must tender all such documents in correct form, except as provided in this Article with respect to bills of lading in a set (subsection (2) of Section 2—323); and

    (b) tender through customary banking channels is sufficient and dishonor of a draft accompanying the documents constitutes non-acceptance or rejection.

§ 2—504. **Shipment by Seller.**

Where the seller is required or authorized to send the goods to the buyer and the contract does not require him to deliver them at a particular destination, then unless otherwise agreed he must

(a) put the goods in the possession of such a carrier and make such a contract for their transportation as may be reasonable having regard to the nature of the goods and other circumstances of the case; and

(b) obtain and promptly deliver or tender in due form any document necessary to enable the buyer to obtain possession of the goods or otherwise required by the agreement or by usage of trade; and

(c) promptly notify the buyer of the shipment.

Failure to notify the buyer under paragraph (c) or to make a proper contract under paragraph (a) is a ground for rejection only if material delay or loss ensues.

§ 2—505. **Seller's Shipment under Reservation.**

(1) Where the seller has identified goods to the contract by or before shipment:

    (a) his procurement of a negotiable bill of lading to his own order or otherwise reserves in him a security interest in the goods. His procurement of the bill to the order of a financing agency or of the buyer indicates in addition only the seller's expectation of transferring that interest to the person named.

    (b) a non-negotiable bill of lading to himself or his nominee reserves possession of the goods as security but except in a case of conditional delivery (subsection (2) of Section 2—507) a non-negotiable bill of lading naming the buyer as consignee reserves no security interest even though the seller retains possession of the bill of lading.

(2) When shipment by the seller with reservation of a security interest is in violation of the contract for sale it con-

stitutes an improper contract for transportation within the preceding section but impairs neither the rights given to the buyer by shipment and identification of the goods to the contract nor the seller's powers as a holder of a negotiable document.

§ 2—506. **Rights of Financing Agency.**

(1) A financing agency by paying or purchasing for value a draft which relates to a shipment of goods acquires to the extent of the payment or purchase and in addition to its own rights under the draft and any document of title securing it any rights of the shipper in the goods including the right to stop delivery and the shipper's right to have the draft honored by the buyer.

(2) The right to reimbursement of a financing agency which has in good faith honored or purchased the draft under commitment to or authority from the buyer is not impaired by subsequent discovery of defects with reference to any relevant document which was apparently regular on its face.

§ 2—507. **Effect of Seller's Tender; Delivery on Condition.**

(1) Tender of delivery is a condition to the buyer's duty to accept the goods and, unless otherwise agreed, to his duty to pay for them. Tender entitles the seller to acceptance of the goods and to payment according to the contract.

(2) Where payment is due and demanded on the delivery to the buyer of goods or documents of title, his right as against the seller to retain or dispose of them is conditional upon his making the payment due.

§ 2—508. **Cure by Seller of Improper Tender or Delivery; Replacement.**

(1) Where any tender or delivery by the seller is rejected because non-conforming and the time for performance has not yet expired, the seller may seasonably notify the buyer of his intention to cure and may then within the contract time make a conforming delivery.

(2) Where the buyer rejects a non-conforming tender which the seller had reasonable grounds to believe would be acceptable with or without money allowance the seller may if he seasonably notifies the buyer have a further reasonable time to substitute a conforming tender.

§ 2—509. **Risk of Loss in the Absence of Breach.**

(1) Where the contract requires or authorizes the seller to ship the goods by carrier

   (a) if it does not require him to deliver them at a particular destination, the risk of loss passes to the buyer when the goods are duly delivered to the carrier even though the shipment is under reservation (Section 2—505); but

   (b) if it does require him to deliver them at a particular destination and the goods are there duly tendered while in the possession of the carrier, the risk of loss passes to the buyer when the goods are there duly so tendered as to enable the buyer to take delivery.

(2) Where the goods are held by a bailee to be delivered without being moved, the risk of loss passes to the buyer

   (a) on his receipt of a negotiable document of title covering the goods; or

   (b) on acknowledgment by the bailee of the buyer's right to possession of the goods; or

   (c) after his receipt of a non-negotiable document of title or other written direction to deliver, as provided in subsection (4)(b) of Section 2—503.

(3) In any case not within subsection (1) or (2), the risk of loss passes to the buyer on his receipt of the goods if the seller is a merchant; otherwise the risk passes to the buyer on tender of delivery.

(4) The provisions of this section are subject to contrary agreement of the parties and to the provisions of this Article on sale on approval (Section 2—327) and on effect of breach on risk of loss (Section 2—510).

§ 2—510. **Effect of Breach on Risk of Loss.**

(1) Where a tender or delivery of goods so fails to conform to the contract as to give a right of rejection the risk of their loss remains on the seller until cure or acceptance.

(2) Where the buyer rightfully revokes acceptance he may to the extent of any deficiency in his effective insurance coverage treat the risk of loss as having rested on the seller from the beginning.

(3) Where the buyer as to conforming goods already identified to the contract for sale repudiates or is otherwise in breach before risk of their loss has passed to him, the seller may to the extent of any deficiency in his effective insurance coverage treat the risk of loss as resting on the buyer for a commercially reasonable time.

§ 2—511. **Tender of Payment by Buyer; Payment by Check.**

(1) Unless otherwise agreed tender of payment is a condition to the seller's duty to tender and complete any delivery.

(2) Tender of payment is sufficient when made by any means or in any manner current in the ordinary course of business unless the seller demands payment in legal tender and gives any extension of time reasonably necessary to procure it.

(3) Subject to the provisions of this Act on the effect of an instrument on an obligation (Section 3—802), payment by check is conditional and is defeated as between the parties by dishonor of the check on due presentment.

§ 2—512. **Payment by Buyer Before Inspection.**

(1) Where the contract requires payment before inspection non-conformity of the goods does not excuse the buyer from so making payment unless

(a) the non-conformity appears without inspection; or

(b) despite tender of the required documents the circumstances would justify injunction against honor under the provisions of this Act (Section 5—114).

(2) Payment pursuant to subsection (1) does not constitute an acceptance of goods or impair the buyer's right to inspect or any of his remedies.

§ 2—513. **Buyer's Right to Inspection of Goods.**

(1) Unless otherwise agreed and subject to subsection (3), where goods are tendered or delivered or identified to the contract for sale, the buyer has a right before payment or acceptance to inspect them at any reasonable place and time and in any reasonable manner. When the seller is required or authorized to send the goods to the buyer, the inspection may be after their arrival.

(2) Expenses of inspection must be borne by the buyer but may be recovered from the seller if the goods do not conform and are rejected.

(3) Unless otherwise agreed and subject to the provisions of this Article on C.I.F. contracts (subsection (3) of Section 2—321), the buyer is not entitled to inspect the goods before payment of the price when the contract provides

(a) for delivery ''C.O.D.'' or on other like terms; or

(b) for payment against documents of title, except where such payment is due only after the goods are to become available for inspection.

(4) A place or method of inspection fixed by the parties is presumed to be exclusive but unless otherwise expressly agreed it does not postpone identification or shift the place for delivery or for passing the risk of loss. If compliance becomes impossible, inspection shall be as provided in this section unless the place or method fixed was clearly intended as an indispensable condition failure of which avoids the contract.

§ 2—514. **When Documents Deliverable on Acceptance; When on Payment.**

Unless otherwise agreed documents against which a draft is drawn are to be delivered to the drawee on acceptance of the draft if it is payable more than three days after presentment; otherwise, only on payment.

§ 2—515. **Preserving Evidence of Goods in Dispute.**

In furtherance of the adjustment of any claim or dispute

(a) either party on reasonable notification to the other and for the purpose of ascertaining the facts and preserving evidence has the right to inspect, test and sample the goods including such of them as may be in the possession or control of the other; and

(b) the parties may agree to a third party inspection or survey to determine the conformity or condition of the goods and may agree that the findings shall be binding upon them in any subsequent litigation or adjustment.

Part 6 **Breach, Repudiation and Excuse**

§ 2—601. **Buyer's Rights on Improper Delivery.**

Subject to the provisions of this Article on breach in installment contracts (Section 2—612) and unless otherwise agreed under the sections on contractual limitations of remedy (Sections 2—718 and 2—719), if the goods or the tender of delivery fail in any respect to conform to the contract, the buyer may

(a) reject the whole; or

(b) accept the whole; or

(c) accept any commercial unit or units and reject the rest.

§ 2—602. **Manner and Effect of Rightful Rejection.**

(1) Rejection of goods must be within a reasonable time after their delivery or tender. It is ineffective unless the buyer seasonably notifies the seller.

(2) Subject to the provisions of the two following sections on rejected goods (Sections 2—603 and 2—604),

(a) after rejection any exercise of ownership by the buyer with respect to any commercial unit is wrongful as against the seller; and

(b) if the buyer has before rejection taken physical possession of goods in which he does not have a security interest under the provisions of this Article (subsection (3) of Section 2—711), he is under a duty after rejection to hold them with reasonable care at the seller's disposition for a time sufficient to permit the seller to remove them; but

(c) the buyer has no further obligations with regard to goods rightfully rejected.

(3) The seller's rights with respect to goods wrongfully rejected are governed by the provisions of this Article on Seller's remedies in general (Section 2—703).

§ 2—603. **Merchant Buyer's Duties as to Rightfully Rejected Goods.**

(1) Subject to any security interest in the buyer (subsection (3) of Section 2—711), when the seller has no agent or place of business at the market of rejection a merchant buyer is under a duty after rejection of goods in his possession or control to follow any reasonable instructions received from the seller with respect to the goods and in the absence of such instructions to make reasonable efforts to sell them for the seller's account if they are perishable or threaten to decline in value speedily. Instructions are not reasonable if on demand indemnity for expenses is not forthcoming.

(2) When the buyer sells goods under subsection (1), he is entitled to reimbursement from the seller or out of the proceeds for reasonable expenses of caring for and selling them, and if the expenses include no selling commission then to such commission as is usual in the trade or if there is none to a reasonable sum not exceeding ten per cent on the gross proceeds.

(3) In complying with this section the buyer is held only to good faith and good faith conduct hereunder is neither acceptance nor conversion nor the basis of an action for damages.

§ 2—604. **Buyer's Options as to Salvage of Rightfully Rejected Goods.**

Subject to the provisions of the immediately preceding section on perishables if the seller gives no instructions within a reasonable time after notification of rejection the buyer may store the rejected goods for the seller's account or reship them to him or resell them for the seller's account with reimbursement as provided in the preceding section. Such action is not acceptance or conversion.

§ 2—605. **Waiver of Buyer's Objections by Failure to Particularize.**

(1) The buyer's failure to state in connection with rejection a particular defect which is ascertainable by reasonable inspection precludes him from relying on the unstated defect to justify rejection or to establish breach

(a) where the seller could have cured it if stated seasonably; or

(b) between merchants when the seller has after rejection made a request in writing for a full and final written statement of all defects on which the buyer proposes to rely.

(2) Payment against documents made without reservation of rights precludes recovery of the payment for defects apparent on the face of the documents.

§ 2—606. **What Constitutes Acceptance of Goods.**

(1) Acceptance of goods occurs when the buyer

(a) after a reasonable opportunity to inspect the goods signifies to the seller that the goods are conforming or that he will take or retain them in spite of their non-conformity; or

(b) fails to make an effective rejection (subsection (1) of Section 2—602), but such acceptance does not occur until the buyer has had a reasonable opportunity to inspect them; or

(c) does any act inconsistent with the seller's ownership; but if such act is wrongful as against the seller it is an acceptance only if ratified by him.

(2) Acceptance of a part of any commercial unit is acceptance of that entire unit.

§ 2—607. **Effect of Acceptance; Notice of Breach; Burden of Establishing Breach After Acceptance; Notice of Claim or Litigation to Person Answerable Over.**

(1) The buyer must pay at the contract rate for any goods accepted.

(2) Acceptance of goods by the buyer precludes rejection of the goods accepted and if made with knowledge of a non-conformity cannot be revoked because of it unless the acceptance was on the reasonable assumption that the non-conformity would be seasonably cured but acceptance does not of itself impair any other remedy provided by this Article for non-conformity.

(3) Where a tender has been accepted

(a) the buyer must within a reasonable time after he discovers or should have discovered any breach notify the seller of breach or be barred from any remedy; and

(b) if the claim is one for infringement or the like (subsection (3) of Section 2—312) and the buyer is sued as a result of such a breach he must so notify the seller within a reasonable time after he receives notice of the litigation or be barred from any remedy over for liability established by the litigation.

(4) The burden is on the buyer to establish any breach with respect to the goods accepted.

(5) Where the buyer is sued for breach of a warranty or other obligation for which his seller is answerable over

(a) he may give his seller written notice of the litigation. If the notice states that the seller may come in and defend and that if the seller does not do so he will be bound in any action against him by his buyer by any determination of fact common to the two litigations, then unless the seller after seasonable receipt of the notice does come in and defend he is so bound.

(b) if the claim is one for infringement or the like (subsection (3) of Section 2—312) the original seller may demand in writing that his buyer turn over to him control of the litigation including settlement or else be barred from any remedy over and if he also agrees to bear all expense and to satisfy any adverse judgment, then unless the buyer after seasonable receipt of the demand does turn over control the buyer is so barred.

(6) The provisions of subsections (3), (4) and (5) apply to any obligation of a buyer to hold the seller harmless against infringement or the like (subsection (3) of Section 2—312).

§ 2—608. **Revocation of Acceptance in Whole or in Part.**

(1) The buyer may revoke his acceptance of a lot or commercial unit whose non-conformity substantially impairs its value to him if he has accepted it

(a) on the reasonable assumption that its non-conformity would be cured and it has not been seasonably cured; or

(b) without discovery of such non-conformity if his acceptance was reasonably induced either by the difficulty of discovery before acceptance or by the seller's assurances.

(2) Revocation of acceptance must occur within a reasonable time after the buyer discovers or should have discovered the ground for it and before any substantial change in condition of the goods which is not caused by their own defects. It is not effective until the buyer notifies the seller of it.

(3) A buyer who so revokes has the same rights and duties with regard to the goods involved as if he had rejected them.

§ 2—609. **Right to Adequate Assurance of Performance.**

(1) A contract for sale imposes an obligation on each party that the other's expectation of receiving due performance will not be impaired. When reasonable grounds for insecurity arise with respect to the performance of either party the other may in writing demand adequate assurance of due performance and until he receives such assurance may if commercially reasonable suspend any performance for which he has not already received the agreed return.

(2) Between merchants the reasonableness of grounds for insecurity and the adequacy of any assurance offered shall be determined according to commercial standards.

(3) Acceptance of any improper delivery or payment does not prejudice the party's right to demand adequate assurance of future performance.

(4) After receipt of a justified demand failure to provide within a reasonable time not exceeding thirty days such assurance of due performance as is adequate under the circumstances of the particular case is a repudiation of the contract.

§ 2—610. **Anticipatory Repudiation.**

When either party repudiates the contract with respect to a performance not yet due the loss of which will substantially impair the value of the contract to the other, the aggrieved party may

(a) for a commercially reasonable time await performance by the repudiating party; or

(b) resort to any remedy for breach (Section 2—703 or Section 2—711), even though he has notified the repudiating party that he would await the latter's performance and has urged retraction; and

(c) in either case suspend his own performance or proceed in accordance with the provisions of this Article on the seller's right to identify goods to the contract notwithstanding breach or to salvage unfinished goods (Section 2—704).

§ 2—611. **Retraction of Anticipatory Repudiation.**

(1) Until the repudiating party's next performance is due he can retract his repudiation unless the aggrieved party has since the repudiation cancelled or materially changed his position or otherwise indicated that he considers the repudiation final.

(2) Retraction may be by any method which clearly indicates to the aggrieved party that the repudiating party intends to perform, but must include any assurance justifiably demanded under the provisions of this Article (Section 2—609).

(3) Retraction reinstates the repudiating party's rights under the contract with due excuse and allowance to the aggrieved party for any delay occasioned by the repudiation.

§ 2—612. **"Installment Contract"; Breach.**

(1) An "installment contract" is one which requires or authorizes the delivery of goods in separate lots to be separately accepted, even though the contract contains a clause "each delivery is a separate contract" or its equivalent.

(2) The buyer may reject any installment which is non-conforming if the non-conformity substantially impairs the value of that installment and cannot be cured or if the non-conformity is a defect in the required documents; but if the non-conformity does not fall within subsection (3) and the seller gives adequate assurance of its cure the buyer must accept that installment.

(3) Whenever non-conformity or default with respect to one or more installments substantially impairs the value of the whole contract there is a breach of the whole. But the aggrieved party reinstates the contract if he accepts a non-conforming installment without seasonably notifying of cancellation or if he brings an action with respect only to past installments or demands performance as to future installments.

§ 2—613. **Casualty to Identified Goods.**

Where the contract requires for its performance goods identified when the contract is made, and the goods suffer casualty without fault of either party before the risk of loss passes to the buyer, or in a proper case under a "no arrival, no sale" term (Section 2—324) then

(a) if the loss is total the contract is avoided; and

(b) if the loss is partial or the goods have so deteriorated as no longer to conform to the contract the buyer may nevertheless demand inspection and at his option either treat the contract as voided or accept the goods with due allowance from the contract price for the deterioration or the deficiency in quantity but without further right against the seller.

§ 2—614. **Substituted Performance.**

(1) Where without fault of either party the agreed berthing,

loading, or unloading facilities fail or an agreed type of carrier becomes unavailable or the agreed manner of delivery otherwise becomes commercially impracticable but a commercially reasonable substitute is available, such substitute performance must be tendered and accepted.

(2) If the agreed means or manner of payment fails because of domestic or foreign governmental regulation, the seller may withhold or stop delivery unless the buyer provides a means or manner of payment which is commercially a substantial equivalent. If delivery has already been taken, payment by the means or in the manner provided by the regulation discharges the buyer's obligation unless the regulation is discriminatory, oppressive or predatory.

§ 2—615. **Excuse by Failure of Presupposed Conditions.**

Except so far as a seller may have assumed a greater obligation and subject to the preceding section on substituted performance:

(a) Delay in delivery or non-delivery in whole or in part by a seller who complies with paragraphs (b) and (c) is not a breach of his duty under a contract for sale if performance as agreed has been made impracticable by the occurrence of a contingency the nonoccurrence of which was a basic assumption on which the contract was made or by compliance in good faith with any applicable foreign or domestic governmental regulation or order whether or not it later proves to be invalid.

(b) Where the causes mentioned in paragraph (a) affect only a part of the seller's capacity to perform, he must allocate production and deliveries among his customers but may at his option include regular customers not then under contract as well as his own requirements for further manufacture. He may so allocate in any manner which is fair and reasonable.

(c) The seller must notify the buyer seasonably that there will be delay or non-delivery and, when allocation is required under paragraph (b), of the estimated quota thus made available for the buyer.

§ 2—616. **Procedure on Notice Claiming Excuse.**

(1) Where the buyer receives notification of a material or indefinite delay or an allocation justified under the preceding section he may by written notification to the seller as to any delivery concerned, and where the prospective deficiency substantially impairs the value of the whole contract under the provisions of this Article relating to breach of installment contracts (Section 2—612), then also as to the whole,

(a) terminate and thereby discharge any unexecuted portion of the contract; or

(b) modify the contract by agreeing to take his available quota in substitution.

(2) If after receipt of such notification from the seller the buyer fails so to modify the contract within a reasonable time not exceeding thirty days the contract lapses with respect to any deliveries affected.

(3) The provisions of this section may not be negated by agreement except in so far as the seller has assumed a greater obligation under the preceding section.

Part 7 Remedies

§ 2—701. **Remedies for Breach of Collateral Contracts Not Impaired.**

Remedies for breach of any obligation or promise collateral or ancillary to a contract for sale are not impaired by the provisions of this Article.

§ 2—702. **Seller's Remedies on Discovery of Buyer's Insolvency.**

(1) Where the seller discovers the buyer to be insolvent he may refuse delivery except for cash including payment for all goods theretofore delivered under the contract, and stop delivery under this Article (Section 2—705).

(2) Where the seller discovers that the buyer has received goods on credit while insolvent he may reclaim the goods upon demand made within ten days after the receipt, but if misrepresentation of solvency has been made to the particular seller in writing within three months before delivery the ten day limitation does not apply. Except as provided in this subsection the seller may not base a right to reclaim goods on the buyer's fraudulent or innocent misrepresentation of solvency or of intent to pay.

(3) The seller's right to reclaim under subsection (2) is subject to the rights of a buyer in ordinary course or other good faith purchaser under this Article (Section 2—403). Successful reclamation of goods excludes all other remedies with respect to them.

§ 2—703. **Seller's Remedies in General.**

Where the buyer wrongfully rejects or revokes acceptance of goods or fails to make a payment due on or before delivery or repudiates with respect to a part or the whole, then with respect to any goods directly affected and, if the breach is of the whole contract (Section 2—612), then also with respect to the whole undelivered balance, the aggrieved seller may

(a) withhold delivery of such goods;

(b) stop delivery by any bailee as hereafter provided (Section 2—705);

(c) proceed under the next section respecting goods still unidentified to the contract;

(d) resell and recover damages as hereafter provided (Section 2—706);

(e) recover damages for non-acceptance (Section 2—708) or in a proper case the price (Section 2—709);

(f) cancel.

§ 2—704. **Seller's Right to Identify Goods to the Contract Notwithstanding Breach or to Salvage Unfinished Goods.**

(1) An aggrieved seller under the preceding section may

(a) identify to the contract conforming goods not already identified if at the time he learned of the breach they are in his possession or control;

(b) treat as the subject of resale goods which have demonstrably been intended for the particular contract even though those goods are unfinished.

(2) Where the goods are unfinished an aggrieved seller may in the exercise of reasonable commercial judgment for the purposes of avoiding loss and of effective realization either complete the manufacture and wholly identify the goods to the contract or cease manufacture and resell for scrap or salvage value or proceed in any other reasonable manner.

§ 2—705. **Seller's Stoppage of Delivery in Transit or Otherwise.**

(1) The seller may stop delivery of goods in the possession of a carrier or other bailee when he discovers the buyer to be insolvent (Section 2—702) and may stop delivery of carload, truckload, planeload or larger shipments of express or freight when the buyer repudiates or fails to make a payment due before delivery or if for any other reason the seller has a right to withhold or reclaim the goods.

(2) As against such buyer the seller may stop delivery until

(a) receipt of the goods by the buyer; or

(b) acknowledgment to the buyer by any bailee of the goods except a carrier that the bailee holds the goods for the buyer; or

(c) such acknowledgment to the buyer by a carrier by reshipment or as warehouseman; or

(d) negotiation to the buyer of any negotiable document of title covering the goods.

(3) (a) To stop delivery the seller must so notify as to enable the bailee by reasonable diligence to prevent delivery of the goods.

(b) After such notification the bailee must hold and deliver the goods according to the directions of the seller but the seller is liable to the bailee for any ensuing charges or damages.

(c) If a negotiable document of title has been issued for goods the bailee is not obliged to obey a notification to stop until surrender of the document.

(d) A carrier who has issued a non-negotiable bill of lading is not obliged to obey a notification to stop received from a person other than the consignor.

§ 2—706. **Seller's Resale Including Contract for Resale.**

(1) Under the conditions stated in Section 2—703 on seller's remedies, the seller may resell the goods concerned or the undelivered balance thereof. Where the resale is made in good faith and in a commercially reasonable manner the seller may recover the difference between the resale price and the contract price together with any incidental damages allowed under the provisions of this Article (Section 2—710), but less expenses saved in consequence of the buyer's breach.

(2) Except as otherwise provided in subsection (3) or unless otherwise agreed resale may be at public or private sale including sale by way of one or more contracts to sell or of identification to an existing contract of the seller. Sale may be as a unit or in parcels and at any time and place and on any terms but every aspect of the sale including the method, manner, time, place and terms must be commercially reasonable. The resale must be reasonably identified as referring to the broken contract, but it is not necessary that the goods be in existence or that any or all of them have been identified to the contract before the breach.

(3) Where the resale is at private sale the seller must give the buyer reasonable notification of his intention to resell.

(4) Where the resale is at public sale

(a) only identified goods can be sold except where there is a recognized market for a public sale of futures in goods of the kind; and

(b) it must be made at a usual place or market for public sale if one is reasonably available and except in the case of goods which are perishable or threaten to decline in value speedily the seller must give the buyer reasonable notice of the time and place of the resale; and

(c) if the goods are not to be within the view of those attending the sale the notification of sale must state the place where the goods are located and provide for their reasonable inspection by prospective bidders; and

(d) the seller may buy.

(5) A purchaser who buys in good faith at a resale takes the goods free of any rights of the original buyer even though the seller fails to comply with one or more of the requirements of this section.

(6) The seller is not accountable to the buyer for any profit made on any resale. A person in the position of a seller (Section 2—707) or a buyer who has rightfully rejected or justifiably revoked acceptance must account for any excess over the amount of his security interest, as hereinafter defined (subsection (3) of Section 2—711).

§ 2—707. **"Person in the Position of a Seller".**

(1) A "person in the position of a seller" includes as against a principal an agent who has paid or become re-

sponsible for the price of goods on behalf of his principal or anyone who otherwise holds a security interest or other right in goods similar to that of a seller.

(2) A person in the position of a seller may as provided in this Article withhold or stop delivery (Section 2—705) and resell (Section 2—706) and recover incidental damages (Section 2—710).

§ 2—708. **Seller's Damages for Non-Acceptance or Repudiation.**

(1) Subject to subsection (2) and to the provisions of this Article with respect to proof of market price (Section 2—723), the measure of damages for non-acceptance or repudiation by the buyer is the difference between the market price at the time and place for tender and the unpaid contract price together with any incidental damages provided in this Article (Section 2—710), but less expenses saved in consequence of the buyer's breach.

(2) If the measure of damages provided in subsection (1) is inadequate to put the seller in as good a position as performance would have done then the measure of damages is the profit (including reasonable overhead) which the seller would have made from full performance by the buyer, together with any incidental damages provided in this Article (Section 2—710), due allowance for costs reasonably incurred and due credit for payments or proceeds of resale.

§ 2—709. **Action for the Price.**

(1) When the buyer fails to pay the price as it becomes due the seller may recover, together with any incidental damages under the next section, the price

(a) of goods accepted or of conforming goods lost or damaged within a commercially reasonable time after risk of their loss has passed to the buyer; and

(b) of goods identified to the contract if the seller is unable after reasonable effort to resell them at a reasonable price or the circumstances reasonably indicate that such effort will be unavailing.

(2) Where the seller sues for the price he must hold for the buyer any goods which have been identified to the contract and are still in his control except that if resale becomes possible he may resell them at any time prior to the collection of the judgment. The net proceeds of any such resale must be credited to the buyer and payment of the judgment entitles him to any goods not resold.

(3) After the buyer has wrongfully rejected or revoked acceptance of the goods or has failed to make a payment due or has repudiated (Section 2—610), a seller who is held not entitled to the price under this section shall nevertheless be awarded damages for non-acceptance under the preceding section.

§ 2—710. **Seller's Incidental Damages.**

Incidental damages to an aggrieved seller include any com-

mercially reasonable charges, expenses or commissions incurred in stopping delivery, in the transportation, care and custody of goods after the buyer's breach, in connection with return or resale of the goods or otherwise resulting from the breach.

§ 2—711. **Buyer's Remedies in General; Buyer's Security Interest in Rejected Goods.**

(1) Where the seller fails to make delivery or repudiates or the buyer rightfully rejects or justifiably revokes acceptance then with respect to any goods involved, and with respect to the whole if the breach goes to the whole contract (Section 2—612), the buyer may cancel and whether or not he has done so may in addition to recovering so much of the price as has been paid

(a) "cover" and have damages under the next section as to all the goods affected whether or not they have been identified to the contract; or

(b) recover damages for non-delivery as provided in this Article (Section 2—713).

(2) Where the seller fails to deliver or repudiates the buyer may also

(a) if the goods have been identified recover them as provided in this Article (Section 2—502); or

(b) in a proper case obtain specific performance or replevy the goods as provided in this Article (Section 2—716).

(3) On rightful rejection or justifiable revocation of acceptance a buyer has a security interest in goods in his possession or control for any payments made on their price and any expenses reasonably incurred in their inspection, receipt, transportation, care and custody and may hold such goods and resell them in like manner as an aggrieved seller (Section 2—706).

§ 2—712. **"Cover"; Buyer's Procurement of Substitute Goods.**

(1) After a breach within the preceding section the buyer may "cover" by making in good faith and without unreasonable delay any reasonable purchase of or contract to purchase goods in substitution for those due from the seller.

(2) The buyer may recover from the seller as damages the difference between the cost of cover and the contract price together with any incidental or consequential damages as hereinafter defined (Section 2—715), but less expenses saved in consequence of the seller's breach.

(3) Failure of the buyer to effect cover within this section does not bar him from any other remedy.

§ 2—713. **Buyer's Damages for Non-Delivery or Repudiation.**

(1) Subject to the provisions of this Article with respect to proof of market price (Section 2—723), the measure of

damages for non-delivery or repudiation by the seller is the difference between the market price at the time when the buyer learned of the breach and the contract price together with any incidental and consequential damages provided in this Article (Section 2—715), but less expenses saved in consequence of the seller's breach.

(2) Market price is to be determined as of the place for tender or, in cases of rejection after arrival or revocation of acceptance, as of the place of arrival.

§ 2—714. Buyer's Damages for Breach in Regard to Accepted Goods.

(1) Where the buyer has accepted goods and given notification (subsection (3) of Section 2—607) he may recover as damages for any non-conformity of tender the loss resulting in the ordinary course of events from the seller's breach as determined in any manner which is reasonable.

(2) The measure of damages for breach of warranty is the difference at the time and place of acceptance between the value of the goods accepted and the value they would have had if they had been as warranted, unless special circumstances show proximate damages of a different amount.

(3) In a proper case any incidental and consequential damages under the next section may also be recovered.

§ 2—715. Buyer's Incidental and Consequential Damages.

(1) Incidental damages resulting from the seller's breach include expenses reasonably incurred in inspection, receipt, transportation and care and custody of goods rightfully rejected, any commercially reasonable charges, expenses or commissions in connection with effecting cover and any other reasonable expense incident to the delay or other breach.

(2) Consequential damages resulting from the seller's breach include

(a) any loss resulting from general or particular requirements and needs of which the seller at the time of contracting had reason to know and which could not reasonably be prevented by cover or otherwise; and

(b) injury to person or property proximately resulting from any breach of warranty.

§ 2—716. Buyer's Right to Specific Performance or Replevin.

(1) Specific performance may be decreed where the goods are unique or in other proper circumstances.

(2) The decree for specific performance may include such terms and conditions as to payment of the price, damages, or other relief as the court may deem just.

(3) The buyer has a right of replevin for goods identified to the contract if after reasonable effort he is unable to effect cover for such goods or the circumstances reasonably indicate that such effort will be unavailing or if the goods have been shipped under reservation and satisfaction of the security interest in them has been made or tendered.

§ 2—717. Deduction of Damages From the Price.

The buyer on notifying the seller of his intention to do so may deduct all or any part of the damages resulting from any breach of the contract from any part of the price still due under the same contract.

§ 2—718. Liquidation or Limitation of Damages; Deposits.

(1) Damages for breach by either party may be liquidated in the agreement but only at an amount which is reasonable in the light of the anticipated or actual harm caused by the breach, the difficulties of proof of loss, and the inconvenience or nonfeasibility of otherwise obtaining an adequate remedy. A term fixing unreasonably large liquidated damages is void as a penalty.

(2) Where the seller justifiably withholds delivery of goods because of the buyer's breach, the buyer is entitled to restitution of any amount by which the sum of his payments exceeds

(a) the amount to which the seller is entitled by virtue of terms liquidating the seller's damages in accordance with subsection (1), or

(b) in the absence of such terms, twenty per cent of the value of the total performance for which the buyer is obligated under the contract or $500, whichever is smaller.

(3) The buyer's right to restitution under subsection (2) is subject to offset to the extent that the seller establishes

(a) a right to recover damages under the provisions of this Article other than subsection (1), and

(b) the amount or value of any benefits received by the buyer directly or indirectly by reason of the contract.

(4) Where a seller has received payment in goods their reasonable value or the proceeds of their resale shall be treated as payments for the purposes of subsection (2); but if the seller has notice of the buyer's breach before reselling goods received in part performance, his resale is subject to the conditions laid down in this Article on resale by an aggrieved seller (Section 2—706).

§ 2—719. Contractual Modification or Limitation of Remedy.

(1) Subject to the provisions of subsections (2) and (3) of this section and of the preceding section on liquidation and limitation of damages,

(a) the agreement may provide for remedies in addition to or in substitution for those provided in this Article and may limit or alter the measure of damages recoverable under this Article, as by limiting the buyer's remedies to return of the goods and repayment of the price or to repair and replacement of non-conforming goods or parts; and

(b) resort to a remedy as provided is optional unless the remedy is expressly agreed to be exclusive, in which case it is the sole remedy.

(2) Where circumstances cause an exclusive or limited remedy to fail of its essential purpose, remedy may be had as provided in this Act.

(3) Consequential damages may be limited or excluded unless the limitation or exclusion is unconscionable. Limitation of consequential damages for injury to the person in the case of consumer goods is prima facie unconscionable but limitation of damages where the loss is commercial is not.

§ 2—720. **Effect of "Cancellation" or "Rescission" on Claims for Antecedent Breach.**

Unless the contrary intention clearly appears, expressions of "cancellation" or "rescission" of the contract or the like shall not be construed as a renunciation or discharge of any claim in damages for an antecedent breach.

§ 2—721. **Remedies for Fraud.**

Remedies for material misrepresentation or fraud include all remedies available under this Article for non-fraudulent breach. Neither rescission or a claim for rescission of the contract for sale nor rejection or return of the goods shall bar or be deemed inconsistent with a claim for damages or other remedy.

§ 2—722. **Who Can Sue Third Parties for Injury to Goods.**

Where a third party so deals with goods which have been identified to a contract for sale as to cause actionable injury to a party to that contract

(a) a right of action against the third party is in either party to the contract for sale who has title to or a security interest or a special property or an insurable interest in the goods; and if the goods have been destroyed or converted a right of action is also in the party who either bore the risk of loss under the contract for sale or has since the injury assumed that risk as against the other;

(b) if at the time of the injury the party plaintiff did not bear the risk of loss as against the other party to the contract for sale and there is no arrangement between them for disposition of the recovery, his suit or settlement is, subject to his own interest, as a fiduciary for the other party to the contract;

(c) either party may with the consent of the other sue for the benefit of whom it may concern.

§ 2—723. **Proof of Market Price: Time and Place.**

(1) If an action based on anticipatory repudiation comes to trial before the time for performance with respect to some or all of the goods, any damages based on market price (Section 2—708 or Section 2—713) shall be determined according to the price of such goods prevailing at the time when the aggrieved party learned of the repudiation.

(2) If evidence of a price prevailing at the times or places described in this Article is not readily available the price prevailing within any reasonable time before or after the time described or at any other place which in commercial judgment or under usage of trade would serve as a reasonable substitute for the one described may be used, making any proper allowance for the cost of transporting the goods to or from such other place.

(3) Evidence of a relevant price prevailing at a time or place other than the one described in this Article offered by one party is not admissible unless and until he has given the other party such notice as the court finds sufficient to prevent unfair surprise.

§ 2—724. **Admissibility of Market Quotations.**

Whenever the prevailing price or value of any goods regularly bought and sold in any established commodity market is in issue, reports in official publications or trade journals or in newspapers or periodicals of general circulation published as the reports of such market shall be admissible in evidence. The circumstances of the preparation of such a report may be shown to affect its weight but not its admissibility.

§ 2—725. **Statute of Limitations in Contracts for Sale.**

(1) An action for breach of any contract for sale must be commenced within four years after the cause of action has accrued. By the original agreement the parties may reduce the period of limitation to not less than one year but may not extend it.

(2) A cause of action accrues when the breach occurs, regardless of the aggrieved party's lack of knowledge of the breach. A breach of warranty occurs when tender of delivery is made, except that where a warranty explicitly extends to future performance of the goods and discovery of the breach must await the time of such performance the cause of action accrues when the breach is or should have been discovered.

(3) Where an action commenced within the time limited by subsection (1) is so terminated as to leave available a remedy by another action for the same breach such other action may be commenced after the expiration of the time limited and within six months after the termination of the first action unless the termination resulted from voluntary discontinuance or from dismissal for failure or neglect to prosecute.

(4) This section does not alter the law on tolling of the statute of limitations nor does it apply to causes of action which have accrued before this Act becomes effective.

Appendix D

Restatement (Second) of Torts (Excerpts)

Section 402 A. Special liability of seller of product for physical harm to user or consumer.

(1) One who sells any product in a defection condition unreasonably dangerous to the consumer or to his property is subject to liability for physical harm thereby caused to the ultimate user or consumer, or to his property, if

(a) the seller is engaged in the business of selling such a product, and

(b) it is expected to and does reach the user or consumer without substantial change in the condition in which it is sold.

(2) The rule stated in Subsection (1) applies although

(a) the seller has exercised all possible care in the preparation and sale of his product, and

(b) the user or consumer has not bought the product from or entered into any contractual relation with the seller.

Section 402 B. Misrepresentation by seller of chattels to consumer.

One engaged in the business of selling chattels who, by advertising, labels, or otherwise, makes to the public a misrepresentation of a material fact concerning the character or quality of a chattel sold by him is subject to liability for physical harm to a consumer of the chattel caused by justifiable reliance upon the misrepresentation, even though

(a) it is not made fraudulently or negligently, and

(b) the consumer has not bought the chattel from or entered into any contractual relations with the seller.

Appendix E

Sherman Antitrust Act (Excerpts)

The Sherman Antitrust Act (1890, as amended)

Section. 1 Every contract, combination in the form of trust or otherwise, or conspiracy, in restraint of trade or commerce among the several States, or with foreign nations, is hereby declared to be illegal. Every person who shall make any such contract or engage in any such combination or conspiracy shall be deemed guilty of a felony, and, on conviction thereof, shall be punished by fine not exceeding one million dollars if a corporation, or, if any other person, one hundred thousand dollars or by imprisonment not exceeding three years, or by both said punishments in the discretion of the court.

Section 2. Every person who shall monopolize, or attempt to monopolize, or conspire with any other person or persons, to monopolize any part of the trade or commerce among the several States, or with foreign nations, shall be deemed guilty of a felony, and, on conviction thereof, shall be punished by fine not exceeding one million dollars if a corporation, or, if any other person, one hundred thousand dollars or by imprisonment not exceeding three years, or by both said punishments, in the discretion of the court.

Appendix F

Clayton Act (Excerpts)

The Clayton Act as Amended

Section 2. This section is also known as the Robinson-Patman amendment to Section 2 of the Clayton Act. (a) That it shall be unlawful for any person engaged in commerce, in the course of such commerce, either directly or indirectly, to discriminate in price between different purchasers of commodities of like grade and quality, where such * * * commodities are sold for use, consumption, or resale within the United States or any Territory thereof * * * and where the effect of such discrimination may be substantially to lessen competition or tend to create a monopoly in any line of commerce, or to injure, destroy, or prevent competition with any person who either grants or knowingly receives the benefit of such discrimination, or with customers of either of them: Provided, That nothing herein contained shall prevent differentials which make only due allowance for differences in the cost of manufacture, sale, or delivery resulting from the differing methods or quantities in which such commodities are to such purchasers sold or delivered: Provided, however, That the Federal Trade Commission may, after due investigation and hearing * * * fix and establish quantity limits, * * * as to particular commodities or classes of commodities, where it finds that available purchasers in greater quantities are so few as to render differentials on account thereof unjustly discriminatory or promotive of monopoly in any line of commerce; and the foregoing shall then not be construed to permit differentials based on differences in quantities greater than those so fixed and established: And provided further, That nothing herein contained shall prevent persons engaged in selling goods, wares, or merchandise in commerce from selecting their own customers in *bona fide* transactions and not in restraint of trade: And provided

further, That nothing herein contained shall prevent price changes from time to time where in response to changing conditions affecting the market for or the marketability of the goods concerned, such as but not limited to actual or imminent deterioration of perishable goods, obsolescence of seasonal goods, distress sales under court process, or sales in good faith in discontinuance of business in the goods concerned.

(b) Upon proof being made, at any hearing on a complaint under this section, that there has been discrimination in price or services or facilities furnished, the burden of rebutting the *prima facie* case thus made by showing justification shall be upon the person charged with a violation of this section, and unless justification shall be affirmatively shown, the Commission is authorized to issue an order terminating the discrimination: Provided, however, That nothing herein contained shall prevent a seller rebutting the *prima facie* case thus made by showing that his lower price or the furnishing of services or facilities to any purchaser or purchasers was made in good faith to meet an equally low price of a competitor, or the services or facilities furnished by a competitor.

(c) That it shall be unlawful for any person engaged in commerce, in the course of such commerce, to pay or grant, or to receive or accept, anything of value as a commission, brokerage, or other compensation, or any allowance or discount in lieu thereof, except for services rendered in connection with the sale or purchase of goods, wares, or merchandise, either to the other party to such transactions or to an agent, representative, or other intermediary therein where such intermediary is acting in fact for or in behalf, or is subject to the direct or indirect control, of any party to such transaction other than the person by whom such compensation is granted or paid.

(d) That it shall be unlawful for any person engaged in commerce to pay or contract for the payment of anything of value to or for the benefit of a customer of such person in the course of such commerce as compensation or in consideration for any services or facilities furnished by or through such customer in connection with the processing, handling, sale, or offering for sale of any products or commodities manufactured, sold, or offered for sale by such person, unless such payment or consideration is available on proportionally equal terms to all other customers competing in the distribution of such products or commodities.

(e) That it shall be unlawful for any person to discriminate in favor of one purchaser against another purchaser or purchasers of a commodity bought for resale, with or without processing, by contracting to furnish or furnishing, or by contributing to the furnishing of, any services or facilities connected with the processing, handling, sale, or offering for sale of such commodity so purchased upon terms not accorded to all purchasers on proportionally equal terms.

(f) That it shall be unlawful for any person engaged in commerce, in the course of such commerce, knowingly to induce or receive a discrimination in price which is prohibited by this section.

Section 3. That it shall be unlawful for any person engaged in commerce, in the course of such commerce, to lease or make a sale or contract for sale of goods, wares, merchandise, machinery, supplies, or other commodities, whether patented or unpatented, for use, consumption, or resale within the United States or *   *   * other place under the jurisdiction of the United States, or fix a price charged therefor, or discount from, or rebate upon, such price, on the condition, agreement, or understanding that the lessee or purchaser thereof shall not use or deal in the goods, wares, merchandise, machinery, supplies, or other commodities of a competitor or competitors of the lessor or seller, where the effect of such lease, sale, or contract for sale or such condition, agreement, or understanding may be to substantially lessen competition to tend to create a monopoly in any line of commerce.

Section 4. That any person who shall be injured in his business or property by reason of anything forbidden in the antitrust laws may sue therefor in any district court of the United States in the district in which the defendant resides or is found, or has an agent, without respect to the amount in controversy, and shall recover threefold the damages by him sustained, and the cost of suit, including a reasonable attorney's fee.

Section 4A. Whenever the United States is hereafter injured in its business or property by reason of anything forbidden in the antitrust laws it may sue therefor in the United States district court for the district in which the defendant

resides or is found or has an agent, without respect to the amount in controversy, and shall recover actual damages by it sustained and the cost of suit.

Section 4B. Any action to enforce any cause of action under sections 4 or 4A shall be forever barred unless commenced within four years after the cause of action accrued. No cause of action barred under existing law on the effective date of this act shall be revived by this Act.

*   *   *   *

Section 6. That the labor of a human being is not a commodity or article of commerce. Nothing contained in the antitrust laws shall be construed to forbid the existence and operation of labor, agricultural or horticultural organizations, instituted for the purposes of mutual help, and not having capital stock or conducted for profit, or to forbid or restrain individual members of such organizations from lawfully carrying out the legitimate objects thereof; nor shall such organizations or the members thereof, be held or construed to be illegal combinations or conspiracies in restraint of trade, under the antitrust laws.

Section 7. That no person engaged in commerce shall acquire, directly or indirectly, the whole or any part of the stock or other share capital and no corporation subject to the jurisdiction of the Federal Trade Commission shall acquire the whole or any part of the assets of another corporation engaged also in commerce, where in any line of commerce in any section of the country, the effect of such acquisition may be substantially to lessen competition, or to tend to create a monopoly.

No person shall acquire, directly or indirectly, the whole or any part of the stock or other share capital and no corporation subject to the jurisdiction of the Federal Trade Commission shall acquire the whole or any part of the assets of one or more corporations engaged in commerce, where in any line of commerce in any section of the country, the effect of such acquisition, of such stocks or assets, or of the use of such stock by the voting or granting of proxies or otherwise, may be substantially to lessen competition, or to tend to create a monopoly.

This section shall not apply to persons purchasing such stock solely for investment and not using the same by voting or otherwise to bring about, or in attempting to bring about, the substantial lessening of competition . . .

Section 8. *   *   * No person at the same time shall be a director in any two or more corporations any one of which has capital, surplus, and undivided profits aggregating more than $1,000,000 engaged in whole or in part in commerce, *   *   * if such corporations are or shall have been theretofore, by virtue of their business and location of operation, competitors, so that the elimination of competition by agreement between them would constitute a violation of any of the provisions of the antitrust laws. *   *   *

Appendix G

Federal Trade Commission Act (Excerpts)

The Federal Trade Commission Act (1914) [Excerpts]

Section 5. (a)(1) Unfair methods of competition in or affecting commerce, and unfair or deceptive acts or practices in or affecting commerce, are hereby declared unlawful.

(2) The Commission is hereby empowered and directed to prevent persons, partnerships, or corporations from using unfair methods of competition in or affecting commerce and unfair or deceptive acts or practices in or affecting commerce.

(l) Any person, partnership, or corporation who violates an order of the Commission after it has become final, and while such order is in effect, shall forfeit and pay to the United States a civil penalty of not more than $10,000 for each violation, which shall accrue to the United States and may be recovered in a civil action brought by the Attorney General of the United States. Each separate violation of such an order shall be a separate offense, except that in the case of a violation through continuing failure to obey or neglect to obey a final order of the Commission, each day of continuance of such failure or neglect shall be deemed a separate offense. In such actions, the United States district courts are empowered to grant mandatory injunctions and such other and further equitable relief as they deem appropriate in the enforcement of such final orders of the Commission.

Appendix H

The Robinson-Patman Act (Excerpts)

Section 2. Discrimination in Price, Services, or Facilities—Price; Selection of Customers

(a) It shall be unlawful for any person engaged in commerce, in the course of such commerce, either directly or indirectly, to discriminate in price between different purchasers of commodities of like grade and quality, where either or any of the purchases involved in such discrimination are in commerce, where such commodities are sold for use, consumption, or resale within the United States or any Territory thereof or the District of Columbia or any insular possession or other place under the jurisdiction of the United States, and where the effect of such discrimination may be substantially to lessen competition or tend to create a monopoly in any line of commerce, or to injure, destroy, or prevent competition with any person who either grants or knowingly receives the benefit of such discrimination, or with customers of either of them; *Provided,* That nothing herein contained shall prevent differentials which make only due allowance for differences in the cost of manufacture, sale, or delivery resulting from the differing methods or quantities in which such commodities are to such purchasers sold or delivered: *Provided, however,* That the Federal Trade Commission may, after due investigation and hearing to all interested parties, fix and establish quantity limits, and revise the same as it finds necessary, as to particular commodities or classes of commodities, where it finds that available purchasers in greater quantities are so few as to render differentials on account thereof unjustly discriminatory or promotive of monopoly in any line of commerce; and the foregoing shall then not be construed to permit differentials based on differences in quantities greater than those so fixed and established: *And provided further,* That nothing herein contained shall prevent persons engaged in selling goods, wares, or merchandise in commerce from selecting their own customers in bona fide transactions and not in restraint of trade: *And provided further,* That nothing herein contained shall prevent price changes from time to time where in response to changing conditions affecting the market for or the marketability of the goods concerned, such as but not limited to actual or imminent deterioration of perishable goods, obsolescence of seasonal goods, distress sales under court process, or sales in good faith in discontinuance of business in the goods concerned.

Burden of Rebutting Prima-Facie Case of Discrimination

(b) Upon proof being made, at any hearing on a complaint under this section, that there has been discrimination in price or services or facilities furnished, the burden of rebutting the prima-facie case thus made by showing justification shall be upon the person charged with a violation of this section, and unless justification shall be affirmatively shown, the Commission is authorized to issue an order terminating the discrimination: *Provided, however,* That nothing herein contained shall prevent a seller rebutting the prima-facie case thus made by showing that his [or her] lower price or the furnishing of services or facilities to any purchaser or purchasers was made in good faith to meet an equally low price of a competitor, or the services or facilities furnished by a competitor.

Payment or Acceptance of Commission, Brokerage, or Other Compensation

(c) It shall be unlawful for any person engaged in commerce, in the course of such commerce, to pay or grant, or to receive or accept, anything of value as a commission, brokerage, or other compensation, or any allowance or discount in lieu thereof, except for services rendered in connection with the sale or purchase of goods, wares, or merchandise, either to the other party to such transaction or to an agent, representative, or other intermediary therein where such intermediary is acting in fact for or in behalf, or is subject to the direct or indirect control, of any party to such transaction other than the person by whom such compensation is so granted or paid.

Payment for Services or Facilities
for Processing or Sale

(d) It shall be unlawful for any person engaged in commerce to pay or contract for the payment of anything of value to or for the benefit of a customer of such person in the course of such commerce as compensation or in consideration for any services or facilities furnished by or through such customer in connection with the processing, handling, sale or offering for sale of any products or commodities manufactured, sold, or offered for sale by such person, unless such payment or consideration is available on proportionally equal terms to all other customers competing in the distribution of such products or commodities.

Furnishing Services or Facilities for Processing,
Handling, etc.

(e) It shall be unlawful for any person to discriminate in favor of one purchaser against another purchaser or purchasers of a commodity bought for resale, with or without processing, by contracting to furnish or furnishing, or by contributing to the furnishing of, any services or facilities connected with the processing, handling, sale, or offering for sale of such commodity so purchased upon terms not accorded to all purchasers on proportionally equal terms.

Knowingly Inducing or Receiving Discriminatory Price

(f) It shall be unlawful for any person engaged in commerce, in the course of such commerce, knowingly to induce or receive a discrimination in price which is prohibited by this section.

Section 3. Discrimination in Rebates, Discounts, or Advertising Service Charges; Underselling in Particular Localities; Penalties

It shall be unlawful for any person engaged in commerce, in the course of such commerce, to be a party to, or assist in, any transaction of sale, or contract to sell, which discriminates to his [or her] knowledge against competitors of the purchaser, in that, any discount, rebate, allowance, or advertising service charge is granted to the purchaser over and above any discount, rebate, allowance, or advertising service charge available at the time of such transaction to said competitors in respect of a sale of goods of like grade, quality, and quantity; to sell, or contract to sell, goods in any part of the United States at prices lower than those exacted by said person elsewhere in the United States for the purpose of destroying competition, or eliminating a competitor in such part of the United States; or, to sell, or contract to sell, goods at unreasonably low prices for the purpose of destroying competition or eliminating a competitor.

Any person violating any of the provisions of this section shall, upon conviction thereof, be fined not more than $5,000 or imprisoned not more than one year, or both.

Appendix I

Securities Act of 1933 (Excerpts)

Definitions

Section 2. When used in this title, unless the context requires—

(1) The term ''security'' means any note, stock, treasury stock, bond, debenture, evidence of indebtedness, certificate of interest or participation in any profit-sharing agreement, collateral-trust certificate, preorganization certificate or subscription, transferable share, investment contract, voting-trust certificate, certificate of deposit for a security, fractional undivided interest in oil, gas, or other mineral rights, any put, call, straddle, option, or privilege on any security, certificate of deposit, or group or index of securities (including any interest therein or based on the value thereof), or any put, call, straddle, option, or privilege entered into on a national securities exchange relating to foreign currency, or, in general, any interest or participation in, temporary or interim certificate for, receipt for, guarantee of, or warrant or right to subscribe to or purchase, any of the foregoing.

Exempted Securities

Section 3. (a) Except as hereinafter expressly provided the provisions of this title shall not apply to any of the following classes of securities:

*   *   *   *

(2) Any security issued or guaranteed by the United States or any territory thereof, or by the District of Columbia, or by any State of the United States, or by any political subdivision of a State or Territory, or by any public instrumentality of one or more States or Territories, or by any person controlled or supervised by and acting as an instrumentality of the Government of the United States pursuant to authority granted by the Congress of the United States; or any certificate of deposit for any of the foregoing; or any security issued or guaranteed by any bank; or any security issued by or representing an interest in or a direct obligation of a Federal Reserve Bank. *   *   *

(3) Any note, draft, bill of exchange, or banker's acceptance which arises out of a current transaction or the proceeds of which have been or are to be used for current transactions, and which has a maturity at the time of issuance of not exceeding nine months, exclusive of days of grace, or any renewal thereof the maturity of which is likewise limited;

(4) Any security issued by a person organized and operated exclusively for religious, educational, benevolent, fraternal, charitable, or reformatory purposes and not for pecuniary profit, and no part of the net earnings of which inures to the benefit of any person, private stockholder, or individual;

*   *   *   *

(11) Any security which is a part of an issue offered and sold only to persons resident within a single State or Territory, where the issuer of such security is a person resident and doing business within, or, if a corporation, incorporated by and doing business within, such State or Territory.

(b) The Commission may from time to time by its rules and regulations and subject to such terms and conditions as may be described therein, add any class of securities to the securities exempted as provided in this section, if it finds that the enforcement of this title with respect to such securities is not necessary in the public interest and for the protection of investors by reason of the small amount involved or the limited character of the public offering; but no issue of securities shall be exempted under this subsection where the aggregate amount at which such issue is offered to the public exceeds $5,000,000.

Exempted Transactions

Section 4. The provisions of section 5 shall not apply to—

(1) transactions by any person other than an issuer, underwriter, or dealer.

(2) transactions by an issuer not involving any public offering.

(3) transactions by a dealer (including an underwriter no longer acting as an underwriter in respect of the security involved in such transactions), except—

(A) transactions taking place prior to the expiration of forty days after the first date upon which the security was bona fide offered to the public by the issuer or by or through an underwriter.

(B) transactions in a security as to which a registration statement has been filed taking place prior to the expiration of forty days after the effective date of such registration statement or prior to the expiration of forty days after the first date upon which the security was bona fide offered to the public by the issuer or by or through an underwriter after such effective date, whichever is later (excluding in the computation of such forty days any time during which a stop order issued under section 8 is in effect as to the security), or such shorter period as the Commission may specify by rules and regulations or order, and

(C) transactions as to the securities constituting the whole or a part of an unsold allotment to or subscription by such dealer as a participant in the distribution of such securities by the issuer or by or through an underwriter.

With respect to transactions referred to in clause (B), if securities of the issuer have not previously been sold pursuant to an earlier effective registration statement the applicable period, instead of forty days, shall be ninety days, or such shorter period as the Commission may specify by rules and regulations or order.

(4) brokers' transactions, executed upon customers' orders on any exchange or in the over-the-counter market but not the solicitation of such orders.

* * * *

(6) transactions involving offers or sales by an issuer solely to one or more accredited investors, if the aggregate offering price of an issue of securities offered in reliance on this paragraph does not exceed the amount allowed under Section 3(b) of this title, if there is no advertising or public solicitation in connection with the transaction by the issuer or anyone acting on the issuer's behalf, and if the issuer files such notice with the Commission as the Commission shall prescribe.

Prohibitions Relating to Interstate Commerce and the Mails

Section 5. (a) Unless a registration statement is in effect as to a security, it shall be unlawful for any person, directly or indirectly—

(1) to make use of any means or instruments of transportation or communication in interest commerce or of the mails to sell such security through the use or medium of any prospectus or otherwise; or

(2) to carry or cause to be carried through the mails or in interstate commerce, by any means or instruments of transportation, any such security for the purpose of sale or for delivery after sale.

(b) It shall be unlawful for any person, directly or indirectly—

(1) to make use of any means or instruments of transportation or communication in interstate commerce or of the mails to carry or transmit any prospectus relating to any security with respect to which a registration statement has been filed under this title, unless such prospectus meets the requirements of section 10, or

(2) to carry or to cause to be carried through the mails or in interstate commerce any such security for the purpose of sale or for delivery after sale, unless accompanied or preceded by a prospectus that meets the requirements of subsection (a) of section 10.

(c) It shall be unlawful for any person, directly, or indirectly, to make use of any means or instruments of transportation or communication in interstate commerce or of the mails to offer to sell or offer to buy through the use or medium of any prospectus or otherwise any security, unless a registration statement has been filed as to such security, or while the registration statement is the subject of a refusal order or stop order or (prior to the effective date of the registration statement) any public proceeding of examination under section 8.

Appendix J

Securities Exchange Act of 1934 (Excerpts)

Definitions and Application of Title

Section 3.   (a) When used in this title, unless the context otherwise requires—

* * * *

(4) The term "broker" means any person engaged in the business of effecting transactions in securities for the account of others, but does not include a bank.

(5) The term "dealer" means any person engaged in the business of buying and selling securities for his own account, through a broker or otherwise, but does not include a bank, or any person insofar as he buys or sells securities for his own account, either individually or in some fiduciary capacity, but not as part of a regular business.

* * * *

(7) The term "director" means any director of a corporation or any person performing similar functions with respect to any organization, whether incorporated or unincorporated.

(8) The term "issuer" means any person who issues or proposes to issue any security; except that with respect to certificates of deposit for securities, voting-trust certificates, or collateral-trust certificates, or with respect to certificates of interest or shares in an unincorporated investment trust not having a board of directors or the fixed, restricted management, or unit type, the term "issuer" means the person or persons performing the acts and assuming the duties of depositor or manager pursuant to the provisions of the trust or other agreement or instrument under which such securities are issued; and except that with respect to equipment-trust certificates or like securities, the term "issuer" means the person by whom the equipment or property is, or is to be, used.

(9) The term "person" means a natural person, company, government, or political subdivision, agency, or instrumentality of a government.

Regulation of the Use of Manipulative and Deceptive Devices

Section 10.   It shall be unlawful for any person, directly or indirectly, by the use of any means or instrumentality of interstate commerce or of the mails, or of any facility of any national securities exchange—

(a) To effect a short sale, or to use or employ any stop-loss order in connection with the purchase or sale, of any security registered on a national securities exchange, in contravention of such rules and regulations as the Commission may prescribe as necessary or appropriate in the public interest or for the protection of investors.

(b) To use or employ, in connection with the purchase or sale of any security registered on a national securities exchange or any security not so registered, any manipulative or deceptive device or contrivance in contravention of such rules and regulations as the Commission may prescribe as necessary or appropriate in the public interest or for the protection of investors.

A-85

Appendix K

Title VII of the Civil Rights Act of 1964 (Excerpts)

Title VII of the Civil Rights Act of 1964—The Employment Discrimination Section

Section 703. Unlawful Employment Practices. (a) It shall be an unlawful employment practice for an employer—

(1) to fail or refuse to hire or to discharge any individual, or otherwise to discriminate against any individual with respect to his compensation, terms, conditions, or privileges of employment, because of such individual's race, color, religion, sex, or national origin; or

(2) to limit, segregate, or classify his employees or applicants for employment in any way which would deprive or tend to deprive any individual of employment opportunities or otherwise adversely affect his status as an employee, because of such individual's race, color, religion, sex, or national origin.

(b) It shall be an unlawful employment practice for an employment agency to fail or refuse to refer for employment, or otherwise to discriminate against, any individual because of his race, color, religion, sex, or national origin, or to classify or refer for employment any individual on the basis or his race, color, religion, sex, or national origin.

(c) It shall be an unlawful employment practice for a labor organization—

(1) to exclude or to expel from its membership, or otherwise to discriminate against, any individual because of his race, color, religion, sex, or national origin;

(2) to limit, segregate, or classify its membership or applicants for membership, or to classify or fail or refuse to refer for employment any individual, in any way which would deprive or tend to deprive any individual of em-

ployment opportunities, or would limit such employment opportunities or otherwise adversely affect his status as an employee or as an applicant for employment, because of such individual's race, color, religion, sex, or national origin; or

(3) to cause or attempt to cause an employer to discriminate against an individual in violation of this section.

(d) It shall be an unlawful employment practice for any employer, labor organization, or joint labor-management committee controlling apprenticeship or other training or retraining, including on-the-job training programs to discriminate against any individual because of his race, color, religion, sex, or national origin in admission to, or employment in, any program established to provide apprenticeship or other training.

(e) Notwithstanding any other provision of this subchapter.

(1) it shall not be an unlawful employment practice for an employer to hire and employ employees, for an employment agency to classify, or refer for employment any individual, for a labor organization to classify its membership or to classify or refer for employment any individual, or for an employer, labor organization, or joint labor-management committee controlling apprenticeship or other training or retraining programs to admit or employ any individual in any such program, on the basis of his religion, sex, or national origin in those certain instances where religion, sex, or national origin is a bona fide occupational qualification reasonably necessary to the normal operation of that particular business or enterprise, and

(2) it shall not be an unlawful employment practice for a school, college, university, or other educational institution

or institution of learning to hire and employ employees of a particular religion if such school, college, university, or other educational institution or institution of learning is, in whole or in substantial part, owned, supported, controlled, or managed by a particular religion or by a particular religious corporation, association, or society, or if the curriculum of such school, college, university, or other educational institution or institution of learning is directed toward the propagation of a particular religion.

(f) As used in this subchapter, the phrase "unlawful employment practice" shall not be deemed to include any action or measure taken by an employer, labor organization, joint labor-management committee, or employment agency with respect to an individual who is a member of the Communist Party of the United States or of any other organization required to register as a Communist-action or Communist-front organization. * * *

(g) Notwithstanding any other provision of this subchapter, it shall not be an unlawful employment practice for an employer to fail or refuse to hire and employ any individual for any position, for an employer to discharge any individual from any position, or for an employment agency to fail or refuse to refer any individual for employment in any position, or for a labor organization to fail or refuse to refer any individual for employment in any position, if—

(1) the occupancy of such position, or access to the premises in or upon which any part of the duties of such position is performed or is to be performed, is subject to any requirement imposed in the interest of the national security of the United States * * * and

(2) such individual has not fulfilled or has ceased to fulfill that requirement.

(h) Notwithstanding any other provision of this subchapter, it shall not be an unlawful employment practice for an employer to apply different standards of compensation, or different terms, conditions, or privileges of employment pursuant to a bona fide seniority or merit system, or a system which measures earnings by quantity or quality of production or to employees who work in different locations, provided that such differences are not the result of an intention to discriminate because of race, color, religion, sex, or national origin, nor shall it be an unlawful employment practice for an employer to give and act upon the results of any professionally developed ability test provided that such test, its administration or action upon the results is not designed, intended or used to discriminate because of race, color, religion, sex, or national origin. * * *

(j) Nothing contained in this subchapter shall be interpreted to require any employer, employment agency, labor or-

ganization, or joint labor-management committee subject to this subchapter to grant preferential treatment to any individual or to any group because of the race, color, religion, sex, or national origin of such individual or group on account of an imbalance which may exist with respect to the total number of percentage of persons of any race, color, religion, sex, or national origin employed by any employer, referred or classified for employment by any employment agency or labor organization, or admitted to, or employed in, any apprenticeship or other training program, in comparison with the total number or percentage of persons of such race, color, religion, sex, or national origin in any community, State, section, or other area, or in the available work force in any community, State, section, or other area.

* * * *

Section 704. Other Unlawful Employment Practices. (a) It shall be an unlawful employment practice for an employer to discriminate against any of his employees or applicants for employment, for an employment agency, or joint labor-management committee controlling apprenticeship or other training or retraining, including on-the-job training programs, to discriminate against any individual, or for a labor organization to discriminate against any member thereof or applicant for membership, because he has opposed any practice made an unlawful employment practice by this subchapter, or because he has made a charge, testified, assisted, or participated in any manner in an investigation, proceeding, or hearing under this subchapter.

(b) It shall be an unlawful employment practice for an employer, labor organization, employment agency, or joint labor-management committee controlling apprenticeship or other training or retraining, including on-the-job training programs, to print or publish or cause to be printed or published any notice or advertisement relating to employment by such an employer or membership or any classification or referral for employment by such a labor organization, or relating to any classification or referral for employment by such an employment agency, or relating to admission to, or employment in, any program established to provide apprenticeship or other training by such a joint-labor-management committee, indicating any preference, limitation, specification, or discrimination, based on race, color, religion, sex, or national origin, except that such a notice or advertisement may indicate a preference, limitation, specification, or discrimination based on religion, sex or national origin when religion, sex, or national origin is a bona fide occupational qualification for employment.

Appendix L

Americans with Disabilities Act of 1990 (Excerpts)

TITLE I—EMPLOYMENT
Sec. 101. Definitions.

As used in this title: * * *

(8) **Qualified individual with a disability.**—The term "qualified individual with a disability" means an individual with a disability who, with or without reasonable accommodation, can perform the essential functions of the employment position that such individual holds or desires. For the purposes of this title, consideration shall be given to the employer's judgment as to what functions of a job are essential, and if an employer has prepared a written description before advertising or interviewing applicants for the job, this description shall be considered evidence of the essential functions of the job.

(9) **Reasonable accommodation.**—The term "reasonable accommodation" may include—

(A) making existing facilities used by employees readily accessible to and usable by individuals with disabilities; and

(B) job restructuring, part-time or modified work schedules, reassignment to a vacant position, acquisition or modification of equipment or devices, appropriate adjustment or modifications of examinations, training materials or policies, the provision of qualified readers or interpreters, and other similar accommodations for individuals with disabilities.

(10) **Undue Hardship.**—

(A) **In general.**—The term "undue hardship" means an action requiring significant difficulty or expense, when considered in light of the factors set forth in subparagraph (B).

(B) **Factors to be considered.**—In determining whether an accommodation would impose an undue hardship on a covered entity, factors to be considered include—

(i) the nature and cost of accommodation needed under this Act;

(ii) the overall financial resources of the facility or facilities involved in the provision of the reasonable accommodation; the number of persons employed at such facility; the effect on expenses and resources, or the impact otherwise of such accommodation upon the operation of the facility;

(iii) the overall financial resources of the covered entity; the overall size of the business of a covered entity with respect to the number of its employees; the number, type, and location of its facilities; and

(iv) the type of operation or operations of the covered entity, including the composition, structure, and functions of the workforce of such entity; the geographic separateness, administrative, or fiscal relationship of the facility or facilities in question to the covered entity.

Sec. 102. Discrimination.

(a) **General Rule.**—No covered entity shall discriminate against a qualified individual with a disability because of the disability of such individual in regard to job application procedures, the hiring, advancement, or discharge of employees, employee compensation, job training, and other terms, conditions, and privileges of employment.

(b) **Construction.**—As used in subsection (a), the term "discriminate" includes—

(1) limiting, segregating, or classifying a job applicant or employee in a way that adversely affects the opportunities

or status of such applicant or employee because of the disability of such applicant or employee;

(2) participating in a contractual or other arrangement or relationship that has the effect of subjecting a covered entity's qualified applicant or employee with a disability to the discrimination prohibited by this title (such relationship includes a relationship with an employment or referral agency, labor union, an organization providing fringe benefits to an employee of the covered entity, or an organization providing training and apprenticeship programs);

(3) utilizing standards, criteria, or methods of administration—

(A) that have the effect of discrimination on the basis of disability; or

(B) that perpetuate the discrimination of others who are subject to common administrative control;

(4) excluding or otherwise denying equal jobs or benefits to a qualified individual because of the known disability of an individual with whom the qualified individual is known to have a relationship or association;

(5)(A) not making reasonable accommodations to the known physical or mental limitations of an otherwise qualified individual with a disability who is an applicant or employee, unless such covered entity can demonstrate that the accommodation would impose an undue hardship on the operation of the business of such covered entity; or

(B) denying employment opportunities to a job applicant or employee who is an otherwise qualified individual with a disability, if such denial is based on the need of such covered entity to make reasonable accommodation to the physical or mental impairments of the employee or applicant;

(6) using qualification standards, employment tests or other selection criteria that screen out or tend to screen out an individual with a disability or a class of individuals with disabilities unless the standard, test or other selection criteria, as used by the covered entity, is shown to be job-related for the position in question and is consistent with business necessity; and

(7) failing to select and administer tests concerning employment in the most effective manner to ensure that, when such test is administered to a job applicant or employee who has a disability that impairs sensory, manual, or speaking skills, such test results accurately reflect the skills, aptitude, or whatever other factor of such applicant or employee that such test purports to measure, rather than reflecting the impaired sensory, manual, or speaking skills of such employee or applicant (except where such skills are the factors that the test purports to measure). * * *

Sec. 104. Illegal Use of Drugs and Alcohol. * * *

(b) **Rules of Construction.**—Nothing in subsection (a) shall be construed to exclude as a qualified individual with a disability an individual who—

(1) has successfully completed a supervised drug rehabilitation program and is no longer engaging in the illegal use of drugs, or has otherwise been rehabilitated successfully and is no longer engaging in such use;

(2) is participating in a supervised rehabilitation program and is no longer engaging in such use; or

(3) is erroneously regarded as engaging in such use, but is not engaging in such use;

except that it shall not be a violation of this Act for a covered entity to adopt or administer reasonable policies or procedures, including but not limited to drug testing, designed to ensure that an individual described in paragraph (1) or (2) is no longer engaging in the illegal use of drugs. * * *

Sec. 107. Enforcement.

(a) **Powers, Remedies, and Procedures.**—The powers, remedies, and procedures set forth in sections 705, 706, 707, 709, and 710 of the Civil Rights Act of 1964 (42 U.S.C. 2000e-4, 2000e-5, 2000e-6, 2000e-8, and 2000e-9) shall be the powers, remedies, and procedures this title provides to the Commission, to the Attorney General, or to any person alleging discrimination on the basis of disability in violation of any provision of this Act, or regulations promulgated under section 106, concerning employment.

(b) **Coordination.**—The agencies with enforcement authority for actions which allege employment discrimination under this title and under the Rehabilitation Act of 1973 shall develop procedures to ensure that administrative complaints filed under this title and under the Rehabilitation Act of 1973 are dealt with in a manner that avoids duplication of effort and prevents imposition of inconsistent or conflicting standards for the same requirements under this title and the Rehabilitation Act of 1973. The Commission, the Attorney General, and the Office of Federal Contract Compliance Programs shall establish such coordinating mechanisms (similar to provisions contained in the joint regulations promulgated by the Commission and the Attorney General at part 42 of title 28 and part 1691 of title 29, Code of Federal Regulations, and the Memorandum of Understanding between the Commission and the Office of Federal Contract Compliance Programs dated January 16, 1981 (46 Fed. Reg. 7435, January 23, 1981)) in regulations implementing this title and Rehabilitation Act of 1973 not later than 18 months after the date of enactment of this Act.

Sec. 108. Effective Date.

This title shall become effective 24 months after the date of enactment.

Appendix M

The Uniform Partnership Act

(Adopted in forty-nine States [all of the states except Louisiana], the District of Columbia, the Virgin Islands, and Guam. The adoptions by Alabama and Nebraska do not follow the official text in every respect, but are substantially similar, with local variations.)

The Act consists of 7 Parts as follows:

I. Preliminary Provisions

II. Nature of Partnership

III. Relations of Partners to Persons Dealing with the Partnership

IV. Relations of Partners to One Another

V. Property Rights of a Partner

VI. Dissolution and Winding Up

VII. Miscellaneous Provisions

An Act to make uniform the Law of Partnerships

Be it enacted, etc.:

Part I Preliminary Provisions

Sec. 1. Name of Act

This act may be cited as Uniform Partnership Act.

Sec. 2. Definition of Terms

In this act, "Court" includes every court and judge having jurisdiction in the case.

"Business" includes every trade, occupation, or profession.

"Person" includes individuals, partnerships, corporations, and other associations.

"Bankrupt" includes bankrupt under the Federal Bankruptcy Act or insolvent under any state insolvent act.

"Conveyance" includes every assignment, lease, mortgage, or encumbrance.

"Real property" includes land and any interest or estate in land.

Sec. 3. Interpretation of Knowledge and Notice

(1) A person has "knowledge" of a fact within the meaning of this act not only when he has actual knowledge thereof, but also when he has knowledge of such other facts as in the circumstances shows bad faith.

(2) A person has "notice" of a fact within the meaning of this act when the person who claims the benefit of the notice:

(a) States the fact to such person, or

(b) Delivers through the mail, or by other means of communication, a written statement of the fact to such person or to a proper person at his place of business or residence.

Sec. 4. Rules of Construction

(1) The rule that statutes in derogation of the common law are to be strictly construed shall have no application to this act.

(2) The law of estoppel shall apply under this act.

(3) The law of agency shall apply under this act.

(4) This act shall be so interpreted and construed as to effect its general purpose to make uniform the law of those states which enact it.

(5) This act shall not be construed so as to impair the obligations of any contract existing when the act goes into

effect, nor to affect any action or proceedings begun or right accrued before this act takes effect.

Sec. 5. **Rules for Cases Not Provided for in This Act.**

In any case not provided for in this act the rules of law and equity, including the law merchant, shall govern.

Part II Nature of Partnership

Sec. 6. **Partnership Defined**

(1) A partnership is an association of two or more persons to carry on as co-owners a business for profit.

(2) But any association formed under any other statute of this state, or any statute adopted by authority, other than the authority of this state, is not a partnership under this act, unless such association would have been a partnership in this state prior to the adoption of this act; but this act shall apply to limited partnerships except in so far as the statutes relating to such partnerships are inconsistent herewith.

Sec. 7. **Rules for Determining the Existence of a Partnership**

In determining whether a partnership exists, these rules shall apply:

(1) Except as provided by Section 16 persons who are not partners as to each other are not partners as to third persons.

(2) Joint tenancy, tenancy in common, tenancy by the entireties, joint property, common property, or part ownership does not of itself establish a partnership, whether such co-owners do or do not share any profits made by the use of the property.

(3) The sharing of gross returns does not of itself establish a partnership, whether or not the persons sharing them have a joint or common right or interest in any property from which the returns are derived.

(4) The receipt by a person of a share of the profits of a business is prima facie evidence that he is a partner in the business, but no such inference shall be drawn if such profits were received in payment:

(a) As a debt by installments or otherwise,

(b) As wages of an employee or rent to a landlord,

(c) As an annuity to a widow or representative of a deceased partner,

(d) As interest on a loan, though the amount of payment vary with the profits of the business,

(e) As the consideration for the sale of a good-will of a business or other property by installments or otherwise.

Sec. 8. **Partnership Property**

(1) All property originally brought into the partnership stock or subsequently acquired by purchase or otherwise, on account of the partnership, is partnership property.

(2) Unless the contrary intention appears, property acquired with partnership funds is partnership property.

(3) Any estate in real property may be acquired in the partnership name. Title so acquired can be conveyed only in the partnership name.

(4) A conveyance to a partnership in the partnership name, though without words of inheritance, passes the entire estate of the grantor unless a contrary intent appears.

Part III Relations of Partners to Persons Dealing with the Partnership

Sec. 9. **Partner Agent of Partnership as to Partnership Business**

(1) Every partner is an agent of the partnership for the purpose of its business, and the act of every partner, including the execution in the partnership name of any instrument, for apparently carrying on in the usual way the business of the partnership of which he is a member binds the partnership, unless the partner so acting has in fact no authority to act for the partnership in the particular matter, and the person with whom he is dealing has knowledge of the fact that he has no such authority.

(2) An act of a partner which is not apparently for the carrying on of the business of the partnership in the usual way does not bind the partnership unless authorized by the other partners.

(3) Unless authorized by the other partners or unless they have abandoned the business, one or more but less than all the partners have no authority to:

(a) Assign the partnership property in trust for creditors or on the assignee's promise to pay the debts of the partnership,

(b) Dispose of the good-will of the business,

(c) Do any other act which would make it impossible to carry on the ordinary business of a partnership,

(d) Confess a judgment,

(e) Submit a partnership claim or liability to arbitration or reference.

(4) No act of a partner in contravention of a restriction on authority shall bind the partnership to persons having knowledge of the restriction.

Sec. 10. **Conveyance of Real Property of the Partnership**

(1) Where title to real property is in the partnership name, any partner may convey title to such property by a conveyance executed in the partnership name; but the partnership may recover such property unless the partner's act binds the partnership under the provisions of paragraph (1) of section 9, or unless such property has been conveyed by the grantee or a person claiming through such grantee to a holder for value without knowledge that the partner, in making the conveyance, has exceeded his authority.

(2) Where title to real property is in the name of the partnership, a conveyance executed by a partner, in his own name, passes the equitable interest of the partnership, provided the act is one within the authority of the partner under the provisions of paragraph (1) of section 9.

(3) Where title to real property is in the name of one or more but not all the partners, and the record does not disclose the right of the partnership, the partners in whose name the title stands may convey title to such property, but the partnership may recover such property if the partners' act does not bind the partnership under the provisions of paragraph (1) of section 9, unless the purchaser or his assignee, is a holder for value, without knowledge.

(4) Where the title to real property is in the name of one or more or all the partners, or in a third person in trust for the partnership, a conveyance executed by a partner in the partnership name, or in his own name, passes the equitable interest of the partnership, provided the act is one within the authority of the partner under the provisions of paragraph (1) of section 9.

(5) Where the title to real property is in the names of all the partners a conveyance executed by all the partners passes all their rights in such property.

Sec. 11. **Partnership Bound by Admission of Partner**

An admission or representation made by any partner concerning partnership affairs within the scope of his authority as conferred by this act is evidence against the partnership.

Sec. 12. **Partnership Charged with Knowledge of or Notice to Partner**

Notice to any partner of any matter relating to partnership affairs, and the knowledge of the partner acting in the particular matter, acquired while a partner or then present to his mind, and the knowledge of any other partner who reasonably could and should have communicated it to the acting partner, operate as notice to or knowledge of the partnership, except in the case of a fraud on the partnership committed by or with the consent of that partner.

Sec. 13. **Partnership Bound by Partner's Wrongful Act**

Where, by any wrongful act or omission of any partner acting in the ordinary course of the business of the part-

nership or with the authority of his co-partners, loss or injury is caused to any person, not being a partner in the partnership, or any penalty is incurred, the partnership is liable therefor to the same extent as the partner so acting or omitting to act.

Sec. 14. **Partnership Bound by Partner's Breach of Trust**

The partnership is bound to make good the loss:

(a) Where one partner acting within the scope of his apparent authority receives money or property of a third person and misapplies it; and

(b) Where the partnership in the course of its business receives money or property of a third person and the money or property so received is misapplied by any partner while it is in the custody of the partnership.

Sec. 15. **Nature of Partner's Liability**

All partners are liable

(a) Jointly and severally for everything chargeable to the partnership under sections 13 and 14.

(b) Jointly for all other debts and obligations of the partnership; but any partner may enter into a separate obligation to perform a partnership contract.

Sec. 16. **Partner by Estoppel**

(1) When a person, by words spoken or written or by conduct, represents himself, or consents to another representing him to any one, as a partner in an existing partnership or with one or more persons not actual partners, he is liable to any such person to whom such representation has been made, who has, on the faith of such representation, given credit to the actual or apparent partnership, and if he has made such representation or consented to its being made in a public manner he is liable to such person, whether the representation has or has not been made or communicated to such person so giving credit by or with the knowledge of the apparent partner making the representation or consenting to its being made.

> (a) When a partnership liability results, he is liable as though he were an actual member of the partnership.

> (b) When no partnership liability results, he is liable jointly with the other persons, if any, so consenting to the contract or representation as to incur liability, otherwise separately.

(2) When a person has been thus represented to be a partner in an existing partnership, or with one or more persons not actual partners, he is an agent of the persons consenting to such representation to bind them to the same extent and in the same manner as though he were a partner in fact, with respect to persons who rely upon the representation. Where all the members of the existing partnership consent to the

representation, a partnership act or obligation results; but in all other cases it is the joint act or obligation of the person acting and the persons consenting to the representation.

Sec. 17. **Liability of Incoming Partner**

A person admitted as a partner into an existing partnership is liable for all the obligations of the partnership arising before his admission as though he had been a partner when such obligations were incurred, except that this liability shall be satisfied only out of partnership property.

Part IV Relations of Partners to One Another

Sec. 18. **Rules Determining Rights and Duties of Partners**

The rights and duties of the partners in relation to the partnership shall be determined, subject to any agreement between them, by the following rules:

(a) Each partner shall be repaid his contributions, whether by way of capital or advances to the partnership property and share equally in the profits and surplus remaining after all liabilities, including those to partners, are satisfied; and must contribute towards the losses, whether of capital or otherwise, sustained by the partnership according to his share in the profits.

(b) The partnership must indemnify every partner in respect of payments made and personal liabilities reasonably incurred by him in the ordinary and proper conduct of its business, or for the preservation of its business or property.

(c) A partner, who in aid of the partnership makes any payment or advance beyond the amount of capital which he agreed to contribute, shall be paid interest from the date of the payment or advance.

(d) A partner shall receive interest on the capital contributed by him only from the date when repayment should be made.

(e) All partners have equal rights in the management and conduct of the partnership business.

(f) No partner is entitled to remuneration for acting in the partnership business, except that a surviving partner is entitled to reasonable compensation for his services in winding up the partnership affairs.

(g) No person can become a member of a partnership without the consent of all the partners.

(h) Any difference arising as to ordinary matters connected with the partnership business may be decided by a majority of the partners; but no act in contravention of any agreement between the partners may be done rightfully without the consent of all the partners.

Sec. 19. **Partnership Books**

The partnership books shall be kept, subject to any agreement between the partners, at the principal place of business of the partnership, and every partner shall at all times have access to and may inspect and copy any of them.

Sec. 20. **Duty of Partners to Render Information**

Partners shall render on demand true and full information of all things affecting the partnership to any partner or the legal representative of any deceased partner or partner under legal disability.

Sec. 21. **Partner Accountable as a Fiduciary**

(1) Every partner must account to the partnership for any benefit, and hold as trustee for it any profits derived by him without the consent of the other partners from any transaction connected with the formation, conduct, or liquidation of the partnership or from any use by him of its property.

(2) This section applies also to the representatives of a deceased partner engaged in the liquidation of the affairs of the partnership as the personal representatives of the last surviving partner.

Sec. 22. **Right to an Account**

Any partner shall have the right to a formal account as to partnership affairs:

(a) If he is wrongfully excluded from the partnership business or possession of its property by his co-partners,

(b) If the right exists under the terms of any agreement,

(c) As provided by section 21,

(d) Whenever other circumstances render it just and reasonable.

Sec. 23. **Continuation of Partnership beyond Fixed Term**

(1) When a partnership for a fixed term or particular undertaking is continued after the termination of such term or particular undertaking without any express agreement, the rights and duties of the partners remain the same as they were at such termination, so far as is consistent with a partnership at will.

(2) A continuation of the business by the partners or such of them as habitually acted therein during the term, without any settlement or liquidation of the partnership affairs, is prima facie evidence of a continuation of the partnership.

Part V Property Rights of a Partner

Sec. 24. **Extent of Property Rights of a Partner**

The property rights of a partner are (1) his rights in specific partnership property, (2) his interest in the partnership, and (3) his right to participate in the management.

Sec. 25. **Nature of a Partner's Right in Specific Partnership Property**

(1) A partner is co-owner with his partners of specific partnership property holding as a tenant in partnership.

(2) The incidents of this tenancy are such that:

(a) A partner, subject to the provisions of this act and to any agreement between the partners, has an equal right with his partners to possess specific partnership property for partnership purposes; but he has no right to possess such property for any other purpose without the consent of his partners.

(b) A partner's right in specific partnership property is not assignable except in connection with the assignment of rights of all the partners in the same property.

(c) A partner's right in specific partnership property is not subject to attachment or execution, except on a claim against the partnership. When partnership property is attached for a partnership debt the partners, or any of them, or the representatives of a deceased partner, cannot claim any right under the homestead or exemption laws.

(d) On the death of a partner his right in specific partnership property vests in the surviving partner or partners, except where the deceased was the last surviving partner, when his right in such property vests in his legal representative. Such surviving partner or partners, or the legal representative of the last surviving partner, has no right to possess the partnership property for any but a partnership purpose.

(e) A partner's right in specific partnership property is not subject to dower, curtesy, or allowances to widows, heirs, or next of kin.

Sec. 26. **Nature of Partner's Interest in the Partnership**

A partner's interest in the partnership is his share of the profits and surplus, and the same is personal property.

Sec. 27. **Assignment of Partner's Interest**

(1) A conveyance by a partner of his interest in the partnership does not of itself dissolve the partnership, nor, as against the other partners in the absence of agreement, entitle the assignee, during the continuance of the partnership, to interfere in the management or administration of the partnership business or affairs, or to require any information or account of partnership transactions, or to inspect the partnership books; but it merely entitles the assignee to receive in accordance with his contract the profits to which the assigning partner would otherwise be entitled.

(2) In case of a dissolution of the partnership, the assignee is entitled to receive his assignor's interest and may require an account from the date only of the last account agreed to by all the partners.

Sec. 28. **Partner's Interest Subject to Charging Order**

(1) On due application to a competent court by any judgment creditor of a partner, the court which entered the judgment, order, or decree, or any other court, may charge the interest of the debtor partner with payment of the unsatisfied amount of such judgment debt with interest thereon; and may then or later appoint a receiver of his share of the profits, and of any other money due or to fall due to him in respect of the partnership, and make all other orders, directions, accounts and inquiries which the debtor partner might have made, or which the circumstances of the case may require.

(2) The interest charged may be redeemed at any time before foreclosure, or in case of a sale being directed by the court may be purchased without thereby causing a dissolution:

(a) With separate property, by any one or more of the partners, or

(b) With partnership property, by any one or more of the partners with the consent of all the partners whose interests are not so charged or sold.

(3) Nothing in this act shall be held to deprive a partner of his right, if any, under the exemption laws, as regards his interest in the partnership.

Part VI Dissolution and Winding up

Sec. 29. **Dissolution Defined**

The dissolution of a partnership is the change in the relation of the partners caused by any partner ceasing to be associated in the carrying on as distinguished from the winding up of the business.

Sec. 30. **Partnership not Terminated by Dissolution**

On dissolution the partnership is not terminated, but continues until the winding up of partnership affairs is completed.

Sec. 31. **Causes of Dissolution**

Dissolution is caused:

(1) Without violation of the agreement between the partners,

(a) By the termination of the definite term or particular undertaking specified in the agreement,

(b) By the express will of any partner when no definite term or particular undertaking is specified,

(c) By the express will of all the partners who have not assigned their interests or suffered them to be charged for their separate debts, either before or after the termination of any specified term or particular undertaking,

(d) By the expulsion of any partner from the business bona fide in accordance with such a power conferred by the agreement between the partners;

(2) In contravention of the agreement between the partners, where the circumstances do not permit a dissolution under any other provision of this section, by the express will of any partner at any time;

(3) By any event which makes it unlawful for the business of the partnership to be carried on or for the members to carry it on in partnership;

(4) By the death of any partner;

(5) By the bankruptcy of any partner or the partnership;

(6) By decree of court under section 32.

Sec. 32. Dissolution by Decree of Court

(1) On application by or for a partner the court shall decree a dissolution whenever:

(a) A partner has been declared a lunatic in any judicial proceeding or is shown to be of unsound mind,

(b) A partner becomes in any other way incapable of performing his part of the partnership contract,

(c) A partner has been guilty of such conduct as tends to affect prejudicially the carrying on of the business,

(d) A partner wilfully or persistently commits a breach of the partnership agreement, or otherwise so conducts himself in matters relating to the partnership business that it is not reasonably practicable to carry on the business in partnership with him,

* (e) The business of the partnership can only be carried on at a loss,

(f) Other circumstances render a dissolution equitable.

(2) On the application of the purchaser of a partner's interest under sections 28 or 29 [should read 27 or 28];

(a) After the termination of the specified term or particular undertaking,

(b) At any time if the partnership was a partnership at will when the interest was assigned or when the charging order was issued.

Sec. 33. General Effect of Dissolution on Authority of Partner

Except so far as may be necessary to wind up partnership affairs or to complete transactions begun but not then finished, dissolution terminates all authority of any partner to act for the partnership,

(1) With respect to the partners,

(a) When the dissolution is not by the act, bankruptcy or death of a partner; or

(b) When the dissolution is by such act, bankruptcy or death of a partner, in cases where section 34 so requires.

(2) With respect to persons not partners, as declared in section 35.

Sec. 34. Rights of Partner to Contribution from Co-partners after Dissolution

Where the dissolution is caused by the act, death or bankruptcy of a partner, each partner is liable to his copartners for his share of any liability created by any partner acting for the partnership as if the partnership had not been dissolved unless

(a) The dissolution being by act of any partner, the partner acting for the partnership had knowledge of the dissolution, or

(b) The dissolution being by the death or bankruptcy of a partner, the partner acting for the partnership had knowledge or notice of the death or bankruptcy.

Sec. 35. Power of Partner to Bind Partnership to Third Persons after Dissolution

(1) After dissolution a partner can bind the partnership except as provided in Paragraph (3).

(a) By any act appropriate for winding up partnership affairs or completing transactions unfinished at dissolution;

(b) By any transaction which would bind the partnership if dissolution had not taken place, provided the other party to the transaction

(I) Had extended credit to the partnership prior to dissolution and had no knowledge or notice of the dissolution; or

(II) Though he had not so extended credit, had nevertheless known of the partnership prior to dissolution, and, having no knowledge or notice of dissolution, the fact of dissolution had not been advertised in a newspaper of general circulation in the place (or in each place if more than one) at which the partnership business was regularly carried on.

(2) The liability of a partner under paragraph (1b) shall be satisfied out of partnership assets alone when such partner had been prior to dissolution

(a) Unknown as a partner to the person with whom the contract is made; and

(b) So far unknown and inactive in partnership affairs that the business reputation of the partnership could not be said to have been in any degree due to his connection with it.

(3) The partnership is in no case bound by any act of a partner after dissolution

(a) Where the partnership is dissolved because it is unlawful to carry on the business, unless the act is appropriate for winding up partnership affairs; or

(b) Where the partner has become bankrupt; or

(c) Where the partner has no authority to wind up partnership affairs; except by a transaction with one who

(I) Had extended credit to the partnership prior to dissolution and had no knowledge or notice of his want of authority; or

(II) Had not extended credit to the partnership prior to dissolution, and, having no knowledge or notice of his want of authority, the fact of his want of authority has not been advertised in the manner provided for advertising the fact of dissolution in paragraph (1bII).

(4) Nothing in this section shall affect the liability under Section 16 of any person who after dissolution represents himself or consents to another representing him as a partner in a partnership engaged in carrying on business.

Sec. 36. Effect of Dissolution on Partner's Existing Liability

(1) The dissolution of the partnership does not of itself discharge the existing liability of any partner.

(2) A partner is discharged from any existing liability upon dissolution of the partnership by an agreement to that effect between himself, the partnership creditor and the person or partnership continuing the business; and such agreement may be inferred from the course of dealing between the creditor having knowledge of the dissolution and the person or partnership continuing the business.

(3) Where a person agrees to assume the existing obligations of a dissolved partnership, the partners whose obligations have been assumed shall be discharged from any liability to any creditor of the partnership who, knowing of the agreement, consents to a material alteration in the nature or time of payment of such obligations.

(4) The individual property of a deceased partner shall be liable for all obligations of the partnership incurred while he was a partner but subject to the prior payment of his separate debts.

Sec. 37. Right to Wind Up

Unless otherwise agreed the partners who have not wrongfully dissolved the partnership or the legal representative of the last surviving partner, not bankrupt, has the right to wind up the partnership affairs; provided, however, that any partner, his legal representative or his assignee, upon cause shown, may obtain winding up by the court.

Sec. 38. Rights of Partners to Application of Partnership Property

(1) When dissolution is caused in any way, except in contravention of the partnership agreement, each partner, as against his co-partners and all persons claiming through them in respect of their interests in the partnership, unless otherwise agreed, may have the partnership property applied to discharge its liabilities, and the surplus applied to pay in cash the net amount owing to the respective partners. But if dissolution is caused by expulsion of a partner, bona fide under the partnership agreement and if the expelled partner is discharged from all partnership liabilities, either by payment or agreement under section 36(2), he shall receive in cash only the net amount due him from the partnership.

(2) When dissolution is caused in contravention of the partnership agreement the rights of the partners shall be as follows:

(a) Each partner who has not caused dissolution wrongfully shall have,

(I) All the rights specified in paragraph (1) of this section, and

(II) The right, as against each partner who has caused the dissolution wrongfully, to damages for breach of the agreement.

(b) The partners who have not caused the dissolution wrongfully, if they all desire to continue the business in the same name, either by themselves or jointly with others, may do so, during the agreed term for the partnership and for that purpose may possess the partnership property, provided they secure the payment by bond approved by the court, or pay to any partner who has caused the dissolution wrongfully, the value of his interest in the partnership at the dissolution, less any damages recoverable under clause (2a II) of the section, and in like manner indemnify him against all present or future partnership liabilities.

(c) A partner who has caused the dissolution wrongfully shall have:

(I) If the business is not continued under the provisions of paragraph (2b) all the rights of a partner under paragraph (1), subject to clause (2a II), of this section,

(II) If the business is continued under paragraph (2b) of this section the right as against his co-partners and all claiming through them in respect of their interests in the partnership, to have the value of his interest in the partnership, less any damages caused to his co-partners by the dissolution, ascertained and paid to him in cash, or the payment secured by bond approved by the court, and to be released from all existing liabilities of the partnership; but in ascertaining the value of the partner's interest the value of the good-will of the business shall not be considered.

Sec. 39. **Rights Where Partnership Is Dissolved for Fraud or Misrepresentation**

Where a partnership contract is rescinded on the ground of the fraud or misrepresentation of one of the parties thereto, the party entitled to rescind is, without prejudice to any other right, entitled,

(a) To a lien on, or right of retention of, the surplus of the partnership property after satisfying the partnership liabilities to third persons for any sum of money paid by him for the purchase of an interest in the partnership and for any capital or advances contributed by him; and

(b) To stand, after all liabilities to third persons have been satisfied, in the place of the creditors of the partnership for any payments made by him in respect of the partnership liabilities; and

(c) To be indemnified by the person guilty of the fraud or making the representation against all debts and liabilities of the partnership.

Sec. 40. **Rules for Distribution**

In settling accounts between the partners after dissolution, the following rules shall be observed, subject to any agreement to the contrary:

(a) The assets of the partnership are:

  (I) The partnership property,

  (II) The contributions of the partners necessary for the payment of all the liabilities specified in clause (b) of this paragraph.

(b) The liabilities of the partnership shall rank in order of payment, as follows:

  (I) Those owing to creditors other than partners,

  (II) Those owing to partners other than for capital and profits,

  (III) Those owing to partners in respect of capital,

  (IV) Those owing to partners in respect of profits.

(c) The assets shall be applied in the order of their declaration in clause (a) of this paragraph to the satisfaction of the liabilities.

(d) The partners shall contribute, as provided by section 18(a) the amount necessary to satisfy the liabilities; but if any, but not all, of the partners are insolvent, or, not being subject to process, refuse to contribute, the other partners shall contribute their share of the liabilities, and, in the relative proportions in which they share the profits, the additional amount necessary to pay the liabilities.

(e) An assignee for the benefit of creditors or any person

appointed by the court shall have the right to enforce the contributions specified in clause (d) of this paragraph.

(f) Any partner or his legal representative shall have the right to enforce the contributions specified in clause (d) of this paragraph, to the extent of the amount which he has paid in excess of his share of the liability.

(g) The individual property of a deceased partner shall be liable for the contributions specified in clause (d) of this paragraph.

(h) When partnership property and the individual properties of the partners are in possession of a court for distribution, partnership creditors shall have priority on partnership property and separate creditors on individual property, saving the rights of lien or secured creditors as heretofore.

(i) Where a partner has become bankrupt or his estate is insolvent the claims against his separate property shall rank in the following order:

  (I) Those owing to separate creditors,

  (II) Those owing to partnership creditors,

  (III) Those owing to partners by way of contribution.

Sec. 41. **Liability of Persons Continuing the Business in Certain Cases**

(1) When any new partner is admitted into an existing partnership, or when any partner retires and assigns (or the representative of the deceased partner assigns) his rights in partnership property to two or more of the partners, or to one or more of the partners and one or more third persons, if the business is continued without liquidation of the partnership affairs, creditors of the first or dissolved partnership are also creditors of the partnership so continuing the business.

(2) When all but one partner retire and assign (or the representative of a deceased partner assigns) their rights in partnership property to the remaining partner, who continues the business without liquidation of partnership affairs, either alone or with others, creditors of the dissolved partnership are also creditors of the person or partnership so continuing the business.

(3) When any partner retires or dies and the business of the dissolved partnership is continued as set forth in paragraphs (1) and (2) of this section, with the consent of the retired partners or the representative of the deceased partner, but without any assignment of his right in partnership property, rights of creditors of the dissolved partnership and of the creditors of the person or partnership continuing the business shall be as if such assignment had been made.

(4) When all the partners or their representatives assign their rights in partnership property to one or more third persons who promise to pay the debts and who continue

the business of the dissolved partnership, creditors of the dissolved partnership are also creditors of the person or partnership continuing the business.

(5) When any partner wrongfully causes a dissolution and the remaining partners continue the business under the provisions of section 38(2b), either alone or with others, and without liquidation of the partnership affairs, creditors of the dissolved partnership are also creditors of the person or partnership continuing the business.

(6) When a partner is expelled and the remaining partners continue the business either alone or with others, without liquidation of the partnership affairs, creditors of the dissolved partnership are also creditors of the person or partnership continuing the business.

(7) The liability of a third person becoming a partner in the partnership continuing the business, under this section, to the creditors of the dissolved partnership shall be satisfied out of partnership property only.

(8) When the business of a partnership after dissolution is continued under any conditions set forth in this section the creditors of the dissolved partnership, as against the separate creditors of the retiring or deceased partner or the representative of the deceased partner, have a prior right to any claim of the retired partner or the representative of the deceased partner against the person or partnership continuing the business, on account of the retired or deceased partner's interest in the dissolved partnership or on account of any consideration promised for such interest or for his right in partnership property.

(9) Nothing in this section shall be held to modify any right of creditors to set aside any assignment on the ground of fraud.

(10) The use by the person or partnership continuing the business of the partnership name, or the name of a deceased partner as part thereof, shall not of itself make the individual property of the deceased partner liable for any debts contracted by such person or partnership.

Sec. 42. **Rights of Retiring or Estate of Deceased Partner When the Business Is Continued**

When any partner retires or dies, and the business is continued under any of the conditions set forth in section 41 (1, 2, 3, 5, 6), or section 38(2b) without any settlement of accounts as between him or his estate and the person or partnership continuing the business, unless otherwise agreed, he or his legal representative as against such persons or partnership may have the value of his interest at the date of dissolution ascertained, and shall receive as an ordinary creditor an amount equal to the value of his interest in the dissolved partnership with interest, or, at his option or at the option of his legal representative, in lieu of interest, the profits attributable to the use of his right in the property of the dissolved partnership; provided that the creditors of the dissolved partnership as against the separate creditors, or the representative of the retired or deceased partner, shall have priority on any claim arising under this section, as provided by section 41(8) of this act.

Sec. 43. **Accrual of Actions**

The right to an account of his interest shall accrue to any partner, or his legal representative, as against the winding up partners or the surviving partners or the person or partnership continuing the business, at the date of dissolution, in the absence of any agreement to the contrary.

Part VII Miscellaneous Provisions

Sec. 44. **When Act Takes Effect**

This act shall take effect on the ____ day of ____ one thousand nine hundred and ____.

Sec. 45. **Legislation Repealed**

All acts or parts of acts inconsistent with this act are hereby repealed.

Appendix N

A Guide to Research in Legal Environment

A business student who wishes to do research on legal environment topics can consult many sources. Depending on the focus of the research, different types of sources should be consulted. For example, if the researcher only wants a general overview of the law and legal environment, he or she could look at a secondary legal source—such as a legal encyclopedia, a *Restatement of the Law,* or a treatise. If the student wants to consult a primary source of law, such as an actual court case, then he or she might look at a judicial reporter. Other primary sources include constitutions, statutes, and regulations. If a researcher wants to look at commentaries on the status of the law today, there are a plethora of law reviews and topical legal journals that provide scholarly articles on current issues of legal interest.

Any person undertaking legal research will want to become familiar with the "finding tools" of legal research—computer data bases, law digests, looseleaf services, bar association publications, weekly bulletins, and so on—that are available today. These services and publications not only assist the researcher in locating legal documents but also keep the researcher abreast of recent legal developments.

The summary below explains how these and other legal research tools can be used to assist you in learning more about the topics discussed in this text.

◼ Legal Encyclopedias

Legal encyclopedias cover topics of law in a general manner. They explain subjects, define terms, and offer historical as well as current coverage. They are also helpful in finding primary sources of authority. The two major legal encyclopedias are *Corpus Juris Secundum* (C.J.S.), published by the West Publishing Company, and *American Jurisprudence 2d* (Am.Jur.2d)—"2d" means second edition—published by the Lawyers Co-Operative Publishing Company. Each of these encyclopedias divides the law into more than four hundred topics. Although legal discussions in these encyclopedias give broad statements of accepted law, because the discussions are extensively footnoted, the encyclopedias are valuable sources for research.

Some states also have encyclopedias, such as *Texas Jurisprudence 3d.* A less technical reference is *The Guide to American Law: Everyone's Legal Encyclopedia,* which is published by West Publishing Company.

◼ Restatements of the Law

The *Restatements of the Law* are compilations of the common law covering various legal areas. There are *Restatements* of the law of agency, conflict of laws, contracts, judgments, property, restitution, security, torts, trusts, foreign relations law, and landlord-tenant law. A student wishing more information on the law of contracts, for example, might consult the *Restatement (Second) of Contracts.* (The word "second" in parenthesis means second edition.) Similarly, if a student is interested in studying the law of agency in more detail, he or she could look at the *Restatement (Second) of Agency.* The title of each *Restatement* follows this same format. The *Restatements* include a summary of the "black letter" law on a particular topic, an explanatory comment on the general principles underlying that law, and examples of particular cases and variations on the general proposition.

Treatises

Treatises are like encyclopedias; they are written by specialists on certain subjects. Longer treatises are frequently published in multiple volumes. There are treatises for virtually all of the major topics of law. When updated, treatises are usually accurate explanations of the law in a particular area, and, at the same time, they are usually easy to read and a good source to turn to when beginning one's legal research. For example, *Prosser and Keeton on Torts* would assist a student in researching those topics introduced in Chapters 7 and 8 of this text. *Collier on Bankruptcy* outlines the law presented in Chapter 12 of this text.

Digests of Case Law

Digests are indexes to American case law. There are digests for both the federal and state court systems. Digests consist primarily of case summaries, which are arranged topically, from each jurisdiction. The advantage of a digest is that researchers can review cases from, for example, all appellate courts for a ten-year period. The American Digest System is the master index giving access to all cases published in the National Reporter System. The American Digest System includes the *Decennial Digest Series,* which is published every ten years, and the *General Digest Series* that is issued periodically between publications of the *Decennial Digest Series.*

There are also a number of subject-matter digests and jurisdictional digests, which are simply extractions of digested cases from the master index.

When one is researching a relatively narrow legal topic such as patent law, which was presented in Chapter 26 of this text, the *U.S. Patents Quarterly Digest* would be a promising source of information.

Judicial Reporters

Judicial reporters are volumes for various jurisdictions that contain reported appellate decisions and opinions. As discussed in Chapter 1 of this text, there are reporters published by jurisdiction (for example, the *Federal Reporter* includes all cases from the federal courts of appeals, and the *Federal Supplement* contains cases selected for publication from the U.S. district courts and other federal courts), and there are also reporters that cover specific geographical regions (for example, the *Southern Reporter* covers state appellate cases for the states of Louisiana, Mississippi, Alabama, and Florida). In these reporters, cases are reported chronologically, according to the date of the decision.

In addition to general reporters, some subject reporters are also published. For example, a student who wishes to learn more about bankruptcy and reorganization (discussed in Chapter 12 of the text) would be able to find cases on that subject in the *American Bankruptcy Reports.*

Annotated Statutes

The *United States Code* (U.S.C.) contains the text of the U.S. Constitution and current federal legislation. There are two annotated versions of the U.S. Code: the *United States Code Annotated* (U.S.C.A.) and the *United States Code Service* (U.S.C.S.). The textual arrangement in these annotated volumes is identical to that found in the official U.S. Code. Unlike the U.S. Code itself, however, as explained in Chapter 1, these annotated volumes provide summaries of cases that have interpreted the statutory sections. If there are numerous case annotations, an outline of the annotations is also provided to make the research easier.

Looseleaf Services

Looseleaf services collect legal source material in certain subject areas and are kept current by frequent supplementation (often, once a week). They offer another practical means of access to the law in particular areas of interest. Two of the primary publishers of looseleaf services are the Bureau of National Affairs (BNA) and the Commerce Clearing House (CCH). The *BNA Corporate Practice Series* would be useful for a researcher who wants to study those topics introduced in Chapter 13 of this text (on business organizations). The *BNA International Trade Reporter* would supplement the materials presented in Chapter 27 (on international law). The *CCH Employment Practices Guide* would be useful in researching employment and labor relations law (introduced in Chapter 16). The *CCH Congressional Index* would assist research on administrative law (discussed in Chapter 5). This two-volume set indexes bills, committee reports, and hearings. It also includes sections on pending bills, bill status tables, members of Congress and their voting records, and so on.

■ Law Reviews

Law reviews are scholarly publications edited by law students or legal associations. Law reviews are published periodically (some once a year, others two or more times a year) and cover a broad range of legal topics. The contents of most law reviews include (1) commentaries about the law, usually written by law professors, judges, or practicing attorneys; (2) reviews of books recently written about the law; (3) comments by a student writer explaining the meaning of five or six recent cases; and (4) student notes on specific topics of law. Almost every accredited law school publishes a law review. A scholarly article or review can be found on virtually every topic of law in some issue of a law review, and depending on the topics covered in a particular review, it may assist the researcher in finding further information on any of the subjects presented in this book. The *Harvard Law Review* is one of the most prestigious law reviews. There are many more of equal quality.

■ Topical Law Journals

In addition to the general law reviews, many law schools also publish law journals on specific topics. The contents of the journals are similar to those of the law reviews—scholarly articles, book reviews,

case comments, and student notes—but the range of topics is limited to a specified area. The list of topical journals is quite extensive, and there is likely to be an individual journal on almost every topic covered in this text.

For instance, *Environmental Law* focuses on the impact of various laws on the environment; this journal would therefore assist the student in obtaining a more comprehensive understanding of Chapter 19 of this text (on environmental law). The *Antitrust Law Journal* would offer further detail on the materials presented in Chapters 20 and 21 (on antitrust). The *Journal of Products Liability* focuses on the materials presented in Chapter 11 (on product liability). A number of law journals focus specifically on international law. Students interested in researching topics in this area might consult the *American Journal of Comparative Law,* the *American Journal of International Law,* or a number of other topical journals on this subject published by law schools.

■ Weekly Newsletters/Bulletins

To keep abreast of recent developments in the judicial and executive branches of the government, one should consult the following weekly publications:

1. *United States Law Week*—This is a weekly looseleaf service published in two volumes. The first volume is designed specifically to provide coverage of the United States Supreme Court. The second volume covers topics of general law; the items presented concern legal developments that, although they are unrelated to the Supreme Court, are of national significance.

2. *United States Supreme Court Bulletin*—This is a weekly looseleaf set designed specifically to provide coverage of the United States Supreme Court. This set contains a copy of the Supreme Court opinions rendered during the current term. In addition, there are sections that provide subject access to everything on the court's docket and a copy of the docket. Other sections include rules of the Supreme Court and a tentative calendar for arguments before the Court.

3. *Weekly Compilation of Presidential Documents*—This weekly publication includes executive orders, proclamations, reorganization plans, speeches, and press conferences. All official presi-

dential documents, except executive agreements, are included. Everything found in this compilation is arranged in chronological order. A student wishing to learn more about administrative law (covered in Chapter 6 of this text) would find this publication useful.

■ Computerized Research Assistance

The days of the hunched-over law clerk searching through copious volumes of dusty tomes filled with ancient cases are not completely over, but, as could be expected, computers have streamlined legal research techniques. Today, there are a number of data bases—collections of information useful to anyone doing legal research—that can be accessed through several high-speed data-delivery systems. The two major legal research systems are LEXIS, owned by Mead Data Central, Inc., and WESTLAW, offered by West Publishing Company.

LEXIS and WESTLAW allow for access to the full text of cases, statutes, and regulations—both state and federal—with a minimum of physical effort and time delay. Both systems are kept extremely current, and often the latest cases can be retrieved through these systems before they are available in the printed reporters. The systems also include specialized libraries of materials on specific topics, such as criminal law, legal ethics, and other topics, which can provide assistance to the student researcher.

■ Bar Association Publications

Bar associations also issue legal materials of various kinds, including newletters and periodicals, that may be useful for the researcher. The *American Bar Association Journal* and the *National Bar Journal,* for example, both contain reports on association activities, articles on legal topics, and notices of recent developments in the law. Additionally, many of the specialized sections of the bar publish their own quarterly newsletters, such as *American Patent Law Association Quarterly Journal,* which provides the members of the section with an update of the most recent developments in this area of the law.

■ Form Books

If a business student had to draft a contract or some other document, or wanted to see the "typical language" found in a legal instrument, he or she would want to look at one of the many form books available. These books frequently offer instructions on how to fill in the sample forms included in the books. An example of a form book is *American Jurisprudence Legal Forms 2d,* a twenty-volume set that contains legal forms of every kind for a commercial transaction. The *American Jurisprudence Pleading and Practice Forms,* in contrast, provides forms that are essential to litigation.

■ List of Selected Research Sources

Administrative Law Bulletin
American Bankruptcy Law Journal
American Business Law Journal
American Civil Law Journal
American Journal of Comparative Law
American Journal of Criminal Law
American Journal of International Law
American Journal of Tax Policy
American Journal of Trial Advocacy
American Judicature Society Journal
American Jurisprudence Forms Proof of Facts
American Jurisprudence Legal Forms 2d
American Jurisprudence Pleading and Practice
    Forms
American Lawyer
American Patent Law Association Quarterly
    Journal
American Society of International Law
    Proceedings
Annals of Air and Space Law
Annual Review of Banking Law
Annual Survey of Bankruptcy Law
Antitrust Law Journal
Arbitration Law
Banking Law Journal
Bender's Uniform Commercial Code Service
BNA Antitrust and Trade Regulation Reporter
BNA Collective Bargaining and Negotiations
    and Contracts
BNA Corporate Practice Series
BNA International Trade Report
BNA Labor Relations Reporter
BNA Media Law Reporter

BNA Patent, Trademark and Copyright Reporter
BNA Securities Regulations and Law Reporter
BNA United States Law Week
Boston University International Law Journal
Business Law Journal
CCH Bankruptcy Law Reporter
CCH Congressional Index
CCH Consumer Products Safety and Health
    Guide
CCH Contract Cases
CCH Copyright Law Reporter
CCH Employment Practices Decisions
CCH Labor Law Reporter
CCH Products Liability Reporter
CCH Secured Transactions Guide
Chicago Legal Forum
Clearinghouse for Civil Rights Research
Code of Federal Regulations
Computer Law Journal
Congressional Information Service Index
Congressional Record
Criminal Law Bulletin
Decennial Digest
Environmental Law
Federal Register
Federal Reporter
Federal Rules Decisions
Federal Rules of Civil Procedure
Federal Supplement
Federal Trade Commission Reports
General Digest
George Washington Journal of International Law
    and Economics
Harvard Environmental Law Review
Harvard International Law Journal
Harvard Journal of Law and Public Policy
Index to Legal Periodicals
Insurance Law Journal
Intellectual Property Journal
International and Comparative Law Bulletin
International Journal of Medicine and Law
International Journal of Politics
International Journal of the Sociology of Law
International Law Reporter
International Review of Law and Economics
International Social Science Journal
International Trade Reporter
Journal of Contemporary Law
Journal of Corporate Taxation
Journal of Energy and Natural Resources Law

Journal of Law and Commerce
Journal of Law and Economics
Journal of Law and Politics
Journal of Law and Technology
Journal of Products Liability
Journal of Real Estate Taxation
Journal of the American Medical Association
Law and Contemporary Problems
Legal Times of Washington
Loyola Entertainment Law Journal
Maryland Journal of International Law and
    Trade
Media Law Reporter
Mediation Quarterly
Moore's Federal Practice
National Bar Journal
New Republic
North Atlantic Regional Business Law Review
Northwestern Journal of International Law and
    Business
Notre Dame Journal of Law, Ethics and Public
    Policy
Patent and Trademark Review
Performing Arts Review
Prentice Hall: Securities Regulation
Quarterly Journal of Economics
Real Estate Law Journal
Real Property Probate and Trust Journal
Restatement (Second) of Agency
Restatement (Second) of Contracts
Restatement (Second) of Torts
Restatement (Second) of Trusts
Restatement of Property
Review of Litigation
Rutgers Journal of Computers, Technology and
    the Law
Shepard's Acts and Cases by Popular Names
    Citations
Social Sciences and Humanities Index
Stanford Environmental Law Journal
Stanford Journal of International Law
Student Lawyer
Supreme Court Bulletin
Supreme Court Reporter
Texas International Law Journal
Trademark Law Handbook
U.S. Attorney General Opinions
U.S. Code Annotated
U.S. Code Congressional and Administrative
    News

U.S. Code Service
U.S. Patents Quarterly Digest
U.S. Statutes at Large
Uniform Commercial Code Series (Callaghan)
Virginia Journal of International Law
Wall Street Journal

West's Bankruptcy Reporter
Women's Law Journal
Yale Journal of International Law
Yale Journal of World Public Order
Yearbook of Law—Computers and Technology

Appendix O

Spanish Equivalents for Important Legal Terms in English

Abandoned property: bienes abandonados
Acceptance: aceptación; consentimiento; acuerdo
Acceptor: aceptante
Accession: toma de posesión; aumento; accesión
Accommodation indorser: avalista de favor
Accommodation party: firmante de favor
Accord: acuerdo; convenio; arregio
Accord and satisfaction: transacción ejecutada
Act of state doctrine: doctrina de acto de gobierno
Administrative law: derecho administrativo
Administrative process: procedimiento o metódo administrativo
Administrator: administrador (-a)
Adverse possession: posesión de hecho susceptible de proscripción adquisitiva
Affirmative action: acción afirmativa
Affirmative defense: defensa afirmativa
After-acquired property: bienes adquiridos con posterioridad a un hecho dado
Agency: mandato; agencia

Agent: mandatorio; agente; representante
Agreement: convenio; acuerdo; contrato
Alien corporation: empresa extranjera
Allonge: hojas adicionales de endosos
Answer: contestación de la demande; alegato
Anticipatory breach: anuncio previo de las partes de su imposibilidad de cumplir con el contrato
Appeal: apelación; recurso de apelación
Appellate jurisdiction: jurisdicción de apelaciones
Appraisal right: derecho de valuación
Arbitration: arbitraje
Arson: incendio intencional
Articles of partnership: contrato social
Artisian's lien: derecho de retención que ejerce al artesano
Assault: asalto; ataque; agresión
Assignment of rights: transmisión; transferencia; cesión
Assumption of risk: no resarcimiento por exposición voluntaria al peligro
Attachment: auto judicial que

autoriza el embargo; embargo

Bailee: depositario
Bailment: depósito; constitución en depósito
Bailor: depositante
Bankruptcy trustee: síndico de la quiebra
Battery: agresión; física
Bearer: portador; tenedor
Bearer instrument: documento al portador
Bequest or legacy: legado (de bienes muebles)
Bilateral contract: contrato bilateral
Bill of lading: conocimiento de embarque; carta de porte
Bill of Rights: declaración de derechos
Binder: póliza de seguro provisoria; recibo de pago a cuenta del precio
Blank indorsement: endoso en blanco
Blue sky laws: leyes reguladoras del comercio bursátil
Bond: título de crédito; garantía; caución
Breach of contract: incumplimiento de contrato
Brief: escrito; resumen; informe
Burglary: violación de domicilio

Business judgment rule: regla de juicio comercial
Business tort: agravio comercial

Case law: ley de casos; derecho casuístico
Cashier's check: cheque de caja
Causation in fact: causalidad en realidad
Cease-and-desist order: orden para cesar y desistir
Certificate of deposit: certificado de depósito
Certified check: cheque certificado
Charitable trust: fideicomiso para fines benéficos
Chattel: bien mueble
Check: cheque
Chose in action: derecho inmaterial; derecho de acción
Civil law: derecho civil
Close corporation: sociedad de un solo accionista o de un grupo restringido de accionistas
Closed shop: taller agremiado (emplea solamente a miembros de un gremio)
Closing argument: argumento al final
Codicil: codicilo
Collateral: garantía; bien objeto de la garantía real
Comity: cortesía; cortesía entre naciones
Commercial paper: instrumentos negociables; documentos a valores commerciales
Common law: derecho consuetudinario; derecho común; ley común
Common stock: acción ordinaria
Comparative negligence: negligencia comparada
Compensatory damages: daños y perjuicios reales o compensatorios
Concurrent conditions: condiciones concurrentes
Concurrent jurisdiction: competencia concurrente de varios tribunales para entender en una misma causa
Concurring opinion: opinión concurrente

Condition: condición
Condition precedent: condición suspensiva
Condition subsequent: condición resolutoria
Confiscation: confiscación
Confusion: confusión; fusión
Conglomerate merger: fusión de firmas que operan en distintos mercados
Consequential damages: daños y perjuicios indirectos
Consideration: consideración; motivo; contraprestación
Consolidation: consolidación
Constructive delivery: entrega simbólica
Constructive trust: fideicomiso creado por aplicación de la ley
Consumer-protection law: ley para proteger el consumidor
Contract: contrato
Contract under seal: contrato formal o sellado
Contributory negligence: negligencia de la parte actora
Conversion: usurpación; conversión de valores
Copyright: derecho de autor
Corporation: sociedad anónima; corporación; persona juridica
Co-sureties: cogarantes
Counterclaim: reconvención; contrademanda
Counteroffer: contraoferta
Course of dealing: curso de transacciones
Course of performance: curso de cumplimiento
Covenant: pacto; garantía; contrato
Covenant not to sue: pacto or contrato a no demandar
Covenant of quiet enjoyment: garantía del uso y goce pacífico del inmueble
Creditors' composition agreement: concordato preventivo
Crime: crimen; delito; contravención
Criminal law: derecho penal
Cross-examination: contrainterrogatorio
Cure: cura; cuidado; derecho de

remediar un vicio contractual
Customs receipts: recibos de derechos aduaneros

Damages: daños; indemnización por daños y perjuicios
Debtor: deudor
Debt securities: seguridades de deuda
Deceptive advertising: publicidad engañosa
Deed: escritura; título; acta translativa de domino
Defamation: difamación
Delegation of duties: delegación de obligaciones
Demand deposit: depósito a la vista
Depositions: declaración de un testigo fuera del tribunal
Devise: legado; deposición testamentaria (bienes inmuebles)
Directed verdict: veredicto según orden del juez y sin participación activa del jurado
Direct examination: interrogatorio directo; primer interrogatorio
Disaffirmance: repudiación; renuncia; anulación
Discharge: descargo; liberación; cumplimiento
Disclosed principal: mandante revelado
Discovery: descubrimiento; producción de la prueba
Dissenting opinion: opinión disidente
Dissolution: disolución; terminación
Diversity of citizenship: competencia de los tribunales federales para entender en causas cuyas partes intervinientes son cuidadanos de distintos estados
Divestiture: extinción premature de derechos reales
Dividend: dividendo
Docket: orden del día; lista de causas pendientes
Domestic corporation: sociedad local
Draft: orden de pago; letrade cambio

Drawee: girado; beneficiario
Drawer: librador
Duress: coacción; violencia

Easement: servidumbre
Embezzlement: desfalco; malversación
Eminent domain: poder de expropiación
Employment discrimination: discriminación en el empleo
Entrepreneur: empresario
Environmental law: ley ambiental
Equal dignity rule: regla de dignidad egual
Equity security: tipo de participación en una sociedad
Estate: propiedad; patrimonio; derecho
Estop: impedir; prevenir
Ethical issue: cuestión ética
Exclusive jurisdiction: competencia exclusiva
Exculpatory clause: cláusula eximente
Executed contract: contrato ejecutado
Execution: ejecución; cumplimiento
Executor: albacea
Executory contract: contrato aún no completamente consumado
Executory interest: derecho futuro
Express contract: contrato expreso
Expropriation: expropriación

Federal question: caso federal
Fee simple: pleno dominio; dominio absoluto
Fee simple absolute: dominio absoluto
Fee simple defeasible: dominio sujeta a una condición resolutoria
Felony: crimen; delito grave
Fictitious payee: beneficiario ficticio
Fiduciary: fiduciaro
Firm offer: oferta en firme
Fixture: inmueble por destino, incorporación a anexación
Floating lien: gravamen continuado

Foreign corporation: sociedad extranjera; U.S. sociedad constituída en otro estado
Forgery: falso; falsificación
Formal contract: contrato formal
Franchise: privilegio; franquicia; concesión
Franchisee: persona que recibe una concesión
Franchisor: persona que vende una concesión
Fraud: fraude; dolo; engaño
Future interest: bien futuro

Garnishment: embargo de derechos
General partner: socio comanditario
General warranty deed: escritura translativa de domino con garantía de título
Gift: donación
Gift *causa mortis:* donación por causa de muerte
Gift *inter vivos:* donación entre vivos
Good faith: buena fe
Good-faith purchaser: comprador de buena fe

Holder: tenedor por contraprestación
Holder in due course: tenedor legítimo
Holographic will: testamento ológrafico
Homestead exemption laws: leyes que exceptúan las casas de familia de ejecución por duedas generales
Horizontal merger: fusión horizontal

Identification: identificación
Implied-in-fact contract: contrato implícito en realidad
Implied warranty: guarantía implícita
Implied warranty of merchantability: garantía implícita de vendibilidad
Impossibility of performance: imposibilidad de cumplir un contrato

Imposter: imposter
Incidental beneficiary: beneficiario incidental; beneficiario secundario
Incidental damages: daños incidentales
Indictment: auto de acusación; acusación
Indorsee: endorsatario
Indorsement: endoso
Indorser: endosante
Informal contract: contrato no formal; contrato verbal
Information: acusación hecha por el ministerio público
Injunction: mandamiento; orden de no innovar
Innkeeper's lien: derecho de retención que ejerce el posadero
Installment contract: contrato de pago en cuotas
Insurable interest: interés asegurable
Intended beneficiary: beneficiario destinado
Intentional tort: agravio; cuasi-delito intenciónal
International law: derecho internaciónal
Interrogatories: preguntas escritas sometidas por una parte a la otra o a un testigo
Inter vivos trust: fideicomiso entre vivos
Intestacy laws: leyes de la condición de morir intestado
Intestate: intestado
Investment company: compañia de inversiones
Issue: emisión

Joint tenancy: derechos conjuntos en un bien inmueble
Joint tenancy: derechos conjuntos en un bien inmueble en favor del beneficiario sobreviviente
Judgment *n.o.v.*: juicio no obstante veredicto
Judgment rate of interest: interés de juicio
Judicial process: acto de procedimiento; proceso jurídico

Judicial review: revisión judicial
Jurisdiction: jurisdicción

Larceny: robo; hurto
Law: derecho; ley; jurisprudencia
Lease: contrato de locación; contrato de alquiler
Leasehold estate: bienes forales
Legal rate of interest: interés legal
Legatee: legatario
Letter of credit: carta de crédito
Levy: embargo; comiso
Libel: libelo; difamación escrita
Life estate: usufructo
Limited partner: comanditario
Limited partnership: sociedad en comandita
Liquidation: liquidación; realización
Lost property: objetos perdidos

Majority opinion: opinión de la mayoría
Maker: persona que realiza u ordena; librador
Mechanic's lien: gravamen de constructor
Mediation: mediación; intervención
Merger: fusión
Mirror image rule: fallo de reflejo
Misdemeanor: infracción; contravención
Mislaid property: bienes extraviados
Mitigation of damages: reducción de daños
Mortgage: hypoteca
Motion to dismiss: excepción parentoria
Mutual fund: fondo mutual

Negotiable instrument: instrumento negociable
Negotiation: negociación
Nominal damages: daños y perjuicios nominales
Novation: novación
Nuncupative will: testamento nuncupativo

Objective theory of contracts: teoria objetiva de contratos

Offer: oferta
Offeree: persona que recibe una oferta
Offeror: oferente
Order instrument: instrumento o documento a la orden
Original jurisdiction: jurisdicción de primera instancia
Output contract: contrato de producción

Parol evidence rule: regla relativa a la prueba oral
Partially disclosed principal: mandante revelado en parte
Partnership: sociedad colectiva; asociación; asociación de participación
Past consideration: causa o contraprestación anterior
Patent: patente; privilegio
Pattern or practice: muestra o práctica
Payee: beneficiario de un pago
Penalty: pena; penalidad
Per capita: por cabeza
Perfection: perfeción
Performance: cumplimiento; ejecución
Personal defenses: excepciones personales
Personal property: bienes muebles
Per stirpes: por estirpe
Plea bargaining: regateo por un alegato
Pleadings: alegatos
Pledge: prenda
Police powers: poderes de policia y de prevención del crimen
Policy: póliza
Positive law: derecho positivo; ley positiva
Possibility of reverter: posibilidad de reversión
Precedent: precedente
Preemptive right: derecho de prelación
Preferred stock: acciones preferidas
Premium: recompensa; prima
Presentment warranty: garantía de presentación
Price discrimination: discriminación en los precios

Principal: mandante; principal
Privity: nexo jurídico
Privity of contract: relación contractual
Probable cause: causa probable
Probate: verificación; verificación del testamento
Probate court: tribunal de sucesiones y tutelas
Proceeds: resultados; ingresos
Profit: beneficio; utilidad; lucro
Promise: promesa
Promisee: beneficiario de una promesa
Promisor: promtente
Promissory estoppel: impedimento promisorio
Promissory note: pagaré; nota de pago
Promoter: promotor; fundador
Proximate cause: causa inmediata o próxima
Proxy: apoderado; poder
Punitive, or exemplary, damages: daños y perjuicios punitivos o ejemplares

Qualified indorsement: endoso con reservas
Quasi contract: contrato tácito o implícito
Quitclaim deed: acto de transferencia de una propiedad por finiquito, pero sin ninguna garantía sobre la validez del título transferido

Ratification: ratificación
Real property: bienes inmuebles
Reasonable doubt: duda razonable
Rebuttal: refutación
Recognizance: promesa; compromiso; reconocimiento
Recording statutes: leyes estatales sobre registros oficiales
Reformation: rectificación; reforma; corrección
Rejoinder: dúplica; contrarréplica
Release: liberación; renuncia a un derecho
Remainder: substitución; reversión
Remedy: recurso; remedio; reparación
Replevin: acción reivindicatoria; reivindicación

Reply: réplica
Requirements contract: contrato de suministro
Rescission: rescisión
Respondeat superior: responsabilidad del mandante o del maestro
Restitution: restitución
Restrictive indorsement: endoso restrictivo
Resulting trust: fideicomiso implícito
Reversion: reversión; sustitución
Revocation: revocación; derogación
Right of contribution: derecho de contribución
Right of reimbursement: derecho de reembolso
Right of subrogation: derecho de subrogación
Right-to-work law: ley de libertad de trabajo
Robbery: robo
Rule 10b-5: Regla 10b-5

Sale: venta; contrato de compreventa
Sale on approval: venta a ensayo; venta sujeta a la aprobación del comprador
Sale or return: venta con derecho de devolución
Sales contract: contrato de compraventa; boleto de compraventa
Satisfaction: satisfacción; pago
Scienter: a sabiendas
S corporation: S corporación
Secured party: acreedor garantizado
Secured transaction: transacción garantizada
Securities: volares; titulos; seguridades
Security agreement: convenio de seguridad
Security interest: interés en un bien dado en garantía que permite a quien lo detenta venderlo en caso de incumplimiento
Service mark: marca de identificación de servicios
Shareholder's derivative suit: acción judicial entablada por un

accionista en nombre de la sociedad
Signature: firma; rúbrica
Slander: difamación oral; calumnia
Sovereign immunity: immunidad soberana
Special indorsement: endoso especial; endoso a la orden de una person en particular
Specific performance: ejecución precisa, según los términos del contrato
Spendthrift trust: fideicomiso para pródigos
Stale check: cheque vencido
Stare decisis: acatar las decisiones, observar los precedentes
Statutory law: derecho estatutario; derecho legislado; derecho escrito
Stock: acciones
Stock warrant: certificado para la compra de acciones
Stop-payment order: orden de suspensión del pago de un cheque dada por el librador del mismo
Strict liability: responsabilidad unconditional
Summary judgment: fallo sumario

Tangible property: bienes corpóreos
Tenancy at will: inguilino por tiempo indeterminado (según la voluntad del propietario)
Tenancy by sufferance: posesión por tolerancia
Tenancy by the entirety: locación conyugal conjunta
Tenancy for years: inguilino por un término fijo
Tenancy in common: specie de copropiedad indivisa
Tender: oferta de pago; oferta de ejecución
Testamentary trust: fideicomiso testamentario
Testator: testador (-a)
Third party beneficiary contract: contrato para el beneficio del tercero-beneficiario
Tort: agravio; cuasi-delito
Totten trust: fideicomiso creado por un depósito bancario
Trade acceptance: letra de cambio aceptada

Trade name: nombre comercial; razón social
Trademark: marca registrada
Traveler's check: cheque del viajero
Trespass to land: ingreso no authorizado a las tierras de otro
Trespass to personal property: violación de los derechos posesorios de un tercero con respecto a bienes muebles
Trust: fideicomiso; trust

Ultra vires: ultra vires; fuera de la facultad (de una sociedad anónima)
Unanimous opinion: opinión unámine
Unconscionable contract or clause: contrato leonino; cláusula leonino
Underwriter: subscriptor; asegurador
Unenforceable contract: contrato que no se puede hacer cumplir
Unilateral contract: contrato unilateral
Union shop: taller agremiado; empresa en la que todos los empleados son miembros del gremio o sindicato
Universal defenses: defensas legitimas o legales
Usage of trade: uso comercial
Usury: usura

Valid contract: contrato válido
Venue: lugar; sede del proceso
Vertical merger: fusión vertical de empresas
Void contract: contrato nulo; contrato inválido, sin fuerza legal
Voidable contract: contrato anulable
Voir dire: examen preliminar de un testigo a jurado por el tribunal para determinar su competencia
Voting trust: fideicomiso para ejercer el derecho de voto

Waiver: renuncia; abandono
Warranty of habitability: garantía de habitabilidad
Watered stock: acciones diluídos; capital inflado

White-collar crime: crimen administrativo

Writ of attachment: mandamiento de ejecución; mandamiento de embargo

Writ of *certiorari*: auto de avocación; auto de certiorari

Writ of execution: auto ejecutivo; mandamiento de ejecutión

Writ of mandamus: auto de mandamus; mandamiento; orden judicial

Glossary

A

Abandoned property Property with which the owner has voluntarily parted, with no intention of recovering it.

Abandonment In landlord-tenant law, a tenant's departure from leased premises completely, with no intention of returning before the end of the lease term.

Acceleration clause A clause in an installment contract that provides for all future payments to become due immediately upon the failure to tender timely payments or upon the occurrence of a specified event.

Acceptance (1) In contract law, the offeree's notification to the offeror that the offeree agrees to be bound by the terms of the offeror's proposal. Although historically the terms of acceptance had to be the mirror image of the terms of the offer, the UCC provides that even modified terms of the offer in a definite expression of acceptance constitute a contract. (2) In commercial paper law, the drawee's signed agreement to pay a draft when presented.

Acceptor The person (the drawee) who accepts a draft and who engages to be primarily responsible for its payment.

Accession The changing (for example, through manufacturing) of one good into a new good (for example, flour into bread); the right, upon payment for the original materials, to keep an article manufactured out of goods that were innocently converted.

Accommodation party A person who signs an instrument for the purpose of lending his or her credit to another party on the instrument.

Accord and satisfaction An agreement and payment (or other performance) between two parties, one of whom has a right of action against the other. After the agreement has been made and payment or other performance has been tendered, the "accord and satisfaction" is complete.

Accredited investors In the context of securities offerings, "sophisticated" investors, such as banks, insurance companies, investment companies, the issuer's executive officers and directors, and persons whose income or net worth exceeds certain limits.

Act of state doctrine A doctrine that provides that the judicial branch of one country will not examine the validity of public acts committed by a recognized foreign government within its own territory.

Actual malice Real and demonstrable evil intent. In a defamation suit, a statement made about a public figure normally must be made with actual malice (with either knowledge of its falsity or a reckless disregard of the truth) for liability to be incurred.

Actus reus A guilty (prohibited) act. The commission of a prohibited act is one of the two essential elements required for criminal liability, the other element being the *intent* to commit a crime.

Adequate protection doctrine In bankruptcy law, a doctrine that protects secured creditors from losing their security as a result of an automatic stay on legal proceedings by creditors against the debtor once the debtor petitions for bankruptcy relief. In certain circumstances, the bankruptcy court may provide adequate protection by requiring the debtor or trustee to pay the creditor or provide additional guaranties to protect the creditor against the losses suffered by the creditor as a result of the stay.

Adhesion contract A "standard form" contract, such as that between a large retailer and a consumer, in which the stronger party dictates the terms.

Adjudication The act of rendering a judicial decision. In administrative process, the proceeding in which an administrative law judge hears and decides on issues that arise when an administrative agency charges a person or a firm with violating a law or regulation enforced by the agency.

Administrative law A body of law created by administrative agencies—such as the Securities and Exchange Commission and the Federal Trade Commission—in the form of rules, regulations, orders, and decisions in order to carry out their duties and responsibilities. This law can initially be enforced by these agencies outside the judicial process.

Administrative law judge (ALJ) One who presides over an administrative agency hearing and who has the power to administer oaths, take testimony, rule on questions of evidence, and make determinations of fact.

Administrative process The procedure used by administrative agencies in the administration of law.

Administrator One who is appointed by a court to handle the probate (disposition) of a person's estate if that person dies intestate (without a will).

Adverse possession The acquisition of title to real property by occupying it openly, without the consent of the owner, for a period of time specified by state statutes. The occupation must be actual, open, notorious, exclusive, and in opposition to all others, including the owner.

Affidavit A written or printed voluntary statement of facts, confirmed by the oath or affirmation of the party making it and made before a person having the authority to administer the oath or affirmation.

Affirmative action Job-hiring policies that give special consideration or compensatory treatment to minority groups in an effort to overcome present effects of past discrimination.

Affirmative advertising Providing specific information in an advertisement so as to prevent consumers from being misled. May be required of a firm by the Federal Trade Commission if the FTC, after investigation, decides that the firm has engaged in deceptive advertising.

Affirmative defense A response to a plaintiff's claim that does not deny the plaintiff's facts but attacks the plaintiff's legal right to bring an action. An example is the running of the statute of limitations.

After-acquired property Property of the debtor that is acquired after a secured creditor's interest in the debtor's property has been created.

Agency A relationship between two persons in which, by agreement or otherwise, one is bound by the words and acts of the other. The former is a *principal;* the latter is an *agent.*

Agent A person authorized by another to act for or in place of him or her.

Agreement A meeting of two or more minds. Often used as a synonym for contract.

Alien corporation A designation in the United States for a corporation formed in another country but doing business in the United States.

Allonge A piece of paper firmly attached to a negotiable instrument, upon which transferees can make indorsements if there is no room left on the instrument itself.

Alterations In the context of leaseholds, improvements or changes made that materially affect the condition of the property. Thus, for example, erecting additional structures probably would (and painting interior walls would not) be considered making alterations.

Alternative dispute resolution (ADR) The resolution of disputes in ways other than those involved in the traditional judicial process. Mediation and arbitration are forms of ADR.

Amend To change and improve through a formal procedure.

Analogy In logical reasoning, an assumption that if two things are similar in some respects, they will be similar in other respects also. Often used in legal reasoning to infer the appropriate application of legal principles in a case being decided by referring to previous cases involving different facts but considered to come within the policy underlying the rule.

Annuity An insurance policy that pays the insured fixed, periodic payments for life or for a term of years, as stipulated in the policy, after the insured reaches a specified age.

Answer Procedurally, a defendant's response to the complaint.

Antecedent claim A preexisting claim. In negotiable instruments law, taking an instrument in satisfaction of an antecedent claim is taking the instrument for value—that is, for valid consideration.

Anticipatory breach An assertion or action by a party indicating that he or she will not perform an obligation that the party is contractually obligated to perform at a future time.

Antitrust law The body of federal and state laws and statutes protecting trade and commerce from unlawful restraints, price discrimination, price fixing, and monopolies. The principal federal antitrust statutes are the Sherman Act (1890), the Clayton Act (1914), and the Federal Trade Commission Act (1914).

Apparent authority Authority that is only apparent, not real. In agency law, a person may be deemed to have had the power to act as an agent for another party if the other party's manifestations to a third party led the third party to believe that an agency existed when, in fact, it did not.

Appellant The party who takes an appeal from one court to another; sometimes referred to as the petitioner.

Appellee The party against whom an appeal is taken—that is, the party who opposes setting aside or reversing the judgment; sometimes referred to as the respondent.

Appraisal right A dissenting shareholder's right, if he or she objects to an extraordinary transaction of the corporation (such as a merger or consolidation), to have his or her shares appraised and to be paid the fair market value of his or her shares by the corporation.

Appropriate bargaining unit A designation based on job duties, skill levels, etc., of the proper entity that should be covered by a collective bargaining agreement.

Appropriation In tort law, the act of making a thing one's own or exercising or making use of an object to subserve one's own interest. When the act is wrongful, a tort is committed.

Arbitration The settling of a dispute by submitting it to a disinterested third party (other than a court), who renders a legally binding decision.

Arbitration clause A clause in a contract that provides that, in case of a dispute, the parties will determine their rights by arbitration rather than through the judicial system.

Arbitrator A disinterested party who, by prior agreement of the parties submitting their dispute to arbitration, has the power to resolve the dispute and (generally) bind the parties.

Arson The malicious burning of another's dwelling. Some statutes have expanded this to include any real property regardless of ownership and the destruction of property by other means—for example, by explosion.

Articles of partnership A written agreement that sets forth each partner's rights in, and obligations to, the partnership.

Artisan's lien A possessory lien given to a person who has made improvements and added value to another person's personal property as security for payment for services performed.

Assault Any word or action intended to make another person fearful of immediate physical harm; a reasonably believable threat.

Assignee The person to whom contract rights are assigned.

Assignment of rights The act of transferring to another all or part of one's rights arising under a contract.

Assignor The person who assigns contract rights.

Assumption of risk A doctrine whereby a plaintiff may not recover for injuries or damages suffered from risks he or she knows of and assents to. A defense against negligence that can be used when the plaintiff has knowledge of and appreciates a danger and voluntarily exposes himself or herself to the danger.

Attachment (1) In a secured transaction, the process by which a security interest in the property of another becomes enforceable. (2) The legal process of seizing another's property in accordance with a writ or judicial order for the purpose of securing satisfaction of a judgment yet to be rendered.

Attempt to monopolize The deliberate attempts by a company possessing substantial market power both to raise barriers to entry into its product market and drive existing competitors out of business so that it may charge monopoly prices for its product.

Attractive nuisance doctrine A common law doctrine under which a landowner or landlord may be held liable for injuries incurred by children who are lured onto the property by something dangerous and enticing thereon.

Authorization card A card signed by an employee that gives a union permission to act on his or her behalf in negotiations with management once a majority of the employees has signed such cards.

Automated teller machine (ATM) An electronic customer-bank communication terminal that, when activated by an access card and a personal identification number, can conduct routine banking transactions.

Automatic stay A suspension of all judicial proceedings upon the occurrence of an independent event. Under the Bankruptcy Code, the moment a petition to commence bankruptcy proceedings is filed, all litigation by creditors against a debtor and the debtor's property is suspended.

Award As a noun, the decision rendered by an arbitrator or other extrajudicial decider of a controversy. As a verb, to give or assign by sentence, judicial determination, or otherwise after a careful weighing of evidence, as when a jury awards damages.

B

Bailee One to whom goods are entrusted by a bailor.

Bailment An agreement in which goods or personal property of one person (a bailor) are entrusted to another (a bailee), who is obligated to return the bailed property to the bailor or dispose of it as directed.

Bailor One who entrusts goods to a bailee.

Bait-and-switch advertising Advertising a product at a very attractive price (the "bait") and then informing the consumer, once he or she is in the store, that the advertised product is either not available or is of poor quality; the customer is then urged to purchase ("switched" to) a more expensive item.

Bank draft A check, draft, or other order for payment of money drawn by a bank on itself (such as a cashier's check) or on another bank.

Barriers to entry Restrictions on the ability to enter into business in a given industry, sometimes resulting from the fact that the market for that industry is controlled by just a few firms with which an entrant into the industry could not compete effectively.

Battery The unprivileged, intentional touching of another.

Bearer A person in the possession of an instrument payable to bearer or indorsed in blank.

Bearer instrument In the law of commercial paper, any instrument that runs to the bearer, including instruments payable to the bearer or to "cash."

Bequest A gift by will of personal property (from the verb *to bequeath*).

Beyond a reasonable doubt The standard used to determine the guilt or innocence of a person criminally charged. To be guilty of a crime, one must be proved guilty "beyond and to the exclusion of every reasonable doubt." A reasonable doubt is one that would cause a prudent person to hesitate before acting in matters important to him or her.

Bilateral contract A contract that includes the exchange of a promise for a promise.

Bill of lading A document that serves both as evidence of the receipt of goods for shipment and as documentary evidence of title to the goods.

Binder A written, temporary insurance policy.

Blank indorsement An indorsement made by the mere writing of the indorser's name on the back of an instrument. Such indorsement causes an instrument, otherwise payable to order, to become payable to bearer and negotiated only by delivery.

Blue sky laws State laws that regulate the offer and sale of securities.

Boards of adjustment Public agencies that consider appeals by individuals and other entities regarding zoning matters.

Bona fide occupational qualification Under Title VII of the Civil Rights Act of 1964, identifiable characteristics reasonably necessary to the normal operation of a particular business. These characteristics can include gender, national origin, and religion, but not race.

Bond A certificate that evidences a corporate debt. It is a security that involves no ownership interest in the issuing corporation.

Breach of contract Failure, without legal excuse, of a promisor to perform the obligations of a contract.

Bribery The offering, giving, receiving, or soliciting of anything of value with the aim of influencing an official action or an official's discharge of a legal or public duty—or, in the case of commercial bribery, a business decision.

Brief A written summary or statement prepared by one side in a lawsuit to explain its case to the judge; a typical brief has a facts summary, a law summary, and an argument about how the law applies to the facts.

Bulk zoning Zoning regulations that restrict the amount of structural coverage on a particular parcel of land.

Burglary The unlawful entry into a building with the intent to commit a felony. (Some state statutes expand this to include the intent to commit any crime.)

Business ethics Ethics in a business context; a consensus of what constitutes right or wrong behavior in the world of business and the application of moral principles to situations that arise in a business setting.

Business judgment rule A rule that immunizes corporate management from liability for actions that are undertaken in good faith, when the actions are within both the power of the corporation and the authority of management to make.

Business necessity defense A showing that an employment practice that discriminates against members of a protected class is related to job performance.

Business tort A tort occurring within the business context; typical business torts are wrongful interference with the business or contractual relationships of others and unfair competition.

Buy-sell agreement A buy-out agreement. In the context of partnerships, an express agreement made at the time of partnership formation for one or more of the partners to buy out the other or others should the situation

warrant—and thus provide for the smooth dissolution of the partnership.

C

Case law Rules of law announced in court decisions. Case law includes the aggregate of reported cases that interpret judicial precedents, statutes, regulations, and constitutional provisions.

Cash surrender value The amount that the insurer has agreed to pay to the insured if a life insurance policy is canceled before the insured's death.

Cashier's check A draft drawn by a bank on itself.

Causation in fact An act or omission without which an event would not have occurred.

Cease-and-desist order An administrative or judicial order prohibiting a person or business firm from conducting activities that an agency or court has deemed illegal.

Certificate of deposit (CD) An instrument evidencing a promissory acknowledgment by a bank of a receipt of money with an engagement to repay it.

Certificate of limited partnership A certificate that is required for the establishment of a limited partnership. The certificate must be filed with the designated state official (usually the secretary of state).

Certification mark A mark used by one or more persons, other than the owner, to certify the region, materials, mode of manufacture, quality, or accuracy of the owner's goods or services. When used by members of a cooperative, association, or other organization, such a mark is referred to as a *collective mark*. Examples of certification marks include the ''Good Housekeeping Seal of Approval'' and ''UL Tested.''

Certified check A check drawn by an individual on his or her own account but bearing a guaranty (acceptance) by a bank that the bank will pay the check regardless of whether the drawer's account contains adequate funds at the time the check is presented.

Chain-style business franchise A franchise that operates under a franchisor's trade name and is identified as a member of a select group of dealers that engages in the franchisor's business. The franchisee is generally required to follow standardized or prescribed methods of operations. Examples of this type of franchise are McDonald's and most other fast-food chains.

Chancellor An advisor to the king at the time of the early King's Courts of England. Individuals petitioned the king for relief when they could not obtain an adequate remedy in a court of law, and these petitions were decided by the chancellor.

Charging order In partnership law, an order granted by a court to a judgment creditor that entitles the creditor to attach profits or assets of a partner upon dissolution of the partnership.

Charitable trust A trust in which the property held by a trustee must be used for a charitable purpose, such as the advancement of health, education, or religion.

Chattel A tangible piece of personal property or an intangible right therein.

Check A draft drawn by a drawer ordering the drawee bank or financial institution to pay a certain amount of money to the holder on demand.

Choice-of-language clause A clause in a contract designating the official language by which the contract will be interpreted in the event of a future disagreement over the contract's terms.

Choice-of-law clause A clause in a contract designating the law that will govern the contract. For example, two contracting parties from different countries may choose the law of a third country to govern their agreement.

Citation A citation indicates where a particular constitutional provision, statute, reported case, or article may be found; also an order for a defendant to appear in court or indicating that a person has violated a legal rule.

Civil law The branch of law dealing with the definition and enforcement of all private or public rights, as opposed to criminal matters.

Civil law system A system of law derived from that of the Roman Empire and based on a code rather than case law; the predominant system of law in the nations of continental Europe and the nations that were once their colonies. In the United States, Louisiana is the only state that has a civil law system.

Close corporation A corporation whose shareholders are limited to a small group of persons, often including only family members. The rights of shareholders of a close corporation usually are restricted regarding the transfer of shares to others.

Closed shop A firm that requires union membership by its workers as a condition of employment. The closed shop was made illegal by the Taft-Hartley Act of 1947.

Closing The final step in the sale of real estate—also called settlement or closing escrow. The escrow agent coordinates the closing with the recording of deeds, the obtaining of title insurance, and other concurrent closing activities. Several costs must be paid, in cash, at the time of closing, and they can range from several hundred to several thousand dollars, depending on the amount of the mortgage loan and other conditions of sale.

Closing argument An argument made after the plaintiff and defendant have rested their cases. Closing arguments are made prior to the jury charges.

Codicil A written supplement or modification to a will. Codicils must be executed with the same formalities as a will.

Collateral In a broad sense, any property used as security for a loan. Under the UCC, property of a debtor in which a creditor has an interest or a right.

Collateral promise A secondary promise that is ancillary to a principal transaction or primary contractual relationship, such as a promise made by one person to pay the debts or discharge the duties of another if the latter fails to perform. A collateral promise normally must be in writing to be enforceable.

Collecting bank Any bank handling an item for collection, except the payor bank.

Collective bargaining The process by which labor and management negotiate the terms and conditions of employment including such things as hours, workplace conditions, etc.

Collective mark A mark used by members of a cooperative, association, or other organization to certify the region, materials, mode of manufacture, quality, or accuracy of the specific goods or services. Examples of collective marks include the labor union marks found on tags of certain products and the credits of movies, which indicate the various associations and organizations that participated in the making of the movies.

Comity A deference by which one nation gives effect to the laws and judicial decrees of another nation. This recognition is based primarily upon respect.

Comment period A period of time following an administrative agency's publication of a notice of a proposed rule during which private parties may comment in writing on the agency proposal in an effort to influence agency policy. The agency takes any comments received into consideration when drafting the final version of the regulation.

Commercial impracticability A doctrine under which a seller may be excused from performing a contract when (1) a contingency occurs, (2) the contingency's occurrence makes performance impracticable, and (3) the nonoccurrence of the contingency was a basic assumption on which the contract was made. Despite the fact that UCC 2-615 expressly frees only sellers under this doctrine, courts have not distinguished between buyers and sellers in applying it.

Commercial paper Under UCC Article 3, negotiable instruments (signed writings that contain an unconditional promise or order to pay an exact sum of money, either when demanded or at an exact future time), including drafts, promissory notes, certificates of deposit, and checks.

Common areas In landlord-tenant law, the portion of the premises over which the landlord retains control and maintenance responsibilities. Common areas may include stairs, lobbies, garages, hallways, and other areas in common use.

Common law That body of law developed from custom or judicial decisions in English and U.S. courts, not attributable to a legislature.

Common situs picketing The illegal picketing of an entire construction site by workers who are involved in a labor dispute with a particular subcontractor.

Common stock Shares of ownership in a corporation that are lowest in priority with respect to payment of dividends and distribution of the corporation's assets upon dissolution.

Community property A form of concurrent ownership of property in which each spouse owns an undivided one-half interest in property. This type of ownership applies to most property acquired by the husband or wife during the course of marriage. It generally does not apply to property acquired prior to the marriage or to property acquired by gift or inheritance during the marriage. After a divorce, community property is divided equally in some states and according to the discretion of the court in other states.

Comparable worth A doctrine that aims to correct for past employment discrimination against women by advocating comparable pay for comparable work. The concept of comparable worth involves equal pay for different kinds of jobs that require the same degree of education, training, or effort.

Comparative negligence A theory in tort law under which the liability for injuries resulting from negligent acts is shared by all persons who were guilty of negligence (including the injured party), on the basis of each person's proportionate carelessness.

Compensatory damages A money award equivalent to the actual value of injuries or damages sustained by the aggrieved party.

Complaint The pleading made by a plaintiff or a charge made by the state alleging wrongdoing on the part of the defendant.

Computer crime Any wrongful act that is directed against computers and computer parts, or wrongful use or abuse of computers or software.

Concentrated industry An industry in which a large percentage of market sales is controlled by either a single firm or a small number of firms.

Concurrent conditions Conditions that must occur or be performed at the same time; they are mutually dependent. No obligations arise until these conditions are simultaneously performed.

Concurrent jurisdiction Jurisdiction that exists when two different courts have the power to hear a case. For example, some cases can be heard in a federal or state court.

Concurrent ownership Joint ownership.

Condition A qualification, provision, or clause in a contractual agreement, the occurrence of which creates, suspends, or terminates the obligations of the contracting parties.

Condition precedent In a contractual agreement, a condition that must be met before the other party's obligations arise.

Condition subsequent A condition in a contract that, if not met, discharges an existing obligation of the other party.

Confession of judgment A judgment entered against a debtor by a creditor, with the debtor's permission and for an agreed sum, without the use of legal proceedings.

Confiscation A government's taking of privately owned business or personal property without a proper public purpose or an award of just compensation.

Conforming goods Goods that conform to contract specifications.

Confusion The mixing together of goods belonging to two or more owners so that the independent goods cannot be identified.

Conglomerate merger A merger between firms that do not compete with each other because they are in different markets (as opposed to horizontal and vertical mergers).

Consent Voluntary agreement to a proposition or an act of another. A concurrence of wills.

Consequential damages Special damages that compensate for a loss that is not direct or immediate (for example, lost profits). The special damages must have been reasonably foreseeable at the time the breach or injury occurred in order for the plaintiff to collect them.

Consideration That which motivates the exchange of promises or performance in a contractual agreement. The consideration, which must be present to make the contract legally binding, must result in a detriment to the promisee (something of legal value, legally sufficient, and bargained for) or a benefit to the promisor.

Consignment A transaction in which an owner of goods (the consignor) delivers the goods to another (the consignee) for the consignee to sell. The consignee pays the consignor for the goods when the consignee sells the goods.

Consolidation A contractual and statutory process whereby two or more corporations join to become a completely new corporation. The original corporations cease to exist, and the new corporation acquires all their assets and liabilities.

Constructive delivery An act equivalent to the actual, physical delivery of property that cannot be physically delivered because of difficulty or impossibility; to illustrate, the transfer of a key to a safe constructively delivers the contents of the safe.

Constructive eviction Depriving a person of the possession of rental property that he or she leases by rendering the premises unfit or unsuitable for occupancy.

Constructive trust A trust created by operation of law against one who wrongfully has obtained or holds a legal right to property that the person should not, in equity and good conscience, hold and enjoy.

Consumer-debtors Debtors whose debts are primarily consumer debts—that is, debts for purchases that are primarily for household or personal use.

Contingency fees Attorneys' fees that are based on a percentage of the final awards received by their clients as a result of litigation.

Contract A set of promises constituting an agreement between parties, giving each a legal duty to the other and also the right to seek a remedy for the breach of the promises/duties owed to each. The elements of an enforceable contract are competent parties, a proper or legal purpose, consideration (an exchange of promises/duties), and mutuality of agreement and of obligation.

Contract implied in law A contract imposed upon parties by law, in the absence of justice, to prevent unjust enrichment even though the parties never intended to voluntarily enter into a contract; sometimes referred to as a quasi contract.

Contract under seal A formal agreement in which the seal is a substitute for consideration. A court will not invalidate a contract under seal for lack of consideration.

Contractual capacity The threshold mental capacity required by the law for a party who enters into a contract to be bound by that contract.

Contributory negligence A theory in tort law under which a complaining party's own negligence contributed to or caused his or her injuries. Contributory negligence is an absolute bar to recovery in a minority of jurisdictions.

Convenant of the right to convey A grantor's assurance that he or she has sufficient capacity and title to convey the estate that he or she undertakes to convey by deed.

Conversion The wrongful taking or retaining possession of personal property that belongs to another.

Cooperative An association that is organized to provide an economic service to its members (or shareholders). An incorporated cooperative is a nonprofit corporation. It will make distributions of dividends, or profits, to its owners on the basis of their transactions with the cooperative rather than on the basis of the amount of capital they contributed. Examples of cooperatives are consumer purchasing cooperatives, credit cooperatives, and farmers' cooperatives.

Copyright The exclusive right of "authors" to publish, print, or sell an intellectual production for a statutory period of time. A copyright has the same monopolistic nature as a patent or trademark, but it differs in that it applies exclusively to works of art, literature, and other works of authorship (including computer programs).

Corporation A legal entity created under the authority of the laws of a state or the federal government. The entity is distinct from its shareholders/owners.

Correspondent bank A bank in which another bank has an account (and vice versa) for the purpose of facilitating fund transfers.

Cost-benefit analysis A way to reach decisions in which the costs of a given action are compared with the benefits of the action.

Counteradvertising New advertising that is undertaken pursuant to a Federal Trade Commission order for the purpose of correcting earlier false claims that were made about a product.

Counterclaim A claim made by a defendant in a civil lawsuit that in effect sues the plaintiff; it can be based on entirely different grounds than those given in the plaintiff's complaint.

Counteroffer An offeree's response to an offer in which the offeree rejects the original offer and at the same time makes a new offer.

Course of dealing A sequence of previous conduct between the parties to a particular transaction that establishes a common basis for their understanding.

Course of performance The conduct that occurs under the terms of a particular agreement; such conduct indicates what the parties to an agreement intended it to mean.

Court of equity A court that decides controversies and administers justice according to the rules, principles, and precedents of equity.

Court of law A court in which the only remedies that could be granted were things of value, such as money damages. In the early English King's Court, courts of law were distinct from courts of equity.

Covenant against encumbrances A grantor's assurance that on land conveyed there are no encumbrances—that is, that no third parties have rights to, or interests in, the land that would diminish its value to the grantee.

Covenant not to sue An agreement to substitute a contractual obligation for some other type of action.

Covenant of quiet enjoyment A promise by the grantor (or landlord) that the grantee (or tenant) will not be evicted or disturbed by the grantor or a person having a lien or superior title.

Covenant of seisin An assurance to the purchaser that the grantor has the very estate in the quantity and quality that the grantor purports to convey.

Covenant running with the land An executory promise made between a grantor and a grantee to which they and subsequent owners of the land are bound.

Cover Under the UCC, a remedy of the buyer that allows the buyer, on the seller's breach, to purchase the goods from another seller and substitute them for the goods due under the contract. If the cost of cover exceeds the cost of the contract goods, the breaching seller will be liable to the buyer for the difference.

Crashworthiness doctrine A doctrine that imposes liability for defects in the design or construction of motor vehicles that increase the extent of injuries to passengers if an accident occurs. The doctrine holds even when the defects do not actually cause the accident.

Creditor beneficiary A creditor who has rights in a contract made by the debtor and a third person, in which the terms of the contract obligate the third person to pay the debt owed to the creditor. The creditor beneficiary can enforce the debt against either party.

Creditors' composition agreement An agreement formed between a debtor and his or her creditors in which the creditors agree to accept a lesser sum than that owed by the debtor in full satisfaction of the debt.

Crime A broad term for violations of law that are punishable by the state and are codified by legislatures. The objective of criminal law is to protect the public.

Criminal law Law that governs and defines those actions that are crimes and that subject the convicted offender to punishment imposed by the government.

Cumulative voting A method of shareholder voting designed to allow minority shareholders to be represented on the board of directors. With cumulative voting, the number of members of the board to be elected is multiplied by the total number of voting shares held. The result equals the number of votes a shareholder has, and this total can be cast for one or more nominees for director.

Cumulative zoning A zoning classification scheme that permits higher uses such as single-family residences to be built in the same zone as lower uses such as factories.

Cure The right of a party who tenders nonconforming performance to correct his or her performance within the contract period [UCC 3-508].

D

Damages Money sought as a remedy for a breach of contract or for a tortious act.

Debtor A person who owes a sum of money or other obligations to another.

Debtor in possession In Chapter 11 bankruptcy proceedings, a debtor who is allowed, for the benefit of all concerned, to continue in possession of the estate in bankruptcy (the business) and to continue business operations.

Deed A document by which title to property (usually real property) is passed.

Defamation Anything published or publicly spoken that causes injury to another's good name, reputation, or character.

Default judgment A judgment entered by a clerk or court against a party who has failed to appear in court to answer or defend against a claim that has been brought against him or her by another party.

Defendant One against whom a lawsuit is brought; the accused person in a criminal proceeding.

Defense That which a defendant offers and alleges in an action or suit as a reason why the plaintiff should not recover or establish what he or she seeks.

Deficiency judgment A judgment against a debtor for the amount of a debt remaining unpaid after collateral has been repossessed and sold or after foreclosure proceedings.

Delegation of duties The act of transferring to another all or part of one's duties arising under a contract.

Delivery order A written order to deliver goods directed to a warehouser, carrier, or other person who, in the ordinary course of business, issues warehouse receipts or bills of lading [UCC 7-102(1)(d)].

Demand deposit Funds (accepted by a bank) subject to immediate withdrawal, in contrast to a time deposit, which requires that a depositor wait a specific time before withdrawing or pay a penalty for early withdrawal.

Demurrer See Motion to dismiss.

Depositary bank The first bank to which an item is transferred for collection, even though it may also be the payor bank.

Deposition A generic term that refers to any evidence verified by oath. As a legal term, it is often limited to the testimony of a witness taken under oath before a trial, with the opportunity of cross-examination.

Deregulation The removal of regulatory restraints; the opposite of regulation.

Devise To make a gift of real property by will.

Disaffirmance The repudiation of an obligation.

Discharge The termination of one's obligation. In contract law, discharge occurs when the parties have fully performed their contractual obligations or when events, conduct of the parties, or operation of the law releases the parties from further performance.

Discharge in bankruptcy The release of a debtor from all debts that are provable, except those specifically excepted from discharge by statute.

Disclosed principal A principal whose identity and existence as a principal is known by a third person at the time a transaction is conducted by an agent.

Discovery A method by which opposing parties may obtain information from each other to prepare for trial. Generally governed by rules of procedure, but may be controlled by the court.

Disparagement of property Economically injurious falsehoods made about another's product or property. A general term for torts that are more specifically referred to as slander of quality or slander of title.

Disparate-impact discrimination In an employment context, discrimination that results from certain employer practices or procedures that, although not discriminatory on their face, have a discriminatory effect. For example, a requirement that all employees have high school diplomas is not necessarily discriminatory, but it may have the *effect* of discriminating against minority groups.

Disparate-treatment discrimination In an employment context, intentional discrimination against individuals on the basis of color, gender, national origin, race, or religion.

Dissolution The formal disbanding of a partnership or a corporation. It can take place by (1) agreement of the parties or the shareholders and board of directors, (2) the death of a partner, (3) the expiration of a time period stated in a partnership agreement or a certificate of incorporation, or (4) court order.

Distribution agreement A contract between a seller and a distributor of the seller's products setting out the terms and conditions of the distributorship.

Distributorship A business arrangement that is established when a manufacturer licenses a dealer to sell its product. An example of a distributorship is an automobile dealership.

Diversity of citizenship Under Article III, Section 2, of the Constitution, a basis for federal court jurisdiction over a lawsuit between citizens of different states.

Divestiture The act of selling one or more of a company's parts, such as a subsidiary or plant; often mandated by the courts in merger or monopolization cases.

Dividend A distribution to corporate shareholders, disbursed in proportion to the number of shares held.

Document of title Paper exchanged in the regular course of business that evidences the right to possession of goods (for example, a bill of lading or warehouse receipt).

Domestic corporation In a given state, a corporation that does business in, and is organized under the laws of, that state.

Domestic relations courts Courts that deal with domestic (household) relationships, such as adoption, divorce, support payments, child custody, and the like.

Donee beneficiary A third party to whom the benefits of a contract flow as a direct result of an intention to make a gift to that person.

Double taxation A feature (and disadvantage) of the corporate form of business. Because a corporation is a separate legal entity, corporate profits are taxed by state and federal governments. Dividends are again taxable as ordinary income to the shareholders receiving them.

Draft Any instrument drawn on a drawee (such as a bank) that orders the drawee to pay a certain sum of money.

Drawee The person who is ordered to pay a draft or check. With a check, a financial institution is always the drawee.

Drawer A person who initiates a draft (including a check), thereby ordering the drawee to pay.

Due diligence A required standard of care that certain professionals, such as accountants, must meet to avoid liability for securities violations. Under securities law, an accountant will be deemed to have exercised due diligence if he or she followed generally accepted accounting principles and generally accepted auditing standards and had, ''after reasonable investigation, reasonable grounds to believe and did believe, at the time such part of the registration statement became effective, that the statements therein were true and that there was no omission of a material fact required to be stated therein or necessary to make the statements therein not misleading.''

Due negotiation The transfer of a document of title in such form that the transferee becomes a holder [UCC 7-501].

Dumping Selling goods in a foreign country at a price below the price charged for the same goods in the domestic market.

Duress Unlawful pressure brought to bear on a person, overcoming that person's free will and causing him or her to do (or refrain from doing) what he or she otherwise would not (or would) have done.

E

Easement A nonpossessory right to use another's property in a manner established by either express or implied agreement.

Easement appurtenant A right to use the land of another in some way that passes with the benefitted land rather than the landowner.

Easement in gross A right to use the land of another in some way that is personal to the easement holder and not dependent on his or her ownership of a particular parcel of land.

Eighty-day cooling-off period A provision of the Taft-Hartley Act that allows federal courts to issue injunctions against strikes that might create a national emergency.

Ejectment The eviction of a tenant from leased premises. A remedy at common law to which the landlord can resort when a tenant fails to pay rent for leased premises. To obtain possession of the premises, the landlord must appear in court and show that the defaulting tenant is in wrongful possession.

Electronic fund transfer A transfer of funds with the use of an electronic terminal, a telephone, a computer, or magnetic tape.

Electronic fund transfer system (EFTS) A system used to transfer funds electronically.

Embezzlement The fraudulent appropriation of money or other property by a person to whom the money or property has been entrusted.

Eminent domain The power of a government to take land for public use from private citizens for just compensation.

Employee A person who works for an employer for salary or wages.

Employment-at-will doctrine A common law doctrine under which employer-employee contracts are considered to be "at will"—that is, either party may terminate an employment contract at any time and for any reason, unless the contract specifies otherwise. Although several states still adhere to the employment-at-will doctrine, exceptions are frequently made on the basis of an implied employment contract or public policy.

Enabling legislation Statutes enacted by Congress that authorize the creation of an administrative agency and specify the name, composition, and powers of the agency being created.

Endowment insurance A type of insurance that combines life insurance with an investment so that if the insured outlives the policy, the face value is paid to him or her; if the insured does not outlive the policy, the face value is paid to his or her beneficiary.

Entrapment In criminal law, a defense in which the defendant claims that he or she was induced by a public official—usually an undercover agent or police officer—to commit a crime that he or she would otherwise not have committed.

Entrepreneur One who initiates and assumes the financial risks of a new enterprise and who undertakes to provide or control its management.

Entrustment The transfer of goods to a merchant who deals in goods of that kind and who may transfer those goods and all rights to them to a buyer in the ordinary course of business [UCC 2-403(2)].

Environmental impact statement (EIS) A statement required by the National Environmental Policy Act for any major federal action that will significantly affect the quality of the environment. The statement must analyze the action's impact on the environment and alternative actions that might be taken.

Environmental law All statutory, regulatory, and common law relating to the protection of the environment.

Equal dignity rule In most states, a rule stating that express authority given to an agent must be in writing if the contract to be made on behalf of the principal is required to be in writing.

Equal protection clause The clause in the Fourteenth Amendment to the Constitution that guarantees that no state will "deny to any person within its jurisdiction the equal protection of the laws." This clause mandates that the state governments treat similarly situated individuals in a similar manner.

Equitable principles and maxims Propositions or general statements of rules of law that are frequently involved in equity jurisdiction.

Equitable servitudes Restrictions on the use of land that are enforceable in a court of equity.

Equity of redemption The right of a mortgagor who has breached the mortgage agreement to redeem or purchase the property prior to foreclosure proceedings.

Escheat The transfer of property to the state when the owner of the property dies without heirs.

Escrow account An account that is generally held in the name of the depositor and escrow agent; the funds in the account are paid to a third person only upon fulfillment of the escrow condition.

Establishment clause The clause in the First Amendment to the Constitution that prohibits Congress from creating any law "respecting an establishment of religion."

Estop To bar, impede, or preclude.

Estoppel The principle that a party's own acts prevent him or her from claiming a right to the detriment of another who was entitled to, and did, rely on those acts. *Agency by estoppel* arises when a principal negligently allows an agent to exercise powers not granted to the agent, thus justifying others in believing that the agent possesses the requisite agency authority. *See also* Promissory estoppel.

Estray statutes Statutes dealing with finders' rights in property when the true owners are unknown.

Ethics Moral principles and values applied to social behavior.

Eviction Depriving a person of the possession of land or rental property that he or she owns or leases.

Exclusionary rule In criminal procedure, a rule under which any evidence that is obtained in violation of the accused's constitutional rights guaranteed by the Fourth, Fifth, and Sixth Amendments, as well as any evidence derived from illegally obtained evidence, will not be admissible in court.

Exclusive dealing contract An agreement under which a producer of goods agrees to sell its goods exclusively through one distributor.

Exclusive distributorship A distributorship in which the seller and distributor of the seller's products agree that the distributor has the exclusive right to distribute the seller's products in a certain geographic area.

Exclusive jurisdiction Jurisdiction that exists when a case can be heard only in a particular court.

Exculpatory clause A clause that releases a party (to a contract) from liability for his or her wrongful acts.

Executed contract A contract that has been completely performed by both parties.

Executor A person appointed by a testator to see that his or her will is administered appropriately.

Executory contract A contract that has not as yet been fully performed.

Executory interest A future interest, held by a person other than the grantor, that either cuts short or begins some time after the natural termination of the preceding estate.

Export To sell products to buyers located in other countries.

Express authority Authority expressly given by one party to another. In agency law, an agent has express authority to act for a principal if both parties agree, orally or in writing, that an agency relationship exists in which the agent had the power (authority) to act in the place of, and on behalf of, the principal.

Express contract A contract that is oral and/or written (as opposed to an implied contract).

Express warranty A promise, ancillary to an underlying sales agreement, that is included in the written or oral terms of the sales agreement under which the promisor assures the quality, description, or performance of the goods.

Expropriation The seizure by a government of privately owned business or personal property for a proper public purpose and with just compensation.

Extension clause A clause in a time instrument extending the instrument's date of maturity. An extension clause is the reverse of an acceleration clause.

Externalities The costs or benefits of an action that are not known or properly accounted for by the parties to that action. An example of an externality is environmental pollution.

F

Featherbedding A requirement that more workers be employed to do a particular job than are actually needed.

Federal question A question that pertains to the U.S. Constitution, acts of Congress, or treaties. A federal question provides jurisdiction for federal courts. This jurisdiction arises from Article III, Section 2, of the Constitution.

Fee simple A form of property ownership entitling the property owner to use, possess, or dispose of the property as he or she chooses during his or her lifetime. Upon death, the interest in the property descends to the owner's heirs.

Fee simple absolute An estate or interest in land with no time, disposition, or descendibility limitations.

Fee simple defeasible An estate that can be taken away (by the prior grantor) upon the occurrence or nonoccurrence of a specified event.

Felony A crime—such as arson, murder, rape, or robbery—that carries the most severe sanctions, usually ranging from one year in a state or federal prison to the forfeiture of one's life.

Felony murder A common law doctrine under which the intent to commit a felony unrelated to a resulting homicide was sufficient to meet the *mens rea* requirement for murder. Because of the many new statutory

felonies that pose little threat of death or bodily harm to anyone, this doctrine has been limited by courts and legislatures.

Fictitious payee rule A rule under which indorsements by fictitious payees (a payee on a negotiable instrument whom the maker or drawer does not intend to have an interest in the instrument) will not be deemed forgeries.

Fiduciary relationship A relationship founded upon trust and confidence.

Final order The final decision of an administrative agency on an issue. If no appeal is taken, or if the case is not reviewed or considered anew by the agency commission, the administrative law judge's initial order becomes the final order of the agency.

Financial institutions Organizations authorized to do business under state or federal laws relating to financial institutions. For example, under the Electronic Fund Transfer Act, financial institutions include banks, savings and loan associations, credit unions, and any other business entities that directly or indirectly hold accounts belonging to consumers.

Financing statement A document prepared by a secured creditor, and filed with the appropriate state or local official, to give notice to the public that the creditor claims an interest in collateral belonging to a certain named debtor. The financing statement must be signed by the debtor, contain the addresses of both the debtor and creditor, and describe the collateral by type or item.

Firm offer An offer (by a merchant) that is irrevocable without consideration for a period of time (not longer than three months). A firm offer by a merchant must be in writing and must be signed by the offeror.

Fixture A thing that was once personal property but that has become attached to real property in such a way that it takes on the characteristics of real property and becomes part of that real property.

Float time The time between the issuance of a check and the deduction of the amount of the check from the drawer's account.

Floating lien A security interest retained in collateral even when the collateral changes in character, classification, or location.

Floating zones A particular land use designation that specifies that a parcel of land be set aside for a particular purpose within a zoning district even though the exact site may not be selected at the time the zoning scheme is enacted.

***Force majeure* clause** A clause in a contract stipulating that certain unforeseen events—such as war, political upheavals, acts of God, or other events—will excuse a party from liability for nonperformance of contractual obligations.

Foreclosure A proceeding in equity whereby a mortgagee either takes title to, or forces the sale of, the mortgagor's property in satisfaction of a debt.

Foreign corporation In a given state, a corporation that does business in the state without being incorporated therein.

Foreign exchange market A worldwide system in which foreign currencies are bought and sold.

Foreign exchange rate The price of a unit of one country's currency in terms of another country's currency. For example, if today's exchange rate is 100 yen for $1, that means that anybody with 100 yen can obtain $1, or that 1 yen equals $0.01.

Foreseeable risk In negligence law, the risk of harm or injury to another that a person of ordinary intelligence and prudence should have reasonably anticipated or foreseen when undertaking an action or refraining from an action.

Forfeiture The termination of a lease, according to its terms or the terms of a statute, when one of the parties fails to fulfill a condition under the lease and thereby breaches it.

Forgery The false or unauthorized signature of a document, or the false making of a document, with the intent to defraud.

Formal contract An agreement or contract that by law requires for its validity a specific form, such as executed under seal.

Formal rulemaking Agency rulemaking that is much more extensive than informal rulemaking and in which a public hearing is conducted in the manner of a trial. After the hearing is concluded, the agency is required to prepare a formal written statement describing its findings based on the evidence presented by both sides. Also referred to as rulemaking-on-a-record.

Forum-selection clause A clause in a contract designating the forum (the nation, state, or jurisdiction) in which a dispute will be litigated.

Franchise A written agreement whereby an owner of a trademark, trade name, or copyright licenses another to use that trademark, trade name, or copyright, under specified conditions or limitations, in the selling of goods and services.

Franchisee One receiving a license to use another's (the franchisor's) trademark, trade name, or copyright in the sale of goods and services.

Franchisor One licensing another (the franchisee) to use his or her trademark, trade name, or copyright in the sale of goods or services.

Fraud Any misrepresentation, either by misstatement or omission of a material fact, knowingly made with the intention of deceiving another and on which a reasonable person would and does rely to his or her detriment.

Free exercise clause The clause in the First Amendment to the Constitution that prohibits Congress from making any law ''prohibiting the free exercise'' of religion.

Frustration of purpose A court-created doctrine under which a party to a contract will be relieved of his or her duty to perform when the objective purpose for performance no longer exists (due to reasons beyond that party's control).

Fungible goods Goods that are alike by physical nature, by agreement, or by trade usage. Examples of fungible goods are wheat, oil, and wine that are identical in type and quality.

Future interest An interest in real property that is not at present possessory but will or may be possessory in the future. Remainders and reversions are future interests.

G

Garnishment A legal process whereby a creditor appropriates the debtor's property or wages that are in the hands of a third party.

General duty clause A requirement of the Occupational Safety and Health Act that businesses be maintained free of known hazards that could cause serious injury to workers.

General partner In a limited partnership, a partner who assumes responsibility for the management of the partnership and liability for all partnership debts.

General plan A comprehensive document that local jurisdictions are often required by state law to devise and implement as a precursor to specific land-use regulations.

Generally accepted accounting principles (GAAP) The conventions, rules, and procedures necessary to define accepted accounting practices at a particular time. The source of the principles is the Federal Accounting Standards Board.

Generally accepted auditing standards (GAAS) Standards concerning an auditor's professional qualities and the judgment exercised by him or her in the performance of an examination and report. The source of the standards is the American Institute of Certified Public Accountants.

Genuineness of assent Knowing and voluntary assent to the terms of a contract. If a contract is formed as a result of a mistake, misrepresentation, undue influence, or duress, genuineness of assent is lacking, and the contract will be voidable.

Gift Any voluntary transfer of property made without consideration, past or present.

Gift *causa mortis* A gift made in contemplation of death. If the donor does not die of that ailment, the gift is revoked.

Gift *inter vivos* A gift made during one's lifetime and not in contemplation of imminent death, in contrast to a gift *causa mortis*.

Good faith purchaser A purchaser who buys without notice of any circumstance that would put a person of ordinary prudence on inquiry as to whether the seller has valid title to the goods being sold.

Grand jury In criminal cases, a body of citizens that decides whether a person accused of a crime should be prosecuted. If the jury concludes that the evidence against the individual is sufficient to justify a trial, the individual will be indicted and a trial held. Called a ''grand'' jury because it consists of a greater number of jurors than the ordinary trial jury, or ''petit'' jury.

Grant deed A deed that simply recites words of consideration and conveyance. Under statute, a grant deed may impliedly warrant that at least the grantor has not conveyed the property's title to someone else.

Group boycott The boycott of a particular person or firm by a group of competitors; prohibited under the Sherman Act.

Guarantor One who agrees to satisfy the debt of another (the debtor) *only* if and when the debtor fails to pay the debt. A guarantor's liability is thus secondary.

H

Holder A person ''who is in possession of a document of title or negotiable instrument or a certificated investment security drawn, issued, or indorsed to him or his order or to bearer or in blank'' [UCC 1-201(20)].

Holder in due course Any holder who acquires a negotiable instrument for value; in good faith; and without notice that the instrument is overdue, that it has been dishonored, or that any defense or claim to it exists on the part of any person.

Holding zone A designated parcel of land that may be restricted to unusually low levels of development activity to give planners time to formulate a more detailed long-term zoning scheme.

Holographic will A will written entirely in the signer's handwriting and usually not witnessed.

Homestead exemption A law allowing an owner to designate his or her house and adjoining land as a homestead and thus exempt it from liability for his or her general debt.

Horizontal market division A market division that occurs when competitors agree to divide up the market for their products or services among themselves, either geographically or by functional class of customers (such as retailers or wholesalers). Such market division constitutes a *per se* violation of the Sherman Act.

Horizontal merger A merger between two businesses or persons competing in the marketplace.

Horizontal restraint Any agreement that in some way restrains competition between rival firms competing in the same market. Price fixing and horizontal market division are examples of horizontal restraints on competition.

Hot-cargo agreement An agreement in which em-

ployers voluntarily agree with unions not to handle, use, or deal in non-union-produced goods of other employers. A type of secondary boycott explicitly prohibited by the Landrum-Griffin Act of 1959.

Hybrid rulemaking A set of loosely defined procedures for agency rulemaking that incorporate advantages of both the formal and informal procedures. As with formal rulemaking, there is an opportunity for direct participation through a public hearing, but the right of interested parties to cross-examine witnesses is much more restricted. Also, the standard applied by an independent court in reviewing an agency's procedures is different.

I

Identification Proof that a thing is what it is purported or represented to be. In the sale of goods, the express designation of the goods provided for in the contract.

Immunity A status of being exempt, or free, from certain duties or requirements. In criminal law, the state may grant an accused person immunity from prosecution—or agree to prosecute for a lesser offense—if the accused person agrees to give the state information that would assist the state in prosecuting other individuals for crimes. In tort law, freedom from liability for defamatory speech. *See also* Privilege.

Implied authority Authority that is created not by an explicit oral or written agreement but by implication. In agency law, implied authority (of the agent) can be conferred by custom, inferred from the position the agent occupies, or implied by virtue of being reasonably necessary to carry out express authority.

Implied warranty A warranty that the law implies through either the situation of the parties or the nature of the transaction.

Implied warranty of fitness for a particular purpose A presumed promise made by a merchant seller of goods that the goods are fit for the particular purpose for which the buyer will use the goods. The seller must know the buyer's purpose and know that the buyer is relying on the seller's skill and judgment to select suitable goods.

Implied warranty of habitability A presumed promise by the landlord that rented residential premises are fit for human habitation—that is, free of violations of building and sanitary codes.

Implied warranty of merchantability A presumed promise by a merchant seller of goods that the goods are reasonably fit for the general purpose for which they are sold, are properly packaged and labeled, and are of proper quality.

Implied-in-fact contract A contract formed in whole or in part from the conduct of the parties (as opposed to an express contract).

Impossibility of performance A doctrine under which a party to a contract is relieved of his or her duty to perform when performance becomes impossible or totally impracticable (through no fault of either party).

Imposter One who, with the intent to deceive, pretends to be somebody else.

In pari delicto At equal fault.

In personam **jurisdiction** Court jurisdiction over the "person" involved in a legal action.

In rem **jurisdiction** Court jurisdiction over a defendant's property.

Incidental beneficiary A third party who incidentally benefits from a contract but whose benefit was not the reason the contract was formed; an incidental beneficiary has no rights in a contract and cannot sue the promisor if the contract is breached.

Incidental damages Damages resulting from a breach of contract, including all reasonable expenses incurred because of the breach.

Indemnify To compensate or reimburse another for losses or expenses incurred.

Independent contractor One who works for, and receives payment from, an employer but whose working conditions and methods are not controlled by the employer. An independent contractor is not an employee but may be an agent.

Indictment A charge or written accusation, issued by a grand jury, that a named person has committed a crime.

Indorsee The one to whom a negotiable instrument is transferred by indorsement.

Indorsement A signature placed on an instrument or a document of title for the purpose of transferring one's ownership in the instrument or document of title.

Indorser One who, being the payee or holder of a negotiable instrument, signs his or her name on the back of it.

Industrywide liability Product liability that is imposed on an entire industry when it is unclear which of several sellers within the industry manufactured a particular product.

Informal contract A contract that does not require a specified form or formality for its validity.

Informal rulemaking A procedure in agency rulemaking that requires (1) notice; (2) opportunity for comment; and (3) a general statement of the basis for, and purpose of, the proposed rule. Also referred to as notice-and-comment rulemaking.

Information A formal accusation or complaint (without an indictment) issued in certain types of actions by a prosecuting attorney or other law officer, such as a magistrate. The types of actions are set forth in the rules of states or in the Federal Rules of Criminal Procedure.

Information return A tax return submitted by a partnership that only reports the income earned by the business. The partnership as an entity does not pay taxes on the income received by the partnership. A partner's profit from the partnership (whether distributed or not) is taxed as individual income to the individual partner.

Initial order In the context of administrative law, an agency's disposition in a matter other than a rulemaking. An administrative law judge's initial order becomes final unless it is appealed.

Injunction A court decree ordering a person to do, or refrain from doing, a certain act or activity.

Innkeeper's lien A possessory or statutory lien allowing the innkeeper to take the personal property of a guest, brought into the hotel, as security for nonpayment of the guest's bill (debt).

Innocent misrepresentation A false statement of fact or an act made in good faith that deceives and causes harm or injury to another.

Insider A corporate director or officer, or other employee or agent, with access to confidential information and a duty not to disclose that information in violation of insider-trading laws.

Insider trading Purchasing or selling securities on the basis of information that has not been made available to the public.

Insolvent A term describing a person whose liabilities exceed the value of owned assets *or* a person who "either has ceased to pay his debts in the ordinary course of business or cannot pay his debts as they come due" [UCC 1-201(23)].

Installment contract A contract in which payments due are made periodically. Also may allow for delivery of goods in separate lots with payment made for each.

Insurable interest An interest either in a person's life or well-being or in property that is sufficiently substantial that insuring against injury to the person or damage to the property does not amount to a mere wagering (betting) contract.

Insurance A contract in which, for a stipulated consideration, one party agrees to compensate the other for loss on a specific subject by a specified peril.

Intellectual property Property resulting from intellectual, creative processes—the products of an individual's mind.

Intended beneficiary A third party for whose benefit a contract is formed; intended beneficiaries can sue the promisor if such a contract is breached.

Intentional tort A wrongful act knowingly committed.

Inter vivos **gift** *See* Gift *inter vivos.*

Inter vivos **trust** A trust created by the grantor (settlor) and effective during the grantor's lifetime (that is, a trust not established by a will).

Intermediary bank Any bank to which an item is transferred in the course of collection, except the depositary or payor bank.

International law The law that governs relations among nations. International customs and treaties are generally considered to be two of the most important sources of international law.

International organization In international law, a term that generally refers to an organization composed mainly of nations and usually established by treaty. The United States is a member of more than one hundred multilateral and bilateral organizations, including at least twenty through the United Nations.

Interpretative rules Administrative agency rules that are simply statements and opinions issued by an agency explaining how the agency interprets and intends to apply the statutes it enforces. Such rules are not automatically binding on private individuals or organizations.

Interrogatories A series of written questions for which written answers are prepared and then signed under oath by a party to a lawsuit (the plaintiff or the defendant).

Intestacy laws State laws determining the division and descent of the property of one who dies intestate (without a will).

Intestate One who has died without having created a valid will.

Investment company A company that acts on behalf of many smaller shareholders/owners by buying a large portfolio of securities and managing that portfolio professionally.

Invitee A person who, either expressly or impliedly, is privileged to enter upon another's land. The inviter owes the invitee (for example, a customer in a store) the duty to exercise reasonable care to protect the invitee from harm.

Irrevocable offer An offer that cannot be revoked or recalled by the offeror without liability. A merchant's firm offer is an example of an irrevocable offer.

Issue The first transfer, or delivery, of an instrument to a holder.

J

Joint and several liability A doctrine under which a plaintiff may sue, and collect a judgment from, any of several jointly liable defendants, regardless of that particular defendant's degree of fault. In partnership law, joint and several liability means a third party may sue one or more of the partners separately or all of them together, at his or her option. This is true even if the partner did not participate in, ratify, or know about whatever it was that gave rise to the cause of action.

Joint liability Shared liability. In partnership law, partners incur joint liability for partnership obligations and debts. For example, if a third party sues a partner on a partnership debt, the partner has the right to insist that the other partners be sued with him or her.

Joint stock company A hybrid form of business organization that combines characteristics of a corporation (shareholder-owners, management by directors and of-

ficers of the company, and perpetual existence) and a partnership (it is formed by agreement, not statute; property is usually held in the names of the members; and the shareholders have personal liability for business debts). Usually, the joint stock company is regarded as a partnership for tax and other legally related purposes.

Joint tenancy The ownership interest of two or more co-owners of property whereby each owns an undivided portion of the property. Upon the death of one of the joint tenants, his or her interest automatically passes to the others and cannot be transferred by the will of the deceased.

Joint venture A joint undertaking of a specific commercial enterprise by an association of persons. A joint venture is normally not a legal entity and is treated like a partnership for federal income tax purposes.

Judgment *n.o.v.* A judgment notwithstanding the verdict; may be entered by the court for the plaintiff (or the defendant) after there has been a jury verdict for the defendant (or the plaintiff).

Judgment rate of interest A rate of interest fixed by statute that is applied to a monetary judgment from the moment the judgment is awarded by a court until the judgment is paid or terminated.

Judicial process The procedures relating to, or connected with, the administration of justice through the judicial system.

Judicial review The authority of a court to reexamine a previously considered dispute; the process by which a court decides on the constitutionality of legislative acts.

Jurisdiction The authority of a court to hear and decide a specific action.

Jurisprudence The science or philosophy of law.

Justice of the peace courts Courts of limited civil and criminal jurisdiction, presided over by judicial magistrates of inferior rank (called justices of the peace).

Justiciable Appropriate for court review. A justiciable controversy is one that is not hypothetical or academic but real and substantial.

K

King's Court A medieval English court. The King's Courts, or *Curia Regis,* were established by the Norman conquerors of England. The body of law that developed in these courts was common to the entire English realm and thus became known as the common law.

L

Laches The equitable doctrine that bars a party's right to legal action if the party has neglected for an unreasonable length of time to act upon his or her rights.

Laissez-faire A doctrine advocating government restraint in the regulation of business.

Landlord's lien A landlord's remedy for a tenant's failure to pay rent. When permitted under a statute or the lease agreement, the landlord may take and keep or sell whatever of the defaulting tenant's property is on the leased premises.

Land-use control The control over the ownership and uses of real property by authorized public agencies.

Larceny The act of taking another person's personal property unlawfully. Some states classify larceny as either grand or petit, depending on the property's value.

Last clear chance A doctrine under which a plaintiff may recover from a defendant for injuries or damages suffered, notwithstanding the plaintiff's own negligence, when the defendant had the opportunity—a last clear chance—to avoid harming the plaintiff through the exercise of reasonable care but failed to do so.

Lease A transfer by the landlord/lessor of real or personal property to the tenant/lessee for a period of time for consideration (usually the payment of rent). Upon termination of the lease, the property reverts to the lessor.

Lease agreement An agreement between a landlord and tenant setting forth the terms of the lease.

Leasehold estate An estate in realty held by a tenant under a lease. In every leasehold estate, the tenant has a qualified right to possess and/or use the land.

Legacy A gift of personal property under a will.

Legal rate of interest A rate of interest fixed by statute as either the maximum rate of interest allowed by law or a rate of interest applied when the parties to a contract intend, but do not fix, an interest rate in the contract. In the latter case, the rate is frequently the same as the statutory maximum rate permitted.

Legal realism A school of legal thought of the 1920s and 1930s that challenged many existing jurisprudential assumptions, particularly the assumption that subjective elements played no part in judicial reasoning. The legal realists, as the term implies, generally advocated a less abstract and more realistic approach to the law, an approach that would take into account customary practices and the circumstances in which transactions take place. The school left a lasting imprint on American jurisprudence.

Legatee A person who inherits personal property under a will.

Legislative rules Administrative agency rules that carry the same weight as congressionally enacted statutes.

Lender liability The liability of lenders to their borrowers or for the actions of their borrowers.

Lessee A person who pays for the use or possession of another's property.

Lessor A property owner who allows others to use his or her property in exchange for the payment of rent.

Letter of credit A written instrument, usually issued by a bank on behalf of a customer or other person, in which the issuer promises to honor drafts or other demands for payment by third persons in accordance with the terms of the instrument.

Leveraged buy-out (LBO) A corporate takeover financed by loans secured by the acquired corporation's assets or by the issuance of corporate bonds, resulting in a high debt load for the corporation.

Libel A written defamation of one's character, reputation, business, or property rights. To a limited degree, the First Amendment to the Constitution protects the press from libel actions.

License A revocable privilege to use another's intellectual property or to enter onto another's real property.

Licensee One who receives a license to use, or enter onto, another's property.

Lien An encumbrance upon a property to satisfy or protect a claim for payment of a debt.

Lien creditor One whose claim is secured by a lien on particular property, as distinguished from a general creditor, who has no such security.

Life estate An interest in land that exists only for the duration of the life of some person, usually the holder of the estate.

Limited partner In a limited partnership, a partner who contributes capital to the partnership but has no right to participate in the management and operation of the business. The limited partner assumes no liability for partnership debts beyond the capital contributed.

Limited partnership A partnership consisting of one or more general partners (who manage the business and are liable to the full extent of their personal assets for debts of the partnership) and of one or more limited partners (who contribute only assets and are liable only up to the amount contributed by them).

Limited-payment life A type of life insurance for which premiums are payable for a definite period, after which the policy is fully paid.

Liquidated damages An amount, stipulated in the contract, that the parties to a contract believe to be a reasonable estimation of the damages that will occur in the event of a breach.

Liquidation The sale of the assets of a business or an individual for cash and the distribution of the cash received to creditors, with the balance going to the owner(s).

Litigant A party to a lawsuit.

Loan workout A common law or bankruptcy composition (agreement) with creditors under which a debtor enters into an agreement with a creditor or creditors for a payment or plan to discharge the debtor's debt(s).

Lockout The closing of a plant to employees by an employer to gain leverage in collective bargaining negotiations.

Long arm statute A state statute that permits a state to obtain jurisdiction over nonresident individuals and corporations. Individuals or corporations, however, must have certain ''minimum contacts'' with that state for the statute to apply.

Lost property Property with which the owner has involuntarily parted and then cannot find or recover.

M

Mailbox rule A rule providing that an acceptance of an offer becomes effective upon dispatch (upon being placed in a mailbox), if mail is, expressly or impliedly, an authorized means of communication of acceptance to the offeror.

Maker One who issues a promissory note or certificate of deposit (that is, one who promises to pay a certain sum to the holder of the note or CD).

Manufacturing or processing-plant franchise A franchise that is created when the franchisor transmits to the franchisee the essential ingredients or formula to make a particular product. The franchisee then markets the product either at wholesale or at retail in accordance with the franchisor's standards. Examples of this type of franchise are Coca-Cola and other soft-drink bottling companies.

Market concentration A situation that exists when a small number of firms share the market for a particular good or service. For example, if the four largest grocery stores in Chicago accounted for 80 percent of all retail food sales, the market clearly would be concentrated in those four firms.

Market power The power of a firm to control the market for its product. A monopoly has the greatest degree of market power.

Market share test The primary measure of monopoly power. A firm's market share is the percentage of a market that the firm controls.

Marshalling assets The arrangement or ranking of assets in a certain order toward the payment of debts. In equity, when two creditors have recourse to the same property of the debtor, but one has recourse to other property of the debtor, that creditor must resort first to those assets of the debtor not available to the other creditor.

Mask work A series of images related to the pattern formed by the many layers of a semiconductor chip product.

Material facts Those facts to which a reasonable person would attach importance in determining his or her course of action. In regard to tender offers, for example, a fact is material if there is a substantial likelihood that a reasonable shareholder would consider it important in deciding how to vote.

Mechanic's lien A statutory lien upon the real property of another, created to ensure priority of payment for work performed and materials furnished in erecting or repairing a building or other structure.

Mediation A method of settling disputes outside of court by using the services of a neutral third party, who acts as a communicating agent between the parties; a method of dispute settlement that is less formal than arbitration.

Mediator A person who attempts to reconcile the differences of two or more parties.

Mens rea Mental state, or intent. A wrongful mental state is as necessary as a wrongful act to establish criminal liability. What constitutes a mental state varies according to the wrongful action. Thus, for murder, the *mens rea* is the intent to take life; for theft, the *mens rea* must involve both the knowledge that the property belongs to another and the intent to deprive the owner of it.

Merger A contractual process by which one corporation (the surviving corporation) acquires all the assets and liabilities of another corporation (the merged corporation). The shareholders of the merged corporation receive either payment for their shares or shares in the surviving corporation.

Minimum-contacts requirement The requirement that before a state court can exercise jurisdiction over a foreign corporation, the foreign corporation must have sufficient contacts with the state. A foreign corporation that has its home office within the state or has manufacturing plants in the state meets this requirement.

Mini-trial A private proceeding that assists disputing parties in determining whether to take their case to court. During the proceeding, each party's attorney briefly argues the party's case before the other party and (usually) a neutral third party, who acts as an adviser. If the parties fail to reach an agreement, the adviser renders an opinion as to how a court would likely decide the issue.

Mirror image rule A common law rule that requires, for a valid contractual agreement, that the terms of the offeree's acceptance adhere exactly to the terms of the offeror's offer.

Misdemeanor A lesser crime than a felony, punishable by a fine or imprisonment for up to one year in other than a state or federal penitentiary.

Mislaid property Property that the owner has voluntarily parted with and then cannot find or recover.

Mitigation of damages The rule requiring the party suing to have done whatever was reasonable to minimize the damages caused by the defendant.

Money laundering Falsely reporting income that has been obtained through criminal activity as income obtained through a legitimate business enterprise—in effect, ''laundering'' the ''dirty money.''

Monopolization The possession of monopoly power in the relevant market and the willful acquisition or maintenance of the power, as distinguished from growth or development as a consequence of a superior product, business acumen, or historical accident. A violation of

Section 2 of the Sherman Act requires that both of these elements be established.

Monopoly A term generally used to describe a market for which there is a single seller.

Monopoly power An extreme amount of market power.

Mortgage A written instrument giving a creditor (the mortgagee) an interest (lien) in the debtor's (mortgagor's) property as security for a debt.

Mortgagee The creditor who takes the security interest under a mortgage agreement.

Mortgagor The debtor who pledges collateral in a mortgage agreement.

Motion for a directed verdict In a jury trial, a motion for the judge to take the decision out of the hands of the jury and direct a verdict for the moving party on the grounds that the other party has not produced sufficient evidence to support his or her claim.

Motion for judgment on the pleadings A motion, which can be brought by either party to a lawsuit after the pleadings are closed, for the court to decide the issue without proceeding to trial. This motion may be used when only questions of law are at issue.

Motion to dismiss A pleading in which a defendant admits the facts as alleged by the plaintiff but asserts that the plaintiff's claim fails to state a cause of action (that is, has no basis in law) or that there are other grounds on which a suit should be dismissed. Also called a demurrer.

Multiple product order An order issued by the Federal Trade Commission to a firm that has engaged in deceptive advertising by which the firm is required to cease and desist from false advertising not only in regard to the product that was the subject of the action but also in regard to all the firm's other products.

Municipal courts City or community courts with criminal jurisdiction over traffic violations and, less frequently, with civil jurisdiction over other minor matters.

Mutual assent The element of agreement in the formation of a contract. The manifestation of contract parties' mutual assent to the same bargain is required to establish a contract.

Mutual fund A specific type of investment company that continually buys or sells to investors shares of ownership in a portfolio.

Mutual rescission An agreement between the parties to cancel their contract, releasing the parties from further obligations under the contract. The object of the agreement is to restore the parties to the positions they would have occupied had no contract ever been formed. *See also* Rescission.

N

National law Law that pertains to a particular nation (as opposed to international law).

Natural law school The oldest and one of the most significant schools of legal thought. Adherents of the natural law school believe that government and the legal system should reflect universal moral and ethical principles that are inherent in human nature.

Negligence The failure to exercise the standard of care that a reasonable person would exercise in similar circumstances.

Negligent misrepresentation Any manifestation through words or conduct that amounts to an untrue statement of fact made in circumstances in which a reasonable and prudent person would not have done (or failed to do) that which led to the misrepresentation. A representation made with an honest belief in its truth may still be negligent due to (1) a lack of reasonable care in ascertaining the facts, (2) the manner of expression, or (3) the absence of the skill or competence required by a particular business or profession.

Negotiable instrument A written and signed unconditional promise or order to pay a specified sum of money on demand or at a definite time to order (to a specific person or entity) or to bearer.

Negotiation The transferring of a negotiable instrument to another in such form that the transferee becomes a holder.

No-par shares Corporate shares that have no face value—that is, no specific dollar amount is printed on their face.

No-strike clause A provision found in some public employee labor contracts, especially those involving essential services, which prohibit the employees from going out on strike.

***Noerr-Pennington* doctrine** A series of cases that permits competitors to lobby for changes in the law to gain greater protection from competition.

Nominal damages A small monetary award (often one dollar) granted to a plaintiff when no actual damage was suffered.

Nonconforming use A land use that was lawful prior to the adoption of new zoning regulations or laws but which now does not comply with the newly adopted laws.

Noncumulative use Zoning designations in which higher uses such as single family residential homes are excluded from lower-use zones allowing such things as factories.

Note A written instrument signed by a maker unconditionally promising to pay a sum certain in money to a payee or a holder on demand or on a specific date [UCC 3-104].

Notice of Proposed Rulemaking A notice published (in the *Federal Register*) by an administrative agency describing a proposed rule. The notice must give the time and place for which agency proceedings on the proposed rule will be held, a description of the nature of the proceedings, the legal authority for the proceedings (which is usually the agency's enabling legislation), and the terms of the proposed rule or the subject matter of the proposed rule.

Notice-and-comment rulemaking A procedure in agency rulemaking that requires (1) notice, (2) opportunity for comment, and (3) a general statement of the basis for, and purpose of, the proposed rule. Also referred to as informal rulemaking.

Novation The substitution, by agreement, of a new contract for an old one, with the rights under the old one being terminated. Typically, there is a substitution of a new person who is responsible for the contract and the removal of the original party's rights and duties under the contract.

Nuisance An act that interferes unlawfully with a person's possession or ability to use his or her property.

Nuncupative will An oral will (often called a deathbed will) made before witnesses; usually limited to transfers of personal property.

O

Objective theory of contracts The view taken by American law that contracting parties shall only be bound by terms that can actually be inferred from promises made. Contract law does not examine a contracting party's subjective intent or underlying motive.

Offer An offeror's proposal to do something, which creates in the offeree accepting the offer a legal power to bind the offeror to the terms of the proposal by accepting the offer.

Offeree A person to whom an offer is made.

Offeror A person who makes an offer.

Omnibus, or other-driver, clause A provision in an automobile insurance policy that protects the vehicle owner who has taken out the insurance policy and anyone who drives the vehicle with the owner's permission.

Opinion A statement by the court expressing the reasons for its decision in a case.

Option contract A contract under which the offeror cannot revoke his or her offer for a stipulated time period, and the offeree can accept or reject the offer during this period without fear of the offer's being made to another person. The offeree must give consideration for the option (the irrevocable offer) to be enforceable.

Order for relief A court's grant of assistance to a complainant. In the context of bankruptcy, relief consists of discharging a complainant's debts.

Order instrument A negotiable instrument that is payable to the order of a specific person.

Output contract A binding agreement in which a seller agrees to deliver/sell the seller's entire output of a good (an unspecified amount at the time of agreement) to a buyer, and the buyer agrees to buy all the goods supplied.

P

Par-value shares Corporate shares that have a specific face value, or formal cash-in value, written on them, such as one penny or one dollar.

Parol evidence rule A substantive rule of contracts under which a court will not receive into evidence prior statements or contemporaneous oral statements that contradict a written agreement when the court finds that the written agreement was intended by the parties to be a final, complete, and unambiguous expression of their agreement.

Partially disclosed principal A principal whose identity is unknown by a third person, but the third person knows that the agent is or may be acting for a principal at the time the contract is made.

Partnership An association of two or more persons to carry on, as co-owners, a business for profit.

Past consideration An act done before the contract is made, which ordinarily, by itself, cannot be consideration for a later promise to pay for the act.

Patent A government grant that gives an inventor the exclusive right or privilege to make, use, or sell his or her invention for a limited time period. The word *patent* usually refers to some invention and designates either the instrument by which patent rights are evidenced or the patent itself.

Payee A person to whom an instrument is made payable.

Payor bank A bank on which an item is payable as drawn (or is payable as accepted).

Penalty A sum inserted into a contract, not as a measure of compensation for its breach but rather as punishment for a default. The agreement as to the amount will not be enforced, and recovery will be limited to actual damages.

Per capita A Latin term meaning *per person*. In the law governing estate distribution, a method of distributing the property of an intestate's estate by which all the heirs receive equal shares.

Per se In itself; inherent.

Per se **violation** A type of anticompetitive agreement—such as a price-fixing agreement—that is considered to be so injurious to the public that there is no need to determine whether it actually injures market competition; rather, it is in itself (*per se*) a violation of the Sherman Act; economic practices that are themselves considered to be inherently harmful to competition.

Per stirpes A Latin term meaning *by the roots*. In the law governing estate distribution, a method of distributing an intestate's estate in which a class or group of distributees take the share to which their deceased ancestor would have been entitled.

Perfect tender rule A common law rule under which

a seller was required to deliver to the buyer goods that conformed perfectly to the requirements stipulated in the sales contract. A tender of nonconforming goods would automatically constitute a breach of contract. Under the UCC, the rule has been greatly modified.

Perfection The method by which a secured party obtains a priority by notice that his or her security interest in the debtor's collateral is effective against the debtor's subsequent creditors. Usually accomplished by filing a financing statement at a location set out in the state statute.

Performance In contract law, the fulfillment of one's duties arising under a contract with another; the normal way of discharging one's contractual obligations.

Periodic tenancy A lease interest in land for an indefinite period involving payment of rent at fixed intervals, such as week to week, month to month, or year to year.

Personal defenses Defenses that can be used to avoid payment to an ordinary holder of a negotiable instrument. Personal defenses cannot be used to avoid payment to a holder in due course (HDC) or (under the shelter principle) to a holder through an HDC.

Personal identification number (PIN) A number given to the holder of an access card that is used to conduct financial transactions in electronic fund transfer systems. Typically, the card will not provide access to a system without the number, which is meant to be kept secret to inhibit unauthorized use of the card.

Personal property Property that is movable; any property that is not real property.

Personalty Personal property.

Petition in bankruptcy An application to a bankruptcy court for relief in bankruptcy; filing for bankruptcy. The official forms required for a petition in bankruptcy must be completed accurately, sworn to under oath, and signed by the debtor.

Petitioner The party who presents a petition to a court, initiates an equity proceeding, or appeals from a judgment.

Petty offense In criminal law, the least serious kind of wrong, such as a traffic or building-code violation.

Plaintiff One who initiates a lawsuit.

Plea bargaining The process by which the accused and the prosecutor in a criminal case work out a mutually satisfactory disposition of the case, subject to court approval. Usually involves the defendant's pleading guilty to a lesser offense in return for a lighter sentence.

Pleadings Statements by the plaintiff and the defendant that detail the facts, charges, and defenses. Modern rules simplify common law pleading, often requiring only the complaint, an answer, and sometimes a reply to the answer.

Pledge The bailment of personal property to a creditor as security for the payment of a debt.

Point-of-sale system An electronic customer-bank-merchant communication terminal that, when activated by an access card and a personal identification number, can debit the customer's account to cover a purchase from the merchant.

Police powers Powers possessed by states as part of their inherent sovereignty. These powers may be exercised to protect or promote public health, safety, or morals, or the general welfare.

Policy In insurance law, the contract of indemnity against a contingent loss between the insurer and the insured.

Positive law The objective laws legally created by a society, as opposed to natural law or the unwritten laws arising from social customs; also called *black-letter law.*

Positivist school A school of legal thought that holds that there can be no higher law than a nation's positive law—law created by a particular society at a particular point in time. In contrast to the natural law school, the positivist school maintains that there are no ''natural'' rights; rights come into existence only when there is a sovereign power (government) to confer and enforce those rights.

Possibility of reverter A future interest in land that a grantor retains after conveying property subject to a condition subsequent (for example, if a certain future event occurs, the interest in the estate will terminate automatically).

Potential competition doctrine A doctrine under which a conglomerate merger may be prohibited by law because it would be injurious to potential competition. Potential competition is the competitive effect that a firm has on a market even though the firm does not operate in the market. The firm's effect is felt by its ''waiting in the wings''—ready to enter the market if firms already in the market begin to earn supranormal profits by charging noncompetitive prices. This potential competition is lost if the firm that is waiting in the wings merges with a dominant firm in the industry.

Power of attorney A document or instrument authorizing another to act as one's agent or attorney.

Preauthorized transfer A transaction authorized in advance to recur at substantially regular intervals. The terms and procedure for preauthorized electronic fund transfers through certain financial institutions are subject to the Electronic Fund Transfer Act.

Precedent A court decision that furnishes an example or authority for deciding subsequent cases in which identical or similar facts are presented.

Predatory pricing The pricing by a company of its products with the intent of driving its competitors out of business.

Preemptive rights Rights held by shareholders that entitle them to purchase newly issued shares of a corporation's stock, equal in percentage to shares presently held, before the stock is offered to any outside buyers.

Preemptive rights enable shareholders to maintain their proportionate ownership and voice in the corporation.

Preference In bankruptcy proceedings, the debtor's favoring of one creditor over others by making payments or transferring property to that creditor at the expense of the rights of other creditors in the bankruptcy estate. The bankruptcy trustee is allowed to recover payments made both voluntarily and involuntarily to one creditor in preference over another.

Preferred stock Classes of stock that have priority over common stock both as to payment of dividends and distribution of assets upon the corporation's dissolution.

Prejudgment interest Interest that accrues on the amount of a court judgment from the time of the filing of the suit to the issuing of the judgment.

Premium In insurance law, the price for insurance protection for a specified period of time.

Presentment warranty An implied warranty, made by any person who seeks payment or acceptance of a negotiable instrument to any person who in good faith pays or accepts the instrument, that the party presenting the instrument has good title to the instrument or is authorized to obtain payment or acceptance on behalf of a person who has good title, has no knowledge that the signature of the maker or the drawer is unauthorized, and has no knowledge that the instrument has been materially altered [UCC 3-417(1), 3-418].

Pretrial motion A written or oral application to a court for a ruling or order, made before trial.

Price discrimination Setting prices in such a way that two competing buyers pay two different prices for an identical product or service.

Price fixing Fixing—by means of an anticompetitive agreement between competitors—the prices of products or services.

Prima facie **case** A case in which the plaintiff has produced sufficient evidence of his or her conclusion that the case can go to a jury; a case in which the evidence compels the plaintiff's conclusion if the defendant produces no evidence to rebut it.

Principal In agency law, a person who, by agreement or otherwise, authorizes an agent to act on his or her behalf in such a way that the acts of the agent become binding on the principal.

Private law Law governing the behavior of individual members of society as that behavior affects other individuals. Examples of private law are contract law and tort law.

Privilege In tort law, the ability to act contrary to another person's right without that person's having legal redress for such acts. Privilege is usually raised as a defense.

Privity of contract The relationship that exists between the promisor and the promisee of a contract.

Probable cause Reasonable grounds to believe the ex-

istence of facts warranting certain actions, such as the search or arrest of a person.

Probate The process of proving and validating a will and the settling of all matters pertaining to administration, guardianship, and like matters.

Probate court A court having jurisdiction over proceedings concerning the settlement of a person's estate.

Procedural rules Rules that define the manner in which the rights and duties of individuals may be enforced.

Proceeds In secured transactions law, whatever is received when the collateral is sold, exchanged, collected, or otherwise disposed of, such as insurance payments for destroyed or lost collateral. Money, checks, and the like are *cash proceeds,* whereas all other proceeds received are *noncash proceeds.*

Product liability The legal liability of manufacturers and sellers to buyers, users, and sometimes bystanders for injuries or damages suffered because of defects in goods purchased. Liability arises when a product has a defective condition that makes it unreasonably dangerous to the user or consumer.

Product misuse A defense against product liability that may be raised when the plaintiff used a product in a manner not intended by the manufacturer. If the misuse is reasonably foreseeable, the seller will not escape liability unless measures were taken to guard against the harm that could result from the misuse.

Professional corporation A corporation formed by professional persons, such as physicians, lawyers, dentists, and accountants, to gain tax benefits. Subject to certain exceptions (when a court may treat a professional corporation as a partnership for liability purposes), the shareholders of a professional corporation have the limited liability characteristic of the corporate form of business.

Profit In real property law, the right to enter upon and remove things from the property of another (for example, the right to enter onto a person's land and remove sand and gravel therefrom).

Profit appurtenant The right to take something from a parcel of land such as minerals or timber that passes with the benefitted land itself rather than the owner.

Profit in gross A right to take something from a parcel of land such as minerals or timber that is personal to the profit holder and not dependent on his or her ownership of a particular parcel of land.

Promise A declaration that binds the person who makes it (promisor) to do or not to do a certain act. The person to whom the promise is made (promisee) has a right to expect or demand the performance of some particular thing.

Promisee A person to whom a promise is made.

Promisor A person who makes a promise.

Promissory estoppel A doctrine that applies when a promisor reasonably expects a promise to induce definite and substantial action or forbearance by the promisee, and that does induce such action or forbearance in reliance thereon; such a promise is binding if injustice can be avoided only by enforcing the promise. *See also* Estoppel.

Promissory note A written instrument signed by a maker unconditionally promising to pay a certain sum in money to a payee or a holder on demand or on a specified date.

Promoter An entrepreneur who participates in the organization of a corporation in its formative stage, usually by issuing a prospectus, procuring subscriptions to the stock, making contract purchases, securing a charter, and the like.

Property The legally protected rights and interests a person has in anything with an ascertainable value that is subject to ownership. *See also* Personal property; Real property.

Protected class A class of persons with identifiable characteristics who historically have been victimized by discriminatory treatment for certain purposes. Depending on the context, these characteristics include age, color, gender, national origin, race, and religion.

Proximate cause The "next" or "substantial" cause; in tort law, a concept used to determine whether a plaintiff's injury was the natural and continuous result of a defendant's negligent act. If the negligent act of a defendant was the sole cause or a substantial cause of injuries to a plaintiff, the defendant will be liable.

Proxy In corporation law, a written agreement between a stockholder and another under which the stockholder authorizes the other to vote the stockholder's shares in a certain manner.

Public figures Individuals who are thrust into the public limelight. Public figures include government officials and politicians, movie stars, well-known businesspersons, and generally anybody who becomes known to the public because of his or her position or activities.

Public law Law governing the relationships between individuals and their government. Examples of public law are administrative law, constitutional law, and criminal law.

Puffing A salesperson's often exaggerated claims concerning the quality of the goods offered for sale. Such claims involve opinions rather than facts and are not considered to be legally binding promises or warranties.

Punitive damages Compensation in excess of actual or consequential damages. They are awarded in order to punish the wrongdoer and usually will be awarded only in cases involving willful or malicious misconduct.

Purchase-money security interest A security interest to the extent that it is (1) taken or retained by a seller of the collateral to secure all or part of the price of the collateral or (2) taken by a creditor who, by making advances or incurring an obligation, gives value to en-

able the debtor to acquire rights in, or use of, the collateral, if such value is in fact so used.

Q

Qualified indorsement An indorsement on a negotiable instrument by which the indorser disclaims to subsequent holders secondary liability on the instrument; the most common qualified indorsement is "without recourse."

Quantum meruit Literally, "as much as he deserves"—an expression describing the extent of liability on a contract implied in law (quasi contract). An equitable doctrine based on the concept that one who benefits from another's labor and materials should not be unjustly enriched thereby but should be required to pay a reasonable amount for the benefits received, even absent a contract.

Quasi contract An obligation or contract imposed by law, in the absence of agreement, to prevent unjust enrichment. Sometimes referred to as an implied-in-law contract (a legal fiction) to distinguish it from an implied-in-fact contract.

Questions of fact In lawsuits, issues involving factual disputes that can be decided by a jury.

Questions of law In lawsuits, issues involving the application or interpretation of law; therefore, the judge, and not the jury, decides the issues.

Quitclaim deed A deed intended to pass any title, interest, or claim that the grantor may have in the premises but not professing that such title is valid and not containing any warranty or covenants of title.

R

Ratification The approval or validation of a previous action. In contract law, the confirmation of a voidable act (that is, an act that without ratification would not be an enforceable contractual obligation). In agency law, the confirmation by one person of an act or contract performed or entered into on his or her behalf by another, who assumed, without authority, to act as his or her agent.

Reaffirmation agreement An agreement between a debtor and a creditor in which the debtor reaffirms, or promises to pay, a debt dischargeable in bankruptcy. To be enforceable, the agreement must be made prior to the discharge of the debt by the bankruptcy court.

Real property Immovable property consisting of land and buildings thereupon, as opposed to personal property, which can be moved. In the absence of a contract, real property includes things growing on the land before they are severed (such as timber), as well as fixtures.

Reasonable care The degree of care that a person of ordinary prudence would exercise in the same or similar circumstances.

Reasonable doubt *See* Beyond a reasonable doubt.

Reasonable person standard The standard of behavior expected of a hypothetical ''reasonable person.'' The standard against which negligence is measured and that must be observed to avoid liability for negligence.

Rebuttal The refutation of evidence introduced by an adverse party's attorney.

Receiver A court-appointed person who receives, preserves, and manages a business or other property that is involved in bankruptcy proceedings.

Recording statutes Statutes requiring that deeds, mortgages, and other real property transactions be recorded so as to provide notice to future purchasers, creditors, and encumbrancers of an existing claim on the property.

Red herring A preliminary prospectus that can be distributed to potential investors after the registration statement (for a securities offering) has been filed with the Securities and Exchange Commission. The name derives from the red legend printed across the prospectus stating that the registration has been filed but has not become effective.

Redemption A repurchase, or buying back. In secured transactions law, a debtor's repurchase of collateral securing a debt after a creditor has taken title to the collateral due to the debtor's default but before the secured party disposes of it.

Reformation A court-ordered correction of a written contract so that it reflects the true intentions of the parties.

Regulation E A set of rules issued by the Federal Reserve System's board of governors under the authority of the Electronic Fund Transfer Act to protect users of electronic fund transfer systems.

Regulation Z A set of rules promulgated by the Federal Reserve System's board of governors to implement the provisions of the Truth-in-Lending Act.

Rejoinder The defendant's answer to the plaintiff's rebuttal.

Release The relinquishment, concession, or giving up of a right, claim, or privilege, by the person in whom it exists or to whom it accrues, to the person against whom it might have been enforced or demanded.

Remainder A future interest in property, held by a person other than the grantor, that occurs at the natural termination of the preceding estate.

Remanded Sent back. If an appellate court disagrees with a lower court's judgment, the case may be remanded to the lower court for further proceedings, in which the lower court's decision should be consistent with the appellate court's opinion on the matter.

Remedy The relief given to innocent parties, by law or by contract, to enforce a right or to prevent or compensate for the violation of a right.

Remedy at law A remedy available in a court of law. Money damages are awarded as a remedy at law.

Remedy in equity A remedy allowed by courts in situations where remedies at law are not appropriate. Remedies in equity are based on settled rules of fairness, justice, and honesty.

Rent escalation An increase in rent during a lease term according to a lease clause.

Repair-and-deduct statutes Statutes providing that a tenant may pay for repairs and deduct the cost of the repairs from the rent, as a remedy for a landlord's failure to maintain leased premises.

Replevin An action brought to recover the possession of personal property unlawfully held by another.

Reply Procedurally, a plaintiff's response to a defendant's answer.

Requirements contract An agreement under which a promisor promises to supply the promisee with all the goods and/or services the promisee might require from period to period.

Res ipsa loquitur A doctrine under which negligence may be inferred simply because an event occurred, if it is the type of event that would not occur absent negligence. Literally, the term means *the thing speaks for itself.*

Resale price maintenance agreement An agreement between a manufacturer and a retailer in which the manufacturer specifies the minimum retail price of its products. Resale price maintenance agreements are illegal *per se* under the Sherman Act.

Rescission A remedy whereby a contract is terminated and the parties are returned to the positions they occupied before the contract was made; may be effected through the mutual consent of the parties, by their conduct, or by the decree of a court of equity.

Respondeat superior In Latin, ''Let the master respond.'' A principle of law whereby a principal or an employer is held liable for the wrongful acts committed by agents or employees while acting within the scope of their agency or employment.

Respondent In equity practice, the party who answers a bill or other proceeding. In appellate practice, the party against whom an appeal is taken (sometimes referred to as the appellee).

Restitution An equitable remedy under which a person is restored to his or her original position prior to loss or injury, or placed in the position he or she would have been in had the breach not occurred.

Restraints of trade Any conspiracy or combination that unlawfully eliminates competition or facilitates the creation of a monopoly or monopoly pricing.

Restrictive indorsement Any indorsement of a negotiable instrument that purports to condition or prohibit further transfer of the instrument. As against payor and intermediary banks, such indorsements are usually ineffective.

Resulting trust A trust implied in law from the intentions of the parties to a given transaction. A trust in which a party holds legal title for the benefit of another, although without expressed intent to do so, because the presumption of such intent arises by operation of law.

Retaliatory eviction The eviction of a tenant because of the tenant's complaints, participation in a tenant's union, or similar activity with which the landlord does not agree.

Reversible error An error by a lower court that is sufficiently substantial to justify an appellate court's reversal of the lower court's decision.

Reversion A future interest under which a grantor retains a present right to a future interest in property that the grantor conveys to another; usually the residue of a life estate. The reversion is always a vested property right.

Revocation In contract law, the withdrawal of an offer by an offeror; unless the offer is irrevocable, it can be revoked at any time prior to acceptance without liability.

Rezoning The reclassifying of an existing zoning designation.

Right of contribution The right of a co-surety who pays more than his or her proportionate share upon a debtor's default to recover the excess paid from other co-sureties.

Right of entry The right to peaceably take or resume possession of real property.

Right of first refusal The right to purchase personal or real property—such as corporate shares or real estate—before the property is offered for sale to others.

Right of reimbursement The legal right of a person to be restored, repaid, or indemnified for costs, expenses, or losses incurred or expended on behalf of another.

Right of subrogation The right of a person to stand in the place of (be substituted for) another, giving the substituted party the same legal rights that the original party had.

Right-to-work laws State laws generally providing that employees are not to be required to join a union as a condition of receiving or retaining employment.

Risk A specified contingency or peril.

Risk management Planning that is undertaken to protect one's interest should some event threaten to undermine its security. In the context of insurance, transferring certain risks from the insured to the insurance company.

Robbery Theft from a person, accompanied by force or fear of force.

Rule of four A rule of the United States Supreme Court under which the Court will not issue a writ of *certiorari* unless at least four justices approve of the decision to issue the writ.

Rule of reason A test by which a court balances the reasons (such as economic efficiency) for an agreement against its potentially anticompetitive effects. In antitrust litigation, most practices are analyzed under the rule of reason.

Rule 10b-5 A rule of the Securities and Exchange Commission that makes it unlawful, in connection with the purchase or sale of any security, to make any untrue statement of a material fact or to omit a material fact if such omission causes the statement to be misleading.

Rulemaking The actions undertaken by administrative agencies when formally adopting new regulations or amending old ones. Under the Administrative Procedures Act, rulemaking includes notifying the public of proposed rules or changes and receiving and considering the public's comments.

Rulemaking-on-a-record Agency rulemaking that is much more extensive than informal rulemaking and in which a public hearing is conducted in the manner of a trial. After the hearing is concluded, the agency is required to prepare a formal written statement describing its findings based on the evidence presented by both sides. Also referred to as formal rulemaking.

S

S corporation A close business corporation that has met certain requirements as set out by the Internal Revenue Code and thus qualifies for special income-tax treatment. Essentially, an S corporation is taxed the same as a partnership, but its owners enjoy the privilege of limited liability.

Sale The passing of title to property from the seller to the buyer for a price.

Sale on approval A type of conditional sale that becomes absolute only when the buyer approves, or is satisfied with, the good(s) sold. Besides express approval of goods, approval may be inferred if the buyer keeps the goods beyond a reasonable time or uses the goods in any way that is inconsistent with the seller's ownership.

Sale or return A type of conditional sale wherein title and possession pass from the seller to the buyer; however, the buyer retains the option to rescind or return the goods during a specified period even though the goods conform to the contract.

Scienter Knowledge by the misrepresenting party that material facts have been falsely represented or omitted with an intent to deceive.

Searches and seizures The searching or taking into custody of persons or private property by the government. Unreasonable and unwarranted searches and seizures are prohibited by the Fourth Amendment. In the context of administrative law, searches and seizures may be undertaken by administrative agencies to gather information and necessary evidence to prove that a regulation has been violated.

Secondary boycott A union's refusal to work for, purchase from, or handle the products of a secondary employer, with whom the union has no dispute, with the object of forcing that employer to stop doing business with the primary employer, with whom the union has a labor dispute.

Secured party A lender, seller, or any other person in whose favor there is a security interest, including a person to whom accounts or chattel paper has been sold.

Secured transaction Any transaction, regardless of its form, that is intended to create a security interest in personal property or fixtures, including goods, documents, and other intangibles.

Securities Stock certificates, bonds, notes, debentures, warrants, or other documents given as evidence of an ownership interest in the corporation or as a promise of repayment by the corporation.

Security agreement The agreement that creates or provides for a security interest between the debtor and a secured party.

Security interest Every interest "in *personal property or fixtures* [emphasis added] that secures payment or performance of an obligation" [UCC 1-201(37)].

Self-defense The legally recognized privilege to protect one's self or property against injury by another. The privilege of self-defense only protects acts that are reasonably necessary to protect one's self or property.

Service mark A mark used in the sale or the advertising of services, such as to distinguish the services of one person from the services of others. Titles, character names, and other distinctive features of radio and television programs may be registered as service marks.

Severance pay Funds in excess of normal wages or salaries paid to an employee upon termination of his or her employment with a company.

Sham transaction A false transaction without substance that is undertaken with the intent to defraud a creditor or the government. An example of a sham transaction is the sale of assets to a friend or relative for the purpose of concealing assets from creditors or a bankruptcy court.

Shareholder's derivative suit A suit brought by a shareholder to enforce a corporate cause of action against a third person.

Shelter principle The principle that the holder of a negotiable instrument who cannot qualify as a holder in due course (HDC), but who derives his or her title through an HDC, acquires the rights of an HDC.

Short-form merger A merger between a subsidiary corporation and a parent corporation that owns at least 90 percent of the outstanding shares of each class of stock issued by the subsidiary corporation. Short-form mergers can be accomplished without the approval of the shareholders of either corporation.

Signature The name or mark of a person, written by that person or at his or her direction. In commercial law, any name, word, or mark used with the intention to authenticate a writing constitutes a signature.

Slander An oral defamation of one's character, reputation, business, or property rights.

Slander of quality Publication of false information about another's product, alleging it is not what its seller claims; also referred to as trade libel.

Slander of title The publication of a statement that denies or casts doubt upon another's legal ownership of any property, causing financial loss to that property's owner.

Small claims courts Special courts in which parties may litigate small claims (usually, claims involving $2,500 or less). Attorneys are not required in small claims courts, and in many states, attorneys are not allowed to represent the parties.

Sole proprietorship The simplest form of business, in which the owner is the business; thus, anyone who does business without creating a formal business entity has a sole proprietorship. The owner of a sole proprietorship reports business income on his or her personal income tax return and is legally responsible for all debts and obligations incurred by the business.

Sovereign immunity A doctrine that immunizes foreign nations from the jurisdiction of U.S. courts when certain conditions are satisfied.

Special indorsement An indorsement on an instrument that specifies to whom or to whose order the instrument is payable.

Special warranty deed A deed in which the grantor only covenants to warrant and defend the title against claims and demands of the grantor and all persons claiming by, through, and under the grantor.

Specific performance An equitable remedy requiring *exactly* the performance that was specified in a contract. Usually granted only when money damages would be an inadequate remedy and the subject matter of the contract is unique (for example, real property).

Spendthrift trust A trust created to protect the beneficiary from spending all the money to which he or she is entitled. Only a certain portion of the total amount is given to the beneficiary at any one time, and most states prohibit creditors from attaching assets of the trust.

Spot zoning Granting a zoning classification to a parcel of land that is different from the classification given to other land in the immediate area.

Stale check A check, other than a certified check, that is presented for payment more than six months after its date.

Standing The requirement that an individual must have a sufficient stake in a controversy before he or she can bring a lawsuit. The plaintiff must demonstrate that he or she either has been injured or threatened with injury.

Stare decisis A flexible doctrine of the courts, recognizing the value of following prior decisions (precedents) in cases similar to the one before the court; the courts' practice of being consistent with prior decisions based on similar facts.

Statute of Frauds A state statute under which certain types of contracts must be in writing to be enforceable.

Statute of limitations A statute of the federal government or state government setting the maximum time period during which certain actions can be brought or rights enforced. After the time period set out in the applicable statute of limitations has run, no legal action can be brought.

Statute of repose Basically, a statute of limitations that is not dependent upon the happening of a cause of action. Statutes of repose generally begin to run at an earlier date and run for a longer period of time than statutes of limitations.

Statutory law Laws enacted by a legislative body (as opposed to constitutional law, administrative law, or case law).

Statutory period of redemption A time period (usually set by state statute) during which the property subject to a defaulted mortgage, land contract, or other contract can be redeemed by the debtor after foreclosure or judicial sale.

Stock In corporation law, an equity or ownership interest in a corporation, measured in units of shares.

Stock certificate A certificate issued by a corporation evidencing the ownership of a specified number of shares at a specified value.

Stock warrant A certificate commonly attached to preferred stock and bonds that grants the owner the right to buy a given number of shares of stock, usually within a set time period.

Stop-payment order An order by the drawer of a draft or check directing the drawer's bank not to pay the check.

Strict liability Liability regardless of fault. In tort law, strict liability is imposed on a merchant who introduces into commerce a good that is unreasonably dangerous when in a defective condition.

Sublease A lease executed by the lessee of real estate to a third person, conveying the same interest that the lessee enjoys, but for a shorter term than that held by the lessee (as compared with an assignment of a lease, in which the lessee transfers the entire unexpired term of the leasehold to a third party).

Submission An agreement by two or more parties to refer any disputes they may have under their contract to a disinterested third party, such as an arbitrator, who has the power to render a binding decision.

Subpoena A document commanding a person to appear at a certain time and place to give testimony concerning a certain matter.

Substantive law Law that defines the rights and duties of individuals with respect to each other, as opposed to procedural law, which defines the manner in which these rights and duties may be enforced.

Summary judgment A judgment entered by a trial court prior to trial that is based on the valid assertion by one of the parties that there are no disputed issues of fact that would necessitate a trial.

Summary jury trial A relatively recent method of settling disputes in which a trial is held but the jury's verdict is not binding. The verdict only acts as a guide to both sides in reaching an agreement during the mandatory negotiations that immediately follow the trial. If a settlement is not reached, both sides have the right to a full trial later.

Summons A document informing a person that a legal action has been commenced against him or her and that he or she must appear in court on a certain date to answer the plaintiff's complaint. The document is delivered by a sheriff or other official.

Supremacy clause The clause in Article VI of the Constitution that provides that the Constitution, laws, and treaties of the United States are ''the supreme Law of the Land.'' Under this clause, state laws that directly conflict with federal law will be rendered invalid.

Surety One who agrees to be primarily responsible for the debt of another, such as a cosigner on a note.

Suretyship A contract in which a third party to a debtor-creditor relationship (the surety) promises that the third party will be primarily responsible for the debtor's obligation.

T

Target corporation The acquired corporation in a corporate takeover; a corporation to whose shareholders a tender offer is submitted.

Technology licensing Allowing another to use and profit from intellectual property (patents, copyrights, trademarks, innovative products or processes, and so on) for consideration. In the context of international business transactions, technology licensing sometimes is an attractive alternative to the establishment of foreign production facilities.

Tenancy at sufferance Tenancy by one who, after rightfully being in possession of leased premises, continues (wrongfully) to occupy the property after the lease has been terminated. The tenant has no estate in the land and occupies it only because the person entitled to evict has not done so.

Tenancy at will The right of a tenant to remain in possession of land with permission of the landlord until either the tenant or the landlord chooses to terminate the tenancy.

Tenancy by the entirety The joint ownership of property by husband and wife. Neither party can alienate or encumber the property without the consent of the other. The property is inherited by the survivor of the two, and dissolution of marriage transforms a tenancy by the entirety into a tenancy in common.

Tenancy for years A nonfreehold estate/lease for a specified period of time, after which the interest reverts to the grantor.

Tenancy in common Co-ownership of property in which each party owns an undivided interest that passes to his or her heirs at death.

Tender A timely offer or expression of willingness to pay a debt or perform an obligation.

Term insurance A type of life insurance policy for which premiums are paid for a specified term. Payment on the policy is due only if death occurs within the term period. Premiums are less expensive than for whole life or limited-payment life, and there is usually no cash surrender value.

Testamentary trust A trust that is created by will and therefore does not take effect until the death of the testator.

Testator One who makes and executes a will.

Third party beneficiary contract A contract between two or more parties, the performance of which is intended to benefit a third party directly, thus giving the third party a right to file suit for breach of contract by either of the original contracting parties.

Tippee A person who receives inside information.

Title insurance Insurance commonly purchased by a purchaser of real property to protect against loss in the event that the title to the property is not free from liens or superior ownership claims.

Tombstone ad An advertisement, in a format resembling a tombstone, of a securities offering. The ad informs potential investors of where and how they may obtain a prospectus.

Tort Civil (as opposed to criminal) wrongs not arising from a breach of contract. A breach of a legal duty owed by the defendant to the plaintiff; the breach must be the proximate cause of the harm done to the plaintiff.

Tortfeasor One who commits a tort.

Totten trust A trust created by the deposit of a person's own money in his or her own name as a trustee for another. It is a tentative trust, revocable at will until the depositor dies or completes the gift in his or her lifetime by some unequivocal act or declaration.

Trade libel The publication of false information about another's product, alleging it is not what its seller claims; also referred to as slander of quality.

Trade name A name used in commercial activity to designate a particular business, a place at which a business is located, or a class of goods. Trade names can be exclusive or nonexclusive. Examples of trade names are Sears, Safeway, and Firestone.

Trade secrets Information or processes that give a business an advantage over competitors who do not know the information or processes.

Trademark A word or symbol that has become sufficiently associated with a good (at common law) or has been registered with a government agency. Once a trademark is established, the owner has exclusive use of it and has the right to bring a legal action against those who infringe upon the protection given the trademark.

Tradeoff A desired result that one must sacrifice (trade off) to obtain another desired result.

Transfer warranties Warranties (guaranties) made by the indorser and transferor of a negotiable instrument to all subsequent transferees and holders who take the instrument in good faith that (1) the transferor has good title to the instrument or is otherwise authorized to obtain payment or acceptance on behalf of one who does have good title; (2) all signatures are genuine or authorized; (3) the instrument has not been materially altered; (4) no defense of any party is good against the transferor; and (5) the transferor has no knowledge of any insolvency proceedings against the maker, the acceptor, or the drawer of an unaccepted instrument.

Transferee In negotiable instruments law, one to whom a negotiable instrument is transferred (delivered).

Transferor In negotiable instruments law, one who transfers (delivers) a negotiable instrument to another.

Traveler's check An instrument purchased from a bank, express company, or the like, in various denominations, that can be used as cash upon a second signature by the purchaser. It has the characteristics of a cashier's check.

Treasure trove Money or coin, gold, silver, or bullion found hidden in the earth or other private place, the owner of which is unknown; literally, treasure found.

Treble damages Damages consisting of single damages determined by a jury and tripled in amount in certain cases as required by statute.

Trespass to land At common law, the intentional or unintentional passing over another person's land uninvited, regardless of whether any physical damage is done to the land. Today a majority of courts find trespass only in cases of intentional intrusion, negligence, or some "abnormally dangerous activity" on the part of the defendant.

Trespass to personal property Any wrongful transgression or offense against the personal property of another.

Trust (1) A form of business organization somewhat similar to a corporation. Originally, the trust was a device by which several corporations that were engaged in the same general line of business combined for their mutual advantage to eliminate competition and control the market for their products. The term *trust* derived from the transfer of the voting power of the corporations' shareholders to the committee or board that controlled the organization. (2) An arrangement in which title to property is held by one person (a trustee) for the benefit of another (a beneficiary).

Trustee One who holds title to property for the use or

benefit of another (the beneficiary).

Tying arrangement An agreement between a buyer and a seller under which the buyer of a specific product or service is obligated to purchase additional products or services from the seller.

U

Ultra vires A Latin term meaning *beyond the powers.* Activities of a corporation's managers that are outside the scope of the power granted them by the corporation's charter or the laws of the state of incorporation are *ultra vires* acts.

Unconscionable contract or clause A contract or clause that is void on the basis of public policy because one party, as a result of his or her disproportionate bargaining power, is forced to accept terms that are unfairly burdensome and that unfairly benefit the dominating party.

Underwriter In insurance law, the one assuming a risk in return for the payment of a premium; the insurer. In securities law, any person, banker, or syndicate that guarantees a definite sum of money to a business or government in return for the issue of stock or bonds, usually for resale purposes.

Undisclosed principal A principal whose identity is unknown by a third person, and the third person has no knowledge that the agent is acting in an agency capacity at the time the contract is made.

Unenforceable contract A valid contract having no legal effect or force in a court action.

Unilateral contract A contract that includes the exchange of a promise for an act.

Union shop A place of employment in which all workers, once employed, must become union members within a specified period of time as a condition of their continued employment.

U.S. trustee A government official who performs appointing and other administrative tasks that a bankruptcy judge would otherwise have to perform.

Universal defenses Defenses that can be used to avoid payment to all holders of a negotiable instrument, including a holder in due course (HDC) or (under the shelter principle) a holder through an HDC. Also called *real defenses.*

Universal life A type of insurance that combines some aspects of term insurance with some aspects of whole life insurance.

Unlawful detainer The unjustifiable retention of the possession of real property by one whose right to possession has terminated—as when a tenant holds over after the end of the lease term in spite of the landlord's demand for possession.

Unreasonably dangerous product In product liability, a product that is defective to the point of threatening a consumer's health and safety. A product will be considered unreasonably dangerous if it is dangerous beyond the expectation of the ordinary consumer or if a less dangerous alternative was economically feasible for the manufacturer, but the manufacturer failed to produce it.

Usage of trade Any practice or method of dealing having such regularity of observance in a place, vocation, or trade as to justify an expectation that it will be observed with respect to the transaction in question.

Use zoning Zoning classifications within a particular municipality that may be distinguished based upon the uses to which the land is to be put.

Usury Charging an illegal rate of interest.

Utilitarianism An approach to ethical reasoning in which ethically correct behavior is not related to any absolute ethical or moral values but to an evaluation of the consequences of a given action on those who will be affected by it. In utilitarian reasoning, a "good" decision is one that results in the greatest good for the greatest number of people affected by the decision.

V

Valid contract A properly constituted contract having legal strength or force.

Variances Official grants of permission by the relevant public agencies to landowners to depart from the strict requirements of the zoning laws so as to avoid undue hardship.

Venue The geographical district in which an action is tried and from which the jury is selected.

Vertical merger A combining of two firms, one of which purchases goods for resale from the other. If a producer or wholesaler acquires a retailer, it is a *forward* vertical merger. If a retailer or distributor acquires its producer, it is a *backward* vertical merger.

Vertically integrated firms Firms that operate on more than one level of the production and distribution process for a particular product.

Vested right A right possessed by an owner who is building a structure in conformity with zoning laws that have since been revised that will permit him or her to use the structure as was originally contemplated under the original zoning laws.

Vesting The creation of an absolute or unconditional right or power.

Void contract A contract having no legal force or binding effect.

Voidable contract A contract that may be legally annulled at the option of one of the parties.

Voir dire From the French, meaning "to speak the truth." A phrase denoting the preliminary questions that attorneys for the plaintiff and the defendant ask prospective jurors to determine whether potential jury members are biased or have any connection with a party to the action or with a prospective witness.

Voting trust The transfer of title by stockholders of shares of a corporation to a trustee who is authorized to vote the shares on their behalf.

W

Waiver An intentional, knowing relinquishment of a legal right.

Warranty deed A deed under which the grantor guarantees to the grantee that the grantor has title to the property conveyed in the deed, that there are no encumbrances on the property other than what the grantor has represented, and that the grantee will enjoy quiet possession.

Waste The abuse or destructive use of real property by one who is in rightful possession of the property but who does not have title to it. Waste does not include ordinary depreciation due to age and normal use.

Watered stock Stock issued by a corporation as if fully paid for, when in fact less than par value has been paid.

Whistleblowing Telling the government or the press that one's employer is engaged in some unsafe or illegal activity.

White-collar crime Nonviolent crime committed by corporations and individuals. Embezzlement and commercial bribery are two examples of white-collar crime.

Whole life A life insurance policy in which the insured pays a level premium for his or her entire life and in which there is a constantly accumulating cash value that can be withdrawn or borrowed against by the borrower. Sometimes referred to as straight life insurance.

Wildcat strike A strike that is not authorized by the union that ordinarily represents the striking employees.

Will An instrument directing what is to be done with the testator's property upon his or her death, made by the testator and revocable during his or her lifetime. No interests pass until the testator dies.

Winding up The second of two stages involved in the dissolution of a partnership or corporation. Once the firm is dissolved, it continues to exist legally until the process of winding up all business affairs (collecting and distributing the firm's assets) is complete.

Workers' compensation laws State statutes establishing an administrative procedure for compensating workers' injuries that arise out of, or in the course of, their employment, regardless of fault. Instead of suing the employer, an injured worker files a claim with the administrative agency or board that administers the local workers' compensation claims.

Working papers The various documents used and developed by an accountant during an audit. Working papers include notes, computations, memoranda, copies, and other papers that make up the work product of an accountant's services to a client.

Workout A common law or bankruptcy out-of-court negotiation with creditors in which a debtor enters into an agreement with a creditor or creditors for a payment or plan to discharge the debtor's debt(s).

Workout team Individuals specifically designated by a lending institution to negotiate the terms of a workout arrangement with a major debtor when the debtor is in default. The team normally does not include the loan officer who approved the loan that is in default.

Writ of attachment A writ employed to enforce obedience to an order or judgment of the court. The writ may take the form of taking or seizing property to bring it under the control of the court.

Writ of *certiorari* A writ from a higher court asking the lower court for the record of a case.

Writ of execution A writ that puts in force a court's decree or judgment.

Z

Zoning law A law passed by the relevant public authority that relates to the local zoning plan.

Zoning map A map of a municipality or other political subdivision that designates the various zoning classifications given to the lands within its boundaries.

Zoning ordinance A municipal law or statute that specifies the restrictions to which a designated parcel of land is subject.

Zoning The political process by which varied land use designations are given to specific lands within a municipality or other political subdivision.

Zoning variance The granting of permission by a municipality or other public board to a landowner to use his or her property in a way that does not strictly conform with the zoning regulations so as to avoid causing the landowner undue hardship.

Table of Cases

The principal cases are in bold type. Cases cited or discussed are in roman type. Cases that can also be retrieved on West's LEGAL CLERK Research Software System are indicated by a colored dot. To determine which of the three versions of LEGAL CLERK a particular case appears on, please turn to the text page cited and refer to the color-coded computer symbol printed with the case citation.

A black computer symbol with a white background indicates that the case appears on *Uniform Commercial Code Article 2 Sales-Version 1.0.* A black computer symbol with a grey background indicates that the case is on *Government Regulation and the Legal Environment of Business-Version 1.0.* A black computer symbol with a light red background identifies the case as appearing on *Contracts-Version 1.0.*

Index

requirements, 230
requirements of, 200–201
for the sale of goods. *See* Sales contracts
to sell, versus sale, 234
Statute of Frauds and, 216–217
suretyship, 278–280
terms of,
    additional, in acceptance, 231
    definiteness in, 202, 204
    openness of, in sales contracts, 229–230
third party rights in, 217–220
types of, 201–202
unconscionable, 215–216
unenforceable, 202
unilateral, 201
"union security clauses" in, 405
valid, 202
void, 202
voidable, 202
warranties and. *See* Warranties
Contractual relationship, wrongful interference with. *See* Wrongful interference
Contribution, right of, 280
Contributory negligence, 162, 258, 269
Control premium, 340–341
Convention on Contracts for the International Sale of Goods (CISG), 13, 14
compared to Article 2 of the UCC, 651, 658
Conversion, 153–155
Conyers, John, Jr., 183n
Cooperation:
principal's duty of, 367
in sales contracts, 242
Cooperative, 319–320
Copyright, 618–624
for computer software, 622–623
defined, 618
expression protected by, 620–622
fair use doctrine and, 619
infringement of, 619–620
international issues concerning, 623–624
in works created by independent contractors, 360–361
Copyright Act of 1976, 360, 619, 620, 621, 622
Core proceedings, 282
Corporate crime, 169, 183–186, 195–196
Corporate raiders, 598, 643–644
Corporate takeovers. *See* Takeovers
Corporate veil, piercing of, 78, 312–314
Corporation(s), 303–318, 327–353

acquiring, 609
aggressor, 598
alien, 304
assets of,
    distribution of, on dissolution, 338
    purchase of, 609–611
business records of. *See* Corporation(s), records of
C, 308
capital structure of, 311
charter of, 312
classification of, 304–308
commercial speech by, 109–113, 192. *See also* Speech, freedom of
consolidation of. *See* Consolidation
constitutional rights of, 108–111, 112–113, 116–117, 192–194
contracts of, with directors, 330
as creature of statute, 303
crimes by, 169, 183–186, 195–196
de facto, 312
defined, 303
    under Bankruptcy Code, 283n
de jure, 312
directors of. *See* Directors, corporate
disregarding entity of, 312–314
dissolution of,
    shareholders' rights on, 338
    for violating antitrust laws, 482
divestiture of, for violating antitrust laws, 482
dividends issued by, 304, 318, 334–336
domestic, 304
dummy, 598
duration of, 311
eleemosynary, 306
by estoppel, 312
financing of, 312, 519–521. *See also* Securities regulation
foreign, 304–306
formation of, 308–312. *See also* Incorporation
having common directors, contracts between, 330, 482
incorporation of. *See* Incorporation
internal organization of, 311
as legal person, 108, 303–304
liability of,
    for crimes, 183–186, 195–196
    improper incorporation and, 312
    limited, 303
    for preincorporation contracts, 309
    vicarious, 186
    for violating health and safety laws, 427

management of,
    by directors, 304
    shareholders and, 314–317
merger of. *See* Mergers
name of, 311
nature of, 193–194, 303–304
nonprofit, 306
officers of. *See* Officers, corporate
parent, 606
political speech by, 109
private, 306
public, 306
records of,
    director's right to inspect, 332
    Fifth Amendment protection for, 115–117
    shareholder's right to inspect, 336
    stock ownership recorded in, 338
registered office and agent of, 311, 363
S, 308
Section 12, 534, 612
securities of. *See* Bonds; Securities; Stock
shareholders of. *See* Shareholders
shares of. *See* Shares; Stock
subsidiary, 606
successor, liability of, under Superfund, 469–471
surviving, 604
takeover of. *See* Takeovers
target, 598
taxation of, 304, 308
Corporations commissioner, 538
Correspondent banks, 659
Cost(s):
clean-up, liability for,
    of lenders, 591–592
    of successor corporations, 469–471
of litigation, 55
of product liability, reform measures combating, 270–271
search, of consumers, trademarks and, 624
Counteradvertising, 445–446
Counterclaim, 42, 45
Counterfeit Access Device and Computer Fraud and Abuse Act of 1984, 635, 637
Counteroffer, 204–205
Course of dealing, implied warranty arising from, 251
Court(s), 31–54
appellate, 34–37
arbitration compelled by, 71–73
caseload management by, 56–57
chancery. *See* Court(s), equity
constitutional authority for, 10, 103

decisions by
Declaration of Independence, 5
Dedication of land, 553
Deed, easement or profit created by, 557
De facto corporation, 312
Defamation, 103, 147–150. *See also* Libel; Slander
  in business context, 175–178
  by computer, 175–176
  defenses against, 148–150
  defined, 148
  of public figures, 109, 148–150
  publication requirement for, 148
Default, by debtor, 351
  creditors remedies on, 275–280
  ethical aspects of, 563
Default judgment, 42
Defective product, 256, 262, 263
Defendant, 42
Defense(s):
  affirmative, 45
  to assault and battery, 145
  bona fide occupational qualification (BFOQ), 415
  business necessity, 415
  to contract enforcement, 201, 213
  to conversion, 155
  to defamation, 148–150
  to employment discrimination, 415
  of guarantors, 279–280
  to negligence, 162–163e, 258
  of others, 145
  of property, 145
  to product liability, 258, 269
  seniority system, 415
  to strict liability, 269
  of sureties, 279–280
  to takeovers, 599–604
  to trespass to land, 153
  to wrongful interference, 173
Defense Production Act of 1950, 485
Deferred posting, 575
Deficiency judgment, 278
Definiteness of contract terms, 202, 204
  in sales contracts, 229–230
De jure corporation, 312
Delegated powers, 103
Delivery:
  to buyer, 235
  without movement of goods, 234–235, 238
  place of, 239
  tender of, as seller's obligation, 239–242
  term of, 230
Demand draft, 571
Demurrer, 45
De novo review, 71, 135
Department of. *See* U.S. Depart-

ment of
Depositary bank, 575
Depositions, 42
Deposits:
  bank's duty to accept, 574
  direct, 578
Derivative authority, of agent, 357
Derivative suit, shareholder's, 304, 338–339
DES (diethylstilbestrol) cases, 265
Destination contracts, 234, 235
Destruction of subject matter:
  and contract discharge, 221
  and perfect tender rule, 242
  and termination of offer, 206
Detrimental reliance, 206–207, 209–211, 217
Differently abled persons, 421
Direct deposits and withdrawals, 578
Direct examination, during trial, 48
Direct exporting, 654
Directed verdict, motion for, 48, 49
Directors, corporate:
  antitrust law and, 482
  approval by, of merger or consolidation, 605
  compensation of, 332
  contracts of, with corporation, 330
  corporate management by, 317–318
  criminal liability of, 183–186
  dividends declared by, 334. *See also* Dividends
  due care required of, 327–328, 352
  election and removal of, 315, 317
  fiduciary duties of, 315, 317, 327–330, 345
    business judgment rule and, 330–332
    conflict of interests and, 330
    ethics and, 352–353
  indemnification of, 332
  inspection rights of, 332
  loyalty of, to corporate interests, 328–329, 352
  management of corporation by, 304
  meetings of, 318, 327–328
  participation rights of, 332
  qualifications and compensation of, 317
  rights of, 332
  term of, 315, 317
  of two or more corporations, 330, 482
Disabled persons, 421
Disaffirmance, by minor, 211
Discharge:
  in bankruptcy, 291, 295, 296–297
    exceptions to, 290–293
    "hardship," 297
  of a contract, 219–222
    by agreement, 221

    by operation of law, 221–222
    by performance. *See* Performance
Disclaimers, warranty, 250–252
Disclosed principal, 373
Discovery, 46
Discrimination:
  employment. *See* Employment discrimination
  labor unions and, 403–405
  price, 88, 479, 514, 564
  racial, in housing ads, 112–113
  reverse, 89, 416–417, 437–439
  in zoning ordinances, 546
Dismiss, motion to, 45
Dismissal, pretrial, 45–46
Disparagement of property, 176–178
Disparate-impact discrimination, 413–415
Disparate-treatment discrimination, 411–413
Dispute resolution:
  alternative. *See* Alternative dispute resolution
  in court. *See* Court(s); Litigation
  in international transactions, 662–664
Dissenting opinion, 25
Dissolution of corporation:
  as antitrust sanction, 482
  shareholders' rights on, 338
Distribution agreement, 655
Distributor, foreign, 655
Distributorship, 321
  exclusive, 655
District courts. *See* Court(s), district
Diversity of citizenship, 38–39
Divestiture, 482
Dividends, 304, 318
  illegal, 336, 339
  shareholder's right to, 334–336
  sources of funds for, 334
Doctrine of sovereign immunity, 652–654
Documents:
  request for, during discovery, 46
  of title, 235–238
Domestic corporation, 304
Domestic relations courts, 33
Door-to-door sales contracts, 225n, 447
Double taxation, of corporate income, 304
Douglas, Michael, 643
Drafts, 570
  demand, 571
  sight, 571
  time, 571
Drawee, 570
Drawer, 570
Drinking water, 468

communication of, 204
contractual, 202–207
defined, 202
firm, 206, 229n, 230
irrevocable, 206–207
rejection of, by offeree, 204
requirements of, 202–204
revocation of, 204
for sales contract, 229–230
serious intent to make, 202–203
tender, 330, 599
termination of, 204–207
Offeree, 201
counteroffer by, 204–206
rejection of offer by, 204
Offeror, 201
revocation of offer by, 204
Office of Interstate Land Sales
Registration (HUD), 448
Officers, corporate:
as agents of corporation, 318
appointment and removal of, 318
criminal liability of, 183–186
defined under securities law,
534–536
duties of, 318, 352–353. *See also*
Fiduciary duties, of corporate
directors and officers
rights of, 318, 332–333
Oil marketing, antitrust law and, 485
Old Age, Survivors, and Disability
Insurance (OASDI), 430
Older Workers Benefit Protection Act
of 1990, 88
Omission, act of, as crime, 179
Omnibus Crime Control Act of 1968,
422
One year, contract performance
within, 217
"Open field" doctrine, 128
Open terms, in sales contracts,
229–230
Opening statements, during trial, 48
Operation of law:
agency created by, 363
agency terminated by, 381
contract discharged by, 219–222
offer terminated by, 204, 206–207
Opinion:
statement of,
express warranty versus,
248–250
offer versus, 203
statement of fact versus, 152,
judicial, types of, 24–25
Option contract, 206, 230
Oraflex, 97
Oral contracts:
admission of, 233
between merchants, 232. *See also*
Confirmatory memoranda
partial performance of, 233

for specially manufactured goods,
233
Statute of Frauds and. *See* Statute
of Frauds
Order:
cease-and-desist, 134, 386, 444,
482
final, 134
initial, 133–134
multiple product, 445
for relief, in bankruptcy, 283
stop-payment, 573–574
Ordinances:
growth-management, 553
zoning, 549. *See also* Zoning
as source of law, 10
Organized Crime Control Act of
1970, 186
Original jurisdiction, 32, 40
Output contract, 230
Over-the-counter (OTC) securities,
523
Overdrafts, 571–574
Overseas Private Investment
Corporation (OPIC), 665

P

Pac-man defense, 600–601
Packaging laws, 446–447
Pacta sunt servanda, 198
Parallel citations, 19
Federal Supplement, 19
Parent-subsidiary merger, 606
Paris Convention, 668
Partial acceptance, 243
Partial performance:
estoppel based on, 206–207
of oral sales contract, 233
Partially disclosed principal, 373
Participation, director's right of, 332
Partners:
general, 301
limited, 301
Partnerships, 301–303
defined, 301
general, 301
liability in, 301
limited, 301–303
records of, Fifth Amendment
protection and, 115n
taxation of income from, 301
Par-value shares, 340
Passage:
of risk of loss, 235–239
of title, 234–239
Passwords, computer, 632, 635, 636
Patents, 618
for computer software, 618
infringement of, 618
international protection for, 618,
668–669

Pay, severance, 392
Pay-by-telephone systems, 578
Payee, 570
Payment:
as buyer's obligation, 242
for franchise, 321
"grease," 666. *See also* Bribery
in international transactions,
658–661
by letter of credit, 659–661
monetary systems and, 658–659
partial, under oral sales contract,
233
stopping,
on check, 573–574
electronic fund transfers and,
582
term of, in sales contract, 230
Payor bank, 575
Pension plans. *See* Retirement plans
Per se, defined, 82
Per se rule, in antitrust law, 500, 501,
503–505, 511, 512, 515, 666
Peremptory challenge, 48
Perfect tender rule, 240–242
Perfection, of security interest, 282
Performance, 219–222
agent's duty of, 364–365
complete (strict), 220
failure in, as breach of contract,
200
impossibility of, 221–222, 240, 346
monitoring of, by employer, 90,
422–423, 428–429
in one year, Statute of Frauds and,
217
partial, 206–207
of oral sales contract, 233
required degree of, 220–221
of sales contract, 233, 239–244
specific. *See* Specific performance
substantial, 220–221
tender of, 220
time for, 221
Permanent Court of Arbitration, 650
Person(s):
differently abled, 421
foreign, 666
intentional torts against, 144–152
jurisidiction over, 32
legal, 108, 303–304
natural, 108
reasonable, 156
Personal property. *See also* Goods
artisan's lien on, 276–277
defined, 152
intangible, 333, 634. *See also*
Intellectual property
Personal-services contracts:
for undisclosed principal, 374
nonassignability of, 219
Personalty. *See* Property, personal